The Oxford Handbook of
International Psychological Ethics

OXFORD LIBRARY OF PSYCHOLOGY

EDITOR-IN-CHIEF

Peter E. Nathan

AREA EDITORS:

Clinical Psychology
David H. Barlow

Cognitive Neuroscience
Kevin N. Ochsner and Stephen M. Kosslyn

Cognitive Psychology
Daniel Reisberg

Counseling Psychology
Elizabeth M. Altmaier and Jo-Ida C. Hansen

Developmental Psychology
Philip David Zelazo

Health Psychology
Howard S. Friedman

History of Psychology
David B. Baker

Methods and Measurement
Todd D. Little

Neuropsychology
Kenneth M. Adams

Organizational Psychology
Steve W. J. Kozlowski

Personality and Social Psychology
Kay Deaux and Mark Snyder

OXFORD LIBRARY OF PSYCHOLOGY

Editor in Chief PETER E. NATHAN

The Oxford Handbook of International Psychological Ethics

Edited by

Mark M. Leach

Michael J. Stevens

Geoff Lindsay

Andrea Ferrero

Yeşim Korkut

OXFORD
UNIVERSITY PRESS

Oxford University Press, Inc., publishes works that further
Oxford University's objective of excellence
in research, scholarship, and education.

Oxford   New York
Auckland   Cape Town   Dar es Salaam   Hong Kong   Karachi
Kuala Lumpur   Madrid   Melbourne   Mexico City   Nairobi
New Delhi   Shanghai   Taipei   Toronto

With offices in
Argentina   Austria   Brazil   Chile   Czech Republic   France   Greece
Guatemala   Hungary   Italy   Japan   Poland   Portugal   Singapore
South Korea   Switzerland   Thailand   Turkey   Ukraine   Vietnam

Copyright © 2012 by Oxford University Press, Inc.

Published by Oxford University Press, Inc.
198 Madison Avenue, New York, New York 10016
www.oup.com

Oxford is a registered trademark of Oxford University Press

All rights reserved. No part of this publication may be reproduced,
stored in a retrieval system, or transmitted, in any form or by any means,
electronic, mechanical, photocopying, recording, or otherwise,
without the prior permission of Oxford University Press

Library of Congress Cataloging-in-Publication Data
The Oxford handbook of international psychological ethics/edited by Mark M. Leach ... [et al.].
     p. cm. — (Oxford library of psychology)
  ISBN-13: 978–0–19–973916–5
  ISBN-10: 0–19–973916–1
  1. Psychology—Moral and ethical aspects.   2. Psychologists—Professional ethics.   I. Leach, Mark M.
  BF76.4.O94 2012
  174'.915—dc23
  2011042325

9 8 7 6 5 4 3 2
Printed in the United States of America
on acid-free paper

SHORT CONTENTS

Oxford Library of Psychology vii–viii

About the Editors ix

Contributors xi–xiii

Table of Contents xv–xvii

Foreword xix–xxi

Preface xxiii–xxvii

Chapters 1–470

Index 471

OXFORD LIBRARY OF PSYCHOLOGY

The *Oxford Library of Psychology*, a landmark series of handbooks, is published by Oxford University Press, one of the world's oldest and most highly respected publishers, with a tradition of publishing significant books in psychology. The ambitious goal of the *Oxford Library of Psychology* is nothing less than to span a vibrant, wide-ranging field and, in so doing, to fill a clear market need.

Encompassing a comprehensive set of handbooks, organized hierarchically, the *Library* incorporates volumes at different levels, each designed to meet a distinct need. At one level are a set of handbooks designed broadly to survey the major subfields of psychology; at another are numerous handbooks that cover important current focal research and scholarly areas of psychology in depth and detail. Planned as a reflection of the dynamism of psychology, the *Library* will grow and expand as psychology itself develops, thereby highlighting significant new research that will impact on the field. Adding to its accessibility and ease of use, the *Library* will be published in print and, later on, electronically.

The *Library* surveys psychology's principal subfields with a set of handbooks that capture the current status and future prospects of those major subdisciplines. This initial set includes handbooks of social and personality psychology, clinical psychology, counseling psychology, school psychology, educational psychology, industrial and organizational psychology, cognitive psychology, cognitive neuroscience, methods and measurements, history, neuropsychology, personality assessment, developmental psychology, and more. Each handbook undertakes to review one of psychology's major subdisciplines with breadth, comprehensiveness, and exemplary scholarship. In addition to these broadly conceived volumes, the *Library* also includes a large number of handbooks designed to explore in depth more specialized areas of scholarship and research, such as stress, health and coping, anxiety and related disorders, cognitive development, or child and adolescent assessment. In contrast to the broad coverage of the subfield handbooks, each of these latter volumes focuses on an especially productive, more highly focused line of scholarship and research. Whether at the broadest or most specific level, however, all of the *Library* handbooks offer synthetic coverage that reviews and evaluates the relevant past and present research and anticipates research in the future. Each handbook in the *Library* includes introductory and concluding chapters written by its editor to provide a roadmap to the handbook's table of contents and to offer informed anticipations of significant future developments in that field.

An undertaking of this scope calls for handbook editors and chapter authors who are established scholars in the areas about which they write. Many of the nation's and world's most productive and best-respected psychologists have agreed to edit *Library* handbooks or write authoritative chapters in their areas of expertise.

For whom has the *Oxford Library of Psychology* been written? Because of its breadth, depth, and accessibility, the *Library* serves a diverse audience, including graduate students in psychology and their faculty mentors, scholars, researchers, and practitioners in psychology and related fields. Each will find in the *Library* the information they seek on the subfield or focal area of psychology in which they work or are interested.

Befitting its commitment to accessibility, each handbook includes a comprehensive index, as well as extensive references to help guide research. And because the *Library* was designed from its inception as an online as well as a print resource, its structure and contents will be readily and rationally searchable online. Further, once the *Library* is released online, the handbooks will be regularly and thoroughly updated.

In summary, the *Oxford Library of Psychology* will grow organically to provide a thoroughly informed perspective on the field of psychology, one that reflects both psychology's dynamism and its increasing interdisciplinarity. Once published electronically, the *Library* is also destined to become a uniquely valuable interactive tool, with extended search and browsing capabilities. As you begin to consult this handbook, we sincerely hope you will share our enthusiasm for the more than 500-year tradition of Oxford University Press for excellence, innovation, and quality, as exemplified by the *Oxford Library of Psychology*.

Peter E. Nathan
Editor-in-Chief
Oxford Library of Psychology

ABOUT THE EDITORS

Mark M. Leach
Mark M. Leach, Ph.D., is a Professor and Director of Training of the Counseling Psychology program at the University of Louisville. He is an Associate Member of the APA Ethics Committee and has published and presented on international issues of psychological ethics. His ethics research focuses on comparing ethics standards across countries.

Michael J. Stevens
Michael J. Stevens, Ph.D., is a Professor of Psychology at Illinois State University, where he was named Outstanding University Researcher. He also is an honorary professor at The Lucian Blaga University in Romania, where he completed a Fulbright grant and received the Doctor Honoris Causa degree. He has served as President of APA's Division of International Psychology and Director-at-Large of the International Council of Psychologists.

Geoff Lindsay
Geoff Lindsay, Ph.D., is Director of the Centre for Educational Development, Appraisal and Research at the University of Warwick, UK, where he is also Professor of Educational Psychology and Special Needs Education. He is a past president of the British Psychological Society and led the Society's campaign to secure statutory regulation of practitioner psychologists for over 15 years. He was the Convenor of the European Federation of Psychologists' Associations Standing Committee on Ethics for 10 years until 2009.

Andrea Ferrero
Andrea Ferrero, Ph.D., is a clinical psychologist and Professor of Psychology at San Luis University, Argentina. She is also a Full Researcher on ethics in psychology by the National Education Ministry of that country, and led the Ethics Task Force of the Interamerican Psychological Society for two periods (2005–2009). She is involved in the revision of Latin and South American ethics codes in psychology, and in teaching in psychology in the Mercosur countries.

Yeşim Korkut
Yeşim Korkut, Ph.D., is clinical psychologist and an associate professor at Bahçeşehir University Psychology Department, Istanbul, Turkey. She is a member of the European Federation of Psychologists Association Ethics Board. She has worked extensively in the last decade for the Turkish Psychological Association in the development of a national psychology ethics code and an ethics system for the association, and served as ethics committee chair for two terms.

CONTRIBUTORS

An-Magritt Aanonsen
European Federation of Psychologists' Associations
Hubro Kompetanse, Norway

Norman Abeles
Department of Psychology
Michigan State University
East Lansing, MI

Adeyinka M. Akinsulure-Smith
Department of Psychology
The City College of New York
New York, NY

Alfred Allan
School of Psychology and Social Science
Edith Cowan University
Perth, Australia

Katharina Althaus
Center for Anxiety and Obsessive-Compulsive Disorders
Bern, Switzerland

Rubén Ardila
National University of Colombia
Bogotá, Colombia

Dave Bartram
SHL Group Ltd.
Thames Ditton, UK

Stephen Behnke
Director, Ethics Office
American Psychological Association
Washington, DC

Pedro Chacón
Department of Philosophy
Complutense University
Madrid, Spain

Charles C. Chan
Department of Applied Sciences
The Hong Kong Polytechnic University
Hung Hom, Kowloon
Hong Kong

Andrés J. Consoli
Department of Counseling
San Francisco State University
San Francisco, CA

Saths Cooper
Psychological Society of South Africa
Killarney, South Africa

Steve Discont
Department of Psychology
University of Louisville
Louisville, KY

Ian M. Evans
School of Psychology
Massey University
Palmerston North, New Zealand

Andrea Ferrero
Department of Psychology
National University of San Luis
San Luis, Argentina

David Foster
Kryterion, Inc.
Surrey, UK

Alison F. Garton
School of Psychology
Edith Cowan University
Perth, Western Australia

Janel Gauthier
Department of Psychology
Université Laval
Sainte Foy, Québec, Canada

Thomas Hadjistavropoulos
Department of Psychology
University of Regina
Regina, Canada

Averil M. L. Herbert
University of Waikato
Hamilton, New Zealand

Michelle Hilgart
Department of Psychiatry and Neurobehavioral Sciences
University of Virginia
Charlottesville, VA

Benjamin Jeppsen
Department of Educational and Counseling Psychology
University of Louisville
Louisville, KY

Stan Jones
Former Director, Ethics Office
American Psychological Association
Washington, DC

Basak Kacar Khamush
Department of Psychology
Cleveland State University
Cleveland, OH

Casper Koene
Psychologenpraktijk Bos en Lommer
The Netherlands
Centre International de Thérapies
Belgium

Gerald P. Koocher
Associate Provost and Professor
Simmons College
Boston, MA

Yeşim Korkut
Department of Psychology
Bahcesehir University
Istanbul, Turkey

Mark M. Leach
Department of Educational & Counseling Psychology
University of Louisville
Louisville, KY

Peter W. Lee
University of Wisconsin, Milwaukee
Milwaukee, WI

Frederick T. L. Leong
Department of Psychology
Michigan State University
East Lansing, MI

Alvin S. Leung
The Chinese University of Hong Kong
Hong Kong

Geoff Lindsay
Director, CEDAR
University of Warwick
Coventry, UK

Brent J. Lyons
Department of Psychology
Michigan State University
East Lansing, MI

Nicole Mamotte
African AIDS Vaccine Programme's Co-ordinating and Resource Facility on Ethics, Law and Human Rights
Pietermaritzburg, South Africa

Carolina Marín
Complutense University
Madrid, Spain

Polona Matjan
Institute of Clinical Psychology and Psychotherapy
Department of Psychology
University of Ljubljana
Ljubljana, Slovenia

Harold L. Miller, Jr.
Department of Psychology
Brigham Young University
Provo, UT

Raymond Nairn
University of Auckland
Auckland, NZ

Thomas Oakland
College of Education
University of Florida
Gainesville, FL

Haldor Øvreeide
Institute for Family and Relationships Development (IFRU)
Oslo, Norway

Jose Pardo
Department of Psychiatry
University of Minnesota
Minneapolis, MN

Jean L. Pettifor
University of Calgary
Calgary, Alberta, Canada

Ype H. Poortinga
Tilburg University
Tilburg, The Netherlands

José M. Prieto
Faculty of Psychology
Complutense University of Madrid
Madrid, Spain

Lee M. Ritterband
Department of Psychiatry and Neurobehavioral Sciences
University of Virginia Health System
Charlottesville, VA

Mihaela Robila
Department of Family, Nutrition, and Exercise Sciences
Queens College, City University of New York
Flushing, NY

Fred Seymour
Department of Psychology
University of Auckland
Auckland, NZ

Carole Sinclair
The Hincks-Dellcrest Treatment Centre
Toronto, Canada

Ann-Charlotte Smedler
Institute of Psychology
University of Stockholm
Stockholm, Sweden

Karel A. Soudijn
School of Social and Behavioral Sciences
Tilburg University
Tilburg, The Netherlands

Michael J. Stevens
Department of Psychology
Normal, IL
Illinois State University
The Lucian Blaga University
Sibiu, Romania

Alyssa A. Sondalle
Department of Psychology
Illinois State University
Normal, IL

Natasha A. Tassell
School of Psychology
Massey University
Palmerston North, New Zealand

Frances P. Thorndike
Department of Psychiatry and
  Neurobehavioral Sciences
University of Virginia
Charlottesville, VA

Boris B. Velichkovsky
Department of Psychology
Moscow State University
Moscow, Russia

Li-fei Wang
National Taiwan Normal University
Taipei, Taiwan

Douglas R. Wassenaar
Biomedical Research Ethics Committee
University of KwaZulu-Natal
Durban, South Africa

Elizabeth Reynolds Welfel
Department of Counseling, Administration,
  Supervision & Adult Learning
Cleveland State University
Cleveland, OH

Patricia TeW. A. Young
Victoria University of Wellington
Wellington, New Zealand

Alexander I. Yuriev
Department of Political Psychology
St. Petersburg State University
St. Petersburg, Russia

Houcan Zhang
Department of Psychology
Beijing Normal University
Beijing, China

Kan Zhang
Chinese Psychological Society
Institute of Psychology
Chinese Academy of Sciences
Beijing, China

CONTENTS

Foreword xix
Preface xxiii

Part One • Overview of International Psychological Ethics

1. Ethical Principles, Values, and Codes for Psychologists: An Historical Journey 3
   Carole Sinclair
2. An International Perspective on Ethics Codes for Psychology: A Focus on Test Development and Use 19
   Thomas Oakland, Mark M. Leach, Dave Bartram, Geoff Lindsay, Ann-Charlotte Smedler, and *Houcan Zhang*
3. Ethical Dilemmas, Cultural Differences, and the Globalization of Psychology 28
   Jean L. Pettifor and *Andrea Ferrero*
4. Professional Ethics and Enhancement of Competent Practice 42
   Karel A. Soudijn and *Ype H. Poortinga*
5. Ethical Perspectives and Concepts 53
   Haldor Øvreeide and *Polona Matjan*
6. Ethical Decision Making 74
   Geoff Lindsay
7. When Things Go Wrong: On Mediation, Arbitration, Corrective Actions, and Disciplinary Sanctions 90
   Casper Koene

Part Two • Current and Emerging International Ethical and Professional Development Issues

8. Ethical Standards, Credentialing, and Accountability: An International Perspective 103
   Elizabeth Reynolds Welfel and *Basak Kacar Khamush*
9. The Tale of Two Universal Declarations: Ethics and Human Rights 113
   Janel Gauthier and *Jean L. Pettifor*
10. The Search for Common Standards: A Case of Research Standards 134
    Mark M. Leach, Benjamin Jeppsen, and *Steve Discont*
11. A Call for Ethical Standards and Guidelines for Cross-Cultural Research Conducted by American Psychologists 149
    Brent J. Lyons and *Frederick T. L. Leong*

12. Ethical Issues of Web-Based Interventions and Online Therapy   161
    Michelle Hilgart, Frances P. Thorndike, Jose Pardo, and
    Lee M. Ritterband
13. Principles of Indigenous Ethics and Psychological Interventions   176
    Natasha A. Tassell, Averil M. L. Herbert, Ian M. Evans,
    and *Patricia TeW. A. Young*
14. Psychological Ethics and Immigration   191
    Mihaela Robila and *Adeyinka M. Akinsulure-Smith*
15. Principles, Standards, and Guidelines that Impact Test
    Development and Use and Sources of Information   201
    Thomas Oakland
16. Global Test Security Issues and Ethical Challenges   216
    David Foster and *Harold L. Miller, Jr.*
17. Psychologists and Prisoner Interrogations   233
    Norman Abeles

Part Three • Psychological Ethics in Wider Contexts

18. Ethical/Deontological Issues in Work and Organizational Psychology   243
    José M. Prieto, Pedro Chacón, and *Carolina Marín*
19. Ethical Issues and Ethics Reviews in Social Science Research   268
    Douglas R. Wassenaar and *Nicole Mamotte*
20. Ethics and Law from an International Perspective: The Relationship between
    National Psychological Association Ethics Codes and Civil Law   283
    Stephen Behnke and *Stan Jones*

Part Four • Psychological Ethics by Region: Convergence and Divergence

21. Ethics and South African Psychology   299
    Saths Cooper
22. Latin and South America   308
    Andrés J. Consoli, Rubén Ardila, and *Andrea Ferrero*
23. North America: Canada and the United States   321
    Gerald P. Koocher and *Thomas Hadjistavropoulos*
24. Psychological Ethics in Chinese Societies   328
    Charles C. Chan, Alvin S. Leung, Peter W. Lee, Li-fei Wang, and *Kan Zhang*
25. Psychological Ethics in Europe: Convergence and Divergence   337
    An-Magritt Aanonsen and *Katharina Althaus*
26. Psychological Ethics in Oceania: Convergence and Divergence   358
    Alison F. Garton and *Alfred Allan*

Part Five • Economic, Political, and Social Influences on Psychological Ethics and Ethics Code Development

27. Psychological Ethics and Macro-Social Change   375
    Michael J. Stevens

28. Argentina   394
    Andrea Ferrero
29. Aotearoa/New Zealand   405
    Fred Seymour and *Raymond Nairn*
30. Russia   424
    Boris B. Velichkovsky and *Alexander I. Yuriev*
31. Turkey   443
    Yeşim Korkut
32. Taking Stock and Looking Forward   451
    Geoff Lindsay, Michael J. Stevens, Mark M. Leach, Andrea Ferrero, and *Yeşim Korkut*

Appendix   464
    Michael J. Stevens and *Alyssa A. Sondalle*
Index   471

FOREWORD

We live in times of rapid social change: the new millennium began with a unique combination of political transformation to more democratic rule in many countries, especially in Europe, overlaid by globalization that has generally affected all societies through the opening up of world markets and the free circulation of goods and services. Recently, however, the globalized world has been challenged by financial crises that many would say arose in no small part through a lack of ethical conduct. The world also faces deepening divides between political and cultural systems, not to speak of threats by radical and militant ideologies. Yet despite all this, most people would agree that since the 1990s the world has become a better place for many citizens, who can now strive to fulfill their aspirations under conditions that offer better prospects with regard to human rights.

As a discipline, psychology aims at understanding of how people can strive to fulfill their aspirations, how they can realize their true potential concerning their thoughts and actions, and it does this by describing, predicting, explaining, and optimizing psychological adaptation and development in the human ecology. This raises an interesting question: did the social change just described, which has had such a profound impact on the world, also have an impact on the development of the discipline of psychology, a field of research and practice that ultimately wants to serve the well-being of humankind? Based on some intriguing facts found in *The Oxford Handbook of International Psychological Ethics*, the tentative answer is yes. In particular, according to the chapter by Michael Stevens (Chapter 27), it would seem that more prosperous and democratic countries have a higher share of psychologists in the population and a higher publication output of relevant research, and that this effect is mediated largely by the advantage of a market economy and political freedom for human achievements, such as high life expectancy, widespread literacy, and adequate living standards. If this is the case, then the logical assumption is that, as more countries become prosperous and take on democracy, so the discipline will expand and increase. Added to this, globalization brought with it an emerging view that individuals not only pursue their own goals, but also negotiate them in close alignment with the aims of their social reference groups, thereby establishing a synthesis between individualistic and collectivist orientations. This is also fertile soil for the ongoing growth of the discipline.

The need for quality standards and rules of conduct concerning all aspects of the activities of psychology has long been acknowledged. Indeed, as the book explains, modern codes of ethics have been in existence since the mid-20th century, and ethical principles articulated with regard to respect for persons and social responsibility can be traced back across time almost to the ancient world. However, over the last few years there has been a growing awareness of the need for and the advantage of internationally recognized ethical standards, particularly concerning research and practice and the well-being of individuals and societies: this volume is the most comprehensive assembly of facts and visions across the entire field that one could imagine. Of particular importance, it discusses the history and aims of ethical meta-codes, such as the 2008 *Universal Declaration of Ethical Principles for Psychologists*, already adopted by the two world organizations of psychology, the International Union of Psychological Science (IUPsyS) and the International Association of Applied Psychology (IAAP). As discussed in the chapter by Janel Gauthier and Jean Pettifor (Chapter 9), this declaration holds respect for the dignity of persons and peoples, competence in their care, integrity of psychological action, and professional and scientific responsibilities to societies to be guiding principles for all psychological work. This is compared and contrasted with the older *Universal Declaration of Human Rights*, issued by the United Nations in 1948, following the end of World War II, and the case is made for how these two declarations—one on human rights and one on ethics—complement each other and provide a framework for addressing many of today's global problems.

With regard to the development of an internationally agreed code of ethics, the hope is that psychologists and their scientific and professional organizations will refer to the *Universal Declaration of Ethical Principles for Psychologists* and use it to help develop their ethical codes to include standards of conduct that take cultural and other specific characteristics of their countries and societies more into account. Naturally, most national associations of psychology represented in the IUPsyS, and there are more than 70 worldwide, have already implemented such standards and have long been engaged in adapting them to the new challenges arising from developments in the discipline, such as the growing role of methods and concepts from molecular genetics and neuroscience. Moreover, consideration has been given to new developments in society at large, such as the increasingly multicultural orientation in many countries and the formation of multinational bodies like the European Union.

Interestingly, the social change that has happened or is happening in various corners of the world has already left a clear mark on many recent versions of ethical codes. In many areas, developments signaling a break with the past can be seen especially concerning higher legal or constitutional protections, the prohibition of inhuman and degrading treatment, greater sensitivity to diverse and vulnerable communities, more openness to multiple viewpoints, and responsible ways of decision making. Thankfully, this is no case for any one region of the world to feel superior over another—these examples of amendments and improvements in reaction to deficits and threats refer to various countries in the North and South, West and East, including the highly reputed powerhouses of psychology, such as the United States.

With regard to the scope of the book, it over 30 chapters, which means that it is truly comprehensive and addresses almost all aspects of psychological ethics one can think of. However, among the many, several are worthy of particular note: the history of ethical standards of psychology, certification of psychologists, research ethics for various fields, hot new topics such as immigration, culturally adequate interventions, research utilizing the new media, psychological testing in times of confidentiality concerns, psychologists and the legal system, and ethical standards in various regions of the world at various stages to and from democratization. As one would expect, the book concludes with a full synopsis, including recommendations on how to implement ethical standards and what open questions research might pursue.

Readers will learn about paradigmatic negative cases, such as the obvious misuse of psychology for maintaining divisions among peoples, but also about the fresh positive impetus psychology can give to national development and the improvement of the human condition. The book is written in a nontechnical language that conveys a framework of ethical principles, values, and rules that allows psychologists to see their work and life as honorable.

As president of the IUPsyS, I welcome *The Oxford Handbook of International Psychological Ethics* as a source of knowledge and wisdom for our discipline.

Rainer K. Silbereisen

PREFACE

Ethics and ethics codes are designed to serve multiple purposes, such as protecting the general public and promoting public trust, educating members of professions and students undergoing professional training about ethical ideals and expected standards of conduct, and reflecting legislative initiatives that link ethics to the law and to government policy. The purpose of *The Oxford Handbook of International Psychological Ethics* is to be the state-of-the-art source for information on psychological ethics worldwide, and to offer a comprehensive international review of contemporary and emerging ethical issues within psychology as a science and profession. There is no comparable book on the market, notwithstanding the importance and timeliness of the topics to be covered in the *Handbook*.

Evidence is increasing that the future of psychological ethics and ethics codes will be grounded in an international perspective, as evidence by the following examples. First, the *Meta-Code of Ethics* was developed in Europe in 1995 (and revised in 2005) as a document intended to highlight principles that European countries should consider when constructing or revising their national codes of psychological ethics. Although these national codes differ in content, they are consistent with the fundamental principles contained in the Meta-Code. Similarly, the Mercosur countries of South America developed a common economic agreement in the mid-1990s that allowed for greater commercial access among these countries. Such access has opened artificial boundaries in other areas, including the discipline of psychology. To wit, the Mercosur countries have discussed common ethical issues that arise across nations (and in 1997 developed the only regional declaration of ethical principles for psychology in South America: the *Ethics Framework for Professional Practice of Psychology in the Mercosur and Associated Countries*).

Second, while on a much grander scale, other international documents have appeared which further testify to the growing internationalization of psychological ethics. One such document is the *Universal Declaration of Ethical Principles for Psychologists*, which was developed through a joint effort among the International Union of Psychological Science (IUPsyS), International Association of Applied Psychology (IAAP), and International Association for Cross-Cultural Psychology (IACCP). The objectives of the Universal Declaration are to provide a generic set of morally based principles that enable national psychological organizations to formulate or revise their ethics codes, to assess progress in the ethical and moral relevance of such codes, to evaluate alleged unethical behavior by their members, and to speak with collective authority on matters of ethical concern. The Universal Declaration deliberately avoids prescribing specific standards of conduct because of its sensitivity to the cultural variation in how generic ethical principles are expressed. With its approval at the 2008 meeting of the IUPsyS's General Assembly, the Universal Declaration has clear-cut implications for the ethical practice of psychology around the globe.

Third, certificate programs in psychology, such as those derived from the DaVinci project in Europe (i.e., the EuroPsy), are being designed so that their graduates can work across European borders. This development has implications for quality assurance of the training provided in psychological ethics and for the uniform ethical practice of psychology in its various specialties. Countries in close proximity (e.g., Canada and the United States) often have psychologists residing across borders given similar training programs, yet their ethics codes differ significantly.

Fourth, over the past 20 years there has been an increase in the number of national and international psychological associations that have focused their priorities and resources on psychological ethics, with multiple countries developing or revising their codes over the past decade. For example, both the Turkish and Iranian codes have been developed in the past five years, and the Chinese code was revised during that time. The International Test Commission is currently developing an ethics code to be used in conjunction with their test guidelines. Fifth, there has been a strong movement to restore, include, or expand the focus within psychological ethics codes on social justice and human rights issues. A growing number of national ethics codes from such diverse countries as Canada, New Zealand, South Africa, and Uruguay feature aspirational principles and standards of conduct that emphasize psychologists' sense of social responsibility and call upon psychologists not only to respect, but also to advocate for the disempowered and marginalized.

Finally, unlike countries in other geographic regions (South America, Europe) that historically have adopted an international orientation, the United States, through the American Psychological Association (APA), has relatively recently turned its attention to a variety of international issues that bear on psychological science and practice. For example, in 2008 the membership of the APA approved a petition resolution stating that U.S. psychologists may no longer work in settings where individuals are held outside of or in violation of international law or the U.S. constitution unless they are working directly for detained persons or for a third party engaged in the protection of human rights.

Beyond the developments and trends just described, there are numerous cultural, educational, and social dimensions of psychological ethics that have gained international attention and thus demand substantive examination. For example, test security has become a global issue, as psychological tests and even college entrance and graduate school admission tests have found their way online. Given growing international collaboration, there has been a call for better ethical guidance in responding to the multitude of issues that surround the implementation of international research. Ethical issues concerning licensure and certification, indigenous interventions, competent transnational practice, interdisciplinary cooperation, and diverse approaches to ethical decision making are all important topics that increasingly will have an impact on psychological research, practice, and training.

Ethical developments and issues within geographical regions (e.g., Africa, Asia) are on the rise and are being dealt with on regional as well as national levels. One of the purposes of the *Handbook* is to offer international guidance to psychologists from or working in various geographic regions in resolving ethical dilemmas.

As noted at the outset, the intent of *The Oxford Handbook of International Psychological Ethics* is to be the much-needed comprehensive source of information on psychological ethics from an international perspective, with material related to recent, current, and future international developments and issues regarding psychological ethics. These developments and issues have yet to be discussed in significant depth in the professional literature, although they have been presented to a small degree in the form of conference symposia and scattered journal articles. The chapters of the *Handbook* are organized into five sections, which we now describe. The chapter authors include acknowledged experts from around the globe who have provided diverse and authoritative perspectives on the ethical issues covered.

Part One: Overview of International Psychological Ethics

This section includes a survey of the history of professional ethics from which current ethical principles in psychology obtain, conceptual guidelines and case-study vignettes to facilitate the resolution of ethical dilemmas that may arise when working across cultures and national borders, a discursive analysis of complementary and competing value systems intended to raise awareness of the multiple dimensions that undergird ethical practice, the importance of ethical decision-making skills in addition to knowledge of psychological ethics, and an examination of disciplinary versus mediational approaches to remedying ethical infractions and achieving just outcomes for the victim, perpetrator, and psychological community.

Part Two: Current and Emerging International Ethical and Professional Development Issues

This section surveys a wide array of cutting-edge developments and challenges in international psychological ethics, such as the effectiveness of diverse national credentialing standards in psychology, the role of the *Universal Declaration of Ethical Principles for Psychologists* in facilitating human rights and social justice, the search for universal ethical standards, ethical ambiguities in carrying out international and cross-cultural research, the need for a framework to guide ethical online research and practice across national jurisdictions, ethical issues and requirements when applying and evaluating interventions in aboriginal communities and when administering indigenous interventions, perspectives for addressing ethical dilemmas when working cross-nationally with immigrants and refugees, efforts to codify international ethical guidelines for psychological tests and their cross-national applications, ethical responses to security risks that increasingly impact international testing, and proposed responses to ethical issues that arise in national security operations.

Part Three: Psychological Ethics in Wider Contexts

Psychological phenomena, especially those which manifest cross-culturally and cross-nationally, are rightly construed as being multiply determined, and their understanding necessitates inquiry that transcends mainstream disciplinary and structural boundaries. Calls for an internationalized psychology often reference the importance of more inclusive interdisciplinary and multisectoral approaches to scientific research and applied practice. In keeping with this view, this section includes three chapters that relate and/or evaluate psychological ethics in the context of issues and practices that are germane to business and industry, medical research, and the law.

Part Four: Psychological Ethics by Region: Convergence and Divergence

Ethical developments and issues within geographical regions have become more prominent. Over the past 20 years, regional and national psychology associations have prioritized the establishment or revision of their ethics codes. This trend has implications for more uniformity in the ethical practice of psychology and in ethics training. The chapters nested within this section identify and examine areas of convergence and divergence in dominant countries within a particular geographic region that pertain to psychological ethics, specifically ethics codes, laws that regulate psychology, the existence of professional associations and adjudicating committees, ethics training, research on ethics, and future challenges with respect to ethics and ethics codes.

Part Five: Economic, Political, and Social Influences on Psychological Ethics and Ethics Code Development

Given the nature of psychology as a science and profession, it follows that economic, political, and social events and forces shape psychological ethics codes, especially when such events and forces are of sufficient magnitude as to transform the structure and dynamics of society. Following an overview of the relationship of psychological ethics and ethics codes to macro-level change, each of the remaining chapters applies this theme to a particular country that has or is currently undergoing a distinctive form of economic, political, and/or social transformation. These distinctive transformations include: from military dictatorship to representative government (Argentina), from monoculturalism to multiculturalism (New Zealand), from communism to free-market economy (Russia), from racial segregation to pluralism (South Africa), and from secular to religious (Turkey). Each chapter illustrates how national ethics codes in psychology are historically constructed, sample from the general principles and specific standards of its country's ethics codes or from rights and obligations as codified by law, and conclude with questions about the relationship between economic, political, and social transformation and psychological ethics that may guide future research on this topic.

With its broad scope and perspective informed by a synthesis of international scholarship and practice, the *Handbook* will inform readers from around the world of existing and emerging issues and trends that confront psychological ethics and will. The primary audiences for the *Handbook* include graduate-level ethics courses in such fields as psychology (clinical, counseling, industrial-organizational, school), counselor education/guidance and counseling, marriage and the family, pastoral counseling, and social work. The *Handbook* may also be adopted as an adjunct text in disciplines allied to psychology, such as anthropology, sociology, law, medicine, and politics and government. Other audiences include undergraduate students enrolled in psychology courses that may use the *Handbook* as a reference (e.g., cross-cultural psychology, international psychology, multicultural counseling, psychology of diversity) or in general studies courses that emphasize ethics within an international context. Other possible audiences include academic and applied psychologists who are increasingly engaged in international teaching, research, practice, and consulting, as well as international psychology organizations (e.g., national associations such as the APA, regional associations such as the European Federation of Psychologists Associations [EFPA], and international associations such as the IUPsyS).

Mark M. Leach
Michael J. Stevens
Geoff Lindsay
Andrea Ferrero
Yeşim Korkut

PART 1

Overview of International Psychological Ethics

CHAPTER 1

Ethical Principles, Values, and Codes for Psychologists: An Historical Journey

Carole Sinclair

Abstract

In this chapter, a review is provided of the efforts and methods used by professions, from the time of the ancient world to the present, to articulate their ethical principles and values to guide members of the professions. The evolution of the concepts of respect for persons, doing good and avoiding harm, truth-telling, and responsibility to society are traced across time, cultures, and professions. The purpose and role of ethics codes also are described, demonstrating the influence of culture, politics, and historical events. In addition, the history (since the mid-20th century CE) of the development of modern-day codes of ethics for psychologists is outlined, including the possible impact of the *Universal Declaration of Ethical Principles for Psychologists* on this development.

Key Words: history of ethics codes, *Universal Declaration of Ethical Principles for Psychologists*, ethical standards, ethical principles, *Meta-Code*

"Ethics is at the core of every discipline."
—*Universal Declaration of Ethical Principles for Psychologists*, 2008

For all professions, a sense of ethical duty and the need to articulate that duty in a way that can guide members has a long history (Sinclair, 1993; *Universal Declaration of Ethical Principles for Psychologists*, 2008). From ancient times to the present, people throughout the world have struggled to define right and wrong behavior for professionals. The history of this struggle and its current manifestations have been shaped by the evolution of society and its various structures, values, and expectations. To understand and appreciate modern-day codes of ethics as more than simply lists of "rules," and to be able to apply them and their underlying ethical principles meaningfully in everyday professional life, it is important to understand that history.

In the first four sections of this chapter, the history of ethics codes and ethical principles for psychologists is traced using 13 documents from the 18th century BCE[1] to the mid-20th century CE. As the discipline of psychology has a relatively short history, only the latest of the documents is drawn from psychology. All of the other documents relate to the practice of medicine, which has the longest documented history of all professions and provides us with the most relevant information about the history of ethics codes and ethical principles and values. These documents vary from a set of laws for physicians, to formal oaths taken by new physicians, to sets of instructions for physicians, to, in one case, a physician's prayer. Each provides information about ethical principles, values, attitudes, and expectations held by physicians who practiced at the time and place in which they were written, or by the society in which they worked. In the fifth section of the chapter, the development of ethics codes developed specifically for psychologists from the mid-20th century CE to the present is outlined.

To provide a framework for the historical review to the mid-20th century CE, the four ethical principles of the 21st-century *Universal Declaration of Ethical Principles* for psychologists (2008), which is the most recent ethics document for psychologists, are used. During the development of the *Universal Declaration*, a comparison of various 21st-century CE codes of ethics for psychologists was used to help identify the ethical principles and related values of the *Declaration* (Gauthier, 2006). Principle I (Respect for the Dignity of Persons and Peoples) includes the related values of respect for the unique worth and inherent dignity of all human beings; respecting diversity, customs, and beliefs; free and informed consent; privacy and confidentiality; and fairness and justice. Principle II (Competent Caring for the Well-Being of Persons and Peoples) includes the related values of active concern for well-being; taking care not to do harm; maximizing benefits and minimizing harm; correcting or offsetting harm; developing and maintaining competence; self-knowledge; and respect for the ability of persons and peoples to care for themselves and others. Principle III (Integrity) includes the related values of honesty; truthfulness and openness; avoiding incomplete disclosure; maximizing impartiality and minimizing biases; and avoiding conflicts of interest. Principle IV (Professional and Scientific Responsibilities to Society) includes the related values of increasing knowledge in ways that promote the well-being of society and all its members; using psychological knowledge for beneficial purposes and preventing it from being misused; conducting its affairs in a way that promotes the well-being of society and all its members; adequately training its members in their ethical responsibilities and required competencies; developing ethical awareness and sensitivity; and being as self-correcting as possible.

In each of the four time periods to the mid-20th century CE, selected statements from historical documents of the period are presented and compared to the above four ethical principles and related values.

Before the Common Era (BCE): The Ancient World

Three major documents from the ancient world are examined below: (1) the *Code of Hammurabi* (King, 2004); (2) the *Ayurvedic Instruction* (Post, 2003; Reich, 1995); and (3) the *Hippocratic Oath* (Post, 2003; Reich, 1995).[2]

The *Code of Hammurabi* (Babylon, 18th century BCE) was a set of laws carved into a black stone monument discovered in 1901. It is recognized as the earliest known written body of laws that communicated to those living in a region what was expected of them and what punishments would ensue if they did not live up to those expectations. Hammurabi was king of the Babylonian empire from 1795–1750 BCE and is best known for promulgating this set of laws (American College of Physicians, 1984). The laws covered such matters as the sale of property, management of slaves, rules regarding marriage and inheritance rights, and theft. However, the laws also covered expectations for the members of various occupational groups (e.g., tavern keepers, builders, and physicians), and sometimes detailed very harsh punishments (e.g., having one's hands cut off, or having one's child killed) for poor technical performance or harming others when engaged in such occupations. Nine of the 282 laws related to physicians.

The *Ayurvedic Instruction* (India, circa 6th century BCE) was a set of instructions to medical students at their consecration ceremony (Pandya, 2000). Ayurvedic medicine has over 4000 years of history. Originating in India during the Vedic period, it continues to be practiced in the modern world. The *Instruction* was contained in Sanskrit documents written and edited over several centuries and may have been part of the Ayurvedic tradition prior to the 6th century BCE.

The *Hippocratic Oath* (Greece, 4th century BCE) is believed to have been part of a rite of induction into a specific Greek guild-like community of physicians. It is part of a much larger work called the *Hippocratic Corpus*, which contained seven sections (Oath, Precepts, The Art, Epidemics, The Physician, Decorum, and Law). Unlike the oaths taken to enter other guild-like communities of the day, which outlined the responsibilities of members to their "craft" and to the guild community, the *Hippocratic Oath* specified the responsibilities of physicians to persons outside the guild community—namely, persons served by physicians. The *Oath*, translated into many different languages, with wording adapted to different cultures and religions, served as the foundation of medical ethics off and on through many centuries. The *Corpus* was studied and the *Oath* taken by physicians in many countries of the world through to the 20th century CE.

Below are statements from the above three documents, selected for comparison with the four ethical principles of the 21st-century CE *Universal Declaration of Ethical Principles for Psychologists*. Each statement is followed by reference to the most relevant related value subsumed by the particular ethical principle. Both similarities and differences are evident.

Respect for the Dignity of Persons and Peoples

If a physician... saves the eye, he shall receive ten shekels in money... If the patient be a freed man, he receives five shekels... If he be the slave of someone, his owner shall give the physician two shekels.
(*Code of Hammurabi*, Laws 215–217) (Value: unique worth and inherent dignity of all human beings)

If a physician... kill him, or open a tumor with the operating knife, and [accidentally] cut out the eye, his hands shall be cut off... if... the slave of a freed man, and kill him, he shall replace the slave with another slave.
(*Code of Hammurabi*, Laws 219–220) (Value: unique worth and inherent dignity of all human beings)

It is the duty of all good physicians to treat gratuitously with their own medicines, all Brahmins, spiritual guides, paupers, friends, neighbours, devotees, orphans and people who come from a distance as if they are his own friends.
(*Ayurvedic Instruction*) (Value: unique worth and inherent dignity of all human beings)

Whilst entering the family dwelling-place of the patient, you should do it after giving notice to the inmates and with their permission...
(*Ayurvedic Instruction*) (Value: free and informed consent)

You should never give out to others the practices of the patient's home.
(*Ayurvedic Instruction*) (Values: privacy and confidentiality)

What I see or hear in the course of treatment or even outside of the treatment in regard to the life of men, which on no account [ought to be] spread abroad, I will keep to myself, holding such things shameful to be spoken about.
(*Hippocratic Oath*) (Values: privacy and confidentiality)

Whatever houses I may visit, I will come for the benefit of the sick, remaining free of all intentional injustice...
(*Hippocratic Oath*) (Value: fairness and justice)

...I will keep [the sick] from... injustice.
(*Hippocratic Oath*) (Value: fairness and justice)

Competent Caring for the Well-Being of Persons and Peoples

You should, with your whole heart, strive to bring about the cure of those that are ill.
(*Ayurvedic Instruction*). (Value: active concern for well-being)

There is no end to medical science, hence, heedfully devote yourself to it.
(*Ayurvedic Instruction*) (Value: developing and maintaining competence)

I will apply dietetic measures for the benefit of the sick according to my ability and judgment...
(*Hippocratic Oath*) (Value: maximizing benefit)

...I will keep them from harm...
(*Hippocratic Oath*) (Value: taking care to do no harm)

I will not use the knife, not even on sufferers from stone, but will withdraw in favour of such men as are [skilled] in this work.
(*Hippocratic Oath*) (Value: taking care to do no harm)

Integrity

You shall speak words that are... truthful, beneficial, and properly weighed and measured.
(*Ayurvedic Instruction*) (Value: truthfulness and openness)

You should give up... deception, falsehood... and other reprehensible conduct.
(*Ayurvedic Instruction*) (Values: truthfulness and openness; avoiding incomplete disclosure)

Even if possessed with sufficient knowledge, you should not boast of that knowledge.
(*Ayurvedic Instruction*) (Value: avoiding conflicts of interest)

Whatever houses I might visit, I will come for the benefit of the sick, remaining free of... all mischief, and in particular of sexual relations with both male and female persons, be they free or slaves.
(*Hippocratic Oath*) (Value: avoiding conflicts of interest)

Professional and Scientific Responsibilities to Society

...you should always seek, whether standing or sitting, the good of all living creatures.
(*Ayurvedic Instruction*) (Value: promoting the well-being of society and all its members)

...to give a share of precepts and oral instruction and all the other learning to my sons and the sons of him who has instructed me, and to pupils who have signed the covenant and who have taken an oath according to the medical law...

(*Hippocratic Oath*) (Value: training members in their ethical responsibilities and required competencies)

Summary and Conclusions: Before the Common Era (BCE)

Many of the laws in the *Code of Hammurabi* indicate that not all persons were considered of equal worth in the society of the day. Physician's fees were to be set according to the status of patients, with slaves viewed as chattel and of low value, and former slaves (free men) of more value that slaves, but not as valuable as regular citizens. Expectations that physicians should benefit and not harm those they serve are evident in the designation of specific payments for benefit and punishments for harm, and it could be argued that developing and maintaining competence would be encouraged by the harsh punishments that would be incurred if a citizen were harmed. However, there is nothing in the laws that specifically refers to such values. Although the *Code* provides evidence of very early societal concern about governing the members of various occupational groups, and an expectation of responsibility to society, it was written by lawmakers. Little is known about whether the values reflected in the *Code* were espoused by members of those occupational groups.

On the other hand, 12 centuries later, in the *Ayurvedic Instruction* developed by physicians for new inductees, beliefs about the unique worth and inherent dignity of all human beings seems to have taken a sharp turn, with an expectation that most persons (if not all) should be treated "as friends" without regard to their means, their station in life, or their origins. In addition, specific statements are made related to the values of informed consent (to enter a household), privacy, confidentiality, active concern for well-being, developing and maintaining competence, truthfulness and openness, avoiding incomplete disclosure, avoiding conflicts of interest, and promoting the well-being of society and all its members. Similarly, two centuries after the *Ayurvedic Instruction*, the *Hippocratic Oath* makes statements related to the values of maximizing benefit, taking care to do no harm, avoiding conflicts of interest, and training members in their ethical responsibilities.

Although their emphasis, application, and interpretation vary, it is evident that the ethical principles and many of the related values of the 21st-century CE *Universal Declaration of Ethical Principles* have roots that go back at least 26 centuries.

From the 1st to 17th Centuries of the Common Era (CE)

Six major documents from this 17-century span are examined below: (1) the *Ayurvedic Oath of Initiation*; (2) the *Oath of Asaph*; (3) *Haly Abbas' Advice to a Physician*; (4) the *Daily Prayer of a Physician*; (5) the *Seventeen Rules of Enjuin*; and (6) the *Five Commandments and Ten Requirements*. All of these documents, and information about their origins, can be found in Reich (1995) and Post (2003).[3]

The *Ayurvedic Oath of Initiation* (India, circa 100 CE) was a later development for those being initiated into the practice of Ayurvedic Medicine. It appeared in a medical text written by the Indian physician Caraka. In addition to the elements reflected below, it contains several uniquely Hindu elements, including requirements to be celibate and eat no meat.

The *Hebrew Oath of Asaph* (Middle East, unknown country, circa 600 CE) appeared in the "Book of Medicine," written by the physician Osaph, a Hebrew physician from Syria or Mesopotamia. This *Oath* was taken by medical students when they received their diplomas.

Haly Abbas' Advice to a Physician (Persia, circa 950 CE) can be found in the first chapter of Haly Abbas' work, "Liber Regius." Haly Abbas was a leading Persian figure in medicine and medical ethics. The first chapter of his work was dedicated entirely to the topic of ethics.

The *Daily Jewish Prayer of a Physician* (Egypt, circa 1150 CE) is generally attributed to Moses Maimonides, a 12th-century CE Jewish physician in Egypt, although some question that attribution, believing that it was written much later by a German physician. In addition to addressing the physician's responsibilities to patients, it asks for courage and determination, and places the physician's healing in subordination to divine authority.

The *Seventeen Rules of Enjuin* (Japan, circa 1500 CE) were developed for students of the Ri-shu school of medicine in Japan, and draws from Buddhist thought and indigenous Shinto tradition and reflects the "priestly role" of the physician.

The *Five Commandments and Ten Requirements* (China, 1617 CE) represents the most comprehensive document regarding medical ethics in China prior to the 20th century CE. It was written by Chen Shih-Kung, and appeared in his work, "An Orthodox

Manual of Surgery." It draws from Confucianism, including the Confucian virtue of compassion.

Below are statements from the above six documents, selected for comparison with the four ethical principles of the 21st-century CE *Universal Declaration of Ethical Principles for Psychologists*. Each statement is followed by reference to the most relevant related value subsumed by the particular ethical principle. Once again, both similarities and differences are evident.

Respect for the Dignity of Persons and Peoples

No persons who are hated by the king or who are haters of the king, or who are hated by the public shall receive treatment.
(*Ayurvedic Oath of Initiation*) (Value: unique worth and inherent dignity of all human beings)

Similarly, those who are extremely abnormal, wicked and of miserable character or conduct...shall not receive treatment.
(*Ayurvedic Oath of Initiation*) (Value: unique worth and inherent dignity of all human beings)

Do not harden your heart [and turn it away] from pitying the poor and healing the needy.
(*Hebrew Oath of Asaph*) (Value: unique worth and inherent dignity of all human beings)

In the sufferer let me see only the human being.
(*Daily Prayer of a Physician*) (Value: unique worth and inherent dignity of all human beings)

You should rescue even such people as you dislike or hate.
(*Seventeen Rules of Enjuin*) (Value: unique worth and inherent dignity of all human beings)

Physicians should be ever ready to respond to any calls of patients, high or low, rich or poor. They should treat them equally...
(*Five Commandments and Ten Requirements*) (Value: unique worth and inherent dignity of all human beings)

Prostitutes should be treated just like patients from a good family...
(*Five Commandments and Ten Requirements*) (Value: unique worth and inherent dignity of all human beings)

Mocking should not be indulged for this brings loss of dignity.
(*Five Commandments and Ten Requirements*) (Value: unique worth and inherent dignity of all human beings)

The peculiar customs of the patient's household shall not be made public.
(*Ayurvedic Oath of Initiation*). (Values: privacy and confidentiality)

Do not divulge the secret of a man who has trusted you.
(*Hebrew Oath of Asaph*) (Values: privacy and confidentiality)

A physician should respect confidences and respect the patient's secrets. In protecting a patient's secrets, he must be more insistent than the patient himself.
(*Haly Abbas' Advice to a Physician*) (Values: privacy and confidentiality)

You should not tell what you have learned from the time you enter a woman's room.
(*Seventeen Rules of Enjuin*) (Values: privacy and confidentiality)

The secret diseases of female patients...should not be revealed to anybody, not even to the physician's own wife.
(*Five Commandments and Ten Requirements*) (Values: privacy and confidentiality)

He must never expect remuneration from the poor but rather provide them with free medicine.
(*Haly Abbas' Advice to a Physician*) (Value: fairness and justice)

Medicine should be given free to the poor. Extra financial help should be extended to destitute patients, if possible.
(*Five Commandments and Ten Requirements*) (Value: fairness and justice)

Competent Caring for the Well-Being of Persons and Peoples

Day and night, however thou mayest be engaged, thou shall endeavour for the relief of patients with all thy heart and soul.
(*Ayurvedic Oath of Initiation*) (Value: active concern for well-being)

May no strange thoughts divert my attention at the bedside of the sick, or disturb my mind in its silent labours, for great and sacred are the thoughtful deliberations required to preserve the lives and health of Thy creatures.
(*Daily Jewish Prayer of a Physician*) (Value: active concern for well-being)

You should be delighted if, after treating a patient without success, the patient receives medicine from another physician and is cured.
(*Seventeen Rules of Enjuin*) (Value: active concern for well-being)

Thou shalt not desert or injure thy patient for the sake of thy life or thy living.
(*Ayurvedic Oath of Initiation*) (Value: taking care not to do harm)

Do not attempt to kill any soul by means of a potion of herbs.
(*Oath of Asaph*) (Value: taking care not to do harm)

[A physician] should never use or prescribe a harmful drug...
(*Haly Abbas' Advice to a Physician*) (Value: taking care not to harm)

In our school, teaching about poisons is prohibited, nor should you receive instructions about poisons from other physicians.
(*Seventeen Rules of Enjuin*) (Value: taking care not to harm)

Remedies should be prepared according to the pharmaceutical formulae but may be altered to suit the patient's condition.
(*Five Commandments and Ten Requirements*) (Value: maximizing benefit)

Thou shalt act always with a view to the acquisition of knowledge and fullness of equipment.
(*Ayurvedic Oath of Initiation*) (Value: developing and maintaining competence)

There is no limit at all to the Science of Life, Medicine. So thou shouldst apply thyself to it with diligence.
(*Ayurvedic Oath of Initiation*) (Value: developing and maintaining competence)

[A physician] must study medical books constantly... He has to learn what he is studying and repeat and memorize what is necessary. He has to study in his youth because it is easier to memorize the subject at this age than in old age, which is the mother of oblivion.
(*Haly Abbas' Advice to a Physician*) (Value: developing and maintaining competence)

A medical student should be constantly present in the hospital so as to study disease processes and complications under the learned professor and proficient physicians.
(*Haly Abbas' Advice to a Physician*) (Value: developing and maintaining competence)

Should those who are wiser than I wish to improve and instruct me, let my soul gratefully follow their guidance, for vast is the extent of our art.
(*Daily Jewish Prayer of a Physician*) (Value: developing and maintaining competence)

Never allow the thought to arise in me that I have attained to sufficient knowledge, but vouchsafe to me the strength, the leisure and the ambition ever to extend my knowledge.
(*Daily Jewish Prayer of a Physician*) (Value: developing and maintaining competence)

A physician or surgeon must first know the principles of the learned. He must study all the ancient standard medical books ceaselessly day and night, and understand them thoroughly so that the principles enlighten his eyes and are impressed on his heart. Then he will not make any mistake in the clinic.
(*Five Commandments and Ten Requirements*) (Value: developing and maintaining competence)

The physician should improve his knowledge by studying medical books, old and new, and reading current publications.
(*Five Commandments and Ten Requirements*) (Value: developing and maintaining competence)

Integrity

Even knowing that the patient's span of life has come to its close it shall not be mentioned by thee there, where if so done, it would cause shock to the patient or to others.
(*Ayurvedic Oath of Initiation*) (Value: truthfulness and openness)

Do not say of [what is] good; it is bad, nor of [what is] bad; it is good.
(*Oath of Asaph*) (Value: truthfulness and openness)

No offering of presents by a woman without the behest of her husband or guardian shall be accepted by thee.
(*Ayurvedic Oath of Initiation*) (Value: avoiding conflicts of interest)

[A physician] should not look upon women with lust and never go to their home except to visit a patient.
(*Haly Abbas' Advice to a Physician*) (Value: avoiding conflicts of interest)

A physician is to prudently treat his patients with food and medicine out of good and spiritual motives, not for the sake of gain.
(*Haly Abbas' Advice to a Physician*) (Value: avoiding conflicts of interest)

Do not allow thirst for profit, ambition for renown and admiration, to interfere with my profession, for these are the enemies of truth and love for mankind

and they can lead astray in the great task of attending to the welfare of Thy creatures.
(*Daily Jewish Prayer of a Physician*) (Value: avoiding conflicts of interest)

You should not exhibit avarice and you must not strain to become famous.
(*Seventeen Rules of Enjuin*) (Value: avoiding conflicts of interest)

If the case improves, drugs may be sent, but physicians should not visit them again for lewd reward.
(*Five Commandments and Ten Requirements*) (Value: avoiding conflicts of interest)

Professional and Scientific Responsibilities to Society

...thou shalt pray for the welfare of all creatures...
(*Ayurvedic Oath of Initiation*) (Value: promoting the well-being of society and all its members)

Support me, Almighty God, in these great labours that they may benefit mankind...
(*Daily Jewish Prayer of a Physician*) (Value: promoting the well-being of society and all its members)

Be kind to the children of your teachers and if one of them wants to study medicine you are to teach him without any remuneration.
(*Haly Abbas' Advice to a Physician*) (Value: training members in their ethical responsibilities and required competencies)

Summary and Conclusions: The 1st to the 17th Centuries of the Common Era (CE)

Although the documents reviewed are from several different cultures, religions, geographic locations, and centuries, considerable similarity can be found. With the exception of the 1st-century CE *Ayurvedic Oath of Initiation*, where certain categories of persons were considered unworthy of medical treatment (which seems to contradict the earlier *Ayurvedic Instruction*, possibly due to interceding political influences), all of the documents seem to reflect strong support for the ethical value of respecting the unique worth and inherent dignity of all human beings regardless of social status, origins, or ability to pay. In addition, there is similar support for protecting the privacy and confidentiality of persons served. On the other hand, unlike the earlier *Ayurvedic Instruction*, none of the documents specifically mentions the importance of consent. However, there is no evidence that it was considered acceptable to do anything against the will of an individual.

The ethical values of active concern for well-being and avoidance of harm also show substantial similarity over the centuries. In addition, the importance of developing and maintaining one's competence is a strong theme throughout the documents studied. Moving to the ethical principle of integrity, the documents are similar in their statements about the importance of telling the truth (with the possible exception of a dying patient) and avoiding conflicts of interest (putting patients' interests first).

The least similarity to ethical values related to the ethical principles of the *Universal Declaration of Ethical Principles for Psychologists* was with respect Principle IV (Professional and Scientific Responsibilities to Society). Although statements could be found about the concept of being concerned about all of humanity, the concept was not tied to responsibility to develop knowledge for this purpose. Also, only one statement could be found regarding the responsibility to adequately train new members in their ethical responsibilities and required competencies. This does not mean that such values did not exist over the 1st to 17th centuries, only that the selected guiding documents do not reflect them. It is possible that other documents (e.g., for physicians who taught medicine) might have addressed them.

The 18th and 19th Centuries of the Common Era (CE)

Two major documents from this two-century span are examined below: (1) *A Physician's Ethical Duties* (Reich, 1995); and (2) the *Medical Code of Ethics of the American Medical Association* (1847).

A Physician's Ethical Duties (Persia, 1770 CE) was part of the first chapter of the work, "Kholasah al Hekmah," written by Mohamed Hosin Aghili, a physician from Shiraz, Persia, during Persia's Islamic era. Included in the 23 duties is the admonishment that physicians should not be conceited, but rather remember that "the actual healer is God."

The *Medical Code of Ethics of the American Medical Association* (United States, 1847) was the first code of ethics for physicians developed in the United States. It was heavily based on the work *Medical Ethics* written in England by Thomas Percival in 1794. This latter document had been criticized severely in some quarters as more "a manual of medical etiquette" than a guide to medical ethics (Leake, 1927), and for ignoring the writings of ethicists such as Thomas Gisborne, who promulgated the concept of an unwritten, but voluntary and mutual, contract between physicians and those they served (Chapman, 1984). Of the *Medical Code of Ethics*' eleven sections, only two address the ethical responsibilities of physicians to their patients and the public. All other sections relate to physicians' responsibilities to each other and the profession, or the responsibilities of patients and the public to physicians.

Below are statements from the above two documents, selected for comparison with the four ethical principles of the 21st-century CE *Universal Declaration of Ethical Principles for Psychologists*. Each statement is followed by reference to the most relevant related value subsumed by the particular ethical principle. Once again, both similarities and differences are evident.

Respect for the Dignity of Persons and Peoples

He must not be proud of his class or his family and must not regard others with contempt.
(*A Physician's Ethical Duties*) (Value: unique worth and inherent dignity of all human beings)

A physician... must protect the patient's secrets and not betray them.
(*A Physician's Ethical Duties*) (Values: privacy, and confidentiality)

...none of the privacies of personal and domestic life, no infirmity of disposition or flaw of character observed during attendance should ever be divulged by him except when he is imperatively required to do so.
(*Medical Code of Ethics of the American Medical Association*) (Values, privacy, and confidentiality)

...such professional services should always be cheerfully and freely accorded.
(*Medical Code of Ethics of the American Medical Association*) (Value: fairness and justice)

Competent Caring for the Well-Being of Persons and Peoples

A physician should not only be ever ready to obey calls of the sick, but his mind ought also to be imbued with the greatness of his mission, and the responsibility he habitually incurs in its discharge.
(*Medical Code of Ethics of the American Medical Association*) (Value: active concern for well-being)

Every case committed to the charge of a physician should be treated with attention, steadiness and humanity.
(*Medical Code of Ethics of the American Medical Association*) (Value: active concern for well-being)

A physician... should never recommend any kind of fatal, harmful, or enfeebling drug.
(*A Physician's Ethical Duties*) (Value: taking care to do no harm)

He must never be tenacious in his opinion, and continue in his fault or mistake, but, if it possible, he is to consult with proficient physicians and ascertain the facts.
(*A Physician's Ethical Duties*) (Values: maximizing benefits, minimizing harm)

Consultations should be promoted in difficult or protracted cases, as they give rise to confidence, energy, and more enlarged views of practice.
(*Medical Code of Ethics of the American Medical Association*) (Values: maximizing benefits, minimizing harm)

A physician ought not to abandon a patient because the case is deemed incurable; for his attendance may continue to be highly useful to the patient, and comforting to the relatives around him, even in the last period of a fatal malady, by alleviating pain and other symptoms, and by soothing mental anguish.
(*Medical Code of Ethics of the American Medical Association*) (Values: maximizing benefits, minimizing harm)

Human life and human happiness must not be endangered by the incompetency of presumptuous pretenders.
(*Medical Code of Ethics of the American Medical Association*) (Value: developing and maintaining competence).

Integrity

Practice medicine with integrity... Do not replace precious herbal materials provided by the family of patients with inferior ones.
(*A Physician's Ethical Duties*) (Value: honesty)

A physician... must not hold his students or his patients under his obligation.
(*A Physician's Ethical Duties*) (Value: avoiding conflicts of interest)

...unnecessary visits are to be avoided as they... render him liable to be suspected of interested motives.
(*Medical Code of Ethics of the American Medical Association*) (Value: avoiding conflicts of interest)

He must never claim that he can cure an impoverished patient who has gone to many physicians...
(*A Physician's Ethical Duties*) (Value: truthfulness and openness)

But he should not fail, on proper occasions, to give to the friends of the patient timely notice

of danger... and even to the patient himself if absolutely necessary.
(*Medical Code of Ethics of the American Medical Association*)
(Value: truthfulness and openness)

Professional and Scientific Responsibilities to Society

On them devolves, in a peculiar manner, the task of noting all the circumstances affecting public health, and of displaying skill and ingenuity in devising the best means for its protection.
(*Medical Code of Ethics of the American Medical Association*) (Value: increasing knowledge in ways that promote the well-being of society and all its members)

As good citizens, it is the duty of physicians to be ever vigilant for the welfare of the community, and to bear their part in sustaining its institutions and burdens.
(*Medical Code of Ethics of the American Medical Association*) (Value: conducting its affairs in ways that promote the well-being of society and all its members)

He must not withhold medical knowledge; he should teach it to everyone in medicine without discrimination between poor and rich, noble or slave.
(*A Physician's Ethical Duties*) (Value: adequately training members in their ethical responsibilities and required competencies)

Summary and Conclusions: The 18th and 19th Centuries CE

Once again, although the two documents from the 18th and 19th centuries reviewed in this section are from two different parts of the world, and are different in structure and the sociopolitical context in which they were developed, examples of values related to the four ethical principles of the 21st-century CE *Universal Declaration of Ethical Principles for Psychologists* can be found. Both documents address the importance of privacy and confidentiality, active concern for well-being, maximizing benefits and minimizing harm, avoiding conflicts of interest, and truthfulness. *A Physician's Ethical Duties* further addresses inherent dignity, and taking care to do no harm. The *Medical Code of Ethics of the American Medical Association* further addresses fairness and justice, competence, increasing knowledge, and promoting the well-being of society and its members. Consent is not addressed in either document; however, there is no indication in either document that services could be administered without consent.

Early to Mid-20th Century of the Common Era (CE)

Two major documents from the beginning to the middle of the 20th century CE are examined below: (1) the *Nuremberg Code of Ethics in Medical Research* (Mappes & Zembaty, 1981); and (2) the American Psychological Association's 1958 *Ethical Standards of Psychologists* (APA, 1959). Due to the profound impact these documents had on the development of codes of ethics during the rest of the 20th century CE and into the 21st century CE, including codes of ethics for psychologists, the sociopolitical context of their development is outlined, and they are explored below in more detail than the other documents reviewed above, with interspersed commentary and explanation.

Prior to the development of either of the above documents, the early 20th century CE saw a burgeoning number of occupational groups being designated as professions (Sinclair, 1993; Sinclair, Simon, & Pettifor, 1996). Until the 19th century CE, the designation "profession" had been limited primarily to medicine, law, and theology. By the end of that century, the designation had been broadened to include a few other occupational groups (e.g., veterinary medicine, architecture, and engineering). However, due to an unprecedented explosion of specialized knowledge in the 20th century CE, and the need for a more structured division of labor in the application of that knowledge, increasingly more occupational groups were established. Many of these occupational groups claimed the designation "profession." The 20th century CE became known as the time of the "professionalization of society." One of the key requirements to such a claim is the generation of a code of ethics (Kultgen, 1988). The new professions looked primarily to existing examples to help them establish their own codes. The best known were those in the medical profession. Even so, very few of the new professions, including psychology, had their own codes of ethics by the beginning of the Second World War in 1939.

Events of the Second World War, in particular the research carried out primarily by physicians on the inmates of concentration camps, acted as a catalyst for the development of professional codes of ethics following the war. The research in concentration camps had been carried out without informed consent, on unwilling participants, and almost invariably was harmful, often resulting in the death of the participant. When these events came to light, the *Nuremberg Code of Ethics in Medical Research* was developed in 1946 for judicial use in the war crimes trials in Germany, to judge the physicians who had been involved in the research (Kanovitch, 1998; Mappes & Zembaty, 1981). Medical codes of ethics had been available to the physicians involved in the concentration camp research; however, such codes dealt primarily with ethical principles as applied to the provision of service, not as applied to research. The physicians tried to justify their actions as beneficial in that they were increasing scientific knowledge that would benefit society. They argued that this was more important than the harm to their research participants.

The atrocities in concentration camps acted as a wakeup call to all existing professions regarding the need to codify their ethical principles, values, and behavioral expectations, and to clarify what must take precedence when competing principles and values come into play. Shortly after the Second World War, the American Psychological Association (APA) started work on what was to become the first major code of ethics for psychologists. Hobbs (1948) described the 1947 appointment of the Committee on Ethical Standards for Psychologists by the president of the APA and the criteria to be used in the development of a code of ethics. A second article (APA, 1949) described the 2-year plan for developing such a code. The first year was to be devoted to collecting and classifying descriptions of incidents requiring ethical choices; the second year was to be devoted to a critical examination of these incidents, and the formulation and testing of ethical principles derived from them. By 1952, the APA had developed and adopted provisional ethical standards based on the work of the Committee. In 1958, the APA gave final approval (for a 3-year trial period) of a revision of the 1952 draft (APA, 1959). Organized under 18 headings called "principles," ethical standards described the responsibilities and expected behaviors of psychologists. Even before its final adoption, however, this code, the process used to develop it, and its draft versions had served and were continuing to serve as a model for the development of ethics codes for psychologists in other countries, and for other disciplines (Bloom, 1964; Bondy, 1959; Hall, 1952; Lee, 1953; Pacaud, 1954). The 1958 version contained more detailed articulation of each of the ethical principles being discussed in this chapter than any of the other documents reviewed above. It also addressed responsibilities as they related to the different roles of psychologists; namely, teacher, practitioner, and researcher.

Respect for the Dignity of Persons and Peoples

Although the *Nuremberg Code of Ethics in Medical Research* is different from the other codes discussed in this paper, insofar as it was written for a judicial purpose and was directed to physicians' roles in research rather than in service, some of the key ethical values related to each of the ethical principles of *Universal Declaration of Ethical Principles for Psychologists* were addressed, sometimes in a unique way.

For instance, the *Nuremberg Code* made one of its most profound contributions to today's professional codes of ethics by combining truthfulness and consent into the concept of free and informed consent (Sinclair, 1993), challenging the primary reliance up to that time on an ethic of professional "beneficence":

> The voluntary consent of the human subject is absolutely essential. This means that the person involved should have the legal capacity to give consent; should be so situated as to be able to exercise free power of choice, without the intervention of any element of force, fraud, deceit, duress, overreaching, or other ulterior form of constraint or coercion; and should have sufficient knowledge and comprehension of the elements of the subject matter involved to enable him to make an understanding and enlightened decision. This latter element requires that before the acceptance of an affirmative decision by the experimental subject there should be made known to him the nature, duration, and purpose of the experiment; the method and means by which it is to be conducted; all inconveniences and hazards reasonably to be expected; and the effects upon his health or person which may possibly come from his participation in the experiments.
> (Article 1)

Unlike the *Nuremberg Code of Ethics in Medical Research*, which did not mention privacy or confidentiality, the APA 1958 *Ethical Standards of Psychologists* devoted an entire section or "principle" to confidentiality, providing significantly more detail about a professional's duties with respect to this value than had been provided in any other of the documents reviewed above.

> Safeguarding information about an individual that has been obtained by the psychologist in the course of his practice or investigation is a primary obligation of the psychologist.
> (Principle 6)

Information received in confidence is revealed only after most careful deliberation and when there is clear and imminent danger to an individual or to society...
(Principle 6a)

Clinical and other case materials are used in classroom teaching and writing only when the identity of the person involved is adequately disguised.
(Principle 6c)

Only after explicit permission has been granted is the identity of research subjects published...
(Principle 6e)

Although the APA 1958 *Ethical Standards of Psychologists* never used the term "informed consent," it clearly espoused the concept, and extended it beyond research:

The psychologist who asks an individual to reveal personal information...does so only after making certain that the responsible person is fully aware of the purposes...and of the ways in which the information might be used.
(Principle 7d)

The psychologist informs his prospective client of the important aspects of the potential relationship that might affect the client's decision to enter the relationship.
(Principle 8)

When a possibility of serious after effects exists, research is conducted only when the subjects or their responsible agents are fully informed of this possibility and volunteer nevertheless.
(Principle 16b)

Competent Caring for the Well-Being of Persons and Peoples

A second major contribution of the *Nuremberg Code of Ethics in Medical Research* to professional ethics was its codification of the need to consider the balance of risks and benefits, the unacceptability of doing harm to research participants, and clearly stating that when benefits and harm to society are in conflict with benefits and harm to an individual research participant, concern for the research participant must be given precedence; for instance:

The experiment should be such as to yield fruitful results for the good of society, unprocurable by other methods or means of study, and not random and unnecessary in nature.
(Article 2)

The experiment should be so conducted as to avoid all unnecessary physical and mental suffering and injury.
(Article 4)

No experiment should be conducted where there is an *a priori* reason to believe that death or disabling injury will occur...
(Article 5)

During the course of the experiment the scientist in charge must be prepared to terminate the experiment at any stage, if he has probable cause to believe...that a continuation of the experiment is likely to result in injury, disability, or death to the experimental subject.
(Article 10)

With respect to the values of active concern for well-being, doing no harm, maximizing benefit and minimizing harm, and offsetting or correcting harm, the following examples can be found in the APA 1958 *Ethical Standards of Psychologists*:

The psychologist...protects the welfare of the person or group with whom he is working.
(Principle 7)

When there is a conflict among professional workers, the psychologist is concerned primarily with the welfare of any client involved and only secondarily with the interest of his own professional group.
(Principle 7b)

The psychologist attempts to terminate a clinical or consulting relationship when it is reasonably clear to the psychologist that the client is not benefiting from it.
(Principle 7c)

The psychologist...protects the examinees by insuring that the tests and test results are used in a professional manner.
(Principle 7f)

The psychologist seriously considers the possible harmful after effects and removes them as soon as permitted by the design of the experiment.
(Principle 16c)

With respect to the value of developing and maintaining competence, the *Nuremberg Code* states that only those who are competent should be engaged in any particular research study:

> The experiment should be conducted only by scientifically qualified persons. The highest degree of skill and care should be required through all stages of the experiment of those who conduct or engage in the experiment.
> (Article 8)

The APA 1958 *Ethical Standards of Psychologists* devotes an entire section to competence, delineating a positive duty to be competent, as well as to stay within the limits of one's competence.

> The maintenance of high standards of professional competence is a responsibility shared by all psychologists...
> (Principle 2)

> The psychologist recognizes the boundaries of his competence and the limitations of his techniques and does not offer services or use techniques that fail to meet professional standards established in particular fields.
> (Principle 2b)

> ...he refrains from undertaking any activity in which his personal limitations are likely to result in inferior professional services or harm to a client; or, if he is already engaged in such an activity when he becomes aware of his limitations, he seeks competent professional consultation.
> (Principle 2c)

Integrity

As noted above, in its demand for and definition of free and informed consent, the *Nuremberg Code of Ethics in Medical Research* combined both the value of truthfulness and consent.

Truthfulness also was emphasized in the APA 1958 *Ethical Standards of Psychologists*, with a level of detail that went beyond most previous guiding ethics documents. For instance:

> The psychologist...places high value on objectivity and integrity...
> (Principle 1)

> The psychologist avoids misrepresentation of his own professional qualifications, affiliations, and purposes, and those of the institutions and organizations with which he is associated.
> (Principle 4)

> Psychologists who interpret the science of psychology or the services of psychologists to clients or to the general public have an obligation to report fairly and accurately. Exaggeration, sensationalism, superficiality, and other kinds of misrepresentation are avoided.
> (Principle 5a)

On the other hand, unlike the *Nuremberg Code*, the APA 1958 *Ethical Standards of Psychologists* allowed temporary misinformation to be given to research participants in some limited circumstances:

> Only when a problem is significant and can be investigated no other way is the psychologist justified in giving misinformation to research subjects...
> (Principle 16)

Professional and Scientific Responsibilities to Society

Insofar as the *Nuremberg Code of Ethics in Medical Research* was used to judge physicians in the Nuremberg military tribunals, responsibility to society can be inferred. However, responsibility also is addressed in relationship to consent, as follows:

> The duty and responsibility for ascertaining the quality of the consent rests upon each individual who initiates, directs, or engages in the experiment. It is a personal duty and responsibility which may not be delegated to another with impunity.
> (Article 1)

The 1958 APA code makes several strong statements about psychologists taking responsibility for both the quality and outcomes of their activities. Although structures for external accountability to society were only in their infancy (Sinclair, Simon, & Pettifor, 1996), it is clear that psychologists were viewed as accountable not just to their professional community, but to society as a whole. For instance:

> As a practitioner, the psychologist knows that he bears a heavy social responsibility because his work may touch intimately the lives of others.
> (Principle 1c)

> As a teacher, the psychologist recognizes his primary obligation to help others acquire knowledge and skill...
> (Principle 1b)

> ...When a psychologist or a person identifying himself as a psychologist violates ethical standards, psychologists who know firsthand of such activities attempt to rectify the situation. When such a situation cannot be dealt with informally, it is called to the attention of the appropriate local, state, or

national committee on professional ethics, standards, and practices.

(Principle 2a)

The psychologist in the practice of his profession shows sensible regard for the social codes and moral expectations of the community in which he works…

(Principle 3)

…He is willing to contribute a portion of his services to work for which he receives little or no financial return.

(Principle 12a)

Summary and Conclusions: Early to Mid-20th Century CE

The first half of the 20th century CE saw rapid and significant changes in the professional and political landscape. An increasing number of professions developed throughout the world, including psychology, yet codes of ethics were primarily limited to the practice of medicine until the Second World War. Although there is evidence that psychology organizations in various countries saw the need for codifying their ethical principles and values to guide members (e.g., Dunbar, 1998), little was done until after the Second World War (Sinclair, 1993). The atrocities of harmful experiments, carried out without consent in concentration camps during the war, led to the seminal *Nuremberg Code of Ethics in Medical Research* and served as a wakeup call to all professions. The American Psychological Association provided leadership at the time, beginning a comprehensive and lengthy process in 1948 that eventually led to the approval of a detailed code of ethics in 1958. This code served as a model for other psychology organizations in many other countries. However, much more was to come.

Mid-20th Century CE to the Present

Over the latter half of the 20th century CE and the first decade of the current century, over 40 national psychology organizations developed their own codes of ethics. (For a list, see http://www.iupsys.net/index.php/resources/ethics/131-list-of-codes-of-international-organizations). During the first four decades, most of these codes adopted the basic structure of the APA 1958 *Ethical Standards of Psychologists*. However, during the last two decades, partly due to the work of the Canadian Psychological Association (CPA), the structure of new and revised codes of ethics began to change.

Canada was one of a few countries that adopted the American Psychological Association code for use in its own country. With only a few wording changes (e.g., "state" changed to "province"), the 1958 APA code and its 1963 and 1977 revisions were adopted and used. However, after about a decade, signs of discontent among Canadian psychologists became evident when various revisions were suggested or occurred, some of which CPA Board meeting minutes described as "clearly designed for the current American social and moral climate, and geared to American traditions and law" (Dunbar, 1998). Rather than adopt the 1979 revision of the APA code, the Canadian Psychological Association began the development of its own code, the *Canadian Code of Ethics for Psychologists* (CPA, 1986, 1991, 2000).

The steps taken to develop the *Canadian Code* are detailed elsewhere (Sinclair, Poizner, Gilmour-Barrett, & Randall, 1987; Sinclair, 1998). However, in summary, the process first involved a review of the international and interdisciplinary literature regarding codes of ethics, and the identification of four main purposes for such codes: (a) to help establish a group as a profession; (b) to act as a support and guide to individual professionals; (c) to help meet the responsibilities of being a profession; and (d) to provide a statement of moral principle that helps individual professionals resolve ethical dilemmas. It was noted that many codes of ethics, including the APA code, were organized around "principles" that were sometimes areas of practice (e.g., Assessment Techniques) and sometimes ethical principles (e.g., Welfare of the Consumer). In addition, they did not always tie standards to specific ethical principles, and offered little guidance when ethical principles or ethical responsibilities conflicted with one another. Early in the development of the *Canadian Code*, a decision was made to try to provide a code organized around a moral framework that could give more guidance to psychologists, including guidelines for action when ethical principles or responsibilities are in conflict. In a study that involved Canadian psychologists resolving hypothetical ethical dilemmas, four umbrella ethical principles were derived: I. Respect for the Dignity of Persons; II. Responsible Caring; III. Integrity in Relationships; and IV. Responsibility to Society. Ethical standards were grouped into four main sections, each related to one of the ethical principles. In each section, the ethical principle first was explained in terms of the ethical values subsumed by the principle, and in terms of psychological activities impacted by the values. In addition, the *Canadian Code* ordered the four main sections according to the weight each generally should be given when the principles are in conflict, and included a suggested set of decision-making steps for ethical decision making. First adopted in 1986, these elements remained constant across the two revisions of the *Code* (adopted in 1991 and 2000), indicating that the moral-framework path taken in developing the *Canadian Code* had worked well for Canadian psychologists.

The formal ordering of ethical principles has remained unique to the *Canadian Code*. However, use of a moral-framework format (i.e., specifying four to six broad ethical principles, explaining each ethical principle in terms of subsumed values, and organizing all behavioral-expectation standards around the ethical principles) has been adopted by some other national psychology organizations since the 1990s when developing or revising their ethics codes. Examples include Ireland (Psychological Society of Ireland, 1999) and New Zealand (New Zealand Psychological Society, 2002).

A further significant use of the moral-framework format has been the development of templates designed to be used in the development of country-specific codes by organizations representing countries that are different in culture, religion, and/or politico-legal context. Two examples are the *Meta-Code of Ethics* developed by the European Federation of Professional Psychologists' Associations[4] (EFPPA, 1995) and the *Universal Declaration of Ethical Principles for Psychologists* adopted in 2008 by the International Union of Psychological Science and the International Association of Applied Psychology. Both of these documents arose from a recognition similar to the Canadian Psychological Association's recognition; namely, that the specific standards of behavior in one country's ethics code, while based primarily on ethical principles that had broad acceptance across countries, were also influenced by the "social and moral climate" and the "traditions and laws" that are specific to that country and not necessarily appropriate or acceptable in another country.

In 1990, EFPPA established a Task Force on Ethics with the initial aim of developing a common ethics code for European psychologists. However, it was quickly evident that differences in culture, worldview, history, and legal structure across member countries were barriers to the consensus that would be required to agree on specific ethical standards of behavior across all countries (Lindsay, 2008). Instead, the Task Force decided to concentrate on developing a moral-framework template of ethical principles and values about which consensus could be found and which could (and was expected) to be used by member psychology organizations to revise or develop their own more specific codes of ethics. The resulting *Meta-Code of Ethics* was organized around four ethical principles, each in its own section: (a) Respect for a Person's Rights and Dignity; (b) Competence; (c) Responsibility, and (d) Integrity. Each ethical principle is explained briefly, and then followed by a series of brief statements outlining more specific values related to the principle (e.g., the section titled Respect for a Person's Rights and Dignity contains statements related to confidentiality and privacy, informed consent and freedom of consent, etc.) The first version of the *Meta-Code* was adopted by EFPPA in 1995. A revised version, highly similar to the first, was adopted in 2005. The *Meta-Code* has been used since its first adoption as a framework for developing or revising European countries' codes of ethics for psychologists. The majority of such use has been within individual countries. One exception, however, is the Nordic countries (Denmark, Finland, Iceland, Norway, and Sweden) which, probably due to a shared history and overlap in culture, had been able to develop and agree to a common code of ethics in 1988. In 1998, this code, the *Ethical Principles for Nordic Psychologists*, was revised to be in accordance with the *Meta-Code* (Aanonson, 2003).

At about the same time as the *Meta-Code* was first approved, a similar development was occurring in South America where, in 1997, six countries signed the *Protocol of the Framework Agreement of Ethical Principles for the Professional Practice of Psychology in the Mercosur and Associated Countries* (Gauthier & Pettifor, 2011). In this situation, no common association of psychology organizations existed. However, representatives of organizations from the six countries (Argentina, Bolivia, Brazil, Chile, Paraguay, and Uruguay) came together to both define the scope of practice of psychology in their countries and to develop a moral-framework template for psychological practice. The *Protocol* contained five general ethical principles: (a) Respect for People's Rights and Dignity, (b) Competence, (c) Professional and Scientific Commitment, (d) Integrity, and (e) Social Responsibility. As with other documents that used the moral-framework format, each ethical principle is followed by a few statements outlining subsumed values. For instance, the principle of Respect for People's Rights and Dignity includes statements about not engaging in discriminatory practice and respecting privacy and confidentiality.

The most recent, distinct, and challenging contribution to ethics in psychology has been the development of the *Universal Declaration of Ethical Principles for Psychologists*, which was unanimously adopted in 2008 by the International Union of Psychological Science (IUPsyS) and the International Association of Applied Psychology (IAAP) (Gauthier, 2008a, 2008b, 2009; Ferrero & Gauthier, 2009). The *Universal Declaration* was the result of a 6-year process "involving careful research, broad international consultation, and numerous revisions in response to feedback and suggestions from the international psychology community" (Gauthier & Pettifor, 2011). Led by Dr. Janel Gauthier, a working group of psychologists representing different continents, cultures, and worldviews developed the *Declaration*. The final document contains the following four principles: (a) Respect for the Dignity of Persons and Peoples; (b) Competent Caring for the Well-being of Persons and Peoples; (c) Integrity; and (d) Professional and Scientific Responsibilities to Society. It is these four principles that are used above to review ethics documents from ancient times to the middle of the 20th century CE.

The objectives of the *Universal Declaration*, as articulated in its preamble, are to assist psychologist organizations across the world to: (a) evaluate the ethical and moral relevance of their codes of ethics; (b) serve as a template to guide the development or evolution of their codes of ethics; (c) encourage global thinking about ethics, while also encouraging action that is sensitive and responsive to local needs and values; and (d) speak with a collective voice on matters of ethical concern. Its intent is to support ethical behavior by psychologists that is appropriate to local culture(s), but also to encourage psychologists to see themselves as part of a global psychological community with a commitment to the betterment of society as a whole:

> It reaffirms the commitment of the psychology community to help build a better world where peace, freedom, responsibility, justice, humanity, and morality prevail.
> (*Universal Declaration of Ethical Principles for Psychologists*, Preamble)

Summary and Conclusions: Mid-20th Century CE to the Present

The past five decades have been a period of rapid development in the articulation of ethical principles, values, and codes for psychologists. Building on the work of the American Psychological Association, psychologists in many countries began developing their own codes of ethics. However, as the world became more global, and as individual countries became more multicultural in nature, it became increasingly difficult to rely on ethics codes that were based on a single worldview. A partial solution to this was developing templates for codes of ethics. Such templates provided a moral framework that emphasized ethical principles and values held in common. In this way, specification of behavioral standards in particular codes of ethics is left to local regions or individual countries, ensuring that the specific behavioral expectations are respectful of and consistent with local cultures and worldviews.

Conclusion

And so our historical journey has now arrived at 2012. As with all journeys, there are people and places that remain unexplored due to limitations of time or space, or both. However, it is hoped that the overview provided in this chapter has allowed us to see that there has been considerable similarity in ethical principles and values since ancient times. Although the vehicles used to articulate them in a way that can guide professionals have varied widely—from laws, to oaths, to prayers, to formal codification—it is evident that the ethical principles and values we espouse as psychologists in today's world were not "invented" by us; rather, they have deep roots to the past and reflect our common humanity.

Notes

1. Centuries and approximate years are identified either as BCE (before the Common Era) or as CE (of the Common Era). Exact years are not identified in this way and can be assumed to be CE.

2. Post (2003) and Reich (1995) refer to the 3rd and 2nd editions, respectively, of *Biomedical Ethics*. As this encyclopedia comprises five volumes and the later edition may not be available in all libraries, both editions are referenced. All historical ethics documents appear in Volume 5 of these two editions. They also can be retrieved from http://www.bioethics.org.au/

3. See Footnote 2.

4. Now called the European Federation of Psychologists' Associations (EFPA).

References

Aanonson, A. (2003). EFPA Meta-Code on ethics and the Nordic Code. In D. Wedding & M. J. Stevens (Eds.), *Psychology: IUPsyS Global Resource*. (2008 ed.). [Computer software]. Hove, UK: Psychology Press.

American College of Physicians, Ad Hoc Committee on Medical Ethics. (1984). Part I: History of medical ethics, the physician and the patient, the physician's relationship to other physicians, the physician and society. *Annals of Internal Medicine, 101*, 129–137.

American Psychological Association, Committee on Ethical Standards for Psychologists. (1949). Developing a code of ethics; a first report of progress. *American Psychologist, 4,* 17.

American Psychological Association. (1959). Ethical standards of psychologists. *American Psychologist, 14,* 279–282.

Bloom, B. L. (1964). The code of ethics of the French Psychological Society. *American Psychologist, 19,* 183–185.

Bondy, C. (1959). Die ethischen Grenzen psychologischor Arbeit [Ethical limits of psychological investigations]. *Psychologische Rundschau, 10,* 237–250.

Canadian Psychological Association. (1986). *Canadian code of ethics for psychologists.* Ottawa, ON: Author.

Canadian Psychological Association. (1991). *Canadian code of ethics for psychologists. Revised.* Ottawa, ON: Author.

Canadian Psychological Association. (2000). *Canadian code of ethics for psychologists* (3rd ed.). Ottawa, ON: Author.

Chapman, C. B. (1984). *Physicians, law, and ethics.* New York: New York University Press.

Dunbar, J. (1998). A critical history of CPA's various codes of ethics for psychologists (1939–1986). *Canadian Psychology, 39,* 177–186.

European Federation of Professional Psychologists Associations. (1995). *Meta-code of ethics.* Brussels, Belgium: Author.

Gauthier, J. (2006). Onward toward a universal declaration of ethical principles for psychologists: Draft and progress report. In M. J. Stevens & D. Wedding (Eds.), *Psychology: IUPsyS Global Resource* [Computer software]. Hove, UK: Psychology Press.

Gauthier, J. (2008a). IAAP adopts the Universal Declaration of Ethical Principles for Psychologists. *The IAAP Bulletin: The International Association of Applied Psychology, 20*(4), 110–112.

Gauthier, J. (2008b). The Universal Declaration of Ethical Principles of Psychologists presented at the United Nations DPI/NGO Conference in Paris. *Psychology International, 19*(4), October. Retrieved from *http://www.apa.org/international/pi/1008gauthier.html.*

Gauthier, J. (2009). Ethical principles and human rights: Building a better world globally. *Counselling Psychology Quarterly, 22,* 25–32.

Gauthier, J., & Pettifor, J. L. (2011). The evolution of ethics in psychology: Going international and global. In P. R. Martin, F. M. Cheung, M. C. Knowles, L. Littlefield, J. B. Overmeier, & J. M. Prieto (Eds.), *IAAP handbook on applied psychology* (pp. 700–714). Oxford, UK: Blackwell Publishing Limited.

Hall, L. K. (1952). Group workers and professional ethics. *Group, 15,* 3–8.

Hobbs, N. (1948). The development of a code of ethical standards for psychology. *American Psychologist, 3,* 80–84.

Kanovitch, B. (1998). The medical experiments in Nazi concentration camps. In U. Tröhler & Stellas Reiter-Theil (Eds.), *Ethics codes in medicine: Foundations and achievements of codification since 1947* (pp. 60–70). Brookfield, VT: Ashgate Publishing.

King, L. W. (2004). *The code of Hammurabi.* Whitefish, MT: Kessinger Publishing.

Kultgen, J. (1998). *Ethics and professionalism.* Philadelphia, PA: University of Pennsylvania Press.

Leake, C. D. (1927). *Percival's medical ethics.* Baltimore, MD: Williams & Wilkins.

Lee, A. M. (1953). Responsibilities and privileges in sociological research. *Sociology and Social Research, 37,* 367–374.

Lindsay, G. (2008). Professional ethics and psychology. In G. Lindsay, C. Koene, H. Øvreeide, & F. Lang (eds.), *Ethics for European psychologists* (pp. 1–14). Gottingen, Germany: Hogrefe & Huber Publishers.

Mappes, T. A., & Zembaty, J. S. (1981). *Biomedical ethics.* Toronto, ON: McGraw-Hill.

New Zealand Psychological Society. (2002). *Code of ethics for psychologists working in Aotearoa/New Zealand.* Wellington, New Zealand: Author.

Pacaud, S. (1954). La deontologie et l'organization de la profession. [Ethics and the organization of the profession.] *Revue de Psychologie Appliquée, 4,* 13–19.

Pandya, S. K. (2000). History of medical ethics in India. *Eubios Journal of International Bioethics, 10,* 40–44.

Post, S. G. (Ed.) (2003). *Encyclopedia of bioethics* (Vol. 5, 3rd ed.). New York, NY: MacMillan.

Psychological Society of Ireland. (1999). *Code of professional ethics.* Dublin, Ireland: Author.

Reich, W. T. (Ed.). (1995). *Encyclopedia of bioethics* (Vol. 5, rev. ed.). New York, NY: MacMillan.

Sinclair, C. (1993). Codes of ethics and standards of practice. In K. S. Dobson & D. J. G. Dobson (Eds.), *Professional psychology in Canada* (pp. 167–199). Germany: Hogrefe & Huber.

Sinclair, C. (1998). Nine unique features of the Canadian Code of Ethics for Psychologists. *Canadian Psychology, 39,* 167–176.

Sinclair, C., Poizner, S., Gilmour-Barrett, K., & Randall, D. (1987). The development of a code of ethics for Canadian psychologists. *Canadian Psychology, 28,* 1–8.

Sinclair, C., Simon, N. P., & Pettifor, J. L. (1996). The history of ethics codes and licensure. In L. J. Bass, D. T. DeMers, J. R. Ogloff, C. Peterson, J. L. Pettifor, R. P. Reaves, T. Rétfalvi, N. P. Simon, C. Sinclair, & R. M. Tipton (Eds.), *Professional conduct and discipline in psychology* (pp. 143–154). Washington, DC: American Psychological Association, & Montgomery, AL: Association of State and Provincial Psychology Boards.

Universal Declaration of Ethical Principles for Psychologists. (2008). Retrieved from http://www.iupsys.org/ethics/univdecl2008.html

CHAPTER 2

An International Perspective on Ethics Codes for Psychology: A Focus on Test Development and Use

Thomas Oakland, Mark M. Leach, Dave Bartram, Geoff Lindsay, Ann-Charlotte Smedler, and Houcan Zhang

Abstract

The purpose of this chapter is to describe and discuss the international status of ethics codes and other documents that address test development and use in light of fundamental characteristics of such codes. The selection of issues associated with test development and use to assist in a discussion of ethics codes was due, in part, to the early onset and international nature of their development and use. Models of ethics codes and documents are examined, including similarities and differences in their emphasis on principles and standards, as well as professionals impacted by a code. Test issues are discussed in light of codes and documents that apply to individual countries, a regional code for countries that have considerable diversity, a regional code for countries that have considerable cultural consistency, and internationally. Information in this article may assist national psychological associations engaged in developing or revising their ethics codes.

Key Words: international ethics codes, test development, EFPA, ITC, ethical standards, ethical principles

A professional association and the people its members serve form an implied social contract. The people, through their public and private support, establish institutions utilized by professions to educate and prepare students for service, to conduct research, to engage in public policy, and in other ways prepare to serve the public good. In turn, people expect professions to serve society well, including persons from diverse backgrounds and various locations. Minimally, members of a profession are expected to do no harm.

The presence of a strong professional association generally signifies the presence of relatively large numbers of psychologists who are qualified to serve the public. In turn, the public recognizes the value of their testing, teaching, research, clinical, public policy, and other services (e.g., often through legislation that restricts the use of titles and services). Mature professional associations assume leadership for the development of ethics codes. Psychological associations have been formed in more than 70 countries, including those that hold membership in the International Union of Psychological Science. Many of these associations have developed ethics codes that address practice issues. However, most countries do not have a professional association for psychology. Thus, psychologists practicing in many countries are unlikely to be bound by a nationally approved ethics code.

Purposes of Ethics Codes

Ethics codes generally serve four purposes. First and foremost, they educate members of the profession and the public as to behaviors consumers can expect from a profession. Second, ethics codes promote public trust of members of a profession, a quality indispensable to the provision of effective professional services. Third, ethics codes often embody legislative, administrative, and judicial policy, thus linking ethics and laws, public policy, and practice. Fourth, ethics codes enable professionals working in institutions that may not have ethics codes to advocate for high ethical standards. Additionally, professionals who violate the public trust through an ethics code violation may be sanctioned and even barred from practice in countries that have such enforcement mechanisms (Koocher & Keith-Spiegel, 2008; Ritchie, 2008).

Virtues, Principles, and Standards

Ethics codes differ in their reliance on virtues, principles, and standards. These terms differ in their specificity.

Virtues. The term *virtue*, the broadest term, generally refers to moral excellence. Thus, persons who are virtuous display exemplary morals honored by the society in which they practice. Few ethics codes emphasize virtues.

Principles. The term *principles* refers to broad rules of conduct and is aspirational. Examples may include doing no harm (nonmaleficence), acting benevolently, displaying fidelity and integrity, respecting the rights of others, and promoting justice. Principles-based codes encourage professionals to reflect on what may be the correct thing to do; such codes do not address specific required behaviors.

Standards. The term *standards* refers to specific behaviors established by general consent that professionals are obligated to demonstrate. For example, in reference to test use, standards may *require* a psychologist to obtain informed consent prior to testing, use measures that reflect high standards of reliability and validity, explain test results to examinees, and maintain test security. Ethics codes that emphasize standards require more detailed and specific behaviors and are more enforceable than those that emphasize principles. Although some ethics codes include only principles, many codes include both principles and standards (e.g., the ethics code from the American Psychological Association, APA). Compared to principles-based codes, standards-based codes may need to be revised more frequently due to their focus on specific behaviors that may be subject to change.

Standards versus Guidelines. An understanding of differences between *standards* and *guidelines* is important. The term *standards* generally is used in ethics codes when the professional association and/or licensing bodies that adopt the code have an infrastructure to enforce the code by receiving and resolving ethical complaints. Ethical standards can be implemented effectively only following the establishment of this administrative infrastructure. In contrast, the term *guidelines* refers to laudatory and desired behaviors. This term may be used when a professional association and/or licensing bodies have not developed an administrative infrastructure and thus lack the ability to enforce the code. Some professional associations at the national and regional levels, and all associations at the international level, lack this infrastructure and thus tend to use the term *guidelines* rather than *standards*. The International Organization for Standardization (ISO) is an exception. It uses the term *standard* to specify what shall and shall not be done (e.g., the ISO standard of assessment in work and organizational settings; http://www.iso.org/iso/home.htm).

To Whom Ethics Codes Apply

National ethics codes are developed by national psychological organizations and vary significantly as to their breadth, content areas, and structure. Persons who are members of the profession that developed the code, as well as those who are certified or licensed by agencies that have adopted the code, are expected to adhere to the code. However, a code's impact may be broader, including those whose professional practices include the provision of services that rely on the discipline's knowledge and technology (e.g., tests). Although they may not be members of the profession that developed the code or governed by agencies that adopt it, their practices may be held to its principles and/or standards.

Test Use, Development, and International Ethics

Test development and use have a long history and predate most if not all other common psychological services. Approximately 3000 years ago China developed a system that relied heavily on tests to identify civil servants. It continued until the beginning of the 20th century and became a model for civil service examination systems in other countries (Higgins & Sun, 2002).

National ethics codes reflect a country's culture, including its history, customs, and practices. For example, countries differ in their acceptance and use of clinical services, including test use. Although test use is universal, test availability is most abundant in Western European countries as well as Australia, Canada, Israel, New Zealand, and the United

States. Historically, their use has been less frequent in Central and South American, African, Middle Eastern, Asian, and Russian Federation countries (Hu & Oakland, 1991). However, the pattern of test use globally is changing, in part due to Internet delivery and increased test use in China, India, and the Russian Federation.

National ethics codes differ considerably in the extent to which they address test development and use. Ethics issues associated with test development and use are found in some but not all countries that have well-established codes. Moreover, the ethics codes in some countries that commonly use tests do not address testing issues. For example, a review of ethics codes from 35 countries found wide variations in the extent to which they addressed test development and use (Leach & Oakland, 2007). Ethics codes from approximately one-third of the countries did not address test development or use, including codes from four Western countries (i.e., Canada, Great Britain, Spain, and Switzerland). Ethics codes from countries with specific standards for test development and use ranged from giving these issues little to considerable attention. Ethics standards commonly require an explanation of test results and proper test use, limit test use by unqualified individuals, and restrict test purchase and reproduction. In contrast, few codes address issues related to test construction and restricting the use of obsolete tests.

However, an absence of test standards within national ethics codes may not indicate that test ethics documents do not exist in those countries. Some codes rely heavily on principles and therefore are not likely to include specific standards for any practice domain (e.g., psychotherapy, testing). Nevertheless, these principles are intended to address all common practice areas, including testing. In addition, some national codes may not include specific domain areas such as testing because they are addressed in other documents. For example, although the British Psychological Society's ethics code does not address test issues, its Division of Occupational Psychology adopted an ethics code that includes testing. Canada's national code does not address test use and instead encourages psychologists engaged in testing to use the *Standards for Educational and Psychological Testing* (American Educational Research Association, American Psychological Association, and National Council for Measurement in Education, 1999), albeit a document that addresses professional rather than ethical issues.

Ethics Code Models and Their Geographic Impact

Ethics codes differ in their models and geographic impact. A code may be developed by an association in one country, associations in a larger number of countries that are unified in other ways, associations in a small number of countries with shared cultural values and a somewhat common history, and international associations. The major features of ethics codes in psychology, including their similarities and differences, are described below. The codes typically highlight principles and some include standards. Test issues are used as examples.

Two Single Country Codes: The People's Republic of China and the United States of America. The ethics codes from the Chinese Psychological Society (CPS) and the American Psychological Association (APA) are two single country codes among the 44 codes included on the International Union of Psychological Science's web page (http://www.iupsys.net/). These two were selected for discussion due to their potential impact on large numbers of persons served by the profession of psychology; their vastly different histories, cultures, and ethics code development; and their relatively comprehensive coverage of ethics issues. In addition, the CPS code is rather new, discussed rarely in the literature, and deserves broader recognition. The APA code was the first national psychological ethics code. A summary of some relevant conditions in the People's Republic of China and the United States that stimulated the development of these codes is likely to promote an understanding of them.

Historic and Cultural Conditions in the People's Republic of China. Although some may cite the history of psychology in China as long and distinguished, most scholars consider psychology's modern history was established in the late 1970s after a 10-year hiatus during Mao Zedong's imposed Cultural Revolution. China's economic reforms during the early 1980s resulted in economic progress and triggered many social and personal changes, including the move of large numbers of people from rural to urban areas resulting in family dislocation and personal disharmony. The need for psychological services, including counseling and psychotherapy, grew rapidly. However, few professionals were prepared to respond to this need. Thus, others began providing counseling and psychotherapy services. Some lacked an academic degree and received only brief training (e.g., 1 to 3 months) in clinical methods. Additionally, test development and use again became important, in part to support the country's organizational and industrial expansion.

In 1992 the CPS developed its first codes of ethics: *Regulation for the Management of Mental Tests* and the *Ethical Code for Psychologists of Mental Tests*. This code addressed both regulatory and ethical issues related to test use (e.g., registering all tests with the CPS's Specialized Committee for Mental Tests, establishing qualifications of users, and controlling tests) and emphasized principles (e.g., psychologists must be aware of their social responsibilities and the importance of cooperation and respect). A few ethics standards also were included (e.g., "When using mental tests as the reference basis for diagnosis...or other important policy decisions, those using the tests must choose an appropriate test and adopt specified examination steps..." III.8). The Chinese government endorsed the code, thus mandating its use.

During a similar time period the China Mental Health Association adopted the 1993 Regulations of Psychological Counseling and Psychotherapy that addressed professional responsibility as well as professional qualifications and requirements (e.g., loving one's country and maintaining a calm, professional demeanor). This code lacked organization and continuity. Importantly, the Chinese government did not endorse it, thus resulting in its limited use.

In 2007 the CPS adopted an ethics code for psychotherapy and psychological counseling services, thus updating and expanding the 1992 code (http://www.cpsbeijing.org/en/index.php). This new code addresses various psychological practices found commonly in other ethics codes (e.g., therapy, testing, teaching, research) and mirrors the growth of psychology in China. Those individuals developing the Chinese code examined ethics codes from other national professional associations (e.g., Psychological Society of South Africa and the APA) while tailoring one that is consistent with desired directions for psychology and China's culture. As seen below, the CPS's code strongly resembles the APA's code. The CPS is attempting to institutionalize and legalize it through government endorsement, similar to its earlier code.

Historic and Cultural Conditions in the United States. In contrast to the People's Republic of China, the history of psychology in the United States has been briefer and more continuous. Its origins occurred in the early 20th century through the development of academic psychology (e.g., research, theory development, and teaching). The aftermath of World War II (WWII) signaled the need for the emergence of clinical practices, first in clinical psychology to meet the needs of returning military personnel who exhibited mental and physical health problems. Other specialties soon emerged, first counseling, industrial/organizational, and school psychology, and later others.

A need to regulate the professional practice of psychology within the United States was made evident, in part, by the discovery of Nazi atrocities during WWII. The APA adopted the first ethics code in psychology in 1953. Its development benefitted from four prior codes: the Code of Hammurabi (1795–1750 BC), the Hippocratic Oath (400–500 BC), the first American Medical Association Code of Ethics in 1847, and the Nuremberg Code of Ethics in Medical Research following WWII (Koocher & Keith-Spiegel, 2008). The 1953 APA code has been revised nine times, with its most current form adopted in 2002 (*www.apa.org/ethics/code2002.html*). This code, along with others internationally, has been influenced by a number of broader and more global ethics documents (e.g., United Nations Declaration of Human Rights, World Medical Association Declaration of Helsinki).

Code Similarities. The APA code was examined while developing the CPS code. Thus, some overlap between the CPS and APA codes can be expected. Both codes begin by discussing five general principles: beneficence (and nonmaleficence), responsibility (and fidelity), integrity, justice, and respect (Table 2.1). The codes then proceed to discuss ethical standards. The two national codes are structured similarly and use the same or similar titles for five standards: Privacy and Confidentiality, Assessment, Education and Training, Research and Publication, and Resolving Ethical Issues. Issues discussed within these commonly titled standards generally are similar. Some examples follow. Many issues discussed in the CPS code under Professional Relationships are discussed in the APA code under Therapy, Human Relations, and Record Keeping and Fees. Many issues discussed in the CPS code under Professional Responsibility are discussed in the APA code under Competence, as well as Advertising and Other Public Statements. Specific to testing, the CPS section on Assessment and Evaluation includes six standards related to test use, all of which are included in the APA code.[1]

Code Differences. Historic, cultural, and professional differences between the two countries resulted in some code differences. The APA code is

Table 2.1 General Principles and Ethical Standards in Ethics Codes from the Chinese Psychological Society (CPS) and the American Psychological Association (APA)

CPS	APA
General Principles	
Beneficence	Beneficence and Nonmaleficence
Responsibility	Fidelity and Responsibility
Integrity	Integrity
Justice	Justice
Respect	Respect for the People's Rights and Responsibility
Ethical Standards by Title (and Number of Standards)	
Privacy and Confidentiality (7)	Privacy and Confidentiality (7)
Professional Responsibility (8)	Competence (6) Advertising (6)
Assessment and Evaluation (6)	Assessment (11)
Teaching, Training, and Supervision (7)	Education and Training (7)
Research and Publication (9)	Research and Publication (15)
Resolving Ethical Issues (8)	Resolving Ethical Issues (8)
Professional Relationships (13)	Human Relationships (12), Therapy (10), and Record Keeping and Fees (7)

broader than the CPS code. The former addresses all psychologists, including those in academic as well as in all practice areas, while the latter seemingly addresses two specialty practice areas in psychology: counseling and clinical psychology. The APA code's added breadth and specificity can be seen by the number of included standards: 89 in the APA code versus 58 in the CPS code. These differences in the number of standards may reflect the culturally based structure of the codes. For example, the larger number of standards found in the APA code may be due, in part, to the litigious nature of the United States combined with its emphasis on reductionism (e.g., Leach & Harbin, 1997). Although differences in these two national codes exist, their similarities clearly outweigh them.

A Regional Code for Countries that have Considerable Diversity (i.e., EFPA's Meta-Code)

Psychological associations in most, but not all, European countries have national ethics codes. In addition, the European Federation of Psychologists' Associations (EFPA) established a Meta-Code designed to identify and standardize a set of ethical principles common to psychological practices. Rather than serving as a common code of ethics, it was designed to include principles on which national association codes should be based or should contain. EFPA's 1995 and 2005 Meta-Codes underscore four principles: respect for a person's rights and dignity, together with professional competence, responsibility, and integrity. The Meta-Code acknowledges the interdependence of the four principles and encourages psychologists to reflect on them when engaged in ethical decision making. Ethical standards and reference to specific psychological practices (e.g., therapy, testing, teaching, research) are not included. The Meta-Code's development, discussion of principles, and specifications are discussed in detail elsewhere (Lindsay, Koene, Øvreeide, & Lang, 2008). Psychological associations in some European countries (e.g., Greece) do not have their own national code and thus rely solely on the EFPA Meta-Code (Maria Malikiosi-Loizos, personal communication, December 11, 2007).

Although the Meta-Code does not directly address test use, EFPA, in conjunction with the

European Association of Work and Organization Psychologists, has established standards for test use for this specialty: *European Test User Standards for Test Use in Organizational and Work Settings*. These standards are based on the International Test Commission (ITC) Guidelines on Test Use (ITC, 2001) and frequently address ethical practice issues. This document includes contextual information that addresses ethical test practices. The goal of EFPA is to develop these and other documents to minimize country boundaries and increase professional access multinationally. EFPA is exploring a process for accrediting national test user qualification procedures in relation to its standards.

The European Certificate in Psychology (EuroPsy) also exemplifies this goal. Although not directly related to ethics, it does have ethics implications. The EuroPsy is a system of education and training standards available to psychologists who meet these eligibility standards in their home country (Lindsay, 2006). Professionals applying for the EuroPsy must have met common education, competence, and ethical conduct requirements. Its intent is to enable awardees to practice anywhere in the European Union. The EuroPsy does not license holders of this certificate to practice psychology. National regulations governing licensure differ and are met by provisions beyond the receipt of this certificate.

The EuroPsy is in an experimental stage and exists within only six European member countries (Finland, Germany, Hungary, Italy, Spain, and the United Kingdom). This certificate program has important implications for the cross-border preparation of psychologists practicing ethically. Awardees must understand and respect the ethic code of the country in which they work.

A Regional Code for Countries that have Similar Cultures (Scandinavian Code)

The five Scandinavian countries (Denmark, Finland, Iceland, Norway, Sweden) co-developed an ethics code, originally in the mid-1980s, during a period when a number of national psychological organizations were developing ethics codes. For decades, Nordic laws have allowed individuals to live and work in other Nordic countries, thus paving the way for psychologists to be guided by one ethics code. Additionally, licensure of psychology was established in these countries from the late 1970s through the mid-1980s, leading to a need for more regulated and common practice, including common ethical principles. This work became solidified in the mid-1980s. In order to harmonize with the 1995 EFPA Meta-Code[2], the Nordic code was last revised in 1998. The code highlights principles intended to promote reflection on ethical dilemmas rather than specifying standards.

With the exception of the Meta-Code, the Nordic ethics code is the only code that has been developed and promulgated by two or more sovereign countries. Given the increased professional mobility among countries, other countries in close proximity also may begin to develop common ethics codes.

International Codes

The International Union of Psychological Science (IUPsyS) and the International Association of Applied Psychology (IAAP) are two of the largest broad-based associations. Each has the potential to assume leadership for developing an ethics document in the style of EFPA's Meta-Code. However, they have been reluctant to develop an ethics code.

International Union of Psychological Science (IUPsyS). The IUPsyS membership consists of national psychological associations, not individual members. IUPsyS together with the International Association of Applied Psychology and the International Association of Cross-Cultural Psychology have supported the development of a document outlining principles: the *Universal Declaration of Ethical Principles for Psychologists* (Gauthier, 2008; retrieved from http://www.am.org/iupsys/resources/ethics/univdecl2008.html). The Universal Declaration was approved by IUPsyS in July 2008. Although not an ethics code, this Universal Declaration represents an important step toward developing an internationally agreed-upon statement that links values to four broad principles: respect for the dignity of persons and people, competent care for the well-being of persons and people, integrity, and professional and scientific responsibilities to society.

The Universal Declaration is intended to provide a moral framework based on shared human values and identifies common ethical principles for possible inclusion in ethics codes of national psychological associations. More specifically, it was developed "(a) to evaluate the ethical and moral relevance of their codes of ethics; (b) to use as a template to guide the development or evolution of their codes of ethics; (c) to encourage global thinking about ethics, while also encouraging action that is sensitive and responsive to local needs and values; and (d) to speak with a collective voice on matters of ethical concern" (pp. 4–5, http://www.am.org/iupsys/resources/ethics/univdecl2008.html).

During its development, the Universal Declaration identified and included common principles from national ethics codes, other disciplines (e.g., medicine), and other international documents (e.g., Universal Declaration of Human Rights). Historic documents that identify the roots of modern psychological ethical practices also were examined.

International Association of Applied Psychology (IAAP). Unlike the IUPsyS, whose membership consists of national organizations, the IAAP membership consists of individuals. The organization has supported the development of the Universal Declaration and recently confirmed its acceptance in July 2008.

Thus, international associations committed to provide leadership for the broad profession of psychology rely on codes based on principles. This reliance reflects their lack of an enforcement infrastructure, their respect for different cultural values and traditions, and recognition that the profession of psychology is unevenly developed internationally. In contrast, codes from international associations that represent specialties in psychology (e.g., sports psychology, school psychology) may include both principles and standards.

International Test Commission (ITC)

The International Test Commission (www.intestcom.org) exemplifies international associations that represent specialties in psychology. The ITC has a long-standing commitment to promote suitable practices governing test development and use (Oakland, Poortinga, Schlegel, & Hambleton, 2001). Its *International Guidelines on Test Use* (ITC, 2001) includes the fair and ethical use of tests with the intent to provide an internationally agreed-upon framework from which standards for training and test user competence and qualifications could be derived.

These ITC guidelines emphasize two broad obligations. These are to assume responsibility for ethical test use and to follow good practices in test use by (1) acting in a professional and ethical manner, (2) ensuring they and others display the competence needed to use tests, (3) assuming responsibility for their test use, (4) ensuring test security, and (5) ensuring test results remain confidential. Good practices in test use are evidenced by (1) evaluating the potential utility of test use, 2) selecting technically sound tests in light of their intended use, (3) recognizing the importance of fairness in testing, (4) preparing for the testing session, (5) administrating the tests properly, (6) scoring and analyzing the test results accurately, (7) interpreting the results properly, (8) communicating the results clearly and accurately, and (9) reviewing the appropriateness of the test and its uses. These international guidelines also address issues associated with developing an organizational policy on test use, developing contracts between parties involved in the testing practice, testing persons with disabilities, and translating tests. A number of countries have translated and adopted these ITC guidelines, including the EFPA Standing Committee on Tests and Testing.

ITC Guidelines on Adapting Tests. Test adaptations (www.intestcom.org/itc_projects.htm) are relevant to test use, particularly in countries that import tests. The topic of test adaptations includes ethics, yet it is much broader than ethics and thus is not reviewed in this chapter. Nevertheless, readers are encouraged to consult these guidelines when engaged with test translations and adaptations, including Oakland (2005) for a discussion of ethical issues associated with test adaptations.

The ITC also has developed guidelines on *Computer-Based and Internet-Delivered Testing* (Bartram & Hambleton, 2006; ITC, 2006). The goal of these guidelines is to raise awareness, among all stakeholders in the testing process, of internationally recognized guidelines that highlight good practice issues in computer-based testing and testing delivered over the Internet. The development of these guidelines drew on common themes that are found in other existing guidelines, codes of practice, standards, scholarship, and other sources, leading to the creation of a coherent structure within which they can be used and understood. In addition, these guidelines are specific to computer-based testing and the Internet. Again, readers are encouraged to consult these guidelines when engaged in computer-based and Internet-delivered testing.

Additional International Organizations

Other international associations have developed codes of ethics that are specific to their member's interests. For example, the International School Psychology Association (http://www.ispaweb.org/) and the International Society of Sport Psychology (www.issponline.org/p_codeofethics.asp?ms=3) have codes of ethics that govern their members' professional conduct. These and other codes from numerous other national associations can be found at www.kspope.com.

Summary

The purpose of this chapter was to describe and discuss the international status of ethics codes and other documents that address test development and use in light of fundamental characteristics of such codes. Although some forms of psychological services may be provided in most countries, ethical provisions of such services often are not guided by codes. Most countries do not have psychological associations and thus lack an ethics code.

A number of countries interested in developing or revising their ethics codes have contacted APA's Ethics Office for consultation (Steve Behnke, personal communication, July 24, 2008) and perhaps other professional associations (e.g., British Psychological Society, Canadian Psychological Association). In addition, a review of existing ethics codes (www.am.org/iupsys/ethics/ethic-com-natl-list.html), along with other information on common ethical test practices standards (e.g., ITC 2006; Leach & Oakland, 2007; Oakland, 2005), may be of assistance when developing or revising codes.

Associations developing or revising their codes should consider the following issues. Decisions must be made as to whether the general code will highlight virtues, principles, standards, or a combination of these three broad options. Moreover, professional associations that develop standard-based codes should have or be prepared to develop an infrastructure that provides for an adjudication of charges of ethics violations. National associations that develop virtue-based or principle-based codes also should consider the value of developing such an infrastructure. The emphasis placed on prevention or adjudication deserves discussion. That is, what is the proper balance between promoting ethical conduct through education and training versus through adjudication? These issues may be particularly pertinent for emerging associations and international bodies for whom an adjudication system is impractical.

This chapter narrows the discussion to four ethics code models: those for an association in one country, for associations in a large number of culturally diverse countries that are unified in other ways, for associations in a small number of countries with shared cultural values and a somewhat common history, and internationally. The decision to use one or more of these models will depend on the degree of independence or interdependence desired by the national professional association(s), as well as the degree of shared cultural values, a somewhat common history, views as to the desired future of psychology within a given region, as well as the presence of trade or other economic agreements that may characterize professional services as commodities. Ethical statements must be developed in light of local cultures, laws, public policy, and the nature of psychological services. Additionally, such statements must acknowledge international copyright laws and trade agreements that pertain to psychologists, regardless of nation of origin.

Most ethics codes are devised for a specific country. This trend is likely to continue. Those countries that desire a multi-country code may find the five-country Scandinavian code or the multi-country Meta-Code to be desirable models. Countries that develop a single country code also may participate in developing a multi-country code.

For example, in 1994 the Mercosur (Mercado Comun del Cono Sur; Southern Cone Common Market) countries in South America (i.e., Argentina, Brazil, Paraguay, and Uruguay, with other countries as associate members) formed a common market. This resulted in the formation of a committee of psychologists in these countries (Psychologists Committee of Mercosur and Associated Countries) that developed a brief declaration of principles in 1997 (*Ethical Principles Framework for the Professional Practice of Psychology in the Mercosur and Associated Countries*) in addition to national and local ethics codes (Andrea Ferrero, personal communication, September 24, 2008). As the title of this document suggests, it is intended to be a possible precursor to a joint ethics code, not a code itself.

Whether a universal ethics code acceptable to each country can or should be developed deserves continued discussion. Such discussions will benefit from information obtained from research that identifies the degree to which ethics principles and standards are common across countries (e.g., see Leach & Harbin, 2008, as well as the methods used by Gauthier). Additionally, a universal code may need to be delayed until additional national psychological associations are formed and involved in this process. Increased test development and use warrant ethical guidance on these issues. Codes and other documents from the ITC and other international professional associations, as well as regional and national associations, establish a firm basis to guide current ethical test practices and serve as a basis for code revisions.

Notes

1. The 2007 CPS code was approved after Leach & Oakland's (2007) research on test ethics internationally.

2. The 1998 Nordic code also corresponds well with the 2005 version of the EFPA Meta-Code.

References

American Educational Research Association, American Psychological Association, and National Council on Measurement in Education. (1999). *Standards for Educational and Psychological Testing*. Washington DC: American Psychological Association.

Bartram, D., & Hambleton, R. (Eds.) (2006). *Computer-based testing and the Internet: Issues and advances*. West Sussex, England.

Chinese Psychological Society (2007). *Code of ethics for counseling and clinical practice*. Beijing: Author.

Comité Coordinador de Psicólogos de; Mercosur y Países Asociados [Psychologists Committee of Mercosur and Associated Countries] (1997). *Protocolo de Acuerdo Marco de Principios Éticos para Psicólogos del Mercosur y Países Asociados* [Ethical Principles Framework for the Professional Practice of Psychology in the Mercosur and Associated Countries]. In Conselho Federal de Psicologia [Federal Board of Psychology] A psicologia no Mercusol [Psychology in the Mercuror] (pp. 11–14). Brasilia, Brazil: Author.

Gauthier, J. (2008). Universal declaration of ethical principles for psychologists. Retrieved from *http://www.am.org/iupsys/ethics/univdecl2008.html*.

Higgins, L.T., & Sun, C.H. (2002). The development of psychological testing in China. *International Journal of Psychology, 37*, 246–254.

Hu, S., & Oakland, T. (1991). Global and regional perspectives on testing children and youth: An empirical study. *International Journal of Psychology, 26*, 329–344.

International Test Commission. (2001). International guidelines on test use. *International Journal of Testing, 1*, 93–114.

International Test Commission. (2006). International guidelines on computer-based and Internet-delivered testing. *International Journal of Testing, 6*, 143–172.

Koocher, G., & Keith-Spiegel, P. (2008). *Ethics in psychology and the mental health professions* (3rd ed.). New York: Oxford University Press.

Leach, M. M., & Harbin, J. J. (1997). Psychological ethics codes: A comparison of twenty-four countries. *International Journal of Psychology, 32*, 181–192.

Leach, M. M., & Oakland, T. (2007). Ethics standards impacting test development and use: A review of 31 ethics codes impacting practices in 35 countries. *International Journal of Testing, 7*, 71–88.

Lindsay, G. (2006) Testing practices: Ethical codes, standards and dilemmas. Paper presented at the International Testing Commission Conference on Psychological and Educational Tests Adaptation Across Language and Culture, July 6–8, Brussels.

Lindsay, G., Koene, C., Øvreeide, H., & Lang, F. (2008). *Ethics for European psychologists*. Gottingen, Germany and Cambridge, MA: Hogrefe.

Oakland, T. (2005). Selected ethical issues relevant to test adaptations. In R. Hambleton, P. Merenda, & C. Spielberger (Eds.), *Adapting educational and psychological tests for cross-cultural assessment* (pp.65–92). Mahwah, NY: Erlbaum Press.

Oakland, T., Poortinga, Y., Schlegel, J., & Hambleton, R. (2001). International Test Commission: Its history, current status, and future directions. *International Journal of Testing, 1*(1), 3–32.

Ritchie, P. L. J. (2008). Codes of ethics, conduct, and standards as vehicles of accountability. In J. E. Hall & E. M. Altmaier (Eds.), *Global promise: Quality assurance and accountability in professional psychology* (pp. 73–97). New York: Oxford University Press.

3

Ethical Dilemmas, Cultural Differences, and the Globalization of Psychology

Jean L. Pettifor *and* Andrea Ferrero

Abstract

As the world becomes globalized, psychologists more frequently encounter ethical dilemmas based on differences in worldviews. Enlightened globalization may lead to greater harmony, while unilateral globalization by dominant cultures will not. This chapter presents practical examples for psychologists of culture-based ethical dilemmas around such themes as respect, competency, professional boundaries, the status of women, the law, and social justice. Today, psychologists and counselors may come from different cultures, train in different countries, and practice with a diversity of clients and in a diversity of locations. When cultural beliefs appear to clash with ethical rules of conduct, ethical decision making must focus on the well-being of clients individually and collectively. Respect and caring for clients takes priority over Western concepts of rule-compliance. The vignettes of ethical dilemmas illustrate some of the complexities of working across cultures. Psychologists are urged to support an enlightened globalization.

Key Words: ethics, ethical dilemmas, globalization, rule compliance, worldviews

This chapter on ethical dilemmas, cultural differences, and the globalization of psychology addresses ethical dilemmas that psychologists encounter in working across cultures in a world that is rapidly becoming global rather than local or regional. The process of globalization for psychology involves complex interactions of a number of variables, such as the goals of globalization, cultural differences in worldviews, power relationships, and the implications of cultural differences for psychologists in all aspects of their work. Vignettes of ethical dilemmas put a real-life face on crosscultural dilemmas and illustrate similarities and differences in belief systems across cultures. Thus, we use vignettes to identify culturally sensitive issues that cannot be resolved by merely applying codified rules, but rather need to be negotiated in the interests of a positive process and outcome of globalization.

Globalization is seen as both beneficial and destructive, as "enlightened" or "unilateral" (Kim & Park, 2007). Conflicting forces are at work like huge tectonic plates rubbing together, sometimes peaceful and sometimes resulting in earth-quaking disaster. On the one hand, communication, population mobility, trade, weapons of war, and financial systems have become global, sometimes for better and other times for worse. Economic and technological forces push for globalization. Psychological and sociopolitical forces may resist globalization inasmuch as the concept of "one world" may be viewed as a threat to the maintenance of different cultural identities and different worldviews. The professions, such as psychology, strive for global standards, mobility, and accountability in psychological research, professional training, and practice. A part of the search is for common ethical guidelines and regulatory standards (Hall & Altmaier, 2008; Hall & Lunt, 2005; Stevens & Gielen, 2007; *Universal Declaration of Ethical Principles for Psychologists*, 2008). Universality of ethical guidelines for psychologists requires worldwide agreement on valuing human life and rejection of oppression. "Enlightened" globalization is based on a sharing of common values. "Unilateral" globalization is based on the worldwide imposition of the values and worldviews of dominant groups over the beliefs and practices of others. For psychology, globalization must be enlightened to be ethical; that is, it must be respectful, fair, and beneficial across nations and cultures.

In the past, people emigrated from a home country to a new country, and were relatively stable in maintaining their residence there. Today, there is less geographical stability in that people may work in many countries over a lifetime, or may move freely back and forth in pursuit of professional, business, or recreational interests. National boundaries are a historical reality, but in many ways are becoming an anachronism. I can sit in my living room and see, hear, and make judgments on what I see in other parts of the world. I can sit at my computer and communicate with persons at other computers worldwide. It is possible within hours to travel to any part of the world.

In the "melting pot" scenario, people on the move are expected to replace old identities with new. In the "mosaic" scenario, people retain their old identities, at least for the first generation, and adjust to living peacefully in a new land with those from other cultures. When different cultural beliefs come together, globalization may provide the context for a positive merging with a wider scope of understanding and respect for others; or societies may become fragmented by competing diversities; or globalization may be a recipe for misunderstanding and violence as peoples fight to protect their own cultural identities. Moghaddam (2008) describes the competing forces for and against globalization as resulting in a "fractured" globalization that may feed terrorism.

The problem facing psychology organizations in attempting to develop international standards, including codes of ethics, is to find the universal values that are accepted worldwide, while at the same time recognizing and accommodating a variety of cultural beliefs and practices. The achievement of a positive and enlightened globalization of psychology will require confidence among psychologists of different beliefs that those with the greatest power and resources do not attempt to unilaterally impose their models. Moghaddam (2009) introduces the concept of "omniculturalism" to replace "multiculturalism." Instead of addressing many cultures, the practice of omniculturalism would encourage all individuals to develop a primary identity first that is based on universal human similarities. Then, people could develop secondary identities that are based on subgroups honoring cultural differences, such as ethnicity, religion, and social practices. If clashes occurred between the primary and secondary identities, the primary universal values would take priority. Many of the ethical dilemmas demonstrated in this chapter result from different subgroup views on what are right and wrong ways of living. The goal of ethical decision making across cultures may become one of finding and negotiating solutions that are consistent with the primary values.

The Language of Dominance

Politics, history, and geography contribute to the language we use in reference to culture. For example, the usage of terms "the West" and "Western," "the East" and "Eastern," and "Middle East," are well established when referencing countries, cultures, beliefs, and worldviews, despite being geographically inaccurate. The terminology of "the West" and "the East" appears to have been determined by the powerful European colonizing powers of the past. For those who were formerly conquered and oppressed, the word *Western* may still be perceived as implying that the West is superior and dominant over the non-West.

The dictionary definition of "the West" that is most relevant to a discussion of globalization is that the West consists of that part of the globe that encompasses the cultures and countries in Europe west of the former communist states and including the hemisphere that contains North and South America, otherwise called *the Occident*. "The East" and "Eastern" is defined as countries east of the Mediterranean including Asian countries of Japan and China, otherwise called *the Orient*. The use of the term "American" for the United States does not acknowledge Canada, Mexico, and Central and South America. For psychologists in South America, the North–South differentiation is more relevant.

If our starting point were in China, the Americas would be to the east, unless one preferred to look west across the "Middle East," Europe, and the Atlantic Ocean to reach the Americas. Christopher

Columbus sailed west from Spain to discover a new world blocking his way to the far east, or was it the far, far west? Since he thought that he had come to India, the land he found became the West Indies and its aboriginal inhabitants became Indians. In the age of imperialism and colonization it appears that the conquerors chose the language of the "new world" even though the societies and cultures described were long-standing and "old." The history of those who have been conquered and oppressed in the past is not forgotten. When we use the West–East terminology in this chapter, we do not imply that the West is superior to or better than the non-West.

Adair, Coelho, and Luna (2002) present evidence that, although psychology is growing internationally, it has no presence in many parts of the world. In addition, English is the dominant language for international discourse. Hogan and Vaccaro (2007) describe the historical shift in the cultural embeddedness of psychology from Europe to the United States. They believe that, although the monolithic power of the United States in international psychology is being eroded today by the strengthening of psychology in some nations and the emergence of psychology in others, the United States, because of its sheer size and breadth of resources, will continue to be a strong influence internationally. It follows that how the greater power and resources of psychology in the West are used will be an important factor in how psychology is able to incorporate ethical principles and guidelines within an enlightened globalization. Many of the vignettes of ethical dilemmas that we use in this chapter reflect differences between Western and non-Western cultures. We write in English with full knowledge that it is the dominant language for international discourse, but that it is not a universal language.

Indigenous Psychology

Of vital importance in the development of global psychology is the resolution of questions surrounding the meaning of indigenous psychology, the indigenizing of psychology, and of traditional healing. Indigenous psychology, as described from the point of view of science, is a complementary, scientifically credible approach to research that is very different from that advanced in general psychology (Adair, 2006; Kim & Park, 2007; Kim, Yang, & Hwang, 2006; Moghaddam, Erneling, Montero, & Lee, 2007). Jilek and Draguns (2008) believe that traditional healing and modern psychotherapies will continue to coexist and that there is an urgent need for better understanding between these two main approaches, as well as a need for flexible qualitative and quantitative research.

Adair (2006) describes the process of indigenization as a sequence of steps: importation (of models), implantation (recruitment of scholars and research), indigenization (critique and adaptation of Western models), and autochthonization (establishment of local structures to self-perpetuate). Kim and Park (2007) describe unilateral globalization as one culture dominating and subjugating another, which historically is the most common approach to defining common standards. On the other hand, enlightened globalization is based on understanding, dialogue, respect, and integrating knowledge to foster cultural development. Recent literature in the English language on indigenous psychology focuses largely on science and research, and less frequently on issues of practice in health, education, and other applied services. However, Jilek and Draguns (2008) have provided case studies of indigenous counseling, and Moodley and West (2005) have provided brief summaries of some two dozen cultural worldviews that are relevant to integrating traditional healing practices into counseling and psychotherapy.

Some differences across cultures may be seen as difficult or impossible to resolve. The World Psychiatric Association adopted the Declaration of Madrid in 1996, along with several position papers that outlined the ethical responsibilities of psychiatrists to provide competent mental health care for all persons without discrimination or political interference. Okasha (2000) presents the dilemma of choosing to practice in accordance with high scientific Western standards as compared to the indigenous traditional beliefs of the local population. "How can we practice without showing disrespect or disregard for local values?... how can we ensure that respect for the local culture does not become a pretext for bypassing ethical guidelines to the detriment of our patients' rights?" (Okasha, 2000, p. 18).

The relationship between psychology and traditional or indigenous healing has not been resolved. An enlightened global psychology must bring together different psychologies without one culture or country dominating or subjugating the views of another (Kim & Park, 2007; Kim et al., 2006). Communication is essential to foster understanding. Moghaddam (2008) reports that the West is unaware of a great deal of literature on indigenous psychology because it is not available in the English language. A careful review seems necessary on what psychology is, what indigenous practice is, and how the two relate to each other.

The Search for Multicultural Competencies

Ethical psychologists strive to be competent in all their work because to be incompetent puts others at risk. Competency is a major issue in cross-cultural counseling, inasmuch as professionals will inevitably encounter clients with worldviews that are different from their own. A common ethical dilemma is determining whether a professional is competent to offer services in a specific situation. A strong counseling movement developed in the United States to define multicultural competencies (i.e., knowledge, skills, and attitudes). The focus was primarily on the competencies of a mainstream counselor in the North American context working with a minority client. The competencies are based on the counselor's awareness of self, the counselor's awareness of the culture of the nondominant "other," and the development of a positive working alliance between them. Recent authors emphasize the importance of in-depth analysis of the cultural identities of the counselor and counselee in order to negotiate what is in the best interests of the client (Arthur & Collins, 2010; Houser, Wilczenski, & Ham, 2006; Thomas & Schwarzbaum, 2006; Stevens, 2008).

With the increasing multicultural composition of the populations in many countries, there are more cross-cultural role combinations, including non-Western psychologists trained in different countries working with both non-Western and Western clients. There also is more emphasis on reducing the power differential between counselor and client, increasing the sharing of information on an equal basis, and negotiating goals and procedures. The resolution of ethical dilemmas based on cultural differences also may require negotiation on how to achieve the best outcome for the client rather than strict compliance with the rules. The realization is growing that the competencies developed for multicultural counseling are relevant for all counseling (Arthur & Collins, 2010). Pedersen (2001) predicted that a "fourth" force is emerging in counseling in which all counseling will be understood as culture-centered.

At the same time that the counseling profession was defining multicultural competencies in order to better serve the public, psychology associations were establishing regulatory boards under state legislation in order to better protect the public. Among other requirements, a profession had to adopt a code of ethics or conduct that contained specific rules for practice, and also procedures for adjudicating complaints of misconduct. The legalistic rule-of-law approach at times seemed to run counter to a value base of placing the first priority on the well-being of the client.

Major codes of ethics in the United States have come under criticism for focusing on specific rules rather than on more generic human values. Pack-Brown and Williams (2003) raise questions about the adequacy of three major mental health codes of ethics in the United States (i.e., those of the American Psychological Association, American Counseling Association, and National Association of Social Work) to provide a practical text and support for practitioners to make culturally appropriate and sensitive decisions. They offer strategies for thinking and acting ethically in a multicultural context. They suggest that bending the codified rules is necessary if not doing so would harm the client. Stevens (2008) evaluates the same three codes on how well the wording facilitates or impedes effective multicultural and/or international practice and finds that the codes require additional interpretation to be helpful in the international arena. He concludes that ethics codes need to be revised in order to ensure quality services in multicultural and international practice.

Gallardo, Johnson, Parham, and Carter (2009) state that when psychologists have a conflict between obeying the ethics rules and serving the multicultural client, they give priority to obeying the rules in order to protect themselves against complaints. These authors maintain that to be culturally responsive, ethical psychologists must make the welfare of the client the first priority in everything that they do; to do so requires a shift in the definition of the profession of psychology, its training, and its codes of ethics. Examples of this type of dilemma are presented below.

If and when all counseling is understood as culture-centered, the emic (culture-specific) versus the etic (universalist) debate in psychology may be resolved in favor the universalist. Currently, a combination of the two positions is developing in which ethical principles that approach universal acceptance provide an overall moral framework, under the umbrella of which subgroups may develop culture-specific behaviors or rules of conduct. Approaches to universality are seen in such documents as the *Universal Declaration of Human Rights* (United Nations, 1948), *Toward a Universal Declaration of a Global Ethic* (1993), and *Universal Declaration of Ethical Principles for Psychologists* (2008). Increasingly professional codes of ethics in psychology are describing the ethical principles that provide the moral foundation for their ethical standards.

Social Responsibility and Social Justice

Social justice as an ethical responsibility is gaining attention in the counseling and psychology professions, and is especially cogent in the global context. Social justice means that the advantages and disadvantages of society are shared equally and fairly. Global problems are often societal, political, and life-threatening to the extent that individual counseling and therapy are insufficient interventions. Poverty, crime, war, genocide, terrorism, disease, natural disasters, and human trafficking are examples of gross injustices that require macro-strategies for social change.

Codes of ethics in psychology include responsibility to contribute to the welfare of society. Also included are respect for all people and the prohibition of unfair discriminatory practices. General statements of responsibility to society are open for interpretation, from taking care to be competent in research, teaching, and practice, to taking collective action to eliminate unjust aspects of society. *Social justice* is considered a stronger statement than *responsibility to society* inasmuch as it recognizes that there is injustice in many aspects of society, such as unequal access to education, public health services, and employment. Those who have suffered most from oppression may be the most vocal and proactive in their commitment to human rights, social justice, democracy, freedom, and dignity of persons and peoples. For example, psychology in many South American countries that suffered a painful past under cruel dictatorships in the mid-1970s now place a strong emphasis on human rights in their codes of ethics (Ardila, 2004; Colegio de Psicólogos de Chile, 1999; Comité Coordinador de Psicólogos del Mercosur y Países Asociados, 1997; Consejo Federal de Psicología de Brasil, 2005; Coordinadora de Psicólogos del Uruguay, 2001; Federación de Psicólogos de la República Argentina, 1999; Ferrero, 2006). In another example, the New Zealand code of ethics includes "social justice and responsibility to society" as one of its overarching ethical principles, one that recognizes the need to eliminate unjust practices in society (New Zealand Psychological Society, 2002).

Toporek, Gerstein, Fouad, Roysircar, and Israel (2006) view social justice as an integral part of counseling psychologists' practice both at home and internationally. Collins and Arthur (2010) include social justice as a core competency in their culture-infused counseling competencies framework under the heading of "Engage in social justice activities to directly influence the systems that negatively affect the lives of non-dominant populations" (p. 63). They describe in detail the attitudes and beliefs, knowledge, and skills that comprise social justice competencies. Wessells and Dawes (2007) describe strategies for psychologists to contribute internationally with macro-social interventions directed toward real-world problems, and urge psychologists to engage with cultural and ethical sensitivity in political and social change processes. The *Universal Declaration of Ethical Principles for Psychologists* (2008) includes Professional and Scientific Responsibilities to Society in its moral framework and states that these responsibilities are considered in culturally appropriate ways that are consistent with the ethical principles and related values of this Declaration. In this chapter, some of the vignettes that are presented as individual dilemmas are the result of macro-issues of injustice that require macro-solutions.

Vignettes of Ethical Dilemmas

We present ethical dilemmas in the form of vignettes to illustrate types of ethical situations that may arise when psychologists work cross-culturally. All of the vignettes have a cultural component that complicates the situation so that a clear right or wrong answer is unlikely. The rules on ethical conduct may require extra interpretation of what is respectful and caring, and the solutions may require negotiation with the affected parties on what is in their best interests individually and collectively.

Of the many ways in which vignettes can be used to illustrate ethical dilemmas, we have chosen to create vignettes that illustrate the dilemmas that occur for psychologists when there are differences between ethical principles, between principles and the rules, or between the interests and worldviews of different parties. The stories are relatively brief, which allows room for many "what if" questions to be considered in exploring the best response to the situation. There may be more than one ethical way to resolve a problem.

We have also chosen to represent different ethnic combinations of the psychologist/counselor-client dyad. For example, a Western white counselor practicing cross-culturally in either the country of origin or abroad, a non-Western counselor trained in the West returning home to practice, and a professional from a non-Western country who chooses to practice in the West.

The vignettes are organized roughly according to the nature of the dilemma, specifically competence, respect for the dignity of persons and peoples, professional boundaries, the status of women, legal restrictions, and human justice issues. In real life each vignette will involve more than one issue (e.g., competency combined with consent and confidentiality, respect combined with dual relationships and exploitation, respect combined with compliance with the law and responsibility to society). The ethical issues may overlap in a given vignette. The vignettes are intended to stimulate discussion that brings people together in understanding their common human values.

Competence

Practice within the boundaries of one's competence (at most benefiting others and at least doing no harm) appears to be the overarching ethical concern for psychologists who work across cultures and beyond national boundaries. In the West, two different approaches have been taken to define and measure competency. The general approach used by regulatory boards is to define the educational preparation requirements (e.g., university degrees, supervision, and examinations). A second, more specific approach is to define the competencies for multicultural practice; namely, the required knowledge, skills, and attitudes.

Vignette. You make a special visit to a remote northern community to meet with two white nurses from the south and a local aboriginal man who is also an employee of the health center. You are to discuss how to help his community grieve the accidental death of three teenagers. You are doing your best to be respectful and not talk like white folk who come to tell the local people that they are wrong in some way. You ask, "What can I do to help?" He is clearly uncomfortable. You ask again, "What do you suggest?" He looks away and speaks so you can scarcely hear him, but you pick up the words, "Be with the people." You persist, "What exactly should I do to help?" He finally turns to you and says, "Look, if you are here with the people you just know what to do. If you are not here with the people you will never know." Your job responsibilities cover an immense geographical area. How can you be with the people?

Comment. What does it mean to be "with the people?" Is there more emphasis on collective than on individual well-being? Is there more emphasis on being than on doing? What are the implications for the meaning of cross-cultural competencies? Are the expectations on you as an employee of the health center culturally appropriate? What can you do?

Vignette. The supervisor, trained in another continent, has taken a position in a clinic in the United States. The supervisor told the supervisee, who has come from Puerto Rico, that she is relying heavily on her for her competence with Mexican-American children who make up the majority of referrals to the clinic. The supervisee is very uncomfortable with this statement and attempts to clarify that these two countries are very different. The supervisor discounts this and says, "I am relying on you."

Comment. What is the ethical dilemma for the supervisee? What is the ethical dilemma for the supervisor? In this situation, cultural beliefs from at least three sources are coming together with no plan for sharing or understanding the similarities and differences. If your agency were to employ you to oversee the clinical supervision and training program, you would potentially add a fourth set of views. How, within the organizational structure, could you ensure cross-cultural competency in the program?

Vignette. Child Protective Services refers a refugee woman to you for assessment of her mental abilities and possible therapy. She is suspected of welfare fraud, in that she may be earning money for domestic services that she is not reporting. Neighbors have reported that the children are neglected. She is afraid of police. Her brother disappeared in her homeland. Her husband was tortured. On arriving in this country, her husband left her. Ethically, should you accept this referral?

Comment. You have done considerable work for this agency over the years and believe that you are competent to assess her abilities. However, you have not worked with refugee and torture survivors before, and you know very little about circumstances in her homeland. You do not know if you are expected to work for the woman's welfare or to investigate for potential neglect of children and fraud. You do not know how much you need to know. Would you be competent if you accepted this referral?

Respect for the Dignity of Persons and Peoples

Respect for the inherent worth of all human beings individually and collectively is fundamental to a global ethic. Respect for the dignity of persons and peoples is expressed in different ways in different communities and cultures. Ethical guidelines regarding consent, confidentiality, and privacy are subsumed under respect.

Vignette. In your position as head of a psychology department in a country of your choice, you recruit an internationally renowned scholar who now expresses concerns that student attendance in his classes is very poor, and he wonders if such disrespectful behavior is the result of racial bias. When you question the students, they tell you that they learn more from the textbook than the lectures because his accent is too difficult to understand.

Comment. This cross-cultural situation could arise in any country. How can you resolve this problem in ways that are respectful of all parties and are culturally sensitive? What choices do you have?

Vignette. A psychologist, who has returned to her own country from abroad after completing her doctoral training, says that she has learned about professional ethics codes and guidelines. However, some of the standards are not respectful and may even be harmful for some of her clients. She does not comply if she believes doing so would cause harm. For example, she never suggests that a woman has the option of leaving an abusive husband if it means possible death, starvation, or loss of her children. If appropriate, she might try conflict resolution, meditation, religious exercises, or referral to an indigenous healer. She and the client may find that reconnecting with the spiritual world through local customs is more helpful than medication or psychotherapy.

Comment. What she is doing may be called the indigenization of psychology, or a modification of what she has learned in her training in order to be relevant for her clientele and culture. Do you believe that she is acting competently and respectfully? How does your answer reflect your own cultural identity?

Vignette. You have volunteered to spend six weeks assisting in the provision of mental health services in a refugee camp crowded with people who have fled civil war in their homeland. You try to treat people with respect and competent caring. You work out of tents with no soundproofing or air conditioning. There is little confidentiality. You manage to have a large sign removed that reads, "Rape victims line up here." A man approaches you to see if you have talked to his wife without his consent, and what you talked about. To protect her from further harm, you lie that you only talked about the children and where to find food. You hear more horrific stories of suffering and abuse than you can tolerate. Your code of ethics seems more relevant to an office practice at home than to the crisis conditions in the camp.

Comment. What do you do for the mental health of people under these circumstances? Are you prepared for this kind of work? Lack of consent, confidentiality, privacy, and safety is a reality. What do you do to take care of yourself? What cross-cultural dilemmas do you encounter?

Professional Boundaries

The issues around professional boundaries, dual and multiple relationships, and conflict of interest arise frequently in working across cultures. Western guidelines for ethical practice separate the professional relationship from other types of relationships, whereas other cultures may emphasize "being with the people" rather than remaining professionally distant. Guidelines for using good judgment that bends the rules and avoids doing harm may be more useful than specific rules that do not address cultural differences.

Vignette. A new employee in your clinic has come to your country as a refugee. He is employed specifically to provide services to his own immigrant ethnic community. He lives in this community and attends religious and social events there. He provides services by visiting the clients in their homes. His Western-born and trained supervisor reprimands him for having "multiple relationships" that she says interfere with his being objective. And besides, he can see more clients each day if he schedules appointments in the office. He is very sad because he knows that his people generally do not believe in science as a source of knowledge, and they are unlikely to use established mental health services. He must be with his people in their community in order to help. You see him as very respectful of authority to the point of avoiding confrontation, and as a refugee very grateful for having a job that enables him to send money home and eventually be reunited with his family. He tells you that he cannot tell his supervisor what he thinks, but he seeks your advice because he believes that you will understand.

Comment. What are the issues of respect, and for whom? There are possibly three cross-cultural issues: the interpretation of professional boundaries, the lack of adequate communication between supervisor and supervisee, and possibly whether his likely indigenization of services is acceptable to the agency. What do you see as a useful role for yourself as a colleague?

Vignette. The territorial government in the far north invites you to present a workshop on ethics for their departmental employees, who are responsible for services over a very large territory. Most of the employees are aboriginal, while most of the government managers are of white European descent.

You are asked what you think of a recent directive from the central government prohibiting employees from accepting gifts when they visit villages on government business. The aboriginal woman asking the question says that it would be insulting to her people if she refused a gift of reindeer meat or a piece of Arctic char.

Comment. To take sides without a shared understanding of the reasons for accepting or not accepting gifts would contribute to the conflict, while refusing to respond to a local dilemma would be seen as disrespectful. Would it be appropriate to ask questions about what process is available to understand both the concerns of government managers and the cultural concerns of employees, and how agreement can be reached on appropriate guidelines? Could you suggest a process for a win–win solution? How would you reply?

Vignette. Your therapy with a 9-year-old immigrant boy who has suffered serious discrimination and bullying at school has been successful. He and his parents are deeply grateful and, as a special token of appreciation, invite you to attend a three-day celebration to which "outsiders" are rarely invited. You are not comfortable with attending, but you are also concerned that declining would be interpreted as racial discrimination. How do you respond?

Comment. Your problem appears to be how to decline such a special invitation in a culturally sensitive way. A simple explanation of your code of ethics is not enough. If it is essential culturally to give a gift, perhaps the donation could be made to the school or to the community. What options can you negotiate?

Status of Women

There are huge differences in the status of women in various parts of the globe. When we strip the vignette of the specific name of country, culture, or religion, the conflicting views on equality for women can be found in almost every country. The more severe the restrictions placed on women and the more severe the punishments for nonconformity, the greater is the dilemma in achieving satisfactory solutions.

Vignette. You are a white female psychologist who has assessed a preschool boy as having a severe learning disability that requires a special-needs remedial program. The mother is cooperative. She says that the father claims that there is nothing wrong with his son who is lazy and just needs a "good hiding." You believe that in their culture, women have little status or credibility. You are concerned that as a white female psychologist the father is unlikely to listen to you.

Comment. How do you obtain special help for the boy? Is there a way of presentation that the father would find credible? Can the necessary information be provided from a source that he would find more acceptable? Are there other ideas?

Vignette. You are a male counselor with excellent credentials from your own country and are now taking some courses to ensure that you are aware of standards and practices in your adopted country. You consider yourself a family counselor, but now feel that you must reevaluate your beliefs about family relationships in your respective countries. In your own culture there are many restrictions on the activities of women that serve to protect them from harm. At a professional level, will you need to modify how your values are put into practice? At a personal level, how will you protect your daughters from harm when as adolescents they will want the same freedom as other young women in this country?

Comment. How do you resolve your professional and personal concerns with respect, caring, and fairness? It will require reflection on how your values are demonstrated in daily living, and it will require respectful discussion and negotiation within the family. There is no checklist of what to do.

Vignette. You are a psychologist working in a trauma clinic in one of the most violent areas in the world. Most of your clients are women who live in traditional homes. A young woman who lives at home seeks help, but unlike most of her peers she also attends a nearby university. She is torn between the vastly different expectations for women in the two settings. When she was gang-raped by her brothers and their friends, culturally she could not report them for criminal behavior. However, she now has access to a world where women are expected to have equal rights. She does not know where she belongs.

Comment. How do you address her issues, the trauma, gender roles, and cultural identity? How does your cultural identity interact with hers?

Legal Restrictions

Usually ethical principles and the law are mutually supportive. When they are in conflict, some argue that the law takes priority while some assert that ethical principles must trump the law. Others may want to do a risk analysis of any proposed actions. Still others will look for opportunities to negotiate,

Vignette. You work for a government public assistance program. You are expected to counsel clients who are considered employable to find employment. You have just seen a 50-year-old woman who has been informed that her benefits will be discontinued if she does not look for paid employment. She tells you that she is the only family member left in this country who can take care of her 88-year-old mother. She has promised her mother that she will never abandon her in an institution like many people do in this country.

Comment. What are your issues around culture, government policy, and respect? How do you negotiate a culturally appropriate solution for this dilemma? Do special circumstances ever warrant an exception to government policies? Are there other options?

Vignette. You have an internship in forensic psychology in another country that has the death penalty and prides itself on being tough on crime. However, a person may not be executed unless he is competent enough to be aware of the penalty and the reason for it. You are assigned a therapy case in which the objective is for the prisoner to become competent enough that the death penalty can be implemented. You believe that this is wrong. Distressed by this situation, you go to your supervisor, who points out that this is a good learning experience for you and that continuing to provide therapy for this purpose is sound legally and clinically.

Comment. How much are your concerns based on a different view on the value of human life, your understanding of your code of ethics in your own country, its laws, your commitment to helping people, and your guilt in enabling someone to be executed? How do you resolve your ethical dilemma?

Vignette. You are a clinical psychologist employed one week per month to provide mental health services in an aboriginal community. The people are generally satisfied with your services, with one exception. One of the local leaders tells you that you must stop reporting child sexual and physical abuse to outside authorities, as is required by law, because it only makes things worse to have the white man's oppressive judicial system involved. These situations should be handled locally and in culturally appropriate ways. You need to comply before your contract comes up for renewal.

Comment. What are the legal and ethical issues for you? Larger systems are involved. Is it possible to facilitate a process whereby a mutually acceptable solution might be negotiated?

Social Justice

Social injustice can range in severity from genocide to ethnic or gender discrimination in employment practices. Some dilemmas occur when the client suffers from unjust discrimination and the counselor questions whether the purpose of counseling is to accept what cannot be changed through counseling, or to become an advocate for the elimination of injustice in society. We have chosen three vignettes in which the counselor may encounter situations of culture-related injustice.

Vignette. You are a member of an oral examination committee that is interviewing an international candidate for his ability to practice ethically and legally in your country. He tells you that his home country is in a prolonged civil war based partly on ethnic differences. The government has directed that school psychologists assess all male students over 14 years of age for competency to serve in the military. This was a very disturbing dilemma for him since he knew the military had few resources and meager training, so that his assessments reports were the equivalent of death sentences. He explained that he falsified his reports to indicate that most of the young men had disabilities that would preclude them from military service.

Comment. Was his behavior admirable and ethical, or did it indicate dishonesty and manipulation that failed to meet the ethical obligations of the profession? Was he on a slippery slope to greater deceit and dishonesty? Do some ethical principles carry greater weight than others?

Vignette. You are a career counselor working with a young woman regarding vocational training. She says that she trusts you enough to seek help on something else. She has resisted getting married because she is not a virgin. Five years ago she was raped by her cousin, and her family does not know. Now, there is a young man who wishes to marry her and take her abroad. She wants your help in finding a doctor who will medically restore her virginity so that her prospective husband does not know. You both know that in this country, what she is requesting is a criminal offense and you could both be severely punished.

Comment. How can you reconcile these conflicting interests? Do you distance yourself, refer, consult, address her anxiety, involve family, offer premarital counseling, and/or check your code of ethics? What ethical options do you have?

Vignette. You have received a grant from an international health organization to use your counseling skills in an economically disadvantaged part of the world to educate the local women to breastfeed their infants instead of using a well-marketed brand of condensed milk. Aside from the normal benefits of breastfeeding, mixing canned milk with unclean water is dangerous to their health and costs more money than they can afford. A government official warns you that if you do not cease speaking against canned milk, you will be asked to leave the country. The government appears to share in the profits of the sale of condensed milk.

Comment. You may have thought that you had a clear mandate for making a difference. How do you respond—such as comply, carry on as long as possible, find a powerful advocate, negotiate? You lack information about what else is going on, and whether there is room to craft a solution. Your sponsoring organization also has responsibility for negotiating their contact with the government and supporting you in whatever way is deemed appropriate.

Underlying Tensions

Sometimes one is alerted to an ethical dilemma by a feeling of discomfort that something is wrong, without knowing clearly why. That feeling needs to be explored in an attempt to clarify and address the problem. An effective working relationship between counselor and client is open and trusting, allowing for an understanding of their respective belief systems. Here are examples in which there may be underlying tensions related to culture.

Vignette. The client is an African-American 4-year-old child who hit another child with a brick. The parents of the assaulted child demand that the child be expelled from kindergarten. The supervisee is white and from a very conservative part of the country. The supervisor describes herself as African. Her father came to the United States from Kenya. The supervisee, who has been seeing the child in the school setting, believes that the supervisor's recommended interventions are not working. The supervisor is angry and blames the supervisee for the continuing bad behavior of the child. When the supervisee tries to discuss her feelings with the supervisor, she is told that feelings are not relevant. What is relevant is the intervention with the child.

Comment. What is the ethical dilemma for the supervisee? What is the appropriate role for the supervisor? What cross-cultural dynamics may be operating?

Vignette. You have been asked to offer a professional training seminar in the department of psychology at a university in a very conservative religious country. The topic of your seminar is sexual issues in therapy; that is one of your specialties in North America. You deal with a wide range of sexual problems, some of which are particularly sensitive cross-cultural issues, including homosexuality (which is forbidden and illegal although prevalent in your host country). One of your seminar attendees describes a problem she is having in her family therapy with a husband and his two wives. Someone then asks your opinion on the "family bed," where the children and the parents sleep in the same bed until the children are grown and leave home.

Comment. There are unspoken tensions in the group and a confusing lack of focus in the questions. You do not know what different interests are represented among the attendees. How might you respond to the questions when you perceive that you are consulting in a culture with laws and customs that are unfamiliar to you? Have you made a mistake in accepting the invitation to present before knowing more about the culture and expectations?

Vignette. You are asked to assess an aboriginal boy who is doing poorly in school. The grandmother insists that she be present. The grandfather died recently and the boy continues to hear his grandfather talking to him. The grandmother has bad dreams that she believes predict the future. She keeps him close and fears that he will soon join his grandfather. You inform them that you are considering a referral for a psychiatric evaluation in the closest urban center because you are worried about their mental health. You request that they return for another appointment. You feel uncomfortable, inasmuch as you do not want to miss psychotic symptoms, but neither do you understand their spiritual beliefs and customs surrounding death. They do not show for the next appointment, and you do not know why.

Comment. Your discomfort alerts you that you have a problem. You are not connecting with the clients or sharing their worldviews, and referral for psychiatric evaluation seems based more on your anxiety than on helping them. What do you think is the problem and what can you do next?

Ethical Decision Making

We have presented many vignettes without discussing ethical decision-making models. Although such models are rarely included in codes of ethics, various authors in the West have described linear and rational steps for solving ethical dilemmas (Fisher, 2003; Koocher & Keith-Spiegel, 2008; Pope & Vasquez, 2007). Generally, psychologists are asked to identify the problem, the parties who are involved, the relevant rules, codes, and guidelines, the probable consequences of alternative courses of action, and then to take action on what seems most appropriate. Reflection and consultation are recommended.

This approach is useful for the psychologist in focusing on compliance with both the moral principles and the rules of conduct, but it may fall short of the negotiation and sharing of worldviews that is required in resolving issues in cross-cultural counseling. A moral framework and open communication may have greater potential to be effective in working across cultures than are specific rules that may not serve the needs of the client. More exploration of alternate approaches to ethical decision making is essential in the realization of an enlightened globalization. Relevant models must be grounded in an overarching moral framework in which the first priority is respect and responsible caring for the well-being of others.

Recent authors propose greater sharing of worldviews and of the decision-making process. Houser et al. (2006) present a hermeneutic model of ethical decision making in counseling in which elements of the client's and counselor's horizons are considered in a back-and-forth manner so as to develop a level of understanding sufficient to resolve the core ethical dilemma. These elements are as follows:

- client values, race, gender, history, etc.;
- professional knowledge;
- ethical theories;
- supervisor's values and agency policies;
- counselor's values, race, gender, history, etc.;
- geographic region and culture;
- local, state, and federal laws; and
- professional codes of ethics.

These elements are placed on a circle or sphere wherein one is not more important than another. Continuing dialogue and sharing of experiences is seen as leading to meaning and meaningful action.

Stevens (2008) proposes a social-constructionist approach to ethical decision making as more useful for multicultural and international practice. The decision making depends on dialogue in sharing worldviews and finding meaning relative to the context and persons involved. This approach is value driven rather than rule driven. Arthur and Collins (2010) emphasize the positive working alliance between the counselor and the client as the context for the open shared exploration of the cultural identities of both the counselor and the person being counseled, and how together this understanding contributes to an effective therapeutic process that includes the resolution of ethical dilemmas. The Feminist Therapy Code of Ethics (Feminist Therapy Institute, Inc., 1999) would be equally relevant if the words *feminist therapist* were changed to *multicultural* or *cross-cultural,* inasmuch as the code addresses cultural diversities and oppressions, power differentials, overlapping relationships, and social change. The feminist ethical decision-making model (Hill, Glaser, & Harden, 1995), intended to supplement but not replace general codes of ethics, endorses intuition, awareness of feelings of self and others, collaboration, openness, and empowerment.

Barriers and Opportunities for International and Global Ethics in Psychology

The vignettes of ethical dilemmas in this chapter, through the telling of stories, suggest potential barriers for the application of global ethics. At the same time, recent work on multicultural competencies that emphasize the sharing of worldviews and sharing in making culturally appropriate ethical decisions provide hope for the enlightened globalization of psychology.

The potential barrier that receives the most attention in the literature is the degree of emphasis that is placed on individualist as opposed to collectivist values. This issue appears to be a matter of emphasis more than a dichotomy, inasmuch as people in individualist societies are still interested in the good of society, and those in collectivist societies do not wish to deliberately diminish the individual. However, many psychologists who have been trained within a perspective of individual rights may have to adapt to a client's special valuing of interpersonal relationships and mutuality. Many of the vignettes address cultural conflict over family, gender, and intergenerational relationships. The roles of women and the incidents of violence are issues frequently encountered in our examples. The oppression of women may occur in any society, but bringing about change becomes more difficult in states in which women are devalued by religion, law, and oppressive governments. Some of the vignettes reflect these issues.

Positions taken by governments can inhibit or support the growth of psychology globally. Oppressive regimes may define and enforce political and ideological priorities to the point that there is no room for individual questioning, reflection, or options in decision making. Even countries that are perceived to be open and democratic may become more restrictive in wartime in the interests of national security. In general, democratic governments are more compatible with the global expansion of psychology.

One of the potentially difficult problems when contemplating an enlightened globalization of psychology is that psychology, as a Western science-based profession, has not accommodated indigenous psychologies in science and practice. The vast inequality in the power, privilege, and resources among the world's nations also presents a challenge to achieving an enlightened globalization. Psychologists have reason to address social justice issues and social problems worldwide lest globalization remain fractured, fragmented, and unilateral as described by Moghaddam (2008). There are many factors beyond the scope of this chapter to address with regard to the globalization of psychology, not the least of which is terrorism and counterterrorism.

Despite the above problems, there have been many attempts to bring nations and peoples together in peace and harmony and with a common moral ethical framework, such as the *Universal Declaration of Human Rights* (United Nations, 1948), plus many associated documents, including *Toward a Universal Declaration of a Global Ethic* (1993) and the *Universal Declaration of Ethical Principles for Psychologists* (2008). The latter document reflects changing times, the increasing interconnections of all parts of the globe, the continuing desire for peace, harmony, and productivity, and the removal of threats to human life. The Universal Declaration provides a moral framework and generic set of ethical principles for psychology organizations worldwide. It does not address the behavioral manifestations of these principles, inasmuch as these will and must be culture-appropriate.

What is the significance of the *Universal Declaration of Ethical Principles for Psychologists* (2008) in the consideration of ethical dilemmas that are complicated by cultural issues? For each dilemma there are alternative actions that may be considered. The proposed action needs to be compatible with local culture and consistent with moral guidelines, such as articulated in the Universal Declaration; namely, Respect for the Dignity of Persons and Peoples, Competent Caring for Persons and Peoples, Integrity, and Professional and Scientific Responsibility to Society. In this way there is a unifying ethic based on universal principles, while at the same time honoring the practical differences in cultural interpretation. The Universal Declaration can be considered an application of the "omnicultural" approach described by Moghaddam (2009). The declaration may represent the most recent statement of ethical principles for professional disciplines that are dedicated to the global betterment of humankind.

Reflections

Ethics codes and ethical thinking evolve over time (Gauthier & Pettifor 2011; Sinclair, 2005) as demonstrated in the current linking of standards to principles that obtain from a moral framework, the adoption of ethical decision-making models, the recognition and appreciation of diversity, the impact of new developments in technology, and the movement to develop global standards for psychological education, research, and practice. Psychological literature on ethics and ethical thinking across different countries, cultures, and regions is in early stages of development. Psychologists can expand on the existing work of the counseling profession in North America on defining multicultural competencies. Examples of vignettes of ethical dilemmas across different cultures and countries are needed in order to understand real-life dilemmas. In addition, a variety of counselor–client combinations need to be represented in such vignettes, such as counselors from different countries who were trained and now practice in different countries and whose clients come from a variety of backgrounds. These considerations are important in the promotion of an enlightened globalization rather than a unilateral one.

When we remove from the ethical dilemmas the identifying names of places, religions, associations, and individuals, we find that most of the dilemmas and issues that had been viewed as culture-specific actually occur in many cultures (e.g., the status of women, parental concern for children, defining professional boundaries, complying with the law, protection of one's cultural identity). The stronger the identification of people with culture-specific beliefs and practices, the greater the potential threat that globalization will result in a loss of cultural identity. The greater the recognition that respect, caring, and integrity can be expressed in diverse ways across cultures, the greater the potential for an enlightened globalization of psychology.

Western psychology's attempt to codify the rules for ethical behavior has limitations when working cross-culturally, inasmuch as the rules do not always reflect the cultural beliefs of different parties. We have shown in the vignettes that the resolution of most cross-cultural ethical dilemmas involve dialogue, sharing, negotiating, and genuine collaboration more than compliance with rules.

Gallardo et al. (2009) questions whether psychology as a discipline needs to redefine its purpose, mandate, and potential contributions to society, which in turn impacts professional training, research, practice, and ethics. They believe that psychologists must shift their first commitment and priority from compliance with rules to providing culturally sensitive responses that contribute to the well-being of clients. This commitment takes priority over compliance with predetermined rules of conduct and predetermined theories and intervention methods.

Ethical decision making across cultures has to be shared and negotiated. An accommodation with indigenous psychology is needed. A commitment to social justice, to building a society that is fair, just, and peaceful, is essential. The process and dialogue thrives on trust, respect, caring, and seeking common values that are endorsed and differences that are accommodated.

This chapter has focused primarily on ethical dilemmas as a practical way of identifying issues to be addressed by psychologists in coping with the drive toward globalization. The literature and the vignettes support the belief that the well-being of persons and peoples who are intended to benefit from the work of psychologists must be the first ethical priority. Therefore, psychologists need the flexibility and commitment to adhere to the moral principles that place the beneficiaries first. Varying degrees of conversation and exploration are required to understand the cultural meanings for the persons involved, and how those persons can best serve and be served. There is much room for continued listening and dialogue on the road to global understanding and to an acceptance of multiple cultures. Vignettes of ethical dilemmas across cultures illustrate some of the challenges. There are no cookbook answers to the dilemmas that are presented, but, instead, discussion may stimulate an in-depth exploration of human values.

Listen to the stories that people tell about what is important in life, and seek meaning and harmony. Possibly the next major development in professional ethics will center on global and international practice.

Limitations

Each coauthor has a cultural existence and perspective that, no matter what the effort, cannot fairly represent all the other cultures in the world. As authors we recognize the personal limitations of our life experiences and our need to be vigilant in learning about worldviews and cultural identities, including our own. There are limitations in terms of the information available to us. The data presented in the vignettes cannot be understood as psychology's snapshot of the world today. These vignettes are qualitative examples of different kinds of dilemmas encountered by psychologists, but they do not provide a comprehensive global survey of international ethical dilemmas. From where we stand now, we reach and aspire to a global perspective. Our hope is for continuing dialogue that brings psychologists from around the world together to work toward a better world.

Author Note

We wish to acknowledge with thanks the many students and colleagues who have generously shared their knowledge on ethical dilemmas encountered by psychologists in working across different cultures and worldviews. These include in alphabetical order: Nicole Aube, Beth Hedva, Carol Falender, Veronica Horn, Pumla Gobodo-Madikizela, Teresita Jose, Nicole Rosendorff, Mohammed Sadiq, and Carole Sinclair. Thank you.

Correspondence concerning this chapter should be addressed to Jean L. Pettifor, 2731 Crawford Road NW, Calgary, AB T2L1C9, Canada; E-mail: pettifoj@telus.net

References

Adair, J. G. (2006). Creating indigenous psychologies: Insights from empirical social studies of the science of psychology. In U. Kim, K-S. Yang, & K-K. Hwang (Eds.), *Indigenous and cultural psychology: Understanding people in context* (pp. 467–485). New York: Springer.

Adair, J. G., Coelho, A. E. L., & Luna, J. R. (2002). How international is psychology? *International Journal of Psychology, 37*, 160–170.

Ardila, R. (2004). Psychology in Colombia: Development and current status. In M. J. Stevens & D. Wedding (Eds.), *Handbook of international psychology* (pp. 169–178). New York: Brunner-Routledge.

Arthur, N., & Collins, S. (Eds.). (2010). *Culture-infused counseling* (2nd ed.). Calgary: Counselling Concepts.

Colegio de Psicólogos de Chile. (1999). *Código de ética profesional* [Code of professional ethics]. Santiago: Author.

Collins, S., & Arthur, N. (2010). Culture infused counselling: A framework for multicultural competence. In N. Arthur & S. Collins (Eds.), *Culture-infused counseling* (2nd ed., pp. 45–65). Calgary: Counselling Concepts.

Comité Coordinador de Psicólogos del Mercosur y Países Asociados. (1997). Protocolo de acuerdo marco de principios éticos para el ejercicio profesional de los psicólogos en el Mercosur y países asociados [Agreement protocol on the framework of ethical principles for the professional practice of psychologists in the Mercosur and associated countries]. En Conselho Federal de Psicologia (Ed.), *A psicologia no Mercosul* (pp. 11–14). Brasilia: Conselho Federal de Psicologia.

Consejo Federal de Psicología de Brasil. (2005). *Código de ética profesional de los psicólogos* [Code of professional ethics for psychologists]. Brasilia: Author.

Coordinadora de Psicólogos del Uruguay. (2001). *Código de ética del psicólogo* [Code of ethics for psychology]. Montevideo: Author.

Declaration of a Global Ethic (1993) www.religioustolerance.org/parliane.htm

Federación de Psicólogos de la República Argentina—FePRA. (1999). *Código de ética* [Code of ethics]. Buenos Aires: Author.

Feminist Therapy Institute, Inc. (1999). *Feminist therapy code of ethics*. San Francisco: Author.

Ferrero, A. (2006). Human rights and psychology ethics codes in Argentina. In A. Columbus (Ed.), *Advances in psychology research* (Vol. 41, pp. 129–135). New York: Nova Publishers.

Fisher, C. (2003). *Decoding the ethics code: A practical guide for psychologists*. Thousand Oaks, CA: Sage.

Gauthier, J., & Pettifor, J.(2011). The evolution of ethics in psychology: Going international and global. In P. R. Martin, F. Cheung, M. Kyrios, L. Littlefield, M. Knowles, J. B. Overmier, & J. M. Prieto (Eds.), *The IAAP handbook of applied psychology* (pp 700–714). Oxford, UK: Blackwell.

Gallardo, M. E., Johnson, J., Parham, T., & Carter, J. (2009). Ethics and multiculturalism: Advancing cultural and clinical responsiveness. *Professional Psychology: Research and Practice, 40*, 425–435.

Hall, J., & Altmaier, E. M. (2008*)*. *Global promise: Quality assurance and accountability in professional psychology*. New York: Oxford University Press.

Hall, J., & Lunt, I. (2005). Global mobility for psychologists: The role of psychology organizations in the United States, Canada, Europe, and other regions. *American Psychologist, 60*, 712–726.

Hill, M., Glaser, K., & Harden, J. (1995). A feminist model for ethical decision-making. In E. J. Rave & C. C. Larsen (Eds.), *Ethical decision-making in therapy: Feminist perspectives* (pp. 18–37). New York: Guilford.

Hogan, J. D., & Vaccaro, T. P. (2007). International perspectives on the history of psychology. In M. J. Stevens & U. P. Gielen (Eds.), *Toward a global psychology: Theory, research, intervention, and pedagogy* (pp. 39–68). Mahwah, NJ: Erlbaum.

Houser, R., Wilczenski, F., & Ham, M. A. (2006). *Culturally relevant ethical decision-making in counseling*. Thousand Oaks, CA: Sage.

Jilek, W., & Draguns, J. G. (2008). Interventions by traditional healers: Their impact and relevance within their cultures and beyond. In U. P. Gielen, J. G. Draguns, & J. M. Fish (Eds.), *Principles of multicultural counseling and therapy* (pp. 353–371). New York: Taylor and Francis.

Kim, U.,Yang, K-S., & Hwang, K-K. (Eds.). (2006). *Indigenous and cultural psychology: Understanding people in context*. New York: Springer Science and Business Media.

Kim, U., & Park, Y-S. (2007). Development of indigenous psychologies: Understanding people in a global context. In M. J. Stevens & U. P. Gielen (Eds.), *Toward a global psychology: Theory, research, intervention, and pedagogy* (pp. 147–172). Mahwah, N.J: Erlbaum.

Koocher, G. P., & Keith-Spiegel, P. (2008). *Ethics in psychology: Professional standards and cases* (3rd ed.). New York: Oxford University Press.

Moghaddam, F. M. (2008). *How globalization spurs terrorism: The lopsided benefits of one world and why that fuels violence*. London: Praeger Security.

Moghaddam, F. M. (2009). Commentary: Omniculturalism: Policy solutions to fundamentalism in the era of fractured globalization. *Culture and Psychology, 15*, 337–347.

Moghaddam, F. M., Erneling, C. E., Montero, M., & Lee, N. (2007). Toward a conceptual foundation for a global psychology. In M. J. Stevens, & U. P. Gielen (Eds.), *Toward a global psychology: Theory, research, intervention, and pedagogy* (pp. 179–206). Mahwah, NJ: Erlbaum.

Moodley, R., & West, W. (Eds.). (2005). *Integrating traditional healing practices into counseling and psychotherapy*. Thousand Oaks: Sage.

New Zealand Psychological Society. (2002). *Code of ethics for psychologists working in Aotearoa/NewZealand*. Auckland: Author.

Okasha, A. (2000). The impact of Arab culture on psychiatric ethics. In A. Okasha, J. Arboledo Florez, & N. Sartorius (Eds.), *Ethics, culture, and psychiatry* (pp. 15–28). Washington, DC: American Psychiatric Press.

Pack-Brown, S. P., & Williams, C. B. (2003). *Ethics in a multicultural context*. Thousand Oaks: Sage.

Pedersen, P. (2001). Multiculturalism and the paradigm shift in counselling: Controversies and alternative futures. *Canadian Journal of Counselling, 35*, 15–25.

Pope, K., & Vasquez, M. (2007). *Ethics in psychotherapy and counseling: A practical* guide (3rd ed.). San Francisco: Jossey-Bass.

Sinclair, C. (2005). A brief history of ethical principles in professional codes of ethics. In M. J. Stevens & D. Wedding (Eds.), *Psychology: IUPsyS global resource* [Computer software] (6th ed.). Hove, UK: Psychology Press.

Stevens, M. (2008). Professional ethics in multicultural and international context. In U. P. Gielen, J. G. Draguns, & J. M. Fish (Eds.), *Principles of multicultural counseling and therapy* (pp. 135–166). Mahwah, NJ: Erlbaum.

Stevens, M. J., & Gielen, U. P. (Eds.). (2007). *Toward a global psychology: Theory, research, intervention, and pedagogy*. Mahwah, NJ: Erlbaum.

Thomas, A., & Schwarzbaum, S. (2006). *Culture and identity: Life stories for counselors and therapists*. Thousand Oaks, CA: Sage.

Toporek, R., Gerstein, L., Fouad, N., Roysircar, G., & Israel, T. (Eds.). (2006). *Handbook for social justice in counseling psychology: Leadership, vision, and action*. Thousand Oaks, CA: Sage.

United Nations. (1948). *Universal declaration of human rights*. Retrieved from http://www.un.org/en/documents/udhr.

Universal Declaration of Ethical Principles for Psychologists. (2008). Retrieved from http://www.iupsys.net/index.php/ethics/declaration.

Wessells, M. G., & Dawes, A. (2007). Macro-social interventions: Psychology, social policy, and societal influences processes. In M. J. Stevens & U. P. Gielen (Eds.), *Toward a global psychology: Theory, research, intervention and pedagogy* (pp. 267–298). Mahwah, NJ: Erlbaum.

World Psychiatric Association. (1996). *Madrid declaration on ethical standards for psychiatric practice*. Retrieved from *http://w.panet.org/content/madrid-ethic-english.shtml*.

CHAPTER 4

Professional Ethics and Enhancement of Competent Practice

Karel A. Soudijn *and* Ype H. Poortinga

Abstract

Professional codes of ethics are meant to set standards for the competence of psychologists and the quality of their professional actions (for which we will also use the term *interventions*). The codes encourage psychologists to continuously improve their level of competence. This chapter presents arguments as to how the standards or rules in such codes can contribute to the overall objective of competent practice and to the enhancement of competence practice.

First we show that standards of competence can never be absolute. We also mention some distinctions between categories of rules in professional codes of ethics, adding one further distinction to existing categorizations; namely, between constituent rules that define a game and the tactical rules that are used by players. We see tactical rules as indicating ways in which psychologists can improve the level of quality of their actions.

We then address the question of what constitutes the foundation for the competence of psychologists in some of the internationally better known codes. We subsequently describe four ways of anchoring ethically competent actions. Three of these are a matter of the profession and its members, viz: (i) the fund of scientific knowledge that exists in psychology and the psychologist's familiarity with this through education; (ii) the fund of professional knowledge and expertise; and (iii) professional experience. The fourth mode of anchoring places competence in broader contexts, referring to clients, sponsors, the public at large, and the legislation in a country that applies to the profession of psychology. This mode refers to the interactions between the profession and stakeholders from outside.

In the concluding section we list four questions that refer to four sets of stakeholders. These questions set a frame for competent practice of psychologists; they are interrelated in the sense that an answer to one of them imposes constraints on how the others should be answered.

Key Words: professional ethics, standards of competence, standards of conduct, EFPA Meta-Code, stakeholders

Standards of Competence

Competence as a quality or characteristic of professional interventions presumes standards in terms of which such competence can be assessed. For professional actions of psychologists there are no absolute yardsticks. Most explicit are standards formulated as rules in codes of professional ethics and these are less than absolute for three reasons.

First, principles and rules in ethical codes tend to be subject to revision from time to time; there is a relationship with historical time. For example, the *Ethical Principles of Psychologists and Code of Conduct* of the American Psychological Association (APA) was published for the first time in 1953. This code has been revised a few times before the most recent version, which is from 2002 (APA, 2002). There have been evident changes over time.

Second, a code is meant to apply to psychologists who practice in a certain country or region. Although there tends to be a good deal of similarity between national codes, there are numerous differences in details and in the emphasis on certain principles and standards of good practice. In part, these reflect broader societal concerns about civil rights and dignity of clients. Thus, there are cultural dependencies. This can be illustrated with the *Meta-Code of Ethics* approved by the European Federation of Psychologists Associations (EFPA, 2005). This Meta-Code is meant as the basis for the codes of national psychological associations in the countries of Europe (e.g., Lindsay, Koene, Øvreeide, & Lang, 2008). The idea is that the elaboration of the principles laid down in the Meta-Code can differ; the national associations in the various countries will include their own emphases and express local concerns in the formulation of specific rules.

Third, the understanding and implementation of standards is to some extent dependent on the perceptions of judges whose interpretations of the rules determine whether a certain action by a psychologist amounts to a breach of the rules. There is almost always space for interpretation; only in extreme cases are rules defined so precisely that the boundary between transgressing and keeping a rule is sharp. Such precise rules are the outcome of processes of decision making and negotiation in conflicts. They are the crystallization of a majority opinion about appropriate action in particular situations or circumstances that have become salient at some moment in time, often because complaints have been lodged about the behavior of a psychologist deemed inappropriate by others that cannot be sanctioned under the existing code.

To reduce inadvertent consequences of differences in interpretation, there is usually an appeal procedure when a psychologist has been sanctioned by a committee on professional ethics for a transgression of the standards that are in force at some time and place. For example, in the Netherlands complaints about interventions of psychologists can be submitted to the "board of supervision" of the Netherlands Institute of Psychologists (NIP). This board will assess the complaint in the light of the professional code of the NIP (2007). After the complainant and the psychologist at whom the complaint was directed have been informed of the verdict of the board, either of them can turn to the Board of Appeal. As in the case of a court of justice, the Board of Appeal can revise the original decision.

As an illustration of fairly dramatic changes over the course of a few decades in what is considered ethically acceptable, we like to refer to a project called the "phobia project," that was started at the University of Amsterdam in 1966 (e.g., Van Krogten, Hanewald, & Soudijn, 1984). Master's level students had to complete an internship. In this context each student provided treatment to a patient suffering from complaints of phobia. The treatment was given for free, but in exchange the patient had to be prepared to participate as a "subject" in a scientific project. A limited number of staff members was assigned the task to supervise the activities of each student as therapist and researcher. The treatments often had an experimental character; the investigations of the students were meant, among other goals, to provide information about the effectiveness of various forms of therapy.

Apparently, in 1966 it was deemed ethically acceptable to let students combine the roles of therapist and researcher. Moreover, it was considered efficient to approach those in search of help as research subjects. By limiting the supervision of the students to a single type of clients (suffering from phobias), the supervision by more experienced psychologists could be limited, a distinct advantage at a time when the number of staff positions at universities was clearly lagging behind the rapid growth in the number of psychology students.

In terms of the current professional code of the NIP (2007) such a project would be totally inacceptable. Much more than before, it is emphasized that there are severe objections to engaging with a client in a combination of different professional roles. In addition, nowadays great value is attached to freedom of choice within a professional relationship. Participants in research projects must be able to terminate their participation at any moment in time. With financial payments this can be realized much more easily than when reimbursement is in the form of professional services. Moreover, it would be considered inadmissible to allow inexperienced professionals (students) to work with treatment methods that are still in development. The minimal amount of supervision that was provided would also be seen as totally inadequate.

Categories of Principles and Standards

To avoid an endless and unmanageable array of rules covering specific situations, ethical codes tend to be based on more inclusive, higher-order principles. One example is the distinction in the ethical code of the APA (2002) between *general principles* and *ethical standards*. The principles are "aspirational in nature" (APA, 2002, p. 3); and: "Their intent is to guide and inspire psychologists toward the very highest ethical ideals of the profession." It is mentioned that these general principles "do not represent obligations and should not form the basis for imposing sanctions"; the ethical standards serve that purpose. Thus, in the APA code there are goals that one should strive for, and concrete obligations. The aspirational goals require that the psychologist makes an effort, but it is difficult to evaluate to what extent this actually has been done in any given situation. In contrast, the standards should be formulated in such a way that it can be assessed whether or not a psychologist has been acting in accordance with the prescriptions of the code. The APA code distinguishes five principles: (1) Beneficence and Nonmaleficence, (2) Fidelity and Responsibility, (3) Integrity, (4) Justice, (5) Respect for People's Rights and Dignity. There are ten categories of standards; evidently there is no one-to-one relationship, in the sense that standards are categorized according to principles.

The Meta-Code of the EFPA (2005) follows a somewhat different organization. Right at the start, four ethical principles are formulated: (1) Respect for a Person's Rights and Dignity, (2) Competence, (3) Responsibility, and (4) Integrity. In subsequent paragraphs each of these principles is expanded in standards for professional conduct. In the professional codes of the respective countries, one finds further elaboration in more details. Hence, the Meta-Code and the national codes in Europe following the Meta-Code have a clearly hierarchical structure. If a psychologist wishes to know what action is prescribed, s/he can best begin to search at the most specific level to determine whether any standard has been formulated. If there are no such standards, the search can be extended to a higher level of inclusiveness to determine whether there are prescriptions that pertain to the situation at hand. Thus, it should be possible to sanction a psychologist for transgression of a principle, even if there is no specific standard which covers the action that is being challenged.

Also, the *Universal Declaration of Ethical Principles for Psychologists* adopted in 2008 by the International Union of Psychological Science and the International Association of Applied Psychology (see the website of either of these two organizations) distinguishes four general principles: (1) Respect for the dignity of persons and peoples; (2) Competent caring for the well-being of persons and peoples: (3) Integrity (based on honesty and transparency); and (4) Professional and scientific responsibilities to society. The elaboration of these principles in the declaration is in general terms, amounting to an elucidation of the principles. Here, specific rules are largely avoided, which fits the objective to define an ethical framework for global psychology—but as a consequence, the Universal Declaration provides few concrete boundaries between acceptable and unacceptable actions of psychologists.

The three codes mentioned differ in the degree to which both principles and concrete standards are made explicit. In the APA code, where standards are listed, a direct link with one of the (aspirational) principles is not always specified. In the Universal Declaration the operationalization of principles in concrete standards is left open. The EFPA Meta-Code occupies an intermediate position, leaving to national codes the detailed specification of principles into standards. To some extent all three codes remain incomplete; they are not closed systems unambiguously linking ethical principles to concrete rules of conduct.

Constituent and Tactical Rules

The openness allows for another possible categorization that we would like to introduce. Standards are rules that apply to psychologists' interventions. Metaphorically speaking these are the rules of the psychologists' game. With games one can distinguish between constituent and tactical rules. The former define the essentials of a game (e.g., in chess there are pawns). Such rules impose constraints on the players (e.g., pawns can only move forward). There are also tactical rules, which apply within the space of opportunities or affordances left by the constituent rules (of all the moves allowed in chess, some are clearly better than others). Within that space participants are free to vary the tactical rules (there are voluminous books on opening theory or on end games in chess). Competence and the enhancement of competence can be linked meaningfully to tactical rules, but not to constituent rules. Players of checkers follow rules that differ from chess, but we cannot say that players of chess display more or less competence in their game than players of checkers do. However, within either game higher competence can be gained by further developing certain tactics.

Is the distinction between constituent and tactical rules meaningful in the context of ethical codes?

At first sight it might appear that all standards in a code are constituent rather than tactical rules. However, constituent rules imply a closed system. A certain game can be played at any time and place without contextual influences on the constituent rules. In contrast, ethical codes clearly are intended not only to maintain but also to enhance competent practice; they encourage psychologists to continually improve the level of their functioning; in other words, they also serve as a framework for tactical rules. We shall return to this point later on.

Anchoring of Competence

Psychologists' competence is said to be based on academic knowledge of psychology, professional training, and professional experience (e.g., Lindsay, 2008). In ideal circumstances the three components of scientific education, professional training, and experience will be complementary, but reality tends to be different. From time to time new techniques of diagnosis and treatment are embraced by practitioners, which are considered with skepticism by most researchers in psychology as to their validity and demonstrated effectiveness. On the other hand, new scientific findings are often met with skepticism in professional circles, especially if they question the validity of existing methods and techniques.

Competence in the EFPA Meta-Code

Competence is one of the four principles that form the top of the hierarchy of rules according to the EFPA Meta-Code. The moral obligation to act competently is a basic constituent rule of the profession, and permeates the other three principles. The following definition is provided:

> Psychologists strive to ensure and maintain high standards of competence in their work. They recognise the boundaries of their particular competencies and the limitations of their expertise. They provide only those services and use only those techniques for which they are qualified by education, training or experience
> (*EFPA*, 2005, p. 2).

In the elaboration of this ethical principle the Meta-Code distinguishes four themes for which national associations might formulate more specific rules. The first theme is ethical awareness; it is elucidated as follows: "Obligation to have a good knowledge of ethics, including the Ethical Code, and the integration of ethical issues with professional practice."

It is noteworthy that competence is linked to the entire code. Apparently it is not a theme that should be seen as standing on its own. In a discussion on competence, the standards mentioned with other principles also need to be considered.

In addition to ethical awareness the Meta-Code mentions four further themes that have to do with competence; namely, limits of competence, limits of procedures, continuing development, and incapability. In the context of the present chapter we would like to refer to the difference between the first two themes. With "limits of competence" the emphasis is on the education, training, and experience; psychologists have to stay within the limits set by these three parameters. With "limits of procedures" the focus is on an additional aspect; it is argued that psychologists in their work must be aware of "the psychological community's critical development of theories and methods." In other words, on the one hand the psychologists' scope for interventions is bounded by their personal background, whether in an educational context, such as a university curriculum in psychology, or in a professional context, such as interactions with clients. On the other hand, boundaries are also set by the current state of affairs in psychological science, as interpreted by the community of psychologists.

Competence in the APA Code

In the EFPA code, competence is one of the principles that need to be detailed further. In the APA code (APA, 2002) competence is not formulated as a principle, but is reflected in a set of standards forming one of ten sections. The section has six articles. In various articles it is emphasized that psychologists should be aware of the boundaries of their own competence and stay within the limits set by their training and experience. Psychologists should actively seek to keep their competence up to date and to increase it, but in the article setting this standard (2.03) it is not made explicit how this effort should be realized. The next article (2.04) mentions: "Psychologists' work is based upon established scientific and professional knowledge of the discipline." A clause between brackets contains cross-references to some other standards.

The APA code appears to impose a stricter standard than the EFPA (2005) Meta-Code. The EFPA code requires that psychologists should remain *aware* of scientific development (as interpreted by the community of psychologists). The APA code requires that psychologists' interventions have to be *based* on established scientific and professional knowledge. Article 2.04 stipulates the boundaries within which psychologists have to operate: it is inacceptable if psychologists justify their professional actions with reference to knowledge, including that of other disciplines, unless that knowledge has been accepted as such within the community of psychologists.

Psychological Science

As we indicated already, the relationship between science and competence is not without problems. Science is geared toward the building of theories and the testing of hypotheses, with the realization that the knowledge gained is not absolute. In the widely endorsed approach of Popper (1959), science progresses through the falsification of established insights; knowledge can be refuted but never confirmed as being definite. Popper (1963) has compared the conduct of science with driving piles into a swamp. Too much reliance on the carrying capacity of such piles is questionable; research findings should be treated with caution. Moreover, there is the problem for practitioners whether methods for which treatment efficacy has been supported also will be effective in the actual circumstances in which an intervention is needed (Shadish, Cook & Campbell, 2002). In other words, the practitioners who want to apply scientific findings should be able to argue why the circumstances are similar to those for which treatment efficacy was demonstrated. This requires an interpretation that in itself is a source of uncertainty. A perspective on science as briefly outlined here makes clear that scientific knowledge cannot serve as an absolute standard.

At the same time, the scientific method is geared toward critical appraisal of existing notions. It continually seeks to drive more piles into the swamp when the existing ones succumb under the weight of empirical evidence. In our reading of the sections of the EFPA Meta-Code and the APA code just mentioned, as well as numerous national codes, psychology tends to be portrayed as a science-based profession, and knowledge of this science is the primary basis for legitimating psychologists' claims to expertise.

Previously (Poortinga & Soudijn, 2003) we have argued that our profession does not have a good record when it comes to abandoning reliance on obsolete theories and the use of methods that have not stood up to critical scrutiny. We cited two examples of continued use and endorsement of methods on which the volume of negative scientific evidence far outweighed the positive evidence. One example was the continued widespread use of the Rorschach as a diagnostic device despite consistent negative psychometric evidence (e.g., Lilienfeld, Wood & Garb, 2001). The other example was the endorsement of "anatomically detailed dolls" by the APA Council of Representatives (Fox, 1991) and by the Council of the Netherlands Institute of Psychologists (NIP, 1989) at a time when critical evidence had already been accumulating.

Currently there are trends in a number of countries toward the use of more "evidence-based" methods, especially in the area of health. Rising costs of health care are a driving force, and the interventions of (highly educated) psychologists tend to be time-consuming and costly. One way in which the profession can react is to strengthen the reliance of interventions on scientific evidence. This implies closer links between practice and science, the use of efficacious interventions, and the phasing out of obsolete methods and theories (e.g., Baker, McFall, & Shoham, 2009). As we have seen in this section, this certainly is a direction that is in line with the perspectives taken in ethical codes.

In our experience and from our reading of literature, not only associations of psychologists but also ethics boards leave ample space for professionals to choose their own methods and theories. If methods are questioned on scientific grounds, it is usually in the context of professional conduct that violates other ethical standards. For example, a few years ago the Board of Supervision of the NIP dealt with a complaint of sexual intimidation. The psychologist defended his actions as part of a therapy in which bodily interaction with the client was an essential ingredient. He argued that this therapy was based on scientific research, and referred to publications of which he was the author in a journal of which he happened to be the editor. Among the reasons given by the Board of Supervision for rejecting this defense was the argument that the journal was not recognized as a scientific journal by Dutch universities. Unfortunately, there is no answer to a question that we would like to raise; namely, whether a sanction would have been imposed if the complaint had been directed at some obscure method that did not have any sexual (or otherwise threatening) connotations.

Professional Knowledge

Ethical codes seek to anchor competence in scientific knowledge, but this is possible only up to a point. We would argue that the fund of currently established scientific knowledge in psychology is more limited than in several other professions. Engineers have standard principles in design. Medical practitioners have handbooks that prescribe diagnostic procedures and the treatment of several illnesses for which there are recognized cures. As an illustration of what we mean, please compare a medical handbook (outside psychiatry) with a handbook in some field of applied psychology. Of course, the extent to which there is a "canon" of well-tested methods and practices differs per area; for example, there is more of a canon for assessing cognitive abilities than for organizational consultancy or therapy. One reason for the lack of canonization is that psychologists are often confronted with issues for which there is not an unambiguous diagnosis or treatment, even in the light of the best available scientific evidence. Such issues tend to be fuzzy and to form a rather open problem space. A second reason lies in the dynamic nature of interventions, in the course of which interactions with clients are changing.

It cannot be expected that psychologists should limit themselves to methods and practices for which there is sufficient scientific evidence (in whatever way this might be defined). Most professional psychologists would argue that this would place too much confidence on knowledge that is preliminary in the sense of Popper (1959). Also, the scope of the profession would be so severely restricted that the ethical principle of social responsibility of psychologists might suffer. In any case, reliance on science only is not the direction taken in the professional codes. Rather, an appeal is made to professional competence or knowledge. In professional codes this tends to appear next to scientific evidence. Article 2.04 of the APA code, to which we referred before, states: "Psychologists' work is based upon established scientific and *professional* [emphasis added] knowledge of the discipline."

As we have seen, the Meta-Code of the EFPA (2005) is less explicit. It stipulates an obligation to practice within the limits of competence derived from education, training, and experience (article 3.2.2), and an obligation to be aware of the limits of procedures (article 2.4.4). However, in neither of these two codes is there any indication to the effect that scientific evidence, given its higher methodological rigor, takes precedence over professional insights. It also is not mentioned what should be done when scientific knowledge is in conflict with professional insight and practices. Our understanding is that the two are seen as always compatible, at least in principle, even though the examples just given show that such conflict can occur. At the same time, the respect for professional insights shown in the codes leaves much space for practitioners to apply and develop tactical rules in shaping their interventions.

A Reflection on Rawls

The notion of professional knowledge implies that a psychologist can justify a course of action better if she or he can refer to procedures or practices that fellow practitioners see as competent. The emphasis in codes on professional knowledge amounts to a tactical rule aimed at promoting competent practice. It stimulates psychologists to do their work using methods and procedures similar to those used by fellow professionals. A consequence of this tactical rule is that acceptable practices become less individual, and that existing practices are more likely to become seen as competent practices. A rationale for accepting professional knowledge can be derived from ideas in philosophy of law formulated by Rawls (1971). He addressed the question of how judicial rules can be justified. When there are no absolute standards (independent of time and context), it becomes important to consider under which conditions people feel themselves to be bound by rules. Rawls did not solve this problem through empirical research; he made use of a thought experiment. Whoever likes to introduce a certain rule, according to Rawls, has to imagine being in a social position totally different from one's present position. What this position will be like is unpredictable; we do not know how our position may change. However, we can imagine what it will be like to be subjected to the proposed rule.

According to Rawls, a rule is acceptable if one would like to see the rule applied to oneself in all imaginable situations. In professional codes for psychologists, an idea similar to that of Rawls can be found (Soudijn, 2007). An action of a psychologist is justifiable insofar as it can be separated from this individual practitioner; it is acceptable if any other (well educated) psychologist in similar circumstances might have carried out the same action. Thus, professional codes are conducive to promoting practices that are in agreement with what fellow professionals would do in similar situations. Such practices acquire, rightly or wrongly, an appearance of competence, or at least an aura of acceptability, as illustrated by the following case.

The Board of Supervision of the NIP received a complaint lodged by an applicant who was rejected for a senior position on the basis of a psychological report. The report reflected the results of an assessment procedure conducted by a reputable consulting company, which had been asked to establish the suitability of a few applicants for the position. As required by the NIP code of ethics, a draft of the report was shown to the applicant for comments before it was sent to the prospective employer. The responsible psychologist made clear on that occasion that the conclusion about the applicant's suitability for the job would not be changed. The applicant raised an objection but did not stop the submission of the report. The complaint lodged with the Board of Supervision after he had been rejected for the job was that the report did not mention the margin of uncertainty in the interpretation of test scores in terms of his fitness for the position. The omission of this uncertainty had been misleading, it was argued, as the prospective employer might have realized insufficiently the potential capabilities of the applicant.

The psychologist mentioned three arguments in defense. The first referred to the relevant literature, which was said to show ample evidence that assessment will lead to a better judgment than other forms of selection. The second argument was that the sponsor was not interested in the merits of the instruments and other methods. Third, other senior selection agencies in the Netherlands also prepared concise reports on assessments for job selection without details about margins of uncertainty and alternative interpretations.

The Board of Supervision rejected the complaint, but drew attention to a dilemma. On the one hand, the argument about common practices was accepted as valid; on the other hand, the Board noted that such a concise report was not in line with the requirements for reporting in other fields of applied psychology. Especially in the area of mental health, the requirements about justifying interpretations are much stricter. Therefore, the Board included in its verdict a recommendation for the work and organization psychologists in the Netherlands to the effect that a better underpinning of conclusions about the suitability of applicants for certain kinds of jobs might be advisable.

Professional Experience

Of the three sources of competence referred to in professional codes and mentioned by Lindsay (2008)—academic knowledge of psychology, professional training, and professional experience—the third is the least accessible to independent empirical scrutiny. Personal experience is a method of gaining knowledge that, almost by its very nature, tends to seek convergent evidence supporting an individual's perceptions, rather than discriminant evidence that seeks to falsify existing perceptions and beliefs. By and large, professional codes radiate respect for the insights of psychologists obtained in the course of their work; experience is portrayed as an asset. Exploration of novel approaches as a way of improving tactical rules is looked upon favorably. The EFPA (2005) Meta-Code is explicit on this when mentioning, under the principle of competence, that "new areas of practice and methods will continue to emerge and this is a positive development."

The relationship between experience and outcomes in psychotherapy is not very clear (Beutler et al., 2002). Also, studies in which professional judgments of more experienced and less experienced psychologists are compared have found that experience, at best, has a limited impact on the quality of professional judgments in diagnosis (see, for example, Spengler et al., 2009). Such findings may seem surprising in light of the perspective on experience taken in the ethical codes. On the other hand, when dealing with an alleged transgression, a board of ethics will tend to accept references to scientific evidence and/or to professional practices as justification for a course of action, but not references to personal experience. If challenges are raised, references to personal experience are trumped by both scientific and professional knowledge.

Competence in Broader Context

The codes refer to competence as a quality of psychologists' interventions. The ultimate rationale for such interventions is the care for the well-being of humans, especially the clients of psychologists. Clients (individuals for whose well-being interventions are conducted), sponsors (individuals or organizations who commission the interventions), and the public at large (social responsibility) are all mentioned in the codes. In this section we refer to some dilemmas arising from the interactions of psychologists with these various stakeholders.

Entitlements of Clients

Clients appear primarily as targets of interventions and as recipients of psychologists' professional actions, but codes of ethics also refer to more active roles. As in medicine, psychologists' codes attach great value to *informed consent*. Clients need to be informed in sufficient detail about the intended course of action in interventions. In general the psychologist can only start a planned intervention after the permission of the client has been obtained. Legal prescriptions can preempt this requirement, but exceptions are few (see for example article 3.10 in the APA code and article 3.1.3 and 3.1.4 in the EFPA Meta-Code). A rule in the code of the NIP (2007) extends informed consent to reports about clients. Psychologists can submit a report to a third party, including the sponsor of the intervention, after the client has had the opportunity to read the report and has given explicit consent to send it. The refusal to have the report dispatched is to be respected unless the intervention was commissioned by a court of law.

Forty years ago the Dutch psychologist De Groot (1970) argued that with the use of tests, not only psychometric criteria (validity, reliability) should be taken into account, but also a criterion that he called "acceptability." According to this criterion a test could only be administered if the most direct stakeholders agreed to the use of this instrument. This implied that psychologists would have to convince their clients that a certain test would be an acceptable method in a given situation. At the time there was not much support for this idea, which was seen as a subversion of the expertise and authority of the psychologist. Standards in contemporary codes that emphasize informed consent can be seen as an operationalization of the principle of acceptability.

Standards about informed consent, or acceptability, respect the right of the client to make decisions about intervention methods, but make it necessary for psychologists to step out of their professional boundaries in order to convince others beyond fellow psychologists of the value and significance of such methods. Here, enhancement of competence entails that psychologists reflect on the position and perspective of the client. This is a concrete instance of competence extending well beyond areas of expertise that are associated with psychology as a science and/or profession. The European Certificate (*EuroPsy*) of the EFPA (2009), meant as a diploma for independent practice for psychologists in the European Union (see Gauthier & Pettifor, Chapter 9, this volume), mentions this as one of the enabling competences that are needed to render services effectively.

There is another aspect of informed consent to which we would like to draw attention; namely, a possible incompatibility with another standard. It is imaginable that a psychologist is of the opinion that method A should be used rather than method B, because of evidence of better validity or effectiveness/efficacy, but that the client rejects this method. How much loss in expected results can be accepted before the use of treatment B becomes ethically unacceptable? We have seen that ethical codes attach importance to the scientific basis of methods, as well as to the agreement of clients (informed consent). However, we do not see that one could derive any concrete prescription on how much loss of validity or effectiveness a psychologist could accept, a point to which we will return.

A further, rather common, instance is a possible tension between confidentiality and transparency. Openness or transparency is a hallmark of science (Popper, 1959). At the same time, psychologists are bound strictly to confidentiality. The code of the APA (2002) has a category of standards on "privacy and confidentiality" and the EFPA (2005) Meta-Code mentions confidentiality as part of the principle of respect for a person's rights and dignity. Under either of these two codes it is difficult to imagine that a psychologist having difficulties with a diagnosis would present a client to a group of colleagues for interviewing, even if the client would agree to this. Thus, the emphasis on confidentiality can make it difficult to make interventions testable and controllable.

The apparent contrast between demands of science and confidentiality can also be used to illustrate that professional codes contain rules to neutralize possible disadvantages of incompatible conditions. Psychologists are free to discuss with colleagues interesting information derived from individual clients, and even publish this, provided the anonymity of the client can be guaranteed. The disadvantage of this arrangement is that a lack of openness hampers accountability, although this disadvantage also holds in scientific research that is based on anonymous "participants" or "subjects." In actual fact, there is only a single constraining principle: disadvantage to the client has to be avoided. It is up to psychologists to find tactical rules that optimize other goals while respecting this constraint.

Ethics Codes as a Coat-of-Arms

Through their work, psychologists are meant to contribute to the well-being of individuals and of the society at large. But it is also of interest to psychologists that their profession is respected. One of the functions of codes of ethics is that they serve as coats-of-arms that are meant to impress the public at large with the quality of psychological services. A sound reputation of psychologists is an asset for the profession. Psychologists are held to protect this asset by refraining from actions that could damage the reputation of the profession. Notably, they have to treat their fellow professionals with respect. For example, in the code of the German Society of Psychologists (DGP, 2005, article B.II.2.1) there is a standard that reads: "Psychologists owe their professional colleagues respect and refrain from nonfactual criticisms about the way in which these colleagues conduct their profession" (our translation).

It may appear at first sight that such standards do not contribute to the competence of psychologists or the enhancement of competence. Still, relationships are not hard to find. Self-protection of the profession serves to increase the confidence of the public in the profession. It is difficult for psychologists to work competently and effectively if (potential) clients are suspicious of psychologists and their interventions.

In the code of the NIP this is mentioned explicitly: psychologists have to refrain from actions which they know or reasonably can foresee "may damage the confidence in the science of psychology, the practicing of psychology, or psychologists" (NIP, 2007, article III.1.1.1). Scientific research generally will benefit from a critical attitude (Popper, 1959). Theories should be tested sharply and the results of investigations should be interpreted with a fair deal of scepsis. Mutual criticism is seen as the engine propelling scientific research. However, the NIP code prescribes Dutch psychologists to exercise constraint in their criticisms; the confidence in psychology should not be undermined. Again we see a dilemma: science functions on the basis of disagreement, but the Dutch code restricts this principle; the credibility of the profession should not suffer.

Self-protection can also be found in the APA code (2002). Several articles contain qualifiers like "reasonable" and "appropriate." Such qualifiers lead to fuzziness; it is difficult for outsiders to see whether a choice of action has been "reasonable" or whether measures have been "appropriate." In any case, qualifiers make it more difficult to challenge psychologists in a court of law on the basis of a transgression if the standards are subject to reservations. It is mainly the professionals themselves who can judge what is appropriate and reasonable (Bersoff, 1994).

Standards need not be defensive when it comes to the public image of psychologists and their profession; they can also be proactive. In a previous illustration we have seen that an applicant in the Netherlands has the right to read his assessment report and prohibit submission to the sponsor. In the same country the right of patients in the healthcare system to examine their own records is entrenched in the law. In the code of ethics of the NIP (2007) this right is extended to all clients of psychologists, also outside the area of health care. As soon as a professional relationship has been established between a psychologist and a client, the psychologist is obliged to keep a formal record. The client is entitled to examine the record and to demand a copy. The extension of the legal right to examine one's record from patients in health care to all clients, also serves as a signal that the profession can be trusted; the interventions of psychologists are transparent.

The image of psychology as a socially concerned and ethically responsible profession is reflected in the principle of integrity. Honesty, fairness, and respect are part of this, according to the EFPA (2005) Meta-Code. This code does not refer to financial arrangements between psychologists and clients, contrary to the other ethical document with an international perspective that we have referred to, the *Universal Declaration of Ethical Principles for Psychologists*. This declaration states under the principle of integrity that psychologists accept not to exploit persons or peoples for personal, professional, or financial gain. Numerous national codes also contain standards on responsibilities of psychologists in their financial arrangements. How far does this responsibility go?

For example, a Dutch psychologist followed an advanced training course for registration as a healthcare psychologist. As part of this course he worked under supervision in a hospital and, in addition to client reports, he had to write case analyses which were more extensive. In one of these analyses he gave a detailed but anonymous account of a client, who had been informed and had agreed to this. After approval by his supervisor the psychologist arranged with the client to read and discuss this document. The client felt unable to read and comprehend the entire document, including the theoretical elaborations, and asked for a copy. The psychologist agreed to this but charged extremely high copying costs. The client considered this unacceptable and submitted a formal complaint to the NIP.

As we have seen before, according to the NIP (2007) code, clients have access to reports written about them. They can also ask for a copy and the psychologist can only charge a reasonable amount of copying costs. In the present instance the amount the psychologist asked for was much higher. However, the psychologist had prepared an anonymous case analysis. According to the Board of Supervision, which judged the merits of the complaint, this implied that the document should not be considered part of the records of the client or the report about the intervention, which are never anonymous. Therefore, the rule that clients are entitled to a copy of their report did not apply. The psychologist made a clear arrangement that entitled the client to an examination of the document with the case analysis. At that occasion the client asked for something more. As the psychologist was not bound by the code to meet this request, she or he could charge her or his own price, even if this might be considered unreasonably high. The Board of Supervision was of the opinion that the psychologist was not violating any standard in the NIP code (2007) when acting in the way described.

In this section we have come across various instances where ethical standards impose conditions on professional actions that are incompatible or at least difficult to reconcile with each other in specific instances. In this last example there is an obvious tension between the high ethical principles of the profession, and the extent to which deviations of such principles can be sanctioned. Apparently, psychologists can also use their competence to operate close to the limits of what ethical standards allow, and find protection under their professional code as long as they do not contravene clearly formulated standards. Tactical rules leave freedom of action even when the course of action chosen by a psychologist is frowned upon by most fellow professionals.

Conclusions

By and large, codes provide rules about (un)acceptable professional conduct as if in any situation only one standard applies. In reality there are dilemmas that the psychologist will have to resolve individually or in consultation with communities of psychologists. In this chapter we have discussed various themes of competence and enhancement of competence. Standards of conduct that pertain to these themes sometimes result in conflicting demands or lack of clarity as to how they can be interconnected. Professional codes may be meant to maintain and enhance the professional competence of psychologists, but how this can be realized becomes unclear if standards appear to be at variance with each other.

According to the codes referred to in this chapter, psychologists have to deal with four kinds of actors or stakeholders: (a) researchers contributing to the fund of knowledge reflected in the scientific literature; (b) clients and others who need to be informed about the interventions of psychologists and whose approval is required; (c) fellow professionals who will endorse or disapprove of a course of action and would or would not follow a similar course in a similar situation; and (d) the broader society in which psychologists function and which forms a judgment about their reputation.

The themes raised in this chapter can be summarized in a set of four interrelated questions that a practicing psychologist continually will have to address:

1. Is a planned course of action justifiable in the light of available knowledge from scientific research?
2. Can this course of action be explained to clients and sponsors, and do they agree to this?
3. Will this course of action find approval in the eyes of a substantive part of the community of professionals working in the same area of application?
4. Is the course of action possibly detrimental to the reputation of fellow psychologists or the profession at large?

Professional codes of ethics are subject to revision from time to time. This implies that new directions are given about the ways in which psychologists should answer these four questions. There will be shifts in balance, leading to more emphasis on one question and less on some other question. We can formulate this in another manner. Each question imposes boundaries on how the other three questions can be answered, and these boundaries are shifting. Each question refers to constraints that are to be considered when answering another question. There is a complex dynamic equilibrium; as we mentioned before, ethical rules are dependent on time, location, and observer.

References

American Psychological Association. (2002). Ethical principles of psychologists and code of conduct. *American Psychologist, 47*, 1597–1611.

Baker, T. B., McFall, R. M., & Shoham, V. (2009). Current status and future prospects of clinical psychology. *Psychological Science in the Public Interest, 9*, 67–103.

Bersoff, D. N. (1994). Explicit ambiguity: The 1992 Ethics Code as an oxymoron. *American Psychologist, 25*, 382–387.

Beutler, L. E., Talk, M., Alimohamed, S., Harwood, T. M., Talebi, H., Noble, S. & Wong, E. (2002). Therapist variables. In M. J. Lambert, (Ed.), *Bergin and Garfield's handbook of psychotherapy and behavior change* (pp. 227–306). New York: Wiley.

De Groot, A. D. (1970). Some badly needed non-statistical concepts in applied psychometrics. *Nederlands Tijdschrift voor de Psychologie, 25*, 360–367.

DGP (Deutsche Gesellschaft für Psychologie). (2005). *Ethische richtlinien der DGPs und des BDP* [Ethical rules for members of the German Psychological Association]. Münster: Deutsche Gesellschaft für Psychologie e.V. und Berufsverband Deutscher Psychologinnen und Psychologen.

EFPA (European Federation of Professional Psychologists' Asssociations). (2005). *Meta-code of ethics*. Brussels, EFPA.

EFPA. (2009). *EuroPsy: European certificate in psychology; EFPA rules on EuroPsy and appendices*. Revised June 2009. Brussels: European Federation of Psychologists' Associations.

Fox, R. E. (1991). Proceedings of American Psychological Association, incorporated, for the year 1990: Minutes of the meeting of the council of representatives. *American Psychologist, 46,* 689–726.

Lilienfeld, S. O., Wood, J. M., Garb, H. N. (2001). What's wrong with this picture? *Scientific American, 284*(5), 73–79.

Lindsay, G. (2008). The principle of competence. In G. Lindsay, C., Koene, H., Øvreeide, & F. Lang (Eds.), *Ethics for European psychologists* (pp. 79–102). Göttingen: Hogreve.

Lindsay, G., Koene, C., Øvreeide, H., & Lang, F. (2008). *Ethics for European psychologists*. Göttingen: Hogreve.

NIP (Netherlands Institute of Psychologists) (1989). Verklaring van het Hoofdbestuur inzake Bolderkar-affaire [Declaration of the executive concerning the "Bolderkar" affair]. *De Psycholoog, 24,* 43.

NIP (2007). *Beroepscode voor psychologen 2007 van het Nederlands Instituut van Psychologen* [Ethical code for psychologists 2007 of the Netherlands Institute of Psychologists]. Amsterdam: Nederlands Instituut van Psychologen.

Poortinga, Y. H., & Soudijn, K.A. (2003). Ethical principles of the psychology profession and professional competencies. In W. O'Donohue, & K. Ferguson (Eds.), *Handbook of professional ethics for psychologists: Issues, questions, and controversies* (pp. 67–80). Thousand Oaks, CA: Sage.

Popper, K. R. (1959). *The logic of scientific discovery*. London: Hutchinson.

Popper, K. R. (1963). *Conjectures and refutations: The growth of scientific knowledge*. London: Routledge & Kegan Paul.

Rawls, J. (1971). *A theory of justice*. Cambridge, MA: Belknap.

Soudijn, K. A. (2007). *Ethische codes voor psychologen* (2nd ed.) [Ethical codes for psychologists]. Amsterdam: Nieuwezijds.

Shadish, W. R., Cook, T. D., & Campbell, D. T. (2002). *Experimental and quasi-experimental designs for generalized causal inference*. Boston: Houghton Mifflin.

Spengler, P. M., White. M. J., Ægisdóttir, S., Maugherman, A. S., Anderson, L. A., Cook, R. S., et al. (2009). The meta-analysis of clinical judgment project: Effects of experience on judgment accuracy. *The Counseling Psychologist, 37,* 350–399.

Van Krogten, I. A. M. H., Hanewald, G. J. F. P., & Soudijn, K.A. (Eds.), (1984). *Fobieën: Het Amsterdamse fobieënproject* [Phobias: The Amsterdam phobias project]. Deventer: Van Loghum Slaterus.

CHAPTER 5

Ethical Perspectives and Concepts

Haldor Øvreeide *and* Polona Matjan

> **Abstract**
> This chapter gives an outlook on ethics and provides a discussion of some relevant concepts that may deepen the understanding of the text in ethical codes, and provide assistance in solving ethical dilemmas and challenges. The topics discussed are not discrete, independent entities that add up to a comprehensive ethical theory, or one perspective on ethics. They are to be understood more as ways of looking at similar questions from different social and intellectual positions. Some of the ideas presented have sprung from discussions in the group of European colleagues who developed the text of the *Meta-Code of Ethics for European Psychologists* (European Federation of Psychologists Associations, 2005).
>
> **Key Words:** ethical dilemmas, ethical discourse, Meta-Code, morals, ethics, dialogic

Ethical Perspectives and Concepts
Ethical Discourses

Moral questions are at the base of all small or larger social projects and conflicts. Morals are both core and unavoidable complementary issues in all political and social processes, in the single dyad, as well as in larger social systems and societies. All human interactions are thus embedded in discourses on ethics—What will be the right thing to do? How do we achieve the good and the best? How do we share and distribute resources? How do we relieve pain and avoid harm?, and—How do we evaluate what happened from a moral perspective? This last question, however, refers to *moralizing* practices and discourses, in contrast to *ethics*, which refers to a proactive testing of values for an optimal future practice. On the other hand, if the main issue is "to do better next time," and not only an argument about who is to blame, moral testing of our historic practices can be important contributions to an ethical discourse.

These discourses are practiced in many different arenas, one of which is when psychologists, in a continuous flow of communication, develop their own sectional, professional ethics. This book is a contribution to this discourse, as well as a source for solving actual dilemmas. However, many of the important ethical discourses and developments take place without us being really aware that this is so, since they are embedded in all kinds of social interactions and problem solving. Changes in our personal perspectives on values, as well as in our professional choices and preferences, are often deeply affected by moral discourses that give options that earlier were closed or limited. Reading a novel, seeing a film, listening to a lecture, being contested by a client, can all become instances that heighten and change our ethical awareness and perspectives both in personal and professional encounters.

As humans we have different needs, interests, dependencies, loyalties in our relationships, and contextual frames. Thus we often arrive at different answers to moral questions and dilemmas when they arise. Despite differences, we still have to be in dialogue and engage in ethical discourse because we also have mutual dependencies and common interests and goals, in groups and as humanity in general. Thus we have an overriding common interest in resolving the dilemmas that arise. The formulation and awareness of ethical principles for guidance are necessary and serve as roadmaps for human coherence and conflict management. However, once established, the perpetual societal change and developments demand that moral and ethical principles are continually scrutinized and discussed as to how they are to be understood and applied at different times and in differing situations. This ongoing moral testing of our practices is a prerequisite for cooperation and unity within human systems, and life on Earth in general. For example, in the last decades a growing moral awareness has been on the fact that survival of the human race is strongly connected to how we as humans protect both inanimate and living nature as a whole. This discourse has also changed psychology to hold a more ecological perspective. Such a perspective opens new ethical implications for how psychologists in their professional roles care for their clients. Cooperation, openness, and informed consent have, for example, become more focused values in treatment and consultation, as well as in research. Correspondingly, the paternalistic position of professional practice has declined.

In the first essay some typical areas for ethical discussions and developments will be described. These discourses might be relevant when we, as psychologists, establish and understand our ethical obligations and principles and use them in more nuanced ways to monitor our practice.

Moral Philosophy

Moral questions have been the most central issues in philosophy as an academic discipline, as well as in religious philosophical thinking and writing. Moral philosophy, seen as an intellectual testing of basic moral issues is, and should be, an integral part of all scientific endeavors. Intellectual pondering on ethical questions has been an important base for scientific as well as social and educational programs, and thus the development of society. Moral philosophy as an academic discipline can also be seen the study of morals in ongoing social processes. It is putting morality into words and concepts, a description of the process, as well as offering critical perspectives on contemporary moral phenomena and dilemmas.

Moral philosophy can be seen as an intellectual expression of central moral themes in contemporary society, as well as in historical social processes. Important philosophical texts and discussions on morals flourished, for example, in the aftermath of the Second World War, and older philosophical contributions were revisited and criticized. Both intellectual and political endeavors contributed to the formulation of international declarations of human rights, an important basis also for professional ethics. None of the existing professions came through the war times without flaws being identified in their professional integrity.

Lately the academic philosophical discourse has had a deconstructive perspective on social practice with its moral implications (Bauman, 1993). This perspective has given space to, or has been a reflection of, a more liberal social practice with the individual "on stage" in pursuing self-fulfillment, as opposed to a social practice structured by more fundamental and collectivistic ideas. And in the last decade, migration and the "war against terror" have challenged liberal democracies, and even the psychological profession, with our adherence to ethical principles derived from declarations on human rights.

Developments in sciences other than philosophy and scientifically based professions are important contributions to unraveling the phenomena and processes that are of interest to moral philosophers. Contributions from psychology have been central. The Adorno studies (Adorno, 1950) on the authoritarian personality had an impact on philosophy, as well as the Milgram study (Milgram, 1974) and Zimbardo's later studies and writings (Zimbardo, 2007).

Today, biotechnological possibilities raise many new ethical questions within a broad range of human practice. This could become of acute interest to psychologists who might be asked to identify psychological criteria and consequences of the biotechnological possibilities for manipulating human capacities. Also, the discovery of the socially competent baby (Trevarten & Aitkin, 2001), and neuroscience's parallel detection of a system of mirror neurons (Iacoboni, 2008) shed new light onto empathic and intersubjective processes, important for understanding how moral questions and the ethics of "the primary dyad"—baby and caregiver—are solved. This is an example where scientific contributions might have impact on ethical thinking and practice in encounters with children and perhaps on human relationships at large. When individual competence for relationships, right from the child's first cry, is understood as innate and central to human development, then dialogue and consciousness on cooperation are necessary to solve the ethical challenges of the primary dyad (further discussed in the next essay on ethical dimensions). This invites philosophical rethinking and adjustment of earlier answers to moral questions in the socializing practice in family and school, albeit philosophers had foreseen some of these later discoveries of dialogical processes in their discussions on the moral appeals and contradictions that exist in the human encounter (Arendt, 1978; Levinas, 1981). Sometimes it can be said that the task of philosophy is to pose questions, and other sciences "see" and describe the phenomena foreseen and advised by philosophy, as well as the other way round.

Without input from moral philosophy to guide scientific progress and practice, science loses an important compass for its development as legitimate and valuable social practice. That does not mean that the compass is always right; it must continuously be tested and adjusted. Intellectually marvelous moral ideas and constructs can go terribly wrong when they are seen as *the solution* and put into practice, whether in politics or in professional practice.

This applies, for example, to late communist and socialist systems, in which one of the authors grew up, where morally acceptable ideas of a truly just society were constantly abused in different ways. The declared social equality was perverted into enormous social differences between the political elite and the rest of the population. In reality the proclaimed liberty of an individual meant subordination to the social and political system. In short, asserted values were in real life almost completely voided of their sense. In many ways this political manipulation also shaped manipulative behavior in social relationships in general. The ethical position of an individual in these systems became questionable and limited because political and social violence fostered individuals to subordinate and remain in a dependent position. The individual's voice on moral values and ethical conflicts had no standing. The main value became belonging to a specific social group or ideology without any examination of the moral values of that ideology.

Today's world has been changing very quickly. Social systems have been moving forward, but at the same time genocides have been implemented, not standing back and learning from earlier atrocities. The production and sale of weapons has been growing; we have been manipulated by very sophisticated marketing knowledge, where methods of technology, including psychotechnology, have been used for exerting power in a social context. The nonrestricted economic growth and freedom at the turn of the millennium sent millions of people in 2008 into deep poverty, and many countries like Iceland woke to an economic nightmare. An individual, psychologically weak and dependent, can easily feel alienated and as such be prepared to adapt in any situation Amati Sas 1992. The Milgram study revealed important information about human nature—that most of us have in our personality a fragile and dependent part, so in a specific situation we might behave in an immoral way.

Religious texts have important intellectual contributions to understanding and solving moral dilemmas and, historically, many important moral philosophical contributions, both from Eastern and Western cultures, are hybrid philosophical texts on religious and moral questions. The problem when moral text and thinking are too closely connected to religion and political ambitions is that they often imply or are accompanied by intolerance for other perspectives. In the same way as ideal political solutions can become perverted, excellent religious moral advice in the frame of being "the right solution" constitutes some of today's world's greatest challenges.

At the edge of moral philosophy are art and literature, which are also often in-depth intellectual examinations of moral questions. An important part of the intellectual consciousness and development of moral questions is to be found in the works of artists, novelists, and in the interpretations and discussions of their texts and artistic expressions. Dostoyevsky, Ibsen, Kafka, Picasso, Munch, and an endless line of other authors and artists have made significant contributions to the moral discourse and to our understanding of ethical dilemmas, and our human fragilities and successes.

It is important that ethical principles formulated by the psychological profession and the practice that follows have resonance in moral philosophy, so that professional practice is intellectually well founded also on values. Reasoning and arguing for best practice are needed to lift it from the flaws of feelings and popular trends. Ethical principles and their derivations should be anchored on solid intellectual ground, contestable for their relevance and limitations.

Common Ethics. While philosophy can be seen as an intellectual effort to answer general ethical questions in depth, there is always an ongoing here-and-now discussion in newspapers, on the Internet, in schools, in the parliament, at the work place, etc. All these discussions will be mirroring ad hoc events and their moral issues, what might be seen as local discourses on ethics: these may be called *common ethics* in groups, in social classes, and in society. Everybody may have a say in common ethics.

The common ethics comes close to the timely ethical problem solving in society at large. It is the moral here-and-now context for ethical problem solving, a continuous evolving of consensuses and divergences on value issues. It is embedded in the actual attitudes, values, prejudices, and meanings at a certain place and time. Common ethics shows what issues are in front and how the moral thinking, the ethics, is reflected in these discussions and their corresponding practices. In contrast to what later is called *personal ethics*, the common ethics discourses can be seen as the striving for moral consensuses at a given time and place. It is situated in a "now" and in a definable social context. As such, it can be observed and empirically studied. It reflects how people feel, think, and behave in relation to certain values and how these values should be practiced. Political campaigns, elections, polls, and many different social studies can be seen as catching and exposing the common ethics at the time. Likewise essays, columns, blogs, and debates in newspapers, journals, and on the Internet, all expose thinking and feeling on how different ad hoc issues are related to values.

The diverse common discourses are of interest for the profession and the individual psychologist to be aware of. This is because *these will be the discourses that our clients may be engaged in, and out of which they understand their own moral position, rights, and responsibilities.*

Personal Ethics. Personal ethics can be seen as the result of how the individual's upbringing and experiences are related to moral issues. It contains both a cognitive structure of social stances and, not least, an emotional inclination for responding to what is "right," the moral "gut-feeling." All behaviors, both in private as well as in professional practice, will be related to personal attitudes and moral tendencies for responding—to what feels right, what fosters inclusion or rejection, and what generates guilt and shame, as well as feelings of coping and success. Early childhood experiences of being supported and taken care of form the cornerstone of the capacity of the individual as an adult to give support and take care of the Other. This may be seen as the individual's basis for an ethical position. If the social world is dangerous, aggressive, and full of conflicts, the individual may remain in a dependent position and learn to adapt in any situation to be able to survive. The individual may recognize the cruel reality, but is unable to be critical in adequate ways to that same reality. Thus the person becomes alienated from his or her own feelings and may consequently be unable to take an ethical position of support and care of the Other.

This means that due to differences in upbringing, subcultural standing, and individual experiences, moral values will be ordered in differing personal hierarchies and dispositions. These individual dispositions will apply both in private as well as professional settings. One person will be notably sensitive to the Other's needs for care, a second will be acutely conscious of respecting the integrity of the Other. The third may be occupied with avoiding negative consequences for the Other, while the fourth is seeking to support the long-term best interests of the Other, and for the fifth, aesthetics and convention in the relationship to the Other are important. Individual differences in temperament and reactivity can also be expected to influence one's moral inclinations. In professional practice it will be important to be aware of how one's personal values and tendencies are aggregated and how they may enter and affect practice.

Personal ethics can be seen as largely a set of emotionally organized dispositions derived from experiences in family and social life. This will be a very local and emotionally charged discourse. As such it may be unconsciously triggered and it can be a challenge to bring this often-masked discourse into reason and intellectual scrutiny. Thus personal ethics can come to interfere with a sound ethical assessment of a specific professional challenge. For example, when psychologists enter into dual relationships with clients many ethical dilemmas arise. And entering such relationships is often fostered by following an emotionally based personal ethics without proper reflection on the consequences of multiple relationships with a client.

Personal ethics should, however, first of all be seen as a resource. The emotionally based sensitivity for values and moral issues is often necessary for catching ethical dilemmas and to pose relevant questions. One "feels" a value in a social encounter as much as it can be intellectually deduced, and in the last instance one "feels" if the action was "right or wrong." This occurs without it necessarily being the best action taken according to common ethics, or especially when considered from the perspective of professional ethics. Professional ethics, its principles and specifications, are important for balancing, correcting, and advising the impulses from personal ethics, which always will be the base for ethical acuity and responding. The first impulse will, however, need support or correction following reflective consideration. Thorough knowledge of professional ethical codes, and the discourses from which they are derived, will be essential when entering the professional context. Discussing ethical dilemmas and options with colleagues are important ways to counterbalance the first impulses to act—impulses that often stem from a more or less conscious and nonarguable personal value system.

Sector Ethics and Professional Ethics. Sector ethics refers to the highlighting of certain values and practices within a special social grouping. It can be within a firm, a religious grouping, a sports organization, a professional group, etc. Specific guidelines or norms for the members' behavior are discussed, developed, and formulated by and for the members or practitioners of the group or organization. To become a *sector ethics*, apart from the more free-floating processes in common ethics, the values and principles for practice must be focused and explicated by the members within the sector themselves. It is thus the discourse within the group concerning members' own behavior and practice that constitutes a sector ethics, and not what might be specified through laws and regulations by governments or other sources of external constraints. Sometimes, however, processes concerning ethical issues within the sector might bring forward statutory regulations, and then sector ethics and outside directives might to some extent become paralleled. Apart from regulating the behavior of its affiliates, an explicit sector ethics can be an important base for the sector's autonomy and legitimate place within the larger society.

Professional ethics for psychologists is a typical sector ethics. Due to the societal importance of professions and the importance of competent practitioners, governmental regulations of the professions have been implemented in many countries. At the base of these regulations is often solid work on an explicit ethics within the profession itself. When psychologists' associations formulate ethical principles for their members, two main motives can be explicated.

First, the profession wants to signal that the practice to be expected will be in line with important social values, so as to safeguard its clients from exploitation. Second, this safeguarding also gives societal legitimacy for the profession. In relation to moral philosophy, there must be a resonance between professional ethics and basic concepts from moral philosophy and central declarations of human rights. So also there must be a reverberation with, or an openness and communicability to, the common ethics of the time. In the professional encounter with the client it is necessary to understand the moral position of the client in order to respect and communicate on important issues. The client will be embedded in the ongoing discourses in common ethics. That does not mean that professional ethics should be seen as, or be a simple derivative of or extract from, common ethics. Quite the opposite— professional ethics should include, but at the same time, from the professional perspective, take a critical stand regarding common ethical solutions and practices, as well as with respect to the imperfection of personal ethics, as discussed above. A relevant question to raise is: How do both personal and common ethics enhance or limit reaching the profession's goals, and how do they support or undermine the trust and legitimacy of the profession?

Example:
The client of a psychologist wrote a furious letter to one of the authors serving as chair of the ethical board for psychologists. The board had intervened in a couple of cases where colleagues had sexually abused clients. These cases had also come to the notice of the tabloid press. In her letter the woman strongly argued that she felt that the ethical board itself was behaving unethically when reprimanding therapists for having sex with their clients. She claimed to be a responsible adult, and what happened between consenting adults was their right to engage in as long as no one else was damaged. Somewhat similar views appeared in readers' columns.

This example brings out a second, and possibly the most important, motive for formulating sector ethics for psychologists. This motive is an awareness that the profession itself must take the responsibility for the practice that is derived from the specific and privileged knowledge that psychologists uphold. It is not obvious that outsiders will understand the limitations, effects, and the range of consequences of professional practice. The example shows that mechanisms of counter-power protecting clients from exploitation and repressions are not always there. It is not for all clients, like the woman in the example, to understand the power difference and its risks in the psychologist–client relationship. By focusing on ethical issues that are not obvious to outsiders, professional ethics has an important function to regulate situations where the client could be at hazard for deliberate as well as fortuitous abusive or degrading practices by the psychologist. The potential ethical pitfalls connected with psychological practice must be contemplated by the practitioners themselves, preferably in a proactive process and always by an ethical evaluation of their effects on the ongoing practice. This is what sound ethical discourses and development of ethical codes and regulations within the profession are about.

In sector ethics, like common ethics, there is a direct link between formulated values and actual practice. As such, how it is understood and practiced can be observed, registered, and empirically assessed. For example, in professional ethics for psychologists: What cases are filed for ethical complaint? What and how have formulations in the codes been interpreted and applied, and what have been the ethical boards' reactions? What ethical dilemmas do psychologists experience in their practice? What do they seek consultation on, and what issues with ethical components are discussed in different professional forums? Unlike common ethics, which may consist of an array of different opinions and maybe inconsistencies, more explicit codes advising practice are developed by the profession and must show a high degree of consistency and wide applicability. Such standards can be used not only for guidance but also to evaluate actual practice.

Although meant for advising and disciplining, psychologists' professional ethics will also contribute to the wider discourse of common ethics. When professional ethics is exposed outside the professional sector, both by its codifications and when shown as a base for practice and analysis—in articles, reports and discussions, showing how clients are met and described, for example in cooperative settings with other professionals—it may contribute to a more general ethical awareness of current issues as well as of the case at hand. A challenge is for psychologists to maintain self-reference in ethical assessments and evaluations, and not fall into moralizing. The psychologist is no moral expert, but strives toward an ethical practice in scientific extraction and application of psychological knowledge.

Ethics and Law. In most countries professional psychological practice will be regulated by professional ethics, as well as by law and statuary regulations. Thus it is necessary to explore the relationship between ethics and law. The two often apply to the same situations, may be practiced concurrently, and may raise similar questions. Consequently they are not always easy to keep apart. It is, however, important to separate the two, as they have different bases for legitimization, different coverage, and should pose different challenges. One cannot be considered as a substitute for the other. For example, a professional psychological organization cannot protect itself and a psychologist by not reacting to an ethical complaint if there is a contemporary legal procedure going on.

Example:
A 25-year-old woman files a complaint about sexual abuse by her therapist/psychologist. In her letter to the ethical board of the psychologist's association, she states that she also will take legal steps against her therapist. The ethical board decides that since the alleged behavior will be assessed by police and court, there is no special need to have another procedure on the same act. The board argues the decision by the fact that one cannot be punished twice for the same act.

This ethical board may be confounded on the relationship between ethics and law. Simply put: ethics challenges us to come to a personal, responsible decision of what is right or best to do—practice guided and monitored by values. Law obliges us to be aware of and find what behavior the lawmaker or law-enforcing authorities would expect in the present situation—practice guided and monitored by legal obligations. Professional ethics, when formulated in codes, are a somewhat mixed entity. Like law, they give a set of norms by which actual professional behavior can be evaluated. However, they comprise self-enforced norms which should first of all be formulated as guiding principles of high generality, and not as specific rules for practice. The evaluation of an ethical dilemma resides with the practitioner, even if later it might be reevaluated by an ethical board after a complaint. The ethical norms laid down in professional codes might also be used for a legal evaluation of a psychologist's behavior—for an evaluation of "good practice." It will, however, still be the text of the law to be enforced that has the final word—for example, in withdrawing a license or deciding on a reimbursement of fees. This cannot be the other way around, like the board in the example above seemed to believe. Referring to law can never be an argument for not assessing behavior from an ethical perspective, although the ethical board may decide to delay its own deliberations until after the conclusion of the legal process.

It is also necessary to note that an ethical evaluation will often present the challenge of balancing several ethical principles, while complying with law is a more simple process of finding if the rule set by law applies to the situation or not. Most law texts strive to have a high degree of specificity, in contrast to ethical principles. For example: A psychologist who comes to know about a child being maltreated finds that he has the obligation by law to inform child protection authorities. His own ethical evaluation according to the ethical principles of the profession came to the same conclusion, an obligation to protect the weaker part—the child. However, the ethical evaluation adds much to his practical solution; for example, how and when to inform his client. This is not specified by law but advised by ethical principles of respect and responsibility. At other times one can come close to, or even to an opposing ethical conclusion compared with the legal position.

Examples:
1) The client of a psychologist was a depressed man of 55, with the secondary sequelae of divorce, social isolation, a drinking problem, and problems with staying in work. His only daughter had been molested and killed some years ago, and that was when his life problems all started. Now, after a period with stomach pain, his condition was diagnosed as cancer. He soon revealed suicidal plans to the psychologist. He could not bear the thoughts of going through harsh treatments and being left to be cared for by strangers. He felt responsibility to nobody, and would not want to be a burden on anybody. He explained how he was planning a quiet and undramatic exit.

The psychologist found the man's suicidal intent to be very realistic. He discussed the client's options and admitted that the client had a very strong and appealing case for his right to decide if and how he could end his life. On the other hand, as a health professional the psychologist had the legal responsibility to protect life; an obligation that gave no options. On the basis of the information the client had given, and his own evaluation of the probability of a suicidal episode, he decided to take action to submit the client to a secure ward. After three weeks in a protective ward, the therapeutic relationship survived, and so did the client for half a year. The client refused life-lengthening but accepted pain-relieving treatment, and he came to reconciliation with his ex-wife.

In this example the psychologist communicated his ethical evaluation, but acted on a legal obligation. One can easily follow the psychologist's ethical evaluation and share his appraisal of the client's appeal for the right to decide to live or not, thus respecting his right to self-determination, but at the same time this would be in conflict with the legal responsibility. Acting on a legal obligation gives high legitimacy for the decision taken. However, the ethical evaluation undertaken by the psychologist will always be important for the relationship, whether it is in line with or at variance with the legal requirement. Sometimes, like here, a differing ethical evaluation to the legal imperative might save a relationship, although the psychologist here acted on his legal obligation.

2) At the very end of a communist state, a law was passed, allowing army authorities access to psychological files in mental health and in health services of all young men. The aim was to gather relevant data on recruits for military service. Besides that, the same law obliged psychologists working in health services to make a psychological assessment of cognitive and emotional capacities of the whole generation of young men, with specific psychological tests and a specific cutoff point. The cutoff point was determined by the army. This turned out to be inappropriate because it was defined in a population of young men with significantly lower educational level than the population in the region to be assessed. Even mentally retarded young men passed the cutoff point and could come to enter military service. It could have been a disaster. Psychologists organized themselves and, with the aid of their professional organization, refused to give the results of the psychological assessments to the army authorities and also refused to allow the army access to the psychological files. For the single psychologist, this was a very difficult decision to act against the law and to be afraid of the consequences for not obeying. Not all psychologists had the courage to follow their ethical evaluation and ignore the law. The situation became morally so complicated that it later became difficult to discuss among colleagues.

The problem that arose at that time, and which to some extent is still present in the aftermath of the communist systems, is that psychologists, other professionals, and people in general took justice into their own hands. Under the earlier regimes people often found law and morals to be in conflict, as the law did not have democratic legitimization. What was right and morally courageous 20 years ago may, however, not be so today. But the same professionals and people still live and work with an emotionally strong experience that laws should not be obeyed, and that not following laws could be morally right. In the late communist systems, democratic process is still partly running outside the political system, and the trust in and loyalty to democratically developed laws are not yet fully integrated as parts of personal beliefs and values.

In a democratic process many laws and statutory regulations can be seen as solutions to ethical dilemmas that have gone from ethical considerations to become explicit legal norms—a problem area is assessed, a proposal is raised, a democratic process is initiated and a legitimate body makes a decision, and a law regulating the problem area is established. It is through a democratic process that the solution is found to what one should or should not do. When a proposal for a law has passed this process and has been instigated, you just have to follow the law. If uncertain of its relevance to a specific situation, you may consult a person or body competent in law, and assess if it applies to the situation you are in. The moral thinking, the ethics, is done in the lawmaking process and later interpreted by courts. You have not much to say but to obey, or oppose with the legal consequences that may follow.

Say the psychologist in the above example with the suicidal man had not acted to prevent the client's suicide plans and they were carried out. On ethical grounds, the psychologist considered that the existential situation for the client was such that he found that no other values could be weighed in favor to intervene on the client's plans, after having given him a chance to discuss the options. The cancer specialist, or the client's ex-wife, might have charged the psychologist for not acting according to his legal obligation, and he may have been reprimanded for this or even punished in some way. That does not mean that his ethical evaluation was wrong. The psychologist had, however, weighed ethics heavier than the legal requirement. This might in some instances be the best moral stand, but that does not free the psychologist from the consequences of not following legal demands.

The differentiation of law and ethics may be especially delicate, but particularly more important, in clinical and health psychology. When psychologists are dealing with clients who have psychological problems that can be understood and classified in medical diagnostic schemas as normal on the one hand, or disorder and illness on the other hand, there is a danger that the psychologist may equate legal and healthy, and unhealthy and illegal, behavior. If this happens more or less unconsciously, the psychologist's practice may become part of a nonlegitimate repressive system. For example, in assessing sexual or antisocial conduct this may happen, as these behaviors may be of relevance to legal questions and assessment as well as being health issues. However, in a democratic system only legally defined persons and bodies have the right to constrain citizens' behavior. When health professionals and the judicial system interact, the roles and different obligations should be very clearly defined. This is not always so—with ethical consequences. For example, the integrity of the psychologist can become blurred for the client if the roles are not well defined.

Just to follow the law, leaving out an independent ethical evaluation which might end in a divergent appraisal to that which the law prescribes, can be seen as self-protective for the psychologist. Self-protection as a motive is relevant in the legal domain, but not within ethics. While many laws and regulations have moral challenges as primary intents, others are self-protective and interest-based. For example, laws regulating imports and immigration are often explicitly self-protective. Professional laws also have elements of protecting the interests of the profession. In this way there is a fundamental divergence from ethics. Ethics are solely aiming at the best interests of the Other—setting the client, not the psychologist, first. That does not mean that the psychologist's own interest should not also be weighed, if the behavior and claims of the client are too invasive and exceeding the limits and resources at hand with reference to the professional role. In such situations laws and other protective measures are important to lean on. Use of such instruments is not part of an ethical evaluation, but might be legitimate and necessary, as no one has the right to threaten or damage others. Law can thus be an important contextual element that makes nuanced ethical evaluations and practice possible.

From one point of view, the law can be seen as yesterday's solutions to moral problems. An ethical problem has arisen and, as earlier underlined, a democratic process has brought forward a law that in the aftermath must be obeyed, also by any minority that might have been in opposition to passing such a law. This might be seen as an inherent ethical problem with law, especially if the law in unpredicted ways overrules the interests of and respect for minorities. Laws can thus create ethical problems, not only in repressive and nondemocratic systems. A free press and the protection of the freedom to speak are indispensable for reducing and explicating when yesterday's moral solutions, intrinsic in law, create unethical dilemmas today. Law should thus always be scrutinized for unethical effects. Psychologists may have an important perspective on such issues as our profession comes close to observing the negative effects of repressive and unjust social structures.

When a law is enacted, then the general discussions of the moral issues will usually lessen, at least for the time being, although there might be many battles in court on how the law is to be understood and applied. Thus law is foremost a conservative social element, and when first instituted discussions mostly go on among legal representatives and experts. Ethical evaluations are, on the other hand, freer and catch the dilemmas of the here and now as well as trends for the future by discussing and assessing situations, without relying on the conservative element of the legal system, to say what is right. Ethical discussions might, as stated above, sometimes be about the archaic structures in laws which do not match the information and challenges of today. For example, not many years ago homosexual practice was forbidden and punished in many European countries. It took a long time, however, from the vigorous raising of this as an ethical issue, until laws were changed. When such laws were abolished it had strong liberating effects. Ethical discourses on the effects of law might result in a process that changes laws that are found not to function according to new or a modern understanding of ethical dilemmas. As such, lawmaking, in abolishing, changing and establishing new laws will often have a radical and progressive function for solving moral issues. The point here is that once instigated, the good intentions in law might come to function conservatively with respect to social progress. This is not necessarily negative. However, it must not be left alone, but always be supplemented by here- and-now ethical assessments. Certainly, ethical discussions will arise about laws and legal practices of today that will be viewed as discriminatory when seen in the aftermath. For example, laws keeping immigrants for years in camps or as illegal work resources, excluding them from workers' rights, education, and health services, as is the practice today in many European countries, will presumably not survive.

From the ethical perspective, norms are not fixed in the same way as law. Ethical norms may change and are reassessed through dynamic and open discourses. This happens in philosophical thinking as well as in the common ethics in a democratic society, in the socialization of children, and so also in the discussions and in the formulation of the ethical codes and declarations, both general and sectorial. Like law, established ethical codes are norms—but they are principles with higher generality, and strive to be close to universal adherence and reflect human development and unity.

Two final remarks on the relationship between law and ethics: First, many actions may be legal, or rather not illegal, but might be unethical to do. Ethics thus helps to advise behavior and regulate relationships to a much wider extent than law does.

Example:
The psychologist coaching a group of leaders in a firm was attacked by one of the members for the way he handled the group process. The psychologist answered by making a rather sarcastic remark, and went into a more open conflict with the group member. The trust in the psychologist was reduced for the whole group after this incident. He did not manage to recover the situation and the engagement came to an early end.

Of course, such behavior is far from being illegal; it was, however, unethical, and thus unprofessional to respond sarcastically toward a client, with the effect of isolating the psychologist and undermining his work.

Secondly, when a person feels he has or is given a legal and formal civil right, the refusal or denial to fulfill this right will, for most people, be felt as abusive. The psychologist's knowledge of the client's legal rights, and behaving with respect and in line with these, are important to prevent a strain in the professional relationship. This connects to the preventive idea in law. For example, laws addressing violence and abuse within the family, and the corresponding right to be protected by society also in private relationships, will heighten the acuity and reactivity when such violations happen. Through the formal formulation of a right, a person may be helped to understand and register when they are abused or exploited. The development and proliferation of patients' legal rights within the health system have helped, and will help psychologists' clients to be more aware of and able to react when meeting unethical procedures and behavior.

Ethical Dimensions

The second essay in our chapter highlights different dimensions or angles to consider in finding the best ethical solutions. In many instances none of these will alone be adequate when faced with an ethical dilemma. It may be necessary to give them differential weight in the consideration and final choice of action. But first we will formulate a basic conception of:

The Ethical Position

The primary ethical challenge will always be in a "me" in relation to a "you" in an unique event of interaction, where the degree and character of dependency will generate power issues and hence the distribution of responsibilities within the relationship. The one with most power and least dependency will have the greater responsibility, and this defines what we will name as *the ethical position*. This position represents an ethical obligation to give priority to the needs and interests of the Other in the relationship—not only in theory, but in the daily lived practice.

By looking at the relationship between caregiver and the newborn baby, we may find in this a fundamental model for the ethical position in a human relationship and its basic qualities. It is characterized by three clear premises or challenges, all of which must be met by the caregiver to secure the existence, well-being, and development of the child.

• First, this caring relationship is characterized by the baby's total dependency on a caring person. The baby's vital needs can only be met by a caregiver's orientation and resources to meet these needs.
• Second, the relationship must build on cooperation. The competence to cooperate is an intrinsic capacity of the child. Dialogue, jointly attuned interaction, and mutual adaptation are prerequisites for the caring process to be optimal and for the child's development.
• Third, the caregiver/child relationship is culturally embedded in multiple relationships. The caring process must from the beginning be oriented toward the cultural inclusion of the child.

These basic premises for the ethical position can serve as a starting point for analyzing the caregiver's ethical challenges—challenges that will require different dimensions for consideration to come to the best ethical behavior toward the child. For the first two premises, dependency and cooperation, the legitimization for the caregiver's behavior must be found within the relationship. For the third, the cultural inclusion, the caregiver's behavior must be justified externally in the expectations from the social context of the relationship.

Internal legitimacy for the caregiver's behavior will be found if the caregiver:

• is giving priority to the child—takes the ethical position toward the weaker Other—and acts on a prosocial intention in line with the child's dependency;
• acts on the child's observed needs—assesses and delivers in line with actual needs and resources in the relationship—according to an assessment of consequences;
• acts in a cooperating mode with the child—respecting the capacity, competence, and individuality of the child;
• acts in a predictable and transparent way—with integrity.

External legitimacy for the caregiver's behavior will be found if the caregiver:

• is culturally accepted in the role as caregiver—does not interfere with others who might have a more legitimate place in the caring role;
• builds a necessary base to be of value for the child in an extended perspective—seeks competence and takes extended responsibility in line with expectations in the culture and local social network;
• gives space and respect to other relationships for the child—thus respecting the child's biological, cultural, and multi-relationship, structure of the child's identity;
• acts according to cultural expectations assumed to be of value for the child, and for protection of the child—assuming responsibility for the child's safe inclusion into the society within which the relationship exists.

To some degree and in various ways we will find this structure and challenges of the primary caregiver's ethical proto-position in all human relationships. Since the professional relationship will always be characterized by some difference in power and other asymmetrical aspects, these challenges will also apply for professional relationships. We shall look closer at some of the dimensions that will be needed for an ethical assessment when we are in an ethical position. Being professional will always imply being in an ethical position in a professional relationship.

Ethics of Intention

The ethics of intention can be seen as taking a prosocial position—to put the Other first. It means to have the best intentions and to be nonjudgmental and accepting of the Other in the relationship. All ethics are based on a willingness to see and meet the Other's needs and interests, and to be committed to the Other even if it should demand abstaining from one's own needs and interests. As such, ethics of intention is a starting point—"the will to do good and best." This position is for most persons connected to their personal ethics and corresponding empathic capacity. However, attitudes and personal prejudices might jeopardize attaining a prosocial stand in all situations. As indicated earlier, personal ethics may be seen as traits and competences that can mature and develop in line with the person's experiences and development: for example, by being critical and reflective in our own social encounters and experiences. The prosocial challenge might be a question of having integrated the "right" values, virtues, and character. This connects to the individual's upbringing and the cultural expectations of not only the intention to do right, but also internalized ideas of "what is right." Intentional ethics are thus not independent of the next dimension—*ethics of duty*, to be discussed later.

Professional ethics does not exist outside the person—it should be well connected with our personal ethics. To attain such a connection our personal ethics must be scrutinized for prejudices that might hinder us being able to have the general prosocial, positive intentional starting point in all our professional relationships. The individual psychologist's intentional ethical position can be seen as a competence that can develop through teaching, training, and collegial reflection and discussions on ethical dilemmas. Thus the prosocial intentions may become generalized, and well integrated in professional practice.

As mentioned above, ethics of intention might be seen as primary and a premise for ethical awareness; that one has an inclination and willingness to let moral values guide one's behavior. However, ethics of intention draw attention to the actor, not to the act or behavior, nor to the relationship and its context. The question of intentions or moral character of the actor are thus not of much help in evaluating a dilemma, or as an argument for the actions taken. Most people will say, and probably experience, that in general they have the best intentions and a prosocial stand. If, however, these intentions have strong connections to norms and duties that are highly valued by the intending person, the individual's "good will" can be an argument or excuse for transgressions and offense. For example, a strong norm saying that children should behave respectfully in relationship to parents might be an argument for belittling and offending a child's integrity—with the best intentions in the eyes of the offender. In professional practice "the good intentions to help" can end up becoming an ethical problem and offense. A single focus on one's "best intensions" may often end in patronizing and disrespectful behavior, as well as in conflicts and unforeseen consequences.

Example:

A psychologist worked in a child protection institution assessing the needs of the children and advising on placements in foster care. After six months, a 5-year-old boy previously assessed by the psychologist came back to the institution after placement in foster care. The foster parents had separated and neither of them wanted to go on taking care of the child. The psychologist felt very badly for the boy, who already had experienced several grave rejections and traumas in his life. After discussion with his own family, they applied and became the foster family for the boy and he thrived. One year later the biological mother brought the placement of the child to court. The psychologist's different roles came into focus in the proceedings and were also criticized by colleagues acting as witnesses. He was accused of having misused his position for his own interests. The boy was taken out of his care and brought back to a rather miserable situation with his mother and her new fiancé, who was seen by the court as having a "caring potential." The boy lost all connection with the psychologist and his family.

When questions and criticisms are raised about behavior and actions, it is not uncommon that the person whose actions are questioned responds by claiming to have had the best intentions. "I did not mean to…" is an often heard rhetorical phrasing when confronted with negative consequences or criticism of one's behavior. It is a tip of the tongue phrase that is early attained by the child and follows the person through life. By claiming the best intentions one tries to avoid rejection and other negative responses for wrongdoing. When arguing with the best intentions, this is also an appeal for forgiveness. This diverts attention from the wrong to the intended good.

When evaluating complaints for the board of ethics it was the experience of one of the authors that in response to filed complaints, psychologists often stated: "It was absolutely not my intention..." It is, of course, not possible to argue against a person's intentions, or, for that matter, to question them. In the aftermath the intention was a totally private and bygone state, not observable or assessable to others. For ethical evaluations the claim for having had the best intentions should not be an excuse and divert attention from the unethical result, although it might be part of an honest explanation that could contribute to consolation.

As mentioned, statements of positive intentions may sometimes be seen as manipulative acts to divert the attention from the negative effects of the behavior to a question of forgiveness—the offender or wrongdoer is issuing an appeal to the injured party. Strong engagement, out of the best intentions, can end in transgressions which set others aside who might have more legitimate qualifications to give support and care. In voluntary work, but also in professional practice, one can sometimes question whether or not helpers strongly want to demonstrate their good intentions, thus ignoring or blocking other resources that might be helpful. The helping project may become a project for the helper, where showing off may be an important part of the motivation and dynamics of the helper. In such instances the ego-related motivation may come to create unhealthy dependencies and cover up a misuse of power; and "the best intentions" have become a source for an unethical practice.

Example:
A client, with the support of her psychologist, complained against a civil organization that was, as in many countries, founded with the intention to help victims of different culpable acts. The client, mother of a young child, had protected her child from alleged sexual abuses from her father by withholding the child from visiting the father. A legal procedure was ongoing. In the meantime contacts between the father and the girl were forbidden by the social service authorities. With support from the civil organization, the father presented himself as the victim in the situation. The organization was led by very engaged individuals from different professions, with best intentions. They helped him vigorously to fight the social service authorities. Without checking and taking into consideration the security of the child, they managed to force through a change so the father got the right to see his daughter, even though the case still was pending in the court.

The best-intention project alone can, as mentioned, become a paternalistic position: *This is for your best interest!* If not the psychologist, many consigning instances may have this attitude toward primary clients; this may occur in contracting for the psychologist's assistance in reorganizing a workplace, or in referring a client for psychotherapy. For the psychologist it is important to try to communicate with the parties and to analyze one's own motives, so that the best intentions of others do not come to patronize the client in the relationship with the psychologist. Sometimes professionals, psychologists included, work for "the good course." In such programs and projects the best intentions can come to override more nuanced ethical evaluations. The psychologist must make a clear distinction between his/her own intentions and the referral agency's motives.

Paradoxically, the idea of *having the best intentions and interests of the client* in mind can foster distance from the client, and the client's responsibilities. One can come to overlook clients' competences, needs, feelings, and responsibilities, and the intentions of the helper in a professional position can even become cynical. It is often astonishing to register that personnel in institutions, especially when they are to administer restrictions on clients' freedom, can develop degrading attitudes and illegitimate limitations on top of the legal restrictions they are expected to uphold. The whole staff can lose their ability to react to moral misbehavior by colleagues. Lobotomy, sterilizing, isolation of disabled people, etc., have been upheld in the not so distant past as being "in the best interests" of the individuals abused. In such instances the "best interests of whom" can become unclear. Such ambiguity might still happen. For example, this may occur in some countries when social authorities find a father being a violent or sexual offender in the family. Instead of removing him out of the family, small children and their mothers have to leave their home and they may have to stay in protective care in order to be shielded from the violent father. A thorough analysis of the dependency issues is always important, in order to discover whether it really is the interests of the weaker Other which are being given priority.

This discussion should show that although being a necessary base for ethical practice, the best intentions do not help the psychologist much in ethical assessment and evaluations. Quite the contrary:

strong reliance on ethics of intention can grow into an unethical position. On the other hand, having a prosocial and open mind to the needs of others can be seen as a prerequisite for being able to behave ethically. It will, however, require communication and other guiding principles to find the ethically best solutions.

Ethics of Duty

One widespread and central way of looking at ethics is the claim that there are some universal, natural principles for responsible behavior in human relationships with which it is mandatory that the individual comply. These principles have the status of being imperative in their conceptualization: *you should/must/ought—should/must/ought not*—much in line with how laws and regulations are formulated. However, different from legal regulations, which are democratically decided, the ethics of duty, or of nature, are seen as embedded in the human condition, and as such above humans to decide on. In religious contexts, such principles are seen as given by God. In a more humanistic context, many of the same principles are seen as knowledge-based implications. When reflecting on, and getting more knowledge about the human function and existence, our relationships, and dependencies to our environmental context, some ethical issues and imperatives arise. As such, they are seen as given by nature and may also be called an *ethics by nature* or *duty*. Such principles of duty or of nature are formulated in religious texts, in the Koran and the Bible for example, in UN declarations, and in different ethical codes. Most codes of professional ethics, like the EFPA Meta-Code of ethics, have some formulations of this character. For example: in the first principle on respect: "The psychologist accords appropriate respect to, and promotes the development of fundamental rights, dignity and worth of all people." As we see, there is no option; psychologists must just behave in this way, it is a fundamental duty to do so.

The human condition, which is our natural human capacities and our contextual realities, social and others, can be said to be the basis for an ethics of duty. Our common destiny and dependencies will demand and appeal to the individual to make efforts so that the necessary community and loyalties can be upheld, without which the individual will not be able to exist. There is a need for a basic human solidarity, and this basic premise of human nature implies social duties from the individual. If you refuse to act on the appeals of others you lose your moral right to make appeals to others when you are in need—a position every human being will encounter.

While ethics of duty were formulated in earlier times in religious texts, the more modern versions are motivated by knowledge, understanding of, and a claim for respect for the "natural" preconditions for human life. More modern ethical declarations can also be seen as reflecting an ecological understanding of the individual human being. As such, the ethical principles of duty can be argued by empirically derived information and a rational approach to human and inter-human phenomena and mutual dependencies. Acquired psychological knowledge about what conditions are necessary for healthy human development, for example by secure attachments and minimization of threats, can be seen as information supporting an ethics of duties toward children and how they should be respected and treated.

It is often claimed that ethics of duty or nature and their derived principles are universal. At the same time, such principles may be vigorously debated for their implications, interpretations, range of validity, and application at different times and under different conditions. For example, there is much debate and many disputes and conflicts within and between religious groups and traditions on how to apply imperative texts of duty within the context of modern living. There are also discussions on humanistic or secular principles of human rights, challenged by different interpretations and contextual conditions. Globalization and secularization have fostered declarations and codes to secure reciprocal respect and care cross-culturally. At the same time, this confronts traditional principles of duties embedded in local cultures and religions. What are seen as universal can be seen very differently from differing local perspectives.

"Universal truth" is often used to protect the system that is producing it, either in religion, politics, or science. Humans strive to discover universal truths that could solve problems and dilemmas and offer knowledge for what is right. But all data, including scientific data, need to be understood within a specific cultural and temporal context. Science brings new knowledge very rapidly, so actions from these conclusions will always have a limited duration and validity. One should always be cautious when postulating and using ethical principles as absolutely universal and timeless.

In modern media, single cases and events are often exposed in relation to how ethics of duty has been neglected or is challenged. This often creates important discussions on value issues and how duties and responsibility for the individual's dignity are managed in the case that has been publicized; for example, on issues including ethnicity, sex, childhood, immigration, and the like. However, the problem with exposing ethical issues primarily by single cases, as modern media often do, is that this can come into conflict with an approach to the same issue based on solidarity. Focus on the individual case may hide or repress the interests of other individuals or groups living under the same conditions. Ethics of duty can become an overriding dimension that focuses on the single event. The symptom may come into focus while the underlying dynamics and systemic defects are still unchanged. Many people can become occupied with the one media-exposed child victim of war, or in poverty, while the other children's faces in the shadow of that exposure are never recognized. And when the TV camera is turned off, or focuses on a new face and event, the interest for the former exposure is gone.

In modern discourse, ethics of duty is much related to the rights and dignity of the single individual. Human attachments and the corresponding multi-relational characteristics of human identity can become undervalued. If the rather absolute character of ethics of duty is taken too literally, other perspectives and valued interests can be set aside. Following only one "duty" to the individual might end in an unethical position. For example, there might be a tension between respecting the individual's freedom to choose and the protection of others. Therefore, all duties have their practical and timely domain of validity. If taken only on its literal and aspirational level, and not evaluated on the practical level, ethics of duty, as with ethics of intentions, will lose its value for practical ethical guidance.

While ethics of nature has its motivation in scientific "truths," discussions will also arise on what these facts are. While religious and tradition-based duties must be interpreted and implemented according to the stage of development of the relevant society, so also will knowledge-based principles, as already mentioned, be discussed according to the actual knowledge available. Despite the claim for universality, the understanding and validity of ethics of duty or ethics of nature are embedded in the general discourse on common ethics, as well as in the ongoing discourse in moral philosophy (Vetlesen, 2005).

Ethics of Consequence and Utility

An important corrective to ethics of intention and ethics of duty and nature is what might be called *ethics of consequence*. What are the possible foreseen or expected consequences of our professional acts and interventions? How we attain the very best benefits for our clients should, of course, be the primary goal for professional work. However, simultaneously we should reflect on what may be possible negative effects. From the age of Hippocrates, *primo non noccere*—"First of all do no harm"—is an old and primary principle in the ethical code of medicine. It has since been used as a principle of attention and vigilance in most professions. A proactive analysis of possible negative effects should also be central in psychologists' practice. Therefore, this principle is also included as central in the EFPA Meta-Code of Ethics.

Focusing on possible negative effects can, however, be misconceived as a principle of self-protection. As ethical guidance, ethics of consequence refer to the effects for the Other (client), not for the actor (psychologist). In professional contexts it is sometimes observed that being cautious is understood as: "I must see to it that I am not criticized." Being in a professional role includes the possibility of having worries, taking some risks, being criticized, complained about, and even sued. It takes some courage to be a professional. Being too occupied with negative consequences for oneself can lead to an approach that is influenced or even driven by self-protection. This is not an ethical position; quite the contrary, it can lead to an unethical position if safeguarding oneself is the main motive in the thinking of possible consequences. One will not be able to utilize one's full potential as a professional in the interests of the client if one's own safeguarding is put first.

Example:
"I try to avoid clients that are, or might be involved in legal matters. Then I don't do any harm. I hate being summoned as a witness and to appear in court. You never know, people like that might also one day sue yourself."

This statement from a colleague in a seminar on ethics raised a heated discussion on the balancing of the responsibility for clients against the interests of the psychologist, avoiding tasks that might be unpleasant for her. Avoidance, and not acting, can be unethical if the psychologist had the potential to act in a way that might enhance the well-being of or reduce harm to the Other.

As ethical guidance, ethics of consequence are concerned with the optimization of the utility and positive effects of the relationship, and having awareness of and acting to limit the possible negative effects for the Other. For the psychologist this is the primary client. It is, of course, legitimate also to be aware of the possible consequences for oneself in the assessment. It is the total weighing of utility or negative effects, and who is given priority, that is the ethical issue. An important turning point in the balancing of consequences and interests is when there is a threat to the psychologist's personal integrity and legitimate role that might undermine the ability to uphold a professional position: for example, by being gravely threatened, or getting sick or burned out by the workload in the professional relationship. Sometimes, however, taking risks and accepting personal strain can be necessary for the psychologist to attain the best and protect a client from negative consequences.

Example:
During a family therapy session a young girl discloses that her father had abused her friend during an overnight stay with the family. This had happened during one of the father's drinking periods, and had become an unmentionable event within the family until the moment it was revealed. The girl was afraid that her friend would tell other friends about her father's drinking and what had happened. When the psychologist asks the parents what they feel they must do now that the episode is out in the open, both parents say that nothing more needs to be done. The mother says she has talked with the abused child and told her that the father regretted very much what happened, and that they all should forget about the incident. If anything more should be done they would sort it out themselves. The psychologist then says that she has both a legal and an ethical obligation to inform the appropriate authorities when having knowledge about a child being abused and under possible pressure. The parents strongly protest and claim to be protected by the psychologist's confidentiality. After some discussion the psychologist informs the child protection authorities. The abused child confirms the information disclosed and is protected from further contact with the family. Legal proceedings are started against the father and complaints about the psychologist's actions are filed. The psychologist is also for some time disturbed by nightly telephone calls with only breathing on the line.

The primary concern for the psychologist was to protect the probably maltreated girl from being threatened and possibly becoming re-victimized. This girl became an ethically relevant secondary client—a "third face" (see later discussion) in danger of negative consequences if the psychologist did not act. The total consequences of the psychologist's action were extensive: the family went into a crisis, the child protection authorities acted on two families, the father was jailed, and the therapeutic relationship was broken. The parents reacted toward the psychologist, claiming that their right to self-determination and confidentiality was broken. If, however, the psychologist had refrained from acting on the information, the alleged abused girl might have been further repressed and victimized by the abuser and his family. Giving ethical priority to the possible negative consequences for the abused girl did, however, have dramatic outcomes for others in the client system, and was an unpleasant process for the psychologist.

Ethics of consequence does not only address being attentive to minimize negative consequences. As mentioned, the primary goal of all professional practice is the expectation that it should have some positive consequence or be of value for the client—utility. For psychologists, as science-based professionals, that means that utility should be scientifically describable. Utilitarian anticipations are thus implicit in professional practice. Some kind of evidence for positive effects is demanded and anticipated by clients, employers, and referral agencies. The questions then also arise: who is to define what is useful, and for whom? From an ethical point of view this is not a simple question. Two domains can be differentiated in answering these questions.

First, these questions can be said to be scientific: are scientifically established theories and methods available and valid for the effect sought and observed? This is a question of scientific evidence that can be defined and answered solely by scientists. When trying to answer this part, it is important to keep in mind that scientific answers are always contestable, as this is a key hallmark of scientific process. So also is the professional use of scientific evidence. A precondition for the use of scientific evidence is the ability to understand the level of uncertainty in all scientific answers, to be critical toward the answers, and still to endure this and be able to apply the uncertain answers to solve practical problems and challenges. That also means a willingness to change when evidence changes. It can be difficult to maintain this professional stance as professional methods and even scientific theories and "schools" are often branded and marketed with economic interests connected to their professional application and dissemination. To be critical of the understanding and the limits for generalization of the effects and consequences observed is a permanent ethical challenge for the individual psychologist, as well as for the professional community.

The second domain for defining utility or negative consequences of professional actions is not a scientific question. It is rather a question of values that must be assessed in the relationships of the individuals involved. For example, the relationship between a psychologist and client may be valued highly by the client although no "objective" effect can be observed: no change, just stability. And, in a developmental perspective, an experience of today might not have an observable impact in the short term, but may still gradually change a developmental trajectory. The questions will thus be: How much should the client's experience of an understanding human encounter at the right moment be valued as part of a professional practice? Is it the right of the client to define what is developmentally useful for himself or herself? In giving weight to the client's right to evaluate the professional relationship it is, however, important that client feedback and the professional practice are well linked in sound scientific theory, even though it is not possible to observe a direct link between the psychologist's practice and short-term change in the client's behavior. For the psychologist, it is important that practices are always open to what the outcomes and consequences may be, even if the client has the most to say on the worth of interacting with the psychologist. The practice still must have a scientific basis. Otherwise the professional relationship can slide into a private relationship, and become a dual relationship with all its ethical hazards.

In using ethics of consequence as guidance it may be important to separate the concept of *utility* from the concept of *productivity*. The latter may be of most interest to employers, funding agencies, and governmental planning of services, while the first comes closer to assessing the usefulness, the good, for the individual client. There may be a conflict between utility and productivity. Whereas productivity is often seen in short-term and directly observable effects, or in economic calculable terms, utility may be seen in a more long-term and developmental perspective. The two can foster different and conflicting theories and practices.

A further question may be whether the observed or valued effects come about and can be attributed to the privileged knowledge determining the psychologist's interventions, or be attributed to the client's competence to make sense and use of the psychologist's expertise. It is not without ethical relevance how effects are explained. Psychologists (as other humans!) may have a tendency to attribute failure in attaining sought results and negative effects to a lack of motivation, personality traits of the client, or other factors external to themselves. Similarly, positive results and successes may be described as being in line with and attributed to the psychologist's theory, interventions, and competence. What kind of evaluation of utility and evidence is this from an ethical perspective? It can be argued that the ethical qualities in the relationship between the psychologist and clients are what is significant for the client in making use of the psychologist's competence—a joint effort. The question of utility is thus connected to how the effects are explained, and explaining is part of the power issue between client and psychologist. *To optimize the ethical qualities of the relationship should be considered important for enhancing the utility of professional practice.*

A final point, however: even if the psychologist lets the client set goals, make priorities, and evaluate outcomes, the responsibility for the process will reside with the psychologist. It is for the psychologist to ensure that the approach to the problem and the goals set are reachable and within with the methods and competence of the psychologist; so also must the psychologist assess and explain limitations and possible negative outcomes. The practice must always be in a frame that is supported by describable professional experience, evidence-based theory, and ethical responsibility.

Ethics of Procedure

Righteousness and what is fair are central issues in ethics. This is very often a question of distribution—how resources, goods, rights, needs, and freedom to choose are distributed. Avoiding discrimination is important, but sometimes unbalanced distribution or positive discrimination can be seen as fair, due to the lack of other opportunities—for example, an exclusive parking zone for disabled close to the entrance of a building, or giving priority to women and immigrants for certain employment in governmental institutions, etc. These are actions to bring about more equality in areas that have been closed or limited for some groups, or that recognizes the special needs of individuals. Positive discrimination may be seen as a balancing against other or earlier discriminations. Questions of fairness are often central in political issues and debates—how resources and degrees of freedom should be distributed. It is typical in addressing such questions, either by democratic or bureaucratic processes, that solutions are found in setting up some kind of fixed procedure for how the just distribution, or positive discriminations, should be implemented. Procedures based on specific criteria and rules may be seen as necessary if resources and goods are limited or unevenly allocated.

Specific procedures are also relevant for exploring how positive effects might or should be enhanced and negative effects reduced. Ethics of procedure thus often has links to ethics of duty or of consequence, where ethics of procedure is a method for reaching and upholding these values. One chooses to conform to a specific norm for behavior in solving an ethical challenge. As such, it becomes an ethical method much in line with laws and legal regulations. There is, however, an important difference. While legal regulations have their legitimate basis in democratic representative decisions, ethics of procedure do not have such a base. The norms for practice are set up by the practitioner(s) themselves to solve ethical challenges. Surgeons, for example, will have some standard procedures to avoid accidental complications, and the surgeons will have to bear the responsibility themselves for these procedures.

Procedural ethics is typical for professional practice where the client in the relationship is passive or has little opportunity to contribute to or influence the process—a comatose patient, an air flight passenger, a psychologist's client being tested, and the like. However, while both passenger and test-taker have previously agreed to engage, what is to happen thereafter lies totally in the hands of the professional. If the client was invited to influence what should happen when landing an airplane, one would be unsure how the result would come out. Uncertainty of outcome is reduced by not involving the client, and is for the interest of the client. "Do not disturb the driver!" is the mantra.

The idea and expectations behind procedural ethics are that if, over time and situations, we meticulously follow a specified procedure this will lead us to obtain the most just, best results and fewest failures. By extensive use of manuals for practice and interactions one does not have to rely on the single practitioner's creativity or imperfection, only on the practitioner's compliance with an evidence-based procedure. How to act if the unexpected situation arises might even be built into the procedure. The "human factor" is to be minimized.

Like ethical solutions, procedures and rules will always be relative and must be argued and defensible in the specific situation and compared to other ways of solving a dilemma. If one becomes used to solving challenges by procedures, it might become a habit. Then the procedure becomes a goal in itself. It might even lose connection to values behind developing the procedure in the first place. Our tendency to engage in repetitive, conservative, and "safe" behaviors can be a strong element in procedural ethics. Using standardized practices can become a comfortable way to practice, a manner of avoiding personal responsibility by seeking safety within a generally accepted procedure. However, responsibility for professional practice will always stay with the individual psychologist. This demands a double perspective when applying procedural solutions as ethical solutions. One must both follow the procedure and at the same time be critical to its application and its consequences in the actual situation. For example, one should evaluate whether there might be vicarious or self-protective elements dominating when applying the procedure. .

One argument for using procedures for practice is the need for scientific and evidential support for theories and methods. This has been a steady argument within psychological professional practice in recent years, when different funding agencies have been setting criteria for the funding. Governmental institutions, insurance companies, and other large firms with bureaucratic structure often use psychologists' expertise, contracting for larger or more limited tasks, assessments, and interventions. The product delivered by the psychologist will often be part of procedures set up by the contracting agency. One ethical quandary for the psychologist is to reflect on how one's own contribution fits into the total procedure in an ethically acceptable way. Consider the following example:

> A university student with dyslexic problems applied to the national social security for a scholarship making it possible to have reading support and, if necessary, to extend the stipulated standard time for completing the curriculum for which she had been accepted. The student

had excellent grades from the sixth-form college where she had been supported by special teaching programs. She had passed by good margins the inclusion criteria for the university course. The social security office demanded that before her application would be evaluated she had to be tested by a psychologist to prove her intellectual capacity to cope with the curriculum. She felt offended, as for a time she had felt misconceived as mildly mentally retarded, being wrongly assessed by a school psychologist when she was in second grade. She hoped that the psychologist who was contracted by social security authorities would write a recommendation based on the earlier diagnostic information about her dyslexia and her study success so far. The psychologist, however, insisted on making a full intellectual assessment, as this was what he was asked to do, and argued that this was standard procedure in such cases. The student felt herself to be discriminated against by such a procedure. She let herself be interviewed on national television, and she later complained to the ethical board for psychologists. The board found that the psychologist would have enough documentation to conclude that she had the capacity to manage further studies and to be in need of special support for the dyslexic problem. Further assessment of intellectual capacity could be seen as redundant and thus unnecessary for the question at hand. Understandably, it might be experienced as unfair, as other students who entered the course would not have to be tested. The student got her scholarship, and the procedures for obligatory psychological assessment were changed.

This example demonstrates that procedures that might have a general positive goal—to ensure that those in most need should receive proper support—can be inappropriate in specific cases. This is not an unusual contradiction in using procedures. It demands that when such an incongruity arises, a new assessment is needed of what ethical dilemmas are at stake—a review that the psychologist in the example did not do. What in the next section is called *ethics by proxy* will be an important supplement when such situations arise.

Dialogical/Proximal Ethics[1]

It can sometimes be difficult for the psychologist to establish and maintain a dialogical connectedness with the client, and at the same time uphold a second, scientific and professional perspective on the client's behavior, thoughts, and feelings. The first perspective demands being in an interactive process with the client; the second requires a detached position. There is often a tension between closeness and distance. The least complicated is to take on the position of distance and to give responses, answers, and interventions that are solely based on psychological interpretations and explanations. This, however, isolates the client as an object of the psychologist's study and interventions. However, as earlier shown in the model of the prototypical ethical position, responding ethically requires letting the Other maintain the position of being a self-organized and cooperating actor in the relationship to the greatest extent possible: this even when dependency is almost total, as with the baby. In the cooperating frame, both the caretaker and the baby are on the same human level. It is a question of how one reacts and respects the Other in the human encounter as cooperating actors, under the limitations of differing dependencies and in a context of multiple relationships.

Dialogical ethics, or ethics of proximity, means to find the ethically most sound solutions through being in communication and cooperation in the close, face-to-face frame. Most human encounters can be seen as dialogically organized. It is through dialogue that distance and closeness and intersubjectivity and mutual understanding are developed. This view looks at ethics as taking a responsible ethical position in response to the actual closeness and dialogue that will develop in any relationship. The dialogue will influence and determine what could be *right* or *best*, because it is here, in the transactions of the relationship, that needs, states of mind, initiatives, meanings, and responses can and will be exposed, hidden or distorted, accepted or refused. A central philosophical perspective for this way of looking at ethics is that of Levinas (Levinas, 1981; Bauman, 1993). This proximal perspective takes as a starting point that in the human encounter *the Face of the Other* cannot refrain from expressing itself, to convey an appeal. Any face-to-face encounter is characterized by mutual appeals, as feelings and sentiments are exposed and reacted to by each other's bodily expressions.

According to this view, it is the interaction and construction of meanings in the relationship that can foster a mutual understanding of the demands and needs exposed, as well as misunderstandings and rejection. The challenge for ethical behavior is thus to come into an interaction that truly assesses the needs and states of the Other, through the proximity of the dialogue in the face-to-face interaction. Such a searching dialogue is not possible without mutual trust and safety. It is only within a trusting and non-rejecting relationship that one can expose oneself. This means that one cannot abstain from entering the emotional, not always understandable in a rational sense, experience that all human encounters entail. Both parties will react to each other's emotional expressions, and trust is thus not something that can be demanded or given as a permanent state. Rather, it must be developed and upheld all the way during the interaction. The mutual trust will always be tested in the actual dialogue. "Can I dare to expose myself?"—is a question permanently embedded in the exchange. If you try to control the Other's expressions, this will be contrary to the goal of the dialogue to expose oneself with authenticity. An open dialogue demands that the Other is respected as a self-organized actor, with the right to freely choose and form his/her own initiatives and reactions.

When ethics are seen through a dialogical lens, one can never know if one's initiative or action is ethically proper until the Other has presented a reaction. However, as mentioned, openness can only be based on mutual trust because *being open and authentic also implies being vulnerable*. Trust can only be achieved if being open is not exploited by the other. Denied dependencies and corresponding hidden power issues are the most central threats to authentic self-exposure, and can foster unethical practice. Assessing and communicating dependencies and their power derivations are, therefore, important issues for reaching sound and supportive ethical practice in any relationship.

At first glance, a proximal perspective on ethics can seem individualistic in its suggestions for solutions to challenges: "What is good for us is right." If, however, we look closer at what is implied in being open and authentic, it will first of all be to expose one's dependencies and responsibilities to others. An awareness of the Other is, as mentioned earlier, a corresponding awareness of the multi-relational identity of any individual and the cultural inclusion of all relationships. We are all in multiple relationships, and the *third faces*, meaning our obligations to others in other relationships, will enter and make demands in the actual Me–You relationship and its dialogical process. Shame, guilt, feelings of attachment, loyalty, love, and responsibility all point to relevant Third Faces in our encounters with the actual Other. In a proximal perspective, a full understanding of You will thus reveal our multi-relationship identities and lives—your Third significant relationship will be a contextual premise for Our relationship.

An individualistic or non-dialogical perspective on ethics can be seen as distancing from the reality that we all have many relationships that count in our lives. However, a proximal view on ethics confirms the responsibilities that also are relevant in the relationships to third persons. For example, if a psychologist listens to a leader complaining about his employees, the indirect appeal from them may expose itself through a growing uneasiness that these people are not heard, and this uneasiness will be part of the actual relationship with the leader. The depressed mother who feels worthless for her children will expose an appeal from her children; what is the developmental condition for them?

Such indirectly exposed appeals from Third Faces can lead to moralizing and communicative problems in the dyadic process. "What do you think your mother would say!" can be a representative phrase for this position that can arise. In this way, we always meet our own, or the Other's others in the dyadic dialogue—and they have a say. For example, the psychologist's colleagues can often be relevant Third Faces in his/her relationship to a client. Some of our other relationships will almost always indirectly be part of any ongoing relationship. One may say that "dialogue is dyadic in process but triadic in consequence." What I do and expose in one relationship will be of relevance for other relationships of mine. This is an ethical challenge that the proximal ethical perspective helps us to uphold. It exposes the often experienced doubt and ambivalence: Who should be given priority and how should support be weighed, handled, and distributed? The psychologist who privatizes the relationship with a client will expose his/her disrespect for colleagues and undermine other clients' general trust in psychologists; but most of all, it can hurt and damage other important relationships of the client.

Responsibility always follows when we enter relationships. This is clearly relevant in professional relationships where the roles, status, and dependencies of the psychologist and client are different. Thus there will always be a need for the psychologist to find the right degree of responsibility to take. The dialogue within the relationship, including the revealing of the most relevant Third Faces, can uncover resources, contradictions, conflicting issues, needs, and dependencies that are not obvious from outside the relationship. Responsibility may thus best be assessed in the proximal process with the client. In the EFPA Meta-Code of Ethics, clients are defined sometimes to be "persons indirectly affected" (third faces).

A proximal or dialogical ethical perspective can help in being attentive to the following concerns:

• *The unique* character of the person encountered and the situation in which the encounter occurs, and the distinctive emotional manifestation of the encounter. This is an important corrective or supplement to standardized classifications and methods that are part of a scientific, more distanced approach to human phenomena. Encounters that imply, for example, diagnosing human behavior, can be seen as unethical if simultaneously no space is given for those diagnosed to present themselves on their own terms. All kinds of objectifying and generalizing of the individual will entail an unethical potential that might reduce the unique humanity of the individual.

• *The basic human appeal;* a mutual need for respect and care where the most independent in the relationship will ethically be the most challenged. That person will have the greatest degree of freedom to choose to follow or not the appeals. For the more dependent, compliance or rejection will be the alternatives. An appeal and its response can only be issued individually—*from me to you,—I want,—I respond.* Ignoring an appeal is also a response, a rejection with its consequence for the relationship. In the perspective of proximal ethics, one can say that the individual appealing and the one to whom the appeal is issued are bound in a joint destiny, both being in need of human relationships and thus in need for ethics for these relationships.

• *Dialogue* is the means necessary in relationships to sort out needs, resources, values, and obligations that are relevant in the relationship; including expectations and consequences for third parties with which the two in interaction have relationships. Dialogue gives the individual the possibility to express individuality and uniqueness. Only through dialogue in a trusting relationship can authentic information about oneself, not catchable by the Other's observation alone, be expressed.

• *Power* and corresponding differences in responsibility are central in relationships. In a professional relationship the most power, and thereby responsibility, will be with the professional. Through dialogue the power issues can be exposed and sorted so that both parties can express themselves in understandable ways within a shared meaning of the contextual limitations and options. In this process, appeals from relevant "third faces" will become visible as important elements in the context of the relationship, and must be brought into the professional's ethical assessments.

Concluding Remarks

In these essays we have discussed some of the broader ethical discourses that must be considered in the formulation of any ethical code. We have also pointed to a necessary differentiation and often a preferable tension between ethics and law. Finally, a basic model for the ethical position and some ethical dimensions has been explored. These discussions demonstrate the complexity and importance of continuous thinking, assessing, and evaluation in coming to a best ethical practice. Considering only one dimension in one's assessment may end in an unethical practice. The text of professional codes, for example the Meta-Code of Ethics for European Psychologists, which the authors have worked on, is important guidance. However, awareness of the different dimensions and discourses underlying the text are important supplements in application of the text to one's general practice, as well as in solving the more challenging ethical dilemmas.

Author Note

This chapter is developed from: Øvreeide, H. (2008). Ethical discourses and dimensions. In Lindsay, F., Koene, C., Øvreeide, H., & Lang, F. *Ethics for European Psychologists.* Gottingen, Germany: Hogrefe.

Note

1. One of the authors has coined this term, *ethics of dialogue* (Øvreeide & Backe-Hansen, 2002), meaning that a central place for sorting out ethical issues and dilemmas is in the dialogical, dyadic process between people; between psychologist and client. This will also expose the nature of the individual's multiple relationships, both client and psychologist, further discussed in the text.

References

Adorno, T. W., Adorno, T., Frenkel-Brunswick, E., Levinson, D. J., Sanford, R. N. (1950). *The authoritarian personality.* New York: Harper & Row.
Amati Sas, S. (1992). Ethics and shame in the countertransference. *The International Journal of Psychoanalysis, 12,* 570–579.
Arendt, H. (1978). *Life of the mind.* London: Secker & Warburg.
Bauman, Z. (1993). *Postmodern ethics.* Cambridge: Blackwell.
European Federation of Psychologists Associations. (2005). *Meta-code of ethics for European psychologists.* Retrieved from: www.efpa.be.

Iacoboni, M. (2008). *Mirroring people: The new science of how we connect with others*. New York: Farrar, Straus & Giroux.

Jogan, E. (2008). *Etika in psihoanaliza v teoriji in praksi* [Ethics and psychoanalysis in theory and practice]. Morality, Proceedings of the 11th Meeting of Slovenian Psychotherapists with International Participation, 8–22.

Levinas, E. (1981). *Otherwise than being: Or beyond essence*. The Hague: Martinus Nijehov.

Lindsay, G., Koene, C., Øvreeide, H., & Lang, F. (2008). *Ethics for European psychologists*. Gottingen, Germany and Cambridge MA: Hogrefe

Milgram, S. (1974). *Obedience to authority: An experimental view*. New York: HarperCollins.

Trevarthen, C., & Aitken, K. J. (2001). Infant intersubjectivity: Research, theory, and clinical applications. *Journal of Child Psychology and Psychiatry, 42*(1), 3–48.

Øvreeide, H., & Backe-Hansen, E. (2002). *Fagetikk i psykologisk arbeid*. Kristiansand: Høyskoleforlaget. (Swedish 2004 ed.).

Øvreeide, H. (2008). Ethical discourses and ethical dimensions. In Lindsay, G., Koene, C., Øvreeide, H., & Lang, F. *Ethics for European psychologists* (pp. 15–38). Gottingen, Germany and Cambridge MA: Hogrefe.

Vetlesen, A. J. (2005). *Evil and human agency*. Cambridge: Cambridge University Press.

Zimbardo, P. G. (2007). *The Lucifer effect: Understanding how good people turn evil*. New York: Random House.

CHAPTER
6

Ethical Decision Making

Geoff Lindsay

Abstract

This chapter explores the use of ethical codes to support ethical decision making. The nature of codes is examined with reference to ethical principles, domains of practice, cultural factors, and function. Distinctions are made between using codes for developmental/educative purposes, as working to assist decision making, as a basis for regulatory bodies' decision making, and as public statements. Three levels of complexity for decision making are proposed, from relatively automatic responses based on experience to analysis of ethical dilemmas. A model of decision making is proposed, drawing upon that of the Canadian Psychological Association. Its use is exemplified by a vignette describing decision making using the European Federation of Psychologists' Associations' Meta-Code of ethics.

Key Words: ethical decision making, Meta-Code of ethics, ethical dilemmas, regulation

Psychological practice requires a number of discrete but overlapping sets of knowledge and skills. This applies whether the psychologist is engaged in research or professional practice, for example, as a clinical or educational (school) psychologist. There are a number of common elements across the different branches of psychological practice. One example is their foundation in a scientific approach to the discipline, whereby research findings are fundamental to forming the basis of practice. In the United States, following the Boulder Conference of 1949, the term *scientist-practitioner* captured this approach. Another common element is the necessity to practice ethically, in whatever domain of the discipline.

Applied psychological practice is characterized by particular elements specific to a subdiscipline within the overall applied discipline of psychology, and also a large degree of commonality at a superordinate level across all subdisciplines. For example, all psychologist practitioners are trained in psychometric principles and the nature of methods of assessment; furthermore, assessment in a broad sense typically forms an important element of practice of a psychologist whatever his or her specific role. At the level of subgroups of practitioners, such as forensic psychologists, clinical psychologists, or counseling psychologists, these general domains are differentiated into more specific aspects. For example, specific assessment measures will vary to reflect different demands. These relate to domains of practice (e.g., clinic, factory, school), age of client (e.g., child, adult) and the purpose of the intervention (e.g., assessment alone compared with assessment linked directly to a treatment program, whether direct intervention or indirect, such as consultancy).

Also fundamental to psychological practice is decision making. The focus of this chapter is ethical decision making but there are overlaps with, for example, technical questions regarding practice. One instance concerns the technical quality of the methods to be used. The question of fitness for purpose is important here. Issues of reliability and validity, for example, are essentially technical issues and psychologists must be aware of these factors when using any instruments. However, there is also an ethical dimension concerning the use of measures which includes, but goes beyond, their technical quality.

This chapter explores ethical decision making. A worked example is provided in the latter section, drawing upon the European Federation of Psychologists Associations' (EFPA) Meta-Code of ethics. I argue that an ethical code is an important and useful aid to ethical decision making, but also that it is not sufficient. Furthermore, ethical codes vary in their conceptual framework, organization, and level of detail. Consequently, I first explore the nature of ethical codes and the implications for ethical decision making. I then set out an ethical decision-making model before using a vignette of an ethical dilemma as a worked example.

The Nature of Ethical Codes
The Purpose of Ethical Codes

The existence of an ethical code may be seen as one of the necessary characteristics of a profession. It is a clear indicator that its practitioners are expected to meet ethical standards. A second factor is more variable, namely that the ethical code forms the basis upon which the practitioner will also be held to account for his/her practice. Historically, using ethical codes for regulatory purposes has not necessarily followed the former, or at least not until some time later. This is because the holding to account of an individual requires a system of investigation, evaluation, and administration of sanctions as appropriate.

Ethical codes may be used to achieve different ends: I suggest that there are four main purposes. First, the code may be *educative*. Psychologists use the code to develop their understanding of the ethical dimensions of their practice. This is an important element in the initial training of psychologists, as researchers or applied professional practitioners. Both philosophical and practical issues may be explored to assist each psychologist to develop ethical awareness and develop the basis for ethical practice. However, initial training cannot provide all the preparation a professional needs. Rather, it is more useful to consider a long-term process of professional development, starting with initial training but continuing throughout a professional's working life.

The second purpose of an ethical code, therefore, is as a *working tool*. Initial training will lay a foundation but it is the engagement as a practitioner that leads to the need for psychologists to use ethical decision making in a real life setting. Interestingly, this is not always recognized. In the 1980s, Pope and Vetter (1992) undertook a study which asked members of the American Psychological Association (APA) about ethical dilemmas encountered in the previous year or two. It is of interest that 134 of the 679 who responded to the survey claimed that they had not had an ethically troubling issue to deal with over that period. This paradigm was utilized in the United Kingdom by Lindsay and Colley (1995) with members of the British Psychological Society (BPS), and also by Lindsay and Clarkson (1999) with U.K. psychotherapists. Subsequently, researchers from various other countries also replicated the study. In all cases, a sizeable minority of respondents decided that they had not had an ethically troubling incident to deal with in the previous year or two. (NB: It may also be speculated that a proportion of the nonrespondents to each survey had a similar view and so did not take part.)

The third purpose of an ethical code is to provide a *basis for regulatory bodies* to consider allegations of unethical conduct by a psychologist. For example, the BPS was until 2009 the nonstatutory regulatory body of member psychologists in the United Kingdom. Complaints about a psychologist that were heard by a disciplinary committee were presented as violations of the BPS ethical code, rather than in terms of the behavior per se, which became the specification of the substance for offending the ethical code. It is often argued that for this purpose it is preferable to have a code that is as specific as possible, so that it is more clear whether an offense has been committed or not (see below.) The problem with this approach, however, is that increased specificity brings its own limitations, as the allegation must also be framed specifically. Compare this with a charge of "bringing the profession into disrepute" as a result of specified activities, which may provide more freedom of interpretation for the disciplinary committee/tribunal.

Finally, the fourth purpose of an ethical code for psychologists is to provide a *public document* for use by nonpsychologists. This may be essentially for information, to inform the lay public that psychologists have an ethical code (important in itself) and what it comprises. Or, it may assist a client who is unsure what to expect of a psychologist's practice. That is, there is a political purpose to indicate the status of a profession, in that it has an ethical code and also a purpose of direct public benefit to provide information to those who may have an interest. These include the public who want to know the ethical standards expected of the profession with whom they will deal, and any person who has concern about the ethical behavior of the professional with whom they are or have been working.

The Style of Ethical Codes

Ethical codes vary in style and content. When the EFPA Meta-Code was being developed, I reviewed seven national codes and identified both similarities (e.g., all addressed confidentiality) but also significant variations (e.g., guidance about billing, which is not relevant in state-funded systems [Lindsay, 1992]). Some variations, therefore, concern specific content domains, while others are more fundamental.

Aspirational vs. "Bottom Line." Some codes provide guidance designed to help the psychologist to develop "best practice." Such aspirational codes seek to raise psychologists' sights to the highest ethical standards to which they should always aspire. An alternative is to identify the "bottom line" below which practice should not fall. The former is especially challenging, of course, but has the benefit of stressing positive standards. The latter may be particularly helpful in the early days of a psychologist's practice. However, there is the danger of seeing these standards not as a baseline from which to develop but rather a "good enough" level at which to remain. A developmental perspective may see the "bottom line" approach as level 1, to establish basic ethical practice, to be followed throughout the psychologist's career by an aspirational approach, always seeking optimal practice. This is an appropriate model for a psychologist's development, but an ethical code, as a written document, is not so easily constructed to meet each purpose unless the continuing professional development rationale is clearly woven through the document.

Principles and Standards

The EFPA Meta-Code and the ethical codes of the APA (2002) and Canadian Psychological Association (CPA, 2003) each comprise ethical principles followed by exemplifications of these through specifications or standards. The *Universal Declaration of Ethical Principles for Psychologists* (International Union of Psychological Science and International Association of Applied Psychology, 2008) also follows this model, whereas the previous BPS ethical code (actually a "code of conduct": British Psychological Society, 1985) comprised five sections without any statement of specific ethical principles. The influence of the EFPA Meta-Code has also led to the codes of its constituent national associations following the same model, as it is an EFPA requirement that a national code must be in accord with the Meta-Code. Although this requirement is essentially one of compliance with the content, many EFPA member associations have revised their codes to follow the same organizational model as the Meta-Code, including the BPS (2009). However, this is still work in progress and many associations within the EFPA are still working to develop other codes. At the 2009 General Assembly 11, the codes of national associations of the 35 members were approved as compliant with the Meta-Code. Also, new associations' codes are judged for their compliance with the Meta-Code when a national association seeks membership, but not all are structured in the form of principles and standards. For example, the Russian association was also accepted in 2009, although its code is organized in sections that do not match the principle-driven structure of the Meta-Code; the Russian association is expected to develop its code further to be fully compliant.

This is not simply a cosmetic issue. Rather, the organization and structure of an ethical code are important dimensions in addition to the code's content, and have implications for its use as an aid to ethical decision making. Codes that are driven by ethical principles have a coherent, intellectually driven structure. The specification of particular standards follows from the principles. Without this approach an ethical code may be rather more pragmatic, including elements which have a salience, but perhaps one that is partial for the profession as a whole, being rather more specific to particular groups of psychologists. For example, some such codes, from countries developing their systems of applied psychological practice, tend to focus on clinical psychology, as this is often the most developed. Starting with principles helps to ensure that the ethical guidance is widely applicable, especially if the standards are not written at too high a level of specificity. Clinical psychology is not only likely to be the subdiscipline developed earliest in countries with an emerging psychological practitioner community, it is also typically the largest grouping of the discipline in countries in which there is a more established profession of psychologist practitioners. This can lead to codes being developed to support practice in this domain at the expense, potentially, of other subdisciplines. However, the *essential* elements of psychological practice are largely generalizable, even if specifics such as location, actual measures, and particular interventions will vary between sub-disciplines. This problem is not insurmountable, but organizing the ethical code around principles and their exemplifications provides a sound framework for inclusion of all current, and indeed potential, subdisciplines of psychologists.

Another reason to develop an ethical code which is principle-led is that there is less danger of it becoming outdated. Codes that are organized around specific behaviors may be exposed as a new development appears that was not previously the subject of a standard in the code. For example, the use of the Internet has raised many ethical issues (e.g., Eynon, Schroeder, & Fry, 2009). Lindsay (2008, 2009) has explored the ethical challenges raised by states developing a concern for "national security," and Koocher (2007) has provided a comprehensive overview of new ethical challenges facing psychologists. It is of interest that the EFPA Standing Committee on Ethics was able to develop guidance on the use of the Internet, using the Meta-Code as a foundation, with relatively little problem. The principles and the specifications were found to cover the ethical issues of Internet use and other methods of working at a distance ("telepsychology").

Principles vs. Domains of Practice

Cultural Factors and Ethical Codes. Psychology cannot be "value-free." It is applied in the context of a world of values and rights of individuals (Lindsay, 1995). Furthermore, values and rights may be areas for debate and disagreement. If values and rights vary, then moral absolutes are rare. Ethical codes must, therefore, reflect their societal and cultural context. Ethical codes are typically developed by expert committees of a psychological association. In this case, experienced psychologists draw upon experience and other codes to develop a new code; subsequent revisions are then made by a committee building upon the original code and experience gained from its use. This was not, however, the origin of the APA code. Rather, the first edition of the code was developed using *critical incidents* of ethical issues gleaned from practice (American Psychological Association, 1952). This helped to ensure the ecological validity of the ethical code: it was immersed in real practice.

The EFPA Meta-Code (see below) was developed by a specialist taskforce drawn from a number of constituent associations, to ensure that the expertise was drawn from across the whole of Europe. This reflected a recognition of the number of European states and their variety in many cultural dimensions. This inclusive approach was both philosophical and pragmatic: to optimize the appropriateness and usefulness of the Meta-Code for Europe as a whole. This raises a further issue concerning the breadth of material on which codes may draw, in addition to domains within psychology itself. In particular, it is important when developing an ethical code to ensure that the results reflect the cultural, religious, and ethnic diversity that exists in the constituency for which the code is designed. Some countries, at least until recently, have been highly homogeneous, whereas others (e.g., England) are characterized by a long tradition of immigration from many countries, bringing a diversity of cultures and languages. The *Universal Declaration of Ethical Principles for Psychologists* may be seen as the extreme case. Its development was specifically designed to be inclusive with the ad hoc development group comprising psychologists from across the world. Furthermore, cultural diversity, specificity, and sensitivity were all seen as fundamental issues to address.

Patterns of migration have varied across nations and time. The United States has a long tradition of immigration of a large number of specific groups, and more recently an issue of immigration particularly from its neighboring country, Mexico. The United Kingdom's tradition has been driven by its having had the British Empire (now Commonwealth). Citizens from many colonies had the right to move to the United Kingdom and exercised that right. In addition, the United Kingdom has been the host to groups of refugees seeking safety, escaping various forms of persecution (for example, the Huguenots and Jews from Europe and, more recently, many war zones in Eastern Europe, Africa, and beyond). Mainland Europe has had a different pattern: a long history of wars, invasions, annexing parts of states, and the creation of large groupings (e.g., Austrian-Hungarian empire, Yugoslavia) which later split. More recently the collapse of the USSR has resulted in its constituent states gaining greater autonomy, and hence a further increase in diversity.

Reasons for migration, therefore, vary, and this has implications for ethical codes. First, the *specific groups* that join a host country are important. These may be similar to or very different from the host country on key dimensions. Religion has been an important dimension, in particular the difference between the Protestant and Catholic Christian traditions. Now, Islam is an important religious tradition in many countries. In addition, the Jewish religion has been a significant, if minority, religious grouping across most of Europe and the United States. Second, there is a question of the *status* of the migrant group. Whereas some immigrate to take up high-status positions, many others come to escape economic hardship and violence. The latter often immigrate with little support and join a lower level of the socioeconomic strata, with lower levels of attributed status and esteem.

Associated with this issue of status at migration is the developmental trajectory of subsequent status. In some instances, the first or possibly second generation to be born in the new host country take available opportunities and tend to "merge" successfully into the dominant culture; in other cases, successor generations remain at a low socioeconomic level, not sharing the benefits of citizenship in an equitable manner.

These various cultural factors associated with the development of modern-day societies have a direct relevance to ethical codes. It is necessary to consider whether the cultural assumptions of the dominant culture that may be shaping the development of a new code are applicable to subgroups or new immigrant groups. One important dimension is the distinction between the primacy of the individual versus the group. The former is strong in Western, particularly capitalist, cultures with an emphasis on individual responsibility for one's own actions. Therapy in the Western tradition typically seeks to support the development and autonomy of the individual client, but this may clash with the expectations of a person from a culture that promotes the need of the group (family, village, etc.) rather than those of the individual.

It is also important to recognize that these are not simple patterns of variation. There are differences between but also within groups, whether religious, national, or cultural. It is not as easy as having a "cultural sensitivity" by undertaking broad, generalized knowledge of various groups. Rather, the challenge is to develop an ethical code that is appropriate to a *diverse* society; and this applies to the diversity among psychologists as well as among client groups.

Statutory Regulation

So far the emphasis has been on ethical codes developed by psychological associations. However, in countries where there is a statutory regulatory system for practitioners, that system may well be separate from that of the national association. Regulatory bodies have a different function from professional associations, and this has an impact on the nature of the code. In the United States and Canada, licensing of psychologists to practice is the responsibility of individual states and provinces. The Association of State and Provincial Psychology Boards (ASPPB) is the association of the licensing boards for individual states and provinces in the two countries. The ASPPB has a code of conduct (revised edition 2005) for use by individual state/province boards. In the foreword, Kim Jonason, ASPPB President, distinguishes an ethics code produced by a professional association from that of a regulator. The former is the association's own guidance for its members to protect the public, and it may have elements of a regulatory code of conduct, but these "Rules of conduct in a professional association ethics code may be less specific, however, than is desirable from a regulatory code." Jonason goes on to note that the ethics code may also include advisory or aspirational as well as regulatory issues. The ASPPB code of conduct is designed to be specific and detailed. This approach is also taken in the United Kingdom by the new (since 2009) regulator of practitioner psychologists (not those who are engaged solely in research or teaching), namely the Health Professions Council (HPC). The HPC currently regulates a total of 16 "health professions," of which psychology is the latest addition. The HPC has responsibility for approving training programs and dealing with complaints against its registrants: it is mandatory by law that a practitioner psychologist is registered with the HPC. Unless registered, use of a protected title, such as "clinical psychologist," "forensic psychologist," or "educational psychologist," is illegal.

The HPC does not have an ethics code as such, but rather "Standards of Conduct, Performance and Ethics" (Health Professions Council, 2008).

There are no *ethical principles* specified. Rather, 14 standards are presented as required behaviors with narrative elaborations. These include:

• You must respect the confidentiality of service users.
• You must keep high standards of personal conduct.
• You must get informed consent to give treatment (except in an emergency).
• You must behave with honesty and integrity and make sure that your behavior does not change the public's confidence in your profession.

Inspection of these standards and their elaborations confirms that these are essentially absolutist statements of what a psychologist (or other HPC registrant) *must* do. This is an example of a "bottom line" approach to ethical codes indicating minimum standards of practice. There is no suggestion of aspiration. There is a lack of recognition of the subtleties of ethical decision making. Furthermore, the document has *no* content on ethics per se. The only reference to ethics is self-referential to the title of the document itself. Nevertheless, U.K. practitioner psychologists must comply with these standards. The BPS *Code of Ethics and Conduct* (British Psychological Society, 2009), by contrast, has been written to comply with the EFPA Meta-Code and presents ethical principles from the Meta-Code plus associated standards, just as the CPA and APA codes do for psychologists in Canada and the United States, respectively.

A system of ethical oversight separate from that of the psychological association may also exist for research ethics. In the United Kingdom, for example, research carried out in universities is subject to oversight by the institution's research ethics committee. Typically there may be several subcommittees to cover broad disciplinary domains (e.g., social sciences rather than psychology alone). The development of a formal research ethics approval system has been contested. Some regard it as over-bureaucratic and criticize its implementation, but others offer more strident fundamental critiques. Dingwall (2008), for example, argues that ethical regulation of research if fundamentally wrong. On the other hand, bodies such as the Economic and Social Research Council (n.d.) in the United Kingdom have produced an ethical framework that has been generally adopted by universities. Central to its conceptualization is the notion of degree of *risk*, as a major driver to ethical decision making. There are now attempts to develop a European approach to research ethics, partly in response to the large multistate research programs funded by the European Union (Fitzgerald, 2007).

Ethical Decision Making: Codes or Principles?

The previous sections have described the development of and variation in ethical codes. In the last section, I introduced a "joker" into the pack: a statutory set of guides for professional conduct, not emanating from psychologists. In this section I shall address a final question before considering examples of ethical decision making. Put simply, how is the individual psychologist expected to develop and implement ethical thinking and practice? I have explored a developmental approach, from the start of a career and initial training, through the career itself. But what will guide and support the development of ethical practice?

The CPA (1991, revised 2000) took a very clear decision on this many years ago. Their code is accompanied by extensive vignettes to assist in training and development of psychologists. The EFPA Standing Committee on Ethics also took this approach after the Meta-Code had been reviewed and its revision approved in 2005 (EFPA, 2005). The focus of activity switched to the development of guidance in the form of a book, *Ethics for European Psychologists* (Lindsay, Koene, Øvreeide, & Lang, 2008). Written by long-standing members of the EFPA Standing Committee on Ethics, this was designed to provide discussion of the Meta-Code and extensive examples of dealing with ethical dilemmas by using the Meta-Code. In the United States, a number of texts have been produced over the past decade to support psychologists, some of which are based on the APA ethical code specifically (Fisher, 2003; Koocher & Keith-Spiegel, 1998), and the APA has a fine tradition of publishing books on ethics (e.g., Bersoff, 2003). Its head of Ethics Office Stephen Behnke also publishes a monthly column in the *APA Monitor*, sent to all APA members, with examples to stimulate thinking about ethical decision making. There have also been capacity-developing activities supported by the APA, EFPA, and CPA directly, or by senior psychologists from the organizations, to promote ethical practice internationally and to assist newly developing psychological associations to develop their own ethical codes and to set up systems within the associations to support further development (e.g., Gaulthier, Lindsay, Korkut, & Behnke, 2009).

The approach advocated here, and exemplified by such initiatives, is to engage with ethical principles and then—by a process of exploration, reflection, and discussion, aided by information about past cases—to help psychologists to develop their own ethical thinking. This is, of course, very different from the model used by the United Kingdom's Health Professions Council, which sets out standards to be followed. A fundamental reason for the approach advocated here is that psychological practice is not always so clear-cut. For example, the exhortation to maintain confidentiality is a reasonable starting point, but professional life may throw up challenges to a categorical decision, the most commonly identified being the tension caused when information provided puts the client or another (or even the psychologist) at risk (Rae, Sullivan, Razo, & de Alba, 2009). For a useful introduction to the landmark case of Tarasoff v. Regents of the University of California (1976), see Bersoff (2003). That said, however, it is also important to stress that some ethical decisions are straightforward.

Consequently, in the next section I shall explore the question of models of ethical decision making and then move on to examples of such a decision-making model in practice, using the EFPA Meta-Code. I shall give examples of how an ethical code (the EFPA Meta-Code) may *assist* in decision making but *not* in a purely didactic manner; rather, by identifying the nature of the decisions and the decision-making process that will optimize ethical decision making.

Ethical Decision Making

Ethical decisions differ in their degree of complexity and challenge. Furthermore, the resources a psychologist is able to bring to the decision-making process will differ, especially with respect to prior experience and thinking about ethical issues. It is useful to consider ethical decisions operating at three levels.

At the first level, decision making is *relatively automatic*. The range of issues to be considered is narrow and the preferred options limited. Also, and an important dimension that will be considered at each level, the level of *risk* may be very low. An example is the selection of an appropriate measure for the assessment of a client where the selection is from a limited range of instruments whose technical quality is known to be acceptable. Another example may be the need to gain informed consent, which is an automatic request in a high proportion of work.

At the second level, the issue may not be quite so straightforward such that an automatic response is possible, but *referring to the ethical code* will provide a very helpful resource. Also, the process of reference to the code will itself provide the psychologist with the opportunity to ensure that all relevant ethical issues are covered.

The third level is the most challenging: true *ethical dilemmas*. Here, a decision may not be clear, possibly because different options appear to support one, but also to be in conflict with another ethical principle. Take for example the issue of gaining informed consent when a client is an adolescent. In which case should the parent give consent, the young person give consent, or should each give consent? What factors, such as developmental age, intellectual capacity, or the risk related to the focus of the concern, for example, and the legal framework, apply, and to what degree?

These three levels may be seen as the overall framework for a decision-making model. The main focus to be explored in detail below will be at level 3, where an elaborated model will be presented. With respect to levels 1 and 2 it is worth conceptualizing these as part of initial and very early career training. Frequent and focused discussions between trainee psychologist and supervisor/mentor, and also peer discussions between trainees, supported by knowledge of the ethical code, can provide a solid basis for automatic ethical decision making in a large proportion of the early work faced by newly qualified psychologists and during their professional training program. Also, this is the time to set up positive habits, three of which will be stressed here.

First, the ethical code should be seen as an important support tool, to be readily available to the psychologist for checking with respect to a particular challenge from practice. Second, this is the time to set up an expectation of consultation with another psychologist to discuss practice. Typically this is formalized during training and during the initial period of post-qualification practice by a specified system of supervision by a senior psychologist. However, this formal process varies greatly and is not evident or elaborated in many countries. Nevertheless, informed peer consultations can be set up to serve a similar purpose. It is important that the "other" psychologist is a "critical friend" and not simply somebody who will collude in uncritical agreement: this is unhelpful to professional development. This is important whether informal or formal systems apply. In the latter case, the psychologist must see these as professionally helpful and necessary, rather than bureaucratic processes to "tick boxes."

The third process to be set up is that of *reflection*. The more complex and challenging the ethical challenge, the more that reflection will be needed in addition to any peer discussion. However, reflection is also important at levels 1 and 2. For example, too rigid a categorization of issues as having an "automatic" action may lead to overgeneralization outside the original range of specificity. Taking informed consent as an example, it may be that a psychologist's work typically requires the client to sign a form that confirms the client gives informed consent. But what should the psychologist do if the client states they do not wish to sign such a form? Reflection may include whether the form is really for client protection, or rather for the safeguarding of the psychologist in case of a client complaint. What are the factors relevant to the client's position? Is this *really* a position of strong autonomy, of a well-informed client operating their preference? Or is it an uncertain client who is taking a position that may not be in their best interest? The point here is that even with apparently automatic issues, variants may arise that require reflection. Therefore, reflection should be part of the overall decision-making model from level 1 onward, increasing in importance at level 3.

A Decision-Making Model

A number of decision-making models have been developed (see Pryzwansky & Wendt, 1999, for a review). They vary in complexity, partly as some have built upon earlier models. This is a potential danger of which to be aware: if the decision-making model becomes too complex or time-consuming it is less likely to be used, or unacceptable shortcuts may be taken. The model presented here draws on a number of earlier models, especially that of the Canadian Psychological Association (2003). This has also been amended by the British Psychological Society in its most recent Code of Ethics and Conduct (British Psychological Society, 2009). The model is presented in Figure 6.1.

1. The first stage is one of analysis. Recall, this elaborated model is expected typically to be limited to complex, challenging cases where ethical principles may be in conflict. Analysis, therefore, is presented as a single stage, rather than sequential as in some models, to stress that the different dimensions must be analyzed both *in parallel* and *iteratively*. Ethical principles are the first and driving domain, but the more detailed specifications of each principle are also important in a full analysis. These must also be considered in relation to questions of *values* and *rights* as they apply to those affected, directly and indirectly, by the potential decision. Also, the *cultural context* is crucial. Ethical codes vary in their sensitivity or recognition of the relevant cultural dimensions, so this needs explicitly to be brought into the analysis.

The distinction between ethical and legal matters is not simple. Unethical behavior may not necessarily be designated illegal in any particular country, but often it is necessary to take account of legal factors. For example, decisions on whether a young person may give informed consent, rather than that this must be the responsibility of the parent(s), is linked to the child's age and the country's legal definition of the age of majority, when independent judgments are recognized in law. It may also be linked to the concept of intellectual capacity rather than chronological age, as in England. However, from an ethical point of view the situation may be more subtle. Even if a parent is not legally required to give consent to a particular action by a psychologist, perhaps from an ethical perspective this would be judged important to secure, for example, recognizing the principle of respect (to the parent).

Finally among the elements in the analysis are those persons for whom the decision will have direct or indirect influence. This concerns the

---

1. Analysis of the presenting ethically challenging dilemma;
    - The ethical principles that apply
    - The ethical standards that apply
    - Any values or rights issues that have not so far been identified
    - The cultural context
    - The legal context
    - The person(s) directly and indirectly affected
2. Consideration of how self interest, personal biases or personal stress may influence the decision-making.
3. Proposal of possible courses of action and determination of preferred option.
4. Examination of potential impacts on the client and other relevant parties
    - Short- and long-term
    - Positive and negative
5. Consultation with colleague(s) to take place at this point, and perhaps also earlier in the process.
6. Ethical decision to be confirmed and implemented.
7. Monitoring of the effects of the decision.
8. Reflection on the decision and subsequent monitoring
    - Is revision, further action needed?
    - What lessons can be learned and generalised for future practice?
9. Consideration of dissemination of the learning through input to Ethics Committee, teaching and workshops, publications.

Figure 6.1 An Ethical Decision-Making Model.

question of first and second order clients. In some cases the relationship of the psychologist is with a single client. Often, however, there may be more than one "client." In some cases this is clear, for example family therapy, where the family is specified as client(s). In the case of a school referring a child for a psychological assessment and possible intervention, with the agreement and support of the parent(s), there are already three "clients": the child, the parent(s) and "the school," whether seen as an individual (the principal/head teacher) or a corporate body. Complexities also arise when dealing with industrial and commercial organizations about individuals or groups of individuals (e.g., personnel assessments), the military, and the prison/justice systems. The question of first and second order client is particularly important to clarify, along with the ethical considerations that follow. For example, is the commissioning company the first order client for psychometric data, with the individual the second order client? If so, does the individual have any right to access the results of the evaluation? Whose rights have primacy when a prisoner is evaluated on behalf of the prison/justice services? Does the psychologist have any say in the determination of these rights? Can the psychologist withdraw if it is judged that the lack of a prisoner's rights to information, for example, is unethical?

This stage of analysis, therefore, is essential in order to explore all of these different elements and their interrelationships. It is not uncommon, as a consequence, to identify different implications for different persons concerned, and an ethical decision-making process must result in these different implications being set out.

2. Having fully analyzed the issue, the psychologist must stand back and consider whether there is any degree of self-interest or bias that may be influencing the decision or, indeed, the analysis. Will a particular ethical decision be more advantageous for the psychologist? If so, is this by chance, or as an inappropriate element in the analysis and proposed decision? Some types of self-interest are clearly identifiable, including inappropriate financial gain or personal gratification through an inappropriate relationship. Others are more subtle and may relate to professional standing and prestige, for example. It is important to stress that the issue here is not whether the psychologist derives some form of gain, but whether it is identified, and hence transparent in the analysis and, if there is a gain, is it unethical? For example, a highly competent and ethical psychologist may gather a high reputation for his work: this is acceptable. A psychologist who gains a high reputation from providing the "right answer" for particular assessment enquiries would not be acting ethically if her results were skewed to the "right answer" category inappropriately.

3. Following this further analysis and reflection, proposed course(s) of action are required. Setting out a preferred option is often the easiest first step; alternatives may then be listed relative to the main proposal, identifying tensions that exist. An option appraisal may then follow, to check the original choice against possible alternatives and decide the action to be taken.

4. After the actions are set out, so next must be the potential impacts. These may be positive and/or negative, and for different persons in the scenario. Short-term impacts may differ from those in the long term. All of these will, of course, be judgments of the future, and their reliability limitations must be recognized. Again, these will need to be balanced one with another.

5. So far in this model, the psychologist has produced an elaborated analysis with transparent examination not only of the ethical issues but also matters of rights, values, and cultural issues, as well as the psychologist's own place in the scenario. Consultation with a peer may have occurred earlier in the process, and this is often advisable in order to optimize the analysis. In any case, whether that has occurred or not, now is a time for the psychologist to draw upon the involvement of another psychologist.

As noted above, a system of supervision may be in place, such that this process of consultancy with a peer is expected and built into practice. If not, an informal system is required. In whichever case, the role of the colleague is not simply to listen and concur, but also to question, challenge, and seek explanation and justification: to be a "critical friend." To work well, this approach requires a sound relationship built on respect and objectivity and a recognition that this is *normal* practice: problems are more likely to arise if this is a rare process only undertaken when a practitioner is having difficulty, as defensiveness and reduced receptivity may occur. On the contrary, this should be an open, transparent, and supportive process designed to assist the psychologist to come to the best (not necessarily the only) decision that is available, given the evidence.

6. Following confirmation of the ethical decision, together with alternative actions if deemed appropriate, the psychologist confirms and implements the decision. At this point it is advisable that the decision will be recorded, backed up by the prior analysis, and with a brief report of the consultation with the colleague including disagreement if any. Such recording is useful for several reasons. There is a record if the psychologist must account for the actions taken but, in addition and importantly, this forms part of the accumulating self-development record and may provide a useful resource for the psychologist faced with a similar challenge at a later date.

7. Implementation may be a one-off event (e.g., an assessment report) or take place over time (e.g., a decision regarding certain characteristics of therapy). In either case, there is an obligation on the psychologist to monitor the effects of the ethical decision, just as the effects of the assessment or therapy will be monitored.

8. The psychologist should reflect on the total ethical decision-making process and its outcomes. The primary reason is to check against the impact on the client(s) involved, as identified in this analysis. In some cases there may be an indication that a revision could be helpful, which would need further consideration of the impact on others before action. The psychologist should also reflect on the lessons learned that will influence future practice. Just as experience with psychological instruments, for example, will shape later practice, so too should the ethical decision made. In this context it is worth stressing that not all decisions will in fact turn out to be "right" or "the best." Despite high professionalism, careful analysis, and peer discussion, a reasonable decision may turn out to have deficiencies. This is a good reason for reflection: What, if anything, did I miss? What would I do differently next time; or even, was this a real outlier, and so very exceptional, and should not necessarily lead to a different action next time?

9. The final step in this ethical decision-making model is not typically found in other models. However, there is a benefit in sharing such vignettes with colleagues. Some psychological associations have a forum for presenting vignettes. The psychologist may be able to contribute, through teaching, to initial training of new practitioners or on continuing professional development courses. This is not to argue that every such case should be written up for presentation more widely, but rather to stress that it is an ethical stance to seek to disseminate ethical practice and to provide useful information and experience to colleagues.

Use of the EFPA Meta-Code

In this final section I shall provide a detailed example by means of a vignette of ethical decision making. Prior to that, I shall set the scene by presenting a brief history of the European Federation of Psychologists Associations' Meta-Code and its present use.

In 1990, the EFPA[1] set up a task force whose first meeting was in Copenhagen. Our task was to create a European code of ethics. We quickly decided this was certainly impossible and probably unwelcome. A number of countries had an ethical code and would not necessarily wish to change it. Many countries in Europe, particularly in the east, did not have a code. We foresaw many practical problems trying to secure votes at national conferences for not only a new code, but one which had to be the same across many countries: a single amendment in one association would destroy the whole enterprise. We therefore redefined our task and spent the next 5 years creating the original Meta-Code approved at the General Assembly in Athens, Greece, 1995. The Task Force was then changed into a Standing Committee on Ethics, and during the next decade we reviewed the effectiveness of the Meta-Code. We found it to be very popular and, perhaps surprisingly, in need of minimal changes. The current revised Meta-Code was approved by the General Assembly in Granada, Spain, 2005.

The Meta-Code is unusual, as it was not designed as an ethical code for individual psychologists; rather, it specified what a national association code should cover. From the beginning, and with the benefit of a group comprising psychologists from all over Europe, we stressed the need for universality and recognition of cultural variations. We also decided at the start to develop a code based on four ethical principles, using the format you will see below. We developed specifications or standards to explicate in more detail the ethical issues derived from each principle. Furthermore, we stressed (see the opening sections of the Meta-Code) that other dimensions are important. All professional practice, we argued, must be conceptualized as a stage in the development of the professional relationship. Ethical principles often interacted and could be in conflict.

The Meta-Code became popular among many individual psychologists who did not have access to a national code in their own country. After 2005, the Standing Committee on Ethics decided on a program to disseminate ethical practice, the main outcome of which is the book, *Ethics for European Psychologists* (Lindsay, Koene, Øvreeide, & Lang, 2008) written by four long-standing members of the Standing Committee. This has a large selection of vignettes of ethical issues.

This final section of the chapter provides an in depth example of the analysis of an ethical dilemma using the Meta-Code's four ethical principles and the related specifications/standards. The four principles are:

RESPECT FOR A PERSON'S RIGHTS AND DIGNITY

Psychologists accord appropriate respect to and promote the development of the fundamental rights, dignity, and worth of all people. They respect the rights of individuals to privacy, confidentiality, self-determination, and autonomy, consistent with the psychologist's other professional obligations and with the law.

COMPETENCE

Psychologists strive to ensure and maintain high standards of competence in their work. They recognize the boundaries of their particular competencies and the limitations of their expertise. They provide only those services and use only those techniques for which they are qualified by education, training, or experience.

RESPONSIBILITY

Psychologists are aware of the professional and scientific responsibilities to their clients, to the community, and to the society in which they work and live. Psychologists avoid doing harm and are responsible for their own actions, and assure themselves, as far as possible, that their services are not misused.

INTEGRITY

Psychologists seek to promote integrity in the science, teaching, and practice of psychology. In these activities psychologists are honest, fair, and respectful of others. They attempt to clarify for relevant parties the roles they are performing and to function appropriately in accordance with those roles.

The example has been deliberately selected to emphasize the cultural dimensions of practice and how conflict can arise if this is not handled appropriately. The focus of this section is on stage 1 in the decision-making model above, the analysis of the ethical issues relevant to the presenting dilemma, as the previous section explored in detail the processes involved in the other stages of the model.

An Example of Decision Making with the EFPA Meta-Code

The rest of this chapter takes a vignette and considers how the Meta-Code may be used to aid ethical decision making. The most pertinent clauses (specifications) in the Meta-Code are considered:

A mental health service in a large (European/North American) city hires, for a temporary position, an Asian-trained male psychologist newly arrived in the country to provide mental health services in his native language to immigrants from his country of origin. The psychologist is a refugee himself, and is trying to obtain permission for his family to join him. He is deeply grateful for having been given the position in the mental health clinic.

After he has been on the job for six weeks, his supervisor reprimands him for visiting his clients in their homes and attending social functions in the immigrant community. She informs him that there is a strict policy about doing this because it is important to maintain good boundaries with clients and not enter into dual relationships with them. Also, she points out that he can see more clients in a day if he makes appointments to see his clients in the office.

The psychologist is very upset and not sure what to do. He feels great respect for persons in authority, and deep gratitude for having employment and money to send home to his family. He cannot afford to lose his employment. He was unable to explain his position to his supervisor. However, he lives in the immigrant community and knows that his people have very different beliefs about the nature of mental health problems and they find services in this country very strange.

He also knows that if he does not participate in community events, he will not be accepted by them and will not be able to help them.

He comes to you as an understanding friend and colleague. How can you help?

Process Issues. All four principles in the Meta-Code must be considered for salience, and will be discussed individually. But first there is also a need to consider *process* issues. The Meta-Code sets out the following key points:

• Psychologists' professional behavior must be considered within a professional role, characterized by the professional relationship.

- Inequalities of knowledge and power always influence psychologists' professional relationships with clients and colleagues.
- The larger the inequality in the professional relationship and the greater the dependency of clients, the heavier is the responsibility of the professional psychologist.
- The responsibilities of psychologists must be considered within the context of the stage of the professional relationship.

These four elements are presented separately in the Meta-Code and before discussing the principles, in order to provide a framework within which to interpret the application of ethical principles to the particular case.

The first statement refers to the *professional* role. However, in this case the boundary between professional and personal is somewhat blurred, although often this is not the case and the psychologist has a clear role. Note also the reference to "professional relationship." When a psychologist works with a client there is always some form of professional (as opposed to personal) relationship. The nature of this relationship may vary, influenced by such factors as personal style and cultural norms. For example, we British are often regarded as "formal" in our professional behavior compared with some cultures. In the example below, cultural expectations of the nature and boundaries of the *professional relationship* are important.

Second, the psychologist must appreciate the element of power that is always present in a professional relationship. This is typically viewed as the psychologist being more powerful, and in one respect at least this is certainly the case. The psychologist is the one with the formal power by nature of the role, and this brings with it important responsibilities not to abuse that power. However, in practice there may also be subtle (and even not so subtle) additional power dynamics. For example, perhaps the head teacher/principal of a school overtly says that they want to assist a student but the agenda may also include seeking to influence the psychologist into decisions that remove the young person from the school ("for the good of the others"). Hence, power must be recognized as a complex issue, and inequalities of power may operate in different ways. Ultimately, however, it is the psychologist who has the responsibility to act ethically after appropriate analysis.

Third, the degree of power inequality must be identified: contrast the distressed client of limited resources seeking a psychologist's help with the school principal mentioned above, or the fund-holding head of a company who could influence access to future contracts for the psychologist depending, perhaps, on the outcome of the presenting case.

Finally, there is the question of the stage of the professional relationship. Sometimes this is limited and somewhat transitory, as in the instance of a single assessment session. Other times the psychologist may work with a client over weeks or years, for example as a therapist or a psychologist working with children who maintains engagement throughout childhood and/or adolescence. These examples indicate the likelihood of different types of relationships including degrees of professional intimacy (the detailed knowledge of the client's history, their hopes and fears, their personal views shared with a trusted psychologist over the years, perhaps changing over time) and dependency: clients (or parents of a primary client) may come to rely on the psychologist, beyond the main focus of the psychologist's involvement, to provide support and advice.

In this vignette, the expectations of the professional relationship are central. Boundary issues are not so straightforward. Power inequalities are also important— between the psychologist and supervisor, his clients, and the community. With respect to level of inequality the vignette provides an opportunity not only to think this out as a psychologist–client issue but also as a supervisor–psychologist issue. This stresses again the complexity of such dilemmas, and also the need to be comprehensive in consideration of such factors. Finally, stage of relationship is also important, as the psychologist in the vignette is a recent arrival not only in the psychological service but also in the country (and is a temporary employee), and so there are issues of new learning by all concerned. Both interpretation of actions and judgments of their meaning from an ethical perspective are influenced by the stage of the relationship of the psychologist with a client and, in this vignette, particularly with the supervisor.

Now, let us consider the relevance of each principle to the vignette presented above. In the analysis I shall propose how specifications of each principle may be relevant to decision making in this case.

Respect for a Person's Rights and Dignity
GENERAL RESPECT
- Awareness of and respect for the knowledge, insight, experience and areas of expertise of clients, relevant third parties, colleagues, students, and the general public.

This psychologist, by nature of his cultural background, had experience and insights not shared by the supervisor. These could provide important assistance to practice. Thus, even though he is new and of limited experience in his new job, respect for what he potentially has to offer is necessary.

- Awareness of individual, cultural, and role differences, including those due to disability, gender, sexual orientation, race, ethnicity, national origin, age, religion, language and socioeconomic status.

This supervisor may be aware and welcoming of the psychologist's potential to contribute to service delivery on the basis of his linguistic competence. Unfortunately, she does not demonstrate awareness of or sensitivity to cultural differences relating to ethnicity—it may be the case that religious differences are also present. Not only is this problematic with respect to her dealings with the psychologist, it is also potentially a missed opportunity to learn from him and his engagement with the community.

- Avoidance of practices which are the result of unfair bias and may lead to unjust discrimination.

The supervisor may consider she is simply treating the psychologist like everyone else—"rules are rules" and the service has a set of procedures and protocols. This may be so, but equality does not necessarily mean sameness. In this case, although unintended, the psychologist's strengths are not recognized sufficiently and the instructions do impose a restriction on what he might reasonably regard as appropriate behavior. Consequently, unjust discrimination occurs.

Competence
ETHICAL AWARENESS
- Obligation to have a good knowledge of ethics, including the Ethical Code, and the integration of ethical issues with professional practice.

Both the supervisor and psychologist would do well to consider this specification. It appears from what has been analyzed so far that the supervisor is not sufficiently aware of the ethical code (or at least the Meta-Code, used here). But what of the psychologist? He has important strengths and a potential contribution, but should he not have considered the expectations and protocols of the service? As a new immigrant he also has much to learn if he is to operate optimally. By not checking and discussing differences in expectation before he acted, he contributed to the problems that arose.

LIMITS OF PROCEDURES
- Obligation to be aware of the limits of procedures for particular tasks, and the limits of conclusions that can be derived in different circumstances and for different purposes.

The service appears to have recognized particular strengths in this new colleague that could help in the delivery of a psychological service to a community that may have been poorly served in the past. In this sense, those responsible for hiring the psychologist may have been aware of the requirements of this clause. The supervisor's actions suggest that she may not have been as sensitive to the matter of validity of engagement, as she had not considered the psychologist's perspective on maximizing acceptance by the community and individual clients before engaging in specific intervention.

- Obligation to practice within, and to be aware of the psychological community's critical development of theories and methods.

Again, we might ask whether the supervisor was sufficiently thoughtful about the importance of awareness of cultural factors in psychological practice. But the same could be said to apply to the psychologist—did he consider the requirements on professional practice expected of personnel in this service? His focus on the community he knew came at the expense of awareness of the community, the dominant community, into which he was socializing.

- Obligation to balance the need for caution when using new methods with recognition that new areas of practice and methods will continue to emerge, and that this is a positive development.

Was the supervisor sufficiently aware of the need to have an open mind? What would this new colleague bring? In addition to the behavior reported here, what would he bring to the specific practice with clients? The arrival of a new colleague has potential for existing staff to learn and develop from the ideas that colleague brings. In this case, there were other cultural and linguistic elements to consider, with great potential benefit to the existing staff. The psychologist also, however, appears not to have thought about this—he was practicing on the basis of what seemed appropriate from past experience—fine, but what more he could learn from exploring the practice of those new colleagues he was joining?

CONTINUING DEVELOPMENT
• Obligation to continue professional development

As both supervisor and psychologist were qualified, the issue raised is that of CPD—each has much to give but much also to learn. This may be an opportunity where CPD could be collaborative and collegial, with the new colleague contributing to the development of his colleagues and they, in turn, reciprocating.

Responsibility
GENERAL RESPONSIBILITY
• For the quality and consequences of the psychologist's professional actions.
• Not to bring the profession into disrepute.

These clauses are pertinent to both. The psychologist was in danger of creating a significant problem, and that could lead to concern in the service. The supervisor meanwhile could be taking action that would offend not only the psychologist but the minority community who would welcome this new, enlightened practice. Neither psychologist was deliberately flouting good practice requirements, but neither was sufficiently thoughtful to ensure good practice occurred.

EXTENDED RESPONSIBILITY
• Assumption of general responsibility for the scientific and professional activities, including ethical standards, of employees, assistants, supervisees and students.

The supervisor had an important responsibility to induct her colleague into practice in this service. Induction is a crucial stage even for an experienced practitioner. It is a period of adjustment, recalibration of expectations and norms against which to regulate your own expectations and behavior. The supervisor could have prevented the difficulties from arising if her approach to supervision had been more sensitive.

RESOLVING DILEMMAS
• Recognition that ethical dilemmas occur, and responsibility is placed upon the psychologist to clarify such dilemmas and consult colleagues and/or the national association, and inform relevant others of the demands of the ethical code.

Each had an ethical dilemma but it is not clear that either recognized this. Rather, the psychologist appears to have acted in a way he assumed was correct, and not appreciated that there was a dilemma regarding practice. The supervisor also seems to have adopted a "head down" approach playing by the "rules"—the strict agency policy on not visiting homes. No doubt this was a well-intentioned policy and may have been developed by all staff after much consultation, but its implementation in this case was insufficiently thought through. This is the problem with simply adopting and then requiring all staff to follow policies and protocols.

Psychologists, as professionals, should have a high degree of autonomy. Policies can be helpful but even the best are rarely universally appropriate. Indeed, a critical aspect of being a professional rather than a technician is the obligation and ability to think outside the set procedures. The Meta-Code recognizes this by highlighting the ethical principles first—the specifications are intended to focus thinking on more specific issues. The Meta-Code was also written for associations, not individuals, but in fact many psychologists find it helpful by the nature of its "meta" framework. It does not specify precise and absolute standards. Rather, it specifies issues to consider. The original purpose was to use this method to allow associations freedom to devise a local code that met their national requirements, but within a European consensus; the approach also facilitates and indeed encourages individual psychologists to *think* about ethics and not simply follow a "cookbook" approach.

Integrity
RECOGNITION OF PROFESSIONAL LIMITATIONS
• Obligation to be self-reflective and open about personal and professional limitations and a recommendation to seek professional advice and support in difficult situations.

Neither of our psychologists thought to be self-reflective or seek further advice until the psychologist came to his friend after the confrontation. This was a wise move, but it is a pity it did not occur sooner. One might wonder whether the supervisor had also thought to take similar action—she seems to need to have the opportunity to explore her own thinking on the subject. In fact, as has become evident, each had limitations in their practice—as psychologist and supervisor. Each appeared to have acted in good faith, but nevertheless the outcome was problematic. By each opening up about *why* they were adopting their chosen approach, then, perhaps with a third person to facilitate, a greater sense of understanding on both sides could be engendered.

CONFLICT OF INTERESTS AND EXPLOITATION

• Awareness of the problems which may result from dual relationships and an obligation to avoid such dual relationships which reduce the necessary professional distance or may lead to conflict of interests, or exploitation of a client.

This is at the heart of the vignette, at least as seen by the supervisor. Protecting against inappropriate dual or multiple relationships is generally seen as good practice—but note the word "generally." In fact this is a much more complex issue. Many psychologists have dual/multiple relationships. This is particularly obvious in small communities where we must shop, take health care, have cars repaired, etc., and indeed, generally live our lives. Our children may be friends with the children of clients or, in the case of educational/school psychologists, with the children who are our primary clients. The important issue to recognize is that dual relationships are not necessarily inherently wrong. Rather, it is the nature of the relationship, its purpose, and the degree to which the psychologist considers the ethical implications. There is a wide difference between the therapist who abuses power to seduce a client compared with the psychologist who attends the same church congregation or school parent–teacher association in community activities.

In this case, the service was no doubt correct to give this issue careful consideration, but there was a need to be less rigid and to think through the particular circumstances. The psychologist, however, should also consider this issue carefully. Visiting homes and attending social functions may well be normal, even expected or necessary in the culture, but the same concerns that led the service to develop its policy are pertinent. The psychologist must still consider where is the appropriate boundary in this community for him as a member of the community, as opposed to a psychologist in a professional capacity.

• Obligation to give a reasonable critique of the professional actions of colleagues, and to take action to inform colleagues and, if appropriate, the relevant professional associations and authorities, if there is a question of unethical action.

The supervisor had the opportunity to offer a reasonable critique—this could have been helpful if done in a particular way. But it seems the critique was not an intellectual appraisal influenced by a social/emotional awareness of the dynamics of the situation. Rather, it was a negative attack, as seen by the psychologist, on what he thought was not only acceptable but indeed good practice. In this case, was the psychologist acting unethically? Was it not rather a case of differences of view? But in any case, the important issue is that neither acted in the best way. If each had adopted a position of reviewing the situation from the principles of good, ethical practice, the confrontation that ensued could have been avoided.

Conclusions

In this chapter I have argued that ethical practice must require an awareness of an appropriate code and set of ethical principles. In addition, there must be an interpretation relevant to the cultural context. This applies at the major level of national identities, laws, and values, right down to local communities. In many countries there is a decreasing sense of unidimensionality with respect to identity and culture. Countries such as the United Kingdom have benefited from centuries of immigration to enrich the culture. But this process also brings challenges, which may change over time. The task for psychologists, therefore, is to have a firm grounding in ethical decision making but to have the capacity to be flexible in interpretation and action.

The EFPA Meta-Code was used in this chapter as the basis for considering how ethical decision-making could operate. As noted above, its framework and style actually provide a useful, rather freer model than many national codes. Rather than setting out firmer "bottom line" behaviors to follow, the Meta-Code encourages psychologists to think about interpretation of principles and specifications. In this example it is important to note that *both* participants had responsibilities—it was not simply one psychologist who would benefit from a better consideration of ethical decision making. This is not the case normally when a complaint is made about an alleged unethical conduct to an association, but it is quite likely to be the case when psychologists have disagreements or conflicts, at least when these occur for reasons of limited understanding rather than deliberate flouting of the ethical code, or from indifference.

In terms of using the Meta-Code, a simple approach might be characterized as follows. Action requires:

• Identifying each relevant element
• Analyzing each element in terms of the pertinent issues

- Separating each of these from other factors; for example, service conventions which are not specifically ethical issues

The primary messages to take away are, perhaps, simple. First, ethical decision making should be an integral part of professional practice. Second, it is a developmental process, shaped and developed both by practical experience and information from formal training and personal research. Third, ethical codes can provide a very useful support not only by providing information (their content) but also as a tool to support the analysis of ethical dilemmas and decision making regarding action. My last point is to stress the necessity to develop a mindset that places ethical decision making appropriately. With good initial training, supervised practice (especially early on in a career), and reflection, much practice is relatively straightforward with respect to ethical decision making. Some issues, however, are not, and require careful thought and analysis. So, my final comment is to keep a reasonable perspective and to continue to engage in dialogue, whether formally or informally, with a "critical friend" to support the maintenance and development of ethical decision making throughout the professional career.

Note

1. Then known as the European Federation of Professional Psychologists Associations (EFPPA).

References

American Psychological Association. (1952). A little recent history. *American Psychologist, 7*, 426–428.

American Psychological Association. (2002). *Ethical principles of psychologists and code of conduct.* Washington, DC: Author. Retrieved from www.apa.org/ethics/code2002.pdf.

Association of State and Provincial Psychology Boards. (2005). *ASPPB code of conduct.* Retrieved from http://www.asppb.net/i4a/pages/index.cfm?pageid=3353.

Bersoff, D. N. (2003). *Ethical conflicts in psychology* (3rd ed.). Washington DC: American Psychological Association.

British Psychological Society. (1985). *Code of conduct.* Leicester, England: Author.

British Psychological Society. (2009). *Code of ethics and conduct.* Leicester, England: BPS. Retrieved from http://www.bps.org.uk/the-society/code-of-conduct/.

Canadian Psychological Association. (2003). *Canadian code of ethics for psychologists* (3rd ed.) Ottawa, Ontario: Author. Retrieved from http://www.cpa.ca/cpasite/userfiles/Documents/Canadian%20Code%20of%20Ethics%20for%20Psycho.pdf.

Dingwall, R. (2008). The ethical case against ethical regulation in humanities and social science research. *21st Century Society, 3*, 1–12.

Economic and Social Research Council. (n.d.). *Research ethics framework.* Swindon: Author. Retrieved from http://www.esrc.ac.uk/_images/Framework_for_Research_Ethics_tcm8-4586.pdf

European Federation of Psychologists Associations. (2005). *Meta-code of ethics.* Retrieved from http://www.efpa.eu/ethics/ethical-codes.

Eynon, R., Schroeder, R., & Fry, J. (2009). New techniques in online research: Challenges for research ethics. *21st Century Society, 4*, 187–199.

Fisher, C. B. (2003). *Decoding the ethics code: A practical guide for psychologists.* London: Sage.

Fitzgerald, M. (2007). The EU gets tough on ethics. *Technology Ireland, 38*, 27–30.

Gauthier, J., Lindsay, G., Korkut, Y., & Behnke, S. (2009). *How to use ethical principles for creating or reviewing a code of ethics.* South Eastern Europe Regional Conference of Psychology. Sofia, Bulgaria.

Health Professions Council. (2008). *Standards of conduct performance and ethics.* London: Author. Retrieved from http://www.hpc-uk.org/assets/documents/10002367FINALcopyofSCPEJuly2008.pdf

International Union of Psychological Science and International Association of Applied Psychology. (2008). *Universal declaration of ethical principles for psychologists.* Retrieved from http://www.am.org/iupsys/resources/ethics/univdecl2008.pdf

Koocher, G. P., & Keith-Spiegel, P. (1998). *Ethics in psychology: Professional standards and cases* (Rev. ed.). Oxford: Oxford University Press.

Koocher, G. P. (2007). Twenty-first century ethical challenges for psychology. *American Psychologist, 62*, 375–384.

Lindsay, G. (1992). Educational psychologists and Europe. In S. Wolfendale, T. Bryans, M. Fox, A. Labram, & A. Sigston (Eds.), *The profession and practice of educational psychology* (pp. 185–197). London: Cassell.

Lindsay, G. (1995). Values, ethics and psychology. *The Psychologist: Bulletin of the British Psychological Society, 8*, 448–451.

Lindsay, G. (2008). Ethical challenges for the future. In G. Lindsay, C. Koene, H. Øvreeide, & F. Lang (Eds.), *Ethics for European psychologists* (pp. 181–189). Gottingen, Germany and Cambridge MA: Hogrefe.

Lindsay, G. (2009). Ethical dilemmas of psychologists: How are these affected at times of national security? In V. Claudio et al. (Eds.), *III coloquio Europeu de psicologica e etica* (pp. 213–220). Lisbon, Portugal: Instituto Superior de Psicologica Aplicada.

Lindsay, G., & Clarkson, P. (1999). Ethical dilemmas of psychotherapists. *The Psychologist: Bulletin of the British Psychological Society, 12*, 182–185.

Lindsay, G., & Colley, A. (1995). Ethical dilemmas of members of the Society. *The Psychologist: Bulletin of the British Psychological Society, 8*, 214–217.

Lindsay, G., Koene, C., Øvreeide, H., & Lang, F. (Eds.). (2008). *Ethics for European psychologists.* Gottingen, Germany and Cambridge MA: Hogrefe.

Pope, K. S., & Vetter, V. A. (1992). Ethical dilemmas encountered by members of the American Psychological Association. *American Psychologist, 47*, 397–411.

Pryzwansky, W. B., & Wendt, R. N. (1999). *Professional and ethical issues in psychology.* London: W.W. Norton.

Rae, W. A., Sullivan, J. R., Razo, N. P., & de Alba, R. C. (2009). Breaking confidentiality to report adolescent risk-taking behavior by school psychologists. *Ethics and Behavior, 19*, 449–460.

CHAPTER 7

When Things Go Wrong: On Mediation, Arbitration, Corrective Actions, and Disciplinary Sanctions

Casper Koene

Abstract

Sometimes, psychologists' conduct may lead to discomfort. Sometimes, expectations about their interventions and professional evaluations might have been inadequate. But things can go wrong, too. Errors are made. Unethical conduct will occur. Psychologists need to face this. Individual psychologists need to be open to look critically into their own behavior and thus to be loyal in having their professional conduct scrutinized. In this chapter, the different modalities of dealing with possible infringements of ethics are described. Coming to a settlement with the complainant as a result of a mediation process might be a preferable option to restore the relationship. However, in criticizing the psychologist's professional conduct in retrospect, the imposition of sanctions by the professional association or a legal disciplinary board may be unavoidable.

Yet, to take corrective actions (e.g., requiring additional training) might be more constructive to improve the ethical quality of future professional conduct.

Key Words: Mediation, arbitration, disciplinary sanctions, corrective actions

Helene Smith felt depressed. Because of her heavy alcohol abuse, her husband had left her, divorced, and got the custody of their young daughter. In order to get her life in a reasonable order somehow, and to live more or less peacefully with her loss, Helene sought help and found Marion Sluyters, PhD, willing to take her in for psychotherapy. In the second session Marion found out that in the course of Helene's legal divorce procedure her ex-husband had presented a letter from his psychologist, stating that Helene's recurrent alcohol abuse and her dependent personality disorder could be seen as highly unfavorable conditions for the upbringing of her child. Although Helene's lawyer at the time strongly advised to counteract and to lodge a complaint against the husband's psychologist because he had made statements about Helene's psychological condition without her consent, and without even having seen her face-to-face, Helene had decided to leave it as it was. After all, the psychologist's conclusion was probably right, and she herself felt incompetent deep down to properly raise her daughter, being a single mother now.

Psychologists' doings do not always lead to happy faces. Sometimes expectations about psychologists' interventions are too high, sometimes an assessment's outcome is disappointing, sometimes some doubt has been cast upon the ethical level of the psychologist's behavior, and sometimes the psychologist's action is experienced as bluntly crossing boundaries of decent professional behavior.

If this occurs, clients or others involved, like Helene Smith, may want to talk about their unhappy feelings with the criticized psychologist, if they didn't already decisively slam the door in leaving the psychologist's office. Otherwise, they might like to speak to one of the psychologist's colleagues, or they may just want to raise a complaint to get the psychologist severely punished.

In such a situation, psychologists are faced with possible infringements of their ethical standards. First of all, the alleged trespassing psychologist is infringing, obviously, *if* he or she knows.

In the latter case, it demands some professional maturity and courage to critically look inside oneself to see whether the other person could be right, and to not too easily slide into defensiveness by deliberately searching for justifications and excuses, or blaming the other. Such critical self-reflection might not only improve the ethical quality of one's work, but also lead toward the best condition to honestly face the other person and to show understanding of his or her objections.

However, it could very well be that psychologists stay ignorant about others' grudges. For example, Helene Smith didn't inform her ex-husband's psychologist about hers, if she bore any.

As it was the case in Helene's story, other psychologists may become involved, as a consequence of their professional relationship with offended persons, like Marion Sluyters, or just as fellow psychologists. If so, they are challenged to take action as the consequence of their ethical duty to take signs of possible infringements seriously. After all, it is not only right to show people who have been possibly unjustly treated the ways to get things cleared, but it is also of importance to further adherence to ethical standards in the profession's interest.

That's not all. As one shouldn't stay idle, just looking at someone who apparently isn't a swimmer, fallen into the water, one cannot let colleagues down by staying silent when one knows of possible unethical acts—not just to prevent others from being harmed in the future and to prevent the profession from being compromised, but also to help colleagues to find right ways. Moralistic? It surely is, and precisely what professional ethics is about.

Codes of ethics ask for taking such actions. For instance, the American Psychological Association's standard on informal resolution of ethical violations (APA, 2010) requires psychologists, when they believe that there may have been an ethical violation by another psychologist, to attempt to resolve the issue by bringing it to the attention of that individual, if an informal resolution appears appropriate and the intervention does not violate any confidentiality rights that may be involved.

The European Federation of Psychologists Association (EFPA, 2005a) Meta-Code expects its member associations' national codes to oblige psychologists to give a reasonable critique of the professional actions of colleagues and to take action to inform colleagues and, if appropriate, the relevant professional associations and authorities, if there is a question of unethical action.

The Dutch national psychologists association's code of ethics (NIP, 2007) only allows lodging complaints against colleagues if the colleague who has supposedly contravened the code of ethics is not willing to justify his or her professional conduct in a fraternal dispute, or doesn't want to change this behavior. Doing so, the Dutch code actually emphasizes the value of the fraternal appeal.

Obviously, it is not primarily the bystander colleague who should not stay passive when things go wrong. First of all, as the logical counterpart of the obligation to *give* a reasonable critique of the professional actions of colleagues, psychologists should be open to *receive* critiques of their own professional actions and to faithfully cooperate with the evaluation of these actions, if these are questioned. Lack of maturity or courage doesn't free them from the moral responsibility to take complaints or critical remarks seriously, regardless of where these critical remarks or questions come from.

Such questions may come from the professional association. Faced with allegations of infringement of their ethical standards, psychologists' associations cannot ignore them and not take any action. For example, in the preamble to its Meta-Code, the EFPA demands that its European national member associations have procedures to investigate and decide upon complaints against their members. Taking into account the nature and seriousness of the complaint, this may lead to mediation, to corrective actions, or a disciplinary sanction. Although worldwide the majority of psychologists' associations seem to have some sort of investigatory and disciplinary system, detailed information is lacking. In this chapter, only available figures will be used illustratively.

The core of the matter is whether or not an association chooses to bind its members to act in accordance with the association's ethical standards. Some associations seem to regard ethical guidance more as aspirational, thus leaving the full responsibility for adhering to codes of ethics to the individual psychologists.

However, if their professional association chooses to take institutional responsibility, psychologists are obliged to justify their professional conduct in case of a complaint being lodged.

A refusal to cooperate in evaluation procedures can be seen as an offense, as stated in the EFPA

Recommendations on Evaluative Procedures and Corrective Actions (EFPA, 2005b) and effectively laid down in, for example, the American, Dutch, and Turkish codes of ethics.

Penny Asscher, industrial psychologist, terminated her membership in the psychologists' association at the moment it became clear that a complaint would be raised against her. Nevertheless, the disciplinary board decided the complaint was admissible, because termination of membership only can be effected at the end of the year, which was not the case here. Mrs. Asscher did not respond to any correspondence from the disciplinary board.

After hearing the complainant, the disciplinary board decided to expel Mrs. Asscher from membership, not only because of the nature of the primary infringement—which had not happened for the first time—but also because of her immediate termination of her membership and her failure to respond to any of the board's letters to her. This was regarded as an attempt to withdraw from the evaluation of her professional action.

Psychologists' associations may by statute forbid their members from terminating membership during a complaint procedure to ensure that the evaluation of their professional actions can occur, with or without their cooperation. Although not quite irrelevant for *individual* psychologists reading this handbook on professional ethics, it particularly shows whether and to which extent *collectives*, i.e., the psychologists' associations, take responsibility for safeguarding the ethical norms and standards and the protection of clients by preventing members from fleeing the consequences of a misdemeanor, which could be seen as "disciplinary hit-and-run" (Koene, 2004).

Openness to critique and willing cooperation in having one's professional conduct evaluated can be seen as major conditions for the upholding of ethical standards in the profession.

Nevertheless, one may wonder if such an evaluation always will give enough satisfaction to complainants, who are often clients. This brings into question the main issue in this present chapter: whose interests have been infringed in cases of unethical behavior, whose interests have actually been damaged most seriously, and what is consequently the most appropriate answer to this?

Are the client's interests really most harmed, being the primarily injured party, or those of the psychologists' community, whose professional ethics rules are violated and whose reputation might be at stake? Is a client really served by disciplinary evaluation and eventual sanction?

Evaluative and disciplinary procedures are, to a certain extent, comparable to criminal law procedures. In spite of the fact that complainants usually are the accusatorial party in front of the disciplinary tribunal[1]—unlike criminal law cases, where the public prosecutor and not the complainant is the antagonist of the accused—the outcome of the evaluative and disciplinary procedures exclusively concerns the relationship between the censured psychologist and the professional collective. Be it a warning, a reproach, a suspension, or an expulsion from membership, gaining satisfaction from these sanctions is all the complainant may get out of it.

Basically, disciplinary systems are not meant for individual atonement. Those who do not primarily wish to prevent others from having the same bad experiences, but instead are driven by disappointment, grief, anger, or need for revenge, will be dissatisfied if their complaint is turned down.

There may be violations of norms that justify a community to take action in order to protect others against being victimized. There also may be violations of norms that justify a community feeling deeply harmed and determined to impose punishment because of the fundamental unacceptability of such a crime, even if this punishment is not, or is no longer in the victim's interest nor in the interest of others in his or her direct environment; for example, avenging the murder of a lonely vagabond. Upholding norms by the collective is meant to prevent individuals feeling victimized, and this is even more important if it concerns individuals in a relatively weak and vulnerable position. The psychologists' associations' disciplinary procedures may find their raisons d'être especially in this last condition.

However, presuming the complainant's interests are to be regarded as equally important to those of the psychologists' association, one may wonder whether the individual client is served in the best possible way by disciplinary procedures, even if client vulnerability provides justification for special complaint procedures.

In the event that a sanction is imposed after a disciplinary procedure—which is often long and drawn out, and in which discrepancies will be accentuated rather than diminished—will such a sanction bring the satisfaction the complainant is waiting for? Sometimes it does, sometimes certainly not, far from it. Some complainants want to see blood, but not all of them. Some of these could feel more satisfied and better understood in their complaint if a well-meant apology was given. Nevertheless, after a formal evaluative and disciplinary process, an explanation and apology—if appropriate as such—will often be further away than ever. And how often could this count for the psychologist as well?

Carrie Winter had not worked for quite some time. She had even given up having small temporary jobs, because of the problems with her back. On her general practitioner's advice, she applied eventually for a job in sheltered employment, where her impairment would be taken into consideration. But, to be admitted to this kind of employment is not a simple matter in her country. An assessment needs to be done to verify whether the person has physical, mental, or intellectual disabilities to such an extent that working in a normal job in competitive society is impossible.

When the authorities finally let Carrie Winter know the outcome of the assessment, it turned out that she was considered to belong to the target group for sheltered employment. However, Carrie's joy was tempered, to put it mildly, because of the basis of this decision. Not only was she supposed to have physical impairments due to her back issues—during the examination, some evidence was found that Carrie had had special education and had suffered from severe test anxiety. The psychologist involved in the assessment procedure reported on the basis of these findings that Carrie Winter was intellectually and mentally impaired as well.

To be seen as a "cretin" and a "nut" was too much for Carrie, and she raised a complaint against the psychologist. According to Carrie, he should never have drawn such conclusions without conducting his own psychological examination, and the report should never have been sent to the authorities without her permission.

It eventually did not become a disciplinary court case, since after further reflection Carrie decided to withdraw her complaint.

About the quality of the psychologist's judgment we may only guess, as we may guess about the procedure, in which the judgment was based purely upon documents. And we may wonder if Carrie Winter had been given the opportunity to read the report before it was sent to the admission committee.

Yet, what could have brought Carrie to her decision to withdraw—was she afraid of repercussions?

After all, she had been put on the waiting list for getting a job in the sheltered workshop, which she have yet. Or, did she have a talk with the psychologist, who might have made clear to her that the probability of eventually getting a job in sheltered employment only had increased by also being labeled mentally impaired as well as intellectually handicapped? We do not know.

Mediation

For a client, having a conversation with the psychologist about experienced unethical behavior could be seen as the *via regia*, the preferred way to get rid of his or her grudges. However, it takes some determination, which certainly not everyone has, even if the psychologist is open to it. There might be another way.

In mediation, the complaint can be seen as an expression of a problem or conflict between the complainant and the accused psychologist. Seen from that point of view, the interests of the psychologists' association are not at stake. In an informal, semistructured process, an impartial mediator assists the disputing parties to work through and resolve problems or conflicts together. It is a nonjudgmental, voluntary process that focuses on helping parties to find mutually satisfying resolutions to their problems, consistent with the interests of each party. Whether or not by one's own initiative, participation in mediation is on a voluntary basis. Both complainant and psychologist are autonomous and able to determine their own actions. This requires that each party is free to close the mediation process at any moment, if they no longer consider the mediation as helpful. Mediation may thus end with the insight of the complainant that no ethical violation took place, it may end with the psychologist's expression of remorse, or it may end with any other formal, written agreement between parties to "close the books," or with a recompense. However, as parties are free to close mediation at any time, mediation may end without any result being satisfactory to both parties.

As conflicting parties are facilitated to come to a solution themselves, and have the freedom to terminate this process at any time, mediation conditions are essentially different from binding oneself beforehand to a final decision of any authority, as in arbitration.

The involvement of a third party may be seen as a complicating factor. Such a person may have their own interests in the solution of the conflict and may interfere, or perhaps their approval of the outcome must be required. Therefore, possible juridical or complaint procedures, which had already been started, must be deferred in order to be able to start with mediation.

Solutions found in mediation may well be better—for both the complainant and the accused—than a judicial judgment. After all, both parties carry the outcome, which is certainly not the case if the disciplinary tribunal rules against one party. Therefore, for the client to be understood in his or her complaint by the psychologist involved, it might be preferable to choose mediation instead of a formal complaint procedure, which only may lead to an acknowledgement by the profession.

In Carrie Winter's case, for instance, the psychologist's recognition of blame and his atonement would give a better opening for redeeming and reconciliation than would a conviction for a "crime" and an imposed punishment. However, even if there is no violation of any professional ethics principle, mediation will probably give the psychologist a better opportunity to come to an understanding of the client's objections, and to be able to show this, than standing in front of a tribunal.

Obviously, people are free to choose mediation, as they are free to just arrange a face-to-face encounter. This regards both the persons with complaints and the psychologists against whom they hold any grudges.

However, mediation within the framework of an ethics complaint procedure begins with the psychologists' association's willingness to refrain from further investigation and evaluative procedures during the period of mediation, and to recommend the opportunity for mediation to the complainant and the accused psychologist. This implies that the association only decides about proper conditions of the process— for example, the impartiality of the mediator, the power balance during the mediation, the limits of the feedback to the association—and will not interfere in the process nor demand to be asked for agreement on the mediation outcome (EFPA, 2007). As a party of indirect interest, the association puts itself, so to speak, on the "reserve bench."

In considering whether or not the opportunity for mediation should be offered, the fundamental question arises: how should the client's individual interest of atonement be weighed against the psychologists' association's interest in upholding norms by evaluating the professional behavior and eventually sanctioning trespassers?

This consideration should have regard for the seriousness of the alleged infringement. Therefore, the nature of the complaint should be taken into account, as well as the potential for further risk to the public and the reputation of the profession. This means that in certain cases the profession—embodied in the psychologists' association—may decide that its collective responsibility doesn't allow it to stay passive. This is the case when the possible infringement of the profession's ethical standards is such a serious offense that other clients' welfare or the profession's standing are seriously at stake. In that case the association will not abstain from formal evaluation of the alleged misconduct.

Not to take away the vital importance of what just has been stated, nor questioning its eventual impact, it is challenging to reflect upon another perspective. Seen from a moral point of view, one may wonder whether, in its ultimate consequence, the complainant and the accused shouldn't *always* be offered the opportunity to come to an agreement by themselves. In its ultimate consequence, it could be taken for granted that, for instance, even serious breaches could be compensated financially, and psychologists thus have a lucky escape from being sanctioned heavily. After all, it is not unthinkable that some complainants will choose such options. One may wonder which objections might arise against such a solution. Doesn't a direct atonement for distress or compensation for harm outweigh formal sanctions? Isn't a direct paying-off of the debt superior to punishment for breaching norms? And why should the possibility of a more satisfactory settlement be given to someone who raises a minor complaint, and not to someone raising a serious one? One might argue that cases of serious harm in particular deserve the best possible atonement.

Until now, these reflections were focused on the significance mediation could have for the complainant. However, for the psychologist involved, the significance of mediation might be as large. To nondefensively explain one's own point of view, and to show understanding for the complainant's angle, is more easily done if one is not being put in a vindicative position. Thus, mediation gives opportunities that are less likely in a formal exchange of documents or a hearing in front of a tribunal. This is especially so if the real motives to complain are hidden behind formal objections: the implosion of high expectations, the disappointment about the outcome of an examination, the confrontation with painful developments in life. Sometimes the client holds the psychologist, the messenger, responsible for these, and seeks pretexts for a complaint.

The fact that in cases of mediation the profession steps back and doesn't have any influence on the outcome doesn't mean that the outcome of the mediation is not in the interest of the profession. After all, mediation could well contribute to restoring the complainant's confidence in the profession and, moreover, it is conceivable that more understanding for the complainant's point of view could bring the psychologist to an improved reflection on the ethical dimensions of their professional actions, maybe more than disciplinary sanctions will do.

Up to this point mediation seems to be the morally ideal means to bring conflicting parties together in order to find a solution, agreed by both of them. By its nature mediation could contribute to raise the psychologist's ethical awareness and the client's appreciation of the psychologist's profession's ethics. However, this is a wishful view. Realistically, expectations should unfortunately not be too high. Only a minority of the complainants chooses options for mediation that are offered in running complaint procedures. The majority prefers to lodge a formal complaint. Moreover, certainly not all mediations lead to an end that is acceptable for both parties. As mentioned before, parties are free to close the mediation process at any moment if they no longer consider the mediation as helpful. Therefore, there will be instances where a mediation procedure is closed in an untimely manner, and consequently a formal complaint procedure is opened or reopened.

For an exploratory psychological assessment, Anna Fischer's general practitioner referred her to a psychologist. At her first appointment, Mrs. Fischer arrived 20 minutes late because of problems in finding the location of the practice. Shortly before the set hour of the second appointment, Mrs. Fischer cancelled because her child was suffering from a headache. During this phone conversation, the psychologist told her that she would be charged the fee for this appointment, whether she arrived or not. Then, she decided to come anyway, albeit with substantial delay.

A few days later, Anna Fischer received the psychologist's invoice.

In her complaint, Anna Fischer contended that she had been under the impression that the psychological diagnosis would be established under the national health insurance scheme and thus would not be payable by her. In the complaint investigation, the psychologist stated that the appointment with Mrs. Fischer for a clinical-psychological diagnostic assessment had been made by phone. A time period from 10 a.m. to noon was reserved for her, and she had been requested to be punctual. In this very telephone call the psychologist had told Mrs. Fischer that if she were unable or unwilling to keep the appointment, she should cancel the set appointment 48 hours in advance; otherwise the full fee of the session would be charged.

After Mrs. Fischer arrived at her first appointment with a 20-minute delay, the psychologist had again called her attention to the aforementioned cancellation conditions. To accommodate Mrs. Fischer, the psychologist did not charge any fee for this 20-minute delay. Furthermore, the second appointment was cancelled by phone, 40 minutes before its scheduled beginning. Mrs. Fischer claimed that she could not attend because she had to appear in court. The psychologist had reminded her again that appointments should have been called off 48 hours before, underlining that appearances in court are not communicated only 30 minutes before the beginning of a hearing. Then, Mrs. Fischer decided to keep her appointment after all and arrived at 11.30 a.m.

The psychologist charged her only for 90 instead of 120 minutes.

After several phone conversations with both parties, the arbitration board decided that Anna Fischer should pay the outstanding fee.

Arbitration

This possibility to open or reopen formal complaint procedures will not be the case after arbitration, if an association has chosen to offer this instead of mediation. In arbitration, too, the situation is seen as a conflict between the complainant and the accused psychologist. As in mediation, in arbitration also the position of the profession is formally marginalized and evidence of an infringement of ethical principles will not lead to disciplinary measures. The fundamental difference between mediation and arbitration is that the latter will give an outcome, whether or not parties find it agreeable, since both parties bind themselves beforehand to accept the arbiter's decision.

Disciplinary Procedures

Whether or not after a complainant's or a psychologist's refusal of mediation, an untimely closed mediation, or the association's decision not to offer mediation, a lodged complaint may lead to formal disciplinary procedures.

Then, an investigation will take place through the formal complaint procedure, be it a separate stage in the process or not. The investigation will involve gathering evidence from the complainant, the psychologist who is the subject of the complaint, and any other source that will provide information relevant to the complaint.

From the very beginning of the complaint procedure, the psychologist needs to be aware of the prevailing ethical principles and code regulations that still pertain in such a challenging situation.

> Anton Berg, clinical psychologist, was not amused when he got a letter from the disciplinary committee that Mrs. Schmidt had raised a complaint against him for breaching confidentiality in his contact with her general practitioner. Berg was invited to give a first reply, in the context of the investigation.
>
> Berg wrote an angry letter, stating that such a complaint by "someone with clear histrionic personality characteristics, which the disciplinary committee indubitably must have recognized, has to be seen evidently as a revengeful acting out of despair due to a collapse of her erotomaniac fantasies (see Mrs. Schmidt's enclosed record). Thereby Mrs. Schmidt's complaint should immediately be dismissed."

Justified by the principle of equal arms[2], psychologists may decide to breach confidentiality to be able properly to found their defense against allegations. However, psychologists aren't completely free in doing so. Ethical principles should still guide actions, and psychologists are still subject to their code of conduct. Therefore, revealing data from the client's record should be done respectfully and restricted to those relevant and necessary for the defense. However, using psychopathological labels in this context can only be seen as complainant-bashing by inappropriately attempting to disqualify complainants and bluntly neglecting to pay appropriate respect.

It does not only happen that psychologists try to disqualify complainants in such a blatant way. At least as serious are attempts to exclude more categorically certain people from raising complaints in the first place.

> Cora Hermanides, forensic psychologist and manager of a large forensic experts' bureau, contacted her association claiming immunity for the members of her team, since forensic expertise too easily leads to disciplinary complaints. Cora Hermanides argued that it happens all the time that unsatisfied parties, supported by their lawyers, try to seek ways to disqualify unfavorable forensic reports by misusing disciplinary procedures. These procedures bring along an excessive extra workload and a substantial strain for the psychologists involved. In her opinion, this should be an argument for the psychologists association no longer to burden the staff members of this respectable expert bureau with disciplinary procedures.
>
> The association's reply was not particularly welcomed. It said that the association's members are obliged to cooperate faithfully if there is any reason to evaluate their professional conduct. This obligation is fully incompatible with any claim on immunity. As the association did acknowledge the higher complaint rates in forensic psychology, it recommended Mrs. Hermanides to set up special ethics courses for her staff members, in order to sensitize her colleagues to the special pitfalls in the practice of forensic psychology. In this way the ethical quality of their work could be improved and the prevention of complaints could be maximized. An additional recommendation contained initiating in corporate trainings to prepare her colleagues to appropriately defend their cases in front of the tribunal.

The second recommendation, given to Cora Hermanides, brings us to the point that many psychologists are ill-prepared when faced with a complaint. The idea of having to show up for a hearing is often rather emotionally disturbing for many colleagues. Arguments that disciplinary procedures could be seen as part of one's personal quality assurance system may be valid in theory, but in practice having one's conduct scrutinized easily brings highly uncomfortable feelings, even in case of a good conscience.

Standing in front of a tribunal *is* standing in front of a tribunal. This is a situation where one cannot count on just friendly fraternal understanding, as some lay people may think. On the contrary, there are indications that fellow professionals might be stricter in keeping the standard of their ethics high.

Nearly 20-year-old research findings in The Netherlands—not necessarily outdated, though—showed more than once a more lenient attitude in university educated nonpsychologists compared to psychologists in solving ethical dilemmas for psychologists presented to both categories (Koene, 1993). On some topics this was also the case in research results a few years later, where respondents were asked to give their "disciplinary verdict" on psychologists' conduct, decribed in 18 vignettes (Koene, 2007).

Nevertheless, psychologists better rely upon fair trial of their associations. After all, important law procedure principles, such as the presumption of innocence and the equality of arms, are widely adopted. Undoubtedly, psychologists' associations too will strive to base their investigatory and evaluative procedures on such principles. The tribunal's impartiality, hearing both parties, and principles of laying the burden of proof upon the plaintiff (*actori incumbit probatio*) and upon him who affirms (*affirmanti incumbit probatio*), all ensure a fair trial. However, this *affirmanti incumbit probatio* contains a special dimension. Psychologists do have an obligation to implement proper recordkeeping, which may shift some of the onus of proof to them. This does not diminish the fact that as long as the tribunal is not convinced by the plaintiff's arguments and evidence, the complaint should be regarded as unproven.

The standard of proof in a tribunal's operation may vary. In the United Kingdom, for example, the standard is the "balance of probabilities," unlike in criminal cases in court where the standard is "beyond reasonable doubt." Also, there is a requirement that the implementation of this standard takes into account the seriousness of the case for the psychologist. So, if a guilty verdict will lead in all probability to the psychologist being struck off the register, the bar is set higher.

Back to real ethics! What does it actually mean, hearing about a complaint being lodged against a colleague? Do we tend to avoid him or her, not referring clients anymore, or are we still open to give fraternal support? Being supportive to colleagues could be seen as a consequence of the general responsibility for the profession—not to protect colleagues unduly, but to contribute personally to the support system of the profession. From this perspective, it is not fair to ostracize colleagues just because of complaints being raised against them. As the Turkish Association states in its ethics code: "Psychologists do not discriminate against people who are being investigated nor jeopardize their employment. However, they take the necessary steps following the conclusion of the ethical investigation according to the requirements of the verdict."

Unproven complaints may not be untrue. However, we must rely on the tribunal's verdict. Please, no "where-there's-smoke-there's-fire" bias!

Be that as it may, even evidence doesn't necessarily mean that it was more than just an error. After all, "...practitioners may make errors of judgment, and...such errors are distinct from malpractice" (Psychological Society of Ireland's recommended procedure for ethical decision making). Furthermore, there is no justification to see minor infringements as capital sins. After all, a warning doesn't imply more than the word says: "a suitable reprimand, which posits the incorrectness of the conduct, without qualifying it as reprehensible" (explanatory memorandum on the Dutch Individual Health Care Professions Act).

When Things Go Wrong

Professional errors, remorse, infringements, atonement, malpractice and disciplinary measures—one may wonder how often actually things go wrong, and then what happens eventually. Unfortunately only some figures are available, not enough to get a reasonable reliable impression of the facts worldwide. As mentioned earlier, they cannot be regarded as more than illustrative.

The earlier mentioned study on this subject (Koene, 1997) is over 10 years old, and published in Dutch after being orally reported at the 5th European Psychology Congress, held in Dublin, July 1997. Though disciplinary procedures may have progressed since, and the questionnaire response doesn't allow drawing firm conclusions anyway, it might be noteworthy to get an impression of the results, together with some results from a questionnaire as sent out "worldwide" in preparing this present chapter.

The 1997 questionnaire was sent to all 31 EFPA member associations[3], in order to get information about their disciplinary procedures and sanctions. In a second part of this inquiry, statistical information was gathered. In the third part, 18 short vignettes were presented, giving "facts" of possible violations of professional ethics. The associations were requested to give their opinion about the appropriate measures to be taken in the given cases. Outcomes of this third part were compared with data gathered from samples of Dutch psychologists and civil servants at the Dutch Ministry of Social Affairs, giving their opinion on the same vignettes.

The 2009 questionnaire was meant to get minimum background information—more updated—about the associations' state of affairs on mediation and disciplinary procedures. This questionnaire was sent "worldwide" to all EFPA member associations, as well as to colleagues involved in the setup of this present handbook. At the same time they were asked to forward the questionnaire to anyone else who could give useful information.

Fourteen associations filled out the first part of the 1997 questionnaire. Nearly all of these had a disciplinary committee to investigate and decide upon alleged infringements of their ethical codes.

Also, on the 2009 questionnaire, 14 associations responded—from Argentina, South Africa, the United States, and 11 from Europe. All of these have procedures to evaluate alleged unethical actions of their members.

In 1997, in a small number of associations it wasn't possible to have a hearing attended by both parties; their disciplinary committees only decided on the basis of circulated documents above. In 2009 this was the case in only one of the respondents.

Half of the responding associations in 2007 formally forbade their members to terminate membership during a complaint procedure. However, a third of the associations didn't even require their members to cooperate with the scrutiny of their professional conduct.

Both in 1997 and in 2009, 2 out of 14 associations did not have power to impose a sanction on members for proven infringement of their ethical code, although one of these could, like the others, expel from membership in case of serious infringements.

Even though disciplinary actions may have quite some impact for psychologists, and therefore access to a review of the verdict is important, in 1997 a nonmarginal minority of the associations did not have an appeal procedure. In 2009 this was only the case in 2 associations out of 14.

In 2009, apart from formal complaint procedures, 8 out of 14 associations can offer mediation in case of complaints about alleged unethical behavior.

Three out of the fourteen 2009 respondents evaluate even alleged unethical acting of psychologists who are not members of the association, and hence give their opinion or advice.

Considering all these measures, one may wonder how often people lodge complaints, and thereby to what number of complaints these measures serve. After all, every year psychologists all over the world see millions of clients in over a hundred million sessions.[4]

Publications about the Dutch legal healthcare disciplinary system stated that the number of complaints is substantially fewer than the estimated number of medical errors made. It is not very likely that there would be a considerable difference in complaining about psychologists.

An experience of being unjustly treated seems certainly not always to be a sufficient reason to decide to complain. In our daily life we often take certain miseries for granted. The burden of writing a letter... claiming a guarantee for something we bought somewhere far away. After all, the expected retribution should be in reasonable balance with the invested effort, as is the case with the expected probability of retribution. Obviously, the extent to which we are aggrieved or hurt plays a role, too. On top of it, dependency and loyalty often play a role in client–psychologist relationships, which may put up an extra barrier against complaining.

The European associations responding to the 1997 survey *and* having procedures to evaluate alleged unethical acting of their members, received 360 complaints in the year of the inquiry; i.e., 0.4% of the 96,740 psychologists being members of these associations.

In the 2009 survey, it was reported that 320 complaints were lodged in 12 of the 14 responding associations, or 0.1% of the 281,797 member psychologists.

In 1997, evidence for unethical behavior was found in just half of the cases. In three occasions—i.e., 0.8% of the complaints and thereby 1.7% of the cases found culpable—the psychologists (3 out of 96,740) were expelled from membership of their association.

In the 2009 survey, evidence for unethical behavior was found in only 25% of the complaints, but at least[5] 15 out of 281,497 psychologists were expelled in the 14% of the complaints where the psychologist's conduct was blamed.

It is noteworthy to underline that, where available numbers show psychologists' membership rates from over 90% down to less than 50%, these figures pertain not to nations but to national associations. One should further note that these national associations differ in the extent of complaints being lodged and in disciplinary measures taken by them. Most influential could be whether practicing psychology is bound by legal licensing and whether legal evaluative and disciplinary procedures exist. If the latter is the case, complaining to a legal disciplinary board may decrease the number of complaints lodged to the association, and leave increased dark numbers of unreported cases. However, taking into account the small number of countries without any legal licensing, available figures don't convincingly show such a relationship. In countries where licensing isn't at a national level, like the United States or Argentina, the way to nationwide organized psychologists associations may be seen by the public as more troublesome and less profitable than the one to regional bodies, however. This could explain the even lower incidence of complaints in those associations.

May Justice be Done

A psychologist consulting to a secondary school was asked to give counseling to a 15-year-old girl. Before the start of the professional contact the girl insisted on absolute confidentiality as *conditio sine qua non*. Even her parents weren't allowed to get any information.

Rather soon, the girl turned out to be suicidal. The psychologist consulted a colleague and a psychiatrist and found that the situation wasn't so dangerous that other interventions were necessary. Nor did he find a reason to breach confidentiality by contacting the parents.

After a while, the guidance of the girl could be finished successfully.

Later on, the parents found out what had happened. They furiously lodged a complaint to the disciplinary committee.

As argued before, in mediation cases the psychologist and the offended person are the only *dramatis personae*. The outcome of the mediation is exclusively their business, and by its nature it may differ from case to case, from time to time, from place to place.

In formal evaluation of the psychologist's professional conduct on the other hand, not only the psychologist and the offended person are interested parties, but the psychologists' association or the legal disciplinary body, too. In those procedures one would wish the outcome of the evaluation of similar cases not to be too different from time to time, from place to place.

To my knowledge, there isn't any comparable study worldwide on disciplinary sanctioning in the psychology profession. In the third part of the aforementioned 1997 questionnaire, 18 vignettes were presented to disciplinary committees of European national psychologists associations, and later on to Dutch psychologists and ministry civil servants. They were all asked to regard all the shown details as—the only—facts of the cases, and to come to a sanction to be chosen out of the following tariff:

• the psychologist's conduct should be regarded as being within the ethical standards;
• the reason for the complaint should be acknowledged, but no sanction will be imposed;
• the psychologist needs to be given some advice on professional ethics;
• a warning should be given;
• a reprimand should be given;
• a reprimand should be given, as well as a conditional suspension of membership;
• a fine should be given;
• the psychologist should be expelled from his association's membership;
• other....

For several reasons only six associations responded on this part of the questionnaire, reason why the results should be seen as highly tentative. Nevertheless the results may give some insight into how disciplinary board members at the time thought about ethics infringements.

The overall interrater agreement was very reasonable. Not surprisingly, the psychologists were more coherent in their opinions than the nonpsychologists. As a group, the latter were more lenient about issues such as sexual relationships with clients immediately after termination of therapy. Apart from a striking discordance on the case described in the vignette at the beginning of this paragraph, the interrater agreement between disciplinary board members of different countries was higher than the Dutch psychologists', whereas cultural differences easily could have interfered. Compared to Dutch psychologists, the disciplinary board members' opinions were generally expressed in somewhat milder terms.

Although the presented findings aren't up to date, and are restricted to the European context, they may promise the likelihood of fairly equal treatment of complaints against psychologists, wherever they practice, in Europe. Let's hope that crosscultural differences in moral standards for psychologists worldwide won't be much larger than in Europe.

And what about Helene Smith, who was introduced at the beginning of this chapter? Would she feel better in the long run by letting go of her feelings of being unjustly treated by her ex-husband-to-be's psychologist making statements about her psychological condition, even if his opinion might have been right? Would it have been better after all to look into one another's eyes, giving and receiving apologies? Or would she have felt most satisfied with a formal evaluation by the psychologist's association or legal disciplinary board, to prevent others from being put down by unethical psychologists' conduct? Who knows.

Anyhow, the preventive role of disciplinary actions may remain merely ritualistic, if actions are not properly followed up by information and education of the professional community. Not by pillorying psychologists, but by regularly and accessibly publicizing case studies.

Conclusions

Things can go wrong. Errors are made. Infringements will occur. Psychologists need to face this and to take the consequences. Individual psychologists need to be open to look critically into their own behavior, and thus to be loyal in having their professional conduct scrutinized if a complaint is raised. Or, sometimes better, to come to a settlement as a result of a mediation process.

If the profession decides to take responsibility to maintain its high standards of professional ethics by having procedures to investigate and to decide upon complaints, may these be solid ones.

In criticizing the psychologist's professional conduct in retrospect, the imposition of sanctions may be unavoidable. However, to take corrective actions—for example, requiring additional training—to improve the ethical quality of future professional conduct might be more constructive in promoting good ethical behavior.

Looking into the future, it would be a good thing for the profession if upholding its ethical standards could be equally good, worldwide.

Author Note

The author chose to use the title of his Chapter 9 in Lindsay et al. (2008), on which content the present one is largely based.

Notes

1. This is not always and not everywhere the case. For instance, in the Netherlands, the Health Inspector may act as prosecutor in legal disciplinary pursuits, and in the British Psychological Society, after the preliminary investigation the individual complainant is no longer a party in front of the tribunal. At that point, the BPS takes the role of public prosecutor.

2. The term *equal arms* is adopted from the European Convention of Human Rights. It is one of the principles in this Convention that ensure a fair trial for defendants.

3. In 2010 the European Federation of Psychologists Association had 35 member associations, representing about 250,000 psychologists.

4. One could roughly estimate 60 clients and 600 client contacts per psychologist per year on average (10 contacts per client, 15 client contacts a week, 40 weeks a year).

5. Some information is given on a regional level, while national data are lacking.

References

American Psychological Association. (2010). *Ethical principles of psychologists and code of conduct*, 2010 amendments. Washington DC: APA. Retrieved from www.apa.org

European Federation of Psychologists Associations. (2005a). *Meta-code of ethics* (2nd ed.). Brussels: EFPA. Retrieved from http://www.efpa.eu.

European Federation of Psychologists Associations. (2005b). Recommendations on evaluative procedures and disciplinary actions in case of complaints about unethical conduct. Brussels: EFPA. Retrieved from http://www.efpa.eu.

European Federation of Psychologists Associations. (2007). Guidelines on mediation in the context of complaints about unethical conduct. Brussels: EFPA. Retrieved from www.efpa.eu.

Koene, C. (1993). Het hemd nader dan de rok? Resultaten van een enquête beroepsethische dilemma's. *De Psycholoog 28*, 128–132.

Koene, C. (1997). Op de stoel van de tuchtrechter. *De Psycholoog 32*, 511–517.

Koene, C. (2004). Opgezegd. *De Psycholoog 39*, 569–573.

Koene, C. (2007). Blame and atonement. *European Psychologist, 39*, 235–237.

Lindsay, G., Koene, C., Øvreeide, H., & Lang, F. (2008). *Ethics for European psychologists*. Göttingen: Hogrefe & Huber Publishers.

Nederlands Instituut van Psychologen. (2007). *Beroepsethiek voor psychologen*. Amsterdam: NIP. Retrieved from http://www.psynip.nl.

PART 2

Current and Emerging International Ethical and Professional Development Issues

CHAPTER 8

Ethical Standards, Credentialing, and Accountability: An International Perspective

Elizabeth Reynolds Welfel *and* Basak Kacar Khamush

Abstract

Across the globe, the existence of formal standards for credentialing of psychologists is tied to a nation's economic wealth (or at least economic stability) and the vibrancy of the academic discipline of psychology there. Countries with long-standing stable governments, and with the opportunity for free and fair elections, also appear to have a more formal system for the education, credentialing, and oversight of psychological practice. In nations where governments are autocratic and dictatorial, and economies are unstable, the profession is largely invisible and certainly without formal governmental recognition. Nations that have been isolated from international contacts may also lag behind in availability of well-trained mental health professionals and in the regulation of mental health practice (Sanchez-Sosa & Riveros, 2007). China is one example of this dynamic, though it no longer has an unstable economy and is catching up rapidly. In this chapter we will examine the commonalities and variability in professional identity, licensing standards, and measures of accountability in 13 countries across the globe, representing six continents, and address general global trends. Specifically, we will highlight the state of regulation of psychology and related professions in each nation, the vibrancy of the profession and the professional associations in each country, and, whenever regulations exist, the procedures for licensing aimed at protecting the public from harm. Finally, we will identify points of convergence and divergence in licensing standards and discuss the fundamental issues and values that appear to underlie those similarities and differences.

Key Words: ethical standards, credentialing, accountability, licensing

Africa

Ten African countries have active professional associations of psychologists: Botswana, Egypt, Ethiopia, Kenya, Morocco, Namibia, Nigeria, South Africa, Sudan, and Uganda. With the exception of South Africa and Zimbabwe, which have both regulated psychological practice for several decades, no country has any level of governmental regulation of professional psychology (Lunt, 2000). Because it is typical of the state of psychological regulation in this continent, we will first highlight the current status of the mental health professions in Kenya. Then we will describe the credentialing and accountability mechanisms available in South Africa.

Kenya

In Kenya the majority of those who offer mental health services are counselors or psychologists, and they number approximately 3,000 individuals in a population of 36.1 million (http://www.kenya-information-guide.com/kenya-population.html). In other words, there is one graduate-level counselor or psychologist for every 120,000 people. The master's degree is typically the highest degree attained, but some have earned doctorates. Others practice as counselors at the bachelor's level, and still others offer counseling services without benefit of any degree (Koinange, 2004). Most of those with graduate degrees in psychology work as university professors, not in mental health care. A professional association has been established (Kenya Psychological Association) and it offers ethics guidelines for its members, but it has no authority to regulate professional practice. A parallel organization for professional counselors (Kenya Association of Professional Counselors) was founded in 1990. No national or regional licensing laws for form of mental health practice are in force. According to Koinange (2004), many psychologists in Kenya tend to look to the codes of the British Psychological Association and the American Psychological Association to address ethical questions. Much of the professional service activity of mental health professionals in this country is coordinated with the work of the nongovernmental organizations (NGOs) and focuses on service to populations needing assistance with basic needs and health care. Many counselors provide service to those with health issues, especially those with HIV spectrum disorders. According to Jimerson, Skokut, Cardenas, Malone, and Stewart (2008), some professionals practice as school psychologists, but no separate professional organization or credentialing of school psychologists has been established here.

South Africa

South Africa has had several iterations of its professional association in the last 60 years but currently, the Psychological Society of South Africa (PSSA) is the organization representing the profession. In 2010 the association counted approximately 3,500 members spanning any of the seven membership levels, with full membership reserved for individuals with at least a master's degree in psychology (Health Professions Council of South Africa, 2004; Watts, 2010). A board of psychology was established in 1994, and this body has been granted the authority to register psychologists and suspend the registration of psychologists who violate the code of conduct. To register as a psychologist in South Africa, an applicant must have successfully completed a master's degree in psychology and an internship. The title itself is protected, and can only be used by those who are appropriately registered with the board. An applicant can register in one of four categories: clinical, counseling, educational, and industrial psychology. Any psychologist registered before the current standards went into effect can maintain the license. Both the code of ethics and regulations for practice have been regularly updated, with the most recent change being the publication of a statement of the scope of practice of psychology (South African Professional Board for Psychology, 2007). No breakdown exists of the percentages of psychologists engaged in the various practice settings, but 6,469 South African psychologists registered for professional practice appear to be employed in the same variety of activities as those in Europe and North America (Stead, 2004; Watts, 2010).

The practice of professional counseling in South Africa is also regulated, with specific criteria developed for multiple practice settings from career counseling to sports counseling. The minimum requirement is a bachelor's degree in psychology and an internship (see http://psychologyinfo.co.za/regs.htm for a list of these regulations). School psychology in South Africa is regulated as well, and its rules are subsumed under the licensing laws for psychologists; its professional association is a division of PSSA.

Asia

Asia has 60% of the world's population and more than 4 billion inhabitants. Psychological services as organized and provided in the Western hemisphere are relatively scarce, and the ratio of psychologists to the overall population is one of the lowest on the planet. Seeking mental health service typically carries with it stigma, but that stigma is changing, especially in highly industrialized countries like China and Japan (Stevens & Wedding, 2004). Most countries have little governmental regulation of psychology or other mental health professions, but nearly all have active professional associations.

China

China's mental health professionals have organized both national and regional professional associations for psychology (Chinese Psychological Society [CPS]), school psychology (Chinese Society of School Psychologists), and for other mental health professions with ties to medical settings (Chinese Mental Health Association [CMHA]) (Yang, 2004). The Chinese Psychological Society first developed a code of ethics in 1993, and the current revision was published in 2007 (Han & Zhang, 2007). CPS also oversees the registration of psychologists, and has also stipulated extensive criteria for registration as a psychologist (CPS, 2009) and for training in clinical and counseling professions, the minimum of which is a master's degree in psychology or a related field. These criteria also enumerate criteria for psychological supervision, internship experiences, and continuing education programs and instructors. Each of these organizations claims 2,000 to 3,000 members and Yang (2004) indicates that approximately 10,000 psychologists are practicing in China. With a population of 1.3 billion, these figures suggest that extremely few mental health professionals are available to serve the needs of the population. Han and Zhang (2007) report that at the time of publication of their article, more than 300 students were pursuing doctorates in psychology in China.

Aside from the registration procedures identified by CPS and CMHA, no other licensing processes exist for psychologists or other mental health professionals. These registration procedures mirror the qualifications identified in Western licensing and accreditation standards. Chinese psychologists are employed in schools, universities, medical centers, and in NGOs that provide free psychological services. Positions in industrial and forensic psychology settings are also available for professionals with appropriate training.

India

The Indian Association of Clinical Psychologists (IACP) has been in existence since 1968 and is the organization that is informally recognized for setting professional standards for practice and for offering credentials to members. There is no governmental licensing of psychologists in India, but those who obtain membership in IACP appear to have better employment prospects in mental health settings (Barnes, 2004). The 2009 annual report of the organization indicates that there are 852 members (http://www.iacp.in/2010/03/iacp-annual-report-2009.html) divided among three membership categories: fellowship, professional membership, and associated membership, paralleling the membership categories in APA. The criteria for membership are not clearly stated in the public materials on the IACP website, but it appears that the criterion for professional membership is a 2-year master's degree and an internship in psychology. Training opportunities at the doctoral level are available, but limited. In 2001, four students were enrolled in doctoral training at the All Indian Institute of Mental Health, a program that uses the American scientist-practitioner model for doctoral study. The most recent estimate of the number of psychologists working in mental health in India was offered by Prabhu in 1998, and it shows only 300–350 practitioners, although 600 psychologists have received graduate degrees in the discipline in India. According to Prasadarao and Sudhir (2001) most practitioners are female, and the disparity between the number trained and the number practicing is best explained by emigration of psychologists to other nations. Given the recent increase in the membership in IACP, it is likely that the number of practitioners has increased, though it is still clearly inadequate to meet the needs of India's huge population.

The IACP uses the APA Code of Ethics (2002) as its code of conduct, but according to Barnes (2004) it has struggled to obtain any real authority to monitor professional practice or to discipline psychologists who violate the standards. The organization has been lobbying to secure licensing laws but thus far has had no success.

South America

Several South American countries have procedures for credentialing and monitoring the professional practice of psychology, though this circumstance is not universal. In Chile, for example, no governmental regulation of professional practice exists, although the Chilean Society of Clinical Psychology (Sociedad Clilena de Psicologia Clinica) provides a registration process for the practice of psychology and publishes a code of ethics (Makrinov, Scharager & Diaz, 2006). In contrast, both Argentina and Brazil, described in the following paragraphs, have long-established professional associations and licensing procedures.

Argentina

Argentina has a substantial number of psychologists for its population; in fact, according to Bell (2010) it has the highest proportion of clinical psychologists for its population of any nation on the planet. Its government, through the Ministry of Education and Justice, has licensed psychologists with appropriate training and competencies in practice and research since 1985. Its model of licensing is fairly unique, however. A psychologist must become a member of the regional division of the Federation of Psychologists, the national association. Moreover, a psychologist must reside/practice in that region to be eligible for licensing. In order to practice in different region the professional must petition the Minister for permission. Requirements for licensing include a graduate degree in a government-approved psychology program. Each region of the country offers at least one approved training program. No licensing examination is required by law; graduation from an approved program with sufficient field experience during the training appears to be sufficient for eligibility to practice. The licensing law also specifies that those who teach psychology must meet the licensing requirements as well. In short, the licensing law gives more authority to universities to decide whether its graduates are competent to practice.

There is also discussion of enforcement in the licensing law, indicating that violations of the law and the ethics code may result in discipline, and that the regional bodies of the federation have responsibility for enforcing the stipulations of the licensing law. For example, the Association of Psychologists of Buenos Aires lists an ethics committee, a complaint procedure, and a history of complaints received (http://www.psicologos.org.ar). The most current version of its code of ethics was published in 1999 (Psychology Federation of Argentina, 1999). Its contents and organization appear very similar to the current APA code.

Brazil

While Argentina has more psychologists per capita than any other Country in the world, the total number of psychologists in Brazil is second in the world to the United States. According to Hutz, McCarthy, and Gomes (2004) there are 140,000 licensed psychologists in Brazil. Eligibility for licensing includes the successful completion of an accredited 5-year university curriculum that includes two years of internship, resulting in what would be considered a master's degree in the United States. The number of psychologists with doctoral degrees working in Brazil is very small, however, numbering only 900 in 2004 (Hutz et al., 2004).

Brazil governs the practice of psychology primarily through 15 regional councils, first established by the Brazilian Congress in 1971. These elected councils have responsibility for monitoring and regulating professional practice through the umbrella organization, the Federal Council of Psychology. Licenses are granted by each state, but requirements for licensing are consistent throughout the country and once a license is obtained, a psychologist can practice anywhere in Brazil provided they become members of the regional council in which they work. Licensing is based on successful completion of the 5-year curriculum—no licensing examination is required. A national code of ethics has been published and it is the responsibility of the councils working together in the Federal Council to update that code. Enforcement activities are located in the regional councils and they have the authority to address and adjudicate complaints.

There is no national association equivalent to the American Psychological Association or Canadian Psychological Association in Brazil. The Brazilian Psychological Society is similar to APA in goals, however. Psychological societies with specialized missions also exist. For example, the National Association for Graduate Research and Study in Psychology, established in 1983, is at the center of accreditation of training programs in psychology.

Europe

Virtually all European countries have well-established professional psychological associations and regulations of mental health practice. Currently 19 of the 27 member countries in the European Union have enacted laws to regulate the use of the title of psychologist. In addition, the European Federation of Psychologists Associations (EPPA) has developed a certification program for psychologists who qualify, in order to facilitate professional mobility among countries in the European Union (Lunt, 2008). Currently, there are four standards for qualification for the EPPA certificate: five years of formal education in recognized psychology training program, one year of successful professional practice, a statement on ethical conduct, and a commitment to continuing education. Psychologists who meet qualifications are listed in the European Register of Psychologists (See http://www.efpa.eu/europsy/what-is-europsy for a full description of the program). According to Lunt (2008) European governmental involvement in the licensing of psychologists is tied to the number of psychologists employed in governmentally controlled health care settings. The greater the number of psychologists working in such settings the greater the likelihood for government control of licensing (Lunt, 2008). To illustrate the typical structures European nations use for credentialing and accountability, we refer to Poland and Spain as examples from Eastern and Western Europe. Added to this list is a country new to the European Union, Turkey, which borders the Middle East.

Poland

Recent estimates suggest that Poland has 26 psychologists per 100,000 citizens and that most of these professionals practice in urban areas. Approximately half of its 10,000 psychologists are members of the Polish Psychological Association (PPA) (Heszen-Niejodek, 2004). The PPA has numerous local chapters and several sections of members with common research and practice interests (e.g., psychotherapy, forensics, developmental, and health psychology) (Heszen-Niejodek, 2004). However, the PPA is not the primary body that aims at setting high standards for the practice of psychology in Poland—the

Committee of the Psychological Sciences of the Polish Academy of Sciences (KANPAN) also serves that function. The latter body sets standards for the education and training of psychologists, publishes a professional journal, and sponsors conferences to advance the science of psychology in the country.

Even though Poland has a long tradition of psychological science and psychotherapy practice, its government did not formally recognize the profession until 2001 when it passed legislation that established the professional status of the profession and the protection of the profession from practice by unauthorized individuals (Heszen-Niejodek, 2004). The publication of a code of ethics for the profession significantly predates the legislation. The first code of ethics was published in 1988 and was updated in 1991. The current version of the code can be found at http://www.am.org/iupsys/resources/ethics/poland-code-eng.pdf. In addition to the preamble it contains 50 statements divided into four major sections: General Principles, The Practicing Psychologist, Psychologist as Researcher, and Psychologist as Teacher and Disseminator.

The responsibility for enforcement of the code of ethics does not fall to the government; it is the province of the PPA to adjudicate alleged violations and to discipline violators. The specific body that addresses complaints is the Fellow Court of the Board of Directors of the PPA (Heszen-Niejodek, 2004). Ethics complaints are investigated by regional officers for professional conduct and adjudicated by a regional disciplinary committee. Disciplinary actions range from warnings to revocation from the registry. When ethical complaints have arisen from health or mental health problems, a special commission of medical professionals is formed to evaluate the capacity of the psychologist to practice competently. It is important to note that in Poland two titles exist for those with graduate training in professional psychology—psychotherapists and clinical psychologists. Those with the latter title are typically employed in hospital settings.

Spain

The Spanish Psychological Association, the Colegio Oficial de Psicologos (http://www.cop.es), was formed in 1980. The term *colegio* refers to "a self-governing body of a profession in which higher education is a prerequisite" (Prieto & Garcia-Rodriguez, 2004, p. 353). The body was granted the status of a *colegio* by an act of the Spanish parliament in 1979, and one of its primary functions is to prevent unqualified individuals from the practice of psychology. The specific qualifications for the title of clinical psychologist were established by law in 1998. Counseling psychology and school psychology were not included by name in this legislation. This statute identifies the scope of practice (psychological diagnosis, assessment, and treatment) and stipulates that only individuals with education in psychology are allowed to participate in clinical psychology training programs (Prieto & Garcia-Rodriguez, 2004). In spite of repeated legal challenges from psychiatry professionals, in 2002 the Supreme Court of Spain upheld the right of psychologists to practice on equal footing with psychiatry.

Turkey

The development of psychological study and practice in Turkey has been significantly influenced by the models of psychological practice and training in its European neighbors. Currently, however, the title of psychologist is not regulated and any individual with an undergraduate degree in psychology can use the title. The Turkish Psychological Association (TPA) is working to establish a formal credentialing procedure for the profession and a set of accreditation guidelines for training programs, although these efforts have not yet come to fruition (Cinarbis & Ciftci, 2009). Turkey is a nation of 67 million but there is only one mental health professional per 168,000 people, a ratio that helps explain why efforts to obtain formal regulation and credentialing of psychology have moved so slowly through the legislature. Nearly half of those who have psychological training work in healthcare settings (46%) and only 8% work in other psychological settings. Private practice of psychology is still rare in Turkey (Boratav, 2004), and receiving mental health services still carries with it significant stigma (Cinarbis & Ciftci, 2009).

The only legislation that exists in Turkey subsumes psychological services under health services and does not differentiate between psychology and psychiatry. Thus, physicians are the only professionals formally authorized to administer psychological services at this point. (Cinarbis & Ciftci, 2009).

The Turkish Psychological Association is actively working to obtain more independence of practice for psychologists in healthcare settings. The organization was founded in 1976 and currently has approximately 2,500 members or associate members. TPA also monitors the practice of psychology to the extent possible without formal legislation, developing principles for the professional practice of psychology, publishing an ethics code (http://www.am.org/iupsys/resources/ethics/turkey-code-eng.pdf), and providing Turkish translations of the APA *Ethical Principles* (2002) and other APA guidelines for practice. TPA also sponsors professional conferences and continuing education programs to help assure competent psychological practice.

Middle East

Not surprisingly, the practice of psychology and other mental health professions has been substantially affected by the political unrest and frequent violence in the region. Many professionals in countries affected by such events work in settings with those who have suffered the consequences of the unrest.

Israel

The law governing the use of the title of psychologist and the regulations regarding practice were enacted in 1977 and have been revised several times since. The law recognizes five distinct specialties: clinical, educational, social/vocational, rehabilitation, and developmental psychology (Barak & Golan, 2000). The authority responsible for implementing the law is called the Council of Psychologists (COP). The council acts in an advisory capacity to the Minister of Health on any psychology-related issues. The COP also has a role in assuring the quality of psychology training programs, internships, supervisors of trainees, and professional examinations. The Israeli Psychological Association (IPA) is the organization that promotes the professional practice and the science of psychology in Israel (Jacoby, 2004), and it has been in existence since 1957. The IPA publishes a code of ethics which its members must agree to follow. Its structure and content closely parallels the code of the American Psychological Association, beginning with general principles of the profession, followed by ethical standards. (See http://www.am.org/iupsys/resources/ethics/israel-code.eng.pdf). As is true with most countries around the globe, the minimum credential for practice as a psychologist is a master's degree in professional psychology and an internship. Those who have reached this milestone are eligible to register with the Minister of Health, referred to as "signing the registration book." No additional licensing examination is required. In other words, the determination of competence to practice is left to the faculties in the psychology departments. Registered psychologists practice in a variety of public and private settings. Those in nongovernmental work settings have substantially more freedom to determine therapeutic procedures and treatments than those in public service. For example, the Ministry of Health can decide length of outpatient therapy sessions (currently 30 minutes) and the amount of time in total that will be allotted to mental health care in the public health system (Jacoby, 2004).

Iran

In this country of 65.4 million people, most of those who work as psychologists operate with bachelor's or master's degrees and the majority reside in urban centers (Ghobari & Bolhari, 2001). Although the BA is the minimum requirement for practice in the helping professions, most mental health clinics give preferential hiring to those with more advanced degrees (Ghobari & Bolhari, 2001). Iran has no centralized system for credentialing of psychologists, though advanced academic degrees are valued by employers and rigorous training programs for mental health providers have been developed at the Iranian Psychiatric Institute and Tehran University (Birashk, 2004). Ghobari and Bolhari (2001) indicate that in order to engage in clinical practice in Iran, a person must complete specific coursework in clinical or counseling psychology that includes psychological assessment, as well as practica and internship at psychiatric hospitals. However, no formal system exists for ensuring competence to practice. The role of admitting patients to hospitals and prescribing medications is the sole province of physicians. Mental health counseling for graduates of counselor education programs is also emerging in Iran, but no credentialing exists for these practitioners, either (Priester, 2008).

The Iranian Psychological Society was founded in 1968 but is work was ended by the Iranian revolution in 1979. Currently, four psychological organizations operate in the country, the most notable of which is the Iranian Psychological Association, which has 4,200 members and numerous divisions, including clinical and counseling psychology (Birashk, 2004). This body has been working to establish minimum competencies for work in mental health settings but no outcome documents have yet been published. The organization also published a code of ethics, closely modeled after the APA document (http://www.am.org/iupsys/resources/ethics/iran-code-eng.pdf).

Oceania

The regulation of psychology in this part of the globe is a study in contrasts. In some nations regulation is either newly adopted or nonexistent, and opportunities for advanced training are limited, while other countries have some of the strictest and most comprehensive regulation of psychological practice on the planet. Indonesia represents the former and New Zealand the latter.

Indonesia

The qualifications of those who treat clients with mental and emotional disorders has been a topic of significant controversy in recent years in Indonesia. Historically, academic psychologists have been allowed to practice without specific training in clinical or counseling psychology, and this group resisted for some time efforts to set standards that included clinical training (Sarwono, 2004). The Indonesian Alliance of Psychologists (HIMPSI), an organization of 6,800 members, used its influence to ensure that academic psychology training is distinguished from clinical training, and that a regulatory body was established to monitor malpractice and work with faculties in universities to set criteria for mental health training programs. These new criteria became effective in 2004 and include a master's degree in the field. HIMPSI also has the authority to adjudicate ethics complaints based on the code of ethics it established, using a committee structure that includes representation from the profession and related professions (Sarwono, 2004). It is important to note that HIMPSI is not a governmental body and no statutory regulation of professional practice exists in Indonesia, so the efforts of the organization to credential and monitor professional practice have limited effectiveness.

New Zealand

The New Zealand Psychological Society (NZPsS) was organized in 1947, but the professional practice of psychology was not a major focus of the group for the first 20 years of its existence. Substantial change began in the 1960s when the first graduate training program in clinical psychology was established (Stanley & Manthei, 2004) and a Division of Clinical Society was recognized within the larger organization. Currently, the professional practice of psychology is regulated by the Health Practitioners Competence Assurance Act, passed by the legislature and signed into law in 2003. This act replaces the former licensing law, the Psychologists Act, which was enacted in 1981 after lengthy lobbying efforts by the NZPsS. The Health Practitioners Competence Assurance Act not only regulates the practice of psychology, but all health professions.

According to Stanley and Manthei (2004), it "provides a standard framework for initial registration, renewal of registration, and challenges to registration (complaints) in the interest of consistency, flexibility, transparency, efficiency, simplicity, and economy" (p. 305). The scope of practice for the profession and the standards for accreditation of training programs are defined by the New Zealand Psychologists Board. It has established standards for cultural competence, clinical practice, and ethical conduct (see http://www.psychologistsboard.org.nz/ for detailed information about processes and procedures for registration as a psychologist in New Zealand). It defines the master's degree and a 1500-hour internship as the minimum credential for registration, and identifies the scope of practice for counseling, clinical, and educational psychologists, and psychological trainees. The board also specifies core competencies for professional practice, emphasizing cultural competency along with scientific, ethical, assessment, and intervention competencies.

Complaints against psychologists are adjudicated by the Health Professions Disciplinary Tribunal, a body composed of health professionals from a variety of disciplines. They post extensive information about complaint procedures and about the outcomes of disciplinary actions on their website (http://www.hpdt.org.nz/Default.aspx?tabid=166). Since the establishment of the tribunal, nine psychologists have been found guilty of professional misconduct.

The New Zealand Psychologist Board takes a very comprehensive approach to monitoring a professional's competence to practice. Not only does it require continuing education of all registered psychologists, it has also initiated a procedure for review of the competence of any practitioner. These reviews are meant to be educative and facilitative of more competent practice and can be instigated by colleagues, employers, the board, or the Health and Disability Commissioner and Professional Conduct Committees of the Health Professions body. However, their primary function is to ensure that a psychologist is not practicing below the standard of care for the profession, and if the findings of the review indicate substandard practice, the psychologist can be mandated to undertake a program of continuing education, and his or her practice can be curtailed until competency standards are met. See http://www.psychologistsboard.org.nz/conduct/competence.html#ask%20review for a detailed description of the program.

Based on this extensive set of regulations for professional psychology, it is clear that this country's approach to protecting the public from incompetent or irresponsible practice is one of the most comprehensive and aggressive in the world.

North America

Not only has the U.S. model of regulation of professional practice greatly influenced both the nature of regulations and the structure and function of professional associations in other parts of the world, the United States has also been a major force in the models for psychology regulation used by its neighbors on the North American continent.

Mexico

Mexico developed national standards and procedures for licensing psychologists in 1964, and since that date more than 68,000 psychologists have obtained professional licenses, most of whom practice in health-related areas (Dirección General de Profesiones, Subdirección de Colegios Profesionales, 2003). The entry level for professional practice is the *Licenciatura*, a credential granted after 5–6 years of psychology study at the university level, including both a publicly defended thesis and a practicum. In Mexico the divisions between clinical, counseling, and school psychology typically do not exist, with most programs fitting what is referred to in the United States as a combined model (Sanchez-Sosa, 2004, 2009). The Council for the Accreditation of Higher Education, a body funded by the Ministry of Education but otherwise separate from it, accredits professional psychology training programs. If a program is not accredited its graduates are not license-eligible. Graduates from accredited programs register with the Mexican Ministry of Education to obtain a license, and this body has the authority to revoke licenses for those found to violate ethical standards of practice. A master's program in this system provides specialization training, while the doctorate is strictly a research degree (Sanchez-Sosa, 2009).

The Mexican Psychological Society publishes a code of ethics for its members, the most recent version of which appeared in 2007. The first version was published 30 years earlier. The current version of the code was the product of a survey of Mexican psychologists on the ethical issues they encountered in their practice, and a process of collaboration with the Canadian Register of Health Care Providers (Hernandez-Guzman & Ritchie, 2001). Its structure and content parallel the Canadian code of ethics (Sanchez-Sosa, 2009).

Canada

As in the United States, the license to practice as a psychologist is governed by the provinces not the federal government. In some provinces, the minimum requirement for licensing is the master's degree, and in others it is the doctorate. In the more highly populated provinces, such as Quebec and Manitoba, the minimum requirement is the doctorate, but in Nova Scotia and Newfoundland/Labrador a master's degree is sufficient to earn a license. In British Columbia, a licensee with a doctorate is referred to as a "registered psychologist" and a professional with a master's degree is referred to as a "registered psychological associate," but there is no distinction in the scope of practice for the two groups, although associates must complete three years of post-degree supervised experience to be eligible for the register (College of Psychologists of British Columbia, 2011). Only the Yukon Territories has no licensing law in psychology. Most provinces also require post-degree supervised experience and a passing score on the Examination for Professional Practice in Psychology (EPPP). Approximately 14,600 psychologists are licensed in Canada, nearly half of them in Quebec. Clinical, counseling, and school psychology are recognized specialties in Canada (Jordan, Hindes, & Saklofske, 2009; Ritchie & Sabourin, 2004; Young, & Nicol, 2007). Nearly 3,000 psychologists are listed in the Canadian Register of Health Care Providers in Psychology, the only national form of registration of psychologists in the country (Canadian Register of Health Care Providers in Psychology, 2009).

Most provinces with licensing laws publish a code of ethics for psychologists. Generally, they follow the organization of the APA Ethics Code (2010, although some are more detailed and offer fuller definitions of terms. The code for British Columbia psychologists is one example of a more detailed code. British Columbia also produces "practice advisories" from time to time. These advisories serve the same function as the guidelines APA publishes regarding ethical practice.

Provincial boards have the responsibility for adjudicating ethics complaints against psychologists and psychologist associates. In addition to revocation of registration, the College of Psychologists in British Columbia can place a psychologist on the "limited register," which limits the scope of practice of a practitioner either because of an ethics violation, some other problem with competency, or a personal decision to restrict practice because of health or other personal reasons (College of Psychologists in British Columbia, 2011). The Ordre du Psychologues du Quebec is authorized not only to adjudicate complaints against psychologists but also to conduct an annual inspection program, in which random psychologists registered there have a mandatory in-person visit by an inspector. According to the Ordre, the purpose of the inspection is to help psychologists to reflect on their careers, take a look at their practice, evaluate their skills, be advised on how to improve their practice, and establish a personal continuous training program (Ordre du Psychologues du Quebec, 2010).

The Canadian Psychological Association (CPA) listed 6,755 members in 2010 (CPA, 2010a) and is a vibrant force in the profession in Canada. The organization not only promotes the science and practice of psychology in the country, it also accredits doctoral programs and internships. Currently 25 clinical psychology programs, four counseling psychology programs, one clinical neuropsychology program, and one school psychology doctoral program are accredited. Canada's approach to internship accreditation differs somewhat from that of the United States. CPA accredits internships by specialization, with the great majority of these in clinical psychology (n = 25) and a few in counseling psychology (n = 3) and clinical neuropsychology (n = 3). The practice of concurrently accrediting internships and training programs in both the United States and Canada is being phased out and will end in 2015 (CPA, 2010b). As is typical of most psychological associations across the globe, CPA publishes a code of ethics (CPA, 2000), appoints an ethics committee to adjudicate complaints against members, and offers consultation to members about ethical issues. The ethics committee is also involved in the publication of a number of policy statements and ethical guidelines for responsible practice. See http://www.cpa.ca/publications/ for a listing of these statements.

Summary

Depending upon one's location on the planet, psychology appears either as a well-established and influential influence on mental health practice and social policy regarding that practice, or as a fledgling profession working hard to get a foothold in countries where mental health care is seen as the province of other professionals or of spiritual or religious interventions. The models of psychological practice in the United States and Western Europe have been dominant forces in how other countries view the ethical standards for practice and the nature of the regulations that ought to be put into place. Some psychological associations are laboring to establish their own identities for the profession, integrated with the cultural and social fabric unique to them. The energy that is being devoted to that task across the globe is exciting for the future of the profession.

References

American Psychological Association. (2010). *Ethical principles and code of conduct of psychologists*. Retrieved from http://www.apa.org/ethics/code/index.aspx.

Barak, A., & Golan, G. (2000). Counseling psychology in Israel: Successful accomplishments in a non-existent specialty. *The Counseling Psychologist, 28*, 100–116.

Barnes, B. (2004). Psychology in India. In M. J. Stevens & D. Wedding (Eds.), *Handbook of international psychology* (pp.225–242). New York: Brunner-Routledge.

Bell, V. (2010). Psychology in Argentina. *National Psychologist, 19*, 3–4.

Birashk, B. (2004). Psychology in Iran. In M. J. Stevens & D. Wedding. (Eds.), *Handbook of international psychology* (pp.405–418). New York: Brunner-Routledge.

Boratav, H. B. (2004). Psychology at the cross-roads: The view from Turkey. In M. J. Stevens & Wedding, D. (Eds.), *Handbook of international psychology* (pp.311–330). New York: Brunner-Routledge.

Canadian Psychological Association. (2000). *Canadian Code of Ethics for Psychologists*. Retrieved from http://www.cpa.ca/cpasite/userfiles/Documents/Canadian%20Code%20of%20Ethics%20for%20Psycho.pdf.

Canadian Psychological Association. (2010a). *Associate director's report*. Retrieved from http://www.cpa.ca/cpasite/userfiles/Documents/AR2010English.pdf.

Canadian Psychological Association. (2010b). *APA accreditation of Canadian programmes*. Retrieved from http://www.cpa.ca/education/accreditation/apaaccreditationofcanadianprograms

Canadian Register of Health Care Providers in Psychology. (2009). *Executive director's report*. Retrieved from http://www.crhspp.ca/Docs/exrep.htm.

Chinese Psychological Society. (2007). *Code of ethics for clinical and counseling practice*. Retrieved from http://www.am.org/iupsys/resources/ethics/china-code-eng.pdf.

Chinese Psychological Society. (2009). *Registration criteria*. Retrieved from http://softexpublishing.com/index2.php?option=com_content&do_pdf=1&id=213.

Cinarbis, D. C., & Ciftci, A. (2009). Counseling in Turkey. In L. H. Gerstein, P. P. Heppner, S. Ægisdttir, S. A. Leung, & K. L. Norsworthy,. (Eds.), *International handbook of cross-cultural counseling: Cultural assumptions and practices worldwide* (pp. 475–485). Thousand Oaks, CA: Sage.

College of Psychologists of British Columbia. (2011). *Registration requirements*. Retrieved from http://www.collegeofpsychologists.bc.ca/docs/Registration%20Requirements.pdf.

Dirección General de Profesiones, Subdirección de Colegios Profesionales. (2003). Total de profesionistas registrados en la carrera de psicologia de 1945 [Total professionals registered in the psychology program in 1945]. Mexico City: Author.

Ghobari, B., & Bolhari, J. (2001). The current state of medical psychology in Iran. *Journal of Clinical Psychology in Medical Settings, 8,* 39–43.

Han, B., & Zhang, K. (2007). Psychology in China. *The Psychologist, 20.* Retrieved from http://www.thepsychologist.org.uk/archive/archive_home.cfm/volumeID_20-editionID_154-ArticleID_1280-getfile_getPDF/thepsychologist%5C1207chin.pdf.

Health Professions Council of South Africa. (2004). *Professional board for psychology.* Retrieved from http://www.hpcsa.co.za/board_psychology_registration.php.

Hernandez-Guzman, L., & Ritchie, P. L. J. (2001). Hacia la transformacion y actualización empiricas del codigo etico de los psicologos mexicanos [Toward the transformation and empirical updating of the ethics code for Mexican psychologists]. *Revista Mexicana de Psicologia, 18,* 347–357.

Heszen-Niejodek, I. (2004). Psychology in Poland: A country in transition. In M. J. Stevens & D. Wedding,. (Eds.), *Handbook of international psychology* (pp. 273–292). New York: Brunner-Routledge.

Hutz, C. S., McCarthy, S., & Gomes, W. (2004). Psychology in Brazil: The road behind and the road ahead. In M. J. Stevens & D. Wedding (Eds.), *Handbook of international psychology* (pp. 151–168). New York: Brunner-Routledge.

Jacoby, R. (2004). Psychology in Israel. In M. J. Stevens & D. Wedding (Eds.), *Handbook of international psychology* (pp.419–435). New York: Brunner-Routledge.

Jimerson, S. B., Skokut, M., Cardenas, S., Malone, H., & Stewart, K. (2008). Where in the world is school psychology: Examining evidence of school psychology across the globe. *School Psychology International, 29,* 131–144.

Jordan, J. J., Hindes, Y. L., & Saklofske, D. H. (2009). School psychology in Canada: A survey of roles and functions, challenges and aspirations. *Canadian Journal of School Psychology, 24*(3), 245–264.

Koinange, J. W. (2004). Psychology in Kenya. In M. J. Stevens & D. Wedding (Eds.), *Handbook of international psychology* (pp. 25–42). New York: Brunner-Routledge.

Lunt, I. (2000). Psychology as a profession. In K. Pawlik & M. R. Rosenzeig (Eds.), *International handbook of psychology* (pp. 534–548). Thousand Oaks, CA: Sage.

Lunt, I. (2008). Professional mobility and quality assurance within the European Union. In J. E. Hall, & E. M. Altmaier (Eds.). *Global Promise: Quality assurance and accountability in professional psychology* (pp. 128–139). New York: Oxford University Press.

Makrinov, N., Scharager, J., & Diaz, R. (2006). Psychology in Chile. *National Psychologist, 19,* 596–598.

Mexican Psychological Society. (2007). *Codigo etico del psicologo* [Code of ethics of psychologists]. Mexico City: Trillas.

Ordre du Psychologues du Quebec. (2010). *Professional code.* Retrieved from http://www.ordrepsy.qc.ca/en/psychologue/obligations/code-of-ethics.sn

Prabhu, G. G. (1998). Psychotherapy in India. *Indian Journal of Psychological Medicine, 11,* 155–159.

Prasadarao, P. S. D. V., & Matam Sudhir, P. (2001). Clinical psychology in India. *Journal of Clinical Psychology in Medical Settings, 8*(1), 31–38.

Priester, P. E. (2008). Mental health counseling in the Islamic Republic of Iran: A marriage of religion, science, and practice. *Counseling and Values, 52*(3), 253–264.

Prieto, J. M., & Garcia-Rodriguez, Y. (2004). Strengthening psychology in Spain. In M. J. Stevens & D. Wedding (Eds.), *Handbook of international psychology* (pp. 351–369). New York: Brunner-Routledge.

Psychology Federation of Argentina. (1999). Code of ethics. Buenos Aires: Author.

Ritchie, P. L. J., & Sabourin, M. E. (2004). Psychology in Canada. In M. J. Stevens & D. Wedding (Eds.), *Handbook of international psychology* (pp. 75–92), New York: Brunner-Routledge.

Sanchez-Sosa, J. J. (2004). Psychology in Mexico: Recent developments and perspective. In M. J. Stevens & D. Wedding (Eds.), *Handbook of international psychology* (pp. 93–107), New York: Brunner-Routledge.

Sanchez-Sosa, J. J. (2009). Psychology in Mexico: Background and current status. *IUPsyS Newsletter, 8.* Retrieved from http://www.am.org/iupsys/newsletter/2009-v8-2/2009-8-2-mexico.htm.

Sanchez-Sosa, J. J., & Riveros, A. (2007). Theory, research, and practice in psychology in the developing (majority) world. In M. J. Stevens & U. P. Gielen (Eds.), *Toward a global psychology: Theory, research, intervention, and pedagogy* (pp. 101–146). Mahwah, NJ: Lawrence Erlbaum.

Sarwono, S. W. (2004). *Psychology in Indonesia.* In M. J. Stevens & D. Wedding (Eds.), *Handbook of international psychology* (pp. 59–74). New York: Brunner-Routledge.

South African Professional Board for Psychology. (2007). Practice framework adopted by the professional board for psychology: September 2007. Retrieved from http://www.psyssa.com/documents/scope-of-practice.pdf.

Stanley, P., & Manthei, R. (2004). Counselling psychology in New Zealand: The quest for identity and recognition. *Counselling Psychology Quarterly, 17*(3), 301–315.

Stead, G. B. (2004). Psychology in South Africa. In M. J. Stevens & D. Wedding (Eds.), *Handbook of international psychology* (pp.59–74). New York: Brunner-Routledge.

Stevens, M. J. & Wedding, D. (2004). International psychology: A synthesis. In M. J. Stevens & D. Wedding (Eds.), *Handbook of international psychology* (pp. 481–500). New York: Brunner-Routledge.

Watts, A. (2010). Psychology in South Africa. *IUPsyS Newsletter, 9,* 12–19. Retrieved from http://www.iupsys.net/images/newsletter/2010-newsletter-v9-1.pdf.

Yang, Y. (2004). Advances in psychology in China. In M. J. Stevens & D. Wedding (Eds.), *Handbook of international psychology* (pp. 173–192). New York: Brunner-Routledge.

Young, R. A., & Nicol, J. (2007). Counselling psychology in Canada: Advancing psychology for all. *Applied Psychology: An International Review, 56,* 20–32.

CHAPTER 9

The Tale of Two Universal Declarations: Ethics and Human Rights

Janel Gauthier *and* Jean L. Pettifor

> **Abstract**
>
> In 1948, in the aftermath of WWII, and before the development of ethics codes in psychology, the United Nations adopted the Universal Declaration of Human Rights to protect people of all nations from harm. In 2008, 60 years later, in an increasingly globalized world, the International Union of Psychological Science and the International Association of Applied Psychology adopted the Universal Declaration of Ethical Principles for Psychologists. This latter declaration commits psychologists world-wide to be guided by fundamental ethical principles of respect and caring in all of psychology's interactions with persons and peoples. This chapter demonstrates how fundamental human rights in the world and ethical principles in psychology were each recognized through a universal declaration, how the approach to building a better world has evolved over time, and how the two universal declarations complement and strengthen each other in meeting today's global challenges for achieving freedom, justice, and peace in the world.
>
> **Key Words:** Universal Declaration, declaration, ethics, rights, human rights, ethical principles, globalization

In 2008, the General Assembly of the International Union of Psychological Science[1] and the Board of Directors of the International Association of Applied Psychology[2] adopted the *Universal Declaration of Ethical Principles for Psychologists* as "a common moral framework that guides and inspires psychologists worldwide toward the highest ethical ideals in their professional and scientific work" (Universal Declaration of Ethical Principles for Psychologists, 2008). This important historical event happened 60 years after the General Assembly of the United Nations proclaimed the *Universal Declaration of Human Rights* (UDHR) "as a common standard of achievement for all peoples and all nations, to the end that every individual and every organ of society, keeping this Declaration constantly in mind, shall strive by teaching and education to promote respect for these rights and freedoms and by progressive measures, national and international, to secure their universal and effective recognition and observance, both among the peoples of Member States themselves and among the peoples of territories under their jurisdiction" (United Nations, 1948).

In this chapter, we demonstrate how the *Universal Declaration of Ethical Principles for Psychologists* (2008) and the *Universal Declaration of Human Rights* (United Nations, 1948) have a common purpose in building a better world, how they differ in reflecting specific issues of their time and place in history, and how they complement and strengthen each other in meeting the worldwide challenges for human life in the 21st century. Ethics and human rights provide a much needed moral framework for addressing today's global problems.

Human societies over the centuries have been in a constant process of transformation. The pace of transformation has dramatically increased since World War II (WWII), especially sociopolitical problems associated with the process of globalization. Money, technology, raw materials, and products move ever more freely and swiftly across national borders. So do people, ideas, and cultures. As a result, societies are confronted with challenging crosscultural issues, particularly with respect to cultural diversity, social injustice, and indigenous practices. Close proximity of people with diverse views of the world can lead to understanding, tolerance and cooperation, but often leads to fear, distrust, and even violence and killing to protect what people believe is theirs. The economic, political, social, and technological developments that are accelerating in the early 21st century represent macro-level forces that are moving psychology toward a science and profession without borders. Stevens and Gielen (2007) offer rich and varied evidence for the globalizing of psychology. We also know that with or without globalization, large numbers of the world's population live under horrific conditions of poverty, oppression, disease, exploitation, environmental degradation, and harm that can only be seen as gross injustice and a violation of human rights. With easy access and broad exposure to today's media reports, psychologists and nonpsychologists alike cannot remain unaware of such injustices.

Our continuous existence as a species on this planet depends on how we act in relationship to ourselves, to other persons, and to nature. We call on psychologists as human beings to contribute their knowledge and skills to resolving societal problems, to creating just societies, and eliminating global threats to our very existence. We call on psychologists to keep their connectedness to a moral framework as the foundation for all their work as psychologists. Both ethics and human rights help to keep the spirit of these ideals alive.

This chapter is organized in the following sections: Recognizing Fundamental Human Rights through a Universal Declaration, Recognizing Fundamental Ethical Principles through a Universal Declaration, and Ethics and Human Rights: Together in Serving Humankind. This organization reflects the order in which fundamental human rights in the world and ethical principles in psychology were each recognized through a universal declaration; it also helps to highlight the historical context in which each document came about, and how the approach to meeting worldwide challenges for human life and achieving freedom, justice, and peace in the world has evolved over time.

Recognizing Fundamental Human Rights through a Universal Declaration

With a history of just over 60 years, the UDHR (United Nations, 1948) has come to be regarded as the single most important document in the 20th century to establish a worldwide standard for human rights, and a foundation for building a world that enables all people to live in dignity and peace. The UDHR enjoys a high level of worldwide support.

The purpose of the UDHR (United Nations, 1948) is to promote respect for the rights and freedoms of all people, and, by progressive measures, to secure their universal and effective recognition and observance nationally and internationally, both among the peoples of states which are members of the United Nations and among the peoples of territories under their jurisdiction.

The Concept of Human Rights

The core concept of human rights is the belief that every person should be accorded a sense of value, worth, and dignity, and that every person should be protected from infringements and abuses of fundamental rights. Human rights are based on moral rights, and our moral duties and obligations are inherent in what it means to be a person born equal in dignity, and with the freedom to make individual choices. Human rights are moral rights that are inherent in the nature of being human. Therefore, human rights are unalienable in that they cannot be denied, changed, or neglected.

Human rights are moral imperatives inasmuch as they are unavoidable obligations that must be acted on because they are correct, regardless of opposition or difficulty. They take priority over all other issues.

What is the relationship between *human* rights and *legal* rights? Is there a distinction to be made between human rights and legal rights? Human rights cannot be denied or changed, whereas legal rights can be changed by changing the law. Legal rights (sometimes also called "civil rights" or "statutory rights") are defined by the different states and governments, whereas moral rights are natural. Human rights are considered "natural" in that they are an inherent part of every person. Because they are natural and unalienable, human (moral) rights are necessarily universal, whereas legal rights are culturally and politically relative. Legal rights may or may not be consistent with human (moral) rights. Human (moral) rights thus take priority if they conflict with legal rights.

When nations ratify the UDHR (United Nations, 1948), they are committed to incorporating human rights into their own legislation. Therefore, when human rights become part of a nation's laws, moral and legal rights will appear to be the same, but they are not to be confounded. Human rights are subject to no particular system of law or religious or political administration, although they express the political objective that governments must respect, protect, and promote.

When embedded in law, human rights become binding and the law can be used to monitor and enforce compliance. Since the adoption of the UDHR in 1948, the development in the field of international human rights law has been wide-ranging, placing the UDHR and the many covenants, conventions, and protocols adopted during the last 60 years, in the forefront of international political and social discourse.

Historical Context

The historical background of moral discourse leading to the UDHR (United Nations, 1948) is lengthy. The Ten Commandments are perhaps one of the oldest examples of a list of religious and moral imperatives that are recognized (with minor differences in wording) as a moral foundation in Judaism, Christianity, and Islam. Over 1,200 years before the birth of Christ, these commandments were delivered directly to man from God[3] to guide the behavior of humans. In the first half of the document, allegiance is commanded to the one and only God, who is loving of the faithful and punishing of the disobedient. The remaining commandments address human relationships on earth, primarily around doing no harm, such as prohibiting murder, adultery, bearing false witness, stealing, and coveting that which belongs to the neighbor. While you should not do harm to others, you and others should also be free of being harmed. The Ten Commandments, although not using the language of human rights, are still honored today as a basic foundation for ethical human behavior. In addition to moral conduct issues, the early prophets of all the world's great religions were deeply concerned about the oppression and abuse suffered by the common people at the hands of the ruling classes. Within the context of their time and place in history, they preached love and compassion, and they demanded justice from ruling powers (Pettifor, 1996; Smith, 1991).

Throughout much of history, people acquired rights and responsibilities through their membership in a group: a family, indigenous nation, religion, class, community, or state. Most societies have had traditions similar to the "Golden Rule" of "Do unto others as you would have them do unto you." The Hindu Vedas, the Babylonian Code of Hammurabi, the Hebrew Bible (which includes only texts of the Old Testament) and the Christian Bible (which includes texts of both the Old and the New Testaments), the Qur'an, and the Analects of Confucius are among the oldest written sources which address questions of people's duties, rights, and responsibilities.

The Magna Carta, also called the "Great Charter of Freedom (1215), was the first attempt by a group of the English king's subjects to protect their own interests and privileges by forcing a legal document on the king that would limit his powers (Howard, 1998). Perhaps the most important legacy of the Magna Carta was establishing the foundation for the principle of habeas corpus, protecting the individual against illegal imprisonment. Along with revisions, the Magna Carta continued to be a force in the development of laws and constitutions until late in the 18th century (Holt, 1992).

The English Bill of Rights (1689), which grew out of what has been called the "bloodless revolution" or the "glorious revolution" of 1688, set out strict limits on the royal family's legal prerogatives. It was designed to control the power of kings and queens and to make them subject to laws passed by parliament. As part of their oaths, the new King William III and Queen Mary were required to swear that they would obey the laws of parliament, a significant move from the rule of man to the rule of law. When the English Bill of Rights was given royal assent, it represented the end of the concept of divine right of kings.

The United States Declaration of Independence (1776) states "We hold these truths to be self-evident, that all men (sic) are created equal, that they are endowed by their Creator with certain unalienable Rights, that among these are Life, Liberty and the pursuit of Happiness" (http://www.ushistory.org/declaration/document/index.htm). The American declaration provided a moral justification for an otherwise illegal war of independence from British colonization.

From the French Revolution came the Declaration of the Rights of Man and of the Citizen [In French: *Déclaration des droits de l'homme et du citoyen*] (1789) and the slogan "liberty, equality and fraternity." The French declaration affirmed the natural rights of man (sic) to liberty, property, security, and resistance to oppression. It called for the destruction of aristocratic privileges, since all men were created equal before the law. The strongest emphasis was on equality. While it set forth fundamental rights, not only for French citizens but for "all men without exception," it did not make any statement about the status of women, nor did it explicitly address slavery. The recognition of "resistance to oppression" as a fundamental natural right provided moral justification for the French Revolution including violence against unjust rulers and unjust laws.

Documents asserting individual rights, such the Magna Carta (1215), the English Bill of Rights (1689), the American Declaration of Independence (1776), and the French Declaration of the Rights of Man and of the Citizen (1789) are the written precursors to many of today's human rights documents. Yet many of these documents, when originally translated into policy, excluded women, people of color, and members of certain social, religious, economic, and political groups.

Until the 17th century, attempts to establish a framework for rules, laws, and codes, whether in social, legal, secular, or theological debate, emphasized duties and privileges that arose from peoples' status or relationships, rather than from abstract rights. Then, attention moved from social responsibilities to individual needs and participation. These rights were called "natural rights," or "the rights of man."

Although the concept of "human rights" is essentially the product of 17th- and 18th-century European thought, the term "human rights" has only come into common currency in the 20th century. The concept of "human rights" became especially important after the Nuremberg Trials disclosed to the world the extent of war crimes and crimes against humanity committed by the Nazis during WWII. Human rights became a core objective of the United Nations when it was founded in 1945 (Mann, Gruskin, & Grodin, 1999; Power, 2002).

The violation of human rights continues to be a major concern in many parts of the world today, and is used as a moral justification for protest and sometimes violence against what are perceived as corrupt and oppressive governments. As a reaction against the gross abuses perpetrated against individuals, it is natural to focus on the rights of individuals. However, in a global world, the importance of also focusing on harmony and cooperation for the collective good cannot be overemphasized.

Adoption of the Universal Declaration of Human Rights

The UDHR (United Nations, 1948) was a direct response to the exposure of WWII atrocities, and its message was that all nations must commit to protecting human rights of its citizens. The UDHR was the first universal statement on the basic principles of inalienable human rights to which all persons are entitled. It is regarded today as the greatest statements of "natural" or human rights.

The UDHR was adopted by the General Assembly of the United Nations on the 10th of December 1948, after a long and sometimes difficult process to obtain agreement on the content. None of the 58 member states of the United Nations voted against the Declaration. However, eight nations chose to abstain (Belorussian Soviet Socialist Republic, Czechoslovakia, Poland, Saudi Arabia, South Africa, the Soviet Union, the Ukrainian Soviet Socialist Republic, and Yugoslavia) and two were absent. The six communist countries abstaining claimed that the Declaration did not provide enough emphasis on economic rights. Saudi Arabia cited conflict with Islamic law to justify its decision not to vote in favor of the Declaration. South Africa claimed that the Declaration was going too far (Morsink, 1999).

The road to adoption was not an easy one. The final text was a compromise; many controversial issues were excluded and broad language was used, omitting references to specific religious or philosophical doctrines (Glendon, 2001). By the time the Declaration (United Nations, 1948) was brought before the United Nations General Assembly in Paris, the document had been the subject of dozens of meetings and proposed amendments. To complicate matters, the United States and the Soviet Union were in the beginning stages of the Cold War, an ideological battle with serious implications for human rights around the world.

Eleanor Roosevelt of the United States played a key role in leading the process of developing the UDHR (United Nations, 1948). At the time, she was chairing the newly created Commission on Human Rights. The membership of the Commission was designed to be broadly representative of the global community with representatives of the following countries serving: Australia, Belgium, Byelorussian Soviet Socialist Republic, Chile, China, Egypt, France, India, Iran, Lebanon, Panama, Philippines, United Kingdom, United States, Union of Soviet Socialist Republics, Uruguay, and Yugoslavia.

Many prominent people provided drafts to the Commission for its consideration (Glendon, 2001; Morsink, 1999). Canadian law professor John Peter Humphrey was called upon by the United Nations Secretary-General to work on the project. In this role, he produced the first draft of a list of rights that were to form the basis of the Declaration (United Nations, 1948). The underlying structure of the Declaration was introduced in its second draft, which was prepared by French jurist René Cassin, who worked from the Humphrey blueprint. Also instrumental in the drafting of the UDHR were Eleanor Roosevelt; Chang Peng-chun, a Chinese playwright, philosopher, and diplomat; and Charles Habib Malik, a Lebanese philosopher and diplomat.

During the process of developing the UDHR (United Nations, 1948), the Commission solicited contributions from all over the world (Glendon, 2001; Morsink, 1999). The United Nations Educational, Scientific and Cultural Organization (UNESCO), at the behest of the Human Rights Commission, sent questionnaires to prominent thinkers in every corner of the globe, including Mahatma Gandhi (India) and Aldous Huxley (England). Respondents offered their thoughts on human rights ideals given their distinct ethnic, philosophical, and religious backgrounds.

Subsequently, with the goal of establishing mechanisms for enforcing the UDHR (United Nations, 1948), two other human rights covenants were adopted by the General Assembly of the United Nations on December 1966: the *International Covenant on Civil and Political Rights* (United Nations, 1966a) and the *International Covenant on Economic, Social and Cultural Rights* (United Nations, 1966b) It took almost another 20 years to reach an agreed-upon legally binding text, and another 10 years before a sufficient number of states had acceded to it. These two documents, together with the UDHR, represent today what is known as the *International Bill of Human Rights* (Smith, 2010).

The historical development of the covenants can be linked to classical civil rights struggles of workers, peasants, and various oppressed people for political and civil participation in governance from the 18th to the early 20th century. For example, the civil and political rights enshrined in the *International Covenant on Civil and Political Rights* (United Nations, 1966a), whose purpose is to protect the liberty of the individual against the tyranny and abuse of the state, were first proclaimed in the declarations of the French and American revolutions. The economic, social, and cultural rights proclaimed in the *International Covenant on Economic, Social and Cultural Rights* (United Nations, 1966b) can be viewed against the background of Mexican and Russian revolutions in opposing capitalistic exploitation of workers, and more generally the injustice of social inequality (Wellman, 2000).

A concept that is frequently used to describe and capture the significance of the historical context of human rights and their development over time is the notion of "generations of human rights" as advanced in 1979 by French jurist Karel Vasak (Steiner & Alston, 1996). Vasak's model of three generations was inspired by the three ideals of the French Revolution: liberty, equality and fraternity.

The "first" generation of human rights, enshrined in both the UDHR (United Nations, 1948) and the *International Covenant on Civil and Political Rights* (United Nations, 1966a), covers civil and political rights (liberty rights). These rights include freedom of speech, freedom of religion, and the right to a fair trial. First-generation rights are concerned chiefly with protection of persons against the fiat of draconian states, and oppose government interventions that compromise human dignity (Weston, 2002). Most Western scholars and critics consider first-generation rights as the standard against which subsequent claims of rights should be measured (Charlesworth, 1994).

The "second" generation of rights deals with equality, and encompasses economic, social, and cultural rights. The definitions of these rights are set out in the *International Covenant on Economic, Social and Cultural Rights* (United Nations, 1966b), and include the right to health, work, social security, and education. While the first-generation rights are "negative rights," since they serve to protect citizens from the excesses of the state, second-generation rights are "positive rights," and represent the state's obligations to ensure that these rights are progressively realized (Mann et al., 1999).

The "third" generation of rights, sometimes referred to as "new" rights (Cook, 1994) are solidarity rights, and cover group and collective rights, such as the right to self-determination, to development, to control over resources, to a clean environment, to protection against ecological ravages, and to peace. Third-generation rights have been championed within the United Nations by developing nations (Cook, 1994), but have not been fully accepted by the mainstream. No international covenants exist at this stage to aid their acceptance and recognition at an international level.

Structure and Content of the Universal Declaration of Human Rights

The UDHR (United Nations, 1948) includes a preamble followed by 30 articles, of which 17 could be regarded as relating to civil and political rights and 8 to economic and social rights.

The document was structured by René Cassin. He wanted people to see the way the articles of the UDHR (United Nations, 1948) were organized as a coherent set of rules clustering around various organizing ideas that are simple to understand, even if the rules are somewhat complex. His vision was that of the portico of a Greek temple, with a foundation, steps, four columns, and a pediment erected on the four columns (Ishay, 2008).

In Cassin's model, articles 1 and 2 are the foundation blocks, with their principles of dignity, equality, brotherhood, and freedom. The seven paragraphs of the preamble, setting out the reasons for the Declaration (United Nations, 1948), are represented by the steps. The main body of the Declaration forms the four columns. The first column (articles 3–11) constitutes rights of the individual, such as the right to life, liberty, security, justice, and the right not to be subjected to torture. The second column (articles 12–17) constitutes the rights of the individual in civil and political society (e.g., the rights to privacy of family life and to marry, to freedom of movement within the national state or outside it, to have a nationality, to asylum in case of persecution, to property, to practice a religion). The third column (articles 18–21) is concerned with spiritual, public, and political freedoms (e.g., freedom of conscience, thought and expression, freedom of assembly and association, the right to vote and to stand for election, the right of access to government). The fourth column (articles 22–27) sets out social, economic, and cultural rights (i.e., those rights which operate in the sphere of labor and production relationships and in that of education; rights to work and social security and to free choice of employment, to just conditions of work, to equal pay for equal work, to form and join trade unions, to rest and leisure, to health care, to education and to participate freely in the cultural life of the community). The last three articles of the Declaration (articles 28–30) provide the pediment which binds the structure together. They place rights in the context of limits, duties, and the social and political order in which they are to be realized.

Significance of the Universal Declaration of Human Rights

In the course of a half century, the UDHR (United Nations, 1948) has become possibly the most important document in the world to define a standard for human rights. The UDHR expands on human justice messages from the past, and is seen as an essential foundation for building a world in which all human beings can look forward to a life of dignity and peace. Even countries that have been doubtful about the whole human rights enterprise feel bound to defend themselves when they are accused of being in breach of the UDHR. Human rights have achieved an important political and moral status. Although a declaration is not a legally binding document, the UDHR has achieved the status of "customary international law" because people regard it as a common standard of achievement for all people and all nations (Glendon, 2001). Its foundation of moral and practice terms makes it virtually unchallengeable as a part of "customary international law."

The Charter of the United Nations[4] (United Nations, 1945) established at the end of WWII that how a government treats its own citizens is a matter of legitimate international concern, and not simply a domestic issue. The UDHR (United Nations, 1948) has reinforced this revolutionary change by spelling out the meaning of the fundamental rights and freedoms proclaimed in the Charter. Now, it is often referenced in resolutions of the United Nations General Assembly and in its debates. To some extent, it has become "the international Magna Carta for all men everywhere," as Eleanor Roosevelt had predicted in her speech before the General Assembly of the United Nations on December 10, 1948.

Judges of the International Court of Justice have invoked principles contained in the *International Bill of Human Rights* as a basis for their decisions. The UDHR (United Nations, 1948) continues to be widely cited by governments, academics, advocates, and constitutional courts, and individual human beings who appeal to its principles for the protection of their recognized human rights.

The UDHR (United Nations, 1948) has been translated into at least 375 languages and dialects (http://www.ohchr.org/en/udhr/pages/introduction.aspx), making it one the most widely translated documents in the world. The principles of the UDHR have been incorporated into the national constitution of most of the 192 member states of the United Nations. They also serve as the foundation for a growing number of international treaties, national laws, and international, regional, national and subnational institutions protecting and promoting human rights (Glendon, 2001).

Nearly all international human rights instruments adopted by the United Nations bodies since 1948 elaborate on principles set out in the UDHR

(United Nations, 1948). These universal principles today are embedded in numerous international human rights conventions, declarations, and resolutions, expressing the obligations and rights of states in a more specified and detailed way than what was possible within the framework of the UDHR. The conventions have all been developed on the basis of the principles in the UDHR, followed often by lengthy processes of drafting and negotiation before adoption (Ishay, 2008). States are then invited to sign, and thereafter ratify, making them party to the conventions and all that they entail. Through ratification of the treaties, the government in each state is required to make domestic measures and legislation comparable with their treaty obligations and duties (Smith, 2010).

There are nine core international human rights treaties: The International Convention on the Elimination of All Forms of Racial Discrimination (United Nations, 1965); the International Covenant on Civil and Political Rights (United Nations, 1966a), and the International Covenant on Economic, Social, and Cultural Rights (United Nations, 1966b); the Convention on the Elimination of All Forms of Discrimination against Women (United Nations, 1979); the Convention against Torture and Other Cruel, Inhuman, or Degrading Treatment or Punishment (United Nations, 1984); the Convention on the Rights of the Child (United Nations, 1989); the International Convention on the Rights of All Migrant Workers and Members of their Families (United Nations, 1990); the International Convention for the Protection of All Persons from Enforced Disappearance (United Nations, 2006b); and finally, the Convention on the Rights of Persons with Disabilities (United Nations, 2006a). To each of these treaties committees have been established to monitor nations' implementation of the provisions of the conventions (for further details, see http://www.ohchr.org/en/hrbodies/Pages/HumanRightsBodies.aspx). The committees consist of a number of independent experts who regularly examine compliance and implementation, based on the periodic reports from the governments themselves and from other independent sources.

Over the past 60 years, the UDHR (United Nations, 1948) has acquired the status of "customary international law" because most states treat it as though it were law (Smith, 2010). However, governments have not applied this customary law equally. Socialist and communist countries of Eastern Europe, Latin America, and Asia have emphasized social welfare rights, such as education, jobs, and health care, but often have limited the political rights of their citizens. The United States has focused on political and civil rights and has advocated strongly against regimes that torture, deny religious freedom, or persecute minorities. On the other hand, the United States government has rarely recognized health care, homelessness, environmental pollution, and other social and economic concerns as human rights issues, especially within its own borders.

The dramatic changes in Eastern Europe, Africa, and Latin America since 1989 have powerfully demonstrated a surge in demand for respect of human rights. Popular movements in China, Korea, and other Asian nations reveal a similar commitment to these principles. In Europe, the Americas, and Africa, regional documents for the protection and promotion of human rights extend the *International Bill of Human Rights*. For example, the African states have created their own *African Charter of Human and Peoples' Rights* (African Commission on Human and Peoples' Rights, 1981), and Muslim states have created the *Cairo Declaration on Human Rights in Islam* (1990). Notice that some of those documents have been developed because the concept of human rights presented in the UDHR (United Nations, 1948) is seen as incompatible with fundamental cultural or religious beliefs. For example, in the Muslim world, states recognize no authority or power but that of God, and no legal tradition apart from Islamic law. Most of them object to the universal character and indivisibility of human rights, as interpreted in the UDHR, which according to them, is a "Western secular concept of Judeo-Christian origin," incompatible with the sacred Islamic *shari'ah* (Littman, 1999).

To sum up, the UDHR (United Nations, 1948) is an increasingly powerful instrument for the achievement of human dignity and peace for all. Both its achievements and challenges are great. Through the promotion and implementation of inalienable rights for all people, the UDHR leaves an abiding legacy for humankind.

Recognizing Fundamental Ethical Principles Through a Universal Declaration

The most recent and arguably the single most important international development in the history of psychology ethics is the unanimous adoption of the *Universal Declaration of Ethical Principles for Psychologists* by the General Assembly of the International Union of Psychological Science and the Board of Directors of the International

Association of Applied Psychology during the International Congress of Psychology in Berlin in 2008 (Gauthier, 2008a, 2009; Ferrero & Gauthier, 2009).

The rationale for developing a universal declaration of ethical principles for psychologists was to provide a universal moral framework and generic set of ethical principles to guide psychologists worldwide in meeting the ethical challenges of rapid globalization, a set of principles that encompasses all their scientific and professional activities as psychologists in a manner that also recognizes and may be used to address culture-specific interpretations.

The objectives of the *Universal Declaration of Ethical Principles for Psychologists* (2008) are clearly defined in the second paragraph of the Preamble, which reads as follows:

> The objectives of the *Universal Declaration* are to provide a moral framework and generic set of ethical principles for psychology organizations worldwide: (a) to evaluate the ethical and moral relevance of their codes of ethics; (b) to use as a template to guide the development or evolution of their codes of ethics; (c) to encourage global thinking about ethics, while also encouraging action that is sensitive and responsive to local needs and values; and (d) to speak with a collective voice on matters of ethical concern.

It is important to note that the *Universal Declaration of Ethical Principles for Psychologists* (2008) is not a worldwide code of ethics or code of conduct. A declaration of ethical principles reflects the moral principles and values that are expected to be addressed in a code of ethics or a code of conduct. Codes of conduct define what one *must* or *must not* do as a psychologist, whereas codes of ethics are more aspirational, and link standards to the overarching principles and values. Codes of conduct are enforceable, while aspirational principles without further elaboration are not.

The Concept of Ethical Principles

In ethics, the term *ethical principle* refers to an overarching generic and widely held moral belief of what is "right" in interactions between human beings and with the environment. Ethical principles are deeply rooted in our view of the purpose and meaning of life or existence in general. This question has been the subject of much philosophical, theological, and scientific speculation throughout history, and has yielded a large number of answers from many different cultural and ideological backgrounds.

Ethical principles are expected to be reasonably permanent, although there will be differences in how they are described and translated into practice. Some common terminology for ethical principles includes respect for the dignity of persons and peoples; autonomy; self-determination, beneficence, nonmaleficence, responsible caring; welfare of others; integrity; welfare of society; and social justice. Each ethical principle has associated values that bring one's attention a step closer to applying the principle in practice. For example, in considering how we show respect for the dignity of persons and peoples, we may identify such values as informed consent, confidentiality of personal information, and privacy. Standards or behavioral rules on what specific behavior is required to comply with ethical values and principles is usually defined locally and/or by psychology regulatory boards, and is consistent with the nature of practice and clientele, resources available, cultural context, interagency relationships, and so on. For example, in protecting the confidentiality of client information, there are rules regarding the storage of records, access to records, and the content of records; physical barriers between offices and reception area; and rules relative to seeking consultations. The specific rules must be compatible with the local setting, but also be consistent with the overarching ethical principles.

Historical Context

Ethics have developed as people have reflected on the moral intentions and consequences of their acts. From this reflection on the nature of human behavior, ethical systems have developed, giving direction to much ethical thinking, which has greatly influenced the development of ethical standards of conduct that individuals have constructed for themselves, or the body of obligations and duties that a particular society requires of its members.

Codes of ethics that decree desired professional and societal behaviors have been around since antiquity (e.g., Code of Hammurabi, Hippocratic Oath). Prior to WWII, psychology was a relatively new discipline and did not yet have codes of ethics. The convergence of several factors following WWII contributed to the development of codes of ethics for psychologists and, more recently, the *Universal Declaration of Ethical Principles for Psychologists* (2008).

From 1946 through 1947, the Nuremberg trials disclosed to the world the extent of the barbarous acts committed in Nazi Germany during WWII. People across the globe were outraged. Numerous charges were brought against the defendants. One of these charges involved the conducting of medical experiments on thousands of concentration camp prisoners without their consent, experiments during which the defendants also committed murders and all kinds of brutalities and other cruel, inhuman acts. The trial drew attention to the lack of international standards on research with human participants, and resulted in the establishment of the Nuremberg Code of Ethics on Medical Research (1947), which stated that "The voluntary consent of the human participant is absolutely essential," making it clear that participants should give consent and that the benefits of research must outweigh the risks. Although it did not carry the force of law, the Nuremberg Code was the first international document which advocated voluntary participation and informed consent. It had tremendous influence on the subsequent development of professional codes of ethics.

In 1948, in view of the medical crimes which had been committed in Nazi Germany, the World Medical Association (WMA) adopted the Declaration of Geneva (WMA, 1948) to declare the dedication of physicians to the humanitarian goals of medicine. The Declaration of Geneva, also named "Physician's Oath," was intended as a revision of the Oath of Hippocrates to a formulation of the moral truths contained in the oath that could be more easily comprehended and acknowledged in modern times. This document was adopted only three months before the United Nations General Assembly adopted the UDHR (United Nations, 1948). The Declaration of Geneva was amended in 1968, 1984, 1994, 2005, and 2006.

In 1964, the WMA adopted the Declaration of Helsinki (WMA, 1964), which established ethical and operational guiding principles for the medical community regarding biomedical research involving human participants. It developed the 10 principles first stated in the Nuremberg Code (1947), and linked them to the Declaration of Geneva (WMA, 1948). The Declaration governs international research ethics and defines rules for "research combined with clinical care" and "nontherapeutic research." The Declaration is an important document in the history of research ethics, as it represents the first significant effort of the medical community to regulate research itself, and is widely regarded as the cornerstone document of human research ethics. Since its original adoption, the Declaration of Helsinki was revised in 1975, 1983, 1989, 1996, 2000 and 2008.

The Nuremberg Code (1947), the Declaration of Geneva (WMA, 1948), and the Declaration of Helsinki (WMA, 1964) formed the foundation for modern psychological research ethics in many countries.

After the atrocities committed by medical doctors during WWII, the public demanded greater professional scrutiny and stricter standards (Lindsay, Koene, Øvreeide, & Lang, 2008; Sinclair, Simon, & Pettifor, 1996). In 1945, the first legislation in North America for the regulation of psychological practice for the purpose of protecting the public from harm was passed in Connecticut (Pettifor, Estay, & Paquet, 2002). The remaining states in the United States and provincial/territorial jurisdictions in Canada all followed suit. Psychological practice gained credibility during WWII.

With legislated regulation, it was also essential to develop codes of ethics and the means for handling disciplinary complaints. In 1948, the American Psychological Association (APA) began working on the first code of ethics for psychologists, again to protect the public from harm. In the development of its first code of ethics, the APA depended heavily on consultation with its members on the kinds of ethical dilemmas that they encountered in practice. A final draft was adopted on a trial basis by APA in 1952 and published in 1953 (American Psychological Association, 1953; Fisher, 2003). Since then, the APA code has been revised nine times. The APA Council of Representatives adopted the latest revision in 2002 (American Psychological Association, 2002). Over the years, the APA ethics code has been used as a model for the development of codes in other psychology jurisdictions, albeit with modifications consistent with local needs.

Since the development of the first APA ethics code, there have been over 50 national codes of ethics developed globally (see http://www.iupsys.net/index.php/ethics/compendium-of-codes-of-ethics-of-national-psychology-organizations for a list), with the majority being developed in the past quarter-century. Within the last decade, many psychological organizations have been developing or revising their codes. For example, Iran and Turkey have developed their own codes, while China has revised its code of ethics for counseling and clinical practice.

Ethics documents intended to be applied across national boundaries in psychology have been developed to meet new needs. In 1988, the Nordic countries (Denmark, Finland, Iceland, Norway, and Sweden) were among the first psychology regions to adopt a common code of ethics (Aanonsen,

2003). They revised their code in 1996 and 1997. The revised version was adopted in 1998. It is entitled *Etiske Prinsipper for Nordiske Psykologer* [In English: Ethical Principles for Nordic Psychologists] (1998). In 1995, the European Federation of Psychologists' Associations (EFPA; formerly EFPPA—European Federation of Professional Psychologists' Associations) adopted a meta-code (European Federation of Professional Psychologists' Associations, 1995) that set out what each member association should address in their codes of ethics, but left it to the member associations to produce their own specific codes. Another regional initiative is the development of the *Protocolo de Acuerdo Marco de Principios Éticos para el Ejercicio Profesional de los Psicólogos en el Mercosur y Paises Asociados* [In English: Protocol of the Framework Agreement of Ethical Principles for the Professional Practice of Psychology in the Mercosur and Associated Countries] (1997) by the Comité Coordinador de Psicólogos del Mercosur y Paises Asociados [In English: Coordinating Committee of Psychologists of the Mercosur and Associated Countries] in South America.

The development of regional ethical guidelines was driven by politics and economics resulting from the creation of a common market. In Europe, for example, the EFPA *Meta-Code of Ethics* was first adopted in 1995, 38 years after the creation of a common market called the European Economic Community and three years after the Treaty on European Union was signed.[5] In South America, the Protocol of the Framework Agreement of Ethical Principles (1997) was endorsed six years after the Mercosur was formed. The Nordic countries adopted their regional code of ethics in 1988, 34 years after a common Nordic labor market was established[6] and seven years after the agreement on the common Nordic labor market in health care was signed.[7]

By the end of the second millennium, psychology had ethical rules. Since WWII, most countries had become increasingly multicultural, and people moved more freely across the globe. A universal declaration of ethical principles was needed to address the new issues and challenges. To enjoy widespread support and to be of worldwide value, such a declaration would have to be relevant to local communities, respect indigenous values, and be sensitive to cultural differences. However, specific rules for the practice of psychology are not sensitive to cultural differences, and therefore, for one part of the world to impose its rules on another would in itself violate principles of respect and caring for diversity. The application of ethical principles and values to the development of specific standards of conduct varies across cultures, and must occur locally or regionally in order to ensure their relevance to local or regional cultures, customs, beliefs, and laws.

Adoption of the Universal Declaration of Ethical Principles for Psychologists

The *Universal Declaration of Ethical Principles for Psychologists* (2008) was developed some 55 years after the first APA code of ethics (American Psychological Association, 1953). The rapid globalization of today's world means that isolation is impossible, that traditional national borders are rapidly fading, and that many countries are increasingly multicultural. On the one hand, technology has opened the possibilities for global peace and harmony, while on the other hand it has increased the potential for universal suffering and destruction. The Universal Declaration was developed at a time when, for the sake of the future of our world, global consensus on what constitutes "good" is urgently needed. Looking for universality also means that the Universal Declaration does not address specific behaviors and rules for psychologists, for the simple reason that these are not universal.

The *Universal Declaration of Ethical Principles for Psychologists* (2008) is the product of a 6-year process involving careful research, broad international consultation, and numerous revisions in response to feedback and suggestions from the international psychology community (Gauthier, 2008b, 2008c; Gauthier & Pettifor, 2011; Leach & Gauthier, in press).

An international ad hoc joint committee, working under the auspices of the International Union of Psychological Science and the International Association of Applied Psychology, developed the *Universal Declaration of Ethical Principles for Psychologists* (2008). The committee was chaired by Canadian psychology professor Janel Gauthier, and it included scientists and practitioners in psychology from China, Colombia, Finland, Germany, Iran, New Zealand, Singapore, South Africa, United States, Yemen, and Zimbabwe. All countries that have membership in the International Union of Psychological Science were given the opportunity to review and discuss progress reports, and drafts of the Universal Declaration were presented for review and discussion at many international conferences and in many parts of the world. Focus groups of psychologists were held at international meetings in Asia,

Europe, India, North America, South America, and the Middle East. International symposia were organized in Athens, Beijing, Berlin, Granada, Kolkata, Prague, Singapore, and Vienna.

Further information regarding the development of the *Universal Declaration of Ethical Principles for Psychologists* (e.g., background papers, progress reports, and discussions on important issues) is available from the International Union of Psychological Science website (http://www.iupsys.net/index.php/background-documents).

Structure and Content of the Universal Declaration of Ethical Principles for Psychologists

The *Universal Declaration of Ethical Principles for Psychologists* (2008) includes a preamble followed by four sections in which each of the ethical principle identified in the Universal Declaration are described. Each description is followed by a list of basic values that are associated with that principle. The statements that define each principle are presented in Table 9.1. The values associated with each

Table 9.1 Statements Defining the Four Ethical Principles Contained in the Universal Declaration of Ethical Principles for Psychologists

Principle I: Respect for the Dignity of Persons and Peoples

Respect for the dignity of persons is the most fundamental and universally found ethical principle across geographical and cultural boundaries, and across professional disciplines. It provides the philosophical foundation for many of the other ethical principles put forward by professions. Respect for dignity recognizes the inherent worth of all human beings, regardless of perceived or real differences in social status, ethnic origin, gender, capacities, or other such characteristics. This inherent worth means that all human beings are worthy of equal moral consideration.

All human beings, as well as being individuals, are interdependent social beings that are born into, live in, and are a part of the history and ongoing evolution of their peoples. The different cultures, ethnicities, religions, histories, social structures and other such characteristics of peoples are integral to the identity of their members and give meaning to their lives. The continuity of peoples and cultures over time connects the peoples of today with the peoples of past generations and the need to nurture future generations. As such, respect for the dignity of persons includes moral consideration of and respect for the dignity of peoples.

Respect for the dignity of persons and peoples is expressed in different ways in different communities and cultures. It is important to acknowledge and respect such differences. On the other hand, it also is important that all communities and cultures adhere to moral values that respect and protect their members both as individual persons and as collective peoples.

Principle II: Competent Caring for the Well-Being of Persons and Peoples

Competent caring for the well-being of persons and peoples involves working for their benefit and, above all, doing no harm. It includes maximizing benefits, minimizing potential harm, and offsetting or correcting harm. Competent caring requires the application of knowledge and skills that are appropriate for the nature of a situation as well as the social and cultural context. It also requires the ability to establish interpersonal relationships that enhance potential benefits and reduce potential harm. Another requirement is adequate self-knowledge of how one's values, experiences, culture, and social context might influence one's actions and interpretations.

Principle III: Integrity

Integrity is vital to the advancement of scientific knowledge and to the maintenance of public confidence in the discipline of psychology. Integrity is based on honesty, and on truthful, open and accurate communications. It includes recognizing, monitoring, and managing potential biases, multiple relationships, and other conflicts of interest that could result in harm and exploitation of persons or peoples.

Complete openness and disclosure of information must be balanced with other ethical considerations, including the need to protect the safety or confidentiality of persons and peoples, and the need to respect cultural expectations. Cultural differences exist regarding appropriate professional boundaries, multiple relationships, and conflicts of interest. However, regardless of such differences, monitoring and management are needed to ensure that self-interest does not interfere with acting in the best interests of persons and peoples.

(continued)

Table 9.1 (Continued)

Principle IV: Professional and Scientific Responsibilities to Society

Psychology functions as a discipline within the context of human society. As a science and a profession, it has responsibilities to society. These responsibilities include contributing to the knowledge about human behavior and to persons' understanding of themselves and others, and using such knowledge to improve the condition of individuals, families, groups, communities, and society. They also include conducting its affairs within society in accordance with the highest ethical standards, and encouraging the development of social structures and policies that benefit all persons and peoples.

Differences exist in the way these responsibilities are interpreted by psychologists in different cultures. However, they need to be considered in a way that is culturally appropriate and consistent with the ethical principles and related values of this *Declaration*.

---

principle contained in the Universal Declaration are presented in Table 9.2.

The ethical principles in the *Universal Declaration of Ethical Principles for Psychologists* (2008) are numbered from I to IV. This ordering of the principles is meant to facilitate reference to various parts of the content of the Universal Declaration. It is not intended to reflect the ethical priorities of the discipline. Although there is no hierarchy involved in the numbering of the principles, there is relationship among them. Out of respect we treat others fairly and compassionately, provide competent care, practice with integrity, and seek the collective good of society. A lack of ethical commitment is the foundation for many of the world's gravest societal problems, past and present. Therefore, in the structure chosen for the *Universal Declaration of Ethical Principles for Psychologists*, one principle has no priority over another, since all are manifestations of *respect*.

This is why Respect for the Dignity of Persons and Peoples (Principle I) is described as "the most fundamental and universally found ethical principle across geographical and cultural boundaries, and across professional disciplines." All human beings are of inherent worth and all human beings are deserving of equal moral consideration. The Universal Declaration also acknowledges that "all human beings, as well as being individuals, are interdependent social beings that are born into, live in, and are a part of the history and ongoing evolution of their peoples." Accordingly, it proclaims that "respect for the dignity of persons includes moral consideration of and respect for the

Table 9.2 Ethical Principles and Related Values Contained in the Universal Declaration of Ethical Principles for Psychologists

Principle I	Principle II	Principle III	Principle IV
Respect for the Dignity of Persons and Peoples	Competent Caring for the Well-Being of Persons and Peoples	Integrity	Professional and Scientific Responsibility to Society
Values	*Values*	*Values*	*Values*
Respect for dignity and worthiness of all human beings	Caring for health and well-being	Accuracy/Honesty	Development of knowledge
Non-discrimination	Maximize benefits	Maximizing impartiality	Use of knowledge for benefits of society
Informed consent	Minimize harm	Minimizing biases	Avoid misuse of knowledge
Freedom of consent	Offset/Correct harm	Straightforwardness/Openness	Promotion of ethical awareness and sensitivity
Privacy	Competence	Avoidance of incomplete disclosure	Promotion of highest ethical ideals
Protection of confidentiality	Self-knowledge	Avoidance of conflict of interest	Ethical responsibilities to society
Fair treatment/Due process			

dignity of peoples." It acknowledges that respect for the dignity of persons and peoples may be expressed in different ways in different communities and cultures, while at the same time it highlights the necessity for societies to adhere to shared moral values.

In the statement on Competent Caring for the Well-Being of Persons and Peoples (Principle II), emphasis is placed, above all, on doing no harm. The statement highlights the need to maximize benefits, minimize potential harm, and offset or correct harm. It pronounces that competent caring requires the application of knowledge and skills that are appropriate for the nature of a situation, as well as the social and cultural context; the ability to establish interpersonal relationships that enhance potential benefits and reduce potential harm; and adequate self-knowledge of how one's values, experiences, culture, and social context might influence one's actions and interpretations. Competent caring for the well-being of persons and peoples is an essential component of respect in providing services for others.

In the statement on Integrity (Principle III), integrity is based on honesty, and on truthful, open and accurate communications. Integrity also includes recognizing, monitoring, and managing potential biases, multiple relationships, and other conflicts of interest that could result in harm and exploitation of persons or peoples. Complete openness and disclosure of information must be balanced with other ethical considerations, including the need to protect the safety or confidentiality of persons and peoples, and the need to respect cultural expectations. It is acknowledged that cultural differences exist regarding appropriate professional boundaries, multiple relationships, and conflicts of interest. Integrity is an essential component of respect in psychologists' professional relationships with others.

The statement defining Professional and Scientific Responsibilities to Society (Principle IV), declares that psychology functions as a discipline within the context of human society and that, as a science and a profession, it has responsibilities to society. These responsibilities include contributing to the knowledge about human behavior and to persons' understanding of themselves and others, and using such knowledge to improve the condition of individuals, families, groups, communities, and society. Psychologists are also responsible for conducting their affairs within society in accordance with the highest ethical standards, and encouraging the development of social structures and policies that benefit all persons and peoples. While the statement acknowledges that differences exist in the way these responsibilities are interpreted by psychologists in different cultures, it also stresses that these responsibilities need to be considered in a way that is culturally appropriate and consistent with ethical principles and related values, such as those endorsed in the *Universal Declaration of Ethical Principles for Psychologists* (2008). A sense of responsibility to society and the collective good is an essential component of respect for peoples as well as individuals.

Significance of the Universal Declaration of Ethical Principles for Psychologists

Psychologists in the 21st century are faced with expanding their scope of practice and competency in order to work multi-culturally within their own country and culture, as well as to work internationally and globally. The *Universal Declaration of Ethical Principles for Psychologists* (2008) describes ethical principles based on shared human values across cultures. It reaffirms the commitment of the psychology community to help build a better world where peace, freedom, responsibility, justice, humanity, and morality will prevail. It provides a universally acceptable moral framework to guide psychologists in conducting their professional and scientific activities anywhere in the world, whether in research, direct service, teaching, administration, supervision, consultation, peer review, editorial consultation, expert witness, social policy, or any other role related to the discipline of psychology.

The *Universal Declaration of Ethical Principles for Psychologists* (2008) speaks to a common moral framework that guides and inspires psychologists worldwide toward the highest ethical ideals in their professional and scientific work. It states:

> Psychologists recognize that they carry out their activities within a larger social context. They recognize that the lives and identities of human beings both individually and collectively are connected across generations, and that there is a reciprocal relationship between human beings and their natural and social environments. Psychologists are committed to placing the welfare of society and its members above the self-interest of the discipline and its members. They recognize that adherence to ethical principles in the context of their work contributes to a stable society that enhances the quality of life for all human beings.

The *Universal Declaration of Ethical Principles for Psychologists* (2008) has an empirical basis to the extent that research was conducted to identify the most fundamental principles deemed to be based on shared human values across cultures. For example, many of psychology's professional codes of ethics from around the world were reviewed to identify commonalities in ethical principles (Gauthier, 2002, 2003, 2004, 2005). Ethical principles espoused by other disciplines and communities were also examined (Gauthier, 2005). Eastern and Western history of modern-day ethical principles and values were explored (Gauthier, 2006; Sinclair, 2005a, 2005b, 2005c). Internationally accepted documents such as the UDHR (United Nations, 1948) and the Universal Declaration of a Global Ethic (Center for Global Ethics, 1998) were reviewed (Gauthier, 2003, 2004).

According to our knowledge, the *Universal Declaration of Ethical Principles for Psychologists* may be the only universal declaration with a research-based framework. It was necessary to overcome a number of impediments in undertaking this project, not the least of which was a lack of resources. There was no funding, and all work and resources were pro bono. Communications among members of the ad hoc joint committee were limited to mostly email. Occasionally, some members of the committee had the opportunity to meet at an international congress. Attempts were made to have a meeting of the committee as a whole in 2004 and 2006, but only a few members were able to attend. However, consultations were held in many countries and continents in order to obtain a global perspective. Furthermore, many sources of information were reviewed in the search for common principles and values. Strong committed leadership was crucial for the success of this project. Because this leadership came largely from Western societies, because many non-Western countries have used North American models to develop their own codes of ethics, and because English is the language for international discourse, one must be alert to the possibility of some degree of unintentional cultural bias. Hopefully, dialogue, research, and practice will continue to be used in refining universal ethical principles.

It is important to note that the *Universal Declaration of Ethical Principles for Psychologists* (2008) is not a code of ethics or a code of conduct, inasmuch as such codes suggest or prescribe specific behaviors that are influenced by and reflect the particular cultural, social, and political beliefs of the cultures in which they are created. One of the goals in developing the *Universal Declaration* was to encourage the development of culture-sensitive codes based on universal ethical principles.

Gauthier, Pettifor, and Ferrero (2010) have presented a "culture-sensitive" model to assist psychologists in applying the *Universal Declaration of Ethical Principles for Psychologists* to creating or reviewing a code of ethics. The first step that is recommended is to consider the reasons for wanting a code of ethics (e.g., for whom is it intended, why is it needed, how will it be used, are unique or cultural aspects to be addressed?) The second step is to consider what each of the four ethical principles means within the given culture and context. The third step is to define culture-specific standards or behaviors that are relevant to local objectives and also reflect proposed universal ethical principles. Throughout the process, which may take longer than anticipated, it is highly desirable to consult with those whose work will be most affected by the code of ethics that you endorse. Their input is invaluable in creating a relevant document, and their support is invaluable in accepting the guidance provided in the code of ethics. Gauthier et al. (2010) emphasizes that models from different cultures need to be considered as well. Time will tell how well this goal will be achieved.

Another major development in ethics documents is the articulation of a moral ethical framework or philosophical foundation that is not only aspirational, but is clearly demonstrated in all value and standards statements that may follow. In the *Universal Declaration of Ethical Principles for Psychologists* (2008), for example, the ethical principle of Respect for Persons and Peoples is demonstrated in such values as confidentiality, consent, and privacy, which may be defined further in specific behaviors or standards according to local or regional cultures, customs, beliefs, and laws. Linking the moral framework directly to the standards has been embraced in countries such as Canada (Canadian Psychological Association [CPA], 1986, 1991, 2000), Ireland (Psychological Society of Ireland, 1999), New Zealand (New Zealand Psychological Society, 2002), and Mexico (Sociedad Mexicana de Psicología, 2002, 2007). The EFPA Meta-Code of Ethics (European Federation of Professional Psychologists' Associations, 1995; European Federation of Psychologists' Associations, 2005) is another example of this recent development. In order to link behavior to ethical principles internationally and globally, it is essential to seek universal principles and shared values. The *Universal Declaration of Ethical Principles for Psychologists* (2008) has built on the growing practice of defining a moral or philosophical foundation of what has been identified as universally shared values. This development is important in considering the relationship between universal ethical principles and the corresponding standards, rules, and articles.

The *Universal Declaration of Ethical Principles for Psychologists* (2008) states, "The significance of the *Universal Declaration* depends on its recognition and promotion by psychology organizations at national, regional and international levels. Every psychology organization is encouraged to keep this *Declaration* in mind and, through teaching, education, and other measures to promote respect for, and observance of, the *Declaration*'s principles and related values in the various activities of its members." Psychology organizations have already begun to endorse, ratify, or adopt the Universal Declaration. In 2008, for example, it was adopted by the Psychological Society of South Africa, and ratified by the Canadian Psychological Association. It was also adopted in 2008 by the Interamerican Society of Psychology, which went one step further than any other psychology organization: in 2009, it approved an amendment to its constitution to require from its membership compliance with the Universal Declaration. A culture-sensitive model has been developed to guide psychologists in the development of a national code of ethics (Gauthier et al., 2010). In 2009, the first workshop on how to use the *Universal Declaration of Ethical Principles for Psychologists* to develop or revise a code of ethics was presented at the First South-Eastern Europe Regional Conference of Psychology in Sofia, Bulgaria (Gauthier, Lindsay, Korkut, & Behnke, 2009). The Universal Declaration has been used by national psychology organizations to develop or revise codes of ethics. Although in development at the time, it was used by the Australian Psychological Society to revise its code of ethics from 2005 to 2007. The 2008 adopted version of the Universal Declaration was used by the College of Psychologists of Guatemala [In Spanish: *Colegio de Psicológos de Guatemala*] to develop its first code of ethics from 2009 to 2010 (Colegio de Psicológos de Guatemala, 2011).

New applications of the *Universal Declaration of Ethical Principles for Psychologists* (2008) are emerging. Indeed, researchers and practitioners have begun to use the Universal Declaration as a framework for discussing ethical issues from an international perspective, and to offer recommendations of global value. One fine example of such an application can be found in a recent article by Fitzgerald, Hunter, Hadjistavropoulos, and Koocher (2010). In their article, the authors examine ethical issues relating to the growing practice of Internet-based psychotherapy through the lens of the Universal Declaration. Furthermore, on the basis of their findings, they make recommendations intended to guide mental health practitioners who are considering involvement in the provision of Internet-based services.

The *Universal Declaration of Ethical Principles for Psychologists* (2008) is very new. It holds promise for extending psychological practice globally in ways that maintain the highest level of ethical practice, and that incorporate advocacy to eliminate misuse and abuse. The process of developing declarations and guidelines requires much listening and discussion that in itself supports integration and cooperation across national and cultural boundaries. Such processes on an international level make it easier to recognize what we have in common and to recognize what is culture-specific.

Ethics and Human Rights: Together in Serving Humankind

Professional ethics and human rights both support the highest standards of respect, liberty, equality, and well-being of all peoples. The *Universal Declaration of Ethical Principles for Psychologists* (2008) and the *Universal Declaration of Human Rights* (United Nations, 1948) are each a product of their times. Although there is a span of 60 years in their creation, both are highly relevant in the 21st century. The effectiveness of each declaration in building a better world may be greater because their roles complement each other, but are not the same.

The *Universal Declaration of Ethical Principles for Psychologists* (2008) reflects a concern that psychologists in a rapidly globalizing world need ethical guidelines that address global issues and can encompass working cooperatively across worldviews in ways that were not included in their professional training, their practice standards, their codes of ethics, or their past experiences. The larger context is the desire that the rapid globalization of life on the planet contributes to a better life for persons and peoples generally, rather than contributes to increased suffering. While technology makes possible "one world," the needs of people to maintain their cultural identities demand respect and, in addition, negate rules and prescriptions imposed from the outside on how they should conduct their lives. In this context, guidance from a moral framework that approaches universality leaves room for local initiative in defining culture-specific interpretations. The *Universal Declaration of Ethical Principles for Psychologists* supports globalization that is "enlightened" (i.e., based on sharing and respect for cultural differences and commonalities), and is not "unilateral" (i.e., imposed to serve political and economic interests of a few to the detriment of the others). The Universal Declaration addresses professional relationships of psychologists and emphasizes respect and caring for individuals, families, groups, and communities, as well as respecting cultural differences that do not violate its moral framework.

The *Universal Declaration of Human Rights* (United Nations, 1948) was developed by the United Nations to ensure that state-sponsored horrific acts of cruelty and racism such as those that occurred under the Nazi regime would never happen again in the world. The document proclaims that all human beings have unalienable rights and entitlements to freedom and dignity, to be free of specified harms, and to enjoy the benefits of society equally with others. The rights are specific and the same for all societies and do not vary with different political, religious, or cultural entities. The UDHR is directed primarily at all nations and states to ensure freedom and justice for its citizens, and to protect them from oppression and harm. There continue to be grave violations of human rights in many parts of world today, and in many countries, work involving the UDHR is highly valued.

Both universal declarations share the fundamental goals of protecting society from harm and the enhancement of the quality of life of its members. Both rely on moral imperatives of respect and valuing of human life. However, there are important differences between these two declarations. The ethics document addresses primarily individual professionals, while the human rights document addresses the responsibilities of states and nations. The ethics document carefully avoids authoritative language, such as, *should, must, obey, comply, endorse, ratify*, whereas the language of human rights is legalistic and prescriptive in tone.

The term *human rights* was also avoided in the ethics document because, although similarity in the expression of values exists, the term "human rights" has a negative connotation in some countries. In some parts of the world, human rights as defined in the UDHR (United Nations, 1948) are perceived as a political tool for harassing or controlling other nations, or as a lack of understanding and respect for different cultures, religions, or political systems. The use of the term "human rights" in the *Universal Declaration of Ethical Principles for Psychologists* (2008) would have made it impossible for some countries to adopt and apply the declaration. The *Universal Declaration of Ethical Principles for Psychologists*, in its recognition of cultural diversity, is compatible with current developments in psychology to define multicultural competencies. The ethics document is aspirational and has no mechanisms for enforcement, whereas human rights may be implemented and if necessary enforced through the ratification of individual nations. Despite these differences, there is a high level of congruence between the ethical principles and the human rights articles, as shown in Table 9.3.

What authority is there for accepting the human rights and the ethical principles as described in these two universal declarations? The historical antecedents of the UDHR (United Nations, 1948) included the Ten Commandments and other religious documents from ancient times believed to be received directly from the Creator or God. Revolutions in the 17th and 18th centuries invoked the concept of natural law or God's natural law, thus maintaining a powerful supernatural authority. Today, the UDHR is declared to consist of unalienable and inherent natural rights that are beyond human intervention, even though the UDHR itself was created with wide consultation by a United Nations Commission on Human Rights. Today, God, by whatever name, is less frequently mentioned, but the divine authority over humankind appears to be implicit in the UDHR.

The authority for the *Universal Declaration of Ethical Principles for Psychologists* (2008) also lies in a consensus on the nature of ethical principles. As mentioned earlier in this chapter (see the Significance of the Universal Declaration of Ethical Principles for Psychologists subsection), the Universal Declaration used a research strategy to identify human values that are shared across cultures. The research conducted to identify those values yielded data showing general support for the content of human rights. For example, in one of the studies (Gauthier 2003, 2004), Gauthier found a high level of similarity between the ethical principles

Table 9.3 Connecting Human Rights and Ethics

The *Universal Declaration of Human Rights* recognizes that everyone has…	The *Universal Declaration of Ethical Principles for Psychologists* recognizes as fundamental…
• the right to recognition of dignity	• respect for the dignity of persons and peoples
• the right to recognition of inherent worth	• respect for the inherent worth of all human beings
• the right to non-discrimination	• the recognition that all human beings are worthy of equal moral consideration, regardless of perceived or real differences in social status, ethnic origin, gender, capacities, or other such characteristics
• the right to justice	• fairness and justice in the treatment of persons and peoples
• the right to freedom	• respect for the ability of individuals, families, groups, and communities to make decisions for themselves and to care for themselves and each other
• the right to education, health and well-being	• caring for the well-being of persons and peoples, developing and maintaining competence
• the right to protection, security and social order	• informed consent, protection of confidentiality
• the right to privacy	• privacy for individuals, families, groups, and communities
• the right to free and full consent	• free and informed consent
• duties to the community	• the principle of professional and scientific responsibilities to society

most commonly found in psychology ethics codes and the fundamental rights set out in the UDHR (United Nations, 1948). As shown in Table 9.3, comparisons between the *Universal Declaration of Ethical Principles for Psychologists* and the *Universal Declaration of Human Rights* reveal differences in the choice of language, but similarities in content. In the consideration of ethical principles in today's climate, it is generally seen as culturally inappropriate to prescribe the same specific behaviors across the globe. In the *Universal Declaration of Ethical Principles for Psychologists*, it is stated that the application of the principles and values to the development of specific standards of conduct must occur locally or regionally in order to ensure their relevance to local or regional cultures, customs, beliefs, and laws.

A major difference between the two declarations is that the UDHR (United Nations, 1948) is primarily for nations and the *Universal Declaration of Ethical Principles for Psychologists* (2008) for members of the psychological community. That said, human rights agendas that target primarily nations and governments, and universal ethical principles that guide professional associations and their members, are both required in achieving a better life for the inhabitants of a global world. The UDHR names serious abuses of human rights, from which everyone should be free, and the elimination of which few could disagree, such as torture, slavery, arbitrary arrest, and persecution. Promoting positive rights both locally and globally is also important, such as ensuring standards of living, social security, social services, opportunities for education and work, and so on. Both are required in achieving a better life for the inhabitants of a global world. Both have a role to play, and both appear to be based on a general consensus of human thinking on what is morally right in addressing human problems.

Globalization is a major development in the 21st century, and one that has, and will have, a major impact on the discipline of psychology. Globalization increases the need for psychologists to accept an active role in changing the conditions in society that contribute to the suffering and dehumanization of persons and peoples. Psychologists can actively contribute to "enlightened globalization," in which persons and peoples can enjoy a more harmonious world based on human rights and a renewed commitment to moral principles.

Psychology continues to explore the possibilities of common global standards in training, research, practice, and ethics (e.g., Hall & Altmaier, 2008; Stevens & Gielen, 2007). The UDHR (United Nations, 1948) has charted the rights and entitlements of all human beings, and named abuses that must be eliminated (largely by governments). Universal ethical principles provide a moral framework to guide psychologists in maintaining common human values while also honoring and understanding culture-specific differences. Work continues within the profession on developing multicultural competencies that not only truly respect and honor differences in cultural beliefs and practices, but also help to resolve dilemmas imposed by a perceived clash of cultures (Gielen, Draguns, & Fish, 2008). A knowledge of ethical decision making and of human rights is needed. Most psychology codes of ethics include responsibility to society and a commitment to work in respectful ways to change those aspects of society that pose serious violations of their ethical principles. Many codes fall short of using the language of social justice.

It is also recognized that a few nations have put forward two major reasons for not adopting the UDHR (United Nations, 1948). First is the idea that the UDHR defines human rights in the Judeo-Christian tradition that fails to take into account the culture and religious context of all nations. Second is the belief that some powerful nations accuse other nations of human rights violations for political gains rather than genuine concern for the well-being of persons and peoples. The details of these concerns are beyond the scope of this chapter.

Globalization can be both beneficial and destructive. The positive globalization of psychology must be based on collaboration and understanding, and not be perceived as imposed by outside powerful or dominant forces, be the cause of an increasing divide between the rich and the poor, or be a sufficient threat to cultural identity, such that some may turn to violence and terrorism to protect their way of life. At the present time, Moghaddam (2008) sees the future of globalization as more fractured and fragmented than enlightened. Globalization that is positive in people's lives is an objective on which psychologists and human rights activists have much to contribute and much to share. Violations of human rights often may be considered acts of social injustice, and therefore social justice and human rights issues become similar. We need not be fractured and fragmented in working together for the larger common good.

The debate between extreme universalism and extreme cultural relativism is nonproductive. It should be possible to maintain independent moral standards, as in the UDHR (United Nations, 1948), as well as apply moral principles as in the *Universal Declaration of Ethical Principles for Psychologists* (2008) with respect for both cultural differences and social political contexts. To do so requires discussion, collaboration, and mutual sense of purpose. The *Universal Declaration of Ethical Principles for Psychologists* may be a first step to bridging the perceived divide. The recent flurry of publications addressing international and global issues for ethical professional practice is also an impetus to undertake a process of greater collaboration.

From the Nobel laureate and author of the *Ethics for the New Millennium* bestseller comes a passionate and exquisitely argued call for a spiritual and ethical revolution that may inspire all of those interested in ethics and human rights:

> Compassion is one of the principal things that make our lives meaningful. It is the source of all lasting happiness and joy. And it is the foundation of a good heart, the heart of one who acts out of a desire to help others. Through kindness, through affection, through honesty, through truth and justice toward all others we ensure our own benefit. This is not a matter for complicated theorizing. It is a matter of common sense.
> (The *Dalai Lama*, 1999, p. 234)

In conclusion, the *Universal Declaration of Human Rights* (United Nations, 1948) and the *Universal Declaration of Ethical Principles for Psychologists* (2008) strengthen and complement each other; they are enriched by their differences. In human rights, we envision a free, just, and peaceful world when abuses and injustices are eliminated. In ethical principles, we envision a free, just, and peaceful world in accordance with the highest humanitarian values of our existence. Both universal declarations are remarkable documents, with their full impact yet to be achieved.

Author Note

We are grateful to Dr. Nora Sveaass (Associate Professor at the University of Oslo, Norway and Vice-Chair of the United Nations Committee against Torture) for her comments and suggestions during the preparation of this manuscript. We admire her knowledge and dedication to human rights.

Notes

1. The International Union of Psychological Science is to psychology what the United Nations is to the world, in that members of the Union are national psychology organizations and only one organization per country can join the Union.

2. The International Association of Applied Psychology represents the largest international body of psychologists and its board of directors has about 45 members.

3. Different names are given to the divine in different religions. Sometimes, numerous names are given to the divine within the same religion. However, the word *God* is used by multiple religions to refer to the deity.

4. The Charter of the United Nations (United Nations, 1945) is the foundational treaty of the United Nations. All members of the United Nations are bound by its articles. A member of the *United Nations* which has persistently violated the principles contained in the *Charter* may be expelled from the organization.

5. The Treaty on European Union (TEU) was signed in Maastricht in 1992 and entered into force in 1993. It represented a new stage in European integration since it opened the way to political integration. It created a European Union, introduced the concept of European citizenship, reinforced the powers of the European Parliament, and launched economic and monetary union (http://europa.eu/legislation_summaries/economic_and_monetary_affairs/institutional_and_economic_framework/treaties_maastricht_en.htm).

6. The agreement establishing a common Nordic labor market was concluded in 1954. This agreement, amended in 1982, enables Nordic nationals to work and to settle in another Nordic country without a work permit or permanent residence permit (http://www.norden.org/en/about-nordic-co-operation/agreements/treaties-and-agreements/labour-market/agreement-concerning-a-common-nordic-labour-market/).

7. The agreement on the common Nordic labor market in health care was signed in 1981 and reformed in 1993. Under the terms of this agreement, most educational qualifications completed in the healthcare field are recognized without any additional requirements (http://www.norden.org/en/about-nordic-co-operation/agreements/treaties-and-agreements/social-and-health-care/gemensam-nordisk-arbetsmarknad-foerviss-haelso-och-sjukvaardspersonal-och-veterinaerer)

References

Aanonsen, A. (2003). EFPA Metacode on ethics and the Nordic Code. In J. B. Overmier & J. A. Overmier (Eds.), *Psychology: IUPsyS global resource* [Computer software] (4th ed.). Hove, UK: Psychology Press.

African Commission on Human and Peoples' Rights. (1981). *African Charter on Human and Peoples' Rights*. Retrieved from http://www.achpr.org/english/_info/charter_en.html.

American Psychological Association. (1953). *Ethical standards of psychologists*. Washington, DC: Author.

American Psychological Association. (2002). Ethical principles of psychologists and code of conduct. *American Psychologist, 57*, 1060–1073.

Bill of Rights (1689). In M. R. Ishay (2008). *The history of human rights from ancient times to the globalization era* (2nd ed., p. 86). Berkeley and Los Angeles, CA: University of California Press. Also retrieved from http://www.britannia.com/history/docs/rights.html

Cairo declaration on human rights in Islam. (1990). Retrieved from http://www.unhcr.org/refworld/docid/3ae6b3822c.html.

Canadian Psychological Association. (1986). *Canadian code of ethics for psychologists*. Ottawa, ON: Author.

Canadian Psychological Association. (1991). *Canadian code of ethics for psychologists* (2nd ed.). Ottawa: Author.

Canadian Psychological Association. (2000). *Canadian code of ethics for psychologists* (3rd ed.). Ottawa: Author.

Center for Global Ethics. (1998). Toward a Universal Declaration of a Global Ethic. Retrieved from http://globalethic.org/Center/declarel.htmhttp://astro.temple.edu/~dialogue/Center/declarel.htm

Charlesworth, H. (1994). What are "women's" international human rights? In R. J. Cooke (Ed.), *Human rights of women: National and international perspectives* (pp. 58–84). Philadelphia: University of Pennsylvania Press.

Colegio de Psicológos de Guatemala. (2011). *Código de Ética* [Code of Ethics]. Ciudad de Guatemala: Servisa Litografía.

Cook, R. (1994). *Human rights of women: National and international perspectives*. Philadelphia: University of Pennsylvania Press.

Declaration of Independence (1776). In M. R. Ishay (2008). *The history of human rights from ancient times to the globalization era* (2nd ed., p. 95). Berkeley and Los Angeles, CA: University of California Press. Also retrieved from http://www.ushistory.org/declaration/document/index.htm.

Declaration of the Rights of the Man and the Citizen [*Déclaration des droits de l'homme et du citoyen*]. (1789). In M. R. Ishay (2008). *The history of human rights from ancient times to the globalization era* (2nd ed., pp. 82–83). Berkeley and Los Angeles, CA: University of California Press. Also retrieved in French from http://www.assemblee-nationale.fr/histoire/dudh/1789.asp.

European Federation of Professional Psychologists' Associations. (1995). *Meta-code of ethics*. Brussels: Author.

European Federation of Psychologists' Associations. (2005). *Meta-code of ethics* (2nd ed.). Brussels: Author.

Etiske Prinsipper for Nordiske Psykologer [Ethical principles for Nordic psychologists]. (1998). Retrieved from http://www.psykologforeningen.no/pf/Fag-og-profesjon/For-fagutoevere/Etikk/Etiske-prinsipper-for-nordiske-psykologer.

Ferrero, A., & Gauthier, J. (2009). Desarrollo y adopción de la Declaración Universal de principios Éticos para Psicólogas y Psicólogos [The development and adoption of the Universal Declaration of Ethical Principles for Psychologists]. *Boletín de la SIP, 90* (March), 8-10. Retrieved from http://issuu.com/sipsych/docs/sip_newsletter_v90_march_2009.

Fisher, C. (2003). *Decoding the ethics code: A practical guide for psychologists*. Thousand Oaks, CA: Sage.

Fitzgerald, T. D., Hunter, P. V., Hadjistavropoulos, T., & Koocher, G. P. (2010). Ethical and legal considerations for internet-based psychotherapy. *Cognitive Behavior Therapy, 34*, 1–15.

Gauthier, J. (2002). Ethics and human rights: Toward a universal declaration of ethical principles for psychologists. In J. L. Pettifor (Chair), *Professional codes of ethics across national boundaries: Seeking common grounds*. Symposium conducted at the 25th International Congress of Applied Psychology, Singapore.

Gauthier, J. (2003). Toward a universal declaration of ethical principles for psychologists. In J. B. Overmier & J. A. Overmier (Eds.). *Psychology: IUPsyS Global Resource* [Computer software] (4th ed.). Hove, UK: Psychology Press.

Gauthier, J. (2004). Toward a universal declaration of ethical principles for psychologists. *International Association of Applied Psychology/Newsletter, 16*(4), 10–24.

Gauthier, J. (2005). Toward a universal declaration of ethical principles for psychologists: A progress report. In M. J. Stevens & D. Wedding (Eds.), *Psychology: IUPsyS global resource* [Computer software] (6th ed.). Hove, UK: Psychology Press.

Gauthier, J. (2006). Onward toward a universal declaration of ethical principles for psychologists: Draft and progress report. In M. J. Stevens & D. Wedding (Eds.), *Psychology: IUPsyS global resource* [Computer software] (7th ed.). Hove, UK: Psychology Press.

Gauthier, J. (2008a). IAAP adopts the universal declaration of ethical principles for psychologists. *The IAAP Bulletin: The International Association of Applied Psychology, 20*(4), 110–112.

Gauthier, J. (2008b). The universal declaration of ethical principles for psychologists presented at the United Nations DPI/NGO conference in Paris. *Psychology International, 19*(4). Retrieved from http://www.apa.org/international/pi/2008/10/gauthier.aspx.

Gauthier, J. (2008c). Universal declaration of ethical principles for psychologists. In J. Hall & E. Altmaier (Eds.), *Global promise: Quality assurance and accountability in professional psychology* (pp. 98–109). London: Oxford University Press.

Gauthier, J. (2009). Ethical principles and human rights: Building a better world globally. *Counselling Psychology Quarterly, 22*, 25–32.

Gauthier, J., Lindsay, G., Korkut, Y., & Behnke, S. (2009). How to use ethical principles for creating or reviewing a code of ethics: A step-by-step approach. Workshop presented at the South-Eastern Europe Regional Conference of Psychology, Bulgaria, Sofia.

Gauthier, J., & Pettifor, J. (2011). The evolution of ethics in psychology: Going international and global. In P. R. Martin, F. Cheung, M. Kyrios, L. Littlefield, M. Knowles, B. Overmier, & J. M. Prieto (Eds.), *The IAAP handbook of applied psychology* (pp. 700–714). Oxford, UK: Blackwell Publishing.

Gauthier, J., Pettifor, J., & Ferrero, A. (2010). The universal declaration of ethical principles for psychologists: A culture-sensitive model for creating and reviewing a code of ethics. *Ethics and Behavior, 20*(3&4), 1–18.

Gielen, U., Draguns, J., & Fish, J. (Eds.). (2008). *Principles of multicultural counseling and therapy*. New York: Routledge/Taylor and Francis Group.

Glendon, M. A. (2001). *A world made new: Eleanor Roosevelt and the Universal Declaration of Human Rights*. New York, NY: Random House.

Hall, J., & Altmaier, E. (Eds.). (2008). *Global promise: Quality assurance and accountability in professional psychology*. London: Oxford University Press.

Holt, J. C. (1992). *Magna Carta* (2nd ed.). Cambridge: Cambridge University Press.

Howard, A. E. D. (1998). *Magna Carta: Text and commentary* (rev. ed.). Charlottesville & London: The University Press of Virginia.

Ishay, M. R. (2008). *The history of human rights: From ancient times to the globalization era*. Berkeley, CA: University of California Press.

Leach, M. M., & Gauthier, J. (in press). Internationalizing the professional ethics curriculum. In F. T. L. Leong, A. Marsella, M. M. Leach, & W. Pickren (Eds.), *Internationalizing the psychology curriculum in the United States: Meeting the challenges of globalization*. New York: Springer.

Lindsay, G., Koene, C., Øvreeide, H., & Lang, F. (2008). *Ethics for European psychologists*. Cambridge, MA: Hogrefe & Huber Publishers.

Littman, D. (1999). Universal human rights and human rights in Islam. *Midstream, 42*(2), 2–7. Retrieved from http://www.dhimmi.org/Islam.html.

Magna Carta (1215). In D. Danziger, & J. Gillingham (2003). *1215: The year of Magna Carta* (p. 275). London: Hodder & Stoughton. Retrieved from http://www.bl.uk/treasures/magnacarta/index.html.

Mann, J. M., Gruskin, S., Grodin, M. A., & Annas, G. J. (1999). *Health and human rights: A reader*. New York: Routledge.

Moghaddam, F. M. (2008). *How globalization spurs terrorism: The lopsided benefits of "one world" and why that fuels violence*. Westport, CT: Praeger Security International.

Morsink, J. (1999). *The Universal Declaration of Human Rights: Origins, drafting & intent*. Philadelphia: University of Pennsylvania Press.

New Zealand Psychological Society. (2002). *Code of ethics for psychologists working in Aotearoa/New Zealand*. Wellington: Author.

Nuremberg Code. (1947). *Trials of war criminals before the Nuremberg military tribunals under Control Council Law No. 10: Vol. 2* (pp. 181–182). Washington, DC: U.S. Government Printing Office.

Pettifor, J. (1996). Ethics: Virtue and politics in the science and practice of psychology. *Canadian Psychology, 37*, 1–12.

Pettifor, J. L., Estay, I., & Paquet, S. (2002). Preferred strategies for learning ethics in the practice of a discipline. *Canadian Psychology, 42*, 260–269.

Power, S. (2002). *A problem from hell: America and the age of genocide*. New York: Harper Collins.

Protocolo de Acuerdo Marco de Principios Éticos para el Ejercicio Profesional de los Psicólogos en el Mercosur y Paises Asociados [Protocol of the framework agreement of ethical principles for professional practice of psychology in the Mercosur and associated states]. (1997). Santiago, Chile: Author.

Psychological Society of Ireland. (1999). *Code of Professional Ethics*. Dublin: Author.

Sinclair, C. (2005a). A brief history of ethical principles in professional codes of ethics. In J. B. Overmier & J. A. Overmier (Eds.), *Psychology: IUPsyS global resource* [Computer software] (6th ed.). Hove, UK: Psychology Press.

Sinclair, C. (2005b). The eastern roots of ethical principles and values. In M. J. Stevens & D. Wedding (Eds.), *Psychology: IUPsyS global resource* [Computer software] (6th ed.). Hove, UK: Psychology Press.

Sinclair, C. (2005c). The roots of ethical principles and values in codes of ethics. In J. L. Pettifor (Chair), *Cultural implications for a universal declaration of ethical principles*. Symposium conducted at the European Congress of Psychology, Granada, Spain.

Sinclair, C., Simon, N. P., & Pettifor, J. L. (1996). The history of ethical codes and licensure. In L. J. Bass, S. T. DeMers, J. R. P. Ogloff, C. Peterson, & J. L. Pettifor (Eds.), *Professional conduct and discipline in psychology* (pp. 1–15). Washington, DC: American Psychological Association.

Sociedad Mexicana de Psicología. (2002). *Código ético del psicólogo* [Psychologist's code of ethics] (3rd ed.). Mexico City: Editorial Trillas.

Sociedad Mexicana de Psicología. (2007). *Código ético del psicólogo* [Psychologist's code of ethics] (4th ed.). Mexico: Editorial Trillas.

Smith, H. (1991). *The world's great religions: Our great wisdom traditions*. San Francisco: Harper.

Smith, R. K. M. (2010). *Textbook on international human rights* (4th ed.). New York: Oxford University Press.

Steiner, H. J., & Alston, P. (1996). *International human rights in context: Law and politics morals*. Oxford: Clarendon Press.

Stevens, M. J., & Gielen, U. P. (Eds.). (2007). *Toward a global psychology: Theory, research, intervention, and pedagogy*. Mahwah, NJ: Erlbaum.

The Dalai Lama (1999). *Ethics for the new millenium*. New York: Riverhead Books.

United Nations. (1945). *Charter of the United Nations*. Retrieved from http://www.un.org/en/documents/charter/.

United Nations. (1948). *Universal declaration of human rights*. Retrieved from http://www.un.org/en/documents/udhr.

United Nations. (1965). *International convention on the elimination of all forms of racial discrimination*. Retrieved from http://www2.ohchr.org/english/law/cerd.htm.

United Nations. (1966a). *International covenant on civil and political rights*. Retrieved from http://www2.ohchr.org/english/law/ccpr.htm.

United Nations. (1966b). *International covenant on economic, social and cultural rights*. Retrieved from http://www2.ohchr.org/english/law/cescr.htm.

United Nations. (1979). *Convention on the elimination of all forms of discrimination against women*. Retrieved from http://www2.ohchr.org/english/law/cedaw.htm.

United Nations. (1984). *Convention on torture and other cruel, inhuman or degrading treatment or punishment*. Retrieved from http://www2.ohchr.org/english/law/cat.htm

United Nations. (1989). *Convention on the rights of the child*. Retrieved from http://www2.ohchr.org/english/law/crc.htm.

United Nations. (1990). *International convention on the rights of all migrant workers and members of their families*. Retrieved from http://www2.ohchr.org/english/law/cmw.htm.

United Nations (2006a). *Convention on the rights of persons with disabilities*. Retrieved from http://www2.ohchr.org/english/law/pdf/disabilities-convention.pdf.

United Nations. (2006b). *International convention for the protection of all persons from enforced disappearance*. Retrieved from http://www2.ohchr.org/english/law/disappearance-convention.htm.

Universal Declaration of Ethical Principles for Psychologists. (2008). Retrieved from http://www.iupsys.net/index.php/ethics/declaration.

Wellman, C. (2000). Solidarity, the individual, and human rights. *Human Rights Quarterly, 22*, 639–657.

Weston, B. H. (2002). The United States: Imperial rogue state. *World Editorial and International Law, 1(1),* 1.

World Medical Association. (1948). *Declaration of Geneva*. Retrieved from http://www.wma.net/en/30publications/10policies/g1/.

World Medical Association. (1964). *Declaration of Helsinki*. Retrieved from http://www.wma.net/en/30publications/10policies/b3/.

CHAPTER 10

The Search for Common Standards: A Case of Research Standards

Mark M. Leach, Benjamin Jeppsen, *and* Steve Discont

Abstract

Research on the comparisons of ethics standards across ethics codes has increased over the past decade, with the goal of determining common standards. Finding these common standards may help assess the degree to which psychology shares common values, as well as help ascertain what psychology considers good ethical practices regardless of country. The purpose of this chapter was to uncover ethical standards common to research practices across national codes of ethics. This study did not use a particular code as the foundation from which to compare other codes, reducing ethnocentric bias. Results indicated common research standards across countries, with additional trends for consideration.

Key Words: common standards, research ethics, international ethics, national codes of ethics

In 1995 the European Federation of Psychologists' Associations (EFPA) adopted the *Meta-Code of Ethics,* which was developed to provide guidance to member psychological associations. It was designed to specify what ethics codes should incorporate into their national psychological codes, while maintaining flexibility so that each national organization could modify its code to be most relevant for its needs. In essence, each member association can create or revise its own code of ethics but must maintain compliance with the four fundamental principles outlined in this Meta-Code. Prior to this, the five Scandinavian countries (Denmark, Finland, Iceland, Norway, and Sweden) decided to develop only one code of ethics to be used by each country's psychological association. These were the first attempts by psychological organizations to adopt common principles (the Meta-Code) across countries (and in the case of the Scandinavian countries, also their standards).

The development of the *Universal Declaration of Ethical Principles for Psychologists* (Gauthier, 2008) represented a leap forward for psychology and psychological ethics around the world. It includes four principles commonly found in psychology that can be used to guide psychologists to act ethically regardless of cultural context. It can also assist current and future ethics code developers, as the principles act as the cornerstone for professional ethical standards that are typically included in psychological ethics codes. Principles, by definition, are aspirational and not easy to assess and enforce, whereas standards are typically considered more enforceable. When considering enforcement, though, standards are also much more likely to be contextually and culturally interpretable than principles, raising the question of whether common standards are possible to consider in the same manner as principles. In this chapter we will address the question of whether common ethical standards are possible, first by presenting previous ethics research that may include common standards, followed by the present study investigating the inclusion of common research standards found in psychological ethics codes internationally.

Our argument is that common standards are possible and have been found in the literature across national ethics codes. These standards are manifestations of common ethical values that psychology shares internationally.

Many psychologists are now aware of the *Universal Declaration of Ethical Principles for Psychologists*. This document provides a moral framework that guides psychologists to act in the highest professional manner. What is most relevant to note for this chapter regarding the Universal Declaration is not the final outcome of the document, but the process itself. The principles are based on shared human values. However, it can be argued that values are culturally bound and any document resulting from values are, by extension, culturally bound. Gauthier initially recognized this limitation and delved into geographically broad ancient and recent historical documents from a variety of secular and religious influences and from various professions (see http://www.iupsys.org/ethics/univdecl2008.html for a review). The idea was to examine common principles and values, and the underlying moral imperatives gleaned from these documents that humans appear to share. Once a draft of the Universal Declaration was developed it was presented in all geographic regions of the world over a period of years, with comments accepted that would help refine the final document. This document embeds human values that transcend times in history, geographic locations, and cultures, and includes four principles (Respect for the Dignity of Persons and Peoples, Competent Caring for the Well-Being of Persons and Peoples, Integrity, Professional and Scientific Responsibilities to Society). If desired, national psychological organizations can apply the Universal Declaration as a foundation from which to develop or refine their codes of ethics (though Stevens [2010] presents interesting questions regarding the relationship between universal ethical principles and local norms and professional activities). Thus, a value-based foundation can be established when developing these codes (though stating common values is not without discussion of further questions; see Blickle, 2004; Pettifor, 2004). A question arises that if common principles can be employed in ethics codes, can common standards be equally employed? The Universal Declaration has also been envisioned as a tool for adjudicating ethical violations, which implies that there may be common standards based on shared values across contexts and cultures.

Common Standards

Professional psychology has been increasingly characterized within a regional and global framework (e.g., Arnett, 2002, 2008; Hall & Lunt, 2005). Geographic boundaries are becoming more porous, and technological advances that almost force greater international considerations have enabled more psychologists to both consider and practice outside of their home countries. Increased virtual and physical mobility among psychologists is desired and beginning to occur. Hall and Lunt (2005) outlined four components to achieving this mobility: professional consensus on recognition standards (i.e., the educational level required by psychologists across countries), demand by psychologists for mobility, advocacy efforts by psychological organizations to promote multiple pathways (to achieving seamless mobility), and cooperation across member jurisdictions/states/countries. The first of these, professional consensus on recognition standards, has implications for ethical standards, though adoption of common standards across national organizations will require active efforts and cooperation of not only the national organizations but also international psychological associations. For example, the International Test Commission developed international standards for test development and use, in conjunction with the Joint Commission on Testing Practices and the National Council on Measurement in Education. Until national organizations work together more closely when developing or revising standards within their codes of ethics, a place to begin could rest with results of a series of empirical studies highlighting existing common standards.

Standards of conduct, which are considered more enforceable than principles, both prescribe and proscribe ethical behaviors. Standards assist in professions being recognized and foster trust and confidence by the community, and can also include mechanisms for monitoring and sanctioning professional behaviors (Blickle, 2004). Codes of ethics across national psychological organizations differ broadly regarding their structure and format. For example, some include large numbers of standards (e.g., Germany, South Africa), while others are shorter and primarily principled (e.g., Malta). Some include language with a tone that has been considered "legalistic" (e.g., United States), while others use language that allows for greater contextual considerations (e.g., Australia, Canada). Most include a few standards that are unique to their cultural context, whereas other standards overlap significantly across codes of ethics (see Leach, Glosoff, & Overmier, 2001; Leach & Harbin, 1997; Leach & Oakland, 2007). With all of the unique features found in codes of ethics internationally, questions arise as to whether common standards can be agreed upon. In essence, to what degree is there agreement as to common standards of practice across countries? Agreement in content becomes more complex given the multiple ethical algorithms available (see Nagy, 2011) to assist psychologists to engage in good psychological practices. Add cultural variables, and the issue becomes even more complex. Combining principles and standards into one document, the structure found in the majority of ethics codes has implications regarding the amount of emphasis placed on these principles and standards within the codes, their specificity, and their relationships to local and national laws. For example, the American Psychological Association (APA) code includes three standards regarding informed consent, but laws differ across U.S. states regarding the actual content contained in informed consent documents. Thus, while the code offers some guidance regarding the importance of informed consent, its interpretations differ based on local laws. That said, we believe that research into common standards across countries is necessary given the increasing numbers of ethics codes that have been developed over the past two decades and the increased recognition of psychology in national jurisdictions.

Common standards found within ethics codes can be determined in at least two ways. First, representatives from ethics committees of each national organization can meet and discuss their standards, eventually arriving at some agreement. Second, individual or small-team researchers can examine each code and make comparisons empirically to determine which standards are consistent among countries. From a methodological perspective the first approach is clearly superior, as both cultural and language interpretations can be made and presented. More detailed and culturally nuanced information can be gleaned also regarding each standard. For example, debriefing research participants after completion of a research project may be listed as "debriefing" in two codes, yet differ in meaning. One may imply only simple instruction as to what the project actually entailed, particularly if there was deception, whereas another could include the offering of full study results. However, this detailed approach is both costly and impractical. To gather representatives from all countries that have psychological ethics codes would require hundreds of thousands of U.S. dollars. Additionally, inviting those who are bilingual or multilingual would be necessary for many countries, and the time involved to complete the project could be prohibitive.

A more realistic means to determine common standards is for individuals or small research teams to examine each ethics code and determine common standards. A limitation includes the increased chance for misinterpretation and misrepresentation based on either the original intent behind the language, or how a particular standard is determined based on how conservative or liberal the methodology. For example, informed consent can be included in therapy sections, research sections, or other intervention sections. Without specific reference to research, however, informed consent may not be considered for a project on determining common research standards, although the original intent may have included research participants. A benefit of using small research groups is that it is much more financially manageable and geographically practical. Taken together, until representatives can convene to discuss common standards, individual research groups may be the best solution. A brief review of research considerations and previous research investigating common standards will be presented next.

Research Considerations when Investigating Ethical Standards

Previous authors (i.e., Leach & Harbin, 1997) used the term *universal* to describe standards that met a 75% cutoff criterion, meaning that 75% of the codes examined included a particular standard. After further consideration and discussion with other ethics researchers it was determined that "common" standards may be a more accurate phrase. The term *universal* implies that a standard is accepted in all countries and in all codes. When we indicate that standards are "common," we do not mean that the meaning behind the language is consistent across the board. We mean that the themes of the statements are consistent. For example, consider the following two standards related to duty to protect: The Italian code states, "Should a report or declaration be required by law, the psychologist shall refer what he has known during his/her professional relation to the minimum extent, in order to guard his/her patient's psychological state. In other cases he shall carefully evaluate the need to make a total or partial exception to the confidentiality he is bound to, when serious dangers for the patient's or third party's life or psychophysical well-being of the patient or others arise (Article 13)." Similarly, the Puerto Rican code states, "The confidential information received is revealed only to professional and/or pertinent public authorities when the client threatens or infers irreparable damage to him/herself and/or to third parties"(Standard 3). Additionally, many countries, even some with national psychological organizations, have not developed an ethics code, so to state that a standard is universal would be inaccurate. Thus, we will use the term *common* to better reflect standards found across the codes examined.

Standards are more amenable to cultural interpretations than principles. Most codes of ethics are composed of principles and standards, with standards representing the bulk of the codes themselves. For example, the U.S. code has five principles and 88 standards. Standards are developed within a contextual framework, interpreted within that framework, and are enforced within the same framework. The framework is embedded within a culture. Since cultures differ it would be expected that codes of ethics differ with regard to their standards. However, a common value base within psychology is also expected to show some common standards regardless of cultural context. Thus, there will be common standards based on values that psychology shares, and these common values may translate into commonly agreed-upon practices regardless of country and culture. However, the behavioral expression of these standards may also have interpretable differences. For example, confidentiality may be derived from a common value, yet the limits of confidential information may differ based on cultural context. Additionally, there are standards that are unique to a country based on cultural values. Though framed from a psychological value perspective, Blickle's (2004) statements could easily be applied to common standards, given that standards are derived from values: "Psychology cannot, however, give up this value base. With regard to these values, no cultural adaptation is possible. If psychology were to lose these values, it would simultaneously lose its identity" (p. 274). Thus, if psychology is indeed becoming a global field then it should share certain values, and these values can be reflected as standards (and principles) within ethics codes.

Comparisons of standards have recently gained some attention in the psychological ethics literature. The purpose of these studies was to determine the extent to which national psychological organizations' codes of ethics share common standards, and which are culturally dependent. Though a fully agreed-upon code of ethics is unlikely, examination of common standards can offer similar guidance to that found with the *Universal Declaration of Ethical Principles for Psychologists*. Just as the Universal Declaration offers a framework from which to develop or update codes of ethics, standards found in the majority of countries offers psychologists a means to determine some agreement within our collective beliefs surrounding good, ethical practices. For example, if informed consent is a standard found in the majority of ethics codes, then we can make assumptions that informed consent is a standard valued by the majority of the psychology community internationally. Eventually a core of common standards can be presented to the international psychology ethics community for their consideration when developing or revising their codes. It should be noted that there is already significant overlap among some national ethics codes (e.g., Ireland, New Zealand) because these countries examined a third code and either included significant portions of the code or were guided by it (in this case, Canada).

Though small, there is a growing literature on studies investigating standards common across ethics codes. Certain caveats must be presented prior to presenting a brief sampling of this literature. First, language equivalence has not been guaranteed. It cannot be guaranteed that the same meaning for confidentiality, both in initial intent and interpretation, is found in both the German and Singapore codes of ethics. Though the literature presented below can offer some guidance regarding common standards, the only way to fully understand the relationships among standards is to have native speakers work together on projects, offering not just to interpret the meaning of language but to offer context from which the standards were developed. For example, a few countries (e.g., Chile) offer standards against the use of torture, included because of national histories of oppressive regimes in which psychologists were complicit in or forced to comply with those regimes' ideologies (Part Five of this volume explicates the relationships among cultures, histories, and psychology). These standards are unique to these few countries, but the context allows readers to better understand their inclusion.

Second, standards may be included or lacking from codes of ethics because of the relationship between national laws and ethics within professional psychological associations. Chapter 20 by Steve Behnke in this volume expands on the relationship between law and ethics. For example, the American

Psychological Association's *Ethical Principles of Psychologists and Code of Conduct* (2002) includes the need for informed consent across human relations, clinical, and research categories so that clients can make good, informed choices. However, as indicated above, states' laws differ regarding the information to be included in consent forms. Thus, while informed consent is included in the APA code of ethics, its meaning and ramifications cannot be fully understood without understanding the interaction between law and ethics. The extent to which ethics standards are enforced also differ among countries. For example, clients who believe they have been ethically wronged in South Africa and the United States can have their concerns heard in court fairly easily. In the Netherlands, ethics complaints are often heard by ethics committees with less sanctioning power.

Previous Research Attempting to Determine Common Standards

Schuler (1982) was probably the first researcher to compare standards among national ethics codes, by comparing research guidelines set forth in nine national psychological organizations' codes of ethics. Kimmel (1996) followed up with an informal survey of research standards but did not examine them in depth, and focused only on research standards. Leach and Harbin (1997) investigated all standards and principles among codes represented in over 20 countries, and found 10 standards approaching common agreement. A caveat is needed here. When developing or revising codes of ethics, many countries will first examine codes from other countries. For example, the current New Zealand code drew heavily from the current Canadian code. Thus, some overlap is expected. Though the number of studies comparing codes of ethics across nations is small, they have implications for a potential common core of standards in future codes of ethics.

Leach, Glosoff, and Overmier (2001) conducted a follow-up study to determine culture-specific differences among national ethics codes' standards, and identified standards generally reflective of a country's licensure provisions, political history, or government policies. Leach and Oakland (2007) found that one-third of 31 codes representing 35 countries indicated no test use standards, while there was significant overlap with the APA code governing test use among the remaining two-thirds of countries. Thus, of those codes with test use standards, there were a significant number of common standards. Methodologically the Leach and Harbin (1997) and Leach and Oakland (2007) studies were limited. Each examined standards from codes of ethics through the lens of the American Psychological Association code of ethics. Essentially, the APA code was used as the reference code by which all other codes, and thus standards, were measured. The intent of using this method was not to present the APA code as the standard, but simply to use it as a guide to make data analysis more manageable given the large number of standards from an increasing number of countries with ethics codes. The authors recognized the ethnocentric limitation.

Leach (2009) examined the standards and principles pertaining to duty to protect within 34 codes of ethics representing 38 countries using a different methodology, which consisted of simply examining each code for duty to protect standards within code categories of confidentiality and disclosure. He found duty to protect principles and standards were included in codes of 70% of countries, while acknowledging cultural and legal variations across countries. Again, there appeared to be a growing number of common standards found in psychological ethics codes.

Research Ethics as Common Standards

Ethics within the field of psychology grew, in part, from the atrocities that occurred during World War II and the resultant Nuremberg Trials. The Nuremberg Code of 1947 outlined 10 standards to which physicians must conform when including human participants in research studies. Primary among them was voluntary informed consent, a research standard found common in Leach and Harbin (1997). Though the first code of ethics in psychology, the 1953 APA code, was broader in scope than research ethics, it nonetheless grew from the post-WWII professional climate. Since then codes from other countries have included research content, though the full extent to which this content is included has yet to be determined. As stated above, both Schuler (1982) and Kimmel (1996) assessed research standards across countries. Leach and Harbin (1997), comparing all standards from 19 codes, found a range of research standards in the codes they examined. However, other than limiting methodological issues described by Leach and Harbin (1997), there are two reasons for the necessity of an update on common research standards found across countries.

First, since the 1980s there has been growing recognition of psychology as a science internationally (Rosenzweig, 1992), as defined by research publication output. With increased recognition comes increased methodological complexity and sophistication, leading to greater needs for good ethical practices. It would benefit the profession to determine common research standards among national codes in order to offer some guidance for future iterations of codes and to assist research internationally with engaging in good research practices. Second, the majority of codes included in Leach and Harbin (1997) were published in the 1980s and early 1990s. Ethics code development in psychology has increased significantly over the past few decades, with countries either developing new documents or revising dated documents. Additionally, with increased use of technology countries can view others' codes when developing or revising, including ideas they deem ethically and culturally appropriate while not including others deemed less relevant. Also, through better access to ethics codes via technology the number of codes included in this chapter far exceeds that found in other studies of standards (e.g., Leach & Oakland, 2007; Leach & Harbin, 1997). Thus, the findings will be more robust than those found in previous studies. Given these two reasons for the necessity of an update on research ethics, standards, we have decided to assess the psychology research ethics field in terms of common standards found across national codes.

As a means to continue the search for common standards, the remainder of this chapter will focus on common research standards within codes of ethics from 39 countries. The 39 countries are: Argentina, Australia, Bolivia, Bulgaria, Canada, Chile, China, Columbia, Costa Rica, Croatia, Estonia, Germany, Great Britain, Hong Kong, Hungary, Iran, Ireland, Israel, Japan, Latvia, Lithuania, Malta, Netherlands, New Zealand, Paraguay, Peru, Philippines, Poland, Romania, Serbia, Singapore, Slovenia, South Africa, South Korea, Spain, Turkey, United States, Uruguay, and Venezuela. In addition, four codes (Czech-Moravia, Dominican Republic, Lithuania, and Scandinavia [which includes Denmark, Finland, Iceland, Norway, Sweden]) included only either ethical principles and not standards, or standards with no specific research language. Nonetheless, since the purpose of this chapter is to compare all codes, instead of those only containing specific research standards, these four codes were included. Results will include percentages of research standards found in all 43 codes of ethics, as well as research standards contained only in codes with specific reference to research standards. Using both levels of inclusion allows for a more robust understanding of the field.

The purpose of this study was to determine ethical standards common to research practices across national codes of ethics. As in previous studies (i.e., Leach & Harbin, 1997), standards included in 75% or more of national codes will be considered common across codes. Readers can consider percentages close to 75% as trends.

Method

A content analysis method was used for this study. Ethics codes included in the study were gathered from the International Union of Psychological Science (IUPsyS) website, in addition to eight codes not yet included on the site and others in the first author's possession. Each of these codes had been translated to English, with some received from English-speaking countries, some by translators within other countries, and the rest via bilingual speakers within the United States.

As indicated above, previous research comparing ethics codes (e.g., Leach & Harbin, 1997) used the American Psychological Association's *Ethical Principles of Psychologists and Code of Conduct* as the foundation, though the researchers discussed the ethnocentric bias embedded within their method. To use any one code of ethics (in that case the APA code) implies some bias in that all other codes will be compared to that initial code. We sought to eliminate this bias in this study in two ways. First, in order to develop a final framework within which to code the standards without bias, the process began without any predetermined categories or countries. In addition to this bias, content analysis studies are time-limited due to changes among codes over time. Even within countries but across code iterations, the number of section categories (if countries include them) can change. For example, the 1992 APA code included 21 standards specific to research, whereas the 2002 code includes 15 standards. Thus, to include a code from a specific country as the framework from which to determine common standards seemed methodologically inappropriate. It should be noted that only the latest iteration of a country's code was included.

Countries were coded in alphabetical order to mitigate any potential bias that could occur by using a familiar country's code as a standard. Research content within each code was examined. When a country introduced a new standard that was not listed previously, a new category was listed on the coding spreadsheet. In this way, no one country was viewed through a lens that would restrict the scope of their standards. Second, national organizations tend to organize their standards in different ways. For example, two almost exact standards can be listed individually in one code of ethics but subsumed within a general heading, or in combination with another standard, in another code. By examining each research-related sentence regardless of whether it was listed individually or subsumed, organization bias is reduced. Thus, we did not feel constrained to include a standard only if it fell within a predetermined category.

Data analysis involved four steps. First, the coding process involved reviewing the ethics standards and listing any standards that referenced ethical research. This included standards that were grouped under a research or publication heading, in addition to statements regarding research practices contained within other headings. Some countries included research participants as part of the definition of "clients" or research in general as part of the definition of "psychological services." Standards that were broadly worded as, for example, "psychological services" were not included as a specific research standard, unless under a research subheading. As another example, due to its structure the Scandinavian code included language that indicated the following standards related to a variety of psychological responsibilities (e.g., general acknowledgement of clinical work, research, teaching) but were not specific to research. They were included in the analyses though not perceived to include specific research standards. Thus, a conservative approach was taken when including standards that were not explicit in their reference to research.

Second, each sentence was examined for content themes. Some sentences included one research-related theme, whereas others included more than one theme. If the latter, these themes were initially given separate categories, because to subsume them together under a specific category would increase the potential for miscategorization. Third, categories and standards placed into those categories were developed independently as each code of ethics was examined independently by the two raters. Fourth, the two coders met together to discuss any differences in coding (initial interrater agreement >.85). If a solution was not found, the content (standard) was reviewed by the lead author for the final decision to determine in which category the standard belonged. Categories were examined by the lead author and discussed with the raters to determine whether some initial standards could be collapsed into another. Final decisions were not made until a unanimous decision among all three was reached.

Consistent with Leach and Harbin (1997) an inclusion criterion of five countries was used for a general category to be listed. Standards found in fewer than five countries were considered unique to those cultures and will be examined at a later date. It should be noted that "five countries" was subjectively derived in the earlier study, and readers should feel free to use their own criteria. Continuing to use a cutoff of five in this study was simply to maintain consistency. Finally, after common standards were agreed upon, coders reviewed all ethical codes again through the final framework to check for any overlooked or mislabeled standards. The results can be found in Table 10.1.

Results

Seventeen standards themes emerged from the 43 countries assessed and were placed into 17 categories. We titled them based on common nomenclature found in the research ethics literature. They are Informed Consent, Confidentiality, Debriefing, Data, Delegation, Accuracy in Reporting, Plagiarism, Authorship Credit, Conflicts of Interest, Animal Rights, Avoiding Harm, Compensation, Right to Withdraw, Scientific Standards, Ethical Review, Verification, and Confidentiality of Proposal.

Category Development

As indicated earlier, if five or more countries shared the same standard it became a general category. In some cases we believed that two categories fit into the same general theme, so we merged them into one. As an example, during the coding process there was an initial category entitled "Dual Relationships" to describe the standards that prohibited researchers from engaging in dual relationships with research participants. These dual relationships could occur in a variety of different contexts and were often described in the context of business relationships. Other standards included explicit statements that prohibited research that would directly benefit the researcher financially or for business purposes, so another category entitled "Conflicts of Interest" was included. Upon final determination it was decided that the term *conflicts of interest* could describe dual relationships in research, and they were collapsed into one category. As another example, many standards encouraged researchers to consider the potential risks to participants before conducting research, and others stated that researchers should avoid harm to participants wherever possible. Again, it was decided that these two categories were similar conceptually, and were collapsed.

Table 10.1 Countries with Standards of Ethical Research Consistent with Common Standards

Research Standards listed in more than five countries' official standards of ethics

Informed Consent	Confidentiality	Debriefing	Data	Delegation	Accuracy in Reporting	Plagiarism	Authorship Credit	Conflicts of Interest
Argentina	Argentina	Australia	Australia	Australia	Argentina	Argentina	Argentina	Australia
Australia	Australia	Bolivia	Canada	Britain	Australia	Australia	Australia	Bolivia
Bolivia	Bolivia	Canada	Chile	Bulgaria	Bolivia	Bulgaria	Bolivia	Canada
Canada	Canada	Croatia	Columbia	Canada	Britain	China	Canada	Columbia
Chile	China	Great Britain	Great Britain	Chile	Canada	Columbia	China	Germany
China	Columbia	New Zealand	Hungary	Germany	Chile	Costa Rica	Columbia	Great Britain
Columbia	Croatia	Peru	Iran	Great Britain	China	Croatia	Costa Rica	Hungary
Costa Rica	Germany	Serbia	Israel	Hong Kong	Columbia	Great Britain	Croatia	Ireland
Croatia	Great Britain	South Africa	Netherlands	Hungary	Croatia	Hong Kong	Germany	Japan
Germany	Hong Kong	South Korea	New Zealand	Iran	Estonia	Hungary	Great Britain	Latvia
Great Britain	Iran	Turkey	Romania	Ireland	Germany	Iran	Hong Kong	New Zealand
Hong Kong	Ireland	USA	Serbia	Israel	Hong Kong	Israel	Hungary	Peru
Hungary	Israel	Venezuela	South Korea	Peru	Hungary	New Zealand	Iran	South Africa
Iran	Japan		USA	Poland	Iran	Paraguay	Ireland	
Ireland	Latvia			Serbia	Ireland	Peru	Israel	
Israel	Malta			Slovenia	Latvia	Philippines	New Zealand	
Japan	Netherlands			South Africa	Netherlands	Poland	Paraguay	

(*continued*)

Table 10.1 (Continued)

Research Standards listed in more than five countries' official standards of ethics

Informed Consent	Confidentiality	Debriefing	Data	Delegation	Accuracy in Reporting	Plagiarism	Authorship Credit	Conflicts of Interest
Latvia	New Zealand			South Korea	New Zealand	Singapore	Peru	
Malta	Paraguay			USA	Paraguay	South Africa	Philippines	
Netherlands	Peru				Peru	South Korea	Poland	
New Zealand	Poland				Philippines	Turkey	Romania	
Paraguay	Serbia				Poland	USA	Singapore	
Peru	Singapore				Romania	Venezuela	South Africa	
Poland	South Africa				Serbia		South Korea	
Romania	South Korea				Singapore		Turkey	
Serbia	Turkey				South Africa		USA	
Singapore	USA				South Korea		Uruguay	
Slovenia	Uruguay				Turkey		Venezuela	
South Africa	Venezuela				USA			
South Korea					Uruguay			
Spain					Venezuela			
Turkey								
USA								
Uruguay								
Venezuela								
N=35	30	13	14	18	31	24	28	13
RSO =90%	77	33	36	46	80	62	72	33
All=81%	70	30	33	42	72	56	65	30

Note: RSO = Research Standards Only, N=39; All = All codes including those without explicit research standards, N = 43

Research Standards listed in more than five countries' official standards of ethics

Animal Rights	Avoiding Harm	Compensation	Right to Withdraw	Scientific Standards	Ethical Review	Verification	Confidentiality of Proposal
Argentina	Argentina	Canada	Argentina	Argentina	Argentina	Australia	Australia
Canada	Bolivia	Croatia	Canada	Canada	Canada	Canada	Canada
Chile	Canada	Great Britain	Chile	Chile	Chile	Croatia	Croatia
Columbia	Chile	Ireland	China	China	Columbia	Germany	Germany
Croatia	China	Israel	Columbia	Columbia	Costa Rica	Hungary	Israel
Germany	Columbia	Romania	Croatia	Croatia	Croatia	Peru	South Africa
Great Britain	Costa Rica	South Africa	Germany	German	Great Britain	Romania	Turkey
Hong Kong	Croatia	South Korea	Great Britain	Hong Kong	Hungary	South Africa	USA
Hungary	Germany	Turkey	Hong Kong	Iran	Iran	South Korea	
Iran	Great Britain	USA	Hungary	Ireland	Ireland	Turkey	
Ireland	Hong Kong	Venezuela	Iran	Japan	New Zealand	USA	
Israel	Hungary		Israel	Latvia	Peru	Venezuela	
Japan	Iran		Japan	New Zealand	Romania		
New Zealand	Ireland		Latvia	Paraguay	Serbia		
Paraguay	Israel		Paraguay	Poland	South Africa		

(continued)

Table 10.1 (Continued)

Research Standards listed in more than five countries' official standards of ethics

Animal Rights	Avoiding Harm	Compensation	Right to Withdraw	Scientific Standards	Ethical Review	Verification	Confidentiality of Proposal
Philippines	Japan		Peru	Romania	Turkey		
Poland	Malta		Poland	Serbia	USA		
Romania	New Zealand		Romania	South Korea			
Singapore	Peru		Serbia	Spain			
South Africa	Philippines		South Africa	Uruguay			
Spain	Poland		Spain	Venezuela			
Turkey	Serbia		Turkey				
USA	Singapore		USA				
	Slovenia		Uruguay				
	South Africa		Venezuela				
	South Korea						
	Spain						
	Turkey						
	USA						
	Uruguay						
	Venezuela						
23	32	11	25	21	17	12	8
59	82	28	64	54	44	31	21
54	74	26	58	49	40	28	19

Note: RSO = Research Standards Only, N=39; All = All codes including those without explicit research standards, N = 43

There were other situations in which it was determined that very similar categories remain separate. One example is *Informed Consent* and *Confidentiality*. The *Informed Consent* category refers to the importance of research participants consenting with an understanding of the nature of the research and their roles in the research process. This category includes standards referencing the use of deception in research as well. One example is found in Croatia's Standard 4.4 Test Takers Consent under the Research and Scientific Work section, "4.4 Potential test takers must be given an opportunity to decide for themselves whether or not they wish to take part in the study after they have been informed of their obligations, limitations, possible consequences and the risks." *Confidentiality*, conversely, refers to the importance of ensuring that all findings are kept confidential, and that participants identifying information not be connected to their data. One example of this category can be found in Singapore's code 6.5, "Only after explicit permission has been granted is the identity of research subjects published. When data have been published without permission for identification, the psychologists assume responsibility for adequately disguising their sources." One might see how the above standard could be considered a part of informed consent; however, we thought the distinction was important, in that some countries had specific standards for informed consent but not for confidentiality. Chile, Costa Rica, Hungary, Slovenia, and Spain all identified Informed Consent but not confidentiality as specific standards of ethical research. This was an important enough distinction that we did not want to blend them into one and lose the distinction.

The next two categories revolve around the rights of the participants. *Debriefing* refers to the participants' rights to information and results following the study. The New Zealand Code is a good example of both of these standards:

> 2.6.6. Psychologists have a responsibility to debrief research participants and do so in such a way that any harm caused can be discerned. They act to correct such harm. Such communication should be comprehensible.
>
> 2.6.7. Psychologists communicate findings of research to participants in ways that value and respect their contribution.

The category, *Data*, is similar to confidentiality; however, it refers specifically to standards for collection and storage of data only necessary for the study. Canada's code includes good examples:

> I.39 Record only that private information necessary for the provision of continuous, coordinated service, or for the goals of the particular research study being conducted, or that is required or justified by law.
>
> I.42 Take all reasonable steps to ensure that records over which they have control remain personally identifiable only as long as necessary in the interests of those to whom they refer and/or to the research project for which they were collected, or as required or justified by law (e.g., the possible need to defend oneself against future allegations), and render anonymous or destroy any records under their control that no longer need to be personally identifiable.

Next, *Delegation* refers to the ethical responsibilities of a researcher when he/she delegates work to research assistants. This typically means that the primary researcher is responsible for the ethical behavior of his/her subordinates, and is responsible for determining whether delegation is ethical at all given the context of the project. Germany Standard C.III.6 illustrates both principles:

> C.III.6 Psychologists are also responsible for ensuring that research work on people conducted by persons under their supervision or other forms of control and monitoring is ethically sound. Tasks involved in research with human participants may only be assigned to persons who have been appropriately trained and prepared for such work. Psychological experiments may only be conducted in appropriate institutional settings.

The next three categories could be referred to as published research findings. Standards under the *Accuracy in Reporting* heading refer to the manipulation of data in a manner that presents favorable results. This includes ignoring data contrary to one's hypotheses or misrepresenting one's findings publicly. Estonia's standard 8 is an example of this principle. In research the psychologist follows the scientific ethics (including truthful reporting of data, following publication rules, etc.).

Though considered published research findings, the next two categories are examples of two very similar categories that were separately maintained. First, *Plagiarism* refers to the importance of not publishing work that was previously published. An example of this standard is in Bulgaria's code:

> 2.4 Respectability—In these activities the psychologists are honest, impartial and respect the

others, don't allow any form of misappropriation of somebody else's achievements in science and applied science, of somebody else's copyright, the theft of other people's ideas, and the falsification of somebody else's work.

Other countries included standards that emphasized the importance of acknowledging the work of all those who helped with research projects, as well as the authorship order being proportional to the amount of work provided. This category was titled *Authorship Credit*, and an example can be found in Canada's code III.7, "Take credit only for the work and ideas that they have actually done or generated, and give credit for work done or ideas contributed by others (including students), in proportion to their contribution." Next is the category discussed earlier, *Conflicts of Interest*; Latvia standard number 1 under Professional Relationships states, "Psychologists do not exploit their professional relationship with their clients, or research, for personal gains."

The next few categories involve the safety of research participants, animal and human alike. *Animal Rights* is referred to in countries that have specific standards of ethical research involving animals. Stipulations usually refer to the protection of animals or restricting the use of animals to cases where research is considered necessary. Iranian Standard 8.10 includes an example, "Psychologists and counselors should carry out research projects on animals only if doing so would be necessary and essential, and when the results obtained from such studies would be effective and beneficial to the advancement of psychology and the promotion of quality in people's lives." The next category is *Avoiding Harm*. This category was discussed earlier, and represents the standards that require researchers to consider the risks involved with their research and protect the physical and emotional safety of the participant. In cases where risk is involved, these standards require researchers to make clear the risks during the informed consent process. China standard 6.1 provides a good example:

> 6.1 Clinical and counseling psychologists who conduct research with human participants should respect the basic human rights. They should conduct research in a manner that is consistent with pertinent ethical principles, laws, host institutional regulations and scientific research standards with human participants. They should take responsibility to ensure the security of their participants and take reasonable precaution to avoid causing harm to participants' interests.

In cases where risk is involved, some countries included a statement that prohibited researchers from using excessive rewards or other *Compensation* that would increase participation through the manipulation of individuals. Standard 5.6 from Israel provides an example, "Psychologists must refrain from excessive or inappropriate incentives for their research participants in order to obtain their consent of research participation, especially when these incentives might coerce participation." The *Right to Withdraw* includes standards indicating that participants can withdraw from participation at any time, regardless of its effects on the research project. The United States includes a statement that represents this right in their informed consent standard 8.02:

> (a) When obtaining informed consent as required in Standard 3.10, Informed Consent, psychologists inform participants about (1) the purpose of the research, expected duration, and procedures; (2) their right to decline to participate and to withdraw from the research once participation has begun; (3) the foreseeable consequences of declining or withdrawing; . . .

The next category, *Scientific Standards,* refers to statements that instruct researchers to conduct research according to accepted scientific standards or methods. Research should be conducted properly and objectively, as in Poland's standard 30:

> The psychologist implementing scientific research will only undertake topics not violating the ethical standards of his profession. He is responsible for choice of research methods enabling reliable results to be achieved and for the integrity of the results announced. Making decisions on these points, the psychologist will not be swayed by pressure exerted by persons or circumstances.

Some countries' codes mandate researchers to account to themselves about the ethical nature of their research. Those listed in the *Ethical Review* category require that researchers obtain institutional approval from an objective ethical review board, as well as statements about the truthful reporting of the research intent in such research proposals. Ireland standard 3.3.14 is an example, "Seek an independent and adequate ethical review of the balance of risks and potential benefits of all research which involves procedures of unknown consequence, or where pain, discomfort, or harm are possible, before making a decision to proceed."

The next category, *Verification*, refers to the importance of replication of research to confirm findings. In order to prevent dishonest research, some countries require that researchers be transparent about their data and procedures so that other investigators can verify their findings, as in the Turkish code, standard 9.14:

> After research results are published, psychologists do not withhold the data on which their conclusions are based from other professionals who wish to reanalyze the data, and permit such reanalysis after ensuring the confidentiality of the participants. Psychologists who would like to have access to the data for the above mentioned reasons use the data accordingly and do not submit the data as original data.

The final category also refers to inter-researcher relations. *Confidentiality of Proposal* refers to countries that include statements about the importance of maintaining researcher confidentiality when proposing research. Australia standard A.2.5 is a good example, "Psychologists who review grant or research proposals or material submitted for publication respect the confidentiality and proprietary rights of those who made the submission."

Discussion of Common Standards

We have used research standards as a means to continue the examination of common standards and common ethical research practices across countries. Rather than begin with a framework of a particular code of ethics known to have a significant number of included research ethics standards (e.g., American Psychological Association, British Psychological Society, Psychological Society of South Africa), we decided to simply alphabetize the codes and develop the final list of standards using this method. So, rather than determine how many standards fell within the 11 research standards from the APA *Ethical Principles of Psychologists and Code of Conduct*, for example, we created separate categories based on the themes noted throughout the 43 codes.

When considering all codes, including those without specific research standards, only one met the conservative criteria of a 75% inclusion rate, Informed Consent (81%). Three others—Avoiding Harm, Accuracy in Reporting, and Confidentiality—all fell between 70%–74% of codes and can be considered trends. When considering only codes that included specific research standards (four codes did not), all four of the above standards exceeded the 75% inclusion rate. Additionally, Authorship was found in 72% of codes that included research standards.

Thus, five either met or are approaching common standard status among codes internationally for those reporting specific research standards (depending on which criteria are used). As Table 10.1 indicates, three others, Right to Withdraw, Plagiarism, and Animal Rights, were found in the approximately 60% range, and Scientific Standards was found in approximately 50% of all codes. While not meeting the common criteria standard, they are interesting nonetheless. The psychological research community has been growing at a rate faster than that in the United States, which for years dominated psychological research (Rosenzweig, 1992). The results indicate that eight or nine (depending on criteria) of the 17 research standards found in this study were included in over 50% of the countries. Those standards that fell below 50% are still interesting nonetheless, as they have been deemed important enough by multiple national associations to merit their inclusion. These include Debriefing, Data, Delegation, Conflicts of Interest, Compensation, Ethical Review, Verification, and Confidentiality of the Proposal. Future researchers can determine whether these standards become more common across codes as ethics committees reevaluate their own codes and examine others for ideas. They can also determine the extent to which these standards are considered important for their organization and code of ethics.

Final Thoughts

A question arises as to whether common standards are possible? Our response to this question is an unequivocal yes. The number and focus areas of common standards are still in need of study, but Leach and colleagues have found enough evidence over the years to signify that the profession of psychology is founded on at least some common standards and common ethical practices. An argument could be made that common standards are unlikely because they are culturally based to a greater extent than principles. Cultures may contribute to specific standards found only in a particular (or few) national code (see Leach, Glosoff, & Overmier, 2001), or they may influence the interpretation of common standards. In order to be considered a credible profession, organizations often develop ethics codes early in their development. The rise in the profession of psychology internationally has resulted in an increasing number of ethics codes, and both common standards and common principles lend themselves to unifying psychology as a reputable profession internationally. These unifying themes help solidify common features and common beliefs of psychology internationally. Granted, cultures can agree or disagree with principles, such as free choice, yet Gauthier (2008) developed the *Universal Declaration of Principles for Psychologists* based on historical and contemporary documents of morals and principles from all geographic regions of the globe. This does not mean that all national psychological organizations, and especially all psychologists, agree with these principles, but that movement toward common principles that psychologists can adhere to is being discussed among national, regional, and international psychological organizations. The same can occur for ethical standards. There are certain stated ethical standards, derived from a common value base, in which diverse psychological organizations agree, regardless of cultural variations. Interpretations may differ (e.g., the cultural meaning of confidentiality in a particular code of ethics) but the standard itself is maintained regardless of culture. Thus, these ethical standards are manifestations of common values found within psychology regardless of cultural context.

Limitations

Cross-cultural studies like this one have limitations that must be considered. First, many of the ethics codes have been translated into English, most prior to the authors receiving them. Others were translated over the years by different individuals associated with the first author. Given the multiple translators and the lack of back-translations, the potential for translation error is unknown. Second, words and phrases have different meanings and interpretations in different cultures, so when comparing standards without the benefit of indigenous collaborators the potential for interpretation differences increases. For example, definitions of data, or what constitutes informed consent, may differ across national codes. The current study attempted to determine the intent of the standards and categorize them accordingly. As mentioned earlier, the best way to conduct a study of this type is to have individuals representing each country's code discuss the meaning of the standards, yet inclusion of these individuals given the number of codes would be costly. Some standards may have simply been imported from more established codes, so their adherence in other countries is not currently known. Reviewing the table, readers can determine that there are vastly different cultures, values, geographic regions, and government structures represented within the standards. Questions can arise regarding whether a particular standard is meaningful and valued similarly across these countries.

References

American Psychological Association. (2002). Ethical principles of psychologists and code of conduct. *American Psychologist*, 57, 1060–1073.-066X.57.12.1060

Arnett, J. (2002). The psychology of globalization. *American Psychologist*, 57(10), 774–783. Arnett, J. (2008). The neglected 95%: Why American psychology needs to become less American. *American Psychologist*, 63(7), 602-614.-066X.63.7.602

Blickle, G. (2004). Commentaries on "Professional ethics across national boundaries" by Jean L. Pettifor: Professional ethics needs a theoretical background. *European Psychologist*, 9(4), 273–274. Gauthier, J. (2008). Universal declaration of ethical principles for psychologists. In J. E. Hall & E. M. Altmaier (Eds.), *Global promise: Quality assurance and accountability in professional psychology* (pp. 98–105). New York: Oxford University Press.

Hall, J. E., & Lunt, I. (2005). Global mobility for psychologists: The role of psychology organizations in the United States, Canada, Europe, and other regions. *American Psychologist*, 60(7), 712–726.

Kimmel, A. J. (1996). *Ethical issues in behavioral research: A survey*. Cambridge, MA: Blackwell Publishing.

Leach, M. M. (2009). International ethics codes and the duty to protect. In J. R. Werth, E. Welfel, & G. H. Benjamin (Eds.), *The duty to protect: Ethical, legal, and professional considerations for mental health professionals* (pp. 41–58). Washington, DC: American Psychological Association.

Leach, M. M., Glosoff, H., & Overmier, J. B. (2001). *International ethics codes: A follow-up study of previously unmatched standards and principles.* In J. B. Overmier & J.A. Overmier (Eds.), *Psychology* [CD-Rom]. IUPsyS Global Resource.

Leach, M. M., & Harbin, J. (1997). Psychological ethics codes: A comparison of twenty-four countries. *International Journal of Psychology*, 32(3), 181–192.

Leach, M. M., & Oakland, T. (2007). Ethics standards impacting test development and use: A review of 31 ethics codes impacting practices in 35 countries. *International Journal of Testing*, 7(1), 71–88.

Nagy, T. F. (2011). *Essential ethics for psychologists: A primer for understanding and mastering core issues.* Washington, DC: American Psychological Association.

Pettifor, J. L. (2004). Professional ethics across national boundaries. *European Psychologist*, 9(4), 264–272.

Rosenzweig, M. R. (1992). Psychological science around the world. *American Psychologist*, 47(6), 718–722.

Schuler, H. (1982). *Ethical problems in psychological research* (translated by M. S. Woodruff & R. A. Wicklund). New York: Academic Press.

Stevens, M.J. (2010). Etic and emic in contemporary psychological ethics. *Europe's Journal of Psychology*, 4, 1–7.

CHAPTER 11

A Call for Ethical Standards and Guidelines for Cross-Cultural Research Conducted by American Psychologists

Brent J. Lyons *and* Frederick T. L. Leong

Abstract

In light of expansive globalization, the lack of ethical guidelines regulating the cross-cultural international research of American psychologists reflects an emerging ethical challenge. The American Psychological Association (APA) code of ethics (2002) is silent on ways to cope with cross-cultural ethical dilemmas, and the *Universal Declaration of Ethical Principles for Psychologists* (Gauthier, 2008), though a useful framework for shedding light on the issue, offers no practical recommendations for researchers. Considering the cross-cultural ethical gaps that exist, in this chapter we provide examples of ethical dilemmas faced by American psychologists conducting cross-cultural international research, such as dilemmas with institutional approval, informed consent, participant inducement, research involving deception, and the dissemination of research results. We conclude with a "Call to Action" and present frameworks that may aid in the APA's development of a code of ethics specific to American psychologists who conduct cross-cultural international research.

Key Words: international research, cross-cultural research, ethical dilemmas, globalization, ethical guidelines

During the last decade, the impact of globalization on the roles of social scientists has received increasing recognition. Its impact is clear when exchange and educational opportunities for academics are considered. In recent years the number of graduate students and faculty within the social sciences participating in some kind of international cross-cultural exchange program has increased dramatically; the number of U.S. students, including Fulbright scholars, studying abroad has increased by 150% over the past 10 years (Institute of International Education, 2008).

The phenomenon of globalization is attracting the interest of psychologists in particular. For psychology and other health professions that provide services across countries, learning from colleagues who are working in different cultural contexts is critically necessary for developing knowledge and understanding of human behavior that will be maximally useful to practitioners and researchers alike (Ritchie, 2008). As psychologists are becoming more involved globally, psychology worldwide is benefiting from enhancements in global thinking and dialogue (Pettifor, 2007). However, in order for psychological knowledge and skills to be used sensitively and effectively, psychologists need to be aware of how its benefits and detriments can vary depending on cultural context. With more and more psychologists practicing abroad in communities with diverging values and expectations, the scope of problems related to cross-cultural ethics in research is expected to increase. Ethical standards inform researchers of appropriate conduct, and the importance of establishing ethical guidelines for appropriate practices in international cross-cultural psychological research is thus of crucial importance.

Ethical codes are not created in vacuums but are instead contextualized and reflect the culture of the country in which the codes have been developed. Psychologists know very little about the cultural conflicts and ethical dilemmas that arise when these culture-specific ethical codes are utilized across cultures in international psychological research. One common problem relates to cross-cultural ethical dilemmas created by value or belief conflicts between an American psychologist and the country in which the cross-cultural research is being conducted. With no guidelines in place, psychologists have limited awareness as to how their practices can lead to ethical dilemmas in other cultures. Examples of potential ethical conflicts include: The institutional review board (IRB) requirement of written consent may be problematic in societies that possess no written language, or in societies with a strong relationship between the legal system and ethical codes. In order to provide access to samples, U.S. values concerning bribery are discrepant with other culture's expectations of gifts. Appropriate levels of financial inducements (i.e., neither excessive nor diminutive) will differ in less economically resourced countries with high poverty rates. Also, it is unclear as to whom is monitoring the potential abuse of participants in less economically resourced countries in order the advance the scientific careers of psychologists in more economically resourced countries.

The lack of ethical standards for cross-cultural and international research reflects an emerging ethical challenge. In order to establish a clear set of ethical guidelines for conducting international research, American psychologists require a better understanding of cross-cultural issues. Ritchie (2008) argues that that an understanding of cross-cultural issues is rooted in respect for and acceptance of diversity. Instead of American psychologists conducting international research by simply focusing on means to satisfy their own ethical standards, it is important to recognize that understanding meaningful differences between cultures enhances the likelihood that people will be respected and services will be more adapted to their respective needs (Ritchie, 2008). The American Psychological Association (APA) code of ethics (2002) (herein referred to as the APA code) is silent on ways to cope with such cross-cultural ethical dilemmas and leaves major gaps when applied to international and cross-cultural research situations. The APA code is primarily behaviorally based, providing standards relevant to psychologists conducting research throughout various countries and world regions (e.g., Canada, South Africa, parts of Asia, and Oceana). However, the standards are specific to ethical conflicts psychologists face in one cultural context (particularly in the United States) and are silent to ethical dilemmas that may emerge when American psychologists conduct research in countries for which the standards do not resonate. Further, the APA code is not responsive to cross-cultural conflicts that are often subtle and invisible to many American psychologists when researching across cultures internationally.

In recent years, international collaborators have called for the creation of ethical codes that guide psychological research and practice across differing cultures. An example of such a multinational ethical framework—or meta-code—is one adopted by the European Federation of Psychologists Association (EFPA, 1995), bringing together national psychology bodies of 32 European countries (Ritchie, 2008). Meta-codes are intended to be complimentary to the codes of the national organizations that have specific values and principles to be included in their respective codes. Specification is important because ethics codes are socially constructed and derived from factors characteristic of the society from which they emerge (Lindsay, 1996; Ritchie, 2008). For example, complimentary to the EFPA's (1995) four principle meta-codes, 19 further specifications are articulated accounting for the diverse pedagogical, philosophical, political, theological, and socioeconomic distinctions between various regions of Europe. The eventual goal is a single set of guidelines that will guide ethical code development for all countries in the world. In order to do so, the International Association of Applied Psychology (IAAP) and the International Union of Psychological Science (IUPsyS) established a joint work group on the development of the *Universal Declaration of Ethical Principles* in 2002 (Gauthier, 2008; this will be discussed below in further detail). Indeed, the Universal Declaration incorporated values and ethics from diverse cultures' historical and contemporary documents, emphasizing the existence of core ethical values worldwide.

Thus, American psychologists conducting cross-cultural research internationally could consult ethical codes in other countries, but there may be particular value in consulting the Universal Declaration (Gauthier, 2008) and APA codes (2002) to help guide their cross-cultural research. However, even when considering both the APA Code and the Universal Declaration, specific ethical dilemmas faced by American psychologists researching abroad will not be adequately addressed. The APA code is generally ethnocentric to American values and beliefs, whereas the Universal Declaration was not designed to offer behaviorally specific recommendations and offers no practical guidance for researchers. The Universal Declaration instead introduces a framework by which more behaviorally specific guidelines can be developed for American psychologists researching across cultures and abroad.

APA Code of Ethics

The APA has documented ethical guidelines related to the practice of psychology for American psychologists. The APA Ethical Principles of Psychologists and Code of Conduct (i.e., American Psychological Association's own Code of Ethics, 2002) provides a detailed outline of ethical standards for research practices. Within its preamble, the APA code (2002) states that "Psychologists respect and protect civil and human rights and the central importance of freedom of inquiry and expression in research, teaching, and publication…providing specific standards to cover most situations encountered by psychologists" (p. 3). Highlighting five general ethical principles, the code suggests that psychologists should strive to conduct themselves with beneficence and nonmaleficence, fidelity and responsibility, integrity, justice, and respect for people's rights and dignity. Its intent is to promote accountability among American psychologists conducting research. However, the code itself is ethnocentric to American and a select number of related belief systems and value systems, focusing on behaviors that may only be relevant to a subset of psychologists. The APA guidelines do not specifically address international and cross-cultural research.

As the introduction to the APA code (2002) indicates, "The ethical standards set forth enforceable rules for conduct as psychologists" (p. 2). While such enforceable standards are important in setting minimum thresholds of acceptable behavior, and making it possible to legally enforce the standards if any psychologists violate them, such specific statements leave unaddressed certain problems created in international cross-cultural research situations. By urging psychologists to "eliminate the effect of biases in their work," the code provides a framework for culturally sensitive practices and incites an awareness of cultural considerations. However, the behavioral specificity of the APA code ignores an entire range of ethical challenges faced by American psychologists when conducting cross-cultural research in other countries. It is thus apparent, while balancing the behavioral specificity of the APA code (2002), additional ethical codes for American psychologists conducting cross-cultural research would benefit from a broader, more idealistic, and culturally sensitive set of regulations such as those highlighted by collaborators establishing a worldwide Meta-Code of the *Universal Declaration of Ethical Principles for Psychologists* (Gauthier, 2008).

Universal Declaration of Ethical Principles for Psychologists

As noted earlier, the rapid globalization of research conducted by social scientists in recent years has highlighted a need to develop a meta-code specifying guidelines for researchers around the world. In 2002, the General Assembly of the International Union of Psychological Science (IUPsyS) assembled an Ad Hoc Joint Committee, consisting of members from five countries, to develop a universal declaration of ethical principles for psychologists. Their primary goal was to articulate principles and values that provide a common moral framework for psychologists around the world, and a framework that can also aid in the development of more specific standards as appropriate for particular cultural contexts (Gauthier, 2008). In order to establish the principles, the committee made comparisons with existing codes of ethics for psychologists and other disciplines around the world to identify commonalities in ethical principles and values. The Universal Declaration aspires to inspire world psychological organizations to develop and evaluate the ethical and moral relevance of their codes of ethics:

> This Universal Declaration describes ethical principles and related values for the international psychology community. It provides a shared moral framework that will help members of the psychology community to recognize that they carry out their activities within a larger social context, and that they need to act with integrity in the development and application of psychological knowledge and skills and in a manner that benefits humanity and does not harm or oppress persons or peoples.
> (see http://www.sagepub.com/cac6study/pdf/UniversalDeclaration.pdf).

The focus of the Universal Declaration is aspirational rather than specific and prescriptive. The specific application of its principles will vary across cultures, and must occur at a local level to ensure their relevance to local beliefs and values (Gauthier, 2008). The Universal Declaration proposed four general principles to help aid international organizations in their evaluation and development of ethical codes: (i) Respect for the Dignity of Persons and Peoples, (ii) Competent Caring for the

Well-Being of Persons and Peoples, (iii) Integrity, and (iv) Professional and Scientific Responsibilities to Society.

Respect for the Dignity of Persons and Peoples

This principle aspires that all individuals, regardless of social status, demographics, or other capacities, are entitled to equal moral consideration and respect for the dignities of people. Examples of related values include: fair and just treatment of others, privacy for individuals, free and informed consent, and respect for customs and beliefs of cultures. Respect for the dignity of persons and peoples is expressed differently in different cultures. It is thus important to acknowledge and respect such differences.

Competent Caring for the Well-Being of Persons and Peoples

This principle aspires that psychologists will work for the benefit of others and do no harm, including maximizing benefits, minimizing harm, and correcting undue harm. This requires that psychologists apply their knowledge and skills that are appropriate for the nature of a situation, as well as the social and cultural context.

Integrity

This principle aspires that psychologists are honest and engage in truthful, open, and accurate communication. It also includes managing and correcting for potential biases and other conflicts that could result in harm to others. However, complete disclosure should be balanced with considerations of cultural expectations (e.g., appropriate professional boundaries) and desires for privacy.

Professional and Scientific Responsibilities to Society

Finally, this principle aspires that psychologists will contribute to knowledge of human behavior and to use this knowledge to improve the well-being of individuals, communities, and society. The ways in which such responsibilities are interpreted in various cultures differ and thus the advancement in knowledge needs to be interpreted in a way that is culturally appropriate.

Gaps in Ethical Guidelines

The principles proposed by the Universal Declaration provide a framework for the development of culturally sensitive ethical guidelines, but they do not specify standards for behaviors of American psychologists researching abroad, nor are the specific ethical dilemmas that these psychologists face captured by the specific and ethnocentric nature of the APA code (2002). As recommended by the Universal Declaration and as implemented by the EFPA's (1995) Meta-Code, ethical standards and regulations need to be contextualized within the value and belief frameworks of the culture of interest and will thus vary across regional, cultural, and political systems (Ritchie, 2008). No current code exists for the unique struggles of American psychologists practicing and conducting cross-cultural research internationally. Guidance that the APA code offers only goes so far, and serious gaps exist when addressing the specific ethical dilemmas faced by American researchers.

What follows are examples of specific ethical dilemmas that American researchers have faced when conducting research internationally. Each is an example of a dilemma regarding the research practices of psychologists outlined in section eight of the APA's code (2002). For example, dilemmas regarding institutional approval (standard 8.01); informed consent to research (8.02); client/patient, student, and subordinate research participants (8.04); offering inducements for research participation (8.06); deception in research (8.07); and reporting research results (8.10) will be discussed as specific standards outlined by the APA code that create dilemmas for American cross-cultural researchers. In this review we have included only those examples of dilemmas that researchers have noted as challenging in a cross-cultural context, focusing specifically on instances with human participants. For each challenge related to a specific APA standard, principles of the Universal Declaration will be applied to illustrate how a culturally sensitive meta-code can provide guidance for American psychologists, but how the Universal Declaration may not be completely sufficient to provide guidance for a variety of ethical dilemmas.

8.01 Institutional Approval

Before beginning any research, the APA code (2002) requires that research proposals are approved by an institutional review board (IRB) to ensure that no ethical standards are violated in the proposed research. IRBs also ensure that research is conducted in accordance with the approved research protocol (APA, 2002). Most U.S. IRB guidelines require that researchers obtain informed consent from participants before collecting data. However, these procedures do not exist in most countries outside the United States (Matsumoto & Jones, 2008; White, 2007). In some countries, submitting a research proposal for review is not necessary and obtaining informed consent is often unnecessary or even frowned upon (Matsumoto & Jones, 2008). Citing a similar concern in cross-cultural medical research, White (2007) raised the question of how to maintain Western ethical standards when research is conducted in countries with differing values. In cultures with different values, political systems, and economic systems, it may be imposing to insert U.S.-centric ethics in a research setting (White, 2007). In developing countries, the responsibility of the IRB to safeguard the rights and welfare of research participants is complicated when there is inadequate health care provision, high levels of social inequality, and social systems that fail to respect U.S. notions of human rights (London, 2002; White, 2007). Medical ethicists argue that a disparity in social power between researchers and participants, the complexity of information, and subjects' often desperate need for medical treatment may make risks associated with ethics violations in obtaining informed consent problematic (White, 2007). There is no doubt that American psychologists conducting cross-cultural research will face similar issues in obtaining informed consent (more specific examples are to follow). For U.S. IRBs, it is unclear by what ethical or legal standards research protocols should be evaluated. Such concerns are voiced by the Universal Declaration's principle of Respect for the Dignity of Persons and Peoples, in which psychologists are asked to attend to social context when obtaining informed consent (Gauthier, 2008). However, the APA code does not provide guidance on how the U.S.-based IRB can account for such culturally variant and contextually specific provisions.

Additionally, the APA code (2002) largely reflects a U.S. concept of human rights, emphasizing beneficence and nonmaleficence, fidelity and responsibility, integrity, and justice as its core ethical principles. If U.S. IRBs evaluate research proposals of psychologists conducting research in other countries, it is likely that the values and beliefs of those research participants will not be recognized in the research process. For example, U.S. IRBs place great emphasis on autonomy in informed consent as a right of participants (i.e., individual agency in choice to participate in research or not) instead of as a value, particularly when related to groups identified as vulnerable or in need of protection.

Constructions of autonomy differ across cultures and should thus have implications on how informed consent is operationalized (London, 2002). The process of ethical review can be biased as it takes place within the contexts of the varying interests of stakeholders (e.g., government, academic institutions, funding agencies, communities). In general, in many countries U.S. IRBs are at a disadvantage for having little familiarity with some key contextual issues necessary for assessing the ethical standards of a research protocol (London, 2002). No ethics code is currently in place that provides guidance for IRBs so that they are able to account for contextually relevant factors in evaluating a research protocol without including American ethnocentric assumptions and biases in the decision-making process.

8.02 Informed Consent to Research

Standard 8.02 of the APA code (2002) requires researchers to obtain informed consent from their prospective participants, using language (or other form of communication) that is understandable to the persons involved, before they collect any data. Persons are expected to be informed of the purpose of the research, expected duration, and procedures; their right to decline to participate and to withdraw from the research once participation has begun; benefits and risks in participating; and contact information if they have questions about the research (APA, 2002). Although the APA code emphasizes the importance of obtaining informed consent and how it is documented, no processes associated with obtaining informed consent are concerned with participants' actual understanding of their obligations or other implications associated with participating in the project. Even though some countries may find informed consent unnecessary (White, 2007), in those countries that do find it necessary, efforts of translating informed consent are of little use in regions with low levels of literacy. Even in regions with adequate literacy, there may be poor understanding of the nature of the research (Bhutta, 2004). In traditional societies, the strategy and risks associated with research may be difficult for researchers to explain to participants (Bhutta, 2004). For example, Bhutta (2004) references a study by Karim, Qurraishi, Coovadia, and Susser (1998), who evaluated the consent process for HIV testing in an antenatal clinic in South Africa. Karim et al. (1998) found that, even if researchers followed standard procedures for obtaining informed consent, 84% of participants perceived participation to be mandatory.

Similarly, Molyneux, Wassenaar, Peshu, and Marsh (2005) held discussions with members of a Kenyan community living in the rural study area associated with the Kenyan Medical Research Institute (KEMRI), a large research unit in Kenya associated with the United Kingdom–based Wellcome Trust. They noted that the practical difficulties associated with obtaining informed consent for medical research common to high-income countries are multifaceted in low-income communities due to low levels of formal education, poor access to adequate biomedical services, and a variety of different values, priorities, and understandings of health and illness (Molyneux et al., 2005). In the Kenyan communities, community members had widespread agreement that chiefs and elders could give permission for research to be carried out in the area, but these leaders could not decide for specific households or individuals. For children aged less than 18 years, parents were to be asked for informed consent, and it is generally the father who has primary decision-making authority. If the father is absent, the mother obtains the decision-making authority, or that authority becomes that of the other males or elders in the extended households (Molyneux et al., 2005). Additionally, in China reports surfaced of American researchers having difficulty obtaining true informed consent. A report by the United States Embassy Beijing on human research subject protection (2000) highlighted differences in political climate and literacy levels between certain regions of China and the United States as problematic for American researchers. Depending on the development of a specific region in China, county officials have varying degrees of influence. In the report, a prominent Chinese epidemiologist warned that money paid by a foreign researcher to a county official may result in those county officials using the money to buy a car and order health workers in the villages to do work without compensation (United State Embassy Beijing, 2000). In less developed regions of China, local officials can have such great power that village farmers are often unwilling to say no to their requests (United States Embassy Beijing, 2000).

Granting consent due to perceived coercion is in violation of APA codes, but both the APA code of ethics and Universal declaration do not offer specific and practical instructions for how American psychologists can overcome ethical concerns associated with government control in less developed regions of China. Further, the U.S. Embassy Beijing (2000) notes that due to China's history of frequent political campaigns and reversals in political power, many individuals are unwilling to put any information down on paper. In such regions, true informed consent is difficult to obtain, as subjects may not be willing to sign a document but may be willing to participate in a study anyway (United States Embassy Beijing, 2000). In more prosperous regions of China, heads of counties are often college graduates, who do not merely accept orders from local governments (United States Embassy Beijing, 2000). The epidemiologist notes that foreign researchers are more likely to obtain true informed consent in more developed areas of China, and effective supervision of the research projects is also more easily accomplished (United States Embassy Beijing, 2000). American psychologists need to attend to political and community differences in varying regions of China, ensuring that literate or illiterate individuals living in less developed regions are not victim to exploitation.

Indeed, both the Universal Declaration's (Gauthier, 2008) principles of Respect for the Dignity of Persons and Peoples and Integrity highlight that informed consent is culturally defined and relevant for individuals, families, groups, and communities, and should avoid the incomplete disclosure of information pertinent to the research, respectively. It is clear that authority hierarchies, community-based decision making, ranges in literacy levels, and language barriers are culturally sensitive factors that American psychologists need to consider when obtaining true informed consent in some African communities, regions of China, and abroad. As mentioned earlier, issues of informed consent are considered crucial in IRB evaluations of research proposals, yet the APA code (2002) does not specifically regulate informed consent strategies used by American psychologists obtaining consent in some communities abroad.

8.04 Client/Patient, Student, and Subordinate Research Participants

Issues pertaining to the power dynamic between psychological researchers and their subjects are exacerbated when researcher and participant cultural, political, and economic systems differ (London, 2002; Matsumoto & Jones, 2008; White, 2007). Standard 8.04 of the APA code (2002) requires that American psychologists take steps to protect participants from adverse consequences of declining or withdrawing from participation. Like medical researchers, psychologists are often charged with understanding a phenomenon that has great implications for the lives of those they are researching. Given the power imbalance between researchers and participants, it is important that American psychologists have the appropriate knowledge of the phenomenon they are researching so they can disseminate informed knowledge, allowing their participants to have appropriate information to make the most beneficial choices. As such, the Professional and Scientific Responsibilities to Society principle of the Universal Declaration (Gauthier, 2008) recommends that psychologists will use their knowledge to improve the well-being of individuals, communities, and society.

American psychologists' attempts to provide aid for victims of trauma in various countries will likely be ineffective if culture-specific considerations are not taken into account. For example, Giller (1998) found that her Western individualized approach to counseling interventions was culturally inappropriate when developing a center for survivors of torture with post-traumatic stress disorder (PTSD) in Uganda. When Tantink (2004) surveyed individuals within the Mbarara district of Uganda, subjects complained of sleeping problems, nightmares, and other symptoms of PTSD. However, Tantink questioned how effective a diagnosis of PTSD would be in the specific Mbarara societal context. By using an individual diagnosis paradigm, instead of a social paradigm, the group of American psychologists overlooked the role of the social environment's interaction with individuals' exposure to trauma. Daily life in Mbarara is more focused on relationships with family and community members than individuals alone. In order to aid the victims of Uganda in "healing," the community and culture first needed "social healing" (i.e., connectedness; Tantink, 2004). The Western-influenced tendency to focus on the individual victims discounted the detrimental effects that pervasive poverty can have on the social functioning of Mbarara community members. To develop more culturally congruent treatment methods, Giller (1998) turned to community members to help develop acceptable approaches to treatment. Without considering the crucial role of community in some cultures, American psychologists face high risk of harming individuals through inappropriate diagnoses or prescribing ineffective therapy.

8.06 *Offering Inducements for Research Participation*

In order to motivate subjects to participate in research, psychologists often pay them to do their work. The APA code (2002) requires that psychologists not offer excessive or inappropriate financial (or other types of) inducements to participants when such inducements could be construed as coercion for participation. However, issues of appropriate levels of payment become more complicated for American psychologists conducting research internationally. Goodwin (2002) highlighted the dilemmas he experienced while conducting cross-cultural research in Eastern Europe. For example, he claimed that in some regions of Russia, five dollars is seen to be a lot of money in a country where monthly wages are less than $25, which can cause resentment among those people not chosen as participants. But, five dollars can also offend business people who earn many hundreds of dollars an hour.

Goodwin (2002) also found paying children in schools to participate in research to be complicated. Requiring parental permission to participate, many children were often motivated to lie and sign the forms themselves, pretending to be their parents in order to obtain the payment. As a result, Goodwin had to follow a rather extensive consent process through which the researchers telephoned participant parents to ensure they had given their permission. To effectively maintain ethical standards when conducting cross-cultural international research in Eastern Europe, Goodwin (2002) suggests that foreign researchers closely collaborate with trusted researchers who are familiar with a specific region. The APA code (2002) provides no guidance to American psychologists in determining appropriate recruiting and payment methods in countries with highly variable economic climates. In line with Goodwin's (2002) suggestion, the Universal Declaration (Gauthier, 2008) also acknowledges that psychologists should attend to specific cultural penchants to correct for and minimize potential harm caused by research activities, as outlined in the principle of Competent Caring for the Well-Being of Persons and Peoples.

8.07 *Deception in Research*

Deception is used in many studies in the United States, and the APA code (2002) requires that psychologists do not conduct a study involving deception unless they can justify its use by the study's significant scientific, educational, or applied value, and if effective nondeceptive alternatives are not possible (APA, 2002). IRBs in the United States treat deception seriously in order to prevent it from introducing undue risks to participants, particularly in terms of trust violations, in the hope of preserving the respect and dignity of participants (Matsumoto & Jones, 2008). Following participation in a study involving deception, it is typically required that participants be fully debriefed about the true nature of the study, and they are often asked for their consent to use the data. That is, for research conducted within the United States there are specific guidelines and regulations for researching involving the use of deception.

However, IRBs do not exist in many other countries, making the use of deception in such countries easier (Matsumoto & Jones, 2008). Confounded with language barriers and an elevated power imbalance between researchers and participants (Bhutta, 2004; Karim et al., 1998), potential for exploitation due to participant misunderstanding is higher in other cultures. With an elevated ease in using deception and risk of exploitation, Matsumoto and Jones (2008) argue that American psychologists conducting international cross-cultural research have greater obligation to exercise caution. International cross-cultural research involving deception needs to be conducted with additional care and caution, possibly by collaborating with cultural informants who can gauge the necessity of the deception, and by obtaining true informed consent and using full debriefing procedures for participants to preserve individual participant integrity (Matsumoto & Jones, 2008).

The Universal Declaration (Gauthier, 2008) highlights Integrity as a key principle to which psychologists should aspire. Fundamentally rooted in being honest, for psychologists to ensure integrity they must recognize, monitor, and manage potential conflicts of interest that could result in the exploitation of participants. Psychologists' own self-interest in deception may interfere with the best interests of the participants (Gauthier, 2008). Cultural differences in necessary levels of disclosure exist (Gauthier, 2008; Matsumoto & Jones, 2008) and the Universal Declaration recommends that psychologists should avoid incomplete disclosure of information unless complete disclosure is culturally inappropriate, violates confidentiality, or may be harmful to the participants themselves, their family, group, or community. However, no current ethical guidelines exist that set standards for what is considered "culturally inappropriate" or harmful to participants in countries that do not have IRBs. Culturally sensitive requirements for researchers' justification of deception, similar to those outlined by the APA code (2002), are necessary for American psychologists researching abroad.

8.10 Reporting Research Results

A primary concern with the reporting of research results is how the results will be subsequently interpreted and used by the academic community. The APA code of ethics (2002) is vague on specifying standards for using research results. That is, standard 8.10 merely requires that psychologists do not fabricate their research, and if errors are made in published data, they are corrected. Standard 5.01a of the APA code of ethics, however, requires that psychologists do not make public (e.g., publish) work that is knowingly false, deceptive, or fraudulent (APA, 2002). Several ethical dilemmas associated with cross-cultural research jeopardize the validity of inferences that can be drawn from research conducted on groups with which American psychologists are not familiar.

Ethical dilemmas can arise in the administering of surveys or tests in cultures unfamiliar to American psychologists and for which the instruments were not designed. More specifically, Foxcroft (2002) noted that in testing situations, particular attention needs to be paid to the testing context to ensure that the test-taker does not perceive the test, or its outcomes, to be unfair or in violation of some ethical standard (Foxcroft, 2002). Imposing a Westernized testing system on a community within an African region, whose members have no experience with "test-taking," is problematic when decisions are made or research is developed based on the test results (Foxcroft, 2002, Gil & Bob, 1999). In response to such concerns, the International Test Commission (ITC; 2001) has highlighted key ethical testing practices that assessment practitioners should follow when conducting analyses in cross-cultural international research in their "International Guidelines for Test Use." The ITC (2001) indicates key competencies necessary for assessment practitioners to have, spanning an entire range of testing processes: strong knowledge of psychometrics and testing, an understanding of the broader social context in which the test is being used and the manner in which such contextual factors may influence test results, results interpretation, and the way in which the results are used (Foxcroft, 2002; Gil & Bob, 1999; ITC, 2001).

If an assessment practitioner or researcher wants to follow ethical testing practices, the extent to which a test or survey is administered to a particular sample should be decided before administration and after issues of bias and re-norming have been addressed (Foxcroft, 2002). Additionally, for some cultures it is important for practitioners and researchers to have knowledge about the test-takers in relation to their family, community, and general cultural environment in order for fair, valid, and ethical conclusions to be drawn (Foxcroft, 2002).

Gil and Bob (1999) argued that culturally sensitive researchers should only select tests based on cultural orientation information. Cultural factors affect the interpretation of many standardized psychological tests, and misinterpretations occur when a psychologists uses a test on a population for which no normative data exists. Psychologists often conduct research in cultures for which no information is available on how to provide meaningful interpretation. The APA ethics code does not prohibit such research, but warns researchers to use caution and discretion when interpreting results.

Additionally, cross-cultural researchers are often interested in studying differences between cultures. One consequence of this interest is that the reporting of differences may help perpetuate stereotypes of differences held by consumers of the research (Matsumoto & Jones, 2008). For example, as Matsumoto and Jones (2008) suggest, it is fairly easy to take research findings documenting differences between Americans and South Koreans and make statements that overgeneralize those findings to all members of those groups. The incorrect interpretation of results of cross-cultural research can be used to ignore individual differences within those cultural groups. Often times, interpretation of cultural differences are not based on empirical evidence and are, instead, based on assumptions of the researchers that are not empirically grounded (Matsumoto & Jones, 2008). For example, Matsumoto and Jones cite a study conducted by Iwata and Higuchi (2000), who compared Japanese and Americans using the State-Trait Anxiety Inventory (STAI). Iwata and Higuchi (2000) found that Japanese were less likely to report positive feelings, and more likely to report higher state and trait anxiety than Americans. Iwata and Higuchi (2000) make one assumption, among many others, that Japanese—as a collective culture—are more likely to put the well-being of their group over that of themselves. However, Matsumoto and Jones note that this assumption has no empirical basis and is simply a stereotype of Japan as a collectivist society.

In addition to stereotypical interpretations of research findings, cross-cultural research findings are also susceptible to biased and ethnocentric interpretations. Researchers interpret their data through their own "cultural filters" (Matsumoto & Jones, 2008) and in particular for American psychologists, interpretation of American results compared against those of another country are often influenced by an implicit assumption that the American results are "normal" and the other country's scores are "deviant."

In light of these concerns, Matsumoto and Jones (2008) argue that researchers have an obligation to be aware of their own biases and, to avoid any inappropriate usage of their findings, should take steps such as carefully describing their findings in their own writings and correcting misinterpretations of their findings made by others. Indeed, the Universal Declaration's principles of Integrity and Professional and Scientific Responsibilities to Society suggest that psychologists conducting cross-cultural research should maximize impartiality and minimize bias, and should also be as sensitive, aware, and self-correcting as possible. By aspiring to these principles, psychologists would ameliorate concerns of unethical inferences made about cross-cultural comparisons. However, no such standards guiding these aspirations have been implemented for American psychologists.

Recommendations

Thus far, ethical dilemmas stemming from section 8—Research and Publication—of the APA's code (2002), related to conducting international cross-cultural psychological research, have been examined. Whether it be through issues of IRB approval, obtaining true informed consent, participant inducement, the researcher-subject relationship, deception, or use of results, it is clear that the APA code is not sufficient to guide the cross-cultural international research of American psychologists. In light of expansive globalization and international education and exchange, the need for ethical guidelines to regulate cross-cultural international research is ever-pressing. Though the Universal Declaration (Gauthier, 2008) provides a values framework and attempts to shed light on the issue, it does not offer specific or practical guidelines for international research, nor was it intended to do so. Below, a series of frameworks are described that may aid in the development of a code of ethics specific to American psychologists who conduct cross-cultural international research.

In response to a pressing need for culturally sensitive ethical guidelines, the APA "Resolution on Culture and Gender Awareness in International Psychology" was formulated by the Council of Representatives on July 28, 2004. This APA resolution can serve as another framework to guide an understanding of the ethical challenges inherent in conducting cross-cultural research. The passing of this resolution was largely influenced by a set of astounding figures and a growing awareness of a set of issues facing the world of psychology. That is, an estimated 60% (or more) of the world's psychologists now live outside the United States (Hogan, 1995). These psychologists have generated perspectives, methods, practices, and collected data that correspond to the specific needs of the people in their societies, relevant to the development of a more complete "psychology" of people (Bhopal, 2001; Espin & Gaweleck, 1992; Martin-Baro, 1994; Weiss, Whelan & Gupta, 2000; Winslow, Honein, & Elzubeir, 2002). However, U.S. leadership in world psychology is sometimes perceived as disproportionably influential, partly because of access to research funds, an abundance of American publication outlets, and the wide acceptance of the English language (Kağitçibasi in Sunar, 1998; Sloan 2000). As a result, American-grounded, normed, and structured measures dominate American empirical psychology, while internationally based, qualitative methods, such as community action research, are less known or valued in the United States (Denzin & Lincoln, 2001; Murray & Chamberlain, 1999; Robson, 1993). Additionally, American assessment procedures, tests, and normative standards have been used extensively in other countries, sometimes without consideration of cultural differences that affect reliability and validity (Dana, 2000), as methods of clinical diagnosis are exported to other cultures based on U.S. norms and values (Foa, Keane, & Friedman, 2000; Mezzich, 2002; Nakane & Nakane, 2002; Thorne & Lambers, 1998). Ultimately, there is a need to develop and disseminate materials that will facilitate the training of psychologists to conduct culturally appropriate research and practice around the world (diMauro, Gilbert, & Parker, 2003; Friedman, 1997; Hays, 2001).

With the passing of the APA "Resolution on Culture and Gender Awareness in International Psychology" it is resolved that the APA will abide by the following ten guidelines: (1) advocate for more research on the role that cultural ideologies have in the experience of women and men across and within countries on the basis of sex, gender identity, gender expression, ethnicity, social class, age, disabilities, and religion; (2) advocate for more collaborative research partnerships with colleagues from diverse cultures and countries, leading to mutually beneficial dialogues and learning opportunities; (3) advocate for critical research that analyzes how cultural, economic, and geopolitical perspectives may be embedded within U.S. psychological research and practice; (4) encourage more attention to a critical examination of international cultural, gender, gender identity, age, and disability perspectives in psychological theory, practice, and research at all levels of psychological education and training curricula; (5) encourage psychologists to gain an understanding of the experiences of individuals in diverse cultures and their points of view, and to value pluralistic world views, ways of knowing, organizing, functioning, and standpoints; (6) encourage psychologists to become aware of and understand how systems of power hierarchies may influence the privileges, advantages, and rewards that usually accrue by virtue of placement and power; (7) encourage psychologists to understand how power hierarchies may influence the production and dissemination of knowledge in psychology internationally and to alter their practices according to the ethical insights that emerge from this understanding; (8) encourage psychologists to appreciate the multiple dilemmas and contradictions inherent in valuing culture and actual cultural practices when they are oppressive to women, but congruent with the practices of diverse ethnic groups; (9) advocate for cross-national research that analyzes and supports the elimination of cultural, gender, gender identity, age, and disability discrimination in all arenas—economic, social, educational, and political; and (10) support public policy that supports global change toward egalitarian relationships and the elimination of practices and conditions oppressive to women. Based on this resolution, a call to action to consider cross-cultural ethical practices is imperative. Work on cross-cultural ethics has emerged in related disciplines.

An additional framework that may provide some guidance to U.S. psychologists conducting international research comes from the International School Psychology Association (ISPA). The ISPA executive committee approved this ethical code in July, 1990, and recommended its adoption as a statement of ethics for the association by the membership at its 1991 Colloquium (Oakland, Goldman, & Bischoff, 1997).

The ISPA code of ethics for research (section III) has general (part A) stipulations that include: School psychologists strive to avoid cultural, racial, social class, or ethnic biases in their research (stipulation 1), and school psychologists consider unintended direct and indirect consequences of research activities for various members of the community (stipulation 13). Further, under Cross-Cultural Research (part B), stipulations concern cross-cultural issues directly: (1) School psychologists abide by the research ethics of the country in which they are performing their studies, (2) school psychologists demonstrate a respect for the host culture and avoid actions that violate cultural expectations or reveal culturally biased perspectives while formulating the research problem, executing the study, or reporting findings; (3) school psychologists undertaking cross-cultural research are knowledgeable in cross-cultural methodology and familiar with the cultural context of the research setting. The investigator should exercise care while selecting measuring instruments, particularly when these are to be used for cross-cultural comparisons and while interpreting cultural differences (Oakland, Goldman, and Bischoff, 1997).

Conclusion

Much in the same way that the ISPA has evolved their own code of ethics to deal with the ethical challenges created by international and cross-cultural research, the same process has to occur within APA as it deals with the challenges of globalization. The Universal Declaration (Gauthier, 2008) can provide a culturally sensitive framework that can aid in the development of more specific APA standards for American psychologists conducting international cross-cultural research. It is our position that ethical principles like those in the Universal Declaration (Gauthier, 2008) need to be supplemented with ethical standards that provide clear and specific guidance in the conduct of international research undertaken by American psychologists. In conclusion, a major purpose of this chapter is a "Call to Action" for the American Psychological Association, particularly their Committee on International Relations in Psychology (CIRP) and the Division of International Psychology, to begin to assess and evaluate the nature and extent of ethical problems in conducting cross-cultural research among its members.

A useful place to start would be to conduct a census among psychology faculty in the United States who are currently (last 12 months) conducting or have during the last 5 years conducted international or cross-cultural research outside of the United States. Such a survey would help us obtain an idea of the degree of the challenges we are facing, and also serve as a baseline for monitoring future increases or decreases in international psychological research. Since the APA Office of Workforce Analysis routinely collects data on its members, it should not be difficult to add a few questions into their survey to obtain this information. A variation of this association-wide approach within APA would be a census conducted among the members of the APA Division of International Psychology (Division 52).

While the APA Resolution on Culture and Gender Awareness in International Psychology and the ISPA ethical codes can provide some guidance in the interim, the American Psychological Association needs to provide much more systematic attention to the ethical challenges created by the increasing international and cross-cultural research being conducted by its members.

References

American Psychological Association. (2002). Ethical principles of psychologists and code of conduct, *American Psychologist*, 57, 1060–1073. Bhopal, K. (2001). Researching South Asian women: Issues of sameness and difference in the research process. *Journal of Gender Studies*, 10, 279–286.

Bhutta, V. A. (2004). Beyond informed consent, *Bulletin of the World Health Organization*, 82, 771–777.

Dana, R. H. (2000). An assessment-intervention model for research and practice with multicultural populations. In R. H. Dana (Ed.), *Handbook of cross-cultural and multicultural personality assessment* (pp. 5–16). Mahwah, NJ: Lawrence Erlbaum.

Denzin, N., & Lincoln, Y. (Eds.) (2001). *Handbook of qualitative research*. Thousand Oaks, CA: Sage Publications, Inc.

European Federation of Professional Psychologists Associations (EFPA). (1995). *Metacode of ethics*. Brussels: Author.

Foa, E. B., Keane, T. M., & Friedman, M. J. (Eds.) (2000). *Effective treatments for PTSD: Practice guidelines from the International Society for Traumatic Stress Studies*. New York: Guilford Press.

Foxcroft, C. D. (2002). Ethical issues related to psychological testing in Africa: What I have learned (so far). In W. J. Lonner, D. L. Dinnel, S. A. Hayes, & D. N. Sattler (Eds.), *Online Readings in Psychology and Culture*. International Association for Cross-Cultural Psychology, Retrieved from http://orpc.iaccp.org/index.php?option=com_content&view=article&id=45%3Afoxcroft&catid=23%3Achapter&Itemid=2

Friedman, S. (Ed.) (1997). *Cultural issues in the treatment of anxiety*. New York: Guilford.

Gauthier, J. (2008). Universal declaration of ethical principles for psychologists. In J. E. Hall & E. M. Altmaier (Eds.), *Global promise: Quality assurance and accountability in professional psychology* (pp. 98–105). New York: Oxford University Press.

Gil, E. F., & Bob, S. (1999). Culturally competent research: An ethical perspective. *Clinical Psychology Review*, 19, 45–55.

Giller, J. (1998). Caring for victims of torture in Uganda: Some personal reflections. In P. Bracken & C. Petty (Eds.), *Rethinking the trauma of war* (pp. 128–145). London: Free Association Books.

Goodwin, R. (2002). Conducting cross-cultural psychological research in changing cultures: Some ethical and logistical considerations. In W. J. Lonner, D. L. Dinnel, S. A. Hayes, & D. N. Sattler (Eds.), *Online readings in psychology and culture*. International Association for Cross-Cultural Psychology, Retrieved from http://orpc.iaccp.org/index.php?option=com_content&view=article&id=49%3Arobingoodwin&catid=3%3Achapter&Itemid=2

Hays, P. A. (2001). *Addressing cultural complexities in practice: A framework for clinicians and counselors*. Washington, DC: American Psychological Association Books.

Hogan, J. D. (1995) International psychology in the next century: Comment and speculation from a U.S. perspective. *World Psychology, 1*, 9–25.

Institute of International Education (2008). 2008 Annual Report. Retrieved from http://www.iie.org/en/Who-We-Are/Annual-Report/-/media/Files/Corporate/AR/2008-IIE-Annual-Report.ashx

International Test Commission (ITC). (2001). International guidelines for test use. *International Journal of Testing, 1*, 93–114.

Iwata, N., & Higuchi, H. R. (2000). Responses of Japanese and American university students to the STAI items that assess the presence or absence of anxiety. *Journal of Personality Assessment, 74*(1), 48–62.

Karim, A., Qurraishi, S. S., Coovadia, H. M., & Susser, M. (1998). Consent for HIV testing in a South African hospital: Is it truly informed or truly voluntary? *American Journal of Public Health, 88*, 637–640.

Lindsay, G. (1996). Psychology as an ethical discipline and profession. *European Psychologist, 1,* 79–88. London, L. (2002). Ethical oversight of public health research: Can rules and IRBs make a difference in developing countries? *American Journal of Public Health, 92*, 1079–1084.

Matsumoto, D., & Jones, C.A.L. (2008). Ethical issues in cross-cultural psychology. In D. M. Mertens & P. E. Ginsberg (Eds.), *The handbook of social research ethics*. (pp. 323–336). Thousand Oaks, CA: SAGE Publications.

Mezzich, J. E. (2002). International surveys on the use of ICD-10 and related diagnostic systems. *Psychopathology, 35*(2–3), 72–75.

Molyneux, C., Wassenaar, D., Peshu, N., & Marsh, K. (2005). Community voices on the notion and practice of informed consent for biomedical research. *Social Science & Medicine, 61*, 443–454.

Murray, M., & Chamberlain, K. (Eds.). (1999). *Qualitative health psychology theories and methods*. London: Sage Publications Ltd.

Nakane, Y., & Nakane, H. (2002). Classification systems for psychiatric diseases currently used in Japan. *Psychopathology, 35*(2–3), 191–194.

Oakland, T., Goldman, S., & Bischoff, H. (1997). Code of ethics of the International School Psychology Association. *School Psychology International, 18*, 291–298.

Pettifor, J. L. (2007). Toward a global professionalization of psychology. In M. J. Stevens & U. P. Gielin (Eds.), *Toward a global psychology: Theory, research, intervention, and pedagogy* (pp. 229–331). Mahwah, NJ: Laurence Erlbaum.

Ritchie, P. L. J. (2008). Codes of ethics, conduct, and standards as vehicles of accountability. In J. E. Hall & E. M. Altmaier (Eds.), *Global promise: Quality assurance and accountability in professional psychology* (pp. 73–97). New York: Oxford University Press.

Robson, C. (1993). *Real world research*. Oxford, UK: Blackwell.

Sloan, T., (Ed.). (2000). *Critical psychology: Voices for change*. Hampshire, England: Palgrave.

Sunar. D. (1998). An interview with Cigdem Kağitçibasi. *World Psychology, 2*, 139–152.

Tantink, M. (2004). Not talking about traumatic experiences: Harmful or healing? Coping with war memories in southwest Uganda. *Intervention, 2*, 3–17.

Thorne, B., & Lambers, E. (Eds.). (1998). *Person-centered therapy: A European perspective*. London: Sage Publications, Ltd.

United States Embassy Beijing. (2000). *Human research subject protection in China: Implications for U.S. collaborators*. Retrieved from the library Institute of Chinese Studies, University of Heidelberg website: http://www.usembassy-china.org.cn/sandt/humanresearchsubjectprotection.htm.

White, M. T. (2007). Guidelines for IRB review of international collaborative medical research: A proposal. *The Journal of Law, Medicine, and Ethics, 27*, 87–94.

Winslow, W., Honein, G., Elzubeir, M. (2002). Seeking Emirati women's voices: The use of focus groups with an Arab population. *Qualitative Health Research, 12*, 566–576.

CHAPTER 12

Ethical Issues of Web-Based Interventions and Online Therapy

Michelle Hilgart, Frances P. Thorndike, Jose Pardo, *and* Lee M. Ritterband

Abstract

Increased access to and use of the Internet is significantly impacting health care, psychological practice, and clinical research, leading to the development of a new field called *eHealth*. This chapter highlights the ethical issues associated with providing psychological interventions over the Internet, in the context of both research trials and delivery of clinical services. It covers both the ethical benefits of eHealth (greater access to treatment, increased options for communication, enhanced convenience, potential cost savings, and improved data collection) and the challenges surrounding the delivery of eHealth (informed consent, privacy and confidentiality, appropriateness of online treatment, online assessment, identity verification, data validity, communication, competence, crisis intervention, and legal concerns). By more clearly defining eHealth interventions, the inherent ethical challenges can become more transparent and ethics codes can be more aptly developed. While ethics codes will be challenged to keep pace with evolving technologies, researchers should continue to investigate the ethical benefits and challenges of delivering eHealth interventions and then work to make these benefits and risks known through evolving codes of practice.

Key Words: eHealth, ethics, Internet intervention, online treatment, psychological intervention

The advent of the Internet and other information-communication technologies (ICTs) such as computers, information networks and software, as well as telephony, cable, satellite, and radio, have brought a wide range of changes that have profoundly influenced how people view the world and with whom they communicate and interact regularly (Barnett & Scheetz, 2003; Jerome & Zaylor, 2000). These new technologies have influenced not only individual lifestyles, but have had far-reaching implications for global connectivity and the availability of information, including health information (Fox, 2006). Internet usage has increased worldwide in the past decade, from under 400 million users in 2000 to nearly 2 billion users in 2010 (Internet World Stats, 2010), becoming an integral component of everyday life for many people worldwide (Barak, 1999; Midkiff & Wyatt, 2008; Tate & Zabinksi, 2004). Growth in usage from 2000–2010 has been particularly dramatic in Africa, the Middle East, and Latin America/Caribbean countries. Europe, North America, and Oceania/Australia have reached over 50% penetration as a percent of population.

This increased access to and usage of the Internet is having a significant impact on health care (Eysenbach, 2001) and psychological practice (Barnett & Scheetz, 2003), and has led to the new field of eHealth. In 2001, Gunther Eysenbach defined eHealth as:

> ...an emerging field in the intersection of medical informatics, public health and business, referring to health service and information delivered or enhanced through the Internet and related technologies. In a broader sense, the term characterizes not only a

technical development, but also a state-of-mind, a way of thinking, an attitude, and a commitment for networked, global thinking, to improve health care locally, regionally, and worldwide by using information and communication technology.
(*Eysenbach*, 2001, p. e20)

A particularly promising component of eHealth is the way that the Internet can be used to deliver psychotherapeutic and behavioral health interventions (Childress, 2000). Scientists and practitioners now have the ability to provide highly specialized psychological and health interventions to people all over the world (Ritterband et al., 2003). Benefits include: greater access to treatment (Barak, Hen, Boniel-Nissim, & Shapira, 2008; Barak, Klein, & Proudfoot, 2009; Griffiths, Lindenmeyer, Powell, Lowe, & Thorogood, 2006; Manhal-Baugus, 2001; Ritterband et al., 2003), increased options for communication (Abbott, Klein, & Ciechomski, 2008; Manhal-Baugus, 2001; Midkiff & Wyatt, 2008), increased convenience (Abbott et al., 2008; Griffiths et al., 2006; Mallen, Vogel, & Rochlen, 2005; Midkiff & Wyatt, 2008), potential cost savings (Griffiths et al., 2006; Tate, Finkelstein, Khayjou, & Gustafson, 2009), and improved data collection (Eyde, Robertson, & Krug, 2010). However, there are also ethical challenges surrounding the delivery of eHealth care, including issues of informed consent (Campbell, Vasquez, Behnke, & Kinscherff, 2010; Fisher, 2009; Fisher & Oransky, 2008; Manhal-Baugus, 2001), privacy and confidentiality (Campbell et al., 2010; Fisher, 2009; Kraus, Zack, & Stricker, 2004), appropriateness of online treatment (Campbell et al., 2010; Fisher, 2009; Kraus et al., 2004), online assessment and diagnoses (Abbott et al., 2008; Manhal-Baugus, 2001), identity verification (Manhal-Baugus, 2001), data validity (Mallen et al., 2005; Midkiff & Wyatt, 2008), communication (Abbott et al., 2008; Koocher, 2007; Kraus et al., 2004; Maheu & Gordon, 2000), competence (Bersoff, 2008), crisis intervention (Bersoff, 2008), and legal concerns (Koocher, 2007; Mallen et al., 2005). This chapter addresses the ethical issues associated with providing psychological interventions over the Internet, either through research trials or through direct care.

Defining Online Psychological Treatment

There are two primary ways in which the Internet is being used to deliver psychological care: web-based interventions and online counseling and therapy. A web-based intervention is defined as, "A primarily self-guided intervention that is executed by means of a prescriptive online program operated through a website and used by consumers seeking health- and mental-health related assistance" (Barak et al., 2009, p. 5). The program attempts to create positive change and/or improve and enhance knowledge, awareness, and understanding by the use of reliable health-related material and web-based components, including content, multimedia, interactivity, and guidance/feedback. Some consider purely education-based websites (e.g., health education websites providing educational content without a structured behavior-based component) as web-based interventions. And, in fact, some recent meta-analyses found that web-based education interventions can achieve medium to high mean effect sizes (Barak et al., 2008; Spek et al., 2007). However, more typically, web-based interventions focus on content that is formulated in a comprehensive manner and presented in a highly structured format. The content is informed by theory—for example, cognitive behavioral theory (CBT)—and modeled on evidence-based, face-to-face treatment and prevention programs that have been operationalized for Internet delivery (Ritterband et al., 2003). These programs range from fully automated systems to programs backed by significant human support. There is now strong evidence of the efficacy of web-based interventions (Barak et al., 2008; Murray et l., 2005; Spek et al., 2007).

Online counseling and therapy is defined as "the use of Internet-based communication for therapeutic purpose…" (Barak et al., 2009, p. 9). Online counseling allows clinicians to conduct treatment with clients using the Internet, without regard to geographical location and with expanded convenience. In online therapy, the traditional "office appointment" is no longer the primary method of interaction, and writing may support or even replace talking as the primary means of communication. Barak and colleagues identify four communication modalities used in online counseling and therapy: (1) individual, (2) group, (3) synchronous (being online at the same time and communicating in real time), and (4) asynchronous (being online at separate times without communicating in real time). In the use of individual, synchronous communication, a clinician and client interact online simultaneously in real time, for example by using instant messaging. In group use, members of a group may communicate with one another and the clinician using electronic communications at separate times (asynchronous communication), for example by using an online discussion group. These modalities significantly shape the ways clinicians and clients communicate and interact with one another during treatment. Despite methodological difficulties, published quantitative studies provide some support for the effectiveness of online therapy (Barak et al., 2009).

Ethical Benefits in Delivering eHealth Care

As psychological and behavioral treatments take advantage of the Internet and other ICTs, the human interactions and relationships that surround these treatments will likely change. As ethical researchers and practitioners, it is important to consider the kinds of personal practices, social interactions, legal and political norms, and lasting principles that will emerge from these changes in psychology practice. To guide this inquiry, the specific ethical benefits, or the advantages and opportunities surrounding eHealth care, are considered.

Expanded Access

Expanded Access to Treatment. As the Internet continues to become available to more users, eHealth interventions have the potential to reach ever-greater numbers of people (Barak et al., 2008, 2009; Ritterband et al., 2003; Sampson, Kolodinsky, & Greeno, 1997). Web-based interventions and online therapy offer the potential to increase access to care by helping clients overcome many of the barriers encountered with obtaining traditional care. Individuals can seek treatments that are not constrained by geographical location of providers, the number of specialty providers, or the higher costs that can be associated with more traditional psychological services (Ritterband et al., 2003). Individuals also have increased opportunities to participate in clinical research when the intervention being examined occurs online and they are able to participate without a face-to-face component.

eHealth care may also have the potential to reduce health disparity, particularly disparity caused by geographical isolation. Global health disparities are particularly common in mental health (Tomlinson et al., 2009). Mental health disorders make a substantial contribution to the burden of disease worldwide, are costly to treat, and are linked to other health conditions (Prince et al., 2007). Yet, health systems around the world face a scarcity of financial resources and qualified staff to treat mental and behavioral health problems. The situation is exacerbated in low-income and middle-income countries by lack of public health policy and funding for mental health initiatives (Tomlinson et al., 2009).

In Griffiths et al.'s (2006) systematic review of healthcare interventions delivered over the Internet, reaching isolated groups was one of the purposes for the intervention cited by the authors of 13 of the 28 interventions included in the review. The authors of five studies stated overcoming geographical isolation as their primary reason for delivering their intervention via the Internet (Griffiths et al., 2006) The ability to increase global access to treatment is a significant ethical benefit of web-based interventions and online counseling, and allows additional treatment opportunities that would not otherwise be available (Barak et al., 2009; Manhal-Baugus, 2001; Sampson et al., 1997).

Expanded Access to Assessment. Currently, the testing industry is a multibillion-dollar sector of the economy, and psychological assessments are widely used in clinics, schools, and the workplace for decision making and diagnosis. Test use has expanded substantially during the past decade, and much of the recent increase in test use has resulted from access to ICTs and the increased use of psychological assessments as tools for decision making in clinical assessment (Eyde et al., 2010). A benefit of web-based interventions is the ability to expand and facilitate access to assessments; that is, making assessments that have been proven valid and reliable available to people who can benefit from greater access to the results of the assessment.

Increased Communication and Convenience

Communication. The Internet allows for greater communication with the web-based program, clinician, support person, or researcher, than may be possible in a weekly, face-to-face session. This increased communication, in turn, has the potential to increase a client's continuity of care and to encourage levels of therapeutic alliance that may be comparable to face-to-face treatment (Abbott et al., 2008). In the delivery of web-based, human-supported interventions and online counseling, clients may have an arrangement where no appointment is needed and they may contact their therapist by email whenever they have access to an Internet-connected computer (Manhal-Baugus, 2001). This allows clients increased opportunities for communication with their clinician, more freedom and time to compose messages to their therapist or support person, and more time to reflect on their therapist's messages. Email also provides an automatic record of communications, which can be referred to as often as needed (Midkiff & Wyatt, 2008). In the case of web-delivered interventions without support, there are still increased opportunities to engage with the program that are not dependent on schedule or availability of a clinician.

Communication can also be enhanced by enabling clinicians, using online therapy or web-based interventions, to assign and monitor homework that is stored online (Midkiff & Wyatt, 2008; Wiggins Frame, 1997). This has the potential to allow the tracking of progress over time because the full record of homework, completed online assignments or questionnaires, and email or other electronic communication is saved online and can be accessed and reviewed by the clinician and client as needed. In face-to-face or telephone contact, communication that is not recorded is not available for future review.

Convenience. Clients may also benefit from the comfort and convenience of being in their own space when they are interacting with their clinician or web-based intervention program (Abbott et al., 2008; Griffiths et al., 2006; Midkiff & Wyatt, 2008). This can potentially allow clients to feel less inhibited and more willing to disclose feelings and experiences that could potentially accelerate the rate of therapeutic change (Manhal-Baugus, 2001). The increased convenience of online counseling and web-based interventions may also provide another way to maintain contact with those who would otherwise drop out (including those who move). Examples of people who may benefit from increased mobile interactions are students who move away to college and people who travel frequently for business (Mallen et al., 2005).

Increased convenience (combined with reducing cost) was also identified as a rationale for development of Internet interventions in 20 of the 28 interventions studied in Griffiths et al.'s (2006) systematic review. With respect to increased convenience, users specifically noted saving time, requiring less effort, and receiving more accessible interventions (Griffiths et al., 2006).

Cost Effectiveness

Cost effectiveness is one of the most frequently cited reasons for developing Internet-delivered interventions (Griffiths et al., 2006; Tate et al., 2009). However, a review of Internet interventions between 1995 and 2008 (Tate et al., 2009) identified only eight studies that specifically reported on the cost effectiveness or cost benefit associated with an Internet intervention, thus demonstrating how few studies have looked at the economic analysis of Internet interventions despite the growing body of outcome research. While it may appear obvious that eHealth care options will save costs, additional research is necessary.

Case Example 1
Ethical Dilemma: Access to Treatment

This example demonstrates increased access to treatment, increased convenience, and cost savings in providing treatment over the Internet.

Sharon, a 52-year-old widow and mother of four children, lives in a rural, southeastern community in the United States. She has experienced sleep problems for more than 10 years. Over this time she has followed the advice of her family doctor for good sleep hygiene (e.g., no napping) and tried over-the-counter medications, natural sleep remedies, and even prescription sleep medicine. Despite these efforts, Sharon found only brief periods of relief that eventually resulted in a relapse and continued sleep problems. Sharon complained that she was not able to concentrate and believed her work performance worsened when she was sleeping poorly. She was eager to find a solution to her sleep problems and found a psychologist who specialized in cognitive behavioral therapy for insomnia (CBT-I), a treatment proven to be effective for insomnia. Sharon was very interested in the treatment, but it was a 2-hour drive from her home to the therapist's office. Sharon knew she would not be able to take time off work and arrange childcare for her children in order to regularly engage in the treatment. There was no one closer to Sharon's home offering the type of treatment she needed. The therapist told Sharon about an Internet intervention, SHUTi (Sleep Healthy Using the Internet), which delivers personalized and tailored CBT-I recommendations and has been shown to be efficacious in adults with insomnia. Sharon, who was comfortable using computers and had Internet access at home, wanted to try the program. Sharon was a good candidate for using a self-guided Internet intervention. She felt comfortable reading text on the computer and did not mind entering personal information into the program. She used a unique login ID and password to access the program. Sharon appreciated that she could use SHUTi when it was most convenient for her, and the program was more affordable than face-to-face sessions that would require taking time off work, finding and paying for childcare, and making the long drive to the therapist's office. Sharon successfully completed the SHUTi program over 9 weeks and followed program recommendations. Assessments completed by Sharon at the end of the program indicated that she had improved her sleep and no longer met the clinical definition of insomnia. Sharon was sleeping well regularly and felt better than she had in years. She also felt confident that she had learned the strategies she would need to prevent a relapse in her sleep problems.

Enhanced Data Collection for Research

One of the clear advantages of using the Internet in the collection of research data is the ability to reach samples that have been difficult to access in the past (Birnbaum, 2004; Bull, Vallejos, Levine, & Ortiz, 2008; Chiasson et al., 2006; Grazina Johnston, Trummal, Lohmus, & Ravalepik, 2009; Ramo, Hall, & Prochaska, 2010). In the United States, these groups also include rural populations, people living with chronic illness or disability, and people who work evening or night shifts. Globally, people living in low-income and middle-income developing countries may have inadequate local or regional opportunities to participate in health research. Yet, people in such countries have increased their use of the Internet through smart phones and other wireless connection options, thus making the Internet a viable option for the collection of research data with these populations (Kim, Kelly, & Raja, 2010). Reaching and assessing outcomes in more diverse populations will allow less biased conclusions to be reached in research.

In 2006, a 10-year study of the global mental health research literature showed that between 1992–2001, 94% of the mental health research was contributed by countries representing 15% of the world's population, whereas 85% of the world's population contributed just 6% to the internationally accessible mental health literature. Countries not represented and underrepresented in the database were mid-sized countries with populations above 5 million people (e.g., Chad, Guinea, Honduras, Rwanda, Somalia; see Saxena, Paraje, Sharan, Karam, & Sadana, 2006).

In addition, Internet studies reduce other barriers to research participation, such as scheduling appointments or having to return questionnaires by mail. Studies of response rates and reviews of recruitment methods have typically shown that efforts to recruit online yield similar or higher response rates than traditional methods (Whitehead, 2007).

Efficacy of eHealth Care

Not only are there clear ethical advantages to web-based interventions and online therapy, but the findings of meta-analyses (see Ritterband & Palermo (2009) for a list) provide strong support for the adoption of online interventions as legitimate therapeutic activities. In 2004, Wantland, Portillo, Holzemer, Laughter, and McGhee published a meta-analysis of behavioral change outcomes in web-based versus non-web-based interventions. They reported finding a "12-fold increase in MEDLINE citations for 'web-based therapies'" (p. e40) during the 7-year period of 1996–2003. Their meta-analyses on 22 studies with aggregated participant data totaling 11,754 participants (5,841 women and 5,729 men) and an average age of 41.5 years, showed an improvement in outcomes for individuals using web-based interventions in the attainment of specified knowledge and/or behavior change for studied outcome variables (Wantland et al., 2004). These outcome variables included, among others, 18-month weight-loss maintenance, increased exercise time, increased knowledge of nutritional status, and increased knowledge of asthma treatment.

In 2008, a comprehensive review and meta-analysis of the effectiveness of Internet-based psychotherapeutic interventions was conducted (Barak et al., 2008). Including intervention studies that had been published up to 2006, 92 studies with a total of 9,764 participants who were treated through various Internet-based psychological interventions were analyzed. The overall mean weighted effect size was 0.53 (medium effect), which is similar to the average effect size of traditional, face-to-face therapy (Barak et al., 2008).

While many web-based interventions and online counseling should not be considered a replacement of face-to-face interventions, they can be viewed as a method for providing access to individuals who would not otherwise seek or obtain treatment (Barak et al., 2008, 2009; Ritterband et al., 2003). In other cases, Internet-delivered care may serve as an adjunct to more traditional psychological services. As evidence continues to support the effectiveness of eHealth care, more interventions will likely be created and tested, providing an evidence base for future development and paving the way for further widespread dissemination of effective interventions. Although the benefits of eHealth care appear significant, this potential for increased access to Internet-delivered psychological and behavioral health programs forces us to also consider the ethical challenges that arise with this mode of delivering treatment.

Ethical Challenges in Delivering eHealth Care

As with all healthcare interventions, the evaluation of potential benefit from using the Internet and other ICTs to provide care must be balanced against potential harm (Childress & Asamen, 1998). The presence of risk or ethical challenges should not preclude the use of an intervention if it is balanced by likely benefits. For web-based interventions and online therapy that have a reasonable likelihood of providing benefit to clients, the guiding principle should be ensuring that practitioners providing these interventions understand the risks, communicate these risks to potential clients or users, and minimize the risks to the extent possible (Childress, 2000).

This section evaluates the specific ethical challenges in the delivery of web-based interventions and online therapy. The challenges presented serve to highlight ethical considerations, at this point in time, in the dissemination and delivery of eHealth care. It should be recognized that new technologies are developing and evolving rapidly, necessitating frequent review of these issues. Ethical cases should be evaluated in light of existing technologies (and their capabilities), rather than using written standards alone, which may quickly become outdated (Bersoff, 2008; Fisher, 2009).

Informed Consent

For clients to elect to participate in a web-based intervention or online therapy, they need to be able to make an informed choice about their participation. As with all treatments, every effort should be made to ensure that the client understands the treatment process, any risks inherent in that process, the safeguards that have been taken to mitigate those risks, and alternative treatment options (Campbell et al., 2010; Fisher & Oransky, 2008; Manhal-Baugus, 2001). When psychological treatment is being delivered through the Internet or another ICT (which is substantively more complex than viewing content on a website), informed consent and documentation of the informed consent process must occur. Encouragingly, eHealth care is moving toward acceptance of electronic signatures to document that the informed-consent process occurred.

As part of informed consent, clients should be clearly notified of the known risks in web-based interventions or online therapy. These risks are explained in greater detail in the subsequent sections, but include: limits to privacy/confidentiality, procedures for electronic record-keeping, concerns with data validity, and procedures for handling high-risk situations. The informed consent process necessitates that care providers possess knowledge of existing laws and regulatory statutes that apply to their own provision of eHealth care so they can appropriately inform potential clients of relevant laws and statues (e.g., mandates about reporting child abuse). Given that regulations can differ from state to state and country to country, practitioners must be familiar with their unique regulations and how it will impact clients participating in their web-based interventions or receiving online therapy (Campbell et al., 2010).

Privacy and Confidentiality

Two of the most complex ethical issues confronting eHealth care, and the delivery of web-based interventions and online therapy, are those of privacy and confidentiality (Campbell et al., 2010; Fisher, 2009; Kraus et al., 2004; Nickelson, 1998). Clients should be informed that their privacy is limited by the security of the technology being used. The process of electronic transfer of client communication and information should be explained, and clients should understand how electronic communications are recorded and stored (Manhal-Baugus, 2001). Practitioners and researchers who deliver web-based interventions and online therapy must be knowledgeable about where and how breeches of privacy could occur within their respective technologies (Campbell et al., 2010; Fisher, 2009).

Safeguards are available to increase privacy when delivering web-based interventions and online therapy, and practitioners should take these steps. Efforts should be focused on protecting the security of the data being transferred between the client and the therapist or online program. Security can be enhanced by requiring the use of passwords, adding encryption, and placing communications and content behind firewalls (American Psychological Association, 2002; Campbell et al., 2010; Fisher, 2009). Without employing adequate technological security measures, Internet communication may retain confidential status only as long as no one is interested enough and knowledgeable enough to access the information (Campbell et al., 2010). Providers of web-based interventions or online therapy are ethically bound to disclose these risks to privacy and confidentiality inherent in online interactions (Baltimore, 2000; Manhal-Baugus, 2001; Midkiff & Wyatt, 2008).

Records

Psychologists must protect the confidentiality of clinical and research records from the time they are created through maintenance, dissemination, and disposal (Fisher, 2009). In the United States, the Health Insurance Portability and Accountability Act (HIPAA) of 1996 regulates the ways in which protected health information should be treated when it is delivered and stored online (Kraus et al., 2004). Practitioners should comply with HIPAA security rules (Campbell et al., 2010) and inform clients of efforts to protect confidentiality of data stored on databases and other records systems. Clients and participants in research should also be notified of the limitations of confidentiality in recordkeeping (Fisher, 2009). A significant difference between more traditional psychological treatment and online therapy is that in online therapy, verbatim records are often kept. In web-based interventions, all exchanges (e.g., email, online input) are typically captured, saved, and stored electronically.

Financial Arrangements

Those who provide online therapy or web-based interventions should clearly explain the current fee and billing policies (Kraus et al., 2004). Arrangements should be made as early as is feasible in the professional relationship (Fisher, 2009) and should safeguard the best interests of, and be understood by, all parties (Australian Psychological Society, 2007). When online treatment is covered in whole or part by third-party payers, clients and users should be notified and may need to agree to release their protected health information (Fisher, 2009; Campbell et al., 2010; Kraus et al., 2004). When online treatment and web-based interventions are not covered by clients' insurance, clients should have "secure" ways to pay for services. This may entail obtaining credit card information by phone or mail, or allowing clients to pay by check (Australian Psychological Society, 2007).

Appropriateness of Online Treatment

Potential participants in web-based interventions or online therapy should initially complete an intake, where the needs of the client can be evaluated (Manhal-Baugus, 2001). The intake procedure should help determine whether the needs of the person seeking help can potentially be met through a web-based intervention or online therapy. In certain situations, web-based interventions or online therapy may not be appropriate. For example, individuals with psychotic disorders, those with significant suicidal ideation, or current victims of violence or sexual abuse may not be appropriate candidates for Internet-delivered programs (unless the programs have been specifically targeted to these populations; see Abbott et al., 2008). The section titled "Crisis Intervention" provides more guidance on how these high-risk situations should be handled within web-based interventions and online therapy.

Individuals with limited computer knowledge, experience, or access may not be well-suited to web-based interventions or online therapy. Thus, despite increasing numbers of people with Internet access and technological capabilities, it is important to inquire about computer skills and Internet access during an intake or screening procedure (Abbott et al., 2008; Mallen et al., 2005).

The literacy level of a potential user of web-based interventions should also be considered. The ability to read and write and have comfort with text-based communication can clearly impact the client's experience with online treatment. It has been recommended that web-based interventions deliver text targeted to a 6th–8th grade reading level (Abbott et al., 2008) to allow for greater intervention adoption.

In sum, the appropriateness of web-based interventions and online therapy, as well as the efficacy of these interventions, is influenced by a variety of factors, including diagnosis, comfort with the technology, access to the Internet, and literacy level. Appropriate screening, intake, and introduction to the online treatment are essential (Sampson et al., 1997), and adequate steps should be taken to help clients similarly evaluate whether they believe online treatment can best suit their needs.

Online Assessment and Diagnosis

Clinicians using online assessments to measure and diagnose clients must understand the inherent challenges to completing evaluations through this medium. The inappropriate use of online assessments can lead to harmful diagnostic decisions based on inaccurate and misleading information (Fisher, 2009). Particular attention should be given to the risks associated with administering measures that have not yet been validated for online use. Providers must ensure that the technical aspects of the testing are appropriate, especially considering which hardware and software are required to complete the evaluations. Ideally, tests and assessments should be first validated for online use, or, in the absence of validated material, clients should be made aware that the tests being used are modeled after validated paper-based measures, but have not yet been validated for use online. Clinicians must maintain the security of testing materials and control the delivery of tests (American Psychological Association, 2002; Campbell et al., 2010). Practitioners are expected to uphold their field's standards of privacy, data protection, and confidentiality, and they must take appropriate steps to authenticate test-takers. Finally, eHealth care providers should inform clients that while online psychological assessment can offer many benefits, it is not a substitute for face-to-face evaluation (American Psychological Association, 2002; Fisher, 2009).

Identity

In fully automated web-based interventions, the lack of face-to-face contact and the reliance on primarily text-based interactions can limit the clinician or researcher's ability to verify a client's identity (Manhal-Baugus, 2001). In some cases, the inability to confirm a user's identity can be problematic, particularly when it results in unknowingly providing treatment to minors or when a clinical crisis arises and needs to be managed. In some cases, additional steps will need to be taken to authenticate the client's identity. For example, this would be necessary when providing online therapy to a minor and guardian consent is required. Some researchers and providers have opted to deal with these situations by obtaining users' local telephone or mobile phone numbers, as well as their physical addresses, as part of the intake process to allow for direct contact in the event of a clinical crisis.

Data Validity

Researchers and practitioners should recognize and mitigate the risk of delivering invalid information, both about the intervention itself and the actual intervention content. Information provided about the web-based intervention or online therapy (whether online or elsewhere) should be reviewed for accuracy and clarity (Midkiff & Wyatt, 2008). In online therapy, providers should include their degree, licensure information, years of experience, and expertise, to allow clients to evaluate the provider (Mallen et al., 2005). In web-based interventions, the creators of the intervention should be identified and their contact information should be provided. Inclusion of this information allows clients to evaluate the intervention.

Boundaries of Competence

Ethical codes of conduct guide providers to practice only within the area of competence that is achieved through their training and experience (American Psychological Association, 2002). Providers trained in traditional psychotherapy must consider whether they are competent to practice online therapy, and pursue the necessary training and supervision to competently provide this service. Similarly, developers and providers of web-based interventions must have the appropriate training, knowledge, and skills to create and manage web-based interventions. For example, providers should understand what safeguards can be taken to protect client privacy and confidentiality. Professional associations have begun to establish clear guidelines that prohibit providers from treating any problem online that they would not treat face-to-face (International Society for Mental Health Online, 2000). However, these guidelines are insufficient to enforce compliance with ethical standards (Koocher, 2007). Researchers and practitioners should consistently monitor the competencies needed to deliver their respective eHealth care interventions, given rapidly evolving technologies, and pursue additional training when needed.

Training

Closely connected to the domain of competence is training. Providers of web-based interventions and online therapy need technology-focused training to appreciate the unique demands and differences of delivering treatment through different modalities. Providers of web-based interventions and online therapists must have adequate training in the technologies in which they will be delivering care. They must understand the security precautions that are necessary to adequately protect client data, and have competence in implementing and maintaining these safeguards (Bersoff, 2008). In order to adequately support clients using these technologies, practitioners, researchers, and professionals managing web-based interventions need to know the entire scope of ethical issues that could potentially occur with each technology they use, and develop plans to help protect against known risks (Campbell et al., 2010). As the eHealth care field expands, graduate training programs will need to provide training in this field to prepare competent providers and researchers.

Crisis Intervention

Individuals who are in a crisis and need immediate clinical attention may not be best served with a web-based intervention or online therapy, unless the therapy or program has been designed specifically for such use (Abbott et al., 2008; Manhal-Baugus,

2001). Online therapists must prepare and plan for crisis intervention in the event of high-risk situations, such as risk of suicide, harm to others, and obligation to report child abuse or neglect. As in face-to-face therapy, the plan for high-risk situations should be discussed at the onset of online therapy: emergency contact numbers should be made available to the online client, including provision of contact numbers for the online therapist as well as a review of how to access to local community resources. This clearly necessitates the need for online clinicians to have some knowledge of the local community resources for each of their clients. Online therapists should also obtain contact information for their online clients should these clients require additional monitoring, follow-up, or coordination with local resources. As in face-to-face therapy, risk assessment occurs through interview with the client and additional steps are taken as indicated by the information gathered (e.g., contact with local Child Protective Services if child abuse or neglect is reported).

In a similar vein, the researchers or clinicians who manage web-based interventions and possess information about a client's identity have the responsibility for planning how clinical emergencies will be handled, should they arise. With some interventions (e.g., an intervention to manage tinnitus), it is unlikely that the professionals managing the intervention will become aware of a high-risk situation that necessitates intervention. Other interventions, however, are much more likely to assess, and therefore have knowledge of, a potentially high-risk situation (e.g., an intervention targeting depression that assesses suicidal ideation). In the latter case, safeguards should be built into the web-based intervention to ensure that a clinician can be made aware of the high-risk situation and then respond appropriately. For example, some web-based interventions have put into place a system that sends automated emails to the professionals managing the intervention when a user endorses suicidal ideation on an online questionnaire.

In both web-based interventions and online therapy, the researchers and clinicians administering the intervention have the responsibility of managing a high-risk situation should they become aware of that situation. In some cases, management of a high-risk situation could entail contact outside of the automated intervention, including having licensed clinicians conduct assessments by phone. The phone call may include referral to appropriate local resources, and follow-up contact may occur if it is needed to ensure that the patient has been able to access local treatment. Anonymous clients should be informed that if it becomes known that there is a potential for harm to themselves or others, steps may be taken to try to establish their identity and intervene to prevent harm (American Psychological Association, 2002).

Case Example 2
Ethical Dilemma: Crisis Intervention

This example demonstrates best ethical practice in confirming identity, informed consent, privacy, and crisis intervention in research providing an Internet intervention.

Researchers conducting a clinical trial examining the efficacy of an Internet intervention for adolescent depression are recruiting a sample of national adolescents in the United States. During recruitment, a self-reported 16-year-old submits an email declaring her interest in the program. The researchers inform her that, to be eligible to participate, both she and a parent/legal guardian will have to consent to participating in the trial. Later, a phone interview is conducted with the child and parent, during which the investigator discloses all potential benefits and risks to both parties. The pair is informed about limits to confidentiality and privacy, including mandates to report child abuse or neglect should it become known. The researcher obtains local telephone numbers for both the child and parent. At the conclusion of the informed consent process, both the child and parent indicate their consent through an online mechanism that allows them to access and digitally "sign" an online consent form. Several weeks into the intervention, the adolescent discloses in an email that she has been sexually assaulted by a teacher at her school. After receiving the email, the investigator contacts the participant by phone using the local phone number obtained at the outset of the trial, further assesses the situation by phone, informs the participant and parent of the requirements for disclosure, and then ultimately makes the disclosure to Child Protective Services.

Communication

With both human-supported web-based programs and online therapy, a therapeutic relationship is typically established between the client and the online clinician. Although there are many ways technology can facilitate this relationship, Internet-delivered communications may also hinder the therapeutic relationship (Abbott et al., 2008; Kraus et al., 2004; Koocher, 2007; Sampson et al., 1997).

Lack of face-to-face interactions with clients in eHealth care can create increased opportunities for miscommunication and misunderstanding over the course of treatment (Manhal-Baugus, 2001). Although some clients may even prefer the increased anonymity that comes with seeking eHealth care, the disadvantage in seeking care through the Internet or ICTs is that many of the cues used in an in-person evaluation, including tone of voice, facial cues and body language, are not available. These attributes can all inform the diagnostic picture and yield valuable information about the person seeking care (Abbott et al., 2008; Kraus et al., 2004).

This challenge can often be overcome by researchers and providers appropriately assessing potential clients during the intake and informed consent process, allowing a complete clinical picture despite the lack of many of the nonverbal cues. When possible, part of the screening and intake process should entail an assessment of the client's ability to communicate via technology. Online clients need to be clearly informed of the communication channels that exist within web-based interventions or online therapy. Researchers and practitioners can also work to establish formal ways to avoid miscommunication in text and set up protocols for handling misunderstandings when they do occur (Campbell et al., 2010; Fisher, 2009).

Because online practitioners and researchers can deliver treatment without regard to geographic location, they can easily be unaware of location-specific conditions, events, and cultural practices that may affect clients (Maheu & Gordon, 2000; Sampson et al., 1997). This could potentially result in missing important information that affects clients, and could potentially impact clients' engagement with and outcome in treatment. For example, differences in regional cultural norms may lead to potential misunderstandings or misinterpretations between the client and online therapist. The online therapist may not be able to distinguish ethnic or racial differences and adjust treatment accordingly. Similarly, the web-based intervention may contain scenarios and vignettes that are not applicable to all clients from diverse geographies. This may be particularly salient when interventions are accessed by an international audience.

As is the case with all potential risks in web-based interventions or online therapy, researchers and practitioners should be aware of the risk for miscommunication and misunderstanding, and attempt to mitigate these risks by having an appropriate intake process that helps identify gaps in understanding. By realizing the potential for miscommunication and taking steps to identify it, misunderstandings may be avoided or more quickly discovered and resolved (Childress, 2000; Sampson et al., 1997).

Legal Aspects

Ethical issues surrounding the dissemination of web-based interventions and online therapy extend to the legal realm as well. Many of the benefits and challenges discussed also raise legal concerns. For example, the ability of web-based interventions and online therapy to be delivered without geographic constraints allows increased access to treatment, thereby making it more equitable for clients to receive care. However, this flexibility of providing treatment without regard to geographic location also presents legal questions. If disputes arise in web-based interventions or online therapy, it is not always clear which state's or country's regulations take precedence regarding delivery of the service (Mallen et al., 2005). Although several U.S. state licensing boards have adopted guidelines for those practicing online therapy, some regulations dictate that providers cannot practice beyond state lines in the United States (Koocher, 2000), and insurance carriers may not cover clinicians who practice beyond certain geographic restrictions (Kraus et al., 2004). This, of course, means that online clinicians and professionals managing web-based interventions could potentially be practicing outside of covered areas. Professionals must be aware of their affiliated licensing board and insurance carrier to determine the laws and policies that apply to ethical practice. Similarly, researchers and providers need to be aware of clients' or users' local regulations of age of consent, requirements for reporting child abuse, and requirements for parental consent when treating minors (American Psychological Association, 2002). In sum, providers need to ensure that the use of the technology to deliver care does not violate the laws of any local, state, national, or international entity, and observe relevant statutes (American Psychological Association, 2002; Koocher, 2007). At the same time, however, professionals should advocate that existing codes and statutes be revised in consideration of the changing landscape of how care can be provided, and eHealth providers are encouraged to work together, and across disciplines, to form stronger, more persuasive advocacy groups.

Codes and Guidelines for Delivering eHealth Care

Ethical and legal regulatory bodies have not kept pace in establishing guidelines for web-based interventions and online therapy (Barak, 1999; Maheu & Gordon, 2000; Midkiff & Wyatt, 2008). However, a number of comprehensive ethical guidelines for psychologists and others delivering eHealth care have been developed globally. The guidelines range from outlining explicit ethical Internet practices, such as those of the Australian Psychological Society (Australian Psychological Society, 2007), and the American Psychological Association (American Psychological Association, 2002), whose code implies coverage for Internet practices in certain areas but does not provide explicit or implied coverage in others. International social work and counseling organizations, such as the National Association of Social Workers and Association of Social Work Boards (2005), National Board for Certified Counselors (2005), and Commission on Rehabilitation Counselor Certification (2009), have also developed specific guidelines for the ethical provision of online counseling. The American Mental Health Counselors Association (2010) and American Counseling Association (2005), U.S.-based organizations, each address ethical practices in delivering psychological services over the Internet. The International Society for Mental Health Online (2000) and Association for Counseling and Therapy Online (2010) are international groups that have specifically addressed ethical issues in delivering Internet interventions in their ethical guidelines.

Figure 12.1 summarizes the issues covered in this chapter. Codes of ethics were reviewed and categorized as having explicit coverage of the ethical issue, implied coverage, or no coverage of the issue within the guidelines. Several codes, including the Australian Psychological Society, the International Society for Mental Health online, and the Commission on Rehabilitation Counselor Certification, all have created specific guidelines to address Internet-delivered treatment, yielding a comprehensive set of guidelines for ethical issues. The majority of ethical codes, however, either more generally address ethical issues in these areas or fail to cover them at all. Here is a brief description of each of the organizations identified in the chart with their relevant ethical guidelines and codes related to the use of the Internet and provision of mental health services:

Australian Psychological Society (APS)

The Australian Psychological Society (APS) is the largest professional association for psychologists in

	Informed Consent	Privacy and Confidentiality	Records	Financial Arrangements	Appropriateness of Online treatment	Online Assessment and diagnosis	Identity	Data Validity	Boundaries of Competence	Training	Crises Intervention	Communication	Legal Aspects
Australian Psychological Society	●	●	●	●	●	●	●	●	●	●	●	●	●
American Psychological Association	◐	◐	●	○	○	◐	●	●	●	◐	○	○	●
The National Association of Social Workers/ The Association of Social Work Boards	◐	●	●	○	○	●	●	●	●	●	○	●	●
The National Board of Certified Counselors	●	●	●	○	●	●	●	●	●	●	●	●	●
Commission on Rehabilitation Counselor Certification	●	●	●	○	●	●	●	●	●	●	●	●	●
American Mental Health Counselors Association	●	●	●	●	◐	●	○	●	○	●	○	●	●
American Counseling Association	●	●	●	○	●	●	●	●	●	○	●	●	●
International Society for Mental Health Online	●	●	●	●	○	●	●	●	●	●	●	●	◐
Association for Counseling and Therapy Online	●	○	●	●	●	○	○	●	●	●	○	○	●

Legend: ● Explicit coverage ◐ Implied coverage ○ No coverage

Figure 12.1 Guidelines for Ethical Practice in Delivering Web-based Interventions and Online Counseling

Australia, representing more than 18,500 members. Its mission is to represent, promote, and advance psychology within the context of improving community well-being and scientific knowledge. The APS has developed a comprehensive set of *Guidelines for Providing Psychological Services on the Internet* (Australian Psychological Society, 2007), covering both the ethical and general delivery of online services. The purpose of the APS Ethical Guidelines is to clarify and amplify the application of the general principles and specific standards contained in the APS code of ethics, and to facilitate their interpretation in contemporary areas of professional practice. An Ethical Guidelines Committee coordinates the development, implementation, evaluation, review, and revision of the APS ethical guidelines. The committee works in consultation with key stakeholders inside and outside the Society.

American Psychological Association (APA)

Based in Washington, DC, the American Psychological Association is a scientific and professional organization that represents psychology in the United States with roughly 150,000 members (American Psychological Association, 2002). The APA's *Ethical Principles of Psychologists and Code of Conduct* is a set of principles taken from biomedical ethics literature (Campbell et al., 2010; Childress, 2000). The ethics code has 89 ethical standards that apply to a variety of complex practice situations and settings, including Internet and other electronic transmissions (Campbell et al., 2010). There is an APA ethics committee that is tasked to receive, initiate, and investigate complaints of unethical conduct of members, associate members, and affiliates (American Psychological Association, 2002).

National Association of Social Workers (NASW)/Association of Social Work Boards (ASWB)

The National Association of Social Workers describes itself as the largest membership organization of professional social workers in the world, with 150,000 members. NASW works to enhance the professional growth and development of its members, to create and maintain professional standards, and to advance sound social policies. The NASW code of ethics serves as a guide to the everyday professional conduct of social workers.

The Association of Social Work Boards is the association of boards that regulate social work. ASWB develops and maintains the social work licensing examinations used in the United States and in several Canadian provinces, and is a central resource for information on the legal regulation of social work. The *NASW and ASWB Standards for Technology and Social Work Practice* was published in 2005 by the NASW and ASWB, with the NASW code of ethics and the ASWB Model Social Work Practice Act (National Association of Social Workers Ethics Committee, 2005) serving as foundation documents. The National Association of Social Workers ethics committee is responsible for educating NASW membership and the larger professional community to standards of ethical professional practice (National Association of Social Workers Ethics Committee, 2005).

National Board for Certified Counselors (NBCC)

NBCC is an independent, not-for-profit credentialing body for counselors that was incorporated in 1982 to establish and monitor a national certification system, to identify those counselors who have voluntarily sought and obtained certification, and to maintain a register of those counselors. NBCC asserts that its certification program recognizes counselors who have met predetermined standards in their training, experience, and performance on the National Counselor Examination for Licensure and Certification. According to NBCC, it has more than 44,000 certified counselors who live and work in more than 40 countries. Its code of ethics was developed by counseling experts and reviewed by a committee of professional and licensed counselors (J. DiBacco, personal communication, November 12, 2010).

Commission on Rehabilitation Counselor Certification

The Commission on Rehabilitation Counselor Certification (CRCC) is an independent, not-for-profit organization dedicated to improving the lives of persons with disabilities. The CRCC provides leadership in advocating for the rehabilitation counseling profession. As of 2010, the CRCC adopted a code of professional ethics that covers both its certified rehabilitation counselors and its Canadian certified rehabilitation counselors. The CRCC ethics committee is a standing committee of the Commission and is responsible for periodically reviewing and recommending changes, as well as educating CRCC members and the general public as to the provisions of the ethics code and guidelines (Commission on Rehabilitation Counselor Certification, 2009).

American Mental Health Counselors Association (AMHCA)

The American Mental Health Counselors Association is the U.S.-based professional organization of mental health counselors, with approximately 6,000 mental health counselor members. The AMHCA subscribes to rigorous standards for education, training, and clinical practice, and establishes and promotes the highest professional standards. Mental health counselors subscribe to and pledge to abide by the principles identified in the code of ethics. The AMHCA code of ethics was revised in 2010, and has a section on "Technology-Assisted Counseling" that provides explicit ethical guidelines (AMHCA, 2010).

American Counseling Association (ACA)

The American Counseling Association is a not-for-profit, professional and educational organization dedicated to the growth and enhancement of the counseling profession. ACA provides leadership training, publications, continuing education opportunities, and advocacy services to over 40,000 members, and has helped set professional and ethical standards for the counseling profession. In 2002, the ACA president created an ACA Ethics Code Revision Taskforce that resulted in an update, in 2005, of the ACA's code of ethics and includes a section explicitly covering online therapy and counseling (American Counseling Association, 2005).

International Society for Mental Health Online (ISMHO)

The International Society for Mental Health Online was formed in 1997 to promote the understanding, use, and development of online communication, information, and technology for the international mental health community. The Society has crafted *Suggested Principles for the Online Provision of Mental Health Services* aimed at students, teachers, researchers, clinical practitioners, and others interested in using Internet technologies to provide mental health interventions. These principles were developed by a joint committee of the International Society for Mental Health Online and the Psychiatric Society for Informatics. The committee made use of previously published online guidelines and websites, including the Code of Conduct for Medical and Health Web Sites and Health On the Net Foundation (International Society for Mental Health Online, 2000).

Association for Counseling and Therapy Online (ACTO)

The Association for Counseling and Therapy Online was formed in 2006 as an umbrella organization in the United Kingdom for therapists who practice online. ACTO asserts a commitment to setting and maintaining the highest standards of therapy in online work (see http://acto-uk.org/). ACTO's Professional Conduct Panel generated its code of ethics to help promote safe professional practice for those therapists who work online. All ACTO members are required to adhere to and follow the code of ethics of the organization with whom they hold membership or accreditation, in addition to the ethical framework within the ACTO code of ethics (Association for Counseling and Therapy Online, 2010).

Conclusion of Codes and Guidelines for Delivering eHealth Care

The codes of these organizations tend to focus on similar ethical challenges from both practice and research perspectives. Given this, it is foreseeable that a set of universal ethical guidelines may be considered in the future. To that end, an influential organization in the field, the International Society for Research on Internet Interventions—a group of researchers, clinicians, policy makers, and industry partners focused on the development, evaluation, and dissemination of Internet interventions—has published 10 aims and directions for Internet interventions that could serve as a basis for the development of a universal set of ethical guidelines (Ritterband, Andersson, Christensen, Carlbring, & Cuijpers, 2006).

Implications for Delivering Online Psychological Treatment

Technological advances and increased access to the Internet and other ICTs have dramatically changed how psychological treatment can be delivered. The rapidly developing field of eHealth enables practitioners and researchers to improve psychological care on a public health level by increasing access to treatment and assessment, enhancing client convenience, improving communication with care providers, and reducing treatment expenses. These improvements, however, also force the psychology and behavioral health fields to reevaluate the standards for how to provide care and conduct research ethically. Toward that end, the purpose of this chapter is to help readers develop a greater sensitivity to the ethical issues inherent in delivering online treatment, and facilitate more informed choices with respect to developing and delivering web-based interventions and online therapy.

In addition to being aware of the many ethical issues raised here, including how best to provide informed consent, protect against breeches of privacy and other potential risks in online treatment, and assess a client's appropriateness for online treatment, practitioners and researchers need to stay abreast of the frequent changes in technology and understand how these changes impact clients and participants. Researchers and practitioners have the responsibility to identify risks in delivering psychological treatment online and provide protection against those risks to the extent possible.

Future Directions

The eHealth field is rapidly changing, and these changes will continue to impact all aspects of the field. Researchers and providers should continue to work to better define their particular interventions (and associated technologies) to allow clear communication regarding their online interventions. With increased clarity, the ethical challenges connected to various online interventions can become more transparent and ethics codes can be more aptly developed. As previously noted, ethics codes will have difficulty keeping pace with evolving technologies, necessitating frequent review and update. Furthermore, in many cases, ethics codes do not always provide adequate coverage or explicit guidelines to offer clear direction. Graduate training programs will need to intensify training in the delivery of online treatment and research to prepare more competent researchers and providers. Similarly, continuing education opportunities need to be developed that allow providers of web-based interventions and online therapy to remain competent.

Licensing boards and insurance carriers also need to work to understand how providing and evaluating online interventions necessitates a new approach to research and provision of care, and that some statutes and regulations are antiquated and need to be reconsidered. For example, preventing a provider from practicing beyond state or national lines severely limits the reach of online interventions that would otherwise be available to clients across national and international lines. Regulatory bodies need to determine which boundaries and limits are appropriate given innovative ways of delivering care. Existing legal and political norms should also be challenged in light of the transformation in the delivery of psychological treatment, as significant changes may be warranted. In closing, researchers and providers must continue to evaluate how new directions in using the Internet and ICTs impact their research and practices in order to ensure the continued delivery of psychological treatment that is ethical and effective.

References

Abbott, J. M., Klein, B., & Ciechomski, L. (2008). Best practices in online therapy. *Journal of Technology in Human Services, 26,* 360–375.

American Counseling Association. (2005). *ACA code of ethics.* Alexandria, VA: Author.

American Mental Health Counselors Association. (2010). *Principles for AMHCA code of ethics.* Retrieved from https://www.amhca.org/assets/content/AMHCACodeOfEthics2010Final.pdf.

American Psychological Association. (2002). *Ethical principles of psychologists and code of conduct.* Washington, DC: American Psychological Association. Retrieved from http://www.apa.org/ethics/code/index.aspx.

Association for Counseling and Therapy Online. (2010). *ACTO code of ethics.* Retrieved from http://acto-uk.org/codeofethics.htm.

Australian Psychological Society. (2007). *Code of ethics: Guidelines for providing psychological services on the Internet.* Retrieved from http://www.psychology.org.au/Assets/Files/Code_Ethics_2007.pdf.

Baltimore, M. L. (2000). Ethical considerations in the use of technology for marriage and family counselors. *The Family Journal: Counseling and Therapy for Couples and Families, 8,* 390–393.

Barak A. (1999). Psychological applications on the Internet: A discipline on the threshold of a new millennium. *Applied and Preventive Psychology, 8,* 231–245. Barak, A., Hen, L., Boniel-Nissim, M., & Shapira, N. (2008). A comprehensive review and a meta-analysis of the effectiveness of internet-based psychotherapeutic interventions. *Journal of Technology in Human Services, 26,* 109–160.

Barak, A., Klein, B., & Proudfoot, J. G. (2009). Defining internet-supported therapeutic interventions. *Annals of Behavior Medicine, 38,* 4–17.

Barnett J. E., & Scheetz, K. (2003).Technological advances and telehealth: Ethics, law, and the practice of psychotherapy. *Psychotherapy: Theory, Research, Practice, Training, 40,* 86–93.

Bersoff, D. N. (Ed.) (2008). *Ethical conflicts in psychology* (4th ed.). Washington, DC: American Psychological Association.

Birnbaum M. (2004). Human research and data collection via the Internet. *Annual Review of Psychology, 55,* 803–832.

Bull, S. S., Vallejos, D., Levine, D., & Ortiz, C. (2008). Improving recruitment and retention for an online randomized controlled trial: Experience from the youthnet study. *AIDS Care, 20*(8), 887–893.

Campbell, L., Vasquez, M. J., Behnke, S. H., & Kinscherff, R. (2010). *APA ethics code commentary and case illustrations.* Portland, OR: American Psychological Association.

Chiasson, M. A., Parsons, J. T., Tesoriero, J. M., Carballo-Dieguez, A., Hirshfield, S., & Remien, R. H. (2006). HIV behavioral research online. *Journal of Urban Health, 83*(1), 73–85.

Childress, C. A. (2000). Ethical issues in providing online psychotherapeutic interventions. *Journal of Medical Internet Research, 2,* e5.

Childress, C. A., & Asamen, J. K. (1998). The emerging relationship of psychology and the internet: Proposed guidelines for conducting internet intervention research. *Ethics and Behavior, 8,* 19–35.

Commission on Rehabilitation Counselor Certification. (2009). *Code of professional ethics for rehabilitation counselors.* Schaumburg, IL: Author.

Eyde, L. D., Robertson, G. J., & Krug, S. E. (2010). *Responsible test use: Case studies for assessing human behavior* (2nd ed.). Washington, DC: American Psychological Association.

Eysenbach, G. (2001). What is e-health? *Journal of Medical Internet Research, 3,* e20.

Fisher, C. B. (2009). *Decoding the ethics code: A practical guide for psychologists* (2nd ed.). Thousand Oaks, CA: Sage.

Fisher, C. B., & Oransky, M. (2008). Informed consent to psychotherapy: Protecting the dignity and respecting the autonomy of clients. *Journal of Clinical Psychology, 64,* 576–588.

Fox, S. (2006). *Online health search.* Washington, DC: Pew Internet & American Life Project.

Grazina Johnston, L., Trummal, A., Lohmus, L., & Ravalepik, A. (2009). Efficacy of convenience sampling through the internet: Challenges reaching a hidden population. *AIDS Care, 21*(9), 1195–1202.

Griffiths, F., Lindenmeyer, A., Powell, J., Lowe, P., & Thorogood, M. (2006). Why are health care interventions delivered over the internet? A systematic review of the published literature. *Journal of Medical Internet Research, 8,* e11.

International Society for Mental Health Online. (2000). *Suggested principles for the online provision of mental health services.* Retrieved from https://www.ismho.org/suggestions.asp.

Internet World Stats. (2010). *Internet usage statistics, the Internet big picture: World Internet users and population stats.* Retrieved from http://www.internetworldstats.com/stats.htm.

Jerome L. W., & Zaylor, C. (2000). Cyberspace: Creating a therapeutic environment for telehealth applications. *Professional Psychology Research and Practice, 31,* 478–483.

Kim, Y., Kelly, T., & Raja, S. (2010). *Building broadband: Strategies and policies for the developing world.* Washington, DC: World Bank. Koocher, G. P. (2007). Twenty-first century ethical challenges for psychology. *American Psychologist, 62,* 375–384.

Koocher, G. P., & Morray, E. (2000). Regulation of telepsychology: A survey of state attorneys general. *Professional Psychology Research and Practice, 31,* 503–508.

Kraus, R., Zack, J. S., & Stricker, G. (Eds.). (2004). *Online counseling: A handbook for mental health professionals.* San Diego, CA: Elsevier.

Maheu, M. M., & Gordon, B. L. (2000). Counseling and therapy on the Internet. *Professional Psychology Research and Practice, 31,* 484–489.

Mallen, M. J., Vogel, D. L., & Rochlen, A. B. (2005). The practical aspects of online counseling: Ethics, training, technology, and competency. *The Counseling Psychologist, 33,* 776–818.

Manhal-Baugus, M. (2001). E-therapy: Practical, ethical, and legal issues. *Cyberpsychology and Behavior, 4,* 551–563.

Midkiff, D. M., & Wyatt, W. J. (2008). Ethical issues in the provision of online mental health services (etherapy). *Journal of Technology in Human Services, 26,* 310–332.

Murray, E., Burns, J., See, T. S., Lai, R., & Nazareth, I. (2005). Interactive health communication applications for people with chronic disease. *Cochrane Database of Systematic Reviews,* CD004274.

National Association of Social Workers and Association of Social Work Boards. (2005). *NASW and ASWB standards for technology and social work practice.* Washington, DC: NASW Press.

National Board for Certified Counselors. (2005). *Code of ethics.* Retrieved from http://www.nbcc.org/Assets/Ethics/nbcc-codeofethics.pdf.

Nickelson, D. W. (1998). Telehealth and the evolving health care system: Strategic opportunities for professional psychology. *Professional Psychology: Research and Practice, 29*(6), 527–535.

Prince, M., Patel, V., Saxena, S., Maj, M., Maselko, J., Phillips, M. R., & Rahman, A. (2007). No health without mental health. *Lancet, 370,* 859–877. Ramo, D. E., Hall, S. M., & Prochaska, J. J. (2010). Reaching young adult smokers through the internet: Comparison of three recruitment mechanisms. *Nicotine & Tobacco Research, 12*(7), 768–775.

Ritterband, L. M., Andersson, G., Christensen, H. M., Carlbring, P., & Cuijpers, P. (2006). Directions for the international society for research on internet interventions (ISRII). *Journal of Medical Internet Research, 8*(3), e23.

Ritterband, L. M., GonderFrederick, L. A., Cox, D. J., Clifton, A. D., West, R. W., & Borowitz, S. M. (2003). Internet interventions: In review, in use, and into the future. *Professional Psychology Research and Practice, 34,* 527–534.

Ritterband, L. M., & Palermo, T. M. (2009). Introduction to the special issue: eHealth in pediatric psychology. *Journal of Pediatric Psychology, 34,* 453–456.

Sampson, J. P., Kolodinsky, R. W., & Greeno, B. P. (1997). Counseling and the information highway: Future possibilities and potential problems. *Journal of Counseling and Development, 75,* 203–212.

Saxena, S., Paraje, G., Sharan, P., Karam, G., & Sadana, R. (2006). The 10/90 divide in mental health research: Trends over a 10-year period. *British Journal of Psychiatry, 188,* 81–82.

Spek, V., Cuijpers, P., Nyklicek, I., Riper, H., Keyzer, J., & Pop, V. (2007). Internet-based cognitive behavior therapy for symptoms of depression and anxiety: A meta-analysis. *Psychological Medicine, 37,* 319–328.

Tate, D. F., Finkelstein, E. A., Khayjou, O., & Gustafson, A. (2009). Cost effectiveness of Internet interventions: Review and recommendations. *Annals of Behavioral Medicine, 38,* 40–45.

Tate, D. F., & Zabinski, M. F. (2004). Computer and internet applications for psychological treatment: Update for clinicians. *Journal of Clinical Psychology, 60,* 209–220.

Tomlinson, M., Rudan, I., Saxena, S., Swartz, L., Tsai, A. C., & Patel, V. (2009). Setting priorities for global mental health research. *Bulletin of the World Health Organization, 87,* 438–446.

Wantland, D., Portillo, C., Holzemer, W., Laughter, R., & McGhee, E. (2004). The effectiveness of web-based vs. non-web-based interventions: A meta-analysis of behavioral change outcomes. *Journal of Medical Internet Research, 6,* e40.

Whitehead, L. C. (2007). Methodological and ethical issues in internet-mediated research in the field of health: An integrated review of the literature. *Social Science and Medicine, 65,* 782–791.

Wiggins Frame, M. (1997). The ethics of counseling via the internet. *The Family Journal: Counseling and Therapy for Couples and Families, 5,* 328–330.

CHAPTER
13
Principles of Indigenous Ethics and Psychological Interventions

Natasha A. Tassell, Averil M. L. Herbert, Ian M. Evans, *and* Patricia TeW. A. Young

Abstract

The importance of indigenous principles in undertaking psychological assessment, interventions, and applied research is increasingly being recognized and acknowledged in most formal codes of ethics for psychologists. Nevertheless, specific ethical guidelines still tend to reflect the established assumptions of the dominant academic cultures. This chapter highlights additional principles and relevant issues at different levels of ethical judgment. At the deepest level are fundamental concerns over power differentials, especially when interventions are designed, controlled, and evaluated by practitioners from majority populations (colonization). At other important levels there are questions concerning the recognition of indigenous knowledge, alternative worldviews regarding psychological well-being, and different cultural values with respect to privacy, consent, and the rights to effective treatment. At a more practical level are issues of treatment acceptability and access, adequacy of the evidence base, prioritization of treatment targets, and training and career development opportunities for indigenous practitioners.

Key Words: psychology, ethics, intervention design, indigenous knowledge

Aotearoa[1] New Zealand has a bicultural heritage based on the foundation document of the Treaty of Waitangi—signed in 1840 between indigenous Māori *iwi* and the British government. The formal parliamentary enactment of the Treaty in 1975 established a forum for redressing historical Treaty breaches and offered a model for relationships between groups and individuals in legal, political, sociological, and psychological contexts. This chapter will examine practice and ethical issues in the light of this experience, as well as considering current opinion on indigenous ethics in psychological interventions worldwide. Most contemporary psychological interventions—treatments such as psychotherapy, counseling, community-based programs, and consulting—have been developed within the framework of modern psychological theories, principles, and empirical paradigms. Insights and findings from this core psychological research are then translated into practical clinical and educational interventions. This knowledge base is almost exclusively North American or European, and implicitly accepted as mainstream and progressive (Pickren, 2009). To be sanctioned by the profession, interventions are piloted and tested for efficacy on volunteers or carefully selected clients who usually share a cultural identity similar to that of the investigators. They are then evaluated for their effectiveness with a possibly broader range of typical clients willing to seek services, but using the standard empirical methods of Western social science.

When considering the value and usefulness of such "validated" interventions or "evidence-based" services for indigenous peoples, who are often in a numerical minority, ethical issues take on a special and unique importance. Among the more obvious concerns are the following questions: (a) What is the cultural relationship between therapist and client (service and consumer), and what are the effects of likely power differentials? (b) Is there sufficient recognition of the value of indigenous knowledge? (c) Are the worldviews and habits of mind of the likely recipients of standard interventions adequately considered in the translation of psychological principals to practical procedures? (d) Are the methods for evaluating treatment outcomes—both at the individual client level and at the group level—appropriate when the clients are indigenous people, having possibly different goals, as well as self-determined criteria for deciding benefits and judging outcomes? (e) To what extent does training and cultural awareness mitigate possible professional misunderstandings, abuse, or exploitation? (f) When assessing the need for psychological intervention, or diagnosing clients' psychological pain, has adequate attention been directed to sources of distress and disadvantage that may be attributable to past injustices, exploitation, discrimination, prejudicial treatment, and collective loss?

The purpose of this chapter is first to explore the principles and values of ethical (best) practice from an indigenous perspective, and second to analyze their implications for psychological intervention. We consider ethical concerns and their ramifications for appropriate professional practice regardless of whether treatment is being delivered by psychologists from the same indigenous group as the clients or by psychologists representing mainstream, majority groups. There are valuable ethical lessons that can be learned from indigenous practice that could benefit all psychological treatment practices. In this chapter we will draw particularly on the experiences of Māori in Aotearoa New Zealand, where the organizational history and formal development of the applied psychology profession essentially mirrors that of Great Britain, Canada, Australia, and the United States.

Foundations of Indigenous Ethics
Delineation

Walker (1987) described indigenous cultures as "generally small-scale in size and ranging from family units to tribes [with] mythology and spiritual beliefs credit[ing] them with divine origin and descent through culture heroes" (p. 228). The United Nations defines an indigenous people as "a politically underprivileged group, who share a similar ethnic identity different to the nation in power, and who have been an ethnic entity in the locality before the present ruling nation took over power" (United Nations Declaration on the Rights of Indigenous Peoples, 2007). Not all indigenous ethnic groups are in a statistical minority. Many majority populations are striving to establish national identities after extensive (e.g., South Africa) or successive (e.g., the Philippines) periods of colonial domination.

The term *indigenous* is itself diverse and varies in acceptability among the very people to whom it might be applied. Aboriginal people in Australia prefer the names of the specific national and linguistic groups to which they belong (National Health and Medical Research Council, 2003). "First Nation" Canadians prefer the more inclusive term *aboriginal*. The commonly used term *Pasifika* implies that Pacific peoples are a homogenous group. While Pacific nations do share similarities, their political and sociocultural histories differ, and Pacific peoples are best described according to ethnic specificity (i.e., Cook Island, Samoan, Niuean, Tongan; Mila-Schaff & Hudson, 2009). In addition to varying levels of current independence, a number of these island communities have never, in fact, been colonized.

Different histories and social and political experiences remind us of "diverse realities" (Durie, 2008). Many Māori in Aotearoa New Zealand are influenced by Christian principles, and historical missionary influences contributed to the establishment of essentially "Māori-fied" Christian religious followings (Elsmore, 1989); within the Māori world these are accepted as mainstream and significant movements. Urban dwellers may have very different views than people living in rural settings. Young Māori in Aotearoa New Zealand may have perspectives that reflect the global youth culture more than their ethnicity (Durie, 2008). Portrayal of the Filipino value system as revolving harmoniously around the extended family, kinship, and the *compadrazgo* system, ignores power relationships based on property, the economy, and American-dominated political institutions (San Juan, 2006).

Enduring Values: Contexts and Relationships

Despite this diversity, indigenous cultures have an enduring perspective on eco-connectedness that highlights ethical principles of sustainability, balance between people and environments, and an interconnected life force that links the living as well as inanimate objects (Kim, Yang, & Hwang, 2006). Walker (1987) suggests "The distinguishing feature of indigenous cultures is the relationship between the people, the earth and its resources... Indigenous people think of themselves as an integral part of the natural order" (p. 228). Psychological health and well-being are products of these interconnections and cannot be conceptualized outside of their wider environmental context (Durie, 2008).

Within Māori culture, *whakapapa*, or genealogy in its widest sense, is the foundation of an individual's identity, providing links not only to one's ancestors (*tupuna*), but also to the land (*whenua*), traditional meeting places (*marae*), and environment (mountains—*maunga*, river—*awa*) (Tassell & Lock, 2011). Understanding people in context is an ethical requirement that, if embraced, will guide interventions which are systemic and give recognition to the individual's physical region—mountain, river, forest, island, seashore, or plain.

Sharing, collective responsibility, and collective ownership explicitly and implicitly pervade ways of doing things and understandings for indigenous cultures (Ermine, Sinclair, & Jeffrey, 2004; Herbert & Morrison, 2007). Ermine et al., in their position paper outlining the ethics of research involving indigenous peoples in Canada, emphasized shared ownership of collective knowledge and data obtained from indigenous communities. Individuals are identified in the context of the collective. So, for Māori in Aotearoa New Zealand, individuals are defined not only by historical links through their genealogy but also through current links underpinned by the values of *kotahitanga* (unity) and *whanaungatanga* (relationships), which heighten the importance of sharing resources and engaging in collectively beneficial actions (Tassell & Lock, 2011). Māori knowledge (*mātauranga Māori*) and genealogy are deemed sacred and not necessarily for dissemination to all individuals. Sometimes only a select few are seen as worthy recipients or guardians of such knowledge (Stewart, 1997).

Australian Aboriginal culture emphasizes the importance of cooperation among its members, and coexistence with the environment for the continuation of peoples (Christie, 1985). Aboriginal knowledge is not something openly available for those who choose to obtain or possess it, but rather is protected by certain people, who serve as guardians to ensure such knowledge is passed on to future generations (Fogarty & White, 1994). These notions of collective responsibility, ownership, and guardianship contrast with the individualism typical of much of Western psychological practices. In more individualistic cultures, relationships tend to be voluntary, contractual, and maintained according to the returns they might bring for advancing academic knowledge and professional standing (Tassell, 2004), although they also demand taking individual responsibility for one's actions.

In summary, these values identify and encompass peoples' genealogy and historical links; relationships and sharing between individuals, families, and communities; cooperation and coexistence with environments and sources of food; and the recognition that some tribal knowledge is not accessible to all. Working within this worldview has implications—to be discussed next—for applied research and psychological practice ethics that prioritize the rights and duties of the individual.

Assumptions in Codes of Ethics

Unless cultural differences are central to the development of ethical principles, certain aspects of professional practice, particularly in connection with interventions, may prove to be less than universal within indigenous contexts. Examples of these widely accepted second-order rules within codes of ethics are rights to privacy, informed consent, avoiding dual relationships, and the assumption that the individual is the unit of professional accountability. Given that many indigenous societies are closely interconnected in collectivist and kinship organizational structures, these "rules" of Western ethical codes may need to be reexamined and modified in keeping with the intent, which is to ensure objective, non-exploitative professional relationships between client and psychologist. Thus, for example, Aboriginal people in Australia, who may see a professional relationship as a personal relationship, are comfortable "yarning," which can as easily take place in the street as in a formal office environment (Vicary, 2003).

The apparently innocuous ethical practice in clinical treatment or research of informed consent is loaded with unexplored cultural assumptions. Asking someone to give consent before they really know you or have an established relationship with you requires the client or participant to surrender their autonomy and adopt a subordinate role. Individuals who feel that their understanding, their being, or their time are essentially gifts that they are willing to bestow on a clinician or a researcher cannot be expected to surrender that privilege simply on being requested to sign a form. Participants are, of course, told that they can withdraw at any time, but how easily is this action performed by socially disadvantaged individuals who may also depend heavily on the financial, educational, or health services delivered by the clinician's or researcher's organization? Consenting to reveal personal and sometimes sacred (culturally privileged) information may require reciprocal self-disclosure by the psychologist (Taiwhati, Toia, Te Maro, McRae, & McKenzie, 2010).

Privacy is another complex issue. Fontes (1998) described a disadvantaged indigenous community in Chile, who expressed that disguising their names and identifying information failed to give them recognition for their contribution. Small communities in rural areas, especially those emphasizing extended kinship relationships or linked by common church membership, are inevitably going to experience dual relationships—professional and personal. The highly desirable strategy of encouraging family support members to attend assessment meetings and treatment sessions completely vitiates standard assumptions of the importance of confidentiality. Conventional ethical rules need to be pared back to their fundamental professional purpose: trust in the professional, safety for the client, and protection of personal rights despite cultural pressures, unless the definition of who is the client is expanded to the group.

Ethics is about values, and indigenous values may not be commensurate with those of Western or European societies. These differences are complicated by language differences. There are no words in Hawaiian for *values, morals,* or *ethics*; however, there are words describing core values such as *aloha* (compassion), *ha'aha'a* (humility), and *ahonui* (patience) (Chun, 2006a). In Māori, the word *respect* has several different translations, all of them with the prefix *whaka* that suggests a relational dimension felt by two parties. From a Māori perspective, respect is a way of being—not something gained by reputation, but judged and felt as it is performed. Being worthy of respect is associated with actions benefitting the culture, rather than those benefitting the individual (Tassell & Lock, 2011). Furthermore, the delineation of indigenous peoples highlights the importance of knowledge of past histories not only from the perspective of understanding positive cultural values, but also from recognizing negative impacts of colonization.

The Psychological Effects of Colonization

Here we use the concept of colonization quite broadly to represent the negative social and emotional consequences that often result from one ethnic or cultural group subjugating another. Across many historical contexts—Native Americans in the United States, First Nation people in Canada, Aboriginal people in Australia, indigenous minority tribes in Botswana—processes that can collectively be described as colonization have resulted in many types of loss for indigenous peoples: loss of tribal lands and traditional means of economic support, destruction of social patterns, loss of power, prestige, and self-respect, loss of language and cultural practices, loss of autonomy and self-determination. Stigma and racism have deep, usually underestimated, psychological effects. The social, economic, and psychological consequences of these losses are being increasingly recognized in professional practice.

Loss

When a leading Māori politician described the effects of European colonization on Māori people in New Zealand as a "holocaust" (Turia, 2000), she was widely criticized in the mainstream media. Yet, if one looks objectively at the result of new European diseases, land confiscations, and destruction of natural resources as means of support, the effects simply on numbers of the Māori population would certainly resemble, proportionately, the outcome of the Holocaust in Europe (Nairn, 2007). By the end of the 19th century the Māori population was less than a quarter its size a hundred years earlier: 42,000 and nearing extinction.

In Australia, where indigenous people were not recognized as citizens until 1967, Aboriginal and Torres Strait peoples experience infant mortality rates almost three times that of other Australians and have 15–20 years lower life expectancy (Bishop, Higgins, Casella, & Contos, 2002). Government policy resulting in what is now known as the "stolen generation" attempted to extinguish from mixed-race Aboriginal children any vestiges of their familial and social connections with their indigenous roots.

In South Africa, apartheid, the long period of enforced separation of African people, resulted in massive social disruptions, with attempts to restrict people to tribal homelands, limit work opportunities through the pass system, ensure that influential political figures were unable to exercise any power and authority, and legalized humiliation and insult through laws against interracial sexual contact, restricted educational opportunities, and separate facilities—from toilets, to buses, to access to alcohol.

The limited commercial opportunities on their one million hectares reservation in South Dakota means there is 80% unemployment among the

Oglala Sioux Nation (McGreal, 2010). In Japan, legislation passed in 1899 to enforce the assimilation of the indigenous Ainu people into Japanese culture mandated teachers in Ainu schools to use only Japanese language (Saeki, 2008). Not until 2008, with their language almost extinct, did the Japanese government formally recognize the Ainu as an indigenous people.

The Inuit communities of the Arctic region experience crisis levels of substance abuse, suicide, and violence attributable to the "trauma of colonization" (Kulchyski, 2006, p. 167). In Hawai'i, *Kānaka Maoli* (Native Hawaiians) have experienced negative effects on health and social status which can be attributed to the radical changes in their way of life following the Americanization of the Hawaiian Islands (Kaholokula, Nacapoy, & Dang, 2009). Of special relevance to the present discussion is these authors' argument that public health benefits cannot be achieved without improving social justice for people of native Hawaiian origin.

These are just a few selective examples of injustices that have had devastating and continuing outcomes on the experiences of many population groups around the world. In such contexts it is not plausible to rely entirely on models of mental health and psychopathology that largely attribute causes of mental disorder to organic processes or intrapersonal deficits. Of course not all indigenous people experience mental illness, and so the effects of colonization must be indirect rather than directly causal. However, in most Westernized countries with significantly indigenous populations, the rates of social dysfunction as revealed by psychiatric referrals, crime rates, prison populations, school failure, and suicide, are always higher for the indigenous people. And this creates a double jeopardy, since very often indigenous groups then become defined by their failures (as characterized by Western and European standards), resulting in deficit theorizing regarding indigenous people and the emphasis on their problems rather than their successes.

The ethical implication of this state of affairs for applied research and psychological intervention is to recognize the importance of historical influences and current contextual factors that disadvantage certain people in health, education, and social opportunity. There is an important ethical imperative to ensure that deficit models and interventions that "blame the victim" are not dictating treatment strategies and social services. Thus, programs and interventions, no matter how well intentioned, which link negative statistics directly with ethnic groups are invariably seen as racist. For example, a child abuse prevention policy in Australia targeting aboriginal communities has been condemned as racist for assuming that pornography and alcoholism problems apply only to aboriginal and not white Australians (Anaya, 2010). Similarly, in New Zealand a government policy to support Māori social and educational initiatives, described as "Closing the Gap," was seen as patronizing—presupposing that being Māori equated with being needy.

In light of these observations and the widely acknowledged failure of assimilation policies (Sissons, 2005), it has become accepted that one possible intervention strategy for social and psychological challenges experienced by indigenous people is to focus broadly on helping clients reestablish contact with their cultural roots and traditions. While this would seem to be a valuable goal in its own right, there is as yet insufficient documentation that it alone represents a viable treatment approach for psychological distress. From the normative perspective the evidence is not strong that people who are closely connected to their cultural heritage are less likely to experience psychological difficulties. Streltzer, Rezentes, and Arakaki (1996) found no correlation between Native Hawaiians' acculturation (indigenous knowledge and values, language, and participation in cultural practices) and self-reported psychopathology. A similar nonrelationship was reported for Māori in New Zealand (Pahina, 2006). What Sissons (2005) refers to as the needed "repossession of indigenous identity" incorporates more than enhancing individual self-esteem and should be viewed as not only "access to [one's own] culture and heritage, but also the opportunity for cultural expression and cultural endorsement within society's institutions" (Durie, 2003, p. 68).

Imbalance of Power

One way in which colonization shapes professional psychological services is through the almost inevitable power differential that exists between indigenous clients and mainstream services. Even if the professional is from the same indigenous population, but working within the confines of the service system of the dominant group, similar conditions will exist. Thus, regardless of the cultural background of the psychologist, the system in which he or she operates will dictate the kinds of services offered, how they are delivered, and the extent to which they represent the extant models of psychopathology and the appropriate forms of treatment.

Psychological services are often government funded, bureaucratic, and employ mainstream-trained professionals who are not always considered cultural authorities by other members of their own people (Bishop et al., 2002).

It has long been recognized that even the best-intentioned psychiatric and psychological mental health services have a political as well as a health component. Abuses of psychiatric methods as a form of social control have been well documented, and many forms of intervention involve involuntary treatment or highly restrictive and coercive methods. When the client is a member of an indigenous group, the risks of these powerful influences being abused becomes even stronger. As apartheid came to an end in South Africa in the 1990s, South African psychologists—who were mostly white and middle class—came to recognize both the failure of the mental health system and the interconnection between psychology and politics (Biesheuwel, 1987). Political transformation demanded a radical shift in mental health services, including a greater reliance on traditional healers, greater professional cooperation, and the imparting of functional clinical skills to other, less expensive, professions (Vogelman, 1990). Hard-won political rights and legally binding treaties can serve to offset inequities to some extent, although, as history has shown, offer no guarantees of power sharing.

Treaty Relationships

The basis for biculturalism in Aotearoa New Zealand is the Treaty of Waitangi. Historically, the Treaty consisted in an agreement signed by representatives of the British Crown and *iwi* (tribes) in 1840. Kawharu (1989) pointed out that most treaties are merely agreements, but the Treaty of Waitangi specified partnership with trust and cooperation between British settlers and Māori, with protection for Māori fisheries and forestry resources and all *taonga* (treasures) necessary for continuing Māori self-determination and sovereignty under British governance (Herbert, 2002). Thus, in three articles, the Treaty of Waitangi: (I) recognized the authority of the British Crown; (II) gave Māori full sovereign rights over lands and *taonga*; and (III) conveyed the rights of British citizenship (Orange, 1987).

While these are essentially legal and constitutional provisions that have often been breached, the Treaty of Waitangi Act 1975 established the Waitangi Tribunal as a forum for grievances and mandated to "make recommendation on claims relating to the practical application of the Treaty" (Orange, 1987, p.246). The significance of the Treaty in this context derives from the expression of the articles, not specified in the Act itself, but generally derived from court rulings (Kawharu, 1989) and usually represented as the principles of *partnership, protection,* and *participation*. These key concepts can be translated into ethical research and intervention practices by offering a model for evaluating every aspect of professional work. Thus, decision making on planning, resourcing, and outcomes in psychological settings should be in fair and equal partnership. Input of both non-Māori and Māori must be considered, which may involve consultation with *iwi, hapū, whānau* and Māori communities to ensure services are appropriate, beneficial, and ethically sound. Partnership is an imperative that has organizational and governance implications in research funding and priorities, and agency policy and procedures. Similarly, *participation* has both individual and broader applications. It is expressed and observed as the rights of citizenship with the expectation that services and benefits are equitable and accessible to all individuals. This means Māori have the right to fair and equal participation in psychological research, both as participants and researchers, and to the benefits of that research, which should then underpin psychological services and interventions for indigenous individuals. Until recently, predominantly Western applied research paradigms underpinned psychological services and delivery, and were therefore often neither meaningful nor easily accessible to nondominant and indigenous groups and individuals. The principle of *protection* embodies the spirit and intention of Article II—sovereignty and cultural self-determination for indigenous groups. This means all psychological intervention and research with Māori should have Māori health development and enhancement as the main focus. Māori have the right to the same level of health as other ethnic groups, and this should be ensured. In many instances a lack of resourcing, infrastructure, and a trained workforce can inhibit truly indigenous services and appropriately informed psychological service. Challenges around developing and balancing ethical imperatives in a Treaty framework is further discussed in this volume (see Seymour & Nairn, Chapter 29).

Recognizing the importance of Māori-focused research to prioritize Māori aspirations and psychological needs, Nikora and others (Nikora & Evans, 1998) established a Māori and Psychology Research Unit (MPRU) within a university psychology department. MPRU is one of several Māori research initiatives that have been instrumental in developing and mentoring Māori/indigenous research and contributing to the broader awareness of ethical issues around Māori/indigenous research and practice (Herbert & Morrison, 2007). These authors stated that Māori access to psychological knowledge is through a *Kaupapa Māori* (Māori focused) approach: "It is about Māori values and validating our metaphors as a way for Māori to understand and access research, teaching and practice from a Māori perspective and within a Māori worldview" (p. 41).

One of the most promising antidotes to professional abuses is the development of mental health services not only by indigenous professionals, but within services that are themselves designed, implemented, and controlled by the indigenous community for whom they are intended. This is consistent with the principle of protection in Article II, which recognizes the importance of *tino rangatiratanga* (sovereignty). *Whānau Ora*, for instance, is a health promotion and preventative program conducted under *iwi* authority, supported by a high-level political task force to shape government policy. It is designed to address issues relevant to the family as a unit rather than focusing on the individual, and will be a coordinated effort between mainstream and indigenous agencies should families choose to incorporate both. Although *Whānau Ora* is underpinned by a Māori philosophical framework and aims to be appealing to Māori families, the program is available to both Māori and non-Māori alike. In this sense, it addresses the needs of the indigenous community, while mitigating any discriminatory concerns by being available to all New Zealand families.

Indigenous mental health literature is invariably underpinned by cultural models of good health with central components of spirituality; for example, the Swinomish Tribal Mental Health Project (1991). Intervention programs are based on tribal concepts, metaphors, and understandings, while promoting interaction with support agencies. Duran and Duran (1995) explored psychological worldviews and the importance of indigenous theory, described as "the replacement of Eurocentric models with native idioms" (p. 125). In another example, the Indian Nations within the United States retain the inherent sovereignty to govern their people and their lands, as consistently upheld by the U.S. Supreme Court (Keel, 2010). Tribes have developed innovative practices in telemedicine and dental services; however, progress still has to be made in the autonomous delivery of psychological services. Tribal leaders such as Keel, President of the National Congress of American Indians, point to a direct domino-like connection between lack of jobs, chronic and severe unemployment, school dropout, substance abuse, domestic violence, and suicide. The causal pathways could not be more obvious; self-determination is a first step to solution.

Practitioner Cultural Competence

For nonindigenous practitioners, an understanding of issues of power and cultural determination is an essential underpinning for developing multicultural competence. In many situations it needs to be recognized that within aboriginal communities, clients themselves are in powerless positions vis-a-vis their own national institutions, as well as lacking resources. National child protection agencies and family courts are often seen as a threat by disadvantaged families. With youth suicide being such an endemic problem in many indigenous societies, the practicing psychologist must not only be extra vigilant in anticipating the risks, but also recognize significant deficits in the bureaucratic support systems and community networks one might assume to be in place.

We are not naive regarding issues within some indigenous societies. Whatever the cause, family violence and mistreatment of women and children is an ever-prevalent risk. But it should also be noted that issues of abuse and violence are not part of many traditional indigenous cultures, such as Māori and First Nations, and are not considered acceptable. Imposing Western ideals of gender equality or children's rights poses ethical cautions when it places individual clients at risk of male physical abuse (Fontes, 2004). Some indigenous communities, such as the Mid-Island Tribal Council on Vancouver Island, which represents several indigenous bands in the area, define domestic violence and abuse as a community problem and have developed programs focusing on healing at this level. Other First Nations communities, such as the Mi'kmaq First Nation Communities of Nova Scotia, have developed programs where the focus of healing is aimed largely at women and children, while men are provided with suitable outreach services (Public Health Agency of Canada, 2009). Positive models focused on cultural traditions of multigenerational and diverse households and the importance of Māori women as leaders, eponymous tribal ancestors, and as repositories and transmitters of tribal knowledge have been recognized as enhancing parenting and support programs in Aotearoa New Zealand (Herbert, 2011) The underlying ethos of these programs is that they provide interventions in a culturally appropriate way, and are managed and used by the indigenous communities that designed them.

Awareness in itself is a very preliminary competency and may even have the reverse effect of the practitioner withdrawing from a professional situation, as observed by Selby (2004). Learning about a culture, however, can increase confidence by informing the practitioner of important tribal histories and cultural values (Jahnke & Taiapa, 1999). Nevertheless, indigenous values and perspectives can be all-encompassing, and by their very nature call for understandings significantly more profound, or at least more specialized, than those of didactic learning. Two of Sue's (1998) three elements of culturally competent practice are predicated on familiarity with the mores, values, and beliefs of the "other" culture—*dynamic sizing* and *culture-specific elements*. Such understanding and openness is always beneficial, but the indigenous position seems to mandate something more akin to "lived experience" than intellectual knowledge (Prilleltensky, Walsh-Bowers, & Rossiter, 1999).

The growing practice of falling back on cultural consultants is equally fraught with errors of understanding and expectation (Westerman, 2004). Nonindigenous practitioners need to earn trust and respect through their face-to-face presence and personal commitment to learn. Even a simple strategy, such as personally exploring the land and history of a community—introduced by Herbert (2002) as a component of clinical psychology students' training—has some benefit when working with a culture that relies so heavily on its sense of place, its ancestral sites, and natural *taonga* (Panelli & Tipa, 2007). In a successful program in Australia for training Aboriginal people to work in the hospitality industry, the trainees themselves organized a "cultural tour" of the region for the trainers and mentors (Bishop et al., 2002).

Indigenous Knowledge and Psychological Practice

Practitioners must respect indigenous knowledge and recognize that differences in perspective exist. Obviously, we cannot summarize the knowledge of any specific indigenous group and there are risks in generalizing anything about different worldviews. There are, however, practical ways in which psychologists working within indigenous cultural settings can ensure that existing knowledge and worldviews are recognized and understood.

It has been succinctly noted that indigenous peoples all over the globe have unique perspectives regarding the world, health, and well-being, which are often grounded in a sense of interconnectedness with the environment and balance in environment–human relations. As stated by one Canadian First Nations elder: "A healthy ocean means a healthy state of mind for us. The health of the ocean means assurance that my body is going to stay healthy" (Castellano, 2004, p. 103). Similarly, Nikora (2007) commented that "Māori have their own approaches to health and well-being, which stem from a world view that values balance, continuity, unity and purpose." (p. 80).

Indigenous peoples have taken steps to ensure the continuation and incorporation of their worldviews into traditional Western systems and practices, including psychology. The First Nations University of Canada provides tertiary education in an environment grounded in the traditions, values, and languages of First Nations peoples. Scholars in Korea developed an approach that uses indigenous worldviews as a guiding framework for explaining the behaviors and cognitions of indigenous Koreans (Kim, Park, & Park, 1999). Nikora (2007) observed that a Māori worldview "is not typically thought of as 'psychology' yet is a foundation for shared understandings and intelligible action among Māori." (p. 80).

Thus, best practice for psychological interventions in indigenous settings requires recognition of "cultural values, protocols and ways of learning as a core component" (Bishop et al., 2002, p. 614). But to appreciate fully the extent of difference between a practitioner's worldview and that of a client who is of a different culture, practitioners need to have a good appreciation of their own cultural values, beliefs, and practices (Celano & Kaslow, 2000; Holcomb-McCoy, 2000). Undergraduate programs at Australian universities have endeavored to broaden the perceptions of students in understanding their own cultural views as well as those of indigenous Australians and other immigrant people (Ranzijn, McConnochie, Day, Nolan, & Wharton, 2008). Moving on from the understanding of self (recommended for both the indigenous and the nonindigenous practitioner), an awareness and understanding of implicit and explicit biases and assumptions in Western worldviews can be explored.

Assumptions Regarding Mental Health

When considering psychological interventions, there is a particularly strong professional ethical obligation to recognize the importance of alternative models of psychopathology. Attribution to spiritual and external forces is common in indigenous cultures, but so too in Western European clients. In many ways indigenous models are not incompatible with Western concepts, but are presented metaphorically in a manner that emphasizes multiple causation and cultural metaphors. The popular Māori model, *Te Whare Tapa Whā*, uses the analogy of a traditional meeting house to emphasize the importance of several factors for well-being. Each of the four walls that equally support the stability of the house is symbolic of dimensions deemed important for well-being: *hinengaro* (feelings, emotions), *tinana* (physical body), *wairua* (spirituality), and *whānau* (family; Durie, 2001). Tongan culture has a similar focus (*kainga* is the extended family, with an emphasis on maintaining love and unity), but adds a fifth component: collective and individual contributions to society (*tokoni ki he fonua;* Tu'itahi, 2009).

Another mental health model, rich in symbolism and metaphor, has been developed for Pacific peoples who are migrants. The *popao* model uses the metaphor of the outrigger canoe to assist clients and professionals to develop a shared understanding of the journey toward recovery and strength. The *popao* is used in lagoon fishing, not the open ocean, and the model allows discussion of the hazards that might be in the lagoon, the preparation needed for a successful journey, and the strengths (paddles) and knowledge (of the canoe) that the service user brings (Fotu & Tafa, 2009).

In North America a core group of indigenous elders from separate regions were asked to consider how people conceived of mind, self, and identity before European contact (Mehl-Madrona & Pennycook, 2009). They endorsed a relational theory of mind, existing between individuals as a result of stories about experiences told in the context of that relationship. Conscious awareness, on the other hand, does not involve language. Mehl-Madrona and Pennycook suggested that "ceremony and ritual community interventions, talking circles, and family therapy are more compatible with aboriginal thought than conventional North American biomedicine and psychology" (p. 85). Similarly, narrative therapy may also be an applicable approach as it "takes into account self, family, and cultural stories" (Cole, 2008, p. 428), which seem more congruent with indigenous peoples' collective ways of being and their views regarding the interconnected nature of people and environment.

Psychological Interventions
Goal Setting

Setting goals for formal intervention has always been seen as a cornerstone of professional services. Establishing the client's goals is necessary for guiding treatment planning, decision making, and determining the merits of the outcome. The professional's causal and explanatory models usually dictate the manner in which the client's personal goals are restated as treatment goals. If there are shared assumptions regarding the nature of personality, psychopathology, and even causality itself, this process of negotiation can be relatively straightforward (Vicary & Westerman, 2004). Since psychologists do have the professional responsibility to make known and use their specialized understanding, the likelihood that this knowledge will be very different from the assumptions of indigenous clients poses something of a dilemma.

Indigenous people are very likely to have personal and social goals that are not easily defined within the standard concepts of psychological health and adjustment, particularly when the true causes of discomfort may well be related to broader social issues such as discrimination and subjugation. A domain that comes to mind might be the importance of spiritual beliefs in the setting of goals, although such understanding could well benefit any psychological practice context. The entire idea of setting personal goals can be out of keeping with the indigenous culture's ways of defining needs, change, and future outcomes, in accordance with collective values and ideals. But in Tongan society, for example, having clear strategic direction in the setting and achieving of priority goals, within the fair distribution of community resources, is well recognized as part of wise and prudent leadership (Tu'itahi, 2009)

One useful approach to goal setting is the *Te Pounamu* model, developed within *Kaupapa Māori* mental health services (Manna, 2002). A critical starting point after *mihimihi* (formal introductions) is a full explanation of the process that will occur, assuming that the role of the client and his or her accompanying support persons within a professional context may be differently understood. As the client talks, key words, phrases, or issues are written on a whiteboard under general categories—presenting issues, coping strategies, *whānau* dynamics, underlying and relationship issues, and strengths. These categories should be familiar to most practitioners, but possibly minimized in the need for a diagnostic label rather than a holistic integration of important influences. Action research models, in which clinical researchers and clients work together to establish mutual goals and strategies for change, fit closely with many key principles, such as using indigenous worldviews as normative and relying on indigenous people to deliver services for their benefit (Kerr, Penney, Moewaka Barnes, & McCreanor, 2010).

Treatment Acceptability

Psychological interventions must always be designed with the beliefs, predilections, standards, and expectations of the intended clients in mind. Psychologists typically adjust their description of the rationale for treatment according to their perception of the client's interests, cognitive style, and cognitive ability. This is necessary to obtain "buy in"—or, more technically, compliance with treatment and acceptance of its underlying theory. One of the best ways of ensuring treatment acceptability is to make the context and setting for service delivery comfortable and in keeping with cultural expectations. Cole (2008) suggested that with people of East African cultures, this can be done by sharing personal information and stories prior to commencing the formal treatment process. An invitation to share a meal with the client's family may be extended to the clinician before treatment begins.

In Aotearoa New Zealand, treatment acceptability can be fostered by having a strong Māori *kaupapa* (theme; philosophy). This might include such elementary components as starting the meeting with a *karakia* (prayer), exploring everyone's ancestral *whakapapa* (including the professional's credibility, which would not be defined by degrees, academic status, or seniority in the organization), encouraging supportive participation by extended family members, and having materials that reflect familiar Māori symbols and icons. Simple procedural niceties might include allowing enough time for any professional activity, and recognizing that people may have travelled to the session and need a meal and other refreshments.

Interestingly, many of these conditions represent simple courtesies that would be common across all cultures, and fit the ethical standard of respect for the dignity of all persons. There are some data indicating that when these everyday cultural practices are genuinely respected and made an integral part of the professional service, treatment outcomes are more positive. A good example of this comes from a specialized treatment program for sex offenders implemented by the New Zealand correctional service. One of the two prison units, but not the other, implemented, in addition to standard cognitive behavior therapy (CBT), Māori protocols emphasizing *wairua* (spirituality), *tautoko* (support), and *awhi* (embracing help), in addition to principles mentioned above. Not only did this unit have better outcomes for Māori, it benefitted non-Māori offenders as well (Nathan, Wilson, & Hillman, 2003).

Treatment Design

Adapting formal treatment protocols to the assumed expectations and beliefs of indigenous people, while seemingly necessary for effectiveness, does have an element of deceptiveness and a failure to provide full disclosure regarding the proposed treatment. There have been significant attempts to modify standard treatment approaches, particularly within CBT. This is because such interventions are usually quite well defined in treatment manuals or protocols. There are numerous examples of the sorts of modifications made to standard treatments. In Canada, McCormick (2000), a member of the Mohawk Nation, has described how conventional "evidence-based" treatments for alcohol and drug abuse among the aboriginal people required a context in which traditional cultural practices were revived and communities took ownership of the substance abuse problem as unacceptable individual behavior.

In Aotearoa New Zealand there is emerging evidence for cultural modifications of standard CBT protocols. Bennett (2009) consulted experienced Māori professionals, who suggested that while the broad principles of cognitive behavior therapy were applicable, it was the manner in which these principles were applied that caused their limitations. For example, the formality of the professional relationship needed to be transformed to a more personal connection, sometimes requiring judicious levels of personal self-disclosure by the therapist. Another adaptation was exploring clients' connections with culturally valued resources, including spirituality, and offering a choice of beginning and ending sessions with *karakia*. Extended family members were involved, and explanations of treatment elements were provided in metaphorical and culturally relevant imagery and aphorisms. Bennett's culturally adapted program had unusually low dropout rates and clinically significant benefits in reducing depression.

There are additional ethical considerations in the design of interventions. It is widely recognized that the processes underlying most of psychotherapy relate to learning—learning about oneself (insight), learning about others (social skills), learning to manage feelings (emotional competence), and learning new skills of coping, resilience, and self-regulation. A clearer understanding of indigenous models of learning could make therapeutic interventions more appropriate and successful. Traditional Hawaiian patterns of education, for example, started with skills in observation, followed by an emphasis on listening, then reflecting, and then increasing mastery by actually doing the task. Only after these steps would questioning be considered appropriate (Chun, 2006b). Similarly, in Canada, Iroquoian and Cree people shun argument and advice-giving as a form of normal communication (Castellano, 2004). It is easy to see how psychotherapy might be reoriented from the conventional Western strategy of encouraging questioning and reflection toward processes of observation (modeling), listening, and practicing.

Evaluating Outcomes

In addition to the design of interventions, a second important area of ethical practice is to ensure that evaluation of the outcome of intervention recognizes client values and priorities. Outcomes must be measured against the goals of the client and not against some arbitrary standard of mental health or psychological adjustment. There are many complex aspects to this seemingly obvious assertion. Most critical, as already discussed, is the need to ensure that the client's goals for psychological intervention are developed in accordance with the individual's cultural context. We need to be cautious when evaluating intervention effectiveness using constructs, tools, and instruments developed in one cultural context.

Test instruments are psychometrically inappropriate when based on standardization groups fundamentally different to the recipients of such testing. It is easy to recognize that measurement devices widely used in psychological settings throughout the Western world might be totally unsuitable for an indigenous cultural group with different language and ideas about mental illness. There is considerable distrust of paper and pencil measures, or evaluation by any set of instruments developed outside that particular culture. Such antipathy and mistrust reflects clearly the manner in which indigenous people have been further disadvantaged by the use of tests and testing procedures foreign to their worldviews.

Methodological Requirements

In mainstream psychology, treatment outcome research has evolved a widely accepted (within the profession) set of methodological strategies, including single-case research designs coming from applied behavior analysis, randomized controlled trials from drug research, and qualitative analyses of the meanings clients impose on their disorder and their treatment. Although qualitative and other concepts from critical psychology are presented as in opposition to positivist science, in reality they tend to complement each other and are often combined in "mixed-methods" research designs. Within culturally diverse environments there is a need for an inclusive view of knowledge and evidence. As Macfarlane (2008) has argued:

> A counter narrative proposes that the word "evidence" means different things to different people; that one's culture, worldview and experiences all play a significant part in determining how particular groups interpret and rationalise details around assessment, analysis and programme planning. Conventional streams of knowledge, while having immense merit, might be strengthened if the concepts of *tika* (the protocol of research), *pono* (the validation of cultural expertise) and *manaaki tangata* (humanitarianism) were to be offered authentic locations in the schema. What constitutes evidence—and who decides? Are particular forms of evidence accorded more privilege? I argue for a balanced integration between the conventional and indigenous knowledge systems
> (p. 33).

It is, therefore, possible to conduct sensitive treatment outcome research without throwing the baby out with the methodological bathwater. Rātima and Rātima (2005) have argued that the inherent value of an evidence-based approach to practice can be sustained as long as it is recognized that values and good judgment are always involved, that the validity of indigenous sources of evidence are recognized, and that the building of an evidence base for indigenous interventions and services is adequately resourced. Herbert (2001), for example, followed standard methods for evaluating the effects of a parent training program, while at the same time demonstrating the importance of ensuring the acceptability of the approach and that the rights of the clients were being protected. She demonstrated that features of the ethical practice of treatment outcome research also reflected standards and values of the Māori community (*tika*). She spent considerable time with experienced elders, who, even if not directly involved in the research, needed to know what was planned to give it some level of approval (*pono*). These elders offered wisdom based on past observation and cultural experiences. She also argued that research participants and their community must receive direct benefits in return for their involvement in the research, in recognition that they were sharing their intellectual property (*manaaki tangata*).

Ethical treatment research with indigenous, possibly vulnerable, groups requires that the issue of who will profit from the research be given primary consideration (Battiste, 2002). Indigenous communities all over the globe have been subjected to research not of direct benefit to their communities (Roberts, 2005), which has often been misguided, misinterpreted, and harmful. This has served to reinforce negative stereotypes about deficiencies and pathologies believed inherent to specific indigenous peoples (Castellano, 2004; Ermine et al., 2004).

The Canadian Institutes of Health Research (2007) and the Health Research Council of New Zealand (2008) have both drafted guidelines for undertaking research with indigenous peoples. Various other institutions (e.g., Australian Housing and Urban Research Institute, 2009; EIDOS Institute, 2007; University of Victoria Canada, 2003) have also implemented their own guidelines. While not specific to clinical intervention research, they do provide research frameworks for nonindigenous researchers to work from, which emphasize the importance of who the benefactors of the research will be.

The commonality among these guidelines suggests researchers will need to systematically build relationships rather than simply try to recruit participants, engage with local communities and community leaders, and be prepared to continue a relationship long after the original research project is over. Active involvement by indigenous researchers encourages capability building and future scholarly autonomy as now-experienced researchers. Will the indigenous community truly benefit from the research findings, or will their intellectual property have been given away with no assurance of future benefit? How will findings be communicated to those who generated them, so their people will benefit directly? Taiwhati et al. (2010) have proposed excellent, practical guidelines based on a metaphor of the traditional Māori cloak (*korowai*), the strands of which weave together the researcher and the participants.

Conclusion: Ethical Intervention Practices in Indigenous Settings

A significant challenge is that the most well-meaning practitioners do not always know what they do not know. In this chapter we have offered a mere sample of the many possible strategies whereby the mistakes of the past and misguided perceptions can be avoided in the future. This seems to us to be the ultimate ethical responsibility for the profession of psychology. Ethical codes should recognize the responsibility of nonindigenous practitioners to ensure that guilt or the magnitude of the personal challenge does not lead to avoidance of making positive contributions. Within the specific confines of ethics for psychological interventions, simply having an open mind and goodwill may be insufficient. Aotearoa New Zealand provides an example of a context where a formal treaty, achieving constitutional status, makes sensitivity to the indigenous population a mandated imperative, not just a nice thing to do.

One reason that ethical practice within indigenous communities requires more than acceptance of differences is the significant power imbalance between professional and client. The ethical rules for applied psychology, such as informed procedural consent, client access to all reports and information, and prohibitions on sexual contact, have been developed as recognitions of this power differential. However, the political aspirations of many indigenous peoples add an additional level to the problem of abuse of power, however unintended.

Despite many gains in human rights and economic advancement being made by indigenous people across the globe, there are very few areas where we can point to successes in creating more equitable societies. Psychology, which, as a discipline, has a fine record of defining and upholding ethical practices, has yet to make a serious impression on injustices worldwide. This may be expecting too much from a profession that even in the mainstream exercises very limited political influence. Psychological models of human distress and need are generally overwhelmed by biomedical and legal concepts and institutions. Because psychology has been identified with the oppressive majority, many indigenous groups have little truck with its principles, or are actively antagonistic to what are perceived as its dangers and threats. Truly ethical interventions and treatment research practices, can, however, empower people and support the common indigenous quest for greater autonomy and self-determination. And psychology as a discipline has long recognized the effects of discrimination and racism on development of the self. Now, can its principles also be mobilized to support repossession initiatives in their broadest sense?

Psychology has acknowledged the importance of culture, and has always understood that reality itself is at least partially socially constructed. Cultural psychology is growing in influence and importance, as is positive psychology, which celebrates accomplishments and achievements in a way that will prove beneficial for indigenous people. There continue to be many issues that need resolving, and the apparent clash between positivist science and indigenous ways of thinking and knowing will doubtless persist. Transcending such debates, however, is the importance of methods and processes that, rather than using or exploiting participants and clients, serve to build true partnerships, intellectual, professional, and interpersonal.

Acknowledgment

The authors are grateful for support for the preparation of this chapter provided by a summer studentship, from the Massey University School of Psychology's research fund, for Ms. Fiona Parkes, who assisted with the original literature search and whose valuable contribution is acknowledged with thanks.

Note

1. Aotearoa is a term used to refer to the whole of New Zealand. While it has gained extensive usage in popular culture as an additional or alternative name for the country, it was the original term used to refer to New Zealand by the great Māori chief Kupe, who is believed the first Polynesian to have discovered the country.

References

Anaya, J. (2010). *Observations on the Northern Territory emergency response in Australia.* Report by the Special Rapporteur on the situation of human rights and fundamental freedoms of indigenous people, James Anaya. New York: United Nations Human Rights Council.

Australian Housing and Urban Research Institute. (2009). *Ethical principles and guidelines for indigenous research.* Retrieved from www.ahuri.edu.au/download.asp?RelatedLinkID=322.

Battiste, M. (2002). Decolonizing university research: Ethical guidelines for research involving indigenous populations. In G. Alfredsson & M. Stavropoulou (Eds.), *Justice pending: Indigenous peoples and other good causes* (pp. 33–44). The Hague: Martinus Nijhoff Publishers.

Bennett, S. Te M. (2009). *Te huanga o te ao Māori: Cognitive behavioural therapy for Māori clients with depression—development and evaluation of a culturally adapted treatment programme.* (Unpublished doctoral dissertation). Massey University School of Psychology, Wellington, New Zealand.

Biesheuwel, S. (1987). Psychology: Science and politics. Theoretical developments and applications in a rural society. *South African Journal of Psychology, 17,* 1–8.

Bishop, B. J., Higgins, D., Casella, F., & Contos, N. (2002). Reflections on practice: Ethics, race, and worldviews. *Journal of Community Psychology, 30,* 611–621.

Canadian Institutes of Health Research. (2007). *CIHR guidelines for health research involving aboriginal people.* Ottawa: Canadian Institutes of Health Research.

Castellano, M. B. (2004). Ethics of Aboriginal research. *Journal of Aboriginal Health, 1,* 98–114.

Celano, M. P. & Kaslow, N. J. (2000). Culturally competent family interventions: Review and case illustrations. *American Journal of Family Therapy, 28,* 217–228.

Christie, M. (1985). *Aboriginal perspectives on experience and learning: The role of language in Aboriginal education.* Melbourne, Victoria, Australia: Deakin University Press.

Chun, M. N. (2006a). *Pono: The way of living. (Ka Wana Series, Book 1).* Honolulu, HI: University of Hawaii.

Chun, M. N. (2006b). *A'o: Educational traditions. (Ka Wana Series, Book 3).* Honolulu, HI: University of Hawaii.

Cole, E. (2008). Navigating the dialectic: Following ethical rules versus culturally appropriate practice. *The American Journal of Family Therapy, 36,* 425–436.

Duran, E., & Duran, B. (1995). *Native American postcolonial psychology.* Albany, NY: State University of New York Press.

Durie, M. (2003). *Ngā kāhui pou. Launching Māori futures.* Wellington, NZ: Huia Publishers.

Durie, M. (2008, December). *Bioethics in research: The ethics of indigeneity.* Paper presented at the 9th Global Forum on Bioethics in Research, Auckland, New Zealand.

EIDOS Institute. (2007). *Ethical principles and guidelines for indigenous research.* Brisbane: EIDOS Institute.

Elsmore, B. (1989). *Mana from heaven: A century of Māori prophets in New Zealand.* Wellington, NZ: Moana Press.

Ermine, W., Sinclair, R., & Jeffrey, B. (2004). *The ethics of research involving indigenous peoples: Report of the Indigenous Peoples' Health Research Centre to the Interagency Advisory Panel on Research Ethics.* Regina, SK: Indigenous Peoples' Health Research Centre.

Fogarty, G. J., & White, C. (1994). Differences between values of Australian Aboriginal and non-Aboriginal students. *Journal of Cross-Cultural Psychology, 25,* 394–408.

Fontes, L. A. (1998). Ethics in family violence research: Cross-cultural issues. *Family Relations, 47,* 53–61.

Fontes, L. A. (2004). Ethics in violence against women research: The sensitive, the dangerous, and the overlooked. *Ethics & Behavior, 14,* 141–174.

Fotu, M., & Tafa, T. (2009). The Papao model: A Pacific recovery and strength concept in mental health. *Journal of Community Health and Clinical Medicine for the Pacific, 15,* 164–170.

Health Research Council of New Zealand. (2008). *Guidelines for researchers on health research involving Māori.* Auckland: Health Research Council of New Zealand.

Herbert, A. M. L. (2001). Whānau whakapakari: A Māori-centred approach to child rearing and parent-training programmes. (Unpublished doctoral thesis). University of Waikato, Hamilton, New Zealand.

Herbert, A. M. L. (2002). Bicultural partnerships in clinical training and practice in Aotearoa/New Zealand. *New Zealand Journal of Psychology, 31,* 110–116.

Herbert, A. M. L. (2011). Māori perspectives on parenting in Aotearoa/New Zealand. In M. Mulholland & T. McIntosh (Eds.), *Māori and Social Issues* (pp. 67–87). Auckland, NZ: Ngā Pae o te Māramatanga.

Herbert, A. M. L., & Morrison, L. E. (2007). Practice of psychology in Aotearoa New Zealand: A Māori perspective. In I. M. Evans, J. J. Rucklidge, & M. O'Driscoll (Eds.), *Professional practice of psychology in Aotearoa New Zealand* (pp. 35–47). Wellington, NZ: New Zealand Psychological Society.

Holcomb-McCoy, C. C. (2000). Multicultural counseling competencies: An exploratory factor analysis. *Journal of Multicultural Counseling and Development. 28,* 83–97.

Jahnke, H. T., & Taiapa, J. (1999). Maori and research. In C. Davidson & M. Tolich (Eds.), *An introduction to social science research in New Zealand* (pp. 39–50). Auckland, NZ: Addison Wesley Longman.

Kaholokula, J. K., Nacapoy, A. H., & Dang, K. (2009). Social justice as a public health imperative for Kānaka Maoli. *AlterNative: An International Journal of Indigenous Peoples, 5,* 116–137.

Kawharu, I. H. (Ed.). (1989). *Waitangi: Māori and Pākehā perspectives of the Treaty of Waitangi.* Auckland, NZ: Oxford University Press.

Keel, J. (2010, January). *Sovereignty and the future of Indian Nations.* 8th Annual State of Indian Nations Address, National Press Club, Washington, DC.

Kerr, S., Penney, L., Moewaka Barnes, H., & McCreanor, T. (2010). Kaupapa Maori action research to improve heart disease services, in Aotearoa, New Zealand. *Ethnicity & Health, 15,* 15–31.

Kim, U., Park, Y. S., & Park, D. (1999). The Korean Indigenous psychology approach: Theoretical considerations and empirical applications. *Applied Psychology: An International Review, 48,* 451–464.

Kim, U., Yang, K. S., & Hwang, K. K. (2006). *Indigenous and cultural psychology: Understanding people in context.* New York: Springer.

Kulchyski, P. (2006). Six gestures. In P. Stern & L. Stevenson (Eds.), *Critical Inuit studies: An anthology of contemporary Arctic ethnography* (pp. 165–173). Lincoln: University of Nebraska Press.

Macfarlane, A. H. (2008). Kia hiwa rā! Listen to culture: A counter narrative to standard assessment practices in psychology. *Bulletin of the New Zealand Psychological Society, 111,* 33–36.

Manna, L. (2002). Biculturalism in practice, "Te Pounamu": Integration of a Māori model with traditional clinical assessment processes. *Proceedings of the National Māori Graduates of Psychology Symposium,* 37–44. University of Waikato, Hamilton, NZ.

McCormick, R. M. (2000). Aboriginal traditions in the treatment of substance abuse. *Canadian Journal of Counselling, 34,* 25–32.

McGreal, C. (2010). First Americans come last. *The Guardian Weekly Review,* 25–27.

Mehl-Madrona, L., & Pennycook, G. (2009). Construction of an aboriginal theory of mind and mental health. *Anthropology of Consciousness, 20,* 85–100. Mila-Schaff, K., & Hudson, M. (2009). *Negotiating space for indigenous theorizing in Pacific mental health and addictions.* Retrieved from http://www.leva.co.nz/file/PDFs/090204-le-va-neg-space-occ-paper-low-res.pdf.

Nairn, R. (2007). Ethical principles and cultural justice in psychological practice. In I. M. Evans, J. J. Rucklidge, & M. O'Driscoll (Eds.), *Professional practice of psychology in Aotearoa New Zealand.* (pp. 19–33). Wellington, NZ: New Zealand Psychological Society.

Nathan, L., Wilson, N. J., Hillman, D. (2003). *Te Whakakotahitanga: An evaluation of the Te Piriti special treatment programme for child sex offenders in New Zealand.* Wellington, NZ: Department of Corrections.

National Health and Medical Research Council. (2003). *Values and ethics: Guidelines for ethical conduct in Aboriginal and Torres Strait Islander health research.* Retrieved from http://www.nhmrc.gov.au/_files_nhmrc/file/health_ethics/human/conduct/guidelines/e52.pdf.

Nikora, L. W. (2007). Māori and psychology: Indigenous psychology in New Zealand. In A. Weatherall, M. Wilson. D. Harper, & J. McDowall (Eds.), *Psychology in Aotearoa/New Zealand* (pp. 80–85). Auckland, NZ: Pearson Education New Zealand.

Nikora, L. W., & Evans, I. M. (1998). A Māori and Psychology Research Unit. In Te Pūmanawa Hauora (Ed.), *Proceedings of Te Oru Rangahau Māori Research and Development Conference* (pp. 196–203). Palmerston North, NZ: Massey University, School of Māori Studies.

Orange, C. (1987). *The Treaty of Waitangi.* Wellington, NZ: Allen & Unwin.

Pahina, J. L. (2006). *The relationship between cultural identity and stress, depression, social support and coping.* (Unpublished Master's thesis). School of Psychology, Massey University, Palmerston North, New Zealand.

Panelli, R., & Tipa, G. (2007). Placing well-being: A Māori case study of cultural and environmental specificity. *EcoHealth, 4,* 445–460.

Pickren, W. E. (2009). Indigenization and the history of psychology. *Psychological Studies, 54,* 87–95.

Prilleltensky, I., Walsh-Bowers, R., & Rossiter, A. (1999). Clinicians' lived experience of ethics: Values and challenges in helping children. *Journal of Educational and Psychological Consultation, 10,* 315–342.

Public Health Agency of Canada. (2009). *Family violence in Aboriginal communities: An Aboriginal perspective.* Retrieved from http://www.phac-aspc.gc/ca/ncfvcnivf/familyviolence/html/fvabor_e.html

Ranzijn, R., McConnochie, K., Day, A., Nolan, W., & Wharton, M. (2008). Towards cultural competence: Australian Indigenous content in undergraduate psychology. *Australian Psychologist, 43,* 132–139.

Rātima, M., & Rātima, K. (2005). The ethics of an evidence-based approach to Māori health. In L. T. Smith & M. Walker (Eds.), *Tikanga rangahau mātauranga tuku iho: Traditional knowledge and research ethics* (pp. 187–198). Auckland, NZ: Ngā Pae o te Māramatanga.

Roberts, R. (2005). Caught between two worlds: An aboriginal researcher's experience researching in her home community. *Pimatisiwin: A Journal of Aboriginal and Indigenous Community Health, 3,* 101–108.

Saeki, T. (2008). *Ainu teachers' experiences in reclaiming the value of indigenous culture, language and identity: The call for establishing the new Ainu school in Japanese society.* (Master's thesis). Department of Educational Administration, Foundations and Psychology, University of Manitoba, Winnipeg, Canada.

San Juan, E. Jr. (2006). Toward a decolonizing indigenous psychology in the Philippines: Introducing Sikolohiyang Pilipino. *Journal for Cultural Research, 10,* 47–67.

Selby, J. (2004). Working divides between indigenous and non-indigenous: Disruptions of identity. *International Journal of Qualitative Studies in Education, 17,* 150–164.

Sissons, J. (2005). *First peoples: Indigenous cultures and their futures.* London, UK: Reaktion Books.

Stewart, T. (1997). Historical interfaces between Māori and psychology. In P. Te Whaiti, M. McCarthy, & A. Durie (Eds.), *Mai i rangiatea: Māori well-being and development* (pp. 75–95). Auckland, NZ: Auckland University Press.

Streltzer, J., Rezentes, W. C., & Arakaki, M. (1996). Does acculturation influence psychosocial adaptation and well-being in Native Hawaiians? *International Journal of social Psychology, 42,* 28–37.

Sue, S. (1998). In search of cultural competence in psychotherapy and counseling. *American Psychologist, 53*(4), 440–448.

Swinomish Tribal Mental Health Project. (1991). *A gathering of wisdoms: Tribal mental health—A cultural perspective.* La Conner, WA: Author.

Taiwhati, M., Toia, R., Te Maro, P., McRae, H., & McKenzie, T. (2010). Takina te kawa—laying the foundation: A research engagement methodology in Aotearoa New Zealand. *Australian Journal of Indigenous Education, 39,* 110–137.

Tassell, N. A. (2004). *Individualism/collectivism, cultural identity and self-enhancement: A study of New Zealand Māori.* (Unpublished Master's thesis). Massey University, Palmerston North, New Zealand.

Tassell, N. A., & Lock, A. (2011). Cultural considerations for professional psychology ethics: Te tirohanga ahurea hei whakatakato tika, whakapakari te aro ki te tangata: Te ahua ki Aotearoa. *Ethics and Social Welfare, 1–18.* Retrieved from http://www.tandfonline.com/doi/abs/10.1080/17496535.2011.632429

Tu'itahi, S. (2009). Fakapotopoto—the way of the wise and prudent: A Tongan leadership model for Pasifika development. In R. Gounder (Ed.), *Pacific development perspectives: Meeting our diverse goals* (pp. 60–68). Palmerston North, NZ: Office of the Directorate Pasifika@Massey.

Turia, T. (2000). Keynote address to the annual conference of the New Zealand Psychological Society. *Bulletin of the New Zealand Psychological Society, 99,* 27–29.

United Nations. (2007). *United Nations declaration on the rights of indigenous peoples.* Retrieved from http://www.un.org/esa/socdev/unpfii/en/drip.html.

University of Victoria. (2003). *Protocols & principles for conducting research in an indigenous context.* Retrieved from http://www.hsd.uvic.ca/policies/documents/igovprotocol.pdf.

Vicary, D. A. (2003, October). *Counselling as yarning: Aboriginal insights into Western therapy.* Paper presented at the 38th annual conference of the Australian Psychological Society, Perth.

Vicary, D., & Westerman, T. (2004). "That's just the way he is": Some implications of Aboriginal mental health beliefs. *Australian e-Journal for the Advancement of Mental Health, 3*(3), 9–18.

Vogelman, L. (1990). Psychology, mental health care and the future: Is appropriate transformation in a future South Africa possible? *Social Science and Medicine, 31,* 501–505.

Walker, R. (1987). *Nga tau tohetohe: Years of anger.* Auckland, NZ: Penguin Books.

Westerman, T. G. (2004). Engagement of indigenous clients in mental health services: What role do cultural differences play? *Australian e-Journal for the Advancement of Mental Health, 3*(3), 1–7.

CHAPTER
14

Psychological Ethics and Immigration

Mihaela Robila *and* Adeyinka M. Akinsulure-Smith

Abstract

This chapter examines the unique challenges faced by immigrants, while exploring the ethical questions that arise when conducting research or providing therapeutic services to this population. An exploration of the American Psychological Association's (APA) *Ethical Principles of Psychologists and Code of Conduct* offers guidelines to address ethical challenges encountered in research and service provision to immigrants. The chapter emphasizes the importance of adopting a multicultural perspective to illuminate the key ethical questions from competing perspectives, as well as offering suggestions for consideration in conducting sound ethical research and clinical practice.

Key Words: immigration, immigrants, refugees, ethics, code of ethics

Introduction

Immigration to the United States has experienced a phenomenal increase in the last decades, with the foreign-born population growing from 19.8 million in 1990 (7.9% of population) to 42.8 million in 2010 (13.5% of the U.S. population; IOM, 2010). The United States is the country with the highest number of international migrants, 42.8 million, followed by the Russian Federation with 12.3 million, Germany with 10.8 million, Saudi Arabia with 7.3 million, and Canada with 7.2 million (IOM, 2010). International migration is one of the most complex contemporary issues, demanding important actions and decisions at national and international levels. The increase in international migration is a significant issue and, as such, societies need to find ways to manage migration effectively to enhance its positive and reduce its negative impacts (Gadit, 2008; McKinley, 2007; Storey, 1994).

As the United States continues to experience this phenomenal increase in its foreign-born population, it is important to recognize that all immigrant experiences are not equal. The growing number of armed conflicts and human rights violations around the world has led to a rise in the number of displaced people who are forced to become immigrants (Blanch, 2008; Drachman, 1995; Gorman, 2001). By the end of 2008, the United Nations High Commission on Refugees (UNHCR) noted that there were approximately 15.2 million refugees and 827,000 asylum seekers worldwide (UNHCR, 2009).

Because the experiences of "voluntary" immigrants are so vastly different from "forced" immigrants, in order to provide ethical and effective clinical services and to conduct ethical research it is important for the practitioner to fully understand what type of immigrant population he or she is working with. Unlike "voluntary" immigrants, who choose to leave their countries and relocate in an orderly, planned fashion, forced immigrants—refugees, asylees, asylum seekers, and some undocumented individuals—are people who have been abruptly forced out of their home countries with very little, as a result of harrowing civil and political upheaval (Blanch, 2008; Drachman, 1995;

Gorman, 2001; Keyes, 2000, Sue & Sue, 2008). Given that the United States is the world's largest resettlement country (UNHCR, 2009) and a large number of the forced migrants come from developing countries (Braken & Petty, 1998; Gorman, 2001), understanding the various categories of immigration status and the legal implications of each category is a first step to addressing the needs of this population.

According to the United Nations Refugee Convention (1951), a refugee is a person who "owing to well-founded fear of being persecuted for reasons of race, religion, nationality, membership of a particular social group or political opinion, is outside the country of his nationality, and is unable to or, owing to such fear, is unwilling to avail himself of the protection of that country; or who, not having a nationality and being outside the country of his former habitual residence [as a result of such events], is unable or, owing to such fear, is unwilling to return to it" (Article 1, The 1951 Convention Relating to the Status of Refugees, Center for the Study of Human Rights, 1994, pp. 57–58). Within the U.S. immigration system, refugee status is determined while the person is still outside the United States. Since their applications have been already approved outside of the country, refugees have lawful status upon entering the United States and qualify for a range of benefits (Blanch, 2008; Drachman, 1995; Ingleby, 2005; Wilkinson, 2007).

Although similar to a refugee, an asylee is an individual who traveled to the United States on his or her own and applied for or received a grant of asylum after arrival in the country. This status acknowledges that that person met the definition of a refugee, and allows him or her to remain in the United States. Asylees also become eligible for refugee assistance and services, and eventually they may be eligible for citizenship (Blanch, 2008; Drachman, 1995; Wilkinson, 2007). Unlike those who have already been granted refugee or asylee status, the long and arduous asylum-seeking process brings its own specific challenges and stressors. Asylum seekers are often denied access to work, education, and social welfare benefits. They are constantly in fear of deportation (Drachman, 1995; Ryan, Kelly, & Kelly, 2009; Wilkinson, 2007). Any person who attempts to enter the United States without a valid visa or with false documents can be detained in an immigration detention center if they indicate they wish to seek asylum (US Committee for Refugees and Immigrants, 2002).

Finally, immigrants with "undocumented or no-lawful status" are people who have not yet applied for any lawful immigration status (Drachman, 1995; Ingleby, 2005; Wilkinson, 2007). Those with "undocumented status" have no legal authorization to be in the United States; they either entered illegally or remained in the United States after their visas expired. Undocumented people are subject to deportation and are ineligible for many social services. There are no reliable estimates on the numbers of undocumented immigrants (Drachman, 1995; Ingleby, 2005)

Since most of the work that has been done in this area has centered on the experiences of refugees, asylees, and asylum seekers, the remainder of this chapter will focus on research and therapeutic services for these populations. The term *forced migrant* will be used to include refugees, asylees, and asylum seekers. Although research and empirically based treatment interventions in the field of psychology for this population are limited, it is important to not only identify and document the unique experiences and needs of this population, but to understand the professional and ethical responsibilities of psychologists who conduct research and/or provide mental health services for forced migrants.

For many forced migrants, the exposure to ongoing and extensive traumatic events and chaos (e.g., torture, sexual violence, war, destruction of their families and communities, forced labor, and multiple losses) is distressful. Unfortunately, such experiences often follow individuals from their home countries, during their search for safety, and continue even as they resettle in a new country (Akinsulure-Smith, 2010; Blanch, 2008; Bemak & Chung, 2008; Chung, Bemak, Ortiz, & Sandoval-Perez, 2008; Drachman, 1995; Fazel, Wheeler, & Danesh, 2005, Marshall, Schell, Elliott, Berthold, & Chun, 2005, Pope & Garcia-Peltoniemi, 1991; Ryan, Kelly, & Kelly, 2009).

The American Psychological Association's *Ethical Principles of Psychologists and Code of Conduct* has as its goals the welfare and protection of the individuals and groups with whom psychologists work. The Ethics Code applies to teaching, conducting research, providing social services, such as therapy or social interventions, program design, and evaluation (APA Ethics Code).

The APA Ethics Code has a significant value when working with different immigrant populations. The following sections present specific elements of the code and how they are related with providing education, conducting research, or providing therapeutic services to this diverse population with multifaceted needs. In this chapter we will highlight the ethical standards of Competence, Education and Training, Research and Publication, and Therapy, as they are particularly important to protecting the welfare of this population.

Psychological Ethics and the Training and Teaching of Cultural Diversity

With the significant growth of an increasingly culturally diverse immigrant population in recent years, becoming culturally competent represents a core duty for any psychology professional. Working with immigrant populations requires knowledge about different cultures and people, openness, and cultural sensitivity. As such, it is extremely important for psychologists to prepare themselves to be culturally competent professionals. One of the APA ethical standards is Competence, which stresses that "psychologists provide services, teach and conduct research with populations and in areas only within the boundaries of their competence, based on their education and training..." (APA Ethics Code, p. 4). This standard also suggests that "where scientific or professional knowledge established that an understanding of factors associated with age, gender, race, ethnicity, culture, national origin, religion, language... is essential for effective implementation of their services or research, psychologists have or obtain the training, experience, consultation, or supervision necessary to ensure the competence of their services or they make appropriate referrals..." (APA Ethics Code, p. 5).

Culture influences all aspects of human life, including values, beliefs, and practices (Arnett, 2002). Becoming a culturally competent professional entails gaining awareness, knowledge and skills (Sue & Sue, 2008), and extensive training in cultural diversity, as well as interacting with people with different cultural backgrounds. As such, it is a duty of social science departments in general to provide such courses and training for their students. A review of teaching about international families across the United States indicates that the number of courses on cultural diversity or international families is still limited, regardless of the increased awareness of their importance and the availability of large numbers of teaching materials (Robila, & Taylor, 2005). Books having a global perspective on children and families (e.g., Hamon, & Ingoldsby, 2003; Roopnarine, & Gielen, 2004) or describing specific cultural groups have been published (e.g., for Caribbean families see Roopnarine, & Brown, 1997; for Eastern European families see Robila, 2004). Moreover, specific volumes on different immigrant groups offer more detailed and specific information on cultural issues and patterns (e.g., for Latino families see Falicov, 2000 or Portes, & Rumbaut, 2001; for Eastern European immigrants see Robila, 2009; for a variety of immigrant groups see the volume edited by McGoldrick, Giordano, & Garcia-Preto, 2005).

In their effort to train ethical psychologists, Handelsman, Gottlieb, and Knapp (2005) drew on J. W. Berry's (2003) model of acculturation strategies as a framework for understanding ethical acculturation, a developmental process during which students can use several types of adaptation strategies. The model is intended to improve students' ethical behavior and better prepare them to be more responsive to an increasingly complex and diverse professional world. Integration is the most effective acculturation strategy, and people who adopt integration retain important aspects of their heritage while also adopting what their new culture has to offer. Applied to ethical acculturation, people choosing integration would adopt the ethical values of psychology while understanding and maintaining their own value tradition. This model might be particularly useful in training ethical professionals who work with immigrants, by increasing their awareness and sensitivity to possible differences and providing guidance for a problem solving.

Ethics Issues while Conducting Research with Immigrants

Studies with immigrants encounter unique methodological challenges, such as the different contexts between the host and origin countries, translation of concepts, or adherence to standard Western research methods. Many immigrants coming from developing countries present a lack of familiarity with the research process, having not been involved in research before, not having seen surveys or participated in an interview. Years of political, ideological, and social turmoil in their countries has led to conditioned fear and distrust of inquiries on any topic and, therefore, a major contextual difficulty is the resistance of immigrants to participate in research studies (Pernice, 1994). Moreover, many developing countries do not have funds for research, and as a consequence it is done at a reduced rate compared to Western, developed societies. Therefore, immigrants might perceive the whole research process with suspicion and reservation, not being aware of its goals and usefulness. Developing guidelines specific to these types of studies could respond to the ethical issues of research with immigrants.

As part of the APA Ethics Code (2002a), a requirement that is particularly important for research with immigrants is "obtaining informed consent of the individuals using language that is reasonably understandable to that person" (p.6). Sometimes this issue presents a challenge, when the immigrants are not very proficient in using the host country language. As part of this process, immigrants are also informed about "their right to decline to participate and to withdraw from the research once the participation has begun" (APA Ethics Code, 2002a, p.11). However, their lack of familiarity with the research process and feelings of insecurity about being in a foreign environment might prevent them from declining or withdrawing from participation. Therefore, it is recommended that special consideration and care should be provided while conducting research with immigrants to ensure that they understand their rights.

The financial incentives that sometimes are provided to research participants might seem particularly attractive to immigrants, who are in many instances in need of financial support. As such, special attention needs to be provided to ensure that these incentives are not becoming coercive factors that push immigrants to participate in research because of financial need. Moreover, the code indicates that "psychologists make reasonable efforts to avoid offering excessive or inappropriate financial or other inducements for research participation when such inducements are likely to coerce participation" (p.11). When working with immigrant groups, the professional's perspective on what is "excessive" might be very different than the perspective of people coming from very poor countries, where even a relatively small amount of financial compensation might act as a coercive force. Therefore, the professional's appraisal needs to be adjusted for the specific cultural group.

Another part of the consent form includes information about "whom to contact for questions about the research and research participants' rights." However, again, it is less likely that immigrants will contact these parties; thus, special consideration needs to be put into making the process as clear as possible, providing opportunities for participants to ask questions and receive answers during the data collection procedure. Finally, another challenge encountered is the immigrant's, and especially refugee's, refusal to sign a consent form because of fear of negative repercussions. Thus a practice designed to protect participants can unintentionally cause psychological distress due to previous political and social experiences (Pernice, 1994).

Data collection or the procedure could also encounter challenges in research studies with immigrants. Sometimes the data collection involves recording voices and images, and although an informed consent is obtained prior to that event as an ethical procedure, this method could be particularly challenging for some immigrant groups, especially those coming from oppressive political regimes. In some of these politically rigid and oppressive societies, such as, for example, the former communist regimes in Eastern European countries, recording people's private phone conversations was a frequent practice as part of political intimidation and secret police manipulation (e.g., Robila, 2004). These immigrants might have a particularly hard time accepting the recording; therefore, sensitivity, respect, and care need to be provided by the professional conducting the study. Another difficulty could be sampling (e.g., random, systematic), since the group might be smaller in size or dispersed (Pernice, 1994).

Professionals should use "assessment instruments whose validity and reliability have been established for use with members of the population tested" (APA Ethics Code 9.02 Use of Assessments, p.13). Sometimes this is not possible when assessing immigrant groups, due to the lack of instruments tailored for those particular cultural groups. In these cases, "when such validity or reliability has not been established, psychologists describe the strengths and limitations of test results and interpretation" (APA Ethics Code p.13). Acknowledging the limitations of research conducted with instruments designed for other cultural groups is necessary and it is recommended that ,as much as possible, instruments be developed and tailored for specific groups. The APA Ethics Code (2002a) also indicates that "Psychologists use assessment methods that are appropriate to an individual's language preference and competence..." (p.13). As such, it is strongly recommended that when conducting research with immigrants, the instruments either be developed in their native language, or at the very least be translated in their native language and respondents be offered the choice of responding using their native language. The translation of the instruments brings up other ethical issues, such as equivalence of concepts in different cultures and languages. A method that has been recommended over the years for translation of instruments is the translation/back-translation method (Hambleton, 1994). Through this method an instrument is translated from one language (usually English) to another and then it is translated back, to determine whether there is any drift in meaning on any of the items.

These translations should be conducted by experts fluent in both languages, who should also examine the clarity and meaning of different items. Questionnaires should also be analyzed for cultural appropriateness of words and phrases. Translation could be modified in accordance with the interpreter's emotional and intellectual state, and especially during interviews the respondents might be worried about divulging their details to a third person who might be known in their cultural/ethnic group (Pernice, 1994). In addition to translation difficulties, the use of self-rating scales has several limitations, requiring participants to be able to read and become familiar with this type of testing (Pernice, 1994).

The question of confidentiality is a major concern for many immigrant groups. The APA Code of Ethics indicates that "psychologists...ensure that confidentiality...is maintained" (2002a, p.13). However, many immigrants might not know what confidentiality is, so special care needs to be provided to explain the process. Those coming from oppressive regimes where regular citizens have been watched and followed by secret police might have difficulties believing in confidentiality and might present reservations. Extended time and explanations should be provided to make the respondents comfortable with the research procedure.

Ethical Considerations for Conducting Research with Forced Migrants

As with voluntary immigrants, psychological research with forced migrants is fraught with a number of challenges, including language translation and cultural concerns, the lack of culturally reliable and valid instruments, the use of Western-based constructs, and the inability to identify appropriate control groups. A number of scholars in the field have identified a range of limitations in refugee research, including the emphasis on Western psychiatric symptomatology, a reliance on quantitative methodologies, and a disregard for the significance of transit stressors and the temporal nature of the forced migrant experience (Keyes, 2000; Miller, Worthington, Muzurovic, & Tipping, 2002; Watters, 2001).

In order to conduct ethical research with this population, researchers are challenged to demonstrate an understanding of diverse research methods, while working with an often traumatized and culturally diverse population. Given the diverse backgrounds and range of experiences that this population brings, it has been argued that a wide range of methodologies (including qualitative, quantitative, and mixed methods) is needed to identify and understand cultural variations in forced migrant well-being and distress (Betancourt & Williams, 2008). Increasingly, community-based participatory methods and grounding assessments have been incorporated, offering unique approaches to understanding and working with these individuals.

Additionally, in order to capture the experiences of the population, researchers must develop or use culturally appropriate instruments that have been normed and validated on similar populations, rather than merely using instruments that have been developed for Western populations. It is also important that the instruments are appropriately translated—culturally and linguistically—in order to capture the forced migrant's experience.

One aspect of research that is often taken for granted is Informed Consent to Research. Ethical researchers must understand that for many forced migrants, prior experiences with atrocities, political violence, torture, and abuse can influence their ability to develop trust and their willingness to disclose information. Such concerns hamper participant recruitment and the ability to obtain representative samples. Thus, it is especially important to address issues of trust and consequences of disclosure in great detail. Participants must feel free to participate or to not participate in research, and institutional review boards should carefully examine the ethical dimensions of conducting research with traumatized, vulnerable populations. Addressing both individual and community consent in a refugee population may uphold ethical standards and create a more effective study (Ellis, Kia-Keating, Yusuf, Lincoln, & Nur, 2007).

A final ethical consideration for researchers includes balancing their needs to gather information and make their findings public in the form of articles, against the rights and well-being of the participants. Given the experiences of the population, researchers must have an understanding of the social, historical, and cultural context of their research in the presentation and use of their research findings, as well examining their own underlying political views and motivations (APA, 2002a; Morrow & Smith, 2000).

Leaning (2001) has argued that in situations where existing ethical guidelines are not sufficient, or are seen as less "ethical" in certain cultural groups, it is the researcher's responsibility to promote ethical research by developing appropriate and/or additional ethical approaches.

Psychological Ethics and Providing Social Services to Immigrants

Providing social services to immigrants entails several challenges. One of them is the lack of familiarity with therapy or social interventions and their purpose. Many of the developing countries do not have well-developed social services and, as a result, immigrants coming to the developed societies might not be familiar with these services and might not be willing or comfortable to access them. Therefore, special care needs to be taken to explaining the therapy or social service to be provided, and its goal and usefulness, so that immigrant clients become comfortable with it. Issues such as confidentiality or recording of the session are sensitive and require special emphasis for many immigrant groups. Another problem is a lack of services targeted to specific immigrant groups. Many times this lack of services is due to a lack of professionals trained to provide culturally tailored services.

One of the APA ethics code standards is Human Relations, with specific reference to "Unfair Discrimination: In their work related activities, psychologists do not engage in unfair discrimination based on age, gender, race, ethnicity, culture, national origin..." (p. 5). Immigrants are more vulnerable to discrimination, due to their status, lack of familiarity with the host environment, and/or lack of social or economic resources. The lack of social services that could potentially support these groups makes them even more vulnerable to the challenges of migration.

The APA ethic code's Competence standard also indicates that "When psychologists are asked to provide services to individuals for whom appropriate mental health services are not available and for which psychologists have not obtained the competence necessary, psychologists with closely related prior training or experience might provide such services in order to ensure that services are not denied..." (APA Ethics Code, p. 5). As such, obtaining specific cultural training is strongly recommended as a step in immigrant program development. Another recommendation is for scholars to write applied articles that could be used by other colleagues while working with specific immigrant groups. For example, a Baptiste, Hardy, and Lewis (1997) article provides information on family therapy with English Caribbean immigrant families, while Berg and Jaya (2007) provide specific recommendations for working with Asian-American families. Similarly, Kinzie and colleagues (1998) provided details on conducting group therapy with Southeast Asian refugees, while Robila and Sandberg (2011) developed recommendations for working with Eastern European immigrants and Laszoffy (2005), illustrates effective techniques for working specifically with Hungarian immigrants.

Since immigration can be potentially a very challenging process, many immigrants encounter mental health problems such as increased depression or anxiety, higher levels of mood disturbance, or post-traumatic symptoms. For example, a Jureidini (2004) study showed preschool-age children who were identified with developmental delay or emotional disturbance, high levels of psychopathology in child and adult asylum seekers, much of this being attributable to traumatic experiences in detention, and, for children, the impact of indefinite detention on their caregivers. Therefore, developing social service and delivering interventions and therapy for these groups becomes even more important.

Ethical Considerations for Mental Health Services to Forced Migrants

Forced migrants who have been exposed to traumatic events during their search for safety are often at risk for a range of physical and emotional difficulties and, as such, they are a vulnerable group. Often, even after resettlement in a safe environment, many physical and psychological challenges remain (Blanch, 2008; Bemak & Chung, 2008, Keyes, 2008; Fazel, Wheeler, & Danesh, 2005; Khawaja, White, Schweitzer & Greenslade, 2008; Porter & Haslam, 2005). Those who are in more tenuous situations, such as asylum-seekers and the undocumented, experience further post-migration stressors, including worries about their immigration status (i.e., fear of deportation), lack or absence of basic needs (e.g., food, shelter, clothing), lack of medical care, and ongoing family separation (Bemak & Chung, 2007; Chung, Bemak, Ortiz, & Sandoval-Perez, 2008; Drachman, 1995, Gong-Guy, Cravens & Patterson, 1991; Porter & Haslam, 2005; Ryan, et al., 2009). Despite the multiple traumas that this population has suffered, and their ongoing stressors, it is not surprising that their immigration status affects not only their willingness to seek services but also the availability of needed services.

When providing therapeutic services to forced migrants, early ethical concerns can revolve around

Informed Consent to Therapy. As with any other population, clinicians working with this population must first address expectations about the duration and nature of therapy. It is important to remember that for many forced migrants who come from developing countries, formal psychotherapy is often a new and unfamiliar concept. Thus, extensive psychoeducation regarding the type of treatment offered, the duration, therapist's expectations, and potential outcomes are an important part of Informed Consent to Therapy.

Although there are numerous psychotherapeutic interventions designed to alleviate the impact of the trauma-related disorders, there are very few empirical studies that confirm their effectiveness on forced migrant populations. Currently, researchers have documented the effectiveness of narrative therapy (Neuner, Schauer, & Klaschik, 2004; Neuner, Catani, Ruf, Schauer, Schauer, & Elbert 2008; Weine, Kulenovic, Pavkovic, & Gibbons, 1998), cognitive behavioral therapy (Otto & Hinton, 2006; Paunovic & Ost, 2001; Regel & Berliner, 2007; Schulz, Resick, Huber, & Griffin, 2006), and trauma-focused therapy (Kruse, Joksimovic, Cavka, Wöller, & Schmid, 2009) in forced migrants. Other therapeutic interventions aimed at addressing the needs of forced migrants are informed by psychodynamic, supportive, and expressive arts and movement therapies, and work to address needs at the individual and family (Porterfield & Akinsulure-Smith, 2007; Weine, Raina, Zhubi, Delesi, Huseni, Feetham, & Pavkovic, 2003; Weine, Feetham, Kulauzovic, Knafl, Besic, Kelbic, & Pavkovic, 2006), group (Akinsulure-Smith, Ghiglione, & Wollmershauser, 2009; Harris, 2007; Stepakoff, Hubbard, Katoh, Falk, Mikulu, Nkhoma, et al., 2006; Watters, 2001), and community levels (Hubbard & Pearson, 2004)

Given that major theories in psychotherapy are based on white, Eurocentric, Western cultural norms (Corey, 2009; Sue & Sue, 2008), and the fact that a large number of forced migrants come from non-Western countries (Bracken & Petty, 1998), to truly address the diverse needs of this unique population, mental health professionals must demonstrate flexibility with treatment models and consider integrative methods when deciding which orientations and techniques are best suited to the presenting problems and needs of their particular forced migrant population. For forced migrants, cultural issues such as those around race, ethnicity, religion, and gender take on very important meanings, as often these factors contributed to their forced migration. Although there is a dearth of empirical studies documenting the effectiveness of available therapeutic interventions for this population, the current literature indicates promising therapeutic initiatives.

In order to address the multiple needs of this diverse population, therapeutic interventions aimed and reducing or healing traumatized forced migrants must draw on a range of culturally informed treatment methods that adhere to APAs standards of care and multicultural competence. Furthermore, development of holistic approaches and community-based interventions that foster the creation of new social networks, support resilience, and incorporate traditional modes of healing need to be explored further (Blanch, 2008; Watters, 2001).

In addition to the ethical principles and code of conduct, the APA (2002b) has outlined standards of multicultural competence expected of all psychologists. It is vital that clinicians incorporate these standards when providing therapeutic services to this population. When providing therapeutic services to culturally and linguistically diverse populations, it is important to recognize that clinicians will at times need to rely on an interpreter to facilitate communication and offer additional cultural knowledge about the client's experience. Working with interpreters presents another layer of complexity to an already challenging cultural encounter and gives rise to additional challenges, ranging from questions regarding confidentiality to miscommunication. Thus, it is the ethical responsibility of the clinician to use a competent, professionally trained interpreter during therapeutic sessions that involve interpreters (O'Hara & Akinsulure-Smith, 2011; Gong-Guy, et al., 1991; Gorman, 2001).

Finally, for clinicians who work with asylum seekers, it is important to recognize that they can be called upon to testify in immigration court as their clients endure the long process of attempting to become asylees. It is the clinician's ethical responsibility to conduct psychological assessments, write reports and, during the asylum hearing, to appear as a competent professional who has the prerequisite education and training to be an "expert" or a "fact" witness in such legal proceedings (Akinsulure-Smith & O'Hara, in press).

As researchers and clinicians, adhering to ethical standards may require increased creativity, flexibility, and thoughtfulness when addressing the needs of forced migrants. In order to provide the highest level of care possible, it is the ethical responsibility of the psychologist to provide informed, sensitive, culturally competent services considering all of these multiple needs (Sue, Arredondo, & McDavies, 1992).

Conclusions

The goal of this chapter was to provide an overview of psychological ethics and how they are influenced by immigration. As the number of immigrants is expected to increase worldwide, concerns regarding ethical research about immigrant experiences and ethical mental health service provision also increase. Drawing on the APA's *Ethical Principles of Psychologists and Code of Conduct* regarding competence, the ethical responsibilities of researchers and clinicians were discussed in this chapter in terms of how they impact work with different immigrant populations.

In the field of psychology, the importance for both students and seasoned psychologists to pay close attention to ethical standards regarding research and clinical practice for immigrant populations has become increasingly apparent. Within the research realm, more training and information is needed to develop appropriate research protocols, methodologies, data collection procedures, and instruments. In terms of providing ethical therapeutic interventions, clinicians must move beyond their basic knowledge about trauma treatment to address areas such as cultural diversity, language barriers, consent to treatment, culturally appropriate interventions, and confidentiality when working with traumatized immigrant populations. In order for both researchers and practitioners to provide and maintain the highest standards of care, effectively address research challenges, and provide quality care to this diverse and fast-growing population, research and treatment must take into account the numerous ethical aspects of this type of work.

References

Akinsulure-Smith, A. M. & O'Hara, M. (in press). Working with forced migrants: Therapeutic issues and considerations for mental health counselors. *Journal of Mental Health Counseling*.

Akinsulure-Smith, A. M. (2010). Torture. In C. S. Clauss-Ehlers (Ed.), *Encyclopedia of cross-cultural school psychology* (Vol. 2, pp. 27–29). New York, NY: Springer.

Akinsulure-Smith, A. M., Ghiglione, J., & Wollmershauser, C. (2009). Healing in the midst of chaos: Nah We Yone's African women's wellness group. *Women & Therapy, 32*, 105–150.

American Psychological Association. (2002a). *Ethical principles of psychologists and code of conduct*. Washington, DC: Author. Retrieved from http://www.apa.org/ethics/code/index.aspx.

American Psychological Association. (2002b). *Guidelines on multicultural education, training, research, practice, and organizational change for psychologists*. Washington, DC: Author.

Retrieved from http://www.apapracticecentral.org/ce/guidelines/multicultural.pdf.

Arnett, J. J. (2002). The psychology of globalization. *American Psychologist, 57*, 774–783.

Baptiste, D. A., Hardy, K., & Lewis, L. (1997). Family therapy with English Caribbean immigrant families in the United States: Issues of emigration, immigration, culture and race. *Contemporary Family Therapy, 19*, 337–359.

Bemak, F., & Chung, R. C-Y. (2008). Counseling refugees and migrants. In P. Pederson, J. Dragons, W. Lonner, & J. E. Trimble (Eds.), *Counseling across cultures* (6th ed., pp. 307–324). Thousand Oaks, CA: Sage.

Berg, I. K., & Jaya, A. (2007). Different and same: Family therapy with Asian American Families. *Journal of Marital and Family Therapy, 19*, 31–38.

Berry, J. W. (2003). Conceptual approaches to acculturation. In K. M. Chun, P.B. Organista, & G. Marin (Eds.), *Acculturation: Advances in theory, measurement, and applied research* (pp. 17–37). Washington, DC: American Psychological Association.

Betancourt, T. S., & Williams, T. (2008). Building an evidence base on mental health interventions for children affected by armed conflict. *Intervention, 6*, 39–56.

Blanch, A. (2008) *Transcending violence: Emerging models for trauma healing in refugee communities*. (SAMHSA contract #280-03-2905). Retrieved from http://www.c-r-t.org/content/research/TransViolencepap.pdf

Bracken, P. & Petty, C. (1998). *Re-thinking the trauma of war*. London: Free Association Books.

Chung, R. C-Y, Bemak, F., Ortiz, D. P., & Sandoval-Perez, P. A. (2008). Promoting the mental health of immigrants: A multicultural/social justice perspective. *Journal of Counseling and Development, 86*, 310–317.

Corey, G. (2009). *Theory and practice of counseling and psychotherapy* (8th ed.). Belmont, CA: Brooks/Cole Publishing.

Drachman, D. (1995). Immigration statues and their influence on service provision, access, and use. *Social Work, 40*(2), 188–197.

Ellis, B. H., Kia-Keating, M., Yusuf, S., Lincoln, A., & Nur, A. (2007). Ethical research in refugee communities and the use of community participatory methods. *Transcultural Psychiatry, 44*, 490–512.

Falicov, C. (2000). *Latino families in therapy*: A guide to multicultural practice. New York, NY: Gilford Press.

Fazel, M., Wheeler, J., & Danesh, J. (2005). Prevalence of serious mental disorder in 7000 refugees resettled in western countries: A systemic review. *The Lancet, 265*, 1309–1314.

Gadit, A.M. (2008). International migration of doctors from developing countries: Need to follow the Commonwealth Code. *Journal of Medical Ethics, 34*(2), 67–68.

Gorman, W. (2001). Refugee survivors of torture: Trauma and treatment. *Professional Psychology: Research and Practice, 32*(1), 443–451.

Gong-Guy, E., Cravens, R. B., & Patterson, T. E. (1991). Clinical issues in mental health service delivery to refugees. *American Psychologist, 46*(6), 642–648.

Hambleton, R. K. (1994). Guidelines for adapting educational and psychological tests: A progress report. *European Journal of Psychological Assessment (Bulletin of International Test Commission), 10*, 229–244.

Hamon, R. R., & Ingoldsby, B. (Eds.). (2003). *Mate selection across cultures*. Thousand Oaks, CA: Sage.

Handelsman, M. M., Gottlieb, M. C., & Knapp, S. (2005). Training ethical psychologists: An acculturation model. *Professional Psychology: Research and Practice, 36*(1), 59–65.

Harris, D. A. (2007). Dance/movement therapy approaches to fostering resilience and recovery among African adolescent torture survivors. *Torture, 17,* 134–155.

Hubbard, J., & Pearson, N. (2004). Sierra Leonean refugees in Guinea: Addressing the mental health effects of massive community violence. In K. E. Miller & L. M. Rasco (Eds.), *The mental health of refugees: Ecological approaches to healing and adaptation* (pp. 95–132). Mahwah, NJ: Erlbaum.

Ingleby, D. (2005). Forced Migration and Mental Health. In D. Ingleby (Ed), *Introduction* (pp. 1–28). New York, New York: Springer.

International Organization for Migration. (2010). Migration reports. Retrieved from http://www.iom.org.

Jureidini, M. S. (2004). Psychiatric assessment of children and families in immigration detention—clinical, administrative and ethical issues. *Australian New Zealand Journal of Public Health, 28*(6), 520–526.

Keyes, E. (2000). Mental health status in refugees: An integrative review of current research. *Issues in Mental Health Nursing, 21,* 397–410.

Khawaja, N. G., White, K. M., Schweitzer, R., & Greenslade, J. (2008). Difficulties and coping strategies of Sudanese refugees: A qualitative approach. *Transcultural Psychiatry, 45,* 489–512.

Kinzie, D. J., Leung, P., Bui, A., Ben, R., Keopraseuth, K. O., Riley, C., et al. (1998). Group therapy with Southeast Asian refugees. *Community Mental Health Journal, 24,* 157–166.

Kruse, J., Joksimovic, L., Cavka, M., Wöller, W., & Schmid, N. (2009). Effects of trauma-focused psychotherapy upon war refugees. *Journal of Traumatic Stress, 22*(6), 585–592.

Laszoffy, T. A., (2005) Hungarian families. In M. McGoldrick, J. Giordano, & N. Garcia-Preto, (Eds.), Ethnicity and family therapy (3rd ed., pp. 586–595). New York, NY: Gilford.

Leaning, J. (2001). Ethics of research in refugee populations. *The Lancet, 357,* 1432–1433.

Marshall, G.N., Schell, T.L., Elliot, M.N., Berthold, S.M., & Chun, C.A. (2005). Mental health of Cambodian refugees 2 decades after resettlement in the United States. *Journal of the American Medical Association, 294,* 571–579.

McKinley, B. (2007). International Migration Organization. Retrieved from www.iom.org.

Miller, K. E., Worthington, G., Muzurovic, J., Tipping, S., & Goldman, A. (2002). Bosnian refugees and the stressors of exile: A narrative study. *American Journal of Orthopsychiatry, 72,* 341–354.

Morrow, S. L., & Smith, M. L. (2000). Qualitative research for counseling psychology. In S. D. Brown & R. W. Lent (Eds.), *Handbook of counseling psychology* (pp. 199–230). New York, NY: Wiley.

Neuner, F., Schauer, M., Klaschik, C., Karunakara, U., & Elbert T. (2004). A comparison of narrative exposure therapy, supportive counseling, and psychoeducation for treating posttraumatic stress disorder in an African refugee settlement. *Journal of Consulting and Clinical Psychology, 72*(4), 579–587.

Neuner, F., Catani, C., Ruf, M., Schauer, E., Schauer, M., Elbert, T. (2008). Narrative exposure therapy for the treatment of traumatized children and adolescents (KidNET): From neurocognitive theory to field intervention, *Child and Adolescent Psychiatric Clinics of North America, 17* (3), 641–664.

O'Hara, M. & Akinsulure-Smith, A. M. (2011). Working with interpreters: Tools for clinicians conducting psychotherapy with forced migrants. *International Journal of Migration, Health and Social Care, 7*(1), 33–43.

Otto, M. W., & Hinton, D. E. (2006). Modifying exposed-based CBT for Cambodian refugees with posttraumatic stress disorder. *Cognitive and Behavioral Practice, 13,* 261–270.

Paunovic, N, & Ost, L. G. (2001). Cognitive-behavior therapy vs exposure therapy in the treatment of PTSD in refugees. *Behavioral Research and Therapy, 39,* 1183–1197.

Pernice, R. (1994). Methodological issues in research with refugees and immigrants. *Professional Psychology: Research and Practice, 25*(3), 207–213.

Pope, K. S. & Garcia-Peltoniemi, R. E. (1991). Responding to victims of torture: Clinical issues, professional responsibilities, and useful resources. *Professional Psychology: Research and Practice, 22*(4), 269–276.

Porter, M. & Haslam, N. (2005). Predisplacement and postdisplacement factors associated with mental health of refugees and internally displaced persons. *Journal of the American Medical Association, 294*(5), 602–612.

Porterfield, K., & Akinsulure-Smith, A. (2007). Therapeutic work with children and families. In H. Smith & A. Keller (Eds.), *Like a refugee camp on First Avenue: Insights and experiences from the Bellevue/NYU Program for Survivors of Torture* (pp 299–335). New York City: Bellevue/NYU Program for Survivors of Torture.

Portes, A., & Rumbaut, R.G. (2001). *Legacies: the story of immigrant second generation.* New York, NY: Russell Sage.

Regel, S. & Berliner, P. (2007). Current perspectives on assessment and therapy with survivors of torture: the use of a cognitive behavioral approach. *European Journal of Psychotherapy and Counseling, 9*(3), 289–299.

Robila, M. (2009). *Eastern European immigrant families.* New York, NY: Routledge.

Robila, M. (Ed.). (2004). *Families in Eastern Europe.* San Diego, CA: Elsevier.

Robila, M. & Sandberg, J. (2011). Family Therapy with Eastern European Immigrants: Recommendations for Practice. *International Journal of Migration, Health and Social Care 7*(4).

Robila, M. & Taylor, A. C. (2005). Teaching about international families across the United States. *Marriage and Family Review, 38*(3), 33–45.

Roopnarine, J. L., & Gielen, U. P. (2004). *Families in a global perspective: An introduction.* Boston: Allyn & Bacon.

Roopnarine, J. L., & Brown, J. (Eds.). (1997). *Caribbean families: Diversity among ethnic groups.* Westport, CT: Ablex/Jai/Elsevier.

Ryan, D. A., Kelly, F. E., & Kelly, B. D. (2009). Mental health among persons awaiting an asylum outcome in Western countries. *International Journal of Mental Health, 38*(3), 88–111.

Schulz, P. M., Resick, P. A., Huber, L. C., & Griffin, M. G. (2006). The effectiveness of cognitive processing therapy for PTSD with refugees in a community setting. *Cognitive and Behavioral Practice, 13,* 322–331.

Stepakoff, S., Hubbard, J., Katoh, M., Falk, E., Mikulu, J., Nkhoma, P., & Omagwa, Y. (2006). Trauma healing in refugee camps in Guinea: A psychosocial program for Liberian and Sierra Leonean survivors of torture and war. *American Psychologist, 61,* 921–932.

Storey, A. (1994). The ethics of immigration controls: Issues for development NGOs. *Development in Practice, 4*(3), 199–209.

Sue, D. W., Arredondo, P., & McDavies, R. J. (1992). Multicultural competencies/standards: A call to the profession. *Journal of Counseling and Development, 70*, 477–486.

Sue, D. W. & Sue, D. (2008). *Counseling the culturally diverse: Theory & practice* (5th ed.). Hoboken, NJ: Wiley & Sons.

United Nations High Commissioner for Refugees. (1951). *Article 1, The 1951 Convention Relating to the Status of Refugees.* (United Nations General Assembly A/CONF.2/2/Rev.1). Retrieved from http://unhcr.org.au/unhcr/images/convention%20and%20protocol.pdf

United Nations High Commission for Refugees (UNHCR). (2009). *2008 global trends: Refugees, asylum-seekers, returnees, internally displaced and stateless persons.* Geneva, Switzerland: Author. Retrieved from http://www.unhcr.org/4a375c426.html.

U.S. Committee for Refugees and Immigrants. (2002). *World refugee survey 2002.* Washington, DC: U.S. Committee for Refugees.

Watters, C. (2001). Emerging paradigms in the mental health care of refugees. *Social Science and Medicine, 52*, 1709–1718.

Weine, S.M.; Kulenovic, A. D.; Pavkovic, I.; & Gibbons, R. (1998). Testimony Psychotherapy in Bosnian Refugees: A Pilot Study, *American Journal of Psychiatry, 155,* 1720–1726.

Weine, S., Feetham, S., Kulauzovic, Y., Knafl, K., Besic, S., Kelbic, A., & Pavkovic, I. (2006). A family beliefs framework for socially and culturally specific preventive interventions with refugee youths and families. *American Journal of Orthopsychiatry, 76,* 1–9.

Weine, S., Raina, D., Zhubi, M., Delesi, M., Huseni, D., Feetham, S., & Pavkovic, I. (2003). The TAFES multi-family group intervention for Kosovo refugees: A feasibility study. *Journal of Nervous Mental Disorders, 191,* 100–107.

Wilkinson. J. (2007). Immigration dynamics: Processes, challenges, and benefits. In H. E. Smith, A. S. Keller, & D. W. Lhewa (Eds.), *Like a refugee camp on First Avenue: Insights and experiences from the Bellevue/NYU Program for Survivors of Torture* (pp. 65–81). New York City: Bellevue/NYU Program for Survivors of Torture.

CHAPTER
15
Principles, Standards, and Guidelines that Impact Test Development and Use and Sources of Information

Thomas Oakland

Abstract

Test development and use may constitute psychology's most important technical contribution to the behavior sciences. Tests are found universally, albeit distributed unevenly. Despite their somewhat widespread use, ethics codes from only 20 psychological associations address issues associated with test development and use. However, services from professionals engaged in test development and use are likely to find general guidance from policies promulgated by international (i.e., World Health Organization, International Union of Psychological Sciences, and the International Association of Applied Psychology) and regional professional associations. Guidelines from the International Test Commission specifically address issues important to test adaptation and use. Guidelines from the American Psychological Association, British Psychological Society, and Canadian Psychological Association also are featured. Prominent sources that provide information on tests are identified.

Key Words: test development, International Test Commission, international test use, ethics codes, principles, standards, virtues

This chapter and others in this book are intended to contribute to our understanding of global issues in psychology (Hall & Altamaier, 2008; Hall & Lunt, 2005; Jimerson, Oakland, & Farrell, 2007; Stevens & Gielen, 2007; Stevens & Wedding, 2004). An appreciation of psychology's relatively brief history aids this understanding. Although the discipline of psychology began to emerge centuries ago, informed by Plato, Socrates, and other philosophers (Hunt, 1993; Benjamin, 2007), its scientific roots were set more recently, shaped initially in laboratories in Germany and England approximately 120 years ago. The profession of psychology (i.e., those who provide clinical and related services) is even newer, having gained a strong foothold in some countries approximately 70 years ago. Clinical practices of psychology have not been established in many countries and are unregulated in most countries. As seen later in this chapter, the availability of ethical and other professional codes that impact clinical services is uneven. Such codes exist in fewer than 40 counties. The availability of such codes that specifically address test development and use also is uneven and are found in fewer than 20 countries.

The limited number of codes that address testing issues may be somewhat surprising, in that test development and use constitute psychology's most important technical contribution to the behavioral sciences and society. Thousands of English-language tests together with the hundreds to thousands of tests in other languages provide resources internationally that allow professionals to describe current behaviors and other personal qualities, assist guidance and counseling services, inform intervention methods, estimate future behaviors, evaluate progress, screen for special needs, diagnose disabling disorders, help place persons in jobs or programs, and assist in determining whether persons should

201

be credentialed, admitted/employed, retained, or promoted. Tests also are used widely in research and for various administrative and planning purposes. Tests may be administered to groups or individually to assess aptitudes, achievement, adaptive behavior, intelligence, language, motor, perception, personality, and other personal qualities (American Educational Research Association, American Psychological Association, and the National Council on Measurement in Education, 1999; Oakland, 2004; Mpofu & Oakland, 2010a, 2010b).

The development and use of tests require a cadre of at least 11 components: test authors who compose tests; test companies that develop, fund, publish, and distribute tests; professional associations that establish standards for test development and use; professionals who educate others about proper test use; judges and other triers of fact before whom testing issues may be adjudicated; persons or organizations that need and make use of test information; professionals who administer, score, and interpret tests; persons who are tested and their families; researchers and others who use tests to assist in their work; and consumers of information from these studies. Additionally, when adapting tests, the cadre includes those who adapt them. Test-related activities by each of these eleven components are likely to be influenced by principles, standards, and guidelines that impact test development and use. The purposes of this chapter are to highlight some of the principles, standards, and guidelines that impact test development and use internationally and to provide references that enable readers to locate more specific information on various tests and test-related topics (Oakland, 2005).

Tests are used universally from infancy through the elderly and most commonly with students. Test use is uneven internationally—a fact that helps explain the few number of codes that address test issues. Test use is not frequent in some countries. Thus, their ethics codes, if available, are unlikely to address test use. Test use is emerging in other countries. Thus, their ethic codes, if available, are increasingly likely to address test issues. Countries with more extensive test use can be expected to address test issues either in their codes or through guidelines. Few codes need to address test development issues because these activities occur rarely in most countries.

Although test use is universal, test availability differs considerably internationally. Test use is most abundant in Western European countries, as well as Australia, Canada, Israel, and the United States. Countries that have a stronger testing infrastructure generally display a stronger commitment to individualist and merit-based beliefs than to collectivist and egalitarian-based beliefs. The collective population in these countries is small, about 10% of the world's population.

Test use is less frequent in Central and South American, African, Middle Eastern, Asian, and Russian Federation countries. Test development and use are lower in countries that have or had strong ties to communism or socialism, strongly value collectivism (e.g., People's Republic of China, countries that formed the Soviet Union, as well as Mexico and those in Central and South America), have a lower gross national product, base psychological practices largely on theory rather than research, or have an education system that does not provide services to both males and females through high school, nor offer special services to special needs students. Test development and use are lowest among the 55 African and 22 Arab countries (Bartram & Coyne, 1998; Hu & Oakland, 1991; Muniz, 1999; Oakland, 1995; Oakland & Hu, 1991, 1992, 1993). However, the pattern of test use internationally shows some change recently, in part due to Internet delivery and increased test use in India, the People's Republic of China, and the Russian Federation.

A Brief History of Test Use in the United States

If asked to name the origins of tests, psychologists may focus on events during the late 19th century, including laboratories established by Fechner in Leipzig, Germany, and Galton in London. Although events at these sites constitute important historic milestones, test development and use occurred first approximately 3000 years ago when China developed a system that relied heavily on test information to identify prospective civil servants. This system continued until the beginning of the 20th century (Wang 1993).

Test development and use always occur in response to social and personal needs and resources. Three war-related events during the 20th century in the United States created a need for tests and helped catapult their development and use from obscure laboratories to prominent positions in society.

The need for tests became apparent during World War I when millions of young men were inducted into the U.S. Army. The intellectual abilities of some were thought to be too limited for service. A committee chaired by Dr. Robert Yerkes was commissioned to develop two group measures of general intelligence, one that required reading language skills and another that minimized the use of language. These tests displayed desired psychometric qualities, and their data were found to have practical applications. This successful effort drew the public's attention to the possible value of test use.

A need for tests again became apparent in the early 1940s during World War II, a period when 16 million young men and women entered the U.S. armed forces. This war used more sophisticated technology (e.g., fighter planes, swift submarines, advanced telecommunications) that required the identification of personnel who displayed needed aptitudes. Thus, whereas test development during World War I was directed toward the development and use of measures of general intelligence, test development efforts during World War II focused on measures of specific aptitudes that were sensitive to technological and other job requirements. The use of the Link Trainer to assist in the training of pilots exemplifies this need. The successful use of tests again drew the public's attention to an expanded role and value of test use.

Many of those returning from World War II exhibited mental and emotional disorders, including symptoms of post-traumatic stress disorders if diagnosed using current standards. Some sought services from Veterans Administration hospitals. However, a shortage of professional personnel to treat these and other disorders limited the provision of needed help. Thus, the federal government commissioned graduate schools of psychology to launch an expansion of programs to prepare doctoral-level clinical psychologists. These students often received federal funding with the proviso that they would intern in Veterans Administration hospitals. This expansion of clinical services led to the expansion of tests of personality and other personal attributes for adults—again, drawing attention to the value of tests.

The expansion of clinical psychology fueled the expansion of school and counseling psychology, thus launching further efforts to develop a wide range of tests for children and youth. The race to the moon, starting in 1957, led to the development of programs for gifted and talented students—and led to the further expansion of tests for this important population. Years later, during the 1970s, the passage of federal legislation that required school districts to provide educational services to children with special needs again added to the need for additional tests to serve still another important population.

A Need for Professional Codes to Inform Those Who Develop and Use Tests

During the first half of the 20th century, guidance on test development and use occurred largely through a few textbooks. However, during the 1950s, professional associations in the United States began to assume a more active role in providing guidance on issues pertaining to these topics. For example, the American Psychological Association (APA) adopted the first ethics code for psychologists in 1953 and published its *Technical Recommendations for Psychological Tests and Diagnostic Techniques* in 1954. Its Technical Recommendations evolved into the current *Standards for Educational and Psychological Testing* (American Educational Research Association, American Psychological Association, and the National Council on Measurement in Education, 1999). Codes that address testing issues are needed in a country only when test development and use become prominent—two conditions that occurred later in other countries and are yet to occur in most countries.

Efforts to establish professional standards occurred after World War II, in part in response to the discovery of Nazi atrocities during this war, resulting in trials of physicians and the establishment of the Nuremberg Code of Ethics in Medical Research (Koocher & Keith-Spiegel, 2008). Previous codes helped establish a foundation for professional ethics. For example, the Code of Hammurabi (1795–1750 BC) may have been the first. It established 282 laws that governed a broad range of behaviors, including the sale of property, marriage, inheritance, and theft. This code anticipated unethical practices by professionals, including innkeepers and barbers. The code specified nine laws for physicians.

The Hippocratic Oath (400–500 BC) is the first known code directed exclusively toward professionals. This oath underscored a physician's responsibility to his patients, including the importance of confidentiality, personal integrity, provision of benefits and avoidance of harm, accountability for one's behaviors, and restrictions on one's practice to areas of competence. The oath served as the foundation for medical ethics for centuries. Additional information on the history of ethics codes is found elsewhere (Sinclair, 1996; Koocher & Keith-Spiegel, 2008).

Three Conditions Reflected in Ethics Codes

Ethics codes typically reflect three conditions: their moral basis, grievances and other unsuitable professional behaviors that rise to a level of social concern, and the acceptance of the code by the profession.

The Moral Basis of an Ethics Code

An ethic code's moral basis often reflects four components: moral sensitivity, moral judgment and reasoning, moral motivation and commitment to act, and moral character. Moral sensitivity involves combining our intuitive understanding of right and wrong with values important to a profession. The ability to understand right from wrong develops during the first few years of life. This ability enables us to become aware of and interpret issues as potential or actual problems, to recognize and consider options, and to see issues from another's perspective.

The formation and implementation of an ethics code rely on moral judgment and reasoning, including the identification of behaviors that are moral in character. Clarity of judgment and reasoning are influenced by one's personal interests (e.g., whether decisions are driven by personal responsibility, self-interests, or fear); an understanding of broad concepts of justice, fairness, and duty; and a commitment to maintain and enforce existing norms as seen in laws, codes, and rules. Recognize, too, that these norms differ between cultures and change over time.

Moral motivation and commitment refer to the implementation of behaviors that are moral. This requires one to prioritize moral behaviors over personal values, including one's career, personal relationships, institutional loyalties, and personal pleasure. One's moral character, the fourth component, refers to an important trait that, like others, melds cognitive, affective, and behavioral qualities. The presence of this trait is strengthened by personal integrity, problem-solving skills, professional competence, and interpersonal skills (Bebeau, 2006; Bebeau & Monson, 2007).

Social Grievances and the Acceptance of an Ethics Code

Ethics codes are developed in response to real and documented grievances resulting from unsuitable services delivered by a profession to members of a society. Grievances selected to be addressed in an ethics code violate common standards, occur somewhat frequently, and are evidence-based. Furthermore, a profession's ethics code must be acceptable to and accepted by members of that profession. Thus, the members must agree that the conduct by more than a few in their profession violates common standards, occurs somewhat frequently, and evidence of misconduct has been documented.

Rules imbued with moral standards may unify a society whose members believe in and are governed by the moral standards. Thus, virtue-based or principle-based professional codes are likely to be acceptable and accepted when the majority of members of a psychological society adhere to these standards. The presence of such a code can help unify a profession. However, virtue-based or principle-based professional codes are unlikely to be acceptable and accepted when many members of a psychological society do not adhere to proposed standards. For example, the moral values of persons whose lives are governed strongly by conservative values or liberal values are likely to differ. Thus, those assuming leadership for developing ethics codes attempt to identify commonalities in values among psychologists in a country, region, or internationally. A goal of the code is to bind and unite professionals, not divide them. Additionally, ethics codes reflect a country's culture, including its history, customs, and practices.

Five General Purposes of Ethics Codes

Ethics codes educate members of the profession and the public as to behaviors members of the profession can be expected to display and consumers can expect from a profession. Thus, codes are intended to promote public trust of members of a profession, a quality indispensable to the provision of effective professional services. Ethics codes often reflect a country's laws, codes, and rules, thus linking ethics to broader social issues. Fourth, ethics codes enable professionals to advocate for high ethical standards. Additionally, ethics codes help establish standards that, if violated, may lead to professional sanctions and even being barred from practice in countries that have such enforcement mechanisms (Koocher & Keith-Spiegel, 2008; see also chapter 2 in this book).

Virtues, Principles, Standards, and Guidelines

Codes differ in their emphasis on virtues, principles, standards, and guidelines. The terms differ in the degree of their specificity and enforceability. The term *virtue*, the broadest term, generally refers to moral excellence. Thus, persons who are virtuous display exemplary morals honored by the society in which they practice. The Ten Commandments exemplify a virtue-based code for Jews and Christians.

The term *principles* refers to aspirational conduct (e.g., to do no harm, act benevolently, display fidelity and integrity, respect the rights of others). Principles-based codes encourage professionals to reflect on what may be the correct thing to do; such codes do not address specific required behaviors.

The term *standard* refers to specific required behaviors established by general consent that professionals are obligated to demonstrate (e.g., restrict one's services only to one's areas of competence, do not engage in sexual relationships with current or recent clients, maintain client confidentiality). Standard-based codes are more enforceable than those that emphasize virtues or principles, due to their specificity.

The term *guidelines* refers to laudatory, best-practice, and desired behaviors, albeit those that are unlikely to be enforced. These desired qualities, although important, do not rise to a level that warrants their inclusion in an ethics code.

Within the profession of psychology, few if any ethics codes emphasize virtues. Many emphasize only principles, or both principles and standards. Guidelines are common when a professional association either is not well established or lacks the ability to enforce codes it promulgates.

International Legal Efforts that Impact Testing

Professional conduct generally is governed by three sources of information: legal, ethical, and scholarship. First and foremost, psychologists are expected to know and abide by the laws and administrative rulings in their country. These generally take precedence over the other two. Professional ethics generally forms a second important tier. Professionals are expected to know and follow these codes and to know and practice consistent with scholarship. Thus, some attention to legal issues in light of provisions that protect intellectual property, including tests, as well as agreements arrived at through the work of the International Organization for Standardization, can inform us about test development and use.

International Legal Safeguards for Tests as Intellectual Property

A test is considered to be intellectual property. Many are copyrighted. Authority for its distribution and sale rests with those who own a test. Various national, regional, and international laws and covenants are intended to safeguard intellectual property and copyright. For example, some but not all countries have enacted laws protecting intellectual property, including tests, books, and films.

Tests and other forms of technology contribute to trade and thus may be covered under regional trade agreements (e.g., North American Free Trade Agreement). International safeguards are found in various sources, including the 1952 Universal Copyright Convention, later the Berne Convention[1], and the most recent World Trade Organization's Agreement on Trade-related Aspects of Intellectual Property Rights (often known as the Uruguay Round). It introduced intellectual property rules into the multilateral system for the first time.

However, some persons ascribe to the view that intellectual property should not be protected. They believe such protection violates basic human rights by limiting personal access to needed resources, including the right to food, education, and other daily essentials (Torremans, 2008). The World Intellectual Property Organization has assumed leadership to promote this viewpoint.

Despite legal agreements to safeguard intellectual property, its protection and enforcement vary widely and often are not present. Most countries, especially low-income countries, do not enforce provisions that prohibit the reproduction of tests and other intellectual property. Unspoken is their belief that such restrictions would negatively impact the welfare of their society. Those whose intellectual property is pirated consider such actions to be theft and thus illegal. Although illegal, such actions rarely are prosecuted.

Practices common to the process of translating or adapting tests and their use were reviewed in light of 25 standards from APA's 2002 *Ethical Principles of Psychology and Code of Conduct* (Oakland, 2005). Violations of copyright through plagiarism and the misuse of a psychologist's work were the most common violations. Psychologists and others working in countries that do not have locally developed tests have a history of obtaining tests developed in other countries and translating or adapting them without securing the permission of the test's author and publisher. These actions occur despite regional and international conventions that protect intellectual property. Other common ethical lapses are seen in not acquiring and maintaining competence—especially in reference to test development, failure to document test development and revision work, using obsolete tests, allowing unqualified persons to use tests, failing to maintain test security, lacking informed consent, and failing to report ethical violations.

International Organization for Standardization

The nongovernmental International Organization for Standardization (ISO) is little known yet wields considerable influence as the world's largest developer and publisher of international standards (www.iso.org/iso/about.htm). Its network includes national standards institutes from 162 countries. ISO forms a bridge between the public and private sectors, with the goal to reach consensus leading to solutions that meet the requirements of business and the broader needs of society.

The involvement of the ISO in setting standards for test development and use may be warranted due to the reluctance or inability of professional associations to establish and enforce such standards. Some believe employers and current and potential employees are likely to benefit from international standards that address chronic issues in the delivery of assessment services in commerce and industry (Bartram, 2008). Proposals for test standards are likely to be formed by committees whose members consist of standards specialists and assessment experts drawn from various geographic locations. Standards for test use in work and organizational settings currently are under review.

International Professional Codes in Psychology that Impact Testing

As noted above, ethics codes may be available internationally, regionally, and nationally. Their review follows.

World Health Organization

The World Health Organization's (WHO) International Classification of Functioning, Disability and Health (ICF; World Health Organization, 2001) provides a bio-psycho-social framework that views behaviors from three broad perspectives: (1) body functions and structures (i.e., physiologic, physical, and psychological functions), (2) activities (i.e., the extent persons engage in functional life activities), and (3) participation (i.e., their participation in social settings). A patient's health is understood from knowledge of the interactions between these three broad components. Working in this model, professionals integrate medical and psychological information with knowledge of a person's social and adaptive skills (e.g., personality traits, coping abilities, stress, and social support). The use of tests figures prominently in the use of the ICF (Mpofu & Oakland, 2010a, 2010b).

The ICF acknowledges that tests can be misused and abused, and thus identified three broad ethical principles to guide proper test use in the ICF model: respect and confidentiality (e.g., respect the inherent value and autonomy of individuals, avoid labeling them, and ensure cooperation and consent); proper clinical use (e.g., explain the use of the ICF, involve the person when framing their ICF codes); and proper social use (promote choices and self-control, work to establish social policy that supports personal participation).

International Union of Psychological Sciences and the International Association of Applied Psychology

The International Union of Psychological Sciences (IUPsyS) and the International Association of Applied Psychology (IAAP) are the two most prominent and highly respected professional associations for psychologists. IUPsyS's membership consists of approximately 71 national professional associations of psychologists. IAAP's membership consists of individual psychologists. Each association sponsors a professional journal and international congresses every four years. Neither has developed an ethics code.

However, in 2008 both associations approved the *Universal Declaration of Ethical Principles for Psychologists,* developed under the leadership of Janel Gauthier (2008), IAAP secretary-general and chair of its committee on ethics. This Declaration is not a code, and instead provides a framework that highlights moral principles that lead to ethical ideals and ultimately to principles for the practice of psychology. This Declaration is remarkable by demonstrating a universal commitment among psychologists to a set of common principles. They include respect for the dignity of persons and people, competent care for the well-being of persons and people, integrity, and professional and scientific responsibility to society. Similarities between these principles and those found in WHO's ethical guidelines are apparent.

International Test Commission

The International Test Commission (ITC) is committed to promoting sound testing practices internationally. This commitment is evident in its original charge to establish ways to restrict access to tests by unqualified persons (Oakland et al., 2001). The ITC has assumed a leadership role in promoting best-practice guidelines for using tests fairly, adapting tests, and using computer-based assessment (see www.intestcom.org/guidelines).

Guidelines for Test Use. The ITC's guidelines for test use (2000) discuss the fair and ethical use of tests with the intent to provide an internationally agreed framework from which standards for training and test-user competence and qualifications could be derived (Bartram, 1996, 1998). These guidelines were approved by the ITC in 1999 and have been endorsed by the European Federation of Professional Psychologists Associations' standing committee on tests and testing. A number of countries have translated and adopted these guidelines.

These guidelines underscore the importance of two broad principles:

(1) Assume responsibility by acting in a professional and ethical manner, ensuring competence in test use, assuming responsibility for test use, ensuring test materials are kept securely, and ensuring test results are treated confidentially.

(2) Follow good practices by evaluating the potential utility of testing in an assessment, selecting technically sound tests appropriate for the situation, considering issues of fairness, preparing properly for the testing session, administering the tests properly, scoring and analyzing the results accurately, interpreting the results appropriately, communicating the results clearly and accurately, and reviewing the appropriateness of the test and its use.

Guidelines on Test Adaptations. The ITC's guidelines for test adaptation were required to change a prevalent practice of obtaining tests developed in other countries and translating them from the source language to the local language. Efforts to acquire representative norms and to estimate the newly translated test's reliability and validity occurred rarely. The ITC, with support and participation from other organizations, developed guidelines for adapting educational and psychological tests in an effort to overcome these deficiencies (Hambleton, 1994; Muniz & Hambleton, 1997; van de Vijver & Hambleton, 1996; Hambleton, Merenda, & Spielberger, 2005).

The test adaptation guidelines are intended to provide assistance to persons attempting to transform a test from one originally intended to be used with one population (the source) to one suitable for use with a different population (the target). Two examples include the transformation of a test originally developed in the United States to one revised for use in Hungary, or transforming a test from one developed in Hungary designed to be used with native-born Hungarians to one revised for use in Hungary with nonnative-born Hungarians from Romania. These guidelines discuss cultural and language differences, identify five technical issues and methods, and describe three conditions that possibly impact test interpretations. A number of countries have adopted these guidelines. These guidelines are being revised.

International Guidelines on Computer-Based and Internet-Delivered Testing. The use of the Internet has materially changed the ways in which people access information, conduct business, and in other ways manage their personal and professional lives. The Internet's impact on test development and use, although obscure to some, has become prominent and will continue to expand (Naglieri, et al, 2004). Technology's international reach requires the involvement of organizations that transcend one nation. Efforts by multinational governmental agencies and multinational companies, as well as regional and international associations often are needed to envision, create, revise, promote, regulate, and in other ways assist in forming and reforming services in light of technology changes. Computer use constitutes a pervasive technology that has changed the ways in which we work, shop, communicate, and play.

The legitimate use and potential abuse of computers generally are well known. The potential for abuse warranted guidelines for test administration, security of tests and test results, and control of the testing process. Therefore, the ITC developed international guidelines on computer-based and Internet-delivered testing in its *Computer-Based Testing and the Internet* (British Psychological Society, 2002; http://www.intestcom.org).

The goal of these guidelines is to raise awareness among all stakeholders in the testing process of internationally recognized guidelines that highlight good-practice issues in computer-based testing (CBT) and testing delivered over the Internet. These guidelines are specific to CBT/Internet based testing. Test developers, test publishers, and test users share responsibilities for ensuring the following four guidelines are enforced:

(1) Attend to technological issues in CBT/Internet testing by reviewing hardware and software requirements, ensuring the robustness of the CBT/Internet tests, recognizing human factors issues in the presentation of material by a computer or the Internet, making reasonable adjustments to the technical features of the test for

candidates with disabilities, and providing help and information as well as practice items within CBT/Internet tests.

(2) Attend to quality issues in CBT/Internet testing by ensuring knowledge and competence of CBT/Internet testing, reviewing the psychometric qualities of the CBT/Internet test, ensuring evidence of equivalence that supports the use of the CBT/Internet test when it has been developed from a paper and pencil version, scoring and analyzing CBT/Internet testing results accurately, interpreting results appropriately, providing appropriate feedback, and working to ensure equality of access for all groups.

(3) Provide appropriate levels of control over CBT/Internet testing by ensuring control over the test conditions and their supervision, controlling prior practice and item exposure, and ensuring control over test taker's authenticity and cheating.

(4) Make appropriate provision for ensuring security and safeguarding privacy in CBT/Internet testing by accounting for the security of test materials, ensuring security of test taker's data transferred over the Internet, and maintaining confidentiality of test taker results.

National and Regional Test Standards
National Ethics Codes

National ethics codes reflect a country's culture, including its history, customs, and practices. For example, countries differ in their acceptance and use of clinical services, including test use. Thus, national ethics codes differ in the extent to which they address test development and use (Leach & Harbin, 1997; Leach, Glosoff, & Overmier, 2001; Leach & Oakland 2007, Oakland, 2009; Oakland et al., in press). An understanding of code differences is facilitated by reviewing distinctions between principle-based and standard-based ethics codes. As noted previously, principle-based codes highlight aspirational conduct (e.g., to do no harm, act benevolently) and encourage professionals to reflect on what may be the correct actions to take in all aspects of their practice. Thus, the broad provisions found in principle-based codes can be expected to address a wide range of issues, including those that may impact test use; they are less likely to address test development due to its relative infrequency. In contrast, standards-based codes specify behaviors professionals are obligated to demonstrate (e.g., restrict one's services only to their areas of competence, maintain client confidentiality).

Principles and standards found in ethics codes from 24 countries and the 1992 APA code were compared (Leach & Harbin, 1997). Some of APA's principles were found in 70% of the 24 country codes and all were found in codes from Australia, Canada, Israel, and South Africa. As expected, lower frequencies of agreement were found on standards that address assessment: explain assessment results (74%); maintain test security (58%); use assessments and interventions competently and appropriately (37%); interpret test results accurately (37%); avoid test use by unqualified persons (37%); use of test scoring and interpretation services (32%); use of assessment in general and with special populations (21%); suitability of evaluations, diagnosis, and interventions (16%); constructing tests (16%); and avoid reliance on obsolete tests and outdated test results (11%). A subsequent analysis of this data set (Leach, Glosoff, & Overmier, 2001) found closest agreement in assessment standards between the United States and Australia (14 agreements), the People's Republic of China (10), and Singapore (6).

A review of general ethics codes from 35 countries (Leach & Oakland, 2007) found about one-third rely on principles (e.g., Canada, Great Britain, Spain, and Switzerland). Their principles are meant to embrace all psychological services. Principles-based codes do not address specific test issues. Among standards-based codes, about two-thirds include specific reference to test development and use. Common examples require test users to explain test results, use tests properly, limit test use by unqualified individuals, and restrict test purchase and reproduction. Few codes include standards that impact test construction or restrict the use of obsolete tests.

The APA's 2002 *Ethical Principles of Psychologists and Code Of Conduct* includes both principles and standards, including 11 broad standards within which 21 specific standards are imbedded that address test development and use. It provides the most thorough listing of standards, probably reflecting the widespread use of tests in the United States. A somewhat detailed discussion of ethics codes in the United States and the People's Republic of China is discussed in Chapter 2 of this book (Oakland et al., 2012). Their similarities are apparent.

A few countries rely on documents other than a national code to address testing issues. For example, although the British Psychological Society's general ethics code does not address test issues, its Division of Occupational Psychology adopted an ethics code that includes testing. Additionally, although

Canada's national code does not address test use, it encourages psychologists engaged in testing to use the *Standards for Educational and Psychological Testing* (American Educational Research Association et al., 1999), albeit a document that links academic scholarship to test development and use, is rather silent on ethical issues, and lacks enforcement provisions.

Three Regional Ethics Codes

Psychological associations from three regions have formed principle-based meta-codes. As with other principle-based codes, their provisions are intended to embrace prominent practices in psychology, not to address any one—including test development and use. The largest, the 35-member European Federation of Psychologists Associations (EFPA; www.efpa.eu/), promulgates its Meta-Code of ethics in an effort to standardize ethical principles common to psychological practice in member countries and to encourage member countries to consider the following four principles when developing or revising their national codes: respect for a person's rights and dignity, professional competence, personal responsibility, and personal integrity (Lindsay, 1996; Keene, 1997; Lindsay, Koene, Ovreeide, & Lang, 2008). These four principles are mutually interdependent. They also are found in the *Universal Declaration of Ethical Principles for Psychologists*.

Meta-codes are derived through a consensus-building process among participants. The inclusion of standards in addition to principles in this Meta-Code was considered and rejected, given the belief that obtaining consensus on a set of standards was unlikely. The EFPA commitment to test-related issues also is seen in its establishing a Standing Committee on Tests and Testing, one that emerged from the Task Force on Tests and Testing in 1997.

Although the Meta-Code does not directly address test use, the EFPA, in conjunction with the European Association of Work and Organization Psychologists, has established standards for test use for work and organizational psychology: *European Test User Standards for Test Use in Organizational and Work Settings*. These standards are based, in part, on the International Test Commission guidelines on test use. These standards include contextual information that addresses ethical test practices.

Assessment activities provided under the direction of organizational and work psychologies, also referred to as industrial/organizational psychologists in some countries, seemingly are expanding in Europe and elsewhere, including the People's Republic of China and the Russian Federation. These changes are prompting EFPA efforts, through the work of a 9-country task force, to develop European standards for test users for this specialty in psychology. The EFPA also is exploring a process for accrediting national test user qualification.

The five Nordic countries (Denmark, Finland, Iceland, Norway, and Sweden) also developed a common code that is consistent with the EFPA Meta-Code (Nordic Psychologists' Associations, 1998). Psychological associations in four South American countries (Argentina, Brazil, Paraguay, and Uruguay) that formed a regional common economic market association (the *Mercado Comun del Cono Sur*, Southern Cone Common Market) led to the 1997 publication of a brief declaration of ethical principles: *Ethical Principles Framework for the Professional Practice of Psychology in the Mercosur and Associated Countries*. It is intended to provide guidelines for future multinational ethics codes and is not a code itself (Hernandez-Guzman & Sanchez-Sosa, 2008).

Other Ways Professional Associations May Impact Test Development and Use

Professional associations also may have a profound impact on test development and use by establishing other policy. Three examples are provided.

Brazil's Federal Council of Psychologists

Brazil's professional association of psychologists, the Federal Council of Psychologists, expressed concern about the status of test development and use in its country. Many translated versions of tests, taken without permission from other countries, lacked suitable norms and little evidence of adequate reliability and validity. The Federal Council took the bold step to establish test standard policies largely consistent with those from the International Test Commission. The Federal Council then convened panels of experts who reviewed existing tests. They found few tests met these standards.

Thus, the Federal Council established companion policies that required psychologists to use only those tests that demonstrated adequate standards. Those who violated these provisions could face disbarment. Although many clinicians and test developers opposed what seemed to them to be harsh policies, the implementation of the policies contributed importantly to an expansion of a testing industry and to the development of many excellent tests, thereby elevating assessment practices in Brazil.

Dutch Institute of Psychology

The Commission on Testing Matters in the Netherlands, Dutch Institute of Psychology, was founded in 1959, in part to promote test quality. Its 2001 report, *Assessment System for the Quality of Tests* (2001), if fully implemented, would have had a deleterious impact on testing practices. Its standards were unattainable. The report underscores a need to involve professionals with considerable practical experience, including the clinical use of tests, when formulating policy—not only academics or moralists who insist on attaining an ideal standard.

Standards for Educational and Psychological Testing

Previous references were made to the *Standards for Educational and Psychological Testing* (American Educational Research Association, the American Psychological Association, and the National Council on Measurement in Education, 1999). The 1999 edition of the Standards is consistent with a tradition to provide criteria for the evaluation of tests, testing practices, and the effects of test use. All professionals engaged in test development and use are encouraged to adopt the Standards.

The Standards address 15 topics within three parts and 283 specific standards. Part I, Test Construction, Evaluation, and Documentation, includes chapters on validity; reliability and errors of measurement; test development and revision; scales, norms, and score comparability; test administration, scoring, and reporting; and supporting documentation of tests. Part II, Fairness in Testing, includes chapters on fairness in testing and test use, rights and responsibilities of test takers, testing individuals of diverse linguistic background, and testing individuals with disabilities. Part III, Testing Applications, includes chapters on the responsibilities of test users, psychological testing and assessment, educational testing and assessment, testing in employment and credentialing, and testing in program evaluation and public policy.

These Standards provide the most authoritative single source of standards for test development and use internationally. Frequent citations to it by others signifies the esteem in which it is held. Ironically, although the title suggests its 283 standards are enforced by the three sponsoring associations (American Educational Research Association, the American Psychological Association, and the National Council on Measurement in Education), enforcement rests on individuals and members of the professions, not the professional associations.

Professional Guidelines that Impact Testing

As noted previously, guidelines refer to laudatory, best-practice, and desired behaviors, albeit those that are unlikely to be enforced. Guidelines are common when the professional is not well established or when an association does not want to or lacks the ability to enforce desired codes.

American Psychological Association Guidelines

The American Psychological Association (APA), formed in 1892, is well established, with a large membership, a divisional structure that recognizes more than 50 different member interests, an active publishing agenda that includes more than one hundred books and journals, and an active public policy agenda. The Association's work on test-related issues is carried out through staff and membership associated with its Committee on Psychological Tests and Assessment. The APA governance has approved guidelines and other statements that may inform test use. They include the following and are available at www.apa.org/science/testclearinghs.html.

"The ABC's of School Testing" provides a video designed to help parents understand many uses of testing in schools. APA's "Record Keeping Guidelines" provide guidance on where and how long test data and other records should be kept, as well as on their disposal. The 40-page report on "Questionnaires Used in the Prediction of Trustworthiness in Pre-Employment Selection Decisions" examines pre-employment integrity tests and related instruments. The "Statement on Third Party Observers in Psychological Testing and Assessment: A Framework for Decision Making" addresses the growing problems associated with parents, advocates, attorneys, and others who insist on observing the administration of individually administered tests. The "Statement on the Use of Secure Psychological Tests in the Education of Graduate and Undergraduate Psychology Students" addresses issues of test security while engaging in teaching and training students in psychology. "Specialty Guidelines for Forensic Psychologists" are intended to improve the quality of forensic psychological services (American Psychological Association, 1991).

The APA has approved various guidelines to assist test use. These include its "Record Keeping Guidelines (APA, 1993) and "Guidelines for Child Custody Evaluations in Divorce Proceedings" (American Psychological Association, 1991). The custody guidelines are designed to assist psychologists engaged in assessing children and youth for the purpose of offering testimony that may impact child custody decisions. This work frequently leads to charges of unethical conduct. Thus, the contents of this document have been instrumental in guiding these services.

Joint Committee on Testing Practices Guidelines

The Joint Committee on Testing Practices, of which APA is a member, developed the following four documents related to test development and use. Its *Code of Fair Testing Practices in Education* (2005) provides guidance to professionals who develop or use educational tests. This Code is consistent with the 1999 *Standards for Educational and Psychological Testing*. The document on "Rights and Responsibilities of Test Takers: Guidelines and Expectations" explains the rights and responsibilities of test takers during the testing process, as well as the general expectations of test takers held by those who develop, administer, and use tests. The document on "Responsible Test Use: Case Studies for Assessing Human Behavior" is designed to educate test users on ways to avoid the misuse of data from educational and psychological tests. The 143-page document on "Test User Qualifications: A Data based Approach to Promoting Good Test Use" provides guidelines to inform test users and the general public of the qualifications considered important for the competent and responsible use of psychological tests.

British Psychological Society Guidelines

The British Psychological Society (BPS) also has had a long and distinguished history of providing leadership on testing issues in the United Kingdom. For example, the BSA has established standards for credentialing (aka chartering) occupational (i.e., Level A) and educational (Level B) psychologists. These lead to nationally recognized certificate(s) of competence in testing.

The BSA's Steering Committee on Test Standards has assumed leadership for issues regarding test development and use by psychologists throughout the United Kingdom. Its work on establishing qualifications for psychological testing in health and social care settings is ongoing. The BSA also has established various guidelines to assist its member practitioners. Four are reviewed below and can be found at www.psychtesting.org.uk.

Its 2007 *Code of Good Practice for Psychological Testing Centers* emphasizes the expectation that those who use psychological tests will assure competence, use procedures and techniques well, and are sensitive to client welfare. Competence requires practitioners to meet all standards of competence defined by the BPS for the relevant certificate(s) of competence in testing and to endeavor, where possible, to develop and enhance their competence as test users. They are expected to monitor the limits of their competence in psychometric testing and not offer services that lie outside their competence nor encourage or cause others to do so. They must have mandatory training and the specific knowledge and skills required for each of the instruments they use.

Practitioners are required to use tests in conjunction with other assessment methods only when their use can be supported by the available technical information. Tests are to be administered, scored, and interpreted consistent with the instructions provided by the test distributor and standards defined by the Society. Test materials are to be stored securely to ensure unqualified persons do not have access to them. Data are used only for the purposes agreed to by the test taker. Test results are kept securely in a form suitable for developing norms, validation, and monitoring for bias.

Sensitivity to client welfare requires practitioners to obtain informed consent of potential test takers and ensure they understand why the tests will be used, what will be done with their results, and who will have access to test data. Professionals work to ensure all test takers are well informed, prepared for the test session, and have had access to practice or familiarization materials when appropriate. Personal qualities (e.g., gender, ethnicity, age, disability, special needs, educational background, and level of ability) are considered when interpreting test results. Test takers and other authorized persons are provided information about the test results that promotes understanding of the results, and in a style appropriate to their level of understanding.

The BPS's "Statement on the Conduct of Psychologists Providing Expert Psychometric Evidence to Courts and Lawyers" is directed toward psychologists with specialized knowledge who engage in forensic practice by offering their opinions in court, or before other tiers of fact in an effort to assist in the resolution of legal issues. Psychologists increasingly are engaged in forensic practices, yet often have little training in doing so. This statement sets out guidelines to psychologists and other users of psychological tests concerning obligations when providing evidence or opinion that rests on the results of psychometric testing.

BSA's book, *About Health Testing*, describes test use in a wide range of circumstances for adult, child and family mental health services, people with learning disabilities, neuropsychological disorders, physical and sensory impairments, and emotional and behavioral difficulties. Its book, *About Occupational Testing*, describes the use of tests and other assessments used by employers in recruitment, selection, promotion, and staff development, as well as to facilitate better working practices.

Canadian Psychological Association Guidelines

The Canadian Psychological Association (CPA) also is well established, with a large membership, widely respected journals, established guidelines for test use (Canadian Psychological Association (1987), and an active public policy agenda. CPS also has a widely respected principles-based *Code of Ethics for Psychologists* (http://www.cpa.ca/aboutcpa/committees/ethics/.

The following CPA guidelines include provisions that impact test use. They include its 2001 "Guidelines for Non-Discriminatory Practice," its 2001 "Practice Guidelines for Providers of Psychological Services," its 2007 "Guidelines for Ethical Psychological Practice with Women," its 2007 "Professional Practice Guidelines for School Psychologists in Canada," and 2009 "Ethical Guidelines for Supervision in Psychology: Teaching, Research, Practice, and Administration." See www.cpa.ca/to obtain the aforementioned documents (September 2, 2009).

CPA's statement on "Improving North American Safeguards that Help Protect the Public Against Test Misuse" attempts to fix a set of problems associated with the implementation of a 1950 APA-approved program for the voluntary use of a three-tier system for classifying tests. It was designed to determine who could purchase and use tests in light of training requirements. Level A, the lowest level, includes tests that can be adequately administered, scored, and interpreted with the aid of the manual and a general orientation from the organization in which one is working. Level B, a mid-level, includes tests that require some technical knowledge of test construction and use, as well as an academic background that includes courses in psychological assessment including statistics, individual differences, personnel psychology, and guidance. Level C, the highest level, includes tests that require substantial understanding of testing and supporting psychological subjects together with supervised experience in their use. Simner (1996), working with the CPA's Professional Affairs Committee Working Group on Test Publishing Industry Safeguards, found significant abuses in this system.

This committee recommended the three-level test classification system either should be replaced or supplemented by a purchaser classification system that recognizes tests typically are employed for different purposes, and that these different purposes should determine whether an individual is qualified to purchase a given test. Furthermore, all first-time purchasers, regardless of background, should be required to complete a test user qualification statement. Hence, firms that publish and/or distribute tests should remove from their catalogues all waiver clauses based on occupation, professional membership, and level of graduate training that exempt certain individuals from the need to complete such a statement. Additionally, the responsibilities assumed by test purchasers and by test distributors to safeguard the public against test misuse must be defined clearly. Firms should be encouraged to insert in their catalogues a statement on who may purchase tests, as well a test user qualification statement. Testing companies that reproduce these or similar statements in their catalogues should receive recognition.

Sources of Information on Testing

The importance of test development and use is expressed, in part, by the many and varied sources designed to provide information to those learning how to develop and use tests, to seasoned practitioners, and to the public. Hundreds of books address test development and use. A list of these books exceeds the scope of this chapter. However, other important sources of information known to the chapter author are summarized below.

Internet Searches

Persons engaged in test development and use increasingly rely on Internet searches to acquire needed information. Those seeking information about specific tests should consider starting with the Educational Testing Service's (ETS) Test Locator, a database of more than 25,000 tests and other measurement devices dating from the early 1900s to the present. This test collection is the largest compilation of tests in the world. Information is acquired from various U.S. publishers and individual test authors together with some tests from Australia, Canada, and the United Kingdom.

American Psychological Association. Searches using Google or other search engines will lead to countless other sources.

The use of PsycINFO, a bibliographic database established by the APA, provides a link to research in psychology published during the last 50 years or more. Thus, it assists in identifying tests used in research as reported in peer-reviewed journals, and helps locate literature on specific tests or on topics that may have used tests.

APA's "Finding Information About Psychological Testing" provides information on locating tests by subject area, finding test publishers, and strategies for finding unpublished measures. APA's report on "Psychological Test Usage in Professional Psychology" provides information on current psychological assessment instruments used by clinical psychologists and neuropsychologists The following also are available from the American Psychological Association (ww.apa.org/science/testclearinghs.html): a 23-page bibliography on "Relevant Literature Addressing Testing and Assessment of Cultural, Ethnic, and Linguistically Diverse Populations"; an 8-page reference on testing people of color, women, language minorities, and people with disabilities; and an 8-page bibliography on books and chapters pertaining to neuropsychological assessment cross-culturally, with minorities, and with non-English speaking individuals, including references in non-U.S. journals.

The *Directory of Unpublished Experimental Measures* (Goldman & Mitchell, 2007) provides researchers and students with easy access to recently developed noncommercially available experimental mental measures, tests, and surveys. The first volume of the Directory was published in 1974, with subsequent editions updated regularly. The first six volumes reference 5,363 tests. Professors engaged in research may find these tests to be of value.

Reliable Commercial Sources

The following four sources provide additional information on tests.

Tests in Print (Geisinger, 2006) is a bibliographic encyclopedia of information on every English-language commercially available test in psychology and education. Each entry consists of the test title, intended population, publication date, acronym (if applicable), author, publisher, foreign adaptations, and references.

Mental Measurements Yearbooks (Geisinger, 2006) provide critiques of tests. Each entry provides information on the test's reliability, validity, norming, scoring and reporting services, and foreign language versions. Most entries also include one or more reviews of the test and testing materials (e.g., manuals) by qualified psychologists.

Test Reviews Online, a web-based service of the Buros Institute of Mental Measurements (www.unl.edu/buros), allows individuals to download reviews of more than 2000 tests found in the *Mental Measurement Yearbooks* for a modest price.

Tests: A Comprehensive Reference for Assessment in Psychology, Education, and Business (Maddox, 2008), similar to *Tests in Print*, provides bibliographic information on a test's title and author, the intended population, the test's purpose and major features, administration time, scoring method, costs, availability, and the primary publisher.

Test Critiques (Pro-Ed, 2009), similar to the *Mental Measurement Yearbooks*, includes psychometric information such as reliability, validity, and norm development, together with a critique.

Test Companies

Some countries or regions are fortunate to have well-funded and commercially successful companies that develop and market tests. These companies typically distribute catalogs annually to promote their products, thus informing test users of these resources. Testing companies that are Affiliate Members of the International Test Commission include OPP Ltd. (formerly the Institute of Personality and Ability Testing), Harcourt Assessment, Hogrefe, and SHL Group plc. *Tests in Print, Mental Measurement Yearbooks, Tests,* and *Test Critiques* provide a list of test publishers.

Note

1. The term *convention* is used to signify a legally binding agreement, typically between two or more countries or political entities.

References

American Educational Research Association, American Psychological Association, and National Council on Measurement in Education. (1999). *Standards for Educational and Psychological Testing.* Washington DC: American Psychological Association.

American Psychological Association, (1991). Specialty guidelines for forensic psychologists. *Law and Human Behavior, 15,* 145–155.

American Psychological Association. (2002). Ethical principles of psychology and code of conduct. Retrieved from ww.apa.org/ethics/code2002.html.

American Psychological Association. (1993). Record keeping guidelines. *American Psychologist, 48,* 984–986.

American Psychological Association. (1994). Guidelines for child custody evaluations in divorce proceedings. *American Psychologist, 9,* 677–680

Bartram, D. (1996). Test qualifications and test use in the UK: The competence approach. *European Journal of Psychological Assessment, 12,* 62–71.

Bartram, D. (1998). The need for international guidelines on standards for test use: A review of European and international initiatives. *European Psychologist, 3,* 155–164.

Bartram, D. (2001). The development of international guidelines on test use: The International Test Commission project. *International Journal of Testing, 1,* 33–54. Bartram, D. (2008). An ISO standard for assessment in work and organizational settings. *International Testing, 20,* 9.

Bartram, D., & Coyne, I. (1998). Variations in national patterns for testing and test use: The ITC/EFPPA international survey. *European Journal of Psychological Assessment, 4,* 249–260.

Bebeau, M. (2006) Evidence-based character development. *Advances in Bioethics, 10,* 47–86.

Bebeau, M., Monson, V. (2007). Guided by theory, grounded in evidence: A way forward for professional ethics education. In J. Nucci & D. Narvaez, *Handbook on moral and character education* (pp. 87–101). Mahwah, NJ: Erlbaum.

Benjamin, L. (2007). *A brief history of modern psychology.* Malden, MA: Blackwell.

British Psychological Society Psychological Testing Centre. (2002). *Guidelines for the development and use of computer-based assessments.* Leicester: British Psychological Society.

Canadian Psychological Association. (1987). *Guidelines for educational and psychological testing.* Ottawa: Canadian Psychological Association.

Dutch Institute of Psychologists. (2001). *Assessment System for the Quality of Tests:* (2001). Amsterdam: Dutch Institute of Psychologists' Commission on Test Quality in the Netherlands.

Geisinger K. (2006). *Tests in print.* Lincoln, NE: The Buros Institute

Geisinger, K. (2006). *Mental measurements yearbooks.* Lincoln, NE: The Buros Institute

Goldman, B. & Mitchell, D. (Eds.). (2007). *Directory of unpublished experimental measures.* Washington DC: American Psychological Association

Gauthier, J. (2008). Universal declaration of ethical principles for psychologists. In J. E. Hall, & E. M. Altmaier (Eds.), *Global promise: Quality assurance and accountability in professional psychology* (pp. 98–105). New York: Oxford University Press.

Hall, J., & Lunt, I. (2005). Global mobility for psychology. *American Psychologist, 60,* 712–726.

Hall, J., & Altamaier, H. (2008). Global promise: Quality assurance and accountability in professional psychology. New York: Oxford University Press.

Hambleton, R. K. (1994). Guidelines for adapting educational and psychological tests: A progress report. *European Journal of Psychological Assessment, 10,* 229–244.

Hambleton, R., Merenda, P., & Spielberger, C. (Eds.). (2005). *Adapting educational and psychological tests for cross-cultural assessment.* Mahwah, NY: Erlbaum Press.

Hernandez-Guzman, L., & Sanchez-Sosa, J. (2008) Practice and regulation of professional psychology in Latin America. In J. Hall & H. Altamaier (Eds.). *Global promise: Quality assurance and accountability in professional psychology* (pp. 109–127). Washington DC: American Psychological Association

Hu, S., & Oakland, T. (1991). Global and regional perspectives on testing children and youth: An international survey. *International Journal of Psychology, 26* (3), 329–344.

Hunt, M. (1993). *The story of psychology.* New York: Doubleday.

International Test Commission (ITC). (2000). *International guidelines for test use.* Retrieved from www.intestcom.org/itc_projects.htm.

Jimerson, S., Oakland, T., & Farrell, P. (Eds.). (2007). *The handbook of international school psychology.* Sage: Thousand Oaks, CA.

Joint Commission on Testing Practices. (2005). *Code of fair testing practices in education.* Washington, DC: American Psychological Association.

Koene, C. J. (1997). Tests and professional ethics and values in European psychologists. *European Journal of Psychological Assessment, 13,* 219–228.

Koocher, G., & Keith-Spiegel, P. (2008). *Ethics in psychology and the mental health professions: Standards and cases* (3rd ed.). New York: Oxford University Press.

Leach, M. M., Glosoff, H., & Overmier, J. B. (2001). *International ethics codes: A follow-up study of previously unmatched standards and principles.* In J. B. Overmier & J. A. Overmier (Eds.), *Psychology: IUPsyS Global Resource.* [Computer software].

Leach, M. M., & Harbin, J. J. (1997). Psychological ethics codes: A comparison of twenty-four countries. *International Journal of Psychology, 32,* 181–192.

Leach, M. M., & Oakland, T. (2007). Ethics standards impacting test development and use: A review of 31 ethics codes impacting practices in 35 countries. *International Journal of Testing, 7,* 71–88.

Lindsay, G. (1996). Psychology as an ethical discipline and profession. *European Psychologist, 1,* 79–88.

Maddox, T. (2008). *Tests: A comprehensive reference for assessment in psychology, education, and business.* Austin, TX: Pro-Ed.

National Council on Measurement in Education. (1999). *Code of professional responsibilities in educational measurement.* Washington, DC: Author.

Nordic Psychologists' Associations (1998). *Ethical principles for Nordic psychologists* Oslo: Author.

Mpofu, E., & Oakland, T. (Eds.). (2010a). *Assessment in rehabilitation and health.* Boston, MA: Pearson Allyn & Bacon.

Mpofu, E., & Oakland, T. (Eds.). (2010b). *Rehabilitation and health assessment: Applying the ICF guidelines.* New York: Springer.

Muniz, J., & Hambleton, R. K. (August, 1997). Directions for the translation and adaptation of tests. *Papeles del Psicologo,* 63–70.

Muniz, J., Prieto, G., Almeida, L., & Bartram, D. (1999). Test use in Spain, Portugal and Latin American Countries. *European Journal of Psychological Assessment, 15,* 151–157.

Naglieri, J., Drasgow, F., Schmit, M., Handler, L., Prifitera, A., Margolis, A., & Velasquez, R. (2004). Psychological testing and the internet. *American Psychologist, 59,* 150–162.

Oakland, T. (2005). Selected ethical issues relevant to test adaptations. In Hambleton, R., Merenda, P., & Spielberger, C. (Eds.), *Adapting educational and psychological tests for cross-cultural assessment* (pp. 65–92). Mahwah, NY: Erlbaum Press.

Oakland, T. (1995). Test use with children and youth internationally: Current status and future directions. In T. Oakland & R. Hambleton (Eds.), *International perspectives on academic assessment* (pp. 1–24). Boston, MA: Kluwer Academic Publishers.

Oakland, T. (2004). Use of educational and psychological tests internationally. *Applied Psychology International Review, 53,* 157–172.

Oakland, T., & Hu, S. (1991). Professionals who administer tests with children and youth: An international survey. *Journal of Psychoeducational Assessment, 9*, 108–120.

Oakland, T., & Hu, S. (1992). The top ten tests used with children and youth worldwide. *Bulletin of the International Test Commission, 19*, 99–120.

Oakland, T. & Hu, S. (1993). International perspectives on tests used with children and youth. *Journal of School Psychology, 31*, 501–517.

Oakland, T, Poortinga, Y. H., Schlegel, J., and. Hambleton R. K. (2001). International Test Commission: Its history, current status, and future directions. *International Journal of Testing, 1*, 3–32.

Pro-Ed. (2009). *Test critiques*. Austin, TX: Author.

Simner, M. (1996). Recommendations by the Canadian Psychological Association for improving the North American safeguards that help protect the public against test misuse. *European Journal of Psychological Assessment, 12*, 72–82.

Sinclair, C., Simon, N. P., & Pettifor, J. L. (1996). The history of ethical codes and licensure. In L. J. Bass, S. T. DeMers, J. R. Ogloff, C. Peterson, & J. L. Pettifor (Eds.), *Professional conduct and discipline in psychology* (pp. 1–15). Washington, DC: American Psychological Association.

Stevens, M. J., & Gielen, U. (2007). *Toward a global psychology: Theory, research, intervention, and pedagogy*. Mahwah, NJ: Lawrence Erlbaum.

Stevens, M. J., & Wedding, D. (Eds.). (2004). *Handbook of international psychology*. New York: Taylor & Francis.

Van de Vijver, F. J. R., & Hambleton, R. K. (1996). Translating tests: Some practical guidelines. *European Psychologist, 1*, 89–99.

Wang, Z. M. (1993). Psychology in China: A review. *Annual Review of Psychology, 44*, 87–116.

World Health Organization. (2001). *International classification of functioning, disability and health* (ICF). Geneva, Switzerland: Author.

CHAPTER 16

Global Test Security Issues and Ethical Challenges

David Foster *and* Harold L. Miller, Jr.

Abstract

The lack of adequate test security for important exams is a growing worldwide problem. As tests are relied upon globally more and more for critical educational and work-related decisions, there is a corresponding increase in attempts to steal test content or to cheat on tests. These threats to the valid use of tests have led to important ethical issues within the testing community. Five ethical dilemmas are presented, along with specific recommendations for resolving these issues.

Key Words: ethics, testing, assessment, global, international, technology, test security, cheating, piracy

As the professional ethics of psychologists become more standardized and formalized internationally (see, e.g., Gauthier, 2007) certain educational, political, and psychological issues remain. For example, test security has become a global issue as all types of tests, including psychological tests, college entrance tests, and graduate school admission tests have found their way online.

Increase in Worldwide Testing

More than ever before, the testing of a person's ability or knowledge is a worldwide phenomenon involving children and adults as test takers. The prevalence of technology-based[1] exams—known variously as computer-based testing, computerized testing, electronic testing, digital testing, or online testing—makes it easier to expand the base of test takers. For example, it is an unusual certification or licensure examination that is administered only to candidates within a single country. A mid-term or final exam administered in a college or high school course can be made available to distance education students in far-flung cultures and countries. Distance education programs, such as The Pennsylvania State University World Campus, primarily use the Internet as the vehicle for delivery of course instruction and exams throughout the world.

However, even if a test is not formally available to the citizens of other countries, given current trends in the rapid movement of individuals across national borders for school or work, in a real sense that test may be administered to a global clientele. Nevertheless, high-stakes[2] tests increasingly are taken by individuals from different cultures and from many countries. As a result, many of the same concerns of adaptation, cultural sensitivity, availability, cost, and fairness that apply to tests meant strictly for in-country use also apply to international use.

Technology and Testing

As already noted, new computer technologies are facilitating the growth in worldwide testing. During the late 1980s and early 1990s, networked microcomputers and improved communication technologies allowed test administration in almost any area of the world. Large testing-center networks were established, some consisting of several thousand locations, to coordinate worldwide testing efforts. Test scheduling, the downloading of exam materials, test administration and scoring, test proctoring, and the uploading of test results all occurred routinely regardless of the global location of the test taker.

The growth in computerized testing grew rapidly, partly due to the significant advantages of such exams over traditional paper-and-pencil testing. These benefits are well known, and have been described and discussed in the published literature (see Olsen-Buchanan and Drasgow, 1999, for an overview). Prominent benefits include: (a) immediate scoring and reporting of results to the test taker and to the testing program; (b) flexibility in scheduling exams, with some exams being offered "on demand"; and (c) the use of innovative item designs and test designs for better measurement of the knowledge and skills of the examinee. Technology-based testing is a source of new alternatives to the static paper-and-pencil test design and to the standard multiple-choice item design. At the same time, computerized testing has increased security concerns (Drasgow, 2002; Potenza, 2002; Way, Steffen, & Anderson, 2002). For example, tests that are available on demand may have an extended window of availability, sometimes up to several months or longer. This window allows earlier test takers to capture the content (by memorization, digital camera, etc.) and share it, often for a fee, with others who will take the test later. The Internet has proved to be a useful tool for disseminating stolen test content (Foster & Zervos, 2006). Testing programs that continue to use technology-based delivery systems have increased the number of items used in their exams or the size of item pools in order to deter theft and compensate for potentially compromised items.

During the past decade, online testing has emerged. Tests are delivered through the convenience of a browser and have the advantages of not being limited to a proprietary operating system platform or to fixed testing locations. Tests can be scheduled and administered at any time and anywhere there is an Internet connection. Initially, and because appropriate test security measures were unavailable, this technology was used only to distribute and administer low-stakes tests; that is, tests for which no consequential decisions were made on the basis of test results.

The realm of pre-employment testing has recently seen a debate over the traditional method of test administration (fixed sites, on-site proctoring, and ID-based authentication) against what is termed *unproctored testing*[3] (Tippens et al., 2006)—online testing without any monitoring or other forms of test security. In contrast to the use of testing center networks or paper-and-pencil models, the convenience, lower cost, and other benefits of unproctored testing (Chapman & Webster, 2003) are attractive for job-applicant screening and selection for many reasons, including the ability of an organization to tap into a much broader range and number of applicants. Pre-employment testing has become a de facto business requirement. It is hardly feasible if it can only occur through a limited number of testing centers, raising the cost per test for job applicants to prohibitive levels.

The debate has been openly about the ethics of test security (Chapman & Webster, 2003). For example, should a potential employer trust the results of an Internet test where there was no attempt to authenticate the test taker, or to stop him or her from cheating or from stealing the test content? Can an employer make ethical pre-employment screening decisions based on such tests? Because the unproctored test model doesn't provide for security, the results of such tests may not be valid and may therefore be useless for formal or even informal applicant screening and selection. On the other hand, it is important to remember that the testing center and paper-and-pencil testing models have their own security problems, as they depend on a security model that can be and is often easily breached. We note that a new Internet testing model has been introduced recently as an alternative to unproctored testing: Internet Testing with Online Proctoring[4] (Foster, 2008a). By adding several unique and effective security measures to online testing, it becomes secure enough for high-stakes tests while continuing to provide the convenience and cost savings normally associated with online testing.

Other technologies that affect test security include devices used to cheat, steal items, and communicate through the Internet. These include cell phones, calculators, digital recording devices for audio and video, social communication technologies on the Internet (chat rooms, YouTube™, FaceBook™, forums, e-mail, etc.). Today these technologies, and new ones that emerge with impressive regularity, contribute to mounting test security problems, helping a person cheat or capture and share test content before, during, or after a test. Colton (1998) describes a number of devices that were available a decade ago. A more recent look is available in Caveon Test Security's (2009) *Cheating in the News*, a periodic review of newsworthy test security attempts and breaches across all areas of high-stakes testing.

Although technology has been applied to the development and administration of tests, as well as to the detection and prevention of cheating and item theft, across a diversity of circumstances, the challenge to understand and mitigate the security risks continues. That these risks are shared by programs around the world is apparent. Among the questions that persist are: Is a test as secure when administered in one country as another? Do the social mores of specific cultures contribute to or alleviate security concerns? Are security problems more prevalent in some countries? What can be done to protect tests worldwide and assure their validity—at least in terms of security threats—wherever they are administered?

In 2001, the International Test Commission addressed these questions by creating a set of guidelines for the use of technology in testing. The most recent version of the *International Guidelines for Computer-Based and Internet Delivered Testing* (ITC, 2006) was updated to accommodate the rapid changes in technology for developing, administering, and securing tests.

Areas of Worldwide High-Stakes Testing

By definition, there are life-impacting consequences attached to high-stakes testing, such as getting into college, getting a better job, graduating from college, and obtaining a license to practice a profession. A few examples, and their impact on global audiences, are presented below.

Primary, Secondary, and Higher Education. The steady movement of temporary workers and immigrants within and across national borders means that the demographic makeup of today's primary, secondary, or higher education classroom in almost all countries is changing. Enrollment by relatively fewer students from the traditional local population and more students from other cultures and countries is increasingly the norm. Although testing may be confined to the classroom, the need to consider the cultural and language differences of the students taking the tests grows more pressing.

Distance Education. As distance education programs exploit the Internet to deliver online curricula, there is an attendant need to provide sound, secure tests. Distance education programs now reach an international audience. The Pennsylvania State University World Campus website reports the enrollment of "students residing on all seven continents (including Antarctica), representing a large number of countries." A recent Sloan Consortium survey of online learning (2008) reports that enrollments in online courses grew by more than 12% in the previous year. The survey of more than 2500 colleges and universities in the United States found that nearly 4 million students were enrolled in at least one online course in the fall of 2007.

Educational Admissions. Colleges and universities throughout the world are increasingly drawing applicants from outside of the country where they are located. The U.S. State Department's Bureau of Consular Affairs reported that, in 1979, the number of student visas issued was just over 224,030. In 2005, this number more than doubled to 518,915 (Congressional Research Services, 2006). Students around the world recognize the benefit of applying to the programs in which they are most interested, rather than simply to those in geographic proximity to them. Often, being admitted to a program located elsewhere allows them new opportunities for an education that will upgrade the quality of life for them and their families.

Certification. Competent workers exist in every country. Information technology (IT) companies (such as Microsoft, Cisco Systems, Oracle, Salesforce.com, and many others) require competent technicians and engineers for worldwide sales and deployment of their technology products. In the early 1990s Novell started the first IT certification program, and it quickly grew to require a global solution. Today, there are more than 100 IT organizations with certification programs. Virtually all have international sales efforts, requiring tests to be administered directly in most countries. Certification programs in other industries have no less need. For example, in the financial industry, certification of financial planners and financial analysts is very popular throughout Asia. Obtaining certification, which is voluntary, usually allows the recipient to obtain a new job, obtain a raise or promotion, or simply to retain the job she or he currently holds.

Licensure. Licensure requirements in the United States for specific professions are regulated at the state or federal level. In order to work in these professions in the United States, a competent person living and trained outside of the United States would need to at least pass the licensure exam. Such exams are increasingly available in areas of the world where many of these licensure candidates live. For example, the Philippines remains a prime source of candidates for nursing exams. Their popularity is such that new high-stakes testing centers regularly open to accommodate the growing volume of tests (Pearson, 2007).

Industrial/Organizational Psychology. Transnational businesses use tests to screen job applicants. According to Burke (2006), "Fueled by an aging but mobile and global workforce, identifying and retaining talent will become more critical. If they have not already adopted the mantra 'Spot them early, train them well and keep them longer', then organizations will have to adopt this as a philosophy to stay in the race" (p. 2). Using the Internet, many of these instruments are administered easily to a worldwide clientele, multiplying the applicant base by thousands and more.

High-stakes testing programs have been in existence, on and off, for thousands of years. Suen and Yu (2006) describe civil service testing in China as early as 606 A.D. Such testing, known as the Keju System, was a complex, government-controlled program of testing for employment and education that lasted for nearly 1300 years. Weiner (2008) describes methods of cheating and corresponding methods of deterrents used by applicants and candidates during testing periods. Creative test takers used available "technologies" of the day to cheat, such as carrier pigeons to communicate with outside confederates, cheat sheets, invisible ink, and hiring substitutes. The frequency of the latter was estimated at between 30% and 40% of test takers, according to Weiner. Despite serious deterrents (e.g., caning, prison, armed guards, body searches, and even execution) cheating continued to grow and be effective. Figure 16.1 depicts a cheating jacket that contains sample essays and information on Confucian classics (www.chinaculture.org, 2006).

Security Threats Old and New

As they were nearly 3000 years ago, security problems are divided into two types: Cheating and piracy (or theft). Cheating refers to any effort designed to help a particular test taker achieve a higher score on a test than otherwise would be achieved. Cheating ranges from gaining pre-knowledge about the test, to using proscribed aids during the test, to arranging for someone else to take the test by proxy.

Test piracy is defined as any effort to capture the test content in order to share it with or sell it to someone else. Piracy, or theft, can occur in many ways, such as by obtaining a copy of the test items, by bribing an insider working for a testing program or a test administration company, or by intercepting a copy of the testing file as it is downloaded to a testing center. Also, the test items can be captured during the test using a digital camera, or through transcribing to an audio recording device, or by the time-honored method of memorization. Pirated items are generally made accessible very quickly through the Internet, text messaging, email, cell phone, or other technology-based communications (see Foster & Zervos, 2006).

The Growing Prevalence of Test Security Problems

In a series of surveys and a review of research on trends in cheating among college students, Don McCabe of Rutgers University and his colleagues

Figure 16.1 A jacket used for cheating on Chinese examinations. It is displayed at the Shanghai Museum of the Chinese Keju System.

at the Center for Academic Integrity found that, in 1961, 26% of students admitted to copying from another student during a test (McCabe & Bowers, 1994). That percentage doubled to 52% 30 years later in 1991. In a 1999 study the percentage increased further to 75% (McCabe, Trevino, & Butterfield, 2001). Summarizing earlier research, Cizek (1999) wrote, "...one conclusion from the trend studies is clear: All agree that the proportion (of cheaters) is high and not going down" (p. 35). A more recent survey of almost 30,000 high school students by the Josephson Institute of Ethics found similar figures for that population. The institute's latest *Report Card on the Ethics of American Youth* (2008) reported that 64% of students admitted to cheating at least once in the past year, up from 60% in a similar study in 2004.

The picture is no brighter when describing online education. Harmon and Lambrinos (2006) studied the predictors of cheating in an online economics course. They administered final exams in two sections of the course. One exam was proctored, the other unproctored. They concluded "...that cheating was taking place when the exams were not proctored" (p. 2).

Common sense dictates that unproctored online tests that have substantial value, to test takers or to others, is an invitation to cheat. In reference to personnel assessment, Riley (2007) states the issues clearly:

> The absence of a proctor obviously presents the candidate with the opportunity to cheat or have someone else take the test for him or her. In addition, there is nothing to prevent the candidate from writing down all of the questions or taking photos of the computer screen and sharing them with others, thus compromising the security of the test.
> (p. 11)

Burke's (2006) assertion is consonant with Riley's: "The biggest challenges, indeed threats, to online assessment are piracy and cheating" (p. 5).

Commonly Alleged Justifications for Cheating

There is no lack of justifications offered for cheating. We cite a few of them here:

1. "Everyone does it." David Callahan in *The Cheating Culture* (2004) opines that cheating is caused by the relaxation of ethical strictures in the interest of success. According to Callahan, cheating occurs—and not just in testing—to get ahead, to get a better job and make more money, to get into the better school. Those successes, despite how they are achieved, are held in high regard and become the means for advancing one's social status.

2. "It's what we do here." Some cultures tolerate and even value cheating, such as helping another person do well on a test, because helping others is a good thing. Magnus, Polterovich, Danilov, and Savvateev (2002) compared differences in students' attitudes toward cheating among Russians, Dutch, Americans, and Israelis and found that the differences varied with the students' level of education.

3. "The test is bad." If the tests are indeed bad (i.e., not psychometrically sound), one popular conclusion is that it seems reasonable to cheat in order to score as well as possible (Foster, Maynes, & Hunt, 2006).

4. "If the program doesn't try to stop cheating, it must be okay to cheat." When test security is poor, the test taker may assume that cheating is actually encouraged. Haney and Clarke (2007) found that, in the case of online tests, test takers adapted to the unproctored testing situation by collaborating with each other, usually by gathering around laptops located in student dormitory lounges.

5. "It's a good way to make a living." Testing is big business. Test preparation in the form of capturing and selling test content can be very profitable.

6. "I don't have time to get prepared, but I really need the job." Under intense time pressure, people may feel justified to cheat.

7. "Cheating is easier than getting the experience." This may be true. However, ultimately the lack of experience is exposed.

8. "The tests are too easy. The tests are too hard. The tests are meaningless." While these statements are hardly true of most high-stakes tests, if a person can find fault with the tests (see the earlier justification in the case of "bad" tests), cheating is easier to justify.

9. "The tests are unfair." If this is true—and sometimes it is—then cheating might be seen as a viable alternative to compensate for the unfairness.

Specific Security Threats

Test security threats have been identified and categorized in several ways (Cizek, 1999; Cohen & Wollack, 2006). Among the categories are whether technology is used or not, whether the security problem occurred before or during testing, whether the test taker was involved or someone else was, etc. Table 16.1 and Table 16.2 list behavioral categories of cheating and piracy, respectively, where cheating refers to efforts aimed at increasing a test score and piracy refers to efforts to capture test content. In addition, each table ranks the threats that it lists. The rankings were assigned by the authors, and are meant as a rough gauge of the seriousness of the threat. Our criteria for estimating seriousness included ease or difficulty of the effort involved, cost in dollars, extent of the damage done, frequency of the threat, and effectiveness of the threat.

Ethical Challenges and Solutions
Psychologists as Testing and Security Professionals

Psychologists, including those with training as psychometricians, provide expertise to testing programs for the creation of tests that measure the target constructs validly and reliably. However, the psychologists' responsibility extends to the proper use of test scores as well. If a test score is based on a faulty or poorly designed test, for example, it cannot be used as a means for high-stakes decision making. Even if the test is properly constructed, should

Table 16.1 Types of Cheating

Security Threat	Threat Ranking	Description	Reasons for Ranking
Pre-Exposure to Test Content	1	Obtaining and using information about the test, test items, or test answers before taking the test	Inexpensive. Low risk of detection. Exact content may be available. It is difficult to distinguish the final result from that of an honest test taker.
Using a Proxy Test-Taking Service	2	Hiring an expert to take the test by proxy	Low risk. Convenient. Guaranteed high score. May be expensive. May not be available.
Receiving Help from a Person at the Testing Center, School, or Other Location	3	Receiving answers to test questions from a person during or after completing the test. The person may be a proctor or simply allowed by a proctor to be in the room. Coaching by a knowledgeable person who is present, such as a teacher or instructor. Changing the responses on answer sheets after the test concludes.	Expert help. May involve additional collusion by proctors, teachers, or administrative staff members.
Using Inappropriate Aids During the Test	4	Using one or more of many available inappropriate test aids for assistance with test content or answers.	A variety of aids is available, most of which are very difficult to detect. Information may not be accurate. Moderate risk of detection.
Having a Friend or Colleague Take the Test	5	Arranging for a friend or colleague to take the test by proxy. This is less formal than the proxy services described above.	Moderate risk of detection. Mostly used in education settings where personal identification is not required. High score is not guaranteed.
Hacking into Scoring Databases to Raise Test Scores	6	Accessing the score database illegally and changing the score for a particular test taker.	Requires technical ability. IT systems are generally difficult to access.
Copying from Another Person During the Test	7	Watching another person take the same test and copying the answers he or she provides.	Less effective for computer-based tests, where usually only one item is on the monitor screen at a time. Item order may be randomized.

Table 16.2 Types of Piracy

Security Threat	Threat Ranking	Description	Reasons for Ranking
Test File Capture	1	Capturing and decrypting downloaded test files. Requires collusion with someone at a testing location.	Exact content is captured. Easily made available and sold over the Internet. Quick turnaround. Low risk of detection.
Digital Still Photography	2	Using a camera or cell phone to take a picture of each item during the test.	Exact content is captured. Medium risk of detection. Depends on the collusion of a proctor.
Video Recording of the Test Session	3	Using a digital recording device or a high-resolution video camera to record the entire test session.	Exact content is captured. Requires technical skills. Medium risk of detection. May need the collusion of testing center personnel.
Memorization	4	Using memorization skills as test items appear. Several test takers may be assigned different blocks of questions.	Inexact content. May require multiple confederates. Difficult to detect.
Retake Violations	5	Retaking a test inappropriately in order to see and capture more of the items.	Takes advantage of lax retake monitoring. Easy to detect. May be expensive to retake exams.
Transcription	6	Transcribing the text of the questions to an audio recording device during the test.	Easy to detect. Requires the collusion of proctors or test administrators.
Collusion with an Insider	7	Obtaining a copy of the test directly from a person working at the testing program or test administration services company.	Low frequency. Lack of opportunity.

security problems exist that compromise the test results, the results are hardly useful. Psychologists are also responsible for making sure that proper security procedures are in place so that test scores represent the honest effort of the test taker to display her or his current knowledge or ability level, or both.

Many internationally applicable standards, codes, and guidelines exist for psychologists and psychometricians who are involved with testing. They provide direction in the use of proper methods for developing tests for the intended purposes, and establishing and monitoring the security of the tests no matter where they are administered and whichever technology may be used. They also specify the actions to be taken should a test score be deemed invalid because of poor test design or security failure (see American Educational Research Association, American Psychological Association, & National Council on Measurement in Education, 1999; American Psychological Association, 2002; American National Standards Institute, 2007; International Organization for Standardization, 2003; International Test Commission, 2006; and Society for Industrial and Organizational Psychology, 2003).

Ethical issues arise when professional codes, standards or guidelines are countervened, either inadvertently, out of ignorance, or willfully. When this occurs, test scores become suspect and may need to be discarded, often to the disappointment of educational institutions, governments, professional associations, and businesses, with potential litigable implications for test makers and test administrators.

Psychologists and psychometricians are not alone in their ethical responsibility related to testing. Others involved in the testing program share that responsibility, including organization executives, project managers, and other staff members, teachers and administrators at educational and training institutions who prepare test takers, test preparation companies that provide supplemental materials and courses, and testing center personnel, including proctors.

Ethical Issues Related to Bad Tests

Flaws in test design, poorly written items, erroneous translations or adaptations, and other test-related problems quickly lead to significant errors that are unrelated to a test taker's knowledge or skill. These amount to *construct-irrelevant variance*, a concept introduced by Messick (1989). For example, if a multiple-choice item has been miskeyed, individuals answering the item correctly will have their final test scores reduced nonetheless. If a testing program knowingly produces such tests, or makes no effort to revise them when they become apparent, this constitutes a violation of professional ethics. The remainder of this chapter will focus on ethical challenges that are related solely to security issues and not those attributable to the poor construction of a test. Ironically, one of the reasons cheaters give for cheating is that they quickly discover or have heard that a test is poorly written and impossible to do well on unless the test taker cheats (Cizek, 1999).

Ethical Dilemmas Related to Test Security

As testing programs adopt technology and the Internet increasingly, and as such programs become global, it is paramount that psychologists and psychometricians understand and adhere to a uniform code of ethics. For example, Code 9.11 of the *Ethical Principles of Psychologists and Code of Conduct* states: "Psychologists make reasonable efforts to maintain the integrity and security of test materials and other assessment techniques consistent with law and contractual obligations, and in a manner that permits adherence to this Ethics Code" (p. 14, American Psychological Association, 2002).

In what follows we describe and provide examples of five current ethical dilemmas and the factors that produce them.

Ethical Dilemma 1: Making Important Decisions Based on Tests Where Security Efforts are Ineffective or Nonexistent, Making the Resulting Test Scores Suspect

This dilemma is described well by Tippens et al. (2006). It is one that psychologists and psychometricians who deal with pre-employment screening often struggle with. Some occupational testing organizations use online testing technology on behalf of their customers to locate potential employees from a large and diverse applicant pool. Online technology allows such organizations to cross national borders in their search. An online test such as this is generally offered *without security*, making it more easily administered, especially when the number of applicants approaches hundreds of thousands across many countries. The results are used to screen the applicants and select some for advancement in the application process. The ethical issues should be obvious. They arise simply because the online tests are administered with little or no security. Cheating is possible and easily accomplished. Test content can be easily captured and shared. There is no way to authenticate the test taker as the person who should be taking the test. It is impossible to tell which applicants had access to the pirated materials, if someone provided coaching, or if a surrogate took the test. In this scenario, it is nearly impossible to tell the difference between an honest test taker and a cheater. This renders the test scores meaningless, allowing some individuals to move along in the application process even though undeservedly. Thus, in situations where a fixed number of individuals must advance, it is reasonable to assume that a certain number of qualified individuals were rejected unfairly.

While some critics might scoff at the scenario and consider such testing patently low-stakes, they would be wrong. Especially in difficult economic climates, it is vital that all qualified applicants be considered equitably for employment. Cheating and test theft occur in these circumstances precisely because high-stakes motives operate: Higher scores allow a person to move forward in the application process. While employment is not guaranteed, it becomes more likely.

Ethical Dilemma 2: Continuing to Deliver High-Stakes Computerized Tests When Serious Security Threats are Known

Information technology (IT) certification tests suffer from a serious malignancy referred to as "braindumps." These are websites that gather and sell test content. For example, a person wishing to pass an IT certification exam can buy the test items and answers from hundreds of available braindump sites, and can do so easily within minutes and inexpensively (usually for less than

$100). Research has shown that these sites actually provide the exact items and answers found on the tests (Foster & Zervos, 2006). The evidence suggests that the braindump sites exploit security "holes" in the technology systems of test administration organizations, obtaining the test content by capturing and decrypting the complete test files that are downloaded to testing centers prior to test administration. The pirates can only do this efficiently by colluding with an authorized testing center where the administration occurs. Some braindump operators are very efficient, even offering on-demand test content. This means that the customer orders the test content, which isn't already available at the site. Within a few days, the items and answers are delivered. Most braindump sites operate out of Asia.

Another well-known security issue affecting IT certification programs is proxy test-taking. Businesses specializing in this service, again in collusion with a testing center, will take a candidate's test for a fee. CyberGandhi (2008) reported that Cisco Systems, which operates one of the largest IT certification programs, found that at least 1 in 200 tests administered in India was taken by proxy.

The ethical issues exist partly because IT certification programs and their test administration partners largely have been ineffective in protecting the content of the tests and identifying proxy test-taking. The sites continue to proliferate and operate with impunity, and IT certification programs seem powerless to stop them. Thus, IT certification programs, knowing that the security of the system is compromised, continue: (a) to publish their newly developed tests in a high-risk environment, losing the content to braindump sites almost immediately; and (b) to certify individuals even though there is confusion about which of them earned the certification credential honestly, which used the content available from braindump sites, and which used a proxy service. As a result, officially certified individuals whose actual competence remains unknown continue to access better jobs, raises, and promotions. Unsuspecting employers hire individuals who may or may not be competent. Increasingly, as these security issues are more widely known, employers are ignoring IT certification results and looking more closely at the work products, résumés, and references of their applicants.

Ethical Dilemma 3: Continuing to Use Dated Psychometric Methods When Such Methods Increase Unsecured Item Exposure and Other Known Security Problems

Most current test designs are based on historical adaptations of paper-and-pencil tests. Most tests delivered via technology today can be accurately described as "page turners," simply presenting the same types of items and same types of tests that are, or can be, delivered in paper-and-pencil formats. The cumulative historical use of paper-and-pencil testing is so compelling that many psychologists view paper-and-pencil testing as a "standard," and any departure from it as wrong or suspect or counter to existing test standards. In fact, it is not unusual for testing experts to require that a new technology-based test demonstrate equivalence with its paper-and-pencil counterpart. According to Kingsbury (2002):

Since the early development of computerized adaptive testing, researchers have *strongly suggested* studies comparing performance of computerized adaptive tests (CAT) to their paper-and-pencil counterparts (Green, Bock, Humphreys, Linn, and Reckase, 1984). This is *imperative* in any situation in which an adaptive test is replacing an existing paper-and-pencil test, or in any situation in which paper tests and adaptive tests are being used concurrently. (Italics added; p. 2)

Such a view today is not universal, as some experts see the promise of technology-based testing to lie in actually improving testing. Drasgow and Olson-Buchanan (1999) list and discuss the potential advantages of several technologies, such as audio and video, new item types, compact storage devices, input devices, and devices for measuring item-response latencies. They conclude by stating that "...computers can administer and score tests with greater convenience, reliability, standardization, and affordability than human test administrators" (p. 3). Such a view encourages the development of improved tests, even tests where security is an inherent part of the test and item designs.

The ethical dilemma lies in passing up (or failing to develop) more effective technology-based test and item designs. For example, a testing program may reject new technology-based designs that limit exposure to test content, while at the same time those designs improve or maintain the measurement ability of the test.

One test design feature is the marking of items for later review in a test—a feature included in most technology-based test administration systems. It allows a test taker to "mark" a question, thus placing it on a list for later review. Usually, the test taker's provisional answer is displayed as well, and then perhaps changed upon later review. The benefit of using such a feature is that a test taker may change previous incorrect answers to the correct answer. Not surprisingly, this feature is similar to what is inherent in paper-and-pencil tests. They allow a test taker to answer items in any order and to mark items for later review. As a consequence, testing professionals may consider such a feature an integral component of technology-based tests.

However, even though mark-and-review can be helpful in improving test scores, it may present a serious security risk. Test takers who are sent to a testing center to "harvest" or steal items find the task easier if they can "mass" the items assigned for harvest; that is, memorize them all at once or capture them using a digital camera or other recording device.

Some technology-based test designs, such as CAT, require a forward-only procedure, meaning that the test taker does not have access to a mark-and-review feature. This occurs because the test provides an interim score after each item has been answered and selects the next item based on the test taker's prior response. The operation of the test would be frustrated were test takers allowed to skip items and return to them later.

Technology can provide new designs at the item level as well. We have recently introduced a new multiple-choice item format known as the Discrete Option Multiple Choice (DOMC) format (Foster, 2008b; Foster & Miller, 2009). Rather than presenting the answer options all at once, as is typical in paper-and-pencil and technology-based tests, it presents the options one at a time, requiring the test taker to decide each time if the option is the correct answer or not. Foster and Miller (2009) asserted that the new item format retains strong measurement properties but is more effective in inhibiting cheating and item theft than traditional multiple-choice formats.

Ethical Dilemma 4: Budgeting Funds for Test Development but Not for the Security of the Tests

Testing programs traditionally spend a great deal of money to develop a high-stakes test. At the same time, they spend very little to secure the new test. Recently, one of us (DFF) discussed this issue with a certification program manager whose tests were typically stolen and compromised within days of their publication. Knowing how much the program spent on test development, and that it spent very little or nothing at all on test security, it seemed not unreasonable to pose this question: Why not create one fewer new exam this year, and spend that money to help protect the others? Her answer reflected a mixture of ignorance regarding security solutions, lack of funding allocated for security purposes, and some apathy that solutions would be effective.

Spending too little on test security is a relatively recent problem stemming from at least three sources. First, technology-based test designs have stimulated the introduction of new security threats. On-demand testing is an example, providing lengthy testing windows and giving cheaters and thieves new opportunities for test fraud. Programs, not anticipating such threats, have been slow to develop solutions and to modify their budgets accordingly. Second, thieves and cheaters have at their disposal new and effective technologies that weren't available even a year ago. For example, digital photography allows the easy capture of test content in a way that would not have been possible just a few years ago. Third, testing programs encourage their test administration service vendors to assume complete responsibility for test security, perhaps trusting that security procedures applied at the time of test administration will be effective and sufficient. Most often that hope is disappointed.

Here the ethical dilemma lies in testing programs not allocating sufficient resources to improve the security of new tests.

Ethical Dilemma 5: Not Dealing Properly and Effectively with Known Cheaters and Test Pirates

More often than not, testing programs are hesitant to take action against someone caught cheating or stealing test content, or against websites that traffic in pirated test content. Lack of incentive, ineffective training, and protection by favorable national legal systems may be responsible for at least some of this hesitation in educational settings (see Cizek, 1999). At a basic level, this could occur when a proctor chooses not to confront a test taker who is cheating, and simply "looks the other way." Or a testing program, confronted with a report detailing a security incident, chooses not to pursue it.[5] The program's hesitancy could result from any of several factors:

• No legal assistance is available, or such assistance would be too expensive.
• There is a lack of confidence in the capability of current security methods.
• No prior warnings or instructions have been given to the test taker.
• No specific legal policy is in place that bans cheating or theft.
• There is concern that such a policy may produce legal action against the testing program.
• There is too little evidence of the incident.
• The incident took place in another country, making it difficult to enforce legally.
• It is important to avoid negative public notice.

As a result of these and other reasons, many incidents go unreported and further incidents effectively expand.

The ethical dilemma arises when information indicates a security breach but no reaction occurs. Inaction rewards the cheater and encourages that person and others to continue or increase their efforts. A harmful side effect of such negligence is that the test scores become increasingly untrustworthy.

Resolving the Ethical Challenges Resulting from Security Problems

The ethical issues considered, and the threats to test security described above, may be attributed to a lack of knowledge about the threats, about the available security solutions, about the proper implementation of security procedures that constitute best practices, or to some combination thereof. Each of the ethical dilemmas we previously examined can be resolved by either adopting better test security practice, or by changing the nature or the goals of the testing program. For example, if the tests can be considered low-stakes instead of high-stakes, then the need for security is reduced considerably. Table 16.3 lists each dilemma and, with it, potential remedies and their likely outcomes.

It is important to note that many testing programs end up at the mercy of these ethical dilemmas without intending to be. This occurs because they: (a) are not aware that test security solutions are available, (b) are not trained sufficiently in test security, (c) lack faith in existing security solutions, (d) are knowledgeable about test security procedures but are unwilling to use them, (e) historically allow test administration vendors to take the responsibility for test security, or (f) hope that test security problems will simply disappear.

A Sample of Security Solutions for the Ethical Dilemmas

We assume that, for each dilemma, the preferred choice is to solve the security problems directly and continue to develop and provide high-stakes tests. This section describes possible security solutions for each dilemma.

Ethical Dilemma 1: Making Important Decisions Based on Tests Where Security Efforts are Ineffective or Nonexistent, Making the Resulting Test Scores Suspect

For pre-employment testing, organizations that depend on the tests need to maintain the advantages afforded by the massive reach of the Internet. The simple solution is that the security of those tests must be raised to an acceptable and effective level. Internet-based tests often are considered nonsecure, but that perception may mislead. The Internet actually provides the opportunity for increasing test security, just as it has done for the now-common practices of online banking or online purchasing. There are new security measures that can be applied to Internet-delivered tests to keep the cost of testing low while allowing the tests to be delivered securely worldwide. They include:

• Monitoring test-taker behavior individually using webcams rather than using on-location proctors.
• Locking down the browser so that no computer-based or Internet-based resources can be accessed during the test.
• Using keystroke dynamics (see Monrose & Rubin, 2000) as a strong authentication measure that does not depend on hardware and does not introduce data privacy issues.
• Monitoring response patterns to test items to detect cheating or theft early in the test.
• Immediately intervening when cheating or item theft occurs.
• Using new item and test designs that protect the content and deter cheating and theft.

Table 16.3 Recommendations for Resolving the Ethical Dilemmas

Ethical Dilemma	Potential Remedies	Likely Outcomes
Dilemma 1. Making important decisions based on tests where security efforts are ineffective or nonexistent, making the resulting test scores suspect	Continue to administer Internet tests without proper security, but no longer make high-stakes decisions based on the scores.	The program may be able to use the scores for marketing or research purposes but will not be able to use them as they have in the past.
	Implement effective security procedures to protect the Internet tests.	The test may cost more develop and administer as new security methods are applied, but the ability to use the test scores properly is preserved.
Dilemma 2. Continuing to deliver high-stakes computerized tests when serious security threats are known	No longer develop and administer high-stakes tests.	The testing program may be able to use other methods, such as portfolios or work products, essays or papers, or personal references as the basis for decisions.
	Eliminate or reduce the security risks by implementing effective security measures.	Secured tests will allow the program to make fair and legally defensible high-stakes decisions.
Dilemma 3. Continuing to use dated psychometric methods when such methods increase unsecured item exposure and other known security problems	Improve the traditional security measures for the testing program (e.g., use more proctors, increase user access controls, etc.).	The testing program may continue to use traditional testing methods, designs, and analyses with the expectation that improved security will reduce the risks.
	Upgrade item and test designs, and implement newer security analyses.	Using newer item and test designs and technology will better protect the tests and provide the program with results that lead to more accurate decisions.
Dilemma 4. Budgeting funds for test development but not for the security of the tests	Because the tests are not sufficiently secured, high-stakes decisions should not rely on them.	Low-stakes tests may serve an organization's purposes better than compromised high-stakes tests. It is also possible that test development costs can be saved.
	Budget sufficient funds to develop a strong test security plan.	Assuming the overall budget doesn't change, fewer resources would be applied to high-stakes tests, but the tests that are produced can provide valid scores for decision making.
Dilemma 5. Not dealing properly and effectively with known cheaters and test pirates	Develop low-stakes tests only, tests for which there is little or no motivation to cheat or steal the content.	Low-stakes tests will not result in security breaches of any substance.
	Actively prevent breaches but when they occur, deal decisively with the cheaters and thieves: withhold scores and decisions, take legal action if necessary, etc.	The testing program will create an environment that deters test fraud of all types. The initial expense will lead to increased credibility and overall lower security costs for the testing program.

Given these innovations, it is clear that the effective administration of important tests over the Internet can be improved with a more determined application of security procedures (ITC, 2006).

Ethical Dilemma 2: Continuing to Deliver High-Stakes Computerized Tests When Serious Security Threats are Known

Easy access to the exact test content has given rise to a proliferation of braindumps, websites that traffic in stolen test content. Foster (2006) confirmed that these sites have the exact text and graphics of the items, together with the answers. Moreover, the items were stolen from intercepted (and perhaps, decrypted) files, rather than memorized and shared by test takers. The IT industry suffered initially and continues to bear the brunt of the effects of braindumps, although the problem is spreading to other important areas of high-stakes testing. To date, the efforts by the IT industry to reduce the risk of braindumps has been ineffective. In fact, the problem continues to grow. Efforts to date have focused on threats of legal action and attempting to shut the sites down.

It is unclear why an organization would continue to develop and deliver high-stakes certification exams when it is clear that: (a) the exams are compromised within days of their publication; (b) certification candidates continue to take the exam, although many of them do not earn the high scores they receive; (c) there is no attempt to determine who truly deserves a passing score and who doesn't; and (d) the certification program suffers from lack of credibility in the marketplace.

Solutions to the security problems are available. Some of the more effective ones are described below:

• Quit using risky test administration networks that allow relatively easy access to test items.
• Protect the content of high-stakes certification exams by using more effective distribution and encryption technology.
• Use test and item designs that protect the content, making it difficult to steal. There are test and item designs that protect against exposure and make it difficult to capture, memorize, and share test content. Impara and Foster (2006) described several tactics a testing program might use if the exam is primarily composed of multiple-choice items. As a unique solution, answer options can be presented one at a time, or not displayed at all, in order to secure them from memorization or other forms of capture (Foster and Miller, 2009). At the test level, CAT presents only a fraction of the item pool, reducing the frequency of presentation of any particular item. However, for some items the exposure level actually increases in a CAT (Davey & Pitoniak, 2006).

• Use new forensic methods to determine which candidates are using pre-knowledge[6] obtained from braindumps or other sources.

Ethical Dilemma 3: Continuing to Use Dated Psychometric Methods when Such Methods Increase Unsecured Item Exposure and Other Known Security Problems

Organizations that continue to use paper-based testing systems do so partly because they are concerned about the security of technology-based exams (Drasgow, 2002; Potenza, 2002; Way, Steffen, & Anderson, 2002). Although this may have been a valid decision 20 years ago when computer-based test administration was introduced, much has been done in the meantime to improve the security of these exams, and particularly in the past few years. Today, however, continuing to use outdated test development and administration procedures presents a growing security risk. Cheaters and thieves have discovered how to steal and cheat using new technologies, including cell phones, digital cameras, two-way radios, etc. Tried-and-true cheat sheets and other "tools" have been upgraded as well. Colton (1998) provides a lengthy list of high-tech cheating tools and their uses.

New technology-based testing models, including those that use the Internet exclusively, have introduced a number of new security tools, even for exams that are given on demand with long testing windows. Some examples follow:

• Strong authentication using biometric technologies in addition to, or to replace, the display of multiple forms of government-issued identification documents. Some biometrics use physical devices, such as those that capture and recognize fingerprints or retinal patterns. Some that are available exclusively over the Internet use an application of keystroke dynamics technology (Foster, Mattoon, & Shearer, 2009) to provide strong authentication.
• Browser or computer system lockdown can prevent access to inappropriate cheating aids and prevent copying or transmitting test content.
• Online proctoring, using webcams and highly trained proctors, provides consistent and unbiased monitoring of each test taker (see Foster & Case, 2010), a feature that is not possible with large-scale paper-and-pencil testing.

- Data-forensic methodologies can be used to continuously monitor item performance, alerting the test administrator when an item is not performing as it had originally and is thus eligible for replacement. Han and Hambleton (2008) describe several item-exposure detection algorithms that analyze item p-values to determine if the item is performing at the same level of difficulty as it did when first presented. Recalculated p-values are plotted with upper and lower limits. When the p-value increases (that is, the item gets easier) due to exposure and crosses the upper limit, it may be replaced with a noncompromised alternative. Other organizations have proposed similar tracking systems for technology-based tests (Maynes, 2006).

Ethical Dilemma 4: Budgeting Funds for Test Development but Not for the Security of the Tests

Developing and implementing a testing program for high-stakes purposes can be costly. The new uses of technology test development and administration, as well as new technology-assisted security methods, have increased the need to budget sufficiently for test security. Many testing programs have yet to do so.

One of the first steps in securing a testing program—and in understanding its costs—is to develop and implement a formal security plan. The American National Standards Institute (2007) suggests that a security plan for certification programs should provide for the following critical aspects of test security:

1. *Maintenance.* What is the schedule for updating and approving the security plan?
2. *Roles and Responsibilities.* What are the security-related roles and the responsibilities of each person or entity?
3. *Budgeting and Finance.* Are there sufficient funds to implement proper security and deal with potential breaches when they occur?
4. *Legal Agreements.* Are proper legal agreements in place with test takers, consultants, item writers, reviewers, etc.?
5. *Item and Test Design.* Has the program implemented item and test designs that protect the content and make it difficult for individuals to cheat or steal the items?
6. *Item and Test Development.* During the development and production of the test items, as well as the compilation of the final versions of the exams, are they completely protected from theft?
7. *Test Publication and Distribution.* Are the tests properly protected as they leave the safety of the testing program offices and servers, and until they are needed for distribution?
8. *Test Administration.* Are the tests protected against theft during test administration? Are enough effective security controls in place to keep individuals—test takers and others—from cheating?
9. *Test Scores and Test Results.* Are test results protected after the test is completed? Unauthorized individuals should be unable to access tests and transmitted test-results files.
10. *Physical Security.* Are the physical locations where test program activity occurs secured? Are visitors checked and escorted? Is the equipment secured?
11. *Information Systems.* Are the testing program's servers protected from unauthorized access?
12. *Internet and Media Monitoring.* Does the testing program assure an ongoing effort to discover whether test takers and others are disclosing its intellectual property on the Internet or in other ways?

Ethical Dilemma 5: Not Dealing Properly and Effectively with Known Cheaters and Test Pirates

Often, testing programs are afraid to take action against someone known or suspected to have cheated or stolen test content. There are at least a few reasons for this stance.

First, the program may conclude that it does not have enough evidence to support a claim of cheating or item theft. It may only have anecdotal evidence, or only statistical evidence that a person cheated. Cizek (1999) advises that "In many circumstances, some method of substantiating our observations—or, at least, making the conclusions based on these observations less subjective—is needed" (p. 135). Recent advances in data forensics, or applied statistical analyses of cheating, can provide substantiating evidence, including the test record of a person caught cheating that shows evidence of aberrance, high gain scores, or unusual responding. New online proctoring systems (Foster & Case, 2010) provide time-stamped video and audio records of security incidents which can be used for decision making and supporting legal action if necessary.

Cizek (1999) suggests that statistical evidence alone may be insufficient to support a program's action against a test taker, for example by cancelling her or his test score. In contrast, Hunt (2006) summarized several major relevant court cases and concluded that "The dictum that emerges from these examples for non-governmental testing programs is that the test-use agreements invest testing programs with broad power of investigation and that data forensics can satisfy the program's responsibility to exercise that power in 'good faith'" (p. 5). Hunt recommends that the program's test-use agreements be reviewed and broadened, if necessary, to provide this capability.

Another reason a testing program might hesitate to take action is the belief that legal efforts are expensive and generally end up in favor of the cheater. However, Burgoyne (2007) reviewed a large number of recent court cases in the United States and other countries involving the theft of test items and test-taker cheating, and found that the view is unwarranted. With proper agreements, copyrights, and security measures in place, testing programs acting in good faith to protect their intellectual property and their decisions are rewarded by the courts.

Testing programs that neglect to follow up by cancelling test scores or taking legal action when appropriate may embolden test takers to cheat and steal. On the other hand, swift and effective action will send a message that such behavior will not be tolerated, and this may have a positive impact on greatly reducing such problems in the future.

Conclusion

The future will only bring more challenges to test security. It is critical that they be recognized for what they are: threats to the validity of tests and, therefore, to all that they are designed to accomplish for the larger society. Such threats must be anticipated if they are to be prevented.

The accelerating popularity of worldwide testing, the use of the Internet and other technologies, and new security threats have produced ethical dilemmas for psychologists and psychometricians. It is important for these individuals, and the testing and testing research programs they represent, to address these dilemmas and respond accordingly. Using test security procedures and technologies quickly and efficiently, and relatively inexpensively, will return a program to solid footing.

Notes

1. To avoid confusion, the term *technology-based* will be used throughout this paper to refer to these various types of tests as a group. When referring to them individually, the specific term will be used.

2. In this paper a "high-stakes" test refers to any exam that produces a score that has important consequences for the examinee and/or other stakeholders. In education, these include course midterms and final exams, U.S. state assessments, admissions tests to college or graduate programs, and others. Outside of education, they include certification and licensure exams, pre-employment screening assessments and employment tests, and clinical psychological exams administered for a variety of purposes including employment, educational placement, and to resolve legal arguments. In contrast, low-stakes tests have no important consequence.

3. While it has a more specific definition, for the purposes of this paper, "unproctored" testing will refer to Internet (or online) testing that has very little or no security, including no authentication of the test taker and no monitoring of test taker behavior.

4. *Online proctoring* refers to several technologies meant to discourage cheating, and to immediately detect and deal with it when it occurs. Online proctoring can be divided into three components: (1) strong authentication through keystroke dynamics, (2) machine lockdown and automated monitoring of attempts to breach the system, and (3) human monitoring of test taker behavior through individual webcam viewing.

5. Of course, this hesitancy may also be closely related to laxity in putting stringent security measures in place: If you catch cheaters effectively you then have the unpleasant and risky task of punishment.

6. In personal communication, Dennis Maynes of Caveon Test Security described to the author a new forensics analysis for a certification program that had exams composed of both new items and older, exposed items. He calculated two scores for each test taker and calculated a "difference" statistic that identified those candidates who had taken the test with pre-knowledge of the exam questions. Armed with such information, the program could reliably identify the truly competent candidates.

References

American Educational Research Association, American Psychological Association, & National Council on Measurement in Education. (1999). *Standards for educational and psychological testing*. Washington, D.C.: American Educational Research Association.

American National Standards Institute (2007). Guidance for conformity to ANSI/ISO/IEC 17024 requirements for certification program security. Retrieved from http://publicaa.ansi.org/sites/apdl/Documents/Conformity%20Assessment/Personnel%20Certifier%20Accreditation/Documents%20related%20to%20accreditation%20under%20ANSI-ISO-IEC%2017024/Public%20Documents/ANSI-PCAC-GI-504.pdf.

American Psychological Association (2002). *Ethical principles of psychologists and code of conduct*. Principle 9.11 Maintaining Test Security. Retrieved from http://www.apa.org/ethics/code2002.html.

Burgoyne, R. (2007). *Responding to test irregularities: The need, the methods, and the risks—litigation*. Paper presented at the

Innovations in Testing Conference for the Association of Test Publishers. Palm Springs, CA.

Burke, E. (2006). *Better practice for unsupervised online assessment.* Thames Ditton: SHL

Callahan, D. (2004). *The cheating culture: Why more Americans are doing wrong to get ahead.* New York, NY: Harcourt, Inc.

Caveon Test Security (2009). *Cheating in the News.* Retrieved from http://www.caveon.com/citn/.

Chapman, D. S., & Webster, J. (2003). The use of technologies in the recruiting, screening, and selection processes for job candidates. *International Journal of Selection and Assessment, 11*, 113–120.

Chinaculture.org. (2006). *New museum showcases 1,300-year-old examination system.* http://www.chinaculture.org/gb/en_newupdate/2006-02/23/content_79628.htm.

Cizek, G. (1999). *Cheating on tests: How to do it, detect it and prevent it.* Mahwah, NJ: Lawrence Erlbaum Associates.

Cohen, A. S., & Wollack, J. A. (2006). Test administration, scoring, security and reporting. In R. L. Brennan (Ed.), *Educational measurement* (4th ed., pp. 355–386). Westport, CT: American Council on Education/Praeger.

Colton, G. D. (1998). Exam security and high-tech cheating. *The Bar Examiner, 67(3).* National Conference of the Bar Examiners.

Congressional Research Services. (2006). *Foreign students in the United States: Policies and legislation.* Retrieved from: http://www.fas.org/irp/crs/RL31146.pdf.

CyberGandhi. (2008). *Too many "proxy test takers" prevalent in India.* Retrieved from: http://escapefromindia.wordpress.com/2008/07/24/too-many-proxy-test-takers-prevalent-in-india/.

Davey, T., & Pitoniak, M. J. (2006). Designing computerized adaptive tests. In S. M. Downing, & T. M. Haladyna (Eds.), *Handbook of test development* (pp. 543–574). Mahwah, New Jersey: Lawrence Erlbaum Associates, Publishers.

Drasgow, F., & Olson-Buchanan, J. B. (1999), Blood, sweat, and tears: Some final comments on computerized assessment. In F Drasgow & J. B. Olson-Buchanan (Eds.), *Innovations in computerized assessment* (pp. 249–254). Mahwah, New Jersey: Lawrence Erlbaum Associates, Publishers.

Drasgow, F. (2002). The work ahead: A psychometric infrastructure for computerized adaptive tests. In C. N. Mills, M. T. Potenza, J. J. Fremer, & W. C. Ward (Eds.), *Computer-based testing: Building the foundation for future assessments.* Mahwah, New Jersey: Lawrence Erlbaum Associates, Publishers.

Foster, D. F. (2008a, April). *Secure, online, high-stakes testing: Science fiction or business reality?* Presentation at the SIOP Annual Meeting, San Francisco, CA.

Foster, D. F. (2008b, March). *Psychometric properties and acceptability of the Foster Item format.* Paper presented at the annual meeting of the Association of Test Publishers, Dallas, TX.

Foster, D.F., & Case, R. (2010). Online secured testing works! Evidence from a few thousand test takers. Workshop conducted at Innovations in Testing the Annual Conference for the Association of Test Publishers, Orlando, FL.

Foster, D. F., Mattoon, N., & Shearer, R. (2009). *Using multiple online security measures to deliver secure course exams to test takers.* Retrieved from http://www.kryteriononline.com/pdfs/Kryterion_White_Paper.pdf.

Foster, D. F., Maynes, D., & Hunt, R. H. (2008). Using data forensics methods to detect cheating. In C. L. Wild & R. Ramaswamy (Eds.), *Improving testing: Applying process tools and techniques to assure quality* (pp. 305–321). New York: Lawrence Erlbaum Associates.

Foster, D. F., & Miller, Jr., H. L. (2009). A new format for multiple-choice testing: Discrete-option multiple choice. Results from early studies. *Psychology Science Quarterly, 51,* 355–369.

Foster, D. F., & Zervos, C. (2006). *The big internet heist.* Poster presented at Association of Test Publishers Annual Conference, Orlando, FL.

Gauthier, J. (2007). *Canadian psychology's contribution to the development of a universal declaration of ethical principles.* Presented at the General Assembly of the College of Psychologists of Saskatchewan, Saskatoon, Saskatchewan, March.

Green, B. F., Bock, R. D., Humphreys, L. G., Linn, R. L., & Reckase, M. D. (1984). Technical guidelines for assessing computerized adaptive tests, *Journal of Educational Measurement, 21,* 347–360.

Han, N., & Hambleton, R. (2008). Detecting exposed items in computer-based testing. In C. L. Wild, & R. Ramaswamy (Eds.), *Improving testing: Applying process tools and techniques to assure quality* (pp. 323–348). New York: Lawrence Erlbaum Associates.

Haney, W. & Clarke, M.J. (2007). Cheating on tests: Prevalence, detection, and implications for online testing. In E. A. Anderman, & T. Murdock (Eds.), *Psychological perspectives on academic cheating* (pp. 255–287). San Diego, CA: Elsevier.

Harmon, O. R., & Lambrinos, J. (2006). Are online exams an invitation to cheat? University of Connecticut, *Department of Economics Working Paper Series.* Retrieved from http://www.econ.uconn.edu/working/2006-08r.pdf

Hunt, R. (2006). *Caveon Legal Forensics™: Legal defensibility of scoring decisions.* Retrieved from http://74.220.207.132/~caveonco/articles/df_legal_defensibility.pdf

Impara, J. C., & Foster, D. F. (2006). Designing computerized adaptive tests. In S. M. Downing, & T. M. Haladyna (Eds.), *Handbook of test development* (pp. 91–114). Mahwah, NJ: Lawrence Erlbaum Associates, Publishers.

International Organization for Standardization. (2003). International standard ISO/IEC 17024, *Conformity assessment—general requirements for bodies operating certification of persons.* Geneva, Switzerland: Author.

International Test Commission (2006). International guidelines on computer-based and internet-delivered testing: Version 2005. *International Journal of Testing, 6,* 143–172.

Josephson Institute of Ethics. (2008). *Report Card on the Ethics of American Youth.* Retrieved from http://charactercounts.org/programs/reportcard/index.html.

Kingsbury, G. (2002). *An empirical comparison of achievement level estimates from adaptive tests and paper-and-pencil tests.* Paper presented at the American Educational Research Association Annual Meeting, New Orleans, LA.

Magnus, J. R., Polterovich, V. M., Danilov, D. L., & Savvateev, A. V. (2002). Tolerance of cheating: An analysis across countries. *Journal of Economic Education 33,* 125–135.

Maynes, D. (2006). *Recent innovations in data forensics.* Retrieved from http://caveon.com/articles/df_innovations06.htm.

McCabe, D. L., & Bowers, W. J. (1994). Academic dishonesty among males in college: A thirty year perspective. *Journal of College Student Development, 35*(1), 5–10.

McCabe, D. L., Trevino, L. K., & Butterfield, K. D. (2001). Cheating in academic institutions: A decade of research. *Ethics and Behavior, 11,* 219–232.

Messick, S. (1989). Validity. In R. L. Linn (Ed.), *Educational measurement* (3rd ed., pp. 13–104). New York: American Council on Education and Macmillan.

Monrose, F., & Rubin, A. D. (2000). Keystroke dynamics as a biometric for authentication. *Future Generation Computer Systems, 16*(4), 351–359.

Olson-Buchanan, J. B., & Drasgow, F. (1999), Beyond bells and whistles: An introduction to computerized assessment. In J. B. Olson-Buchanan & F Drasgow (Eds.), *Innovations in computerized assessment* (pp. 2–3). Mahwah, NJ: Lawrence Erlbaum Associates.

Pearson, V. U. E. (2007). NCLEX Examinations scheduling to open for Philippines test center. Retrieved from http://www.pearsonvue.com/about/release/07_07_11_ncsbn.asp.

Potenza, M. (2002). Test administration. In C. N. Mills, M. T. Potenza, J. J. Fremer, & W. C. Ward (Eds.), *Computer-based testing: Building the foundation for future assessments*. Mahwah, NJ: Lawrence Erlbaum Associates.

Riley, N. (2007). Unproctored, internet employment testing—the technological edge: Panacea or Pandora's box. *The Assessment Council News*, October, 2007. Alexandria, VA: The International Public Management Association for Human Resources.

Sloan Consortium. (2008). *Staying the course: Online education in the United States, 2008*. Retrieved from: http://www.sloan-consortium.org/publications/survey/staying_course.

Society for Industrial and Organizational Psychology, Inc. (2003). *Principles for the validation and use of personnel selection procedures* (4th ed.). Bowling Green, OH: Author.

Suen, H. K. & Yu, L. (2006). Chronic consequences of high-stakes testing? Lessons from the Chinese civil service exam. *Comparative Education Review, 50*(1), 46–65.

Tippens, N. T., Beaty, J., Drasgow, F., Gibson, W. M., Pearlman, K., Segall, D. O., & Shepherd, W. (2006). Unproctored internet testing in employment settings. *Personnel Psychology, 59*(1), 189–225.

Way, D. W, Steffen, M., & Anderson, G. S. (2002). Developing, maintaining, and renewing the item inventory to support CBT. In C. N. Mills, M. T. Potenza, J. J. Fremer, & W. C. Ward (Eds.), *Computer-based testing: Building the foundation for future assessments* (pp. 143–144). Mahwah, NJ: Lawrence Erlbaum Associates.

Weiner, J. (2008). *The potential impact of cheating in online testing: Good news, bad news*. Presented at the International Test Commission Annual Conference, Liverpool, England.

CHAPTER 17

Psychologists and Prisoner Interrogations

Norman Abeles

Abstract

Recent estimates suggest that there have been over 300 articles on the topic of detainee interrogations in the last few years. There has been a marked increase in detainee interrogations in the military system accompanied by allegations of abuse and torture of international prisoners and statements that psychologists were directly or indirectly involved. The American Psychological Association authorized a task force to look at the topic of harsh interrogations, with particular focus on ethical concerns. Part of the report of this task force concluded that psychologists must not engage in behaviors that violate the laws of the United States, and may refuse for ethical reasons to follow laws or orders that are unjust or that violate basic principles of human rights. Further, the report stated that psychologists have an ethical responsibility to report acts of torture and other cruel, inhuman, or degrading treatment to the appropriate authorities.

Key Words: detainee interrogations, principles of human rights, ethics, Guantanamo Bay

In a recent paper on this topic, Carter and Abeles (2009) pointed out that the criminal justice system utilizes interrogations as a staple to elicit needed information. One has only to watch popular TV programs in the United States, like *CSI* and *Law and Order*, to witness the interrogation of suspects and prisoners. The overall aim usually is to obtain hopefully relevant and detailed information that will result in confession, apprehension, and conviction of a suspect, prevent additional criminal acts, and reduce local or international criminal behavior (Hartwig, Granhag, & Vrij, 2005). Specific techniques may vary. Thus, state police agencies may utilize simple deception by exaggerating or minimizing how serious the crime might be, or they may utilize a series of structured steps, the first of which may be factual and nonaccusatory, while later steps involve more direct confrontations.

Psychologists may participate in these techniques via consultation (Kassin & Gudjonsson, 2004) as Carter and Abeles (2009) noted. In fact, psychologists who have studied criminal behaviors frequently consult with local, federal, and military organizations. The American Psychological Association has an entire division devoted to forensic matters, called the American Psychology-Law Society (Division 41). In the United Kingdom there is a division of forensic psychology that is part of the British Psychological Society. It was originally named the Division of Criminological and Legal Psychology, but changed its name to the Division of Forensic Psychology in 1999. It aims to represent psychologists whose work includes involvement in the criminal and civil justice system. It includes psychologists working in prisons, in academic settings, and in health, education, and social service settings (Division of Forensic Psychology, 2009).

As Carter and Abeles (2009) noted, there has been a marked increase in the focus on interrogations in the military system "as allegations of the abuse and torture of international prisoners during interrogation have been raised" (p. 12). While many are aware that interrogation and torture are not the same, there has been a blurring of the two when interrogation techniques have been used in an inappropriate manner. Summerfield (2003) raised the question as to whether or not interrogation techniques had been used inappropriately at Guantanamo Bay because they were close to, or actually were, torture. Thus, military personnel, physicians, and psychologists, as well as psychiatrists, were investigated to see if they crossed the line between interrogation and torture. With regard to psychologists and psychiatrists, the question was not whether they actually tortured prisoners but whether or not their consultation to interrogators condoned torture. Stevens (2005) suggested that psychologists have contributed to intelligence gathering by means of behavioral profiling and screenings in order to reduce and prevent terrorist attacks.

The involvement of psychologists in matters of social control has a longer history. As Abeles (2009) pointed out, some commentators actually insist that psychotherapy itself is a means of social control (Hurvitz, 1973) and psychotherapy has even been compared to brainwashing (Dolliver, 1971; Gaylin, 1974). Coercive practices actually receive a good amount of social approval, and the courts have been active in "sentencing" individuals to mandated treatments for issues such as anger management, driving while intoxicated, and sexual acting out. Certainly the question of whether or not certain psychological techniques allow the therapist to manipulate or control clients has been the subject of discussion. In general, it has been agreed that psychotherapists cannot ethically coerce a client into treatment to force certain goals or outcomes against the client's wishes (Abeles, 2009). Recent concerns have dealt with the role of therapists in dealing with alleged terrorist detainees held by military authorities. Special problems have arisen concerning clients in the military or involuntarily confined in prisons.

Psychologists in the Armed Services

As Carter and Abeles (2009) pointed out, there are numerous activities for psychologists who serve in the armed services or are consultants to the military. These can include assessment for fitness for duty, evaluating individuals for leadership positions, organizational productivity, and determining personnel qualifications (Johnson, 2002). Psychologists and psychiatrists have also served as members of behavioral science consultation teams (BSCTs). Rather than providing direct psychotherapy to incarcerated individuals in the military, their task was to observe interrogations and to provide feedback to interrogators (Bloche & Marks, 2005; Okie, 2005). In an article in the *New England Journal of Medicine*, Okie (2005) stated that she talked to two psychologists at Guantanamo Bay and they emphasized that they do not advise interrogators regarding how to increase stress, since those techniques are not effective. Instead, they stated that rapport building is what should be emphasized. Nevertheless, Okie cited a U.S. Army report in which there were incidents at Guantanamo that detailed harsh interrogation techniques in 2002 and 2004, which included sleep disruption, exposure to extreme temperatures, and prolonged exposure to loud music.

There have also been allegations that psychologists who were trained in the Survival, Evasion, Resistance and Escape Program (SERE), used by the military to help prisoners to tolerate abusive enemy tactics, used this program to develop interrogation techniques at Guantanamo. Evidence for this, however, is disputed. One of the difficulties lies in the definition of who is a psychologist. While there are 150,000 members of the American Psychological Association, there are many more individuals who identify themselves as psychologists. Many of these individuals have received training in psychology, and some of them are not involved in the treatment of patients and clients. The public, however, assumes that almost everyone who is a psychologist must be one who provides treatment. Regardless of whether a psychologist works as a clinician treating patients or does nonclinical work, members of APA are bound by the APA *Ethical Principles and Code of Conduct* (APA, 2002). The ethics code contains a number of aspirational principles at the beginning and then moves on toward the enforceable code, the standards. Thus, if psychologists were to observe abusive treatments in the military (or in other work settings) it would be incumbent on them to report such unacceptable practices.

Some have argued that psychologists working at Guantanamo Bay were aware of such practices and did not report them. This would be the case specifically at Guantanamo, since psychologists were assigned to observe interrogations of prisoners. In addition to the APA Code of Ethics, the 1949 Geneva Convention also required that healthcare professionals abide by medical ethical standards (Carter & Abeles, 2009). That would be the case even if psychologists were ordered not to report such violations (Annas, 2005). To complicate things further, in 2002 then President Bush issued an executive declaration stating that al-Qaida prisoners were not protected by the Geneva Convention because they were to be classified as *enemy combatants*, which was a new type of unlawful enemy category (Mayer, 2005). Individuals classified as such were not considered to be American citizens or citizens of any United Nations member. In addition, they were viewed as threats to national security and thus did not have the rights of prisoners of war. Under the Geneva Convention, prisoners of war can refuse to answer questions put to them by interrogators. As Hall (2004) pointed out, this still does not permit the use of torture under the declaration of the United Nations Convention against Torture.

APA's Attempts to Clarify Military Service by Psychologists

Since there was considerable confusion and concern about psychologists serving as consultants to interrogators at Guantanamo Bay, the APA authorized a Presidential Task Force to examine the issues with particular focus on ethical concerns. For those who might have thought that psychologists who consult in the military might not need to adhere as closely to APA ethical standards, the report gave a clear answer. That answer was no! It reemphasized further that intelligence gathering and the protection of individuals is an important role for psychologists, and concluded that the role of psychologists included the "safe, legal and ethical" practice of psychology (Carter & Abeles, 2009, p.16). The specific role for psychologists is detailed in this *Presidential Task Force on Psychological Ethics and National Security* (PENS; APA, 2005). Here are the conclusions from the report:

1. Psychologists are alert to acts of torture and other cruel, inhuman, or degrading treatment and have an ethical responsibility to report these acts to the appropriate authorities.
2. Psychologists who serve in the role of supporting an interrogation do not use health care related information from an individual's medical record to the detriment of the individual's safety and well-being.
3. Psychologists do not engage in behaviors that violate the laws of the United States, although psychologists may refuse for ethical reasons to follow laws or orders that are unjust or that violate basic principles of human rights.
4. Psychologists are aware of and clarify their role in situations where the nature of their professional identity and professional function may be ambiguous.
5. Psychologists are sensitive to the problems inherent in mixing potentially inconsistent roles such as health care provider and consultant to an interrogation, and refrain from engaging in such multiple relationships.
6. Psychologists may serve in various national security-related roles, such as a consultant to an interrogation in a manner that is consistent with the Ethics Code, and when doing so psychologists are mindful of factors unique to these roles and contexts that require special ethical consideration.
7. Psychologists who consult on interrogation techniques are mindful that the individual being interrogated may not have engaged in untoward behavior and may not have information of interest to the interrogators.
8. Psychologists make clear the limits of confidentiality.
9. Psychologists are aware of and do not act beyond their competencies, except in unusual circumstances such as set forth in the Ethics Code.
10. Psychologists clarify for themselves the identity of their client and retain ethical obligations to individuals who are not their clients.
11. Psychologists consult when they are facing difficult ethical dilemmas.

The PENS report was strongly supported by the APA Ethics Office (Behnke, 2006) and others (Solomon, 2005). However, Dr. Rubenstein of Physicians for Human Rights sent Dr. Behnke of the APA Ethics Office a letter on March 12, 2006, commenting on the PENS Report (Rubenstein, 2006). In his introduction he noted that the "...national security setting cannot be established or fully appreciated in a vacuum...A well-documented public record of abusive interrogation practices shows that they include mock drowning, sleep deprivation, exploitation of fears and phobias and much more." (p.1). He stated further that psychologists should restrict their participation in interrogations to providing only general information, nor should they participate in interrogations of an individual and advise on interrogation techniques for such an individual, nor should they be present while interrogation takes place. APA, on the other hand, had argued that observing interrogations provides for a measure of safety since psychologists could "blow the whistle" on inappropriate interrogation techniques. Indeed, as Soldz (2007) pointed out, Michael Gelles, a military psychologist, did complain about interrogation techniques to his superiors. Gelles was a member of the PENS Task Force and, along with Larry James and Robert Fein, worked to prevent detainee abuse as well as abusive interrogations. Rubenstein did note that the authorization for abusive techniques was withdrawn in January 2003, although a working group recommended some of the previously approved techniques. The Secretary of Defense did not approve all of these techniques but permitted latitude on a case-by-case basis (Rubenstein, p. 3).

In the letter to Behnke, Rubenstein indicated that the role played by psychologists in abusive techniques was unclear. There were allegations in the *Washington Post* and in the *New York Times* about the involvement of psychologists. Rubenstein recommended that exacting ethical rules be established to prevent psychologists from becoming involved in abusive techniques. He then went on to propose specific guidelines to ensure compliance with the first statement (psychologists are alert to torture) of the PENS report. Rubenstein also emphasized the need for psychologists to seek training in the area of human rights. Another section dealt with the harms from psychological interrogation practices. It was suggested that psychologists limit their role to providing only general information about interrogation techniques, and focus on gaining rapport with prisoners and limit activities to gaining information. Psychologists should not advise on techniques to be used on specific individuals or assess them for interrogation with a particular technique. Rubenstein stated that this is consistent with the United Nations principles of medical ethics and the role of health personnel for purposes that are not solely designed to evaluate, protect, or improve their physical and mental health (p. 12). He pointed out that the APA Council of Representatives supported the UN Principles of Medical Ethics.

In an invited commentary on the PENS report by former APA President Phil Zimbardo (2008), the contributions of the PENS report were listed. He noted that the application of the APA code of ethics apply to all psychologists serving, whether they are traditional health service providers or behavioral scientists. He reported that the PENS report was quite explicit in fully rejecting torture or other similar activities. He also commended the writers of the report in rejecting the use of health information by psychologists to the detriment of individuals' safety and well-being. Finally, the PENS report makes individual psychologists responsible for particular behaviors, attitudes, perspectives, and sensitivities. These include (among others) behaviors that violate U.S. laws, being aware of the possible innocence of individuals being interrogated, clarifying the identity of the "client," and becoming informed about how culture and ethnicity interact with investigators or information-gathering techniques (p. 4).

On the other hand, Zimbardo pointed to what he saw as limitations of the PENS report. He commented that when one is hired by a government agency the "client" is one's boss, since it is the agency who pays the psychologist. Thus, the individual being interrogated is no longer the client except in those instances when the psychologist is specifically asked to provide clinical services. There are also pressures on agency employees to be part of the "team" and to refrain from whistleblowing. In fact, it may not be clear to whom one should report violations and the consequences of doing so may be fraught with actions against the person reporting. Keeping these and similar factors in mind, Zimbardo questioned the model used in the PENS report, since it appeared to focus on the psychologist functioning as an independent contractor rather than as an employee. He described psychologists working for government agencies as "hired hands" (Zimbardo, 2008) and suggested that the individual being interrogated is no longer the client unless the psychologist is a health service provider. He maintained that it is not possible for a psychologist to evaluate the morality and ethicality of questioning terror suspects, since the available information is opaque or compartmentalized within a range of military or governmental agencies, with a limit on psychologists need to know. For those psychologists who work in career jobs with government agencies, the pressures on them to be team players is great and it is difficult to be a whistleblower. These and other factors lead Zimbardo to conclude that the PENS report does not represent how things really work. He believes that the APA should not permit an ethical standard less strict than that of the American Medical Association or the American Psychiatric Association, though others disagree with that conclusion.

More Recent Developments

As Abeles (2009) pointed out, the 2006 resolution passed by the APA Council of Representatives prohibited cruel, inhuman, or degrading treatments, and cited the United Nations convention. It also cited the McCain amendment, as well as national and international bodies with similar declarations. The resolution also included the assumption that psychologists are required to intervene and stop abusive behaviors such as torture, and included reference to intentional infliction of severe pain or suffering from both a physical and mental standpoint. If psychologists noted such behaviors they were required to intervene, and if unable to do so they should exit. This resolution was reaffirmed in 2008 and a provision was added concerning the stoppage of such abusive behaviors and the requirement to exit. Many criticized the APA, and some raised political issues. For example, Bryant Welch, former Director for Practice within the APA, alleged that the support by the APA of military psychologists traced back to a political relationship between the APA and the Department of Defense (Welch, 2008). He alleged that the relationship between the APA and the Department of Defense goes back to the prescription privileges effort encouraged by Pat DeLeon, who was a past president of the APA and chief of staff for Senator Inouye. Welch alleged that Inouye removed the funding for closing Gitmo. Welch also suggested that the Human Resource Research Organization (HumRRO) developed in 1951 was run by a psychologist who was deeply involved with the APA. Welch implied that because HumRRO now receives 55% of its budget from the military, the APA was and is closely tied to defense interests. He then went on to criticize the APA's interest in prescriptive authority because the Department of Defense provided funds for a demonstration project, which permitted a small number of selected military psychologists to receive training in prescribing medicines.

In his conclusion, Welch stated that APA governance members were naïve about politics and thus continued to support interrogations of prisoners by psychologists because of the influence of the military establishment. Others who have read Welch's article disagreed and thought it strained credulity. For example, one of the former presidents of the APA (Ron Fox) once remarked, "don't try to teach a pig to sing. It won't work and only annoys the pig."

Another criticism was voiced by Stephen Soldz (2008), who alleged that two psychologists helped to train interrogators in brutal techniques, including waterboarding, in 2002 and 2003. Others argued that in addition to those two psychologists there were others who knew about torture occurring during interrogations of prisoners but did not report those violations (Hall, 2004). It is not clear whether these allegations have been proven. In addition, the APA ethics office deals only with complaints against members of APA based on complaints filed against them. Certainly there are some individuals who call themselves psychologists, regardless of whether their training is as psychologists, in contrast to the profession of medicine where calling oneself "doctor" implies having a medical degree and license (Abeles, 2009).

In 2008 for the first time over 10% of APA members signed a referendum provision which required a vote as to whether or not psychologists can continue to work in detention settings that exist in violation of international law or the U.S. Constitution. The petition resolution stated that the equivalent of torture took place at the U.S. Naval Base at Guantanamo Bay, Cuba, in the presence of psychologists. This was reported by the UN special *rapporteur* on mental health. The resolution stated that psychologists may not work in settings where individuals are held in violation of international law and the U.S. Constitution unless they are working to protect human rights or working directly for the persons being detained (APA Petition Ballot, 2008). There was a pro and con statement for this referendum petition. In the pro statement, Dr. Brad Olsen (2008) argued that psychologists have designed and participated in interrogations that equal torture and considered the APA resolutions to be inadequate. He pointed out that Justice Department lawyers in the Bush administration required a diagnosis of post-traumatic stress syndrome (PTSD) in order for interrogation to equal torture and represent prolonged mental harm. He rejected the argument that some psychologists protected detainees from abuse by going to higher authorities to complain about this abuse, and stated that there was evidence to show that psychologists were silent in the face of torture. He argues that psychologists should be excluded from working in settings where international law and human rights are not upheld.

In response, the con statement was filed by Dr. Robert Resnick (2008), who argued that the referendum was excessively broad and would restrict the scope of practice by psychologists. Prohibiting the location of employment instead of prohibiting ethical behavior would interfere with the work of psychologists and is counter to APA ethical principles. He also insisted that the petition is not enforceable if passed, and puts an unnecessary burden on psychologists because they may not know whether or not their work is in violation of APA policy. Many psychologists who work in forensic settings might be affected improperly. In a rebuttal statement by Dr. Ruth Fallenbaum, it was argued that Resnick was wrong in his assumptions, and unintended consequences can occur with any policy. It was instead imperative that the moral issue be addressed.

The referendum was held in September 2008 and the petition passed by a vote of 8792 to 6157. APA has about 92,000 members (not including student members). This vote was slightly lower than the number of votes usually cast for an APA presidential election, though it was the highest turnout for a referendum in APA history. A lot of APA members do not vote even on important issues. As a result of this action, the president of the APA, Alan Kazdin, established an advisory group designed to implement this policy for this resolution. An effective date for this was discussed at the 2009 meeting of the Council of Representatives. In February 2009, President Obama addressed Congress in a joint session and promised to close the Guantanamo Bay prison by the end of the year. As of February 2010 this has not happened, and there is considerable controversy as to where prisoners from Gitmo should be tried and where incarcerated prisoners should be housed.

Final Words

In 2009 it was estimated that over 300 papers had been written on this topic. I suspect that number has risen since then. In view of all the publications on this topic, I have tried to keep this paper relatively brief. I should also note that the actions of the APA ethics committee are not announced until they are finalized. So of this writing there have been no announcements regarding psychologists who were found to be in violation of APA ethical principles on this issue. It should also be noted that the APA code of ethics applies only to members of the Association, even though there has been some informal discussion recently that this policy should be expanded to include all psychologists, not only those who are members of the APA. At this point, implementing such a policy would seem to be far into the future, if possible at all.

References

Abeles, N. (2009) Ethics and the interrogation of prisoners. *Psychotherapy Bulletin, 44*, 41–45.

Abeles, N. (2010). Ethics and the interrogation of prisoners: An update. *Ethics and Behavior, 20*, 243.

American Psychological Association. (2002). Ethical principles of psychologists and code of conduct. *American Psychologist, 57*, 1060–1073.

American Psychological Association. (2005). *Report of the Presidential Task Force on psychological ethics and national security*. Retrieved from http://www.apa.org/releases/PENSTask force ReportFinal.pdf.

American Psychological Association. (2008). 2008 Petition resolution ballot. Retrieved from http://www.apa.org/governance/resolutions/notorture0807.html.

Annas, G. J.(2005) Unspeakably cruel. Torture, medical ethics and the law. *New England Journal of Medicine, 352*, 2127–2132.

Behnke, S. (2006). Psychological ethics and national security. The position of the American Psychological Association. *European Psychologist, 11*, 153–156.

Bloche, M. G., & Marks, J. H. (2005). Doctors and interrogators at Guantanamo Bay. *New England Journal of Medicine,353*, 6–8.

Carter, L. A., & Abeles, N. (2009). Ethics, prisoner interrogation, national security, and the media. *Psychological Services, 6*, 11–21.

Division of Forensic Psychology. (2009). Retrieved from http://www.bps.org.uk/dfp/dfp_home.cfm.

Dolliver, R. H. (1971). Concerning the potential parallels between psychotherapy and brainwashing. *Psychotherapy: Theory, Research and Practice, 8*, 170–174.

Gaylin, W. (1974). On the borders of persuasion: A psychoanalytic look at coercion. *Psychiatry: Journal for the Study of Interpersonal Processes, 37*, 1–9.

Hall, P. (2004). Doctors and the war on terrorism: Everyone must understand doctors don't "do torture." *British Medical Journal, 329*, 66–67.

Hartwig, M., Granhag, P. A., & Vrij A. (2005). Police interrogation from a social psychology perspective. *Policing & Society, 15*, 379–399.

Hurvitz, N. (1973). Psychotherapy as a means of social control. *Journal of Consulting and Clinical Psychology, 40*, 232–239.

Johnson, B. W. (2002) Consulting in the military context: implications of the revised training principles. *Consulting Psychology Journal: Practice and Research, 54*, 233–241.

Kassin, S. M., & Gudjonsson, G. H. (2004). The psychology of confessions: A review of the literature and issues. *Psychological Science in the Public Interest,5*(33), 67.

Mayer, J. (2005) Annals of Justice; Outsourcing Torture. The New Yorker, Digital edition. February 14, 2005, p.106.

Okie, S. (2005). Glimpses of Guantanamo: Medical ethics and the war on terror. *New England Journal of Medicine, 353*, 2529.

Olsen, B. (2008) Pro statement. Retrieved from http://www.apa.org/gpvernance/resolutions/worksettingspro.html.

Resnick, R. (2008) Con statement. Retrieved from http://www.apa.org/governance/resolutions/worksettingscon.html.

Rubenstein, L. S. (2006). Letter to Stephen Behnke, Director of Ethics. Retrieved from http://www.division39.org/sec_com_pdfs/PHRCommentaryonAPAPENSReport.pdf.

Soldz, S. (2007). "Whistle-blower" Michael Gelles throws in lot with American Psychological Association on interrogation issues. Retrieved from http://www.atlanticfreepress.com/news/opinion/11248/Michael-Gelles-throws in-lot-with-APA-on-interrogations html.

Soldz, S. (2008). The torture trainers and the American Psychological Association. In *Counterpunch*. Retrieved from http://www.counterpunch.org/soldz0625008.html.

Solomon, M. Z. (2005) Health care professionals and dual loyalty: technical proficiency is not enough. *Medscape General Medicine,7*(3), 14.

Stevens, M. J. (2005). What is terrorism and can psychology do anything to prevent it. *Behavioral Science and the Law, 23*, 507–526.

Summerfield, D. (2003). Fighting "terrorism" with torture. *British Medical Journal, 326*, 773–774.

Welch, B. (2008). Torture, political manipulation and the American Psychological Association. In Cockburn, A. & St. Clair. J. (Eds.). *Counterpunch*. Retrieved from http://www/counterpunch.org/welchpy282008.html.

Zimbardo, P. (2008). Foreword. In James, L. *Fixing Hell* (pp. xi–xvl). New York: Grand Central Publishing.

Zimbardo, P. (2006). Commentary on the Report of the American Psychological Association's PENS Report. Retrieved from http://www.prisonexp.org/pdf/PENScommentary.pdf.

PART 3

Psychological Ethics in Wider Contexts

CHAPTER 18

Ethical/Deontological Issues in Work and Organizational Psychology

José M. Prieto, Pedro Chacón, *and* Carolina Marín

Abstract

Pragmatism is the prevailing philosophical framework in work and organizational (W/O) psychology and so is an a posteriori perspective, a justification dependent on consequences of psychological actions and values that highlight transactions. Deontological codes are mere descriptions of inappropriate practices, and deontological committees are not final decision makers on ethics in the profession. Conflicts or complaints are examined privately first, and disagreements have recourse to law. Human rights in the workplace have been outcomes of political and legal actions, never based on ethical allegations (too conservative or religious, often). W/O psychology values, issues, and dilemmas were not taken into consideration in the elaboration of deontological codes for decades. Complaints in this area are rare, and controversial issues such as discrimination, plagiarism, and sexual behaviour are understood differently in W/O psychology. Human resources and global economy policies are interconnected and international (ISO) or national standards and norms abound in the field.

Key Words: pragmatism and ethics, business ethics, descriptive ethics, discrimination in the workplace, sexual behavior in the workplace, plagiarism, industrial psychology and ethics, organizational psychology and ethics, work psychology and ethics, personnel psychology and ethics, occupational psychology and ethics, karma.

Terminology is not Neutral in the Identity of this Professional Profile

In the beginning it was *psychotechnics*, the expression created by William L. Stern (1871–1938) in a lecture (published in 1903) that was used by Hugo Munsterberg (1863–1916) to mean that psychological experiments are "systematically to be placed at the service of commerce and industry" (Münsterberg, 1913, p. 3). Later, in Chapter XIX, he made clear the subservient relationship: "The theoretical views of the economists and of the philosophers of value might thus be directly translated into psychotechnical advice" (p.245). The purpose was satisfying economic life demands, and the theoretical framework of psychological action favoring industrial efficiency was axiology, that is, the science of human values as conceived, for instance, by the German philosopher and psychologist Eduard von Hartmann (1842–1906) and Gordon W. Allport (1897–1967), North American psychologist and president of the APA in 1939.

Psychotechnics in Europe was translated as *applied psychology* in the United States, and it meant "the practical application of psychological principles in economics, sociology, and business" (Goldenson, 1984, p. 608). It is the name of the journal (2008 ISI impact factor 3.769, the highest in the ranking) that started to publish on these matters in 1917 under the APA. Another example, the International Association of Psychotechnics founded by Edouard Claparede (1873–1940) in 1919 became, by the end of the Second World War, the International Association of Applied Psychology (http://www.iaapsy.org/) and as such organizes an international congress every four years and has a journal, (*Applied Psychology: An International Review*, with a 2008 Impact factor 1.177). More specific names for this broad discipline started to be used through the second half of the 20th century.

Work and organizational psychology (W/O psychology from now on) is the terminology preferred in Europe as compared to *industrial and organizational psychology* (I/O psychology), used mainly in the United States. In the United Kingdom, *Occupational and Organizational Psychology* is the name that appears in the journal (2008 ISI impact factor 1.361) published by the British Psychological Society since 1918. However, there is agreement in this field: this psychology exists in organizations, and thus public or private institutions and companies set the political and operational framework. "Business ethics" is the notion that started to circulate in the mid-1970s under the influence of theologians analyzing with entrepreneurs the consequence of business practices in the aftermath of natural disasters (for instance, in Bhopal, India, 1984), war disasters, or economic crises such as the fall of Enron in 2001 (Ferrell, Fraedrich & Ferrel, 2006). The *Journal of Business Ethics* is the main reference since 1982: impact factor 1.203 in 2008 and 7th in the rankings of the ethics category.

The other names used—work psychology, occupational psychology and industrial psychology—introduce nuances about the adequate ethical connection. *Work psychology* was the expression emphasized first in France and, for decades, the focus has been on working conditions, which is the setting or scenarios in the workplace. *Occupational psychology* highlights the idea of professions and profiles and therefore employment, positions on which time is spent by persons. *Industrial psychology* relies on manufacturing and processing, where the expected output is products and services, often linked to research, development, or innovation (R+D&I).

Other terminologies may be also linked to this domain of expertise where psychological action and expertise is understood as a behavioral technology; that is, assessment + treatment = problem solving and thereby efficiency:

a. Consultant or Consulting Psychologist, Occupational Health Psychologist: They may be assimilated into the profile of psychotherapist or therapist, and so transactions and interaction are similar to those performed by clinical psychologists. In these contexts conventional deontological codes endorsed by psychological associations make sense, taking into consideration that the client is explicitly an organization and implicitly individuals. Service-centered interventions and transactions (for instance, stress prevention, recruitment, selection, promotion or outplacement, accident analysis, coaching programs) are regulated through highly specific contracts and, in cases of conflict, courses of action and complaints are submitted to the court or negotiated via a mediator.

b. Personnel Psychologist: A profile linked to the journal with that name issued in 1948 that has been the ensign-bearer in the assessment of individuals and teams (2008 ISI Impact Factor 3.222, the third in the ranking). Trade unions have been somewhere around in committees where assessment protocols are examined in decision-making procedures and they have been acting informally as super-ego and moral authority in working class struggles. There are strong differences between working class trade unions in continental Europe and labor unions in the United Kingdom, United States, and Canada, and it would require another chapter to compare trade unions' ethical practices with those in W/O psychology. Herbert Marcuse (1898–1979), in his classic "one-dimensional man" study, insinuated that applied psychologists' knowhow concentrated efforts to single out methods of better management, safer planning, greater efficiency, and closer calculation. The outcome is problem-solving strategies via the assessment of individuals and groups. They know but never use the ideological terminology of trade unions. So any political or ethical analysis becomes immediately practical under the umbrella of positive thinking (Marcuse, 1964).

c. Research Scientists: Ethical standards in research carried out with human participants have been endorsed in many universities, and the manual of Sales and Folkman (2000) is a suitable reference in organizational settings where applied psychologists play a leading role in research and program evaluation programs.

d. Management Psychologist, Business Psychologist: This tag insists on the psychological perspective when planning, organizing, staffing, leading, and controlling an organization occurs. So political priorities in the organization prevail.

e. Psychological engineering, human engineering, ergonomics, and human factors' psychology are terms that may be applied to researchers that develop protocols, standards, prototypes tested for future use. So, again, Sales and Folkman's (2000) book is an advisory resource because human participants are involved in procedures and findings.

What do all these professionals do? They "apply principles of psychology to personnel, administration, management, sales, and marketing problems. Activities may include policy planning, employee screening, training and development plans and organizational development analyses and programs. Top and middle managers often demand the contribution of W/O Psychologists to reorganize work settings and improve workers' productivity." This is the summary of this profile outlined in the online database of the Occupational Network known as O*Net. It may be reached at http://www.onetcenter.org/ exhaustively and free of charge, because it is a research center and web-based laboratory sponsored by public funding in the United States. It has generated an occupational information system for the 21st century, available online, with not only databases and profiles but also instruments. Several leading members of Division 14 in the American Psychological Association were involved in the initial phase as well as in the continuity of annual updates. In a sense it is a Diagnostic and Statistical Manual of normal behavior and performance in the workplace. The contrast with this is the DSM–IV or V, etc., focused on abnormal behavior. O*Net gathers reliable and updated information and statistics on job profiles and normalized personnel assessment demands in organizations. Peterson, Mumford, Borman, Jeanneret, and Fleishman (1999) summarized background research that supported theoretically and operationally the launching of O*Net.

This description already provides some hints of what may be expected under the umbrella of an ethical perspective:

a. If W/O psychologists devote themselves to "applying principles of psychology," then the deontological code of their psychological association makes sense and must be kept in mind, at least, as a reference.

b. When psychological activities include policy planning, then factual plus value-laden judgments are present and combined, often in a rather confused manner. The analysis and decision making is that required by the organization, so this frame of reference prevails in cases of ethical dilemmas.

c. If applied psychologists work with management issues and dilemmas, then the prime concern is the hierarchy and the organizational structure and chart (that is, the *organigramme* in French terms). The CEO or top managers are the government and represent the moral authority in the company or institution. Employed psychologists may avoid tendering their resignation by accommodating and using the deontological code of their psychological association as an argument: it is the "Establishment" in the profession. In other words, a helmet, a bulletproof vest, at hand.

In deontological terms these distinctions are not neutral and entail, for instance, that those organizations where psychological actions occur settle business ethics. It means that the initiative, the ethical focus, corresponds to the organization where applied psychologists are employed. It is the mainland, and the psychological association is, let's say, the peninsula or the island where psychologists spend the weekend. The consequence is that membership of a psychological association is a contingency and that the application of that associations' deontological code is contingent, circumstantial. The organization that hires them may say, "I am the ethical authority" (rarely occurs) and what happens, from time to time, is the insistence of the psychological association: "I am the genuine ethical authority" because membership overrules employment policies and precepts. So *casus belli*, that is, deontological conflict, ho! It denotes loyalty to one organization or to the other, and often it is the psychological association that insists that professional ethical rules prevail over companies' interests. Sometimes the ego is the center, sometimes is the periphery. Degrees of freedom and tolerance often swing, and a strategic choice (center–periphery) may be a momentary choice. "Over a period of several months in 1997/1998 four members of the Dutch Association of Psychologists (NIP), resigned their membership because they thought that they could not compete with non-members who were not tied to ethical guidelines" (Voskuijl, Evers & Geerlings, 2005, p. 100). As will be substantiated later in this chapter, rarely do companies not take into consideration the ethical demands made by the W/O psychologist.

Important differences in perspective may be derived if the ethical focus is (a) on working conditions that affect employees, (b) occupational activities that generate a salary, (c) industrial settings where transformations happen and clients pay for something they like and purchase. This is the domain of economic behavior and, thus, utilitarianism is in the background: transactions exist and so benefits, profit and loss, and returns on investment are the expected targets of the employer and the employee (Lewis, 2008). Jeremy Bentham (1748–1832) and John Stuart Mill (1806–1873) raised the issue of utilitarianism that became, in the 20th century, consequentialism, launched by Gertrude E. M. Anscombe (1919–2001) in ethics: "the morality of our actions is to be judged by the relative goodness of their effects rather than by their inherent rightness or wrongness" (Lefkowitz, 2003, p. 65). Similar views were shared in psychology, for instance, by John Dewey (1859–1952) and William James (1842–1910) under the umbrella of pragmatism. In his 1891 address to the Yale Philosophical Club, James made clear what it entails:

> there is no such thing possible as an ethical philosophy dogmatically made up in advance...there can be no final truth in ethics...the essence of good is simply to satisfy demand...the *highest* ethical life consists at all times in the breaking of rules which have grown too narrow for the actual case
> (*James*, 1891, p. 330, 343, 348).

It is convenient to elucidate what is meant by pragmatism in science and in psychological practice. Ideologies, theories, and models are validated in the context of problem-solving analysis and strategies. Solutions that generate short-term or long-term damage to people, to properties, to quality of life standards, are considered unethical. Practical and theoretical reasons come together, and setting an ontological difference between facts and values is an artefact. Values are hypotheses about what is good in psychological action, and propositions on practical and unpractical consequences of psychological knowledge and expertise are rooted in beliefs about what is appropriate; hence "the good reasons approach" developed, for instance, by Stephen Toulmin (1922–2009). It is also the domain of metaethics as sponsored by Lekan (2003) and the Meta-Code of ethics launched in 1995 by the European Federation of Psychologists' Associations (EFPA). Lindsay, Koene, Øvreeide, and Lang (2008) outline and discuss practical consequences of the updated Meta-Code (2005; http://www.efpa.eu/ethics) by examining examples and commenting on vignettes. Respect, Competence, Responsibility and Integrity are just ethical tools that make psychological practice more intelligent.

Fritzsche and Becker (1984) also used vignettes to discover that industrial psychologists (and business managers and economists) felt more comfortable asserting that an ethically right action is one that generates a good outcome for the organization, teams, or employees. This research was confirmed later by Premeaux and Mondy (1993) among managers.

The Buddhist notion of karma—action understood as a seed that generates the entire cycle of cause and effect—also holds an a posteriori perspective on what may be viewed as right or wrong practice. In Buddhism the master, the abbot, the Dalai Lama, is not the moral authority; they are exemplars of what is meant by a virtuous life. Buddhist precepts are mainly suggestions and community life guidelines. The focus of Buddhist ethics is building the even-tempered character of any awakened individual (Keown, 2001).

Deontological codes endorsed by psychological associations (drafted after the initiative of clinical and experimental psychologists first, and researchers in psychology afterward) insist that the rightness or wrongness of a psychological action derives from the character of the act itself, and this character is advanced a priori in the code of ethics, and interpreted, complaint by complaint, by the deontological committee that is the hermeneutic and moral authority. In other words, casuistry understood as applied ethics, or precepts figured out as commandments.

Deontological Codes and Membership

Do people join organizations as a way of preventing loneliness, or as a stratagem to prevent isolation in professional life? Henry A. Murray (1893–1988) identified the need of affiliation as a social form of motivation, whereas Stanley Schachter (1922–1997) studied it experimentally in the context of the two-factor theory of emotion.

Psychologists may join political parties, trade unions, or scientific or professional associations. What counts is membership, and disagreements regarding outcomes of elections, leadership style, visibility, policies, investments, or manifestos are just internal controversies. Loyalty to the association is expected from members that may start to consider resignation if discrepancies prevail over compliance. The exception seems to be deontological codes in psychology: interpretations made by ad hoc committees are submitted to the governing body, often the president, and, if endorsed, sanctions are implemented. Immediacy is a cultural but also a strategic matter. The consequence may be that membership is cancelled for some time, and the underlying argument is that ethics is the cutthroat razor of good habits, right practice in the profession. The theoretical framework seems to be the Jewish–Christian tradition of Ten Commandments, a list of religious and moral imperatives. Should deontological codes in psychology be considered prescriptive or descriptive? For decades, the large majority have been enacted as prescriptive: moral principles have been postulated as backbones, setting aside the modulating role of explicit or implicit values that make sense in the situation. It is the contrast yes or no (no errors as criterion), versus mercurial variations of values (that is plasticity and resilience).

The origin of scientific societies may be traced back to the 16 century: the Academy of the Mysteries of Nature (*Academia Secretorum Naturae*) was founded in Naples in 1560 by Giambattista della Porta (1535–1615), a mathematician. Candidates had to present a new fact in natural science as a condition of their acceptance as a member (Bruno, 1987). The society was closed down in 1578 by the order of Pope Paul V under suspicion of sorcery. In Catholic countries, scientific societies and royal academies often came into trouble, also during the French Revolution, and thus cleverly avoided producing ethical codes. In the background lay the conflict between science and church. The sponsorship of the Royal House was the nationally valid safe-conduct against inquisitorial institutions. Historical details may be found in Ornstein (1963) and Fisch (1975). Catholic researchers have been invited to deal with ethical principles under the exclusive umbrella of doctrine and obedience for centuries. Spain is a good example. In formal terms, the Spanish Kingdom is nonconfessional, but Catholic moral principles emerge from time to time in ethical statements or reports made public by institutional leaders of several organized professional groups; for instance, in the area of health sciences and law.

A typical example has been Juan Masiá, Jesuit and chair of the bioethics unit at the University of Comillas in Spain. In February 2006 he was condemned to silence by the National Conference of Bishops: his writings on ethical subjects were considered incompatible with Catholic morality, whereas he continues in the advisory board on bioethics of the National Conference of Bishops in Japan, where he lectures on ethics at Sofia University and Kobe University. His research unit was cancelled in Madrid. His research findings and publications are welcome in one country and rejected in another under the same religious umbrella.

Anywhere around the world those psychologists who consider themselves Catholic must follow Catholic moral norms and, in cases of conflict, the deontological code of psychologists is a secondary source. Typical controversial subjects are psychological actions on abortion, homosexuality, adoptions, and terminal diseases, and the solution is behaving as conscientious objectors.

The situation is still more demanding in countries where the Qur'an is the central religious text. Islamic law "governs every aspect of a Muslim life..., and faithful execution of duties and obligations based on the *Shari'ah* is recognized as a form of worship" (Haniffa & Hudaib, 2007, p. 99). *Shari'ah*-based supervisory boards exist in companies, and their decisions come out on top of ethical principles and rules backed by psychological associations and organizations where psychologists are employed. International corporations and networks of companies acknowledge that Western codes of conduct are secondary sources as compared to the Muslim code of behavior (Kelsay, 1997). It was not the case in the United Kingdom, where the head of the Church was the king or the queen, hence the highest moral authority. In 1662 the Royal Society of London was created under the sponsorship of King Charles II of England (1630–1685) and ethical matters started to be raised as a distinctive framework, to keep out of Christian morality issues and dilemmas. The Hippocratic Oath had set the precedent for centuries (Baker, 1993). The concept of duty and the categorical imperative argument of Immanuel Kant (1724–1804) underlie existing deontological codes in psychology: there are lists of absolute principles and unconditional requirements that assert their ascendancy in a large number of circumstances where psychological action occurs. Each statement is required and justified as an end in itself, and there is an ad hoc committee authorized to carry out reliable interpretations, verdicts, and rulings. It is an a priori approach on what is right or wrong. The *Universal Declaration of Ethical Principles for Psychologists*, adopted by the International Union of Psychological Science and International Association of Applied Psychology in 2008 (and in 2010 by the International Association for Cross-Cultural Psychology), is an initiative launched to generate a change in the ethical framework of all areas of psychology, including work and organizational psychology. It is not a code per se; rather, it describes common moral principles and shared values for psychological practice.

Summarizing, ethical codes exist because British scientific societies started to generate them and other societies in many other countries started to translate and accommodate versions and updates. A deontological code without a British aura is a *rara avis*, also in psychology. Somehow it has been an inspiring model, secularized. Even in countries where Marxism was the main ideology, deontological codes in psychology, if they existed, were just variations, translations submitted to the general assembly of IUPsyS or EFPA, to be accepted as standard by member associations from other countries.

The economic and organizational background where these codes prospered for decades is highly specific to the U.K. and U.S. traditions: they still insist on the free market economy and the invisible hand that maximizes benefits as the only framework. This is not the case in continental Europe, for instance, where there prevails a socioeconomic view and an emphasis on social responsibility. The narrow versus the broader view in the organization of businesses is not neutral when examining what is understood as right or wrong in business ethics, and so in the involvement of W/O psychologists. The socially oriented free market economy and welfare economics are based on belief systems about what is ethically adequate that are not shared by competitive profit-only systems; that is, neo-liberalism as favored by Friedman (2000), the headman: "There is one and only one social responsibility of business, to use its resources and engage in activities designed to increase its profits so long as it stays within the rules of the game, which is to say, engages in open and free competition without deception or fraud" (p. 12). That is not business ethics at all, either normative or descriptive. However, they have applied for governmental subsidies silently during the 2008–2009 economic crisis. The main argument has been social responsibility, conceptually distinct from ethics (Fisher, 2004).

It is convenient to emphasize that deontological codes appeared in nonprofit and scientific societies in the context of free market economies, as have other rules of the economic and productive game (Kitson & Campbell, 1996). These rules and those of business ethics belong to different theoretical and operational realms.

Deontological Codes in Psychology: A Persistent Idea and Praxis

The growth in the number of applications of psychology— its use in the world of technology, its social influence, and its role in building institutions—has become associated with a parallel increase in the awareness of specific moral problems inherent within its practice, something which has also occurred in a similar way in other scientific and professional fields. This awareness relates as much to internal issues of practice, such as criteria regulating inter-professional relationships, as it does to external issues, such as criteria regulating the relationships of professionals with service users, clients, and patients. With the growth in the scope of what a psychologist can do, the number of dilemmas about what psychologists must or should do has also increased. Each and every step we take in the quest to increase our knowledge of and ability to influence events in the world around us, be these natural phenomena or human behavior, raises ethical questions about the legitimate use of such abilities and the moral limits of our intervention in such matters. An example illustrating this is the impressive development of bioethics brought into play by the scientific and technological progress of biochemistry and genetic engineering.[1]

The increasing adoption of codes of conduct drafted by certain associations or professional associations of psychologists since the mid-1950s is not surprising. Although the Committee on Scientific and Professional Ethics of the American Psychological Association (APA) was founded in 1939, the first edition of its code of ethics was not published until 1953, and this was done with the title, *Ethical Standards of Psychologists*. Since then it has been revised several times and in 1992 it was renamed the *Ethical Principles of Psychologists and Code of Conduct* by the American Psychological Association (2002).

Inspired by the aforementioned standards, other ethical codes were developed in an attempt to guide professionals in making decisions relating to the specific moral issues which arose in the increasingly influential professional practice of psychologists. Special mention must be made of the attention devoted to such issues by the Canadian Psychological Association (CPA), whose third edition of their code of ethics was published in 2000. The first code of conduct from the Association of State and Provincial Psychology Boards (ASPPB), which has jurisdiction over authorization to practice in the United States and Canada, was approved in 1990 and revised in 2005.[2]

With regard to Europe, it was not until the late 1980s that organizations or professional associations of psychologists began to draft codes of conduct. The British Psychological Society's code of ethics and conduct was initially approved in 1985 and the last revision was very recent, in 2009. The code of ethics of the Spanish psychological association dates from 1987 (Colegio Oficial de Psicólogos, 1987). Currently, a large majority of scientific and professional associations of European psychologists are bound by ethical regulations.[3] In 1995 even the European Federation of Psychologists' Associations (EFPA) approved a Meta-Code of ethics to serve as a reference for the specific codes adopted by its member associations. This was revised in 2005. The International Union of Psychological Science (IUPsyS) saw fit to pass a *Universal Declaration of Ethical Principles for Psychologists* in the assembly it held in Berlin in July 2008.

Alongside this, an impressive array of ethical regulations, analyses, and casebooks were being published, intended to increase understanding of the application of the principles and abstract criteria of such codes in order to resolve the moral dilemmas that psychologists faced in their professional practice (Bersoff, 1995; Wadeley & Blasco, 1995; Sinclair & Pettifor, 2001).

Given the wide diversity of professional activities carried out by psychologists, and the inevitably generic character of the principles and criteria within the codes of ethics, some associations, linked to more specialized areas of psychological intervention, have attempted to develop their own specific regulations. Such is the case of the International School Psychology Association, which published the *ISPA Code of Ethics* (1990), and the Canadian Psychological Association, which developed *Guidelines for Professional Practice for School Psychologists in Canada* (Canadian Psychological Association, 2007a). But without doubt, dedicated case studies of ethical dilemmas have generated most interest in the areas of clinical psychology (Rosenbaum, 1982; Thompson, 1990; Jensen, 1992; Río Sánchez, 2005), forensic psychology, and research methods. Within these particular fields, the majority of codes and casebook manuals tend to devote a whole section to ethical dilemmas.

We cannot conclude this overview of the ethical regulations within the psychology profession without mentioning the fact that some specific research or psychological practice topics, which are especially subject to social awareness, have merited the elaboration of ethical codes or codes of conduct by scientific and professional associations in order to reach agreement on the ethical criteria that psychologists must apply with regard to the following issues: the use of human subjects or animals in research (British Psychological Society 2004, 2007a, 2009a), anti-discriminative practice (Canadian Psychological Association 2001, 2007b), and the application of new technology in professional practice (British Psychological Society, 2007b). The need to supplement the general principles and ethical criteria of such codes with ethical guidelines that serve to clarify their application to specific problems has led the professional associations to compose conduct guidelines, in order to guide the behaviors of each member of the professional association.

W/O Psychology: The Missing Tile in Deontological Codes Display

Industrial psychology was undoubtedly one of the earliest applications of psychology and contributed largely to the consolidation and to the social identification and recognition of professional psychologists. On the other hand, although its differences in objectives and approaches have sometimes led to tension and ruptures with psychological associations dominated by academic and scientific tradition, W/O psychology has been and continues to be an important part of their institutional organization, according to the extent and diversity of their activities.

One might, therefore, expect that the ethical issues arising in W/O psychology have held a prominent place in the ethical codes of professional organizations of psychologists, and that they have been the subject of special attention in both general studies of professional ethics and in the monographic studies devoted to these, and in the major manuals and handbooks of this discipline.

Nothing could be further from the truth. First, a review of the ethical codes of the main associations of psychologists in Western countries confirms that despite being set out as prescriptive, moral guidelines on the professional conduct of all its members, and despite addressing any problems that may arise in different areas of practice, the codes do not reflect any special sensitivity to W/O psychology. The vast majority of these codes are theoretically dependent on the most primitive codes of other professions, particularly medicine and law, which are based on a bilateral relationship between the practitioner and the patient or client who has directly requested their services. The ethical principles, as formulated, take the human being as a subject of moral rights that the psychologist has to uphold and protect during any proceedings as a reference point, not to mention the ethical obligations that the same psychologist may also have drawn up with a group or institution.

Thus, duties universally recognized in the ethical codes of the associations of psychologists, such as those of confidentiality and data protection, are clearly defined from the perspective of the psychologist–patient relationship. It is often implicitly assumed that this is a therapeutic relationship, and ethical standards are not tailored to ensure that patient rights are guaranteed, in the case of an organizational psychologist, to make them compatible with their own obligations regarding the institution or organization for which they work. The aspect of the moral conflict of person–organization loyalties when making decisions is very relevant to W/O psychology. It will be explained later on through several examples.

On the other hand, some codes of ethics, together with information on criteria and standards of conduct relating to general principles that apply to all psychologists, include specific chapters devoted to ethical standards within particular areas of psychology. For example, paragraph 7 of the APA code is devoted to education and training, paragraph 8 to research and publication, and paragraph 10 to therapy. In contrast, under headings such as Consulting Psychologist, Management Psychologist, or Psychological Engineering, no chapter devoted to the ethical problems specific to W/O psychology has been found in either the American Psychological Association or the British Psychological Association.

The same is also true of those handbooks and casebooks generally devoted to the analysis of ethical dilemmas in psychology. This is reflected in the literature review carried out by Bersoff (1995), in which Chapter 7 is devoted to therapy and other forms of intervention, Chapter 8 to research, teaching, and supervision in academia, and Chapter 9 to forensic settings. Once again, there are no chapters devoted to W/O psychology.

It might be thought that this lack of attention is due to the fact that ethical problems are less important in the field of organizational psychology, or that professionals and users in this sector are less concerned about ethical problems. After all, ethical codes and the successive versions of them outline the dilemmas and the complaints regarding professional conduct lodged by users and clients that are of concern to the members of the associations that issue them. Thus, N. Hobbs already reflected in 1948 that the code of the APA was "an empirically developed code," as it was based on research into ethical dilemmas compiled by a representative sample of members from "descriptions of actual situations which required ethical decisions." The small number of references to problems directly linked to W/O psychology speaks volumes on this issue.

The results of a major study carried out by Pope and Vetter (1992) appear to lead to the same conclusion. They analyzed the responses of 679 APA psychologists to a survey regarding the situations in which they found that their professional practice had come into conflict with ethical criteria. Although it was found that the 23 groups into which the 703 reported dilemmas were classified were not homogenous enough to relate moral ethics to particular professional specialties, the study revealed that the ethical dilemmas related to the different areas were as follows: academic field 57 (8%), forensic psychology 35 (5%), research 29 (4%), and educational psychology 15 (2%). In contrast, only 9 (1%) of dilemmas were found to relate to industrial-organizational psychology (Pope & Vetter, 1992).

Apparently, the same bleak picture has also emerged from the review of the most prestigious handbooks of W/O psychology, which have become far more widespread and have played an important role in establishing the scientific and professional identity of this organization. The contents page of the handbook of Dunnette (1976), drawn from a North American perspective, contains no chapter or indeed any reference to ethics or ethical issues. In the four volumes published by Dunnett and Hough (1990–1994) years later, no chapter on ethics has been included. Here and there, certain references relating specifically to the field of cross-cultural research are included (Dunnette & Hough, 1994). An almost identical case is found with the review of the handbook published by Drenth, Thierry, and Wolff. This is drawn from a European perspective, and the contents page of the 1984 edition does not include any chapter or entry on ethics, while the four-volume edition published in 1998 includes only three entries of brief references to ethical code's principles (Drenth, Thierry, & Wolff, 1984, 1998). Finally, to avoid a long list of additional examples, in Cooper's compilation of the 60 best W/O psychology articles in 1991, there is not one single article devoted to ethics or deontological matters (Cooper, 1991). Furthermore, although the prestigious annual *International Review of Industrial and Organizational Psychology* has been published for over 20 years, almost none of its articles have tackled the subject of ethical dilemmas or criteria. The exception seems to be Cascio and Aguinis (2010): Chapter 18 is devoted to ethical issues in human resources management and Evers, Anderson, and Voskuijl (2005) devote Chapter 5 to ethical issues on personnel selection by questioning, "*is the obvious obvious?*". It is an interdisciplinary-oriented book that summarizes research-based know what and knowhow in the area of human resources.

Ethics in W/O Psychology: Does it Make Sense?
Eppur Si Muove

However, something has been moving for some years now; or rather, something has been changing in the relationship between industrial-organizational psychology and the world of ethics. Casebooks specifically dedicated to ethical dilemmas within this professional field have been published. This is certainly the case with the invaluable works by Lowman in 1985 and 1998, which are a benchmark in this area. Studies which, as seen from a general perspective, deal with ethical dilemmas in the profession of psychology have been gradually paying more attention to professionals working in companies or institutions, and showing increased sensitivity to the specific problems they face. This, however, is still not seen as a priority. Finally, even the latest revisions of individual ethical codes of professional associations have included references to the application of their criteria and principles in those professional activities which have been requested by an organization. They have also incorporated references to the possibility of conflict between the rights of individuals, as listed in the code, and the obligations that the psychologist has to the organization.

This does not mean that the reasons behind the mutual omissions previously prevailing in the relationships between W/O psychology and the world of ethics have been addressed. The majority of W/O psychologists, whether working for private companies or public institutions, maintains very lax relationships with their professional associations and, as a result, do not strictly adhere to the rules issued by the latter, unlike other psychology professionals such as therapists or educational psychologists. It is true that they sometimes share the use of assessment and evaluation techniques with these other psychology professionals, but on many occasions they share the problems they encounter in their professional practice, both technical and ethical, more directly with other professionals with no psychology training, who happen to have similar jobs or carry out similar tasks. These professionals may be part of a team within the organization, such as the department responsible for staff recruitment and training. This, undoubtedly, is reinforced by the blurred boundaries of responsibilities and professional duties restricting organizational psychologists, leading to increased blurring of the ethical obligations that may be associated with these. Finally, the fact remains that customary ethical codes have led some organizations and, thus, some W/O psychologists, as consultants, to draw up their own code of conduct, according to their particular organizational field, and, in case of conflict, to strictly comply with the law and judicial rulings.

In the survey conducted by Pope and Vetter (1992), the proportionally small number of cases provided by psychologists working in the field of industrial-organizational psychology highlights one particular type of ethical conflict:

> Dilemmas in this area tended to describe ways in which management interfered with the psychologist's duties, especially instances in which psychologists were expected or pressured to break pledges of confidentiality to employees or survey respondents, or in which a company breaks a pledge (which the psychologist has conveyed in good faith) to remedy problems
> (*Pope & Vetter*, 1992, p. 408).

It is not surprising that in the professional relationships established by many other psychologists with their patients or service users, including those situations where the provision of services has been requested by a third person, e.g., parents, guardians, or a judge, the ethical issue is to adjust activities according to ethical standards, thus safeguarding the ethical rights of the individual. On the contrary, W/O psychologists have to adjust their conduct by attempting to uphold and protect the rights of the individual, while at the same time endeavoring to fulfill their obligations and ethical duties with respect to the organization. Along with adhering to the code of ethics from the particular psychological association to which they are affiliated, W/O psychologists are also committed to respecting the protocols and codes of conduct of the organizations for which they work. This conflict of loyalties will not necessarily occur but is quite likely. The same individual is both a psychologist and a member of an organization. They must adjust their conduct to this dual role, which will often involve discrepancies and incompatibility between the demands of the ethical criteria of one role and the other.

The codes of conduct or ethics developed by professional associations of psychologists have dealt with these ethical conflicts in an increasingly more comprehensive manner over the last 20 years. However, there has been a general tendency of those who edit the code to unilaterally protect the rights of the individual in cases where the assessment or psychological intervention has been undertaken at the request of an institution or organization, rather than at the request of the individual themselves.

The code of ethics established by Spanish Psychological Association, written in 1987 (a few years after the legal constitution of the organization) is of significance in this discussion. The existence of concern over the fact that compliance with fundamental ethical criteria is not guaranteed is very much evident in the code. Regarding the right to information, the code states:

> When the aforementioned assessment or intervention has been requested by a third party, e.g., judges, education professionals, parents, employers or any person other than the individual being assessed, the latter, or his/her parents or guardians, have the right to be informed of both the results of the assessment or intervention, and of who will receive the subsequent psychological report. The subject of a psychological report is entitled to know the contents thereof, providing that this does not place the subject or psychologist in danger, even if the assessment or intervention has been undertaken at the request of a third party (Art. 42).
> (*Colegio Oficial de Psicólogos*, 1987, p. 7).

The same is true of the code's basic criteria for confidentiality:

> The psychological reports prepared at the request of institutions or organizations in general, apart from those indicated in the preceding article, will adhere to the duty of and general right to confidentiality established previously. In addition, both the psychologist and the party requesting the report are obligated to ensure that this information does not pass beyond the boundaries of the strict framework for which it was collected (Art.43).
> (*Colegio Oficial de Psicólogos*, 1987, p. 7).

The emphasis here not only highlights the suspicion that this is not standard practice in psychological assessment and evaluations undertaken in institutional settings, but also that individuals subjected to psychometric testing during company recruitment processes do not subsequently receive a copy of their results, or that the contents of such reports are not adequately restricted and safeguarded "under the psychologist's personal responsibility for security and confidentiality, such that unauthorized persons are unable to access them" (Art. 46).

It is also interesting to note that when Canadian psychologists realized the benefits that could follow the approval of a code of ethics to govern them, with emphasis on the fact that this could actually support professionals, they came up with the following:

> For instance, if a psychologist is employed by an organization that has little familiarity with the principle of confidentiality, that has goals that are in competition with respecting confidentiality, and that cannot be convinced through discussions about the "right to privacy," having the weight of a profession and a professional code of ethics can be a support to the individual psychologist, if not a convincing argument to the employing organization
> (*Sinclair, Poizner, Gilmour-Barrett, & Randall*, 1987, p.2).

This, however, is only one side of the argument. Ethical conflicts in occupational and organizational psychology are not limited only to those situations in which the organization may be violating the ethical conscience of the professional, with professionals relying on the regulations of their particular psychological association in order to justify their behavior and to deflect any pressure they might be experiencing. The other side of the argument is no less important and relates to those situations in which the dilemma lies in choosing between incompatible actions that correspond to different sources of legitimacy or values. Here the conflict occurs within the psychologist's own ethical conscience. Two types of dilemma can be generalized from this internal conflict of loyalties. The first type of conflict arises when the demands of the established legal framework, with which all citizens must comply, clashes with the psychologist's personal interpretation of how specific criteria from their association's ethical code should be applied. This is a general conflict and not specific to W/O psychologists. It is not even exclusive to psychologists. Indeed, highly relevant at this point are the debates over the legitimacy of "civil disobedience" within the spheres of law and journalism. This is concerned with the ethical duty to withhold information about sources, and the conflict here lies between ethical regulations and legal standards.

The second type of dilemma occurs when conflict arises between the ethical requirements derived from belonging to a particular profession, in this case psychology, and those arising from membership with a particular organization: military, education, prison, and business. The conflict here arises from the noncompatibility in a given situation between ethical norms from these different sets. In other words, it is a conflict of values. This second type of dilemma is widespread in W/O psychology and requires special attention and consideration in any approach to ethical problems. The relevance of this will be analyzed in the following sections of the chapter, alongside a review of some fundamental topics which have had certain *quaestiones disputatae* hanging over them within the ethics of W/O psychology in recent years. The chapter will restrict itself at this point to reflect the fact that the importance of this type of conflict has been such that codes of ethics for psychologists have been unable to ignore it. However, the code guidelines on conduct when such conflicts are encountered remain vague.

As a result, the *Ethical Principles of Psychologists and Code of Conduct* of the APA (2002), under the heading of Conflicts Between Ethics and Organizational Demands, states:

> If the demands of an organization with which psychologists are affiliated or for whom they are working conflict with this Ethics Code, psychologists clarify the nature of the conflict, make known their commitment to the Ethics Code, and to the extent feasible, resolve the conflict in a way that permits adherence to the Ethics Code (Art. 103)
> (*American Psychological Association*, 2002, p. 1063).

Disappointing? Insufficient? Vague? In any case, the above sections clearly indicate that the clarification of the ethical issues specific to W/O psychology have been only partially and inadequately dealt with in the ethical codes established by the professional associations or psychological societies.

Deontological Complaints; Only a Few Cases in W/O Psychology

In the abovementioned survey of Pope and Vetter (1992), only 9 out of 703 ethical dilemmas related to incidents pertinent to W/O psychology (1%). One respondent was a military psychologist specialized in instruction and another was a W/O psychologist who insisted: "when the context of our work has been explained to executives/managers relating to confidentiality/conflict of interest etc. . . . no one has *ever* challenged me or asked me to do something that would compromise the ethical standards of the APA" (p. 399). In other words, unethical incidents appear in other areas of psychological expertise.

Lindsay and Colley (1995) randomly sampled 1000 members of the British Psychological Society (BPS) and 284 returned the survey. Seventeen were from W/O psychology, and five did not report any ethical dilemmas. Twelve reported (that is, 4 % of all respondents) and only 5% of the ethically troubling incidents collected came into the category of W/O psychology (as compared to 1% in APA).

Following their steps Colnerud (1997) contacted 300 out 6,000 members of the Swedish psychological association and 147 provided examples (49%) but none was identified as specific to W/O psychology.

In the Spanish Psychological Association during the period 1984–2009, no complaints have been traced that could relate to W/O psychology either in Madrid or Barcelona, and none at the national board (appeals). Until 2009 no member from W/O psychology had been appointed to participate in committees taking care of deontological codes' interpretations, and the first one appointed was the consequence of a "why not" inquisitiveness factor. Examining the issue, applicants or employees (a) do not view the psychological association as an ethical authority in the field of personnel selection, it is the company that matters as authority, (b) do not contextualize ethical dilemmas in the business setting, and it includes the human resources department. In case of conflict they contact trade union delegates or appeal to the labor court.

A completely different situation has been reported by Voskuijl, Evers, and Geerlings (2005) at the Netherland Institute of Psychology (NIP). They did a follow-up of complaints during the period 1993–2002 and 32% were categorized under W/O psychology, focused mainly (29%) on matters related to personnel selection procedures and outcomes. It is the only report based on the analysis of cases evidencing high incidence. The reason seems to be that "critical publications in newspapers and criticism of the trade unions resulted in the Netherlands in questions in the Lower House of Parliament and the adoption of a motion in which psychological selection was described as unnecessary intrusion into personal privacy" (Voskuijl & Evers, 2007, p. 286). Roe (1991) wrote a handbook, in Dutch, on how to deal with personnel selection dilemmas that has been used as a sound reference among W/O psychologists about how to proceed. It followed a rather psychometric approach based on research findings in the discipline known as "Individual Differences Psychology."

The Right to Privacy and Confidentiality

W/O psychologists are not only bound by the codes of ethics of the psychological profession. In many cases they are members of business organizations, and as such are also bound by the codes of ethics or codes of conduct (corporate codes of ethics) drawn up by these business organizations. They have proliferated in recent years and become one of the fundamental elements of corporate social responsibility (Schwart & Carroll, 2003).

To make matters more complex, W/O psychologists carry out professional functions which they share with other members of the organization. These functions or professional duties have been grouped into specific areas of activity that have not only been established separately within the labor market, but have also led to the formation of associations (other than those directly related to psychology) in defense of the common interests of those responsible for undertaking them. These associations also draft their own specific codes of ethics or professional conduct (codes of ethics of professional organizations). This is the case with the following associations in the United States: Society for Human Resources Management (SHRM), Society for Advancement of Management (SAM), American Marketing Association (AMA), and American Society for Training and Development (ASTD).

In both corporate codes of ethics and professional organizations, "confidentiality" is the most widely upheld moral value. This is reflected in comparative studies carried out on ethical codes of Australian and Canadian companies (Kaye, 1992; Lefebvre & Singh, 1992; Montoya & Richard, 1994). The same result was obtained from comparative studies of the ethical codes of organizations of refined groups of professionals, such as that of Wiley (2000), which looked at human resources managers, and the most extensive study carried out by Gaumnitz and Lere (2002), which examined 15 different ethical codes. Of the nine categories of ethical issues discussed in this particular study, the "confidentiality" category was the only one to be consistently mentioned in all of the professional codes reviewed.

On the other hand, "confidentiality" is also the building block or keystone of the ethical criteria present in every single one of the codes of ethics for psychologists. As a result it has been defined as the "primary obligation of professional practice" (Donner, VandeCreek, Gonsiorek & Fisher 2008, p. 369). To quote how this is qualified by the APA Ethics Code: "Psychologists have a primary obligation to protect confidential information" (APA, 2002, Sec 4.01). Nothing seems more obvious, bearing in mind that the trust of the client/patient, or more generally anyone using the services of a psychologist, rests upon the psychologist's ethical duty, and that of his colleagues, to maintain confidentiality with regards to the information obtained. The duty of confidentiality covers both the information obtained from diagnostic techniques and from the various forms of psychological treatment, whether the psychological intervention was requested by the subjects themselves, or by their parents, judges, or other organizations. It even remains in place after the individual has died or after the public or private institution has ceased to exist, as outlined in article 49 of the code of ethics established by the College of Spanish Psychologists.

The conclusion that appears to be reached from available data on the fulfillment of the duty of confidentiality by professional psychologists is of major relevance and is also highly problematic. In the already mentioned study of Pope and Vetter (1992), 128 out of 703 ethical dilemmas were related to confidentiality. This was the largest number of all the categories analyzed. This is not, however, exclusively a concern of psychologists. It is also a concern of service users. Over the years, the number of complaints and allegations brought before the Ethics Committee of the APA regarding the violation of confidentiality has posed a significant problem (Pope & Vazquez, 2007).

Once again, however, most of the literature produced on the difficulties of the ethical duty of confidentiality in the professional practice of psychologists concerns the psychotherapeutic activity, with little attention to the specific area of W/O psychology. Mary A. Fischer (2008) is completely correct when she points out that "Clearly, psychologists' difficulties about confidentiality do not arise from lack of information. Instead, the problem seems to be the absence of a coherent ethical framework on which to hang all the information that is already available" (p. 4). Also her "Ethical Practice Model" remains focused on the psychological activity model, which identifies with psychotherapy being applied to individuals. All in all, these reflections on confidentiality as a general and fundamental ethical duty of psychologists are very relevant, especially those resulting from judicial rulings which, in the United States, placed legal limits on this duty when the rights of a third party are at stake, such as in cases of child abuse. Recognition of the limits of confidentiality guides the ethical obligation to report these limits in order to gain "informed consent" and to introduce clauses in the codes that function to guide the role of psychologists in cases of ethical–legal conflict.

Ethical conflicts surrounding the confidentiality of W/O psychologists have a unique character. These conflicts do not occur through trying to observe two different values, or through attempting to comply with both a legal standard and an ethical criterion. Rather, they occur through the adjustment of one particular ethical criterion, that of confidentiality, pertaining to two different subjects with interests that are sometimes opposing: the individual and the organization. This is a conflict of loyalties with the psychologist being morally bound and committed to both parties, both those that they have to the individuals who are subject to intervention, and those they have to the organization or institution in which they work. The general principles of promoting welfare, not causing harm, faithfulness, responsibility, integrity, and fairness are owed to both parties, and the criterion of maintaining confidentiality is equally incorporated in both the ethical codes of the psychologist and in the corporate codes of conduct of businesses or institutions, such as in the ethical regulations of professional organizations.

The importance of these conflicts has been recognized in the latest edition (2002) of the code of ethics of the APA, which has added the following section regarding "Conflicts Between Ethics and Organizational Demands":

> If the demands of an organization with which psychologists are affiliated or for whom they are working conflict with this Ethics Code, psychologists clarify the nature of conflict, make known their commitment to the Ethics Code, and to the extent feasible, resolve the conflict in a way that permit adherence to the Ethics Code" (Art. 1.03).

Conscious of the fact that it is in the sphere of confidentiality that a great many of these conflicts occur, and after reinforcing the primary function of the obligation as being to protect the confidential information obtained, the APA acknowledges that "the extent and limits and limits of confidentiality may be regulated by law or established by institutional rules or professional or scientific relationships" (Art. 4.01). Just as in the case of conflicts between laws, the procedure for the resolution of potential conflicts within organizations is to establish the ethical obligation to inform both the individual and the organization, in advance, of the limits of confidentiality (Art. 4.02).

The ethical conflicts occurring in the realm of confidentiality in W/O psychology stand out remarkably in two particular areas: (a) the storage and custody of the records and files of psychological information that has been obtained within business or institutional settings, and (b) the "evaluation for personnel decisions" with recognition of the obligations that the psychologist has to the employer (London & Bray, 1980).

The storage and custody of the psychological reports in businesses is one of the least researched aspects in W/O psychology. The reports end up in personnel files, and the number of people who have access to these is quite large. In addition, these reports are spoken about in staff meetings, which managers and union representatives usually attend. Of course, psychological tests form part of the selection process, which includes various professionals contributing to the process of making decisions. Restricted access to this information is not usually in place, given that when the psychologist leaves the company, they do not destroy the records. One of the technical solutions promoted has been encryption of documents, but W/O psychologists rarely have any expertise in this domain. Data compression has been another technical solution, and it means the inclusion of a password to control access to the original text of the psychological report. It entails a control and follow-up of passwords, and the large majority of W/O psychologists are not exposed to this kind of training.

The contractual nature of the relationship maintained by any W/O psychologist and the employer has been the subject of concern from time to time. A typical case is the right to access or get copies of the psychological report that the psychologist will submit to a decision-making team in the company. Medical or legal reports, and sometimes also reports written by private detectives, on a candidate are made available to the final decision maker and it is a common practice in delicate or suspicious circumstances. Another typical situation occurs when the employer requests the psychological assessment of candidates using, for instance, projective techniques because it is what rival companies use, or to test psychological concepts that appear in the press but they haven't been validated. For instance, the large majority of workplace competences identified for years by consultant psychologists are not examined with tests, questionnaires, or surveys that make public validity and reliability indices. It is a kind of internal face validity or content validity that is accepted as adequate by the employer without further scrutiny. This kind of practice is common currency in consumer behavior analysis or economic behavior predictions made by sociologists and economists in the organization. The application of the deontological code in this context may be considered a typical example of eccentricity as compared to other professional groups in the same scenario.

Normative Versus Descriptive Ethics

The distinction between normative and descriptive ethics makes sense in the context of W/O psychology but it is an Achilles heel in contemporary psychology (Voskuijl & Evers, 2007). Reese and Fremouw (1984) highlighted this difference—descriptive (exhibited in practice as normal) versus normative (extolled or exhorted). The distinction between what psychologists cannot do (as a direct consequence of norms set a priori) and what they actually do (subject to ethical judgments and hence cultural biases) is critical to understand what is just needed in W/O psychology ethical practice.

Reese and Fremouw (1984) added another distinction: normative and functional (when it is exhibited) versus normative but nonfunctional (when it is ignored). These two subcategories clarify the situation: deontological codes in psychological associations are normative and functional and, as such, were devised mainly by clinical psychologists and laboratory and field study researchers in university campuses and institutes. These same codes applied to W/O psychology are normative but nonfunctional because there is a preference toward what is known as "descriptive ethics."

"Descriptive ethics refer to the general beliefs, values, attitudes and standards that, as a matter of fact," guide behavior (Desjardins & McCall, 2004, p. 4). It entails that W/O psychologists examine with other teammates the belief system and the set of facts and values (come together) that determine what they do when they provide services to clients; that is, sponsoring organizations, applicants, employees, employers, test developers, test publishers, other colleagues. All these stakeholders are customers, and Voskuijl, Evers, and Geerlings (2005) have identified examples of transactions that may be considered inappropriate if inquired by deontological committees. They bring out the meaning of principles used to sanction; this is the purpose of normative and functional codes.

Descriptive ethics is a bottom-up perspective based on the study of personal beliefs and convictions of practitioners when they consider the ethical pros and cons of their actions and transactions. Ethical conduct is justified if the W/O psychologist has good reasons for that conduct, if services supplied do not cause direct or indirect damage. When interacting with other teammates they identify situations and choices that lead to situational ethics and dilemmas in the professional context.

Iannone (1989) distinguished between personal and group ethics when beliefs and assumptions are made by individuals or teammates, and this is descriptive ethics that operates in W/O psychology. Clients also have beliefs and assumptions to judge if the professional behavior of the W/O psychologist is viewed as ethical or unethical. A face-to-face analysis may then be the immediate approach to introduce corrections, and very rarely is a complaint submitted to the psychological association. If a critical inquiry on that professional activity is made by the deontological committee, the result is "normative ethics." They examine each complaint and consider how psychologists ought to act in accordance with norms and, in decision making, they disregard whatever kind of ethical beliefs and values guided colleagues in that specific professional practice; for instance, W/O psychology.

The origin of descriptive ethics is philosophical; for instance, existentialism. Simone de Beauvoir (1908–1986) coined the expression "ethics of ambiguity" to emphasize that human life is a game that can be won or lost, and ethical statements may be understood as guidelines that teach practitioners the means of winning, of succeeding. Ethics does not furnish principles valid for all kinds of situations, and personal freedom and choice are the key notions. She identified six character types modulated by the will of freedom that is broken and conditioned often in professional life (Beauvoir, 1947). The autonomy of any W/O psychologist is shaped by those degrees of freedom present in the organization where psychological expertise in action operates (individually or as a member of a team) in making those ethical choices that are pertinent. An example of choices in the area of training and development programs will be examined later.

The origin of descriptive ethics is aesthetics as highlighted by Ludwig Wittgenstein (1889–1951), who stressed the existence of a nexus between ethics and aesthetics on the basis of their specific relation to propositional language (Eskin, 2004). This nexus underlies interactions and transactions where communication occurs between client and practitioner. Such a nexus is a combination of taste, art, courtesy, and organizational culture, present in different ways of seeing and of perceiving what is pertinent to satisfy the client in business practice. The goal is the attainment of satisfaction, which is pleasure, so psychological hedonism as formulated by Stuart Mill (Lefkowitz, 2003). This is the intended consequence of many W/O psychological actions and synergies that affect quality of life and well-being in and out of the workplace. Something starts to be considered unethical if it is viewed as shocking by regular customers: it must be avoided because it is disgusting.

The origin of descriptive ethics is psychological, and Lawrence Kohlberg's (1927–1987) contributions to monitoring the stages of moral developmental are crucial to understand ethical and situational reasoning. At first glance, self-interest orientation is the engine of economic behavior and interpersonal accords and conformity rule many transactions between the expert and the client. However, the large majority of products and services supplied by W/O psychologists have a social order–maintaining orientation; they are employed because their expertise is needed by top and middle managers to optimize short-term and long-term outcomes. The acceptance of societal and organizational conventions regarding what is right or wrong is the standard among W/O psychologists and their regular clients, as compared to other professional profiles in psychology where rejections or borderlines predominate. The contractual perspective is the backbone of W/O psychologists' competence, actions, and interactions; autonomy in professional matters is acknowledged institutionally, and so remote controls by the psychological association via normative ethics are non-functional. In the post-conventional stage identified by Kolhberg, the individual's own perspective takes precedence over society's view, including that of the psychological society (Kohlberg, Levine & Hewer 1983). A protocol or standard is the adequate solution if W/O psychologists ought to do something.

The way ethical aspects have been approached among professionals in training and development programs in the area of human resources is a good example of how deontological codes may be based not on prescriptions, but on descriptions of what may be considered troublemaking practices, procedures that should be revised taking into consideration ethical beliefs and values among customers, among colleagues.

In the American Society for Training and Development it was not an ad hoc task force that, after the analysis of critical incidents in the profession, generated a list of principles and normative actions (it was the case in APA in 1953 when ethical standards were launched). The ASTD sponsored a survey that invited practitioners to identify ethical attitudes and thus "examples of any behavior you have observed which you consider unethical or improper for a training and development professional" (Clement, Pinto & Walker, 1978, p. 10). It was an a posteriori research on practitioners' ways of doing, which is a checkup, based on individual judgments made by 999 respondents (out of 2,790 members of the ASTD). They answered closed-ended and open-ended questions to pinpoint what set of competencies favored an effective performance and sound praxis. It was the main focus. Ethical matters were also examined and only one out of three respondents (35, 80%) were aware of interactions between trainer and trainee that they considered unethical. It meant that the large majority remained silent; maybe they had not witnessed or did not remember situations they considered questionable.

Main findings were reported in the journal of the association. There was not an ad hoc committee of ethics writing an expert report to be sanctioned afterwards as mandatory to all members. Six categories were grouped after a content analysis of responses and according to their frequency: (a) lack of professional development plans or actions was first in the ranking (194 respondents), (b) violation of confidences (146), (c) use of cure-all programs (121), (d) dishonesty regarding program outcomes (118), (e) failure to give credit (79), and (f) abuse of trainees (75). There was a seventh and Pandora's Box category, endorsed by 170 respondents: "other improper behaviors" (Clement, Pinto, & Walker, 1978, p. 12).

These categories were not used to produce a deontological code; they were just descriptions of procedures, transactions, or interactions that some members considered inconvenient. In fact they were a minority, and their criteria were not used to fix a canon. Individual members of the ASTD (not a deontological committee) decide if the praxis labeled should be continued or discarded, taking into consideration the ethical advice sponsored by the ASTD and ethical comments made by customers or by colleagues.

These categories classify situations where the behavior of trainers may be considered unethical by trainees or instructors, and so provide suggestions about how to proceed. These are not prescriptions, but suggestions describing and highlighting unethical actions, decision making, and events in training and development programs.

The existing deontological code of ASTD provides a generic guidance to individual members. It is a public declaration that highlights responsibilities that affect learning in the workplace and in organizations. This is a descriptive code of ethics (available as "trainer code of conduct" at http://www.astd.org/) accentuating that professionals should (a) recognize the rights and dignities of each individual; (b) develop human potential; (c) provide their employer, clients, and learners with the highest level quality education, training, and development; (d) comply with all copyright laws and the laws and regulations governing one's position; (e) keep informed of pertinent knowledge and competence in the workplace learning and performance field; (f) maintain confidentiality and integrity in the practice of one's profession; (g) support one's peers and avoid conduct which impedes their practicing their profession; (h) conduct oneself in an ethical and honest manner; (i) improve the public understanding of workplace learning and performance; (j) fairly and accurately represent one's workplace learning and performance credentials, qualifications, experience, and ability; (k) contribute to the continuing growth of the profession. In other words, it is a meta-code of ethics similar to that sponsored by EFPA. This is the way descriptive ethics operates in a professional association that deals with matters and subjects where W/O psychologist competitors are in the same domain.

Multifaceted Profile

W/O psychologists face ambiguous situations involving potential conflicts of interest, which can arise where most of the employees belong to different professional groups. In consulting firms where the proportion of W/O psychologists may be high, as compared to the staff, conflicts might arise because they pay attention to different obligations and wear different caps. Their degree is in psychology but their occupational profile points to a large array of tasks: 16 have been identified in the online database of O*net Center (http://online.onetcenter.org/) and 14 appear under the category of core tasks. These are the top ten:

• Develop and implement employee selection and placement programs.
• Analyze job requirements and content to establish criteria for classification, selection, training, and other related personnel functions.
• Develop interview techniques, rating scales, and psychological tests used to assess skills, abilities, and interests for the purpose of employee selection, placement, and promotion.
• Advise management concerning personnel, managerial, and marketing policies and practices and their potential effects on organizational effectiveness and efficiency.
• Analyze data, using statistical methods and applications, to evaluate the outcomes and effectiveness of workplace programs.
• Assess employee performance.
• Observe and interview workers to obtain information about the physical, mental, and educational requirements of jobs as well as information about aspects such as job satisfaction.
• Write reports on research findings and implications to contribute to general knowledge and to suggest potential changes in organizational functioning.
• Facilitate organizational development and change.
• Identify training and development needs.

The term *psychology* appears only once, in "psychological test," and in this context W/O psychologists must follow standards in the profession as well as those contents in deontological codes having to do with psychological assessment. In the other 14 core tasks and two supplemental tasks no reference at all is made to psychology and whatever output might be derived from this scientific discipline. In other words, standards in this professional profile are so specific that in fact, what W/O psychologists do is apply their expertise in psychological knowledge and practice to a large array of activities and programs where other professionals are also involved. They team with other university graduates and each expert shares knowledge and skills, but not deontological codes if they exist in each association. In health sciences deontological codes follow the normative pattern. In other professions under the profile of humanities and social sciences, descriptive ethics predominate because person-to-person interactions and responsibilities with individuals as direct customers are rare.

London and Bray (1980) pointed out that nonpsychologists involved in evaluation tasks are not formally responsible for adhering to the standards and principles for ethical practice set by psychological associations. If they belong to other professional organizations, then they should be expected to follow their standards, often descriptive.

One of the formal obligations of W/O psychologists to their profession, psychology, includes reporting unethical practices and increasing colleagues' sensitivity to ethical issues. Nobody seems to do this, because they have never been educated with this possibility as content in the syllabus and because the wording of deontological codes is far removed from this field of expertise. Keeping informed of advances in the field is done via journals and congresses or seminars, and the profile is "Human Resources" or "Accident Analysis and

Prevention"; thus psychological aspects are circumstantial. There are specific obligations to job applicants that include precautionary actions against the invasion of privacy, guaranteeing confidentiality, obtaining informed consent, respecting the individual right to know evaluation results, and finally, psychologists' duties to their employers, such as conveying accurate expectations, ensuring high-quality test data, and respecting the employer. Sometimes those responsibilities can come into conflict and the professionals have to deal with this conflict, making a decision that might damage one of the parties. Good practice guidance or codes of conduct have been set throughout the first decade of 2000 in multinational companies and networked companies, but the main focus has been on the avoidance of internal corruption, bribery, and sexual misconduct. Quite often is just a mission statement, a declaration of intentions and wishful thinking, not a code of ethics as such. Oberer and Lee (1986) highlighted the point that mainly, conflict might arise if we focus on the primary goal of business versus the psychologist's goal. As those authors pointed out, businesses care most about growth and maintenance, which means profitability, while psychologists, mainly counseling psychologists placed at a work setting, are usually more concerned about humanistic values, caring more about their client's adjustment and satisfaction.

It is important to differentiate between unlawful behavior and unethical issues at work, as pointed out by Voskuijl, Evers, and Geerlings (2005). These authors differentiate two types of behaviors that can arise, especially in personal selection procedures, and that a W/O psychologist needs to deal with Both types of behaviors are under the indirect control of ethical guidelines dealing with what is considered right or wrong behavior in a specific situation in psychology. The specific goal of these guidelines and directives are control of misbehavior and, as their authors comment, the difference between them is a question of degree. Consequences derived from the misbehaviors are different, being more extreme when an unlawful and often unethical behavior is displayed than when an ethical behavior is shown, due to the fact that ethical or guidelines codes work more as advisory guidelines. On the other hand, ethical codes seem to apply to fewer people.

In order to appreciate an ethical dilemma (an unlawful and unethical situation, or only an unethical conflict), and then to undertake good practice when ethical dilemmas arise, a W/O psychologist needs to be aware of the legal directives and ethical codes or guidelines. There is no doubt about the importance of being aware of what is expected in the implementation of the ethics codes. However, some studies highlight the lack of awareness of these codes and ethical guidelines for practitioners, as cited by Holaday and Yost (1993). These authors, after asking pre-doctoral psychologists, members of academia, and medical schools for ethical dilemmas related to publication ethics at the university and medical institutions, reported that only 8% of the respondents were unaware of the existence of ethical guidelines concerning the issues queried. Even though 82% of respondents seemed to be aware of ethical guidelines, none complained and only a few reported complaints submitted to committees in the professional association of the university campus. This fact observed in the study might show that there are other aspects apart from unawareness of ethical codes that may play an important role in maintaining ethical dilemmas. In the same study, qualitative information reported from comments written by respondents highlighted the fact that, on several occasions when an ethical conflict related to a publication undertaken by a former major professor was found by students, they were afraid that if they complained, violators with more authority would respond badly, turning a positive relationship into a negative one. Although this study was carried out in an academic context, this situation might arise in any setting where a hierarchy of power is found.

Literature is scarce concerning W/O psychologists facing ethical dilemmas, but after reviewing some of the studies undertaken in this field, it seems this might be a problem which should be solved, in part, at the university or in graduate programs; presently there is no entry in the syllabus, and no subject is specifically dedicated to examine and discuss the ethics code or guidelines in the specialty of W/O psychology. There is a specific case book on W/O psychology's ethical dilemmas in the APA and this is a rather unknown book abroad, as may be verified searching online via European university libraries: rarely, copies of Lowman (1985, 1998, 2006) are available. Along the same lines, another circumstance is observed and reported by Allegretti and Frederick (1995), where they stress the importance of teaching the students a model of thinking critically about ethical issues. They found higher scores on the Cornell Critical Thinking Test (Ennis, Millman & Tomko, 1985) after having taught a five-part model to the students.

It has also been reported that another aspect which could make it more difficult to face and solve an ethical dilemma is that psychologists sometimes find ethical codes unclear and incomplete (Holaday & Yost, 1993). This author reported a relatively high proportion, 20% of the respondents, that appeared unsure how to behave when they are involved in an ethical problem. Manuals or seminars on standards skills to be improved by psychology students do not report "knowhow" procedures to deal with ethical dilemmas in the campus or in the profession. An analysis of codes of ethics and guidelines does not suggest how to proceed when ethical dilemmas appear.

After considering some aspects related to information, formation, and training in ethical codes and dilemmas, we continue pointing out some controversial issues found in the W/O psychology practice:

Reaching this point, how may an ethical dilemma be solved? Why are the dilemmas which have to be faced by W/O psychologists being so poorly studied and documented? If the specific literature is so scarce, might it be that there is not a real demand? Or might it be because the ethical dilemma is not considered a problem at the organizational level? Or it may be because W/O psychologists know that these kinds of demands are conspicuously absent in the institutional culture, and the main indicator is the fact that no committee of ethics exists in the large majority of companies? Their nonexistence denotes irrelevance.

Three Controversial Issues

Let us analyze briefly three problems that appear mentioned in deontological codes that may be not related at all to ethics in W/O psychology practice.

Discrimination

Discrimination in the workplace has been one of the more fashionable subjects in human resources policy making and psychological action, as examined in a large number of articles and books. It has attracted the attention of many authors due to the socially minded repercussion of discrimination in everyday life complaints. However, a preliminary question must be raised: is it a legal or an ethical concern?

Discrimination and unfairness are somehow linked, and it entails those cases where, critically, employment resources, jobs, and salaries are allocated in a way that is regarded as socially unjust. But this is the domain of distributive justice, and the background is either ethical or political. Criteria used to produce a distribution is a strategic matter (for instance, positive action by sex, age, or background), whereas what is considered fair or unfair is a moral framework, allowing individual or group differences in arguments and interpretations. A cake may be divided in equal or dissimilar portions. If each guest gets an equal portion it entails equality, an equal rights approach. However, if one gets a bigger portion and another smaller (because the contribution was above or below standard performance) it is a typical instance of equity, of meritocracy.

What is expected from W/O psychologists are operational and technical details evidencing that their procedures are impartial (under certain political or market policies). The framework is the nomothetic approach to identify trends and biases. Another interpretation might link discrimination with equity and, thus, natural justice, and again, this is a system of jurisprudence that supplements the common law and not an ethical dilemma. For instance, salaries may be revised as a direct consequence of the cost of living index, the performance index, or the gross profit ratio. Recruitment or selection ratios may be based on the proportionality in the population or on the percentage of past employees' relatives (an indirect benefit of early retirement plans).

However, in the study carried out by Voskuijl, Evers, and Geerlings (2005) in the Netherlands Institute of Psychology, discrimination was reported as an unethical behavioral pattern: rejecting minority candidates regardless of their suitability. Discrimination does not appear as an ethical principle or sub-principle in existing deontological codes of psychology. Nondiscrimination in psychological action is considered an ethical behavior in several ethical codes. However, W/O psychologists must discriminate among candidates and among employees by age or experience. It is the domain of fairness and equity in the allocation of personnel. Egalitarianism is a well-known subject in social psychology, but not in W/O psychology.

Let's accept temporarily that this is an ethical matter. Discrimination has been observed and reported in the workplace. Age discrimination, gender discrimination, and race discrimination are some of the topics that have been studied often and have gained attention among researchers. Let's introduce, however, a different example: retirement age. Is age discrimination an ethical, legal, or union argument? There are strong differences across countries and legislative systems regarding what is considered mandatory retirement age (between 55 and 70). If early retirement is the policy of the company, on what premises should this decision be considered unethical, or against human rights or constitutional rights? The expected contribution of W/O psychologists to this debate is technical, not ethical. What is the right moment of retirement for a given individual? The answer requires an idiographic approach based on the uniqueness of performance and adjustment. In the European Union and United States there are political pressures to postpone retirement age, and arguments are based on economics rather than ethics. However, Ferris and King (1992) carried out research to find out that discrimination did occur when younger candidates were preferred to older candidates, when performance was in fact similar or the same. Early retirement is not related to performance in the large majority of cases.

In a similar vein, the paper of Arvey and Renz (1992) on fairness was published in the *Journal of Business Ethics* but the terminology (unfair, objective, consistent, merit-based, job-related) as well as "modus operandi" used to find out likely solutions were technical, not ethical.

Differential validity is a technical concept used to examine indications of discrimination. Raw scores of a test may have significantly different degrees of validity for males vs. females, ethnic groups, or age cohorts, and used as such and allowed in personnel selection or promotion processes. The Spanish legislation, for instance, does not advocate the use of scoring formulae based on statistical estimates to differentiate the performance of one group versus another in exercises and quizzes. Equal rights lead to the same protocol and the same scoring key. Guessing cannot be penalized, even if there is evidence showing covariation between the number of items answered (versus those omitted) and the cut-off score that discriminates between who is accepted or rejected.

Should assessment methods favoring positive action to counteract the effects of past discrimination be considered unethical or illicit? Positive action measures mean that, for instance, males and females of the same cohort who obtained the same score in a given exercise have differential probabilities of obtaining the job due to weighted estimates. Information from the predictor may be interpreted with or without considering subgroup membership. Positive action arrangements are a good example of the lack of clarity underlying the application of an ethical dilemma when the case is technical and the background lawfulness. Many members in the unfavored subgroup may consider unfair and illicit any decision in personnel assessment based exclusively on positive action. They may base their complaint on legal regulations, not on ethical principles. In these circumstances it makes sense to submit a case in court, not in the professional psychological association, although it is necessary to point out that a legal action doesn't need to exclude the moral matter. In case of conflict, the legal perspective comes up on top in W/O psychology.

Plagiarism

Plagiarism has been identified as a category of scientific and publication misconduct reported to the Committee on Publication Ethics (COPE; Marcovitch, 2007). Albeit that plagiarism has been largely reported in academic contexts (Holaday & Yost, 1993; Kenny, 2007; Loui, 2002) it occurs rarely as such in organizational contexts. It appears with another label: copyright infringement. In legal terms it is a conflict between the copyrights of an author (or the publisher that controls it) and the illegal use of copies made by a person without copying rights. In legal terms, only the person plagiarized may apply to the courts asking for protection. The publisher may also act, but nobody else. Whatever kind of decision is made by the Committee on Publications Ethics in the psychological association or the university, it is a private judgment, ethically wise, but nothing else. If the plagiarist does not accept the sanction nothing can be done legally. A doctoral dissertation may be reviewed by the deontological committee and considered a typical case of plagiarism, but legally the degree obtained remains valid if it obtained the OK in the past. Legal advisors in universities know this and insist to professors of psychology that whatever they have in mind after the deontological code, it is just wishful thinking if the student applies to the court. There have been cases in Spain where magistrates did not consider the existence of similar sentences and exercises in specific psychological tests or questionnaires to be plagiarism. In psychological assessment, these cases were submitted by lawyers as good examples of intertextuality in the domain, the shaping of psychological tools' contents and meanings by other texts, as it has been seen often, for instance, in lying or sincerity scales or in motivational distortion scales in questionnaires. The systematic database of tests devised for decades by Joy P. Guilford (1897–1990) or Raymond B. Cattell (1905–1998), in their psychometric study of human intelligence and personality, is somehow present in many parallel developments in W/O psychology assessment procedures. A comparative study of psychological tests in the same area show overlap; that is, covariation, that is intertextuality.

Intertextuality is a notion—launched in 1966 by Julietta Kristeva, philosopher and psychoanalyst—that has had destabilizing effects on the notions of plagiarism and reinterpretation (Allen, 2000). At first glance it has to do with the juxtaposition of different texts, but in psychological assessment correlations and factor analysis show statistically that there is overlap in contents that is a common corpus. Thus, new terms have been introduced that minimize the importance of plagiarism. Dialogism and paratextuality are brand new rhetoric notions that become technical labels allowing trainers to combine texts and introduce variations in the classroom, in manuals. It is not plagiarism.

The widespread use of the Internet and the access to a multitude of resources in support of manuscripts on what is the state of the art, on what are present trends, has generated plagiarism detection tools that are reliable in one language (but almost unreliable across languages). Such software underlines suspicious paragraphs and then indicates what might be the original source. The background is statistics, similarities, and text-based correspondence. These are technical tools to isolate likely cases of plagiarism, but what about the final authority: (a) deontological committee? (b) economic agreement between lawyers? (c) sentencing? In W/O psychology, (b) and (c) are the normal channels. Option (a) makes sense if (b) and (c) do not occur. Sanctions may be overturned legally, and legal advisory boards in Spanish universities suggest, "do not go too far, ... we do not advise departments in these kinds of problems."

Sexual Behavior

Sexuality is mentioned 35 times in the ethical principles of psychologists of the American Psychological Association (2002), and 5 times in the Code of Ethics and Conduct of the British Psychological Society (2009b). The Australian Psychological Society (2007) in its ethical guidelines has a specific section of four pages on the prohibition of sexual relations with clients. Sexual orientation, sexual harassment, sexual relations, sexual intimacies are just some of the headings of what has been regulated. Should W/O psychologists pay attention to each one of these categories in their professional practice? Is there so much concern about sexual behavior in organizational settings? At first glance there is not, and concern appears only when it surfaces in newspapers or bulletins.

Sexual orientation understood as gender identity plus sexual attraction in the workplace is a rather odd concept in organizations. Asexuality or nonsexuality has been the standard postulate in corporate discourse and mission statements. Bogaert (2004) used data from a national probability sample (N > 18,000) of British residents to investigate asexuality and approximately 1% of the sample indicated they were asexual. It is an extravagance to continue insisting on the idea that "having no sexual attraction to a partner of either sex" is what is considered politically correct in the workplace. It means that sexual orientation is a part of the game of interactions that take place: heterosexuality prevails. The critical category seems to be homosexuality, and the consequence has been that only in democratically advanced societies do homosexuals have rights, as a direct consequence of the sexual revolution in the 1960s. A typical case was the mathematician and cryptanalyst Alan Turing (1912–1954), pioneer in computer and cognitive science (Turing Machine). He was forced to chemical castration because homosexual acts were considered immoral and illegal in the United Kingdom in 1952, under the influence of religious thinking. The consequence was depression and suicide because he was not any longer the head of his project. W/O psychologists in this domain have tools that allow them to identify the sexual orientation of candidates, for instance, and the use they may make of this information has to do with their personal ideology about what entails freedom in sexual life, professional discretion, professional secrets, or religious considerations. Deontological codes are clear: psychologists cannot make decisions based on the sexual orientation of employees in the workplace. The Achilles heel is ideological prejudice.

Sexual harassment is an expression coined in 1975 at Cornell University by a group of female students and activists to identify cases of sexual intimidation, coercion, or exploitation in the workplace, as accounted by Brownmiller (1999). It has been a politically minded label that obtained legal endorsement in a large number of advanced democracies. It has been an ideological notion, and in a large number of theocratic societies it is still ignored. Gutek (1985) was the first researcher who discovered strong differences between employees: 67% of men acknowledged being flattered when a woman made advances, whereas 63% of the women considered it offensive if it was the man who made his desires known. It means that the relative frequency of complaints submitted is biased and so are decisions: males are underrepresented as victims and overrepresented as the accused in imputations. *Disclosure* is the name of a 1994 thriller movie on how easy it is to make allegations of sexual harassment in the workplace and how in the background lies a double-standard approach when such allegations are levied by men or by women. The critical aspect is the use of power to generate forced sexual relations. Is it solved as a legal or as an ethical matter? In the large majority of European and Latin American universities, for instance, it becomes a legal or disciplinary matter (power abuse) because there are not ethical guidelines regarding how to proceed in cases of sexual harassment where professors or students are involved. The student rights office or the trade unions may be sensitive to complaints, but there is no final decision maker on this matter in the campus. It must go to the court, that is all that can be done. It means lawyers and expenses.

Consensus sexual relations have existed traditionally in the workplace, often furtive, but during recent decades the frequency and explicitness of such relations has increased and it seems to be a direct consequence of spending so many hours together and the acceptance of sexual freedom as a quality of life standard in affluent societies. Some companies (Gutek, 1985). Keyton & Rhodes (1997) have identified the key factor in the organizational milieu as the ethical ideology of incumbents and the ability of individuals to identify what they mean by flirting or an improper relationship. Some interactions are critical; for instance, superior–subordinate, small or large age differences, married versus single or divorced. All these nuances make clear that it is a combination of beliefs, manners, and, why not, fashion. Online and offline polls carried out by newspapers here and there report that about one out of three employees admit (in democratic countries) they have had sexual liaisons at work, especially at the Christmas office party, in meeting rooms, in the boss' desk, and in the car park. Time spent together in training programs, far from home and in the same hotel, is another typical occasion. In some Latin American countries "Secretaries' Day" is an institutional celebration and it means a party, a lunch, a private celebration: the initiative corresponds to the secretary, it is a bottom-up contingency.

Sexual intimacy entails emotional attachment, frequent interactions, enduring interdependence, as well as fulfillment of needs and sentiments. Pierce, Byrne, and Aguinis (1996) introduced the expression "workplace romance" and began their article by quoting a sentence of Westhoff (1985) on the subject: "Corporate romance is as inevitable as earthquakes in California." They reviewed 56 studies that purported consequences and 17 researchers included workers' morale as an independent variable (understood as the mood or spirit of the work group). Findings suggest that "the mood of a work group can be raised as well as lowered because of such affairs" (p. 20). A list of 31 of direct or indirect consequences were identified as antecedents or outcomes of workplace romance. However, not a single article explored the ethical perspective. In many companies the practice is to try to set the involved persons apart in the same building or to avoid putting them together in decision-making groups.

Summarizing, W/O psychologists face situations and scenarios where sexuality has visibility and aftereffects. Sexual descriptors in deontological codes may be taken into consideration, but it seems to be wise to consider that other priorities prevail in the organizational milieu. For centuries Greek and Romans understood sexual behavior in institutions in a quite different manner than that of the Christians that came after them. Endogamy was holy and royal among divine Pharaohs in Egypt, whereas it was sinful after the imposition of Jewish moral standards. "Do not be licentious or make others be licentious" is the precept highlighted in Taoism (Kohn, 2004). In Buddhism there are different wordings but, in essence, they call for avoiding sexual misconduct (Powers, 2000). That is a description, not a prescription.

Protocols and Standards

It is not necessary to comment on what is meant by deontological codes in a handbook on ethics. However, the issue of protocols is different because its understanding in health sciences departs, somehow, from that prevailing in computer sciences. A clinical protocol is a decision-making procedure, often branched, that identifies what is understood by good practice in the diagnosis, management, and treatment of patients. It includes consensus statements as well as evidence-based practice. Protocols define, in operational terms, how something must be done and carried out, and somehow it has the weight of law or convention among practitioners in a discipline.

The best example is testing procedures, and in W/O psychology the framework is the International Organization for Standardization (ISO; http://www.iso.org/), which develops standards in all the industrial and service sectors in 159 countries.

Due to the initiative of the German representatives (DIN), a process began in 2008 to elaborate a new ISO standard, 10,667, to regulate everything concerning the assessment of people in the work setting. This new standard has been of great interest to W/O psychologists, given their key role in the occupational assessment of people. Various national organizations of psychology appointed experts to the international commission of the ISO as well as various members of the EFPA Standing Committee on Tests and Testing. The final version in English is available at www.iso.org as ISO 10667-1:2011 and 10667-2:2011 and official versions in other languages are in progress. This ISO standard will be used to certify quality controls in assessment procedures implemented in companies, consulting firms, and institutions, thereby guaranteeing that they meet the standard. It has no real legal status, but it is an important market regulation standard, because being certified will have a totally different meaning from not being certified.

The information obtained in February 2009 via email from one of the co-authors indicates that the goal of this ISO standard is to regulate the process of assessment of people in work and organizational settings, considering the entire assessment process from the establishment of the assessment contract up to the use of the results, running through the methodology of the assessment itself. It will be applicable in the procedures and methods used at the individual (selection, counseling, training , etc.), group (work team climate and cohesion), and organizational levels (work climate, company culture, satisfaction, etc.). The competences, obligations, and responsibilities of clients and providers of the assessment service before, during, and after the assessment process are described in the standard. It also provides guidelines for all parties involved in the assessment process, including the person being assessed and those who will receive the results of the assessment. To sum up, once it is published and the process of certification of this new standard begins, it can be an important step toward good practice in the assessment of people in work and organizational settings. The great advantage of a standard like this is that ethical or aesthetic criteria are pushed into the background.

Final Remarks

This chapter makes clear that W/O psychology's challenges and dilemmas were not taken into consideration when deontological codes were devised in psychological associations. Clinical psychologists' problems when dealing with clients, and questions regarding research in laboratories or field studies carried out in universities, have shaped the type of normative ethics endorsed in scientific societies. The backbone is Jewish and Christian conventions and the tissue grows from British traditions of what is science and profession.

This chapter insists on pragmatism as the philosophical basis that makes sense in work and organizational psychology as a field of expertise. A priori or per se, there is not good and bad practice, nor general norms valid for all kind of psychologists. An analysis of positive and negative consequences of psychological actions makes sense when W/O psychologists deal with ethical dilemmas individually or in teams. Who is the moral authority should remain open in W/O psychology, and if inquiry is needed then beliefs and values endorsed by practitioners in their decision making must be accepted as pertinent in the appraisal procedure.

This chapter accentuates the contrast between normative and descriptive ethics. Up to 2010 normative ethics have prevailed, and a change of framework took place when the Meta-Code of ethics was launched by EFPA in 1995, the code of ethics and ethical guidelines of Australian Psychological Society appeared in 2007, the *Universal Declaration of Ethical Principles for Psychologists* was backed by IAAP and IUPsyS in 2008, and the code of ethics and conduct was endorsed by the British Psychology Society in 2009. It is a change of paradigm toward a descriptive understanding of ethics that is congruent with W/O psychology's practice. However, two of these publications are too long and continue the temptation of casuistry as exemplified in Lindsay et al. (2008).

This chapter highlights that ethical principles and values discussed by philosophers for centuries took root in democratic parliaments and generated legislation and norms binding organizational and psychological practice. It is the domain of legal and social obligations transposed into operational and administrative terms—that is, social responsibility as identified, for instance by De George (1999). The approach of ethics committees is ideographic, focused on specific dilemmas and disasters that must be rectified at present or avoided in the future. What about a nomothetic perspective? It moves as quicksand: there are strong differences and nuances across borders. Corporate social responsibility is a self-regulated way of doing things stemming from highly specific business models that often are situationist, linked to who is the top decision maker in the organizational hierarchy. A socially minded chief executive officer will include public interest in the corporate culture in decision making, whereas a liberally minded CEO may favor benchmarking, for instance—that is, comparisons to the best firms in the productive sector.

This chapter acknowledges that jurisdiction and morality are two different domains. Throughout centuries let's say "conscientious objectors" had used moral principles or values to produce changes in legislation. It means that divergent thinking and dissidence in ethics is an attitude that should be favored among students of psychology, and alternative protocols or statements should be made available (via the Internet, for instance) in the syllabus that introduces orthodox deontological codes in their university training,

This chapter emphasizes that self-regulation and monitoring of appropriate and inappropriate practices is a supplementary task that W/O psychologists cannot set aside when their customers complain to them, to the data protection agency, to trade unions, to the committee of ethics in the company, or to psychological associations. All these paths exist and clients, from time to time, will use them. However, when they make an accusation they tend to submit their case to the court because they consider this is the faster or most reliable path. The psychological association is not what they have in mind in such unacceptable circumstances.

Notes

1. Due to the importance of the ethical issues in this field, UNESCO itself found it necessary to promulgate a declaration of principles. Cfr. United Nations Educational, Scientific and Cultural Organization (2005). UNESCO's Universal Declaration on Bioethics and Human Rights.

2. Of particular interest is the comparative analysis between three codes, conducted by the CPA. The latest version of the *Code of Ethics of the Australian Psychological Society* was published recently (2007); it contains major changes with regard to versions prior to 1997 and 2003.

3. A comprehensive list of the codes of practice applied to psychology that are current in different countries may be viewed at http://www.am.org/iupsys/resources/ethics/ethic-com-natl-list.html.

References

Allegretti, C., & Frederick, N. (1995). A model for thinking critically about ethical issues. *Teaching of Psychology,* 2246–2248.

Allen, G. (2000). *Intertextuality*. London and New York: Routledge.

American Psychological Association (APA). (2002). Ethical Principles of Psychologists and Code of Conduct. *American Psychologist, 57,* 1060–1073. Arvey, R. D., & Renz, G. L. (1992). Fairness in the selection of employees. *Journal of Business Ethics, 11,* 331–340.

Association of State and Provincial Psychology Boards (ASPPB). (2005). Code of Conduct. Retrieved from http://www.asppb.net/i4a/pages/index.cfm?pageid=3353.

Australian Psychological Society (APS). (2007). Code of Ethics. Retrieved from
http://www.psychology.org.au/SiteMap.aspx?ID=1304

Baker, R. (1993). The history of medical ethics. In W.F. Bynum & R. Porter (Eds.), *Companion encyclopaedia of the history of medicine,* (Vol. 2, pp. 852–887). London: Routledge.

Beauvoir, B. (1947). *Pour une morale de l'ambiguïté*. Paris: Gallimard.

Bersoff, D. M. (1995). *Ethical conflicts in psychology* (3rd ed.). Washington, DC: American Psychological Association.

Bogaert, A. (2004). Asexuality: prevalence and associated factors in a national probability sample. *Journal of Sex Research, 41,* 279–287.

British Psychological Society (BPS). (2004). Guidelines for minimum standards of ethical approval in psychological research. Retrieved from
http://www.bps.org.uk/what-we-do/ethics-standards/ethics-standards/

British Psychological Society (BPS). (2007a). Guidelines for psychologists working with animals. Retrieved from http://www.bps.org.uk/the-society/code-of-conduct/support-for-researchers_home.cfm.

British Psychological Society (BPS). (2007b). Conducting research on the internet: Guideline for ethical practice in psychological research online. Retrieved from http://www.bps.org.uk/the-society/code-of-conduct/support-for-researchers_home.cfm.

British Psychological Society (BPS) (2009a). Ethical principles for conducting research with human participants. Retrieved from http://www.bps.org.uk/the-society/code-of-conduct/support-for-researchers_home.cfm.

British Psychological Society (BPS). (2009b). Code of ethics and conduct. Retrieved from http://www.bps.org.uk/what-we-do/ethics-standards/ethics-standards

Brownmiller, S. (1999). *In our time: Memories of revolution.* New York: Dial Press.

Bruno, L. C. (1987). *The tradition of science: Landmarks of western science in the collections of the Library of Congress.* Washington, DC: Library of Congress.

Canadian Psychological Association (CPA). (2000). Canadian code of ethics for psychologists. Retrieved from http://www.cpa.ca/cpasite/userfiles/Documents/Canadian%20Code%20of%20Ethics%20for%20Psycho.pdf.

Canadian Psychological Association (CPA). (2001). Guidelines for non-discriminatory practice. Retrieved from http://www.cpa.ca/cpasite/userfiles/Documents/publications/NOnDiscPractrev%20cpa.pdf.

Canadian Psychological Association (CPA). (2007a). *Professional practice guidelines for school psychologists in Canada*. Retrieved from http://www.cpa.ca/cpasite/userfiles/Documents/publications/CPA%20Guideline%20Practice.pdf.

Canadian Psychological Association (CPA). (2007b). *Guidelines for ethical psychological practice with women.* Ontario. Retrieved from http://www.cpa.ca/cpasite/userfiles/Documents/publications/guidelines%20for%20psychological%20practice%20women.pdf

Cascio, W. F., & Aguinis, H. (2010). *Applied psychology in human resources management* (7th ed.). Upper Saddle River, NJ: Prentice Hall.

Clement, R. W., Pinto, P. R. & Walker, J. W. (1978). Unethical and improper behavior by training and development professional. *Training and Development Journal, 32,* 10–12.

Colegio Oficial de Psicólogos (COP). (1987). Código Deontológico del Psicólogo. *Papeles del Colegio 6,* 4–8. Retrieved from http://www.cop.es/index.php?page=Codigo-completo.

Colnerud, G. (1997). Ethical dilemmas of psychologists: A Swedish example in an international perspective. *European Psychologist. 2,* 164–170. doi: 10.1027/1016-9040.2.2.164

Cooper, C. L. (1991). *Industrial and organizacional psychology.* Hants, England: Edward *Elgar* Publishing.

De George, R. T. (1999). *Business ethics* (5th ed.). Upper Saddle; NJ: Prentice Hall.

DesJardins, J. R. & McCall, J. J. (2004). *Contemporary issues in business ethics.* Belmont, CA: Wadsworth.

Donner, M. B., VandeCreek, L., Gonsiorek, J. C., & Fisher, C.B. (2008). Balancing confidentiality: Protecting privacy and protecting the public. *Professional Psychology: Research and Practice, 39,* 369–376.

Drenth, P. J. D., Thierry, H., & de Wolff, C. F. (1984). *Handbook of organizational psychology.* Chichester, UK: Wiley.

Drenth, P. J. D., Thierry, H., & de Wolff, C. F. (1998). *Handbook of organizational psychology.* East Sussex, UK: Psychology.

Dunnette, M. D. (1976). *Handbook of industrial and organizational psychology.* New York: Rand MacNally.

Dunnette, M. D., & Hough, L. M. (Eds.). (1994). *Handbook of industrial and organizational psychology.* Palo Alto, CA: Consulting Psychologists Press.

Ennis, R. H., Millman, J. & Tomko, T. (1985). *Cornell Critical Thinking Test level X & level Z* (3rd ed.). Pacific Grove, CA: Midwest.

Eskin, M. (2004). The double "turn" to ethics and literature? *Poetics Today. 25,* 557–572.

European Federation of Psychologists Association (EFPA). (2005). Meta-code of ethics. Retrieved from http//www.efpa.eu/ethics/ethical-code.

Evers, A., Anderson, N., & Voskuijl, O. F. (2005). *The Blackwell handbook of personnel selection.* Oxford, UK: Blackwell.

Ferrell, O. C., Fraedrich, J., & Ferrell, L. (2006). *Business ethics: Ethical decision making and cases.* Boston: South-Western College.

Ferris, G. R., & King, T. R. (1992). The politics of age discrimination in organizations. *Journal of Business Ethics, 11,* 341–350.

Fisch, M. H. (1975). The academy of the investigators. In E. A. Underwood (Ed.), *Science, medicine and history: Essays on the evolution of scientific thought and medical practice written in honor of Charles Singer* (pp. 521–563). New York: Arno Press.

Fischer, M. A. (2008). Protecting confidentiality rights: The need for an ethical practice model. *American Psychologist, 63,* 1–13.

Fisher, J. (2004). Social responsibility and ethics: Clarifying the concepts. *Journal of Business Ethics, 52,* 391–400.

Friedman, M. (2000). The social responsibility of business is to increase its profits. In J. R. Desjardins & J. J. McCall (Eds.). *Contemporary issues in business ethics* (pp. 8–12). Belmont, CA: Wadsworth.

Fritzsche D. J., & Becker, H. (1984). Linking management behavior to ethical philosophy: An empirical investigation.

The Academy of Management Journal, 27, 166–175. Retrieved from http://www.jstor.org/stable/255964.

Gaumnitz, B. R., & Lere, J. C. (2002). Contents of codes of ethics of professional business organizations in the United States. *Journal of Business Ethics, 35,* 35–49. Goldenson, R. M. (1984). *Longman dictionary of psychology and psychiatry.* NY: Longman.

Gutek, B. A. (1985). *Sex and the workplace: Impact of sexual behavior and harassment on women, men and organizations.* San Francisco: Jossey-Bass.

Haniffa, R., & Hudaib, M. (2007). Exploring the ethical identity of Islamic banks via communication in annual reports, *Journal of Business Ethics, 76,* 97–116 Hobbs, N. (1948). The development of a code of ethical standards for psychology. *The American Psychologist, 3,* 80–84.

Holaday, M., & Yost, T. E. (1993). Publication ethics. *Journal of Social Behavior and Personality,* (8), 557–566

Iannone, A. P. (1989). *Contemporary moral controversies in business.* New York: Oxford University Press.

International School Psychology Association (ISPA). (1990). *Code of ethics.* Retrieved from http://www.ispaweb.org/Documents/ethics_fulldoc.html.

International Union of Psychological Science (IUPsyS). (2008). *Universal declaration of ethical principles for psychologists.* Retrieved from http://www.am.org/iupsys/resources/ethics/univdecl2008.html.

James, W. (1891). The moral philosopher and the moral life. *International Journal of Ethics, 1*(3), 330–354. Retrieved from http://www.jstor.org/stable/2375309.

Jensen, R. E. (1992). *Standards and ethics in clinical psychology.* Lanham: University Press of America.

Kaye, B. N. (1992). Codes of ethics in Australian Business Corporation. *Journal of Business Ethics. 11,* 857–862. doi:10.1007/BF00872364

Kelsay, J. (1997). Islam and the comparative study of religious ethics: Review of selected materials, 1985–1995. *Religious Studies Review, 23,* 3–9.

Kenny, D. (2007). Student plagiarism and professional practice. *Nurse Education Today, 27,* 14–18.

Keown, D. (2001). *The nature of Buddhist ethics.* Basingstoke, UK: Palgrave Macmillan.

Keyton, J., & Rhodes, S. C. (1997). Sexual harassment: A matter of individual ethics, legal definitions, or organizational policy. *Journal of Business Ethics, 16,* 129–146.

Kitson, A., & Campbell, R. (1996). *The ethical organization.* Houndmills: Macmillan.

Kohlberg, L., Levine, C., & Hewer, A. (1983). *Moral stages: A current formulation and a response to critics.* Basel: Karger.

Kohn, L. (2004). *Cosmos & community: The ethical dimension of Daoism.* Cambridge, MA: Three Pine Press.

Lefebvre M., & Singh, J. B. (1992). The content and focus of Canadian corporate codes of ethics. *Journal of Business Ethics, 11,* 799–808.

Lefkowitz, J. (2003). *Ethics and values in industrial-organizational psychology.* Mahwah, NJ: Lawrence Erlbaum.

Lekan, T. (2003). *Making morality: Pragmatist reconstruction in ethical theory.* Nashville, TN: Vanderbilt University Press.

Lewis, A. (2008). *The Cambridge handbook of psychology and economic behavior.* Cambridge, UK: Cambridge University Press.

Lindsay, G., & Colley, A. (1995). Ethical dilemmas of member of the society. *The Psychologist, 8,* 448–453.

Lindsay, G., Koene, C., Øvreeide, H., & Lang, F. (2008). *Ethics for European psychologists*. Cambridge, MA: Hogrefe.

London, M., & Bray, D. W. (1980). Ethical issues in testing and evaluation for personnel decisions. *American Psychologist, 35*, 890–901.

Loui, M. C. (2002). Seven ways to plagiarize: Handling real allegations of research misconduct. *Science and Engineering Ethics, 8*, 529–539.

Lowman, R. L. (Ed.) (1985). *Casebook on ethics and standards for the practice of psychology in organizations*. Bowling Green, OH: Society for Industrial and Organizational Psychology.

Lowman, R. L. (Ed.). (1998). *The ethical practice of psychology of organizations*. Washington, DC: American Psychological Association.

Lowman, R. L. (Ed.). (2006). *The ethical practice of psychology of organizations* (2nd ed.). Washington, DC: American Psychological Association.

Marcovitch, H. (2007). Malas prácticas de investigadores y autores .[Misconduct by researchers and authors]. *Gaceta Sanitaria, 21*(6), 492–499Barcelona.

Marcuse, H. (1964). *One dimensional man*. Boston: Beacon.

Montoya, I. D., & Richard A. J. (1994). A comparative study of codes of ethics in health care facilities and energy companies. *Journal of Business Ethics, 13*, 713–718.

Münsterberg, H. (1913). *Psychology and industrial efficiency*. London: Constable; Boston: Houghton Mifflin.

Oberer D., & Lee, S. (1986). The counseling psychologist in business and industry: Ethical concerns. *Journal of Business and Psychology, 1*(2), 148–162. doi:10.1007/Bf01018810

Ornstein, M. (1963). *Role of scientific societies in the seventeenth century*. London: Archon Books. (Original work published 1928).

Peterson, N. G., Mumford, M. D., Borman, W. C., Jeanneret, P. R., & Fleishman, E. A. (1999). *An occupational information system for the 21st century: The development of O*Net*. Washington, DC: American Psychological Association.

Pierce, C. A., Byrne, D., & Aguinis, H. (1996). Attraction in organizations: A model of workplace romance. *Journal of Organizational Behavior, 17*, 5–32. doi:10.1002/(SICI)1099-1379(199601)17:1<5::AID-JOB734>3.0.CO;2-E

Pope, K. S., & Vazquez, M. J. T. (2007) *Ethics in psychotherapy and counseling: A practical guide for psychologists* (3rd ed.). San Francisco: Jossey Bass.

Pope, K. S., & Vetter, V. A. (1992). Ethical dilemmas encountered by members of the American Psychological Association: A national survey. *American Psychologist, 47*, 397–411.

Powers, J. (2000). *A concise encyclopedia of Buddhism*. Oxford: Oneworld.

Premeaux, S. R., & Mondy, R. W. (1993). Linking management behavior to ethical philosophy. *Journal of Business Ethics, 12*(5), 349–357.

Reese, H. W., & Fremouw, W. J. (1984). Normal and normative ethics in behavioral sciences. *American Psychologist, 39*, 863–876. doi:10.1037/0003-066X.39.8.863

Río Sánchez, C. Del (2005). *Guía de ética profesional en psicología clínica [Ethical guidelines for practitioners in clinical psychology]*. Madrid: Pirámide.

Roe, R. A. (1991). *Grondslagen der personeelsselektie*. [Foundations of personnel selection] (2nd print). Assen: Van Gorcum.

Rosenbaum, M. (Ed.) (1982). *Ethics and values in psychotherapy*. New York: The Free Press.

Sales, B. D., & Folkman, S. (2000). *Ethics in research with human participants*. Washington: American Psychological Association.

Schwartz, M. S., & Carroll, A. B. (2003). Corporate social responsibility. A three-domain approach. *Business Ethics Quarterly, 13*(4), 503–530.

Sinclair, C., Poizner, S., Gilmour-Barrett, K., & Randall, D. (1987). The development of a code of ethics for Canadian psychologists. *Canadian Psychology, 28*, 1–8.

Sinclair, C., & Pettifor, J. (Eds.). (2001). *Companion manual to the Canadian code of ethics for psychologists*. Ottawa, Ontario: Canadian Psychological Association.

Thompson, A. (1990). *Guide to ethical practice in psychotherapy*. New York: Wiley.

Voskuijl, O. F., Evers, A., & Geerlings, S. (2005). Is the obvious obvious? Considerations about ethical issues in personnel selection. In A. Evers, N. Anderson, & O. Voskuijl (Eds.), *The Blackwell handbook of personnel selection* (pp. 98–118). Oxford: Blackwell Publishing.

Voskuijl, O. F., & Evers, A. (2007). Tensions between the prescriptive and descriptive ethics of psychologists, *Journal of Business Ethics, 72*, 279–291. Wadeley, A., & Blasco, T. (1995). *La ética en la investigación y la práctica psicológicas*. Barcelona: Ariel.

Westhoff, L. (1985). *Corporate romance*. New York: Times Books.

Wiley, C. (2000). Ethical standards for human resource management professionals: A comparative analysis. *Journal of Business Ethics, 25*, 93–114.

CHAPTER
19
Ethical Issues and Ethics Reviews in Social Science Research

Douglas R. Wassenaar *and* Nicole Mamotte

Abstract

Although the ethics of social science research has not enjoyed as much scholarly attention as the ethics of biomedical research, social scientists continue to debate the relevance of research ethics and ethics review to social science research. Like social scientists, biomedical scientists have also objected to ethical review of biomedical research, and much has been gained from the ensuing debates. This chapter reviews much of this recent debate, and proposes the application of a framework developed by Emanuel, Wendler, and Grady (2008). We argue, however, that social scientists are generally inadequately trained in research ethics and may still espouse a dangerous view, common among behavioral scientists in the 1950s, that ethical concerns reflect a kind of methodological or scientific naiveté. We provide grounds for arguing, further, that social science research, with a few clear exceptions, should be rigorously ethically reviewed, and that research ethics committees have an obligation to be competent in the appropriate review of social science research, including qualitative research. Although the chapter refers largely to social science research, we include psychological research as a major domain of social science research.

Key Words: research ethics, social science research, research ethics review

One of the most important aims of research ethics is to protect the welfare of research participants.

Ethics review is increasingly becoming mandatory for social science research globally. Similarly, many editors of leading social science journals are requiring authors to furnish proof of ethics approval before a research article is considered for publication. The growing institutional priorities accorded to research ethics review by large institutions such as science councils, universities, and academic journals should not distract individual researchers from their fundamental obligation to treat research participants ethically and not as simple means to the researcher's ends. Although ethics review is an important contributor to the ethical conduct of social science research, the model we support emphasizes ethics review as one of several factors that promote ethical research. The aim of this chapter is to review recent arguments about the ethical review of social science research and suggest an alternate framework for this debate, including social science research that is sponsored by developed countries and conducted in developing countries. For the purposes of this chapter, social science research is taken to include both quantitative and qualitative methodologies, although more discussion centers on qualitative methodologies because of their differences from quantitative methods. We also acknowledge that "social science" embraces a wide and disparate array of disciplines and methodologies, each of which may generate special ethical questions not addressed by this chapter.

Development of Research Ethics

Most accounts of the history of research ethics attribute the growth of the field to the aftermath of the atrocities committed by Nazi medical researchers in Germany during World War II. The trial of several Nazi doctors in Nuremberg was followed by the publication of the Nuremberg Code in 1948 (Amdur & Bankert, 2007). This code emphasized the importance of individual informed consent in all research with human participants, in order to prevent the recurrence of abuses by scientists in the name of research. The Nuremberg Code is rather restrictive regarding persons incapable of consenting to research, and the World Medical Association published the more detailed Declaration of Helsinki in 1964 (revised in 2008; Williams, 2008). The Declaration of Helsinki is important in the history of research, as it stimulated the implementation of the ethics review process through research ethics committees (RECs) in several developed countries. Also influential is the U.S. Belmont Report of 1979, which provided a framework to guide the resolution of ethical problems in research with human participants (Amdur & Bankert, 2007). The report identifies the three basic ethical principles (respect for persons, beneficence, and justice) that should inform the conduct of ethical research involving human participants, and outlines the procedures (informed consent, risk/benefit assessment, and fair subject selection) that should be followed. Many other guidelines and ethics codes for researchers have been published since World War II, and most of these focus on biomedical research; for example, the U.S. Federal Policy for the Protection of Human Subjects ("Common Rule") Federal Research Regulations Common Rule (45 CFR 46) on the protection of human subjects. The main elements of the Common Rule include requirements for assuring ethical compliance by research institutions, and researchers, ethics committee structure and function, and requirements for additional protection of vulnerable research participants such as pregnant women, prisoners, and children (Amdur & Bankert, 2007; cf. Schrag, 2009). Many disciplines in the social sciences have also developed codes of ethical conduct for researchers and established research ethics committees; these include psychology (c.f. American Psychological Association, 2010), sociology, anthropology, history, and nursing (Callahan, 1988). The 2009 annual report of the American Psychological Association's ethics committee, for example, revealed that there were no violations or cases opened in terms of "inappropriate research, teaching or administrative practices" (American Psychological Association, 2009).

As in medicine, increased awareness of the importance of ethics in social science research has been driven in part by outrage caused by particular studies. Probably the best-known controversial social science study is Milgram's obedience experiment (Amdur & Bankert, 2007; Blass, 1999), where participants were led to believe that they were inflicting lethal electric shocks on other people. In reality the shocks were not being delivered, but if they were, some would certainly have been lethal. In a simulated study of the tensions between prisoners and warders, Zimbardo's participants began to abuse each other as conditions in the study rapidly began to resemble a real-life situation (Blass, 1999). In a 1955 study of jury decision making, a jury was audiotaped while considering a case. The researchers, however, did not inform the jurors that they were part of a study or that their deliberations were being recorded, in order to avoid influencing their behavior. When it became known that the deliberations had been recorded by a researcher, there was a public outcry (Amdur & Bankert, 2007). In Laud Humphreys' 1970s "tearoom trade" study of casual homosexual encounters, Humphreys observed sexual meetings in a public park, then recorded participants' car registration numbers, traced their residential addresses, went to their homes, and interviewed them in order to profile the characteristics of persons in the "tearoom trade" (Humphreys, 1975). This study thus involved intrusive monitoring of public and private behavior, as well as deception about the nature of the interviews conducted (Amdur & Bankert, 2007). Many of these studies reflect an attitude toward research ethics that was prevalent in the behavioral sciences in the 1950s and may be implicit in many current objections to ethical review in the social sciences; namely, that concerns with ethics constitute a form of scientific naiveté (Kimmel, 1996). This attitude was characterized by "real" scientists doggedly pursuing truth no matter what humanistic or ethics concerns might arise en route.

Although it could be argued that none of these examples equals the severity and extent of the atrocities committed by the Nazi doctors, or the tragedy of the infamous Tuskegee syphilis study (Brandt, 1978), all of these studies involve ethical violations of one type or another. While some might argue that the eventual benefits to knowledge outweigh the discomforts of a few participants, major research ethics guidelines since World War II have strongly emphasized that the ends of research do not justify the means.

As one outcome of this concern, systems of ethics review have been implemented in many developed and developing countries. The purpose of the ethics review process is to ensure that research participants' dignity and welfare should always transcend the interest of the research. The exact functions, responsibilities, and procedures of RECs are well described elsewhere (e.g., Amdur & Bankert, 2007; WHO, 2011) and will not be elaborated upon here. Although problematic social science research contributed to the need for guidelines and ethics review, most research ethics committees did not develop specific guidelines or procedures for social science protocols. However, many universities and research institutions now require review of all social science research involving human participants by an independent REC prior to data collection, and some have separate RECs for social science protocols (Wassenaar, 2006). Editors of African journals are also increasingly requiring proof of ethics review prior to acceptance of data-based publications (Cleaton-Jones, 2007), and the South African Human Sciences Research Ethics Council established its own REC in 2003.

Resistance to Ethics Review of Research

The growing emphasis on ethics review of social science research has stimulated vigorous and critical debate. Even where ethics review is mandatory, as it is in South Africa, it is nevertheless important to appraise the guidelines and review mechanisms critically in order to develop appropriate criteria and review processes. We review several recent publications that raise questions about ethics review in social science research.

In general, resistance to ethics review can be divided into principled and pragmatic objections. The main principled objection to ethics review comes from those who might argue that the imposition of ethical constraints on research is a curtailment of academic freedom (Rubin & Sieber, 2006). This argument is only true if academic freedom is construed as the freedom to pursue any academic line of enquiry using any methodology, without consideration of the welfare of the research participants (Herrera, 2003). Academic freedom permits freedom of intellectual enquiry, but cannot sanction particular research methodologies that adversely affect the dignity and the rights of others.

Some authors (Mattingly, 2005; Reissman, 2005) object to the ethical universalism implicit in ethics review. According to Redwood and Todres (2006), the fundamental principles of biomedical research mentioned above have been translated into practical guidelines for risk/benefit analysis, informed consent, and confidentiality, and are assumed to be universal. They argue that such ethical universalism is problematic because ethical guidelines and procedures constructed in one context are exported to other contexts, particularly in the developing world, without modification (Mattingly, 2005; Reissman, 2005). Such a standardized approach to research ethics may not always correspond to the actual ethical issues that arise during research; for example, Hyder et al. (2004) found that 83% of the developing country researchers they surveyed felt that U.S. institutional review board (IRB) regulations were insensitive to local cultures and thus likely to be inadequate or misunderstood.

Other principled and partially pragmatic objections include the argument that ethics review of social science research is generally derived from biomedical review (Cribb, 2004; D'Agostino, 1995; Hoeyer, Dahlager, & Lynöe, 2005; Illinois White Paper, 2003; Israel, 2004; Schrag, 2009; Whittaker, 2005). This argument can, however, only be grounds for changes in pragmatic or institutional forms of ethical review. It cannot be used to argue that social science should be judged on different moral standards than biomedical research (Macklin, 1982). If RECs are not competent in the review of social science proposals, key social science nuances, such as limits of confidentiality in focus group discussions, may be overlooked. A major U.S. review of the ethical review requirements for social and behavioral research makes several recommendations to differentiate social science from biomedical research review, in order to focus on the key ethical issues in social science as opposed to biomedical research—although some issues remain common. In general, most social science research carries lower risk of harm than biomedical research, and should focus on ensuring voluntary informed participation and addressing threats to confidentiality (National Research Council, 2003).

Another principled objection is that ethics review is not necessary in social science research, as social science research carries far lower risks to research participants than biomedical research (Cribb, 2004; Oakes, 2002; Schrag, 2009). A related concern is that when REC resources are limited, REC review of minimal-risk research may lead to less oversight for higher-risk research (Rubin & Sieber, 2006). While social science research is unlikely to cause direct physical harm to participants, the risks of invasion of privacy, loss of confidentiality, psychological trauma, embarrassment, deception, stigma, and stereotyping exist and need to be monitored and prevented. Furthermore, it is possible for low-risk methods, such as focus groups, to be used in a high-risk context, such as with injection drug users (Rubin & Sieber, 2006), resulting in ethically complex social science studies.

However, social science researchers are reminded that there is also ongoing resistance to aspects of ethical review by biomedical researchers, suggesting that the debates in these fields are not as different (cf. Gunsalus, Bruner, Burbules, Murray, et al., 2006; Hedgecoe, 2008; Keith-Spiegel & Koocher, 2005; Keith-Spiegel, Koocher, & Tabachnik, 2006) as some social science objectors (cf. Allen & Waters, 1983; D'Agostino, 1995; van den Hoonaard, 2001; Haggerty, 2004; Hedgecoe, 2008) propose. It would be foolish for social science researchers to ignore the considerable body of literature on ethical aspects of biomedical research that has struggled to deal with issues such as making informed consent more understood and more voluntary, ensuring confidentiality, debating community assent to research, risk-benefit determinations, and access to the benefits of research that are pertinent to social science research. Indeed, because social science research generates fewer direct benefits for research participants than many biomedical studies (cf. Macklin, 1982), the risk-benefit determinations of social science research deserve much closer ethical scrutiny.

Social science researchers' objections and negative experiences with ethics review can primarily be attributed to pragmatic concerns (Mamotte & Wassenaar, 2009). Pragmatic objections to ethics review include the issue of time delays involved in obtaining ethics review, as RECs generally meet monthly at best. Typically, about 50% of proposals are returned for amendment (Jelsma & Singh, 2005), and corrections to proposals may require resubmission in a subsequent month. Slow turnaround time of REC review affects researchers' satisfaction with the ethics review process, as well as their ethics compliance (Ashcraft & Krause, 2007; Liddle & Brazelton, 1996). McNeill, Berglund, and Webster (1992) found that despite general support for the ethics review process, researchers experienced ethics review as slow and taxing. Researchers who had their proposals rejected or were required to make modifications prior to approval were more likely to view ethics review as an impediment to research. It is possible, however, that non-approvals arise from the poor research ethics training of many social scientists. If researchers themselves were more competent in the ethical aspects of research, their proposals would be less likely to be returned for revision (Sieber, 1992; Wassenaar, 2006). Some researchers nevertheless believe that RECs are not competent in their review of the technical aspects of the study, or in some cases, even of the ethical aspects of the study. This second point underlines the fact that REC members must be trained in research ethics and that RECs should have access to consultants who are competent in methodological aspects of the studies they review.

The overriding concern of RECs is to prevent harm and defend the rights of research participants. However, in doing so they have been accused of expanding their bureaucracies (Gunsalus et al., 2006; Haggerty, 2004; Illinois White Paper, 2003; Malouff & Schutte, 2005) while failing to address the more controversial issues, such as the future value of a proposed study, the possible systemic harms arising from the findings of the study (D'Agostino, 1995), the dispersal of benefits derived from the research, and the recognition and rewarding of participants for their invaluable contributions (Whittaker, 2005). Another issue that RECs may fail to address is that of interpretation and analysis (Whittaker, 2005). Researchers have complete freedom in the interpretive process and can impose on the collected data any theoretical perspective over which RECs and participants have no or little control (Whittaker, 2005). Furthermore, as it is the researcher's ethical responsibility to make research findings available to participants the possibility exists, especially in qualitative or community-based research (Flicker, Travers, Guta, McDonald, & Meagher, 2007) where a small number of participants are involved, that participants may recognize themselves and become offended or distressed by the researcher's interpretations of their accounts or actions (Guenther, 2009; Löfman, Pelkonen, & Pietila, 2004; Whittaker, 2005).

A further pragmatic criticism is that most RECs do not have the resources to conduct post-approval monitoring of studies. In effect, this means that ethical compliance relies on the integrity of the researcher, with little active involvement by RECs in ensuring compliance with the approved proposal (Keith-Spiegel & Koocher, 2005; Weijer, Shapiro, Fuks, Glass, & Skrutkowska, 1995). Likewise, many RECs are unable to proactively monitor ethical transgressions in data analysis, such as the analysis of fabricated data and the dropping of data that may contradict the researcher's theory (Rosenthal, 1994). In this regard, it would be interesting to compare approved proposals with all publications arising from a study, to determine the degree of compliance with the approved proposal as evident from the resulting publications. McNeill et al. (1992) found that 14% of researchers had at some point deviated from their proposal without REC approval. Deviations included changes in study design, sampling, and the level and scope of participation required of participants. Some have also argued that the increasing powers of RECs may have the consequence of discouraging creative, innovative, and socially provocative social science research proposals, out of fear that ethics approval is unlikely (Haggerty, 2004; Illinois White Paper, 2003). There is, however, no evidence that this has happened in biomedicine, where RECs have had to deal with protocols reflecting rapid changes in technology, epidemics, stigmatizing illnesses, and complex interventions, such as those associated with new reproductive technologies, genetics, genomics, and preventive HIV vaccines. It would be of interest to survey social science researchers to determine whether they have been "dumbing down" their research proposals to avoid conflict with review systems.

Qualitative researchers have argued that qualitative research is exempt from ethical considerations or ethics review. They argue that the method is conversational (Cribb, 2004) and that qualitative data analysis attempts to preserve the integrity of the data collected. Haggerty (2004) compares qualitative research with investigative journalism, which takes place without ethical review. This comparison is misleading for several reasons, although MacIntyre (1982) concedes that "some inferior social science is not at all unlike journalism" (p. 188). First, journalists inform their interviewees as a matter of course that they are journalists, and interviewees, especially in the developed world, expect their narratives to be recorded and reproduced in the public domain with identifying personal information. Furthermore, it could be argued that journalists, on the whole, are interested in a contemporary "snapshot" of their subject matter, rather than a rigorous, theory-driven, systematic sampling and analysis of the material. It has been argued further that journalism has its primary ethical obligation to the public, rather than to the data source (Illinois White Paper, 2003). Indeed, journalists themselves are currently debating similar ethical issues, suggesting that journalists are not as free of ethical constraints as Haggerty suggests (Hafez, 2002; Starck, 2001; Wasserman & Rao, 2008). Interviewees in social science research, especially in developing countries, are not as clear about the intentions and obligations of researchers (Molyneux, Wassenaar, Peshu, & Marsh, 2005), and even if interviewees understand the study it cannot be assumed that they implicitly grant permission to be quoted directly and identifiably in the public domain. For this reason, and despite several objections to the relevance of informed consent in the qualitative research process (cf. D'Agostino, 1995; van den Hoonaard, 2001; Löfman et al., 2004; Whittaker, 2005), the informed consent process must be as explicit as possible, intended outputs described, and confidentiality assured unless explicitly waived. If risks are low, informed consent need not be in writing. Informed consent as a process should convey respect for participants' dignity, no matter how foreign it might feel as an intrusion in the quest for conversational data. Participants in qualitative research are thus entitled to the same protections and respect as those in quantitative research. The intimacy of qualitative interviews carries far more potential to cause subjective distress than most quantitative methods, and this must be carefully addressed in the risk/benefits section of proposals. RECs reviewing qualitative research should also require evidence of a rigorous analytical process to ensure that valid and supportable conclusions are drawn.

Ethical guidelines and reviews have been criticized for not sufficiently addressing the ethical issues unique to qualitative research. Some authors (Cribb, 2003; van den Hoonaard, 2001; Ramcharan & Cutcliffe, 2001; Redwood & Todres, 2006) question the appropriateness of reviewing qualitative research using guidelines written for quantitative or biomedical research. Many guidelines, for example, make reference to "research protocols" and "research subjects," terms which may be foreign to some qualitative researchers who see their research as a collaboration between themselves and the participants (Cribb, 2004; van den Hoonaard, 2001; Flicker et al., 2007).

More serious, however, is the allegation that RECs see quantitative research as the most valid form of knowledge production and may act as gatekeepers to qualitative research (van den Hoonaard, 2001; Redwood & Todres, 2006).

The act of submitting a fully detailed proposal for ethics review prior to the commencement of research is seen as problematic in some qualitative research (Cribb, 2004; van den Hoonaard, 2001). The collaborative nature of qualitative, particularly participatory, research makes it difficult to specify the exact focus of research, as the research is constantly transformed through the collaborative relationship between the researcher and the participants (van den Hoonaard, 2001). As such research is continuously changing and unpredictable, how then is it possible to consider ethical issues prior to the research, as is required for ethics review (Redwood & Todres, 2006)? Qualitative researchers should inform participants (and RECs) as fully as possible of the intended process, including the predictability of unpredictability, and the possibility of distress or other consequences. Löfman et al. (2004) emphasize the researcher's ethical responsibility to make research findings known to participants. Researchers should anticipate these issues when designing their studies so as to maximize benefits and minimize harm.

These arguments suggest that RECs must be competent in reviewing qualitative research, and that review criteria appropriate to qualitative research need to be developed thoughtfully rather than mechanistically applied. These arguments, however, do not justify judging qualitative research by moral standards that are different from those used in quantitative research, but may be a justification for different review procedures. Similarly, the grounds for the exemption of qualitative research from ethics review are not at all persuasive, unless qualitative research is to be accorded a status akin to espionage (cf. MacIntyre, 1982). The difficulty of doing something ethically is not a sound reason for not persisting in finding a way of doing it. Researchers should address ethical issues in their research with the same intellectual and creative vigor that they use to develop methodologies and analytical methods.

In turn, poorly trained RECs lacking in confidence may want to minimize research participants' and their own exposure to risk, and may thus withhold approval of well-designed, complex, and potentially controversial studies. In this regard, there are several global initiatives to build the capacity of REC members, led primarily by the Fogarty International Center at the National Institutes of Health[1] in the United States. The European Union[2] and EDCTP[3] are also funding research ethics capacity development in developing countries (Wassenaar, 2006). Similarly, if researchers themselves are more competent in the ethical aspects of research, their proposals will be less likely to be returned for revision by RECs. The lack of focus on research ethics training in most social science courses (c.f. Kjellström, Ross, & Fridlund, 2010) may also contribute to researchers' resistance to the ethics review process. Ethics review, if competently conducted, can add value to the proposed study and prevent or reduce harm to the participants and adverse consequences for the researcher. Ethics review could be seen as a process comparable with peer review, a practice accepted by all bona fide researchers seeking research funding or publication, notwithstanding critical concerns about peer review (c.f. Mulligan, 2005). Ideally, ethics review should be done quickly by a committee including persons trained in research ethics and familiar with the spectrum of social science methodologies, from ethnography to controlled behavioral interventions. Familiarity with methodology is essential if the REC is to evaluate the scientific components of the protocol. Ethics review of the scientific components of research, although controversial to some (Mamotte & Wassenaar, 2009), is central to the model of ethical research proposed by Emanuel, Wendler, and Grady (2008) which is advocated in this chapter. The purpose of RECs is to promote the ethical conduct of research. Ethics review should not be a form of normative research governance to obstruct scientific progress and discourage innovative researchers. There is a dual obligation on RECs and researchers to fully and frankly address the ethical dimensions of all research if participants are to be protected from harm (Wassenaar, 2006).

Exemptions from Ethics Review

While guidelines on exemption from ethics review are somewhat ambiguous (Pritchard, 2001), there are some types of study that in most countries would be exempted from ethics review. Studies without human participants or those based on information already in the public domain are the clearest examples of such studies. For example, an analysis of newspaper reports on suicide is exempt, as would be a meta-analysis of published studies on childhood sexual abuse. A study of university graduation statistics by race would not require review if based on data released in public reports by universities. Certain organizational evaluation and quality control audits are exempt from review, though these become complicated if considered for publication and individuals or institutions are identifiable. Research based on data from personal clinical or institutional records, however, although not engaging with human participants directly, is not exempt from review. All RECs should issue clear guidance concerning the types of research that are exempt from review so as not to cause unnecessary delays.

The above section has reviewed some of the debates about ethics review in social science research. However, the moral concerns of social scientists should transcend a narrow preoccupation with ethics review. As the framework below will show, ethics review is only one of eight ethical dimensions that should be applied to social science research. Dissatisfaction with the pragmatics of ethics review does not exempt social science researchers from addressing the inherent and inescapable moral dimensions of their work. We believe that the framework outlined below is more congruent with the essentially moral dimensions of conducting social science research (cf. MacIntyre, 1982) than many alternate frameworks, and is more likely to be seen as a resource rather than as a layer of bureaucratic interference with the search for truth.

The Elements of Ethical Research

Although there are several approaches to ethics (cf. Fulford, Dickenson, & Murray, 2002), there are four widely accepted philosophical principles that are applied in various ways to research ethics. These are: Autonomy and Respect for the Dignity of Persons; Nonmaleficence; Beneficence; and Justice. These four philosophical principles frequently find embodiment in the requirements of informed consent, risk/benefit determinations, and fair subject selection, and form the cornerstone of most REC deliberations (Hemmings, 2006). Because they are well known, they are not detailed here (cf. Beauchamp & Childress, 2008). There is a growing realization that it is difficult to apply abstract, universal ethical principles in practice because context, history, culture, and politics, as well as the social, gender, and economic status of participants, can have implications for how ethical principles are applied in different settings (Molyneux & Geissler, 2008). Recent works have attempted to spell out the ethical obligations of researchers more pragmatically and operationally than has to date been clear from the four philosophical principles or available ethical guidelines. The most useful of these recent works was published by Emanuel, Wendler, and Grady (2008). Emanuel et al.'s (2008) framework, which is structured to match the sequential process of research design, implementation, and reporting, embodies the four philosophical principles as well as their operational implications. The framework synthesizes traditional codes, guidelines, and literature on the ethics of researching human participants. Unlike previous documents, Emanuel et al.'s (2008) framework is not a response to a particular incident and therefore does not focus on specific instigating events at the expense of others. While this widely accepted framework was developed in relation to clinical research in developing countries, we believe that its key components are relevant and useful to social science researchers globally, whatever their funding sources, if any. The framework is based on eight broad practical principles: Collaborative Partnership, Social Value, Scientific Validity, Fair Selection of Participants Favorable Risk-Benefit Ratio, Independent Ethical Review, Informed Consent, and Ongoing Respect for Participants and Study Communities (Emanuel et al., 2008). These practical principles, if considered carefully and applied together, are likely to enhance the ethical standing and the scientific value of social science and psychological research. No single principle is more important than any other. Not all of them are applicable to every conceivable research design. The framework provides researchers and REC members with a coherent set of considerations with which to evaluate the ethical merits of research proposals. An adaptation of Emanuel et al.'s (2008) principles is outlined below, with an emphasis on social science research. We advocate the examination and adaptation of this model, as many of these principles will appear familiar to social scientists and psychologists as they reflect aspirational values inherent in much social scientific research conducted in developed and developing country settings.

Collaborative Partnership

This dimension encourages researchers to develop studies in collaboration with the target community or population and other relevant stakeholders (Emanuel et al., 2008). It is derived from the need to reduce possible exploitation of research participants and communities and ideally to ensure that the participating community also shares the benefits of the research (Lairumbi et al., 2008). Research should arise from an expressed community need, should involve the community in all stages of the research from study planning to implementation, and dissemination of results and should be considerate of the traditions, cultural practices, and values of the community (cf. Molyneux et al., 2005). There is a need to set up a "democratic representation of study communities" in connection to research teams (Marsh et al., 2008). This should involve regular yet varied opportunities for communication, interaction, and partnership-building between researchers and communities (Marsh et al., 2008). A challenge to community participation is deciding how the community should be represented in a manner that is well balanced and fair (Marsh et al., 2008). An exception to this principle could be research intended to reveal destructive processes (e.g., racism or sexism in resource allocation). In such cases a researcher would simply argue that the nature of the study makes collaboration with the target community inappropriate or counterproductive. However, additional weight might be placed on the remaining ethical principles. Furthermore, in terms of collaborative partnerships in social science research, Molyneux et al. (2009) suggest that fieldworkers should also be seen as key collaborative partners in the research endeavor because they play an important role in establishing relationships with participants and informing the nature and quality of the data collected. Researchers therefore have an obligation to promote the personal development of fieldworkers. Researchers' obligation to actively engage and study communities increases as the risks of the proposed research increase.

Social Value

Research should address questions that are of value to society or particular communities in society (Emanuel et al., 2008). While the value of social research to society will remain an endlessly contestable debate (MacIntyre, 1982), the research should specify who the beneficiaries of the research will be, and in what way they might benefit directly and indirectly. The problems being studied should lead to knowledge and/or interventions that will be of value to the participants and/or society (Emanuel et al., 2008). Social researchers should take personal responsibility for addressing the issues of the community they study by including an intervention study, action research, or advocacy efforts into the study design (Nyambedha, 2008). This may have both ethical and epistemological advantages. To this end, it has been argued that conducting social research cannot be separated from researchers' ethical obligation to find solutions to the problems they study (Nyambedha, 2008). Although the subjective, malleable, and variable nature of social value makes it difficult to measure (Mulgan, 2010), the social value of research can be increased by establishing collaborative partnerships with and disseminating research results to participants, policymakers, and implementers (Lairumbi et al., 2008). As the role of research in development is debated, new ways of financing ongoing access to beneficial interventions, ancillary care, and other research-related benefits will be developed (IJsselmuiden, Kass, Sewankambo, & Lavery, 2010). Molyneux and Geissler (2008) caution that it may be more difficult for social science research to influence policy and as such, social scientists may need to form strong networks with policymakers and strategically frame their findings in ways that will maximize impact. This area should be addressed cautiously by RECs, as this principle might be the one most likely to tempt RECs to see their role as research governance and accordingly censor provocative studies (Illinois White Paper, 2003). For several reasons, evaluation of the social value of research in social science may be more complex than in biomedical research and is a subject of further rich debate.

Scientific Validity

The design, sample, method, and analysis of the study should be rigorous, justifiable, feasible, and lead to valid answers to the research question (Emanuel et al., 2008). Unreliable and/or invalid methods are unethical because they waste resources, yield invalid and unusable results, and expose participants to risk and inconvenience for no purpose. Poor science is unethical. Methodology should be rigorous, appropriate, and systematic, whether quantitative or qualitative designs are being used. Some restrictions or underpowering of sample size in quantitative studies may be acceptable if the purpose of the research is partly educational (e.g., junior postgraduate research projects conducted under supervision). Theobald and Nhlema-Simwaka (2008) emphasize the importance of rigorous qualitative methodology in research and highlight widespread concerns about the generalizability and validity of qualitative methods and data. The scientific validity of qualitative social science research should be assured and assessed using strategies appropriate to qualitative research. Silverman (2005), for example, suggests using methods such as comprehensive data treatment and deviant case analysis to ensure the validity of findings. The competence of the researcher and his or her research associates to undertake the research and its subcomponent tasks are also important components of this ethical dimension. In qualitative social science research, the "positionality" of fieldworkers in relation to participants, as well as their grasp of conceptual issues, may impact data quality and the attainment of study objectives (Molyneux et al., 2009). The selection and training of appropriate fieldworkers to conduct interviews and observations is therefore essential for high quality, scientifically valid research (Molyneux et al., 2009).

Fair Selection of Participants

The population selected for the study should be those to whom the research question applies (Emanuel et al., 2008). Convenience samples should be avoided unless in pilot research or studies intended primarily as training exercises. For example, while university students from Western countries may be a convenient, low-cost data pool, they are possibly the least representative population from which generalizations can be made (Henrich, Heine & Norenzayan, 2010). Vulnerable populations should not be used merely because they are accessible to the researcher (Eckstein, 2003). Undue inducements should not be offered, because they may distort perceptions of potential risks of the research, where relevant. Those most likely to benefit from the outcomes of the research are those who should bear the largest burden of the research, and vice versa. Random selection of participants may often be inappropriate for qualitative social science research. When purposefully selecting participants for a study, researchers need to consider the wider community's perception of fairness, as they may feel they are being denied the benefits that accompany research participation (Molyneux et al., 2009). Molyneux et al. (2009) recommend clarity and transparency when explaining to the host community how participants will be selected.

Favorable Risk/Benefit Ratio

A favorable risk/benefit ratio requires the fair distribution of research burdens and benefits (Lie, 2010). In social science, as in biomedical research, researchers should carefully identify all the possible harms and "costs" of the research to the participants (cf. Koocher, 2002), and specify means to minimize these so that the risk/benefit ratio is favorable (Emanuel et al., 2008). There are two general issues to be considered in risk/benefit determinations: (a) the probability of the harm occurring, and (b) the anticipated severity of the harm. D'Agostino (1995) rightly warns that identifying the worst case scenario does not equate to identifying the probability that it will arise. RECs should be mindful of this and not stifle research because of the low probability of relatively minor harms occurring, or even the low probability of serious harms occurring provided that steps are taken to minimize the probability of the harm occurring and there are clear benefits to participants and society. At the same time, it could be argued that the benefits of most social science research, no matter how altruistically packaged, are for the career of the researcher, and that relatively few direct benefits accrue to research participants or society at large. RECs should view this ratio carefully to prevent the exploitation of participants. The risk-benefit ratio can best be balanced by minimizing risks and maximizing benefits related directly to the research question. Benefits to society are secondary to benefits to participants, but are nevertheless an important consideration in determining risk-benefit ratio. However, Molyneux et al. (2009) caution that the benefits from social science research can be more difficult to predict in advance. Safeguards and contingencies should be put in place to deal with foreseeable harms (e.g., access to competent counseling facilities where interviews elicit traumatic material). The payment of money for participation in research to reimburse travel and other practical costs, while not unethical, should not be factored into offsetting risk (cf. Dickert & Grady, 1999; Koen, Slack, Barsdorf & Essack, 2008). It must be noted that harms can include wrongs (MacIntyre, 1982; Macklin, 2002): someone may not be harmed by certain research, but they may nevertheless be wronged. For example, if someone had to covertly observe someone's private behavior and never disclose any details to the observed person, they would not be harmed but would nevertheless have been wronged. Wrongs cannot be offset by benefits (MacIntyre, 1982). If deception is regarded as fundamentally wrong (cf. Macklin, 2002), it should be avoided wherever possible through careful consideration of alternative research designs (Herrera, 2000). Research should minimize harms and avoid wrongs.

Potential participants in developing country contexts may be eager to participate in social science research because they expect to receive some form of assistance or benefit in return. Researchers can cause harm through a failure to take action and address the raised expectations of communities involved in the research (Nyambedha, 2008). The local perspectives that emerge from community involvement in planning and conducting research can reduce both internal (e.g., threats to social identity) and external (e.g., stigmatization) risks to that community (Marsh et al., 2008).

In some forms of qualitative social science research the ethical obligation to protect participants from harm may need to be reconceptualized. Löfman et al. (2004), for example, critically consider the notion of harm in relation to participatory action research. As change and empowerment are central aims of this approach, the notion of harm needs to include the emotional, physical, and social demands that research-related changes may have on those involved. In participatory action research, then, protecting participants from harm requires that all changes are carried out slowly and are seen as necessary and valuable to all participants (Löfman et al., 2004; University of Toronto, n.d.). Moreover, protecting participants from harm often entails protecting participant confidentiality; however, in some qualitative social science research it may be ethically appropriate to name participants if they so wish (Guenther, 2009). Naming participants may empower them, strengthen the collaborative endeavor, and even promote social change (Guenther, 2009).

Independent Ethics Review

An independent and competent REC should subject all proposals to independent ethics review prior to commencement of data collection (Emanuel et al., 2008). Competent ethics review should maximize the protection of the participants and enhance the quality of the research. The REC will also review scientific elements of the study (cf. item 2 above), but it will do so to determine whether the methods are appropriate, carry risk of harm or likelihood of benefit, and will consider alternate, less risky methods of addressing the research question. RECs have an obligation to remain abreast of current developments and debates in research ethics, and should have access to expertise on current developments in research methodology. Theobald and Nhlema-Simwaka (2008) advocate for social scientists to serve on RECs that review social science research, and for all REC members to be trained how to appropriately assess social science, particularly qualitative, research (Mamotte & Wassenaar, 2009). REC processes should also be considered as social phenomena, subject to appropriate social science research to evaluate their functioning and to help develop appropriate performance criteria for RECs in general (Emanuel, Wood, Fleischman et al., 2004).

Informed Consent

Historically, informed consent has often mistakenly been seen as the only determinant of ethical research (cf. D'Agostino, 1995). However, it is only one of eight determinants of ethical research. Participants may not, for example, legally consent to research known to cause harm without accruing benefits. The standard components of consent are (a) provision of appropriate information, (b) participants' competence and understanding, (c) voluntariness in participating and freedom to withdraw after the study has started, and (d) formalization of the consent, usually in writing. This means that researchers must provide potential participants with clear, detailed and factual information about the study, its methods, and its risks and benefits, along with assurances of the voluntary nature of participation and freedom to refuse or withdraw without penalties. Some data suggest that historically oppressed groups do not perceive participation in health research as voluntary (Barsdorf & Wassenaar, 2005), and this should be surveyed further in the social sciences. In contrast to assertions made by van den Hoonaard (2001), signed consent is not necessary if the risks of harm are very low and if the signed consent form constitutes a potential breach of confidentiality (Amdur & Bankert, 2007).

Particular care and special precautions need to be taken in obtaining informed consent from vulnerable populations, including but not limited to psychiatric patients, prisoners, members of disadvantaged groups, illiterate persons, persons in impoverished rural settings, persons in crisis situations such as natural disasters, warfare, or refugee situations (cf. Sumathipala & Siribaddana, 2005). Nyambedha (2008) suggests that continuous community sensitization to the role of research should accompany informed consent, as it may be difficult to determine the protective role of informed consent if the vulnerable participant's expectation of assistance or support from the researcher influences their willingness to participate in the research. In some African settings, it is appropriate to seek permission from gatekeepers of particular communities (e.g., village elders) to conduct research with a particular population, but such permission in general is not a substitute for informed individual consent (cf. Diallo et al., 2005; IJsselmuiden & Faden, 1992; Molyneux, Wassenaar, Peshu, & Marsh, 2005; Nyika, Wassenaar, & Mamotte, 2009; Tindana, Kass, & Akweongo, 2006).

Research with minors is ethically and legally complex and should, as a rule, be done only with the consent of legal guardians and the assent of the minor if risks are acceptable (Leikin, 1993; Schenk & Williamson, 2005; Strode, Slack, Wassenaar & Singh, 2007). The degree of risk involved in the particular study and the maturity of the child influence whether or not independent adolescent consent is acceptable. Risks also have to be weighed against direct benefits of participation. Permission to conduct research in a school or other institution does not substitute for obtaining the informed consent of parents or guardians.

In some forms of qualitative social science research, the research activities are negotiated by all participants at each stage in the research process, and participants can only decide whether to participate or not as the process develops (Boser, 2006). The dynamic and flexible nature of these types of qualitative research makes the possibility of obtaining informed consent problematic, and often requires participants to give consent to the unknown (Löfman et al., 2004). It may therefore be necessary for informed consent in some types of qualitative social science research to be phased. This would require consent to be obtained as each new research activity is negotiated.

Ongoing Respect for Participants and Study Communities

This principle requires that participants be treated with respect during and after a study (Emanuel et al., 2008). This can be achieved by allowing participants to withdraw from the research at any stage, providing participants with any new information obtained during the research, monitoring participants' well-being throughout the research, and respecting participants' privacy by maintaining confidentiality and anonymity (Easter, Davis, & Henderson, 2004; Emanuel et al., 2008).

It is not only considered best practice to keep the identity of participants confidential, but also to protect the identity of communities in research to prevent stigma and discrimination (American Academy of Pediatrics, 2004). As such, protecting institutional identities may also be appropriate (Uys, 2008). Participatory activities and focus groups, commonly used in qualitative social science research, present complications concerning confidentiality, as the researcher cannot guarantee that all participants will keep the information released by other participants confidential (Löfman et al., 2004). It may be appropriate to advise focus group participants not to disclose personally sensitive information but rather to discuss their opinions in general on the topics in question. In such research, particular attention should be given to confidentiality issues and participants should be fully informed about confidentiality risks prior to participation (Wassenaar, 2006). Recently, however, Guenther (2009) has urged social scientists to question the ethical assumption that confidentiality is always best. She argues that naming participants may empower them and that researchers should carefully consider whether or not to use names. The decision to name participants should take into account the participants' wishes and the reasons why they wish to be named; the level and type of foreseeable risk associated with being named; and if/how naming participants will affect the reporting of research findings (Guenther, 2009). The researcher's commitment to a collaborative endeavor and/or social change may also influence their decision to name participants (Guenther, 2009). The American Academy of Pediatrics (2004), however, warns that participants wishing to be named may not adequately anticipate or comprehend the potential harms of being named (e.g., stigma), and for this reason researchers and RECs may need to make a paternalistic decision on their behalf.

There is increasing international concern about what happens to participants and host communities once the research is over. Researchers, at the very least, have an obligation to make findings available to the host community in relevant and appropriate formats, and empower that community with the knowledge that has been collected. A more interactive process of results dissemination is often necessary in order to share results with all interested parties, as research findings are mostly disseminated through publication in academic journals that are inaccessible to the majority of research stakeholders (Lairumbi et al., 2008). Nyambedha (2008) advocates the use of community feedback sessions as a way to negotiate the vested interests of study communities and giving back to the community. Community feedback sessions provide an opportunity for researchers to share study findings with participants, and allows participants to respond to the findings and recount their research experience (Nyambedha, 2008). However, making findings available to participants in social science research can prove ethically problematic. The small number of participants involved in most qualitative studies may result in participants recognizing themselves in the findings. Social scientists will have to consider how they should deal with situations where participants become distressed by self-identification in publications and by the researcher's presentation and interpretation of their views or actions.

In behavioral, psychotherapeutic, or community intervention research, the experimental group should be ensured appropriate access to successful interventions, and the intervention must be made available to any control groups that were involved. This has budgetary implications but prevents exploitation of participants for the sake of science and the career of the researcher. Furthermore, to prevent study communities from feeling exploited, researchers can advocate for necessary support for the study community, or incorporate action research components or interventions into their research designs (Nyambedha, 2008). At the very least, researchers should consider these issues and make whatever arrangements are within their means or powers of advocacy to recommend. There is also the question of the nature and degree of obligation that researchers might have to assist participants with other problems that they become aware of in the course of their research (cf. Belsky & Richardson, 2004; Richardson, 2010).

Consideration and thoughtful implementation of these eight principles in social science and psychological research will increase the likelihood that research is ethical and that knowledge is gained without avoidable harms to participants, without whom new knowledge and interventions cannot be created.

Professional Integrity

While we have hopefully demonstrated that Emanuel et al.'s (2008) framework of ethical principles is a powerful approach to the ethical dimensions of conducting research in the social sciences, like many other ethical frameworks, it fails to address issues of professional ethics (or professional integrity). Professional ethics concerns the researcher's conduct of behavior and practice when carrying out professional work (Davison, 2000). For social science researchers, such professional work may include contracting, consulting, researching, teaching, and writing. Although professional associations help to uphold the integrity of their members, Nyika (2009) argues that there is need to complement the efforts of such associations and sensitize researchers to the ethical implications of their decisions concerning authorship, falsification of data, misuse of research funds, mentorship of junior researchers, conflict of interest in research, plagiarism, and failure to publish research findings, etc. A recent study found that 1.97% of scientists fabricate, falsify, or modify results in some way, and up to 33.7% admit to other questionable research practices (Fanelli, 2009). Conflicts of interest have also characterized much psychiatric research, where corporate sponsorship and compensation from pharmaceutical companies have led researchers to suppress research results or publish biased study outcomes in favor of profits (Sharpe, 2009).

Conclusions

In this chapter, we attempt to review some of the reservations that have been expressed by social scientists about ethical aspects of social science research, including ethics review. In objecting to ethics review, social scientists should not confuse ethics review with their fundamental obligation to conduct their research ethically. We propose that the model developed by Emanuel et al. (2008) be adapted and applied to social science research because many of its inherent values will be familiar to most social scientists. Ethics in social science research is currently not as well developed as in the biomedical sciences, and is not without controversy and dissident voices. Research ethics is a field of vigorous debate and complexity, and this is to be desired. Research ethics, as has hopefully been shown, is neither slavish rule obedience nor blunt bureaucratic interference with scientific progress. Research ethics review is fundamentally concerned with assuring that the dignity of human participants is respected rather than violated in the search for knowledge, scientific progress, and career advancement. Science is not value-free, and research ethics strives to make the value component of research more explicit. Efforts need to be made to increase the ethics education of social scientists at undergraduate and postgraduate levels. Systems of ethics review for social science should be sensitive to the particular risks and methodologies of the social sciences, and not just emulate biomedical structures and procedures (Mamotte & Wassenaar, 2009). RECs should be trained in research ethics, self-observing, open to being researched, and careful not to a priori censor provocative research or overreach their mandate. Researchers enjoy considerable power to sway public and professional opinion, and these powers must be exercised responsibly and with sensitivity to the issues covered in this chapter. Ethical sensitivity can enhance the value of research practice if seen as congruent with the common goal of most social scientists i.e., the understanding and betterment of human existence.

Acknowledgments

Drs. Catherine Molyneux and Wenzel Geissler are thanked for their helpful comments on an earlier draft of this chapter.

Notes

1. http://www.fic.nih.gov/
2. http://europa.eu/
3. European and Developing Countries Clinical Trials Partnership; http://www.edctp.org/

References

Allen, P., & Waters, W. E. (1983). Attitudes to research ethical committees. *Journal of Medical Ethics, 9,* 61–65.

Amdur, R. J., & Bankert, E. A. (2007). *Institutional review board member handbook* (2nd ed.). Sudbury, MA: Jones & Bartlett.

American Academy of Pediatrics. (2004). Policy statement: Ethical considerations in research with socially identifiable populations. *Pediatrics, 113,* 148–151.

American Psychological Association. (2010). *Ethical principles of psychologists and code of conduct.* Retrieved from http://www.apa.org/ethics/code/index.aspx.

American Psychological Association. (2009). Report of the ethics committee. *American Psychologist, 65,* 483–492.

Ashcraft, M. H., & Krause, J. A. (2007). Social and behavioral researchers' experiences with their IRBs. *Ethics & Behavior, 17*(1), 1–17.

Barsdorf, N., & Wassenaar, D. (2005). Racial differences in public perceptions of voluntariness of medical research participants in South Africa. *Social Science & Medicine, 60,* 1087–1098.

Beauchamp, T., & Childress, J. (2008). *Principles of biomedical ethics* (6th ed). New York: Oxford.

Belsky, L., & Richardson, H. (2004). Medical researchers' ancillary clinical care responsibilities. *British Medical Journal, 328,* 1494–1496.

Blass, T. (Ed.). (1999). *Obedience to authority: Current perspectives on the Milgram paradigm.* Mahwah, NJ: Lawrence Erlbaum.

Boser, S. (2006). Ethics and power in community-campus partnership for research. *Action Research, 4,* 9–21.

Brandt, A. M. (1978). Racism and research: The case of the Tuskegee syphilis study. *Hastings Center Report, 8,* 21–29.

Callahan, J. (Ed.). (1988). *Ethical issues in professional life.* New York: Oxford.

Cleaton-Jones, P. (2007). Research ethics in South Africa: Putting the Mpumalanga case into perspective. In J. V. Lavery, C. Grady, E. Wahl, & E. Emanuel (Eds.), *Ethical issues in biomedical research: A casebook* (pp. 240–246). New York: Oxford.

Cribb, A. (2003). Approaching qualitative research. In Eckstein, S. (Ed.), *Manual for research ethics committees* (pp. 40–48). Cambridge: Cambridge University Press.

Cribb, R. (2004). Ethical regulation and humanities research in Australia: Problems and consequences. *Monash Bioethics Review, 23*(3), 39–57.

D'Agostino, F. (1995). The ethics of social science research. *Journal of Applied Philosophy, 12*(1), 65–76.

Davison, R. M. (2000). Professional ethics in information systems: A personal perspective. *Communications of the AIS, 3*(8) 1–34.

Diallo, D., Doumbo, O., Plowe, C., Wellems, T., Emanuel, E., & Hurst, S. (2005). Community permission for medical research in developing countries. *HIV/AIDS, 41,* 255–259.

Dickert, N., & Grady, C. (1999). What's the price of a research subject? Approaches to payment for research participation. *New England Journal of Medicine, 341,* 198–203.

Easter, M., Davis, A., & Henderson, G. (2004). Confidentiality: More than a linkage file and a locked drawer. *Ethics & Human Research, 26,* 13–17.

Eckstein, S. (2003). Research involving vulnerable participants: Some ethical issues. In Eckstein, S. (Ed.), *Manual for research ethics committees* (pp. 105–112). Cambridge: Cambridge University Press.

Emanuel, E. J., Wendler, D., & Grady, C. (2008). An ethical framework for biomedical research. In E. J. Emanuel, C. Grady, R. A. Crouch, R. K. Lie, F. G. Miller, & D. Wendler (Eds.), *The Oxford textbook of clinical research ethics* (pp. 123–133). New York: Oxford University Press.

Emanuel, E. J., Wood, A., Fleischman, A., Bowen, A., Getz, K. A., Grady, C., et al. (2004). Oversight of human participants research: Identifying problems to evaluate reform proposals. *Annals of Internal Medicine, 141*(4), 282–291.

Fanelli, D. (2009). How many scientists fabricate and falsify research? A systematic review and meta-analysis of survey data. *PLoS ONE 4*(5). Retrieved from http://www.plosone.org/article/info:doi/10.1371/journal.pone.0005738.

Flicker, S., Travers, R., Guta, A., McDonald, S., & Meagher, A. (2007). Ethical dilemmas in community-based participatory research: Training IRBs. *Journal of Urban Health, 84*(4), 478–493.

Fulford, K., Dickenson, D., & Murray, T. (Eds.). (2002). *Healthcare ethics and human values.* Oxford: Blackwell.

Guenther, K. M. (2009). The politics of names: Rethinking the methodological and ethical significance of naming people, organizations and places. *Qualitative Research, 9*(4), 411–421.

Gunsalus, C., Bruner, E., Burbules, N., Dash, L., Finkin, J., Goldberg, J., et al. (2006). Mission creep in the IRB world. *Science, 312,* 1441.

Hafez, K. (2002). Journalism ethics revisited: A comparison of ethics codes in Europe, North Africa, the Middle East, and Muslim Asia. *Political Communication, 19,* 225–250.

Haggerty, K. D. (2004). Ethics creep: Governing social science research in the name of ethics. *Qualitative Sociology, 27*(4), 391–413.

Hedgecoe, A. (2008). Research ethics review and the sociological research relationship. *Sociology, 42,* 873–886.

Hemmings, A. (2006). Great ethical divides: Bridging the gap between institutional review boards and researchers. *Educational Researcher, 35,* 12–18.

Henrich, J., Heine, S. J., & Norenzayan, A. (2010). The weirdest people in the world? *Behavioral & Brain Sciences, 33,* 61–83.

Herrera, C. D. (2000). Integrating research ethics and undercover hospital fieldwork. *IRB: A Review of Human Subjects Research, 22,* 1–4.

Herrera, C. D. (2003). A clash of methodology and ethics in "undercover" social science. *Philosophy of the Social Sciences, 33,* 351–362.

Hoeyer, K., Dahlager, L., & Lynöe, N. (2005). Conflicting notions of research ethics: The mutually challenging traditions of social scientists and medical researchers. *Social Science & Medicine, 61,* 1741–1749.

Humphreys, L. (1975). *Tearoom trade: Impersonal sex in public places.* New York: Aldine de Gruyter.

Hyder, A. A., Wali, S. A., Khan, A. N., Teoh, N. B., Kass. N. E., & Dawson, L. (2004). Ethical review of health research: A perspective from developing country researcher. *Journal of Medical Ethics, 30,* 68–72.

Illinois White Paper. (2003). *Improving the system for protecting human subjects: Counteracting IRB "Mission creep."* Illinois: Center for Advanced Study.

IJsselmuiden, C. B., & Faden, R. (1992). Research and informed consent in Africa: Another look. *New England Journal of Medicine, 326,* 830–833.

IJsselmuiden, C. B., Kass, N. E., Sewankambo, K. N., & Lavery, J. V. (2010). Evolving values in ethics and global health research. *Global Public Health, 5,* 154–163.

Israel, M. (2004). *Ethics and the governance of criminological research in Australia*. Sydney: New South Wales Bureau of Crime Statistics and Research.

Jelsma, J., & Singh, S. (2005). Research protocols—Lessons from ethical review. *South African Medical Journal, 95*, 107–108.

Keith-Spiegel, P., & Koocher, G. (2005). The IRB paradox: Could the protectors also encourage deceit? *Ethics & Behavior, 15*, 339–349.

Keith-Spiegel, G., Koocher, G., & Tabachnik, B. (2006). What scientists want from their research ethics committee. *Journal of Empirical Research on Human Research Ethics, 1*, 67–82.

Kjellström, S., Ross, S. N., & Fridlund, B. (2010). Research ethics in dissertations: Ethical issues and complexity of reasoning. *Journal of Medical Ethics, 36*, 425–430.

Kimmel, A. (1996). *Ethical issues in behavioral research*. Cambridge MA: Blackwell.

Koen, J., Slack, C., Barsdorf, N., & Essack, Z. (2008). Payment of clinical trial participants can be ethically sound: Moving past a flat rate. *South African Medical Journal, 98*, 926–929

Koocher, G. (2002). Using the CABLES model to assess and minimize risks in research: Control group hazards. *Ethics & Behavior, 12*, 75–86.

Lairumbi, G. M., Molyneux, S., Snow, R. W., Marsh, K., Peshu, N., & English, M. (2008). Promoting social value of research in Kenya: Examining the practical aspects of collaborative partnerships using an ethical framework. *Social Science & Medicine, 67*(5), 734–747.

Leikin, S. (1993). Minors' assent, consent, or dissent to medical research. *IRB: A Review of Human Subjects Research, 15*, 1–7.

Liddle, B. J., & Brazelton, E. W. (1996). Psychology faculty satisfaction and compliance with IRB procedures. *IRB: A Review of Human Subjects Research, 18*, 4–6.

Lie, R. K. (2010). The fair benefits approach revisited. *Hastings Center Report, 40*, 3.

Löfman, P., Pelkonen, M., & Pietilä. A. (2004). Ethical issues in participatory action research. *Scandinavian Journal of Caring Science, 18*, 333–340. MacIntyre, A. (1982). Risk, harm and benefit assessments as instruments of moral evaluation. In T. Beauchamp, R. Faden, R. J. Wallace, & L. Walters (Eds.), *Ethical issues in social science research* (pp. 175–189). Baltimore: Johns Hopkins Press.

Macklin, R. (1982). The problem of adequate disclosure in social science research. In T. Beauchamp, R. Faden, R. J. Wallace & L. Walters (Eds.), *Ethical issues in social science research* (pp. 193–214). Baltimore: Johns Hopkins Press.

Macklin, R. (2002). Unresolved issues in social science research. In F. Lolas & L. Agar (Eds.), *Interfaces between bioethics and the empirical social sciences* (pp. 67–78). Buenos Aires: World Health Organization and PAHO

Malouff, J. M., & Schutte, N. S. (2005). Academic psychologists' perspectives on the human research ethics review process. *Australian Psychologist, 40*(1), 57–62.

Mamotte, N., & Wassenaar, D. (2009). Ethics review in a developing country: A survey of South African social scientists' experiences. *Journal of Empirical Research on Human Research Ethics, 4*, 69–78.

Marsh, V., Kamuya, D., Rowa, Y., Gikonyo, C., & Molyneux, S. (2008). Beginning community engagement at a busy biomedical research programme: Experiences from the KEMRI CGMRC-Wellcome Trust Research Programme, Kilifi, Kenya. *Social Science & Medicine, 67*, 721–733.

Mattingly, C. (2005). Towards a vulnerable ethics of research practice. *Health, 9*(4), 453–471.

McNeill, P. M., Berglund, C. A., & Webster, I. W. (1992). Do Australian researchers accept committee review and conduct ethical research? *Social Science & Medicine, 35*(3), 317–322.

Molyneux, S., & Geissler, P. W. (2008). Ethics and the ethnography of medical research in Africa. *Social Science & Medicine, 67*, 685–695.

Molyneux, C., Goudge, J., Russell, S., Chuma, J., Gumede, T., & Gilson, L. (2009). Conducting health-related social science research in low income settings: Ethical dilemmas faced in Kenya and South Africa. *Journal of International Development, 21*, 309–326.

Molyneux, C., Wassenaar, D. R., Peshu, N., & Marsh, K. (2005). "Even if they ask you to stand by a tree all day, you will have to do it (laughter)...!": Community voices on the notion and practice of informed consent for biomedical research. *Social Science & Medicine, 61*, 443–454.

Mulgan, G. (2010). Measuring social value. *Stanford Social Innovation Review, Summer*, 38–43.

Mulligan, A. (2005). Is peer review in crisis? *Oral Oncology, 41*, 135–141.

National Research Council. (2003). *Protecting participants and facilitating social and behavioral sciences research*. Panel on institutional review boards, surveys, and social science research. C. F. Citro, D. R. Ilgen, & C. B. Marrett (Eds.), Committee on National Statistics and Board on Behavioral, Cognitive, and Sensory Sciences. Washington, DC: The National Academies Press.

Nyambedha, E. O. (2008). Ethical dilemmas of social science research on AIDS and orphanhood in Western Kenya. *Social Science & Medicine, 67*, 771–779.

Nyika, A. (2009). Professional ethics: An overview from health research ethics point of view. *Acta Tropica, 112*, S84-S90.

Nyika, A., Wassenaar, D. R., & Mamotte, N. (2009). The effect of relationships on decision-making processes of women in Harare, Zimbabwe. *Ethics & Behavior, 19*, 184–200.

Pritchard, I. (2001). Searching for "Research involving human subjects": What is examined? What is exempt? What is exasperating? *IRB: Ethics and Human Research, 23*, 5–13.

Ramcharan, P., & Cutcliffe, J. R. (2001) Judging the ethics of qualitative research: Considering the "ethics as process" model. *Health and Social Care in the Community, 9*, 358–366.

Redwood, S., & Todres, L. (2006). Exploring the ethical imagination: Conversation as practice versus committee as gatekeeper. *Forum: Qualitative Social Research, 7*, Article 26. Retrieved from http://www.qualitative-research.net/index.php/fqs/article/view/129.

Reissman, C. K. (2005). Exporting ethics: A narrative about narrative research in South India. *Health, 9*, 473–490.

Richardson, H. S. (2010). Ancillary-care obligations. *Public Health Ethics, 3*, 63–67.

Rosenthal, R. (1994). Science and ethics in conducting, analyzing, and reporting psychological research. In D. Bersoff (Ed.), *Ethical conflicts in psychology*. (pp. 357–363). Washington, DC: American Psychological Association.

Rubin, P., & Sieber, J. E. (2006). Empirical research on IRBs and methodologies usually associated with minimal risk. *Journal of Empirical Research on Human Research Ethics, 1*, 1–4.

Schenk, K., & Williamson J. (2005). *Ethical approaches to gathering information from children and adolescents in international settings: Guidelines and resources*. Washington, DC: Population Council.

Schrag, Z. M. (2009). How talking became human subjects research: The federal regulation of the social sciences 1965–1991. *Journal of Policy History, 21,* 3–37.

Sharpe, V. A. (2009). Sea change on financial conflicts of interest in health care? *Hastings Center Report, May–June,* 9–10.

Sieber, J. E. (1992). *Planning ethically responsible research: A guide for students and internal review boards.* Newbury Park, CA: Sage.

Silverman, D. (2005). *Doing qualitative research.* London: Starck, K. (2001). What's right/wrong with journalism ethics research? *Journalism Studies, 2,* 133–150.

Strode, A., Slack, C., Wassenaar, D. R., & Singh, J. (2007). One step forward, two steps back: Requiring ministerial approval for all "non-therapeutic" health research with minors. *South African Medical Journal, 97,* 200–202.

Sumathipala, A., & Siribaddana, S. (2005). Research and clinical ethics after the tsunami: Sri Lanka. *Lancet, 366,* 1418–1420.

Tindana, P., Kass, N., & Akweongo, P. (2006). The informed consent process in a rural African setting. *IRB: Ethics & Human Research, 28,* 1–6.

Theobald, S., & Nhlema-Simwaka, B. (2008). The research, policy and practice interface: Reflections on using applied social research to promote equity in Malawi. *Social Science & Medicine, 67,* 760–770.

University of Toronto (n.d.) *Guidelines for ethical conduct in participant observation.* Retrieved from http://www.research.utoronto.ca/wp-content/uploads/2009/03/Participant-Observation-Guidelines.pdf

Uys, L. R. (2008). Should researchers protect the good name and reputations of institutions in which research is done? *South African Journal of Higher Education, 22,* 457–465.

van den Hoonaard, W. C. (2001). Is research ethics review a moral panic? *Canadian Review of Sociology & Anthropology, 38*(1), 19–36.

Wassenaar, D. R. (2006). Ethical issues in social science research. In M. Terre Blanch, K. Durrheim, & M. Painter (Eds.), *Research in practice* (2nd ed., pp. 60–79). Cape Town: Jutas.

Wasserman, H., & Rao, S. (2008). The globalization of journalism ethics. *Journalism, 9,* 163–181.

Weijer, C., Shapiro, S., Fuks, A., Glass, K., & Skrutkowska, M. (1995). Monitoring clinical research: An obligation unfulfilled. *Canadian Medical Association Journal, 152,* 1973–1979.

Whittaker, E. (2005). Adjudicating entitlements: The emerging discourses of research ethics boards. *Health, 9,* 513–535.

Williams, J. R. (2008). Revising the Declaration of Helsinki. *World Medical Journal, 54,* 120–125.

World Health Organization. (2011). *Standards and operational guidance for ethics review of health-related research with human participants.* Geneva: WHO.

CHAPTER 20

Ethics and Law from an International Perspective: The Relationship between National Psychological Association Ethics Codes and Civil Law

Stephen Behnke *and* Stan Jones

Abstract

The authors use a novel methodology to gauge how the ethics codes of national psychology associations define the relationship between psychology and the society in which it is practiced. Using ethics codes available in English through the IUPsyS compendium project, the authors examine how national ethics codes make reference to civil law, an indicator of how psychology associations view their relationship to society. The authors identify several ways in which civil law appears in ethics codes. The five national ethics codes that refer to civil law the most are further scrutinized as to whether they impose an obligation to follow the law, provide a means for adjudicating ethical–legal conflicts, specify domains germane to law, address forensic activities, and incorporate transcendent human rights. Some national associations view ethics and law as inextricably intertwined. Other associations adopt a more detached relationship, whereby ethics and law operate largely in two separate realms.

Key Words: ethics code, American Psychological Association ethics code, APA ethics office, international, law

The opinions in this chapter represent the personal views of the authors and do not represent the official views of the American Psychological Association.

Introduction

Developing an ethics code may be viewed as an important marker in the maturation of a profession. Having an ethics code demonstrates that the profession is oriented toward a set of values that inform the discipline's theory and practice. An ethics code sets the standards to which members of the profession are expected to adhere. Training in the ethics code may be central to training for membership in the profession. Violations of the ethics code can provide the basis for exclusion from the ranks of membership.

An ethics code normally arises out of a profession in a progressive fashion, in the sense that the code is a manifestation of lessons learned from the practice of the discipline. This process may take time. As an example, the American Psychological Association wrote its first ethics code nearly six decades after the association was founded. The Turkish Psychological Association adopted its first ethics code nearly three decades after the founding of the association (Korkut, 2010). One aspect of this developmental arc in the profession entails defining the relationship between the profession and the society in which the profession is practiced. This relationship is important, because a profession is inevitably practiced within the context of a civil society that has its own set of customs, values, and enforceable standards of conduct.

Among the various purposes it serves, an association's ethics code may help the profession define the contours of its relationship with the civil society. The Canadian Psychological Association Code of Ethics (Third edition, Canadian Psychological

Association, 2000) provides an eloquent description of the relationship between the profession of psychology in Canada and Canadian society:

> Every discipline that has relatively autonomous control over its entry requirements, training, development of knowledge, standards, methods, and practices does so only within the context of a contract with the society in which it functions. This social contract is based on attitudes of mutual respect and trust, with society granting support for the autonomy of a discipline in exchange for a commitment by the discipline to do everything it can to assure that its members act ethically in conducting the affairs of the discipline within society; in particular, a commitment to try to assure that each member will place the welfare of the society and individual members of that society above the welfare of the discipline and its own members. By virtue of this social contract, psychologists have a higher duty of care to members of society than the general duty of care that all members of society have to each other.

This quotation describes an ongoing, mutually beneficial relationship between the discipline of psychology and civil society, what the Canadian Psychological Association describes as a "social contract." This term captures the inextricable link between the profession and the societies in which the profession is practiced. This relationship will vary depending upon the association and the society. In some national jurisdictions there may be a close nexus between the profession of psychology and the society. In others, the profession may exist much more independently. As a consequence, each national psychological association will define in a unique way how the association will interact with the society with which it is affiliated. That relationship may be reflected in the association's ethics code.

This chapter provides an overview of how national psychological association codes of ethics define the contours of the relationship between the profession of psychology and the civil society in which the profession is practiced. The overview examines how national psychological association ethics codes make reference to civil law, as an important indicator of how associations view their relationship to civil society. Although psychological associations interact with civil law in many ways other than solely through their ethics codes, ethics codes provide the values and standards of conduct by which members are expected to abide. The presence of references to civil law in an ethics code therefore provides a window into how an association conceptualizes its relationship to the society in which its members work.

For the purpose of the overview, the authors examine several features of how civil law appears in the code. First, the authors examine the number of references to civil law in each code, as indication of the extent to which civil law is present in the code. The authors then select the five codes that have the most references to civil law for further examination: Australia, Ireland, Israel, Philippines, and the United States. These five codes are further examined regarding whether the codes impose an obligation on psychologists to follow the law, whether the codes provide a process to adjudicate conflicts between ethics and law, what specific subject areas the codes mention in relation to law (e.g., disclosures of confidential information, informed consent), and whether the codes address forensic activities. Finally, the authors explore whether each ethics code addresses human rights, which are rights that transcend the specific society in which the ethics code has been written.

To the authors' knowledge, this chapter is the first review of how national psychological association ethics codes make reference to civil law. For this reason, the chapter serves as a preliminary study that will continue and expand as the number of association ethics codes increases and more translations into a common language become available. The chapter gives a detailed description of methodology, so that other commentators interested in this topic may see how the data were collected and analyzed. The authors hope that such transparency in methodology will spur additional study of this topic. The authors rely on the website of the International Union of Psychological Science (IUPsyS), which provides the most authoritative collection of national ethics codes.

Method

IUPsyS is a recognized international organization of national psychological associations. The IUPsyS maintains a compendium of "Codes of Ethics of National Psychology Organizations" (IUPsyS, 2011a), in order "to provide the broadest range of codes, available in their original language and translated into English" (IUPsyS, 2011b). The compendium consists of codes from 44 countries. The data in this chapter are derived solely from the codes of countries listed in the IUPsyS website compendium.

Of the 44 countries from which a code is listed, 26 codes are in English, or are given an English translation. The code listed for Russia is the psychiatric code and is not included. Seven links to English codes or translations were not valid; five of those codes were identified on their association sites, reducing the number to two. The link to the code for South Africa is actually to a list of documents for their licensure board and was therefore not included. Accordingly, our sample is of 22 national psychological association ethics codes that are in English or for which there are English translations. The 22 countries are Australia (Australian Psychological Association, 2007), Britain (British Psychological Society, 2009), Bulgaria (Bulgarian Psychological Society, 2005), Canada (Canadian Psychological Association, 2000), China (Chinese Psychological Society, 2007), Croatia (Croatian Psychological Society, 1996), Czech-Moravia (Czech-Moravian Psychological Society, 1998), Estonia (Union of Estonian Psychologists, No Date), Germany (German Psychological Society, 1999), Hong Kong (Hong Kong Psychological Society, 1998), Iran (Iranian Organization of Psychology and Counseling, No Date), Ireland (Psychological Society of Ireland, 2003), Israel (Israeli Psychological Association, No Date), Latvia (Latvian Association of Professional Psychologists, No Date), Malta (Malta Union Of Professional Psychologists, No Date), New Zealand (New Zealand Psychological Society, 2002), Philippines (Psychological Association of the Philippines, 2009), Poland (Polish Psychological Association, No Date), Singapore (Singapore Psychological Society, No Date), Slovenia (Slovene Psychological Association, No Date), Turkey (Turkish Psychological Association, 2004), and United States (American Psychological Association, 2010). Table 20.1 lists the countries and codes.

Many of the English translations are files on the IUPsyS website rather than on their respective association websites. The IUPsyS compendium project

Table 20.1 Countries of National Psychological Association Codes in English or With English Translations

Country	Code Name	Year
Australia	Code of Ethics	2007
Britain	Code of Ethics And Conduct	2009
Bulgaria	Ethical Code	2005
Canada	Canadian Code of Ethics for Psychologists, Third Edition	2000
China	Code of Ethics for Clinical and Counseling Practice	2007
Croatia	Code of Ethics	1996
Czech-Moravia	Code of Ethics	1998
Estonia	Ethical Principles	Undetermined
Germany	Ethical Principles	1999
Hong Kong	Code of Professional Conduct	1998
Iran	Ethics Code	Undetermined
Ireland	Code of Professional Ethics	1999
Israel	Code of Ethics	Undetermined
Latvia	Code of Ethics	Undetermined
Malta	Charter of Professional Ethics	Undetermined
New Zealand	Code of Ethics	2002

(continued)

Table 20.1 (Continued)

Country	Code Name	Year
Philippines	Code of Ethics	2009
Poland	Code of Professional Ethics for the Psychologist	Undetermined
Singapore	Code of Professional Ethics	Undetermined
Slovenia	Code of Professional Ethics	Undetermined
Turkey	Ethics Code	2004
United States	Ethical Principles of Psychologists and Code of Conduct	2010

Note. This list was accessed between June 14, 2011 and August 27, 2011. The documents available on line were rarely scanned copies of published documents, and the official name and date were not independently confirmed. Efforts were made to determine the year each association adopted the ethics code. Where no date could be ascertained, the table indicates "undetermined." The IUPsyS compendium project is ongoing, and is actively soliciting codes, translations, and corrections.

is ongoing, and is actively soliciting codes, translations, and corrections. Beyond locating a code for which the IUPsyS link was invalid, an effort was made to independently locate English translations, or to determine if there was a revised code or translation. The only additional change identified was the 2008–2009 revision of the ethics code of the Psychological Association of the Philippines.

As a preliminary methodological note, the absence of explicit provisions dealing with a matter does not mean that an ethics code is silent regarding that area. For example, a code may have a general provision requiring psychologists to provide only services for which they are competent. Even if that code does not state explicitly that psychologists only provide forensic assessments for which they are competent, the more specific forensic competency would nonetheless implicitly be required. Because the goal of the chapter is to provide a preliminary overview of how national psychological association ethics codes address civil law, the chapter examines *explicit* rather than *implicit* references to law. Additional studies may explore how civil law is present implicitly in national association ethics codes.

One method for identifying how codes deal with issues of law was to search the codes for number of uses of words and phrases such as "law" and "expert witness." Most of the codes were in portable document format (PDF), which makes searches and management convenient. Documents not in PDF format were converted. Country name was added to the document information to make the documents easier to identify in searches.

Word searches of the ethics codes presented a methodological issue. Many pages in these documents do not consist of substantive, ethics-related content, but are rather identification and reference material, such as title and copyright pages, and would therefore create duplicate occurrences of words, such as tables of content or indexes. Accordingly, such pages were deleted. Pages that were generally deleted were: title, copyright, and blank pages; tables of contents and indexes; and pages that described a revision process or overview. Pages that were retained were introductory sections and overviews of code structure and content, including preambles and introductions, definitions sections, statements of how the code is applied, decision-making sections, and appendices.

As noted above, codes that were identified as the documents of the licensing entity of the country were not included. In some cases, however, it was difficult to separate content that was devoted to a licensing process from the ethics code as such. If such content was in a document that was an association's ethics code, it was not retained.

Word searches were conducted using the Acrobat Reader full search, which provides for searching occurrences of specific words in multiple documents. Such searches do not take context into account. The word "law" is counted whether it is in the title to a section, in a section itself, or in a "see also" in another section. For the authors' immediate purpose, this is acceptable. In a more rigorous exercise, a different method might be desirable. The purpose here was to find a subset of the 22 codes for closer scrutiny, and to identify content related to the law and related areas in these codes.

"Whole word only" searches were used for word counts, meaning that a search for "law" would not find "lawful." The authors also used searches that were not limited to whole words, in which a search for "law" would find all words with those 3 letters in them. This provided tests for completeness of the word list. If a new word search found sections that referred to civil law that had not already been identified, the word was added to the word count list. If a word found no new references to law, it was not added.

The final list of words used was: law, laws, lawful, legal, legally, illegal, and statutory. Words searched that did not identify new sections were legality, statute and statutes, and various forms of regulation and regulatory. The latter two words are used in some codes to refer to licensure board activities and authority. Almost all sections dealing with issues of civil law that contain the word *regulatory* or *regulations* are identified by words in the final list. While there might be some additional sections identified by occurrences of the word *regulations*, there would be many occurrences that are not references to civil law. As an example, the Bulgarian code includes "regulations" in referring to the process for granting licensure to practice psychology. Accordingly, for this review, references to the word *regulations* were not added.

Findings and Discussion

The 22 codes vary greatly in length, the shortest (Estonia) being 234 words, and the longest (Canada) 12,125 words. Word counts were done using the documents in which duplicate materials were deleted. The average length is 5,131.3 words. Table 20.2 indicates the range of total words.

Number of References to Civil Law

Using the searches described above, it was determined that the word *law* is used 123 times in the 22 codes. The other words and the number of times they occurred (in order of magnitude) were: legal (118), laws (28), legally (27), statutory (4), lawful (1), and illegal (1). The total number of occurrences for all words was 298. The range was from 0 (Estonia) to 47 (United States). Tables 20.3, 20.4, 20.5, and 20.6 indicate the range of total words, the number of occurrences by word, the total occurrence of civil law words by country, and the percentage of occurrence in the number of words in each code by country respectively.

Table 20.5 indicates the order of codes in terms of the number of references to civil law. These data indicate the extent to which explicit references to civil law are found in the codes. This order reflects how the association views the relationship between ethics and law; that is, whether the profession's ethics act independently of law or whether professional ethics is viewed as firmly embedded in the context of

Table 20.3 Range of Number of References to Civil Law in Ethics Codes

Number of References	Number of Codes
Zero	1
1–5	6
6–10	3
11–15	4
Over 15	8

Note. Word totals are from the 22 ethics codes used in the searches. The number of references is the total of all occurrences of the words illegal, law, lawful, laws, legal, legally, and statutory.

Table 20.2 Range of Number of Words in Ethics Codes

Number of Words	Number of Codes
Less than 1,000	3
1,000–2,999	1
3,000–4,999	7
5,000–6,999	7
7,000 or more	4

Note. Word totals are from the 22 ethics codes used in the searches, which excluded pages that were defined as not content of the code or as duplication. The program "Translator's Abacus" was used for PDF word counts.

Table 20.4 Number of Occurrences of Civil Law Words in Ethics Codes

Word	Number of Occurrences
Law	123
Legal	118
Laws	28
Legally	27
Statutory	4
Lawful	1
Illegal	1

Note. Word totals are from the 22 ethics codes used in the searches.

Table 20.5 Number of References to Civil Law in Ethics Codes by Country

Country	Number of References
United States	47
Philippines	41
Australia	25
Israel	22
Ireland	21
Canada	19
New Zealand	17
Turkey	17
Germany	15
Hong Kong	15
Iran	15
Britain	14
China	8
Croatia	6
Slovenia	6
Czech-Moravia	4
Bulgaria	3
Latvia	3
Singapore	2
Malta	1
Poland	1
Estonia	0
Total References	302

Note. Word totals are from the 22 ethics codes used in the searches. The number of references is the total of all occurrences of the words illegal, law, lawful, laws, legal, legally, statutory.

Table 20.6 Percentage of References to Civil Law in Ethics Codes by Country

Country	Percentage of References
United States	0.46%
Israel	0.41%
Czech-Moravia	0.41%
Iran	0.39%
Australia	0.38%
Philippines	0.38%
Ireland	0.32%
Turkey	0.26%
Britain	0.26%
Hong Kong	0.26%
New Zealand	0.23%
Germany	0.23%
Malta	0.22%
China	0.20%
Latvia	0.19%
Slovenia	0.19%
Canada	0.16%
Croatia	0.12%
Bulgaria	0.09%
Singapore	0.06%
Poland	0.03%
Estonia	0.00%
Average Percentage	0.26%

Note. Percentages totals are from the 22 ethics codes used in the searches. The percentage of references is the total of each country in Table 20.5 divided by the number of entire words in that country's code.

civil law. It should be noted that neither position is normatively superior to the other. Rather, having no references to civil law or having multiple references to civil law may be a reflection of how the national association views the relationship between professional ethics and civil law. While some national associations see a close relationship between being an ethical professional and following civil law, other associations may view professional ethics quite independently from civil legal obligations.

The five codes having the most references to law are analyzed in greater depth for a deeper understanding of the dimensions of references to civil law in these codes. These are the codes of the national associations from Australia, Ireland, Israel, Philippines, and the United States. First, this examination will include a review of the specific subject areas each ethics code mentions in relation to law (e.g., disclosures of confidential information, informed consent). Then the examination will turn to four areas: whether each code addresses forensic activities (i.e., activities that take place in the context of civil or criminal courts), whether the ethics code imposes an obligation on psychologists to follow the law, whether the ethics code has a process to adjudicate conflicts between ethics and law, and whether each ethics code addresses human rights.

The authors recognize that other commentators might choose to examine different or additional areas. Nonetheless, these areas seemed important for a preliminary overview of how ethics codes incorporate civil law, which is what the authors intend to provide. The authors believe that an overview of these areas will convey a reasonably accurate and comprehensive review of how an ethics code incorporates references to civil law.

Specific Subject Areas the Ethics Code Mentions in Relation to Law

Each of the 156 references to civil law in the five codes were reviewed and categorized as to subject matter. Multiple occurrences of target words in the same passage were treated as duplicates, and not counted. For example, in the code from the Philippines, the passage "In instances where our code of ethics conflicts with the law, regulations or governing legal authority...." includes both "law" and "legal." This is categorized as one occurrence of the category "conflict between ethics and law." There were 37 duplicates, leaving 119 assigned categories.

Table 20.7 lists the number of occurrences of each category in each of the five codes.

As a preliminary review, no attempt was made to create exhaustive categories. In addition, many different systems of categories are possible. For purposes of the table, 28 passages were coded "other" and two coded as not related to content. The content of standards in the "other" category varied widely. For example, these include three standards regarding fees, one each from Israel and the United States regarding legal means to collect fees, and one from the United States requiring that fee practices be consistent with law. Other areas listed in the "other" category include: avoiding harm, competence, conflict of interest, ethics investigations, humane care of animals, multiple relationship, professional liability, professional relationships, public statements, record keeping, sharing data, supervision, and test security. The two coded as noncontent were used in definitions.

What emerges from Table 20.7 is that the five associations with the most references to civil law all address informed consent and confidentiality as areas that involve both professional ethics and law. In addition, the five codes also address compliance with law, which means that each code provides some guidance regarding how a psychologist should view the role of civil law in his or her professional life. This consensus among the five codes indicates that these associations view informed consent and confidentiality as having both ethical and legal

Table 20.7 Number of Occurrences of Subject Areas in Ethics Codes of Five Countries

Subject Area	Country					Total
	Australia	Ireland	Israel	Philippines	United States	
Informed Consent	10	2	4	11	10	37
Confidentiality	1	7	7	5	6	26
Compliance with Law	3	5	2	2	1	13
Conflict between Ethics and Law	0	1	2	1	3	7
Rights	4	1	0	1	1	7
Duplicate	1	1	4	15	16	37
Other	4	4	3	6	10	27
Non-content	2	0	0	0	0	2
Total occurrences	25	21	22	41	47	156

dimensions, and that following civil law in these and other areas should not be left solely in the discretion of individual psychologists without additional guidance from the national association.

Whether the Code Addresses Forensic Activities

In many countries, an important area of practice for psychologists is involvement with the legal system. These involvements range from examining individuals to assess their mental status at the time of an alleged crime, to assessing the nature and extent of psychological damage following a trauma. Examining ethics codes for references to forensic activities indicates the degree to which the psychological association deems it worthwhile to oversee this area of psychological practice. Such an overview thus provides a window into how the association views its role in regulating psychologists' involvement in a country's civil judicial processes.

Word searches are limited in their ability to tease out the nuances of language. However, such searches, as described above, helped to identify words commonly associated with a content area. In the forensic area, the words identified in the 22 codes, with their total occurrences, were court (32), witness (16—also including "expert witness" and "witnesses"), forensic (12), and testimony (4).

Of the 22 codes, five had no occurrences of these words, 14 had from 1 to 5 occurrences, two had from 6 to 10, and one had over 10. Table 20.8 indicates the number of occurrences of these words for the five codes being analyzed, and Table 20.9 provides information about the types of provisions in each of the five codes selected for further analysis.

It is interesting that two countries, the United States and Philippines, have significantly more references to forensic practice than the other three countries identified for further analysis. This discrepancy merits further research. It may be, for example, that the United States and Philippines have a higher number of psychologists involved in forensic practice, or that forensic practice is not viewed as falling under the purview of the national association in other countries so that minimal references to forensic practice are placed in those codes. It is possible, for example, that in certain countries forensic practice is thought to fall more properly under the jurisdiction of the judicial system, rather than that of the professional psychological organization. Despite this discrepancy, there is consensus among the five countries analyzed that ethical practice calls for psychologists to clarify their roles in ambiguous situations that involve the legal system.

Compliance with Law

Each of the five codes analyzed addresses psychologists' compliance with law. Two of the five associations, Australia and Israel, explicitly impose an ethical obligation upon psychologists to follow the law. The three other associations are less clear. Ireland states that psychologists "must take account of the law"; the Philippines states that psychologists must apply ethical principles in a manner that ensures their relevance to local or regional laws; and the United States says that in the process of making their ethical decisions, psychologists must "consider...applicable laws." It is noteworthy that only 40%, or two out of five associations analyzed, impose an explicit obligation on psychologists to follow civil laws. The other three associations give some measure of professional

Table 20.8 Number of References to Forensics in Ethics Codes of Five Countries

Country	Number of Occurrences of Each Word				
	Forensic	Testimony	Court	Witness	Total
Australia	1	0	0	1	2
Ireland	0	0	0	2	2
Israel	0	0	0	1	1
Philippines	1	0	8	1	10
United States	5	2	4	3	14
Total Occurrences	7	2	12	8	29

Table 20.9 Type of Forensic Provisions in Ethics Codes of Four Countries

Type of Provision	Country				
	Australia	Ireland	Israel	Philippines	United States
Clarification of Role/Confidentiality	X		X	X	X
Identifies Role/Activity		X		X	X
Testimony					X
Knowledge of Court Procedures				X	X
Use of Interpreter					X
Exception to Explaining Results					X
Modify Roles					X

Note. If a code has the type of provision listed, it is marked.

discretion to the individual psychologist regarding whether to follow jurisdictional laws.

This area is ripe for further research. In the authors' experience, many psychologists are uncertain about whether their national association ethics code requires adherence to civil law. This initial analysis suggests that the majority may not. It would be interesting to explore the discrepancy between member beliefs and the codes themselves. It would also be worthwhile to ask associations to provide a rationale for why they take a particular position in their ethics code; that is, either requiring psychologists to follow civil law, or leaving this matter to the professional judgment and discretion of the individual psychologist.

Resolving Conflicts between Ethics and Law

A question closely related to compliance with law is the issue of how psychologists should resolve conflicts between ethics and law. Four of the five codes analyzed have provisions that address how a psychologist should act in the face of such a conflict. Australia is the only code that does not contain such a provision.

The language in the Australian code may be helpful in determining why the Australian psychological association alone of the five codes does not have such a provision. In terms of compliance with law (see Table 20.10), the Australian code states "The Code should be interpreted with reference to these laws." It appears that the Australian

Table 20.10 Provisions for Compliance with Law in Ethics Codes of Five Countries

Country	Provision
Australia	Psychologists respect and act in accordance with the laws of the jurisdictions in which they practise. The Code should be interpreted with reference to these laws.
Ireland	Non-members of the Society are not bound by the Code or its associated disciplinary procedures, but like all other citizens, members and non-members alike must take account of the law, and their conduct is subject to legal sanction.
Israel	Psychologists must obey the law and encourage legislation and establishment of social policies to serve the best interest of their client and the public in general.
Philippines	Application of the principles and values to the development of specific standards of conduct will vary across cultures, and must occur locally or regionally in order to ensure their relevance to local or regional cultures, customs, beliefs, and laws.
United States	In the process of making decisions regarding their professional behavior, psychologists must consider this Ethics Code in addition to applicable laws and psychology board regulations.

Psychological Association views civil law as an interpretive lens through which to view the ethics code. If this understanding is correct, the likelihood of a conflict between ethics and law would be minimal, since any such conflict would be viewed from the vantage point of the civil law in question.

Of the other four codes analyzed, Israel and the Philippines direct psychologists to follow the law in case of conflicts between ethics and law. (See Table 20.11.) The United States and Ireland adopt a more process-oriented approach. Ireland acknowledges the possibility of a conflict, and then places the ultimate decision in the professional judgment of the individual psychologist:

> The complexity of ethical issues makes it likely that different principles and subclauses will occasionally clash; in addition, the provisions of the Code may also be at odds with legal provisions and/or other relevant guidelines. Unfortunately, the resolution of ethical dilemmas is not guaranteed to be simple… What is required, in all cases, is a considered professional judgment taken in a systematic way.

In 2010, the American Psychological Association amended the section of its ethics code that addresses conflicts between ethics and law. The previous (2002) version had stated that in cases of such conflicts, psychologists engage in a process of resolving the conflict but may follow the law if the resolution process is unsuccessful. In 2010 this language was amended to state that regardless of the outcome of the resolution process, the American Psychological Association Ethics Code may never "be used to justify or defend violating human rights." Thus, like Ireland, the United States provides for a process of resolving ethical dilemmas, but then places a limit on the psychologists' professional judgment and discretion: no outcome can allow for a violation of human rights.

The issues of compliance with law, and resolving conflicts between ethics and law, have garnered far less attention in the professional literature than

Table 20.11 Provisions for Resolving Conflict between Ethics and Law in Ethics Codes of Five Countries

Country	Provision
Australia	None
Ireland	Appendix A, Recommended Procedure for Ethical Decision Making, next to last paragraph: The complexity of ethical issues makes it likely that different principles and subclauses will occasionally clash; in addition, the provisions of the Code may also be at odds with legal provisions and/or other relevant guidelines. Unfortunately, the resolution of ethical dilemmas is not guaranteed to be simple. However, professional bodies and the law accept that practitioners may make errors of judgment, and that such errors are distinct from malpractice. The formal decision-making procedure is intended to reduce the incidence of decisions which are mistakes because they are taken in the heat of the moment, without consideration of all the relevant factors. What is required, in all cases, is a considered professional judgment taken in a systematic way.
Israel	1.2 The relationship between law and ethics. In case of a conflict between the ethics code and legal instructions, psychologists should honor the law, while emphasizing their commitment to the ethics code, and taking steps to resolve the conflict adequately.
Philippines	I.B Conflicts between Ethics and Law, Regulations or Other Governing Legal Authority. In instances where our code of ethics conflicts with the law, regulations or governing legal authority, our first step is to take appropriate actions to resolve the conflicts while being committed to our code of ethics. However, if the conflicts cannot be resolved by such means, we adhere to the law, regulations or governing legal authority.
United States	1.02 Conflicts between Ethics and Law, Regulations, or Other Governing Legal Authority. If psychologists' ethical responsibilities conflict with law, regulations, or other governing legal authority, psychologists clarify the nature of the conflict, make known their commitment to the Ethics Code, and take reasonable steps to resolve the conflict consistent with the General Principles and Ethical Standards of the Ethics Code. Under no circumstances may this standard be used to justify or defend violating human rights.

their complexity and importance merit. Indeed, many books on professional ethics written by psychologists give scant attention to this important subject, and the authors of this chapter are aware of no comprehensive analysis of how national association ethics codes address these two issues, which are at the heart of ethics and law. Further research and analysis would be highly useful in this area of our professional ethics.

Human Rights in National Association Codes of Ethics

The literatures of professional ethics and human rights have largely remained separate. With the adoption of the *Universal Declaration of Ethical Principles for Psychologists*, there has been considerable interest in how these two discourses relate to one another in the field of psychology. For the purposes of this chapter, human rights are rights that transcend a particular jurisdiction. Human rights belong to individuals by virtue of their humanity, rather than because the individual resides or works in a particular jurisdiction or belongs to a particular group of people.

Certain associations use the terminology "moral rights" rather than "human rights" in this context. The Australian code, for example, in providing definitions states "*Moral rights* incorporate universal human rights as defined by the United Nations Universal Declaration of Human Rights that might or might not be fully protected by existing laws." The Canadian code, in its definitional section, states:

> "Moral rights" means fundamental and inalienable human rights that might or might not be fully protected by existing laws and statutes. Of particular significance to psychologists, for example, are rights to: distributive justice; fairness and due process; and, developmentally appropriate privacy, self-determination, and personal liberty. Protection of some aspects of these rights might involve practices that are not contained or controlled within current laws and statutes. Moral rights are not limited to those mentioned in this definition.

Table 20.12 provides the range of the number of references to human rights and related concepts in the ethics codes. The words used for the total word count among all codes examined in the chapter are human rights (35, including uses that included apostrophes, e.g., humans' rights), moral rights (15), rights and dignity (11), fundamental rights (4), and humanitarian (1). The range of occurrences to human rights is listed in Table 20.12. Each of these words or phrases captures a concept that transcends the jurisdiction's civil law.

Table 20.13 provides the number of occurrences of each word in the five codes selected for further analysis. Table 20.13 indicates significant variation

Table 20.12 Range of Number of References to Human Rights in Ethics Codes

Number of References	Number of Codes
Zero	4
1–5	14
6–10	2
11–15	2

Note. Word totals are from the 22 ethics codes used in the searches. The number of references is the total of all occurrences of the words fundamental rights, human rights, humanitarian, moral rights, and rights and dignity. One use each of "human's rights" and "humans' rights" are included in the totals for "human rights."

Table 20.13 Number of References to Human Rights in Ethics Codes of Five Countries

	Number of Occurrences of Each Word					
Country	Human Rights	Moral Rights	Rights and Dignity	Fundamental Rights	Humani-tarian	Total
Australia	3	4	3	0	0	10
Ireland	4	0	2	1	0	7
Israel	2	0	0	0	0	2
Philippines	1	0	2	0	1	4
United States	4	0	1	0	0	5
Total Occurrences	14	4	8	1	1	28

in the language used to signify the notion of rights that transcend the specific jurisdiction, as indicated above. Table 20.13 also indicates significant variation in the degree to which the concept of human rights is found in the ethics codes. Australia, for example, has twice the number of references as does the United States, which has the least number of references to human rights of the five codes analyzed. The authors believe that these data must be placed in a developmental perspective, insofar as the presence of human rights in the codes is likely to change over time, as associations more deeply explore the relationship between professional ethics and human rights discourse. Additional research could fruitfully explore how the number of references to human rights in ethics codes changes over time.

Table 20.14 provides language from the five ethics codes that invokes concepts of human rights. This language seems to break into two broad categories: language that prohibits infringing upon human rights, and language that obligates psychologists to protect human rights. As an example of language that obligates psychologists to protect human rights, the Australian code states:

> Psychologists regard people as intrinsically valuable and respect their rights, including the right to autonomy and justice. Psychologists engage in

Table 20.14 Passages Including "Human Rights" and related concepts in Ethics Codes of Five Countries

Country	Provision
Australia	Moral rights incorporate universal human rights as defined by the United Nations Universal Declaration of Human Rights that might or might not be fully protected by existing laws. [Definitions] Psychologists engage in conduct which promotes equity and the protection of people's human rights, legal rights, and moral rights. [part of General Principle A]
Ireland	Seek an independent and adequate ethical review of human rights issues and protections for any research involving vulnerable groups and/or persons of diminished capacity to give informed consent, before making a decision to proceed. [1.3.13 in Informed Consent and Freedom of Consent] Make every reasonable effort to ensure that psychological knowledge is not misused, intentionally or unintentionally, to infringe on human rights. [3.1.7 in General Responsibility] Make every reasonable effort to ensure that psychological knowledge is not misused, intentionally or unintentionally, to harm others or infringe human rights. [3.3.5 in Avoiding Harm] Refuse to advise, train, or supply information to anyone who, in their judgement, will use the knowledge or skills to harm others or infringe human rights. [3.3.7 in Avoiding Harm]
Israel	They will honor humans' rights for privacy, confidentiality, self-expression, and autonomy. [part of Principle D—Respect of human's rights]
Philippines	We take reasonable steps to ensure that information to be disclosed will not be misused, misunderstood or misinterpreted to infringe on human rights, whether intentionally or unintentionally. [E.1 in Confidentiality]
United States	If psychologists' ethical responsibilities conflict with law, regulations, or other governing legal authority, psychologists make known their commitment to this Ethics Code and take steps to resolve the conflict in a responsible manner in keeping with basic principles of human rights. [part of Introduction and Applicability] Psychologists respect and protect civil and human rights and the central importance of freedom of inquiry and expression in research, teaching, and publication. [part of Preamble] If psychologists' ethical responsibilities conflict with law, regulations, or other governing legal authority, psychologists clarify the nature of the conflict, make known their commitment to the Ethics Code, and take reasonable steps to resolve the conflict consistent with the General Principles and Ethical Standards of the Ethics Code. Under no circumstances may this standard be used to justify or defend violating human rights. [1.02 in Resolving Ethical Issues] If the demands of an organization with which psychologists are affiliated or for whom they are working are in conflict with this Ethics Code, psychologists clarify the nature of the conflict, make known their commitment to the Ethics Code, and take reasonable steps to resolve the conflict consistent with the General Principles and Ethical Standards of the Ethics Code. Under no circumstances may this standard be used to justify or defend violating human rights. [1.03 in Resolving Ethical Issues]

conduct which promotes equity and the protection of people's human rights, legal rights, and moral rights. They respect the dignity of all people and peoples.

The code from Ireland provides an example of prohibitive language: "Make every reasonable effort to ensure that psychological knowledge is not misused, intentionally or unintentionally, to infringe on human rights."

At this point in the development of national association ethics codes, the incorporation of human rights concepts is fairly limited and not overly nuanced. Events over the past ten years, in particular those related to the treatment of detainees, have heightened psychologists' awareness of the importance of vigilance in protecting human rights. As psychologists become increasingly educated about the nature and role of human rights around the world, especially as human rights are related to psychologists' work, it is expected that this increased knowledge will result in a greater and more nuanced presence of human rights and human rights–related concepts in psychological association ethics codes.

Conclusion

This chapter has provided a preliminary overview of how national psychological association ethics code incorporate civil law. The degree to which an ethics code incorporates civil law may be viewed as one gauge of how the association views the relationship between psychology ethics and law in a given jurisdiction. Some national associations view ethics and law as inextricably intertwined. Other associations appear to see a more distant relationship, in which ethics and law function in two largely separate domains. How an association views this relationship may, in turn, reflect how the association views the relationship of the profession to the society in which the profession is practiced.

This chapter has explored several specific topic areas. Each of these areas merits further research and analysis. Consider, for example, that the data presented here suggest some associations view forensic practice as falling under the purview of the profession, while other associations appear much less inclined to bring forensic practice under the jurisdiction of the ethics code, perhaps because other systems such as courts are seen as providing more appropriate oversight. All of the associations, as reflected in their ethics codes, appear to believe that informed consent and confidentiality have firm footing in both law and ethics. The chapter has thus provided a preliminary view into where there appears to be some consensus on ethical issues, and where the associations appear to think differently about the role of an association's ethics code in regulating the professional behavior of psychologists.

In addition to specific content areas and forensic practice, the chapter explored how ethics codes regulate psychologists' behavior vis-à-vis civil law, and whether the codes provide guidance when an ethics code conflicts with civil law. The codes appear to break into two categories on this issue: Certain codes require adherence to the law, while other codes place this decision making in the professional judgment of the psychologist. One code allows for professional judgment but places a limitation on that judgment by saying that the ethics code does not permit an infringement on human rights. How an association addresses this issue in its ethics code is revealing about a number of issues. First, does the association believe that ethics supersedes law, that law supersedes ethics, or that psychologists should simply be law-abiding citizens? Second, how does the association view the role of professional judgment? That is, does the association believe that psychologists must be given strict guidance, with no role for professional discretion when it comes to negotiating ethical and legal obligations, or rather does the association view psychologists as having the training and judgment to determine for themselves how ethical and legal obligations should be ordered? The ethics code of a national psychological association provides interesting insight into this question.

Finally, the chapter explored the role of human rights and human rights–related concepts in national association ethics codes. These concepts are legal in nature but transcend specific jurisdictions. The psychological associations are at an interesting time on this issue, given the growing awareness of the disjuncture between professional ethics and human rights discourses. At present, the references to human rights and human rights–related concepts in the codes appear limited to requirements to respect human rights, and prohibitions against violating human rights. It should be expected that as these two discourses come together, a more nuanced presence of human rights will begin to appear in ethics codes. This trajectory can be empirically supported or refuted.

The chapter provided a preliminary look at ethics codes available in the English language through the IUPsyS compendium project. Although there are important limitations to the current study, and the authors look forward to reading what other commentators will say on this complex topic, the authors nonetheless believe that this chapter makes a contribution to our understanding of how civil law appears in national psychological association ethics codes. One limitation to the study includes limiting data to that derived from the IUPsyS project. The authors were willing to accept this limitation, given that this review is preliminary in nature and that the IUPsyS project clearly has put considerable effort into gathering and translating national association ethics codes. The International Union of Psychological Sciences is an organization recognized by psychological associations worldwide.

Other limitations include the number of ethics codes analyzed, and topic areas examined in each of the codes. The authors acknowledge these limitations and view them as opportunities for further research in this complex and rich topic area. The authors hope that by providing this preliminary review of how national psychological associations incorporate civil law into their ethics codes, psychologists will be encouraged both to explore this relationship more deeply, and to discuss from a normative perspective what the appropriate relationship between ethics and law should be.

References

American Psychological Association. (2002). Ethical principles of psychologists and code of conduct. *American Psychologist, 57*, 1060–1073.

American Psychological Association. (2010). *Ethical principles of psychologists and code of conduct*. Washington, DC: Author. Retrieved from http://www.apa.org/ethics/code2002.html.

Australian Psychological Society. (2007). *Code of ethics*. Melbourne: Author. Retrieved from http://www.psychology.org.au/Assets/Files/Code_Ethics_2007.pdf.

British Psychological Society. (2009). *Code of ethics and conduct*. Leicester: Author. Retrieved from http://www.bps.org.uk/sites/default/files/documents/code_of_ethics_and_conduct.pdf.

Bulgarian Psychological Society. (2005). *Ethical code*. Retrieved from http://www.iupsys.net/images/resources/ethics/bulgaria-code-eng.pdf.

Canadian Psychological Association. (2000). *Canadian code of ethics for psychologists third edition*. Ottawa, Ontario: Author. Retrieved from http://www.cpa.ca/cpasite/userfiles/Documents/Canadian Code of Ethics for Psycho.pdf.

Chinese Psychological Society. (2007). *Code of ethics for clinical and counseling practice*. Retrieved from http://www.iupsys.net/images/resources/ethics/china-code-eng.pdf.

Croatian Psychological Society. (1996). *Code of ethics*. Retrieved from http://www.iupsys.net/images/resources/ethics/croatia-code-eng.pdf.

Czech-Moravian Psychological Society. (1998). *Code of ethics*. Retrieved from http://cmps.ecn.cz/dl/ethic-code.pdf.

German Psychological Society and Association of German Professional Psychologists. (1999). *Ethical principles*. Bonn: Deutscher Psychologen Verlag GmbH. Retrieved from http://www.bdp-verband.org/bdp/verband/ethic.shtml.

Hong Kong Psychological Society. (1998). *Code of professional conduct*. Hong Kong: Author. Retrieved from http://www.hkps.org.hk/en/code.htm

International Union of Psychological Science. (2011a). *Compendium of codes of ethics of national psychology organizations*. Retrieved from http://www.iupsys.net/index.php/resources/ethics/131-list-of-codes-of-international-organizations-.

International Union of Psychological Science. (2011b). *Introduction to the compendium of codes of ethics of national psychology organizations*. Retrieved from http://www.iupsys.net/index.php/resources/ethics/130-introduction.

Iranian Organization of Psychology and Counseling. (n.d.). *Ethics code*. Retrieved from http://www.iupsys.net/images/resources/ethics/iran-code-eng.pdf.

Israeli Psychological Association. (n.d.). *Code of ethics*. Retrieved from http://www.iupsys.net/images/resources/ethics/israel-code.eng.pdf.

Korkut, Y. (2010). Developing a national code of ethics in psychology in Turkey: Balancing international ethical systems guides with a nation's unique culture. *Ethics and Behavior, 20(3–4)*, 288–296, special issue, "On International Dimensions of Psychological Ethics," edited by Mark M. Leach and Frederick T. L. Leong.

Latvian Association of Professional Psychologists. (n.d.). *Code of ethics*. Retrieved from http://www.iupsys.net/images/resources/ethics/latvia-code-eng.pdf.

Malta Union Of Professional Psychologists. (n.d.). *Charter of professional ethics*. Retrieved from http://www.iupsys.net/images/resources/ethics/malta-code-eng.pdf.

New Zealand Psychological Society, Members of the NZ College of Clinical Psychologists, and NZ Psychologists Board. (2002). *Code of ethics*. Retrieved from http://www.psychologistsboard.org.nz/pdfs/Forms from 3.7.06/Copy of CODE OF ETHICS 2002.pdf.

Polish Psychological Association. (n.d.). *Code of professional ethics for the psychologist*. Retrieved from http://www.iupsys.net/images/resources/ethics/poland-code-eng.pdf.

Psychological Association of the Philippines. (2009). Code of ethics for Philippine psychologists. Retrieved from http://www.pap.org.ph/includes/view/default/uploads/code_of_ethics_pdf.pdf.

Psychological Society of Ireland. (2003). *Code of professional ethics*. Dublin: Author. Retrieved from http://www.psihq.ie/DOCUMENTS/Code of Professional Ethics.pdf.

Singapore Psychological Society. (n.d.). *Code of professional ethics*. Retrieved from http://www.singaporepsychologicalsociety.org/code.cfm.

Slovene Psychological Association. (n.d.). *Code of professional ethics*. Retrieved from http://www.iupsys.net/images/resources/ethics/slovenia-code.slovenian.pdf.

Turkish Psychological Association. (2004). *Ethics code*. Retrieved from http://www.am.org/iupsys/resources/ethics/turkey-code-eng.pdf.

Union of Estonian Psychologists. (n.d.). *Ethical principles*. Retrieved from http://www.iupsys.net/images/resources/ethics/estonia-code-eng.pdf.

PART 4

Psychological Ethics by Region: Convergence and Divergence

CHAPTER 21

Ethics and South African Psychology

Saths Cooper

Abstract

The checkered history of South African psychology and its ethical implications underpin this chapter, from its early organizational origins in 1948, which coincided with the legalization of apartheid, to its present-day postdemocratic liberated form. The burgeoning development of psychology as a profession in the southern African region has resulted in the quest to create ethics frameworks in those countries where psychology has legal recognition, using international benchmarking. The close nexus between these countries' ethical bases is alluded to, and, while providing examples of some of the national ethical dilemmas confronted within the psychology profession during apartheid, the chapter indicates the shortcomings that have to be constantly addressed in a fast-transforming country like South Africa, which has constitutional imperatives that mandate its parliament to bring all statutes in line with its liberal human rights culture.

Key Words: apartheid psychology, professional transformation, political dilemmas

Ethics and South African Psychology

Psychology in Africa, like most professional disciplines, is underdeveloped. This is largely due to the overwhelming demands for economic survival in many African countries. Confronted with legacies of slavery, colonialism, and racism, and the postcolonial responses of military and one-party authoritarianism, ethnic irruptions, and general neglect of the desires and wants of the vast majority of the population, the denouement and visibility of psychology in Africa has been predictably low in the hierarchy of expressed African needs.

As psychology has played almost no perceived role in responding to the basic economic and survival needs of the most underdeveloped continent in the world, its efficacy as a discipline has accordingly been undermined and suffered as a consequence. Where psychology does flourish in Africa, its presence is seemingly directly related to more positive economic development, social security, and political stability. Besides certain notable countries that have enjoyed a history of psychology's presence, psychology as a university offering is scarce and its postgraduate professional representation does not seem to exist in most African countries.

This chapter will therefore concentrate generally on southern African countries that appear to have a more developed psychology presence in society, and, of necessity, will rely on the South African psychology experience specifically, without diminishing psychology's particular form and content in other African countries where it flourishes at both the scientific and professional domains.

A Concise History of South African Psychology

South African organized psychology's form and structure was traditionally white, and any black involvement was vigorously deprecated. Very little attempt was made by psychology to incorporate black concerns and reality into its content (Cooper, Nicholas, Seedat, & Statman, 1990; Holdstock, 2000; Stevens, 2001, 1990). Opposition to mainstream psychology's silence during unremitting state violence against children and youthful protestors began to grow in the mid-1980s, and enlightened psychologists, social workers, medical practitioners, and the clergy offered detainee counseling in the major cities almost surreptitiously. The first fully nonracial psychological organization, the Psychological Society of South Africa (PsySSA), responsive to the country's mental health needs was only established in January 1994, some three months before South Africa's historic nonracial democratic elections that saw Nelson Mandela become President.

Apartheid racism bedeviled the development of psychology in South Africa making it largely the preserve of the white minority (Duncan et al, 2001; Holdstock, 2000; Nicholas & Cooper, 1993; Nicholas, 1993) who comprise just over 9% of the population (Statistics SA, 2011). Given South Africa's terrible history of white minority racial domination, it is perhaps understandable that all professional disciplines have been impacted by the erstwhile oppressive apartheid system that sought to protect and promote white interests to the exclusion and expense of the black, largely African, majority (Cooper, 1990; Magwaza, 2001; Nicholas, 1990, 1993, 2001; Seedat, 1990, 2001; Suffla et al., 2001). Most ethical considerations have been located against this backdrop. The marks of psychology's origin, form, and content have influenced ethics in the discipline and have colored many of the ways that this critical underpinning has been viewed by teachers of psychology and practitioners.

The first South African psychology organization, the South African Psychology Association (SAPA), was formed in 1948 (the same year that the National Party that entrenched apartheid into formal legislation came to power) in Bloemfontein, a city in the center of the country that has been the seat of the Supreme Court of Appeals since the formation of South Africa in 1910. When in 1962, some five years after an application for membership was made, a black psychologist's membership was confirmed, a significant number of psychologists broke away to form the whites-only Psychological Institute of the Republic of South Africa, (PIRSA; Nicholas, 2008) and Prime Minister Verwoerd (who was a psychologist, and a notorious architect of apartheid racism) resigned his honorary membership of SAPA (Louw, 1997). This was arguably one of the major ethical dilemmas faced by organized psychology in the country. Although there was contestation between SAPA and PIRSA, the need to collaborate on certain issues, particularly the formal registration of psychologists (Nicholas 1990), saw them holding joint conferences and subsuming their scholarly publications under the *South African Journal of Psychology* during 1970 and 1983.

The Psychological Association of South Africa was formed in 1983, when the leadership of the breakaway PIRSA group, which enjoyed a larger membership than SAPA, felt that two organizations did not serve the interests of psychology (Nicholas, 2008). Yet, psychology's leadership remained white and overwhelmingly Afrikaner male (Duncan, Stevens, & Bowman, 2004; Seedat & Mackenzie, 2008) until the dawn of democracy in South Africa in 1994 when the Psychological Society of South Africa (PsySSA) was inaugurated. The manner in which ethical issues were formally dealt with reflected the concerns of those in the leadership and control of psychology.

The collaboration between SAPA and PIRSA resulted in the promulgation of the Medical and Dental and Supplementary Health Services Act, Act 56 of 1974, in October 1974. This national Act which came into legislative force in 1976, the same year as the Soweto student uprisings, made the registration and licensing of psychologists, psychometrists, and psychotechnicians compulsory, and provided for the establishment of the Professional Board for Psychology, under the South African Medical and Dental Council. Initially, the focus was on clinical psychology that was regarded as a poor cousin of psychiatry. Despite an appointment process that ensured that white male Afrikaner professors of psychology dominated the Professional Board for Psychology, the South African Medical and Dental Council appointed Dr. Robbertse, a psychiatrist who got licensure as a psychologist, to chair the Professional Board for Psychology from its inception and during its formative years. It was unusual to have within the membership of the Professional Board for Psychology anyone who was even a closet critic of the iniquitous apartheid system—which psychology played a pivotal role in underpinning—until 1994 when PsySSA was formed and democracy in the country was indelibly underway.

It is noteworthy that the ironies of apartheid seemed to play little role in ethical considerations, yet the leadership of South African psychology until the last decade of the last century dealt with apparent contradictions through denying or ignoring their existence, sometimes challenging their veracity (Cooper, 1990). Multiple relationships, third party influences, and conflicts of interest, particularly as these related to the maintenance of apartheid and retention of white minority power and privilege, were nuisance variables that, if considered, were routinely overlooked (TRC, 1998). Little wonder then that South Africa's Truth and Reconciliation Commission, chaired by Nobel Laureate Archbishop Desmond Tutu, had harsh words for medical practitioner and psychologist abuses during the apartheid era, particularly their shameful role in the interrogation and torture of detainees who were opposed to the iniquitous system.

Legal Status of the Discipline

Of the southern African countries, Botswana, Namibia, South Africa, and Zimbabwe have national legislation that regulates the profession and practice of psychology. It may be of interest that these countries are part of the (British) Commonwealth, utilize English as an official language, all (save for Botswana) enjoy membership of the International Union of Psychological Science (whose official language is English), and have a close affinity with psychology in the Western (and particularly English-speaking) world.

Psychology as a distinct field of university study in South Africa can be traced back to the end of the First World War, when the first Professorship in Logic and Psychology was created at the newly formed University of Stellenbosch in 1918 (Nicholas, 2008), to cater to white Afrikaners. Two years later the University of Cape Town, the oldest South African university, established a chair of psychology and psychology's higher education trajectory was determined (Cooper & Nicholas, in press). But it was only in 1976, when the Medical and Dental and Supplementary Health Services Act became legally effective, that psychology as a profession was formally recognized in South Africa (Wassenaar, 1998). Subsequently, psychology gained recognition in the other southern African countries.

Psychology in Namibia is regulated under the Health Professionals Act, which is distinct from the Medical and Dental Professions Act. The majority of Namibian psychologists are South African trained, and certain South African psychologists have itinerant practices in Namibia. The Psychological Association of Namibia has a code of ethics.

The Health Professions Act of 2000 regulates psychology in Zimbabwe. Psychologists adhere to the generic ethical code that is applicable to all health professionals. The Zimbabwe Psychological Association is working on a code of ethics that would be specific to psychology, utilizing the British, North American, and South African ethical codes in psychology (Nyanungo, personal communication, November 2010) as a foundation.

The Botswana Health Professions Council, modeled after its South African counterpart, regulates psychology in Botswana. The Botswana Psychological Association has a nascent code of ethics. The Association of Psychology of Mozambique (APM) was incorporated on June 23, 2004, and its statutes place great store on compliance with the *Universal Declaration of Human Rights* (APM Statutes, 2004). The APM is likely to incorporate an ethical code into its governance statutes.

The few psychologists who work in other Southern African countries, like Lesotho and Swaziland, rely on South African practice benchmarks. Many psychologists who work in those countries, especially as consultants, are South African trained. Should their registration and annual licensing be South African, they would presumably be answerable for ethical infractions to the Professional Board for Psychology and the Health Professions Council of South Africa (HPCSA).

According to the Health Professions Council of South Africa, there were 10217 professionals licensed in the various registers of the Professional Board for Psychology (HPCSA, 2010) as of November 1, 2010. Of the 6469 licensed psychologists reported in the previous year (HPCSA, 2009), 2434 were clinical psychologists, 1406 were counseling psychologists, 1258 were educational psychologists, 1196 were industrial psychologists, and 175 were research psychologists. On 1 November 2010 there were 769 master's level interns, 909 Masters level students, 803 registered counselors, and 1786 psychometrists. Female representation within the profession exceeds 75% (Nicholas & Cooper, 1999; HPCSA, 2009; HPCSA 2010). Licensed black professionals comprise some 25% of the profession. This more than doubles black numbers since the early 1990s (Cooper et al., 1990), with more than 80% of black African clinical psychologists being registered since the advent of democracy (Pillay & Siyothula, 2008) and the creation of the nonracial Psychological Society of South Africa (PsySSA) in 1994 (Cooper, 2010).

Besides master's level psychologists and psychology interns, there are HPCSA registers for licensed registered counselors (with a 4-year honors degree), psychometrists (honors degree professionals who administer and score psychometric tests) and mental health workers (undergraduate). Since 1999 psychology enjoys statutory equality with medicine and dentistry, with even the smallest psychology register surpassing psychiatry and the profile of psychology in the public purview increasing dramatically. Since

1998 clinical psychologists have been referred cases by the courts regarding mental capacity to stand trial in criminal proceedings. (Criminal Procedure Act, 1998).

Entry into master's degree training programs that lead to registration in Southern Africa is highly competitive. Candidates usually have to undergo a selection process and their grades have to be at least 70% in psychology. To satisfy registration requirements in Namibia, South Africa, and Zimbabwe, one usually has to have 4 years of pre-master's university education in psychology, complete an accredited university program in one of the registration categories, and complete an unbroken year's accredited internship in the category of registration. For those registering in South Africa, and who have met all the requirements, an additional professional board examination has to be taken. This latter examination primarily deals with ethical issues and relevant legislation, including cultural factors that practitioners need to take into account when dealing with a multicultural environment like South Africa. In addition, those wishing to practice for their own account as clinical psychologists have to complete a year's community service within the public health system, which all health professionals who intend to practice privately have to do, including medical and dental practitioners.

To retain ongoing licensing as a psychologist (or any other registration category like psychometrist and registered counselor) in South Africa, one has to meet continuing education (CE) requirements within a 2-year cycle. Of the 30 CE credits, 6 must be in ethics (HPCSA, 2011) a requirement that caused serious uproar when it was introduced in 2000. It was noteworthy that many professors of psychology at various, previously white universities, were in the forefront of opposition to this requirement of having ethics as a CPD requirement including some of those who were members of the statutory Professional Board for Psychology. There was general opposition to CE, and particularly to ethics being compulsory. Their clarion call was that practitioners should self-regulate, that ethics was not something that required specific attention, which was borne out by the history of psychological practice in the country, and that practitioners did the right thing. Underlying the clamor was a recrudescence of the erstwhile white control that psychology had unnaturally labored under during the previous century. The Health Professions Council dismissed as spurious the charge of conflict of interest in the leadership of the Professional Board for Psychology, and the incumbent Registrar of the Council interceded to settle the defamation action brought by the Professional Board's leadership.

Discipline of registered persons is a key function of the Professional Board for Psychology (Louw, 1997), which first published *Rules Specifying the Acts or Omissions in respect of which Disciplinary Steps May Be Taken by the Professional Board for Psychology and the Council* in September 1977 and variously amended. The *Rules of Conduct Pertaining Specifically to the Profession of Psychology* (Government Gazette, 2006) is the current legislated code of ethical conduct for psychologists in South Africa.

This legislated ethical code for psychology had its genesis in the 6th Professional Board for Psychology (the same board that introduced CE and other equity measures within the profession) and the Psychological Society of South Africa agreeing to craft an ethics code that resonated with the Bill of Rights as contained in the country's liberal democratic constitution (Constitution, 1996). Academic psychologists do not need to be registered, but cannot practice outside the university context (Health Professions Act, 1974) whereas those psychologists registered in the research category have to meet ethical and CE requirements. Research psychologists, many being academic psychologists, are subject to the disciplinary oversight of the Professional Board for Psychology, like those registered in the other categories of clinical, counseling, educational, and industrial psychology.

Titles such as psychologist, counselor, and psychotherapist are reserved for use by persons who are professionally qualified and trained and who are registered with the HPCSA, making it illegal for anyone not so registered to use any such title. However, in a country with the vast need that South Africa has, pastoral and lay counseling probably exceed that which is available through professional credentialing. The vast majority of the southern African population that is largely Christian cannot afford professional counseling and psychotherapy. Many southern African countries have counseling that is offered by voluntary interest groups, especially in the fields of HIV/AIDS and trauma interventions (the region having been plagued by the struggle against apartheid and consequent civil strife that was fomented by the apartheid regime), which operate outside the ambit of any formal or legislated quality assurance regulatory environment.

In a populace of 50.59 million people (Statistics SA, 2011) the ratio of officially qualified and licensed psychologists in South Africa is approximately

1:9,200 people. Nearly one third of the population is younger than 15 years of age, with some 7.7% being 60 years of age or older, with a life expectancy at birth of 54.9 for males and 59.1 for females. Appropriate psychological services are lacking for this demography of massive social insecurity and economic instability resulting from endemic violence, the effects of historic white privilege and entitlement, huge earnings and wealth differentials, elevated poverty, and high unemployment (Statistics SA, 2011).

Professional Associations

Southern African psychological associations are independent professional bodies that rely on member dues and receive no financial support from their governments. Membership is voluntary and there is no obligation on the part of psychologists to belong to the associations, but many do in order to enable themselves to keep abreast of professional, especially ethical, developments and to network and be exposed to the latest research and intervention techniques that may be relevant to their practice areas. Professional psychology associations interact with appropriate government agencies and departments, with many key departments relying on the advice and insights of psychologists. Psychological associations have their own internal disciplinary processes and provide guidance to members on ethical dilemmas. The ethics committee of the Psychological Society of South Africa, for example, provides confidential assistance to members electronically and as well as personally. The Society holds regular ethics workshops that focus on common infractions, interactions with the law (especially matters that are adjudicated in civil court where child custody is in dispute), and advances in the legislative environment (mandated by the Constitution, 1996) that may have an impact on ethical considerations in practice. Similarly, other psychological associations in the southern African region have ethics committees that provide assistance and support to colleagues in their countries.

Ethics Committees

While ethics committees subsisted within the various organized psychology formations, universities, and the regulatory Professional Board for Psychology, their composition and concerns were narrowly defined according to the prevailing mores of apartheid racism.

White males usually populated these ethics committees, with this provenance assuming the position of normative correctness. Legend abounds of a "*Broerskap*" (brotherhood) that kept close counsel on complaints that affected their own, with no transparency or accountability. The sense that this was a secret cabal without let was preeminent, even when the author was an established member of the Professional Board.

Any disciplinary finding when reported to the Professional Board was so terse as to be cryptic. The laudable rationale was the preservation of confidentiality, which board members were already enjoined by their statutory obligations, and all were registered persons of some standing. The irresistible conclusion was that this was the pretext for precluding scrutiny of committee activities, the Preliminary Committee being the only board committee not to present minutes of its proceedings. In a private meeting in 1998, the then chair, saying that he would deny it, mentioned that there was a complaint against a sitting member of the Preliminary Committee.

Louw states that "obligations toward fellow professionals predominate (restrain competition for clients), while specific service obligations (e.g., client trust) take up a relatively small space" (Louw, 1997, p. 193) within the ethical rules applicable between 1974–1990. Of the 70 ethical provisions only 10 "refer directly to the relationship of the professional with the client" (Louw, 1997.)

An interesting dimension was admission to the profession, which was closely guarded. In the author's case, registration was denied for two years citing imprisonment on Robben Island during 1976 to 1982 for opposition to apartheid.

The Preliminary Committee of the Professional Board remains the first line for an evaluation of ethical complaints against registered practitioners. Should the explanation proffered by the practitioner be accepted, the matter ends there. If the explanation is not acceptable and there is a prima facie case, or if no explanation is proffered, which can happen when a lawyer, incorrectly, advises his client, the matter will go to a hearing.

A controversial matter that arose during the Truth and Reconciliation Commission hearings was the simplistic and convenient diagnosis of post-traumatic stress disorder (PTSD) made by Dr. Robbertse and a few other Afrikaans psychologists, in mitigation of the atrocities committed by former security policemen who had applied for amnesty. Apparently, so traumatized were these perpetrators by the atrocities that they committed that they suffered PTSD. Such tendentious diagnostic conclusions flew in the face of the literature on PTSD. It was also probably the last public defense by those who actively supported the apartheid system, and who went out of their way to find mitigation for white perpetrators of gross human rights abuses against blacks. The Professional Board for Psychology could not act against Dr. Robbertse, as he was a psychiatrist and his psychology licensure had lapsed, but did against two other university-based psychologists, who entered into plea-bargaining arrangements. Similarly, some psychologists with court-based practices often become hired guns for one or the other side, which tends to lower the esteem of the profession and its fundamental ethical foundations.

Ethics Codes

Formal ethical codes for psychologists exist in most southern African countries. As already explained, the *Rules of Conduct Pertaining Specifically to the Profession of Psychology* were promulgated into South African law on August 4, 2006. Most of the southern African national psychology associations have ethical codes that are largely aligned with the American, Canadian, and British national psychology associations' codes, depending on the educational and intellectual proximity and nexus with those countries. Zimbabwe, for example, which had a colonial relationship with Britain, models its educational system on the British system. It is also a member of the Commonwealth (formerly British Commonwealth) and relates to Canada as it does to its neighbor, South Africa. The Psychological Society of South Africa has bilateral relationships through memoranda of understanding with the APA, the BPS, and the CPA. Many in South African psychology's leadership over the decades have had professional collaborations with colleagues from these countries. Some have taught there, and many have graduate degrees from these countries. The exposure to and reliance on the ethical codes from these established psychological dispensations is understandable.

At its annual general meeting on August 27, 2008, the Psychological Society of South Africa adopted the *Universal Declaration of Ethical Principles for Psychologists* (PsySSA, 2008). The Universal Declaration, in the view of many psychologists in southern Africa, needs to be reviewed to consider the important issue of conflict of interest and multiple relationships that may arise, especially when psychologists have to deal with government needs as opposed to the best interests of clients. This becomes even more important for psychologists globally in the changed geopolitical landscape of the 21st century, where narrow nationalism and ethnicity have become articles of faith. The closeness between organized psychology in South Africa and the apartheid leadership is no secret (Nicholas & Cooper, 1993; Nicholas, 1993; Duncan et al, 2001). Their attempts to thwart black entry into the profession in a country where blacks are the majority, their justification and defense of apartheid, even selectively interpreting psychology in the service of apartheid, have made new generations of psychologists sensitive to the subversion of ethical principles and codes of conduct. While the principles of freedom of expression and association are paramount, South African psychologists who have witnessed or otherwise experienced the nefarious effects of apartheid hold that ethical precepts should not succumb to party political interests, however democratic the latter may appear to be. To do otherwise would constitute the slippery slope of returning to the past, where conflictual and multiple relationships were acceptable, thus providing succor to oppressive and exploitative practices and systems.

Ethics Training

Ethics training is mandatory in the master's professional training programs in the southern African region that lead to registration and licensing. However, in most universities this crucial adjunct to professional psychology is taught in the breach, tagging an ethics component toward the end of the training program. With fast-changing legislation the practitioners (rather than academics) who often teach the ethics component are unable to keep abreast of the legislative minefield that practitioners have to confront currently; something that the teachers did not have to contend with when they were exposed to their ethics training. The statutory Professional Board requirement for ethics, cultural sensitivity, and violence intervention has meant that if there are no faculty members with specific interest in these areas, this knowledge has to be sourced from outside the extant faculty and can be seen as a nuisance, if not burdensome. This is revealed in the outcomes of the South African Professional Board for Psychology's entrance examination where a significant minority has to repeat the examination, which largely tests ethics and applied practice issues that have resonance in law and the polity in a multicultural environment.

There is a strong need for better ethical grounding of would-be practitioners during their postgraduate training. A much more integrated ethical understanding throughout the various course offerings of the professional training programs is necessary so that ethics flows seamlessly through all that a practitioner thinks and does. This would also reduce the burden that seems to afflict ethics teaching, which is perhaps the least sexy and exciting part of professional training programs.

Current Research on Psychological Ethics

There is some master's and doctoral level research into contemporary issues in ethics and psychology. The Psychological Society of South Africa and some of the other southern African psychological associations are reviewing their ethical codes to bring them in line with the massive socioeconomic transformations that have occurred in the region.

In South Africa, PsySSA had a code of ethical conduct for psychologists that was essentially relied on by PsySSA members and was referred to in some disciplinary matters heard by the Professional Board for Psychology. The Board tended to make ethical pronouncements on an ad hoc basis, largely in reaction to some actual or potential unethical practice. Although there were rules promulgated by the Professional Board from time to time, there was no consolidated overarching ethical code that was legally enforceable and that applied to all psychologists whether they were PsySSA members or not.

The Professional Board for Psychology at the Health Professions Council, under the leadership of the author, engaged with the Psychological Society of South Africa in 2000 to adopt the Society's ethics code. This was assented to, and a vigorous process ensued of bringing the code in line with a liberal constitutional democracy with a strong Bill of Rights. Each of the specific Bill of Rights provisions was examined for its relevance to an ethical code of conduct for psychologists. Those that had resonance and meaning for psychology became principles under which specific parts of the ethical code were then grouped, thus articulating the applicable Bill of Rights provisions with ethical precepts.

The Professional Board published this ethics code in 2000. Subsequently, the Department of Health's legal advisors interacted with the author and certain Professional Board executive members to re-craft that code into the one that is now included in South African statute books. The Psychological Society of South Africa in 2009 decided to review the ethics code, especially incorporating Bill of Rights issues, as these prove to be quite thorny for psychologists in the legal sphere. Another consideration was to align its ethics code to the *Universal Declaration of Ethical Principles for Psychologists* and to address the multiple-role conflict that psychologists have to contend with in working in conditions of conflict (like the U.S. "war on terror").

Since the notable review of ethical conduct by Louw (1997), there has not been much published on ethics in South Africa. This is probably because of the bewildering array of legislative issues that has to be taken into serious account, and, just as there seems to be some surety, another piece of legislation is promulgated or another lawyer makes a different interpretation. Very few among us would want to challenge eminent lawyers! Yet there is some doctoral research into the advances in ethics since the advent of democracy in South Africa.

The psychological associations in the southern African region are collaborating on reviewing ethical issues that are common to the region. Certain psychologists, specifically South African based, practice cross-border and it is important for uniformity in approach to ethical dilemmas that may be faced in a fast globalizing world. The national psychological associations of Namibia, South Africa, and Zimbabwe have formal memoranda of understanding, which enables such convergence on ethical issues.

Future Challenges for Psychological Ethics and Ethics Codes

In a society in massive transition and transformation, an ethical code must constantly be reviewed to ensure that it is in line with the numerous legislative changes that frequently occur. It is inevitable that the prevailing ethics code will be overtaken by national legislation that is promulgated by the country's parliament, which is mandated to align all laws with that of South Africa's constitution.

A glaring example is the universally controversial issue of child assent and confidentiality. The 2006 *Rules of Conduct* of the Professional Board for Psychology state that "A psychologist shall take special care when dealing with children of the age of 14 years or younger." The Children's Act of 2005 (which came into full force and effect in 2008), states in section 10 (child participation): "Every child that is of such an age, maturity and stage of development as to be able to participate in any matter concerning that child has the right to participate in an appropriate way and views expressed by the child must be given due consideration." Other sections of the Children's Act (e.g., information on health care, major decisions involving a child, disclosure of HIV status) are even more specific and state that where a child is "under the age of 12 years and is of sufficient maturity to understand…the implications of such a disclosure" a child has the right to have access to information and confidentiality regarding the causes, health promotion, prevention, and treatment of his or her health status. It is only when "maintaining such confidentiality is not in the best interests of the child" that confidentiality may be breached. In all matters related to children the applicable standard is that the best interests of the child are paramount, a principle enshrined in the Bill of Rights, which supersedes ethical rules of the profession and the rights of parents.

The issue of appropriate psychometric and psychological test usage in a multicultural context (Wassenaar, 1998) has been a perennial ethical minefield. So incensed were leading trade unions to inappropriate personnel and other test selection during the apartheid era that specific complaints were raised with the Truth and Reconciliation Commission. The trade union lobby succeeded in pushing for the following to be part of the Employment Equity Act: "Psychological testing and other similar assessments of an employee are prohibited." The intercession of PsySSA resulted in this being changed to "Psychological testing and other similar assessments of an employee are prohibited unless the test or assessment being used—(a) has been scientifically shown to be valid and reliable; (b) Can be applied fairly to all employees; and (c) Is not biased against any employee or group." (Employment Equity Act, 1998). Nevertheless, most practitioners relying on test results continue to use tests that are not normed and validated for over 90% of the South African population. International test developers, particularly those involved with multinational corporations, ignore the element of cultural appropriateness and the resultant test bias that emerges.

These complex issues have had an impact on ethics in the South African psychology context and must be realistically addressed to avoid the baby being thrown out with the bathwater, as nearly occurred with the prohibition of all psychological tests. Psychological interest groups and university training programs would do well to continue the critical debates on ethical issues that those outside of psychology have raised, and provide meaningful resolution of these multifaceted dilemmas.

It is most important for psychology to demonstrate its autonomy in these highly political times, and to controvert the notion that "The potential failures or shortcomings of the profession as a whole therefore are weakly addressed (if at all) by codes of ethics" (Louw, 1997, p. 194) and that ethical codes are a confusing set of arcane precepts that tend to protect the profession more than they do the public. "A mark of any discipline's relevance is its ability to keep pace with social dynamics and emerge competent to describe its purview in terms of social relevance." (Cooper, cited by Cavill, 2000)

References

APM, 2004. Projecto de Estatutos, O Ministro da Justica, Republica de Mocambique, 23 June 2004. Maputo: Associacao de Psicologia de Mocambique.

Cavill, S. (2000). Saths Cooper. From prisoner to president. *The Psychologist, 13*, 14–15.

Council on Higher Education. (2009). The state of higher education in South Africa. *Higher Education Monitor*, No. 8, October 2009. Pretoria: Author.

Constitution of the Republic of South Africa. (1996).

Cooper S. & Nicholas, L.J. (in press). Counseling and Psychotherapy in South Africa: Responding to Post-Apartheid Counseling Needs. In Moodley, R., Gielen, U.P. & Wu, R. (Eds.) *Handbook of Counseling and Psychotherapy in an International Context*. New York: Routledge

Cooper, S. (1990). Social control or social empowerment? The psychologist as social activist. In L. J. Nicholas & S. Cooper (Eds.), *Psychology and apartheid* (pp.60–65). Johannesburg: Vision Publications.

Cooper, S., Nicholas, L. J., Seedat, M., & Statman, J. M. (1990). Psychology and apartheid: The struggle for psychology in South Africa. In L. J. Nicholas & S. Cooper (Eds.), *Psychology and apartheid* (pp. 1–21). Johannesburg: Vision Publications.

Criminal Procedure Act, No. 68 of 1998 as amended. Parliament of the Republic of South Africa, Cape Town, 1998.

Duncan, N., Stevens, G., & Bowman, B. (2004). South African psychology and racism: Historical determinants and future prospects. In D. Hook (Ed.), *Introduction to critical psychology* (pp. 360–388). Cape Town: UCT Press.

Duncan, N., van Niekerk, A., de la Rey, C., & Seedat, M. (Eds.). (2001). *Race, racism, knowledge production and psychology in South Africa*. New York: Nova Science Publishers.

Employment Equity Act, Act 55 of 1998. Parliament of the Republic of South Africa, Cape Town, 1998.

Government Gazette. (August 4, 2006). *Rules of Conduct pertaining specifically to the Profession of Psychology*. Annexure 12, No 29079, Government Printer, Pretoria.

Holdstock, L. T. (2000). *Re-examining psychology: Critical perspectives and African insights*. London & New York: Routledge.

Health Professions Act. (1974). Act No. 56 of 1974. Pretoria: Government Printer.

Health Professions Council of South Africa. (2011). *Continuing Professional Development Guidelines for Psychology*, Form 277. Pretoria: Author.

Health Professions Council of South Africa. (2010). *Total No of Qualified Practitioners Registered (As at 01 November 2010)*. Retrieved December 12, 2011 from http://www.hpcsa.co.za/statistics.php

Health Professions Council of South Africa. (2009). *Annual Report*. Pretoria: Author.

Louw, J. (1997). Regulating professional conduct. *South African Journal of Psychology, 27*, 183–195.

Magwaza, A. (2001). Submissions to the South African Truth and Reconciliation Commission: The reflections of a commissioner on the culpability of psychology. In N. Duncan, A. van Niekerk, C. de la Rey, & M. Seedat (Eds.), *"Race,"*

Nicholas, L. J. *racism, knowledge production and psychology in South Africa* (pp. 37–44). New York: Nova Science Publishers.

Nicholas, L. (Ed.) (2008). *Introduction to psychology.* Cape Town: UCT Press.

Nicholas, L. J. (2001). The history of racism in professional South African psychology. In N. Duncan, A. van Niekerk, C. de la Rey, & M. Seedat (Eds.), *"Race," racism, knowledge production and psychology in South Africa* (pp. 37–44). New York: Nova Science Publishers.

Nicholas, L. (Ed.). (1993). *Psychology and oppression: Critiques and proposals.* Johannesburg: Skotaville.

Nicholas, L. J., & Cooper, S. (1999). *Status of psychology in South Africa.* Pretoria: Centre for Science Development.

Nicholas, L. J., & Cooper S. (Eds.). (1993*). Psychology and apartheid: Essays on the struggle for psychology and the mind in South Africa.* Johannesburg: Vision/Madiba.

Nicholas, L. J. (1990). The response of South African Professional Psychology Associations to apartheid. In L. J. Nicholas & S. Cooper (Eds.), *Psychology and apartheid* (pp. 50–59). Johannesburg: Vision Publications.

Pillay A. L., & Siyothula E-T. B. (2008). The training institutions of black African clinical psychologists registered with the HPCSA in 2006. *South African Journal of Psychology, 38*(4), 725–735.

The Children's Act, No. 38 of 2005, Parliament of the Republic of South Africa, Pretoria: Government Printer.

Psychological Society of South Africa. (2008). *PsySSA Council Minutes*, August 26, 2008. Johannesburg: Author.

Seedat, M. (2001). Invisibility in South African psychology (1948–1988). A trend analysis. In N. Duncan, A. van Niekerk, C. de la Rey, & M. Seedat (Eds.), *"Race," racism, knowledge production and psychology in South Africa* (pp. 83–102). New York: Nova Science Publishers.

Seedat, M. (1990). Programmes, trends and silences in South African psychology: 1983–1988. In L. J. Nicholas & S. Cooper (Eds.), *Psychology and apartheid* (pp. 22–49). Johannesburg: Vision Publications.

Seedat, M., & Mackenzie, S. (2008). The triangulated development of South African psychology: Race, scientific racism and professionalisation. In C. van Ommen & D. Painter (Eds.), *Interiors: A history of psychology in South Africa* (pp. 63–91). Pretoria: Unisa Press.

Suffla, S., Stevens, G., & Seedat, M. (2001). Mirror reflections: The evolution of organised professional psychology in South Africa. In N. Duncan, A. van Niekerk, C. de la Rey & M. Seedat (Eds.), *"Race," racism, knowledge production and psychology in South Africa* (pp. 27–36). New York: Nova Science Publishers.

Statistics South Africa. (2011). *Mid-year population estimates, 2011.* Pretoria: Author.

Truth and Reconciliation Commission. (1998). *The final report: Truth and Reconciliation Commission of South Africa.* Cape Town: Author.

Wassenaar, D. (1998). A history of ethical codes in South African psychology: An insider's view. *South African Journal of Psychology, 28*, 135–145.

CHAPTER 22

Latin and South America

Andrés J. Consoli, Rubén Ardila, *and* Andrea Ferrero

Abstract

Ethics in psychology in Latin and South America have become an important, even central area in the discipline. Latin and South American countries have advanced an organized psychological discipline by creating professional societies and *Colegios,* developing ethics codes, and writing laws regulating the practice of psychology. These countries have sought to systematize the training and eventual accreditation in psychology through regional agreements such as NAFTA, Southern Common Market, the Andean Community, and the Central American Council on Accreditation. In this chapter we review the status of psychology and psychological ethics in Argentina, Brazil, Colombia, Mexico, Peru, and Puerto Rico. All countries have developed a national code of ethics applicable to all psychologists in the country, and have instituted an ethics committee to attend possible complaints against professionals. All codes share a similar structure, highlight ethical principles, and articulate a code of conduct.

Key Words: Latin America, South America, organized psychology, ethics code, laws

Latin and South America

Considering the recent and sizable developments of ethics in psychology and the fact that ethics are involved in every academic, scientific, and/or professional action, discipline-specific ethics are becoming a central core of psychology. Ethics in psychology in Latin and South America are no exception to this trend. Framed by the conviction that acquiring knowledge and abilities in psychology should be accompanied by a solid ethical position and that such knowledge and abilities impact the welfare of clients and communities, ethical matters are addressed in most programs of psychology in Latin and South American countries.

Psychology in many Latin and South American countries started as an independent profession with the creation of the first few programs at the end of the 1940s, the bulk of them at the end of the 1950s and the 1960s, and then more in the 1970s. Contemporary programs usually involve a 5-year training sequence that seeks to integrate theoretical knowledge with supervised practice. This approach has been called the "Latin American Training Model," or "Bogota Model," as it was framed during the *I Latin American Conference on Training in Psychology* that took place in that city in 1974 (Ardila, 1975). The inclusion of ethics in the educational programs is related to the aspired integration between theory and practice.

As psychological services became a reality, so did the need to develop ethical rules to advance an ethical, scientific, and professional practice of psychology, to provide answers to an increasingly complex reality, and to address the challenges faced by psychologists in their everyday practice. While there were some psychological associations already in existence, mostly with a scientific emphasis (e.g., social, educational, research, or clinical psychology), other associations were created during the 1960s and the 1970s, this time with a professional focus (Ardila,

1986). Contemporarily, almost all Latin and South American countries have psychological associations that have developed their own ethics codes, and most of them have passed specific professional laws. In some countries, psychologists wishing to become licensed have to join these professional associations, since the associations, which may have a national, state or provincial status, are in charge of providing licensure and exerting control of the profession.

Having been empowered by the state and charged with guaranteeing sound psychological interventions and affirming consumers' welfare, the professional psychological associations developed their own codes of ethics. Over time, these codes have acquired higher levels of specificity, paralleling the discipline's own development. Latin and South American codes of ethics in psychology tend to have a similar structure. Most of them begin with a preamble, an introduction, and/or presentation, then continue with a declaration of ethical principles, and end with the ethical standards that regulate the professional conduct. One specific declaration of ethical principles in psychology in Latin and South America, that of the *Mercado Común del Sur* (Mercosur; Southern Common Market, originally a regional trade agreement that now also applies to diverse areas of society, including professions) has been subscribed to by Argentina, Brazil, Paraguay, and Uruguay as full members, and Bolivia and Chile as associated members (Comité Coordinador de Psicólogos del Mercosur y Países Asociados, 1997). The five ethical principles of the Mercosur's agreement for psychologists are: respect for the rights and dignity of people, competence, professional and scientific commitment, integrity, and social responsibility. This declaration of principles had an important impact on the development of professional codes of ethics in the subscribed countries, as professional associations eventually modified their codes to include these principles in an explicit or implicit way.

Most Latin and South American countries did not enact specific laws until the 1970s and early 1980s for the purpose of providing legal support to the practice of psychology while regulating psychologists' work in science, academics, and professional practice. In comparison to other regions, this relative delay has been associated not only with specific consolidation processes of the profession itself, but with other factors such as extended Latin American military dictatorships that were against the professionalization of psychology, mainly construed as a threat to the dominant ideology (Ferrero, 2009). In some countries there is a national law governing professional psychology, while in other countries there are state or provincial laws regulating psychological practice. In all these laws, professional competence is tied to academic competence; in other words, the competences expected of psychologists are those that should have been acquired within their education (Alonso & Eagly, 1999).

We now analyze the situation in Argentina, Brazil, Colombia, Mexico, Peru, and Puerto Rico. We have selected these countries due to their significant histories of advancing a scientific, academic, and professional psychology, and with an eye toward capturing some of the diversity and variety within the region. We discuss the legal status of the discipline in each country, the main professional associations and their role in the development of the ethics code, the current code of ethics, its relationship to the *Universal Declaration of Ethical Principles for Psychologists* (Universal Declaration), the role and functions of ethics committees, ethics training, the current research on psychological ethics, and future challenges for psychological ethics and ethics codes.

Argentina

Professional psychology in Argentina commenced in the 1950s with the appearance of the first programs in psychology. From the 1950s until the early 1980s, psychologists were considered psychiatrists' assistants, had to receive supervision from a medical professional, and could not offer psychotherapy services. The psychological community perceived this as a great paradox, considering that psychologists had 5 years of training, much of it emphasizing psychotherapy. The legalization of the discipline began in 1974 but this process was interrupted during the military, nondemocratic government that took place between 1976 and 1983. With the return of democratic governments, all the provinces passed their own laws regulating psychologists' labor. There are 24 psychology laws in total, one per province and an additional one for Buenos Aires City, as an autonomous territory, and the Malvinas and South Atlantic Islands. With a few exceptions, each of these territories has its own psychologists' organization called *Colegio de Psicólogos* (College of Psychologists). A *Colegio* grants licensure and exerts legal control over the psychological practice in a given province (Alonso, 1999; Ferrero, 2009).

Psychology laws address all aspects of psychological practice, delegate to the psychological community the power to exert the control over psychological practice by creating the *Colegios*, and ask the *Colegios* to develop a code of ethics and an ethics committee to safeguard the ethical practice of psychology. There are no specific conditions such as exams or any other kind of evaluation by which psychologists obtain their license, nor is there mandatory continuing education (CE) to maintain a license in good standing. A psychologist's license may be revoked for engaging in unethical conduct, as determined by the ethics committee. Being part of a *Colegio* is not a choice, as they are mostly obligatory membership associations (Klappenbach, 2004).

Ethics codes in Argentina were developed in the 1980s and, to a large extent, they were done in accordance with professional laws' recommendations. In 1999, a national ethics code was developed by the *Federación de Psicólogos de la República Argentina* (FePRA, Psychologists' Federation of the Argentine Republic, www.fepra.org.ar), a federation that groups all the *Colegios de Psicólogos* in the country. FePRA has no real legal power, as there is no national license in Argentina. The intention of developing this code was to unify criteria for ethical standards throughout the country, and to be a template for future codes. This code has a similar structure to the ones from the provinces: a preamble which states the objective of the codes, and five general principles: respect for the right and dignity of people, integrity, competence, scientific and professional commitment, and social responsibility (adapted from the Mercosur declaration, see above); and articles with specific norms of conduct (Federación de Psicólogos de la República Argentina, 1999). Considering that most Argentine ethics codes are more than 10 years old, FePRA is planning to revise them all, including its own.

In Argentina, the degree that meets the educational requirements for the professional practice of psychology is called *Licenciatura* (in psychology). Such a degree is obtained through a 5-year training program that includes some pre-professional practice and, in many instances, a thesis consisting of an original essay focusing on theory and/or practice. Once completed, graduates must matriculate with the *Colegio* in their jurisdiction in order to practice.

Ethics training consists mostly of one obligatory course taken in one of the last two years of the *Licenciatura*; the course addresses ethics, deontology, laws, and professional issues. This course is currently offered in 95% of the undergraduate programs in psychology in Argentina, and it will be soon be offered in all universities, both private and public. In this course, students are expected to acquire specific knowledge and to develop an autonomous and reflective position about these topics, while considering ethical dilemmas and relevant situations. In addition to this obligatory course, there is an increasing tendency toward involving students in discussion of ethical issues throughout their *Licenciatura*. Unfortunately, there is no current formal postgraduate or CE training in ethics in psychology in the country.

Current research on psychological ethics in Argentina is mainly developed in psychology departments of public universities. There are several research projects dedicated to ethical issues, focused mostly on training and professional practice. With respect to training, research projects address ethical circumstances in the teaching of psychology, ethical dilemmas that students may face during their pre-professional practicum, and supervisors' duties. With respect to professional practice, research projects on ethics are mainly focused on professional perceptions about ethics in different areas such as education, research, and clinical services, and the relation between ethics and human rights.

The field of ethics in psychology in Argentina is facing some important challenges. For example, it is necessary that all jurisdictions create a *Colegio* with legal control of the licensure, especially in Buenos Aires City where approximately a third of all the psychologists in the country live and work. Another great challenge is the need to revise and update the national and provincial ethics codes; it is anticipated that the revised versions will consider the recommendations of the Universal Declaration (Gauthier, Pettifor, & Ferrero, 2010). It is also necessary to extend the obligatory ethics courses to all undergraduate programs, and to develop postgraduate courses on ethics. Considering that nouns in Spanish are gender-specific and that the masculine noun has always been used to refer to both genders, it will be appropriate to change the traditional name of *Colegio de Psicólogos* (College of Psychologists), as the word *psicólogos* addresses male psychologists, excluding female psychologists (*psicólogas*). Therefore, not just in Argentina, but throughout Spanish-speaking Latin and South American countries, professional associations may consider the name *Colegio de Psicología* (College of Psychology), as the current name perpetuates, unwillingly, a gender-biased position. Finally, Argentina faces another challenge related to the Mercosur's policies, that of updating the terms of the agreement considering current social challenges in the region (e.g., poverty, social exclusion, marginalization, child labor, and sexual exploitation), and psychology's social responsibility to contribute to redress these challenges.

Brazil

The first psychological practices in Brazil were mainly related to professional guidance and psychometrics applied to employment and education. The first formal program in psychology was developed in 1953 in the *Pontifícia Universidade Católica do Rio de Janeiro*. Many psychological societies have been founded since the 1930s in the country. In 1954, a project regarding professional law was presented for the first time. In 1957, the Resolution 412/57 of the *Conselho Federal de Educação* (Federal Council of Education) acknowledged psychology as a specific discipline, different from psychopedagogy and psychiatry. In August 1962, the same institution passed Law 4119, which established particular conditions both for training and for professional practice in any field of psychology. Brazil was the first Latin American country in which psychology was regulated by law. The law established training criteria for the obtainment of a diploma in psychology. In 1966, the *Associação Brasileira de Psicología* (Brazilian Psychological Association) approved the first ethics code, and the *Conselho de Ética Profissional* (Professional Ethics Council) was founded with the aim of helping in the observance of the code (Ardila, 1986; Maluf, 1999). During the last part of almost two decades of dictatorial government, on December 1971, Law 5766 was passed, which created the *Conselho Federal de Psicologia* (Federal Council of Psychology) at a national level, and the *Conselhos Regionais de Psicologia* (Regional Councils of Psychology) for each state of the country. Through the creation of legally empowered professional associations, this law aimed to regulate professional practice within the country. The objectives of the associations were to grant professional licensure to psychologists in each state, to guide, discipline, and supervise the professional practice of psychology, and to insure the observance of the ethical and behavioral standards of the ethics codes. Each *Conselho* has an ethics committee. The *Conselho Federal de Psicologia* is superior to the seventeen existing *Conselhos Regionais de Psicologia*, and has legal power over the entire Brazilian territory. The goals and procedures of the *Conselho Federal* and the *Conselhos Regionais* are established in professional assemblies during the National Congress of Psychology that takes place every 3 years, when professionals either approve or reject different proposals concerning the structure of the *Conselhos* or the guidelines on training, practice, and ethics. In most *Conselhos Regionais*, human rights and ethics are permanent task forces. There is also an *Fórum Nacional de Ética* (National Ethics Forum), a national forum of ethics in psychology, which considers ethical guidelines in psychology throughout the country (Maluf, Valle Cruces, Salazar, & Linard, 2003).

All psychologists have to be part of a *Conselho Regional de Psicologia*, and a *Conselho* can determine if a psychologist is behaving according to ethical standards. A *Conselho* can assign different kinds of sanctions depending on the gravity of a given ethical violation. The sanctions range from a simple warning to suspension or even loss of license, *ad referendum* of the *Conselho Federal de Psicologia*. There are also many special-interest associations in fields such as social, educational, development, political, health, sports, forensic, psychoanalytical, and applied psychology. Additionally, there is a third kind of psychological institution in Brazil, as some psychologists have organized regional syndicates not unlike labor unions that strive to improve psychologists' salaries and working conditions (Hutz, McCarthy, & Gomes, 2004).

In 1997, Brazil joined with other neighboring countries to develop general training and ethical standards for psychologists in the region (see Comité Coordinador de Psicólogos del Mercosur y Países Asociados, 1997). The Brazilian ethics code was developed after two years of democratic debates in professional meetings, and approved by the *Conselho Federal de Psicologia* in August 2005 during an assembly in which the *Fórum Nacional de Ética* had a leading role (Conselho Federal de Psicologia, 2005). The current code specifies *Princípios Fundamentais* (Fundamental Principles) concerning respect for human rights and dignity, integrity, social commitment, and scientific and professional responsibility (www.pol.org.br). During 2009 the *Conselho Federal de Psicologia* and the *Comisão Nacional de Credenciamento e Fiscalização de Serviços de Psicologia pela Internet* (National Commission for Registration and Supervision of Online Psychological Services) developed a licensure system for online websites delivering psychological services, giving clients the possibility to check for legal certification of registered psychologists offering online therapeutic services.

Psychology training in Brazil has a deep commitment to the values of maintaining a scientific perspective, practicing citizenship, ensuring an ethical practice, and considering psychology in close relation to social issues. The 5-year psychology programs include a 2-year internship, in which students engage in supervised practices with a special focus on the ethical conditions of such practices (Maluf et al., 2003). While most psychology programs include specific courses on ethics, this is not the case in postgraduate training, where courses are mainly focused on clinical, social, work, experimental, educational, health, cognitive, psychoanalytic, and behavioral psychology (Maluf, 1999).

Research in psychology in Brazil has significantly increased during the last 20 years, especially with the support of the *Conselho Nacional de Pesquisa Científica* (National Council of Scientific Research) and the *Associação Nacional de Pesquisa e Pós-Graduação em Psicologia* (National Association of Research and Postgraduate Studies in Psychology; Hutz et al., 2004). Currently, research is focused mainly on the more traditional areas of psychology (e.g., social, educational, organizational, clinical), yet there is some focus on ethics. Some research findings have identified students' interest in ethical issues as part of their training. Ethics in Brazilian psychology are presented as being embedded in a social and historical context, which determines present and future psychology ethical standards (Machado Viana, 2000). Brazilian ethical developments are mainly characterized by democratic debates and social sensitivity, highlighting the importance of respecting human rights and promoting the welfare of people, especially of the most disadvantaged sectors of society.

Colombia

The first department of psychology was created on November 20, 1947 at the National University of Colombia. Currently there are 144 professional training programs, 19 master's programs and 3 doctoral programs. The country has approximately 34,000 psychologists and 36,000 students of psychology. The profession is regulated by the national government. The degree that prepares the student for the practice of psychology is that of psychologist. This degree requires 5 years of study, a thesis, and supervised practical training. It is a terminal degree that requires no additional graduate training to practice in the profession. The term *Licenciado/a* in psychology is not used in Colombia as in other Latin American countries. The title of psychologist is similar to a master's degree (MA or MS) of the United States, not a bachelor's degree (BA or BS). It follows what has been called the "Latin American training model" (see above, and Ardila, 2003).

In Colombia, master's programs generally require 2 additional years of training and are offered in many areas of psychology, such as clinical, community, consumer, educational, experimental, forensic, health, industrial/organizational, social, sport psychology, as well as behavior analysis, measurement and evaluation, and neuropsychology. Doctoral psychology programs began in 2002 at the University of Valle in Cali. There are also doctoral training programs at the University of the North in Barranquilla, since 2004, and at the University of the Andes in Bogota, since 2007. There are now several other doctoral programs in the making, in Bogota and Medellin, including at the National University of Colombia. There are currently few psychology PhD graduates in Colombia; the countries where they have obtained their degrees are primarily the United States, Mexico, Belgium, France, United Kingdom, Russia, Spain, and recently in other nearby nations, such as Brazil.

The first professional association organized in the country was the *Federación Colombiana de Psicología* (Colombian Federation of Psychology), created in 1954. It proposed a code of ethics in 1974. This code can be considered one of the earliest efforts of psychology in Latin America to provide an ethical framework for the practice of the profession. Later on, the *Sociedad Colombiana de Psicología* (Socopsi, Colombian Society of Psychology, www.socopsi.com) founded in 1979, proposed a code that followed international standards and used the American Psychological Association (APA) code as a model. This code, adopted in 2000, has the following sections: professional competencies, integrity, scientific and professional responsibility, social responsibility, respect for other people, confidentiality, avoidance of damage and interference in professional activities, delegation and monitoring, fees and financial aspects, presentation and professional promotion, therapeutic relationship, assessment and diagnosis, scientific research, applications and social context, relationships with colleagues and other professionals, relations with society and the state, disciplinary regime (see Sociedad Colombiana de Psicología, 2000).

The Law 58 of 1983 that initially recognized psychology as a profession in Colombia and regulated its practice was replaced by Law 1090 of 2006 (www.colpsic.org.co/resources/Ley1090–06.pdf). The *Colegio Colombiano de Psicólogos* (Colpsic, Colombian College of Psychologists, www.colpsic.org) created in 2006, introduced an ethics code within the law, which is also based on international standards. This code is the ethical framework of the profession, and is accepted by the Colombian psychological community. It replaced the Society's code, and has legal backing. It is called the *Deontological and Bioethical Code for the Practice of the Profession in Colombia*. The basic principles of the codes of ethics of psychology at the international level and those of the Universal Declaration are implicit in the existing Colombian code; namely, professional competence; integrity; scientific, social and professional responsibility; respect for others; avoidance of harm; and confidentiality, among others. The code emphasizes the formation of ethical tribunals with their corresponding legal backing, demonstrates congruence and harmony with Colombian laws and the constitution, and articulates the rules and regulations of many specific aspects of professional practice. The code is very specific and concrete about issues such as procedures, departmental bioethical psychology tribunals, and sanctions.

Colpsic is the supreme association overseeing professional psychology in Colombia, and has regulated the performance of the ethics committees. The ethics committees operate at the national and departmental level and are dedicated to disseminating the code and to monitoring its implementation and observance in the diverse fields of psychological activity in the country.

To obtain the credential to practice psychology in Colombia it is necessary to have completed a training program and to have received the degree of Psychologist issued by universities duly accredited by the national government. This diploma must be registered with Colpsic, which issues the *tarjeta profesional* (professional card, www.colpsic.org.co/sv_tarjeta.asp). It is mandatory to have this card to practice and it can only be issued by Colpsic. The relationship between Socopsi and Colpsic can be considered complementary. Socopsi emphasizes academic aspects (conferences, congresses and conventions, workshops, seminars, continuing education [CE]), while Colpsic handles legal and professional issues.

In regard to ethics training, most of the psychology training programs at Colombian universities offer formal ethics courses for one semester or more. Seminars on ethics are also offered in courses at the graduate level. In addition, ethical issues are explicitly addressed in several other subjects of the psychology curriculum.

Future challenges in relation to ethics involve the proper practice of the profession, the supervision for issuing the professional card, the adherence to the Colpsic ethics code, and the dissemination of the code within and outside of the profession of psychology (i.e., to inform psychiatrists, counselors, educators, and other professionals in allied fields about such ethical standards).

Mexico

While professional training in psychology in Mexico takes place at different levels, the entry-level training is the *Licenciatura* in psychology. The *Licenciatura* is a 4 (private) to 4.5 or 5-year (public institution) degree following high school. Toward the end of their education, *Licenciados/as* complete a thesis, or an essay based on the mandatory social service they conducted while a student, or a culminating exam. The first program granting the *Licenciatura* in psychology was created in Mexico in 1960 at the Universidad Autónoma de México (UNAM, National Autonomous University of Mexico); there are close to 600 programs currently in existence. Hernández-Guzmán and Sánchez-Sosa (2005) have raised serious concerns about the quality of the *Licenciatura*, characterizing it as long on theoretical knowledge, short on applied knowledge, and grounded in a curriculum that is largely disconnected from the realities of professional practice and the psychological needs of the community.

Degree holders (*Licenciados/as*) are eligible to obtain a *cédula profesional* (professional license). Yet, their degree must have been obtained from an officially recognized educational institution, typically a public university; an independent institute housed at a public university; or a private program duly authorized through an RVOE (*Reconocimiento de Validez Oficial de Estudios* or Recognition of Official Validity of Studies, www.rvoe.sems.gob.mx). Close to 70,000 *cédulas* have been granted since the 1970s by the *Dirección General de Profesiones* (General Bureau of Professions) of the Secretary of Public Education (www.sep.gob.mx). In addition to the existing system and starting in 1983, the Mexican government created the *Comisión Interinstitucional para la Formación de Recursos Humanos para la Salud* (CIFRHuS, or Inter-institutional Commission for the Training of Human Resources in Health, www.cifrhs.salud.gob.mx) for the purpose of regulating new programs at private institutions and to recommend RVOE granting to those deemed worthy of it. *Cédulas* are permanent and no CE is required to maintain a given *cédula* in good standing. While there is no specific law regulating psychology, there are many laws that frame professional practice, education, professional associations, and employment, be that at the national or state level, as well as *Normas Oficiales Mexicanas* (Official Mexican Norms) that regulate specific aspects of professional practice (e.g., response to domestic violence, serving people living with disabilities, maintenance of professional records; L. A. Padilla López, personal communication, November 20, 2009).

According to Hernández-Guzmán and Sánchez-Sosa (2008), the evaluation of professional competence among practitioners in Mexico and the accreditation of training programs have been largely based on the traditional terms of education, training, and experience. More recent initiatives by the Mexican ministries of Health and Education have begun to require educational institutions to provide follow-up data on their graduates, such as employment outcomes and professional achievements, in order to substantiate the granting or maintenance of accreditation status. These changes have been due, in part, to Mexico's active participation in the North American Free Trade Agreement (NAFTA) together with the United States and Canada. The Mexican government has called for the accreditation process to be standardized and regulated, and for accredited institutions to be more accountable. As such, Mexico launched a formal accreditation system, first establishing the *Consejo para la Acreditación de la Educación Superior* (COPAES, Council for the Accreditation of Higher Education, www.copaes.org.mx) in 2000. The COPAES is a nongovernmental, civil association that has as one of its many functions to grant formal recognition to independent organizations that will then conduct the examination of academic programs for the purpose of certifying their quality. Such an organization is the *Comité de Acreditación* (Committee on Accreditation) of the *Consejo Nacional de Enseñanza e Investigación en Psicología* (CNEIP, National Council on Teaching and Research in Psychology, www.cneip.org), recognized by the COPAES in 2002 (Figueroa Rodríguez, López Suárez, & Reyes Lagunes, 2005). The accreditation process is quite involved, encompassing a self-study and a site visit. As of December 2009, there are 61 academic programs accredited in Mexico.

There are numerous psychological organizations in Mexico. A recent census by the *Sociedad Mexicana de Psicología* (SMP, Mexican Society of Psychology, www.psicologia.org.mx) found 59 national organizations between associations, societies, *colegios*, and federations (L. A. Padilla López, personal communication, November 20, 2009). Besides the SMP and the CNEIP, other notable organizations include the *Colegio Nacional de Psicólogos* (CoNaPsi, National College of Psychologists), the *Colegio Mexicano de Profesionistas de la Psicología* (CoMePPsi, Mexican College of Professionals in Psychology), the *Asociación Mexicana de Alternativas en Psicología* (AMAPsi, Mexican Association for Alternatives in Psychology, www.amapsi.org), and the *Federación Nacional de Colegios, Sociedades y Asociaciones de Psicólogos de México* (FeNaPsiMe, National Federation of Colleges, Societies, and Associations of Psychologists in Mexico, www.fenapsime.org), among others.

The ethics code for psychologists in Mexico is the product of the SMP. The code is available only as a book, and it is sold exclusively through a publishing company, *Editorial Trillas* (www.trillas.com.mx). All psychologists are accountable to this national code, regardless of their membership in the SMP or their factual or alleged lack of knowledge of the code's existence. The original code, published in 1984, was largely based on the 1977 version of the ethics code of the APA, among other sources. Hernández-Guzmán and Sánchez-Sosa (2005) credit Mexico's involvement with the Trilateral Forum on Professional Psychology in North America as an important impetus for updating the code. The Forum has focused on matters related to psychologists' international mobility within the United States, Canada, and Mexico; the exchanges of students, researchers, and professionals; and the advancement of a North American ethics meta-code for psychologists, among others.

A revised version of the 1984 ethics code was arrived at through a comprehensive process involving two studies (Hernández-Guzmán & Ritchie, 2001). The first study found the 1984 code falling short in many areas. For example, it mostly failed to link the principles with the norms of conduct specified in the code. There were instances where the principle was not accompanied by a norm of conduct, as there were instances where the norm of conduct did not seem to be based on a given principle. Similarly, the original code included many ambiguous statements and was found to be lacking in specificity with respect to the values informing the expected conduct by a psychologist. The code also focused almost exclusively on clinical psychology situations, particularly individual therapy, and neglected other areas of psychology and other forms of service provisions such as group and family therapy. The second study consisted of a national survey of practitioners in Mexico asking participants to describe their activities as psychologists, to specify the contexts of employment, and to share a critical incident involving an ethical concern that the respondent or a colleague experienced in the prior 2 years. The most frequent concerns expressed by participants involved matters related to professional incompetence (34%), inappropriate academic and scientific conduct (23%), sexual harassment or sexual relationships with patients or students (16%), misuse of psychological assessments or misinterpretation of the results (12%), and problematic dual relationships (8%).

The current, revised code sought to overcome the shortcomings of the original version of the code and to be centered around four purposes: to protect consumers of psychological services, to connect general principles with norms of conduct, to address all areas of psychology, and to provide support to psychologists in their ethical decision making. The code is structured into two main parts; the first concerns general principles, while the second involves norms of conduct. The first part makes it clear that the welfare of consumers, be they individuals, groups, or organizations, is the most important guiding principle in psychologists' actions. This guiding principle is operationalized into four interdependent principles that constitute the bases for the norms of conduct in the second part: respect for the rights and dignity of people, responsible care, integrity in relationships, and responsibility to society and humanity. Particularly noteworthy is a value statement contained under the heading on respect for the rights and dignity of people; it holds psychologists responsible for respecting, protecting, and advancing the rights of people to "privacy, self-determination, personal liberty, and justice... informed consent, confidentiality, autonomy..." (Sociedad Mexicana de Psicología, 2007, p. 39). The four principles in this first part parallel those that characterize the *Universal Declaration* (for an overview of the *Universal Declaration* see Chapter 9).

Also in its first part, the code details a range of ways that psychologists may be sanctioned, should they incur any violations of the ethics code. The sanctions extend from admonishments to license suspension or revocation. The main body that recommends the sanctions is the *Comité Nacional de Ética en Psicología* (CoNaEP, National Committee on Ethics in Psychology), which was created in 2000 and it is part of the SMP. The CoNaEP is constituted by a general advisory board including an executive secretary, a specialized technical board, each with nine members and representing the different and diverse areas of psychology in Mexico, and a judicial advisory board of four lawyers (L. A. Padilla López, personal communication, January 14, 2010). Ethical complaints are to be submitted to the presidency of the SMP, which will then seek input and recommendations from the CoNaEP. It should be noted that the code encourages informal resolutions of ethical concerns, as long as such an approach is appropriate vis-à-vis the concern and as long as confidentiality is not compromised. Formal complaints may involve the CoNaEP as well as other pertinent bodies that govern, for example, the granting of *cédulas* (see above).

The second part of the code details the norms of conduct and it is organized into three chapters encompassing 149 articles. The chapters address the quality of the work performed by psychologists that ought to be characterized by competence and honesty, proper communication and confidentiality of the results obtained, and sound relationships. The code discourages dual or multiple relationships, prohibits sexual relationships with clients, students, or supervisees, and emphasizes the importance of informed consent and confidentiality. The norms of conduct address the multiple areas of psychologists' scope of practice including service delivery, consultation, research, publishing, teaching, training, and supervision, among others.

While research on ethics is limited, what is particularly noteworthy in the case of Mexico is the systematic effort in keeping the code of ethics current. The code has been described as a dynamic document and the SMP is presently engaged in the seventh wave of surveys of psychologists in Mexico, utilizing the critical incident technique, for the purpose of revising and updating the code. The input received has been used to modify the code accordingly. For example, forensic psychologists appointed by a court sought to have clarified in the code their allegiances to a judge in the case of child custody evaluations (L. Hernández-Guzmán, personal communication, November 20, 2009). The most recent version of the code reviewed for this chapter (Sociedad Mexicana de Psicología, 2007) maintains language that is gender-exclusive in its title (*psicólogo*) and content (*psicólogos*); the next version of the code ought to address this issue and resort to gender inclusive language.

Colleague experts in Mexico consulted for this chapter identified several future challenges for psychological ethics (see Author Note for experts' names). Specifically, colleagues expressed concern with the proliferation of programs, be they in psychology or in related fields, that claim to train professionals for the practice of psychology but do not properly prepare their graduates. Colleagues highlighted the need to have the teaching of ethics better integrated into all curricula and at all levels of training. A particular goal is to have ethical matters be made a requirement in the curricula of all duly recognized *Licenciaturas*. Mexico has made significant inroads in the formal accreditation of programs, even when approximately only 1 out of 10 programs are currently accredited under the present system; as Mexico moves toward certification and credentialing at the postgraduate level, advanced ethics training needs to be part of such certification and credentialing. A frequently cited matter was the need to better educate the consumer of psychological services to help them discern the quality of the professional services received. The CoNaEP is working on developing new products based on the current ethics code that would help consumers, students, and professional alike (L. A. Padilla López, November 20, 2009, personal communication). It is noteworthy that while the code of ethics is designed to affirm the welfare of the consumer of professional services, the actual code is not freely available to such a consumer. Finally, Mexican colleagues expressed concerns with the *cédula* system, as it is a permanent license that has no CE requirements; mandated CE could include covering changes to later versions of the code, and an assessment of practical, ethical knowledge could be part of such CE.

Peru

Psychology in Peru has a long history and a very positive present situation. The native inhabitants of the territory (pre-Incas and Incas) had ideas about topics that we call psychological before the arrival of Europeans to the current Peruvian territory. This field of research of native psychologies is quite promising in Peru's case, and their study remains a pending task. The contributions of Walter Blumenfeld (1882–1967) to experimental psychology and psychological measurement, and Honorio Delgado (1892–1969) to psychoanalysis in Peru have been well documented (see Alarcón, 2000, for an historical description of psychology in Peru beginning with the Spanish colonial days).

Professional psychology studies began in 1955 at the *Universidad de San Marcos*. There are currently 36 psychology training programs that confer professional degrees that accredit the practice of psychology as a profession. The professional training lasts between 5 and 6 years. It is a generalist training in all the areas of psychology and some related disciplines; it includes a thesis and a professional supervised practice. Depending on the university, the degree granted is that of *Licenciado/a* in psychology, or Psychologist. There are also several master's programs that began in the mid-1980s, and four doctoral programs of international quality. The universities offering a doctoral degree include San Marcos, Inca Garcilaso de la Vega, San Martín de Porres, and Femenina. A master's degree is required to be eligible for admission to the doctoral program. In Peru in 2006 there were approximately 11,500 psychologists and 10,000 psychology students (see Asamblea Nacional de Rectores, 2006). The growth of the profession in recent years has been substantial.

Research and practical work is done by Peruvian psychologists in all areas of psychology as a science and profession. There is a particular emphasis on topics related to the socioeconomic development problems of Peru. Work on nutrition, poverty, child development, the personality of Peruvians, and similar topics have interested psychologists for several decades.

The *Sociedad Peruana de Psicología* (Peruvian Society of Psychology), founded in 1954, was the association and scientific entity that initially brought Peruvian psychologists together. Associations concerning specific emphases such as clinical psychology, behavior analysis, educational psychology, and others were created later and have voluntary membership. These associations, and mainly the *Sociedad Peruana de Psicología*, had a very important role in the organization of the profession, scientific research, publications, congresses, training, and the inclusion of psychology in Peruvian society.

The *Colegio de Psicólogos del Perú* (Peruvian College of Psychologists, www.colegiodepsicologosdelperu.org) is more recent. It was created in 1980, has formal legal backing, and membership in it is required for the practice of the profession. The profession is regulated by the state. Law 23109 of April 30, 1980, officially recognized the profession of psychology and created the *Colegio*. The *Colegio* has legal control of the profession, as in other countries (e.g., Colombia and several others).

Ethics is a field of great relevance to Peruvian psychologists, and specific courses on the subject are offered in several faculties of psychology. There is a professional code of ethics of Peruvian psychologists, which is the work of the *Colegio*. This code begins with a declaration of principles and then refers specifically to responsibility, competence, legal and moral standards, confidentiality, public statements, consumer well-being, utilization of diagnosis techniques, psychological reports, professional relations, relations with institutions, research, intellectual property, appointments, promotions and contests, fees, and working hours, among other matters.

This ethical code, of a mandatory character and based on the law, is similar to other codes and is grounded on agreements and convergences with the profession of psychology at the international level. The ethics code of the APA has been the basis of many codes in other nations of the world, including Latin American nations, among them Peru.

Puerto Rico

While the history of psychology in Puerto Rico can be traced to pre-Columbian times (see González Rivera, 2006), its more recent history can be dated to the earlier part of the 20th century when Puerto Rican nationals travelled to the United States and received graduate training in psychology. Upon their return to Puerto Rico, they sought to teach psychology and began one of the first programs at the Universidad de Puerto Rico in 1943 (Boulon-Díaz, 2006). Professional psychologists have been imparting services in Puerto Rico since the late 1940s, early 1950s.

The Law 96 of June 4, 1983 regulates the practice of psychology in Puerto Rico (www.lexjuris.com/lexmate/profesiones/lex103.htm). The law has been amended since, perhaps most notably to promote psychological services in public schools (Law 170, August 12, 2000), among other changes (Roca de Torres, 2003). Law 96 created the *Junta Examinadora de Psicólogos de Puerto Rico* (JEPPR, Puerto Rican Examining Board of Psychology), which is charged with developing and implementing proper examinations for psychology candidates seeking to obtain a psychology license. The law also establishes the degree and practice requirements, including a number of supervised practice hours, to sit for the examination (Rivera & Maldonado, 2000). A doctoral degree (PhD or PsyD) is required of those candidates seeking licensure as clinical psychologists, while a master's degree (MA or MS) is required for all other areas (e.g., social-community, industrial-organizational, academic-research, school, counseling) (Boulon-Díaz, 2006). Licensed psychologists in Puerto Rico are required to renew their license every three years, and must complete 45 hours of CE to do so. The JEPPR evaluates the CE credits; currently, it requires that three of the 45 hours address content related to the transmission of infectious diseases, specifically AIDS, tuberculosis, and/or hepatitis. As of 2005, over 2600 licenses had been issued in Puerto Rico, 1900 of which were active as of 2006 (Boulon-Díaz, 2006). Supervisors in all areas of psychology must have a license that is in good standing in order to carry out their duties in compliance with the law.

An important duty of the JEPPR is the development and governance of an ethics code. This includes investigating and adjudicating complaints involving licensed psychologists through its ethics committee. The JEPPR's ethics code is applicable to all licensed psychologists in Puerto Rico. The code was published on September 17, 1992, and was included in the document entitled "General Regulations 4785" of the JEPPR. The code contains a preamble and ten principles: responsibility, competence, moral and legal norms, public statements, confidentiality, well-being of the consumer, collegial relationships, psychological evaluations, research with human subjects, and care and use of animals in research. Furthermore, the code specifies a range of penalties. Violations of the code may be punished by revocation or suspension of license, denial of a license to an applicant, fines, or other sanctions. A revised version of the code was arrived at in 2002 but it has not been adopted as yet. The changes proposed include the use of gender-inclusive language and adding a new principle concerning teaching and supervision in psychology. There have been a limited number of publications addressing ethical matters in Puerto Rico (e.g., Colberg, 2008; Rodríguez Arocho, 2005).

Several other laws exist that shape the practice of psychology in Puerto Rico, most notably Law 408, known as the *Ley de Salud Mental de Puerto Rico* (Puerto Rican Mental Health Law, www.lexjuris.com/LEXLEX/Leyes2000/lex2000408.htm), amended by Law 183 of August 6, 2008, and the law concerning intervention in domestic violence, among others. Due to Puerto Rico's status as an *Estado libre asociado* (i.e., commonwealth) of the United States, federal laws such as the Federal Rules of Evidence and the American with Disabilities Act also shape the practice of psychology on the island (I. Belén, personal communication, October 26, 2009).

The largest national organization of psychologists in Puerto Rico is the *Asociación de Psicología de Puerto Rico* (APPR, Puerto Rican Psychological Association, www.asppr.net). Founded in 1954, it is an independent organization supported by membership fees and affiliated with the APA. Membership in the APPR by psychologists is voluntary. The APPR's mission is to "promote the scientific advancement of psychology and a responsible professional practice that contributes to the health and well-being of the Puerto Rican society" (www.asppr.net). The APPR publishes an indexed journal, the *Revista Puertorriqueña de Psicología* (RePS, Puerto Rican Journal of Psychology) once a year. In addition, the APPR has its own ethics code (www.asppr.net/pdf/codigo_etica_appr_07.pdf) and an ethics committee. The ethics code of the APPR consists of a preamble and 17 principles covering responsibility, competence, moral and legal norms, impersonation, public statements, confidentiality, well-being of the person, proper advertisement of services, collegial relationships, remuneration, psychological evaluations (privacy, consent, use, interpretation and dissemination), research considerations, and credit given to authors in publications. This ethics code applies only to APPR's members. Finally, the APPR organizes a well-attended annual conference and is a recognized provider of CE training for psychologists in Puerto Rico.

Ethics training in Puerto Rico takes place mostly at the graduate level. Most commonly, ethical and legal content is infused into courses such as practicum, psychological evaluation, and research. In the case of the latter, there is an emphasis on the protection of human participants, wherein an institutional review board must approve research projects that involve participants. There are some CE opportunities to further knowledge on ethics and laws, yet there is no mandate to cover such topics in license renewals. Coverage of ethical matters in psychology at the undergraduate level is quite limited.

Expert colleagues in Puerto Rico who were consulted for this chapter identified several future challenges for psychological ethics and the Puerto Rican ethics code (see Author Note for experts' names). Specifically, they identified a need to consider and address professional matters such as the complexities of adopting (or not) foreign, evidence-based practices, contemporary issues such as the use of technological communication tools in psychological practice, and social issues such as migration, changing families, and international tensions, among others (F. Boulon-Díaz, personal communication, November 9, 2009). Puerto Rican psychologists are currently concerned about the use of psychological evaluation instruments that have been standardized in other countries, a preoccupation reflected in the 2008 edition of the RePS (http://web.me.com/nvaras/RePS/Vol_19_-_2008.html). Colleagues agreed on the need for licensed psychologists and students alike to increase their exposure to the ethics code and competence in applying ethical principles to problem solving. They believed that more CE courses should be available for licensed psychologists addressing ethical matters. In fact, the JEPPR has considered establishing a required course on ethics among the 45 hours required every 3 years for license renewal. An important pending matter is the update of the ethics code; the draft of October 17, 2002 has not been adopted as of yet, making the 1992 version of the code the one in force. A future revision of the code may want to address its relationship to the Universal Declaration. Meanwhile, the Universal Declaration has been included already as required reading for ethics courses in graduate programs in Puerto Rico.

Another important matter concerns the minimal resources of the Department of Health assigned to the JEPPR, impacting the implementation of ethics regulations. There is currently markedly limited legal and secretarial staff, which affects the ability of the board to investigate and process complaints in a timely manner. Finally, Puerto Rican colleagues expressed a desire to see the institutional review processes for research protocols within and outside universities disseminated, standardized, and implemented across institutions and the country and, most importantly, for these processes to include more systematic training of research assistants and principal investigators on ethical matters.

Conclusion

Congruent with trends in the rest of the world, ethics in psychology in Latin and South America have become an important, even central area in the discipline. Countries in Latin and South America have advanced an organized psychological discipline through the creation of professional societies and *Colegios* that in turn develop ethics codes, and, through political advocacy, culminating in provincial, state, federal, or national laws regulating the practice of psychology. Furthermore, countries in Latin and South America have sought to systematize the training and eventual accreditation in psychology through regional agreements such as NAFTA, Mercosur, the *Comunidad Andina* (CAN, Andean Community, www.comunidadandina.org), and, more recently, the *Consejo Centromericano de Acreditación de la Educación Superior* (CCA, Central American Council on Accreditation of Higher Education, www.cca.ucr.ac.cr).

The legal and ethical status of psychology in the specific countries reviewed for this chapter has many similarities and some differences. Perhaps with the exception of Mexico, all countries have national laws regulating the practice of psychology. Puerto Rico was the only country requiring a doctoral degree for the practice of clinical psychology or a master's degree for all other areas of psychology, and the only one requiring continuing education training as part of the license renewal process.

All countries have developed a national code of ethics applicable to all psychologists in the country, and have instituted an ethics committee to attend possible complaints against professionals. While all countries resorted to expert consensus to arrive at the current code of ethics, it appears that only Mexico has engaged in systematic research to update its code (see Hernández-Guzmán & Ritchie, 2001; Pettifor & Sawchuk, 2006). All codes share a similar structure (see introduction), highlight ethical principles, and articulate a code of conduct. At the center of most codes is the welfare of the people and communities psychologists seek to serve. Not all codes are readily available via electronic means. This matter should be addressed immediately, as it compromises access to the code not only by psychologists but, most importantly, by consumers, and prevents the profession from making good on its commitment to individual and community welfare. Due to the recency of the adoption of the Universal Declaraion, none of the codes have been able to reference it, yet there is a strong similarity in the language of the Universal Declaration and some of the codes. And ethic courses in many Latin and South American countries address the Universal Declaration already.

Author Note

Andrés Consoli would like to acknowledge Jorge Mario Flores Osorio, Martha Givaudán, Laura Hernández-Guzmán, and Luis Alfredo Padilla López (Mexico); Inés Belén, Frances Boulon-Díaz, Domingo Marqués, Wanda Rodríguez, Irma Serrano García, José Toro Alfonso, and Nelson Varas Díaz (Puerto Rico); and Melissa Morgan for their collaboration. Rubén Ardila would like to acknowledge Colpsic, Socopsi, the *Colegio Peruano de Psicólogos* (Peruvian College of Psychologists), the *Sociedad Peruana de Psicología* (Peruvian Society of Psychology), Reynaldo Alarcón, José Anicama, María Mercedes Botero, Diego Castrillón, Nelly Ugarriza, and Gloria Amparo Vélez for their collaboration on Colombia and Peru. Andrea Ferrero would like to acknowledge FePRA, the *Conselho Federal de Psicologia* (Federal Council of Psychology), Modesto Alonso, Ana María Hermosilla, and Ana Jaco-Vilela, for their collaboration on Argentina and Brazil.

References

Alarcón, R. (2000). *Historia de la psicología en el Perú. De la colonia a la república* [A history of psychology in Peru. From the colonial times to the republic]. Lima, Peru: Universidad Ricardo Palma.

Alonso, M. (1999). Argentina. In M. Alonso & A. Eagly (Eds.), *Psicología en las Américas* [Psychology in the Americas] (pp. 25–45). Buenos Aires, Argentina: Sociedad Interamericana de Psicología.

Alonso, M., & Eagly, A. (1999). *Psicología en las Américas* [Psychology in the Americas]. Buenos Aires, Argentina: Sociedad Interamericana de Psicología.

Ardila, R. (1975). The first Latin American conference on training in psychology. *International Journal of Psychology, 10*, 149–158.

Ardila, R. (1986). *La psicología en América latina. Pasado, presente y futuro* [Psychology in Latin America: Past, present, and future]. Mexico, DF: Siglo XXI Editores.

Ardila, R. (2003). ¿Qué tipo de psicólogo queremos formar en América Latina para el nuevo siglo? El "Modelo Bogotá" tres décadas más tarde [What kind of psychologist do we want to train in Latin America for the new century? The "Bogota model" three decades later]. In J. F. Villegas, P. Marassi, & J. P. Toro (Eds.). *Problemas centrales para la formación académica y el entrenamiento profesional del psicólogo en las Américas* [Central problems for the academic formation and professional training of psychologists in the Americas] (Vol. 3, pp. 139–148). Santiago, Chile: Sociedad Interamericana de Psicología.

Asamblea Nacional de Rectores. (2006). *La carrera de psicología en el Perú* [The psychology career in Peru]. Lima, Peru: Grupo de Trabajo de la Carrera de Psicología.

Boulon-Díaz, F. (2006). La psicología como profesión en Puerto Rico: Desarrollo y nuevos retos [Psychology as a profession in Puerto Rico: Developments and new challenges]. *Revista Puertorriqueña de Psicología, 17*, 215–240.

Colberg, E. M. (Ed.) (2008). *Una mirada a la ética: Desde la perspectiva de la psicología en Puerto Rico* [A view on ethics: From the perspective of psychology in Puerto Rico]. San Juan, PR: Publicaciones Puertorriqueñas.

Comité Coordinador de Psicólogos del Mercosur y Países Asociados. (1997). Protocolo de acuerdo marco de principios éticos para el ejercicio profesional de los psicólogos en el Mercosur y Países Asociados [Agreement protocol on the framework of ethical principles for the professional practice of psychologists in the Mercosur and associated countries]. In Conselho Federal de Psicologia (Ed.), *A psicologia no MERCOSUL* [Psychology in MERCOSUL] (pp. 2–5). Brasilia, Brazil: Author.

Conselho Federal de Psicologia. (2005). *Código de ética profissional do psicólogo* [Professional ethics code for psychologists]. Brasilia, Brazil: Author.

Federación de Psicólogos de la República Argentina (1999). *Código de ética* [Ethics code]. Buenos Aires, Argentina: Author.

Ferrero, A. (2009). A South American experience of the transition from dictatorship to democracy. In D. Wedding & M. J. Stevens (Eds.), *Psychology: IUPsyS global resource* (CD-ROM) (10th Ed.). Hove, UK: Psychology Press.

Figueroa Rodríguez, S., López Suárez, A. D., & Reyes Lagunes, I. (2005). Origen, trayectoria y perspectiva del organismo acreditador de programas de psicología en México [Origin, path and perspectives of the entity accrediting psychology programs in Mexico]. *Revista Mexicana de Psicología, 22,* 287–292.

Gauthier, J., Pettifor, J., & Ferrero, A. (2010). The Universal Declaration of Ethical Principles for Psychologists: A culture-sensitive model for creating and reviewing a code of ethics [Special issue]. *Ethics & Behavior, 20,* 179–196.

González Rivera, S. (2006). Apuntes sobre las ideas psicológicas en Puerto Rico: Desde el periodo precolombino hasta el siglo XIX [Notes on the psychological ideas in Puerto Rico: From the pre-Columbian period to the XIX century]. *Revista Puertorriqueña de Psicología, 17,* 3–25.

Hernández-Guzmán, L., & Ritchie, P. L. J. (2001). Hacia la transformación y actualización empíricas del código ético de los psicólogos mexicanos [Toward the transformation and updating of the ethics code of Mexican psychologists]. *Revista Mexicana de Psicología, 18,* 347–357.

Hernández-Guzmán, L., & Sánchez-Sosa, J. J. (2005). El aseguramiento de la calidad de los programas de formación en psicología profesional en México [Quality assurance of profesional psychology in Mexico]. *Revista Mexicana de Psicología, 22,* 271–286.

Hernández-Guzmán, L., & Sánchez-Sosa, J. J. (2008). Latin America. In J. E. Hall & E. M. Altmaier (Eds.), *Global promise: Quality assurance and accountability in professional psychology* (pp. 109–127). New York, NY: Oxford University Press

Hutz, C., McCarthy, S., & Gomes, W. (2004). Psychology in Brazil: The road behind and the road ahead. In M. J. Stevens & D. Wedding (Eds.), *Handbook of international psychology* (pp. 151–168). New York, NY: Brunner-Routledge.

Klappenbach, H. (2004). Psychology in Argentina. In M. J. Stevens & D. Wedding (Eds.), *Handbook of international psychology* (pp. 129–150). New York, NY: Brunner-Routledge.

Machado Viana, F. (2000). Psicología e ética: Mercosul buscando consensos integradores [Psychology and ethics: Mercosur looking for integration agreements]. In O. Calo & A. M. Hermosilla (Eds.), *Psicología, ética y profesión: Aportes deontológicos para la integración de los psicólogos del Mercosur* [Psychology, ethics and profession: Deontological contributions for psychologists' integration in the Mercosur] (pp. 135–137). Mar del Plata, Argentina: Universidad Nacional de Mar del Plata.

Maluf, M. (1999). La psicología en el Brasil [Psychology in Brazil]. In M. Alonso & A. Eagly (Eds.), *Psicología en las Américas* [*Psychology in the Americas*] (pp. 67–83). Buenos Aires, Argentina: Sociedad Interamericana de Psicología.

Maluf, M., Valle Cruces, A., Salazar, R., & Linard, V. (2003). Os procedimentos pra autorização e reconhecimento de cursos de graduação em psicologia no Brasil [Procedures for acceptance and recognition of undergraduate programs in psychology in Brazil]. In J. Villegas, P. Marassi, & J. P. Toro (Eds.), *Problemas centrales para la formación académica y el entrenamiento profesional del psicólogo en las Américas* [Central problems for the academic formation and professional training of psychologists in the Americas] (Vol. 3, pp. 59–84). Santiago, Chile: Sociedad Interamericana de Psicología.

Pettifor, J., & Sawchuk, T. (2006). Psychologists' perceptions of ethically troubling incidents across international borders. *International Journal of Psychology, 41,* 216–225.

Rivera, B., & Maldonado, L. (2000). Revisión histórica de la reglamentación de la Psicología en Puerto Rico: 1954–1990 [Historical review of regulations in psychology in Puerto Rico: 1954–1990]. *Revista Interamericana de Psicología, 34,* 127–162.

Roca de Torres, I. (2003). Educación profesional en psicología en Puerto Rico: Problemas centrales [Professional education in psychology in Puerto Rico: Central problems]. *Revista Puertorriqueña de Psicología, 14,* 147–179.

Rodríguez Arocho, W. (2005). El código de ética profesional en la psicología [The code of professional ethics in psychology]. In G. Bernal & A. Martínez Taboas (Eds.), *Teoría y práctica de la psicoterapia en Puerto Rico* (pp. 318–336). San Juan, PR: Publicaciones Puertorriqueñas.

Sociedad Colombiana de Psicología (2000). *Código ético del psicólogo* [Psychologist's ethics code]. Bogota, Colombia: Editorial ABC.

Sociedad Mexicana de Psicología (2007). *Código ético del psicólogo* [Psychologist's ethics code]. Mexico, DF: Trillas.

CHAPTER 23

North America: Canada and the United States

Gerald P. Koocher *and* Thomas Hadjistavropoulos

Abstract

Professional licensing and ethics codes of psychologists in the United States and Canada have very similar roots, but also many distinctive elements that represent regional and national jurisdictional differences and traditions. Each national psychological association has a distinctive ethics code with foundations in a strong national consensus. Both nations require substantial standardized educational and credential requirements as prerequisites for psychological practice. Few psychologists in the United States have any awareness of the International Union of Psychological Science or its relatively recent *Universal Declaration of Ethical Principles*, although many of the fundamentals of the Canadian code align more homogenously with that document.

Key Words: Canada, ethics, licensing, North America, United States

Many aspects of the regulation of psychology (e.g., types of examinations and credentials required to become a qualified psychological service provider) and matters relating to the use of ethics codes in training and in regulation are similar in the United States and Canada.[1] In this chapter we discuss the legal status of the discipline, professional associations, ethics committees, ethics training, and related challenges in each of the two countries, highlighting similarities as well as differences.

Legal Status of the Discipline

United States of America. The history of the United States reflects ongoing debate about which governmental powers belong to the states and which accrue to the federal government. It should therefore come as no surprise to find that each state, commonwealth, or territory comprising the United States of America has its own regulatory authority for licensing psychologists. These include 54 jurisdictions: the fifty states, District of Columbia, United States Territory of Guam, Commonwealth of Puerto Rico, and the United States Virgin Islands. The American Psychological Association (APA) has strived to establish the doctoral degree as the entry-level profession practice credential and has created model licensing statutes that it hopes states will adopt (APA, 2010); however, the local needs and political interests of the different jurisdictions has led to considerable variability. For example, some states require a full year of postdoctoral experience prior to licensing, while others allow acquiring the requisite number of supervised hours prior to attaining the doctoral degree. Some states with large underserved areas allow some licensing at the master's degree level. In addition, state laws also vary widely on matters that affect day-to-day practice (e.g., limits of confidentiality and continuing education requirements).

The APA has also established a policy of pursuing authority for appropriately trained psychologists to prescribe medication for the treatment of mental conditions (RxP has become a common abbreviation for such prescription privileges in the professional literature). McGrath and Moore

(2010) provide a thorough overview of RxP from the psychologist's perspective. At the time this chapter was completed, psychologists in Louisiana, New Mexico, and Guam can qualify for such privileges, and six other state jurisdictions have enabling legislation pending. Primary opposition has come from medical associations seeking to prevent the extension of RxP among nonphysician provider groups.

The Association of State and Provincial Psychology Boards (ASPPB), founded in 1961, represents an alliance of state, provincial, and territorial agencies responsible for the licensure and certification of psychologists throughout the United States and Canada. The prime impetus for its founding related to increasing the ease of mobility for practitioners by developing and maintaining a standardized written Examination for Professional Practice in Psychology (EPPP) in 1965. Today, the ASPPB also coordinates cooperative efforts of regulatory bodies in the United States and Canada by facilitating communication among bodies, maintaining a data bank of disciplinary actions taken by member boards, and through the creation of a Certificate of Professional Qualification in Psychology (CPQ) and Interjurisdictional Practice Certificate (IPC) that assist psychologists in transferring their licenses across jurisdictions and in temporarily entering jurisdictions for limited practice purposes where they do not hold a license. Because of statutory differences, however, many jurisdictions will require candidates for licensing to pass both the EPPP and an examination on local jurisprudence, or to meet other requirements for full licensing.

Most jurisdictions in the United States regulate only the use of the title "psychologist" or adjective "psychological" with respect to services offered to the public. Some laws regulate specific psychological practice(s) or provide exemptions for categories of individuals (e.g., government employees working in defined roles) who may perform some professional functions without a license or beyond the scope of a general license. Psychologists who offer health services are regulated in every jurisdiction, but no jurisdiction requires a license of psychologists conducting academic activities such as classroom teaching and research. Many, but not all, jurisdictions require licensing of certain applied psychologists who work in industrial or organizational roles.

Licensing boards in the United States, sometimes called *boards of registration* or *boards of examiners*, typically fall under the executive branch of government in a department of business regulation or professional licensing, with members appointed by the governor. In some jurisdictions professional associations nominate or recommend candidates, while in others communication about nominees between professional organizations and the appointing authority is not welcome. Most licensing boards include both members of the profession and representatives of the public, but significant variation exists. In Massachusetts the Board of Registration of Psychologists consists of seven licensed psychologists and two public members. In South Carolina the State Board of Examiners in Psychology consists of three clinical psychologists; two counseling psychologists; one school psychologist; one psychologist who holds a license in experimental, social, industrial/organizational or community psychology (fields in which many states do not even grant licenses); and one "lay member." New Hampshire has an omnibus Board of Mental Health Practice that includes three public members, a pastoral psychotherapist, a mental health counselor, a marriage & family therapist, a psychologist, and an MSW social worker—representing the spectrum of licenses it regulates. Some states also credential school psychologists separately through state departments of education.

In addition to granting licenses, the regulatory boards adjudicate complaints and can impose discipline. A license may be revoked for nonpayment of renewal fees, failure to complete continuing education requirements (in states that have such requirements), or in response to disciplinary complaints. The hearing process differs by jurisdiction, with all having the authority to issue public reprimands, suspensions, or revocation of licenses. Some also have the authority to restrict practice, require continuing education or supervision, or impose costly fines as part of the disciplinary process.

The distinction between law and ethics codes flows from their respective origins with legislative bodies and professional guilds. Governmental licensing authorities may exert disciplinary control over licensees and over those deemed to practice without a required license. In the United States nearly all jurisdictions incorporate the APA's ethics code as an enforceable provision of its regulations along with other local requirements. As one example of local requirements, consider advertising. The APA's ethics code cannot advocate regulation of advertising, as doing so would be deemed an effort by a national tax-exempt scientific organization to influence interstate commerce. However, individual states can impose restrictions on some types of professional advertising within their own boundaries under a "state's interests" doctrine. Other examples of state-specific licensing rules arise from horrific cases that trigger legislative action in a uniquely nongeneralizable context. For example, the state of Colorado considers using or recommending "rebirthing therapy" illegal (Colorado House Bill 01–1238, adopted April 17, 2001). This type of "therapy" refers to the reenactment of the birthing process through techniques that involve restraint or might create physical injury. The relevant statute, known as Candace's Law, memorializes Candace Newmaker, who suffocated during a 70-minute "attachment and rebirthing therapy" session in April 2000.

Canada. In Canada, regulation of psychological practice occurs at the provincial level. At the time of this writing, 10 provinces and two territories had adopted relevant legislation, while the territory of Yukon had not. As such, the practice of psychology was not regulated in Yukon.

Most provincial regulatory acts of legislation are certification or registration acts protecting the title "psychologist," rather than the scope of practice. Nonetheless, within these acts one sometimes finds licensing components protecting a small number of practice activities, usually limited around the communication of diagnoses for mental disorders. No Canadian jurisdiction allows for the possibility of prescription privileges for psychologists. Some jurisdictions (e.g., Alberta) allow registration/certification with a master's degree and others require the doctorate. Many jurisdictions have dual titles for persons with master's degrees (e.g., "psychological associate" in Ontario and "psychologist" in Saskatchewan) and doctoral degrees ("psychologist" in Ontario and "doctoral psychologist" in Saskatchewan). The scope of practice for master's and doctoral level providers tends to be same despite the dual title. However, in some instances psychological associates/assistants must work under the supervision of a psychologist and may have a more limited scope of practice. Several jurisdictions allow certain specific categories of individuals to use the title "psychologist" without becoming registered or certified (e.g., faculty of university psychology departments).

Provincial regulatory bodies (e.g., the College of Alberta Psychologists, the Nova Scotia Board of Examiners in Psychology) are supported primarily through fees charged to the regulated members. Registration/certification with a regulatory body is usually required for use of the title "psychologist." In most Canadian jurisdictions, psychologists who are regulatory governing council[2] members (e.g., the president) are elected by those who are registered/certified by these regulatory bodies, but often other governing council members are appointed. For example, public members of the governing council of the Saskatchewan College of Psychologists may be appointed by the lieutenant governor of the province. Nonetheless, there are exceptions to the practice of electing psychologist governing council members. For instance, according to the Psychologists Act of Nova Scotia (Psychologists Act, 2000), psychologist governing council members of the regulatory body (i.e., the Nova Scotia Board of Examiners in Psychology) are appointed by the Association of Psychologists of Nova Scotia (which is a fraternal and not a regulatory body).

The authority of the bodies regulating the practice of Canadian psychologists is derived from the relevant provincial or territorial acts of legislation (e.g., The Psychologists Act of Prince Edward Island). As is the case in the United States, regulatory bodies have the authority to not only regulate the use of the title "psychologist" but to also adjudicate complaints against psychologists and to impose disciplinary action (e.g., revocation of registration or certification).

In Canada, cross-jurisdictional mobility of psychologists is facilitated through the CPQ, discussed earlier, and a mutual recognition agreement among provinces signed in 2001 by representatives of Canadian regulatory bodies. As in the United States, the EPPP is required as a prerequisite for registration or certification in most jurisdictions, and candidates must typically pass additional examinations (usually oral) covering largely (but not exclusively) ethical issues and jurisprudence. Preregistration and precertification supervision, sometimes postdoctoral, is often required. Registration and certification are maintained through the payment of an annual fee and, usually, the completion of continuing education requirements. As in the United States, continuing education requirements vary across Canadian jurisdictions. The Canadian Psychological Association code of ethics (CPA, 1986, 2000) has been adopted by most Canadian jurisdictions and the relationship of the code with the legislation is similar to that in the United States.

Professional Associations

United States of America. In the United States, professional associations function as private entities without government support. Federal tax and commercial laws regulate professional associations by placing limits on their activities. For example, the APA is considered a tax exempt not-for-profit scientific organization under the Internal Revenue Code's section 501 c(3), enjoying particular tax advantages. In order to effectively advocate for professional practice interests, a separate APA Practice Organization (APAPO) was established as a professional trade association under the Internal Revenue Code's section 501 c(6). All of the scholarly journal operations and ethics enforcement takes place under the APA umbrella, but neither the APA nor APAPO may engage in activities that are deemed anticompetitive, such as attempting to influence the fees charged by members or price fixing.

The APA has earned the ability to accredit education training programs in psychology from the United States Department of Education, and maintains a Commission on Accreditation that carries out its functions with significant regulatory insulation from the APA's elected governance. Accreditation standards require programs seeking accreditation to incorporate formal education and training in the ethical standards of the profession.

In 1938 the APA established a Committee on Scientific and Professional Ethics and began to deal with ethical complaints on an informal basis (Golann, 1969). In 1948, development of a formal ethical code began under the leadership of Nicholas Hobbs (1948). The first provisional *Ethical Standards of Psychologists* ultimately won adoption by the APA Council of Representatives in 1952 for a 3-year trial period (APA, 1953). The codes had undergone periodic tweaks in addition to full revisions, each involving substantial revision and periods for public comment prior to adoption. The most recent full revision of the APA code (2002) took more than 5 years of work, including broad solicitation of critical incidents (i.e., anecdotes of problem situations) against which to compare the current code and potential changes. The code was amended in 2010 in order to address special concerns related to conflicts between the ethical code and law or organizational demands. This change took place in the context of concerns about roles psychologists might have played in military or intelligence agencies during the administration of former President George W. Bush. At the time of this writing a full markup of the relevant sections showing the 2010 changes can be found at: http://www.apa.org/ethics/code/index.aspx.

Canada. In most of Canada there is a clear distinction between professional associations (that serve a "fraternal" function intended to support the networking and the interests of the profession), such as the British Columbia Psychological Association and the Saskatchewan Psychological Society, and regulatory bodies (e.g., the Newfoundland and Labrador Psychology Board and the College of Psychologists of Ontario). Neither regulatory bodies nor professional associations receive significant government funding, and sustain themselves primarily through membership fees. There is no requirement to join any of the fraternal bodies.

The primary national association for psychologists in Canada is the Canadian Psychological Association (CPA), a nonprofit organization organized in 1939 and incorporated under the Canada Corporations Act, Part II, in May of 1950. The *Canadian Code of Ethics for Psychologists* (CPA, 1986; 2000) was developed by the CPA and has been adopted by most Canadian regulatory bodies. L'Orde des Psychologues du Quebec (the body regulating psychology in the province of Quebec) has developed its own code. Codes of ethics serve to guide the evaluation of responses to questions provided by applicants for registration/certification during required examinations, as a tool for ethics training within university-based psychology programs, and is used by disciplinary committees in their decision making.

Much like the APA in the United States, the CPA operates an accreditation system for graduate programs in professional psychology (CPA, 2002). CPA accreditation of one's doctoral degree is not required for registration/certification. Nonetheless, the registration or certification process often accelerates for applicants who completed degrees at CPA-accredited programs, and many employers require CPA accreditation as a condition of employment. APA accreditation is typically recognized as equivalent to CPA accreditation. As in the case of APA's accreditation system, the CPA accreditation criteria explicitly require accredited programs to provide training in ethics.

Ethics Committees

United States of America. The APA and a small number of state psychological associations maintain ethics committees with the authority to discipline their members. However, membership in professional associations in the United States is completely voluntary. As in Canada, one need not ever join a professional association to qualify for or maintain a license. As a result, professional associations can only exert authority over their members and will not entertain an ethics complaint against a nonmember. The most severe sanction the APA can apply in response to an ethical infraction would involve expulsion of the offending member with notification to licensing boards and the public.

Conducting ethics investigations can prove time consuming and costly in terms of staff time and legal expenses, with APA's ethics office operation spending approximately $780,000 in 2010. In this economic context many state psychological associations in the United States have ceased adjudicating ethics complaints against members, but typically take automatic steps to expel any members who have their licenses revoked or who are expelled from the APA.

State licensing boards stand as governmental entities apart from professional associations. As noted earlier, such boards typically include both psychologists and representatives of the public, and the members are typically appointed by state governors. Funding for such bodies comes from governmental budgets or licensing fees. Licensing boards can investigate violations of law (e.g., practice without a license) and ethical infractions, with the authority to revoke a license and in some cases impose financial penalties.

Canada. Both Canadian regulatory bodies and the CPA have ethics committees. For the purposes of disciplinary action for ethics violations, regulatory bodies have the power to place conditions on registration/certification (e.g., insist someone receive additional supervision) or to suspend registration and certification. The CPA will normally defer complaints that fall under the jurisdiction of provincial/territorial/state regulatory bodies to those bodies, and will review the status of CPA membership subsequent to the more local decision (CPA, 1990). Based on its review of the complaint, the CPA ethics committee will make a recommendations to the CPA board (e.g., suspension of membership). Provincial fraternal bodies may also suspend membership as a result of ethics violations. Ethics committees of psychologists' organizations (e.g., CPA) also provide educational advice or guidance to practitioners who request it.

Ethics Codes

United States of America. The APA ethics code is bifurcated into a set of aspirational standards known as the *Ethical Principles of Psychologists* and an enforceable *Code of Conduct* (APA, 2002). The code has evolved as a function of both practices in the field and political events. For example, in the 1960s the code categorized many forms of advertising by practitioners as unethical, but by the 1980s the consumer movement and government regulators led to the demise of most attempts by profession to regulate advertising. As noted earlier in this chapter, when psychologists learned that the administration of former President George W. Bush employed psychologists to assist in the interrogation of alleged terrorist detainees, additional modifications to the code sought to clarify that participation in human rights violations constitutes ethical misconduct.

Few psychologists in the United States have any awareness of the International Union of Psychological Science (IUPsyS) or its *Universal Declaration of Ethical Principles for Psychologists*. The psychologists involved with the IUPsyS within the United States work largely within the academic and scientific communities. These psychologists typically wield minimal influence in professional regulatory practices. Individual licensing jurisdictions in the United States focus solely on their own statutes and national standards. In that context the Universal Declaration seems unlikely to have any meaningful influence on the APA's ethical code or ethics enforcement in the United States for the foreseeable future.

Canada. The Canadian Code of Ethics for Psychologists (CPA, 1986, 2000) was designed to incorporate the collective wisdom of Canadian psychologists. This was accomplished by examining responses that psychologists provided, as part of a survey, to 37 vignettes representing hypothetical ethical dilemmas (Sinclair, Poizner, Gilmour-Barrett, & Randall, 1987). The psychologists' responses were found to represent four superordinate ethical principles which formed the basis of the four principles that comprise the CPA code of ethics (respect for the dignity of persons, responsible caring, integrity in relationships, and responsibility to society). A consultative process with provincial regulatory bodies supported the validity of the document (Sinclair et al., 1987). The code has received considerable praise and has formed the basis for code development in other countries (Frankel et al., 1998; Hadjistavropoulos, 2009). The Canadian code was also one of the codes that influenced the development of the universal declaration of ethical principles (Gauthier, 2004), and the four principles of the *Universal Declaration of Ethical Principles for Psychologists* closely mirror the principles that are articulated in the CPA code.

Ethics Training

United States of America and Canada. In this section, we cover ethics training in the United States and Canada together because of the similar training approaches and regulatory body expectations in the two countries. Ethics enters psychology curricula chiefly at the graduate level. Undergraduate education tends to have a broader disciplinary focus than in the European university tradition. Certainly, the topic of research ethics does come up from time to time in undergraduate classes, particularly when research participation or project planning raises consent or other issues. Courses in clinical psychology, testing, or psychopathology may also trigger a discussion of ethical issues, but coverage would likely prove shallow at the undergraduate level. Graduate programs must incorporate scientific and professional ethics in both educational degree and internship or residency training programs as an accreditation requirement. Regulatory bodies also expect to see formal course work in such topics prior to approving candidates to sit for examination. Many regulatory bodies also require evidence of periodic postgraduate continuing professional education seminars in ethics as a requirement for maintaining licensure

Current Research on Psychological Ethics

American psychologists have been heavily involved in research on ethics for psychologists. Examples of such studies include surveys concerning ethical dilemmas that psychologists encounter, studies involving responding to problematic vignettes, and investigations of psychologists' attitudes about the ethicality of various actions. The journals *Ethics & Behavior, Professional Psychology: Research and Practice*, and the *American Psychologist* are common outlets for this type of work. Prominent recent topical areas include those related to confidentiality (e.g., duty to protect third parties, release of records, and electronic risks to confidentiality), multiple-role relationship conflicts, support for treatment efficacy (e.g., evidentiary bases for practice approaches), and use of telemetry in service delivery. A substantial body of research on ethical issues, similar to those of interest to American psychologists researching ethics, has also been developed in Canada (e.g., Seitz & O'Neil, 1996; Hadjistavropoulos, Malloy, Sharpe, & Fuchs-Lacelle, 2003). The journal *Canadian Psychology* is a frequent outlet for such work.

Future Challenges for Psychological Ethics and Ethics Codes

Several emerging challenges for psychological ethics and ethics codes are the result of technological advances. The provision of psychological services over the Internet is becoming increasingly common and poses challenges (e.g., Fitzgerald, Hunter, Hadjistavropoulos, & Koocher, 2010; Koocher, 2007). For example, psychologists' services may be reaching individuals outside the jurisdiction that regulates their practice and even outside the country in which they live. Such a crossing of jurisdictions may create a situation where there is a need for international standards and regulation. Moreover, the provision of services via the Internet also poses new ethical challenges (e.g., difficulty in the provision of emergency services, questions about the validity of consent, and others).

In light of the development of technologies that allow cross-jurisdictional professional relationships, the development of international initiatives such as the *Universal Declaration of Ethical Principles* could facilitate the resolution of ethical issues. Whether such international initiatives will be accepted and utilized by regulators, however, is less clear and remains to be seen.

Notes

1. Our discussion on aspects of psychological regulation is based on practices at the time that we prepared this chapter. We caution readers that regulatory policies, codes, and legislation are subject to change. As such, we recommend that interested readers obtain any necessary information directly from the regulatory bodies in their jurisdictions of interest.

2. The term *governing council* is used to describe the structure within the regulatory body that oversees and directs the functions of this body. The formal term used to describe this governing structure varies from jurisdiction to jurisdiction (e.g., "governing council," "board").

References

American Psychological Association (1953). *Ethical standards of psychologists*. Washington, DC: Author.

American Psychological Association (2002). *Ethical principles of psychologists and code of conduct*. Washington, DC: Author.

American Psychological Association (2010). Revision of APA's model act for state licensure of psychologists. Council of Representatives Agenda. Washington, DC: Author.

Canadian Psychological Association (2002). *Accreditation standards and procedures for doctoral programs and internships in professional psychology*, 4th Revision. Canadian Psychological Association. Ottawa: Author.

Canadian Psychological Association (2000). *Canadian code of ethics for psychologists*, 3rd Ed. Canadian Psychological Association. Ottawa: Author.

Canadian Psychological Association (1986). *Canadian code of ethics for psychologists*. Canadian Psychological Association. Ottawa: Author.

Canadian Psychological Association (1990). Rules and procedures for dealing with ethical complaints. Ottawa: Author. Retrieved from http://www.cpa.ca/aboutcpa/committees/ethics/rulesandproceduresfordealingwiththicalcomplaints/

Fitzgerald, T. D., Hunter, P. V., Hadjistavropoulos, T., & Koocher, G. P. (2010) Ethical and legal considerations for internet-based psychotherapy. *Cognitive Behaviour Therapy, 39*, 173–187.

Gauthier, J. (2004). *Toward a universal declaration of ethical principles of psychologists. A progress report.* Retrieved from http://www.iupsys.net/images/resources/ethics/ethic-wg-2004-report.pdf.

Golann, S. (1969) Emerging areas of ethical concern. *American Psychologist, 24*, 454–459.

Hadjistavropoulos, T. (2009). Canadian psychology in a global context. *Canadian Psychology, 50*, 1–7.

Hadjistavropoulos, T., Malloy, D.C., Sharpe, D., & Fuchs-Lacelle, L. (2003). The ethical ideologies of psychologists and physicians: A preliminary comparison. *Ethics & Behavior, 13*, 97–104

Hobbs, N. (1948). The development of a code of ethical standards for Psychology. *American Psychologist, 3*, 80–84.

Koocher, G. P. (2007). Twenty-first century ethical challenges for psychology. *American Psychologist, 62*, 375–384.

McGrath, R. E., & Moore, B.A. (Eds.), (2010). *Pharmacotherapy for psychologists: Prescribing and collaborative roles.* Washington, DC: American Psychological Association.

Psychologists Act, Chapter 32 of the Acts of 2000 amended 2008, c 3, s. 15, Retrieved from http://nslegislature.ca/legc/statutes/psychol.htm.

Seitz, J., & O'Neill, P. (1996). Ethical decision making and the code of ethics of the Canadian Psychological Association. *Canadian Psychology, 37*, 23–30.

Sinclair, C., Poizner, S., Gilmour-Barrett, K., & Randall, D. (1987). The development of a code of ethics for Canadian psychologists. *Canadian Psychology, 28*, 1–11.

Colorado House Bill 01–1238. (2001). Retrieved from http://www.state.co.us/gov_dir/leg_dir/olls/sl2001/sl_129.pdf.

CHAPTER 24

Psychological Ethics in Chinese Societies

Charles C. Chan, Alvin S. Leung, Peter W. Lee, Li-fei Wang, *and* Kan Zhang

Abstract

This chapter reviewing the status of psychological ethics will be organized around a coherent concept of the level of receptivity to psychology in the Chinese societies. The common feature of this unified direction of progression of psychology includes three core components. First, the regions' governmental and circumstantial conditions surrounding statutory registration, or the lack thereof, and regulation of psychological practice; second, the strength and the role of the psychological associations in situ; and finally, the maturity of the marketplace in these regions for consumption of professional psychological services. The readers will be able to note the diversities that exist among these regions while not losing sight of Chinese societies as a collective.

Key Words: psychological ethics, Chinese societies, statutory registration, psychological associations, regulation of practice

In the latest *Oxford Handbook of Chinese Psychology*, Blowers (2010) posits the importance of having to make clear whether we are referring to the Chinese mainland, Taiwan, Hong Kong, Singapore, or elsewhere when we talk about Chinese psychology. He further asserts that seeing the work done in these regions as a whole "would be to dismiss the enormous historical and sociopolitical differences between these regions..." (Blowers, 2010, p.6). In the same handbook, when Chan (2010) reviews the state of community psychology, he refers to these regions not as a whole but as "Chinese societies." Thus, for the purposes of this chapter we will refer to Chinese societies as regions with significant Chinese cultures.

On the topic of psychological ethics, the legal status of psychology as a discipline, and therefore how psychological practice, academic, research and applied psychology are being regulated, also turns out to be noticeably different in these Chinese societies. This chapter will review the status of psychological ethics and will be organized around a coherent concept of the level of receptivity to psychology in these Chinese societies. In short, while differences may be emphasized they are but reflections of a unified direction of progression in these regions.

The common feature of this unified direction of progression of psychology includes three core components. First, the regions' governmental and circumstantial conditions surrounding statutory registration, or the lack thereof, and regulation of psychological practice; second, the strength of the psychological associations in situ; and finally, the maturity of the marketplace in these regions for consumption of professional psychological services. For the readers to be able to note the diversities that exist among these regions, while not losing sight of Chinese societies as a collective, these three components should be considered to represent the levels of receptivity to psychology in the respective Chinese societies.

The Legal Status of Psychology

Established in 1921, The Chinese Psychological Society (CPS) is one of the earliest established academic societies in China. By 1928, the Institute of Psychology was founded within the Chinese Academy of Sciences (CAS). However, it was not until the past 30 years, when China's economy has developed rapidly and the Chinese Mainland has undergone significant changes in all aspects of life, that the need for psychological science and service and the number of people who work in this field have increased at an unprecedented pace.

It was not until the end of the Cultural Revolution that colleges and universities began to reestablish psychology as a formal academic discipline. The Department of Psychology of Peking University, founded in 1978, was the first department of psychology in the People's Republic of China (PRC). According to a nongovernmental estimate, at the end of January 2009 there were 245 subspecialties, departments, or schools of psychology and applied psychology in the Chinese Mainland.

Although there has been rapid progress in the education of psychological science, it should be noted that there is not a unified Chinese ethical code developed pertaining to the entire field of psychology in the PRC. This situation may be related to the fact that psychology is not a legally recognized profession in the PRC. In other words, the profession and the work of psychology are not yet regulated by law in the Chinese Mainland.

In Hong Kong, during the British colonial days, psychology was taught in English in the Faculty of Arts at the University of Hong Kong as an adjunct to philosophy until 1967, when the Faculty of Social Sciences was formed (Blowers, 2010). The Hong Kong Psychological Society (the Society) was incorporated in 1981. Despite repeated consultation with the Hong Kong Special Administrative Region (HKSAR) government officials in the last decade, the government's position has remained unchanged and psychology is still not regulated by law. It was more probable for psychology to go through statutory registration as an allied health profession than for the government to draft a separate bill all on its own, due mainly to the small number of members in the Society. The Society, however, is free to present its own private bill to the HKSAR legislature. The prospect of having a private bill passed depends on whether psychology can negotiate through the always congested legislative agenda, as well as engaging in successful lobbying with the legislators.

We have, however, an example of how this can be accomplished, as it was done in Taiwan a decade ago. Among the Chinese societies, Taiwan is the only region where psychology is legally regulated by the government under the "Psychologist Statute," which was formally put into practice in 2001 (Wang, Kwan, & Huang, 2011). We will briefly discuss the background as to how this occurred in Taiwan.

In the late 1990s the necessity for qualified mental health professionals became a public concern when a series of disastrous events and social problems occurred in Taiwan. In 1998, more than 200 people died in a tragic plane crash in Da-Yuan near an international airport in Taiwan. On September 21, 1999, the so-called "921 Earthquake" caused 2,400 deaths and more than 33 billion NT dollars (about one billion US$) of property damage. Many survivors from both events exhibited post-traumatic stress symptoms. In addition, suicide became a major crisis in Taiwan, perhaps due to the various disasters and problems. Between 1997 and 2000, there was a significant increase in suicide rate from 9.57% to 13.59% (Taiwan's Department of Health, 2008). Psychological problems caused by these natural and social disasters alerted the government to the need for mental health services, as well as a national statute to regulate the professional practice of psychologists (Chang, 1998; Chen & Chen, 2000; Lin, 1998).

In response to these traumatic events and mental health needs, clinical psychologists stepped up to draft a statute for clinical psychology, and proposed that it be legally enforced by the government (Chang, 1998). The statute was a much-needed response to a socially identified need. At the same time, many mental health professionals, including school counselors, community counselors, nurses, psychiatrists, and social workers, felt left out of the process, as the terms of the statute would exclude those who were not clinical psychologists from psychological practice. Some mental health professions sensed an urgency to amend the statute (Chen & Chen, 2000; Lin, 1998).

To respond to the potential threat, counseling psychologists negotiated with clinical psychology colleagues and communicated with government officials in administrative and political offices. Beyond differences in training approaches and practice orientations, counseling psychologists had to identify practice domains the two professions shared in common and where they could complement one another, and present the information to the head of the Ministry of Health, relevant legislators, and their assistants. As a result of these political networking and communication efforts, counseling psychologists were included in the statute and granted the right to co-draft the licensure statute. The initial "Clinical Psychologist Statute" was revised to become the *Psychologist Statute* in 2001. The *Psychologist Statute* serves three primary purposes: (a) regulate the training of psychologists; (b) administer the licensure examination and determine eligibility for professional practice (e.g., psychological testing, counseling, and psychotherapy); and (c) provide effective and ethical practice.

The Professional Associations

It is clear by now that the professional associations in the respective regions played a significant if not pivotal role in the process toward statutory registration of psychology. In the region of Taiwan, but not in other Chinese societies, certain divisions of psychologists are obliged to become members of professional associations. The *Psychologist Statute* has one section that applies to counseling psychologists and a separate section for clinical psychologists. According to the *Psychologist Statute*, school counselors, social workers, nurses, occupational therapists, and psychiatrists who are licensed in their respective professions can conduct psychological practice without being considered as violating the *Psychologist Statute*.

The Chinese Psychological Society (CPS) in the Chinese Mainland, on the other hand, has 15 professional committees, including the Clinical and Counseling Psychology Committee. In 2007, the "Registration Criteria for Professional Organizations and Individual Practitioners in Clinical and Counseling Psychology, CPS" and the "Code of Ethics for Counseling and Clinical Practice, CPS" were both published in *Acta Psychologica Sinica* and started to engage in related work. The executive committee of the CPS has decided to set up a new branch to pay more attention to ethics from a view of the entire field of psychology, and also try to encourage Chinese psychologists to conduct in-depth study into scientific ethics in their own discipline.

What is the role of professional associations in ethics code development? A good case in point would be to look at the Hong Kong example. The Hong Kong Psychological Society (HKPS) has most recently gone through two rounds of formal consultation within its membership in an attempt to update and revise the existing code (Hong Kong Psychological Society, 2007, 2009). H. Lau, in his capacity as the Convener of the Working Group (WG) for the Revision of the Code of Professional Conducts,[1] stated clearly in his opening statement to the Society members that, "With or without statutory registration of psychologists, the Code of Professional Conduct is a very important document that binds all members of the Society and protects the interests of the public with whom members have transactions. The Code has not been revised for over twenty years and many changes are needed to bring the document update to cater for the continuous growth in the diversity and complexity of members' activities" (Hong Kong Psychological Society, 2007).

Structurally speaking, based on the original code, which was prepared over 30 years ago, the WG took reference from the ethical codes of the American Psychological Association (APA), the Canadian Psychological Association, the Australian Psychological Society (APS) and the British Psychological Society (BPS). The purpose was to take heed of the trend in the development of codes used by psychological societies in other parts of the world. After much deliberation, the WG decided to use the recently revised BPS Code of Ethics as the blueprint, and started writing the first draft after agreeing on the basic principles and format. The choice to borrow from the BPS code could be traced back to the long history of association between the Society and the BPS, and the fact that for a very long period of time, the local training in psychology had been very much based on the British system.

Notwithstanding this choice, most of the original layout of the Society's code was retained. The WG hoped that by doing so, members of the Society would find it easier to relate to the changes and that it would facilitate the transition to the use of the new code. While the whole code was formulated around the same four basic ethical principles, as in the case of the British code, the WG had specifically retained the sections on the respective specialties (clinical, educational and industrial-organizational psychology) and professional activities in the draft of the new code. This format is actually similar to the codes of the APA, APS, and even the previous versions of the BPS code (Hong Kong Psychological Society, 2009). The emphasis was on the need to supplement the general codes with more specific professional guidelines that are developed by specialty sub-systems (the divisions, in the Hong Kong case).

The choice of language was targeted at both professional and general membership. The WG decided to keep the language general rather than legal. Alongside the development of statutory registration, sooner or later the Code of Professional Conduct would become a crucial document or reference in future disciplinary proceedings, which would become legal, too. Nonetheless, the WG had agreed that the new draft code would not bind only professional psychologists (psychologists that would be registered) but also other general members of the Society. Besides, the draft new code, like the ethical codes used in other professional societies, is meant to guide the conduct or behavior of members and not to act as a penal code by nature. When considering language, this is a noticeable departure from the original code.

The WG went through two rounds of consultation, with written comments received from the professional divisions within the Society. The new draft code would be used as the basic point of reference for each existing division to work out their own more detailed guidelines on their respective professional practices. It was expected that different divisions might have to expand parts of the new draft code to make them more suitable or applicable to their particular field of professional practice. The WG also suggested that there is a need for regular review of the code and the development of a Standing Committee of Professional Ethics to oversee the work in the future.

The Function and Power of the Society-Based Ethics Committees

In the People's Republic of China (PRC), some of the psychological units have their own ethics committees, such as the Institutional Review Board (IRB) of the Institute of Psychology, Chinese Academy of Science, which was founded in 1996 as the first IRB in the Chinese mainland. The regulations for the establishment of the membership of the IRB are as follows: (1) there are 7–8 members, whose primary affiliation and concerns are scientific areas; (2) at least one member whose primary affiliation is nonscientific areas; and (3) at least one member who is not affiliated with the Institute. The latest committee of the IRB, registered in the Department of Health and Human Services of the National Institutes of Health (NIH) of the PRC, consists of 11 members, including two members who are not affiliated with the Institute.

The Institute is guided by the ethical principles regarding all research involving human participants, as well as animals, under the guidelines for the protection of human subjects and animal welfare. The IRB[2] and its ethics committee review the essential informative elements for the ethics of applied research projects and have authority to approve, require modification in, or disapprove research projects or proposed activities before subjects may be involved. For the human participants, particular consideration is given to (1) the risk and benefits to the participants, (2) the informed consent form and process, (3) the provisions to protect the privacy of participants, (4) participants' rights, and (5) the additional safeguards for vulnerable populations. For animal welfare, particular consideration is given to (1) animal species (no admission for using nationally protected animals), (2) the care of animals used in testing, research, and training, and (3) experimental procedures, which are in compliance with the National Institutes of Health Guide for Care and Use of Laboratory Animals.

The ethics committee also plays an important function in the registration process of clinical and counseling psychologists. The Chinese Psychological Society (CPS) has a system in place that might be called "validation of ethical standards of candidates of registered psychologists." The system now comprises two elements: public announcement of the names of candidates of registered psychologists for a 3-month period, and the ethics committee, which is responsible for the validation of any potential complaints against the announced candidates during that 3-month announcement period. This system is instigated as a final step in a professional assessment of the eligibility of the applicants for registration as clinical or counseling psychologists.

In the case where a complaint has been launched against a candidate, the ethics committee will start a process of investigation and assessment. Given positive evidence of such contravention of ethical standards, the said committee handles all necessary procedures according to the ethical code enforced by the registration system. This has the potential of delaying or denying the successful registration of the applicant.

The ethical guidelines of the Taiwan Psychological Association (TPA) are the earliest code of ethics in Taiwan and have served as a blueprint for other psychology-related associations to follow. The ethical guidelines of the TPA corresponded closely with those of the APA and the American Counseling Association (ACA). At the present time, the government does not have an ethics committee to regulate the discipline of psychology. The TPA has a set of ethical guidelines for members and provisions for an ethics committee to investigate alleged violations.

Yet the mechanism was seldom put into operation, as there had been very few complaint cases. The Taiwan Counseling Psychology Association (TWCPA) probably has the most complete set of ethical guidelines on counseling psychology practice (please refer to http://www.guidance.org.tw/ethic.html), yet the most severe punishment/sanction that its ethics committee can impose is termination of membership, as the ethics committee and the ethical guidelines have no legislative power.

Based on the *Psychologist Statute,* the Government of Taiwan can prosecute psychologists who are licensed as either clinical or counseling psychologists for violations of the statute. The *Psychologist Statute* has provisions on the professional behavior of licensed psychologists, and the Department of Health is the government agency to coordinate the investigation. The procedure for prosecution also involves requesting the corresponding psychologist's professional association to conduct an investigation and provide an opinion for the court to consider.

Despite the fact that practice of psychology is not regulated by law, formal and standard procedures are in place in all professional associations of the Chinese societies. A detailed account of how this works in the case of Hong Kong, a society-based ethics committee can serve as an illustration.

Any member of the public may file a complaint against a member of the Hong Kong Psychological Society (the Society). The official webpage of the Society contains specific instructions and guidelines on lodging complaints. The merits of a written complaint are initially reviewed by the secretary and the president of the Society. If the complaint against the member is considered to be adequate for establishing a case that needs to be answered, the secretary will invite the complainant to submit further details, assist the complainant to review the code of ethics of the Society, and try to formulate the complaint in line with specific categories of violation of the Society's code of ethics. The member against whom the complaint is made ("the member") will also be informed, and be invited to submit to the Society his/her responses in writing together with any supplementary information as the member sees fit. The member and the complainant are informed that information and responses submitted will be exchanged, and there will be further opportunities to exchange information and responses.

At the early stage, if the complainant is satisfied with further information and explanation submitted by the member and wishes to withdraw the complaint, further formal procedures of investigation will be terminated. If, however, the complainant wishes to go ahead to have the complaint formally considered and investigated, he/she is informed that a formal Committee of Enquiry (CoE) of the Society will be formed. Formal hearings are held in due course, and the complainant must make him/herself available when any such formal hearings are being held. For the complaint to be fully investigated, the complainant must agree to present his/her complaints in person to the CoE in the presence of the member, and be prepared to subject him/herself to cross-examination by the member or his/her legal representative.

The CoE membership is formed on recommendations from the Society president and agreed by the presiding council members in a council meeting. A chairperson of high standing and repute, and being expert in the relevant field, will be appointed. Four to five individuals are also invited, with at least one member who is not a member of the Society, usually him/herself belonging to another professional group. In past proceedings, medical doctors and social workers have been invited.

Outcomes and Challenges of Society-Based Ethics Committee Investigation

Legal representation may be invited by the Society (to assist the CoE) and/or the member. The processes of enquiry, including cross-examination by the member and/or his/her legal representative, are subject to detailed recording, and all submitted documents are made available and reviewed. During the process, members of the CoE also have ample opportunities to ask the complainant and the member detailed questions so as to properly assess the merits and circumstances of the complaint for subsequent deliberation and judgment.

After all necessary information has been gathered and formal hearings completed, the CoE members meet in private under the direction of the CoE chairperson to consider all aspects of the complaint and in relation to specific codes of ethics being allegedly violated. The CoE is responsible for independently considering the merits of the complaint, deciding on the adequacy of the complaint, and, if considered valid, also recommending necessary sanctions and actions against the member. The sanctions may range from warning, to removal from professional membership of the Society for a set period of time, or complete disbarment.

The chairperson of the CoE communicates the CoE's findings in a formal report in the first instance to the president of the Society. The president makes the report available to council members for prior review, and council members then consider the CoE's report and recommendations in its next council meeting. The council may also invite the chairperson of the CoE to attend the council meeting to explain its findings. Led by the president of the Society, council members will further deliberate on whether or not to accept the CoE's decisions and recommendations.

After a majority decision has been reached, the president writes a formal letter to the member informing the member of the results and recommendations. Should the complaint be considered valid, and sanction be imposed, the member is informed that he/she has the right to challenge and object to the CoE and the council's decision by giving full reasons within the 30 days.

When an objection is received, the president and the council will once again consider the merits of the member's objection, and may resort to one of two options: namely,

a. reject the member's objection with previous sanctions and recommendations reaffirmed, or

b. conduct another enquiry with a fresh CoE if the member's objections are considered worthy to be deliberated further.

When all formal processes have been completed, the final decision may be published in the Society's webpage for access by members and the public.

The complaint procedure is a resource-laden and time-demanding process. Given that the Society does not have any full-time officials, the burden of the whole procedure is reliant on the voluntary services of senior and respected members. Voluntary services are, as a rule, hard, and difficult to solicit. As it is also stipulated that the CoE membership must consist of at least a member from another profession, this makes the formation of a fully functioning CoE even more difficult. Given the lengthy process and duration of any CoE procedures, the successful formation of the CoE is itself a challenge.

In this connection, the president and the council have on various occasions appealed to the Fellows of the Society, inviting them to take on various CoEs in response to increasing complaints from the public. To encourage such voluntary services, the Society has also pledged full legal support in cases where members of the CoE are sued for liability in a court of law by disgruntled members of the public. The Society is not a professional licensing body. At best, it is a professional society attracting the majority, but not all qualified and/or practicing psychologists in Hong Kong. Despite the fact that a member may be suspended from membership or even terminated from membership, the member is not legally barred from offering professional services to the public. This applies particularly to professional psychologists (clinical, educational, counseling) who, even their Society membership is terminated, are still able to practice as respective clinical, educational, or counseling psychologists. The most that a member can be sanctioned for is to no longer claim himself or herself as a member of the Society. If the public still wishes to redress grievances against such individual's services, they could only resort to a court of law to do so.

Given that in Hong Kong there is no statutory registration for psychologists, no other sanctions can be imposed by the Society. There are some within the Society who are disillusioned and feel that dealing with complaints is a futile process. First, the Society is considered as having not enough "teeth" in imposing effective sanctions. Second, given that there is no independent funding available to the Society, and that the bulk of the Society's income comes from membership fees only, involvement of legal professionals in CoE proceedings may eventually prove to be an unsustainable financial burden. However, legal involvement becomes mandatory for the Society when a member seeks his/her own legal representation. Third, as noted previously, only the really enthusiastic and dedicated senior members are willing to take on the work of a CoE; hence, with each complaint being received, successful formation of the CoE has to be solicited almost primarily through the president and the secretary on a somewhat personal basis.

Enormous difficulties thus lie ahead for the Society in upholding the highest levels of ethical standards in its members. All officials of the Society are on voluntary service, with a term of council membership of one to two years. There are no benefits conferred to members taking on the work of the Society, not that this is an important consideration for council members. The hefty work in relation to ethics and complaints is thus likely to rest on a few people, who have difficulty finding support and assistance from other members.

Statutory registration of professional psychologists, while being actively pursued by the Society with the Hong Kong SAR government, is still likely to be some years away before being implemented. For the time being, the sanctions imposed by the Society on its members will only carry weight if the

Society itself can achieve enough prestige and recognition within the society at large.

While the authors have no doubt that the professional associations will continue to strive to uphold the professional ethical standards of psychologists in the Chinese societies, the processes are fraught with limitations and difficulties. Ethical practice of professional psychology, unfortunately, still relies almost solely on formal training and successful instillation of a high value on ethical practice with psychologists in training.

Development of Ethics Codes in Chinese Societies

In 1997, Leach and Harbin published a comparison study on psychological ethics in 24 countries. Both China and Hong Kong were included in that comparison. In terms of ethical principles, the Leach and Harbin (1997) study, which was based on the 1992 version of the APA ethical principles and code of conduct, highlighted that China showed no APA principles similarity. It was noted, however, that this previous version of the Chinese code applied primarily to testing and assessment. The Hong Kong code, on the other hand, showed overlap with the principles of integrity, respect for people's rights, and concern for human welfare, or three of the six ethical principle areas (50%) in the U.S. code. In terms of standards, China's was the most dissimilar ($M = 17\%$) and Hong Kong stood at 46% similar to the U.S. code. Taiwan was not included in that comparative study.

The purpose and therefore value of this kind of comparison was to identify both universal and context-dependent ethical principles and standards across countries. The authors compared ethical codes by analyzing the percent of the United States APA code found in other national codes, and the percent of countries including each U.S. standard in their respective codes. Variations in these ethical codes inform us about the consistency of values important to psychologists in various countries, and suggest greater understanding of the way these psychologists organize information in their world (Leach & Harbin, 1997).

The authors conducted such comparisons based on the following six principles of the 1992 version of the APA code: A = Competence; B = Integrity; C = Professional & Scientific Responsibility; D = Respect for People's Rights and Dignity; E = Concern for Human Welfare; F = Social Responsibility, and eight categorical standards: I: General Standards; II: Evaluation, Assessment, or Intervention; III: Advertising and Other Public Statements; IV: Therapy; V: Privacy and Confidentiality; VI: Teaching, Training, Supervision, Research, and Publishing; VII: Forensic Activities; VIII: Resolving Ethical Issues.

Each principle or standard from each national code was assessed to determine its consistency with a corresponding principle or standard from the U.S. code. The U.S. code was therefore used as a reference frame for organizing the formatting differences of each country's code. According to Leach and Harbin (1997), some

> "...eight US individual standards had no equivalence in other countries surveyed and are considered specific to US legal and psychological culture. These included accuracy in report to payors and funding sources (General Standards); Couple and family relationships (Therapy); withholding records for nonpayment (Privacy and Confidentiality); design of educational and training programs, duplicate publication of data, sharing of data, professional reviewers (Teaching, Training, Supervision, Research, and Publishing); and prior relationships (Forensic Activities). Seven individual US standards were found in only one other country, 11 individual standards in two other countries, and 11 individual standards in three other countries. Therefore, over 36% of the US standards are contained in either zero, one, two, or three countries (although these countries vary depending on the standard). It could be argued, therefore, that 36% of the US individual standards are culture-specific. (p.187)

Based on the above analysis, a general observation may be true that as the profession matures, ethics codes and standards will be revisited. Fisher (2009), for example, pointed out that there were many standards new in the 2002 APA ethics code including: 2.02, providing services in emergencies; 7.04, student disclosure of personal information; 7.05, mandatory individual or group therapy; 9.03, informed consent in assessment; 10.03, group therapy; 10.06, sexual intimacies with relatives or significant others of current therapy clients/patients. One of the reasons these new standards may not be found in other countries or regions was because they were issues appearing relevant to more advanced markets like that of the United States (Nagy, 2005) for psychological services than that of less developed markets such as in the Chinese Mainland. In short, ethics code development often reflects the maturity of the market for psychological service in a certain country or region.

Apart from the cultural argument presented thus far, we wish to posit another reason attributable to the above phenomena. For the code to be taken up by a country or region, it has to reflect a common enough concern among those who are practicing psychology in that country or region or, more specifically, who are active in the professional association which incorporates such code. The stage of development of psychology as a profession, often reflected by the maturity of the market for psychological services, has definitely had an important role to play. Thus, the differences between the countries perhaps could be attributable more to the stage of development, particularly market conditions, than simply to culture.

Ethics Training

Any competent practice of psychology requires an understanding of and adherence to ethical standards, institutional policy, and law. In Taiwan, training in ethics is more fully implemented in counseling and clinical psychology training programs due to the requirements of the *Psychologist Statute* that ethics be a part of the core training. In other psychology-related training programs at the undergraduate and graduate levels, ethics is often synthesized into different training units rather than being dealt with as a separate training component. The *Psychologist Statute* required licensed psychologists to accumulate 180 hours of continuing education every 6 years, including 12 hours of continuing training on topics/content related to ethics.

The situation is similar in Hong Kong and the Chinese Mainland. Psychological ethics, usually, is a half-year, semester-based, formally organized and taught subject and is a required component in professional psychology programs at the master's level and beyond. More recently, universities in Hong Kong have introduced a mandatory taught subject on professional ethics for all research and higher degree students as well. Research students, in particular, will develop discipline-specific skills and knowledge, but the attributes of honesty, integrity, responsibility, accountability, empathy, respect for self and others, high moral standards, and adherence to accepted ethical codes of conduct are also expected to be developed in the course within the research programs.

Major topics covered will include: concepts and guiding principles of ethics in research; learning from the past to enlighten ethical conduct in the 21st century; ethics in research, communication, science, business and industry; ethics, religion, and the law; and current ethical issues and challenges. These areas are addressed through discussions and applications of the respective ethical principles and standards across a range of scenarios. In the case of undergraduate level psychology programs, the ethical principles and the standards are more likely to be introduced in lectures in an integrative manner with other relevant and substantive topics in psychology (Benzie, Au, Fung, and Lai, separate private communications, 2010).

At this juncture, we wish to acknowledge what Pellegrino has said so succinctly: "No course could automatically close the gap between knowing what is right and doing it" (Pellegrino, 1989, p.492) in the context of what and how ethics can be taught to students of psychology.

A Commitment to Ethical Practice of Psychology in Chinese Societies

In addition to formal channels and steps in the ethics code revision efforts, and publication and dissemination of the ethical principles and standards, it is apparent that the Chinese Psychological Society (CPS) is keenly responsive in efforts to promote measures of facilitating the development of a higher standard of observance of good ethical standards among its members. The official website of the CPS brought to the attention of all its members a proposal on the observance of good ethical practice, which was received at its 2007 General and Experimental Psychology Annual Conference and signed by 58 well-respected scholars in attendance. The aim of the proposal was the inculcation of a good culture of scholarly practice through self-discipline and moral examples exhibited by senior scholars and professors in the academic sector. More specifically, it has made declarations on attitudes toward organizing and attending academic conferences. Sanctions have been devised, in the form of making public the names of those who failed to observe such standard practices at a conference and will be barred from speaking at that annual conference. Perhaps this represents a small area of behavior codified among conference-goers, but what really matters is the message that this measure carries. It speaks volumes about the determination and commitment of psychologists toward good and ethical practice in the society at large.

As a developing country, the Chinese Mainland still has a long way to go to promote psychological practitioners' better understanding of ethics, as well as their practice of ethics and social responsibility. While we see convergence in the Chinese societies in working toward statutory registration, updates and major revision efforts, commitment toward more systematic teaching of ethics codes, and observance of ethical practice on multiple fronts, creating environments that facilitate conscious adoption of these codes in psychologists' research and professional practice on a daily basis is our common direction and, hopefully, our common destiny as well.

> In a field so complex, where individual and social values are yet but ill defined, the desire to play fairly must be given direction and consistency by some rules of the game. These rules should do much more than help the unethical psychologist keep out of trouble; they should be of palpable aid to the ethical psychologist in making daily decisions.
> (*Hobbs*, 1948, p.81)

Acknowledgment

We wish to thank Geoff Blowers for comments on an earlier version of this chapter, and the following individuals: Helios Lau, Terry Au, Iris Benzie, Helene Fung, Julian Lai, Fu Siu Lan, and Hwang Tun

Notes

1. The Working Group on the Revision of the code of Professional Conducts was formally established in 2004 chaired by one of the most senior psychologists in the HKSAR government with four members, one each from the clinical, educational and industrial / organizational as well as the academia respectively.

2. The functioning of the IRB in the early years was limited for reviewing Fogarty programs from NIH and some other international cooperative projects. In the recent years, the work of IRB was extended to examine domestic research projects. In 2009, 38 domestic research projects and 2 international cooperative projects were reviewed and approved by the IRB of the Institute of Psychology, Chinese Academy of Sciences.

References

Blowers, G.H. (2010). The continuing prospects for a Chinese psychology. In M. H. Bond (Ed.), *The Oxford handbook of Chinese psychology* (pp. 5–18). Oxford: Oxford University Press.

Chan, C. C. (2010). Community psychology in Chinese societies. In M. H. Bond (Ed.), *The Oxford handbook of Chinese psychology* (pp. 441–456). Oxford: Oxford University Press.

Chang, P. (1998). Expedite the process of clinical psychologists. *Health, Welfare and Environmental Magazine, 5,* 23–25.

Chen, W., & Chen, Y. (2000). Seeking the blossoming of the counseling services: A discussion of the needs and concerns of the Psychologist Statute. *Journal of Medical Hope, 32,* 16–18.

Chinese Psychological Society. (2007). *Code of ethics for counseling and clinical practice.* Beijing: Author.

Fisher, C. B. (2009). *Decoding the ethics code: A practical guide for psychologists.* Thousand Oaks, CA: Sage Publications, Inc.

Hobbs, N. (1948). The development of a code of ethical standards for psychology. *American Psychologist, 3,* 80–84.

Hong Kong Psychological Society. (2007). Working group for the revision of the code of professional conduct (2007). The revision of the code of professional conducts—A consultation paper. HK: Author.

Hong Kong Psychological Society (2009). Working group for the revision of the code of professional conduct (2009). Code of professional conduct consultation draft—2nd draft. HK: Author

Lin, J. (1998). A joint effort to promote the Statute for psychologists. *Guidance Quarterly, 34,* 1–3.

Leach, M. M., & Harbin, J. J. (1997). Psychological ethics codes: A comparison of twenty-four countries. *International Journal of Psychology, 32*(3), 181–192.

Nagy, T. F. (2005). *Ethics in plain English: An illustrative casebook for psychologists* (2nd ed.). Washington, DC: American Psychological Association

Pellegrino, E. D. (1989). Can ethics be taught? An essay. *Mount Sinai Journal of Medicine, 56,* 490–494.

Taiwan's Department of Health. (2008). *The statistics of suicide rate between 1999 and 2005.* Retrieved from http://www.doh.gov.tw/CHT2006/DisplayStatisticFile.aspx?d=69005 (Taiwanese article)

Wang, L., Kwan, K. L. & Huang, S. F. (2011). Counseling psychology licensure in Taiqan: Development, challenges and opportunities. *International Journal for the Advancement of Counseling, 33,* 37–50.

CHAPTER
25
Psychological Ethics in Europe: Convergence and Divergence

An-Magritt Aanonsen *and* Katharina Althaus

> **Abstract**
>
> One characteristic of psychological ethics in Europe is that the continent has very diverse historical, cultural, and professional traditions. This makes the development of a good, visible structure with transparency in matters concerning ethics—i.e., codes of conduct, ethics committees, and sanctioning procedures—rather a challenge. In this chapter we will look, with the structure of the Meta-Code of the EFPA as a template, at the variety of ethical codes throughout the European continent—depending on the development of the profession of psychologists, the different kinds of psychological organizations and regulation of psychologists—and comment on communalities, differences, or special characteristics of the ethical codes of a majority of EFPA member associations.
>
> **Key Words:** Europe, EFPA, association, legal, ethical code, regulation, sanction, consumer protection

In this chapter, we look into the ethics for psychologists in Europe. In the introduction we will list the different topics to be covered in the chapter and discuss how to define Europe in this context. First, the list of topics:

- Legal status of the discipline: is the discipline regulated by law or otherwise?
- Professional Associations: how psychologists are organized
- Ethics Committees: are such committees a regular body in the associations?
- Ethical Codes: to compare them and point to similarities and differences
- Ethical Training: how are psychologists trained in ethics?
- Current Research: the status of research in psychological ethics
- Future Challenges

How should we define Europe in this context? Europe has changed quite a lot during the last decades. The breaking down of the West–East separation made a great change in the picture of the region. Then the war in the Balkan region dissolved the former Yugoslavia, and we got new (or old) independent countries in this region. The European Union has been growing since it started as the European Economic Community in 1957 with six countries (Germany, France, Italy, the Netherlands, Belgium, and Luxembourg). Today the European Union consists of 27 countries, and some more "knocking on its door." According to the Council of Europe, however, that organization has 47 members.

The modern history of Europe has made the region more united, but psychology as science and profession is still characterized by differences in scope and development. The regulation of the profession varies a lot, as we shall see later in this chapter. The science has been growing within very different conditions. In the western part of the continent, many countries have a long tradition both within the science and the profession of psychology. In the United Kingdom and the Nordic countries, the Anglo-American influence has been strong. In the central parts of Europe before the fall of the Berlin Wall, the development was more restricted. Psychology varies from hardly visible as a profession, with no visible association in some of the Central European countries, to a well-established profession with regulations and high status in the Nordic countries.

A way of defining Europe in this context is to take the European Federation of Psychologists Associations (EFPA) as a reference (see next paragraph). One of the characteristics of a profession is to have a code of conduct, and that was the reason for the EFPA to develop a *Meta-Code of Ethics*, a model to be used by the members to develop their own codes. A code of conduct is established by professional associations to give the public an orientation about the guidelines for professional behavior. It is also a guide for the professional, and breaking the code will most often be met by sanctions from a body within the professional association. When the profession is regulated by law, there could also be reactions from a statutory body.

Legal Status of the Discipline
Is Psychology Regulated by the Law?

Looking at psychology in Europe, out of the 47 countries that are members of the Council of Europe, 35 are actually members of the European Federation of Psychologists Associations (EFPA) (see Table 25.1). Only a small minority of countries, either very small ones or former communist countries, are not yet members of EFPA (see Table 25.2).

Thus, from the EU countries, only the Romanian psychologists do not yet belong to the EFPA; neither is Belarus, which is not a member of the Council of Europe, a member of the EFPA. From these 13 countries there is no information available concerning the legal situation of psychologists. Some of them seem not even to have a national psychological association or society. Those who have such a body were contacted, but there were no answers.

In the countries of the EFPA Member Associations, 27 have or are preparing a national law or a legal regulation protecting the title "psychologist" and/or regulations for the profession of psychologists.[1] (see Table 25.3).

Thus, among the EU member states, only five—Bulgaria, Latvia, the Netherlands, Portugal, and Romania—have no basic legal regulation of psychologists either in existence or in process within the government. Outside the European Union, countries lacking a basic legal regulation of psychologists are Liechtenstein, San Marino, Serbia, and Russia. Therefore, even though there are differences in the systems of regulations, most of the countries we know have some kind of regulation of psychologists.

How is Licensure Obtained and Maintained?

Psychology as a profession is regulated in 26 countries, but not licensed in all of them. As we have seen above, in some countries they only give licenses to clinical and/or health psychologists, and in Germany only psychologists as psychotherapists are licensed. There is a licensing procedure in the five Nordic countries, in Spain, Italy, Croatia, Hungary, and Estonia for psychologists in general, and in the United Kingdom the law protects the titles of psychologists within special fields. It also differs what has to be done to maintain the license. In some countries, it is given for lifetime without

Table 25.1 Members of EFPA

Austria	Belgium	Bulgaria	Croatia	Cyprus
Czech Republic	Denmark	Estonia	Finland	France
Germany	Greece	Hungary	Iceland	Ireland
Italy	Latvia	Liechtenstein	Lithuania	Luxembourg
Malta	Netherlands	Norway	Poland	Portugal
Russia	San Marino	Serbia	Slovakia	Slovenia
Spain	Sweden	Switzerland	Turkey	United Kingdom

Table 25.2 Members of the Council of Europe, but Nonmembers of EFPA

Albania	Andorra	Armenia	Azerbaijan
Bosnia-Herzegovina	Georgia	Macedonia	Moldova
Monaco	Montenegro	Romania	Ukraine

any demand for continued education (Nordic countries). Some countries require a minimum of yearly continued education to keep the title. We will give examples from some of those countries where we have information, to illustrate different solutions to the question in the heading.

Nordic Countries. In Norway, Finland, and Iceland, the profession of psychologist is regulated in the Law of Health Professionals. The license will be given when one applies for it after finishing a university program of 5.5 to 6 years, where supervised practice is included. The license is awarded by authorizing authorities within the health department, and the title is, in principle, for a lifetime.

In Sweden, one may practice as psychologist after having finished the university program of 5 years. To get a license one has to practice for one year with supervision, no renewal needed.

In Denmark, one may also practice as psychologist after a 5-year university program. To be licensed as so-called authorized psychologist, one has to practice for 2 years under supervision.

Italy. The title is protected by the law. The license is obtained through a state exam at the end of the study period plus one year of supervised practice, and is automatically maintained in the absence of conviction of malpractice accreted by the Regional Chamber of Psychologists.

United Kingdom. The law concerning the profession in United Kingdom is quite new, from July 2009. The law does not protect the title of psychologist, but seven adjectival titles, like clinical, educational, and so forth. One has to apply for the title to the Health Professional Council after finishing academic and practical training at the master's or doctoral level.

Germany. The academic title is for a lifetime, and psychology is not regulated by professional law but by competition law; therefore, the professional title could not be taken away. Psychologists specialized in psychotherapy are legally recognized by state authorities on the base of a professional legal regulation.

Netherlands. There is no general licensing system for psychologists in the Netherlands. The title of psychologist is not legally protected. Yet, there is a legal system with an act that covers eight healthcare professions including two psychological ones (clinical psychologist and health psychologist). It establishes disciplinary jurisdiction and requires periodic renewal of registration.

There is also a private system established and managed by the professional association, the National Institute of Psychologists (NIP). The NIP keeps a register of psychologists who are qualified to bear the title "Psychologist NIP."

Czech Republic. Except in health services, the only license issued is a trade certificate. This certificate is valid for life. Within the health service, the psychologist has to go through postgraduate specialized education or earn a certain number of credits from continuous education to be registered by the ministry of health. The registration is valid for

Table 25.3 EFPA Members with Legal Regulation for Psychologists

Austria°	Belgium	Croatia	Cyprus	Czech Republic
Denmark	Estonia	Finland	France	Germany**
Greece	Hungary	Iceland	Ireland*	Italy
Lithuania*	Luxembourg	Malta	Norway	Poland
Slovakia	Slovenia°°	Spain	Sweden	Switzerland
Turkey.⁺	United Kingdom			

° Regulation only for health and clinical psychologists
** An example of a different type of regulation is the situation in Germany, where there is no legal act but a decision by the Supreme Court that only persons with specified university training may use the title "Diplom-Psychologe."
°° Regulation for psychologists in the healthcare sector and for counseling
⁺ Legislation process actually stopped

7 years and one has to submit proof of continuing education to get a renewal.

Belgium. In Belgium, there is a law from 1993 regarding the title "psychologist." One must have a university degree of 5 years. Then one asks for the title and the *Commission des psychologues* awards it.

Malta. Malta has a legal regulation through the Malta Psychology Profession Act from 2005. The license is obtained by applying to Malta Psychology Profession Board, which is regulated by the act mentioned above. To maintain the license one must show evidence of supervised practice and continued professional development every second year.

Estonia. The law regulating psychologists is the Profession Act. According to this act, professional councils are formed. Psychologists' professions belong under the jurisdiction of the Professional Council of Social Work and Health. The council guides the recognition of professional qualifications.

Do these Laws Regulate Specific Aspects of Psychological Practice—Academic, Research, Applied?

The laws in the Nordic countries regulate applied psychological practice, and specifically the work as a psychologist in health and client-based practice. In some countries, the law only regulates health or clinical psychologists, like in the Netherlands and Austria. The new law in the United Kingdom regulates psychologists in different fields, not the general title of psychologist. We know of no countries where the law regulates academic or research psychologists.

What is the Relationship between the Law and Psychological Ethics Codes?

It follows from the examples above that there is eagerness within the member associations of the EFPA to have some kind of regulation, even where the state is not yet at the point of regulating the profession by law. The most regulated field of the profession so far seems to be within the health area; see Table 25.3.

The law and the psychological ethical codes are separate, but influence each other in different ways. Complaints may be sent to the associations to be handled, and to the regulating authorities at the same time. In Denmark, all complaints about authorized psychologists will be sent to the statutory body that also uses the ethical code of the Danish association to evaluate the complaint. In Spain, there is no government body charged with receiving complaints about psychologists. The association is a chamber, Colegio Official de Psicólogos (COP), organized as one national COP based on several regional COP's. The function is officially attributed to the ethical committees of regional COPs. As we saw for the Netherlands, the law also establishes its own disciplinary jurisdiction, alongside the associations' ethical codes.

Regulations within the European Union and the EFPA

Within the EU, psychology does not form part of the regulated professions. Consequently, the European institutions have established rules to facilitate the mutual recognition of professional qualifications between the member states in order to stimulate the mobility of professionals, as well as the delivery of services, across national borders. This is the aim of Directive 2005/36/EC of September 7, 2005 on the recognition of professional qualifications. In this directive there is one article of central relevance, Article 15, which proposes "a more flexible and automatic procedure based on common platforms established by professional associations at the European level." *Common platforms* are defined as "a set of criteria of professional qualifications which attest a sufficient level of competence for the pursuit of a given profession." The commission thus is in favor of professions themselves putting up standards for practice.

In 1999, a proposal was developed for a project under the EU Leonardo da Vinci program. The result of this venture, led by Ingrid Lunt, former president of the EFPA, was the "European Framework for Psychologists Training" or EuroPsyT, which was accepted by the EFPA in 2001. In 2001, a second project began aimed at developing the European Certificate in Psychology (EuroPsy). The objective of the EuroPsy is to define standards for psychology training throughout Europe that should enable the bearers of the certificate to be recognized as "having a European-level qualification in psychology." The EuroPsy is built upon a 6-year education and training in psychology that includes one year of supervised practice. Psychologists holding the EuroPsy have been recorded since 2010 in the Register of European Psychologists.

Paralleled, a first EuroPsy Specialist Certificate has been developed. This is a specialist certificate in psychotherapy based on the EuroPsy, and psychologists holding this will be recorded in the EuroPsy register, also beginning in 2010. The next specialist certificate to be developed is in work and organizational psychology.

How is the EuroPsy connected with the European Commission (EC) directive on recognition of professional qualifications? The intention is that the EuroPsy will eventually form part of the "platform" or "professional card" of the new EC directive on recognition of professional qualifications (COM (2002–119).

Important from the ethics point of view is that the EuroPsy Certificate is awarded under the "pledge to act in accordance with the national code of ethics of the country of practice" (all quotes in this chapter are from EFPA, 2006). The Europsy Certificate will be valid for 7 years. Renewal is dependent on continuing education and ethically correct professional behavior.

Professional Associations
How Are Psychologists Organized?

The history of the profession of psychologists shows a great variety in Europe. The oldest is the British Psychological Society (BPS), existing for more than 100 years. To have a professional association is usually one of the criteria of being a profession. It seems quite impossible to get a full view of the situation in all countries, and the variations seem to follow the kinds of organization that are usual in the different countries. In the south, some countries organize professional associations as chambers, organizations regulated by the state with obligatory membership (Italy and Spain). In the Nordic countries, the oldest association is in Norway, established in 1934. It started as an association of common professional interest and worked on the quality of psychologists' education and practice. This resulted, among other things, in developing an ethics code of conduct in 1958 and a postgraduate specialist education of clinical psychologists established in the same year. Later it also became a trade union with negotiation status, which means that the association is both a professional body and a trade union. This is also the situation in the other Nordic countries. It explains the strong position of the associations in these countries, with a very high percentage of membership (80%–90%) in the associations. In the big European countries like Germany and the United Kingdom, there is a single professional association, while in France there are many different associations, which represent different fields of psychology and various schools of psychological treatment. In the United Kingdom, the British Psychological Society also has had the important role of approving the university programs to become a psychologist and to give the greatly respected title of "chartered psychologist."

The most common structure is that there is one association organized as a nongovernmental organization (NGO), with a voluntary membership of psychologists. In some countries there is more than one association, as in France and Latvia. In Switzerland there are as many as 42 different associations, which together form a federation. The different associations could be competing for the same psychologists or organizing psychologists in different fields. Only one association from each country can become member of the EFPA. The EFPA advises that where there is more than one association, they should together form a federation. This has been done successfully in many countries, such as Italy, France, and Germany.

In some of the countries where psychologists are about to become a recognized profession, there seems to be a tendency to develop chambers, as in Portugal and Croatia, even though they have had professional associations for many years, organized as NGOs.

Support

All the associations, whether voluntary or not, are financed by members' fees. Therefore, the financial support seems to be dependent on the relation between the association and its members. Of course, there is a kind of support when the membership is obligatory under the state regulation. In other ways, the associations might have support in undertaking special projects of interest for the public. In many countries, the professional associations will be important in lobbying around questions of interest for psychologists, and will look for political issues that could be promoted by special projects.

Development of Ethics Codes

In Europe, as well as in the United States and Canada, the first ethical codes for psychologists were developed during the 1950s. Developing an ethics code is a characteristic of the development of a profession. It is quite interesting to observe that even some of the member associations that were engaged in establishing the EFPA in 1981 were then lacking an ethical code. Now, after establishing the *Meta-Code of Ethics*, every association should have an ethical code and it should be based on the Meta-Code. A special development took place in the region during the 1980s, when the five Nordic countries (Finland, Sweden, Denmark, Norway, and Iceland) decided to elaborate a common code of ethics. The first common code was sanctioned by the five associations in the years 1988–1990.

It was revised according to the Meta-Code in the late 1990s.

Adjudication of Ethical Violations

In many countries there have been great discussions within the profession about how the associations should handle complaints against their members. A question often raised is to what degree a member association should treat complaints about their own members, and eventually give sanctions. When there is a complaint about a psychologist and it is decided that it is reasonable to look into it, this will mean a lot of work for the accused. He or she has to answer the complaint, and there may be several interchanges with the association when the latter is gathering information. Not answering is, in many associations, seen as breaking an ethical principle in itself. In addition, in the end the psychologist might be subject to disciplinary actions against him/her. These questions have been treated and solved in different ways within the associations.

The safety of clients has been a major argument for the ethics codes, as well as the code's role in providing guidance on how the psychologist should act in different situations. The code itself has a role as an advisor in how the psychologist should behave in different situations. In difficult ethical discussions and dilemmas, the code is an important aid.

Last, but not least, the professional associations and the profession as such gain more credibility in the society by being willing and able to discipline their own members.

The EFPA's standing committee on ethics (SCE) has worked out "Recommendations on Evaluative and Corrective Actions in Case of Complaints about Unethical Conduct" (EFPA, 2005). The recommendations deal with the association's "responsibility to have procedures for the evaluation of members' practice in cases where a complaint is made, and to have the disciplinary procedures which may follow therefrom.... Associations should determine whether and how the three stages of investigation, evaluation and disciplinary action should be related."

In the countries with the "older" associations—for example, the Nordic countries, the Netherlands, Germany, Spain and Italy—the ethics systems for psychologists are well established, with internal bodies to evaluate and investigate complaints. Some will have particular disciplinary bodies, while others have one committee handling both advisory tasks and the task to investigate, evaluate, and give sanctions when there are complaints about their members.

The association alone is fully responsible for building the system, and often it will be the most important democratic body (general assembly or biannual meeting) that decides on the structure and the ethical code, and what sanctions could be given to a psychologist who has violated the ethical code. The role of the professional associations in these matters is restricted to their members. When membership in an association is not obligatory (which is the normal situation) and the country has no laws regulating psychologists, there will be no sanctions against psychologists outside the association.

Ethics Committees
Do They Exist? Are They Part of or Separate from Professional Associations?

We have been in contact about this with the EFPA Standing Committee on Ethics (SCE) and with many of the associations. As indicated above, we have no information so far about the countries that are not members of the EFPA, but we do have information from many of the member associations. Table 25.4 shows the 27 member associations that have an ethics committee.

The Russian Psychological Society, the newest member of the EFPA, has no ethics committee so

Table 25.4 Countries with an Ethics Committee

Austria	Belgium	Czech Republic	Denmark	Estonia
Finland	France	Germany	Greece	Hungary
Iceland	Ireland	Italy	Latvia	Lithuania
Luxembourg	Malta	Netherlands	Norway	Poland
Portugal	Russia	Spain	Sweden	Switzerland
Turkey	United Kingdom			

far. We lack information from the following eight EFPA member associations: Bulgaria, Croatia, Cyprus, Liechtenstein, San Marino, Serbia, Slovakia, and Slovenia), and from the countries outside the EFPA.

The EFPA *Meta-Code on Ethics* specifies the requirements for a member association like this: "National associations should have procedures to investigate and decide upon complaints against members, and mediation, corrective and disciplinary procedures to determine the action necessary taking into account the nature and seriousness of the complaint."

The EFPA SCE is in the process of reviewing the ethical codes of EFPA member associations to see whether they comply with the Meta-Code and whether they have guidelines on evaluation and disciplinary actions. Due to language differences and to the fact that psychology as a profession is at very different stages throughout Europe, this takes some time and illustrates the great differences in the development of the profession and the great variety in its status throughout Europe.

The ethics committees may have different functions. In the abovementioned recommendations of the EFPA SCE, it is emphasized that both psychologists and the public "should have easy access to information explaining the procedures concerning the making of a complaint; the process of evaluating the complaint and the psychologist's behavior; and the decisions and range of sanctions that are available." This underlines the need for the member association to make information about ethics and the procedures available, and to ensure that its members have the possibility to get information and advice on ethical questions. Some of the ethics committees are engaged in developing the ethical code, and most of them do advisory work.

What is the Function and Scope of Authority of Ethics Committees?

The most common function of ethics committees is to deal with evaluating and developing the ethics code and to give information and advice about ethical questions and dilemmas. In some countries there are committees on different levels (national and regional) that have divided these functions. The national committee deals with evaluation and development of the code (for example, Spain), while the regional committees handle the information about procedures and, in many cases, the complaints against psychologists.

Beside the previously mentioned functions of developing ethics codes and doing advisory work, the ethics committees vary in their scope of authority. In the following examples, we will illustrate some of the similarities and differences between the committees regarding function and scope of authority.

In France, the Consultative National Commission on the Deontology of Psychologists (CNCDP) is a commission inside the French federation working independently. It is composed of eight members coming either from universities or from practice. It can only give motivated advice. Its role is consultative and no contradictory investigation is requested.

In the Czech Republic, the association has an independent ethics committee that only provides recommendations.

In Germany, the ethics committee works on the parts of the code related to professional practice and gives statements and recommendations on practical issues. The committee also proposes changes in the disciplinary procedures. In case of complaints, their lawyer writes up the cases and brings them to the disciplinary board, led by a former judge.

In Estonia, the psychological association has an ethics committee with three members. The function of the committee is to investigate, to evaluate, and answer to appeals the Union of Estonian Psychologists has received. Based on these evaluations the committee recommends solutions to the psychologist.

The Belgian Federation has a "Commission Ethique et Déontologie" that only responds to questions and gives advice.

In the United Kingdom, the new law on psychologists has led to a change. Henceforth, a statutory body will handle most of the complaints. The BPS will have a committee to give advice to its members in ethical questions.

In these six examples, it is clear that the task of an ethics committee is advisory work, and some also evaluate and develop ethics codes. One of them, Germany, uses another body when it comes to investigation or sanctioning in case of complaints about their members. It is unclear whether the other five have any procedures within their respective associations to take care of disciplinary actions. There is a statutory body in the United Kingdom.

The ethics committee within the Federation of Swiss Psychologists (FSP) is in charge of investigating and resolving complaints brought against members of the federation. The committee can impose the following sanctions and directives: reprimand, fine (i.e., monetary payment), temporary suspension from the FSP, and expulsion from the FSP. In addition to or instead of a sanction, the committee may also require that the psychologist undergoes more training or supervision.

In Turkey, there are ethics committees in various regions of the country. Their function is to offer information, to investigate/evaluate, and impose some degree of sanctions. There are four levels of sanctions: notification, warning, suspension of membership, and revocation of membership. The committee may also send an educative letter or give advice to take some courses.

The Netherlands Institute of Psychologists (NIP) has a complaint procedure laid down in its Code of Discipline. The disciplinary board deals with the complaint, hearing both parties. Its evaluation is open to appeal to a board of appeals.

In Spain, all regional COPs have their own regional ethics committees that manage all different types of complaints. The regional ethics committees have sanctioning power. Complaints range from light to extremely serious ones, and sanctions can go from private or public warnings to suspension of professional activity for days and even years.

In Italy, the association is also a chamber, and, as in Spain, there are ethics committees at national and regional levels. At the regional level, the ethics committee has the role to investigate/evaluate and give sanctions. The ethics committee at the national level discusses principles and general ethical aspects of the profession. A deontological observatory analyzes deontological legal cases in order to revise and improve the ethical code.

In these five countries, the ethics committee can have advisory functions as well as disciplinary functions. They differ from the first group in their sanctioning power.

Although the Nordic countries have a common code of ethics, they have developed differently when it comes to the function and power of ethics committees.

In Sweden, the ethics committee gives advice. The committee also receives complaints and discusses the complaints with the psychologists involved. If a complaint is very serious, it will be handed over to a national board to decide whether the complaint should be forwarded for further investigation.

In Denmark, the distinction between "psychologist" and "authorized psychologist" has consequences in terms of how complaints are treated. The ethics committee only treats complaints against psychologists, not authorized psychologists. An official state regulated body, where psychologists are also members, handles the latter.

In Norway, the ethics committee gives advice, investigates, evaluates, and issues minor sanctions, such as notes, warnings, or demands for supervision. Serious violations will be passed on to the national board, which could forward the complaint and evaluation to the statutory board for considering withdrawing the license, or the national board can expel the psychologist from the association. There is a board of appeals open to both parties.

The examples above show that the function and the scope of authority vary a lot. All ethics committees deal with providing information and advice about ethical questions and dilemmas. Some committees also do investigations, evaluations, and sanctions when there are complaints about a member. In a few associations, there is a disciplinary body separate from the ethics committee that evaluates and eventually sanctions the psychologist. Some also have lawyers to help with disciplinary actions.

During recent years there has been a trend in some ethical committees to do more active advisory work. To focus on ethical dilemmas, not only on possible violations of the ethical code, has become more common. In some associations the advisory task of the ethical committees is mentioned as the main task (France and Czech Republic). Psychologists contacting the committee are an important part of the ethical committee's work, and give input to the development of the code according to developments in the society. In some member associations (Nordic countries) one of the services that the committee offers is consulting hours when they may be contacted by telephone. (Dalen, 2006).

In the EFPA Meta-Code (EFPA, 2005a), there is a recommendation to have an appeal body that should be independent of the ethical committee. Appeal committees are explicitly mentioned in the codes in Ireland, the Netherlands, Spain, Switzerland, and Norway.

Where there are licensing authorities, they might as well receive complaints directly and will subsequently investigate the case independently of the association. This is more or less the situation in the Nordic countries, the Netherlands, and the United Kingdom.

How could we explain the great differences between the associations' ways of handling ethics? One way of looking at it could be to look into what role and standing psychologists have in the public arena. There are some indications that when there is a great proportion of psychologists employed in the public sector, psychologists seem to be more eager to join into one association. This gives more power to the association and strengthens solidarity within the profession. In the Nordic countries, this is even more so because of the trade union task of the associations. The state probably also has more interest in regulating the profession (for example, the Nordic countries and the United Kingdom) when it uses professional competence in a large scale in the public arena.

Ethical codes and a fixed set of procedures governing information, evaluation, and disciplinary actions are signs of a serious and strong association. We see that in countries where there are still no regulations that the one association has ethics committees and/or disciplinary boards who take actions when there are violations to the ethical code; for example in Switzerland, Lithuania, and Turkey. We can suppose that a longer tradition of a country's association, the existence of only one association, and the standing of psychologists in a country are factors that stimulate well-developed ethics codes, ethics committees, and procedures.

Development of psychological ethics is reflected in the work of the EFPA SCE, which has developed guidelines and recommendations for new areas such as the use of the Internet by psychologists and the use of mediation within the ethics committee. (EFPA, 2007)

To sum up on the questions raised, ethics committees do exist in the European region. The great efforts made within the EFPA and its Standing Committee on Ethics are bringing results in the development of psychological ethics in its member associations, but we still have some way to go before we have a comparable way of organizing and handling ethical matters throughout the region. Members of the Standing Committee have made very important contributions in this direction. Lately, they have also written a book for European psychologists, taking the Meta-Code as a starting point for discussion and giving examples of ethical questions and dilemmas. (Lindsay et al., 2008). The implementation of the EuroPsy will probably strengthen both the development of the profession and the development of psychological ethics.

Ethics Codes
EFPA Meta-Code of Ethics

As we have pointed out above, in Europe the European Federation of Psychologists' Associations (EFPA) is uniting a great majority of national psychological bodies. The EFPA since 1995 has had a Standing Committee on Ethics, which developed out of the task force that drafted the Meta-Code of ethics approved in 1995 during its General Assembly in Athens, and revised it in 2005 (EFPA, 2005a). The aims of the EFPA explicitly mention the promotion of ethics codes for psychologists. Every member association of the EFPA has to commit to the Meta-Code; in addition, they formulate their own ethical codes, which can complement or more clearly define the content of the Meta-Code. According to the EFPA statutes (EFPA, 2005c), "application for membership...must be accompanied by the...*ethical code* [emphasis added]" (5.2.). "Member associations shall inform the Federation about any substantial changes to their statutes or Ethical Code." (7.2.). "A Standing Committee on Ethics helps to support the development of ethical standards and the implementation of a Meta-Code of ethics." (EFPA, 2009)

"Normally, an association's ethical code is written specifying the behavior of the psychologist. The Meta-Code, however, specifies requirements of the association. The reason is that it was decided...not to seek to produce a single ethical code for all psychologists within EFPA.... The Meta-Code was found to be 'fit for purpose'." (EFPA, 2005b).

It was assumed that developing one single code of conduct was too ambitious for such a big federation. One single association voting no would have brought the project to a halt.

The EFPA Meta-Code of ethics has a quite similar structure to that of the *Universal Declaration of Ethical Principles for Psychologists*. It starts with a preamble, which expresses the general concern of improving the condition of individuals and the society. Then it lays down the obligations of EFPA member associations with regard to developing their own ethical codes and the awareness of their members about ethical issues, as well as offering training and support for their members. Another obligation specifically addressed is the establishment of procedures in the case of complaints against members.

In the preamble it is stated that EFPA "has a responsibility to ensure that the ethical codes of its member associations are in accord with the following fundamental principles which are intended to provide a general philosophy and guidance to cover all situations encountered by professional psychologists."

Then follow the four ethical principles that are basically the same as in the Universal Declaration:

- Respect for a Person's Rights and Dignity
- Competence

- Responsibility
- Integrity

Ethical Codes of EFPA Member Associations

On the following pages, we are going to look into commonalities, differences, or special characteristics of the ethical codes of a majority of EFPA member associations. Unfortunately, there is no information available about ethical codes of psychological societies or associations of those countries that are not members of the EFPA; we do not even know whether those bodies have any ethical codes. In Table 25.5 there are listed the EFPA member associations whose codes were available in English or French.

From the following countries, there were no codes available: Cyprus (only in Greek), Latvia (only in Latvian), Liechtenstein (the psychological association yet does not have its own code), Malta (the association is currently elaborating a code), Poland (only in Polish), and San Marino.

In order to organize the information in a helpful way, we take as a template the structure of the Meta-Code. As the codes are quite different in their construction, it is sometimes not easy to decide to which principle a single statement belongs. Some codes pick up exactly the principles of the Meta-Code and construct relevant chapters; others have a different structuring, while a third type, mainly shorter, are rather a collection of demands.

The main guiding principle we used in choosing the quotes was to give a good illustration for a given topic of the Meta-Code; where possible, we cite different examples to show different emphases for significant matters. Another important reason for using quotes is to show different national traditions or cultures, mentioning points that are specific to a single country. Often, these are likely to show specific historical or political influences and developments.

The codes are very diverse with regard to their length. Certainly, the shortest of all is the Estonian code that formulates its 10 values very concisely on a single page. An interesting characteristic we find in the French code, which differentiates not only the four well-known principles but also introduces three more (Scientific quality, Respect of the fixed goal, Professional independence).

The Dutch code, which is probably one of the oldest, as its first version dates back to 1960, says in its introduction, "Because opinions about decency and acceptability change over time, the Code of Ethics is a time bound document, to be revised regularly. For that reason The Netherlands Institute of Psychologists provides a fixed revision procedure, in which an adjusted code will be laid down each five years." Only one other code, the Portuguese, asks for a regular revision.

Several codes put forward in great detail the obligations of psychologists toward society and toward individuals, so the preamble of the German code states: "They are not only committed to respecting the rights of those with whom they work, but also, whenever appropriate, to intervening actively to protect such rights." (…) "They take all appropriate action to protect the welfare of those with whom they work." (…) "The binding nature of these standards is not restricted to the activities of psychologists in professional contexts alone, but also extends to the conduct of members of the profession in their capacity as psychologists in all aspects of their lives." The Italian code explicitly states, "The psychologist shall consider his/her duty to expand the knowledge of human behavior and use it to promote the psychological well-being of the individual, group, and community." In Spain, this reads, "The exercise of psychology strives toward a human and social goal that can be expressed in terms of such aims as well-being, health, quality of life, full development of individuals and groups within the distinct scope

Table 25.5 Ethical Codes of EFPA Member Associations Available for Comparison

Austria	Belgium*	Bulgaria	Croatia	Czech Republic	Estonia
France	Germany	Greece	Hungary	Ireland	Italy
Lithuania	Luxembourg*	Netherlands	Nordic Countries	Portugal	Russia
Serbia	Slovakia	Slovenia	Spain	Switzerland	Turkey
United Kingdom					

*The Belgian and Luxembourg codes exist only in French.

of individual and social lives." The Serbian Code points out: "When doing empirical research, as well as other forms of scientific production, the psychologist has to acknowledge not only his personal interests but also current and important problems of his community and society."

The Belgian code says explicitly that it is based upon Article 2 of the *Universal Declaration of Human Rights*. The Luxembourg code, too, in several passages refers to the *Universal Declaration of Human Rights*. The Spanish code asks its members to inform the *Colegio* about any violation of human rights they may learn about in their work.

The Hungarian code obliges professionals to do voluntary work for the community. "For the cause of public good they contribute a portion of their professional time for little or no compensation or personal advantage" And there is concern about nonprofessional attempts to influence psychologists' work: "They receive guidance or directions only from people who are authorized to do so." This quote might reflect historical experiences, as well as the following from Serbia: "The psychologist strives toward ideological neutrality of his science. Therefore, he is trying to remove any ideological viewpoints from scientific theses and theories."

The first Greek code dates back to 1965. It points out that "an additional reason why it is essential for Greece to form a code [is] the lack of professional tradition, due to the novelty of the profession."

Respect for a Person's Rights and Dignity
General Respect

The Portuguese Code states: "In the exercise of the profession the psychologist must respect the knowledge, insight, and experience of all the persons with whom he relates." The Slovene code reads: "Psychologists respect all people with whom they establish professional relations. In their expert work they respect the dignity, personality, knowledge, cognizance, experience, and the profession of all persons with whom they come into contact."

Several codes explicitly mention the respect that is due to different groups within the population, sometimes together with a clear ban on any discrimination. The Irish code demands that psychologists "...not allow their service to clients to be diminished by factors such as gender, sexual orientation, disability, religion, race, ethnicity, age, national origin, party politics, social standing, or class." Similar wording is contained in the Dutch, British, Hungarian, and Portuguese codes.

The Irish code asks psychologists to "*use language* [emphasis added] that conveys respect for the dignity of others (for example, gender-neutral terms) in all written or verbal communication." In a similar direction goes this requirement in the Spanish code: "Especially in their written reports, psychologists must be extremely cautious, prudent, and critical with respect to ideas that can easily degenerate into derisory and discriminatory labels..."

Respect is also due to colleagues and students. An example is mentioned in the Croatian code: "An honorable psychologist will treat other psychologists in a manner in which he himself would like to be treated." The Italian code expects this: "*Relations between psychologists must* be inspired by the principle of reciprocal respect, loyalty, and solidarity." In several codes, we find passages with an obligation to respect the work of colleagues and not to criticize colleagues publicly in an unfair manner. The German rules require: "Psychologists are expected to treat their professional colleagues with respect and shall not exercise biased criticism of their professional work." And in Spain: "Without prejudicing the scientific criticism deemed necessary..., psychologists must not discredit colleagues or other professionals working with the same or different methods, and should speak with respect of schools and types of intervention that have scientific and professional credibility."

Respect for colleagues includes giving them adequate working conditions. The German code gives quite far-reaching and detailed prescriptions about the obligation to offer employed staff suitable working conditions, written contracts, and to present trainees such tasks that prepare them for their later professional practice: "It is therefore unacceptable to require such staff to carry out monotonous or low-skilled activities." The Austrian code, very briefly: "Where a clinical psychologist employs a colleague..., he/she shall offer to this worker an employment contract corresponding to professional standards." Several codes draw attention to offering trainees adequate possibilities for acquiring relevant professional competences rather than using them for tedious and auxiliary activities.

Privacy and Confidentiality

Under this value, we find a demand for restricting the seeking of information to only that requisite for the given aim. So, the Irish code: "Explore and collect only that information which is germane to the purposes of a given investigation or intervention, or which is required by law."

The Bulgarian code asks the following concerning data storage: "The information and records are kept in an adequate manner in order to secure confidentiality, including taking reasonably precautious measures for the anonymity of the data when this is appropriate, and limiting the access to the data to the persons who have the right to know."

The Spanish code expresses itself about confidentiality in publications or teaching: "Oral, printed, audiovisual, or any other kind of exhibition of clinical or illustrative cases for educational, communicative, or scientific public purposes must be done in such a way that the identification of the person, group, or institution under consideration is impossible." Similar prescriptions are given in the British and Hungarian codes.

The Russian code has very far-reaching demands for the protection of the privacy of the client: "The psychologist shall not indicate the last names, given names, and patronymics of the test persons, but use a code... drawn up as a single copy, [that] is kept separately from experimental materials in a place inaccessible to others."

The Meta-Code mentions limitations of confidentiality. The British code specifies: "Ensure from the first contact that clients are aware of the limitations of maintaining confidentiality, with specific reference to: (a) potentially conflicting or supervening legal and ethical obligations; (b) the likelihood that consultation with colleagues may occur; and (c) the possibility that third parties... may assist..."

Several codes deal with the necessity to break confidentiality in situations where there is imminent danger for the psychologist or other persons. So, in the Nordic code: "Exceptions from this confidentiality may be made in the case of obvious danger for the client or others." The Slovak code presents this as follows: "In exceptional circumstances under which there appears sufficient evidence to raise serious concern about the safety of clients or third persons who may be endangered by the client's behavior, psychologists take action which they consider as inevitable. This includes disclosing confidential information to competent persons without the client's previous consent." The rules further recommend that such a breach of confidentiality should in advance be consulted with a professional colleague whenever there is enough time to do so. The Luxembourg, British, and Dutch codes argue in the same vein. The Greek code adds that communication of information may be made only to relevant persons or institutions (relatives, guardian, justice officials).

The Slovenian code points out the right of clients to have access to records about themselves: "On the demand of patients, psychologists enable them an insight into their dossier. Information from a dossier is the property of the patient."

A particular point is raised in the Hungarian code that stresses the risks of exchanging information via electronic means: "Psychologists providing information or other services through electronic transmission call their clients' attention to the potential risks regarding privacy and confidentiality." In the same direction argues the Belgian Federation, and the Luxembourg code even asks for destruction of data if their safe storage cannot be guaranteed.

The Turkish code emphasizes the necessity to protect the privacy of students, trainees, and supervisees: "Psychologists do not force students or supervisees to disclose personal information in course- or program-related activities... regarding sexual history, history of abuse and neglect, psychological treatment, and relationships with significant others and political preferences." Exceptions to this demand may occur when this requirement was communicated in the announcement, when personal problems of the students make it necessary to offer them special support, or if these present a danger for the student or others. The Irish and German codes, too, care for the privacy of collaborators.

Another issue is the protection of the interests of third parties related to the client. In the Dutch code this reads: "If it is necessary to include in the record information pertaining to other persons..., then this shall be done in such a way that... it may be temporarily removed should the client request an examination of the record."

The Turkish as well as the Hungarian codes are concerned about a possible breaking of confidentiality by reviewers of publications. The German code speaks out for the rights of clients to get consultation from a psychologist without the presence of a third party. In Italy, there is an explicit mentioning of confidentiality in group interventions: "[The psychologist] is also required to bind the members of the group to respect everyone's right to confidentiality."

Informed Consent and Freedom of Consent

The Meta-Code asks psychologists to clarify their professional actions and possible consequences in order to ensure the client is able to give informed consent. In the Irish code, this reads, "View informed consent not just as the signing of a consent form, but as the outcome of a process of agreeing to work collaboratively." At least these issues should be understood: "Purpose and nature of the activity; mutual responsibilities; likely benefits and risks; alternatives; the likely consequences of non-action; the option to refuse or withdraw at any time, without prejudice; over what period of time the consent applies; and, how to rescind consent if desired." Several codes argue similarly.

The Bulgarian code makes clear: "The psychologist explains to the client the procedures, which he (she) follows in making and keeping work records, publications, and reports."

Self-Determination

The Italian code explicitly mentions the right of self-determination: "The psychologist shall respect the dignity and right of self-determination, autonomy, and confidentiality of the ones who use his services; he/she shall respect their opinions and beliefs and shall refrain from imposing his/her system of values." The Turkish wording is this: "Psychologists do not force clients into declaring, denying, or changing their worldview, sexual orientation, political, religious, and moral values." The Austrian code highlights an interesting aspect of self-determination: "Psychological work shall not be defined as a one-sided adjustment of the individual to society."

The Luxembourg code is very detailed about necessary actions of the psychologist in case of temporary incapability for self-determination of the client. In such situations, the psychologist should base his actions on earlier statements of the client; if not possible, the expressed wishes of a person responsible for the client; and if both are not feasible, he should consult with his colleagues.

In the Meta-Code, there is a short reference about the limits of self-determination taking into account such factors as the clients' developmental state. In some codes, for example, the Dutch, we find quite detailed instructions concerning legal minor clients of different ages or legal adults who are deemed incapable of adequately exercising their rights.

Competence
Ethical Awareness

The Hungarian code in its introduction elucidates that "Lack of awareness or misunderstanding of an ethical standard is not itself a defense to a charge of unethical conduct." It widens the circle of those who should know about the professional and ethical standards to employers of psychologists, because, "This prompts respect for the psychological profession and at the same time provides a safeguard for the appropriate conditions necessary for psychologists to maintain their professional work at a high standard, and provides protection against unreasonable expectations which are antagonistic to the standards of the ethical code."

The Nordic code not only obliges the individual psychologist to build up ethical awareness, but also defines duties for psychological organizations. "The Nordic psychologists' associations have the responsibility for arranging conditions for ethical reflection and debate among their members by, for example, educational and guidance measures." The Dutch code expects this: "The psychologist recognizes the necessity of continuous critical reflection on his professional conduct. He raises the matter of his professional conduct in peer supervision regularly. He follows the debate on professional ethics within his profession."

Limits of Competence

In the code of the Czech-Moravian Psychological Society, this appears: "Psychologists shall practice only within the area of their field for which they have the appropriate preparation and have achieved qualifications." In Hungary, they add, "Should these conditions not apply, they require supervision or a handover of their commissions to others." The Serbian code explains a necessary exception to the obligation to practice within the limits of competence: "A psychologist can perform the work he is not yet qualified for, if there is supervision and approval of colleagues with needed qualifications."

The Croatian code raises an important point: "Psychologists will not teach the implementation of specialized techniques or procedures...to persons without a formal education, specialization, work experience, or some other evidence of professionalism." The Italian code argues in the same vein.

Limits of Procedures

For Spanish psychologists, this applies: "They must recognize both the limits of their competence and the limitations of their techniques." The Nordic code offers this: "The psychologist is aware of the limitations that are inherent in methods and procedures, and of the limitations which, on these grounds, must be specified in the conclusions that may be drawn. The psychologist shows extreme caution when using methods, devices, and techniques that are still in the developmental stage and do not satisfy the usual demands of method."

The Hungarian code, too, asks for caution when using new methods: "They do not base any diagnostic or therapeutic work solely on the basis of new procedures." The Slovene code is very succinct: "Psychologists use methods, techniques, and procedures that have been assessed and accepted by the profession." The Croatian Psychological Association reflects on this: "Psychologists will not issue professional assessments and decisions based on outdated or overused assessment procedures, tests with unknown assessment characteristics, and tests that are not standardized or lack norms for the appropriate population."

The Turkish code reflects on therapies with new, unconventional means that bear unknown ethical risks: "Settings in which telephone calls, emails, chat, or videoconference calls are used from the beginning of the psychotherapeutic relationship include risks that are not expected in face-to-face therapies."

The Serbian code is anxious not to give a wrong picture of psychology: "The psychologist is aware of the limitations of psychology as a science. When presenting psychology to the public, he is required to avoid sensationalism and every other exaggeration which could induce the public to believe that possibilities of psychology are bigger, or smaller, than they really are."

Continuing Development

The Slovenian code points out that "Psychologists have an obligation to ongoing education and training for their professional work." Concerning this issue, the Spanish code states, "The continuous effort to maintain their professional competence is part of their work." And the Nordic code: "The psychologist works in accordance with scientific principles and documented experience, and ensures a continual professional development."

The Hungarian code further draws attention to this: "As leaders they take care of the professional development of their colleagues, such as psychologists, trainees, and assistants."

Incapability

The Estonian code deals with this matter as follows: "[The psychologist] provides his/her own working condition by working within the limits of his/her actual capabilities and, in the case of incapability, takes steps to get personal professional help or withdraws from professional activities." The Slovene code requires, "Psychologists take on and perform expert work only if their physical and mental health allow and enable them for professional ability and judgment." The Irish code argues in the same way. In Slovakia, there is explicit mention of the problematic influence of alcohol or drugs on professional competence.

Responsibility
General Responsibility

The Meta-Code postulates that the psychologist is responsible for the quality and consequences of his/her professional actions. In the Bulgarian code, this reads, "The psychologist takes full responsibility for his (her) scientific, research, teaching, and applied professional activity." In Slovenia, very concisely: "Psychologists are responsible for professionalism, quality, and consequences of their professional work." The Nordic countries present it like this: "The psychologist takes independent responsibility for the quality and the consequences of his/her work, but is at the same time aware that he/she is perceived by others as a representative for the entire professional group." The Turkish code expands the demands on behavior toward collaborators and subordinates: "Psychologists have the responsibility to act in an ethical manner to their assistants, students, supervisees, or supervisors in the scientific and professional arena." In Hungary, they specify, "They are aware of the fact that their decisions may affect the lives of others and they make a strong effort that these decisions should be professionally established, void of any personal, financial, social, organizational, or political influence."

Another concern is to act responsibly toward the profession of psychology. Regarding this, the Slovak code states, "Psychologists should avoid personal and professional misconduct that might bring the reputation of the profession and science of psychology into disrepute." The Portuguese code formulates it this way: "In the exercise of the profession the psychologist should contribute to the development of the discipline of psychology." The Greek code accentuates: "Unfavorable comments about colleagues expressed in public…may bring into disrepute and cause damage to the image of the profession in the public opinion."

In Lithuania, the obligation not to bring the profession into disregard is extended even further, comprising the psychologist's lifestyle: "The way of life led by a psychologist must not hinder execution of his/her professional duties, or cause damage to the prestige of psychology or psychologists. Psychologists are to observe the rules of society life and understand that their violation may have negative impact upon their professional competence and their colleagues' prestige."

The Luxembourg code requires liability insurance to be able to cover possible damages.

Promotion of High Standards

The Dutch code emphasizes, "The psychologist imposes high professional standards and ethical norms on his professional practice. He acts in accordance with acknowledged scientific views. To the best of his ability, he strives for the advancement of such norms and standards in his professional field." In Hungary, this reads, "Psychologists make the effort to do their work at the highest standards and in line with their convictions, complying with the standards of the Ethics Code and meeting legal obligations."

The Italian code is concerned about working conditions that might be in disagreement with ethical obligations: "The psychologist shall not accept working conditions that compromise his/her professional autonomy or the compliance with the regulations in this Code and, if such conditions arise, he shall inform the Board." The Belgian code asks psychologists to evaluate their work through adequate methods.

The Estonian code directs its attention toward teaching: "In teaching, the psychologist takes responsibility for a fully updated scientific level of knowledge and for acquisition of the knowledge by students."

Avoidance of Harm

The Meta-Code underlines the necessity to avoid the misuse of psychological knowledge or practice. Most codes explicitly pick up this issue. In the Swiss Code, this reads, "Psychologists undertake appropriate measures to prevent any misuse of their services or products by third parties that violates the Ethics Code." The Slovak code declares, "Psychologists uphold the responsibility to store psychological tests, psycho-diagnostic instruments, and recordings in a safe place in order to prevent them from being misused by incompetent persons." In Lithuania, they emphasize this even more: "The chief obligation of the psychologist is to guarantee that materials relating to psychological investigations, on the grounds of which conclusions about S's (the clients') mental development, his/her mental health are to be made, are not accessible to laypersons.(...) When promoting psychological techniques and equipment publicly, the psychologist shall be careful not to give information that may reduce effectiveness of such aids in professional activities." Several other codes put their attention on the responsibility not to spread knowledge about psychological instruments, for example, the Slovene, Greek, Spanish, Czech-Moravian, and Italian codes.

Most codes contain statements about avoidance or minimization of foreseeable harm. The code of the Spanish *Colegio* states explicitly that the cooperation with, or even more so the direct application, of torture or bad treatment constitutes the most serious violation of professional ethics for psychologists. "Psychologists shall not participate at all in any cruel, inhuman, or degrading procedure regardless of the purpose and situation." The Nordic and the Irish codes, too, explicitly pronounce an absolute ban on using any physically or psychologically forcible means.

In Estonia, we find an interesting prescription: "The psychologist is in service to the society as long as the society stands for the well-being of the individuals. The psychologist does nothing which might harm any individual despite possible financial, ideological, or political justifications of such harmful action." In the Estonian code, we further read a remarkable idea regarding the avoidance of harm, namely the protection not only of the client, but also of the psychologist him/herself: "In practice the psychologist does no harm to his/her client nor himself/herself."

Several codes explicitly mention research using animals. Probably the most detailed rules are in the Irish code: "Use animals in research only where...the research will increase understanding of the structures and processes underlying behavior, or increase understanding of the particular animal species..., or result eventually in benefits to the health and welfare of humans or other animals. (...) Use procedures subjecting animals to pain, stress, or deprivation only if alternative procedures are unavailable and the goal is justified by prospective...gains. (...) Make every effort to minimize discomfort, illness and pain in animals. (...) Use animals in classroom demonstrations only if the instructional objectives cannot be achieved through...other methods, and if the...demonstration is warranted by the...gain." The Russian code emphasizes: "Animal tests are an inextricable part of psychological research. The fundamental obligation of the psychologist to respect human life is also applicable here." The Greek, Italian, Turkish, Spanish, and German codes, too, mention the demand for special care when using animals for experiments. In the Hungarian code, there is a request for the participation of a veterinary surgeon when using animals.

Several codes also deal with potential harm to research participants. In Slovenia, the demand is rather absolute: "If it is impossible to avoid discomfort, harm, or danger in a research, psychologists decline to participate in it." In the Irish code, this reads, "Protect the dignity and well-being of research participants at all times." In Ireland, Germany, and the United Kingdom, we find a requirement for debriefing research participants if appropriate. This reads, in the British code, "Debrief research participants at the conclusion of their participation, in order to inform them of the outcomes and nature of the research, to identify any unforeseen harm, discomfort, or misconceptions, and in order to arrange for assistance as needed." And the Irish: "Provide a debriefing…following studies in which deception…has occurred. Psychologists shall clarify the real nature of and rationale for the study, and seek to remove any misconceptions and reestablish trust." Particular care when undertaking research with persons who are not able to give consent is an issue in the German and Serbian Codes.

Continuity of Care

In France, there is concern about the appropriate termination of services. "In the case when the psychologist cannot pursue his intervention, he should take the appropriate measures so that the continuity of his professional action may be guaranteed by a colleague with the agreement of the concerned persons." The Croatian code records that in such cases the psychologist "should plan and organize further care of the client." The Luxembourg code states that this obligation may include the referral of the client to another professional from outside psychology.

The Meta-Code points out that the responsibility of the psychologist continues after formal termination of the professional relationship. In Portugal, this reads, "The psychologist should take into consideration that after the formal ending of the relationship, he is responsible for those involved, as long as this responsibility derives directly from such a relationship." The Nordic code uses the same argument.

The Turkish code gives explicit permission to end a professional relationship under specific circumstances: "Psychologists may terminate therapy when threatened or otherwise endangered by the client or by another person with whom the client has a relationship."

Extended Responsibility

The Austrian code points out that "teachers shall draw the attention of trainees to the ethical consequences of their work and inform them about the content and importance of the ethical standards." The Nordic code states: "The psychologist takes responsibility for the scientific and professional activity, including the ethical standard, of his/her employees, assistants, candidates in supervision, and students." The Bulgarian and Croatian codes, too, raise this issue. The Belgian Federation asks its members that they require from their nonpsychologist coworkers that they also respect the ethical code. The psychologist has to assume responsibility even for their misdemeanors. The Turkish psychological society points out the responsibility of supervisors for psychotherapies offered by their trainees: "When the therapist is a trainee, the legal responsibility for the treatment provided belongs to the supervisor. The client is informed about this situation in the beginning of treatment." This last demand is considered in the Croatian Code, too.

Resolving Dilemmas

With regard to this subject, the Dutch code writes, "If, in a given situation the psychologist expects that following a stipulation of the code of ethics leads to not following another stipulation of the code, then he weighs up the outcome of the choice for one of the stipulations carefully and considers obtaining advice from his professional association and/or from experienced colleagues." The Austrian code considers, "If a clinical psychologist is faced with a moral conflict between his/her duty to maintain confidentiality on the one hand, and having to report to the authorities on the other hand, he/she shall first weigh different legal interests against each other. (…) A violation…may be excusable as necessary if it helps to ward off an imminent and significant threat…. If the psychologist concerned finds the moral conflict irresolvable, he/she may turn to the ethics committee." The Luxembourg code says that when a psychologist is asked to act in disaccord with the code, he has to direct his actions according to the spirit of the code and, if necessary, seek advice from the psychological society. The Nordic code argues in a similar direction, asking that: "The psychologist acknowledges that there will always exist a strong mutual dependency between the four basic principles and that these…may come in conflict with each other. Such an ethical dilemma demands reflection and often dialogue with clients and colleagues."

Integrity
Recognition of Professional Limitations

In Bulgaria, this requirement reads, "The psychologist is obliged to be self-reflective and to recognize and accept his (her) personal and professional limitations and the recommendations to search professional advice and assistance in difficult situations." The Portuguese code specifies, "The psychologist should look for professional support and/or supervision to resolve personal situations that may hinder the exercise of the profession." The Lithuanian code makes a point of this: "The psychologist shall not enter into professional interaction if:... unsettled emotional conflicts may exercise influence upon [the client]." The Irish code states: "[They] engage in self-care activities which help to avoid conditions (for example, burnout, addictions) which could result in impaired judgment and interfere with their ability to benefit and not harm others. (...) Seek emotional support and/or supervision from colleagues when feeling stressed or vulnerable due to professional dilemmas."

Honesty and Accuracy

The first concern regarding this is to represent the psychologists' qualifications honestly and accurately. The Nordic code asks for this: "The psychologist gives adequate information about own qualifications, education, experience, competence, and professional affiliation, and uses only the professional titles to which his/her education, authorization, and employment give the right." The German code gives these instructions: "Psychologists may make reference to further and advanced psychological training or certificates which they have undertaken or obtained, as well as to specialism, target groups, and language skills. Psychologists may make reference to a maximum of six such differentiating factors." The Estonian code points out that "The psychologist does not use his/her professional titles in his/her private life and civil activities." In Austria, the code gives quite detailed rules for representing professional qualifications. "Entries in telephone directories shall feature solely the name, relevant academic degrees, address, and phone number, possibly also information about psychologists' affiliations with professional organizations and main areas of activity."

The German code is quite detailed in forbidding what it calls "grandiose" advertisements. "In the field of psychological therapy, the practice may not be referred to in any way that may illegitimately suggest that such a practice enjoys or is able to provide preferential treatment; this applies in particular to descriptions such as "advice center," "head office," "center," or similar terms. The term "institute" or similarly grandiose terms may only be used in the field of psychological therapy if the personnel employed and the equipment and working methods used in such a setting genuinely warrant such a description." Similar demands are found in the Russian code aiming at advertising and nameplates for the psychologist's practice. In the Italian code, this is worded very strongly: "The lack of transparency and truthfulness of the advertised message shall be regarded as a breach to the code of ethics."

Honesty and accuracy in representing information in all aspects is laid down in the Netherlands as follows: "The psychologist issues information meticulously and informs those involved of alternative theories, evidence, or explanations, if there might be any, and he makes his professional judgment on these alternatives explicit." The Spanish code writes it like this: "Psychological reports must be clear, precise, rigorous, and intelligible to the addressee. They must state their range and limitations." In Ireland, very short: "(...) not suppress disconfirming evidence of their findings and views, and acknowledge alternative hypotheses and explanations."

Another important aspect of honesty and accuracy is to not profit illegitimately from the scientific work of others, namely plagiarism. The Croatian code makes a point of this: "Psychologists will not present the ideas of others as their own. Plagiarism is the most extreme form of unethical behavior toward the work of others. (...) Psychologists should provide interested scientists access to stored data following the publication of research results. This method allows for the reanalysis and verification of derived conclusions." The German code also mentions plagiarism as unethical. In the Dutch code the issue is stated like this: "In presenting scientific or applied scientific work, or in presentations meant for lay public..., the psychologist adequately refers to his sources, insofar the results or the ideas aren't the results of his own professional activities."

Several codes reflect upon the *financial implications* of the professional relationship. The Slovak association writes this: "Psychologists should ensure that clients are aware from the first contact of costs and methods of payment for the provision of professional services. Payment is based on the mutual agreement of all the participants and it has to be consistent with the Association's payment regulations." The Nordic code adds, "The psychologist...judges carefully the consequences it may have for the professional relationship if he/she receives gifts or other services from the client." In Portugal, attention is focused on an important aspect of the financial arrangements: "In the exercise of the profession the psychologist agrees, in the early stages of the relationship, his fees. These cannot be conditioned by the results of his professional intervention." The same is mentioned in the Italian and Spanish codes.

Some associations are concerned that psychologists might offer their services for free or under tariff, so the Spanish *Colegio* states: "Psychologists must refrain from accepting financial remuneration that may devalue the profession or be in unfair competition. (…) The *Colegio Oficial de Psicólogos* may elaborate guidelines of minimum fees for each professional service…within the practice of psychology." In Greece, this reads, "When psychologists offer remunerated services, the remuneration must not be inferior to the standards specified/established for the profession." This concern depends on the system and is, of course, not relevant for countries where the National Health Service offers psychological services.

Several member associations stipulate ending interventions that do not bring any more benefits to the client, so, for example, the Spanish *Colegio*: "Psychologists must terminate an intervention and not extend it by concealment or deceit, either when the proposed objectives are achieved or when…they are unable to achieve them. In this case the person, group, institution, or community should be informed of which other psychologists or professionals can take charge of the intervention." In Italy, the wording goes in the same direction.

Straightforwardness and Openness

The Dutch code asks that with respect to this matter, "The psychologist refrains from raising unrealistic or unjust expectations regarding the nature, effects, and consequences of the services he provides."

The Hungarian code deals with introducing deception in research. "Psychologists explain any deception that is an integral feature of the design and conduct of an experiment at the conclusion of the data collection, and allow for the discussion of the participants' experiences." The British code stresses, "The nature of the deception is disclosed to clients at the earliest feasible opportunity." The Irish Psychological Society requires, "Avoid using deception (or techniques which might be interpreted as deception) in research or service activities if there are alternative procedures available or if negative effects cannot be predicted or offset." There is an obligation for debriefing when deception has occurred.

Conflict of Interests and Exploitation

Several codes express themselves about the necessity of avoiding dual relationships. There are different aspects to bear in mind. The Turkish code gives definitions of such relationships: "While in a professional relationship with a client, when psychologists take on an additional role or engage in a relationship with someone who is closely associated with their client, it is called a *dual relationship*. In addition, the instances where psychologists promise a future relationship with a client or with someone who is closely associated with the client are also considered a dual relationship." In Greece, a similar point is raised: "Psychologists should not offer their services to members of their family, associates, or close friends." In Germany the emphasis lies in the professional sphere: "Psychologists active as educators may not provide psychotherapeutic or any other form of treatment to postgraduate trainees or junior colleagues who are in a dependent relationship with the psychologist." The Italian code underlines that to offer professional services to a person with whom the psychologist has or had a significant personal relationship is a serious ethical violation.

In the Meta-Code, there is no direct mention of the explicit ban on sexual relations with clients. This issue is dealt with as the "Obligation not to exploit professional relationships to further personal…interests." Several codes mention this point directly and explicitly. Probably the most detailed and far reaching is the regulation in the Swiss code: "Psychologists desist from all conduct towards clients that is sexual in nature. Following the termination of psychotherapy or other treatment, this prohibition remains in effect for an additional period of 2 years during which no therapy sessions are conducted." In the Nordic countries code it reads, "The psychologist is aware of how intimacy and sexuality directly and indirectly may influence the relationship between psychologist and client. (…) Sexual relations between psychologist and client shall not occur." The Turkish code even enlarges the circle of those exempt from sexual relationships: "Psychologists do not engage in sexual intimacies with current therapy clients, as well as with relatives or significant others of current therapy clients." An interesting variation of this issue we find in the Lithuanian code: "The psychologist should not engage into a professional relationship if…he/she strongly dislikes S or is strongly attracted to S."

Conflicts of interest may also consist in *role conflicts* that can occur in the professional relationships with different clients. The Dutch code draws the attention of the professional to incompatibilities between a new contract and a previous one, and the Portuguese code asks psychologists to avoid establishing a professional relationship when there was another kind of relationship before.

An issue raised in the Turkish code is the demand not to exploit students. "When research participation is a course requirement for extra credit, the prospective participant is given a choice of alternatives." Similarly writes the German association, which is further concerned about this: "Psychologists active as educators must be aware of the special role that exists between teachers and students and do not exploit this relationship for their own personal benefit."

Actions of Colleagues

Most codes offer some comment about this issue. German guidelines consider this: "Psychologists concerned that a colleague may be acting in violation of professional standards and principles should initially, and in confidence, draw the colleague's attention to such conduct." The Croatian code continues, "When obvious ethical misconduct cannot be solved in a cooperative and informal manner, the psychologist is obligated to inform the Chamber, which will then undertake the necessary measures." The same states the Dutch code.

REGIONAL COMMONALITIES, STRIKING DIFFERENCES BETWEEN COUNTRIES, DISTINCTIVE AND SIGNIFICANT NATIONAL DEVELOPMENTS?

As we pointed out in the "Ethics Committees" section above, the regulations within the different national associations differ quite considerably. This applies also for the national ethical codes. As one factor that plays a role, we could identify tradition—"older" versus newer associations. This is also evident in the ethics codes. However, when we compare different codes using the dates of their definitions, we cannot find any common tendencies. Looking at the inner structure, the breadth of the issues addressed, and the length of the codes, we can see that they vary significantly but without any recognizable scheme. There are no characteristics that could help us to categorize countries and their codes. There seem to be coincidences of multiple influences of the history of an association, the ethical awareness and commitment of the concerned bodies and persons within the association, and the status of the profession in the country, as well as the political and historical situation. In codes of countries where neither society nor psychology could freely develop for a long time, we can find demands that emphasize the obligation of psychologists to be watchful with regard to undemocratic tendencies in the country.

ARE NATIONAL CODES BECOMING MORE HOMOGENIZED OR STANDARDIZED? IF SO, WHAT IS THE MECHANISM BEHIND THIS TREND?

By now, there is no standardization visible. The codes are as different as are the member associations of the EFPA, and even newer codes show divergent developments concerning structure, emphasis, and issues addressed. There is an intention within the EFPA to elaborate this further in the future.

RELATIONSHIP OF REGIONAL DEVELOPMENTS IN PSYCHOLOGICAL ETHICS TO THE UNIVERSAL DECLARATION?

As the EFPA Meta-Code is the basis of the ethics codes and ethical awareness in the region, and the *Universal Declaration of Ethical Principles for Psychologists* is rather new compared to these, so far there is no visible influence within them of the Universal Declaration.

Ethics Training

TO WHAT DEGREE ARE PSYCHOLOGICAL ETHICS A PART OF A PSYCHOLOGIST'S TRAINING?

It is difficult to get an overview of Europe regarding this question. So far, we have only information from the Nordic countries, Switzerland, and France. The implementation of the EuroPsy as a model and inspiration in the European countries will have an impact on university programs. In the EuroPsy booklet (EFPA, 2006), ethics training is listed under skills training in undergraduate studies. In the year of supervised practice, it is stated that the students will "develop working roles as a professional psychologist based on one's unique training and personality." This can be understood as an implicit form of ethics training, because the development of a professional role is very much emphasized in the Meta-Code.

The EFPA Standing Committee on Ethics has also given recommendations, accepted by the General Assembly in 1999. (EFPA, 1999) They say about the process:

> All educational programs that are organized, sponsored or accredited by the National Association

should be expected to address relevant ethical issues. This should be clearly stated to the teachers. The programs and seminars should always be evaluated in terms of how ethical issues are addressed in addition to other aspects of content and delivery.

In the countries where we have information, ethics seems to be taught at the universities together with themes like the psychologist's professional role and the laws that psychologists have to know about (Nordic countries). In France, the ethical code specifies that ethics should be part of the syllabus from the first year of the educational program. Ethics has also to be taken up within special areas during education, like testing, and in psychotherapy training. According to the scarce information we have on this, it does not seem to be usual to have special courses in ethics as such during university studies.

In many of the ethics codes of EFPA member associations, there is explicit mention of the responsibility of supervisors to teach their trainees an adequate fulfillment of their professional roles. In the Nordic countries, where there are specialist programs as postgraduate education, ethics are dealt with in discussions about ethical dilemmas within the psychologist's day-to-day work.

Current Research on Psychological Ethics

Going through reference lists in some books on ethics, and asking colleagues in different countries, psychological ethics seems to be an undeveloped research area in Europe. Some years ago, there was a survey undertaken, based on a study of APA members by Pope & Vetter (1992). A survey was done first in the United Kingdom (Lindsay, 1995), and later in Sweden, Finland, and Norway (Odland & Dalen, 1997). The survey asked psychologists what kind of and how many ethical dilemmas they had been working on during the last couple of years. The results were compared between the countries, and the main ethical dilemmas of the surveyed psychologists were found to be similar. Ethical dilemmas around confidentiality were the most commonly reported, followed by worries about colleagues and thirdly, dual relationships. It is quite interesting to note that within these four European and two North American countries considered there were such similarities in what psychologists think of as ethical dilemmas they have encountered. Probably this illustrates that these countries share more or less the same cultural values.

The association in Spain, COP, has formulated a policy statement about research in ethical matters:

> To facilitate research work on ethics and psychology, the Secretary shall prepare summaries on each of the cases for scientific and professional use, taking adequate precautions to ensure privacy and confidentiality for use in casuistry. These summaries shall be saved in file by the documentation service of the COP so that they may be consulted by the college members.

An earlier convener of the ethics committee in Norway, now a researcher at the University of Bergen, Knut Dalen, investigated the work of the Ethics Telephone Counseling Service of that committee. (Dalen, 2006). Here again, confidentiality was the dilemma psychologists called up the committee most often to discuss.

Future Challenges

We think that one challenge of psychological ethics in Europe is to make sure that we develop a good, visible structure with transparency in matters concerning ethics, codes of conduct, ethics committees, and sanctioning procedures. The EFPA Standing Committee on Ethics had and still has an eminent role in this process.

As psychology and psychologists are more and more relevant in society, it will be a continuous challenge to update the codes of conduct or develop guidelines according to the development of new fields of psychology and the developments in society as well.

We have only seen the start of the use of the Internet in treatment and testing. Questions concerning this are already handled in guidelines in the EFPA (EFPA 2006, 2007a). Publishing tests through the Internet and thereby possibly destroying their usability is another challenge. It again raises the question of who is competent to test and to interpret the results.

An important discussion came up when "the war against terror" started. Should psychologists help in interrogations of suspects? There was a huge protest against this and so far, the profession seems to agree that such use of psychology is unethical. However, we will probably meet the question again as this "war against terror" continues.

Data protection, the use of electronic journal systems, electronic referrals, and reports on clients/patients open up concerns about confidentiality and it will probably become a great challenge to develop security systems that will conform to the stipulations of ethics codes and secure the clients from the exposure to third parties of confidential material.

The last but not the least challenge is to stimulate more research in the area of psychological ethics. The status of further development within this area depends on research and findings regarding how the work on ethics affects the profession. An interesting question, which needs further consideration, is whether different associations treat similar complaints in similar ways.

Acknowledgements

We are grateful to the members of the EFPA Standing Committee on Ethics for their support, and to many colleagues of EFPA member associations for their willingness to answer our questions and to provide us with their material.

Note

1. We are very grateful to Tuomo Tikkanen, President of the EFPA 1999–2007, who collected these as-yet unpublished data and presented them within the EFPA.

References

Dalen, K. (2006). To tell or not to tell, that's the question: Ethical dilemmas presented by psychologists in telephone counselling. *European Psychologist, 11*(3), 236–243.

European Federation of Professional Psychologists Associations. (1995). *Meta-code of ethics*. Brussels, Belgium: Author.

European Federation of Psychologists Associations. (1999). *Recommendations for teaching ethics for psychologists*. Retrieved from http://www.efpa.eu

European Federation of Psychologists Associations. (2005). *Recommendations on evaluative procedures and corrective actions in case of complaints of unethical conduct*. Retrieved from http://www.efpa.eu

European Federation of Psychologists Associations. (2005a). *Meta-code of ethics* (2nd ed.). Brussels, Belgium: EFPA. Retrieved from http://www.efpa.eu.

European Federation of Professional Psychologists Associations. (2005b). *Standing committee on ethics report*. Brussels, Belgium: EFPA. Retrieved from http://www.efpa.eu

European Federation of Professional Psychologists Associations. (2005c). *Statutes*. Brussels, Belgium: EFPA. Retrieved from http://www.efpa.eu

European Federation of Psychologists Associations EFPA. (2006). *Europsy booklet*. Brussels, Belgium: Author. Retrieved from http://www.efpa.eu

European Federation of Professional Psychologists Associations. (2009). *Groups*. Brussels, Belgium: EFPA. Retrieved from http://www.efpa.eu

European Federation of Psychologists Associations. (2007). *The provision of psychological services via the internet and other non-direct means*. Retrieved from http://www.efpa.eu

European Federation of Psychologists Associations. (2007a). *Guidelines on mediation in the context of complaints about unethical conduct*. Retrieved from http://www.efpa.eu

Lindsay, G., & Colley, A. (1995). Ethical dilemmas of member of the society. *The Psychologist, 8,* 448–451.

Lindsay, G., Koene, C., Øvreeide, H., Lang, F. (2008). *Ethics for European psychologists*. Hogrefe & Huber publishers.

Odland, T., & Dalen, K. (1997). Ethical dilemmas of members of the Norwegian Psychological Association. *Tidsskrift for Norsk Psykologforening, 11,* 989–996.

Pope, K.S., & Vetter, V.A. (1992), *Ethical dilemmas encountered by members of the American Psychological Association: A national survey*. American Psychologist, 47, 397–411.

CHAPTER
26

Psychological Ethics in Oceania: Convergence and Divergence

Alison F. Garton *and* Alfred Allan

Abstract

This chapter describes psychological ethics in Oceania, mainly in Australia and New Zealand. It traces the chronology of the development of formal codes of ethics for practicing psychologists, their rationales, and their applications. The chapter considers specifically the relevance, development and application of codes to the various indigenous populations in the region. The final section of the chapter considers the most recent development in Australia, namely the introduction of national accreditation and registration for health professions, including psychologists and the implications of this for psychological ethics and for New Zealand.

Key Words: codes of ethics, Oceania, national accreditation, registration, psychological ethics

Legal Status of the Discipline: Historical Perspective

The adoption of the *Health Practitioner Regulation National Law Act* (National Act, 2009), which will be discussed later, has brought about the largest transformation since registration of psychologists first occurred in 1965 with the passage of the Victorian *Psychological Practices Act*. The introduction of this act and the subsequent enacting of legislation in each of the eight Australian states and territories effectively marked the regulation of psychologists and psychological practice. One of the last regulatory acts to be introduced was that in New South Wales (NSW; coincidentally the state with the largest number of psychologists) in 1990.

Legislation previously existed in each state and territory in Australia to regulate the practice of psychology and to protect the public (Garton, 1995). These acts provided for no person being able to use the title psychologist or claim to practise psychology unless registered as a psychologist by a registration board (board). The historical reasons for registration being introduced included the need to protect the public from malpractice and the threat (actual or perceived) from nonprofessionals and inadequately trained people engaging in intelligence and personality assessments of the public. While the activities of untrained or inadequately trained people have gone unabated, registration of psychologists has at least ensured that the public can consult a publicly available document that lists those people whose credentials permit them to be registered psychologists. Such registration does not, of course, guarantee professional competence. Incompetence can, however, be dealt with by the board responsible for registration. Registration in one state permits registration in another through mutual recognition legislation to enable movement of expertise throughout Australia, but it is expensive as psychologists must pay a registration fee in each jurisdiction where they are registered.

The minimum qualifications and standards for registration were set by these various acts, and consequently these were not originally the same across all jurisdictions. In 1992 this changed with the introduction of mutual recognition legislation in each state and territory, aimed initially at removing barriers to trade across Australia but expanded to include portability of professional registration. Despite psychology being unregulated in one jurisdiction (the Australian Capital Territory [ACT]) at the time, it was considered fully regulated for the purposes of the application of mutual recognition legislation. The two areas where the psychologists' registration boards agreed on consistency were the minimum academic requirements for registration and the types of disciplinary measures that could be given (and hence transferable if the practitioner moved interstate). The academic requirement was a 4-year degree in psychology plus 2 additional years of either supervised practice or a university 2-year master's degree. This necessitated changes to legislation in some jurisdictions. Most registration boards in Australia took the opportunity to negotiate with state and territory governments to introduce minimum standards for registration that were comparable to international standards; namely, university-based postgraduate training. Available training places in university postgraduate professional courses were very limited, and "...the application of the Trade Practices Act to the professions in 1991 created a climate that was not conducive to limiting the competition for the practice of a profession by raising the minimum qualification standard" (Geffen, 2005, p. 29).

While most jurisdictions were able to amend their legislation to reflect this higher educational requirement, the Northern Territory retained its legislation that enabled registration with membership of the Australian Psychological Society (APS), which has different academic standards for and potential routes to membership than those of the majority of the registration boards. This loophole prevailed for many years and enabled individuals with academic qualifications other than those making them eligible for registration to obtain registration in the Northern Territory and then, through mutual recognition, obtain registration in another jurisdiction. A similar loophole had existed for a period previously, when first NSW and then ACT had no legal provisions for registration and, after legislation had been passed, grandfathered in those recognized psychologists who had been earning an income from professional practice for a number of years prior to the legislation.

Most of the acts were similar in nature, and the issues facing registration boards included discipline and disciplinary procedures, dealing with complaints, codes of conduct, supervision (both in terms of the supervisors and supervisees), standards of practice and competence to practice, assessment of overseas and nonstandard academic qualifications, regulation of various psychological practices (e.g., hypnosis remained in the psychologists' legislation in many jurisdictions) and the issue of unregistered persons, notably people calling themselves counsellors, and the boards' inability to regulate them.

Reviews of the legislation as directed by national competition policy in the late 1990s resulted in some changes to the various acts, in particular removing the capacity of the APS, the largest national professional body, to nominate board members and requiring a greater transparency about the disciplinary procedures. Most states and territories reviewed and revised their acts in the early 2000s and added professional requirements such as, for the non-university route, compulsory supervisor training, supervision programs for trainees requiring them to demonstrate competence in a range of professional activities, mandatory professional development for registrants and a requirement for indemnity insurance for registrants.

Professional Association and the Development of the Code

The APS is the national association for psychologists and currently has over 20,000 members across the country. It is independent and relies on subscriptions and other forms of income for its direct financial support, such as advertising and participation in other fee-for-service activities including membership of a membership referral database and training activities. It receives no government funding for its member functions, though it does receive grants for specific programs and projects.

After the adoption of legislation to register psychologists across states and territories, the APS maintained its own standards of conduct for its members through the promulgation of successive versions of ethical codes and the establishment of the Committee on Ethical and Professional Standards (CEPS), later the Ethics Committee. The first *Code of Professional Conduct* was adopted at the 1949 annual general meeting of the precursor of the APS, the Australian Branch of the British Psychology Society (BPS). This code was largely the outcome of some concerns regarding the publication of names of persons who had been tested by approved psychologists during and after World War II. Some issues had been raised earlier and were commented on by Bill O'Neil in his 1987 history of psychology (O'Neil, 1987) where, with regard to psychological research, he stated:

> Some intrusions on privacy involving deception were so gross that the need for some guidelines was recognised... Few of us, however, saw any objection to testing schoolchildren without parental consent and passing on test data without consent to teachers, administrators and others... We were, nonetheless, deeply disturbed by colleagues who revealed personal details about subjects who could be readily enough identified.
> (p. 83)

So, the issues raised of confidentiality and communication of psychological test data were those that prompted what was then the Victorian Group of the BPS—Australian Branch to consider who should have access to psychological data stored by the Commonwealth Employment Agency (Cooke, 2000). The recommendations from this group regarding access to these data were then shaped into a code about the communication of all psychological data, what information could be communicated, in what form, and to whom. The somewhat lengthy (6-page) set of recommendations was not completely clear, as not only did they protect "the welfare of both the individual subject and society," but they also looked after "the interests of the profession" (Cooke, 2000, p. 94). As Cooke noted, this produced a "sliding scale of confidentiality" (p. 94) in which a subject had no proprietary rights over the psychologist's records and where good tests results were privileged over bad ones and in particular abnormality, illegitimacy and insanity were to be guarded.

Nonetheless, the South Australian Group drew up a *Code of Ethics*, based largely on one from Minnesota (but one that was adopted before the American Psychological Association or the BPS), which was then adopted in 1949 by the Australian Branch of the BPS (BPS, 1949). Its main planks were confidentiality and the need to act ethically as "The practice of psychology affects the intimate lives and well-being of mankind [sic] and should be undertaken only by persons of the highest professional integrity." It exhorted psychologists "[To be] responsible to a high degree of professional competence and... under obligation when handling a psychological problem not to lose sight of the limitations of techniques and his [sic] own skill." It was also the responsibility of a psychologist to "refrain from obtaining in confidence what he [sic] cannot retain in confidence" (The British Psychological Society—Australian Branch, 1949, cited in Cooke, 2000, p. 112). It should be noted, however, that many of the prescriptions and proscriptions in this first code were still evident in subsequent codes up to and including the 1997 revision and some, reworded, remain as principles in the current version.

Not many psychologists were in independent private practice in the 1950s and the uptake of the code was patchy and not without debate. There was general agreement that the code was good for dealing with complaints against members of the BPS—Australian Branch, but was ineffective if the psychologist was not a member of the organization, as it only bound members. A revision of the 1949 code began in the 1950s and was adopted as the *Code of Professional Conduct* in 1960 by what was by now the Australian Psychological Society. This was a more detailed set of prescribed ("should") and proscribed ("should not") principles (or exhortations and prohibitions, Cooke, 2000) plus an exegesis. As well as practitioners ("the application of such [psychological] knowledge in practical service"), the new code was aimed at those members conducting scientific research and those teaching and disseminating psychological knowledge.

The code was again revised in 1968 and published in 1970 (Australian Psychological Society, 1970), reducing the principles from 112 to 36, and with the addition of appendices on the procedures to be followed in complaints made about professional conduct and on the employment of unqualified people in psychological practice. An "Advice to Members" section contained many of the culled principles. In 1971, amendments were made to the Articles of Association of the APS to add breaches of the code that could lead to reprimand, suspension, or expulsion.

A further revision to the code took place in 1986 (Australian Psychological Society, 1986), and cemented the three general principles that guided professional practice for the following 20 years. These were Responsibility, Competence and Propriety, and each was elaborated as to its intended application and meaning. There was a new section on the prohibition of sexual relationships between psychologists and clients.

This new version of code contained additional appendices, which were guidelines on "blind" interpretation of psychological tests, client/psychologist physical contact, the use of aversive therapeutic procedures, and dealing with suicidal clients. The relationship between the code and these guidelines, which were augmented in the next 10 years, was very unclear, although it was always believed that the principles of the code took precedence over any of the recommended actions in the guidelines. A contentious issue at the time was the addition in the code of a section on advertising, which many members felt restrictive (although compared with what is acceptable today under national competition rules, it seems positively liberal). Acceptable standards of advertising continue to be of concern, with many complaints arising from psychologists viewing their competitors' advertising as misleading or false.

The code was revised in 1997 and reverted to the name of the *Code of Ethics*. Various changes occurred, and the most important provision was the prohibition of sexual relations with ex-clients of up to two years' standing. Section B10 read: "No psychologist may engage in a sexual relationship with a former client when less than two years have expired since the ending or termination of the professional relationship" (APS, 1997, p. 3). This was the first time that the APS was prepared to put a timeframe around this prohibition, noting that *client* referred not only to a direct client, but also to a supervisee or any other person in an unequal professional relationship with a psychologist. There was no clear rationale for why two years was chosen, except that it reflected international practice and standards and acceptable Australian conventions. The onus and responsibility was placed firmly on the psychologist to justify any behaviour that deviated from this proscription.

This code was a mixture of prescription and proscription, generally using exhortations such as "must" and "must not." Like many other professional codes, it does not espouse any particular ethical theory, but is written to be practical and to encourage the highest standard of professional behavior. The code then looked as follows:

> Principles
> Section A: Psychological Assessment Procedures
> Section B: Relationships with Clients
> Section C: Teaching of Psychology
> Section D: Supervision and Training
> Section E: Research
> Section F: Reporting and Publication of Research Results
> Section G: Public Statements and Advertising
> Section H: Members' Relationships with Professionals

Procedures for Persons Considering Invoking Sections of the Code

In 1999, there was what could be regarded as a cosmetic revision with a change of the word *psychologist* to *member* on request of the registration boards. The boards argued that the term *psychologist* was a legally protected title, and since not all APS members were in fact registered, nor were the registration boards obligated to pay any attention to the APS *Code of Ethics*, this needed to be changed. The APS Board of Directors, on legal advice, acquiesced and made the amendment. Other editorial changes were made subsequently, each requiring the support of the membership at the annual general meeting.

From 1997, the appendices were removed and a decision made to issue instead ethical guidelines, which would be reviewed and revised if necessary every five years. This eliminated the confusion around the relationship between the *Code of Ethics* and any other advice. The old appendices were reviewed and, if still relevant, revised first and, when rewritten, explicitly linked to the relevant sections of the code. If a guideline was not regarded as current and/or professionally relevant, then it was not updated. Two reasonably contentious guidelines that had been recent—guidelines for psychological practice with women and guidelines for the provision of psychological services for, and the conduct of psychological research with, Aboriginal and Torres Strait Islander people of Australia—and that had never been included with any previous code, were added to the list of guidelines. New guidelines were then developed as professionally necessary, and there are over 25 guidelines on topics such as "guidelines for working with young people," which was introduced in 2009.

The most recent revision of the APS *Code of Ethics* took place in 2007 and involved a complete overhaul of the code, its content, and its structure. This was considered necessary to reflect the organizational changes to the APS and developments in the socio-legal context within which the APS and its members operate (Allan, 2010a). One such factor was the amendments to legislation that impacted on the professional practice of Australian psychologists, such as changes to the Commonwealth privacy legislation (*Privacy Act*, 1988) in 2001. The APS also wanted to ensure that the ethical standards for psychologists in Australia would be comparable with international standards. On the one hand, this meant comparing the *Code of Ethics* with the codes of ethics of one international, one regional and six national psychology professional bodies. This included reviewing the *Universal Declaration of Ethical Principles for Psychologists* (Universal Declaration) being developed by an Ad Hoc Joint Committee of the International Union of Psychological Science and the International Association of Applied Psychology. On the other hand, Australia was entering into free trade agreements with a number of countries, including the United States, in 2005. These agreements all require that the standards, including professional standards, of signatories should be equivalent. The APS was also cognizant that the registration boards were increasingly compelled by legislation to refer disciplinary matters to courts and other legal tribunals. As the APS is the largest professional body in psychology in Australia, its code is frequently used as a yardstick to measure the professional behavior of Australian psychologists in civil and disciplinary matters. It was therefore essential that the *Code of Ethics* should be a document that was clear and accurate, not subject to misinterpretation by nonpsychologists, and useful to regulatory bodies. In this regard the APS took note that some of the bodies regulating psychologists in the Canadian provinces did not use the code of the Canadian Psychological Association because it was "lacking in behavioral specificity and consequently not useful for the purposes of enforcement" (Dobson & Breault, 1998, p. 214–215).

While the APS appreciated that psychologist registration boards will always have discretion regarding whether and how they want to use the code, it decided that it would be to the mutual benefit of all parties to inform the Council of Psychologists Registration Boards (CPRB) of the review process and offer it an opportunity to give input when and if it chose to do so. The CPRB accepted this invitation by nominating two observers to monitor the review process and, where they thought it was appropriate, contribute to the process.

The comprehensive review process included a roundtable conference where members of the review working group first presented research on specific issues, such as ethical developments in other countries, and then mapped out the outline of the new code (Allan & Symons, 2010). Allan and Symons describe the laborious review process that preceded the release of the draft code for public comment on the website of the APS. Copies of the draft code were also sent to people with specific expertise in relevant areas for their comment. All the comments were collated and analyzed, and the draft code further amended. The amended version was then subject to expert legal review. The final draft of the code was adopted by the members at the APS' 41st annual general meeting, held in 2007.

The *Code of Ethics* consists of a preface, preamble and a comprehensive definition section. The group reinstated the word *psychologist*, instead of *member*, in the code. In explaining the application of the code, it is made clear that, unless a legislator provides to the contrary, the *Code of Ethics* is only applicable to members of the APS. The authors of the code also remind readers that the use of the professional title "psychologist" is restricted. The requirement that psychologists should not engage in sexual activity with former clients within two years after termination of the professional relationship was retained after a robust debate by members of the group (Allan & Thomson, 2010). The 2007 code further provides that psychologists who wish to engage in sexual activity with former clients after two years should "first explore with a senior psychologist the possibility that the former client may be vulnerable and at risk of exploitation, and encourage the former client to seek independent counselling on the matter" (Standard C.4.3). The language in the *Code of Ethics* uses descriptive rather than prescriptive terminology and is based on eight principles: Justice, Respect for Rights and Dignity of People and Peoples, Autonomy, Nonmaleficence, Beneficence, Responsibility, Veracity, and Fidelity. For practical reasons these principles were collapsed into three general principles; namely, Respect for the Rights and Dignity of People and Peoples, Propriety, and Integrity (Allan, 2010b). While the nomenclature differs from that used in other codes of ethics, the general principles of the code are similar to those found in other codes, including the Universal Declaration.

The *Code of Ethics* has three tiers. The section for each general principle commences with a brief statement of the general principle followed by an explanatory statement that provides further guidance to members. These two components constitute the aspirational part of the code and are followed by a set of ethical standards derived from the relevant general principle that specifies the minimum expectations with regard to members' professional conduct (Allan, 2010b).

Ethics Committees

The CEPS was established to oversee compliance with the various codes as they were developed. In addition, the CEPS was able to take some, albeit limited, disciplinary action against psychologists (members of the APS) who had transgressed the code. The work of CEPS became increasingly burdensome during the 1980s before NSW and the ACT had any form of legislation. As well as adjudicating on specific complaints that it received, the CEPS provided advice to members of the APS about professional and ethical conduct (despite what could now be considered to be a conflict of interest in some instances, where advice given by a CEPS member was later contradicted by the CEPS, with the member taking part in the discussion). Furthermore, with the greater detail and specificity in the newer codes, it was inevitable that more cases would be presented for resolution or disciplinary action. There were also more psychologists moving into private practice (mainly from government agencies), meaning there were more solo practitioners dealing with more complex issues. This often meant that the CEPS was grappling with ethical and sometimes legal issues for which its main knowledge base was the experience of its membership. Cases taken up by the CEPS remained confidential but, as the first author was a member of CEPS in the early 1990s, issues such as file management, boundaries (including sexual relations with clients) and the use of psychological tests were those for which advice was sought and which most often gave rise to complaints. By the time the second author chaired the APS Ethics Committee in the middle of the 2000s, file management and boundary issues were still prevalent, together with complaints regarding the quality of reports psychologists write for the courts. The workload had, for reasons that will be explained below, become lighter and has been dropping away even more since.

Once all jurisdictions had legislation in place, some registration boards (such as NSW) developed their own codes of ethics; others, such as Western Australia and Queensland, relied on the current APS *Code*. The relationships between the eight boards, each with separate legislation, and the APS needed careful negotiation, with one board unable to speak on behalf of all boards, making consensus rare. Since 1980, an annual meeting of National Council of Psychologists Registration Boards has been held at the same time and location as the APS annual conference, to which the APS executive director is invited, for between one hour and a whole day, depending on the chair at the time. Issues that were constantly raised at these meetings were how to manage complaints that had been submitted simultaneously to a board and to the APS (they were sometimes investigated simultaneously, which is no longer the case; see below), how to deal with psychologists who moved from state to state (sometimes involving a move to ACT and NSW, where there were grandfather clauses enabling practitioners to be registered if they had earned an income from private practice for so many years prior to legislation being enacted), the necessary qualifications for registration, and what disciplinary measures were appropriate for which misdemeanors. Relations between the boards and the APS varied from cordial to cool, and were mainly based on a power imbalance: the boards' statutory power to prevent psychologists from practising and the APS's limited powers to reprimand or expel its members from the APS. Another issue that divided the APS and the boards was the development of competency standards during the 1990s, the resolution of which restored a good working relationship (Cooke, 2000; Garton, 2006).

After a review of the APS in the early 1990s, it was restructured and the role and responsibilities of the CEPS examined. Now that all jurisdictions had registration boards, it was proposed to limit the scope of the CEPS only to matters that did not involve fitness to practice; that is, largely to qualifications for membership and practice-management issues. This restriction was, however, not formally imposed. In addition, an Ethics Appeal Committee was established to offer an option when a member felt aggrieved by a decision of the CEPS.

During the late 1990s, there was formal establishment of the APS Ethics Committee (by the articles of association) to give the Ethics Committee appropriate legal status within the APS, which it had not previously had. In addition, this period saw the adoption and implementation of the *Rules and Procedures for the Ethics Committee and the Ethics Appeals Committee* (*Rules and Procedures*, 1998), which set out more clearly than had ever been the case, the operation of the Ethics Committee and of the newly established Appeals Committee. During a review of the governance documents of the APS in the second half of the current decade, the *Rules and Procedures* were comprehensively reviewed, but the underlying philosophy remains the same.

The APS adopts a conciliatory approach to complaint resolution and discourages its members from obtaining legal advice if they are subject to a complaint. Legal representation is disallowed, but members may consult a lawyer. Most of the work of the Ethics Committee is conducted through written submissions and decisions are made on the basis of the evidence and the facts of the case. Options for discipline include expulsion or suspension from membership, as well as reprimands and educative letters. None of these prevents a psychologist from practicing. Again, the number of complaints received and the number actually investigated are very small and are reported in the APS annual report each year. Those that should be dealt with by the appropriate state or territory registration board are advised of the fact, so the complainant can lodge his or her complaint with the board. The APS does not forward such complaints.

Ethical Codes

As noted above, the APS has the most widely recognized and comprehensive code of ethics in Australia and in the past many of the registration boards have adopted this code. Others, because of legislative or operational requirements, have complemented it with their own code, often a much shorter document but consistent with the principles in the APS *Code of Ethics*. Lewis, Sandquist, Stark, and Grenyer (2009) undertook a content analysis of five of these codes and the APS *Code* and concluded that the latter was the most comprehensive, with only three of the other codes addressing more than half of the APS ethical standards. There was pressure on the inaugural Psychology Board of Australia (Psychology Board), with the other health professions, to adopt the *Good medical practice: A Code of Conduct for Doctors in Australia* that was developed by Australian Medical Council (2009). The Psychology Board instead adopted the APS *Code of Ethics* as the overarching code for the psychology profession in Australia, but plan to develop a new code in the future with the involvement of key stakeholders.

Working Ethically with Indigenous Australians

To understand more fully the multicultural character of Australia, it is important to know about the culture of indigenous Aboriginal Australians. Indigenous Australians are those who originally lived in Australia and now share their homeland with others. There are indigenous people in other countries, like the Inuit of the Arctic and the Māori of New Zealand. They all share a common cultural element of a strong spiritual connection with the land, and many have been oppressed by colonizers. In Australia, there are Aboriginal peoples and Torres Strait Islanders. The Australian Aboriginals lived on the mainland, in many diverse groups. The Torres Strait Islanders live in a small group of islands off the tip of Cape York Peninsula in Queensland.

Indigenous psychology recognizes the cultural contexts of Australian Aboriginal peoples and seeks to develop locally relevant psychological knowledge. Dudgeon, Garvey, and Pickett (2000a) describe the cultural history of indigenous Australia to understand better contemporary cultures and practices. Most Aboriginal communities and people retain some of their traditional culture. There has also been a strong resurgence of identification with traditional Aboriginal culture by those whose upbringing has been predominantly Western and city-based. The traditional cultural values and behaviors which carry some relevance into 21st-century Australian culture include (a) connections to land and country; (b) the significance of sacred sites and stories; (c) creation—the Dreaming, a timeless dimension at the dawn of time; (d) the importance of kinship and family, sharing, and reciprocity as values in Aboriginal life; (e) living a traditional egalitarian lifestyle; and (f) the role of death, grieving, and funeral practices.

Indigenous Australians have been disadvantaged by Western colonization, and many of the actions of Europeans have removed their human rights and traditional land ownership. Working with indigenous populations psychologically has proven to be difficult and cannot be successful until there is recognition by governments of these human, legal, and social rights. Much psychological practice with indigenous people has been unsuccessful for a number of reasons: practices are not culturally sensitive, practitioners are inadequately trained (and may even demonstrate cultural biases), and there is inadequate knowledge of indigenous behavior, customs, and culture (see the values listed in the previous paragraph). The APS began developing a set of ethical guidelines in the mid-1990s to assist psychologists working with Aboriginal and Torres Strait Islander peoples, particularly in the provision of professional services and conduct of psychological assessment. These guidelines were updated to be consistent with the new *Code of Ethics* and provide guidance when conducting research with, providing psychological services to, and conducting psychological testing or other forms of assessment with indigenous people (APS, 2008). In addition, there is a separate section of guidance on providing psychological services in the area of mental health, and some commentary on guidelines for education and training in cultural awareness and procedures for consultation with indigenous communities.

Aboriginal concepts of mental health and illness must be seen in the context of the indigenous concept of health, which embraces the social, emotional and cultural well-being of the whole community. It requires taking a lifespan view, from birth to death, and facilitates the well-being of the individual and of the community more generally. It is argued that this goal has been "systematically thwarted by the policies of forced removal and institutionalisation" (Dudgeon, Garvey, & Pickett, 2000b, p. 85). In effect, this is claiming that the requirements for good mental health have been denied in Aboriginal communities. This has led, directly and indirectly, to the poor mental health of many Aboriginal people. It is seen in high rates of alcohol and drug use, suicide, and child abuse and neglect.

In addition, there has never been a formal analysis of the suitability of the current systems of diagnosis of psychiatric illness for indigenous people. While the presenting problems can be described, and perhaps attributed to socioeconomic, health, and educational disadvantages, it may be culturally inappropriate to attribute a diagnosis of mental ill-health to these conditions. The APS guidelines, inter alia, urge practitioners to ensure they are familiar with indigenous values and behaviors, are aware that indigenous people are at high risk of self-harm, and make use of culturally appropriate services where those are available.

Furthermore, culturally appropriate forms of intervention for poor mental health, Dudgeon et al. (2000b) say, are not provided. Children witness the antisocial behaviors of their parents, families, and communities, and a cycle of harmful behaviors continues. They argue that services for indigenous people are poorly resourced and generally inadequate. There have been calls for programs that address the mental health problems and mental disorders of young people (children and adolescents), women (particularly their sexual and reproductive health), men (to deal with problems of sexism, drug and alcohol use, victim blaming, and destructive and harmful behaviours) and elders, whose valued place in Aboriginal communities ensures they are respected. Older Aboriginal people are few in number, as their life expectancy is some 20 years less that than of other Australians, so they often do not live long enough to suffer from some of the problems of old age such as dementia and depression. Mental health care for Aboriginal elders, both men and women, includes supported accommodation, appropriate dementia care services, and assistance with daily activities that may be causing stress and distress.

It is generally claimed that the mental health of Aboriginal people is neglected, and that their mental illness is poorly understood. Lette, Wright, and Collard (2000) explored Aboriginal understanding of mental illness, or, as it is termed colloquially, "mental." Many of the meanings associated with mental illness come from hearing about a relative's experience with mental health services or seeing the behaviors of someone with a mental illness. The lack of understanding extends to not wishing to include someone with a current or past mental illness in an activity in case "they go off," reflecting a fear. The basis of the fear is not stated, but is probably the unknown, a fear of violence, or even a connection with evil spirits. Aboriginal people with a mental illness or a mental health problem feel teased, marginalized, and reluctant to seek services or help. Attitudes to hospitalization are colored by views about institutionalization, forced removal from the community, and the effects of medication. These attitudes toward mental illness are a result of earlier Aboriginal contact with government departments and their treatment at the hands of the colonists.

Vicary and Bishop (2005) explored the ways in which Aboriginal people can be engaged in culturally appropriate and respectful ways in psychological therapy. It is acknowledged that mainstream mental health services often fail to meet the mental health needs of Aboriginal people, and specialized services are required. While culturally appropriate treatment and counseling services are now more widespread, little has been done to increase the skills of non-Aboriginal clinicians and counselors, the majority of whom have never had any contact with Aboriginal clients. Vicary and Bishop's research examined gaps in knowledge about Aboriginal attitudes toward and beliefs about, among other things, mental health. In general, they found that Aboriginal concepts of mental health were holistic and contained both cultural and spiritual elements. These, they claimed, are the foundations of Aboriginal attitudes toward mental health. They found Aboriginal interpretations of mental illness do not have causal links (e.g., linking smoking to cancer). Instead, they call upon breaking the law or falling foul of a spirit as a cause of illness. Understanding the influence of culture on interpretations of illness can assist counselors to work in culturally sensitive ways and to provide relevant assistance.

Ethics in New Zealand

In New Zealand, psychologists must be registered to practise under the *Health Practitioners Competence Assurance Act* (2003), which aims "to protect the health and safety of members of the public by providing for mechanisms to ensure that health practitioners are competent and fit to practise their profession"(section 3[1]). Registration and the issuing of practicing certificates for health practitioners include prescribed scopes of practice, which in the case of psychologists is registration for education and clinical practice.

The *Code of Ethics for Psychologists Working in Aotearoa/New Zealand* (*NZ Code*; 2002) was prepared by a joint working group of the New Zealand Psychological Society, the New Zealand College of Clinical Psychologists, and the New Zealand Psychologists Board. According to Seymour, Nairn, and Austin (2004), the working group relied heavily on the code then in use and the Canadian code, and also took into account the results of a survey of registered psychologists that asked them to describe ethical dilemmas they or a colleague had recently faced. The working group released a number of versions of the draft code for comments and integrated these comments to produce a final document. It was adopted by all parties in late 2002 and, although it has been criticized (see Williams, 2004), it seems to have been generally well received by New Zealand psychologists. The New Zealand code identifies four ethical principles: Respect for the Persons and Peoples, Responsible Caring, Integrity of Relationships, and Social Justice and Responsibility to Society. Somewhat akin to the APS *Code of Ethics*, subsumed under each principle is a set of values, which are then linked to statements about the appropriate professional behavior of psychologists in relation to that value. Comments are added to draw attention to important practice issues. These practice implications are not exhaustive, but are merely guides to practice.

Under the first three ethical principles, reference is made to the Treaty of Waitangi (*Te Tiriti o Waitangi*), now in place for 170 years, which provides a framework for respect, responsible caring, and integrity in relationships between the two peoples of New Zealand, Māori (*tangata whenua*) and non-Māori. Principle Four reminds psychologists that the Treaty of Waitangi is a foundational document for social justice, and this principle acknowledges psychologists' position of power and influence in relation to individuals and communities with which the psychologist is involved. It addresses and challenges unjust societal norms and behaviors that disempower people at all levels of interaction. The Treaty of Waitangi more generally acknowledges many of the issues that Australian indigenous people consider to be unspoken and unacknowledged, not just in relation to psychological ill-health and subsequent treatment, but also in recognition of human, legal, and social rights by governments.

Specifically, in the New Zealand code, Principle One, Value Statement 3.1 considers relations between Māori and non-Māori, namely "Psychologists practising in New Zealand recognise that the Treaty of Waitangi sets out the basis of respect between Māori and non-Māori in this country." The practice implications are, first, that psychologists need to be informed about the meaning and implications of the Treaty of Waitangi for their work and understand the principles of protection, participation, and partnership with Maori. Second, both non-Māori and Māori psychologists who work with Māori seek advice and undertake training in the appropriate way to show respect for the dignity and needs of Māori in their practice.

It can be seen that these statements appear much stronger in the New Zealand code than those in the Australia counterpart, where, as noted above, any advice to psychologists regarding working with indigenous people is contained not in the *Code of Ethics* but in the guidelines. However, this does not mean that provisions in the guidelines are any less enforceable than either the Australian code or the New Zealand code (New Zealand Psychological Society, 2002), as the former states that, "psychologists who have acted inconsistently with the Guidelines may be required to demonstrate that their behavior was not unethical" (APS, 2007, p. 7).

In relation to practice with Māori people, comments in the New Zealand code about the value statement note that the Treaty of Waitangi is to be given priority as the text that was offered to and signed by the majority of the Māori signatories. The treaty is the cornerstone of values and attitudes in New Zealand and sits, as the declaration to the New Zealand code (New Zealand Psychological Society, 2002), as follows:

> In giving effect to the Principles and Values of this Code of Ethics there shall be due regard for New Zealand's cultural diversity and in particular for the provisions of, and the spirit and intent of, the Treaty of Waitangi.
> (p. 3)

Despite these inclusive statements, concerns are still being expressed about the application of existing models of psychological training and practice to Māori and, like in Australia, the marginalization of Māori (i.e., indigenous) models of understanding of psychology and psychologists, and how these are linked to deeply embedded cultural differences (Milne, 2005). There is interest in developing *kaupapa Māori* (Maori-centered) psychology training, with it becoming perhaps a recognized scope of practice in psychology. Milne reports strong feelings of spirit to care for the wellness of Māori through the declared motivation to care for individuals, and the role psychologists can play in improving outcomes. But, like in Australia, there are problems of establishing rapport and credibility when working with Māori communities and recognizing the importance of relationships, mutuality, and trust that characterize the culture.

There are, thus, similarities and differences between Australia and New Zealand in how the indigenous populations are recognized generally, and how they are integrated (in New Zealand) or separated (in Australia) from ethical codes of practice for psychologists. The Treaty of Waitangi is at the heart of all professional (and other) relationships in New Zealand, and no such formal treaty exists in Australia. A formal apology from the Australian Prime Minister in 2008 was a start, and heralds a renewed and united effort to close the gap between indigenous and non-indigenous Australians in life expectancy, educational achievement, and economic opportunity (Rudd, 2008).

The historical differences between the countries and the distinct differences between the indigenous people of New Zealand and Australia, which includes people in the Torres Strait, make it unlikely that the psychologists in the two countries will ever share a common code of ethics. There has, nevertheless, been frequent consultation between the psychologists of the two countries around ethics and other professional matters, in that the New Zealand Psychologists Board was a member of the CPRB. This collaboration will continue in the future, and the first meeting between the New Zealand Board and Psychology Board of Australia took place on July 4, 2010.

Ethics Training

Ethics training is expected to take place during the first 3 or 4 years of psychology education. The current Australian Psychology Accreditation Council (APAC) standards (2010) contain six graduate attributes that must be attained through the undergraduate curriculum. For example, Graduate Attribute Four requires that students receive a solid foundation in the core attribute of "Values, research and professional ethics." This entails students' ability to evaluate psychologists' behaviour in psychological research and other professional contexts in relation to the APS *Code of Ethics* and complementary ethical guidelines. This graduate attribute also applies to the curriculum in the fourth year.

At the postgraduate level, there are a number of core capabilities and attributes (as well as the knowledge underpinning them) that must be addressed, initially at the 5th-year and 6th-year levels, but also for other advanced postgraduate training years, to ensure students are equipped to practice safely upon registration. Core capability 5.1.12 (B) relates to the ethical, legal, and professional aspects of psychological practice. It contains a comprehensive list of the particular legal and professional matters with which students must be familiar. These include (a) the main provisions of the State and Commonwealth Acts and Regulations of Parliament relevant to psychologists' work; (b) codes of conduct relevant to psychologists' work, including those published by relevant psychologist registration board(s); and (c) the Australian Psychological Society's *Code of Ethics* and *Ethical Guidelines*, followed by a list of areas and issues of which psychologists must be mindful when in practice.

During postgraduate education, students must also demonstrate conduct or behavior consistent with the legal requirements and codes of conduct relevant to psychologists, especially, inter alia, (a) ethical and professional behavior and manner; (b) state, territory and federal codes of behavior for psychologists and statements of clients' rights; and (c) the Australian Psychological Society's *Code of Ethics* and *Ethical Guidelines*, as well as other administrative and professional roles and responsibilities, including self-awareness and identification of the limits of one's own professional competence.

There is, thus, a requirement that students have a thorough grounding in ethics and professional competence during both their undergraduate and postgraduate education, and that they can demonstrate their knowledge and understanding. Further training in professional practice takes place during the compulsory placements in postgraduate courses and also during the early years of professional practice. Students completing a seventh year in a professional doctorate (DPsych) program are also required to undertake supervision training. Supervisors for some of the registration boards undertake further training, which includes professional practice issues, while those registrants who are completing two years' supervision in lieu of postgraduate education have to demonstrate competence (knowledge and skills) in professional conduct and ethics.

Davidson, Garton, and Joyce (2003) undertook a survey of ethics education in schools and departments of psychology throughout Australia. Content analysis was undertaken of the syllabus material submitted for the purposes of accreditation during the 5-year cycle ending in 2000. (All universities undergo accreditation of their psychology programs once every five years; this survey was based on the first such cycle.) The accreditation guidelines that existed at the time (Australian Psychological Society, 1995) introduced a requirement that undergraduate and postgraduate professional training contain components that addressed relevant codes of research and conduct. The material submitted showed that ethics education was included in fewer than one-quarter of the undergraduate courses analyzed, but rose to nearly 90% in subsequent years (years 4, 5, 6, and 7). Ethics was integrated into the curriculum in years 1–3, and roughly equal emphasis on integration into or separation from the core curriculum in subsequent years. There was equal emphasis on philosophical and code-based instruction in the first three years, and a clear emphasis on code-based instruction in subsequent years. While research ethics was the predominant theme in the first three years, the subsequent years placed greater emphasis on professional practice and ethics. It was notable that in the first three years, ethical knowledge was rarely assessed.

The authors acknowledged that a desk audit of the materials submitted for accreditation cannot and do not tell the whole story about how ethics is taught and what is taught at the various year levels. Not only do accreditation site visits allow for assessors to obtain additional information and clarification about courses (not just ethics courses, but all psychology courses), but the submitted material may also not accurately reflect exactly what ethics education students receive. There can also be differences in terminology and level of detail. The 2003 paper lamented the discouraging picture of ethics education in universities at that time. More positive, however, has been the subsequent response to this state of affairs, with universities paying more attention to the teaching of ethics and the strengthening of the graduate attributes in the undergraduate curriculum, and with the core capabilities in the postgraduate curriculum requiring demonstration of ethical knowledge and understanding (APAC, 2010; see preceding section). This also shifts the emphasis on teaching students compliance with research codes and codes of conduct ("mainly slavish attention to professional and research ethics codes," Davidson et al., p. 220) to innovative curricula, introducing students to real-life ethical dilemmas, models of ethical decision making, and issues and pitfalls in professional practice. Students also become aware of their limitations and, more importantly, their prejudices, which can have an impact on professional practice. In addition, current accreditation submissions demonstrate more imaginative approaches to teaching ethics and a greater awareness among academics about the fundamental importance of instilling in students the ethical, professional, and scientific significance of the professional and research codes of conduct and their philosophical bases.

Current Research on Psychological Ethics

The most comprehensive and recent research on psychological ethics is contained in an edited volume published in 2006 (Morrissey & Reddy, 2006). The book was prepared with a number of issues in mind. First, there was a recognition that the settings in which psychologists are practising are increasing in number and diversity. Second, it was also recognized that by far and away the bulk of research on issues in psychological practice and ethics is conducted in countries other than Australia, and its application to Australia is in some instances limited and even wrong. The textbook, therefore, is a compilation of commissioned papers covering the major ethical and professional issues facing psychologists in professional practice in Australia, aimed at promulgating best ethical practice and to be used as a resource for those academics teaching undergraduate and postgraduate courses on professional practice.

Morrissey and Reddy (2006) is divided into three parts, and the contributors come from a number of different perspectives and with different experiences. Many have been a member of the APS Ethics Committee, a registration board, or both. The first part of the edited volume contains chapters on ethical theory, ethical decision making and the legal context of ethical practice. The second section is more practical and reviews some of the major ethical issues for psychologists, including confidentiality, competence, boundaries and diversity. The final part contains chapters on teaching, training, supervision and monitoring of ethical practice. Each chapter concludes with some questions on which readers can reflect. While aimed at students, and providing examples and situations that are Australian, it also provides a useful resource for supervisors, supervisees and practitioners more generally to remind them of their professional roles and responsibilities.

Some of the members of the working group who reviewed the APS *Code of Ethics* worked together to write a book that reflects the research the authors undertook in preparation for, during, and after the review (Allan & Love, 2010). The authors reflect on the review process, describe problems they experienced during the process, explain some of the group's decisions, and examine some aspects of the *Code of Ethics*. Some of the topics specifically examined are: the principles that underlie the 2007 code; consent, privacy, and confidentiality issues; psychologists' social responsibilities; working with young people; boundaries, multiple relationships and the regulation of sexual activity between psychologists and their clients and former clients.

There is currently no book on ethics written specifically for New Zealand psychologists. This is understandable, as the country has a relatively small number of psychologists (just over 2000) and, therefore, the market for such a book will be small. The New Zealand Psychologists Board does, however, have a very useful rubric in its newsletter, in which the lessons that psychologists can learn from recent health practitioners' disciplinary hearings are discussed.

Future Challenges

Psychology in Australia faces a range of challenges, some which may be unique to the country. The country is vast with areas that are sparsely populated and there are many towns that are in remote areas. Many Australian psychologists, therefore, are far from the traditional support services that psychologists can usually rely on and, to compound the problem, many of them are sole practitioners. Country towns are often small and psychologists practising there are also faced with the practical problems such as multiple relationships experienced by all psychologists working in closed and relatively small communities. There may also be issues of working appropriately and sensitively with indigenous populations. In addition, psychologists find it difficult to obtain appropriate supervision and to remain informed about legal and ethical developments. The Psychology Board has increased the requirements around continued professional development for all registered psychologists. In the future, continued professional education will have to be more active and outcome-based, and all psychologists will have to engage in face-to-face peer consultation. While continued professional education has been compulsory for psychologists who are members of the APS for some time, and for continued registration in some jurisdictions for a few years, and is generally welcomed, psychologists in rural and regional areas often find it more difficult and expensive to meet these requirements than do their colleagues in the metropolitan areas, thus creating a potentially inequitable situation.

Another factor that is causing psychologists concern is the apparent increasing shift of Australian psychologists from salaried positions in organizations, typically government, to private practice, where they often work in relative isolation without professional scrutiny of their practices and devoid of proper supervision (Love & Allan, 2010).

The *National Act* (2009) requires the Psychology Board to examine complaints against psychologists. A feature of this act is that it requires health practitioners, employers, and education providers to report what is called "notifiable conduct" (Sections 141–143)—that is, certain forms of conduct and impairment—to the National Agency, which, with the boards of the different health professions regulates health practitioners including psychologists. Many psychologists fear that this may lead to an indiscriminate notification of psychologists, and also that this will have a negative impact on what psychologists may disclose to supervisors. The *National Act* requires the Psychology Board to distinguish between problems that arise because of unprofessional behavior, poor performance and practice, and impairment. A form of impairment that is becoming more common is dementia, and this trend is likely to continue because, while the profession in Australia is attracting a good supply of younger people, the number of older psychologists is also increasing and so is the risk that psychologists may be suffering dementia. The most common form of impairment, however, remains poor emotional functioning due to a life stressor such as a relationship loss. The concern with these forms of impairment is that they often lead to unethical conduct, such as psychologists seeking solace from their clients.

Another emerging concern in both Australia and New Zealand is around the use of electronic media, such as mobile telephones and social networking sites like Facebook, in the provision of psychological services. The size and relatively small population of Australia make the use of electronic media in the provision of psychological services very attractive. One could also argue that psychologists as a group are morally obliged to use electronic media if so doing will allow them to provide psychological services to people who would otherwise not receive services (Allan, 2008). Electronic media are used in Australia to deliver psychological services, but different legal requirements in the eight states and territories hamper a wider use of them to deliver such services. Some of these problems have been alleviated with the commencement of the *National Act* (2009) on July 1, 2010. For instance, under current legislation it is legally possible for a psychologist to render an online service to a client who is at the time in a state or territory where the psychologists in not registered. The *National Act* may therefore, because of its wider jurisdiction, lead to an expansion of psychologists using electronic media to provide psychological services. Unfortunately, psychologists who develop or use electronic media to provide psychological services often ignore basic ethical principles and, to add to the problem, a large number of people may be affected if there is a violation of an ethical principle (Allan, 2008). This was well illustrated by the recent discovery that the private messages of Australians suffering depression to an online counselling service, funded by the federal government, could be accessed by any computer user (Scott, 2009).

At an institutional level many government and nongovernmental health providers are moving to central patient and client record systems, often held electronically, to which a range of people other than the treating clinician has access. This is just one example where government departments have placed psychologists in a position where they feel that they are potentially required to do things that are unethical.

At a meta-ethical level, there are grave concerns in the profession that the move to a national registration and accreditation system may lead to a reduction of standards. The *National Act* (2009) provides that the ministerial council, consisting of the ministers of health of the federal, state and territory governments, must approve the registration standards set by the Psychology Board. An attempt by the Psychology Board to increase the registration requirements to bring them in line with the expectations of all the current state and territory boards and the APS has already been rebuffed (Reid, 2009). The concerns regarding accreditation have to some degree been allayed by provisions in the *National Act* that restrict the role of the Psychology Board, and therefore the ministerial council, in the accreditation process. There is, nevertheless, still a risk of government interference because the ministerial council can give directives to the Psychology Board regarding proposed accreditation standards if it believes any such standard will have a negative impact on the recruitment and supply of psychologists. The profession has clearly entered a new stage where political interference is much more likely than it was in the past. This may prove to have a notable impact on the professional standards of the profession.

New Zealand has identified as one its priorities the maintenance of a watching brief on the Psychology Board of Australia. A review of the current New Zealand legislation (the *Health Practitioners Competence Assurance Act*, 2003) was undertaken in 2009, with some expected legislative developments in 2010, including the need for the Psychologists Board to work more closely with its Australian counterpart, to identify and share best practice principles and make arrangements for accreditation of educational institutions and programs. A major review of the use of scopes of practice by the Psychologists Board led to a reaffirmation of the existing scopes (as noted previously, namely clinical and educational psychology), with a commitment to investigate the progression of a counseling psychology scope.

Finally, there needs to be further development in professional relationships with indigenous populations in both Australia and New Zealand, and greater general recognition of past injustices and how these affect the cultural perceptions held about the role of professional assistance. Practitioners must ensure they are familiar with indigenous values and behaviors, and in these times of increased immigration (including refugees) from African and Asian countries, there needs to be greater awareness of cultural differences and expectations that in turn should be reflected in codes of professional conduct for practicing psychologists. Training psychologists in cultural awareness, sensitivity, and being nonjudgmental is fundamental, and a recent Australian textbook provides a starting point for the development of such cultural competence (Ranzijn, McConnochie, & Nolan, 2009). Cultural competence refers to a set of skills and understandings that enable professionals to move outside their own cultural views and limitations to engage more widely in a range of cultural contexts. With this in mind, the book aims to develop a new generation of psychologists who can work appropriately and effectively with indigenous clients and communities. This is indeed a brave and welcome step forward.

References

Allan, A. (2008). *An international perspective of law and ethics in psychology*. Somerset West, South Africa: Inter-ed.

Allan, A. (2010a). Introduction. In A. Allan & A. W. Love (Eds.), *Ethical practice in psychology: Reflections from the creators of the APS code of ethics* (pp. 1–11). Chichester, UK: Wiley.

Allan, A. (2010b). The principles that underlie the 2007 code. In A. Allan & A. W. Love (Eds.), *Ethical practice in psychology: Reflections from the creators of the APS code of ethics* (pp. 61–76). Chichester, UK: Wiley.

Allan, A., & Love, A. W. (Eds.). (2010). *Ethical practice in psychology: Reflections from the creators of the APS code of ethics.* Chichester, UK: Wiley.

Allan, A., & Symons, M. (2010). The development of the 2007 code. In A. Allan & A. W. Love (Eds.), *Ethical practice in psychology: Reflections from the creators of the APS code of ethics* (pp. 13–24). Chichester, UK: Wiley.

Allan, A., & Thomson, D. M. (2010). The regulation of sexual activity between psychologists and their clients and former clients. In A. Allan & A. W. Love (Eds.), *Ethical practice in psychology: Reflections from the creators of the APS code of ethics* (pp. 149–160). Chichester, UK: Wiley.

Australian Medical Council. (2009). *Good medical practice: A code of conduct for doctors in Australia.* Canberra: Author.

Australian Psychology Accreditation Council. (2010). Rules for accreditation and accreditation standards for psychology courses. Melbourne: Author.

Australian Psychological Society. (1960). *Code of professional conduct.* Melbourne: Author.

Australian Psychological Society. (1970). *Code of professional conduct.* Melbourne: Author.

Australian Psychological Society. (1986). *Code of professional conduct.* Melbourne: Author.

Australian Psychological Society. (1995). Accreditation guidelines. Melbourne: Author.

Australian Psychological Society. (1997). *Code of ethics.* Melbourne: Author.

Australian Psychological Society. (1998). Rules and procedures for the Ethics Committee and the Ethics Appeals Committee. Melbourne: Author.

Australian Psychological Society. (2007). *Code of ethics.* Melbourne: Author.

Australian Psychological Society (2008). Guidelines for the provision of psychological services for, and the conduct of psychological research with, Aboriginal and Torres Strait Islander people of Australia. Melbourne: Author.

British Psychological Society—Australian Branch. (1949). *Code of professional conduct.* Melbourne: Author

Cooke, S. (2000). *A meeting of minds: The Australian Psychological Society and Australian psychologists 1944–1994.* Melbourne: The Australian Psychological Society.

Davidson, G. R., Garton, A.F., & Joyce, M. (2003). Survey of ethics education in Australian schools and departments of psychology. *Australian Psychologist, 38,* 216–222. doi:10.1080/00050060310001707237

Dobson, K. S., & Breault, L. (1998). The Canadian code of ethics and the regulation of psychology. *Canadian Psychology, 39,* 212–218. Dudgeon, P., Garvey, D., & Pickett, H. (2000a). A cultural history. In P. Dudgeon, D. Garvey, & H. Pickett (Eds.), *Working with indigenous Australians: A handbook for psychologists* (pp. 27–30). Perth, Western Australia: Gunada Press.

Dudgeon, P., Garvey, D., & Pickett, H. (2000b). Indigenous mental health across the lifespan. In P. Dudgeon, D. Garvey, & H. Pickett (Eds.), *Working with indigenous Australians: A handbook for psychologists* (pp. 85–90). Perth, Western Australia: Gunada Press.

Garton, A. F. (1995). Registration of psychologists in Australia. Invited chapter prepared for unpublished edited volume.

Garton, A. F. (2006). Competence. In S. Morrissey & P. Reddy (Eds.), *Ethics and professional practice for psychologists* (pp. 63–73). South Melbourne: Thomson Social Science Press.

Geffen, G. (2005). Raising the standard for registration of psychologists in Australia. *InPsych, 27*(3), 29–30.

Health Practitioner Regulation National Law of 2009, Act §45, Queensland, Australia.

Health Practitioners Competence Assurance Act of 2003, New Zealand.

Lette, H., Wright, M., & Collard, S. (2000). Aboriginal youth: mental health. In P. Dudgeon, D. Garvey, & H. Pickett (Eds.), *Working with indigenous Australians: A handbook for psychologists* (pp. 85–90). Perth, Western Australia: Gunada Press.

Lewis, K. L., Sandquist, K. G., Stark, A. M., & Grenyer, B. F. S. (2009). Towards a national psychology ethics code: Systematic analysis of Australian professional and registration board standards. *Australian Psychologist, 44,* 263–269.

Love, A. W., & Allan, A. (2010). Looking forward. In A. Allan & A. W. Love (Eds.), *Ethical practice in psychology: Reflections from the creators of the APS code of ethics* (pp. 161–169). Chichester, UK: Wiley.

Milne, M. (2005). Maori perspectives on kaupapa Maori and psychology: A discussion document. Prepared for the New Zealand Psychologists Board.

Morrissey, S., & Reddy, P. (Eds.). (2006). *Ethics and professional practice for psychologists.* South Melbourne: Thomson Social Science Press.

New Zealand Psychological Society, NZ College of Clinical Psychologists and New Zealand Psychologists Board (2002). *Code of ethics for psychologists working in Aotearoa/New Zealand.* Wellington, NZ: Author.

O'Neil, W. M. (1987). *A century of psychology in Australia.* Sydney: Sydney University Press.

Privacy Act of 1988, §119, Commonwealth of Australia.

Ranzijn, R., McConnochie, K., & Nolan, W. (2009). *Psychology and indigenous Australians: Foundations of cultural competence.* South Yarra: Palgrave Macmillan.

Reid, M. (2009). Australian Health Ministers' Advisory Council's response to Psychology Board of Australia's consultation paper on registration standards. Retrieved from http://www.psychologyboard.gov.au/documents/submissions/AHMAC%20Governance%20Committee%20for%20NRAS.pdf.

Rudd, K. (2008). *Apology to the stolen generations.* Retrieved from http://australia.gov.au/about-australia/our-country/our-people/apology-to-australias-indigenous-peoples-1111115539655.

Scott, S. (2009). *Depression chats leaked on web.* Retrieved from http://www.abc.net.au/news/stories/2009/12/09/2766589.htm.

Seymour, F., Nairn, R., & Austin, J. (2004). Comments on Tim Williams' paper, "Setting impossible standards: The model of ethical decision-making associated with the New Zealand Psychologists' code of ethics." *New Zealand Journal of Psychology, 33,* 33–34.

Vicary, D. A., & Bishop, B. J. (2005). Western psychotherapeutic practice: Engaging Aboriginal people in culturally appropriate and respectful ways. *Australian Psychologist, 40,* 8–19.

Williams, T. (2004). Setting impossible standards: The model of ethical decision-making associated with the New Zealand Psychologists' code of Ethics. *New Zealand Journal of Psychology, 33,* 26–33.

PART 5

Economic, Political, and Social Influences on Psychological Ethics and Ethics Code Development

CHAPTER
27

Psychological Ethics and Macro-Social Change

Michael J. Stevens

Abstract

After empirically demonstrating that the well-being of psychology is tied to fundamental economic and political conditions, I illustrate how psychological ethics codes are socially situated by sampling from the codes or regulatory laws of selected countries that have transitioned or are transitioning from communism to free-market democracy, military dictatorship to representative government, economically and politically divided to unified, internationally isolated to globally interconnected, monarchy to theocracy, racially segregated to pluralistic, bicultural to multicultural, and at peace to wartime status. I also examine how the *Meta-Code of Ethics* reflects the complex, multidimensional integration of Europe. I conclude by identifying features common to the ethics codes of the above countries in transition and compare them to the *Universal Declaration of Ethical Principles for Psychologists*.

Key Words: economic and political systems, social transition, ethics codes

Because psychology is situated within the complex and evolving fabric of society, it is a priori a socially constructed discipline (Gergen, 2001). Codes of ethics in psychology, which articulate the aspirational goals and standards of conduct of psychologists, are themselves outcomes of a collective process of devising and revising normative conventions of professional rectitude. Given the contextually embedded status of psychology as a science and profession, it is not unreasonable to assert that economic and political events and forces shape psychological ethics codes, especially when these macro-social events and forces are of sufficient magnitude as to transform the structure and dynamics of society. It also follows that the values of society, which are mirrored in the ethics codes of psychology, may be strengthened or weakened depending on the particular form and direction of an economic and/or political transition, thereby ensuring or compromising the integrity of psychological research and practice and, ultimately, protecting or threatening the welfare of the general public.

In this chapter, I argue that codes of ethics in psychology are shaped by economic and political transitions to reflect the process and outcomes of such change, as well as exert control over psychologists to varying degrees (Freidson, 1984). I begin with an empirical demonstration that the well-being of psychology as a discipline is related to certain underlying economic and political conditions. I then illustrate how codes of ethics in psychology are socially constructed, by sampling from the general principles and specific standards of ethics codes or from the rights and obligations of psychologists as codified by law in selected countries that have transitioned or are currently transitioning from communism to free-market democracy (e.g., Romania), military dictatorship to representative government (e.g., Chile), economically and politically divided to unified (e.g., Germany), internationally isolated to globally interconnected (e.g., China), monarchy to theocracy (e.g., Iran), racially segregated to pluralistic (e.g., South Africa), bicultural to multicultural (e.g., Canada), and at peace to wartime status (e.g., United States). I also review the psychological ethics code of the Philippines, a country that has undergone and is currently experiencing complex, multiple transitions; specifically, from dictatorship to democracy and from at peace to war. From a regional perspective, I examine how the *Meta-Code of Ethics* (European Federation of Psychologists' Associations, 1995) reflects the economic and political integration of Europe and serves to guide the ethics codes of national organizations belonging to the European Federation of Psychologists' Associations (EFPA). I also identify the substantive and stylistic features common to the psychological ethics codes of the above countries in economic and/or political transitions and compare them to the *Universal Declaration of Ethical Principles for Psychologists* (Ad Hoc Joint Committee, 2008), adopted by the International Union of Psychological Science (IUPsyS) and International Association of Applied Psychology (IAAP) as a moral framework to guide the development of national codes of ethics in psychology worldwide. I conclude with a list of lingering questions about the relationship between economic and political transitions and ethics codes in psychology that may serve to direct future research on this overlooked topic.

Impact of Economics and Politics on Psychology

The worldwide growth of psychology is evident in the increasing numbers of psychologists, the proliferation of scientific and applied specializations, and the expansion of psychological journals, organizations, and training programs (Nair, Ardila, & Stevens, 2007; Stevens, 2007; Stevens & Wedding, 2004a). This trend parallels, and may even be subsumed by, the overarching process of globalization, which is characterized by the transnational movement of goods and capital, human beings, and information, as well as the rise of free-market democracies that have codified their respect for human rights (Stevens, 2007). Psychological research and practice has also experienced a resurgence in countries and regions that have transitioned economically and politically (e.g., Brazil, Poland). Although psychology became established and has evolved in various economic and political contexts (Brock, 2006; Kugelmann & Belzen, 2009), the status and expansion of psychology in these countries have been tied to stable economic and political systems that emphasize and safeguard the freedom of the individual in society (Jing, 2000; Rose, 1999). Such economic and political systems tend to have well-established structural conditions and a civic culture that supports a more or less demand economy and some form of representative government, respectively. The link between economic and political conditions and the status of psychology is due in part to the expectations of governments, business and industry, and the general public that psychology can play an important role in overcoming national challenges and cultivating personal well-being (Jing, 2000; Stevens & Wedding, 2004a). Given these expectations, psychology is likely to be strengthened by the favorable allocation of resources, creation of jobs, and legislation that legitimizes and sustains the profession (Stevens, 2007; Stevens & Wedding, 2004b). The citizens of democratic countries with free-market economies often experience an increase in personal wealth sufficient to propel them into a post-material mindset to improve their quality of life by discovering or creating more intangible and psychologically meaningful avenues for fulfillment (Rose, 1999; Sullivan & Transue, 1999). This individual and collective quest for growth is further supported by the type and level of education often found in countries with decentralized economies and representative governments that nurture the acquisition of knowledge and development of skills with which to mobilize autonomous decision making, as well as by exposure to and valuing of diverse worldviews that often coexist in such open and interconnected societies (Sullivan & Transue, 1999).

Economic and political transitions seldom occur in isolation from one another. Mark Rosenzweig (1982) found that the membership in psychological organizations serving as national representatives to the IUPsyS increased from 53,219 to 101,521 between 1970 and 1980, with new members belonging mostly to industrialized countries. Qicheng Jing showed that the number of psychologists per million population was higher in developed than in developing countries (513 vs. 130, respectively), a finding that dovetails with earlier research (Fu & Jing, 1994). Not surprisingly, Gross National Product (GNP) per capita as an index of overall national development was positively correlated with the ratio of psychologists per million population in 32 countries with national representation in the IUPsyS, $r = .44$ (Jing, 2000). The United Nations Human Development Index

(HDI) is based not only on the market value of all goods and services produced within a country per population, but also on life expectancy and adult literacy, making HDI a measure of national development that is less likely to be confounded by disparities in wealth distribution and more indicative of how wealth serves to improve citizens' lives (United Nations Development Program, 2009). Of the 43 countries ranked high on HDI in 1998, 36 (84%) had national representation in the IUPsyS, whereas of the 37 countries ranked low, only one (3%) had national representation (Jing, 2000). Furthermore, the correlation between the HDI and ratio of psychologists per million population in 32 IUPsyS member countries was $r = .51$ (Jing, 2000). Finally, the 10 IUPsyS member countries with the highest number of psychologists per million population were both economically robust and politically democratic. Notwithstanding the weaknesses in these data (e.g., limited representation of developing countries), they affirm the positive association of a free market and democratic political system to the status of a country's psychology.

In an effort to update and expand upon Jing's (2000) findings, I identified the 71 countries that currently hold national membership in the IUPsyS. I then gathered the following 2007 data for each of the 71 IUPsyS member countries: Gross Domestic Product index (GDPi) (i.e., purchasing power parity against the U.S. dollar), HDI, and population (United Nations Development Program, 2009); the ratio of psychologists per million population (World Health Organization, 2005); and the number of psychology publications abstracted in the PsycINFO database. I chose to use GDPi rather than GNP per capita because domestic measures of national development reflect economic productivity within in a country, whereas national measures include income earned from abroad. I should also note that, although most psychologists worldwide are engaged in various types of applied work (Nair et al., 2007; Stevens & Wedding, 2004a), the World Health Organization's estimates of psychologists per million population draw heavily on data that document the number of psychologists employed in health settings. Lastly, I conducted a PsycINFO institutional search of the authors of books, book chapters, and journal articles abstracted in 2007, which is a more accurate method than an address search for identifying the national affiliation of published authors. As an aside, 63% of the literature abstracted in PsycINFO is published in non-U.S. outlets and 17% in a language other than English (Psychology International, 2009).

To provide a more direct and compelling demonstration of the relationship between the well-being of psychology and the economic and political conditions in which the discipline is situated, I identified indices of economic and political freedom for the 71 member countries of the IUPsyS. Specifically, I obtained 2007 data for each IUPsyS member country on its level of economic freedom, based on 10 components of economic freedom (e.g., freedom from corruption, labor mobility, property rights) that are averaged to yield an overall score for each country (Heritage Foundation and Dow Jones & Company, 2007). Similarly, I obtained 2007 data for each IUPsyS member country on its level of political freedom, as determined by the combination of political rights (e.g., electoral process, functioning of government, political pluralism and participation) and civil liberties (e.g., associational and organizational rights, freedom of expression and belief, rule of law) in each country (Freedom House, 2007).

Of the 38 countries ranked high on the HDI in 2007, 28 (74%) had national representation in the IUPsyS, whereas none of the 24 countries ranked low on the 2007 HDI were represented in the IUPsyS. These findings closely resemble those of Jing (2000) a decade earlier. Tables 27.1–27.4 contain data for the countries with the highest and lowest ratio of psychologists per million population and highest and lowest ratio of publications per million population. GDPi was positively correlated only with publications per million population, $r(68) = .370$, $p = .002$, whereas HDI was positively correlated with both psychologists per million population, $r(60) = .430$, $p < .0005$, and publications per million population, $r(68) = .603$, $p < .0005$. Not only do GDPi and HDI serve as indicators of national development as well as disciplinary health (Jing, 2000), they also predict distinct dimensions of disciplinary well-being: size of occupational membership and research productivity. Level of economic freedom was positively correlated with psychologists per million population, $r(60) = .281$, $p = .027$, and publications per million population, $r(68) = .632$, $p < .0005$. Level of political freedom also was positively correlated with psychologists per million population, $r(61) = .366$, $p = .003$, and publications per million population, $r(69) = .465$, $p < .0005$. The strong associations between indices of freedom and measures of disciplinary well-being provide for the first time direct evidence to support the previously made assertion that free-market economic systems

Table 27.1 Countries with the Highest Ratio of Psychologists per Million Population

Country	Psychologists/ Population	GDPi	HDI	Economic Freedom	Political Freedom
Argentina	106.00	0.82	0.87	54.0	2.0
Denmark	85.00	0.98	0.96	77.0	1.0
Finland	79.00	0.98	0.96	74.0	1.0
Sweden	76.00	0.99	0.96	69.3	1.0
Norway	68.00	1.00	0.97	67.9	1.0
Germany	51.50	0.98	0.95	70.8	1.0
Austria	49.00	0.96	0.96	71.6	1.0
Switzerland	40.80	1.00	0.96	78.0	1.0
Israel	35.60	0.93	0.94	64.8	1.5
Canada	35.00	0.98	0.97	78.0	1.0

Note. GDPi = purchasing power per capita as a proportion of the $US. HDI < 0.5 represents low national development whereas HDI ≥ 0.8 represents high development. Economic Freedom: 0 = least free, 100 = most free. Political Freedom: 1 = most free, 7 = least free.

and representative forms of government are a boon to psychology (Jing, 2000; Rose, 1999).

I was also interested in testing the hypothesis that the relationships of economic and political freedom to the disciplinary well-being of psychology would be mediated by level of national development (see Figure 27.1). That is, I anticipated that indices of economic and political freedom would each have an indirect relationship to the ratios of psychologists per population and to research productivity per population. If national development (i.e., HDI) is the process whereby freedom exerts influence on

Table 27.2 Countries with the Lowest Ratio of Psychologists per Million Population

Country	Psychologists/ Population	GDPi	HDI	Economic Freedom	Political Freedom
Bangladesh	0.002	0.42	0.54	46.7	4.0
Nigeria	0.02	0.50	0.51	55.6	4.0
India	0.03	0.55	0.61	53.9	2.5
Morocco	0.03	0.62	0.65	56.4	4.5
Ukraine	0.06	0.71	0.80	51.5	2.5
Vietnam	0.06	0.54	0.73	49.8	6.0
Sudan	0.17	0.51	0.53	—	7.0
Albania	0.20	0.71	0.82	61.4	3.0
Pakistan	0.20	0.54	0.57	57.2	5.5
Indonesia	0.30	0.60	0.73	53.2	2.5

Note. GDPi = purchasing power per capita as a proportion of the $US. HDI < 0.5 represents low national development whereas HDI ≥ 0.8 represents high development. Economic Freedom: 0 = least free, 100 = most free. Political Freedom: 1 = most free, 7 = least free.

Table 27.3 Countries with the Highest Ratio of Publications per Million Population

Country	Research/Population	GDPi	HDI	Economic Freedom	Political Freedom
Israel	274.64	0.93	0.94	64.8	1.5
Australia	274.11	0.98	0.97	81.1	1.0
Canada	263.62	0.98	0.97	78.0	1.0
New Zealand	258.10	0.95	0.95	81.4	1.0
Netherlands	247.33	0.99	0.96	75.5	1.0
United Kingdom	234.09	0.98	0.95	79.9	1.0
Sweden	223.26	0.99	0.96	69.3	1.0
United States	222.56	1.00	0.96	81.2	1.0
Norway	220.64	1.00	0.97	67.9	1.0
Switzerland	204.53	1.00	0.96	78.0	1.0

Note. GDPi = purchasing power per capita as a proportion of the $US. HDI < 0.5 represents low national development whereas HDI ≥ 0.8 represents high development. Economic Freedom: 0 = least free, 100 = most free. Political Freedom: 1 = most free, 7 = least free.

Table 27.4 Countries with the Lowest Ratio of Publications per Million Population

Country	Research/Population	GDPi	HDI	Economic Freedom	Political Freedom
Georgia	0.00	0.64	0.78	69.3	3.0
Indonesia	0.12	0.60	0.73	53.2	2.5
Sudan	0.12	0.51	0.53	—	7.0
Yemen	0.13	0.53	0.58	54.1	5.0
Bangladesh	0.23	0.42	0.54	46.7	4.0
Pakistan	0.32	0.54	0.57	57.2	5.5
Philippines	0.34	0.59	0.75	56.0	3.0
Vietnam	0.37	0.54	0.73	49.8	6.0
Ukraine	0.43	0.71	0.80	51.5	2.5
Dominican Republic	0.51	0.70	0.78	56.8	2.0

Note. GDPi = purchasing power per capita as a proportion of the $US. HDI < 0.5 represents low national development whereas HDI ≥ 0.8 represents high development. Economic Freedom: 0 = least free, 100 = most free. Political Freedom: 1 = most free, 7 = least free.

disciplinary well-being, then the introduction of HDI should reduce the direct association of economic and political freedom to the ratios of psychologist per population and research productivity per population. The four conditions for mediation were met (Baron & Kenny, 1986): (1) confirmation of a relationship between economic and political freedom and disciplinary well-being that could be mediated, $R^2 = .135$, $F(2, 59) = 4.619$, $p = .014$, $f^2 = 0.156$ and $R^2 = .405$, $F(2, 67) = 22.790$, $p < .0005$, $f^2 = 0.681$, respectively; (2) a relationship between national development (i.e., HDI) and indices of disciplinary well-being, $R^2 = .185$, $F(1, 60) = 13.589$, $p < .0005$, $f^2 = 0.227$ and $R^2 = .363$, $F(1, 68) = 38.791$, $p < .0005$, $f^2 = 0.570$, respectively; (3) a unique relationship between HDI and psychologists per population and publications per population with the effect of economic and political freedom on

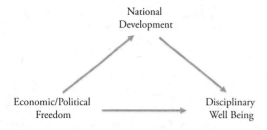

Figure 27.1. Mediation by national development (HDI) of the relationship between economic/political freedom and disciplinary well-being (psychologists and publications per million population)

HDI removed, $R^2 = .195$, $F(3, 57) = 4.594$, $p = .006$, $f^2 = 0.242$, $pr(57) = .264$, $p = .043$ and $R^2 = .502$, $F(3, 65) = 21.875$, $p < .0005$, $f^2 = 1.008$, $pr(65) = .371$, $p = .002$, respectively; and (4) significant Sobel tests that showed diminished direct relationships between indices of freedom and measures of disciplinary well-being with HDI as a mediator. Sobel tests specifically revealed mediation by HDI of level of economic freedom on psychologists per million population, $z = 2.517$, $p = .011$, and on publications per million population, $z = 2.913$, $p = .004$, and by level of political freedom on psychologists per million population, $z = 2.049$, $p = .04$, and publications per million population, $z = 3.518$, $p < .0005$. The discovery that national development, as measured by citizens' literacy, longevity, and standard of living, mediates the relationship of economic and political freedom to disciplinary well-being should give critics pause. The above statistical analyses of transnational empirical data have generated preliminary support for a causal model of how certain economic and political conditions may impact the status of psychology, one which promises to yield a rich vein of research that will further articulate this intricate and important relationship.

Some have argued that any relationship of psychology to free markets and representative government is spurious, and that those who advocate such a relationship confuse correlation with causation (Brock, 2006). These critics must be reminded that the empirical evidence for such a relationship is credible and that statistical demonstrations of mediation imply causality (Baron & Kenny, 1986). Second, these same critics have incorrectly identified various countries' forms of government and then falsely claimed that, because psychology has a weak presence there, a relationship between free-market democracy and disciplinary well-being does not exist. Finally, critics have concluded erroneously that any country without a demand economy or representative government that boasts a thriving discipline of psychology negates any argument, empirically supported or merely logical, in favor of a relationship between economic and political freedom and the status of psychology. Such reasoning belies dichotomous and unscientific thinking. Naturally, there are exceptions to the tendency to find psychology well positioned in free-market democracies. For example (see Stevens, Overmier, & Overmier, 2009), before the 1959 revolution, psychology as a profession did not exist in Cuba. Psychologists' training in Cuba began with the foundation of the school of psychology at the Central University of Las Villas in 1961, followed in 1962 by the school of psychology at Havana University. Psychologists are nationally licensed and abide by a code of ethics. The most recent data indicates that Cuba has nine psychologists per million population, higher than the ratio in Australia, France, and Japan, and equal to that of the United Kingdom (World Health Organization, 2005). Among the developing countries in the Caribbean, Cuban psychologists have published the most research based on a 5-year search of abstracts indexed in PsycINFO (Sanchez-Sosa & Riveros, 2007). Clearly, psychology in Cuba defies the general economic and political trends described above. However, in view of the overall evidence, any success that can be attributed to Cuban psychology, which appears to serve a centralized economy and repressive government, with research and practice directed toward "the regulation of everyday life" (Brock, 2006, p. 158), is but a curious anomaly.

Forms of Economic and Political Transition

Turning to the social construction of ethics that guide the practice of psychology, broadly speaking, I now sample from the principles and standards of ethics codes or from the rights and obligations of psychologists as codified by law in selected countries that have made or are engaged in various forms of economic and political transition. Background information on the economic and political conditions of each country was obtained primarily from *The World Factbook* (Central Intelligence Agency, 2009).

Romania

Romania is a country emerging from communism into free-market democracy. The Soviet occupation of Romania after World War II led to the imposition of a communist regime in 1947. The decades-long rule of Nicolae Ceausescu, who took power in

1965, became increasingly draconian and oppressive through the 1980s. Ceausescu was overthrown and executed in December 1989. Former communists dominated the government until 1996 when they were swept from power in a general election. Successive governments have made substantial economic and political reforms, which have increased the overall quality of life. Romania joined NATO in 2004 and the EU in 2007 and continues to reform its economy. However, political corruption remains widespread and Romania's GDP has been adversely impacted by the worldwide recession. Virtually moribund in 1989, psychology continues its steady course toward renewal (Stevens, 1998).

The most recent legislation governing the practice of psychology in Romania was enacted in 2004 with the adoption of Law No. 213, *Psychologist's Law*. Excerpts from the rights and obligations of psychologists from this law that appear closely tied to Romania's economic and political transition are:

1. Ownership of the right to free practice
2. Ownership of the right to organize
3. Independence from politics
4. Respect for the fundamental rights of humankind
5. Confidentiality is protected and obligatory
6. Rights are extended to EU and bilateral states

The term *ownership* is used repeatedly throughout Law No. 213 and accentuates the legal protections given to individual psychologists to work in their field and to the College of Psychologists, the organization that represents the national and international interests of Romanian psychologists, to function. The term also resonates with Romania's current commitment to capitalism and the privatization of property. The explicit statement that Romanian psychologists are to remain politically independent speaks to the reality of state control during the communist era when employment and professional advancement were tied to membership in and loyalty to the Partidul Comunist Roman (Adler, Mueller, & Ayat, 1993). Respect for the fundamental rights of humankind, specifically the requirement that psychologists maintain the confidentiality of clients and research participants, can also be linked to a time when psychologists were coerced by the Securitate secret police into violating the confidentiality of suspected dissidents (Stevens, 1998). Moreover, under the communist regime, a number of laws, statues, and decrees allowed for the political abuse of professional psychology. For example, in 1978 Law No. 3 was passed legalizing involuntary hospitalization in medical emergencies, enabling the government to incarcerate dissidents during official visits by Western dignitaries (Adler et al., 1993). Similarly, the former penal code contained articles that made possible compulsory medical treatment, as well as prohibition from performing the functions of a professional occupation, both of which served to remove so-called undesirables from circulation. Finally, the legal rights and obligations of Romanian psychologists are extended to psychologists from other nations with whom Romania has bilateral or EU relations, allowing psychologists from those countries to work in Romania under the protection and guidance of the law.

Chile

In Chile the 3-year socialist government of Salvador Allende was overthrown in 1973 by a military coup led by Augusto Pinochet, who ruled the country until a freely elected president was installed in 1990. The country, which had been relatively free of coups, endured one of the harshest Latin American dictatorships of the last century, costing the lives of 3,000 dead and missing. Since the 1980s, sound economic policies not only have reduced poverty by nearly half and contributed to the region's highest GDP per capita, but also have helped to secure Chile's commitment to representative government. Chile's market-driven economy rests on sound fiscal policies and numerous international trade agreements. Within Latin America, Chile leads or ranks high on economic freedom, political stability, and quality of life. Chile also has assumed regional and international leadership roles that reflect its status as a stable, democratic nation.

In 1999 the Colegio de Psicologos de Chile published the most recent iteration of the *Codigo de Etica Profesional*. Excerpts from the rights and obligations of Chilean psychologists that best reflect Chile's political transition from military dictatorship to representative government are contained in the following articles from the country's code of ethics:

1. Do not participate or support practices that commit an outrage against liberty and integrity.
2. Respect the rights and dignities of persons.
3. Improve the well-being and realize the potential of clients.
4. Accept responsibility to transform society for the better.
5. Prevent political and institutional pressures to violate ethics.

The Chilean ethics code explicitly ties its prohibition against harming others to the principles of the *Universal Declaration of Human Rights*, which was adopted in 1948 by the United Nations General Assembly; that is, psychologists are expected to respect the dignity and value of all persons and their rights to autonomy, confidentiality, diversity, privacy, and self-determination. Chilean psychologists are expressly forbidden from engaging in any action that might violate fundamental human rights, and are enjoined from lending indirect or tacit support to such actions. Outrages against liberty and integrity are identified as including, though not limited to, the use of information to the detriment of a client, torture or the infliction of suffering and pain, cruel and degrading treatment, and procedures that aim to break a person's willpower. The significance of excluding these practices by name and incorporating them into the code of professional ethics presumably lies in the mission of the Colegio de Psicologos to prevent a recurrence of the excesses that took place during the dictatorship, in which psychologists may have voluntarily or unwillingly participated.

In addition to being warned against nonmaleficence, Chilean psychologists are encouraged to aspire to beneficent conduct, such as improving the well-being and realizing the potentials of the individual client. The Chilean ethics code further states that psychologists accept personal responsibility to transform society as a whole for the better. Thus, psychologists are guided to cultivate a sense of critical awareness and social justice and to undertake some form of community or national activism, such as political advocacy. Aspiring to improve all of society is an ethical prophylactic to the inherent dangers of acceding to political and institutional pressures to violate professional ethical principles and basic moral values.

Germany

In 1949 the sectors of Germany controlled by allied forces were merged to form the Federal Republic of Germany, or West Germany, while the Soviet-controlled zone became the German Democratic Republic, or East Germany. West Germany was a parliamentary democracy and had a market economy. The country achieved relatively uninterrupted economic growth, as well as military and political integration with the West. East Germany was militarily occupied and politically dominated by the former USSR, as well as economically and militarily integrated with other Warsaw Pact nations. The Socialist Unity Party of Germany maintained exclusive hold on power through the Stasi secret service. A command economy met the basic needs of the population.

In 1989 the disintegration of communist regimes elsewhere in Europe led to mass demonstrations, emigration to the West, and to a series of government decisions and reforms that culminated in the 1990 Two Plus Four Treaty, whereby all occupying powers surrendered their rights and allowed Germany to reunify as a sovereign country.

Germany is now a federal republic. Since reunification, Germany has been engaged in the economic, military, and political unification of Europe and maintains numerous partnerships worldwide. The country has a robust economy and high standard of living, although its economy recently contracted due to the global recession. Compounding matters is the costly long-term process of modernizing and integrating the former East German economy.

East German psychologists were obliged to follow principles of socialist ethics and morality, which directed their practice of psychology toward ideological criteria for social well-being (Rosler, 2009). Today, all German psychologists adhere to the *Ethical Principles* (German Psychological Society and Association of German Professional Psychologists, 1999) in their treatment of clients, conduct of research, relationships with colleagues, and interactions with institutions. The *Ethical Principles* ensures the political freedom of German psychologists, permits economic competition between colleagues and allied professions, and aims to preserve and enhance the well-being of the individual in addition to society (Rosler, 2009). The preamble describes psychology as a "liberal profession"; not only are psychologists committed to protecting and promoting human rights, but they also are reminded explicitly to stand vigilant against economic and political circumstances that could lead to the misuse of their knowledge and skills, and thus compromise the personal freedom to live by one's convictions. To ensure their professional integrity, psychologists are further required to establish standards for the public evaluation of their performance.

Excerpts from the rights and obligations from the *Ethical Principles* that mirror the economic and political dimensions of Germany's unification include:

1. The constitutional right to free scientific inquiry and teaching, along with a complementary duty to prevent partisan external interests from interfering with research and instruction

2. Recognition of dissenting viewpoints, openness to criticism and dialogue, honesty in correcting colleagues, and willingness to acknowledge one's own professional errors

3. Moral responsibility to advance democratic working methods

4. Respect for privacy and protection of privileged information (reinforced by the German Criminal Code)

5. Minimization of threats to the dignity and safety of clients and research participants (e.g., informed consent)

6. Diligence in providing expert opinion, reporting assessment findings, and publishing research that is accurate and scientifically informed

7. Not undermining colleagues by seeking to displace them or prevent them from competing in independent practice

A revision of the current *Ethical Principles* is underway and will take into consideration the *Meta-Code of Ethics* of the EFPA (1995) and the *Ethical Principles of Psychologists and Code of Conduct* of the American Psychological Association (2002). The draft revision emphasizes respect for human rights and dignity as well as the social responsibilities of German psychologists to safeguard the profession, discipline, and greater society from intrusion of the state. The following is written about psychological science as a foundation for professional practice:

> Theories and knowledge of psychology arise from different philosophical understandings about the human being. These are to be considered when interpreting and adapting different concepts.
> (Rosler, 2009)

This strong, ideologically tolerant stance exemplifies the abiding commitment of the German Psychological Society and Association of German Professional Psychologists to educate German psychologists about the risks of ideological perversion of the discipline, which had taken so long to overcome.

China

After World War II, Mao Zedong founded a communist economic and political system that, while ensuring China's sovereignty, imposed strict controls over daily life. Beginning in 1978, Deng Xiaoping and subsequent leaders instituted graduated economic reforms. China's economy during the last quarter-century evolved from a centrally planned system, largely closed to international trade, to a more market-oriented model that features a rapidly growing private sector and which boasts the second largest economy after that of the United States. However, the worldwide economic crisis has reduced the demand for Chinese exports, thereby slowing its meteoric growth in GDP. For much of the population, the standard of living has improved dramatically and opportunities to exert personal choice have expanded. However, political control remains firm. The Chinese government retains virtually complete authority over politics and seeks the elimination of perceived threats to political and social order (e.g., jailing political opponents, censoring the press). Thus, China's "one country, two systems" organization has propelled the country from economic and political obscurity and isolation to worldwide prominence and integration.

The *Code of Ethics for Counseling and Clinical Practice* (Chinese Psychological Society, 2007) was designed to guide the ethical professional practice of clinical and counseling psychology, which is relatively new to China, and to inform the general public about the obligations and responsibilities of psychologists who practice these specialties. The overall purpose of the Chinese ethics code is to enhance mental health and well-being in order to promote the Confucian ideal of a harmonious society. This iteration of the Chinese ethics code appears to follow the principles and standards of the code of ethics of the American Psychological Association (2002) more so than the 1992 version.

Excerpts from the rights and obligations of the principles and standards of the *Code of Ethics for Counseling and Clinical Practice* that seem pertinent to China's transition from global isolation to integration include respect for the individual, which illustrates China's increased exposure to the individualism associated with Western modernity. In sharp contrast with the former jingoistic ethical obligation to love their country, Chinese psychologists are now expected to advance the welfare of the individual for the collective betterment of the nation. Other components of the Chinese code of ethics that possess individualistic qualities to varying degrees are the following protections:

1. Privacy and confidentiality
2. Self-determination
3. Nondiscrimination based on politics and religion

The Chinese code maintains a delicate balance between psychologists' duty not to harm their individual clients and the maintenance of social order as culturally and politically proscribed. Thus, although the ethics code speaks rather ambiguously about the disclosure of confidential information as demanded by various laws and regulations, it encourages psychologists to express their commitment to the code and to resolve conflicts between elements of the code and national law. Specifically, Chinese psychologists are to inform clients of the courts' interests and rights, request documentation from the court regarding the need for disclosure of confidential information, and seek assurance from the court that such disclosure will not jeopardize or harm the professional relationship. Other sections of the Chinese code are somewhat inconsistent and may unwittingly place psychologists in an ethical dilemma that pits the principles of beneficence and respect against potential social gains. For example, although Chinese psychologists are enjoined from forcing people to participate in research, they may use involuntary participants when certain that their research will not cause harm and there is a justifiable need to conduct the research.

Iran

The Islamic Republic of Iran was established in 1979 with the overthrow of the monarchy. Shiite ayatollahs formed a theocratic system of government with ultimate political authority vested in a supreme leader, who vets political candidates and can block legislative reform. The regime enforces public compliance with traditional Islamic law. Nevertheless, a reform movement was launched in response to widespread dissatisfaction over corrupt and repressive leadership, leading to the election of a politically moderate president, Mohammad Khatami, in 1997. Threatened by the prospect of a more open, modern society, conservative clerics regained control over elected government institutions, installing hardliner Mahmoud Ahmadinejad as president in 2005. The 2009 presidential election posed a serious threat to Ahmadinejad's power and to the autocratic system of government by reinvigorating the reform movement. Doubts about the legitimacy the election led to popular demonstrations that were put down violently by government forces. Iran's semi-developed economy hinges on central planning, state ownership of large enterprises, and small private agricultural, trade, and service ventures. The recent drop in oil prices has precipitated a rise in unemployment and a "brain drain." To compound matters, Iran remains subject to economic sanctions due to its sponsorship of terrorism and alleged development of nuclear weapons.

The *Ethics Code* of the Iranian Organization of Psychology and Counseling (n.d.) contains seven general principles that serve as a foundation for 10 derivative sets of standards of conduct. In addition to seeking a balance between the rights of psychologists and those of clients, the introduction to the code explicitly states at the outset that it was designed to preserve the cultural, social, and religious background of Iranians, which reflects the nationalism and fundamentalism on which the Islamic Republic of Iran is founded.

Excerpts from the rights and obligations of the principles and standards of the *Ethics Code* that speak to Iran's transition from monarchy to theocracy are:

1. Respect the orders and rules of society's values
2. Violate confidentiality when ordered by law or a lawful authority
3. Practice within the framework of national law and regulations
4. Participate in activities that contribute to the development of public well-being, including sociopolitical adjustments
5. Take both materialistic and spiritual rights into consideration in all scientific and professional activities

Although the ethical principles and standards of conduct enumerated above appear to bear the imprint of state control, they are vaguely worded and thus open to interpretation. In some ways, these segments from the Iranian code parallel the aspirations and requirements embodied in the ethics codes of secular, democratic societies (e.g., operate within the law). The remaining principles of the Iranian code speak not only of aspiring to widely held human values, but also of adhering to them; these principles include respect for the rights of individuals and groups, nonmaleficence and beneficence, as well as autonomy and equality. Professional integrity appears to be integrated within the code's standards of conduct and covers such issues as approaching clients with sensitivity to their gender, ethnicity, and religion, as well as avoiding injustice in their professional relations, presumably including relations with state authorities. Psychologists are responsible for obtaining informed consent and ensuring that their services are used correctly, such as taking precautions against the misapplication of assessment data and psychological reports. Notwithstanding these injunctions, the Iranian code contains several weakly or ominously worded standards, which suggest the possibility of government intrusion in certain circumstances. For example, psychologists are instructed to take only cautionary steps in maintaining client confidentiality, and are enjoined to minimize possible harm in "unpredictable and inevitable" circumstances. In all, psychologists in Iran seem to have crafted a delicate balance between the secular–religious and democratic–autocratic tensions that pervade their country.

South Africa

In 1961 South Africa achieved independence from British colonial rule. The government legislated a continuation of the official policy of racial segregation, inaugurated by the Boers and later known as apartheid, in spite of opposition from within and outside of the country. In 1990 President F. W. de Klerk began to dismantle this legislation, and in 1994 South Africa held its first democratic, multiracial election. This election brought an end to apartheid and ushered into power Nelson Mandela and the current ruling party, the African National Congress. South Africa, a parliamentary republic, is known for its diversity, with the largest Caucasian, Indian, and racially mixed communities on the continent and with 11 languages recognized by its constitution. In 2008 South Africa placed fifth among sub-Saharan countries on the Ibrahim Index, a measure of the success of a government in delivering healthy economic and political conditions to its citizens. However, economic challenges from the apartheid era persist, including high unemployment and lack of economic empowerment among disadvantaged groups, and the current government struggles with balancing wealth redistribution against economic growth.

The *Rules of Conduct Pertaining Specifically to Psychology* (Health Professions Council of South Africa, 2004) is the most recent version of South Africa's code of ethics in psychology. In updating the 2002 code, the Professional Board for Psychology drew from South African law, relevant sections of the country's constitution, and other widely respected national codes of ethics (e.g., American Psychological Association, Canadian Psychological Association). The South African ethics code is statutorily binding for psychologists who are registered with the Professional Board for Psychology, in that the code is embedded in the country's Health Professions Act.

Excerpts from the rights and obligations of the principles and standards of the *Rules of Conduct Pertaining Specifically to Psychology* that seem especially germane to South Africa's political transition from a racially segregated to a pluralistic country include:

1. Preservation and protection of fundamental human rights
2. Privacy, confidentiality, and access to information
3. Avoiding and preventing the misuse of assessment
4. Truthfulness in forensic testimony and reports
5. Respect for the sociocultural contexts of treatment

The ethics code of South Africa underscores psychologists' primary obligation to ensure the basic rights of clients, research participants, and others with whom they have professional contact. In view of how grievously these basic rights had been violated under apartheid, South African psychologists are directed specifically to guarantee the physical and psychological integrity of their charges and avoid stereotyping based on culture, ethnicity, and race, among other demographic characteristics. Psychologists' obligation to preserve and protect basic human rights also entails commands to preserve privacy, confidentiality, and access to information; to avoid and actively prevent the misuse of psychological assessment results; and to maintain veracity of forensic reports and testimony. The intent of these obligations is for psychologists not to inflict harm, as well as to prevent others from inflicting harm. Respect for the sociocultural contexts of treatment is another prominent feature of the South African code of ethics, revealing sensitivity to potential ethical dilemmas that involve competent practice. The code encourages South African psychologists to expand their scope of applied practice to meet the distinct needs of a diverse population. Suggestions for improving competent practice include the development of indigenized therapeutic methods, use of community-based interventions in responding to shared local concerns, and advocacy to strengthen the voice of the disadvantaged and marginalized. Clearly, the South African ethics code is infused with a social justice perspective, inspiring South African psychologists to bring a proactive beneficent orientation to their professional work.

Canada

Canada has long faced political challenges in responding to the aspirations of its English and French peoples. Since the 1960s there have been periodic separatist movements in predominantly francophone Quebec, culminating in the supreme court ruling that provincial secession is unconstitutional; less than 10 years later, the national parliament passed a motion that symbolically recognized the Quebecois as a nation within Canada. Although bilingual, Canada is rapidly becoming multicultural owing to its changing demography. Canada has the highest per capita immigration in the world, driven by a vibrant mixed economy (although economic growth has slowed due to the slump in housing, automobile, and commodities sectors), and a commitment to provide safe harbor for refugees. Moreover, Canada's aboriginal population is growing at a rate almost twice that of the Canadian average. In 1999 the Canadian government created the territory of Nunavut on a public government model of self-government for the people of the eastern Arctic, and also established a lands claim agreement that ensured Nunavut and the Inuit title to a portion of the land. Under this model, the government serves all residents of Nunavut, whether Inuit or not. However, with the population of Nunavut being primarily Inuit, government is brought closer to the culture and wishes of the Inuit people.

Nunavut offers an unusual illustration of an aboriginal culture applying indigenous Inuit values as guiding principles for the activities of government, including those of psychologists (Pettifor, 2007). This contrasts sharply with the tendency of national psychological associations to model their codes of ethics on those of the Western world. The *Qaujimanituqangit Principles* include the following collectivistic values that are reasonably congruent with the relatively individualistic principles of the Canadian code of ethics: (a) *Pijitsirniq* or the concept of serving, (b) *Aajiiqatigiingniq* or the concept of consensus-making, (c) *Pilimmaksarniq* or the concept of knowledge and skill acquisition, and (d) *Piliriquatigiingniq* or the concept of collaborative relationships.

Although not required to do so, most provincial and territorial bodies have adopted the Canadian code of ethics as a guide for the professional practice of psychology. Excerpts from the rights and obligations of the principles and standards of the *Code of Ethics for Psychologists* that reflect Canada's transition toward multiculturalism are:

1. Inherent worth of persons is independent of culture
2. Moral rights are promoted and protected in culturally distinct ways
3. Moral rights are extended to diverse and collective groupings
4. Oral and nonverbal consent may be acceptable
5. Therapist disclosure may threaten client dignity or well-being
6. Engage cultural communities in research and service delivery
7. Advocate change to social structures and polices that are unjust, especially to vulnerable persons and groups

Not only is the language of the 2000 Canadian code of ethics more inclusive of cultural diversity than either of its predecessors, but also directly acknowledges the fundamental moral protections and rights afforded distinct groups and communities in addition to those given to individuals. The Canadian ethics code is responsive to Canada's increasingly multicultural society in its sensitivity and respect for how Western practices may conflict with, and at times pose risks for, diverse persons and groups if applied uncritically. In this regard, the Canadian code invites respectful horizontal collaboration with local communities in pursuing a more inclusive and meaningful psychological science and practice. In addition, the code of ethics contains a decision-making model to assist Canadian psychologists in resolving ethical dilemmas that may arise from the practice of psychology within a multicultural context. Finally, Canadian psychologists are reminded of their social responsibility to eliminate structural and institutional sources of discrimination and oppression that unjustly contribute to the psychological vulnerabilities and impede the well-being of individuals and communities.

United States

On September 11, 2001, al-Qaida terrorists attacked the World Trade Center in New York City and the Pentagon near Washington, DC, murdering almost 3,000 noncombatants. In response, President George W. Bush enlisted support from the international community in the so-called "war on terrorism," renamed the "overseas contingency operation" in 2009 by the U.S. Department of Defense. Later in 2001, the U.S. military launched Operation Enduring Freedom, toppling Afghanistan's Taliban government and eradicating al-Qaida training camps there. Taliban fighters continue to wage an insurgency against NATO forces, with President Barack Obama authorizing in late 2009 the deployment of an additional 30,000 U.S. troops to stabilize the country. In 2002, appealing to the Iraq Liberation Act of 1998, the Bush administration called for regime change in Iraq. With bipartisan support of the U.S. congress, President Bush formed an international coalition early in 2003 and commenced Operation Iraqi Freedom to remove Saddam Hussein, then president of Iraq, from power. Notwithstanding domestic and foreign pressures to withdraw, the U.S.-led coalition remained in Iraq until President Obama announced the full withdrawal of U.S. combat troops from Iraq by December 31, 2011, while retaining a force of noncombat defense contractors there for an indeterminate period of time.

The war on terrorism been conducted amidst controversy (see Costanzo, Gerrity, & Lykes, 2007). Various groups, including Amnesty International, have demanded that the United States close the detention facility in Guantanamo Bay, Cuba, and rendition centers in other countries, either prosecute detainees under fair trial standards or release them, and reject outright methods of interrogation that involve the use of torture or other forms of maltreatment. Many of the counterterrorism policies enacted by the Bush administration remain in place under the Obama administration (e.g., military commissions, indefinite detention without trial, rendition abroad), while others have been modified to varying degrees. The detention facility at Guantanamo Bay remains open, housing upwards of 200 prisoners, and although President Obama issued an executive order restricting the interrogation of detainees to methods specified in the U.S. Army Field Manual, exceptions may be recommended by the U.S. Attorney General.

The transition of the United States from at-peace to wartime status has been of concern to the American Psychological Association (APA). Allegations by the media and by psychologists of human rights violations in the interrogation of detainees prompted the APA to form a Task Force on Psychological Ethics and National Security (PENS). The task force drafted a report detailing the ethical dimensions of national security activities and the ethical guidance available to psychologists who serve in or consult with the military and security services. The ethical foundation for the PENS report lies mainly in the principles of nonmaleficence and beneficence and of fidelity and responsibility, which demand that psychologists do no harm and commit themselves to advancing the good of society, respectively.

The PENS report (Task Force on Psychological Ethics and National Security, 2005) makes clear that psychologists who engage in, direct, support, facilitate, or offer training in torture or other cruel, inhuman, or degrading treatment stand in violation of the *Ethical Principles of Psychologists and Code of Conduct* (American Psychological Association, 2002). The report adds that psychologists are obligated to disclose such acts to appropriate authorities and permitted to disobey laws or orders that are unjust or violate human rights. The report concludes that psychologists have an important role in ensuring that interrogations are conducted safely, legally, and effectively, noting that psychologists may contribute to effective information-gathering only under such circumstances.

Following intense debate over the PENS report, the APA in 2006 reaffirmed its opposition to all forms of torture as well as other cruel, inhuman, or degrading treatment or punishment regardless of circumstance, and condemned any involvement by psychologists in such activities (American Psychological Association, 2006). The APA's prohibition applies to all psychologists in all settings and makes a stronger statement than the PENS report about the ethical conduct of psychologists involved with national security. The APA extended its no-exceptions stance against torture and cruel, inhuman, or degrading treatment or punishment in 2007 (American Psychological Association, 2007), articulating guidelines for ethical responses both by individuals and organizations to the direct and indirect work of psychologists with detained enemy combatants (e.g., permission for psychologists to engage in civil disobedience, advocacy against using unethically obtained testimony in legal proceedings). Finally, the APA's membership approved a petition resolution stating that, as of August 2009, U.S. psychologists may no longer work in settings where individuals are held outside of or in violation of international law or the U.S. constitution unless they are working directly for detained persons or for a third party engaged in the protection of human rights.

In 2010 the *Ethical Principles of Psychologists and Code of Conduct* (American Psychological Association, 2002) was modified to reflect the PENS report and subsequent APA resolutions prompted by the political transition of the United States from at-peace to wartime status. Two ethical standards (1.02 and 1.03) pertaining to the resolution of conflicts between psychological ethics and both legal regulations and organizational demands were amended to read, "Under no circumstances may this standard be used to justify or defend violating human rights" (American Psychological Association, 2010, p. 493). Plans are underway for a casebook with commentary that will provide U.S. psychologists with detailed guidelines on the appropriate boundaries of their roles in national security activities in a manner that is consistent with international human rights standards.

Philippines

As noted at the outset, economic and political transitions seldom occur in isolation from each other and additional movements that presage social change. How are the complex, multiple transitions of some countries reflected in their psychological ethics codes? The Philippines has experienced such transitions: from oligarchic dictatorship to fragile democracy and from at-peace to war against terrorism.

Aside from periods of Spanish, British, and Japanese rule, the United States has been a dominant economic and political force in the Philippines, which became a sovereign country in 1946. As a constitutional republic, the Philippines has charted a politically stormy course. Prevented from running for a third presidential term in 1972, Ferdinand Marcos imposed martial law and governed from an anticommunist political platform that exploited Cold War fears. Popular demonstrations and military defections that followed the fraudulent election of 1986 forced Marcos into exile, gradually leading to government reforms and the establishment of democratic institutions. However, the dominance and patronage of the elite, political violence (e.g., coup attempts, assassinations of activists and journalists), and both communist and Islamist insurgencies have contributed to economic and political instability. While the relatively decentralized economy continues to grow, albeit more slowly now due to the global financial crisis, the Philippines has not enjoyed enough prolonged growth to ease the country's widespread poverty. With the support of the U.S. military, the Philippines is waging a counterinsurgency against several Islamist terrorist groups, most notably Abu Sayyaf and Rajah Sulaiman, which have received support from international terrorist organizations, including al-Qaida and Jemaah Islamiyah.

The Philippine ethics code applies to clinical psychologists and is composed of three sections that address professional responsibility, interpersonal relationships, and public relations, followed by a set of appendices on the qualifications needed to administer specific psychometric tests, to be employed as a clinical psychologist, and to become grandfathered as a clinical psychologist. Each of the three sections subsumes relevant ethical principles and standards of conduct. The overarching mission of clinical psychologists is to preserve the dignity and welfare of each individual.

Excerpts from the rights and obligations of the principles and standards of the Philippine code of ethics that are particularly relevant to the country's transition from dictatorship to democracy and from at-peace to wartime status include:

1. Commitment to integrity, notwithstanding external or institutional pressures

2. Delineation of the limits of services that can be rendered when engaged by any governmental entity

3. Reasonable regard for the laws of society, with responsibility to avoid the transgression of civil rights

4. Disclosure of privileged information that is pertinent only to the legitimate request of the court

5. Respect for professional organizations, with an obligation to question programs and policies that pose a risk for the individual

Clinical psychologists in the Philippines are expected to ensure the welfare of their clients by, for example, recognizing the right of clients to receive a clear and understandable rationale for the purpose and nature of psychological assessment. In their dealings with the public, clinical psychologists are obliged to assist citizens in forming their own opinions and choices. The mission, ethical principles, and conduct standards of the Philippines code of ethics emphasize the values of autonomy, integrity, and nonmaleficence in guiding the professional activities of clinical psychologists. These values are not worded as strongly as in the ethics codes of other countries that have transitioned from dictatorship to democracy (e.g., Chile) or in the ethics-related documents and resolutions of countries at war with terrorists (e.g., the United States). Nevertheless, the code of ethics of the Philippines appears to maintain a healthy distance from the encroachment by and machinations of government, and articulates with sufficient clarity how clinical psychologists can avoid jeopardizing the public welfare.

European Union

Established in 1993, the European Union (EU) is an economic and political organization of 27 countries committed to regional integration. The emergence of the EU has compelled member countries to pursue a shared economic and political agenda. Through a system of laws that apply in all member countries, the EU has created a single market with a common currency that supports the free movement of goods, capital, services, and people. Politically, the EU functions by a combination of intergovernmentalism and supranationalism. That is, the governments of member states negotiate some decisions, whereas supranational institutions make other decisions without requiring the consensus of member states.

Parallel to the development of the EU were efforts to establish a more cooperative psychology among European countries, which culminated with the founding of the EFPA in 1981 (Nair et al., 2007). At present, the EFPA has 35 national member associations representing approximately 250,000 psychologists. The EFPA provides a forum for European cooperation in such matters as academic training, scientific research, and applied practice. Core aims of the EFPA have been the promotion of psychology as a means to improve the well-being of those whom psychologists serve and the formation of ethics codes that are compatible with the increased uniformity in the professional training and mobility of psychologists throughout the EU (Pettifor, 2007). The EFPA adopted the *Meta-Code of Ethics* in 1995 as the ethical template with which to regulate the content of the ethics codes adopted by its national member associations, as well as to evaluate the professional conduct of their individual members and adjudicate ethical complaints. Since then, many national psychology associations have revised their ethics codes to be consistent with the principles articulated by the Meta-Code. The preeminent authority of the EFPA on psychological ethics is best captured in the preamble of the *Meta-Code of Ethics*:

> The European Federation of Psychologists' Associations has a responsibility to ensure that the ethical codes of its member associations are in accord with the following principles which are intended to provide a general philosophy and guidance to overall situations encountered by professional psychologists.
> (*European Federation of Psychologists' Associations*, 1995)

The four ethical principles of the *Meta-Code of Ethics* include:

1. Respect for a person's rights and dignity (e.g., promoting autonomy and privacy)
2. Competence (e.g., recognizing limits and maintaining high standards)
3. Responsibility (e.g., avoiding harm to the client, community, and society)
4. Integrity (e.g., performing professional roles with honesty and fairness)

Beyond the four principles, there is set of detailed ethical codes, which offer guidance to member associations in developing or revising their national ethics codes in line with the *Meta-Code of Ethics*. In a continent with a long history of strife, these guidelines remind national associations to imbue their ethics codes with an appreciation of individual, cultural, and role differences, as well as recognition of the dangers of unfair biases and unjust discrimination. As a microcosm of the dynamic between the EU and its member countries, the guidelines stress the importance of balancing the individual's right to self-determination against the realities posed by his or her level of dependency on, and the legal constraints imposed by, the larger community. Finally, psychologists in EFPA member countries are enjoined not to exploit any professional relationship for political, religious, or other ideological purposes, thereby making certain that their expert knowledge and services will not be misused and that the welfare of the individual and public remains first and foremost.

Summary: Integration and Comparison

In the main, the moral underpinnings of the ethics codes in psychology examined above appear to have been strengthened by the distinctive economic and political transitions that have or are now taking place in their respective countries of origin. These ethics codes, therefore, enhance the integrity of psychological science and practice and, in turn, function to safeguard the public in these countries. As regards substantive themes common to the psychological ethics codes of selected countries in transition, the following dimensions are most salient:

1. Fundamental human rights (e.g., do no harm)
2. Social responsibility (e.g., correct injustice and improve collective well-being)
3. Independence from politics
4. Nondiscrimination (i.e., based on group membership and/or identity)
5. Privacy, confidentiality, and access to information

Features that distinguish the psychological ethics codes of selected countries in transition include an emphasis on:

1. Legal or constitutional protections (e.g., Romania, Germany, South Africa)
2. Torture and cruel, inhuman, or degrading treatment or punishment (e.g., Chile, United States)

3. Sensitivity to diverse and vulnerable communities (e.g., South Africa, Canada, EFPA)
4. Openness to divergent points of view (e.g., Germany, Canada, Philippines)
5. Ethical decision making (e.g., Iran, Canada)

The articles, principles, and standards of the psychological ethics codes sampled also vary stylistically in their wording, at least in their English translation. Elements of the ethics codes of some countries in transition are at times worded strongly or weakly, and ambiguously or unambiguously. Such variability in tone can function either to protect psychology from the intrusion of economics and politics, or render it, and the general public, more vulnerable to macro-social influence. For instance, ownership of the right to practice psychology freely and the right to organize are direct and specific guarantees provided by Romania's *Psychologist's Law*. Likewise, Germany's *Ethical Principles* explicitly identifies psychology as a "liberal profession" whose members must remain alert to economic and political events and forces that could weaken their moral commitment to the freedom and welfare of the individual and society. South Africa's *Rules of Conduct Pertaining Specifically to Psychology* firmly and clearly communicates the necessity of respecting the sociocultural contexts in which psychological interventions are applied. However, the ethics code of the Philippines cautiously advises clinical psychologists to hold the laws of society in reasonable regard with respect to potential transgressions against the civil (vs. human) rights of citizens.

Conversely, China's *Code of Ethics for Counseling and Clinical Practice* is unclear about the circumstances in which disclosure of confidential information is demanded by law, and inconsistent about how to manage the tension between promoting both individual well-being and social harmony. The *Ethics Code* of Iran directly sets forth its overall nationalistic aim of ensuring the cultural, social, and religious background of Iranians, which unmistakably commits Iranian psychologists to the preservation of a theocratic form of government. The *Ethical Principles of Psychologists and Code of Conduct* remains vague in the guidance offered to U.S. psychologists who serve in or are employed by the military or security services and work with enemy detainees. And, the EFPA's *Meta-Code of Ethics* has the stated purpose of homogenizing the ethics codes of its national member associations and of balancing self-determination against the collective constraints.

The *Universal Declaration of Ethical Principles for Psychologists* (Ad Hoc Joint Committee, 2008), adopted by the IUPsyS and IAAP, provides a common moral framework to guide and inspire psychologists throughout the world toward the highest ethical ideals in their scientific and professional work. The Universal Declaration was derived from shared human values and designed as a template for use in the creation and refinement of national codes of ethics appropriate to a rapidly changing economic and political world. For example, it can serve to guide debate on such macro-social issues as balancing individual versus collective rights, protecting the public from harm versus advocating social change to reduce harm, and respecting the dignity of all versus taking special care when working with vulnerable populations (Gauthier, Pettifor, & Ferrero, 2010). The preamble underscores the relevance of psychological ethics to the welfare of the individual and general public by stating that "adherence to ethical principles in the context of their [psychologists'] work contributes to a stable society" (Ad Hoc Joint Committee, 2008, p. 1).

The Universal Declaration contains four general principles, each with a set of related values; it does not delineate specific standards of conduct, as these vary cross-culturally and cross-nationally and should be developed at the local level to ensure their relevance. The four principles are:

1. Respect for the dignity of persons and peoples
2. Competent caring for the well-being of persons and peoples
3. Integrity
4. Professional and scientific responsibilities to society

These principles dovetail with the overlapping themes extracted from the codes of ethics in psychology of selected countries in economic and political transition. Consistent with the Universal Declaration, the psychological ethics codes of these countries for the most part incorporate a shared moral foundation to guide ethical decision making, emphasize the inherent worth and dignity of all human beings, address the importance of cultural contextualization in the implementation of psychological science and practice, encourage honesty in all professional activities along with the regulation of personal biases that could cause harm, aspire to do no harm, improve the welfare of the person, and in some instances promote structural change for the betterment of society.

Conclusion

There is a clear, empirical connection between the macro-social context in which psychology is situated and the well-being of the discipline (Jing, 2000; Kuglemann & Belzen, 2009; Rose, 1999). In spite of recent anti-globalization rhetoric and criticism of free markets, both of which are tied to democratic governance (see Wall, 2005), the evidence tells a different story: economic freedom, political freedom, and national development are related to the maturity level of national psychology organizations, the proportion of psychologists per population, and their research productivity per population. Furthermore, the impact of economic and political freedom on the occupational membership and research productivity in psychology is mediated by national development. Future research should remedy the shortcomings of the data that were analyzed (e.g., likely underestimates of the ratio of psychologists per million population) and build a multidisciplinary, multisectoral model for explaining how free-market democracies contribute to a healthy psychology. For example, do the governments, businesses and industries, and the general public of such countries expect psychology to play a role in resolving individual and social problems and, if so, do they allocate resources to improving the quality of life (Jing, 2000; Stevens & Wedding, 2004a; Sullivan & Transue, 1999)? Are these expectations and expenditures associated with the creation of jobs and enactment of legislation that sustain and enhance the discipline?

A note of caution is warranted concerning the analysis of the relationship of economic and political transitions to codes of ethics in psychology. First, the types of political transitions examined were somewhat arbitrary; transitions were not matched on dimensions of time, such as the phase or duration of transition, or on direction, as in change from a representative form of government to an autocracy. Second, the ethics codes selected for analysis were essentially a sample of convenience based upon their availability in English; moreover, ethics codes that were translated into English may not convey accurately the meaning or intent of the code as originally conceived. Third, it was not possible to contrast the principles and standards of ethics codes in psychology both before and after political transitions, owing to the general unavailability of the former; however, such an endeavor would serve to identify more precisely the form and degree to which codes of ethics in psychology are affected by larger economic and political events and forces. Finally, notwithstanding the fact that psychologists around the world are guided in their professional conduct not only by codes of ethics, but also by legal statutes, it was not always feasible to identify and analyze laws regulating the practice of psychology in various countries and then to compare their articles with the principles and standards of ethics codes.

The following queries may be useful in directing much-needed research on how codes of ethics in psychology are shaped by economic and political transitions to reflect the process and outcomes of such change. Hopefully, the answers to these queries will contribute to the development of a conceptual framework with which to identify economic and political events and forces, as well as a number of other key variables (e.g., cultural values) that either support or jeopardize the ethical practice of psychology.

1. Although ethics codes center on the preservation of individual and collective rights, can they nevertheless be subverted intentionally or inadvertently to support monolithic economic and political systems (i.e., communism, fascism, extreme ethnocentrism)?

2. What variables predict whether psychologists from countries in economic and/or political transition will accept, reject, or respond ambivalently to ethical guidelines in their professional conduct (e.g., conflicting laws, ideological indoctrination)?

3. How are transitions *from* free markets and representative government reflected in codes of ethics in psychology and the professional conduct of psychologists?

4. How are the ethics codes of non-Western, collectivistic countries in economic and/or political transition similar to or different from the ethics codes of Western, individualistic countries in economic and/or political transition?

5. What is the influence of cultural change relative to economic and/or political transition on psychological ethics codes and the professional conduct of psychologists?

6. How much responsibility and leverage do psychologists and psychological organizations have in bringing about economic and/or political transitions that favor social justice, and what are the rewards, perils, and enduring messages of such efforts?

Author Note

Parts of this chapter were drawn from earlier articles originally published in the Ethics Section of

Psychology: IUPsyS Global Resource (Edition 2009), Wedding, D. & Stevens, M. J. © 2009 International Union of Psychological Science and Psychology Press, and in *Cercetari Filosofico-Psihologice* (Volume 2, Issue 1) © 2010 Academia Romana. Material reproduced with permission.

References

Ad Hoc Joint Committee. (2008). *Universal declaration of ethical principles for psychologists*. Retrieved from http://www.iupsys.net/index.php/ethics/declaration.

Adler, N., Mueller, G. O. W., & Ayat, M. (1993). Psychiatry under tyranny: A report on the political abuse of Romanian psychiatry during the Ceausescu years. *Current Psychology: Research and Reviews, 12,* 3–17.

American Psychological Association. (2010). 2010 amendments to the 2002 "Ethical Principles of Psychologists and Code of Conduct". *American Psychologist, 65,* 493.

American Psychological Association. (2002). *Ethical principles of psychologists and code of conduct*. Washington, DC: Author.

American Psychological Association. (2006). *American Psychological Association reaffirms unequivocal position against torture and abuse*. Retrieved from http://www.apa.org/releases/notorture.html.

American Psychological Association. (2007). *Reaffirmation of the American Psychological Association position against torture and other cruel, inhuman, or degrading treatment or punishment and its application to individuals defined in the United States Code as "enemy combatants."* Retrieved from http://www.apa.org/governance/resolutions/notorture0807.html.

Baron, R. M., & Kenny, D. A. (1986). The moderator-mediator variable distinction in social psychological research: Conceptual, strategic, and statistical considerations. *Journal of Personality and Social Psychology, 51,* 1173–1182.

Brock, A. C. (2006). Psychology and liberal democracy: A spurious connection? In A. C. Brock (Ed.), *Internationalizing the history of psychology* (pp. 152–162.). New York: New York University Press.

Canadian Psychological Association. (2000). *Canadian code of ethics for psychologists*. Ottawa: Author.

Central Intelligence Agency. (2009). *The world factbook*. Retrieved from https://www.cia.gov/library/publications/the-world-factbook/.

Chinese Psychological Society. (2007). *Code of ethics for counseling and clinical practice*. Retrieved from http://www.iupsys.net/index.php/resources/ethics/131-list-of-codes-of-international-organizations-

Colegio de Psicologos de Chile. (1999). *Codigo de etica profesional* [Code of professional ethics]. Retrieved from http://www.colegiopsicologos.cl/el-colegio/comisiones/comision-de-etica/estatutos/.

Costanzo, M., Gerrity, E., & Lykes, M. B. (2007). Psychologists and the use of torture in interrogations. *Analysis of Social Issues and Public Policy, 7,* 7–20.

European Federation of Psychologists' Associations. (1995). *Meta-code of ethics* (revised). Retrieved from http://www.efpa.eu/.

Freedom House (2007). *Freedom in the world 2007*. Retrieved from http://freedomhouse.org/template.cfm?page=363&year=2007

Freidson, E. (1984). The changing nature of professional control. *Annual Review of Sociology, 10,* 1–20.

Fu, X. L., & Jing, Q. C. (1994). The relation between psychology and the development of economy, science and technology. *Acta Psycholgica Sinica, 26,* 208–218.

Gauthier, J., Pettifor, J., & Ferrero, A. (2010). The Universal Declaration of Ethical Principles for Psychologists: A culture-sensitive model for creating and reviewing a code of ethics. *Ethics and Behavior, 20*(3–4), 179–196.

Gergen, K. J. (2001). Psychological science in a postmodern context. *American Psychologist, 56,* 803–813.

German Psychological Society and Association of German Professional Psychologists. (1999). *Ethical principles*. Retrieved from http://www.am.org/iupsys/ethics/ethic-comnatl-list.html.

Health Professions Council of South Africa. (2004). *Rules of conduct pertaining specifically to psychology*. Retrieved from http://www.psyssa.com/aboutus/codeofconduct.asp.

Heritage Foundation and Dow Jones & Company. (2007). *2007 index of economic freedom*. Retrieved from http://www.heritage.org/Index/Download.aspx

Iranian Organization of Psychology and Counseling. (n.d.). *Ethics code*. Retrieved from http://www.iupsys.net/index.php/resources/ethics/131-list-of-codes-of-international-organizations-.

Jing, Q. (2000). International psychology. In K. Pawlik & M. R. Rosenzweig (Eds.), *The international handbook of psychology* (pp. 570–584). Thousand Oaks, CA: Sage.

Kugelmann, R., & Belzen, J. A. (2009). Historical intersections of psychology, religion, and politics in national contexts. *History of Psychology, 12,* 125–131.

Law No. 213, Chamber of Deputies, Official Gazette 492 (2004) (enacted).

Nair, E., Ardila, R., & Stevens, M. J. (2007). Current trends in global psychology. In M. J. Stevens & U. P. Gielen (Eds.), *Toward a global psychology: Theory, research, interventions, and pedagogy* (pp. 69–100). Mahwah, NJ: Erlbaum.

Pettifor, J. L. (2007). Toward a global professionalization of psychology. In M. J. Stevens & U. P. Gielen (Eds.), *Toward a global psychology: Theory, research, interventions, and pedagogy* (pp. 299–331). Mahwah, NJ: Erlbaum.

Psychology International. (2009). PsycINFO database nearing 3 million record. *Psychology International, 20*(4), 14.

Rose, N. (1999). *Governing the soul: The shaping of the private self* (2nd ed.). New York: Cambridge University Press.

Rosenzweig, M. R. (1982). Trends in development and status of psychology: An international perspective. *International Journal of Psychology, 17,* 117–140.

Rosler, H-D. (2009). Political change and professional ethics of psychology in East Germany. In D. Wedding & M. J. Stevens (Eds.), *Psychology: IUPsyS global resource* (10th ed.). Hove, UK: Psychology Press.

Sanchez Sosa, J. J., & Riveros, A. (2007). Theory, research, and practice in psychology in the developing (majority) world. In M. J. Stevens & U. P. Gielen (Eds.), *Toward a global psychology: Theory, research, interventions, and pedagogy* (pp. 101–146). Mahwah, NJ: Erlbaum.

Scientific and Professional Ethics Committee. (2008–2009). *Code of ethics for Philippine psychologists*. Retrieved from http://www.iupsys.net/index.php/resources/ethics/131-list-of-codes-of-international-organizations-

Stevens, M. J. (1998). Professional psychology after communism: The case of Romania. *Professional Psychology: Research and Practice, 29,* 300–304.

Stevens, M. J. (2007). Orientation to a global psychology. In M. J. Stevens & U. P. Gielen (Eds.), *Toward a global psychology: Theory, research, interventions, and pedagogy* (pp. 3–33). Mahwah, NJ: Erlbaum.

Stevens, M. J., Overmier, J. A., & Overmier, J. B. (2009). Psychology throughout the world: A descriptive tour and national contacts. In D. Wedding & M. J. Stevens (Eds.), *Psychology: IUPsyS global resource* [CD-ROM] (10th ed.). Hove, UK: Psychology Press.

Stevens, M. J., & Wedding, D. (2004a). International psychology: A synthesis. In M. J. Stevens & D. Wedding (Eds.), *Handbook of international psychology* (pp. 481–500). New York: Brunner-Routledge.

Stevens, M. J., & Wedding, D. (2004b). International psychology: An overview. In M. J. Stevens & D. Wedding (Eds.), *Handbook of international psychology* (pp. 1–23). New York: Brunner-Routledge.

Sullivan, J. L., & Transue, J. E. (1999). The psychological underpinnings of democracy: A selective review of research on political tolerance, interpersonal trust, and social capital. *Annual Review of Psychology, 50,* 625–650.

Task Force on Psychological Ethics and National Security. (2005). *Report of the American Psychological Association presidential task force on psychological ethics and national security.* Washington, DC: American Psychological Association.

United Nations Development Program. (2009). *Human development report.* Retrieved from http://hdr.undp.org/en/reports/global/hdr2009/.

United Nations General Assembly. (1948). *Universal declaration of human rights* [GA resolution 217 A III].

Wall, D. (2005). *Babylon and beyond: The economics of anti-capitalist, anti-globalist and radical green movements.* London: Pluto Press.

World Health Organization. (2005). *Mental health atlas* (rev.). Retrieved from http://www.who.int/mental_health/evidence/mhatlas05/en/index.html.

CHAPTER 28

Argentina

Andrea Ferrero

Abstract

Political and economic changes shape the development of societies in a process of dialectical feedback. Scientific and professional fields are also affected by these changes, and especially those fields that are strongly related to human sciences (Bourdieu, 1991). In this chapter, the influence of political matters in the development of professional psychologists' associations in Argentina is considered. It establishes how those circumstances affected the legal status of psychology and the definition of professional competencies in the country. It also considers the particular situation of ethics codes that were being developed in the 1970s, and how the return of democracy impacted the course of action in the development of such codes in Argentina..

Key Words: Argentina, ethics code, professional competencies

Psychology was striving to get legal recognition in Argentina when a military coup took place in 1976 and stopped the process. On March 24, military forces overthrew the democratic government of Maria Estela Martínez de Perón, who had become president when her husband had died two years earlier.

From 1976 to 1983, Argentina lived under a dictatorship; not only was the president overthrown, but the House of Representatives and the Senate were closed, and many people were jailed or disappeared. By that time, psychology had become almost a persecuted profession; many training programs in psychology were closed, in addition to most of the few initial psychologists' associations. Psychologists worked without any legal support, as professional laws had not yet been passed, and the ethics codes projects were suspended when the psychological associations had to stop their functions (Ferrero, 2006).

In fact, all of the southeast countries of South America suffered under dictatorship regimes. Beyond some local differences, similar situations occurred in Uruguay, Chile, Bolivia, Brazil, and Paraguay. In all these countries' military forces overthrew the government, restricted political and labor union activities, closed the House of Representatives, suspended democratic elections, as there was no respect for human rights, and those who opposed the regime were severely repressed or even exterminated. State terrorism was a common factor in these countries. From an economic point of view, these countries acquired a large amount of external debt. This debt led to a severe restriction of the financial reserves of the state that were usually intended for subsidizing productive activities. On the other hand, the financial crisis of the state ended in the privatization of big services companies and added thousands of unemployed people to a productive labor system that was already in deficit. Without subsidies for productive activities and with rising unemployment, the levels of social disadvantage dramatically increased. Like other South American countries, since the end of 18th century Argentina had been characterized by a vigorous bourgeoisie supported by a strong state which would be the basis of a highly consolidated middle class by the 1940s. Since 1970, due to the deterioration of the state as guarantor of citizens' welfare, social conditions changed and there were increasing sectors of society with lack of opportunities and resources. In 1983, a new democracy in Argentina allowed the previous process undertaken by psychologists' associations to continue, and finally they were legally recognized. Professional laws were passed and psychologists' associations developed their own ethics codes throughout most of the country.

Psychology as a Science

As in many other countries, the appearance of scientific psychology in Argentina was prior to its development as a profession. The beginning of psychology as a science goes back to the end of the 19th century and its academic development started with two courses: one at the Faculty of Law in 1895 and the other at the Faculty of Philosophy in 1896, both at Buenos Aires University. In 1908, the first association of scientific psychology in South America was formed, the *Psychology Society of Buenos Aires*. Its first journal appeared in the same year and was published from 1908 until 1914. These first developments of psychology in Argentina were strongly influenced by positivism and by the clinical perspectives of French origin, basically the proposals of Ribot, Janet, Binet, and Grasset (Ardila, 1986; Vezzetti, 1988).

At the beginning of the 1930s, an anti-positivistic movement started, marked also by the reception given to German neo-idealistic thought, which concluded in a criticism of the physiological psychology of French roots. From that moment, a complex phenomenon took place. On the one hand, the academic teaching of psychology tried to retake its philosophical affiliation in opposition to the clinical profile that the discipline had acquired, but, on the other hand, the increasing industrialization of the country required a psychology that transcended theoretical speculation and was able to offer an applied perspective of the discipline. A move toward a professionalized psychology began and various changes in its development, both as a science and as a profession, were linked to political processes that determined its direction (Klappenbach, 2004; Paolucci & Verdinelli, 1999; Vilanova, 2000).

In fact, after the creation of undergraduate psychology programs in the 1950s and its growing professionalization, it is necessary to point out two main events which significantly affected its practice: (1) the consequences of two military coups, one in 1966 and the other in 1976, and (2) the consolidation of psychology as a science and a profession after the reinstating of democracy in 1983.

The Answer to Society: Psychology as a Profession—The Coup D'état of 1966

The background of specific university training in psychology included the studies of psychometrics and professional guidance created in the 1930s. Research laboratories were set up and important scientific events and publications were organized. The development of psychology as a profession in Argentina is framed to a great extent within the politics of increasing industrialization of the country, which took place in the mid-1940s.

This growing industrialization generated the need to have professionals whose training could provide answers to a diversity of problems, and went further than the clinical role of the psychiatrist which, up to that time, had traditionally been associated with mental health care in Argentina. However, the field of mental health was linked not only to clinical assistance, but also to the environments of work, school, and other areas that accepted the idea that psychology was a way to promote human welfare in general. It was within the context of a country undergoing clear social and economic growth that the first university undergraduate programs in psychology appeared: the University of Litoral in 1954; the University of Buenos Aires in 1957; the Universities of Cuyo, La Plata, and Córdoba in 1958; and the University of Tucumán in 1959.

The fundamental change that the creation of these psychology programs brought about was the appearance in the 1960s of fully trained professionals in a field which, up to that point, had been almost exclusively in the hands of psychiatrists. The key point of conflict between these two professional areas was related to psychotherapy. Although the university course in psychology was planned over a period of five years, and its training level in the development of skills and abilities to practice psychotherapy was higher than those offered by the medicine colleges, the medical profession was not willing to share this task with the newly born role of psychology as a profession (Klappenbach, 2000, 2004).

In 1966, the democratic government was overthrown by a military coup and Argentina lived under a dictatorship for seven years. This dictatorship, which was by no means the first one in the country during the 20th century, actively persecuted various dissident groups in Argentine society: political parties, workers, professionals, and university scholars.

On July 29, 1966, police attacked students and lecturers of the University of Buenos Aires. This tragic episode is known as "the night of the long batons" because of the wooden sticks used by the police to repress people considered by the dictatorship to be sympathizers of leftwing ideologies, as most opposition members were characterized. A consequence of this was the massive exodus of intellectuals and university scholars to other countries (Aruj, 2004; Moreno, 2002).

In January 1967, responding to the pressure from a sector of the medical profession that wanted to maintain its hegemony over the practice of psychotherapy, the government passed Law 17.132 designed to regulate within the city of Buenos Aires the practice of medicine, dentistry, and all their related areas including psychology (República Argentina, 1967; Viar, 2002). This law prevented the independent professional practice of psychology by subordinating it to the supervision of psychiatry, and specifically prohibited the practice of psychoanalysis and any other psychotherapeutic treatment. It also disregarded psychologists' university training and the level of participation that they had started to achieve in the community (Smith, 1977).

It is important to point out that between the end of the 1960s and the beginning of the 1970s, Buenos Aires had become one of the cities in the world with a very high demand for psychoanalytic therapy. Psychoanalysis impacted not only psychology, psychiatry, and mental health issues, but cultural matters like literature, movies, theatre plays, and many other cultural and intellectual manifestations, as well as in television programs and news features in newspapers (Plotkin, 2002, 2003).

At the same time, even though professional laws had not yet been approved, the professional community ethically backed the practice of psychology. In fact, as early as 1962 the first group of psychology graduates organized themselves and founded the first professional associations in the cities of Rosario, Buenos Aires, and La Plata, called *Colegios* (*Colegios* grant licensure and also exert legal control over psychological practice within a given territory). One of the tasks undertaken by those associations was to establish codes of ethics in order to guarantee competent scientific and professional performance among its members. In 1971 the cities of Córdoba, Mar del Plata, Mendoza, Salta, San Luis, and Tucumán followed this trend. As a result, the *Confederación de Psicólogos de la República Argentina* (COPRA) [Confederation of Psychologists of the Argentine Republic] was created, a federative association which joined all the provincial *Colegios* and it functioned until 1976 when another military coup took place (Klappenbach, 2004).

Democracy was reinstated in 1973, allowing for a positive debate and a vigorous professional struggle, which ended with the approval of the first law regulating the professional practice of psychology, that same year, in the province of Entre Rios. In the following year, the province of Rio Negro passed a similar law (Rébora, 1979). For the first time, it had been possible to defeat the resistance of the traditional and dominant medical profession always in alliance with political power. Both had viewed psychology as an opposing force; a professional competitor with the former, and an ideological threat to the latter.

In 1974, a law was drafted in Buenos Aires by members of the *Asociación de Psicólogos de Buenos Aires* (APBA) [Association of Psychologists of Buenos Aires City] with the objective of giving psychology the recognition to be practiced as an autonomous profession, and intended to replace the existing law that included professional psychology as an "auxiliary" of medical practice. Although this draft law was strongly supported by students, teachers, other professionals, and even many government officials and political parties, it took 11 years before this law was finally enacted (Asociación de Psicólogos de Buenos Aires, 1978a).

Hand in hand with these changes, universities in the country continued offering studies in psychology of a high scientific level, and which were updated according to international trends. Everything indicated that the development of the discipline in Argentina, in both its academic and scientific dimensions, was the result of its consolidation as a legalized profession. However, the military coup in March 1976 dealt a blow to progress.

Years of Terror: The Curtailment of Psychology—The Military Coup of 1976

On March 24, 1976, the armed forces, with the support of some sectors of society linked to economic power, overthrew the democratic government and Argentina entered a period marked by authoritarian rule, repression, and violence in all its forms. This violence was not only physical. There was also the violence resulting from the application of economic policies that dismantled national industries. Factories closed every day, generating hundreds of unemployed people. Destitute families became homeless. Free public education was undermined, while a government-proclaimed "Western and Christian'" model was imposed that bore the unmistakable mark of ruthless capitalism and a dominant ideology. The "Western" adjective was a reference to rightwing ideologies that tried to exert their control over progressive social policies that were being developed in those days. Although dictatorships can never be justified, it is necessary to clarify that there had never been any "eastern" threat in Argentina that might lead to thinking of the need to impose a "Western" ideology, even if that imposition could be acceptable. The "Christian" reference was a continuation of the previous one: any progressive social policy was easily related to Marxist ideology, and therefore to atheism and even to Judaism. This type of rhetoric was a common factor in South American dictatorship ideologies, mostly related to a hegemonic, discriminatory, and authoritarian ideology. Throughout many countries in South and Central America, this ideology received strong support from some powerful countries. This ideological support also implied military training, weapons supply, and external policies that contributed to the overthrow of some South American democratic governments.

The ideological persecution of any political, academic, and even artistic expression that could be interpreted as opposing the ideals of the ruling regime became normal practice. Such opposition was severely punished. Thousands of Argentines were tortured and murdered during those years. Anyone could be a victim of the system—students, teachers, housewives, and professionals—as was demonstrated by the National Commission for Missing People (Comisión Nacional sobre Desaparición de Personas, 1984).

Many university scholars, teachers, and students were kidnapped and disappeared during the years of the military dictatorship. This included university deans and rectors, like Mauricio López. He was kidnapped by military forces on January 1, 1977, when he was Rector of the National University of San Luis. Educated in a Protestant but liberal home, and prior to obtaining his degree in philosophy, he had an important role as general secretary of the World Student Christian Federation (WSCF). He then traveled to Europe and to the United States of America, visiting Christian and ecumenical organizations and also government representatives, promoting the cause of changing an unjust world order. Years later, he led the "Church and Society Commission" at the World Council of Churches, and made a fundamental contribution in the organization of the World Conference on Church and Society, Geneva, Switzerland, in 1966. This important contribution, has been compared in importance to the Catholic Second Vatican Ecumenical Council convened by Pope John XXIII in Rome in the same year. Mauricio López's ideology was related to a strong social commitment, emerging third world ideologies, and social and technological revolutions, all within a framework of Christian dialogue.

As philosophy professor at the National University of Cuyo in Mendoza province, and especially as rector of the National University of San Luis, he promoted education as a way to become not only formally trained, but also an autonomous and more responsible human being. His strong social commitment, his ideas about the different ways in which education can promote social inclusion, and his religious thoughts supporting the idea of a fairer world were the cause of his abduction by military forces in 1977 (Concatti, 2002; Montoya, Klappenbach, Marincevic, & Arias, 1995).

During that time, and apart from the fact that most psychologists in Argentina adhered to progressive ideologies and were against the military government, psychology itself was considered even by the previous dictatorship to be a clearly subversive discipline, exotic in the sense of being different and dangerous. The teaching of psychology was viewed as enhancing the capacity of people to achieve an autonomous view about themselves and society. To be a psychologist meant to be an agent for individual and social change, which was considered highly dangerous as it implied questioning the support given to a style of dominant and hegemonic thought (Bleger, 1966; Sanz Ferramola, 2000).

In 1977, the *Federación de Psicólogos de la República Argentina* (FePRA) [Federation of Psychologists of the Argentine Republic] replaced the Confederación de Psicólogos de la República Argentina (COPRA). This was done in an attempt to recover the links between all the psychological associations in the country, persist in striving toward legislation protections, and continue offering ethical tools to guide professional and scientific practice (Perosio, 1977).

Psychologists, along with many other professionals, were not spared the evils of repression. Many were jailed, tortured, and murdered. Records show that 34 psychologists and a similar number of psychology students disappeared throughout the country. For example, in 1978 while she was working at a kindergarten, military personnel kidnapped Beatriz Perosio, a psychologist and president of the FePRA and the *Asociación de Psicólogos de Buenos Aires* (APBA, Psychologists Association of Buenos Aires] (Asociación de Psicólogos de Buenos Aires, 1978b). She and other colleagues had proposed the 1974 draft law for the professional practice of psychology in the city of Buenos Aires. Only in 1985, in a completely different political context, would the city pass this law (Ares, 1986).

At about the same time as Beatriz Perosio's abduction, two other psychologists were kidnapped: Alfredo Smith, then Secretary of Professional Affairs of APBA, and his wife Celia Kriado. Their disappearance had an enormous impact in the country, as reflected both in the APBA's publications and in national newspapers written in Spanish and English. Two months after being kidnapped, Kriado and Smith were prosecuted and sent to Devoto Prison, where Celia Kriado, who was pregnant when abducted, had her baby. Six months later, in May 1979, the couple and their 5-month-old baby were released (Asociación de Psicólogos de Buenos Aires, 1978c).

No news was given on the whereabouts of Beatriz Perosio, which prompted the local and even international professional community to launch an ongoing complaint, reflected in letters by academics like Bertram Raven and organizations like the Interamerican Society of Psychology and the American Psychological Association (Asociación de Psicólogos de Buenos Aires, 1979a, 1979b). Beatriz Perosio and many other psychologists remain missing today. The APBA remembers its former president at each anniversary of her disappearance (Asociación de Psicólogos de Buenos Aires, 1979c, 1985a, 1988; Cerdá, 1983). The same happens in many other workplaces, such as hospitals and universities, where psychologists still memorialize the names of their disappeared classmates and colleagues on plaques at the entrance of their buildings.

While this was happening, new groups of professional psychologists were graduating from universities and engaged in clinical practice, thus competing with psychiatrists. This led the Ministry of Education in 1980 to give its academic backing to the existing law of professional practice in Buenos Aires, which subordinated psychology to medicine and stipulated that the practice of psychoanalysis and psychotherapy was not within the professional competencies of psychologists. In the same year, one of the two existing professional laws of psychology, the law in Rio Negro province, was sunsetted, causing distress within the professional community (Avelluto, 1980). Subsequent laws regulating professional practice included the creation of a so-called professional college, the *Colegio*. These laws were the means by which the government later delegated control over the scientific and professional practice of psychology to the professional community, including the right to establish its own code of ethics. Because there were no such laws in existence in 1980, professional associations did not have the status of a professional *Colegio* nor did they have authority to issue licenses for professional practice. Up to that time, the few existing professional associations had developed their codes of ethics, but until professional laws were passed and the professional associations were recognized by government, their codes of ethics had only guidance value rather than legal power.

The arbitrary restriction of professional competencies and qualifications by the government had a great impact on the profession and the community in general, particularly in the city of Buenos Aires where psychologists had a relevant presence within society. This impact showed itself through the massive affiliation of psychologists with professional associations in their jurisdictions, and a permanent state of protest as evidenced by numerous public demonstrations and marches demanding a lifting of restrictions on professional competencies. In 1980, the FePRA backed the demand of psychologists for the modification of the competencies and qualifications, with the support of the labor association, General Professionals Confederation. Although the Ministry of Education introduced some changes, the new competencies and qualifications were not substantially different from previous ones. However, they recognized for the first time that psychologists were not a mere auxiliary of medicine (República Argentina, 1980). Nevertheless, there was much more to be done before the criteria for disciplinary mastery that were developed by the psychologists, and which accurately reflected the scientific and professional nature of psychology, would be recognized. This was not to be achieved until 1983 with the restoration of democracy.

The military junta that had seized power was responsible for the implementation of the bloodiest policies of state terrorism ever suffered in Argentina: forced disappearances of people, repression, torture and the death of thousands of people kept in clandestine detention centers, the kidnapping of children born in those centers, and misappropriation of assets belonging to the prisoners or their families.

Those officers responsible were trialed in 1985, found guilty, and sentenced to life imprisonment. However, in December 1990, President Carlos Menem pardoned them. During 1998, they were detained again on charges of kidnapping children and are currently under house arrest.

At the beginning of the 1980s the level of repression, physical violence, and forced disappearances that had been imposed on Argentine society began to ease. Although the wounds inflicted both on individuals and the community were enormous, the military's power began to weaken, particularly after the failure of the Malvinas (Falklands) War. People demanded democracy, and slowly a path toward a transition to political democracy was being charted. The restoration of democracy had a considerable effect on the practice of psychology.

Return to Democracy: The Legalization of Psychology

Parallel to the weakening of the military government, already in its last stages, there was an increasing demand for the approval of laws related to the professional practice of psychology (Aquerreta & Allerand, 1983). Beginning in 1983, there were a multitude of marches by psychologists, which continued until after democracy was reestablished (Asociación de Psicólogos de Buenos Aires, 1984, 1985b; Devries, 1983; Pugliese, 1985). Toward the end of military rule, and in a context of debate about the role of professional organizations in a democratic state, various provinces approved their own laws regulating the practice of psychology: Santiago del Estero in 1978, Misiones in 1980, and four more in 1983 in Salta, Catamarca, Tucumán, and San Luis (Aquerreta & Allerand, 1983).

Free elections were held in October 1983, and in December of that year a new democratic government was inaugurated. Between 1984 and 1986 the federal district of Buenos Aires and 14 provinces (Córdoba, Formosa, Santa Fe, La Pampa, Santa Cruz, Jujuy, La Rioja, Buenos Aires Province, Corrientes, San Juan, Mendoza, Chubut, Neuquén, and Chaco) enacted laws governing the professional practice of psychology. The province of Río Negro reinstated its law, which had been sunsetted in 1974. In 1996, what was then the National Territory of Tierra del Fuego was given the status of province; soon after this change, the new province also passed its own law on professional psychology. By 1985, two years after the return to democracy, all provincial states in the country had included in their legislation a law regulating the professional practice of psychology (Klappenbach, 2000). Current laws define the rights and the obligations of psychologists, especially considering the personal welfare of clients and the welfare of the community involved in any kind of psychological practice within a certain territory. They also are the means by which the national government allows the creation of a *Colegio*. By these laws the national government also delegates control of the professional and scientific practice of psychology to the local psychological community that has organized the *Colegio*. The *Colegios* are also asked by professional laws to develop an ethics code and to create an ethics committee to ensure ethical conditions of psychological practice. The ethics committee can determine that a psychologist's license may be revoked for unethical conduct.

As all 24 jurisdictions (Buenos Aires City as an autonomous territory, with the Malvinas and South Atlantic Islands, and the 23 federal states), have passed their own professional laws of psychology, it can be said that a task initiated 12 years prior with the approval of the first law in 1973, and interrupted by the military takeover, has been achieved within a democratic political system.

All these laws, as it has already been mentioned, finally promoted the creation of professional associations of psychology, which are now legally empowered to regulate the scientific and professional practice of psychology and to develop their own codes of ethics. Each territory, with only a few exceptions, has a local *Colegio* (Alonso, 1999). After difficult political times, democracy in Argentina allowed the consolidation of professional associations of psychology, as well as professional laws and codes of ethics within the whole territory.

The advent of democracy also brought about a process of normalization in the universities, because many of their departments, including psychology, had been closed or had been overrun by military personnel who occupied hierarchical posts.

Psychology in Argentina began to recover the purpose and momentum lost during the last dictatorship. The implementation of laws for professional practice, normalization of the universities, and establishment of codes of ethics in each provincial state created the right climate in which to call again for the legal recognition by the Ministry of Education of new competences and qualifications that reflected the true nature of training received in psychology departments. The professional community again demonstrated massively in the streets, this time supported by ordinary people and the media. Representatives from universities, the FePRA, and the Ministry of Education collaborated for the first time in drafting the new competencies. In 1985 this draft was finally approved, enshrining general and specific criteria for the degree and license in psychology. It incorporated every area of knowledge and skill in which psychologists would be trained during their 5-year program, and established competencies needed for work in science, education, forensic, labor, social, and clinical settings, including psychotherapies of any and all theoretical orientations (República Argentina, 1985; Vilanova, 2000). The approval of the new competencies and professional qualifications gave a boost to psychology in Argentina, and in the nearby region a similar process was going on.

From a regional perspective, the creation of the Mercado Común del Sur (Mercosur; countries signing a regional free trade agreement that also eventually translated to the professions) in 1991 was not only a relevant political and economic fact, but was also related to social, cultural, educational, and scientific shared interests as well. The initial full member countries were Argentina, Brazil, Paraguay, and Uruguay. Another three countries became associated members: Chile in 1996, Bolivia in 1997, and Venezuela in 2006. In 2007, the Mercosur Parliament was created as the political wing of the Mercosur, and it is made up of 72 legislators.

In 1994, around 10 years after the establishment of fully democratically governed systems in South American countries, representatives of psychologists' associations of Argentina, Brazil, Paraguay, and Uruguay created the *Comité Coordinador de los Psicólogos del Mercosur* [Psychologists Committee of Mercosur] with the aim of establishing common criteria for training in psychology, as well as ethical standards for professional practice (Comité Coordinador de Psicólogos del Mercosur y Países Asociados, 1997). With the addition of Chile and Bolivia, the *Comité Coordinador de los Psicólogos del Mercosur y Países Asociados* [Psychologists Committee of Mercosur and Associated Countries], began in 1997 to unify training standards in the region, and in 1998 approved the *Protocolo de Acuerdo Marco de los principios para la formación de Psicólogos en los países del Mercosur y países Asociados* [Agreement protocol on the framework of principles for the training of psychologists in the Mercosur and associated countries]. This document emphasized the need of keeping professional and scientific training in psychology close to ethical values and social interests (Comité Coordinador de los Psicólogos del Mercosur y Países Asociados, 1998; Di Doménico, 1996, 1999; Di Doménico & Vilanova, 1998; Hermosilla, 2000a, 2000b).

In 1997, Mercosur countries also developed common ethical standards through the *Protocolo de Acuerdo Marco de principios éticos para el ejercicio profesional de los psicólogos en el Mercosur y Países Asociados* [Agreement protocol on the framework of ethical principles for the professional practice of psychologists in the Mercosur and associated countries].

The Mercosur's ethical declaration for psychologists considers five ethical principles:

1. Respect for the rights and dignity of people
2. Competence
3. Professional and scientific commitment
4. Integrity
5. Social responsibility

These principles are similar to those included in later foreign ethics codes, such as the code from the American Psychological Association (American Psychological Association, 2002), and those of the more recent European Federation of Psychologists' Associations (European Federation of Psychologists' Associations, 1995). The Mercosur's declaration of principles also shows an important match with those of the *Universal Declaration of Ethical Principles for Psychologists* (Ad Hoc Joint Committee, 2008), adopted in Berlin in June 2008, which was developed as a template for developing new ethics codes or revising those already in existence (Ferrero & Gauthier, 2009; Gauthier, Pettifor, & Ferrero, 2010)

It was not by chance that the first and main principle of the 1997 *Protocolo de Acuerdo Marco de los principios para la formación de Psicólogos en los países del Mercosur y países Asociados* referred to the respect for the rights and dignity of people, which had been systematically violated in the all of those South American countries.

The Mercosur's declaration of ethical principles had an important impact on further development of professional ethics codes in the subscribed countries, as they included them in explicit or implicit ways, especially in the ethics codes of Argentina, Brazil, Chile, and Uruguay (Calo & Hermosilla, 2000).

At a local level, Argentina put in place a permanent process for periodically updating training models not only for the degree in psychology, but also for the postgraduate diploma in psychology. In 2007 national standards on current competencies for the psychology degree were developed through a "degree activities in psychology" document, developed by the *Asociación de Unidades Académicas de*

Psicología (AUAPsi); [Academic Departments of Psychology Associations] and the Federación de Psicólogos de la República Argentina (AUAPsi-FePRA, 2007). This document included three issues: the *Activities Reserved to the Professional Degree*, the *Direct Risk* that involved improper performance of that activity, and the *Curricular Contents* that should be included in training programs. There are 17 specific professional activities, with the primary activities following:

- psychological orientation in community contexts
- mental health prevention
- psychological assessment
- psychotherapy
- use of tests issues
- public mental health policy and its related legislation
- social development
- human rights issues
- research and academic activities
- intervention in specific areas such as labor, counseling, disabilities education, disasters, eating disorders, addictions, communication, forensics, and business.

This document also includes 44 specific curricular content areas that should be acquired during the psychology training program in order to develop each professional future activity in any area of psychology. It is quite remarkable that the only curricular content that is required for all the 17 specific professional activities is related to training in ethics, (deontological and legal issues in psychology), showing the importance that both local academic and professional organizations give to ethical matters (Ferrero & Andrade, 2007).

In 1999, the FePRA developed its *Ethics Code*. This code includes an introduction, a preamble, a declaration of principles and a section of Deontological Dispositions. The introduction expresses the intention and reach of application of the code of ethics. The preamble and the declaration of principles constitute desirable objectives that guide psychologists toward most ideal values of psychology. They express the spirit of this code, and although they are not obligatory rules themselves, they must primarily be considered since they constitute the foundation of ethical conduct of psychologists.

As mentioned earlier, ethical principles included in this code of ethics were exactly the same as those of the Mercosur declaration, again highlighting the importance given by psychology local community for the respect of the rights and dignity of people (Ferrero, 2002). The Deontological Dispositions section of the FePRA ethics code establishes rules of professional conduct that express duties which affect all professional communities. It is considered that neglecting these duties might be detrimental to the rights of people receiving professional services. The primary deontological rules included here are referred to as informed consent; confidentiality; responsibility in professional relationships with consultants, colleagues and community, and also with psychology as discipline and profession; research and academic issues; and public declarations of psychologists.

The code establishes that in the process of decision making relative to their professional conduct, psychologists must consider this code of ethics and the code of the professional association in which they are registered or associated, in addition to current local professional laws (Federación de Psicólogos de la República Argentina, 1999).

Conclusions

As in other South American countries, the legal status of psychology, psychologists' associations, and the development of ethics codes in Argentina were strongly influenced by the process of passing from a dictatorship to a democratically elected political system. Enforcing democratic ideals and policies of democratic governments, as well as economic freedom and social development, directly impacted local psychology associations. This fact allowed the development of national ethics codes and professional laws, also in accordance with universal standards, and regarded both personal and common welfare.

Nowadays, it is possible to affirm that psychology in Argentina has reached an important level of academic and professional development, achieved by the conviction that neither science nor the profession can adequately be developed unless they are in accord with an unbending respect for human rights and a democratic political system.

There are still some queries that may be considered in the enforcement of the ethical practice of psychology regarding political transitions, and particularly when considering current discussions of the universalization of ethical standards as well:

- Is it possible to maintain sustainable ethics agreements in psychology in a given region when some of the involved countries lose their democratic systems of government?
- Considering the incorporation of new country members to the Mercosur, and future

ethics code updates, which challenges will the Mercosur declaration of principles for psychological training and practice have to face?

• How can different current economic policies or political positions among some of the Mercosur countries possibly affect an updating of the Mercosur declaration of principles?

• How can ethics codes be enforced as representative of national scientific interests in a country constrained by economic external interests, as it will probably have to accept foreign conditions to keep on receiving the necessary economic funds for research?

• How can professional associations maintain their policies of respect for human rights in countries with dictatorship government systems?

• How can international associations of psychology give support to national associations in countries under dictatorship government systems?

• How can the *Universal Declaration of Ethical Principles for Psychologists* be considered and eventually adopted in countries under dictatorship government systems?

These are some of the questions that psychologists could take into account to assist in clarifying the effects that dictatorships have had on the scientific and professional practice of our discipline in South America, in this case in Argentina. And especially to highlight the importance of developing a practice that promotes respect for human rights within a national, regional, and international context, which can hardly be achieved without the general framework of democracy.

Author Note

Parts of this chapter were drawn from an earlier article originally published in the Ethics Section of *Psychology: IUPsyS Global Resource* (Edition 2009), Wedding, D. & Stevens, M. J. © 2009 International Union of Psychological Science and Psychology Press. Material reproduced with permission.

References

Ad Hoc Joint Committee. (2008). *Universal declaration of ethical principles for psychologists*. Retrieved from http://www.iupsys.net/index.php/ethics/declaration

Alonso, M. (1999). Argentina. In M. Alonso & A. Eagly (Eds.), *Psicología en las Américas* [Psychology in the Americas] (pp. 25–45). Buenos Aires, Argentina: Sociedad Interamericana de Psicología.

American Psychological Association. (2002). Ethical principles of psychologists and code of conduct. *American Psychologist, 57*(12), 1060–1073.

Aquerreta, M., & Allerand G. (1983). La Ley: ¿Presencia o ausencia? [The Law: Presence or absence?]. *Gaceta Psicológica, 53*, 4–9.

Ardila, R. (1986). *La psicología en américa latina: Pasado, presente y futuro* [Psychology in Latin America: Past, present, and future]. México: Siglo XXI Editores.

Ares, I. (1986). La fuerza de una institución: Crecimiento y participación [The strengh of an institution: Growth and participation]. *Gaceta Psicológica, 68*, 22–23.

Aruj, R. (2004). *Por qué se van: Exclusión, frustración y migración.* [Why they are leaving: Exclusion, frustration and migration]. Buenos Aires: Prometeo.

Asociación de Psicólogos de Buenos Aires. (1978a). Proyecto de Ley [Law Project]. *Gaceta Psicológica, 15*, 2–3.

Asociación de Psicólogos de Buenos Aires. (1978b). Preocupa la situación de Beatriz Perosio, Alfredo Smith y Celia Kriado. [Worried about the situation of Beatriz Perosio, Alfredo Smith and Celia Kriado]. *Gaceta Psicológica, 14*, 2.

Asociación de Psicólogos de Buenos Aires, (1978c). Aparecen dos colegas [Two colleagues appeared]. *Gaceta Psicológica, 15*, 4–5.

Asociación de Psicólogos de Buenos Aires (1979a). Gestiones [Errands]. *Gaceta Psicológica, 19*, 3.

Asociación de Psicólogos de Buenos Aires. (1979b). Beatriz Perosio. *Gaceta Psicológica, 20*, 3.

Asociación de Psicólogos de Buenos Aires. (1979c). Editorial: Beatriz Perosio, a un año de su desaparición [Editorial: Beatriz Perosio, one year of her disappearance]. *Gaceta Psicológica, 21*, 1.

Asociación de Psicólogos de Buenos Aires. (1984). Ley justa para los psicólogos [A fair law for psychologists]. *Gaceta Psicológica, 59*, 9–10.

Asociación de Psicólogos de Buenos Aires. (1985a). Siete años sin Beatriz Perosio [Seven years without Beatriz Perosio]. *Gaceta Psicológica, 68*, 32–33.

Asociación de Psicólogos de Buenos Aires. (1985b). Ejercicio de la profesión [Professional practice]. *Gaceta Psicológica, 65*, 24–25.

Asociación de Psicólogos de Buenos Aires. (1988). ¿Dónde está Beatriz? [Where is Beatriz?]. *Gaceta Psicológica, 83*, 5.

Asociación de Unidades Académicas de Psicología (AUAPsi)—Federación de Psicólogos de la República Argentina (FePRA). (2007). *Actividades reservadas al Título de Psicólogo.* [Activities reserved for the psychologist's degree]. Buenos Aires: Author.

Avelluto, O. (1980). La derogación de la ley del Psicólogo en Río Negro y la APBA [The abolition of the Río Negro Psychology Law and the APBA]. *Gaceta Psicológica, 27*, 11.

Bleger, J. (1966). *Psicohigiene y psicología institucional.* [Psychohygenic and institutional psychology]. Buenos Aires: Paidós.

Bourdieu, P. (1991). The peculiar history of scientific reason. *Sociological Forum, 6*(1), 3–26.

Calo, O. & Hermosilla, A. (2000). Prólogo [Prologue]. In O. Calo & A. M. Hermosilla (Eds.), *Psicología, ética y profesión: aportes deontológicos para la integración de los psicólogos del Mercosur* [Psychology, ethics and profession: deontological contributions for the integration of the Mercosur's psychologists] (pp. 7–11). Mar del Plata: Universidad Nacional de Mar del Plata.

Cerdá, L. (1983). Beatriz Leonor Perosio. *Gaceta Psicológica, 55*, 13.

Comisión Nacional sobre Desaparición de Personas. (1984). *Nunca Más* [Never more]. EUdeBA: Buenos Aires.

Comité Coordinador de Psicólogos del Mercosur y Países Asociados (1997). Protocolo de acuerdo marco de principios éticos para el ejercicio profesional de los psicólogos en el Mercosur y Países Asociados [Agreement protocol on the framework of ethical principles for the professional practice of psychologists in the Mercosur and associated countries]. In Conselho Federal de Psicologia (Ed.), *A psicologia no MERCOSUL* [Psychology in MERCOSUL countries] (pp. 2–5). Brasilia, Brazil: Author.

Comité Coordinador de los Psicólogos del Mercosur y Países Asociados (1998). Protocolo de Acuerdo Marco de los principios para la formación de Psicólogos en los países del Mercosur y países Asociados [Agreement protocol on the framework of principles for the training of psychologists in the Mercosur and associated countries]. Montevideo, Uruguay: Author.

Concatti, R. (2002). Retrato de un hombre solidario. A 25 años de la desaparición de Mauicio López [Portrait of a supportive man. 25 years after the forced disappearance of Mauricio López]. Diario "Los Andes" del 3 de febrero de 2002. Retrieved from http://www.ecumenica.org.ar/docs/MAURICIORetrato.pdf.

Devries, O. (1983). 8 de julio: ¡Misión Cumplida! Ahora: ¡A continuar! [July 8th: The work is done! Now: Let's go on!]. *Gaceta Psicológica, 55*, 2.

Di Doménico, C. (1996). Psicología y Mercosur: acerca de la armonización curricular [Psychology and Mercosur: in reference to curricular standardization]. *Acta Psiquiátrica y Psicológica de América Latina, 42*(3), 230–242.

Di Doménico, C. (1999). Psicología y Mercosur: revisión comparativa de los acuerdos sobre formación de psicólogos [Psychology and Mercosur: comparative revision of training in pscyhology agreements]. *Acta Psiquiátrica y Psicológica de América Latina, 45*(1), 24–33.

Di Doménico, C., & Vilanova, A. (1998). *Formación de Psicólogos en el Mercosur* [Psychologists' training in the Mercosur]. Mar del Plata: Universidad Nacional de Mar del Plata.

European Federation of Psychologists' Associations. *Meta-code of ethics*. (1995). Retrieved from http://www.efpa.eu/.

Federación de Psicólogos de la República Argentina. (1999). *Código de Etica*. [Ethics code]. Buenos Aires: Author.

Ferrero, A. (2002). Importancia de los derechos humanos en los códigos deontológicos de psicología en la Argentina [The importance of human rights in psychology ethics codes in Argentina]. *Revista Argentina de Psicología, 45*, 33–41.

Ferrero, A. (2006). Professional ethics in psychology facing disadvantaged social conditions in Argentina. *Bussiness & Professional Ethics Journal, 25*(1), 81–92.

Ferrero, A., & Andrade, E. (2007). Propuestas vigentes para la formación ético-deontológica en Carreras de Psicología en el contexto del Mercosur. El caso Argentino [Current proposals for ethical and deontological training in psychology programs within Mercosur context. The Argentine case]. *Fundamentos en Humanidades, 8*(15), 163–178.

Ferrero, A., & Gauthier, J. (2009). The development and adoption of the Universal Declaration of Ethical Principles for Psychologists. *SIP Newsletter: Interamerican Psychology, 90*. Retrieved from http://issuu.com/sipsych/docs/sip_newsletter_v90_march_2009

Gauthier, J., Pettifor, J., & Ferrero, A. (2010). The Universal Declaration of Ethical Principles for Psychologists: A culturally-sensitive model for creating and reviewing a code of ethics. *Ethics & Behavior, 20*(3&4), 1–18.

Hermosilla, A. M. (2000a). El Mercosur como contexto de la evolución legal de la psicología argentina [Mercosur as Argentine psychology's legal evolution context]. In O. Calo & A. M. Hermosilla (Eds.), *Psicología, ética y profesión: aportes deontológicos para la integración de los psicólogos del Mercosur* [Psychology, ethics and profession: deontological contributions for the integration of the Mercosur's psychologists] (pp. 119–128). Mar del Plata: Universidad Nacional de Mar del Plata.

Hermosilla et al. (2000b). Psicología, ética y profesión. Aportes deontológicos para la integración de los psicólogos del Mercosur [Psychology, ethics an profession: deontological contributions for the integration of the Mercosur's psychologists]. Mar del Plata: Universidad Nacional de Mar del Plata.

Klappenbach, H. (2000). El título profesional de psicólogo en Argentina: Antecedentes históricos y situación actual [Professional psychologists' degree in Argentina: Historical background and current situation]. *Revista Latinoamericana de Psicología, 32*, 419–446.

Klappenbach, H. (2004). Psychology in Argentina. In M. Stevens & D. Wedding (Eds.), *Handbook of international psychology* (pp. 129–150). New York: Brunner-Routledge.

Montoya, O., Klappenbach, H., Marincevic, J., & Arias, G. (1995). *Crónicas de la vida universitaria en San Luis* [Chronicles of the universitary life in San Luis]. San Luis, Argentina: Universidad Nacional de San Luis.

Moreno, S. (2002). *La noche de los bastones largos* [The night of the long batons]. Buenos Aires: Grupo Editor Latinoamericano.

Paolucci, C., & Verdinelli, S. (1999). La psicología en Argentina [Psychology in Argentina]. In C. Di Doménico & A. Vilanova (Eds.), *Formación de psicólogos en el Mercosur* [Psychologists' training in the Mercosur] (pp. 15–32). Mar del Plata: Universidad Nacional de Mar del Plata.

Perosio, B. (1977). Reorganización nacional de los psicólogos [National reorganization of psychologists]. *Gaceta Psicológica, 4*, 1.

Plotkin, M. (2002). *Freud in the Pampas: The emergence and development of a psychoanalytic culture in Argentina*. Stanford, CA: Stanford University Press.

Plotkin, M. (2003). *Argentina on the couch: Psychiatry, state and society. 1880 to the present*. Albuquerque: University of New Mexico.

Pugliese, S. (1985). Haciendo un balance [Making a balance]. *Espacios y Propuestas, 3*, 10.

Rébora, E. (1979). Legislación del ejercicio de la psicología en la República Argentina [Legislation on psychology practice in the Argentine Republic]. *Gaceta Psicológica, 19*, 7.

República Argentina. (1967). *Ley 17132* [Law 17132]. Buenos Aires: Secretaría de Salud.

República Argentina, Ministerio de Cultura y Educación de la Nación. (1980). *Resolución 1560/80* [Resolution 1560/80]. *Gaceta Psicológica, 30*, 10.

República Argentina, Ministerio de Educación y Justicia de la Nación. (1985). *Resolución 2447/85* [Resolution 2447/85]. Buenos Aires: Author.

Sanz Ferramola, R. (2000). La psicología como ideología exótica en los oscuros años del proceso de desorganización nacional: 1975-1980 [Psychology as an exotic ideology in the dark years of the process of national disorganization: 1975-1980]. *Fundamentos en Humanidades, 1*, 43–62.

Smith, A. (1977). Ley del Libre Ejercicio Profesional [Autonomous Professional Practice Law]. *Gaceta Psicológica, 3*, 2.

Vezzetti, H. (1988). Estudio preliminar [Preliminary study]. In H. Vezzetti (Ed.), *El nacimiento de la psicología en Argentina* [The birth of psychology in Argentina] (pp. 11–34). Buenos Aires: Puntosur.

Viar, J. P. (2002). Algunas cuestiones jurídico-legales relativas al ejercicio profesional de la psicología [Some judicial and legal issues related to professional practice of psychology]. *Revista Argentina de Psicología*, *45*, pp. 99–118.

Vilanova, A. (2000). La formación académica del psicólogo en el mundo y en el país [Academic training of psychologists at international and local level]. In O. Calo & A. M. Hermosilla (Eds.), *Psicología, Ética y Profesión: aportes deontológicos para la integración de los psicólogos del Mercosur* [Psychology, ethics and profession: deontological contributions for the integration of the Mercosur's psychologists] (pp. 107–118). Mar del Plata: Universidad Nacional de Mar del Plata.

CHAPTER 29

Aotearoa/New Zealand

Fred Seymour *and* Raymond Nairn

Abstract

The 2002 Code of Ethics for Psychologists Working in Aotearoa/New Zealand marked a major departure from its predecessor and from codes of other jurisdictions. Following the lead of the Canadian Psychological Association, an aspirational model was adopted in which guidance for ethical decision making is directly related to broad principles and related values. The code explicitly admitted the views of Māori, the indigenous people of New Zealand. As a consequence it reflects a bicultural perspective, including a shift away from an individualized conception of people and their behavior to a stronger acknowledgement of the role of community and culture in people's lives. The social and political influences on the development of this code are described.

Key Words: New Zealand Code, bicultural perspective, social/political influences

---

The Code of Ethics for Psychologists Working in Aotearoa/New Zealand (New Zealand Psychological Society, 2002) marked a major departure from its predecessor in several ways. First, we adopted an aspirational approach in which we recognize ethical decision making as following from broad principles and related values. The previous code (New Zealand Psychological Society Code of Ethics, 1986, 1997) like many others was a "code of conduct" type document that emphasized rules rather than principles and/or values. Several local psychologists contributed to the decision to adopt an aspirational approach, but all acknowledged the lead given by the Canadians in their new code (Canadian Psychological Association, 1992).

Second, unlike its predecessor, the new code explicitly admitted the views of Māori (the indigenous people of New Zealand), making it more compatible with the Treaty of Waitangi, increasingly recognized as the founding document of our society. This step toward recognition of the obligations to and rights of the indigenous people of the country may be seen as the inevitable outcome of adopting a principles-based rather than a "rules" approach to a code, although there were other influences leading in the same direction. Some of those influences were external to the profession, created by changes within the broader New Zealand society and its political institutions. Other influences came from within the profession, particularly within the activities and structure of the New Zealand Psychological Society (NZPsS). The result was a code of ethics that, more than its predecessor or comparable codes from other jurisdictions, reflects a bicultural perspective. Reddy (2006) has observed that three psychology associations that have produced revisions of their codes in recent years (American Psychological Association, 2002; Australian Psychological Society, 2006; British Psychological Society, 2006) had all conveyed greater sensitivity to issues of cultural diversity. By comparison, however, cultural considerations in the New Zealand code are both more prominent in emphasis and more extensive in detail.

Furthermore, the New Zealand code is the only one that distinguishes the situation of the indigenous people from issues of cultural diversity in their wider sense (Seymour, 2002).

Third, the previous code was grounded in an individualized conception of people and their behavior that barely acknowledged the role of community and culture in people's lives. To alter that disparity required a better balance between the individual and the social and communal aspects of human activity, a corollary of which was the clearer obligations for psychologists to demonstrate cultural knowledge and sensitivity in their work.

This chapter gives an account of the development of the 2002 code and attempts to explicitly identify the social and political influences on both the processes followed in the development of the code, and the outcome. The authors of this chapter were closely involved throughout the journey: Fred Seymour as convener of the Working Party and Raymond Nairn as a Working Party member and representative of the National Standing Committee on Bicultural Issues (NSCBI), a standing committee of the NZPsS. Both are psychologists, both are Pākehā (those of non-Māori descent) New Zealanders. Like many New Zealand psychologists we are proud of our current code, and it has given us much pleasure to revisit that work for this chapter. With the benefit of hindsight we believe we have been able to put events and decisions in perspective and identify crucial principles for the development of such a code and for its subsequent revisions.

To tell this story we need to describe the context in which the revision began, identifying major influences and whether or how they changed over the seven years of development before the new code was formally adopted. With the context in place we take the story through four sections: the background to admitting a bicultural perspective, a description of the steps taken in the adoption of an aspirational code and inclusion of a Māori perspective, an outline of the resulting content and structure of the code, and a brief description of how the code reflects the rights of vulnerable populations. In the first of those sections, background to admitting a bicultural perspective, we provide enough detail about the NSCBI and its place in the NZPsS for readers to appreciate how the bicultural perspective in the code was developed and incorporated into psychology. Finally, we look ahead and consider limitations of our current code and future needs.

The Social and Political Context

The late 1980s saw two important developments that continue to affect New Zealand society and, particularly, the activities of service-providing professionals, such as psychologists. First, 1990 was the sesquicentennial of the signing of te Tiriti of Waitangi (the Treaty of Waitangi), the event widely seen as the founding of New Zealand. There were significant efforts by both Māori and Pākehā individuals and communities to ensure the celebrations honored the intentions of the signatories. To do that required informed discussion of the two texts: te Tiriti in Te Reo Māori (Māori language; see Appendix 1) and the Treaty in English (Orange, 1987), the work of the Waitangi Tribunal and other mechanisms for providing restitution for injuries to Māori people arising from colonization, and the racism of the colonizing processes that established modern New Zealand society. Those discussions continue to this day.

Te Tiriti o Waitangi

As Great Britain had recognized Nu Tirani (New Zealand) as a sovereign state following the (New Zealand) Declaration of Independence in 1835, Britain chose to negotiate with Māori before settlement could proceed. The preamble to te Tiriti (see Appendix 1) asserts that Queen Victoria wished to preserve the authority and independence of the "peoples of Nu Tirani" and was seeking the authority to establish "*te Kawanatanga o te Kuini*" (the Queen's exercise of the functions of government). The actual Treaty has three clauses. In the first, Māori agree to the Queen exercising the functions of government. In the second, the Queen "confirms and upholds" the *rangatiratanga* (independence, autonomy) of Māori. In the final clause, Māori are assured that the Queen will protect them and give them the same rights as the people of England (Nairn, 2007). Settlers and colonizers had acted, and continue to act, on the presumption that Māori had ceded their sovereignty, and identifying te Tiriti as the primary text challenges that legitimating presumption. Further, te Tiriti affirmed that Māori, as well as having themselves and their *taonga* (treasures) protected by the Crown, are to be able and entitled to participate in the developing society as partners (Nairn, 2007).

The Waitangi Tribunal

The Waitangi Tribunal was established in 1975 as a permanent commission of inquiry into allegations by Māori individuals that particular actions or inaction of the Crown (government) were in breach of the Treaty (Potaka, 2010). Initially, claims were limited to contemporary breaches, but since 1985 the Tribunal mandate has been to hear claims of breaches occurring after February 6, 1840, the day te Tiriti was first signed (Project Waitangi, 1988). The legislation establishing the Tribunal required it to utilize both texts, te Tiriti and the English draft. Furthermore, the early reports confronted the complacent majority with unpalatable information about actions of Crown agents (e.g., government officials, departments, and local governing bodies) that had violated the Crown's undertakings and been detrimental to Māori. These reports helped all people to learn about te Tiriti, although, as evidenced by the fear and hostility expressed, not everyone welcomed that opportunity.

Racism and Colonial History

Every modern state has its preferred story of how it came into being (Anderson, 1991) and the settler states of Australia, Canada, New Zealand, and the United States are no exception. In New Zealand there is wide familiarity with a standard story of Māori/Pākehā relations as the best in the world. That story says Māori have been respected, their idiosyncrasies tolerated, and they have been integrated into a "harmonious, egalitarian relationship with more recent arrivals" (Nairn & McCreanor, 1991, p. 248). Whenever that story is told it puts a strongly pro-settler gloss on a much less attractive reality. To recognize that the standard story is pro-settler propaganda rather than a trustworthy account requires access to alternative accounts of events and processes, and at least three sources of such alternative accounts became available around the 1980s. There were, as already mentioned, reports from the Waitangi Tribunal; there were critical historians revisiting and, on the basis of their studies, reformulating the story of colonization (Belich, 1986; Walker, 1990; Ward, 1973); and there were increasing numbers of Māori telling their stories through protests, submissions, and in major *hui* (meetings).

Nurses were the first health professionals to engage with te Tiriti, and through that to acknowledge their responsibilities to Māori. The introduction of te Tiriti and colonial history into nursing training was resisted by many students, and their opposition impacted badly on Māori nurse educators who initially led this work. Reflections on such experiences led to the development of cultural safety for patients, students, and staff. Cultural safety, glossed as, "[being] about protecting people from nurses, from our culture as health professionals, our attitudes, our power and how we manage these things whether unintentionally or otherwise" (Ramsden, 2000, p. 4) begins with the individual's self-understanding, their attitudes and culture, and the recognition that they bear the culture of their community and profession. As developed the program was firmly grounded in informed analyses of health practices, emancipatory educational theory, and the language of nursing. Despite such firm foundations, cultural-safety teaching was the target of major media assaults in both 1993 and 1996, with nurses having to appear before the Parliamentary Select Committee on Education and Science on three occasions (Ramsden, 2000; Ramsden, & Spoonley, 1993). Studies of and by the profession confirmed the importance of cultural safety for nursing practice and media interest declined, but other health professionals had been shown what could happen should they, even if pursuing the best interests of their patients or clients, challenge the dominant settler understandings of history and social relations.

The second major development in the social and political context of the psychologists' ethics code revision was a new and vigorous assertion of patient or client rights. Service providers and researchers, if challenged, must be able to show that they took adequate steps to meet the obligations of respect and protection of their clients and research participants. Central to the establishment of that perspective was a major inquiry from 1987 through 1988 into "informal, unregulated cervical cancer research at (the) National Women's Hospital in Auckland" (Moewaka Barnes, McCreanor, Edwards, & Borell, 2009, p. 444). The Cartwright Inquiry, as it was called, found that some women with abnormal cervical smears had, without their knowledge or consent, been merely observed to see what happened rather than receiving the normal treatment. Among the report's recommendations was the establishment of a Health and Disability Commissioner to support patients, clients, and research participants by investigating and acting upon their complaints (Health and Disability Commissioner Act, 1994). As required by that legislation the first Health and Disability Commissioner developed and promulgated a Code of Health and Disability Service Consumers' Rights (Health and Disability Commissioner, 1996). That code of rights has been reviewed three times since then with only a minor amendment, testament to the wide and effective consultation through which it was developed. Of particular significance to psychologists and the development of their new ethical code are that the Office of the Health and Disabilities Commissioner provides both a further code to which psychologists working in health and disability areas are responsible and an alternative route to adjudicate complaints about psychologists' practice and/or conduct.

Admitting a Bicultural Perspective

In this section, we need to help readers appreciate where the bicultural perspective included in the new code came from, how it was developed, and how it came to play such a significant part in that document. Not only was there not a bicultural perspective on psychology waiting to be "downloaded," there also was, as the nursing profession found, significant hostility toward the development of such a perspective and its incorporation into the thinking and practices of a profession. To provide that appreciation readers need to know how the NSCBI, the group in which the bicultural perspective was and continues to be developed, came into being and how its thinking developed prior to the establishment of the Working Party for the new code. Given the significant hostility toward such developments in New Zealand at the time, there needed to be those who welcomed the NSCBI, engaged with the advice and other materials it produced, and provided sufficient shelter from attack for the committee to grow into its task. For that reason, we now tell readers of contributions made by respected psychologists who supported the perspective, helping to make it accessible and attractive to growing numbers of practitioners.

The journey to admit a bicultural perspective began with events that took place within the NZPsS over a few years preceding the establishment of the Working Party that reviewed the code. In 1987 two researchers, Mason Durie and Max Abbott, reported that psychology trained only small numbers of non-Pākehā practitioners (Abbott & Durie, 1987). They found the discipline was proportionately less inclusive than medicine and it did not support any form of affirmative action that might increase the numbers of Māori entering the profession. Concurrently, those Māori who were training in psychology were sharing their dissatisfactions about the content of the courses, the way Māori people, on the occasions they were mentioned, were often constructed as deficient, aggressive failures, and negative experiences of their *whanau* (family) and friends with psychologists. In 1989 a *hui* was organized at Waikato University to discuss these issues. The participants submitted a remit to the NZPsS Annual General Meeting (AGM) seeking a commitment from NZPsS to address this. At the AGM, following some stormy exchanges, a Kaupapa Māori (in accord with a Māori worldview) Working Party was established to advise the NZPsS how to proceed (Duirs, 2005). The members were Professors James Ritchie and David Thomas, and Linda Waimarie Nikora, a Māori woman who had recently been appointed assistant lecturer in psychology at Waikato University. The group was to report to the AGM at the next annual conference.

Prior to the 1990 conference, the Kaupapa Māori Working Party report was presented to a *hui* at Auckland University attended by some members of the NZPsS executive committee, Māori and Pākehā supporters, and members of the Working Party. The *hui* endorsed the report and, when it was announced that Linda Nikora would have to present the report, as she was the only member of the Working Party able to attend the conference, sought support from the NZPsS and the psychology departments at Auckland and Waikato universities to enable a party from the *hui* to accompany Linda and stand with her in support of the *kaupapa* (mission or purpose). Like other incorporated societies, the NZPsS allows nonmembers to attend AGMs but, unless given express permission by the meeting, they may not speak on any matter being considered. As Linda was not a member of the NZPsS there was a real possibility that she could be denied the right to speak, in which case the report would merely be "received." At the AGM the president sidestepped that problem by adjourning the meeting while Linda, flanked by her support group, presented the report. There were strong protests from some members to this course of action being taken. After the report was presented, Linda's support group, following *tikanga Māori* (Māori protocols; Salmond, 1975), sang a *waiata* (song) to *tautoko* (support) her and to endorse the report despite a rumble of protest. The response to the report was an intense and often angry debate. Clearly, at that time and place, there was significant opposition to any moves to relate te Tiriti, institutional racism, and oppression of Māori people to psychology or psychological practice. Yet, the following year, in a different city, the AGM voted to establish the NSCBI to advise the executive and the Council of the NZPsS on bicultural steps and policies, and Treaty of Waitangi issues. The establishment of the NSCBI was the result of the leadership of a number of senior psychologists and the support of a majority of NZPsS members.

It was always envisaged that the NSCBI would include both Māori and Pākehā psychologists to focus on issues in psychology, the NZPsS, and the relationships between Māori and non-Māori that concern Māori. For that to happen there were two sets of problems to be solved. There were the administrative problems around how the committee was set up and supported, and how its work was to affect the decision-making councils of the NZPsS. And, given that there was no blueprint for such a committee, there were issues about how the committee members would, or could, work to perform their assigned tasks. In practice the latter seems to have been easier than the former.

In Te Reo "biculturalism" is *nga tikanga e rua* (two ways) and, looking back over nearly twenty years of NSCBI action, it is clear the committee has explored how to operate in two *tikanga* (cultural traditions) without losing sight of its place within what was, and in large part still is, a monocultural professional organization. Concurrently, the members of the NSCBI had to develop and sustain the relationships of trust and respect that were ultimately what enabled the group to work successfully. Like other standing committees, the NSCBI fulfills the procedural requirements of the NZPsS. It provides minutes of meetings, reports on finances, contributes to NZPsS submissions, and prepares and disseminates educational materials to assist the NZPsS and its members in becoming bicultural. Yet, the NSCBI's ways of doing those things took a recognizably Māori form during the early years when the convenor Linda Nikora and many of the Māori members were not members of the Society. Meetings were like *marae* (meeting place) gatherings (Salmond, 1975), open to anyone who was interested and willing to contribute to the *kaupapa* (purpose). After apologies the first item of business was, and still is, *whakawhanaungatanga* (relationship building), and there is a respect for Māori authority and Māori knowledge in the committee's deliberations. When Ray Nairn represented the NSCBI on the code of ethics Working Party, the relationships built up in those meetings meant he was not alone: *Ehara taku mahi i mahi takutahi, ēngari he mahi takutini* (The work is not mine alone, it is the work of many).

The issues around how the NSCBI was to be set up, supported, and heard in the Executive Committee and other fora of the NZPsS, when there was considerable suspicion about and opposition to committing time and money to "political" issues that were seen as irrelevant, required ongoing support of officeholders and other senior NZPsS members. First, there was the matter of committee membership. According to the rules of the NZPsS, the Executive appoints members of NZPsS to standing committees with each appointee able to serve a maximum of two consecutive 3-year terms. Those rules had to be set aside if the NSCBI was to thrive and the NZPsS was to develop a strong bicultural emphasis as, initially, there were few Māori with the qualifications to be NZPsS members and, of those who had the qualifications, few had chosen to join. There were also relatively few Pākehā psychologists willing and able to engage with these issues. Consequently, senior members of the NZPsS, presidents, and executive members had to be willing to set aside the letter of the rules and face the prospect of challenges from members for doing so. Both the Executive Committee and the NSCBI had to learn how the relationship was to work; that is, how, without undermining the role of the Executive, was the NSCBI to establish priorities and a framework for its work, and to what extent could it be an initiator? Procedures also needed to be put in place to ensure that decisions, once made, were implemented.

Those involved found this learning difficult, and it continues to this day. It was a situation for which no manual existed and the NZPsS found that the familiar languages and practices of administration and psychology carried colonial baggage that often stifled thought and hobbled action. Nairn and Hyde (2010) provide a fuller discussion of examples of this baggage. In colonial practice the cultural character of the dominant or dominating culture is masked by being naturalized as normal practice (Black & Huygens, 2007; Swidler, 2001); consequently, it was often difficult for NZPsS members to recognize how "business as usual" excluded members of nondominant cultures or made it difficult for them to participate. That naturalizing of administration, psychology, and psychological practices obscured the necessity for practitioners to be aware of the impact of the presuppositions and culture embodied in those areas on persons from nondominant cultures. Three instances of such presuppositions are: the nature of knowledge, the role of culture in all people's lives, and the place of spirituality in healthy human life. Psychology has long valorized objective knowledge distinguished from the professional relationships through which it was generated, whereas many cultures understand knowledge to be embedded in and inseparable from personal relationships. As cultures provide the frameworks through which people understand their world and the events within it, we are always "in the cultural world" (McHoul

& Rapley, 2001, p. 433). Naturalization of the dominant culture has made it extremely difficult for psychologists to recognize the cultural character of their therapeutic practice (Taylor & Dickson, 2007) and research (Chamberlain, 2007). Finally, the secular empiricism of mainstream psychology makes it almost impossible for the discipline to respond to issues such as the "fragmentation of identity...and a loss of spirit" (Durie, 1997, p. 32) created by colonial processes like the taking of land.

Despite these problems, key people remained committed to making the changes, and to sustaining the relationships on which they depended, work. A new NZPsS constitution that provided for two "Bicultural Representatives" on the Executive Committee, who were initially seen as responsible for that aspect of NZPsS policies, practices, and initiatives, helped improve communication, although Māori members occupying those positions could find themselves threatened and undermined by the way the NZPsS operated, by being expected to have expertise in *tikanga Māori* that was inappropriate for their age and position in the Māori world, or by demands that they act counter to their own procedures. These were pain-inflicting signs that the dominant group members had yet to make such governing bodies culturally safe for Māori members.

From the first, the NSCBI identified professional psychological practice as a key area of work. The group volunteered to be part of a proposed entity to accredit training programs, and discussed with the convenor of the NZPsS Ethical Issues Committee (EIC) concerns about cultural inadequacies in the then current (1986) code of ethics. As NZPsS members needed to be informed about such concerns and about options for incorporating Māori and bicultural perspectives in teaching and practice, the committee put considerable energy into education. An NSCBI-edited special feature in the *Bulletin* of the NZPsS, written by Māori and Pākehā psychologists (Cram & Nairn, 1993), introduced members to the implications of the Treaty of Waitangi and biculturalism for psychology and for the NZPsS. Later the same year, the committee organized the first bicultural symposium at an annual conference. Linda Nikora ensured that the symposium, "Cultural Justice and Ethics," and the three associated keynote addresses were published (Nikora, 1993). For all such projects the NSCBI sought contributions from NZPsS members.

An early insight of the NSCBI was that bicultural initiatives should be grounded in te Tiriti, and that it would be necessary to keep that understanding before NZPsS members. One way that goal might be achieved would be to add a treaty objective to the existing objectives of the NZPsS, but the committee chose instead to embed the bicultural goal in all activities of the Society by reformulating how the existing objectives of the Society were to be implemented. The NZPsS membership agreed and the 1993 AGM adopted a new "Implementation of Objects" that states:

> In giving effect to the objects for which the Society is established the Society shall encourage policies and practices that reflect New Zealand's cultural diversity and shall, in particular, have due regard to the provisions of, and to the spirit and intent of, the Treaty of Waitangi.
> (*NZPsS*, 1996, p. 2)

That rule, now known as the Bicultural Commitment, provided a focus for NSCBI advice and comment and for Executive initiatives. An early instance of the latter was the changed NZPsS constitution, approved in 1994, that specified an Executive Committee of the President, the President-elect, four Directors (each responsible for an aspect of NZPsS service to members), the Executive Director, and two Bicultural Representatives nominated by the NSCBI. The inclusion of NSCBI-nominated bicultural representatives on the Executive Committee acknowledged the commitment, as did the inclusion of NSCBI representatives among the NZPsS members in two major working parties affecting psychology in New Zealand (NZPsS, 1996).

Steps Taken in the Adoption of an Aspirational Code and Inclusion of a Māori Perspective

The 1986 Code of Ethics had been developed and copyrighted by the NZPsS, and by formal agreement was also used by the Psychologists Board and the New Zealand College of Clinical Psychologists (NZCCP). In contrast, the 2002 code was developed by and is "owned" by all three organizations, although the NZPsS initiated the revision and took the lead role in its production.

There are important differences between NZPsS, NZCCP, and the Psychologists Board bodies. Both the NZPsS and NZCCP are professional organizations, whereas the Psychologists Board is the regulatory body for the discipline. The NZPsS was initially founded in 1947 as a branch of the British Psychological Society (BPS) by members of the fledgling discipline of psychology, many of whom were, and continued to be, members of the BPS. When the NZPsS became an independent Society in 1967, it still showed many of the features of a learned society in the BPS tradition (Whittaker & Seymour, 1997). The Psychologists Board was established via the Psychologists Act 1981 and, like other regulatory bodies, is appointed by government and is answerable to the Minister of Health. It now operates under the aegis of new legislation, the Health Practitioners Competence Assurance Act 2003, which has as its major purpose the protection of the public through regulation of health practitioners. NZCCP was established in 1989 as a professional association independent of NZPsS. Its functions are similar to those of the NZPsS, but confined to practitioners of clinical psychology. In contrast, the NZPsS caters to members from all psychological subdisciplines, including clinical psychology. The NSCBI, although a standing committee within NZPsS effectively became a fourth constituent of the code revision Working Party because of the way it was included and supported by the NZPsS as described below.

The decision to conduct a revision of the 1986 code was made following a symposium of the Ethical Issues Committee of NZPsS at the NZPsS annual conference in 1992. Prior to that conference the chair of the Ethical Issues Committee, Brian Dixon, proposed as a framework for a new code that it should be easily understood by clients and practitioners, responsive to the needs and rights of ethnic and cultural groups in New Zealand society, able to adapt to the needs of an evolving profession, based on clear, well-identified principles rather than providing detailed prescriptions that attempted to anticipate all eventualities, address professional obligations and responsibilities, and focus on preventive ethical practice (Dixon, 1992). His presentation laid the groundwork for the subsequent adoption of an aspirational code that is principles and values–based, and the recognition that the code needed to be culturally responsive. However, the framework did not make any reference to particular responsibilities to Māori arising from the Treaty of Waitangi; nor did it anticipate the subsequent emphasis on biculturalism. Rather, the bicultural and Māori perspectives came from the nascent National Standing Committee on Bicultural Issues which, in response to the news that a revision of the code was imminent, contacted the Ethical Issues Committee stating their desire to be involved in the process (Thomas, 1992). In their initial submission the NSCBI identified four areas of concern: (1) how were practitioners to become culturally competent and who should be responsible for assessing that competence, (2) how could the cultural safety of clients who are not members of the dominant culture be ensured, (3) would the code say anything about the cultural appropriateness of psychological assessment, and (4) the individualized focus of informed consent that for Māori clients needed to include both *whanau* and the client (NSCBI, 1992).

The Working Party, consisting of members of the three professional organizations that used the 1986 code, was established in 1994 to review the code. Consistent with the Bicultural Commitment, NZPsS included a NSCBI representative so that Māori concerns and a bicultural perspective were present in the deliberations of the Working Party. Thus, from the outset, there was a significant commitment by the NZPsS to ensure that the code revision incorporated the views of Māori and adequately captured the obligations that all psychologists have to those from the indigenous culture.

From the first meeting of the Working Party there was broad agreement that the new code would entail a shift from a "code of conduct" to an aspirational document in which ethical decision making is explicitly recognized as following from broad principles and related values; this was never disputed within the Working Party. Several factors contributed to the decision to move away from a "code of conduct" type of document. These included judgments of High Court judges in two appeals of disciplinary decisions by the Psychologists Board in which it was established that a code of ethics served not as the ultimate standard expected for a particular practice, but merely served alongside other documents as an indication of the expected standards of practice at the time of the alleged offense. Consequently, the Psychologists Board now explicitly states that it uses the code as a guideline in considering complaints, rather than treating the code as an exhaustive set of rules against which a psychologist's practice is evaluated. The assessment of the psychologist's practice is guided by the version of the code of ethics in place at the time of the alleged breach, related legislation (e.g., Privacy Act, 1993), and the relevant, published practice guidelines (Evans, Rucklidge, & O'Driscoll, 2007; Maxwell, Seymour, & Vincent, 1996). Clearly, the code remained relevant to, but not determining of, decisions made by regulatory authorities about alleged ethical transgressions by practitioners. However, the code is able to make a significant contribution to this, and by encouraging sound ethical practice, to preventing or reducing the number of complaints made.

A second factor influencing the adoption of an aspirational approach was the personal and financial pressure created by complaints. To some it seemed that the existing code fell well short of effectively preventing poor practice, exposing both the consumers of psychological services and practitioners to unnecessary risk. A values-based code that gave guidance to decision making seemed to have greater potential to prevent poor practice than the rather prescriptive "code of conduct" approach of the 1986 code. This argument applied to practitioners whether they were experienced or newly qualified. Ethics education was becoming more common within university training programs as a means of promoting ethical behaviors within the profession, in professional training programs such as clinical psychology, broader graduate courses (Blampied, 1993), and even undergraduate programs (Tripp, 1993). Examination of ethics education at that time showed that teaching based on broad principles was favored over instruction in a specific code of conduct (Blampied, 1993; Tripp, 1993), thus providing support for a principles and values–based code.

A third influence on the adoption of an aspirational code was the introduction of the Code of Rights (Health and Disability Commissioner, 1996), This is a values-based code and, as already noted, one to which psychologists must also adhere. Within both the Working Party and the constituent organizations it was considered essential that the two codes be compatible in content, reflect similar values, and make similar demands for ethical practice. It also seemed advisable that expressions in the new code are compatible with the Code of Rights, and this has occurred. For example, Right 1 in the code asserts that consumers "should always be treated with respect," which, "…includes respect for your culture, values, and beliefs, as well as your right to personal privacy" (Health and Disability Commissioner, 1996, p. 1). In the 2002 psychologists code, the first principle states: "The principle of respect for the dignity of persons and peoples requires that each person and all peoples are positively valued in their own right, and are shown respect and granted dignity as part of their common humanity" (NZPsS, 2002, p. 4).

Finally, we were impressed with the Canadian code (Canadian Psychological Association, 1992) because it offered an example of how an aspirational approach could be realized. The revision of the New Zealand code drew heavily on the Canadian code and also benefited from inputs from Jean Pettifor, one of the key people in the development of that code, who visited New Zealand and consulted with us both when here and later by correspondence.

An early step in the writing of the 2002 code was to compile a preliminary draft of the new code from a thorough examination of the 1986 code (NZPsS, 1986, 1997), the Canadian code, and an extensive early submission from the NSCBI. That submission noted that examination of the Canadian code showed there was an "almost complete absence of references to culture" and "a total failure to acknowledge culture as a significant factor in social relations or psychological practice" (Nairn, 1995, p. 13). The NSCBI asserted that, to address these deficiencies, the new code would have to counterbalance the almost commonsensical privileging of the autonomous individual by overtly acknowledging the collective, social nature of human life. The submission had as its goal recognition of the fact that people are socially located and socially constituted and, by way of example, recommended that Principle 1 be "respect for the dignity of persons [individuals] and peoples [collectives]" (NZPsS, 2002, p. 4).

The NSCBI was aware that merely adding words or phrases to existing principles, values, and practice implications might achieve the desired outcome, but the change would appear to be an afterthought rather being integral to the operation and use of the code. At that point the committee went back to te Tiriti o Waitangi as the basis for bicultural initiatives and of the importance of collective (i.e., culturally grounded) identities in relationships. That decision does not imply that te Tiriti is a bicultural document; like all treaties it is between two parties—independent nations in this case (Nairn, 2007). What the Treaty does provide is a principled approach to how two peoples, Māori and settler, could share responsibilities for living together in the same land. The NSCBI saw that such a principled approach could guide the efforts to achieve a more prominent place for people's culture in the code. Consequently the submission from the NSCBI showed how both the Treaty of Waitangi and a bicultural perspective could be incorporated. It proposed that the code include specific references to treaty obligations, and offered particular phrasings of the principles, values, and practice implications to realize those obligations (see examples below).

At the next step a national survey of registered psychologists was conducted in a similar manner to that by Pope and Vetter (1992), in which participants were asked to describe an ethical problem they or a colleague had recently faced (Davis, Seymour, & Read, 1997). The purpose here was to identify areas that were not addressed adequately in the 1986 code of ethics or in the draft revision. In addition, complaints received by the Psychologists Board were analyzed, with a focus on Family Courts–related complaints that comprised the most common category of complaints at that time (Walker & Seymour, 1997).

A preliminary draft of the code released for comment in late 1998 resulted in a large number of individual and group submissions. The Working Party also consulted psychologists through workshops conducted by members at NZPsS and NZCCP annual conferences. Reactions to this initial draft, which was very long and not yet clearly organized, included objection to its length and level of detail, which some feared would lead to an avalanche of complaints. Others saw some aspects of the draft as overtly intrusive, as they felt its practice implications reached into psychologists' private lives. Surprisingly, given the hostility that preceded the establishment of the NSCBI, none of the objections related to the strong emphasis on the values and implications attached to cultural competence, or to obligations and rights attached to Māori in particular. It seems likely in hindsight that there were at least some who were uneasy with these developments, but if this was the case they did not express their unease.

Perhaps those who remained silent despite their disquiet sensed there had been widespread change in psychologists' beliefs and practices influenced by changes in New Zealand society. Such change was reflected within the NZPsS in the growing respect for and influence of the NSCBI. Most obvious of the contemporary changes in New Zealand society was government recognition of te Tiriti and the moves to settle historical claims relating to damage suffered by particular *hapu* and *iwi* (subtribes and tribes) because of Crown actions or inaction. Between 1994 and 1998, Treaty Settlements, formal government responses to proven breaches of Treaty responsibilities, were often in the news and were widely discussed. While settlement negotiations required strict confidentiality, evidence that established a breach had occurred could be reported and the "packages" offered the claimants were always described in considerable detail. Packages usually included a formal apology from the Crown for what had been done, transfer of properties from Crown to Māori *iwi* and *hapu* (tribes and sub-tribes), and money or loans. The leader of the government negotiators over this period, the Minister of Justice Douglas Graham, often spoke about the justness of Māori claims, the faithfulness of the claimants, and, of particular importance for Pākehā he asserted that we are not responsible for the breach, but we share the guilt of the perpetrators if, having heard the grievance, we do nothing to resolve it (McCreanor, 1993). New Zealanders were not only being exposed to previously hidden aspects of our history, but the settlements also affirmed the importance of Māori and te Tiriti to our society.

A revised draft was released for comment in August 2000, and further comment was explicitly obtained from the NSCBI and other Māori psychologists outside the NSCBI membership. This led to a further draft in 2001 and, after a final round of submissions in which relatively few comments were received, the definitive version was produced and adopted by the participating bodies in 2002. That version had also benefited from a thorough examination of the ethics codes of the American Psychological Association, Australian Psychological Association, and British Psychological Society that aimed to ensure the listed practice implications were as comprehensive as possible.

Structure and Content of the New Code

In the introduction to the code, three purposes are listed. The first, "To unify the practices of the profession" (NZPsS, 2002, p. 3), recognizes that the identity of a profession is derived from its having a shared knowledge base and competencies, and an expectation that its practitioners will apply that knowledge according to common principles. The second purpose is, "To guide psychologists in ethical decision making," and the third is, "To present a set of guidelines that might be available to the public in order to inform them of the professional ethics of the profession." These purposes emphasize the application of the code to all psychologists, and that its aim is to assist ethical practice by guiding decision making rather than offering an exhaustive list of rules.

As noted above, the 1991 revision of the Canadian code (Canadian Psychological Association, 1992) represented a quite radical departure from their previous code. It grouped standards for psychologist behavior according to overlying ethical principles and values rather than reporting principles and/or values in a section of the document separated from statements of expected conduct (i.e., rules), as is more commonly done. The Canadian code distinguished four principles, "to be considered and balanced in ethical decision making" (Sinclair & Pettifor, 1992, p. 13): Respect for the Dignity of Persons, Responsible Caring, Integrity in Relationships, and Responsibility to Society. An earlier survey of Canadian psychologists found that these principles were used most consistently to resolve hypothetical ethical dilemmas (Sinclair, Poizner, Gilmour-Barrett, & Randall, 1987). Each principle was then elaborated by a statement of those values, "which are included in and give definition to the principle" (Canadian Psychological Association; cited in Sinclair & Pettifor, 1992, p. 13). At a third level, numerous ethical standards were described, "which illustrate the application of the particular principle and values to psychologists" (Sinclair & Pettifor, 1992, p. 13). These ethical standards are similar in content to those commonly described in codes of conduct (see Leach & Harbin, 1997).

For the New Zealand code we adapted the four *principles* from the Canadian code (Sinclair & Pettifor, 1992), as we did not have the resources to conduct our own survey in the style of Sinclair et al. (1987). For each principle, related *values* clarified the import of the principle to guide ethical decision making in relation to practice. Finally, explicit *practice implications* were listed exemplifying appropriate application of these principles and values. These practice implications cover most situations encountered by psychologists that involve ethical issues.

The four ethical principles of the New Zealand code became: Respect for the Dignity of Persons and Peoples, Responsible Caring, Integrity of Relationships, Social Justice and Responsibility to Society. The key elements of the first principle are that all persons (individuals) and peoples (groups) should be valued in their own right, and psychologists should be sensitive to cultural and social diversity (e.g., culture, ethnicity, gender, religion, socioeconomic status). Seven associated values are described, the first being that of general respect: "Psychologists respect the dignity of persons and peoples with whom they relate in their work and are sensitive to their welfare and rights" (NZPsS, 2002, p. 5). Other values are concerned with nondiscrimination, sensitivity to diversity, relations between Māori and non-Māori, responsibilities toward children/young people, confidentiality, and informed consent.

The second principle, Responsible Caring (NZPsS, 2002, p. 9), emphasizes that the practice of psychology is to benefit members of society, promote well-being, and, at the very least, do no harm. Associated values include maintenance of an active concern for peoples' well-being, attaining and maintaining competence in knowledge and skills, and recognizing in one's actions the vulnerability of those with whom one works, including the disadvantaged, children, and animals.

The third principle, Integrity in Relationships (NZPsS, 2002, p. 13), focuses on the professional relationships formed with those with whom the psychologist is engaged. Professional relationships are regarded as "vital to the advancement of social justice, scientific knowledge, and to the maintenance of public confidence in the profession" (NZPsS, 2002, p. 13). Psychologists should, in their professional relationships, act with honesty, maintain an awareness of their own beliefs and values and how these might impact on those with whom they work, maintain appropriate structure (including boundaries) with others, and avoid or at least declare and consider any potential or real conflicts of interest.

The fourth and final principle, Social Justice and Responsibility to Society (NZPsS, 2002, p. 15), is concerned with psychologists' individual and collective responsibility to society, particularly the responsibility to promote its well-being. This principle involves an acknowledgement of psychologists' power and influence in relation to individuals and groups with whom they are involved. Associated value statements include a concern for the welfare of society, respect for the structures and customs of the communities with which the psychologists work, application of psychological knowledge for beneficial purposes, and responsibility to maintain ethical standards and accountability for the actions they take.

Subsumed under each principle and value statement, the practice implications describe the appropriate professional behavior of psychologists in relation to each value. Associated with many of the practice implications are *comments* that draw attention to particular important issues of practice. The practice implications included are considered to be guides that do not exhaust the implications of the associated value for practice. Thus, it is explicitly recognized that there may be circumstances faced by a psychologist for which there is no practice implication that they can refer to, so they must employ a process of ethical problem solving with reference to principles and values. In this process, related practice implications may provide some support but should not be treated as definitive.

The prominent place the code assigns the Treaty of Waitangi exemplifies the discipline's commitment to biculturalism. As declared in the preamble,

"In giving effect to the Principles and Values of this Code of Ethics there shall be regard for New Zealand's cultural diversity and in particular for the provisions of, and the spirit and intent of, the Treaty of Waitangi" (NZPsS, 2002, p. 3).

In relation to each principle of the code—Respect for the Dignity of Persons and Peoples, Responsible Caring, Integrity in Relationships, and Social Justice and Responsibility to Society—there is explicit reference to the Treaty. For example, in relation to Principle 1, the last sentence states, "In New Zealand, the basis for respect between the indigenous people (*tangata whenua*—those who are Māori) and others (those who are not Māori) is set out in the Treaty of Waitangi" (NZPsS, 2002, p. 5). That assertion is repeated as Value Statement 1.3 (NZPsS, 2002, p. 5), and Practice Implication 1.3.1 includes the following, "Psychologists, individually and collectively, seek to be informed about the meaning and implications of the Treaty of Waitangi for their work. This includes an understanding of the principles of protection, participation and partnership with Māori" (NZPsS, 2002, p. 5).

Further practice implications, for example 1.3.2 and 1.4.1, recognize the obligation of psychologists to gain and appropriately demonstrate cultural knowledge and sensitivity in their work with Māori. "Both non-Māori and Māori psychologists who work with Māori seek advice and undertake training in the appropriate way to show respect for the dignity and needs of Māori in their practice" (1.3.2, NZPsS, 2002, p. 6).

In the commonsense of Pākehā New Zealanders (McCreanor, 1989), bicultural relations are seen as excluding or undermining relationships with non-Māori ethnic groups and their cultures. In contrast to that gloomy prognosis, our experience in the NZPsS since the NSCBI was established and the new code adopted is that the focus on biculturalism and on the rights of and obligations to the indigenous people of New Zealand served to clarify and thereby strengthen psychologists' commitment to cultural knowledge and sensitivity in cross-cultural contexts (Rucklidge & Williams, 2007). That stronger, more general commitment is exemplified by Principle 1, Respect for the Dignity of Persons and Peoples, which states:

> Respect requires sensitivity to cultural and social diversity and recognition that there are differences among persons associated with their culture, nationality, ethnicity, colour, race, religion, gender, marital status, sexual orientation, physical or mental abilities, age, socio-economic status, and/or any other personal characteristic, condition, or status. Such differences are an integral part of the person.
> (*NZPsS*, 2002, p. 5)

Practice implication 1.4.1 further states, "Psychologists seek to be responsive to cultural and social diversity and, as a consequence, obtain training, experience and advice to ensure competent and culturally safe service or research" (NZPsS, 2002, p. 6).

The recognition that existing codes are typically grounded in a highly individualistic conception of human behavior and struggle to respond adequately to the role of community and culture in people's lives (Lammers & Nairn, 1999) led to a shift in the balance between the individual and the social and communal aspects of human activity toward the social and communal pole. Throughout the code the language has been carefully designed to accommodate both individual ("persons") and group identity ("peoples"). Explicit recognition of the importance of culture and group membership is provided by practice implication (1.4.2), "Psychologists recognise that people with whom they work have cultural and social needs, and take reasonable steps to help them meet these needs." (NZPsS, 2002, p. 6)

Psychologists' responsibility to community and groups is described under Principle 4, Social Justice and Responsibility to Society:

> The principle of Social Justice is about acknowledging psychologists' position of power and influence in relation both to individuals and groups within communities where the psychologist is involved, and in the broader context. It is about addressing and challenging unjust societal norms and behaviors that disempower people at all levels of interaction.
> (*NZPsS*, 2002, p. 15)

In relation to this principle, the Treaty is described as "a foundation document of social justice" (NZPsS, 2002, p. 15).

Advice on Ethical Decision Making

The code provides a guideline for decision making, encouraging practitioners to identify and consider higher-order principles and values relevant to their situation, relating them to associated practice implications. It is acknowledged that, in practice, many ethical issues are addressed in the practice implications but there will be occasions when an ethical decision will need to be informed by reference to more than one section of the code. To make an informed ethical decision, psychologists are encouraged to proceed through the following six steps when faced with an ethical problem.

1. Identify the issues and practices that are ethically relevant.

2. Develop alternative courses of action, preferably in consultation with a professional colleague or supervisor.

3. For each identified course of action analyze the likely short-term, ongoing, and long-term risks and benefits for the individual(s) and/or group(s) involved or likely to be affected.

4. Conscientiously apply the principles, values, and practice implications to each course of action in the light of the identified risks and benefits and decide which offers the best balance between these.

5. Take the chosen course of action, accepting responsibility for the consequences of the chosen course of action.

6. Evaluate the consequences of the action, correcting negative outcomes if possible and, if the issue(s) originally identified are not resolved, re-engaging in the decision-making process.

While the comments in the preamble to the New Zealand code outline a recommended decision-making process, this does not on its own provide a sufficient discussion of this important issue. Close reading of more extensive treatments, such as those associated with the North American (e.g., Bass et al., 1996) and Australian (Morrissey & Reddy, 2006) codes, are recommended. Other texts have been produced over the last decade that provide further valuable resources on ethics and professional practice, including extensive discussion of ethical problem solving and decision making (e.g., Corey, Corey, & Callanan, 1998; Francis, 1999; Koocher & Keith-Spiegel, 1998; Pryzwansky & Wendt, 1999; Steinman, Richardson, & McEnroe, 1998). In relation to the New Zealand code, Williams (2004) identified various limitations of our six-step approach, and, in so doing provided grounds for its revision (Seymour, Nairn, & Austin, 2004). In particular, the code's preamble should clarify that there is often no need to follow the six steps described. Psychologists are confronted daily with ethical decisions, and on many occasions will be guided by a directly relevant practice implication or previous ethical decisions and, consequently, their practice may appear to be automatic or intuitive (Williams, 2004). The Canadian code provides valuable additional steps, in particular the consideration of personal bias and of actions that may be taken to prevent future occurrences of the dilemma (Sinclair & Pettifor, 1992) that could have, or should have, been retained in the six step-model contained in the New Zealand code.

Rights of Vulnerable Populations

In addition to the emphasis on culture and relationships between the mainstream and indigenous groups, the new code has several other features that distinguish it from the earlier code and that were, at least in part, a response to the prevailing social and political context. For example, the code asserts that, "Psychologists especially provide responsible care to individuals and groups who may be disadvantaged and/or oppressed" (2.4, NZPsS, 2002, p. 11). In an associated comment, vulnerability is recognized as occurring with political or social oppression, age, ethnic origin, ability to communicate, sensory impairments, economic standing, and need for support from others. It is widely acknowledged that people with disabilities often are devalued and disempowered, have little influence on decisions that are made on their behalf, and are often at the mercy of professionals and others who determine what is best for them (Webb & Gates, 1997). For psychologists, the new code draws attention to this issue and provides explicit guidance as, for example, when they are reminded of the need to communicate in plain language or, where relevant, to use interpreters. Psychologists are reminded of the huge impact that psychological opinions can have on where or if people go to school or work, where they might live, and how they might enjoy their leisure time. The new code prompts psychologists to challenge historical stereotypes and practices about the disabled, reminding them to have regard for the dignity of people with disabilities, provide services to them in a caring and supportive way, and relate to them in ways that are positive and in keeping with the framework for social justice that we expect for ourselves.

The writing of these statements in the code was influenced by the fact that New Zealand at the time was undergoing a rapid transformation in the systems of care for those with intellectual and psychiatric disabilities. From the late 1970s, systems for the support of people with intellectual disabilities and/or with psychiatric disorders were moving away from institutionalized care toward the inclusion of such people in community settings (Webb & Gates, 1997). Coinciding with this rapid deinstitutionalization were media reports of abuses within institutional care, both historical and current. Psychologists' use of aversive interventions had attracted criticism from within the profession, both here in New Zealand and in other countries (e.g., LaVigna & Donnellan, 1986; McVilly, 2002). The concerns arose from evidence that aversive interventions do not achieve sustained change, ethical issues involved in subjecting individuals to pain and/or discomfort, and absence of consent to the procedures by the individuals concerned and/or their guardians (Webb & Gates, 1977). From the late 1980s legislation had been introduced (e.g., Mental Health [Compulsory Assessment and Treatment] Act, 1992; Protection of Personal and Property Rights Act, 1988) that recognized that people who have an intellectual disability or psychiatric disorder have rights and responsibilities similar to other citizens. No longer could procedures be carried out with only the consent of institutional authorities (Knight & Linscott, 1997; Webb & Gates, 1997). Poor psychological assessments that may have contributed to some individuals being placed in inappropriate residential or remedial programs also came under close scrutiny. The presence on the Working Party of Olive Webb, a senior psychologist whose career had involved working with people with disabilities, helped the Working Party retain a focus on this population and the practice of psychologists working with such individuals and their families.

No distinction was made between adults and children in the 1986 code of ethics. Although most of the ethical issues addressed in the new code relate to both adults and children, children are regarded as a specific client/research group requiring special consideration. The code recognizes that children are a vulnerable population because of the developing nature of cognitive functioning, their developing emotional maturity, physical size, and social circumstances. It explicitly states the responsibility psychologists have to advocate for and take care of children in ways that optimize their potential for growth and positive development. Along with differences in how children are treated, there are differences in how decisions are implemented (e.g., in relation to informed consent). The new code recognizes that a child's abilities and attributes change as they grow and develop, so that for example, a psychologist's actions regarding a young child will probably differ from those taken with an adolescent. Value statements concerning children include, "Psychologists recognize a responsibility to promote the welfare and best interests of children/young persons" (1.5, NZPsS, 2002, p. 6) and, "Psychologists recognize the vulnerable status of children" (2.5, NZPsS, p. 11).

In the "practice implications" advice is given that the interests and welfare of children are paramount and therefore have precedence over other considerations, and that psychologists have a duty to advocate for a child whose welfare or best interests are threatened. This echoes the "general principle" contained in legislation concerned with the protection of children and young people that states, "In all matters relating to the administration or application of this Act, the welfare and interests of the child or young person shall be the first and paramount consideration" (Children, Young Persons, and their Families Act, 1989, p. 6). The practice implication, that psychologists should be an advocate for children where needed, was influenced by the debate leading to the adoption of the new legislation in which mandatory reporting of child abuse was included in an earlier draft of the Act, but was dropped from the final legislation. Reasons for not adopting mandatory reporting included the argument that an educational approach rather than compulsion was more likely to encourage families to accept help and thereby prevent child abuse. A strong responsibility was thereby placed upon professionals working with children to be self-regulating with respect to reporting child abuse, and working with such families. The code seemed the appropriate place to emphasize a clear position for our profession to adopt.

The Working Party was also mindful that the New Zealand government had ratified the United Nations *Convention on the Rights of the Child* (UNCROC; Office of the United Nations High Commissioner for Human Rights, 1989) in 1993. That ratification has influenced both New Zealand legislation, which must comply with UNCROC, and the practice of professionals who interact with children. UNCROC recognizes that children are entitled to protection, but goes further to recognize that children and young people are to varying degrees autonomous beings with rights, and are therefore to be informed of decisions about their health and well-being and to participate in decisions that affect them. Thus, the ethics code comments that children/young persons' "wishes should be heard, understood, and taken into account, within the context of their needs, general welfare, and wider social environment" (1.5, NZPsS, 2002, p. 6). The implications of the relevant legal frameworks and the code for psychologists' work with children have been described in recent publications (Rucklidge & Williams, 2007; Williams & Rucklidge, 2007).

Conclusion

As described, the Code of Ethics for Psychologists Working in Aotearoa/New Zealand (NZPsS, 2002) reflects both a growing awareness among psychologists and other service providers of rights and obligations conferred by te Tiriti o Waitangi and the rights of those receiving services. That awareness is exemplified by the support for a formal translation of the Code of Ethics into Te Reo Māori, a project that has just begun. Considered in an international context this code can be seen as addressing some of the political and social commitments being made to indigenous peoples, although our government has only recently adopted the *United Nations Declaration on the Rights of Indigenous Peoples* (International Work Group for Indigenous Affairs, 2007). Compared to the code's predecessor, it also is more consistent with the recognition that, to be most effective, mental health and other services should be culturally appropriate.

Our sketch of its origins and development acknowledges the influence of those who sought to resist the destructive effects that cultural imperialism, privilege, power, and oppression have had on relations between social groups, and the consequent adverse impacts on individual well-being. Although this was not explored in the narrative, it also is compatible with a number of developments in the theory and practice of psychology, particularly those identifying psychology as a cultural product and a cultural practice. Members of the Working Party introduced this element into the process of development mainly through submissions and responses to them. Several authors in the recent New Zealand practice handbook (Evans, Rucklidge, & O'Driscoll, 2007), which is structured according to the principles of the code, have drawn out those links and their implications (Black & Huygens, 2007; Kingi-Ulu'ave, Faleafa, & Brown, 2007; Williams & Cleland, 2007). In those chapters the authors hint at possible improvements to the code that will come with subsequent revisions, as does the growing volume of critical scholarship about the nature and implementation of bicultural practice (e.g., Campbell, 2005; Love & Waitoki, 2007). We trust that future revisions of the code will move it more strongly in the bicultural direction. Work remains to be done in some areas. A particular example is that the focus of informed consent remains individualized despite an opinion expressed in early submissions from the NSCBI that for Māori and some other cultural groups, that focus may be inappropriate.

It was our intention to signpost the way for other practitioners and professional organizations wishing to make similar changes in their existing code. Our narrative described three threads wound into the new code: the identification of clients' rights to safe, effective, empowering services; the need for the discipline and practice of psychology to be more culturally appropriate; and the shift from a "code of conduct" to an aspirational document. From our perspective, introducing the first and last of those threads appears to have been reasonably straightforward. However, it is in relation to cultural issues, particularly the grounding of the code on te Tiriti o Waitangi, that we feel the need to emphasize particular features of the process.

First and foremost it must be understood that the NSCBI contribution was not obtained through a routine consultation. We have explained how the NSCBI came into being and outlined the work invested in the committee both by its appointed members and by senior practitioners and office holders of the NZPsS well before the code of ethics Working Party was formed. Central to the eventual success of that Working Party was the creation and maintenance of relationships in which there were high levels of respect and considerable trust among participants. Those relationships created a context in which NSCBI members were motivated to contribute and other psychologists were motivated to listen and engage seriously with what was said. As participants in both the Working Party and the larger struggle to ensure the NZPsS becomes effectively bicultural—a task that continues as we write—we were not aware that our learning to work collegially and to be trustworthy partners in the struggle was creating relationships that would enable the Working Party to be so effective. However, we now agree that the code would not have been realized had responsible relationship-building work not been undertaken.

In this chapter we have shown how social and political issues and events of the last two decades have influenced the development of our code of ethics. In particular this included bicultural issues related to the assertion of Treaty claims and the settlement process, sensitivity to the requirements and expectations of an increasingly multicultural population, and recognition of the rights of and responsibilities to vulnerable populations, including children and those with disabilities. What then are the current and anticipated issues that a future code revision will need to address?

In relation to the Treaty and biculturalism, the New Zealand government is committed to settling all historical Treaty claims by 2020. Is it possible that once this is achieved a substantial group of New Zealanders will believe that te Tiriti o Waitangi no longer has a place in the life of the nation. What are the implications for our code, in which te Tiriti is currently so central?

There is growing evidence that New Zealanders whose working life has been shaped by processes of market liberalization are showing significantly less commitment to egalitarianism and social justice. What are the effects of such changes on future revisions of the code?

New Zealand has traditionally provided social and mental health services through government-funded and managed services. The present government appears to be sympathetic to the privatization of services, as indicated in the recent announcement that some prisons will be "privatized." What are the implications for psychologists working in services managed in such a way, where the profit motive becomes part of one's working life? Related to this is the issue of the self-employed private practice. There have always been some psychologists who work in private practice, but not nearly on the scale of other Western countries. In the present political climate it seems likely that self-employed practitioners will deliver a greater amount of psychological services in this way. What are the implications of this for the code?

Arguably the most pressing international and national issues are concerned with global warming and sustainability of resources, in particular, the environment. In 2010 the NZPsS annual conference carries the title, "Psychology for a Sustainable Future." What will be the contribution of psychology to the huge issues involved here? And, what implications will this have for a future code of ethics?

These questions imply that psychologists and our code of ethics are primarily shaped by social changes in the wider society. The sustainability issue raises the question, what would be needed for psychologists to shape the wider society? And if we do have such influence, what are the implications of this for a future code of ethics?

References

Abbott, M. W., & Durie, M. H. (1987). A whiter shade of pale: Taha Māori and professional psychology training. *New Zealand Journal of Psychology, 16*, 58–71.

American Psychological Association (APA). (2002). Ethical principles and code of conduct. *American Psychologist, 57*, 1060–1073.

Anderson, B. (1991). *Imagined communities: Reflections on the origin and spread of nationalism.* London: Verso.

Australian Psychological Society. (2006). *Code of ethics.* In S. Morrissey & P. Reddy (Eds.), *Ethics and professional practice for psychologists* (pp. 172–189). Melbourne: Thomson.

Bass, L. J., DeMers, S. T., Ogloff, J. R. P., Peterson, C., Pettifor, J. L., Reaves, R. P., et al. (1996). *Professional conduct and discipline in psychology.* Washington, DC: American Psychological Association.

Belich, J. (1986). *The New Zealand wars and the Victorian interpretation of racial conflict.* Auckland: Auckland University Press.

Black, R., & Huygens, I. (2007). Pākehā culture and psychology. In I. Evans, J. Rucklidge, & M. O'Driscoll (Eds.), *Professional practice of psychology in Aotearoa New Zealand* (pp. 49–66). Wellington: New Zealand Psychological Society.

Blampied, N. (1993). Teaching ethics to graduate students. *Bulletin of the New Zealand Psychological Society, 76,* 4–5.

British Psychological Society. (2006). *Code of ethics and conduct.* Leicester: Author.

Campbell, B. M. (2005). *Negotiating biculturalism: Deconstructing Pākehā subjectivity.* (Unpublished doctoral dissertation). Massey University, Palmerston North, New Zealand.

Canadian Psychological Association. (1992). Canadian code of ethics for psychologists, 1991. In C. Sinclair, & J. Pettifor. (Eds.), (1992), *Companion manual of the Canadian Code of Ethics for Psychologists, 1991* (pp. 12–75). Quebec City: Canadian Psychological Association.

Chamberlain, K. (2007). Research ethics and the protection of human participants. In I. Evans, J. Rucklidge, & M. O'Driscoll (Eds.), *Professional practice of psychology in Aotearoa New Zealand* (pp. 163–179). Wellington: New Zealand Psychological Society.

Children, Young Persons, and their Families Act of 1989, 24 Stat., N.Z.

Corey, G., Corey, M. S., & Callanan, P. (1998). *Issues and ethics in the helping professions.* Pacific Grove, CA: Brooks/Cole.

Cram, F., & Nairn, R. (Eds.). (1993). Bicultural issues for psychologists [Special issue]. *Bulletin of the New Zealand Psychological Society, 76,* 6–46.

Davis, G., Seymour, F., & Read, J. (1997). Ethical dilemmas encountered by New Zealand registered psychologists: A national survey. *Bulletin of the New Zealand Psychological Society, 91,* 7–14.

Dixon, B. (1992). Ethics in evolution. *Bulletin of the New Zealand Psychological Society, 72,* 6–9.

Duirs, A. (2005). National Standing Committee on Bicultural Issues (NSCBI): A brief history. *Bulletin of the New Zealand Psychological Society, 105,* 12–13.

Durie, M. H. (1997). Identity, nationhood and implications for practice in New Zealand. *New Zealand Journal of Psychology, 26,* 32–38.

Evans, I., Rucklidge, J., & O'Driscoll, M. (Eds.). (2007). *Professional practice of psychology in Aotearoa New Zealand.* Wellington: New Zealand Psychological Society.

Health and Disability Commissioner Act of 1994, 88 Stat., N.Z.

Health and Disability Commissioner. (1996). *The Code of Rights.* Retrieved from http://www.hdc.org.nz/the-act--code/the-code-of-rights.

Health Practitioners Competence Assurance Act of 2003, 48 Stat., N.Z.

International Work Group for Indigenous Affairs. (2007). *United Nations Declaration on the Rights of Indigenous Peoples.* Retrieved from http://www.iwgia.org/sw248.asp.

Kingi-Ulu'ave, D., Faleafa, M., & Brown, T. (2007). A Pasifika perspective of psychology in Aotearoa. In I. Evans, J. Rucklidge, & M. O'Driscoll (Eds.), *Professional practice of psychology in Aotearoa New Zealand* (pp. 67–84). Wellington: New Zealand Psychological Society.

. Knight, R., & Linscott, R. (1997). Informed consent: Adults. In H. Love & W. Whittaker (Eds.), *Practice issues for clinical and applied psychologists in New Zealand* (pp. 19–31). Wellington: New Zealand Psychological Society.

Lammers, M., & Nairn, R. (1999). Codes and cultures: A resulting ethical dilemma. *Bulletin of the New Zealand Psychological Society, 96,* 8–11.

Lavigna, G., & Donnellan, A. (1986). *Alternatives to punishment: Solving behavior problems with non-aversive strategies.* New York: Irvington Publishers.

Leach, M. M., & Harbin, J. J. (1997). Psychological ethics codes: A comparison of twenty-four countries. *International Journal of Psychology, 32,* 181–192.

Love, C., & Waitoki, W. (2007). Multicultural competence in bicultural Aotearoa. In I. Evans, J. Rucklidge, & M. O'Driscoll (Eds.), *Professional practice of psychology in Aotearoa New Zealand* (pp. 265–280). Wellington: New Zealand Psychological Society.

Maxwell, G., Seymour, F., & Vincent, P. (Eds.). (1996). *The practice of psychology and the law: A handbook.* Wellington: New Zealand Psychological Society.

McCreanor, T. (1993). Settling grievances to deny sovereignty: Trade goods for the year 2000. *Sites, 27,* 45–73.

McCreanor, T. (1989). Talking about race. In H. Yensen, K. Hague & T. McCreanor (Eds.), *Honouring the Treaty: An introduction for Pakeha to the Treaty of Waitangi* (pp. 90–112). Auckland: Penguin Books.

McHoul, A., & Rapley, M. (2001). Ghost: Do not forget this visitation/Is but to whet thy almost blunted purpose. *Culture and Psychology, 7,* 433–451.

McVilly, K. R. (2002). *Positive behavior support for people with intellectual disability: Evidence-based practice promoting quality of life.* Sydney: Australian Society for the Study of Intellectual Disability.

Mental Health (Compulsory Assessment and Treatment) Act of 1992, 46 Stat., N.Z.

Moewaka Barnes, H., McCreanor, T., Edwards, S., & Borell, B. (2009). Epistemological domination: Social science, research ethics in Aotearoa. In D. M. Mertens & P. E. Ginsberg (Eds.), *The handbook of social research ethics* (pp. 442–457). Los Angeles: Sage.

Morrissey, S., & Reddy, P. (Eds.). (2006). *Ethics and professional practice for psychologists.* Melbourne: Thomson.

Nairn, R. (1995). NSCBI and the Canadian Code of Ethics. *Bulletin of the New Zealand Psychological Society, 87,* 13–14.

Nairn, R (2007). Ethical principles and cultural justice in psychological practice. In I. Evans, J. Rucklidge, & M. O'Driscoll (Eds.), *Professional practice of psychology in Aotearoa New Zealand* (pp. 19–34). Wellington: New Zealand Psychological Society.

Nairn, R., & Hyde, P. (2010) New Zealand, Psychology. In I. B. Weiner & W. E. Craighead (Eds.), *The Corsini encyclopedia of psychology* (4th ed., Vol. 3, pp. 1091–1093). Hoboken, NJ: Wiley.

Nairn, R. G., & McCreanor, T. N. (1991). Race talk and commonsense: Patterns in Pākehā discourse on Māori/Pākehā relations in New Zealand. *Journal of Language and Social Psychology, 10,* 245–262.

National Standing Committee on Bicultural Issues. (1992). Newsletter from NSCBI. *Bulletin of the New Zealand Psychological Society, 75,* 6–9.

New Zealand Psychological Society. (2002). *The code of ethics for psychologists working in Aotearoa/New Zealand.* Wellington: Author. Retrieved from http://www.psychology.org.nz/about/Code_of_Ethics_2002.html.

New Zealand Psychological Society Code of Ethics—1986. (1997). In H. Love & W. Whittaker (Eds.), *Practice issues for clinical and applied psychologists in New Zealand* (pp. 431–440). Wellington: New Zealand Psychological Society.

New Zealand Psychological Society. (1996). *Rules.* Wellington: New Zealand Psychological Society.

Nikora, L. W. (Ed.). (1993). *Cultural justice and ethics: Proceedings of a symposium held at the annual conference of the New Zealand Psychological Society.* Hamilton, NZ: Waikato University, Department of Psychology.

Office of the United Nations High Commissioner for Human Rights, (1989). *Convention on the rights of the child.* Retrieved from http://www2.ohchr.org/english/law/crc.htm.

Orange, C. (1987). *The Treaty of Waitangi.* Wellington: Allen and Unwin and Port Nicholson Press.

Pope, K. S., & Vetter, V. A. (1992). Ethical dilemmas encountered by members of the American Psychological Association. *American Psychologist, 47,* 397–411. Potaka, T. W. (2010). Legislation and the legislature. In M. Mulholland & V. Tawhai (Eds.), *Weeping waters: The Treaty of Waitangi and constitutional change* (pp. 83–108). Wellington: Huia Publishers.

Privacy Act of 1993, 28 Stat., N.Z.

Project Waitangi. (1988). *The Waitangi tribunal: Questions and answers.* Wellington: Author.

Protection of Personal and Property Rights Act of 1988, 4 Stat., N.Z.

Pryzwansky, W., & Wendt, R. (1999). *Professional and ethical issues in psychology.* New York: Norton.

Ramsden, I. (2000). Cultural safety/Kawa whakaruruhau ten years on: A personal overview. *Nursing Praxis in New Zealand, 15,* 4–12.

Ramsden, I., & Spoonley, P. (1993). The cultural safety debate in nursing education in Aotearoa. *New Zealand Annual Review of Education, 3,* 161–173.

Reddy, P. (2006). Cultural diversity and professional practice. In S. Morrissey & P. Reddy (Eds.), *Ethics and professional practice for psychologists* (pp. 102–112). Melbourne: Thomson.

Rucklidge, J. J., & Williams, T. (2007). Working with children and youth: issues of consent. In I. Evans, J. Rucklidge & M. O'Driscoll (Eds.), *Professional practice of psychology in Aotearoa New Zealand* (pp. 117–146). Wellington: New Zealand Psychological Society.

Salmond, A. (1975). *Hui: A study of Māori ceremonial gatherings.* Auckland: Heinemann Reed.

Seymour, F. (2002, July). *Cultural considerations in the New Zealand revised code of ethics.* Paper presented at the International Conference of Applied Psychology, Singapore.

Seymour, F., Nairn, R., & Austin, J. (2004). Comments on Tim Williams' paper "Setting impossible standards: The model of ethical decision-making associated with the New Zealand psychologists' code of ethics." *New Zealand Journal of Psychology, 33,* 33–34.

Sinclair, C., & Pettifor, J. (Eds.). (1992). *Companion manual of the Canadian Code of Ethics for Psychologists, 1991.* Quebec City: Canadian Psychological Association.

Sinclair, C., Poizner, S., Gilmour-Barrett, K., & Randall, D. (1987). The development of a code of ethics for Canadian psychologists. *Canadian Psychology, 28,* 1–11.

Steinman, S., Richardson, N., & McEnroe, T. (1998). *The ethical decision-making manual for helping professionals.* New York: Brooks/Cole.

Swidler, A. (2001). What anchors cultural practices. In T. R. Schatzki, K. Knorr Cetina & E. von Savigny (Eds.), *The practice turn in contemporary theory* (pp. 74–91). London: Routledge.

Taylor, J. E., & Dickson, J. A. (2007). Confidentiality and privacy. In I. Evans, J. Rucklidge, & M. O'Driscoll (Eds.), *Professional practice of psychology in Aotearoa New Zealand* (pp. 131–146). Wellington: New Zealand Psychological Society.

Thomas, D. (1992). A report from the National Standing Committee on Bicultural Issues. *Bulletin of the New Zealand Psychological Society, 73,* 8–9.

Tripp, G. (1993). Teaching ethics to undergraduates. *Bulletin of the New Zealand Psychological Society, 77,* 18–19.

Walker, F., & Seymour, F. (1997). Family court related complaints. *Bulletin of the New Zealand Psychological Society, 92,* 9–12.

Walker, R. (1990). *Ka whawhai tonu matou: Struggle without end.* Auckland: Penguin.

Ward, A. (1973). *A show of justice: Racial "amalgamation" in nineteenth century New Zealand.* Auckland: Auckland University Press.

Webb, O., & Gates, S. (1997). Informed consent and people who have an intellectual disability. In H. Love & W. Whittaker (Eds.), *Practice issues for clinical and applied psychologists in New Zealand* (pp. 43–56). Wellington: New Zealand Psychological Society.

Whittaker, W., & Seymour, F. (1997). The New Zealand Psychological Society. In H. Love & W. Whittaker (Eds.), *Practice issues for clinical and applied psychologists in New Zealand* (pp. 396–407). Wellington: New Zealand Psychological Society.

Williams, M. W., & Cleland, A. M. M. M. T. (2007). Asian peoples in New Zealand: Implications for psychological practice. In I. Evans, J. Rucklidge, & M. O'Driscoll (Eds.), *Professional practice of psychology in Aotearoa New Zealand* (pp. 85–102). Wellington: New Zealand Psychological Society.

Williams, T. (2004). Setting impossible standards: The model of ethical decision-making associated with the New Zealand psychologists' code of ethics. *New Zealand Journal of Psychology, 33,* 26–33.

Williams, T., & Rucklidge, J. J. (2007). Confidentiality with children and young people. In I. Evans, J. Rucklidge & M. O'Driscoll (Eds.), *Professional practice of psychology in Aotearoa New Zealand* (pp. 147–160). Wellington: New Zealand Psychological Society.

Appendix 1

TE TIRITI O WAITANGI
(Māori text from the 1985 Schedule to the Treaty of Waitangi Amendment Act)
[Translation provided by the Programme Opposing Racism
of the Conference of Churches of Aotearoa—New Zealand]

HE KUPU WHAKATAKI—Preamble

Ko Wikitoria te Kuini o Ingarani i tana mahara atawai ki nga Rangatira me nga
Victoria, the Queen of England, in her gracious consideration of the authorities and

Hapu o Nu Tirani i tana hiahia hoki kia tohungia ki a ratou o ratou
peoples of New Zealand, and her desire to preserve to them their
rangatiratanga me to ratou wenua a kia mau tonu hoki te Rongo ki a ratou me te
independence and their land, so that Peace may be kept with them, and
Atanoho hoki kua wakaaro ia he mea tika kia tukua mai tetahi Rangatira hei kai
Order, has thought it right to send an authorised person to
wakarite ki nga Tangata Māori o Nu Tirani kia wakaaetia e nga Rangatira Māori
negotiate with the Māori people of New Zealand their agreement to the
te Kawanatanga o te Kuini ki nga wahikatoa o te Wenua nei me nga Motu—na te
Queen's exercising the function of government in all parts of this country and the islands
mea hoki he tokomaha ke nga tangata o tona Iwi Kua noho ki tenei wenua a e
because a great number of her people has settled in this country and more will come here.
haere mai nei.
Na ko te Kuini e hiahia ana kia wakaritea te Kawanatanga kia kaua ai nga kino e
Now the Queen wants to set up the Governorship lest evils
puta mai ki te tangata Māori ki te Pākehā e noho ture kore ana.
should come to the Māori people and to the Pākehā living here without law.

Na, kua pai te Kuini kia tukua ahau a Wiremu Hopihono he Kapitana i te Roiara
Now the Queen has seen fit to send me, William Hobson, a captain in the Royal
Nawi he Kawana mo nga wahi katoa o Nu Tirani e tukua aianei a mua atu ki te
Navy, to be Governor for all parts of New Zealand which are given up today or hereafter to the
Kuini e mea atu ana ia ki nga Rangatira o te wakaminenga o nga hapu o Nu
Queen. And she says to the members of the Confederation of United Tribes of New
Tirani me era Rangatira atu enei ture ka Korerotia nei.
Zealand and the other leaders, these are the aforementioned laws.

KO TE TUATAHI—The First

Ko nga Rangatira o te wakaminenga me nga Rangatira katoa hoki ki hai i uru ki
The members of the Confederation, and all these leaders who have not joined in
taua wakaminenga ka tuku rawa atu ki te Kuini o Ingarani ake tonu atu—te
that confederation transfer to the Queen of England for ever the
Kawanatanga katoa o o ratou wenua.
function of government in their lands.

KO TE TUARUA—The Second

Ko te Kuini o Ingarani ka wakarite ka wakaae ki nga Rangatira ki nga hapu—ki
The Queen of England confirms and upholds for the leaders and peoples—for
nga tangata katoa o Nu Tirani te tino rangatiratanga o o ratou wenua o ratou
all the people of New Zealand, absolute authority over their lands, their
kainga me o ratou taonga katoa. Otiia ko nga Rangatira o te wakaminenga me
homes, and everything which they value. On the other hand, the members of the Confederation and

422 | AOTEAROA/NEW ZEALAND

nga Rangatira katoa atu ka tuku ki te Kuini to hokonga o era wahi wenua e pai ai
the other leaders give to the Queen the right to purchase those pieces of land which the owner wishes to sell
te tangata nona te wenua—ki te ritenga o te utu e wakaritea ai e ratou ko te kai
subject to the arranging of an agreed price between them and the purchaser
hoko e meatia nei e te Kuini hei kai hoko mona.
appointed by the Queen to buy on her behalf.

KO TE TUATORU—The Third

    Hei wakaritenga mai hoki tenei mo te wakaaetanga ki te Kawanatanga o te Kuini
    This is the arrangement for agreement to the function of government of the Queen.

Ka tiakina e te Kuini o Ingarani nga tangata Māori katoa o Nu Tirani ka tukua
The Queen will protect all the Māori people of New Zealand
ki a ratou nga tikanga katoa rite tahi ki ana mea ki nga tangata o Ingarani.
and give them all the same rights as those of the people of England.
Signed, William Hobson
Consul and Lieutenant-Governor

    Na, ko matou ko nga Rangatira o te Wakaminenga o nga hapu o Nu Tirani ka
Now, we the leadership of the Confederation of United Tribes of New Zealand,
huihui nei ki Waitangi ko matou hoki ko nga Rangatira o Nu Tirani ka kite nei i
here assembled at Waitangi, and we, the other leaders of New Zealand,
te ritenga o enei kupu. Ka tangohia ka wakaaetia katoatia e matou, koia ka
see the meaning of these words. We accept and agree to them all and so
tohungia ai o matou ingoa o matou tohu.
sign with our names and our marks.

    Ka meatia tenei ki Waitangi it te ono o nga ra o Pepueri i te tau kotahi mano, e
    This has been done at Waitangi on the sixth day of February in the year one thousand
waru rau e wa te kau o to tatou Ariki.
eight hundred and forty of our Lord.
[Signed by 43 Māori at Waitangi and around 450 further Māori signatures were collected by Hobson's agents across both islands on this Māori language text.]

    PROTOCAL / FOURTH ARTICLE
    E mea ana te Kawana ko nga whakapono katoa o Ingarani o nga Weteriana,
    The Governor says that the several faiths of England, of the Wesleyans,
o Roma, me te ritenga Māori hoki e tiakina ngatahia e ia.
of Rome, and also Māori custom shall alike be protected by him.

CHAPTER 30

Russia

Boris B. Velichkovsky *and* Alexander I. Yuriev

Abstract

Ethical issues are at the core of psychology, both as a science and a profession. By virtue of the subject, psychologists are often dealing with sensitive topics and their words and deeds can exert a profound influence on individuals, organizations, and societies. It is, thus, not surprising that the development of ethical standards and regulations for psychological research and practice has long been given considerable attention by psychological organizations on both the national and international levels. This is clearly documented by the recent development of two unifying ethical frameworks: the *Universal Declaration of Ethical Principles for Psychologists* by the International Union of Psychological Science and International Association of Applied Psychology (Ad Hoc Joint Committee, 2008) and the *Meta-Code of Ethics* by the European Federation of Psychologists' Associations (1995). However, the professional life of psychologists around the world is still dominated by sometimes very different economic, social, historical, and political factors, which often lend a very distinct flavor to the practices of resolving ethical issues in a given country. In the present chapter, the development of psychological ethics in modern Russia will be analyzed with special emphasis on the ideological, societal, and economic forces that have shaped Russian psychology during the last three decades. We will also present the *Ethics Code* adopted by the Russian Psychological Society (2004) and try to explain some of its features in the context of these influences.

Key Words: Russia, Soviet Union, transition, market economy, ethics, psychology, science, ethics code

Psychology in Russia experienced a very turbulent development following the dramatic ups and downs of Russian history in the 20th century. Psychology makes the claim of understanding and possibly influencing the perceptions, feelings, intentions, and so forth, of the people. This had made psychology the target of massive ideological interventions by the Soviet state. Thus, during the Soviet era, Russian psychology, being a very young and relatively immature discipline to begin with, was prevented from using a full range of options to develop the capacity to self-regulate according to the principles of scientific responsibility and priority of universal human values. This stands in stark contrast with the development of psychology in Western democracies, where academic disciplines are traditionally given a free hand to establish mechanisms for achieving high ethical standards. However, it should also be stated that the situation of psychologists was not unique to the Soviet Union, as ethical issues often emerged in Soviet science as a consequence of collisions between scientists' ethical obligations and the goals of Soviet policymakers.

After the massive political and social changes in the late 1980s and early 1990s, Russian psychology had faced a unique opportunity to reorganize itself as a science and a profession. This allowed the opportunity to impose high ethical standards on the professional activities of psychologists and to install a system of principles and mechanisms that would ensure compliance with ethical norms. It was also of extreme advantage at that time that Russian psychologists could draw upon the rich international experience of enforcing high ethical standards at the national level, usually through the ethics codes of national psychological associations. Indeed, some of the world's ethics codes were translated to Russian at that time and published in renowned Russian psychological journals, causing intensive discussions on the necessity and the content of a possible national code for Russian psychology (Eticheskyie standarty..., 1990; Professional'nyi..., 1990).

However, the reorganization of Russian psychology in general, and installing a system of ethical regulations in particular, had to be done under conditions of extreme economic strain, social and political instability, and overall decline in the country's morale. The necessity of ensuring one's bare existence in a country with a collapsing economy and paralyzed government made ethical considerations less important for a significant number of psychological practitioners and even scholars in Russia. Dubious psychological or quasi-psychological services were offered to the public, and violations of research and academic ethics in psychology became commonplace (Eticheskiye problemy..., 2002). Though strongly opposed by the majority of Russian psychologists, these negative developments, propelled by powerful economic and social incentives, are still in place today. Consequently, by the middle of the 1990s, the necessity of creating a system of ethical regulations comparable to those employed in countries with developed psychology became obvious to the Russian psychological community. At the same time it was an extremely difficult thing to do, as part of the psychological community in Russia became economically and socially dependent on conducting unethical practices.

A multitude of factors influencing the ethical aspects of research and practice in Russian psychology had instigated many, often contradictory, processes within the Russian psychological community, the aim of which was to find appropriate ways and means to solve ethical dilemmas with respect to the objective situation in reform-plagued Russia. The outcome of the processes involved is still unclear, despite the efforts many Russian psychologists have made to achieve higher ethical standards for psychological research and practice in Russia. Although the adoption of an ethics code by the Russian Psychological Society in 2003 marked the concern of Russian psychologists for ethical issues, there is still no full-fledged mechanism for enforcing it in practice. It remains to be seen whether the Russian psychological community will manage to overcome the many ethical problems still present in Russian psychology, which seriously undermine the overarching goal of serving Russian people and maintaining the integrity of the profession.

This overview of factors influencing psychological ethics in contemporary Russian psychology is organized as follows. We will reflect on the problems of psychological ethics before the breakdown of the Soviet Union, during the transition to market economy, and in modern Russia. In each case, the analysis of ethical issues in psychology will be preceded by the analysis of the political, economic, and social situation of the reviewed period. The ethics code currently adopted in Russia will be reviewed, and we will try to explain its specifics with respect to the objective situation Russian psychologists must cope with during their daily professional activities. Although the present review is qualitative in nature, mainly due to the lack of relevant empirical evidence on Russian psychological ethics, we will support our reflections with objective data as often as possible.

Psychological Ethics in the Soviet Union
Political, Economic, and Social Context

Soviet Union's communist party ruled the country from 1917 until 1990. The state ideology was based on a variant of Karl Marx's theory of political economy. The influence of ideology on all aspects of political, social, and economic life was immense, and the very artificial social order it produced had to be kept up by a complex system of surveillance and repression. Although the atrocities of the Stalin's regime became a matter of the past relatively quickly after his death in 1953, the Soviet state in its last decades still relied upon suppressing personal freedoms and real democracy. However, covert tensions were present in the Soviet Union, as it fell apart at the first signs of weakness, much to the surprise of the vast majority of Western observers and professional "Sovietologists" (an engaging analysis of the Soviet Union's decline is given in Hollander, 1999).

The Soviet Union had implemented a unique economic model, which was a direct consequence of communist ideology (Hanson, 2003). The economic model had many features that clearly distinguished it from other economies of the world. For example, the Soviet state had a much-reduced notion of private property, which made individual economic activities extremely marginal. Second, the Soviet economy was a planned economy, meaning that the market was completely regulated by the state according to a plan, which prescribed the production of certain goods and services in order to meet certain optimal criteria. A planned economy stands in extreme contrast to a market economy in which economic activities are determined by the laws of supply and demand in a self-regulated manner. Although a planned economy may be (and had been) an advantage under exceptional conditions (e.g., global crises, wars), in peaceful times it turned out to be less effective. Throughout the 1980s, Soviet goods were gradually losing the ability to compete with international products. The decline of the Soviet economy was also accelerated by the resource-consuming arms race with the United States. However, the decline was gradual due to the high price of fossil fuels, of which the Soviet Union quickly became a large exporter.

The social situation in the Soviet Union in the 1980s was marked by a misleading stability. Soviet citizens took advantage of cost-free health care and a competitive system of higher education. Unemployment and layoffs were "unthinkable" to the vast majority of the Soviet population (Eggers, Gaddy, & Graham, 2006). In the 1980s, the Soviet Union had about 12% of its population living under the poverty line (Schroeder, 1993), which was comparable to the poverty level in the European community at that time. The rate of homicides was stable and not excessively high, comparable, for example, to the United States (Pridemore, 2007). The level of psychological health provided evidence of relatively benign conditions of living; suicides and mental disorders were not more prevalent than in the developed countries of the world (Ivanova, 1992). In sum, life in the Soviet Union was reasonably good, and the welfare achieved after the devastating wars of the 20th century sufficed to make the majority of the Soviet population politically passive (Petrenko & Mitina, 2001).

Psychology in the Soviet Union

Russia has a very rich psychological tradition, which was, however, not always visible to the world psychology community (a "firsthand" account of its history and main ideas can be found in Brushlinsky, 1997a). Russian psychology initially developed in full concordance with international psychology. The first psychological laboratory was opened in Russia in 1885 at the Imperial Kazan University. A number of laboratories followed, and this development culminated in 1911 with the opening of the Psychological Institute at the Imperial Moscow University. Many leading Russian psychologists of the first generation had studied under Wilhelm Wundt, and there was a regular scientific exchange between Russian psychologists and their European colleagues. However, after the socialist revolution in 1917 the development of Russian psychology became quite distinctive from that observed in the countries of the West. (Velichkovsky, 2008).

The major factor that determined the uniqueness of Soviet psychology was ideological. All social sciences were obliged to comply with the basic principles of Marxist philosophy, and psychology was not an exception. Soviet psychology suffered a devastating blow in 1936 when a decree of the Central Committee of the Communist Party virtually prohibited all psychology due to alleged negative influence on the Soviet educational system (Brushlinsky, 1997a). It was only in the 1960s that psychology was given a second chance in the Soviet Union. In 1966, concurrent with the International Congress of Psychology held in Moscow, the first Department of Psychology was opened at Moscow State University. New departments of psychology opened at several major universities.

Consequently, Soviet psychology as an institutionalized science was relatively young, but could build upon the groundwork laid by the first generation of Soviet psychologists. Soviet psychology quickly became a developed scientific discipline in which many psychological subfields were represented (Lomov, 1982). Traditionally strong ties with natural sciences and mathematics lent some branches of Soviet psychology a strong quantitative flavor, which subsequently led to an increasing interest by Soviet industry and military. However, psychology as a social science was still influenced by state ideology and often a researcher had to balance the requirements of objectivity with all sorts of ideological constraints. Thus, much of the scientific discourse had become ideological, which significantly hampered the progress of psychological science in Russia (Koltsova, 1996).

Psychological Ethics in Soviet Union

It must be stated in advance that there existed no formal system for ensuring ethical behavior by researchers in Soviet psychology. Nor were there any kind of widely accepted ethical guidelines that would assist researchers in resolving ethical issues that might have arisen in their work. Thus, the ethics of psychological research in the Soviet

Union was heavily dependent on the ethical judgments of researchers themselves, possibly amplified by peer approval or misgivings. One possible cause for the lack of a formal system of ethics regulation is the absence of free public opinion in the Soviet Union, as disciplines often create ethical regulations as a reaction to public outcries (Adair, 2001). Such an arrangement for resolving ethical issues was, of course, insufficient to guarantee high ethical standards when incentives for unethical conduct were applied within the community of researchers. However, under the conditions of relative socioeconomic stability in the late Soviet Union, it fared reasonably well, as no major ethical scandals were documented during this time period.

Aside from the internal regulation of scientific ethics based on researchers' personal conceptions of their ethical responsibilities, there existed two external regulating factors. First, psychologists were formally bound by Soviet legislation, as well as by international norms pertaining to the proper treatment of human beings, which were officially ratified by the Soviet Union. For example, the Constitution of the Soviet Union (Supreme Council of the USSR, 1977) explicitly stated that the dignity of a person and his or her rights and freedoms were to be respected without restrictions (Article 57). On the other hand, the 1964 Declaration of Helsinki (World Medical Organization, 1996) officially served as a basis for Soviet bioethics and was relevant for psychologists involved in human experimentation. Second, and most importantly, due to the totalitarian nature of the Soviet state its representatives were practically unrestricted in interfering in all aspects of Soviet citizens' conduct. To this end, a number of means could be used, of which the local party committees were possibly the most known and feared. An institutional party committee represented the lowest level of organization within the communist party and had the right to impose penalties on the members of the institution. One of the penalties was to deny a membership in the communist party, which signified an end to career advancement, social isolation, and a withdrawal of economic resources. Thus, the Soviet state had an ultimate right to judge the worthiness of the conduct of Soviet scientists, which created an ersatz system for regulating ethical issues. Much too often, however, this system was itself misused to achieve unethical goals.

Article 77 of the 1977 *Constitution of the Soviet Union* guaranteed unrestricted freedom of scientific research. However, in practice this was not the case, as documented by several extreme cases of how freedom of scientific inquiry can be violated. Probably, the best-known example is Lysenkoism, named after Trofim Lysenko, a self-educated biologist who in the 1930s–1950s made the Soviet leadership believe his competence by massive data fabrication and political accusations leveled at his scientific opponents (Graham, 1993). The destruction of several branches of Soviet biology followed. Regarding psychology, a famous case of undermining scientific freedoms were the so-called Pavlovian joint sessions of the Soviet Academy of Sciences and the Soviet Academy of Medical Sciences in 1950–1952 (Brushlinsky, 1997b), which were held with the aim of recasting Soviet physiology, brain sciences, psychology, and psychiatry in terms of Pavlov's theory of reflexes. This paradigm was chosen by the Soviet leadership to be an appropriate materialistic platform in which a crusade against "idealistic" solutions of the mind–body problem could be grounded. During the Pavlovian sessions, leading scientists (including the famous physiologist Nikolai A. Bernstein and neuropsychologist Alexander R. Luria) were to publicly admit having made severe mistakes in their scientific work and to accept Pavlov's theory as the conceptual basis for their future research. In the 1980s the interventions by the state into scientific affairs became less spectacular, but state and party representatives had the last word if the ethical responsibilities of the scientists conflicted with their aims. The absolute dominance of the Soviet state in resolving ethical issues is clearly documented by numerous facts of psychiatric abuse in the Soviet Union, in which political dissidents underwent psychiatric treatments as a consequence of their political attitudes (van Voren, 2010). Thus, scientific self-regulation based on universally accepted ethical norms could easily be overrun by the situational needs of Soviet policymakers.

Retrospectively, several ethical problems were characteristic of Soviet psychology in the last decade of the Soviet Union. First, there existed considerable problems with the methods of conducting research with humans. The very nature of communist ideology made the ultimate ethical principle of preserving human dignity and securing human rights very much a lower imperative for Soviet psychology. A practical consequence of this was the complete absence of mechanisms for ethical review by the institutions where a research project was conducted. There were no institutional ethical committees, nor did there exist any formal guidelines for assessing the ethical value of research proposals or research submitted for publication. Another practical consequence of the reduced sensitivity to the welfare of the individual was that it was highly unusual to collect informed consent from research participants (the problem of introducing ethics committees and procedures for obtaining informed consent for psychological research started to be discussed publicly only in 2000s; see, for example, Eticheskiye problemy..., 2002). The usual practice was to inform the participant either orally or in writing about the general purpose of the research; however, exact prescriptions on how to do this were lacking. In particular, explication of the participant's right to refuse or to quit the research project at any time without negative consequences was often not considered important. It is not surprising, therefore, that there was a complete lack of publications discussing the proper practices of getting informed consent from participants (or even the necessity of it) in the Soviet psychology. This problem can be highlighted by the fact that even in the domain of medicine, which is markedly more sensitive to ethical issues than the domain of psychological research, obtaining voluntary informed consent for medical interventions was legally required in Russia only since 1993. More than a decade later, there still was a considerable debate about how to obtain the informed consent correctly and what its legal and practical implications would be (Varshavsky, Kitaev, & Ershov, 2008).

Today, the lack of ethical committees or established procedures for obtaining informed consent seems especially problematic, as a large amount of research in Soviet psychology was conducted using samples that were dependent on the researcher (students) or had otherwise limited ability to make a free decision about taking part in the study (children, patients, prisoners, and military personnel). No special regulations for handling these special populations are known from the 1980s; it can be safely assumed that no particular care was taken to reduce the potential harm of the psychological research/intervention beyond the common sense of the researcher and his/her ethical judgment. Taking part in psychological examinations was often considered obligatory as long as it was approved by the administration of the institution involved.

Second, there were specific ethical problems in Soviet psychology, which arose from the peculiarities of science–state interactions in the totalitarian Soviet state. As was noted above, freedom of scientific inquiry was largely compromised in the Soviet Union due to the dominance of state ideology.

Thus, a number of unethical practices flourished. For example, scientifically sound criticism was not tolerated if its target was affiliated with the Soviet bureaucracy; otherwise, the scientific work of a psychologist could be heavily criticized if deviant from mainstream Soviet psychological theories. Thus, the ethical obligation of a scientist to be objective in the interpretation of research data was often dropped due to ideological constraints, as breaking these norms almost inevitably meant significant social distress and economic hardship. The consequence was that Soviet psychology became very limited by ideology and constantly lagged behind the developments of international psychology; for example, it definitely missed the cognitive revolution and displayed a weak development in many important applied fields (Barabanshchikov, 2006). It is interesting that the case of Soviet psychology and Soviet science in general can today be considered as a clear example of why the freedom of scientific inquiry is not an ethical requirement in itself, but brings real benefits for the society in the long run (Resnik, 1996).

A third class of ethical problems was comprised of unsound practices in research and publication, which could be found not only in Soviet science, but also internationally (Goodwin, 2004). The most notorious example was the breach of publication merit, as all too often authorship of scientific work was given to those largely uninvolved in the creation of the publication due to a complex network of interdependencies between scientists themselves and even scientific institutions. For example, it was and still remains typical for a publication based on a PhD dissertation to have the doctoral student's advisor's name placed first in the authors list, much to the dismay of the student who had actually completed the study (Bogatov, 2008). On the other hand, plagiarism was less pervasive as the number of professional psychologists in the Soviet Union was relatively small and the modest volume of Soviet psychological literature made it easy to detect such cases (although plagiarism was not at all uncommon to the Soviet science of the 1980s; Fortescue, 1990). Soviet psychologists still mistrusted each other and were typically very reluctant to share primary data (e.g., as encouraged by the APA's 2002 *Ethical Guidelines and Code of Conduct*). No documented cases of data falsification are known, but it can be assumed that this problem was present in a state that constantly falsified its own history and statistics. Data falsification is especially hard to track in the works of Soviet psychologists, as usually few, if any, statistics were reported, making the detection of systematic biases in the results nearly impossible (for a recent analysis of statistics reporting practices in Russian journals see Velichkovsky, 2009).

An exception to the general insensitivity to ethical issues can be found in the field of psychological assessment. The only major handbook on psychological tests and measures (Bodalev & Stolin, 1987) devoted a separate chapter to the description of a project for normative regulation of test usage in the Soviet Union. The proposed norms loosely defined the requirements imposed on psychological tests, formats of their publication, and test users (i.e., professional psychologists and representatives of related disciplines). In particular, the regulations required a formal verification of a test's validity and reliability, and the usage of appropriate test norms according to the testing setting. Professional users of psychological tests were required to ensure the correct application of tests and were made responsible for the decisions made on the basis of psychological testing. Nonprofessional users of psychological tests were to follow the recommendations of a professional psychologist in the correct application of a test and acquire additional competences in psychodiagnostic theory if the usage of a test made this mandatory. All users of psychological tests were required to handle the test results confidentially, and had the obligation to inform respondents about possible disclosures of confidential information and possible decisions which could be made on the basis of the results. It can easily be seen that the project largely paralleled the ethical standards for testing that are ubiquitous in many codes of ethics, which already existed at the time of the handbook's writing. Indeed, the authors made an explicit reference to Sales (1983) as a major source of their proposal. However, the described system of norms was never formally instituted, and there existed no working mechanisms for ensuring that it would have been followed. Violating these norms and internationally accepted best practices, unqualified persons would often conduct psychological assessment, and compromises to test security often occurred when the general public received access to test materials.

Psychological practice was considerably less developed than psychological research in the Soviet Union. However, during the 1980s the necessity of resolving the psychological problems of individuals became more and more obvious, so that the field of professional practice grew (Etkind, 1987). There were two general forms of psychological help that were offered to the population: psychotherapy and psychological counseling. In the Soviet Union, psychotherapy was considered to be a medical specialty and its practice was legally restricted to trained doctors. Thus, the laws and ethical guidelines pertaining to all branches of medicine governed the professional activities of Soviet psychotherapists. Another form of psychological help was psychological counseling, the importance of which constantly grew over the last years of the Soviet Union. The scope of psychological counseling in the Soviet Union was largely equivalent to that in other countries of the world: familial and spousal relationships, personality growth, selection of a career, and so forth. However, counseling psychology was not taught formally at Soviet universities and a practicing psychologist, after getting a degree with a general qualification "psychologist," would usually acquire needed competences by self-study, peer instruction, and workshops and conferences. Ideally, this specialization would take up to several years and, given the relative simplicity with which a psychologist could begin to practice, the quality of professional services provided was not always guaranteed. Needless to say, no structured code of ethics existed for practicing psychologists, although a vast majority of them obviously adhered to the commonsense ethical norms, like the prevention of harm and maintaining confidentiality.

In the last half of the 1980s, an attempt was made to bring the situation under control by founding a section on counseling psychology and nonmedical psychotherapy at the Moscow branch of the Psychologists' Society of the Soviet Union (Butenko, 1988). A committee was formed within the section that was charged with assessing the qualifications of a practicing psychologist and awarding a certificate in the case of a positive evaluation. As Soviet work-related legislation did not permit a public organization to restrict the professional activities of Soviet citizens, such a certificate was not binding. However, it was assumed that the holders of the certificate would be given public support and countenanced by the Psychologists' Society. This attempt to create an internal system for licensing professional psychologists may have resulted in bringing about some ethical standards for practicing psychologists in the Soviet Union. But, the obvious naïveté of the proposal speaks volumes about the development of psychological counseling in the Soviet Union, and it has been quickly forgotten in the socioeconomic perturbations that followed the breakdown of the Soviet Union.

Russian Psychological Ethics in the 1990s
Political, Economic, and Social Context

The breakdown of the Soviet Union in 1991 led to extreme political, economic, and social changes in Russia. The Russian Federation as a new state with a completely different social order emerged. The old one-party political system was replaced with a multi-party democracy aiming at installing a fre -market economy in the country. However, the first years of its existence were marked by a fierce fight for power between the Russian parliament and the first Russian president, Boris N. Yeltsin, which was worsened by separatist movements in several Russian regions. The Russian state system was literally created from scratch, and it is not surprising that the result was, and remains, not fully satisfactory, being a complicated mix of Soviet rudiments, democratic institutions, and ad hoc solutions (Goldman, 1996).

The breakdown of the Soviet Union was mainly initiated by the collapse of the Soviet planned economy. The economic collapse was worsened by the collapse of the political system. The 1990s were a period of "shock reforms," through which an extremely liberal market economy was to replace the previous highly regulated economic model. The consequences of liberating the economic relationships were hyperinflation and massive layoffs. The young Russian economy had to carry the additional burden of substantial Soviet debts, to which new debt was quickly added. It suffices to say that in the middle of the 1990s there was more than a 50% reduction in gross domestic product compared to 1990, and despite some growth afterwards the Soviet level of production was by far not restored by 2000 (EBRD, 2004). The weakness of the Russian economy was clearly demonstrated in 1998, seven years after the beginning of the reforms, when Russia stopped paying its debts and the ruble lost 70% of its value against the U.S. dollar within half a year.

These economic troubles led to an unprecedented level of social and economic tension. At least a third of the population lived below the official poverty line (credible estimates as high as 36% have been reported; Commander, Tolstopiatenko, & Yemtsov, 1999). Average salaries of the Russian population fell to 40%–60% of the Soviet level, and consumer spending fell accordingly (Gokhberg, Kovaleva, Mindeli, & Nekipelova, 2000). The healthcare and education systems struggled for survival, being chronically underfinanced. The mean life expectancy fell from 70 to 65 years, with an exceptional increase in the mortality rate of middle-aged, working men (Walberg, McKee, Shkolnikov, Chenet, & Leon, 1998). There was a doubling of the homicide rate following the breakdown of the Soviet Union (Pridemore & Kim, 2007). The rates of suicide, mental disorders, and substance abuse increased sharply (Mäkinen, 2000). Following miserable economic and social conditions, the demographic situation changed with the birth rate lagging behind the death rate (Heleniak, 1995). High levels of social inequality characterized Russian society in the 1990s, with the vast majority of the population living near poverty versus a small, but extremely influential stratum of very rich (Gustafsson & Nivorozhkina, 2005). Russia also became famous for an exorbitant level of corruption.

Russian Psychology in 1990s

Following the liberalization of political and social life in Russia, the interest in psychology dramatically increased. This was caused by the fall of the ideological monopoly of the Soviet state, to which a natural reaction was a boost in nearly all the humanities. For Russian psychology this meant a revival of theoretical discussions, the establishment of methodological pluralism, and adoption of new paradigms and approaches that were quite distinct from those used before (Barabanshchikov, 2006). Another factor in play was that Soviet politics were characterized by a relative neglect of psychological considerations. In the Soviet Union, psychology was often considered an inexact science of questionable utility. Thus, although Soviet psychology was relatively well developed, in several key respects it was lagging behind the state of the discipline internationally. For example, in the Soviet Union social psychology never had the significance it had in Europe or North America. A series of human-made disasters (of which the Chernobyl catastrophe is but one example) and the breakdown of the Soviet Union itself made the study of beliefs, attitudes, and intentions of people worth considering in making social, economic, and political decisions. Thus, psychology became a respected science in the eyes of policymakers and entrepreneurs. Consequently, in the early 1990s psychologists started to be employed in growing numbers by the education and health systems, and by many Russian state agencies. For example, there was at least a threefold increase in the number of psychologists in Moscow schools throughout the 1990s and the beginning of 2000s (Rubtsov, 2006). Another example was the creation of a psychological service in the Russian federal penitentiary system in 1992 (Debol'sky, 2007), which provided psychological help both to personnel and prisoners; today, it employs over 3500 psychologists.

On the other hand, there was a growing need for psychological services to be offered to the general public (Stepanova, 2004). The rapid transition from one political system to a completely different one evoked a state of existential crisis in large parts of the Russian population. Furthermore, these negative effects were amplified by heavy economic strains and a complete failure of many social services that had been previously taken for granted. The time of economic reforms in Russia, as in many eastern European countries, was an extremely traumatic experience for the vast majority of the population. The overall situation posed a continuing challenge to the population, which had to cope with hardships given the failure of traditional values and norms of behavior. This created a standing demand for psychological counseling and intervention.

Following these trends, Russian psychology rapidly changed during the first half of the 1990s. From being an almost purely academic discipline with only four departments of psychology in the Soviet Union, it quickly became almost a mass occupation with over 100 departments of psychology throughout Russia, training thousands of psychologists by the end of the 1990s (Lyaudis, 1998). For example, the number just of educational psychologists in Russia increased by a factor of five during this time. The structure of psychological education also changed, with programs in psychological practice becoming ubiquitous and a priority for the vast majority of psychology departments in Russia. The major part of graduating psychologists went to work as practicing psychologists in the fields of psychological corrections, counseling, and organizational consulting; according to a survey from 1993, only 10% of psychologists in the Commonwealth of Independent States (CIS) countries reported research as their main professional activity (Nissim-Sabat & Tshedrina, 1995). However, the quality of training was relatively low, as qualified instructors for psychological practice were obviously lacking in Russia because the number of experienced psychologist could not cover the demand for psychological education.

This problem was especially important for the many private universities that had emerged in large numbers in post-Soviet Russia as an obvious reaction to the rigidity of the state system of higher education (Boldov, Ivanov, Suvorov, & Shirokova, 2002). In such universities, up to 75% of the staff were employed part-time, and the quality of education was correspondingly poor. The accreditation procedures for private universities throughout the 1990s were relatively easy to pass, and only in the 2000s did the Russian Ministry of Education begin to exert thoughtful control over the higher education system (Lukashenko, 2003), making accreditation much harder to obtain. In addition, the field of psychological practice was flooded with many unqualified persons providing psychological services without proper education, as the title "psychologist" was not legally protected in Russia.

On the other hand, academic psychology experienced the same problems as other scientific disciplines. Research was chronically underfinanced by the Russian state and financing by industry was extremely rare. The social status of a being a scientist fell extremely low, which prevented many talented youth from pursuing a scientific career. There was a significant brain drain within Russian science, with scientists leaving their occupations for commercial activities or leaving the country to continue their scientific work abroad. As a consequence, the quantity of high-quality research in psychology fell dramatically. For example, a recent search in the ScienceDirect database revealed only about 120 publications from 1996–1999 originated by authors affiliated with Russian institutions. This is roughly comparable to the scientific output of psychologists in Poland, a country with a substantially smaller population (Velichkovsky, 2009).

Psychological Ethics in 1990s

As before, the ethics of psychological research with humans in this reviewed period still suffered from the major flaw that there were no formal rules or obligations to ensure the informed consent of participants. Further, there still was no requirement for institutional approval in conducting research studies. The ethics of human experimentation was still based on the moral judgment of researchers themselves.

Because the ideological intervention of the state into psychological research had completely vanished, no ethical issues arose due to conflicts between a dominating ideology and interpretation of research findings. However, many forms of scientific misconduct became extremely severe as scientists had to compete for financial resources and/or social status under extremely difficult conditions. Plagiarism became commonplace, and its severity was amplified by the emergence of the Internet. Some cases were discussed publicly (e.g., see Kondrat'ev, 1996), but generally there were no means to hold the plagiarist responsible for the misconduct. Plagiarism was especially widespread in dissertations, and although official statistics state that the Higher Attestation Commission of the Russian Federation rejected only 10 of 35,000 dissertations on this ground (Bogatov, 2008), the actual number of faulty citation practices may be several orders of magnitude higher. Further, although there were no documented cases of data fabrication, the very sloppy reviewing policies employed by the majority of Russian psychological journals (Velichkovsky, 2009), as well as general lack of statistical expertise, left little chance for the detection of such cases. Violations of publication merit were still common and did not seem to be viewed as an ethical issue.

It must be stressed that ethical violations in psychological research were of minor importance given the extent of ethical problems in psychological practice. As outlined above, after the breakdown of the Soviet Union a very strong demand for psychological services emerged. The rising demand for psychological services was met with an insufficient number of trained practitioners and a relative lack of experience among formally trained practicing psychologists. There was also a rising sense of disillusionment in the ideals of scientific psychology among Russian psychologists/practitioners, as Soviet scientific psychology seemed to be incapable of handling practical problems (Etkind, 1987). Together, these factors created fertile soil for ethical misconduct by the providers of psychological services.

The low quality of education Russian practicing psychologists had experienced and their inability to stay abreast of modern developments in international psychology led to a generally low quality of services offered. This was worsened by the fact that psychologists had to act in a uniquely historic situation and were confronted with problems for which no ready-made solutions existed in their textbooks. Acquiring additional competences was difficult, as the Soviet system of continuing education expired leaving no substitute. It may be confidently assumed that Russian practicing psychologists in general were aware of their insufficient competences, but were forced to work in traditional ways because this was the only possibility for getting through the economic crisis.

However, the extremely difficult economic situation had a much larger impact on the quality of psychological services. As practicing psychologists, like any economic agents, are to make profit in a market economy, they often reacted by providing services for which there was the most demand. Thus, the structure and content of psychological services was partly dictated by the preferences of ill-educated clients rather than scientifically proven effectiveness. Consequently, many exotic and often dubious practices identified as "psychological" were used in Russia, and sometimes made it into the curricula of Russian universities. One of the most notorious examples is the ontopsychology of Antonio Menegetti, which found a large audience in Russia and was, until very recently, even taught at several Russian universities. In addition, advertisements for many questionable psychological and therapeutic methods often made exaggerated and misleading statements. For example, some providers of psychological services advertised in the Internet that the disputed method of holotropic breathing has the potential to help clients to overcome drug addictions and personal problems in an immediate and almost effortless way via recruitment of not further specified subconscious mental processes.

Psychological practice thus became a method for making a profit with little control exerted by the state or by the psychological community. As the title of psychologist was not and still is not legally protected in Russia, psychological and quasi-psychological services became offered by a significant number of persons with no or questionable training. Acceptance of bogus degrees and scientific titles also became commonplace. One factor which made this possible was that the Russian public generally mistrusted academic science, which was considered to be out of touch with reality and unable to provide quick and effective solutions to real-world problems. These widespread misconceptions were surely supported by some representatives of psychological practice. As a consequence, Russian officials and the public largely ignored experts' opinions that could have stopped professional misconduct. There was little demand for formal research on the effectiveness of psychological interventions; as a matter of fact, the statistical methods of meta-analysis, which can be used for this purpose, are still almost completely unknown in Russia.

Psychological assessment was another area with questionable ethical policies (Lubovsky, Peresleni, & Semago, 1997; Yudina, 2001). The problems of the Soviet period became exaggerated during the 1990s, following the widespread use of various assessment techniques in education, treatment, and organizational settings. Many test materials were freely distributed and their integrity compromised. Test administration and interpretation by incompetent users prevailed. The development of new tests did not meet the requirements of ensuring validity and reliability and, all too often, assessments were applied without respecting the gender, age, or social backgrounds of respondents. For many tests the norms used were those collected during the Soviet period. A specific ethical issue was the use of tests developed outside Russia, which, with only a very few exceptions, were translated and used in violation of copyright law (Balachova, Levy, Isurina, & Wasserman 2001). It should also be stated that the professional community of Russian psychodiagnosticians was well aware of the misconduct and tried persistently to counteract it; for example, some major sources on psychodiagnostics included detailed expositions of ethical issues (e.g., Burlachuk & Morozov, 1999; Shmelev, 1996).

Russian psychology in the 1990s was clearly plagued by severe ethical problems, which emerged when the control by the Soviet state suddenly vanished. Of course, these problems were quite obvious to the Russian psychological community, and the 1990s were marked by an intensive discussion of ethical issues in both psychological science and practice. For example, throughout the 1980s–1990s, several ethics codes of national psychological associations were published in one of best known Russian psychological periodicals, *Voprosy Psikhologii* (for instance, the ethics codes of Spain's Official Collegium of Psychologists and Germany's Federation of German Psychologists' Associations were published in translation in 1990). A series of roundtables were organized by the Russian Academy of Sciences, devoted to ethical problems in psychological research (Etika i psikhologiya, 1996) and practice (Eticheskiye problemy, 2002; Psikhologicheskaya diagnostika, 2000). During this public discussion, the obvious ethical shortcomings of current practices in Russian psychology were acknowledged. The need to develop an ethics code for Russian psychology was almost always stressed. However, the pragmatics of the situation in psychological science and practice made ethical regulation a problem of secondary importance and, given the low level of organization in Russian psychology in the 1990s, no obligatory ethical standards were accepted countrywide.

It is interesting that the need for at least some ethical regulation was so pressing that many local efforts to establish some sort of ethical guidelines for practice took place in the 1990s. Small-scope professional associations of psychologists and even single providers of psychological services and developers of tests compiled surrogate codes of conduct, which were usually made public via the Internet. Most importantly, several federal and regional agencies had developed internal ethical regulations, which were to be followed by psychologists employed by these agencies. Thus, in 1996 the Russian Ministry of Internal Affairs published a *Code of Professional Ethics* for psychologists in service of the Ministry (Stolyarenko, 2001). Furthermore, a code of conduct was discussed for educational psychologists (Eticheskiye printsipy, 1995), and at the end of 1990s several regional Ministries of Education issued documents regulating the professional activities of educational psychologists explicitly referencing ethical principles to be followed. However scattered, these attempts signaled the rising concern about the ethics of psychological practice in Russia. On the other hand, these regulations not only failed to cover practicing psychologists not employed by the state, but also were quite variable across Russian regions and state agencies.

Psychological Ethics in Modern Russia
Political, Economic, and Social Context

The political situation in Russia in the 2000s was characterized by the increasing centralization of power and by an overall strengthening of the state. A peculiar "one-and-a-half-party" political system was installed in the country with one dominant ruling party and a host of opposing, but tolerated parties. The political strategy of Russian policymakers was aimed at avoiding social instability at all costs while preserving the gains made by the new Russian elite during the transitional period (Shlapentokh, 2005). After the years of "shock reform," Russia had completed the transition to a market economy (which, however, was marked by strong state regulation, excessive bureaucracy, and a large share of "grey economics"), and experienced economic growth (Berglof & Lehman, 2009). Throughout the 2000s the Russian economy demonstrated average growth rates of about 7%. This development was initiated by a responsible fiscal policy, substantial foreign capital inflow, the relative weakness of the Russian currency after the 1998 crisis, and the very favorable prices for natural resources, which accounted for almost 80% of Russian exports.

The stabilization of the political and economic situation led to a pronounced improvement in the conditions of living as a consequence (Federal State Statistics Service, 2009a). There was a considerable reduction in unemployment (which sank from about 14% in 1999 to about 7% in 2008) and poverty (the proportion of population living under the official poverty line in 2008 was 18% compared to 36% in 1995). There was a constant increase in real incomes. Importantly, the inequalities in the distribution of income became much less pronounced, as a populous middle class had formed in the country (Gorodnichenko, Sabrianova, & Stolyarov, 2010). State expenses for health care, education, and science increased significantly: for example, state expenses for scientific research in relation to GDP almost doubled between 2000 and 2007, although they were still low to the developed countries of the world). The crime rate stabilized, although it remained relatively high (Gilinsky, 2006). The annual birth rate increased by 35% throughout the 2000s and approached the level of 1990, while the death rate showed a slow but steady decrease in the same period (Federal State Statistics Service, 2009b). Of the causes of death, murder dropped by almost 100% and suicide by 50% in 2008 as compared to 1995. Overall, the socioeconomic situation in Russia showed clear signs of improvement.

Psychology and Psychological Ethics

Psychology was and still is attractive to many students, and the demand for high quality psychological services is still in place in Russia. Due to better financing of Russian universities and strengthening of accreditation procedures, the quality of training and research in psychology has risen significantly. The number of highly qualified psychologists has increased steadily; about 750 doctoral dissertations were completed annually in 2007 as compared to only about 200 in 1996 (Feldstein, 2008). Although the practice of assigning academic titles in psychology was not entirely satisfactory (Tsypin, 2009), the revival of academic psychology clearly improved the overall situation in Russian psychology. One sign of improvement is the marked change in the way psychological ethics is taught to students of psychology. Evidence in support of this is the appearance of the first textbook dedicated to ethical issues in psychology (Protanskaya, 2008). Importantly, the latest federal standard for psychological education (MERF, 2000) makes explicit reference to psychological ethics and ethics of psychological testing as topics that should be formally taught in all accredited Russian universities (in the previous version of the standard from 1996, only ethics as a subdiscipline of philosophy was mentioned).

In the 2000s, the Russian psychological community managed to make clear progress toward self-organization and self-regulation. The Russian Psychological Society was formally created in 1993 as the descendant of the Psychologists' Society of the Soviet Union, and is the largest and most influential association of psychologists in modern Russia. It unites numerous representatives from both academic and professional psychology. The Society was created in order to combat the crises in academic and professional psychology after the breakdown of the Soviet Union, and to help Russian psychology adapt to the dramatic changes in the political and economic environment of modern Russia (Klimov, 1995). Today, the main aim of the Society is to promote psychology in Russia and to ensure high standards of psychological research and practice throughout the country (Velichkovsky, 2008). This, of course, presupposes a concern for ethical issues. Having withstood the troubles of the 1990s, in the 2000s the Society managed to reach a compromise over the introduction of a psychological ethics code in Russia. The ethics code was approved at the Society's Assembly in 2003 (Eticheskiy kodeks Rossiyskogo..., 2004).

Ethics Code of the Russian Psychological Society

Reflecting the severity of ethical issues in psychological practice, the Russian ethics code is primarily intended to advise practicing psychologists in maintaining ethical standards of behavior. It has a specific structure with a special emphasis on topics, some of which are uncommon for many national codes of ethics. For example, it makes a distinction, albeit cumbersome, between a client and a customer; it requires that a psychologist and a customer sign a written agreement that delineates the use of the findings obtained by the psychologist; and it pays considerable attention to the prevention of unfair competition between psychologists, as well as self-promotion by psychologists. On the other hand, the Russian code remains silent on other topics that are addressed by some national codes (e.g., financial and forensic regulations). These specifics were built into the code in order to better cope with the problems that Russian psychology faced after the breakdown of the Soviet Union. However, despite superficial differences with other codes, adherence to many major universal ethical principles, as formulated, for example, in the *Universal Declaration of Ethical Principles for Psychologists* (Ad Hoc Joint Committee, 2008), can easily be found in the Russian code upon closer inspection.

The Russian code is built around an explicit model that describes the professional activities of a psychologist. The model states that a *customer* (which can be a person, an organization, or the state or civil society) initiates the professional activities of a *psychologist* and finances the work of the psychologist. It is the customer to whom the psychologist reports the outcome of the work once completed. The object of the psychologist's activities is a *client* (who can also be the customer), and the interaction with the client produces *results*. Having been obtained, the results are communicated to the customer, who usually uses them to guide action vis-à-vis the client. Consequently, the code is structured as follows: (a) it describes the *requirements* for all entities involved (i.e., psychologist, customer, client, and results); (b) it describes *norms*, which regulate specific interactions between the entities; and (c) it describes ethical principles, which are broad ethical guidelines on which all involved parties should orient themselves. The code also incorporates an introduction and a concluding clause, which regulates the adjudication of alleged *violations* of the code.

Thematically, the code is built around several major topics, which were and still are extremely important for Russian psychology. First, the code is aimed at ensuring that high quality psychological services are offered to the public. This is done through the requirement that the title of psychologist be taken only by a duly trained person. Also, it requires the possession of sufficient professional competencies before entering into a professional relationship. Besides this, it is stressed and required that the effectiveness of methods employed by a psychologist must be scientifically proven. Thus, the code specifically addresses one of the most important ethical issues of contemporary Russian psychology.

Another set of regulations applies when psychologists disrespect the principles of fair competition. For example, considerable emphasis is laid on the prohibition against exaggerated and misleading advertisements about the methods used (e.g., holotropic breathing). It is also prohibited to misuse demonstrations via the mass media, as well as scientific and popular publications, for any form of self-promotion. During the construction of the code, it was even considered important to explicitly prohibit any actions aimed at "driving a colleague out of the professional field and employment" (Section 8.5, Eticheskiy kodeks Rossiyskogo.., 2004).

A significant portion of the code regulates the relationships between the psychologist and the customer. First, and quite atypically, the code tries to prevent possible customer misconduct against the client through the unethical use of the results. Furthermore, the code tries to defend the psychologist against being involved in possibly unethical activities of the customer. Lastly, the code is built to defend the psychologist against unjustified demands by the customer. To these ends, the code prescribes that, before entering a professional relationship, the psychologist makes sure the customer knows and formally agrees to the code's regulations. It is further required that, before the work is conducted, the psychologist and the customer agree on criteria against which the quality of the psychologist's work can be objectively evaluated in order to prevent or resolve conflicts. These regulations were built into the code as a consequence of repeated cases in which unethical customers exploited psychologists and their work.

The code also requires the proper handling of all professional materials created in the course of the psychologist's work. The code demands rigorous documentation of all activities conducted, which can support the conclusions made by the psychologist about the client. The Russian psychological community considered this a very innovative feature, as it opens an opportunity to further increase the quality of psychological service. However, the data collected about the client can be very sensitive. In Russia this means that third parties can easily misuse client data for unethical or even illegal purposes. The code views this as an extremely serious problem and prescribes secure storage and an obligation to keep client materials confidential.

Of course, the code also covers the relationship between the psychologist and the client. The code incorporates a separate principle of the prevention of harm, which in some form or another can be found in the many national ethics codes (Leach & Harbin, 1997). The principle states that no activities of the psychologist or any consequence thereof should endanger the health, psychological state, and material and social standing of the client. It requires that the work of the psychologist begin only after formal consent is given by the client, who has been properly informed about the aims of the psychologists' activities, the methods employed, future usages of the data obtained, and possible risks for the client. Interestingly, the code does not specify the way in which the client should be informed about the *customer's* involvement. The psychologist is obliged to make sure that the client's consent is voluntary and given after thoughtful deliberation; special regulations apply if the client is of reduced capacity to give consent. The psychologist is obliged to respect the dignity and rights of the client, as guaranteed by the Russian Constitution (Constitution of the Russian Federation, 2009). The same principle also excludes the possibility of entering personal relationships with the client, including sexual intimacies. Additionally, the rights of the client are secured by the principle of confidentiality, which requires that no data about the client be disclosed in a way that could be compromising.

Several issues that were identified as problematic for Russian psychology are less well articulated in the code. For example, there are no separate regulations for the proper use of psychological tests. However, inspection of the code reveals that it contains a number of statements relevant to testing. The code requires the usage of duly validated tests. It also requires that the demographic and social characteristics of the client be taken into account when interpreting test data. However, no specific provisions are taken to guarantee the integrity of tests and their not being (mis)used by unauthorized persons. Thus, one of the major ethical problems faced by Russian psychologists is only partly addressed and it is an obvious point of departure for future iterations of the code.

The code also makes several references to the ethics of research and publication. First, the principle of harm prevention obviously also applies in cases of human experimentation. Accordingly, the norm for the psychologist–client relationship states the necessity of properly informing the participant (i.e., the client) about the aims, methods, and risks associated with an experimental study. The psychologist is obliged to monitor the state of the participant and to stop the experiment if a stressful reaction occurs; however, the usual provision for the participant to have the right to quit the experiment anytime without penalty is not mentioned. Deception and covert observation is permitted under the condition of a full debriefing as soon as possible. The code also requires respect to be shown for the order of authorship based on contributions to the preparation of a publication (a chronic problem for Soviet and Russian science), and it makes an explicit requirement to properly identify the sources for any statement not originating with the authors, thereby countering the widespread practice of plagiarism.

Why Is the Russian Code of Ethics Like It Is?

To understand the specifics of any given ethics code, it helps to clarify the functions that such codes are to fulfill. The representatives of any profession share a set of core values, which they strive to achieve and which make the profession respected in the eyes of society and their own. In a professional context, psychologists are often confronted with ethical dilemmas; often they have to select between alternative courses of action which have different risks and benefits for others associated with them. Thus, professionals are often engaged in the process of ethical decision making as an immediate consequence of their professional activities (Pater & van Gils, 2003). Ethical decision making is a complex, multistage process (Jones, 1991) that can go wrong because of many factors. Professional ethics helps professionals to make the "right" decision; that is, it instructs them how to act in a given situation. The "rightness" of an ethical decision is at least partly determined on the basis of core values which form the groundwork of professionals' "conceptions of good practice" (Benson, Cribb, & Barber, 2009, p. 2223). An ethics code is a tool of professional ethics, which makes core values more explicit and often contains specific guidelines for fulfilling them.

The values of a profession may be threatened if its representatives consciously or unconsciously act against them. To prevent this, a profession that has reached maturity and is clear about its core values develops an ethics code, which (a) *suggests some behaviors* and (b) *precludes other behaviors* so that the fit between behavior of the profession's representatives and the values of the profession is maximized. This is needed as professionals' behaviors are obviously also determined by motivational variables other than the profession's values, with the former possibly contradicting the latter. An ethics code never exists in a vacuum, but is a tool with which to facilitate ethical decision making by professionals and should reflect the history and status of the profession in order to be relevant. Therefore, a code of ethics is often a reaction to specific threats to a profession's values, which are characteristic of the context in which the representatives of a profession have to operate. One consequence of the reactive nature of ethics codes is that they are not static, but subject to change that mirrors evolving macrosocial events and forces, as well as values held by the profession itself.

Thus, designers of a code have to identify threats to the profession's values and assign priorities to those ethical problems that should receive focused treatment given the economic and political context of the profession and its level of development. The construction of the Russian code is a clear example of this. Describing the transition to a market economy, we have tried to depict the extremely challenging situation in Russia after the breakdown of the Soviet Union. It was a situation of virtually complete economic collapse and failure of state institutions, after which a decade of totally unregulated "wild capitalism" followed. The almost unbearable pressure to advance economically and socially led to the rejection of the fundamental ethical maxim that one should not gain at another's expense. This was facilitated by the fact that, during the transition, the collectivistic orientation of Soviet society was replaced by an exaggerated individualistic orientation. Individual success was socially rewarded without regard to the means by which it was achieved. Unethical and illegal behavior as a way of securing existence and achieving personal and organizational aims became omnipresent in transitional Russia, leading to a quick degradation of society's moral fabric.

Applied to psychology, this meant conflict with and violation of specific ethical standards. First, psychologists (or persons assuming that title) were tempted to make gains at the expense of clients/customers by providing low quality services. In this vein, scientifically sound methods were applied after insufficient training or even without any training. Moreover, methods were applied that lacked proper scientific justification. This state of affairs was promoted by the fact that, as outlined before, psychological practice was less developed in the Soviet Union, which had left Russian psychology and the Russian public disoriented about the "gold standards" to be used in applied settings. All this created numerous opportunities for incompetent psychologists to operate freely in Russia, and these opportunities were realized to an alarming extent. Also, the style of advertising used by psychologists was extremely aggressive, which was characteristic of the Russian economy generally, thus impeding clients' ability to make reasonable judgments about psychologists' competences.

Second, psychologists were tempted to misuse and mistreat their colleagues to achieve their aims. In psychological research and teaching, this meant that the results and writings of others were appropriated without due reference. This was extremely problematic as entire monographs were, and still are, published that are mainly a compilation of various non-cited Russian and foreign sources. In psychological practice, the ethics of psychologist–psychologist interactions were severely compromised by recurring battles over the methods used, with unfair accusations of unsound practices. In addition, the enormous economic and bureaucratic costs associated with running a practice forced Russian psychologists to establish joint practices, which opened additional possibilities for the exploitation of colleagues.

Finally, gains could be achieved by third parties through the misuse of psychologists and the results of their work. These third parties included unethical customers who would try to influence the ethics of the psychologist–client relationship. Customers could use the findings gathered by a psychologist to take unethical/illegal actions against the clients who, for example, were employed by the customer. One specific instance of this problem was when a customer representing a political entity would try to influence public opinion by misrepresenting the results of a psychologist's study. Russian psychologists were confronted with numerous situations that presented them with the ethical dilemma of whether they are ethically responsible for the subsequent (mis)use of their results by others. Moreover, individuals, commercial and political organizations, and criminal groups could misuse sensitive materials and results obtained by a psychologist in order to influence that psychologist's clients. Due to the weakness of the Russian state and Russian legislation (e.g., laws regulating the use of personal data are being developed at the time of this writing), psychologists could become the target of immense pressure and face extremely challenging ethical dilemmas.

This is why the Russian code repeatedly stresses specific aspects of professional behavior, which in our opinion address many of the issues already presented. First and foremost, the code insists on using scientifically accepted and validated methods of research and practice, and requires their competent application. The application of these methods is to be governed by unbiased professional reasoning, for which a separate principle of impartiality was introduced. All this may sound commonsensical and, indeed, such a principle is absent in the ethics codes of many countries with well-developed psychologies. However, for contemporary Russian psychology the return to scientifically sound professional practices is at the crux of restoring the integrity of the profession and a positive public image. Consequently, the designers of the Russian code have done well by bringing this issue to the fore of the ethical agenda.

The code devotes considerable attention to the quality and quantity of advertisement in psychological practice. It severely restricts the use of professional certificates and public testimonials as means of inflating a psychologist's reputation. It precludes the use of mass-media publications and presentations, which have considerable influence over individual and public opinion in modern Russia, as a platform for self-promotion. Although the code lacks an elaborated position on several important issues typically found in the codes of other countries (e.g., multiple relationships, exploitation of subordinates and colleagues), it is extremely detailed about the regulation of permissible advertising to the point of prescribing the size of a nameplate a practicing psychologist can affix to an office door. While such regulation will probably be replaced in the future by the sensibilities of the plate's owner, its existence is indirect evidence of the intense competition for customers' attention and how easily this can lead to ethical violations.

The code also makes provisions for normalizing relationships within the psychological community, which have hampered the progress of psychology in Russia and created an unhealthy dynamic within the profession. It explicitly requires the due appreciation of others' merits, and quite a few sections of the code address the issue of appropriate criticism of colleagues. The code also extensively addresses the problem of forming and maintaining a joint practice, serving to fill a corresponding gap in Russian legislation.

Last, but not least, the code is cautious about protecting psychologists from being exploited by unethical customers and third parties. For customers, the code requires familiarity and agreement with a psychologist's ethical obligations. Furthermore, the code tries to formalize the psychologist–customer relationship by requiring that specific work to be performed should be agreed upon in writing. While this is rarely done in practice, this approach may give a practicing psychologist an instrument with which to delineate clearly the responsibilities and functions of all parties, and to determine their ethical basis before entering into a binding relationship with the customer. Also, the code clearly states the need for proper preparation and storage of materials, which should minimize the possibility of their being used for unethical/illegal purposes.

In addressing these important issues, the code gives less attention to other significant problems that are typically subsumed by the ethics codes of other countries. For example, the code contains no special provisions for the proper use of psychological testing, withholding records contingent on nonpayment, or proper relationships with agencies that fund research, which can be found, for example, in the codes of the American Psychological Association (2002), British Psychological Society (2009), and Federation of German Psychologists Associations (1998). This may be due to a variety of factors. For example, the lack of extensive coverage of ethical assessment practices is mainly because the vast majority of Russian psychologists are poorly trained in psychometric theory and its application. This is the result of the lack of a well-developed national psychometric tradition in Russia, due to historical reasons. Thus, the dangers associated with improper test use are still not fully appreciated by the Russian psychological community. Other ethical problems are missing from the code because they were not characteristic of Russian psychological research and practice. For example, the code does not try to regulate psychologists' relationships with funding agencies because research funding was relatively unavailable in Russia until very recently. Forensic activities of psychologists are not addressed in the code because Russian psychologists rarely perform these activities. A rather restricted notion of multiple relationships appears in the code owing to the limited experience of Russian practicing psychologists, who have yet to develop a broader formulation of such relationships and their potential for posing ethical dilemmas (e.g., a promise to enter a personal relationship with a person closely associated with the client). Other issues remain unaddressed by the code, as they are considered too "sensitive" in Russian society to be discussed openly (e.g., sexual harassment). There is complete neglect in the code of financial regulations, which surely will remain the case until individual economic activities become more regulated in Russia, perhaps through more mature and transparent legislation.

Given all of these details, how well does the Russian code fare with respect to other national codes? In comparing psychological ethics codes from 24 countries, Leach and Harbin (1997) identified 10 ethical standards that may approach universal significance for psychology. Ignoring the specific structure of the Russian code and inspecting its exact wording, it can be stated that the code matches to an acceptable degree with standards that pertain to disclosure, maintaining confidentiality, boundaries of competence, avoiding harm, refraining from false and deceptive statements, and informed consent to therapy and research (as defined by the APA's 2002 *Ethical Guidelines for Psychologists and Code of Conduct*). However, the Russian code fails to match the APA's standards on exploitative relationships, delegation and supervision of subordinates, and fees and financial arrangements. It is interesting to note that the Russian code seems to have grasped the core values behind psychological ethics: prevention of harm and preserving confidentiality (Schuler, 1982, as cited in Leach & Harbin, 1997). The Russian code also clearly addresses all four ethical principles on which the *Meta-Code of Ethics* (European Federation of Psychologists' Associations, 1995) is built: respect for person's rights and dignity, competence, responsibility, and integrity (although there are some omissions and inconsistencies at the level of implementation of these principles). Thus, the Russian code brings Russian psychology closer to the ideal of high professional responsibility, with a special emphasis on ensuring the welfare of clients and research participants. However, there remains a need to develop and refine the guidelines that cover the more mundane aspects of psychological research and practice.

Summing up, the Russian code of ethics in its present form is a first attempt to articulate ethical issues within Russian psychology at a national level. Its content clearly reflects the concerns of the Russian psychological community about the social responsibility and integrity of psychology in the country. The code addresses complex ethical issues and reflects a compromise among the many competing forces within Russian psychology. However, its very existence is a clear indication that Russian psychology possesses a set of core ethical values that are largely compatible with those of other countries around the world. It is also a sign that Russian psychology is willing to defend its values against contradictory influences arising from strong economic pressures for amoral behavior and the degradation of society's moral fabric. However, as a largely reactive response to the specific circumstances of Russian society, economics, and science after the breakdown of the Soviet Union, the code will not likely remain static but will evolve, hopefully incorporating international best practices in addressing ethical issues in psychology.

Conclusions

From the viewpoint of psychological ethics, two clearly distinct periods can be identified within the history of Russian psychology during the last three decades. Before the breakdown of the Soviet Union, ethical issues were less important in Russian psychology, due to the infrequency of psychological practice, collectivistic societal values, and relative socioeconomic stability in the country. This made ethical misconduct relatively improbable, and there was little pressure for the Russian psychological community to establish formal ethical standards. Additionally, in the Soviet Union questions of professional ethics were traditionally heavily regulated by the state, which left little opportunity psychologists to fashion and implement their own set of professional ethical guidelines.

The situation changed dramatically after the breakup of the Soviet Union. There was an ever-rising demand for publicly offered psychological services. Accordingly, the likelihood of ethical misconduct grew. Generally, professional ethics are compromised if (a) there is pressure for professionals to behave unethically, (b) societal values and reward systems fail to combat unethical behavior at the level of the individual, and (c) professional community/organizations fail to serve a gatekeeping role with respect to ethical misconduct (i.e., by not providing clear ethical guidelines and/or not implementing them rigorously). All three factors were present in Russian psychology during the time of market reforms, the consequence of which was massive ethical problems in psychological practice and, to a lesser extent, in psychological science. From a more conceptual perspective, the ethical situation in Russian psychology can be regarded as a compelling example of how easily safety needs can overcome the higher-order need for behaving ethically, much as Abraham Maslow had theorized.

The ethics code of the Russian Psychological Society reflects the rising concern among Russian psychologists about ethical issues in the years after the disintegration of the Soviet Union. The code was a product of intensive debate within the profession, and the year of its adoption, 2003 (nine years after the founding of the Russian Psychological Society), suggests that the immense economic and social incentives for unethical behavior required the national organization to apply significant effort to ensure adherence to high ethical standards. The fact that the code was adopted years after the first proposal had been made in 1996 clearly mirrored the socioeconomic stabilization in Russia in the new millennium. However, even under these more favorable conditions, it remains to be seen how well the code will fare in maintaining the ethical practice of psychology in contemporary Russia. Without functional mechanisms for its enforcement, without being firmly rooted in society's reward systems, and without being supported by legislation, a code of ethics remains what it actually is: a manifesto of abstract values which are quickly forgotten in the pragmatics of professional life.

The development of psychological ethics in Russia makes a strong case for the dependence of psychological ethics on political and socioeconomic factors. In examining this dependence, many issues and topics are worthy of continued investigation:

- How does the political system of a country affect psychological ethics?
- What are the interactions between state ideology, scientific ethics, and psychological ethics?
- Can an established ethics code assist a psychological community in combating unethical political and/or ideological intrusion?
- Is it altogether possible for a profession to develop a sophisticated ethics code under the conditions of political and/or ideological interventions?
- What is the dependence of psychological ethics on society's ethics, values, and norms? In particular, how does a transition from a collectivistic to an individualistic society affect psychological ethics?
- How can a psychological community prevent ethical misconduct in psychology under the conditions of economic strain? Can an ethics code be instrumental in this respect? What key issues should it address in order to be effective?
- Is there a threshold of economic strain beyond which ethical misconduct is likely to occur on a large scale? Are countries with developed psychologies more resistant to widespread ethical infractions than those with less developed psychologies?
- What are the effects of globalization on psychological ethics and ethics code development?

These questions are not merely of theoretical value. It can surely be expected in the future that some countries in the world will be subject to transitional processes; furthermore, no national economy, as well as world's economy as a whole, is entirely free from the risk of recession. Given the fact that many national psychologies are less developed, psychology in these countries may experience substantial levels of ethical violations at some point in the future, much as Russia experienced throughout the 1990s. By explicating the interactions between psychological ethics, politics, economics, and society, the international psychological community will become more informed as to how to assist national psychological organizations in reducing ethical misconduct in their countries.

References

Ad Hoc Joint Committee. (2008). Universal declaration of ethical principles for psychologists. Retrieved fromhttp://www.am.org/iupsys/resources/ethics/univdecl2008.html .

Adair, J. G. (2001). Ethics of psychological research: New policies, continuing issues, new concerns. *Canadian Psychology, 42*, 25–37.

American Psychological Association. (2002). Ethical guidelines for psychologists and code of conduct. *American Psychologist, 47*, 1597–1611.

Balachova, T. N., Levy, S., Isurina, G. L., & Wasserman, L. I. (2001). Medical psychology in Russia. *Journal of Clinical Psychology in Medical Settings, 8*, 1–68.

Barabanshchikov, V. A. (2006). Russian psychology at the crossroads. In Q. Jing, M. R. Rosenzweig, G. d'Ydewalle, H. Zhang, H-C. Chen, & K. Zhang (Eds.), *Progress in psychological science* (pp. 417–431). Hove, UK: Psychology Press.

Benson A., Cribb, A., & Barber, N. (2009). Understanding pharmacists' values: A qualitative study of ideals and dilemmas in UK pharmacy practice. *Social Science and Medicine, 68*, 2223–2230.

Berglof, E., & Lehman, A. (2009). Sustaining Russia's growth: The role of financial reform. *Journal of Comparative Economics, 37*, 198–206.

Bodalev, A. A., & Stolin, V. V. (1987). *Obshaya psikhodiagnostika* [General psychdiagnostics]. Moscow: Moscow State University.

Bogatov, V. V. (2008). Etika v nauchnoy deyatel'nosti [Ethics in scientific work]. *Vestnik DVO RAN, 1*, 144–157.

Boldov, O. N., Ivanov, V. N., Suvorov, A. V., & Shirokova, T. K. (2002). Dinamika i strktura sfery obrazovaniya v Rossii v 90-e gody [Dynamics and structure of Russian education in 1990s]. *Problemy Prognozirovaiya, 4*, 122–133.

British Psychological Society. (2009). *Code of ethics and conduct*. Leicester, UK: British Psychological Society.

Brushlinsky, A. V. (Ed.). (1997a). *Russian psychology of the XXth century: Problems, theories and histories*. Moscow: Russian Academy of Sciences Press.

Brushlinsky, A. V. (1997b). The Pavlovian sessions of the two academies. *European Psychologist, 2*, 102–105.

Burlachuk, L. F., & Morozov, S.M. (1999). *Slovar'-spravochnik po psikhodiagnostike* [Dictionary and handbook of psychodiagnostics]. St. Petersburg: Piter Press.

Butenko, G. P. (1988). Prakticheskaya konsul'tativnaya psikhologiya [Practical consultative psychology]. *Voprosy Psikhologii, 88*, 180–181.

Commander, S., Tolstopiatenko, A., & Yemtsov, R. (1999). Channels of redistribution: Inequality and poverty in the Russian transition. *Economics of Transition, 7*(2), 411–447.

Constitution of the Russian Federation. Official Edition. (2009). Moscow: Yuridicheskaya literature.

Debol'sky, M. G. (2007). 15 let psikhologicheskoy sluzhbe UIS [15 years of the psychological service of the criminal-penitentiary system]. In *Profilaktika negativnyh yavleniy v uchrezhdeniyakh i organakh ugolovno-ispolnitel'noi sistemy* [Prophylactics of negative phenomena in establishments and institutions of the criminal-penitentiary system] (pp. 12–21). Moscow: FSIN.

EBRD. (2004). *Transition report 2004: Infrastructure*. London: European Bank of Reconstruction and Development.

Eggers, A., Gaddy, C., & Graham, C. (2006). Well-being and unemployment in Russia in the 1990s: Can society's suffering be individuals' solace? *Journal of Socio-Economics, 35*, 209–242.

Eticheskiy kodeks Rossiyskogo psukhologicheskogo obshestva [Ethics code of the Russian Psychological Society]. (2004). *Rossiyskiy Psikhologicheskiy Zhurnal, 1*, 37–54.

Eticheskiye problemy psikhologicheskikh issledovaniy i psikhologicheskoi praktiki [Ethical problems in psychological research and practice]. (2002). *Chelovek, 5*, 5–20 and *6*, 5–20.

Eticheskiye printsipy i pravila raboty prakticheskogo psikhologa [Ethical principles and rules in the work of practical psychologist]. (1995). *Vestnik obrazovaniya, 7*, 37–40.

Eticheskiye standarty dlya psikhologa, Madrid, Ispaniya, 1987 [Ethical standards for psychologists. Madrid, Spain, 1987], (1990). *Voprosy psikhologii, 5*, 158–162.

Etika i psikhologiya: Urovni sopryazheniya [Ethics and psychology: Levels of conjugation]. (1996). *Chelovek, 2*, 5–16.

Etkind, A. M. (1987). Psikhologiya prakticheskaya i akademicheskaya: Raskhozhdeniye kognitivnykh struktur vnutri professional'nogo soznaniya [Practical and academic psychology: Diverging cognitive structures within the professional consciousness]. *Voprosy Psikhologii, 6*, 20–30.

European Federation of Psychologists' Associations. (1995). *Meta-code of ethics* (revised). Retrieved from http://www.efpa.eu/.

Fortescue, S. (1990). Soviet science under Gorbachev. *Prometheus, 8*, 221–239.

Federation of German Psychologists Association. (1998). Ethische Richtlinien des DGPs und des BDP [Ethical guidelines of GDPs and BDP]. Retrieved from http://www.dgps.de/dgps/aufgaben/003.php.

Federal State Statistics Service. (2009a). *Russian statistical yearbook*. Moscow: Author.

Federal State Statistics Service. (2009b). *Russian demographic yearbook*. Federal State Statistics Service. Moscow: Author.

Feldstein, D. I. (2008). O sostoyanii i putyakh povysheniya kachestva dissertatsionnykh issledovaniy po pedagogike i psikhologii [On current quality of dissertations in pedagogics and psychology and ways to improve it]. *Uchenye zapiski, 2*(36), 5–15.

Gilinsky, Y. (2006). Crime in contemporary Russia. *European Journal of Criminology, 3*, 259–292.

Gokhberg, L, Kovaleva, N., Mindeli, L., & Nekipelova, E. (2000). *Qualified manpower in Russia*. Moscow: Center for Science Research and Statistics.

Goldman M. I. (1996). *Lost opportunity: what has made economic reform in Russia so difficult*. New York: W.W. Norton & Company.

Goodwin, C. J. (2004). *Research in psychology: Methods and design* (4th ed.). Hoboken, NJ: Wiley.

Gorodnichenko, Yu., Sabrianova, P. K., & Stolyarov, D. (2010). Inequality and volatility moderation in Russia: Evidence from micro-panel data on consumption and income. *Review of Economic Dynamics, 13*, 209–237.

Graham, L. R. (1993). Stalinist ideology and the Lysenko affair. In L. R. Graham (Ed.), *Science in Russia and the Soviet Union* (pp. 121–136). Cambridge: Cambridge University Press.

Gustafsson, B., & Nivorozhkina, L. (2005). How and why transition made income inequality increase in urban Russia: A local study. *Journal of Comparative Economics, 33*, 772–787.

Heleniak, T. (1995). Economic transition and demographic change in Russia: 1989–1995. *Post-Soviet Geography, 36*, 446–458.

Hollander, P. (1999). *Political will and personal belief: The decline and fall of Soviet communism*. New Haven, CT: Yale University Press.

Hanson, P. (2003). *The rise and fall of the Soviet economy: An economic history of the USSR from 1945*. London: Longman.

Ivanova, A. E. (1992). Sotsial'naya sreda i psikhicheskoye zdorovye naseleniya [Social environment and population's mental health]. *Sotsiologicheskiye issledovaiya, 1*, 19–31.

Jones, T. M. (1991). Ethical decision-making by individuals in organizations: An issue-contingent model. *Academy of Management Review, 16*, 366–395.

Klimov, E. A. (1995). Soobshchestvo psikhologov v Rossii: Sushchee i dolzhnoe [The community of psychologists in Russia: What is and what ought to be]. *Voprosy Psikhologii, 2*, 118–124.

Koltsova, V. (1996). Ideological and scientific discourse in Soviet psychological science. In V. Koltsova, Yu. M. Oleinik, A. R. Gilgen, & K. N. Gilgen (Eds.), *Post-Soviet perspectives on Russian psychology* (pp. 60–70). Westport, CT: Greenwood.

Kondrat'ev, M.Y. (1996). Ostorozhno: Plagiat [Attention: Plagiarism]. *Voprosy Psikhologii, 96*, 154.

Leach, M. M., & Harbin J. J. (1997). Psychological ethics codes: A comparison of twenty-four countries. *International Journal of Psychology, 32*, 181–192.

Lomov, B. F. (1982). Soviet psychology: Its historical origins and contemporary status. *American Psychologist, 37*(5), 580–586.

Lubovsky, V. I., Peresleni, L. I., & Semago, M. M. (1997). O publikatsiyakh psikhodiagnosticheskikh materialov [On publication of psychodiagnostic materials]. *Voprosy Psikhologii, 1*, 133–137.

Lukashenko, M. (2003). Rynok obrazovatel'nykh uslug: 10 let spustya [The market of educational services: 10 years after]. *Vysshee Obrazovaniye v Rossii, 1*, 32–40.

Lyaudis, V. Y. (1998). Psikhologicheskoye obrasovaniye v Rossii: Novye orientiry i tseli [Psychological education in Russia: New landmarks and goals]. *Voprosy Psikhologii, 5*, 148–153.

Mäkinen, H. (2000). East European transition and suicide mortality. *Social Science and Medicine, 51*, 1405–1420.

MERF. (2000). State educational standard for higher professional education, Speciality 020400 "Psychology." Qualification: Psychologist. Lecturer in psychology. Moscow: Russian Federation, Ministry of Education.

Nissim-Sabat, D., & Tshedrina, E. V. (1995). Psikhologi SNG: Anketa zhurnala Voprosy Psikhologii [Psychologists in CIS: The survey by the journal Voprosy Psikhologii]. *Voprosy Psikhologii, 3*, 151–153.

Pater, A., & van Gils, A. (2003). Stimulating ethical decision-making in a business-context: Effects of ethical and professional codes. *European Management Journal, 21*, 762–772.

Petrenko, V. F., & Mitina, O. V. (2001). A psychosemantic analysis of the dynamics of Russian life quality. *European Psychologist, 6*, 1–14.

Pridemore, W. A. (2007). *Ruling Russia: Law, crime and justice in a changing society*. Lanham, MD: Rowman and Littlefield.

Pridemore, W. A., & Kim, S. W. (2007). Socioeconomic change and homicide in a transitional society. *Sociological Quarterly, 48*, 229–251.

Professional'nyi kodeks etiki dlya psikhologov. Bonn, FRG, 1986 [Professional ethics code for psychologists. Bonn, FRG, 1986]. (1990). *Voprosy Psikhologii, 2*, 148–153.

Protanskaya, E. S. (2008). *Professional'naya etika psikhologa* [Professional ethics of psychologist]. St. Petersburg: St. Petersburg State University Press.

Psikhologicheskaya diagnostika v sisteme obrazovaniya i prav rebenka [Psychological diagnostics in educational system and child's rights]. (2000). *Chelovek, 6*, 67–75.

Resnik, D. (1996). Social epistemology and the ethics of research. *Studies in History and Philosophy of Science, 27*(4), 565–586.

Rubtsov, V. V. (2006). Sluzhba prakticheskoi psikhologii obrazovaniya: Sovremennoye sostoyanie i perspektivy [The service of practical educational psychology: Actual state and perspectives]. *Voprosy Sovremennoi Pediatrii, 5*(5), Suppl. 1), 45–48.

Sales, B. D. (1983). *Professional psychologist's handbook*. New York: Plenum.

Schroeder, G. E. (1993). Regional economic disparities, Gorbachev's policies, and the disintegration of the Soviet Union. In R. E. Kaufman & J. P Hardt (Eds.), *The former Soviet Union in transition* (pp. 121–145). New York: M. E. Sharp.

Shlapentokh, V. (2005). The short time horizon in the Russian mind. *Communist and Post-Communist Studies, 38,* 1–24.

Shmelev, A. G. (1996). *Osnovy psikhodiagnostiki* [Basics of psychodiagnostics]. Moscow and Rostov-on-Don: Phoenix.

Stepanova, M. A. (2004). *Prakticheskaya psikhologiya obrazovaniya: Protivorechiya, paradoksy, persperktivy* [Practical educational psychology: Contradictions, paradoxes, perspectives]. Voprosy Psikhologii, 4, 91–101.

Stolyarenko, A. M. (2001). *Prikladnaya yuridicheskaya psikhologiya* [Applied forensic psychology]. Moscow: Unity.

Supreme Council of the USSR, Konstitutsiya (Osovnoy Zakon) Soyuza Sovetskikh Sotsialisticheskikh Respublik [Constitution (Main Law) of the USSR] (July 7, 1977) (enacted).

Tsypin, G. M. (2009). K probleme ekspertizy dissertatsionnykh issledovaniy v oblasty pedagogiki i psikhologii [On the problem of expert evaluation of doctoral dissertations in pedagogy and psychology]. *Mir Obrazovaniya—Obrazovaniye v Mire, 3,* 87–89.

Van Voren, R. (2010). Political abuse of psychiatry: An historical overview. *Schizophrenia Bulletin, 36,* 33–35.

Varshavsky, Yu. V., Kitaev, V. V., & Ershov, V. V. (2008). Dobrovol'noye informirovannoye soglasie patsienta na lutshevoye issledovanye kak eticheskaya i mediko-legal'naya problema [Patient's free informed consent to a radiological examination as an ethical and a medical legal problem]. *Radiologia-Praktika, 3,* 44–49.

Velichkovsky, B. B. (2008). *Psychology in Russia: Its past, present, and future*. Moscow: Russian Psychological Society.

Velichkovsky, B. B. (2009). Open access publishing: A challenge for Russian psychology. *Psychology Science Quarterly, 51*(Supplement 1), 147–159.

Walberg, P., McKee, M., Shkolnikov, V., Chenet, L., & Leon, D. A. (1998). Economic change, crime, and mortality crisis in Russia: Regional analysis. *British Medical Journal, 317,* 312–318.

World Medical Organization. (1996). Declaration of Helsinki. *British Medical Journal, 313,* 1448–1449.

Yudina, E. G. (2001). Eticheskiye problemy psihologo-pedagogicheskoy diagnostiki v obrasovanii [Ethical problems in psycho-pedagogical diagnostics in education]. *Voprosy Psichicheskogo Zdorov'ya Detei i Ppodrostkov, 1,* 14–20.

CHAPTER
31 Turkey

Yeşim Korkut

Abstract

The development of psychological ethics in Turkey is closely related not only to the development of psychology in the country, but also to the trends in psychology in other countries. On a deeper level, political and social changes in the world have influenced both psychology and psychological ethics. In this chapter, therefore, the main aim is first to provide an overview of the history of psychology in Turkey. Furthermore, the influence of Western psychology beginning in the early 1900s, the development of the discipline of psychology in Turkey, and the rapid and systematic development of psychological ethics in Turkey during the most recent decade will be presented. Finally, in light of these interwoven processes, a discussion about the future of psychology and psychological ethics will be provided.

Key Words: Psychology in Turkey, Turkish ethics code

History of Psychology in Turkey

Many authors (Başaran & Şahin, 1990; Sahin, 1997; Toğrol, 1981) agree that the beginning of the official teaching of psychology in Turkey dates back to 1915 with the establishment of the General Psychology Chair in the İstanbul University Philosophy Department by Professor Georg Anschütz. When Anschütz came from Germany, the Ottoman Empire was in the midst of the First World War. Therefore, though he taught some courses at Darülfünün University (which in those years was the name of today's Istanbul University) and helped in the recognition of psychology as a newly rising discipline, he had difficulty in finding students, and nearly all his students were male. This can be due to the fact that it was wartime (Basaran & Şahin 1990), the discipline was very immature all over the world, and that female university students were in general less in number in the Ottoman empire, as was the case elsewhere in that era in the world.

Though there is an agreement about this official beginning to the teaching of psychology, some authors (Başaran & Şahin, 1990; Bilgin, 1981) recollect that in the late years of the Ottoman period there were already many Turkish figures who had written about "the science of soul". These historically important authors, such as Hoca Tahsin and Mustafa Sati, are reported to have written in the late 1880s and early 1900s about pupil aptitudes and intelligence. Unfortunately some of these works had been written in the old Ottoman Turkish language, and are therefore not easy to read today. According to Bilgin (1981), especially during the First and Second Constitutional Era in the history of Ottomans (known as *Meşrutiyet* in Turkish), intellectuals valued social sciences due to the increasing social, economic, and political problems in the empire. As a part of a great desire for modernization, there were attempts to establish new schools and create a more contemporary society out of the Ottoman empire. There were cultural exchange programs with France and Germany, and, according to Başaran and Şahin (1990), this was the main reason for the invitation of Professor Anschütz to give lectures in Istanbul.

For the Western part of the world, and especially for Ottomans, the first two decades of the 1900s were trying years. After the return of Anschütz to Germany in 1918, the Turkish war for independence and the establishment of the Turkish Republic in 1923 took place. A new era began, which initiated a revolutionary transitional period from Ottoman empire to a republic. Through Mustafa Kemal Ataturk, new politics and a social period, which clearly and persistently valued scientific and industrial improvements as well as the modernization in the West, opened up for Turkey. These revolutionary changes, based on the encouragement and representation of women in each area of society and the acceptance of Western clothes and Western letters, created a rapid and strong permanent change at each layer of society. As a consequence, this climate welcomed Western scientists and encouraged the wish to attain similar levels in science to the developed and modern West. In sum, though it had begun during the Ottoman period, relations with the Western sphere of the world replaced the emphasis on the East and Islam, especially after 1923. Turkey could see the effects of modernity on science throughout the world during those years. As a result of this, the admiration of Western and European culture and the rise of modernity allowed the import of the science called "psychology" to Turkey.

In the following years not only Anschütz but also other psychologists, especially from European countries, contributed to the development of psychology in Turkey. Professor Wilhelm Peters from University of Jena, escaping the Third Reich, came to Turkey and established the applied psychology division in Istanbul University (Başaran & Şahin, 1990; Toğrol, 1981). Peters, after 15 years at the University, brought together pedagogy and psychology chairs, which were separate, and established the first experimental laboratory and edited the journal called *Experimental Psychology Studies* [*Tecrübi Psikoloji Çalışmaları*], which today exists under a new name, *Psychology Studies* [*Psikoloji Çalışmaları*].

Many Turkish scholars who had trained abroad came back to their homeland to share their knowledge. Mustafa Şekip Tunc, who studied in Switzerland and returned to Turkey in 1919, is considered to be one of the most prominent figures of psychology (Şahin, 1997; Toğrol, 1981), as is Mümtaz Turhan, who studied in Frankfurt and Cambridge (Toğrol, 1981). According to some authors, psychology as a discipline seems to have developed as a scientific study of human mind and behavior, with that emphasis appearing in Turkey only around the 1930s (Başaran & Şahin, 1990).

Later, the United States influenced the evolution of psychology more strongly than European countries. The legendary Harvard and Columbia trained Turkish social psychologist Muzaffer Sherif conducted research on the autokinetic effect and on realistic conflict theory (e.g., the Robbers Cave Study), and published more than 20 books on a wide range of subjects in psychology (Fine, 2004). Sherif worked and chaired the psychology department in Ankara University between the years of 1939–1945, and contributed immensely to the development of psychology in the country by translating psychological tests into Turkish and producing various books and articles. Başaran and Şahin (1990) state that Istanbul University, which remained the main department at which to teach psychology until the opening of Ankara University in 1939, and later many other universities, profited from American guest lecturers, such as Alexandre Vexliard (Başaran & Şahin, 1990; Toğrol, 1981).

Turkey succeeded in staying as much as possible out of World War II and protected the new republic and all its related endeavors, including social reforms. These were the years of more internal struggles. The political conflicts between parties of the left and the right resulted either in arrests against leftists or short-term, single-party dominance. There was a military coup in the 1960s. Therefore, it is easy to see that from the 1940s through the 1960s there was a relatively slow development in the area of psychology. McKinney (1960) wrote a review of Turkish psychology in those years, and said that in spite of the very early and strong beginning of psychology in Turkey, the rate of development was disappointing due to lack of support by authorities, bureaucratic and cultural problems. By contrast, Başaran and Şahin (1990) stated that actually in those years "whatever existed in the West could easily enter without facing a barrier" (p. 7). In light of these conflicting opinions, it is understood that psychology continued to develop in Turkey, but not at the same speed as it did in the beginning. This was probably stemming from (a) lack of support by authorities and the bureaucracy (McKinney, 1960), (b) the limited function psychology assumed in society (Başaran & Şahin, 1990), (c) only two undergraduate and graduate programs existing for nearly 50 years, and (d) the social and political climate mentioned above. With regard to the last point, it should be borne in mind that psychology grew in a country that changed from an empire to a republic; the compass turned from east to west; that is, from a non-secular country to a secular one. The new and contemporary Turkey, on the road to democracy, went through frequent governmental changes, including strong left wing–right wing struggles, and was interrupted by three military coups.

In the 1960s there were two new state universities and psychology departments in Ankara, namely Middle East Technical University (METU) and Hacettepe University. In the 1970s, Boğazici University in Istanbul and Ege University in İzmir also had psychology departments. Some of these universities provided education in English to their students with a hope of providing them a more contemporary education in a global language. Gradually, psychology became more responsive to the needs of society and consequently more known as a field; increasingly, women joined in the education of the next generation of psychologists, and graduates could find possibilities of work in various areas. Again in the 1960s, Turkey was one of the countries from which workers migrated to various European countries in the hopes of finding better life conditions. This migration wave resulted in a series of adaptation problems for both sides, sender and receiver countries, problems which necessitated extensive study. Acar and Şahin (1990) claim that the internal migration from rural areas of Turkey to the big cities, and the overall changing Turkish family from extended to nuclear, attracted the interest of psychologists, too. In the 1970s, changing family life, gender, migration, and values of children were studied in depth among Turkish psychology academicians.

Beginning with the 1970s the first graduate programs appeared in these universities, though rare in number. Many of these programs were taught by Turkish psychologists, who had taken their degrees in Europe or United States (LeCompte, 1980). These academicians acted like scientific bridges between the Western part of the world and Turkey. The 1970s were, according to LeCompte (1980), the years of rise in psychological research, though in those years funding for research was very weak. On the other hand, political instability due to struggles between the left and the right ended with another military coup in 1980, which resulted with the loss of many leftwing scientists and psychologists either by imprisonment or via "brain drain" to Western countries. There were immense efforts to normalize the politics afterwards. In spite of increasing political conflict, rising inflation, a worsening exchange rate, and a variety of other indications of national crisis, there was clear evidence of growth in the field of psychology in Turkey in those years (LeCompte, 1980). It can be speculated that in those years, in a country determined to become a part of contemporary civilization, establishing psychology as a discipline gave hope to scientists, practitioners, and students, and sustained its development in spite of these difficult events. In the proceedings of the first psychology congress in İzmir, the presentations of Vassaf (1981) and Kağitçibaşi (1981) are full of enthusiasm and vigor in discussing the role and responsibility of psychology in Turkey.

Following this strong tendency toward incorporating psychology as it has developed in the West, in other words through its importation, in the 1980s in Turkey another movement has had a substantial impact, namely cross-cultural psychology. The importance of and search for indigenous values and culture in psychology (Acar & Şahin, 1990) begins especially with the contribution of scholars such as Kağitçibaşi (1980, 1995) and Fişek (1991).

The 1990s and 2000s have been years of more or less political and economic stabilization for Turkey, and this period is characterized by the efforts to enter the European Union (EU). As a matter of fact Turkey has sought membership in the EU for nearly 40 years. This quest can be seen as a culmination of its modernization efforts and is connected to the idea that the West offers a model for a contemporary democratic and liberal state (İnac, 2004). Although as a candidate for EU membership Turkey has worked tirelessly to prepare for the adoption of EU, it still has not been accepted as a permanent member. In connection with these efforts to be a part of Europe and the EU, the TPA (Turkish Psychological Association) has developed close connections with EFPA (European Federation for Psychologists Association) and attempted to adapt itself in many respects to the EFPA's regulations via association-level committee work.

Psychology in Turkey Today

Unofficially founded under the name of Turkish Psychological Society, the association of psychology in Turkey has a tradition with a total of 95 years behind it. In 1996 the Turkish Psychological Association (TPA) in İstanbul, established in 1956, came together with the Association for Psychologists in Ankara, established in 1976. Today, the Turkish Psychological Association (TPA) is the organization that represents psychology in Turkey. The TPA central office is at Ankara and the other branches are in Istanbul, İzmir, Mersin, and Bursa. The main activities of the TPA are legal advocacy, provision of in-service training to its members, encouraging research and quality service in psychology, and public welfare activities. The association organizes biannual psychology congresses, publishes two periodicals (one indexed in the Social Science Citation Index, the other indexed by EBSCO-host), and supports the publication of scientific psychology books. The TPA has representation in, and collaboration at various levels with, the International Union of Psychological Science (IUPsyS) since 1992, the European Federation of Psychologists' Associations (EFPA) since 1993, and the American Psychological Association (APA).

Altogether, the rapidly increasing number of psychology departments (around 40), bodies of research in each area of psychology, biannually organized psychology congresses, two journals indexed in respected indices, and, finally, the acceptance of the ethics code in 2004, are all strong indications of the development of psychology in Turkey. Besides these positive steps, the organized and systematic psychosocial support projects provided by TPA to 1999 Marmara earthquake victims improved the public's perceptions of psychologists.

Specialization in diverse fields of psychology is a developing trend. In addition to already known fields, such as clinical psychology, social psychology, developmental psychology, and experimental psychology, there are rapid developments in relatively new areas of psychology; namely, health psychology and traffic psychology. As Şahin (1997) predicted, psychology is one of the preferred occupations for the younger generation in Turkey today. The great increase in the number of private universities and psychology departments within them is considered as a sign of this interest. Yet, this increase of the number of psychology departments and the students contains certain risks, too.

Feist and Gorman (1998) once claimed that there are three stages in the development of any discipline: in the first stage, individual scientists study similar problems; in the second stage there is an identification with those colleagues, and finally the emergence of conferences, journals, and departments. In this respect, this sequence of steps toward the development of Turkish psychology has been undertaken, a fact that is reflected in the interest of young people in the field. Nowadays, the provision of quality programs is considered to be an extremely important contemporary issue, such that current accreditation attempts of the association are focusing on those needs. Moreover, there are commissions in TPA responsible for the quality of trainings given.

Today, Turkish psychology departments are predominately made up of women, quite different than what Anschütz experienced a century ago. Thanks to Ataturk's new vision of Turkey in the early 1920s, in which a great value was placed on the active role of women in society, Turkish academicians in psychology today are predominantly female, many of whom have served with distinction as presidents of the TPA.

The greatest obstacle facing the association and the profession is the absence of a law that regulates the title and practice of psychology. Possibly due to the negative lobbying activities of various mental health groups, to prevent psychologists rising to a level of professional equality with medical doctors, this law has gathered dust for years in the files of the parliament. The lack of a law for psychology is preventing the TPA from exerting its expert authority on various pending matters. For instance, the increase of the number of psychology departments and rise in the number of graduates stand in contradiction to the relatively few master's and doctoral programs in Turkey. This scarcity in the number of quality graduate programs has created frustration among young, aspiring psychologists. Also, efforts are needed to accredit psychology programs on behalf of TPA, which hopefully will clarify quality-assurance concerns in the future. Other current challenges, according to Bolak-Boratav (2004), are reflected in efforts to understand indigenous culture, as well as in the expansion of new perspectives in academic psychology such as postmodernism, feminist psychology, sexism, and ethnic diversity.

Developments in Ethics

An ethics code is the best means to improve the practices of a science and profession. If ethical dilemmas are not dealt with knowledgeably and sensitively they easily turn into ethical violations, which in the long run hamper the development and recognition of the discipline. A system of ethical guidelines and enforcement adds to and ensures the values of psychological science and practice for academicians, professionals, and the general public. Given the atmosphere portrayed above regarding psychology in Turkey, and as a response to various problems and needs identified in different areas of psychology (Aycan, 1998; Ayvasik, 1999; Eskin,

2000; Köksal, 1994; Korkut, 2001; Kumru, 2001; Sayıl & Yılmaz, 2001; Sümer, 1998), it became clear for everyone that there was a need for an ethics code. Therefore, in the beginning of 2000 a task force on ethics was established in the İstanbul branch of TPA and began to work on the review and analysis of the existing international codes. From the outset, the idea was to create a code suitable to Turkish culture.

In the development phase of this code, a special effort was made to achieve an organic connection between external ethics systems, the needs and problems specific to Turkish culture, and the voice of the members of the association (Korkut, 2010a). These endeavors at the beginning phase included not only an extensive study of international examples of psychological ethics codes, learning from previous articles as mentioned above, but also conducting research about typical cases of ethical violation. The earliest research about the kinds of ethical dilemmas and violations in Turkey, conducted by the same team that prepared the ethics code (Korkut, Müderrisoğlu, & Tanik, 2006), identified the most commonly observed violations, which later found their place in the code. For example, the greatest problems were around competency issues, which later became the first principle of the code. In other words, the rank ordering of the principles was determined by the problems observed and cited in the journal articles mentioned above and through the results of this survey. The text was designed to be compatible with existing international major codes of ethics, but also to have a structure and flow of its own. Drafts of the code of ethics have been presented regularly by the same TPA team at psychology congresses, where the opinions of psychology academicians and practitioners have been collected and presented to the association. The last version of the draft was published in the TPA *Bulletin* and inserted into associations' websites for 6 months in order to obtain comments from as many and diverse an array of psychologists at possible. Finally, the current version of the TPA ethics code (2004a) was accepted in April 2004 by the TPA's General Assembly, by a significant majority of votes of the association members. In order for this ethics code to be implemented in the same year of its adoption by the TPA, Ferhunde Oktem and İhsan Dag constructed a "code for procedures" (TPA, 2004b), which was very much in line with the APA's rules and procedures. This code for procedures is currently under revision.

The idea from the very beginning was not only to create a code, but also to create a working ethics system (Korkut, 2006). After the official acceptance in 2004 of the ethics code and rules and procedures for its implementation, ethics committees established in three branches of the TPA began to evaluate complaints of alleged ethical violations. However, the members of these adjudicating committees needed to benefit from expertise; therefore, guest speakers from the APA Ethics Office (Dr. Stephen Behnke) and EFPA Standing Committee of Ethics (Prof. Dr. Geoff Lindsay) were invited to Turkey to train the ethics committee members and investigators. The committees benefited greatly from these training opportunities. Furthermore, it was important to introduce the ethics code as well as the code for rules and procedures; therefore, attempts have been made in the association to give ethics training to professionals (Korkut, 2006, 2010a,). To increase ethics sensitivity in the younger generation in the last few years, many universities have offered a course in ethics taught at graduate and undergraduate levels. Yet it is not obligatory in all programs, as would be desirable.

Unfortunately, the greatest problem is the persistent lack of a licensing law that regulates the title and practice of psychology, which is creating a long-standing dilemma concerning the adjudication of alleged ethical infractions despite the developments within the TPA. Though ethics codes recognize different levels of sanctions, ethics committees are limited in the sanctions they can apply. Since the association lacks a law on psychology, being a TPA member remains optional. A psychologist who is expelled due to ethical violations can still practice. Although the association has dedicated itself to the realization of this law, the government has yet to approve it. This reluctance is long believed to be related to the lobbying activities of other healthcare professions designed to prevent the empowerment of psychology as a discipline.

If one considers the dates of adoption of ethics codes in various countries around the world, the ethics code developments in Turkey described above are very much on time, and in accordance with the spirit of the times. The TPA has accepted the Ethics Code in 2004 and has been represented in the Standing Committee of Ethics of the EFPA since 2005. In 2009, the Turkish ethics code was accepted as compatible with EFPA (2005) *Meta-Code* of ethics. In sum not only are developments in psychological ethics in Turkey very timely and compatible with EFPA regulations, the Turkish ethics code also is sensitive to local problems and indigenous values and customs, as indicated by the research-based work mentioned previously.

Discussion

From the first decades of the 20th century onward, psychology has shown considerable development in Turkey. Turkey, like all nations, exists in a globalized world. Each country, including its scientific and professional branches, is influenced by the Zeitgeist, by the socioeconomic and sociopolitical events of the time. In addition, countries can influence each other in many different ways. In this respect, Turkey has profited greatly from the developments in the West regarding psychology, and has gained much knowledge and expertise via collaborative relations. In looking back, it can even be asserted that in the past Turkey has incorporated Western knowledge without fully considering whether it would be relevant or applicable in the context of the local social and value system. Now, Turkey is situated in an era in which it must be sensitive to indigenous knowledge. The development of psychology in Turkey teaches that it is not the years of history alone, but rather the overall sociocultural climate, the educational philosophy of the country, and the quality steps taken that are important determinants of the discipline. Turkey has not only experienced positive social and political changes, but also the negative ones, which have dramatically impacted the country. To create a suitable ethical system is important, but to sustain and nurture it in a country where political and economic changes are typical, is vital.

All of the trends described in this chapter point to a dynamic process in the development of psychology in Turkey. It is exactly this dynamism that has led to very systematic and fruitful efforts in establishing an ethics code. As pointed out, the attempts at creating an ethics code for psychology in Turkey necessitated close collaboration with Western psychology, but this time modulated by sensitivity to Turkish needs and values.

Developments in the discipline of psychology and in psychological ethics may be seen as reciprocally influencing each other. It is largely believed that achievements in the area of ethics, in turn, have added to the quality of psychological research and practice in the country. In Turkey, a very recent as yet unpublished survey (Korkut, 2010b) reveals that psychology academicians are more aware of the developments in ethics than are practitioners. The same survey shows that TPA members are aware of basic developments in psychological ethics, yet there is a great need to present all of the updated work of the committees to its members, to create a regular means for training members on possible ethical dilemmas, and to devise and implement a procedure for resolving such dilemmas quickly and effectively so that they do not become cases of ethical violations.

It is very important to keep in mind that there is no endpoint to the development of psychological ethics in Turkey. It should be remembered that any ethical framework ideally should be constructed to achieve as much of an organic unity as possible, that it should grow in response to the problems and needs of the society in which it is situated as well as the to the realities of an increasingly interconnected world. Close ties with larger ethics systems promise to enrich national ethics codes.

To continue to have close ties with members of the national association, to sensitize them on ethical matters, to offer them guidance and support, and to welcome their feedback about the ethics code is of vital importance. In the near future, practitioners should have opportunities to receive free ethics training. We do hope to make ethics training an obligatory part of graduate and undergraduate curricula.

In addition, as mentioned before, a revision to the current ethics code for procedures is being planned. The adoption of a law that governs the practice of psychology in all its branches is more than a necessity, along with the immediate need for additional research related specifically to psychological ethics in Turkey. It is our hope that psychology as a science and profession, along with psychological ethics and ethics code development, continue to keep up with the demands of the association and the global psychological community and contribute to the sociocultural needs of Turkish society.

Finally, this chapter raises several questions that can serve to guide future discussion and research on psychological ethics generally:

1. Is there a "Zeitgeist factor" that has contributed to the rapid development of ethical systems in various countries over the last few decades? What specific events and forces have triggered this development?

2. Can democratic institutions provide a foundation for the development of psychology and psychological ethics in a country?

3. In the globalized world of today, how can psychologists operate within a set of shared values

while remaining connected to local cultural, economic, political, and social conditions?

4. What are the best ways for developing ethics codes so as to preserve a balance between internationally adopted ethical systems and a specific country's local realities?

5. How can we enrich and invigorate psychological ethics in order to increase the level of sensitivity, knowledge, and skill that psychologists bring to various domains in which they practice?

6. As explained in this chapter, although Turkey has identified itself with the West for a long time, Western countries have had great difficulty in viewing Turkey as a part of Europe. Does religion account for the current impasse? Is it not possible that a country whose religious fabric is non-Christian be integrated within European culture and become a member state of the EU? Furthermore, can this external pressure that positions Turkey strongly to the East, equates it with İslam, and, therefore, distances itself from the country, influence a frustrated Turkey to eventually turn away from West? If this occurs, what might its effect be on the development of psychology and psychological ethics in Turkey?

References

Acar, G., & Şahin, D. (1990). Psychology in Turkey. *Psychology in Developing Societies, 2*(2), 241–256.

Aycan, Z. (1998). Turkiye'de psikoloji uygulama, arastırma ve yayımlarında etik ilkeler. Tartısma II: Endustri ve orgut psikolojisi alanında etik uygulamalar [Ethics of psychology practice, research and publications. Discussion II: Ethical practices in the area of industrial and organizational psychology]. *Turkish Journal of Psychology, 13,* 47–51.

Ayvasık, B. (1999). Turkiye'de psikoloji uygulama, arastırma ve yayımlarında etik ilkeler. Tartısma IV: Bilimsel arastırmalarda laboratuar hayvanlarının kullanımı ve bakımına iliskin etik tartısmalar uygulamalar [Ethics of psychology practice, research and publications. Discussion IV: Ethical practices about animal research, their care and use in laboratory]. *Turkish Journal of Psychology, 14,* 79–85.

Başaran, F., & Şahin, N. (1990). Turkey. In G. Shouksmith & E. A. Shouksmith (Eds.), *Psychology in Asia and the Pacific: Status reports on teaching and research in eleven countries* (pp. 7–40). Bangkok, Thailand: UNESCO.

Bilgin, N. (1981). Türkiye'de psikoloji yayın ve arastırmalarinin durumu [The current status of the research and publications in Turkey]. *Ege Universitesi Yayinlari, 9,* 11–27.

Bolak Boratav, H. (2004). Psychology in Turkey. In.M. J. Stevens & D. Wedding, *Handbook of international psychology* (pp. 311–330). New York, NY: Brunner-Routledge.

Eskin, M. (2000). Turkiye'de psikoloji puygulama, arastırma ve yayımlarında etik ilkeler. Tartısma V: Klinik psikolojide etik uygulamalar [Ethics of psychology practice, research and publications. Discussion V: Ethical practices in clinical psychology]. *Turkish Journal of Psychology, 15,* 81–83.

European Federation of Psychologists' Associations (EFPA) (2005). *Meta-code of ethics.* Retrieved from http://www.efpa.eu/ethics.

Feist, G. J. & Gorman, M. E. (1998). The psychology of science: Review and integration of a nascent discipline. *Review of General Psychology, 2*(1), 3–47. Fine, G. A. (2004). Forgotten classic: The Robbers Cave Experiment [Review of the book, *Intergroup Conflict and Cooperation: The Robbers Cave Experiment*, by M. Sherif, O. J. Harvey, B. J. White, W. R. Hood, & C. W. Sherif]. *Sociological Forum, 19*(4), 663–666.

Fisek, G. (1991). A cross-cultural examination of proximity and hierarchy as dimensions of family structure. *Family Process, 30,* 121–133.

İnac, H. (2004). Identity problems of Turkey during the European Union integration process. *Journal of Economic and Social Research, 6*(2), 33–62.

Kağıtçibaşi, C. (1980). *Cocugun degeri: Turkiye'de degerler ve dogurganlik* [The value of children: Values and fertility in Turkey]. İstanbul, Turkey: Bogazici Universitesi Yayinlari.

Kağıtçibaşi, C. (1981). *Sosyal degisme baglaminda sosyal psikolojik arastirmalarin* yeri [The place of social psychology studies in the context of social change]. In N. Bilgin (Ed.), *Ulusal Psikoloji Kongresi* [National Psychology Congress Proceedings] (Vol. 9, pp.140–145). İzmir, Turkey: Ege University Press.

Kağıtçibaşi, C. (1995). Is psychology relevant to global human development issues?: Experiences from Turkey. *American Psychologist, 50*(4), 293–300.

Koksal, F. (1994). Psikoloji arastırmalarında insan ve hayvan denekler ile ilgili ahlak İlkeleri. [Psychology research principles regarding human and animal subjects]. *Psikiyatri, Psikoloji, Psikofarmakoloji (3P) Dergisi, 2,* 66–72.

Korkut, Y. (2001). Bir an önce harekete geçmek zamani: Türkiye'de etik ilke ve kurallara duyulan büyük gereksinim karsisinda neler yapilabilir [The time to make a start: What can we do for the great need for an ethical principles and rules code]? *Turkish Psychological Bulletin, 23,* 220–224.

Korkut, Y. (2006). TPA ethics code: The development "process" of a code. In V. Claudio (Ed.), *II Colloquiu Europeu de Psicologia a Etica. Actas* [2nd European Colloquium of Psychology and Ethics Proceedings] (pp. 233–237). Lisbon, Portugal: ISPA.

Korkut, Y. (2009, July). *Social and political sensitivities of psychologists in times of social and political crisis.* Paper presented at the invited symposium: "Developing ethical codes for a changing world," European Congress of Psychology, Oslo, Norway.

Korkut, Y. (2010a). Developing a national code of ethics in psychology in Turkey: Balancing international ethical systems guides with a nation's unique culture. *Ethics and Behavior, 20*(3–4), 288–296.

Korkut, Y. (2010b, April). *Türk Psikologlar Derneği etik çalışmaları: Son 10 yıldaki vizyon ve etkinliklerimizin değerlendirilmesi* [Turkish Psychological Association ethical work: Vision and effectiveness in the evaluation of the last 10 years]. Paper presented at *Ulusal Psikoloji Kongresi* [National Psychology Congress], Mersin, Turkey.

Korkut, Y., Müderrisoğlu, S., & Tanik, M. (2006). Klinik psikoloji alanında karsilasilan etik ihlal örnekleri ve nasil ele alindiklarinin degerlendirilmesi [Examples of ethical violation cases in clinical psychology and the evaluation of how they are dealt with]. *Turkish Psychological Articles, 9,* 49–61.

Kumru, A. (2001). Turkiye'de psikoloji uygulama, arastırma ve yayımlarında etik ilkeler. Tartısma VII: Çocuklarla çalısan psikologlar için etik standartlar [Ethics of psychology practice, research and publications. Discussion VII: Ethical practices for psychologists who work with children]. *Turkish Journal of Psychology, 16,* 87–91.

LeCompte, W. A. (1980). Some recent trends in Turkish psychology. *American Psychologist, 35*(8), 745–749.

McKinney, F. (1960). Psychology in Turkey: Speculation concerning psychology's growth and area cultures. *American Psychologist, 15,* 717–721.

Sahin, N. (1997). Psikoloji [Psychology]. In *Cumhuriyet doneminde Turkiye'de bilim ve sosyal bilimler* [Science in Turkey during the Republican period: Social sciences] (pp. 203–226). Ankara, Turkey: Tuba.

Sayıl, M., & Yılmaz, A. (2001). Turkiye'de psikoloji uygulama, arastırma ve yayımlarında etik ilkeler. Tartısma VI: Gelisim psikolojisi arastırmalarında etik standartlar ve tartısılan sorunlar [Ethics of psychology practice, research and publications. Discussion VI: Ethical problems and standards in developmental psychology research]. *Turkish Journal of Psychology, 16,* 71–78.

Sumer, C. (1998). Turkiye'de psikoloji uygulama, arastırma ve yayımlarında etik ilkeler. Tartısma I [Ethics of psychology practice, research and publications. Discussion I]. *Turkish Journal of Psychology, 13,* 77–79.

Toğrol, B. (1981). *Turkiye'de psikolojinin gelisim ve tarihcesi* [Development and history of psychology in Turkey] (Vol. 9). İzmir, Turkey: Ege Universitesi Yayinlari.

Turkish Psychological Association. (2004a). Code of ethics. *Turkish Psychological Bulletin, 10,* 20–35.

Turkish Psychological Association. (2004b). Code for ethics procedures. *Turkish Psychological Bulletin, 10,* 35–62.

Vassaf, G. (1981). Dunden yarina Turkiyede Psikoloji [From yesterday to tomorrow: Psychology in Turkey]. In N. Bilgin (Ed.), *Ulusal Psikoloji Kongresi* [National Psychology Congress Proceedings] (Vol. 9, pp.151–153). İzmir, Turkey: Ege University Press.

CHAPTER 32

Taking Stock and Looking Forward

Geoff Lindsay, Michael J. Stevens, Mark M. Leach, Andrea Ferrero, *and* Yeşim Korkut

Abstract

In this chapter we offer a summary and synthesis based on the sections of the *Handbook*, present topics and issues related to psychological ethics that have recently received and will likely continue to receive significant attention worldwide, and address emerging challenges, such as the feasibility of a universal code of ethics, given global events and forces. We describe and evaluate the progress that psychology and psychologists have made in developing an ethical scientific and applied practice, and provide several recommendations on how best to ensure the international adherence to the ethical principles and standards of conduct in the various activities in which psychologists around the world are engaged.

Key Words: historical perspective, critical issues, future challenges

Taking Stock: Psychological Ethics in Historical Perspective

Psychology has come a long way over the past century or so, and this is also true of ethics. This trajectory is not, of course, limited to our own discipline, as others have had much longer to develop an ethical basis for practice. As Sinclair shows in the first chapter of this handbook, we can trace the history of professional ethics to the 18th century BCE, but until recently professional ethics primarily provided a foundation for progress in medicine. The growth in psychology and of psychologists in the 1940s to 1950s stimulated the American Psychological Association (APA) to design its first ethics code. Nevertheless, it is instructive to note Sinclair's analysis, which shows that the four basic ethical principles that form the heart of the *Universal Declaration of Ethical Principles for Psychologists* (Ad Hoc Joint Committee, 2008) can be identified in these early writings: Respect for the dignity of persons and peoples, Competent caring for the well-being of persons and peoples, Integrity, and Professional and scientific responsibilities to society.

There are now over 50 countries whose national psychological associations have a code of ethics (see http://www.iupsys.net/index.php/resources/ethics). Furthermore, specialist organizations such as the International Test Commission (ITC; 2000) have developed their own codes (see Chapter 2 in this volume by Oakland, Leach, Bartram, Lindsay, Smedler, & Zhang). Such codes, however, are not specific to psychologists as they address *activities* rather than members of a specific profession. For example, testing and assessment of human clients are practiced by many other groups whose constituents may include, but not be exclusive to, psychologists. These may be practitioners, such as speech pathologists and audiologists, psychotherapists, and human resources specialists or researchers. Researchers have developed more specific codes, such as codes published to guide qualitative research (Qualitative Research Consultants Association; see http://www.qrca.org/displaycommon.cfm?an=1&subarticlenbr=26).

We have witnessed the forging of both profession-specific and interdisciplinary pathways; that is, ethics codes for distinct professional groups as well as codes based on common activities that are practiced by diverse professions.

With respect to psychology, the role of the APA was fundamental to the development of ethics codes, beginning in the 1940s and continuing into the early 1950s to produce the inaugural edition of the APA's code of ethics in 1953 (Joyce & Rankin, 2010; see Chapter 1 in this volume by Sinclair). This code was built upon and reflected the evolution of professional psychology up to that time. Psychology's scientific research base provided the foundations for the application of disciplinary knowledge to various aspects of society, including education, health, and work. Joyce and Rankin argue that a key factor in psychology's rapid professional growth was the perceived success of "mental tests" in World War I, leading to significant advancements in assessments in different settings, such as business and schools.

It is clear from accounts of the development of the first APA code, *Ethical Standards for Psychologists* (American Psychological Association, 1953) that there was debate about *whether* a code was appropriate (e.g., Hall, 1952) as well as its form. Nevertheless, this pioneering work led to the foundation not only of the APA code of ethics, but also to inroads in psychological ethics in other countries.

Developing Model Codes of Ethics

The early work by the APA can be fast-forwarded to the current ethics code. Examination of the content and language of the ethics codes of other national psychology associations indicates a positive influence in some cases, but also certain opposing reactions motivated by a sense of *not* wanting to follow the APA's model, but rather to formulate a national code that provides a better fit with national circumstances and culture. The development of the European Federation of Psychologists' Associations' (EFPA) *Meta-Code of Ethics* (http://www.efpa.eu/ethics) is an interesting case in point. During the initial period of its construction, there was a proposal to adopt the APA code, but this was resisted by the European Federation of Professional Psychologists' Associations' (EFPPA)[1] Task Force on Ethics (Lindsay, 2011). Instead, the Task Force examined other codes including that of the Canadian Psychological Association (CPA; Canadian Psychological Association, 2000) and the Nordic code (Nordic Committee of Psychological Associations, 1998). There also was a strong view that simply to borrow the code of another country's national organization, however well-regarded, was fundamentally inappropriate. The Task Force therefore decided to use the framework of ethical principles found in the CPA code, which also had an admired companion manual (Sinclair & Pettifor, 1992), as well as that of the APA. South European national psychological organizations had developed the *Carta Etica*, which the Task Force also considered, later becoming an appendix to the first edition of the Meta-Code (European Federation of Professional Psychologists' Associations, 1995).

The development of both the APA code and the EFPA Meta-Code are well documented and informative. First, there is the requirement for a perceived need. This may now seem obvious, but it seems generally the case that ethical codes come later in the maturation of a psychological association than a focus on disciplinary-based science and practice. At some point the need to offer guidance on ethical behavior becomes a priority.

Second, there are differences in the ways in which ethics codes are constructed. The original APA ethics code used ethical dilemmas and issues identified by its members (Bersoff, 2008; Nagy, 2011), whereas later editions have relied upon the expert committee informed by consultation with association members. Third, the structure of a code must be decided. The three common structural models have been areas of practice (e.g., ethical issues concerned with testing and therapy), ethical domains (e.g., confidentiality, informed consent), and ethical principles, each with specifications of associated mandatory behaviors (often called standards). The fourth variable concerns the scope of an ethics code. National associations adopt codes for all of their members and these codes reflect the prevalence and range of member activity (e.g., clinical psychology in its various forms is often the most common professional activity). The development of the Nordic code and *Universal Declaration of Ethical Principles for Psychologists*[2] demonstrate the more recent phenomenon of transnational codes.

The issue of *process* noted in the second point above is arguably even more critical in the development of transnational ethics codes. At a practical level, the task is to ensure adequate evidence of practice in the constituent countries, as well as specialized domains of practice. More than this, however, is the importance of capturing the particulars of the cultural, historical, and indeed political characteristics of each country. This is also true within countries which are often, and increasingly, heterogeneous in their populations.

As we take stock now, we see both the development of ethics codes for specific national organizations and also the establishment of transnational or supranational codes, both of which provide guidance to psychologists, albeit more detailed in the case of national codes. Data from the International Union of Psychological Science (IUPsS) indicate that increasing numbers of national associations have adopted an ethics code; data from the EFPA reveal the impact of the Meta-Code not only in supporting this trend, but also in substantively refining national codes, as each EFPA member must have an ethics code that is compliant with the Meta-Code. This has allowed a fruitful evolution of ethics codes across Europe that address common principles and specified behavioral domains, while at the same time permitting national variation to meet local circumstances. In addition, we see ethics codes and ethical guidance that support more specific practices, such as testing: here, too, transnational, and in some cases such as testing, trans-professional codes have contributed greatly to ethical practice (e.g., International Test Commission, 2000; see http://www.intestcom.org/guidelines/index.php).

The events just summarized are quite positive. The interest in ethical matters is now stronger and becoming more common across the world. As psychology develops as a discipline and its presence grows in different countries, the need for guidance to support an ethical science and practice behavior will likewise grow. As a discipline and profession we can be proud of our progress thus far, but what lies ahead? In the remainder of this chapter we consider some of the key issues that may influence the further international development of psychological ethics.

Specificity Versus Universality in Psychological Ethics

The development of transnational codes and guidance brings to the fore the need to consider diversity. Put simply, to what extent are ethical principles common across the world? Alternatively, to what extent are there specific ethical issues that vary between countries and cultures? Indeed, this task is also applicable to the development and review of national codes, given the demographic heterogeneity of many countries. Whereas some countries have traditionally been relatively homogenous on key dimensions such as ethnicity (e.g., Ireland), others have a history of substantial diversity (e.g., the United States, United Kingdom) or a smaller number of distinct groups, each of which represent a sizeable proportion of the population. The latter case is often found with respect to groups that identify with a certain religion or communicate in a particular language. Furthermore, diversity can be represented by the distinction between indigenous people(s) and later immigrants (e.g., Australia, New Zealand). Hence, diversity may reflect any one or combination of dimensions that include ethnicity, language, religion, and indigenous status. Added to these are the dimensions of history (when peoples become part of a society) and both the current movements and trajectory of acquiring political and socioeconomic status. These situated factors lead to a necessity of ensuring that due consideration is given to the generic and specific aspects of ethics codes and associated systems, including regulation and credentialing, whether they be national or transnational.

The implications of the development of ethics codes lie both in their content and language. For example, the *Universal Declaration of Ethical Principles for Psychologists* (Ad Hoc Joint Committee, 2008) refers to "peoples" in order to inspire psychologists to respect the diversity found within countries, especially those with indigenous populations. Interpretation of practice must also take account of cultural norms and practices. As Pettifor and Ferrero (see Chapter 3 in this volume) argue, the realities imposed by demographic diversity may lead to competing hierarchies of ethical principles. Pettifor and Ferrero argue that respect and caring should take precedence over compliance with rules when there is an ethical conflict between cultural beliefs and standards of conduct. Such value priorities have implications for the interpretation of ethics codes and judgments of psychologists' behavior vis-à-vis such codes; more importantly, perhaps, there are implications for the relevance of ethics codes in guiding decisions in such situations.

Pettifor and Ferrero argue for the importance of resolving questions concerned with evidentiary support for indigenous psychology, specifically the place of indigenous healing within the science-informed professional practice. Again, this is not only a matter of globalization, but also a dilemma for ethically appropriate choices and actions when working with different groups within one nation. A key factor in working with indigenous groups is the ethnocentrism of the dominant culture (Tassell, Herbert, Evans, & Young; see Chapter 13 in this volume). This may be exemplified by interventions designed and administered by the dominant culture that clash with an indigenous culture's perspectives and needs. However, the situation is even more complex. As Tassell et al. show, we cannot assume that external definitions and labels of "indigenous" are appropriate: indigenous peoples in different countries express preferences for different terms, and, no doubt, there are multiple worldviews within each group.

An important distinction that applies to indigenous peoples is the existence of a formal treaty between indigenous people(s) and the government which, in Aotearoa / New Zealand, for example, institutes a statutory bicultural heritage. Such conditions create a different context for framing an understanding of diverse groups within one nation than, alternatively, a country with minority groups all of which are composed of immigrants (see New Zealand Psychological Society, 2002).

Developing a Universal Ethical Practice

Several national associations have elected to collaborate in producing a common ethics code and/or format for considering ethical issues. The Nordic countries developed a common code in 1988, the EFPA created its Meta-Code 1991–1995. These codes differed in purpose, as the Nordic code was a finished product from the constituent member associations of that region whereas the Meta-Code was a model to be used by all member associations in Europe in order to create or modify their national codes. By 2009 one-third of European national ethics codes were known to be compliant, with others in the process of becoming so (Lindsay, 2011). The nature of the relationship between the EFPA and its member associations allowed an expectation of convergence and compliance, but it is interesting to note the willingness of national associations to engage. The Nordic code was revised to be compliant with the Meta-Code (Nordic Committee of Psychological Associations, 1998) and even the British Psychological Society (BPS, 2009), one of the oldest associations, completely changed from a code of conduct with a very different structure to an ethics code firmly based on the Meta-Code. Furthermore, the 2005 revision of the Meta-Code resulted in few, relatively minor changes, reinforcing the fitness in purpose of the original (Lindsay, Koene, Øvreeide, & Lang, 2008). It has been argued that this success was in large part the result of a careful process of constituting the international group of experts which formed the EFPA Standing Committee on Ethics, which drafted the Meta-Code, coupled with the participation of member associations and formal approval by the EFPA General Assembly (Lindsay, 2011).

The task facing the development of the *Universal Declaration of Ethical Principles for Psychologists* was even more daunting. Although this was not intended to be an ethical code, it has a similar aim to the EFPA Meta-Code but without formal expectation of compliance. Its development also required the formation of a committee drawn from experts across the world, along with sensitive and transparent engagement with the psychological community through the three international organizations that sponsored its development, the International Union of Psychological Science (IUPsyS), International Association of Applied Psychology (IAAP), and International Association of Cross-Cultural Psychology (IACCP). Gauthier, Pettifor, and Ferrero (2010) and Gauthier and Pettifor (see Chapter 9 in this volume) have described the development of the Universal Declaration, stressing that it is not a "worldwide code," but rather a statement of aspirational principles that reflect moral values that would be expected of a code of ethics. The development of the Universal Declaration took as a central tenet the need to set forth principles empirically grounded in values that could be considered universal, but equally to avoid the specification of conduct standards, as these are culturally situated. In short, the *Universal Declaration of Ethical Principles for Psychologists* was intentionally designed to be culturally sensitive.

The success of the *Universal Declaration of Ethical Principles for Psychologists,* and of previously mentioned transnational codes, suggests that it is indeed possible to create culturally sensitive ethical guidelines that have broad applicability at the level of values and principles. Evidence following the introduction of the Meta-Code suggests that the model of specifying how general ethical principles may be used at the national level to formulate standards of conduct is also sound.

New and Emerging Challenges

Psychology is a rapidly evolving science and profession, and ethical thinking must be reviewed and often refined as new developments emerge. Furthermore, because psychologists operate in a sociopolitical context, we also need to take account of events and forces external to psychology and our interaction with macro-level factors. In this section we consider some of these issues.

Testing and Assessment

Psychology has a long history in testing and the broader domain of assessment. This history has not always been a comfortable fit from the perspective of ethics. Assessment may be biased and unfair, even if unintended, and well-constructed measures may be abused in practice. The history of the cognitive ability testing is an obvious example of both exemplary and poor quality approaches and of both the well-meaning and not so benign motivations of users or commissioners of assessments. For example, see Neisser (1998) for a critique of *The Bell Curve* (Herrnstein & Murray, 1994), which argued for limits on the intelligence of most of the population: Neisser's edited book argued that, in fact, intelligence scores were rising across the world and examined the complex set of factors involved. Looking to the future, the main challenges in psychological testing and assessment may lie in a continuation of efforts to ensure fairness and in tackling the growing problem of attempts to subvert assessment systems. The former is linked to the increasing diversity and mobility of societies, whether voluntary or as a result of flight from adverse conditions such as war and persecution, scarce resources, and natural disasters. Although long-standing phenomena, the scale of both has increased markedly. As a result, the challenge to create fair methods of assessment has become urgent. Oakland (see Chapter 15 in this volume) argues that national ethics codes tend not to say much about testing and assessment, but that international organizations, such as the ITC (http://www.intestcom.org/itc_projects.htm) have addressed this task; the ITC has posted guidelines on adapting tests and on computer-based and Internet-delivered testing in addition to its more general guidelines on test use. The work of international organizations is clearly positive and complementary to that of national psychology associations. Ethics codes set the main implications of ethical principles and values, but additional guidance can be quite helpful in specific domains of research and practice. The leadership of transnational organizations such as the ITC is crucial, not least because this underscores the need to address cultural diversity and facilitates developments that address issues of cultural diversity in testing and assessment.

The second challenge reflects growth of the Internet. There have always been those prepared to cheat, both assessors and assessed, but the availability of Internet-delivered administration and scoring has vastly increased the use of psychological assessment. Employment selection and educational assessments, for example, are often "high stakes" processes as the outcomes have potential major life implications on test takers. Foster and Miller (see Chapter 16 in this volume) have graphically set out five challenges posed by those seeking to cheat the system. Their specification of these challenges makes clear the responsibilities of psychologists, as researchers developing measures, users of measures in research and practice, and as consultants to others who plan to administer or adapt measures. These include the psychometric quality of assessment approaches, the fairness or nonbiased nature of assessment, and the security of the assessment process.

Telepsychology: Intervention at a Distance

The Internet is a powerful medium for practicing psychology at a distance. There have been earlier versions of telepsychology, as in the case of telephone help lines, which may provide relatively simple information or a vehicle for substantive therapeutic interventions. The Internet, as with testing, raises the potential for ethical concerns and infractions many times. Consequently, a key question is whether these ethical challenges are fundamentally new to the medium or essentially identical to ethical issues that occur in conventional face-to-face methods in a professional workplace.

Hilgart, Thorndike, Pardo, and Ritterband (see Chapter 12 in this volume) have set out the range of ethical challenges that must be addressed as well as the benefits of using the Internet for psychotherapeutic or behavioral interventions. There is evidence for therapeutic effectiveness and cost effectiveness, although research is at a relatively early stage (see also Richardson, Frueh, Grubaugh, Egede, & Elhai, 2009). Using a different medium, Sanders, Montgomery and Brechman-Toussaint (2000) showed positive effects from a randomized control trial of a 12-episode television series designed to reduce children's conduct problems, a Level 1 intervention of the 5-level Triple P parenting program delivered at a distance. More research is needed to examine the comparability of outcomes of face-to-face interventions and delivery of interventions at a distance, of which the Internet is likely to be the main area of growth. Notwithstanding clear practical benefits (e.g., convenience for clients, accessibility for rural residents), Internet-based technology poses risks, including the security (i.e., confidentiality) of digitally transmitted data, difficulties for accurate communication, especially with culturally diverse clientele, and limited access by the poor.

In addition, use of Internet-based therapy is not yet the subject of specific regulation. Koocher (2009) notes that the APA "has not chosen to address teletherapy directly in its ethics code and by this *intentional omission* (emphasis added) has created no rules prohibiting such services" (p. 342). The same action was taken by the EFPA Standing Committee on Ethics, which took the view that telepsychology did not introduce any fundamentally new ethical issues. Rather, the difference between face-to-face and Internet-delivered approaches was seen in the practical implications and relative impact of various challenges, not least articulating an extension of traditional competencies necessitated by use of the medium. There are numerous unresolved ethical challenges to use of the Internet in psychological research and practice, some of which reflect the lack of guidance for psychologists whose activities fall beyond the purview of national ethics codes and laws, and even beyond geographic regions that are regulated by transnational ethics. Moreover, which standards of conduct should be invoked in the adjudication of alleged unethical conduct when such conduct occurs in cyberspace?

Clearly, there are multiple challenges to professional associations and regulators to resolve. With respect to ethical guidance, however, it appears the main approach should be the development of specific guidelines, rather than amending the ethics code. National and transnational bodies have produced such support (e.g. European Federation of Psychologists' Associations, 2006, see http://www.efpa.eu/ethics/efpa-guidelines). Fitzgerald, Hunter, Hadjistavropoulos, and Koocher (2010) have advocated for the application the *Universal Declaration of Ethical Principles for Psychologists* as a means of framing and resolving ethical issues that arise from psychologists' use of the Internet. In addition, both training and continuing education of psychologists must inform scholars and practitioners alike of the ethical issues that arise given the growth of both psychology and the Internet.

Ethical Implementation of Innovative Psychological Approaches

There is increasing recognition by government of the value of science-based practice. In the United Kingdom, for example, the previous New Labour administration funded studies of a large number of new educational initiatives. In one instance, a study was commissioned of parenting programs, three of which were selected as they had evidence of efficacy from research trials. A second study examined the effectiveness of implementing a funded program in 18 local authorities. The success shown led to the funding of a national program in which all local authorities received money to implement programs with demonstrable efficacy; the implementation of these programs was later shown to be effective (Lindsay et al., 2011, Lindsay, Strand, & Davis, 2011). The U.K. government's Allen Review (Allen, 2011) surveyed evidence on the success of early intervention more widely and set forth proposals for evaluating the efficacy of such interventions. Psychologists had been instrumental in devising a number of these interventions and both school and clinical psychologists were engaged in implementing recommended interventions in community settings. On the other hand, a recent study has indicated that the most common intervention programs used by speech pathologists and audiologists in United Kingdom had at best a limited empirical support (Lindsay, Wren, Bakopoulou, & Roulstone, 2011).

Introducing new methods requires careful consideration if psychological practice is to be deemed ethical. Unless the method is effective, fair, and appropriate it could be unhelpful at best or dangerous at worst. The media latch on to many new methods often with little if any firm evidence for their reliability, validity, and usefulness. Ethics codes increasingly recognize the dilemma of when to adopt a new method. A range of evidence may be minimally needed to justify experimental implementation, beyond research trials, in real-world community settings (see Allen, 2011 for a useful framework). Nevertheless, ethical practice requires recognition of a method's scientific status. Responsibility is placed on the psychologist to monitor the administration of innovative interventions and report findings based on measureable outcome. Sadly, such efforts are often poorly designed or variable in quality, as the above examples demonstrate[3]. Section 2.01e of the APA ethics code states that psychologists should take "reasonable steps to ensure the competence of their work and to protect patients, clients, students, research participants, and others from harm" (American Psychological Association, 2002). The EFPA Meta-Code of Ethics (European Federation of Psychologists' Associations, 1995) has a similar clause but recognizes the importance of new methods:

3.2.3 (iii) Obligation to balance the need for caution when using new methods with a recognition that new areas of practice and methods will continue to emerge and that this is a positive development.

Looking ahead, the ethical challenge is relatively simple to identify. It is to have a receptive stance toward to new developments, but also a healthy critical perspective. The use of methods that have accumulated evidence of technical quality, usefulness, and cultural sensitivity requires an analysis of risk. Careful preparation, monitoring, review, and reporting can optimize the likelihood of positive growth in applied psychology and limit the possibility of unethical practice and harm.

Psychological Ethics as Situated in Politics

In this section we consider the potential future impact of political events and forces. We are all citizens of one (or more) country, and as such are subject to the laws and political systems of the society in which we live or work, as mobility increases. Sociopolitical policies have an impact on us as psychologists as well, and some policies raise ethical challenges.

In this regard, a recent controversial topic has been the role of psychologists in times of "war."[4] The events of Abu Ghraib and Guantanamo Bay have shocked the world. There also are specific concerns about the roles of U.S. psychologists[5] and the APA in matters related to national security; the 2002 edition of the APA's *Ethical Principles for Psychologists and Code and Conduct* was criticized as not adequately guiding psychologists engaged in national security operations. The report of the Presidential Task Force on Psychological Ethics and National Security (PENS, 2005; see Abeles Chapter 17) led to much debate within and beyond the association. We will not examine the issues raised by the PENS Report, but note in particular the revision to the ethical code (American Psychological Association, 2010). These amendments were relatively minor in scale, but nonetheless important. They made reference to human rights and may be interpreted to clarify the primacy of the ethics code in matters related to national security. There is recognition of potential conflict between the ethics code and the demands of the organization for or within which a psychologist works or is affiliated. Yet, a psychologist is required to "take reasonable steps to resolve the conflict committed within the General Principles and Ethical Standards of the Ethics Code" (American Psychological Association, 2010, Section 1.02). The amendment further states that, "Under no circumstances may this standard be used to justify or defend violating human rights" (American Psychological Association, 2010, Section 1.03). These changes unambiguously link the ethical practice of psychology to human rights, as has been done even more strongly in the ethics codes and laws of other countries whose histories reveal fundamental violations in human rights through the misuse of psychological science and practice (Colegio de Psicologos de Chile, 1999; Health Professions Council of South Africa, 2004; see Chapter 27 by Stevens in this volume).

The broader point is that in any political system, psychologists may be expected to engage in behavior which appears at odds with ethical practice. Some regimes have severely limited human rights and have had laws (or deliberately misinterpreted or acted beyond de facto laws) that have limited the degree to which psychologists were able to adhere to their ethical principles and standards. The lack of ethics codes in some dictatorships or countries of the former Soviet bloc was recognized by the EFPA Standing Committee on Ethics in its construction of the Meta-Code; that is, the creation of an ethics code was highly sought by psychologists with the newly acquired freedom to practice their profession. However, political constraints may be more subtle. One outcome of the global financial crisis in many countries has been a cutback in support for vulnerable members of society. In the United Kingdom, the provision of most educational and health-related services, including the majority of psychological services in these domains, is funded through taxes and, therefore, free. Current government policy is to reduce substantially public services. There are, of course, arguments for and against this and other political decisions, but political decisions clearly can have major impacts on the practice of psychology, including government-funded research.

The implications for psychologists are first to recognize the potential effect of political decisions on the breadth and depth of psychological research and practice, and second to examine the ethical issues and dilemmas that may arise. The growing interest in ethics, the development of national ethics codes, and the support for transnational ethical initiatives have been salutary in this regard. We cannot, however, assume that the benign ambient circumstances that have allowed, and even supported, these developments will necessarily continue; there may be more rocky paths ahead.

Regulating the Discipline of Psychology

The applications of psychology rest upon their scientific foundations. The development of ethical codes has arguably been driven by applied psychology. The role of regulation and enforcement has been and continues to be more controversial. Revelation of the horrors of medical experimentation during the World War II was a major factor in the development of ethical standards for research with human beings. The 1947 *Nuremburg Code of Ethics in Medical Research* was an important achievement in safeguarding the rights of research participants (see Chapter 1 by Sinclair and Chapter 9 by Gauthier and Pettifor in this volume), and later the Declaration of Helsinki by the World Medical Association in 1964 (World Medical Association, 2008; http://www.wma.net/en/30publications/10policies/b3/). Although formulated by medical institutions, their basic principles have been found useful in guiding others engaged in human- participants research, including psychologists.

Before considering regulation, it may be helpful to consider whether there is a case for ethical guidance. The extreme case (and not just for research) was put by Hall (1952) in his contribution to articles published in the *American Psychologist* when the first edition of the APA ethics code was being developed. He argued that a code was a retrograde step, as "decent mature people do not need to be told how to conduct themselves" (p. 430). In other words, psychologists should be considered to be right-thinking and inherently ethical in their behavior. He went further to argue that "I think it (a formal code of ethics) plays into the hands of crooks on the one hand and because it makes those who are covered by the code feel smug and sanctimonious on the other hand" (p. 430).

However, there is evidence from two main sources that Hall's 1952 assertion does not always apply: studies of psychologists' responses to ethical dilemmas and the data reporting allegations made against psychologists for unethical behavior. For example, data from the American Psychological Association (2009) and the British Psychological Society (2006) indicated 288 and 109 complaints, respectively, against members for alleged unethical conduct, although it should be noted that these represent a very small percentage of the membership of the two organizations, about 91,000 and 45,000 respectively. Investigations of ethical dilemmas have also shown that psychologists in different types of practice, both research and applied settings, sometimes struggle with situations that pose ethical dilemmas (Pope & Vetter, 1992; Lindsay & Colley, 1995). A further source of evidence comprises surveys that provide evidence that respondents have behaved in a manner that could be judged unethical (Lindsay, 1996). This phenomenon is not exclusive to psychologists. Martinson, Anderson, and deVries (2005) conducted a survey of early and mid-career scientists that found nontrivial percentages who admitted to unethical behavior. For example, 20.6% of mid-career respondents admitted to changing the design, methodology, or results of a study in response to pressure from a funding source; small, but still worrisome percentages of 0.5% early-career and 0.2% mid-career scientists reported falsifying or "cooking" their data. Koocher and Keith-Spiegel (2010) conducted a survey of psychologists engaged in research who had suspicions of scientific wrongdoing. Although the survey focused on the actions of these psychologists, it also revealed substantial numbers suspected wrongdoing; over 600 of the 2599 respondents suspected fabrication or falsification of data (the largest category) and over 400 suspected plagiarism.

In summary, there is clear evidence of unethical behavior in both psychological research and applied practice. It is also important to note that the percentage of psychologists who are the target of an ethical complaint is very small, and of those only a small percentage result in an investigation and adjudication (see the APA and BPS reports cited above), although the Koocher and Keith-Spiegel (2010) research suggests that, in the specific domain which they examined, the problem may be much larger. What to do?

Developments up to this point in time have been of two types: self-regulation and institutional regulation. The former stresses the important role of each psychologist in assuming responsibility for his or her behavior. This practice can be informed, maintained, and enhanced by a number of actions. Fundamental is appropriate initial training in ethics, followed by continuing professional education and development. Ethics codes support both professional training and lifelong professional growth by providing a structure with which to gain a formative appreciation of the ethical dimension of professional conduct and guide subsequent decisions when confronted with ethical ambiguities and challenges, respectively. The latter requires the establishment of formal systems of regulatory procedures, which involves financial support and, more importantly, colleagues willing to serve as experts on investigatory panels with the authority to adjudicate allegations of ethical infractions. A related issue concerns whether such a regulatory system should be statutory (i.e., governed by law), operated by the psychological organization, and, if both, how their respective roles and activities are to be coordinated.

There are two approaches that are not mutually exclusive, but which represent different ways of addressing the task of professional regulation. The first may be described as an example of quality assurance, getting it "right" the first time, whereas the latter is quality control—monitoring practice and correcting errors.

If they do so at all, psychological organizations tend to institute regulatory systems as they begin to mature. This is understandable given the need for an ethics code to signal a professional organization's authoritative status. The EFPA Standing Committee on Ethics provided guidance for its member associations to establish systems of evaluation of complaints and determination of corrective actions. These are along the lines of the Meta-Code, namely a general framework and set of principles to inform ethical decision making with latitude for national associations to introduce locally pertinent detail (see http://www.efpa.eu/ethics/efpa-guidelines; Lindsay, Koene, Øvreeide, & Lang, 2008).

An important limitation of an organization's regulatory system is that it can only regulate the organization's members; regulation per se cannot prevent poor practice. Sanctions are limited to reprimands and restrictions on practice if membership is to survive, with expulsion as the ultimate sanction. Statutory regulation, therefore, must be sought in order to secure the power of the law. Such legal regulatory authority may take various forms depending on a country's legal system and conventions. For example, in the United Kingdom regulation of most professionals is *indicative* rather than *functional*. That is, the law regulates who may use a protected title. In the United Kingdom only practitioner psychologists are regulated (i.e., not academics unless they also practice) and protected titles refer to specialist expertise (e.g., clinical psychologist, educational psychologist) rather than the title "psychologist." This is because to regulate this generic title would necessitate bringing nonpractitioner academics into a regulatory system, which is inappropriate. Functional regulation defines who may engage in specified professional activities, such as psychological assessment and psychotherapy. Indicative regulation has the limitation that nonregulated persons may establish themselves by adopting a nonregulated title, whereas functional regulation is exceedingly difficult to implement unless the activity can be clearly operationalized. To add to the confusion, psychological activities may be appropriately and effectively undertaken by professionals other than psychologists (e.g., social workers).

Both self-regulation and regulatory bodies have a vital place in the future. The former is fundamental, and we suggest that this ought to be the primary focus. Self-regulation requires the institutional involvement of psychological organizations at training and post-licensure stages to ensure the acquisition of a positive orientation to professional ethics and an ongoing commitment to further awareness, knowledge, and competencies in professional ethics, respectively. This may well necessitate the articulation of additional guidelines given current gaps. Support for continuing education is another important function of psychological organizations if they are to maintain and enhance the ethical conduct of their members.

Developing regulatory bodies raises separate challenges depending on whether these are statutory or operated within a psychological association. In the latter case, the actions necessary for a psychological association to regulate the ethical conduct of its members are well within its authority. The EFPA guidelines and experience of other psychological organizations can inform national associations that seek to construct a regulatory framework, although the parameters of any regulatory system must fit the legal and cultural characteristics of each country if it is to be meaningful and effective. Where there is a statutory basis for professional regulation, a psychological association's capacity to influence legislative and judicial structures of government is key. In some cases this capacity is well developed and strong. For example, in Canada and the United States, it is the state or provincial psychology licensing board that has responsibility for regulating psychologists, but the APA code of ethics has been used by many states in the United States as the legal basis for a regulating authority's procedures and determinations. In other countries, however, there may not be a direct relationship between a psychological association and statutory regulatory entity. In the United Kingdom, the BPS no longer regulates practitioner psychologists who are members, a task now carried out by a state regulator, the Health Professions Council, whose code is entirely different in conceptualization and structure. It was developed before the Health Professions Council was given responsibility in 2009 for the regulation of psychologists, and was designed to be generically applicable to the 12 professions within its purview at that time. Variants exist in other countries, such as Australia and New Zealand (e.g., Allan & Love, 2010; Garton & Allan, see Chapter 26 in this volume).

Where psychologists seek a statutory regulation system, such a system is more likely to be instituted once a national association becomes well established, respected, and has both an ethics code and in-house regulatory system. Political action then becomes necessary to influence government to implement statutory regulation and to do so in a manner appropriate to the discipline of psychology. Since 1955 the APA has made available a Model Act of State Licensure of Psychologists to guide this legislative process (see American Psychological Association, 2011, for the most recent version). The BPS commissioned the drafting of a psychologist act for the U.K. government when legislation specific to the regulation of psychologists was expected to be the method favored by the government[6]. When government policy changed, the BPS remained engaged in the legislative process by working with the Department of Health officials articulating the details of the professional regulatory law that would be implemented by the Health Professions Council.

Finally, the role of mediation should be considered an integral component of any regulatory system, whether statutory or nonstatutory (for EFPA guidelines on mediation see http://www.efpa.eu/ethics/efpa-guidelines). As Koene (see Chapter 7 in this volume) argues, mediation can be very useful in many cases in reducing the need for formal evaluative and disciplinary action. Moreover, mediation may offer a more satisfactory option for an aggrieved client, provide a path for rehabilitation of a psychologist found to have behaved unethically, and cost less.

The Case of Research

The need for ethics codes to regulate research activities has been more controversial. For example, Dingwall (2008) has argued forcibly that there is an ethical case against the ethical regulation of research in the humanities and social sciences. He suggests that the need for such regulation in biomedical science has been overgeneralized to other disciplines, including psychology. He argues that "ethical regulation is *fundamentally* (original emphasis) wrong because the damage that it inflicts on a democratic society far exceeds any harm that HSS (Humanities and Social Science) research is capable of causing to individuals" (p. 1). Dingwall's case is primarily about the negative impact of regulatory procedures; however, he explores a number of ethical dilemmas that can arise in the research in which psychologists (and others) may engage, albeit of minimal risk.

Generally speaking, there has been resistance by academics in the social sciences in response to efforts to oversee their research. Nevertheless, in many countries research in the social sciences has been brought under a regulatory system when it involves human or non-human participants. Guidance at regional, national, and local (e.g., university) levels have been instituted to varying degrees. For example, the European Commission specifies its research ethics requirements for its 7th Framework Programme (2007–2013) (see Fitzgerald, 2007, and Pauwels, 2007). National criteria for the ethical conduct of research have also been formulated (e.g., UK Research Integrity Office, 2009; see http://www.ukrio.org/ukR10htre/UKRIO-Code-of-Practice-for-Research1.pdf). Guidance on specific research-related topics has been produced that covers copyright issues (British Academy and the Publishers Association, 2008) and retractions in academic journals (UK Research Integrity Office, 2010; see http://www.ukrio.org/ukR10htre/UKRIO-Code-of-Practice-for-Research1.pdf). The main research funding council in the United Kingdom has published its Research Ethics Framework (Economic and Social Research Council, 2006; http://www.esrc.ac.uk/_images/Framework_for_Research_Ethics_tcm8-4586.pdf). Many of the initiatives noted above are in the form of guidance, but other stipulations are clearly regulatory, such as the requirement that research cannot be conducted without ethical approval from an authorized body. It is these regulatory restrictions that have raised concerns (e.g., Dingwall, 2008).

First, there are practical issues related to the time required to approve the ethical foundation of research proposals. This has been a major problem in the United Kingdom and especially in the National Health Service. The bureaucracy that was established contributed to delays, a problem that has been addressed to some extent, but the National Health Service also has research governance procedures which themselves impede the start of research projects. Ironically, therefore, the regulatory system is producing what might be construed as an unethical impact due to increased public cost, delays in much-needed research, and in some cases compromises in the quality of the research (e.g., by reducing the period in which a study may be conducted because of inordinate delays). Second, there have been concerns about the operation of research regulatory committees. Angell and Dixon-Woods (2008) report poor communication by National

Health Service research-ethics committees with researchers in regard to their decisions and the basis on which they were reached. Third, there are concerns about the legitimacy of some research-ethics committees in judging social science (including psychology) research per se, or suitability of certain investigative methodologies (e.g., Jacobson, Gewurtz, & Haydon, 2007). The separation of biomedical from social science research can be helpful in this respect, with disciplinary peers appointed to evaluate research proposals that are fundamentally psychological. Fourth, the need to determine what research should be subject to ethical review creates significant tensions. The American Anthropological Association (2004), for example, produced a statement on whether ethnographic methods or ethnography as a whole should be excluded from the domain of research requiring regulatory oversight, after the Office of Human Research Protection ruled that research methods involved in taking oral histories were to be exempted.

These above concerns include fundamental issues, such as the nature of research and its practical implementation. The former has been addressed in a meaningful way by guidelines, such as the Economic and Social Research Council's (2006) *Research Ethics Framework* (revised 2010), which begins with the premise that all research has ethical components but that there are different levels of risk to participants. Hence, all research should be conducted with the utmost integrity, but the specific actions necessary to administer a research project ethically, and the involvement of an institution's research-ethics committee, should mirror the risk posed to participants. A useful contrast would be statistical analysis of large anonymous datasets versus the qualitative analysis of interviews on highly personal matters with individuals, the protection of whose identity may be difficult if not impossible to guarantee.

In the future, there is likely to be a furtherance of regulatory systems for psychologists in countries that do not yet have them. The lessons learned so far suggest that the primary task is to institute effective training and continuing education for psychologists to anticipate and thereby avoid engaging in unethical behavior. Because some psychologists may still engage in inappropriate behavior, some regulatory framework is necessary to protect the general public. Our recommendation is to base regulation on tried and tested procedures, to modify these as needed to meet local circumstances (e.g., cultural and legal factors), and to limit institutional bureaucracy to a minimum. Furthermore, mediation may prove helpful in satisfying harmed clients and research participants where appropriate, enabling psychologists to correct faulty ethical reasoning and harmful actions, and, hopefully, reducing the likelihood of a recurrence.

Conclusion

This is the first international handbook of psychological ethics. It marks an important development of the standing of ethics in the science and applied practice of psychology. There is now international recognition of the importance of ethical behavior by psychologists in all aspects of their professional work. There also is international agreement of the legitimacy of a core set of ethical principles derived from basic human values. These values reflect fundamental human rights that are enshrined in law.

The future is likely to see an increase in the number of countries that have a national ethical code. This process will be greatly assisted by the *Universal Declaration of Ethical Principles for Psychologists* and, particularly but not exclusively within Europe, by the EFPA Meta-Code. The juxtaposition of the Universal Declaration with a perspectival framework for understanding psychology as a situated discipline raises at least two important issues regarding national ethics codes in psychology and the professional conduct of psychologists in their local milieu (Stevens, 2010):

1. Is it possible for a country's psychological ethics code to mirror universal principles while at the same time embracing local norms; conversely, to what extent are universal principles and local norms irreconcilable?

2. What variables predict whether psychologists from culturally diverse countries accept, reject, or respond ambivalently to universal ethical principles as they engage in professional activities locally?

Fundamental to the task of crafting national ethics codes will be to test the above propositions concerning the interface of universal ethical principles with local specifications.

Psychology finds itself in an ideal position to grow and prosper worldwide. International collaboration is essential to ensure collective understanding and the development of collective wisdom, especially in a world where globalization and diversity at local and national levels are common. The regulation of psychologists is likely to expand as more countries initiate procedures to address public concerns about alleged unethical practice. However, it is of greater importance to ensure that we train ethical psychologists and that high levels of ethical conduct are maintained and strengthened over the course of their careers. Both national and international psychological organizations have a major role to play in supporting the continued development of ethical practice. As a community of psychologists, we owe this to our fellow citizens and to the societies in which we live. Each of us must contribute to the development of ethical principles, standards of conduct, and methods for their application that better serve diverse persons and communities, with diverse problems, in diverse ways and settings, both at home and across national borders.

Notes

1. Now the European Federation of Psychologists' Associations (EFPA), the title to be used for the rest of this chapter.

2. The *Universal Declaration of Ethical Principles for Psychologists* is not an ethics code as such. Indeed, neither is the EFPA Meta-Code, which provides guidance not to individuals but to national associations.

3. The introduction of parenting programs was an example of positive practice, but it should be noted that many other such programs have been developed and are in use with little if any evidence of their efficacy or effectiveness.

4. The quotation marks are used here as recent events have occurred in some instances where there has been no formal declaration of war; this includes the rhetorical "war on terror."

5. Similar concerns apply to and have been raised by members of other professions, in particular physicians and psychiatrists.

6. Previous acts had also been designed to regulate individual professions. As this is very costly in parliamentary time, the 1999 Health Act set up the Health Professions Council for 12 existing health professions (see above) with powers to add to those professions by statutory instrument; psychologists were regulated by this process.

References

Ad Hoc Joint Committee. (2008). *Universal declaration of ethical principles for psychologists*. Retrieved from http://www.am.org/iupsys/resources/ethics/2008-universal-decl-report.pdf

Allan, A., & Love, A. W. (Eds.). (2010). *Ethical practice in psychology: Reflections from the creators of the APS code of ethics*. Chichester, UK: Wiley.

Allen, G. (2011). *Early intervention: The next steps: An independent report to Her Majesty's government*. London: Cabinet Office

American Anthropological Association. (2004). *Statement on Ethnography, and Institutional Review Boards*. Retrieved June 17, 2011 from http://www.aaanet.org/stmts/irb.htm.

American Psychological Association. (1953). *Ethical standards of psychologists*. Washington, DC: Author.

American Psychological Association. (2002). *Ethical principles of psychologists and code of conduct*. Washington, DC: Author.

American Psychological Association (2009). Report of the Ethics Committee, 2008. *American Psychologist, 64*(5), 464–473.

American Psychological Association. (2010). 2010 amendments to the 2002 "Ethical principles of psychologists and code of conduct." *American Psychologist, 65*, 493.

American Psychological Association. (2011). Model act for state licensure of psychologists. *American Psychologist, 66*, 214–226.

Angell., & Dixon-Woods. (2008). Style matters: An analysis of 100 research ethics committee decision letters. *Research Ethics Review, 4*, 101–105.

Bersoff, D.N (2008). A short history of the development of APA's ethics codes. In: D. Bersoff (Ed.), *Ethical conflicts in psychology* (4th ed.) (pp. 10–13). Washington, DC: American Psychological Association.

British Academy and the Publishers Association. (2008). *Joint guidelines on copyright and academic research*. London: Author

British Psychological Society (2006). *The 2006 Annual Report*. Leicester: Author

British Psychological Society. (2009). *Code of ethics and conduct*. Leicester, England: BPS. Retrieved 20 June, 2011 from http://www.bps.org.uk/the-society/code-of-conduct/.

Canadian Psychological Association. (2000). *Canadian code of ethics for psychologists*. Ottawa: Author.

Colegio de Psicologos de Chile. (1999). *Codigo de etica profesional* [Code of professional ethics]. Retrieved from http://www.colegiopsicologos.cl/el-colegio/comisiones/comision-de-etica/estatutos/.

Dingwall, R. (2008). The ethical case against ethical regulation in humanities and social science research. *21st Century Society, 3*, 1–12.

Economic and Social Research Council. (2006). Framework for research ethics. Swindon, UK: Author.

European Federation of Psychologists' Associations. (1995). *Meta-code of ethics* (revised). Retrieved 20 June, 2011 from http://www.efpa.eu/.

Fitzgerald, M. (2007). The EU gets tough on ethics. *Technology Ireland, 38*, 27–30.

Fitzgerald, T. D., Hunter, P. V., Hadjistavropoulos, T., & Koocher, G. P. (2010). Ethical and legal considerations for internet-based psychotherapy. *Cognitive Behaviour Therapy, 39*, 173–187.

Gauthier, J., Pettifor, J., & Ferrero, A. (2010). The universal declaration of ethical principles for psychologists: A culture-sensitive model for creating and reviewing a code of ethics. *Ethics and Behavior, 20*(3&4), 1–18.

Hall, C. S. (1952). Crroks, codes and cant. *American Psychologist, 7*, 430-431.

Health Professions Council of South Africa. (2004). *Rules of conduct pertaining specifically to psychology*. Retrieved from http://www.psyssa.com/aboutus/codeofconduct.asp.

Herrnstein, R. J. & Murray, C. (1994). *The bell curve: Intelligence and class structure in American life*. New York: Free Press.

International Test Commission. (2000). *International guidelines for test use*. Retrieved 20 June, 2011 from http://www.intestcom.org/itc_projects.htm.

Jacobson, N., Gewurtz, R., & Haydon, E. (2007). Ethical review of interpretive research: Problems and solutions. *Ethics and Human Research, 29*, 1–8.

Joyce, N. R., & Rankin, T. J. (2010). The lessons of the development of the first APA ethics code: Blending science, practice, and politics. *Ethics & Behavior, 20*, 466–481.

Koocher, G. P. (2009). Any minute now but far far away: Electronically mediated mental health. *Clinical Psychology: Science and Practice, 16*, 339–342.

Koocher, G., & Keith-Spiegel, P. (2010). Peers nip misconduct in the bud. *Nature, 466*, 438–440.

Lindsay, G. (1996). Psychology as an ethical discipline and profession. *European Psychologist, 1,* 79–88.

Lindsay, G. (2011). Transnational ethical guidance and the development of the EFPA meta-code of ethics. *European Psychologist, 16,* 121–131.

Lindsay, G., & Colley, A. (1995). Ethical dilemmas of members of the Society. *The Psychologist: Bulletin of the British Psychological Society, 8,* 214–217.

Lindsay, G., Koene, C., Øvreeide, H., & Lang, F. (2008). *Ethics for European psychologists.* Ashland, OH: Hogrefe & Huber.

Lindsay, G. Strand, S., Cullen, M. A., Cullen, S., Band, S., Davis, H., et al. (2011). *Parenting Early Intervention Programme evaluation: DFE-R121A.* London: DfE. Retrieved from https://www.education.gov.uk/publications/eOrderingDownload/DFE-RR121A.pdf.

Lindsay, G., Strand, S., & Davis, H. (2011). A comparison of the effectiveness of three parenting programmes in improving parenting skills, parent mental well being and children's behaviour when implemented on a large scale in community settings in 18 English local authorities: The Parenting Early Intervention Pathfinder (PEIP), BMC Public Health 2011, 11:962 doi:10.1186/1471-2458-11-962

Lindsay, G., Wren, Y., Bakopoulou, I., & Roulstone, S. (2011). Interventions for children with speech, language and communication needs in England: Lacking an evidence base? 32nd Annual Conference of the Symposium on Research in Child Language Disorders (SRCLD), June 9–11. Madison, Wisconsin.

Martinson, B. C., Anderson, M. S., & deVries, R. (2005). Scientists behaving badly. *Nature, 435,* 737–738.

Nagy, T. F. (2011). *Essential ethics for psychologists: A primer for understanding and mastering core issues.* Washington, DC: American Psychological Association,

Neisser, U. (Ed.). (1998). *The rising curve: Long-term gains in IQ and related measures.* Washington, DC: American Psychological Association.

New Zealand Psychological Society. (2002). *Code of ethics for psychologists working in Aotearoa / New Zealand.* Wellington: Author.

Nordic Committee of Psychological Associations. (1998). *Ethical principles for Nordic psychologists.* Retrieved from http://www.psykologforbundet.se.

Pauwels, E. (2007). *Ethics for researchers: Facilitating research excellence in FP7.* Luxembourg: Office for Official Publications of the European Communities.

Pope, K. S., & Vetter, V. A. (1992). Ethical dilemmas encountered by members of the American Psychological Association. *American Psychologist, 57,* 397–411. .

Richardson, L. K., Frueh, B. C., Grubaugh, A. L., Egede, L., & Elhai, J. D. (2009). Current directions in videoconferencing tele-mental health research. *Clinical Psychology: Science and Practice, 16,* 323–338. .

Sanders, M., Montgomery, D. T., & Brechman-Toussaint, M. L. (2000). The mass media and the prevention of child behavior problems: The evaluation of a television series to promote positive outcomes for parents and their children. *Journal of Child Psychology and Psychiatry, 41,* 939–948.

Sinclair, C., & Pettifor, J. (1992). *Companion manual to the Canadian code of ethics for psychologists, 1991.* Ottawa: Canadian Psychological Association.

Stevens, M. J. (2010). Etic and emic in contemporary psychological ethics. *Europe's Journal of Psychology, 6*(4), 1–7.

Task Force on Psychological Ethics and National Security. (2005). *Report of the American Psychological Association presidential task force on psychological ethics and national security.* Washington, DC: American Psychological Association.

UK Research Integrity Office. (2009). *Code of practice for research: Promoting good practice and preventing misconduct.* London: Author. Retrieved from: http://www.ukrio.org

UK Research Integrity Office. (2010). *Guidance for researchers on retractions in academic journals.* London: Author. Retrieved from: http://www.ukrio.org

World Medical Association. (2008). *Declaration of Helsinki: Ethical principles for medical research involving human subjects.* Retrieved from http://www.wma.net/en/30publications/10policies/b3/.

APPENDIX

Michael J. Stevens *and* Alyssa A. Sondalle

This appendix contains an annotated list of resources pertaining to international psychological ethics and ethics codes that will be of interest and use to readers of *the Oxford International Handbook of Psychological Ethics*. The list includes an online information clearinghouse; interdisciplinary centers on ethics; international psychology organizations with web links to national and regional codes of ethics; books, CD-ROMS, and special issues of journals; and major ethics journals in psychology.

Online Information
Therapy, Ethics, Malpractice, Forensics, Critical Thinking (and a few other topics)
This psychology site provides free access to a variety of resources, such as:

- over 100 ethics codes and practice standards for assessment, therapy, counseling, and forensic practice developed by professional organizations (e.g., psychologists, psychiatrists, social workers, marriage and family counselors)
- ethics in psychology: 7 essentials
- 8 bogus apologies: ethics, critical thinking, and language
- 21 cognitive strategies to justify any unethical behavior
- informed consent: professional standards, sample forms, and key references
- links to resources on boundary issues in psychotherapy: widely used guides, statistics, trends, research, and resources
- over 300 citations of articles, books, and chapters on the controversy over psychologists and physicians participating in detainee interrogations

Web: http://kspope.com/index.php

Interdisciplinary Ethics Centers
Ethics Center, Department of Applied Ethics, University of Jena (Germany)
The Department of Applied Ethics deals with ethical research and education in key areas of modern societies such as medicine, biology, economics, technology, and sports. The Ethics Center Jena, which is directed by the Chair of Applied Ethics, is responsible for the ethical scholarship in the Faculty of Social and Behavioral Sciences. The Ethics Center, founded in 2002, promotes and coordinates interdisciplinary research and teaching on ethical discussions and conflicts pertinent to issues in Germany and internationally. The Center is located and directed at the offices of the Department of Applied Ethics and focuses on Bioethics/Medical Ethics, Business Ethics, Media Ethics, Sports Ethics, and Ethics in Technology.

ETHICS CENTER JENA
Zwätzengasse 3
Jena 07743, Germany
Tel: +49 (0)3641 / 945 800

Fax: +49 (0)3641 / 945 802
Email: ethikzentrum@uni-jena.de
Web: http://www.ethik.uni-jena.de/eng/index.php?option=com_content&view=article&id=3&Itemid=5

The Oxford Uehiro Center for Practical Ethics (United Kingdom)

The Oxford Uehiro Center for Practical Ethics was established in 2002 with the support of the Uehiro Foundation on Ethics and Education in Japan. It is an integral part of the Faculty of Philosophy at Oxford University. The Center has a threefold mission: research, teaching, and public debate. Its focus is the ethical issues that arise in everyday life and which are related to the changes in society, particularly those related to technological advancement. The Center researches a broad range of topics in practical ethics and moral philosophy, with core areas of expertise in bioethics, medical ethics, neuroethics, just war theory and terrorism, business ethics, and international justice. The Center's research program is interdisciplinary and includes medicine, law, politics, international relations, and religious studies departments, both within Oxford and internationally.

Oxford Uehiro Center for Practical Ethics
Littlegate House, Suite 8
St. Ebbes Street Oxford OX1 1PT, UK
Tel: +44 (0)1865 / 286 888
Fax: +44(0)1865 / 286 886
E-mail: ethics@philosophy.ox.ac.uk
Web: http://www.practicalethics.ox.ac.uk/

THE KENNEDY INSTITUTE OF ETHICS (UNITED STATES)

Founded at Georgetown University in 1971, the Kennedy Institute of Ethics's faculty have expertise in such issues as healthcare reform, death and dying, clinical research ethics, abortion, and environmental ethics. The Institute is committed to a civil dialogue on the pressing questions of the day in a climate of intellectual openness and lively discourse. The Kennedy Institute works in close collaboration with Georgetown's Department of Philosophy to support a variety of graduate degrees that allow advanced work in bioethics.

Joseph and Rose Kennedy Institute of Ethics
Healy Hall, 4th Floor
Georgetown University
Washington, DC 20057, USA
Tel: +202 / 687–8099
Email: kie@georgetown.edu
Web: http://kennedyinstitute.georgetown.edu/

Center for the Study of Ethics in the Professions, Illinois Institute of Technology (United States)

The Center for the Study of Ethics in the Professions (CSEP) was established in 1976 to promote research and teaching on practical moral problems in the professions. The first interdisciplinary center for ethics to focus on the professions, CSEP continues to be one of the nation's leading centers for practical and professional ethics. CSEP promotes innovative teaching. It generates professional ethics courses at IIT and assists faculty at other universities to prepare for teaching professional ethics and to develop courses and programs. The Codes of Ethics Online Collection consists of over 2,000 codes of ethics from professional organizations, businesses, government agencies, and religious and fraternal organizations. The collection includes a guide for using codes of ethics, resources for writing a code of ethics, and links to other collections of codes of ethics on the web.

Center for the Study of Ethics in the Professions at IIT
Hermann Hall, Room 204
241 S. Federal Street
Chicago, IL 60616, USA
Tel: +312 / 567–3017
Fax: +312 / 567–3016
Email: csep@iit.edu
Web: http://ethics.iit.edu/

International Psychology Organizations
International Union of Psychological Science

The ethics pages on the website of the International Union of Psychological Sciences (IUPsyS) contain the *Universal Declaration of Ethical Principles for Psychologists*, adopted by the IUsyS and International Association of Applied Psychology in 2008. It also contains papers describing the origins and development of the Declaration. The site also houses a compendium of ethics codes of national psychology associations in English and in the local language(s) intended for use by researchers, clinicians, instructors, policymakers, and organizations developing or revising their own codes of ethics. Finally, the IUPsyS ethics page has links to declarations of ethical principles from diverse global organizations, such as the United Nations, Center of Global Ethics, and World Medical Association.

> Email: infor@iupsys.org
> Web: http://www.iupsys.net/index.php/resources/ethics

Interamerican Society of Psychology

The Interamerican Society of Psychology (SIP) has a web page devoted to ethics. The page contains links to the national ethics codes of many countries in the Western hemisphere, mainly those of Latin America. In addition, the page has links to the *Universal Declaration of Ethical Principles for Psychologists*, a set of ethical considerations to guide members of SIP that were adopted by SIP in 2008, and a list of ethics codes and practice guidelines for assessment, counseling and psychotherapy, and forensic practice. Finally, the site has links to a diverse set of related resources on ethics.

> Secretario General / SIP
> Universidad de Puerto Rico
> Escuela Graduada de Trabajo Social
> P.O. Box 23345
> San Juan, Puerto Rico 00931–3345
> Tel: 787 / 764–0000, ext. 5974, 7091
> Fax: 787/ 763–4599
> Email: sip@uprrp.edu
> Web: http://www.sipsych.org/index.php?option=com_content&Itemid=55&catid=54&id=49&lang=es&view=article

European Federation of Psychologists' Associations

The European Federation of Psychologists' Associations (EFPA) has web pages on ethics including the 2005 revision of the *Meta-Code of Ethics*. Downloads are available that cover such topics as recommended approaches for teaching ethics, engaging in forensic work and serving as an expert witness, and providing ethical services via the Internet. Additional guidelines are available for the evaluation, mediation, and correction of ethical complaints and misconduct. The site also includes information on conferences around Europe that focus on psychological ethics, along with recommended books and websites on ethics for European psychologists.

> EFPA Head Office
> Grasmarkt 105 / 18
> Brussels B-1000, Belgium
> Tel: +32 (2)503 / 4953
> Fax: +32 (2)503 / 3067
> Web: http://www.efpa.eu/ethics

Books, CD-Roms, Special Journal Issues

Finkel, N. J., & Moghaddam, F. M. (Eds.). (2005). *The psychology of rights and duties: Empirical contributions and normative commentaries.* Washington, DC: American Psychological Association.

This cross-disciplinary book investigates how morality translates into action by presenting original psychological research on human rights and duties. One of the book's goals is to explore the general public's ideas (both in the United States and abroad) about rights versus duties so that legislative and policy changes can be based on solid support, not assumptions. Two strategies are used to lead readers toward a better understanding of human rights and duties. Chapters by empirical researchers present findings on citizens' commonsense understandings of rights and duties, whereas normative chapters by leading social theorists conceptualize rights and duties from many perspectives. By contrasting present-day life circumstances in many social spheres with the world of ideas, the editors expose the debate between what human rights and duties are and what they ought to be. This book may be particularly useful to psychology students and professors in courses on intergroup relations, social justice, psychology and law, ethnic relations and multiculturalism, cross-cultural and cultural psychology, and social psychology.

Goodman, R., & Roseman, M. J. (Eds.). (2009). *Interrogations, forced feedings, and the role of health professionals: New perspectives on international human rights, humanitarian law, and ethics.* Cambridge, MA: Human Rights Program, Harvard Law School.

The involvement of health professionals in human rights and humanitarian law violations has become a lively issue as a consequence of the U.S. prosecution of conflicts with al-Qaida, the Taliban, and Iraq. Health professionals, including MDs trained in psychiatry and PhDs trained in behavioral psychology, have reportedly advised and assisted in coercive interrogation. Such practices are not unique to the United States nor are they the most extreme forms of abuse in the world. The direct involvement of medical professionals in torture, covering up extrajudicial killings, and other extreme conduct is a phenomenon common to many societies and periods of national crisis. The widespread and repeated nature of this problem has led to the development of important legal and ethical codes on the subject. Those codes, however, are insufficient in many cases. A reexamination of international norms, as developed in human rights law, humanitarian law, and professional ethics can shed light on these issues. However, in addition to those instruments, the struggle to end such violations requires an understanding of human behavior and the role of formal and informal institutional pressures. In this volume, a wide range of prominent practitioners and scholars explore these issues. Their insights provide significant potential for reforming institutions to assist health professionals in maintaining their legal and ethical obligations in times of national crisis.

Koocher, G. P., & Keith-Spiegel, P. (2008). *Ethics in psychology and the mental health professions: Standards and cases* (3rd ed.). New York: Oxford University Press.

Now in an expanded edition, the revised volume considers many of the ethical questions and dilemmas that mental health professionals encounter in their everyday practice, research, and teaching. The book has been completely updated and is now also relevant for counselors, marriage and family therapists, social workers, and psychiatrists, and includes the ethics codes of those groups as appendices. Providing both a critical assessment and elucidation of key topics in the American Psychological Association's guidelines, this volume takes a practical approach to ethics and offers constructive means for both preventing problems as well as recognizing, approaching, and resolving ethical predicaments. This edition retains the key features which have contributed to its popularity, including hundreds of case studies that provide illustrative guidance on a wide variety of topics, including fee setting, advertising for clients, research ethics, sexual attraction, how to confront observed unethical conduct in others, and confidentiality.

Leach, M. M., & Leong, F. T. L. (Eds.). (2010). On international dimensions of psychological ethics [Special issue]. *Ethics and Behavior, 2*(3–4).

Psychological ethics has slowly become internationalized, though most psychologists in the United States are unfamiliar with the work and movements in international ethics. Recent national ethics code developments, work on international acceptance of ethical principles, and regional and international codes of ethics highlight this internationalism. The purpose of this special issue is to highlight both international developments and international considerations of psychological ethics. An introduction to the internationalization of psychological ethics is presented, followed by an overview of this special issue. The special issue introduces the reader to a few of the complexities of ethics when considered from an international perspective.

Lindsay, G., Koene, C., Ovreeide, H., & Lang, F. (2008). *Ethics for European psychologists.* Ashland, OH: Hogrefe and Huber.

European national psychology associations have adopted the European *Meta-Code of Ethics* developed by the European Federation of Psychologists, Associations (EFPA) as the basis for national codes, and thus for the standards applying to all psychologists in Europe. This book outlines and discusses the Meta-Code on the basis of practical examples and vignettes. The four ethical principles, Respect, Competence, Responsibility, and Integrity are covered in core chapters. Others give substance to underlying concepts, as well as practical advice and examples for ethical problem solving and for applications of the code. Practicing psychologists can learn how to put their daily practice on a sound ethical foundation and deal with challenging ethical dilemmas. This book is also relevant for teaching and training in both basic courses and advanced education. Further, it provides a basis for psychologists' associations to develop codes and guidelines, monitor national practice, and evaluate ethical complaints, as well as for users of psychologists' services to see what ethical standards they should expect.

Knapp, S. J., & VandeCreek, L. D. (2006). *Practical ethics for psychologists: A positive approach.* Washington, DC: American Psychological Association.

This book helps psychologists clarify what they value, consider how they should behave, and determine what constitutes proper professional conduct. The book is unique in stressing the importance of positive ethics; that is, ways in which psychologists can reach their highest ethical ideals, rather than just avoiding breaking rules. Using the 2002 ethics code of the American Psychological Association as a guide, the authors lay out a five-step model for resolving ethical dilemmas, illustrating the discussion with thumbnail sketches of both ethical and questionable behaviors. Throughout, they stress the importance of self-care, which involves self-regulation, emotional competence, and an understanding of the unique occupational challenges of being a psychologist. Readers will find guidance on dealing with ethically complex issues like competence, multiple relationships, informed consent, confidentiality (including confidentiality with life-endangering patients), fees and financial issues, public statements, and risk management. Individual chapters are devoted to special issues for psychologists working in forensics, teaching, assessment, therapy, and supervision and training.

Nagy, T. F. (2005). *Ethics in plain English: An illustrative casebook for psychologists* (2nd ed.). Washington, DC: American Psychological Association.

This volume is a practical and engaging resource that shows psychologists how to apply the principles of the ethics code of the American Psychological Association to the ethical dilemmas that they encounter in their daily lives. Each ethical standard is reproduced in its entirety. Then, it is translated into everyday language and is followed by a fictional case study that illustrates how the standard might be applied to a real-life situation. Examples of both problematic and exemplary behavior in diverse settings are provided. New to this edition are thought-provoking discussion questions after each case study, making the book even more useful for classroom use or self-study. The chapters cover general principles of ethical decision making as well as a broad range of issues relating to professional competence, human relations, privacy and confidentiality, advertising and other public statements, recordkeeping and fees, education and training, research and publication, assessment, and therapy.

Pimple, K. D. (Ed.). (2008). *Research ethics.* Aldershot, UK: Ashgate.

This volume includes more than 40 important articles on integrity and misconduct, biomedical research, the social and disciplinary contexts of science, research in the social sciences, the social responsibility of science and scientists, and other core issues in research ethics. An introduction by the editor places these articles in their historical and conceptual context. The volume provides a rich library of resources, ideas, and challenges in the ethics of research for scholars concerned with such issues.

Pope, K. S., & Vasquez, M. J. T. (2007). *Ethics in psychotherapy and counseling: A practical guide* (3rd ed.). San Francisco, CA: Jossey-Bass.

Significant changes in the ethics codes both of the American Psychological Association and the Canadian Psychological Association, new legislation and case law, new research findings, and new practice guidelines are among the developments that led to this third edition. Although much of the material is new, this book's fundamental approach to ethics remains unchanged. The approach is grounded in several basic assumptions:

- Ethical awareness is a continuous, active process.
- Awareness of the ethical standards and codes is crucial to competence in the area of ethics, but standards and codes cannot take the place of an active, deliberative, and creative approach to fulfilling our ethical responsibilities.
- Awareness of the scientific and professional literature and evolving research and theory is crucial to competence in the area of ethics, but the claims and conclusions emerging in the literature can never be passively accepted and reflexively applied.
- Clinicians repeatedly encounter ethical dilemmas for which a clear ethical response is elusive. Clinicians must be prepared to actively examine these dilemmas as a normal and expected part of their work.

Wedding, D., & Stevens, M. J. (Eds.). (2009). *Psychology: IUPsyS global resource (10th ed.).* Hove, UK: Psychology Press.

The Ethics in Psychology section of the last edition of this annual CD-ROM includes essays and resources analyzing codes of ethics in psychology. Articles include published comparisons of the principles of national ethics codes, symposia papers on ethics delivered at international conferences (e.g., ethics and ethical decision making across national boundaries and cultures, the impact of political transitions on ethics codes), working drafts and progress reports leading to the adoption of the *Universal Declaration of Ethical Principles of Psychologists*, and the *International Compilation of Human Subject Research Protections* maintained by the U.S. Department of Health and Human Services.

Ethics Journals
Ethical Human Psychology and Psychiatry: An International Journal of Critical Inquiry

Ethical Human Psychology and Psychiatry is a peer-reviewed journal of the International Center for the Study of Psychiatry and Psychology that publishes original research reports, reviews, essays, book reviews, commentaries, and case reports examining the ramifications of the idea that emotional distress is due to an underlying organic disease that is best treated with pharmacological therapy. This view of human nature permeates virtually every area of our society, including medicine, business, law, education, politics, and the media. Thus, the journal welcomes submissions from a broad range of specialties. Over the past several years the journal has published articles about the ethics of medicating children, deficiencies in the biological theory of mental illness, the marketing tactics of the pharmaceutical companies, ethical problems with involuntary treatment, and the benefits of psychotherapy. *Ethical Human Psychology and Psychiatry* will continue its efforts in seeking to raise the level of scientific knowledge and ethical discourse, while empowering professionals who are unsullied by professional and economic interests.

Web: http://www.springerpub.com/product/15594343

The Journal of Ethics: An International Philosophical Review

The Journal of Ethics: An International Philosophical Review publishes articles on a wide range of topics in ethics, philosophically construed, including such areas as ethical theory and moral, social, political, and legal philosophy. Although the journal is primarily an organ of philosophical research, it publishes work on topics of concern to academics and professionals in a wide range of fields. The journal also seeks to publish the highest quality commentaries on works published in its pages.

Web: http://www.springer.com/social±sciences/applied±ethics/journal/10892

Ethics and Behavior

Ethics and Behavior publishes articles on an array of topics pertaining to various moral issues and conduct. These topics may include, but are not restricted to, the exercise of social and ethical responsibility in human behavior, ethical dilemmas or professional misconduct in health and human-service delivery, the conduct of research involving human and animal participants, fraudulence in the management or reporting of scientific research, and public policy issues involving ethical problems. Perspectives are presented occasionally vis-à-vis essays describing challenging dilemmas in ethics and behavior.

Web: http://www.tandf.co.uk/journals/authors/hebhauth.asp

Ethics and Education

Ethics and Education is a new international, peer-reviewed journal that aims to stimulate discussion and debate around the ethical dimensions of education. The journal addresses issues in both formal and informal education and upbringing, and includes within its scope relevant aspects of applied ethics, including:

- Bioethics
- Medical ethics
- Management ethics
- Sex education
- Ethics of therapy and counseling
- Professional ethics

Ethics and Education welcomes all traditions and forms of ethical inquiry from a wide range of philosophical and religious perspectives. As well as appealing to those with a direct interest in ethics and education, the journal will be of interest to philosophers, education specialists, and policy makers.

Web: http://www.tandf.co.uk/journals/titles/17449642.asp

INDEX

A

Abbott, Max, 408
Aboriginal Australians, 364–365
aboriginal people, 176
    in Canada, 386
    cooperation among, 177
    effects of colonization on, 178
About Health Testing (BPS), 211
About Occupational Testing (BPS), 211
ACA. *See* American Counseling Association
Academy of the Mysteries of Nature, 246
accountability, 49, 106, 151
accreditation, 370
    APA and, 324
    in Australia, 367
    in Brazil, 106
    in Canada, 111, 324
    ethics training and, 367–368
    in Mexico, 110, 314, 316
    in New Zealand, 109
    NSCBI and, 410
    in Russia, 1990s, 431
    in Turkey, 107, 446
accuracy in reporting, 140, 145, 147, 353–354
ACTO. *See* Association for Counseling and Therapy Online
Adorno, Theodor, 54
advertising, 353, 432, 437–438
Afghanistan, 386
Africa, 103
African Charter of Human and Peoples' Rights, 119
Ahmadinejad, Mahmoud, 384
Allende, Salvador, 381
Allport, Gordon W., 242
American Counseling Association (ACA), 172, 331
American Medical Association Code of Ethics, 22
American Mental Health Counselors Association (AMHCA), 172
American Psychiatric Association, 235

American Psychological Association (APA), xxiv, 11, 21. *See also Ethical Principles of Psychologists and Code of Conduct*
    accreditation and, 324
    Anatomically Detailed Dolls and, 46
    Committee on Psychological Tests and Assessment, 209
    Committee on Scientific and Professional Ethics, 247, 324
    Council of Representatives, 235
    CPS and, 22, 22–23
    credentialing and, 321
    Division of International Psychology, 158
    eHealth and, 171
    ethical decision-making and, 79
    ethics codes and, 12, 324
    ethics codes development and, 121
    human rights and, 291
    informal resolution of ethical violations and, 91
    Internet searches and, 212
    military service and, 234–235
    Office of Workforce Analysis, 158
    O*NET database and, 244
    PENS report and, 234–235, 387–388
    Perosio and, 398
    sanctions, 324–325
    sexuality and, 261
    test guidelines, 209–210
    test use ethics codes and, 202
    torture at Guantanamo Bay and, 236
American Society for Training and Development (ASTD), 253, 256
AMHCA. *See* American Mental Health Counselors Association
Anschütz, Georg, 443
Anscombe, Gertrude E. M., 245
Aotearoa, 175, 180
APA. *See* American Psychological Association
APAC. *See* Australian Psychology Accreditation Council

APA Code. *See Ethical Principles of Psychologists and Code of Conduct*
APA Practice Organization (APAPO), 324
APA Resolution on Culture and Gender Awareness in International Psychology, 156–157, 157
apartheid, 178, 385
appeals, 43, 98
    basic human, 72
    in Europe, 344
    fraternal, 91
    HKPS and, 333
APS. *See* Australian Psychological Society
arbitration, 95
Argentina, 105–106, 309–311
    competencies in, 398, 399–400
    curtailment of psychology in, 396–399
    democracy in, 399–401
    dictatorship in, 394
    education in, 395, 400–401
    implications of psychology in, 397
    law in, 396, 398
    legalization of psychology in, 399–401
    professional associations in, 396
    provincial law in, 399
    psychological associations in, 399
    psychology as profession in, 395–396
    psychology as science in, 395
    psychotherapy in, 396
    recognition of psychology in, 398
    state terrorism in, 398–399
    torture in, 397
    training in, 395
Asia, 104
ASPPB. *See* Association of State and Provincial Psychology Boards
assessments
    complaints against, 93
    discrimination and, 260
    emerging challenges in, 455
    employee selection, 257
    ethics of procedure and, 69–70
    expanded access to, 162
    grounding, 194

assessments (Cont.)
    growth of psychology and, 452
    for indigenous peoples, 176
    instruments, 193–194, 194
    needs, 62
    online, 166–167
    procedures, 86
    in Russia, 1990s, 432–433
    in Soviet Union, 429
    subdisciplines and, 74
Assessment System for the Quality of Tests, 209
Associação Brasileira de Psicología, 311
Associação Nacional de Pesquisa e Pós-Graduação em Psicologia, 312
Association for Counseling and Therapy Online (ACTO), 172
Association of German Professional Psychologists, 383
Association of Psychologists of Buenos Aires, 106
Association of Social Work Boards (ASWB), 171
Association of State and Provincial Psychology Boards (ASPPB), 78, 247, 322
ASTD. *See* American Society for Training and Development
ASWB Model Social Work Practice Act, 171
asylees, 191
asylum seekers, 190–191, 191, 195, 196. *See also* forced migrants
Ataturk, Mustafa Kemal, 444
atonement, 92, 94, 94, 94
Australia
    accreditation in, 367, 370
    continuing development in, 369
    electronic media in, 369–370
    ethical complaints in, 369
    ethics code development in, 359–361
    ethics codes in, 364–365
    ethics committees in, 362–364
    ethics training in, 367–368
    indigenous cultures in, 364–365, 367, 370
    law in, 358
    literature in, 368–369
    national registration in, 370
    online counseling in, 370
    postgraduate education in, 367
    professional associations in, 359–361
    regional ethics codes in, 363
    registration in, 358–359
    social networking in, 369–370
Australian Medical Council, 364
Australian Psychological Society (APS), 127, 359
    civil law and, 290–291
    eHealth and, 170–171
    ethics code development, 359–361
    Ethics Committee, 359, 363
    invoking ethics code of, 361–362
    membership in, 359
    resolving ethical complaints, 363–364
    restructuring of, 363
    sexuality and, 261
    Universal Declaration of Ethical Principles for Psychologists and, 361–362
Australian Psychology Accreditation Council (APAC), 367
authorship credit, 140, 146, 147
autochthonization, 30
autonomy
    cultural factors and, 78
    as ethical principle, 120
    in ethical research, 273
    indigenous cultures and, 187
    IRBs and, 152
    in mediation, 93
    of psychologists, 87
avoiding harm, 140, 146, 147. *See also* doing no harm
The Ayurvedic Instruction, 4, 6
Ayurvedic Oath of Initiation, 6, 9

B

Beauvoir, Simone de, 255
Behnke, Stephen, 79
Belgium, 340, 343, 347
beneficence, 44, 120, 151, 273
Bentham, Jeremy, 245
Berry, J. W., 192
bias, 86
    in APA Code, 151
    discrimination and, 259
    in ethical decision-making, 82
    ethnocentric, 139
    European, 175
    minimizing, 156
    racial, 33–34
Bible, 115
Bicultural Commitment, 410, 411
biculturalism, 180, 408–410
bioethics, 246, 247
Blumenfeld, Walter, 316
Bond, Michael Harris, 328
Book of Medicine (Osaph), 6
Boulder Conference of 1949, 74
BPS. *See* British Psychological Society
braindump sites, 222–223, 226–227
Brazil, 106, 311–312
bribery, 150
British Psychological Society (BPS), 341
    Australian Branch, 360
    code of conduct, 247
    Code of Ethics and Conduct, 81
    compliance with *Meta-Code of Ethics*, 79
    ethical principles and, 76
    Forensic Psychology division, 232
    sexuality and, 261
    Steering Committee on Test Standards, 210
    test guidelines, 210–211
    test use and, 21

Buddhism, 245
Bush, George W., 233–234, 324, 386

C

Callahan, David, 219
Canada, 110–111
    aboriginal cultures in, 386
    accreditation in, 324
    CPQ and, 323
    current ethics research in, 326
    ethics codes in, 325, 386
    ethics committees in, 325
    ethics training in, 325–326
    immigration in, 190
    legal restrictions in, 323
    legal status of psychology in, 323
    multiculturalism in, 386
    professional associations in, 324
    regulatory bodies in, 323, 324
    statutory regulations in, 78
Canadian Code of Ethics for Psychologists, 15–16, 325, 412, 413–414
Canadian Institutes of Health Research, 186
Canadian Psychological Association (CPA), 15–16, 111, 247, 324
    Code of Ethics, 282–283
    ethical decision-making models and, 81
    ethical principles and, 76
    Guidelines for Professional Practice for School Psychologists in Canada and, 248
    test guidelines, 211
    test use and, 21
    Universal Declaration of Ethical Principles for Psychologists and, 127
Canadian Register of Health Care Providers, 110
CAS. *See* Chinese Academy of Science
Cassin, René, 117, 118
CAT. *See* computerized adaptive testing
Catholic Church, 246
Cattell, Raymond B., 260–261
CBT. *See* cognitive behavioral therapy
CE. *See* continuing education
Ceausescu, Nicolae, 380–381
Center for Academic Integrity, 218–219
Centre for Global Ethics, 31, 39
CEPS. *See* Committee on Ethical and Professional Standards
Certificate of Professional Qualification in Psychology (CPQ), 322, 323
Chang Peng-chun, 117
Charles II, king of England, 246
Charter of the United Nations, 118
cheating, 218, 228–229
    historical, 218
    improper response to, 224–225
    justifications for, 219
    prevalence of, 218–219
    by proxy, 223
    technology, 216–217
    types of, 220

The Cheating Culture (Callahan), 219
Chen Shih-Kung, 6–7
child protection services, 33, 181
children
  advocacy for, 417
  Guidelines for Child Custody Evaluations in Divorce Proceedings and, 209–210
  informed consent and, 276
  in *NZ Code*, 417
  personal ethics and, 56
  as research participants, 154
  test use and, 202
  UNCROC and, 417
  violence among, 37
Chile, 381–382
China, 21, 104–105, 329, 383–384
  cultural conditions of, 21–22
  ethics code, 334
  ethics codes development in, 121
  ethics training in, 335
  good practices in, 335–336
  high-stakes testing in, 218
  informed consent in, 153
  society-based ethics committees and, 331
Chinese Academy of Science (CAS), 329, 331
Chinese Mental Health Association (CMHA), 104
Chinese Psychological Society (CPS), 21, 21–22, 104–105, 329
  APA and, 22, 22–23
  ethical complaints and, 331
  ethical standards and, 331
  professional associations and, 330
Chinese societies, 328
  commitment to good practices in, 335–336
  comparison of ethics codes in, 334–335
  ethics code development in, 334–335
  ethics investigations in, 332–334
  ethics training in, 335
  legal status of psychology in, 329–330
  professional associations in, 330–331
  society-based ethics committees in, 331–332
CIFRHuS. *See* Comisión Interinstitucional para la Formación de Recursos Humanos para la Salud
CIRP. *See* Committee on International Relations in Psychology
civil disobedience, 251
civil law, 283
  Australian Psychological Association and, 290–291
  categories of, 288
  confidentiality and, 288–289
  in ethics codes, 283, 283–286, 286, 287, 286, 287
  informed consent and, 288–289
  literature on, 291–292
  psychological associations and, 294

references to, 286–289
resolving conflicts between ethics codes and, 290–292, 291
specific references to, 288–289
subject areas, 288
Claparede, Edouard, 242–243
clients
  access to records of, 50, 50–51
  customers *versus*, 434–435
  dialogical connectedness with, 70
  in disciplinary evaluations, 92
  entitlement of, 48–49
  familiarity with social services of, 195
  in indigenous cultures, 181
  interest in atonement, 94
  moral position of, 57
  passive, 69
  protection from exploitation of, 57–58
  protection from third party interests, 348
  as research participants, 153–154
  rights of, 407–408
  secondary, 67, 81–82
  sexual relations with, 57, 354
CMHA. *See* Chinese Mental Health Association
CNCDP. *See* Consultative National Commission on the Deontology of Psychologists
CNEIP. *See* Consejo Nacional de Enseñanza e Investigación en Psicología
Code of Ethics (APS), 361
Code of Ethics for Counseling and Clinical Practice, 383–384, 390
Code of Ethics for Psychologists (Canada), 386
Code of Ethics for Psychologists Working in Aotearoa/New Zealand (*NZ Code*), 366–367, 405–406
  adoption of, 413
  aspirational perspective of, 410–413
  biculturalism in, 408–410
  Canadian Code of Ethics for Psychologists and, 412
  children in, 417
  content of, 413–415
  cultural context for, 405–406
  cultural sensitivity in, 415
  ethical decision-making guidelines in, 415–416
  integrity in relationships in, 414
  Maori in, 410–413, 415
  move away from codes of conduct in, 411–412
  political context for, 405–406
  preliminary drafts of, 412, 413
  principles of, 414
  purpose of, 413
  respect for dignity in, 414
  responsibility to society in, 414
  responsible caring in, 414
  social justice in, 414

structure of, 413–415
Treaty of Waitangi and, 412, 414–415
UNCROC and, 417
Code of Good Practice for Psychological Testing Centers (BPS), 210
Code of Hammurabi, 4, 5, 6, 22, 115, 202
Code of Health and Disability Service Consumers' Rights, 407–408
Code of Professional Conduct (APS), 359–360, 360–361
codes of conduct, xix–xx
  Association of State and Provincial Psychology Boards and, 247
  compliance with, 368
  in Europe, 247–248
  HKPS and, 331
  move away from, 411–412
  NZ Code and, 405
  organizational, 258
  regulatory boards and, 31
  universal declarations *versus*, 120
  in W/O Psychology, 250
"Codes of Ethics of National Psychological Organizations" (IUPsyS), 283
CoE. *See* Committee of Enquiry
cognitive behavioral therapy (CBT), 161, 184–185
Colegio official de Psicólogos (COP), 340, 351, 356
Colegios, 396, 399
colleagues
  actions of, 355
  discussing ethical dilemmas with, 57
  ethical complaints against, 97
  mistreatment of, 437
  respect for, 347
  in Russian ethics code, 438
collectivism, individualism *versus*, 391
College of Psychologists in British Columbia, 110–111
Colombia, 312–313
colonialism, 29–30, 178–181, 364, 407–408
Comisión Interinstitucional para la Formación de Recursos Humanos para la Salud (CIFRHuS), 313–314
Comité de Acreditación, 314
Comité Nacional de Ética en Psicología (CoNaEP), 315
Commission on Rehabilitation Counselor Certification (CRCC), 171
Committee of Enquiry (CoE), 332, 332–334, 333
Committee of the Psychological Sciences of the Polish Academy of Sciences (KANPAN), 107
Committee on Ethical and Professional Standards (CEPS), 359, 362–363
Committee on International Relations in Psychology (CIRP), 158
Committee on Publication Ethics (COPE), 260
common markets, 122

common platforms, 340
common practices, 48
common standards, 134–135, 135, 147
   category development of, 140–147
   coding of, 140
   consensus approach to, 136
   countries with, 141–144
   empirical approach to, 136
   across ethics codes, 137
   good practices and, 137
   possibility of, 147
   research ethics as, 138–139
   research limitations on, 148
   research to determine, 138
   test use standards and, 138
   themes, 140
   universal standards *versus*, 136–137
   values and, 137
communication
   eHealth and, 162–163, 168–169
   indigenous psychology and, 30
   in online counseling, 161–162
   in *Universal Declaration of Ethical Principles for Psychologists*, 125
communism, 55, 381, 425–426
community
   assent, 270
   collaborative partnership with, 273–274
   democratic representation of study, 273–274
   feedback sessions, 277
   in *NZ Code*, 406
   after research, 277
   responsibility to, 415
   study, 277–278
compensation, 140, 146, 147. *See also* financial arrangements
competence, 42–43, 86–87
   anchoring of, 45
   appearance of, 47
   boundaries of, for eHealth, 167
   cultural, 181–182, 370
   cultural diversity training and, 192
   enhancement of, 49
   ethical dilemmas of, 33
   in *Ethical Principles of Psychologists and Code of Conduct*, 45–46
   in *Ethical Standards of Psychologists*, 14
   in Europe, 349–350
   intentional ethics as, 63
   in interventions, 48
   limits of, 45, 349
   measuring, 33
   in Mercado Común del Sur, 309
   in *Meta-Code of Ethics*, 16, 23, 44, 45, 84
   moral obligation for, 45
   multicultural, 196
   in New Zealand, 109
   in *Nuremberg Code of Ethics in Medical Research*, 13–14
   promotion of, 47
   in South America, 16
   tactical rules and, 44
competent caring for well-being
   across cultures, 151
   in early to mid-20th century, 13–14
   in *Universal Declaration of Ethical Principles for Psychologists*, 17, 44, 125, 151
complainants, 92, 92–93, 95, 96
Compulsory Assessment and Treatment Act, 417
Computer-Based and Internet Delivered Testing (ITC), 25, 206
computerized adaptive testing (CAT), 223
CoNaEP. *See* Comité Nacional de Ética en Psicología
concentration camps, 11–12
Confederación de Psicólogos de la República Argentina (COPRA), 396
confidentiality. *See also* privacy
   in biomedical research, 270
   breaching, 67, 96, 348
   business ethics and, 253–254
   civil law and, 288–289
   Code of Ethics for Counseling and Clinical Practice and, 390
   before Common Era, 5
   as common standard theme, 140
   cross-cultural, 34
   of data, 145, 348
   duty of, 253
   eHealth and, 165
   ethical dilemmas of, 253
   in *Ethical Standards of Psychologists*, 12–13
   ethics codes and, 253
   in Europe, 347–348
   focus groups and, 277
   inclusion rate of, 147
   indigenous cultures and, 178
   informed consent *versus*, 145
   interpreters and, 196
   limits of, 253, 348
   professional associations and, 253
   of proposal, 140, 147
   psychotherapy and, 253
   of research participants, 277
   in research with immigrants, 194
   Spanish Psychological Association and, 251
   suicide and, 99
   test use and, 205
   transparency *versus*, 49
   W/O Psychology and, 251, 252–254
conflicts of interest, 88, 146
   as common standard theme, 140
   cross-cultural, 34
   dual relationships and, 140
   in Europe, 354–355
   inclusion rate of, 147
   in research, 278
Confucius, 115
Consejo Nacional de Enseñanza e Investigación en Psicología (CNEIP), 314
Consejo para la Acreditación de la Educación Superior (COPAES), 314
Conselho de Ética Profissional, 311
Conselho Federal de Psicologia, 311
Conselho Regionais de Psicologia, 311
consent, freedom of, 348–349. *See also* informed consent
construct-irrelevant variance, 222
Consultative National Commission on the Deontology of Psychologists (CNCDP), 343
consumer behavior analysis, 254
consumers, welfare of, 315
continuing development, 45, 87, 350, 369
continuing education (CE), 45, 318
continuing professional development (CPD), 87
continuity of care, 352
convenience samples, 275
Convention Against Torture and Other Cruel, Inhuman, or Degrading Treatment or Punishment, 119
Convention on the Elimination of All Forms of Discrimination Against Women, 119
Convention on the Rights of Persons with Disabilities, 119
Convention on the Rights of the Child, 119
cooperation, 54
   among Aboriginal people, 177
   across geographic boundaries, 135
   internal legitimacy and, 62
   loyal, 92
Coordinating Committee of Psychologists of the Mercosur and Associated Countries, 122
COP. *See* Colegio official de Psicólogos
COPAES. *See* Consejo para la Acreditación de la Educación Superior
COPE. *See* Committee on Publication Ethics
COPRA. *See* Confederación de Psicólogos de la República Argentina
copyright infringement, 260
Council of Europe, 339
Council of Psychologists Registration Boards (CPRB), 362
counseling. *See also* online counseling
   cultural identities and, 31
   ethical decision-making in, 38
   indigenous, 30
   multicultural competencies and, 31
   rehabilitation, 171
   in South Africa, 104
   in Soviet Union, 429
   universalist *versus* culture-specific, 31
counterterrorism, 387
CPA. *See* Canadian Psychological Association

CPD. *See* continuing professional development
CPQ. *See* Certificate of Professional Qualification in Psychology
CPRB. *See* Council of Psychologists Registration Boards
CPS. *See* Chinese Psychological Society
CRCC. *See* Commission on Rehabilitation Counselor Certification
credentialing
   in Colombia, 313
   in Europe, 106
   in Indonesia, 109
   in Iran, 108
   in Israel, 108
   in Mexico, 110
   in New Zealand, 109
   in South America, 105
   in Turkey, 107
   in US, 321
criminal justice system, 232
crisis intervention
   eHealth, 167–168
   ethical dilemma, 168
   for online counseling, 168
   for web-based interventions, 168
criticism, 50
   openness to, 92
   reasonable, 88
   receiving, 91
cross-cultural exchange programs, 149
Cuba, 380
cultural awareness
   in ethics codes, 126
   indigenous cultures and, 182
   promotion of, 157
   in South African ethics code, 385
   training, 176
cultural beliefs, 29, 39
cultural contexts
   analysis of, 81
   globalization and, 149
   for *NZ Code*, 405–406
   Rules of Conduct Pertaining Specifically to Psychology and, 390
cultural diversity
   ethics codes and, 405–406
   globalization and, 114
   teaching of, 192
   training, 192
   transnational ethics codes and, 453
cultural expectations
   external legitimacy and, 62
   individualism and, 78
   treatment acceptability and, 184
cultural factors
   autonomy and, 78
   awareness of, 85–86
   in eHealth, 169
   ethics codes and, 77–78
   in international research ethical guidelines, 150
   with PTSD, 154
   in test use, 156
cultural identity, 31
   codes of ethics and, 34
   learning, 40
   loss of, 39
   technology and, 127–128
cultural psychology, 187
cultural relativism, 130
cultural respect
   Australian Aborigines and, 365
   external legitimacy and, 62
   government policies and, 36
Cultural Revolution, 21, 329
cultural sensitivity, 40, 78, 86, 415
customers, 434–435
Czech-Moravian Psychological Society, 349
Czech Republic, 339–340, 343

D

Daily Jewish Prayer of a Physician, 6
Dalai Lama, 130, 245
data, 145
   collection, 164, 193
   as common standard theme, 140
   compression, 254
   confidentiality, 145, 348
   exploitation of, 437
   falsified, 278
   forensics, 228, 228–229
   limited, 294–295
   manipulation, 145
   protection, 356–357
   in Russian ethics code, 435
   storage, 348
   validity, 167
death penalty, 36
debriefing, 140, 145, 147
deception, 36, 155–156
Declaration of Geneva, 121
Declaration of Helsinki, 121, 268, 427
Declaration of Independence, 115
Declaration of Madrid, 30
Declaration of the Rights of Man and of the Citizen, 115–116
deinstitutionalization, 416–417
de Klerk, F. W., 385
delegation, 140, 145
DeLeon, Pat, 236
Delgado, Honorio, 316
delineation, 176
della Porta, Giambattista, 246
democracy, 60, 377, 401
Deng Xiaoping, 383
Denmark, 24, 339, 340, 344
Deontological and Bioethical Code for the Practice of the Profession in Colombia, 313
deontological codes, 244, 245
   consulting psychologists and, 243
   discrimination and, 259
   in FePRA ethics code, 401
   membership and, 245–247
   in psychology, 247–248
   W/O Psychology and, 248–249
deontological conflicts, 244
Department of Defense, 236
developing countries, 275
Dewey, John, 245
Diagnostic and Statistical Manual, 244
dialogism, 261
dialogue
   dyadic, 71
   ethics of, 70–72
   proximity to, 70–71
   in relationships, 72
dictatorships
   in Argentina, 394
   in Chile, 381
   human rights and, 402
   ideology of, 397
   in South America, 394
   Universal Declaration of Ethical Principles for Psychologists and, 402
Directory of Unpublished Experimental Measures, 212
disaster, 329
disciplinary evaluations, 91–92
   clients in, 92
   criminal law *versus*, 92
   interested parties in, 99
disciplinary procedures, 95–97
   non-psychologists in, 95–97
   preventative role of, 100
   problems with, 97–99
   psychologist cooperation with, 98
   questionnaires on, 97–98
disclosure, 125, 155
Discrete Option Multiple Choice (DOMC), 224
discrimination, 32, 86
   age, 259–260
   avoidance of, 68–69
   human resources and, 259
   against immigrants, 195
   misinterpretation of, 35
   positive, 68–69
   of research participants, 277
   research to eliminate, 157
   respect in Europe and, 347
disease, 32
diversity, 39, 157. *See also* cultural diversity
doing no harm. *See also* avoiding harm
   in Chile, 382
   in *Ethical Standards of Psychologists*, 13
   in *Nuremberg Code of Ethics in Medical Research*, 13
   qualitative research and, 275–276
   RECs and, 270
   risk-benefit determination and, 275
   social order *versus*, 383–384
   in *Universal Declaration of Ethical Principles for Psychologists*, 125
domains of practice, 77–78

DOMC. *See* Discrete Option Multiple
    Choice
dramatis personae, 99
dual relationships, 140, 354. *See also*
    multiple relationships
Durie, Mason, 408
Dutch Institute of Psychology, 209
duty
    of confidentiality, 253
    ethics of, 65–66
    ethics of procedure and, 69
    Kant and, 246
    professional, W/O Psychology and, 253
    to protect, 138

E

East Germany, 382
Economic and Social Research Council,
    79
economic behavior predictors, 254
economic freedom, 391, 391
    indices, 377
    national development and, 378–380
economic growth, 55, 186
economic transitions, 375, 376–380
    ethics code enforcement in, 402
    forms of, 380–389
    to market economy, 436–437
    social justice and, 391
Editorial Trillas, 314
education
    in Argentina, 395, 400–401
    in Colombia, 312
    distance, 215, 217
    ethics codes for, 75
    ethics training in, 355–356
    high-stakes testing in, 217
    in Mexico, 313
    in modern Russia, 434
    normalization of, in Argentina, 399
    online, 219
    in open societies, 376
    in Peru, 316
    postgraduate, 367
    in Russia, 1990s, 431
    in Turkey, 445
Education and Social Research Council, 461
Education Testing Service (ETS), 211
EFPA. *See* European Federation of
    Psychologists' Associations
EFPPA. *See* European Federation
    of Professional Psychologists'
    Associations
eHealth, 160–161, 162
    as adjunct, 164
    anonymity and, 169
    APA and, 171
    appropriateness of, 166
    APS and, 170–171
    boundaries of competence, 167
    communication and, 162–163,
        168–169
    confidentiality and, 165

cost effectiveness of, 163–164
crisis intervention, 167–168
cultural factors in, 169
data collection and, 164
data validity, 167
efficacy of, 164
ethical challenges for, 165
ethical guidelines for, 170
ethics codes, 170, 172
expanded access and, 162
financial arrangements, 166
identity verification, 167
implications for, 172–173
informed consent and, 165
intakes, 166
law and, 169
licensing, 169
nonverbal cues and, 169
online assessments, 166–167
online diagnoses, 166–167
records, 166
risks, 165
statutory regulations and, 165
training, 167
electronic signatures, 165
e-mail, 162–163
employee performance, 257
employee selection, 257
English *Bill of Rights*, 115
English language, 30
entitlement, of clients, 48–49
EPPP. *See* Examination for Professional
    Practice in Psychology
ergonomics, 243–244
Estonia, 340, 343, 346, 351
ethical awareness, 45, 63, 86, 349
*Ethical Code for Psychologists of Mental
    Tests*, 22
ethical complaints
    adjudicating, 31
    in Australia, 369
    in Canada, 110–111
    against colleagues, 97
    CPS and, 331
    evaluation procedures, 91–92
    frequency of, 98
    in Hong Kong, 332
    incidence of, 98–99
    intentional ethics and, 64
    investigations into, 96
    mediation of, 93–95
    Meta-Code of Ethics and, 91
    in Mexico, 315
    in New Zealand, 109
    NIP and, 344
    process of, 333
    resolving, 363–364
    severity of, 94
    underreported, 98
    unproven, 97
    withdrawal of, 93
ethical decision-making, 37–38, 75,
    80–81, 88–89

bias in, 82
community-based, 153
across cultures, 40
guidelines, 415–416
implementing decisions of, 83
influence of, 81–82
Meta-Code of Ethics and, 84–85
mindset for, 89
models, 39, 81–83
peer consultation in, 82
principles *versus* ethics codes in, 79–80
process issues in, 84–85
proposed courses of action in, 82
reflection in, 80–81, 83
relative automaticity of, 80
Russian ethics code and, 436
self-protection in, 82
social-constructionist approach to, 38
technical quality of, 74–75
ethical dilemmas, 57, 248
    appreciation of, 157
    common interests in, 54
    of competence, 33
    of confidentiality, 253
    crisis intervention, 168
    cross-cultural, 28, 150
    democratic process and, 60
    emotionally-based sensitivity for, 56–57
    ethical decision-making and, 80
    ethical principles in, 59
    ethics committees and, 344
    frequency of, 75
    in international research, 151
    law and, 60–61
    of legal restrictions, 35–36
    limited specificity of, 249
    multicultural competencies and, 31
    of professional boundaries, 34–35
    relating to ethics codes, 249
    resolving, 39–40, 87, 352
    of respect for dignity, 33–34
    section ethics and, 58
    in social justice, 36–37
    of status of women, 35
    with testing security, 222–225
    of underlying tensions, 37
    *Universal Declaration of Ethical
        Principles for Psychologists* and, 39
    vignettes of, 32–33
ethical guidelines, 150, 170, 244
ethical principles, 3–76, 129
    autonomy of psychologists and, 87
    awareness of, 96
    common, 24
    concept of, 120
    context-dependent, 334
    engagement with, 79
    in ethical dilemmas, 59
    history of, 3–4
    Meta-Code of Ethics and, 3–4, 389
    motivations for, 57
    Psychologists Committee of Mercosur
        and Associated Countries of, 400

revisions of, 42–43
universal, 129–130, 334
universal declarations and, 119–120
Ethical Principles for Nordic Psychologists, 16, 122, 134, 341–342, 454
Ethical Principles of Psychologists and Code of Conduct (APA Code), 151, 247, 324, 325
   bias in, 151
   competence in, 45–46
   Conflicts Between Ethics and Organizational Demands, 252
   cross-cultural limitations of, 150
   cross-cultural research and, 150–151
   ethical principles in, 76
   ethical standards *versus* principles in, 44
   ethnocentric bias and, 139
   gaps in, 151
   Germany and, 383
   goals of, 191
   IACP and, 105
   immigration and, 191–192
   informed consent and, 152
   Internet and, 171
   military psychologists and, 233
   multicultural competence and, 196
   PENS report and, 387–388
   professional knowledge in, 47
   as reference code, 138
   research practices in, 151
   revisions to, 42–43
   self-protection in, 50
   test security and, 222
ethical standards
   advocacy for, 203
   CPS and, 331
   principles and, 76–77
   research considerations for, 136–138
   as rules, 44
   in Soviet Union, 426–427
Ethical Standards of Psychologists, 11, 324
   competence in, 14
   confidentiality in, 12–13
   doing no harm in, 13
   ethical principles in, 11
   informed consent in, 13
   responsibility to society in, 14–15
   structure of, 15
   truthfulness in, 14
ethical statements, 26
ethical violations
   adjudication of, 342
   EFPA and, 91
   informal resolution of, 91
   NIP and, 91
   reasonable critique of, 91
ethics. *See also* research ethics
   from 1st to 17th centuries, 6–9
   in 18th and 19th centuries, 9–11
   of ambiguity, 255
   business, 243, 253–254
   common, 55–56, 57, 58
   before Common Era, 4–6

   definition of, 58
   developments, 448
   dialogical, 70–72
   of duty, 65–66
   in early to mid-20th century, 11–15
   in historical perspective, 451–453
   history of, 3–4
   human rights and, 127–130
   indigenous, 175, 176, 176–178
   individualistic, 71
   of intention, 63–65
   international, 20–21, 38
   internationalization of, xxiii–xxiv
   law and, 58–61
   law *versus*, 322–323
   from mid-20th century to present, 15–17
   normative but nonfunctional, 255
   normative *versus* descriptive, 255–257
   personal, 56–57, 63
   personal *versus* group, 255
   professional, 43, 57–58, 58–59, 63
   section, 57–58
   self-protection and, 60
   standards, 20
   test documents, 21
   universality *versus* specificity in, 453–454
   of utility, 66–68
   in W/O Psychology, 250–252
Ethics & Behavior, Professional Psychology: Research and Practice, 326
ethics code development, xx, 247
   APA and, 121
   APS, 359–361
   assistance in, 79
   in Australia, 359–361
   in Chinese societies, 334–335
   for EFPA member associations, 346
   in Europe, 341–342
   increase in, 139
   language and, 453
   model, 452–453
   process of, 282
   in Turkey, 447
ethics codes
   ACA, 172
   acceptance of, 203
   ACTO, 172
   affecting tests, 205–207
   AMHCA, 172
   APA and, 12, 324
   APA and CPS, 22, 22–23
   appearance of competence within, 47
   applicability of, 20
   in Argentina, 106, 310
   aspirational *versus* bottom line, 76
   assistance in, 26
   ASTD, 256
   ASWB and, 171
   in Australia, 364–365
   awareness of, 96, 258
   in Brazil, 311

   British influence on, 246–247
   in Canada, 325, 386
   Canadian, 110
   in Central America, 309
   in Chile, 381–382
   civil law in, 283, 283–286, 286, 287
   as coat-of-arms, 49–51
   Colegios and, 399
   in Colombia, 312
   combining principles and standards in, 136
   commonalities among, 376
   common standards in, 136, 137
   comparisons of, 138, 334–335, 438–439
   compliance with, 368
   compliance with law and, 289–290, 290
   conditions reflected in, 202–203
   confidentiality and, 253
   constituent rules and, 44–45
   construction of, 452
   corporate, 252
   of countries in transition, 389–390
   CPA, 111
   CRCC, 171
   cultural beliefs *versus*, 39
   cultural differences among, 138
   cultural diversity and, 405–406
   cultural factors and, 77–78
   cultural identity and, 34
   cultural sensitivity in, 126
   culture-specific, 149–150
   for education, 75
   of EFPA member associations, 346–347
   eHealth, 170, 172
   emphasis of, 20
   enforcement of, 402
   English-language, 284–285
   in ethical decision-making, 79–80, 80
   ethical dilemmas relating to, 249
   in Europe, 247–248, 345–346
   evolution of, 39
   of FePRA, 401
   financial arrangements in, 50–51
   forensic activities and, 289
   forensic provisions in, 290
   globalization and, 127
   government influence on, 384–385
   history of, 3–4, 120
   HKPS and, 330–331
   homogenization of, 355
   Hong Kong *versus* China, 334
   human rights in, 288, 292–294
   indigenous cultures and, 177–178
   individualism in, 415
   international, xxiii, 24–25, 29
   interpretation of, 43
   in Iran, 108, 384–385
   of ISPA, 157–158
   language of, 330–331
   law references in, 285
   law *versus*, 340

ethics codes (*Cont.*)
  legal conflicts in, 288
  legal obligations and, 288
  length of, 286
  limited specificity in, 249
  loyalties, 250
  in Mexico, 110, 314
  models, 21–23, 26
  moral basis for, 203
  NASW and, 171
  national, 20–21, 43, 44, 319
  in New Zealand, 365–367
  non-compatibility between, 251–252
  organizational psychology and, 249
  in Peru, 316–317
  in Philippines, 388
  in Poland, 107
  principle-based *versus* standards-based, 207
  prioritizing, 31
  professional judgment and, 294
  psychologist-client relationship bias in, 248–249
  as public documents, 75–76
  in Puerto Rico, 317
  purpose of, 19, 75–76, 203
  regional, 23–24, 24, 363
  regulatory bodies and, 75
  regulatory power of, 294
  research-based, 126
  research methods studying, 139–140
  resolving conflicts between civil law and, 290–292, 291
  review of, 343
  revisions of, 42–43, 51, 315, 411
  in Russia, 425, 433, 434–436, 436–439
  for social science research, 268
  society and, 282–283
  in South Africa, 385
  in South America, 309
  specialized, 248
  specific references to civil law in, 288–289
  specific rules *versus* human values in, 31
  statutory regulations *versus*, 78
  structure of, 76
  subject area references in, 288
  subversion of, 391
  as support tool, 80, 89
  sustainable, in political transitions, 401
  for test development, 202
  for test use, 202
  test use and, 20–21
  themes in, 389
  translations of, 148, 390
  transnational, 453
  in Turkey, 107–108, 446–448
  universal, 26, 28–29
  US, 325
  value of, 282
  variation among, 135–136
  vulnerable populations and, 416
  word searches in, 285–286
  as working tools, 75
ethics committees
  in Australia, 362–364
  authority of, 343–345
  in Canada, 325
  countries with, 342
  ethical dilemmas and, 344
  in Europe, 342–345
  function of, 343
  lack of, in Soviet Union, 427–428
  professional associations *versus*, 342–343
  society-based, 331–332
  US, 324–325
Ethics for European Psychologists (Lindsay, Koene, Øvreeide, & Lang), 79, 83–84
Ethics for the New Millennium (Dalai Lama), 130
ethics investigations, 325, 333, 332–334
ethics review, 146, 267
  biomedical, 269
  as common standard theme, 140
  competent, 272
  concerns beyond, 273
  exemptions from, 272–273
  inclusion rate of, 147
  mandatory, 269
  purpose of, 269
  resistance to, 268, 269–272
  universalism in, 269
ethics training, xxiv
  accreditation and, 367–368
  in Argentina, 310
  in Australia, 367–368
  in Brazil, 311–312
  in Canada, 325–326
  in China, 335
  in Chinese societies, 335
  in Colombia, 313
  in Europe, 355–357
  in Hong Kong, 335
  indigenous knowledge in, 182
  in Latin America, 308
  in New Zealand, 412
  postgraduate, 367
  in Puerto Rico, 318
  of RECs, 278
  in South America, 308
  in Taiwan, 335
  in Turkey, 447
  in US, 325–326
ETS. *See* Education Testing Service
EU. *See* European Union
Europe, 106
  accuracy in reporting in, 353–354
  adjudication of ethical violations in, 342
  appeals in, 344
  avoiding harm in, 351–352
  bias, 175
  codes of conduct in, 247–248
  competence in, 349–350
  confidentiality in, 347–348
  conflicts of interest in, 354–355
  continuing development in, 350
  dual relationships in, 354
  ethical awareness in, 349
  ethics code development in, 341–342
  ethics codes in, 247–248, 345–346
  ethics committees in, 342–345
  ethics research in, 356
  ethics training in, 355–357
  exploitation in, 354–355
  extended responsibility in, 352
  honesty, 353–354
  incapability in, 350
  informed consent in, 348–349
  integration of, 376
  integrity in, 352–355
  law in, 338
  law *versus* ethics codes in, 340
  legal status of psychology in, 338–341
  limits of competence in, 349
  limits of procedures in, 349–350
  modern history of, 337
  plagiarism in, 353
  professional associations in, 341–342
  promotion of high standards in, 351
  psychological associations in, 341
  recognition of professional limitations in, 352–353
  regional commonalities in, 355
  research participants in, 352
  resolving ethical dilemmas in, 352
  respect for dignity in, 347–349
  respect in, 347
  responsibility in, 350–352
  sanctions in, 342
  self-determination in, 349
  social responsibility and, 247
  straightforwardness in, 354
  variations across, 337–338
  working conditions in, 347
European Association of Work and Organization Psychologists, 24, 208
European Certificate in Psychology (EuroPsy), 24, 49, 340–341, 355
European Federation of Professional Psychologists' Associations (EFPPA), 16, 16
European Federation of Psychologists' Associations (EFPA), 23–24, 122, 345, 389. *See also* Meta-Code of Ethics
  certification program of, 106
  disciplinary procedures questionnaires and, 91
  ethical violations and, 91
  ethics codes and, 345–346
  ethics training and, 355–356
  European psychological associations and, 341
  member countries, 338, 339
  Meta-Code of Ethics and, 134, 150
  pragmatism and, 245
  regulations within, 340–341
  review of ethics codes, 343

Standing Committee on Ethics, 77, 83–84, 342
Standing Committee on Tests and Testing, 206, 208
European Psychology Congress, 97
European Register of Psychologists, 106
European Test User Standards for Test Use in Organizational and Work Settings, 24, 208
European Union (EU), 337, 340–341, 388–389
EuroPsy. *See* European Certificate in Psychology
evidence-based practices, 46
    context for, 184
    emerging challenges in, 456
    for indigenous peoples, 175–176
Examination for Professional Practice in Psychology (EPPP), 110, 322, 323
existentialism, 255
exploitation, 88
    of data, 437
    in Europe, 354–355
    in international research, 155
    of research participants, potential, 275
    in Russian ethics code, 438
    sexual harassment and, 261–262
    of students, 355

F

fairness, 68–69
Fallenbaum, Ruth, 236
Federación Colombiana de Psicología, 312
Federación de Psicólogos de la República Argentina (FePRA), 310, 397–398, 400–401, 401
Federal Council of Psychology (Brazil), 106, 208
Federal Research Regulations Common Rule, 268
Fein, Robert, 234–235
Feminist Therapy Code of Ethics, 38
FePRA. *See* Federación de Psicólogos de la República Argentina
financial arrangements, 50–51, 166, 353–354. *See also* compensation
Finland, 24
First South-Eastern Europe Regional Conference of Psychology, 127
Fischer, Mary A., 253
Five Commandments and Ten Requirements, 6–7
forced migrants, 191
    interventions for, 196
    mental health services for, 195–197
    research with, 194–195
forensic activities, 288
    ethics codes and, 289
    jurisdiction of, 294
    provisions, 290
forgiveness, 63
Fórum Nacional de Ética, 311
France, 343, 346
fraternity, 117
free market economies, 247, 376, 380, 436–437
French Revolution, 115–116, 117, 246

G

Gandhi, Mahatma, 117
Gauthier, Janel, 4, 17, 122, 205
GDPi. *See* Gross Domestic Product index
Geisinger, Kurt, 212
Gelles, Michael, 234–235
gender, 310, 315
    across cultures, 38
    equality, 181
    identity, 261
genealogy, 177
Geneva Convention, 233–234
genocide, 32
geographic stability, 29
German Psychological Society, 383
German Society of Psychologists, 50
Germany, 382–383
    ethics code of, 346
    ethics committees in, 343
    immigration in, 190
    licensing in, 339
    reunification of, 382
gifts, 34–35, 150
Gisborne, Thomas, 9–10
globalization, xix, 28–29, 113–114, 135
    adoption of Universal Declaration of Ethical Principles for Psychologists and, 122
    benefits of, 130
    cultural contexts and, 149
    enlightened, 29, 30, 128
    ethics codes and, 127
    fractured, 29
    growth of psychology and, 376
    impact of, 129, 149
    indigenous psychology and, 39
    loss of cultural identity and, 39
    social justice and, 39
    unilateral, 29, 30
GNP. *See* gross national product
goal setting, 68, 183–184, 183
Golden Rule, 115
Good Medical Practice: A Code of Conduct for Doctors in Australia, 364
good practices, 138–139
    in China, 335–336
    commitment to, in Chinese societies, 335–336
    common standards and, 137
    ethics codes style and, 76
    organizational, 258
    in test use, 206
governments
    cultural respect and, 36
    influence on ethics codes, 384–385
    licensing and, 106
    oppressive, 38–39
    representative, 380
Graham, Douglas, 413
Greece, 347
Gross Domestic Product index (GDPi), 377
gross national product (GNP), 376
Guantanamo Bay, 232–233, 233, 387
    proposed closing of, 237
    torture at, 236
Guatemalan Psychological College, 127
guidelines, 203–204. *See also* ethical guidelines
    APA, 209–210
    BPS, 210–211
    impacting tests, 209–211
    for Internet tests, 206–207
    Joint Committee on Testing Practices, 210
    standards *versus*, 20
    for technology in testing, 217
    test adaptations, 206
    testing, 221
    test use, 206
Guidelines for Child Custody Evaluations in Divorce Proceedings, 209–210
Guidelines for Professional Practice for School Psychologists in Canada, 248
Guilford, Joy P., 260–261

H

Haly Abbas' Advice to a Physician, 6
Hawaiian Islands, 179
HDI. *See* Human Development Index
Health Insurance Portability and Accountability Act (HIPAA), 166
Health Practitioner Regulation National Law Act, 358
Health Practitioners Competence Assurance Act, 365–366, 411
Health Professions Council (HPC), 78–79, 79–80
Health Professions Disciplinary Tribunal, 109
Health Research Council of New Zealand, 186
Hebrew Oath of Asaph, 6
HIMPSI. *See* Indonesian Alliance of Psychologists
HIPAA. *See* Health Insurance Portability and Accountability Act
Hippocrates, 66
Hippocratic Oath, 4–5, 6, 22, 202, 246
HIV spectrum disorders, 104
HKPS. *See* Hong Kong Psychological Society
HKSAR. *See* Hong Kong Special Administrative Region
homosexuality, 37, 61, 261
honesty, 353–354
Hong Kong, 329
    ethical complaints in, 332
    ethics code, 334
    ethics training in, 335
    professional associations in, 330
    registration in, 333–334
    society-based ethics committees in, 332

Hong Kong Psychological Society
  (HKPS), 329, 330–331
 ethics investigations and, 332–334
 language of ethics code of, 330–331
 limitations of, 333
Hong Kong Special Administrative Region
  (HKSAR), 329
Hosin Aghili, Mohamed, 9
HPC. *See* Health Professions Council
Human Development Index (HDI),
  376–377, 377–378, 380
human engineering, 243–244
Human Resource Research Organization
  (HumRRO), 236
human resources, 259
human rights, 32, 114–115
 APA and, 291
 civil rights *versus*, 114
 declarations on, 54
 demand for, 119
 dictatorships and, 402
 documents, 116
 ethics and, 127–130
 in ethics codes, 288, 292, 293
 ethics codes and, 292–294
 first generation of, 117
 generations of, 117
 history of, 116
 indigenous cultures and, 186
 IRBs and, 152
 language of, 293–294
 in law, 115
 moral framework and, 113
 moral philosophy and, 54
 negative connotation of, 128–129
 PENS report and, 387
 political status of, 118
 second generation of, 117
 social justice and, 130
 third generation of, 117
 training, 235
 treaties, 119
 *Universal Declaration of Ethical
  Principles for Psychologists* and, 292
 through universal declarations, 114
 unjust allegations of violating, 130
 violations, 116, 190–191
human trafficking, 32
Humphrey, John Peter, 116–117
Humphrey, Laud, 268
HumRRO. *See* Human Resource Research
  Organization
Hungary, 347, 348
Huxley, Aldous, 117

I

IAAP. *See* International Association of
  Applied Psychology
IACP. *See* Indian Association of Clinical
  Psychologists
Iceland, 24
ICF. *See* International Classification of
  Functioning, Disability and Health

ICTs. *See* information-communication
  technologies
identity verification, 167, 227
I Latino American Conference on Training
  in Psychology, 308
immigrants
 discrimination against, 195
 mental health services for, 195
 research with, 192–194
 social services for, 195
immigration, 77, 88. *See also*
  undocumented people
 APA Code and, 191–192
 effects of, 195
 forced *versus* voluntary, 191
 international, 190
Immigration Court, 196
imperialism, 29–30, 418
Improving North American Safeguards
  that Help Protect the Public Against
  Test Misuse, 211
incapability, 45, 350
India, 105
Indian Association of Clinical
  Psychologists (IACP), 105
indigenization, 30, 34
indigenous cultures
 assimilation policies and, 179
 in Australia, 364–365, 370
 Australia *versus* New Zealand, 367
 autonomy and, 187
 clients in, 181
 collective responsibility and, 177
 confidentiality and, 178
 cultural awareness and, 182
 definition of, 176
 earning trust of, 182
 economic growth and, 186
 effects of colonization on, 178–181
 ethics codes and, 177–178
 evaluating outcomes of interventions
  in, 185
 evidence-based practices for, 175–176
 goal setting in, 183–184
 health concepts of, 364–365
 human rights and, 186
 interventions in, 182, 183–186
 interventions treatment acceptability
  in, 184
 intervention treatment design in,
  184–185
 loss in, 178–179
 mental health assumptions in, 183
 methodological requirements of
  interventions in, 185–186
 in New Zealand, 370
 power inequalities and, 179–180, 186
 psychological treatment for, 179–180
 racism against, 179
 research guidelines for, 186
 rights of, 405
 rules and, 177
 self-determination and, 181

 sovereignty and, 180–181
 spiritual beliefs of, 183
 sustainability and, 176–177
 test use and, 185
 violence in, 181
indigenous psychology, 30, 453–454
 Aboriginal Australians and, 364
 globalization and, 39
 Maori and, 366–367
 research, 180–181, 186
individual experiences, 56
individualism
 in *Code of Ethics for Counseling and
  Clinical Practice*, 383
 collectivism *versus*, 391
 cultural expectations and, 78
 in ethics codes, 415
Indonesia, 109
Indonesian Alliance of Psychologists
  (HIMPSI), 109
Industrial and Organizational Psychology
  (I/O Psychology), 243
industrial psychology, 105, 218, 243, 248
information-communication technologies
  (ICTs), 160, 165
information technology (IT), 217,
  222–223
informed consent, 48–49
 APA Code and, 152
 in China, 153
 civil law and, 288–289
 before Common Era, 5
 as common standard theme, 140
 components of, 276
 confidentiality *versus*, 145
 cultural assumptions in, 177–178
 eHealth and, 165
 in *Ethical Standards of Psychologists*, 13
 in Europe, 348–349
 for forced migrant mental health
  services, 195–196
 inclusion rate of, 147
 increased focus on, 54
 in international research, 152–153
 Internet and, 165
 IRBs and, 151–152
 law and, 137–138
 minors and, 276
 *Nuremberg Code of Ethics in Medical
  Research* and, 12, 138
 online, 168
 political influence and, 153
 qualitative research and, 271, 277
 research and, 276–277
 in research with forced migrants, 194
 research with immigrants and, 193
 social inequalities and, 153
 in Soviet Union, 428
 standards about, 49
 standards incompatibility and, 49
 from vulnerable populations, 276
Institutional Review Board (IRB), 150,
  151–152, 154–155, 331

480 | INDEX

insurance, 173, 351
integrity, 4, 87–88
    from 1st to 17th centuries, 8–9
    in 18th and 19th centuries, 10–11
    in APA Code, 151
    in *Canadian Code of Ethics for Psychologists*, 15–16
    before Common Era, 5
    across cultures, 151
    in early to mid-20th century, 14
    as ethical principle, 120
    in *Ethical Principles of Psychologists and Code of Conduct*, 44
    in Europe, 352–355
    image of psychology and, 50
    internal legitimacy and, 62
    in Mercado Común del Sur, 309
    in *Meta-Code of Ethics*, 16, 23, 44, 84
    in Mexico, 315
    in relationships, 414
    research, 155, 278
    in South America, 16
    in *Universal Declaration of Ethical Principles for Psychologists*, 17, 44, 50, 125, 151
intellectual disabilities, 416–417
intellectual property, 204
intentions
    best, 63, 64
    ethics of, 63–65
    focus of, 64
Interamerican Society of Psychology, 127, 398
Interjurisdictional Practice Certificate (IPC), 322
International Association of Applied Psychology (IAAP), 16, 17, 24, 122, 150
    adoption of *Universal Declaration of Ethical Principles for Psychologists* by, 113, 119–120
    history of, 242–243
    international ethics codes and, 25
    test use and, 205
International Association of Cross-Cultural Psychology, 24
International Bill of Human Rights, 117, 118
International Classification of Functioning, Disability and Health (ICF), 205
International Convention for the Protection of All Persons from Enforced Disappearance, 119
International Convention on the Elimination of All Forms of Racial Discrimination, 119
International Convention on the Rights of All Migrant Workers and Members of their Families, 119
International Court of Justice, 118
International Covenant on Civil and Political Rights, 117, 119

International Covenant on Economic, Social and Cultural Rights, 117, 119
International Guidelines on Test Use (ITC), 25
International Organization for Standardization (ISO), 20, 204, 205, 262–263
international research
    census of, 158
    collaborative, 157
    disclosure in, 155
    ethical dilemmas in, 151
    ethical guidelines for, 150
    exploitation in, 155
    inducements for, 154
    informed consent in, 152–153
    institutional approval of, 151–152
    ISPA ethics code and, 157–158
    moral frameworks for, 156–158
    over-generalization in, 156
    recommendations, 156–158
    reporting of, 155–156
    Universal Declaration of Ethical Principles for Psychologists and, 150–151
International School Psychology Association (ISPA), 25, 157–158, 248
International Society for Research on Internet Interventions, 172
International Test Commission (ITC), 23–24, 25, 135
    cross-cultural test-taking and, 155
    guidelines for technology in testing, 217
    Guidelines for Test Adaptation, 206
    testing companies and, 212
    test use and, 205–207
International Union of Psychological Science (IUPsyS), 16, 17, 122, 150, 248, 283, 294–295
    Ad Hoc Joint Committee of, 151
    adoption of *Universal Declaration of Ethical Principles for Psychologists* by, 113, 119–120
    "Codes of Ethics of National Psychological Organizations," 283
    HDI and, 377–378
    increased membership in, 376
    international ethics codes and, 24–25
    test use and, 205
Internet, 77, 345, 356. *See also* online counseling; web-based interventions
    APA Code and, 171
    distance education programs and, 215
    emerging challenges in, 455
    experience, 166
    informed consent and, 165
    plagiarism and, 261
    psychotherapy, 127
    research participants and, 164
    searches, 211–212
    security, 165
    testing security tools, 225–226

    tests, guidelines on, 206–207
    Turkey and, 448
    usage, 160
Internet Testing with Online Proctoring, 216
interpreters, 196
interrogations, 232, 356
    complaints about, 234–235
    law and, 235
    Obama and, 387
    torture *versus*, 232–233
    training, 236
intertexuality, 260, 261
interventions. *See also* web-based interventions
    availability of, after research, 277–278
    competence in, 48
    cultural flexibility in, 196
    dynamic nature of, 47
    effect of research on, 51
    eHealth and, 161
    evaluating outcomes of, 185
    for forced migrants, 196
    indigenous, 182, 183–186
    innovative, 456–457
    ritual community, 183
    termination of, 354
    treatment acceptability, 184
    treatment design, 184–185
Inuit people, 179, 386
I/O Psychology. *See* Industrial and Organizational Psychology
IPA. *See* Israeli Psychological Association
IPC. *See* Interjurisdictional Practice Certificate
Iran, 108, 121, 384–385
IRB. *See* Institutional Review Board
Ireland, 16, 291
Islam, 119, 246
Islamiyah, Jemaah, 388
ISO. *See* International Organization for Standardization
ISPA. *See* International School Psychology Association
ISPA Code of Ethics, 248
Israel, 108
Israeli Psychological Association (IPA), 108
IT. *See* information technology
Italy, 339, 344, 346–347
ITC. *See* International Test Commission
IUPsyS. *See* International Union of Psychological Science

J

James, Larry, 234–235
James, William, 245
Japan, 179
JEPPR. *See* Junta Examinadora de Psicólogos de Puerto Rico
Jing Qicheng, 376
Joint Commission on Testing Practices, 135, 210

Jonason, Kim, 78
Journal of Business Ethics, 243, 260
Junta Examinadora de Psicólogos de Puerto Rico (JEPPR), 317, 317
justice, 44, 99–100, 151, 273. *See also* social justice

K

KANPAN. *See* Committee of the Psychological Sciences of the Polish Academy of Sciences
Kant, Immanuel, 246
karma, 245
Kazdin, Alan, 237
Keju System, 218
KEMRI. *See* Kenyan Medical Research Institute
Kenya Association of Professional Counselors, 104
Kenyan Medical Research Institute (KEMRI), 153
Kenya Psychological Association, 104
Keyser, David J., 212
Khatami, Mohammad, 384
kidnapping, 397, 397–398
Koene, Casper, 79, 83–84
Kohlberg, Lawrence, 256
Kriado, Celia, 398
Kristeva, Julietta, 261

L

Lang, Fredi, 79, 83–84
language
 of dominance, 29–30
 equivalence, 137
 ethics code development and, 453
 of ethics codes, 330–331
 gender bias in, 310, 315
 of human rights, 293–294
 indigenous, 178
 interpreters and, 196
 research with immigrants and, 193–194
 respect and, 347
 of translated ethics codes, 390
Latin America, 308–309
law, 60–61. *See also* civil law; statutory regulations
 in Argentina, 309, 396, 398
 in Australia, 358
 changing, 61
 in Colombia, 312
 compliance with, 289–290, 290
 conflicts in ethics codes, 288
 criminal, 92
 culturally conflicting, 36
 customary international, 119
 definition of, 58
 eHealth and, 169
 ethical dilemmas and, 60–61
 ethical discourses about, 61
 ethics and, 5, 58–61
 ethics codes and, 19–20
 ethics codes *versus*, 340
 ethics *versus*, 322–323
 in Europe, 338
 human rights in, 115
 informed consent and, 137–138
 intellectual property and, 204
 interrogation and, 235
 in Latin America, 309
 legitimacy of, 60
 in Mexico, 313–314
 as preventative measure, 61
 professional ethics and, 58–59
 provincial, 399
 psychological associations and, 58–59
 psychological associations *versus*, 137–138
 in Puerto Rico, 317, 317
 references to, in ethics codes, 285
 regulatory reach of, 340
 self-protection and, 60
 sexual harassment and, 262
 in South America, 309
 in Soviet Union, 427
 specificity of, 59
 testing piracy and, 229
 test use and, 204
 in transitioning countries, 375–376
 unethical behavior and, 81
legal obligations
 ethics codes and, 288
 records and, 59–60
legal restrictions
 in Canada, 323
 ethical dilemmas of, 35–36
 ethics of procedure and, 69
 sector ethics and, 57
Liber Regius (Haly Abbas), 6
Licenciatura, 310, 313
licensing
 in Argentina, 105–106, 309, 310
 in Belgium, 340
 boards, 322, 325
 in Brazil, 106, 311
 in Canada, 110
 in China, 104
 in Czech Republic, 339–340
 in Denmark, 339
 eHealth, 169
 in Estonia, 340
 in Europe, 106, 338–340
 EuroPsy and, 24
 in Germany, 339
 government involvement with, 106
 high-stakes testing for, 217–218
 incidence of unethical complaints and, 98–99
 in India, 105
 in Israel, 108
 in Italy, 339
 in Malta, 340
 in Mexico, 110, 313–314, 316
 in Netherlands, 339
 New Zealand, 109
 in Poland, 106–107
 in Puerto Rico, 317
 in South Africa, 104
 in Spain, 107
 state-specific, 322–323
 in Sweden, 339
 transfer of, 322
 in Turkey, 107–108, 447
 in UK, 339
 in US, 322
Lindsay, Geoff, 79, 83–84
literature, 466–469
 in Australia, 368–369
 on civil law, 291–292
 for cultural diversity training, 192
 on ethical decision-making guidelines, 416
 moral philosophy and, 55
 in New Zealand, 369
 W/O Psychology, 258
López, Mauricio, 397
L'Orde des Psychologues du Quebec, 324
Lunt, Ingrid, 340
Luxembourg, 347
Lysenko, Trofim, 427

M

Maddox, Teddy, 212
Magna Carta, 115, 115
Maimonides, Moses, 6
Malik, Charles Habib, 117
Malta, 340
Malvinas War, 399
Mandela, Nelson, 385
Maori, 175
 Christianity and, 176
 effects of colonization on, 178
 genealogy and, 177
 indigenous psychology and, 366–367
 NSCBI and, 409
 NZ Code and, 366–367, 405, 415
 perspective, in *NZ Code*, 410–413
 racism towards, 179, 407–408
 spiritual beliefs, 183
 Treaty of Waitangi and, 366
Maori and Psychology Research Unity (MPRU), 180–181
Mao Zedong, 21, 383
Marcos, Ferdinand, 388
Marcuse, Herbert, 243
Maria Estela Martínez de Perón, 394
mark-and-review, 224
market liberalization, 419
Marxism, 426
Masía, Juan, 246
McCabe, Don, 218–219
McCain amendment, 235–236
mediation, 93–95, 345, 460
 arbitration *versus*, 95
 availability of, 98
 dramatis personae and, 99
 research and, 461
Medical Code of Ethics of the American Medical Association, 9–10

competent caring for well-being in, 10
integrity in, 10–11
respect for dignity in, 10
responsibility to society in, 11
Medical Ethics (Percival), 9–10
medicine, 3, 98
Menegetti, Antonio, 432
mental health
  assumptions, 183
  of Australian Aborigines, 365
  for immigrants, 195
  services, 195–197
Mental Measurement Yearbooks (Geisinger), 212
Mercado Común del Sur, 309, 400
Meta-Code of Ethics, 16, 16, 23–24, 122, 134, 248, 338, 345–346, 389
  BPS compliance, 79
  competence in, 45, 84
  complementary nature of, 150
  creation of, 83–84
  cultural dependencies and, 43
  development of, 452
  ethical complaints and, 91
  ethical decision-making and, 75, 84–85
  ethical principles and, 76
  ethics code development and, 341–342
  gaps in, 151
  Germany and, 383
  inclusiveness of, 77
  integrity in, 84
  Internet and, 77
  limits of confidentiality in, 348
  national ethics codes and, 44
  persons indirectly affected in, 71–72
  pragmatism and, 245
  principle categories in, 44
  professional knowledge in, 47
  regional test standards and, 208
  resolving ethical dilemmas and, 87
  respect for dignity in, 84
  responsibility in, 84, 350
  Russian ethics code and, 439
  self-determination in, 349
  structure of, 345–346
  style of, 76
  Turkey and, 447–448
methods
  canonization of, 47
  civil law in ethics codes, 283–286
  freedom to choose, 46
  for indigenous peoples, 176
  new, 86
  obligation to practice within, 86
  obsolete, 46
  questioning of, 46
  scientific validity of, 274
  as social control, 180
  transparency of, 283
  unscientific, 437
Mexican Psychological Society, 110
Mexican Revolution, 117
Mexico, 16, 110, 313–316

Middle East, 108
Mid-Island Tribal Council on Vancouver Island, 181
migration, 77–78, 195
Mi'kmaq First Nation Communities of Nova Scotia, 181
Milgram, Stanley, 54, 55, 268
military, 233–234, 233–234
Mill, John Stuart, 245, 255–256
mirror-neurons, 54
Mohawk Nation, 184
monarchies, 384
moral authority, 263
moral awareness, 54
moral frameworks, 113
  common, 125
  connectedness to, 114
  for international research, 156–158
moral judgment, 203
moral philosophy, 54–56, 66
moral principals, 38
moral questions, 54
moral rights, 114, 292. *See also* human rights
morals, 53, 54
moral sensitivity, 203
moral standards, 203
moral testing, 53
"mosaic" scenario, 29
MPRU. *See* Maori and Psychology Research Unity
multicultural competencies, 31, 33
multiculturalism, 29, 386
multiple relationships, 34, 84
  conflicts of interest and, 88
  personal ethics and, 56
  Third Faces and, 71
  in *Universal Declaration of Ethical Principles for Psychologists*, 125
Munsterberg, Hugo, 242
Murray, Henry A., 245

N

NASW. *See* National Association of Social Workers
National Association for Graduate Research and Study in Psychology (Brazil), 106
National Association of Social Workers (NASW), 171
National Commission of People Disappearance, 397
National Congress of American Indians, 181
National Council on Measurement in Education, 135
national security, 77, 387
National Standing Committee on Bicultural Issues (NSCBI), 406, 408
  accreditation and, 410
  Bicultural Commitment and, 410
  ethics code revision and, 411
  Maori and, 409
  structure of, 409
Netherlands, 339, 346

Netherlands Institute of Psychologists (NIP), 43, 43
  Anatomically Detailed Dolls and, 46
  assessment procedures and, 47–48
  deontological complaints and, 252
  ethical complaints and, 344
  ethical violations and, 91
  self-protection in, 50
  sexual intimidation and, 46
New Zealand, 16, 109–110, 365–367
  clients' rights in, 407–408
  colonialism in, 407–408
  ethics code revision, 411
  ethics training in, 412
  independence of, 406
  indigenous cultures in, 367, 370
  literature in, 369
  political system, 406–408
  professional associations of, 410–411
  racism in, 407–408
  social justice in, 32
  survey of psychologists in, 412–413
  Treaty of Waitangi, 175
New Zealand College of Clinical Psychologists (NZCCP), 410–411
New Zealand Psychological Society (NZPsS), 109–110
  Bicultural Commitment and, 410
  biculturalism and, 408
  Ethical Issues Committee, 410
  NZ Code and, 405
  procedural requirements of, 409
  structure of, 409
New Zealand Psychologists Board, 109, 369, 410–411
NGOs. *See* non-governmental organizations
Nikora, Linda Waimarie, 408
NIP. *See* Netherlands Institute of Psychologists
non-governmental organizations (NGOs), 104, 341
nonmaleficence, 44, 120, 151, 273
norms, 61, 92
North America, 29, 110, 175
Norway, 24, 344
NSCBI. *See* National Standing Committee on Bicultural Issues
Nuremberg Code of Ethics in Medical Research, 11, 11–12, 22, 120–121, 202
  common standards and, 138
  competence in, 13–14
  doing no harm in, 13
  informed consent in, 12
  research ethics and, 267–268
  responsibility to society in, 14
Nuremberg Trials, 14, 116, 120–121
NZCCP. *See* New Zealand College of Clinical Psychologists
NZ Code. See Code of Ethics for Psychologists Working in Aotearoa/New Zealand
NZPsS. *See* New Zealand Psychological Society

O

Obama, Barack, 237, 386–387, 387
Oceania, 108–109, 358–359, 369–370
Olsen, Brad, 236
omniculturalism, 29, 39
O'Neil, Bill, 359–360
O*NET database, 244
online counseling, 161–162. *See also* eHealth
   in Australia, 370
   communication and, 163
   convenience and, 163
   crisis intervention for, 168
   emerging challenges in, 455–456
   meta-analyses of, 164
   records, 166
ontopsychology, 432
An Orthodox Manual of Surgery (Chen), 6–7
Other
   best interests of, 60
   commitment to, 63
   dispositions towards, 56
   personal ethics and, 56
   prioritizing of, 64
   proximity to, 70
Øvreeide, Haldor, 79, 83–84
Oxford Handbook of Chinese Psychology (Bond, ed.), 328

P

paratexuality, 261
peer consultations, 80, 82, 87–88
peer review, 272
Pennsylvania State University World Campus, 215, 217
PENS Task Force. *See* Psychological Ethics and National Security Task Force
Percival, Thomas, 9–10
Perosio, Beatriz, 397–398
Peru, 316–317
Peters, Wilhelm, 444
Pettifor, Jean, 412
Philippines, 376, 388
A Physician's Ethical Duties, 9
Pinochet, Augusto, 381
plagiarism, 145–146
   as common standard theme, 140
   in Europe, 353
   inclusion rate of, 147
   Internet and, 261
   isolating, 261
   sanctions, 261
   test, 204
   W/O Psychology and, 260–261
Poland, 106–107
Polish Psychological Association (PPA), 106–107
political freedom, 391
   indices, 377
   national development and, 378–380
   research on, 391
political systems

New Zealand, 406–408
   in Russia, 430, 433–434
   in Soviet Union, 425–426
   stable, 376
political transitions, 375, 376–380
   forms of, 380–389
   social justice and, 391
   sustainable ethics codes in, 401
Pontifícia Universidade Católica do Rio de Janeiro, 311
post-traumatic stress disorder (PTSD), 154, 195, 236
power
   awareness of, 157
   dialogic ethics and, 72
   hierarchies, 157
   inequalities, 85, 85, 152, 179–180, 186
   over research participants, 153–154
   professional relationships and, 85
PPA. *See* Polish Psychological Association
pragmatism, 245, 263
prescriptions, 49
principles, 20, 203–204
   based on values, 134–135
   categories of, 43–44
   combined with standards, 136
   common, 135
   cultural interpretation of, 136–137
   domains of practice *versus*, 77–78
   enforcement of, 134
   in ethical decision-making, 79–80
   ethical standards *versus*, 44
   in *NZ Code*, 366, 414
   standards and, 76–77
   universal, 65
privacy, 348. *See also* confidentiality
problem-solving, 243
procedures, 68–70. *See also* disciplinary procedures
   appeals, 43
   limits of, 45, 86, 349–350
   relativity of, 69
process, 84–85, 452–453
productivity, utility *versus*, 68
professional associations, 19. *See also* psychological associations
   in Argentina, 396
   in Australia, 359–361
   authoritative status of, 459
   in Canada, 324
   in Chinese societies, 330–331
   confidentiality and, 253
   ethics committees *versus*, 342–343
   in Europe, 341–342
   evaluation tasks and, 257
   impact on test development and use of, 208–209
   loyalty to, 245
   of New Zealand, 410–411
   US, 323–324
   for W/O Psychology, 253
professional boundaries, 34, 34–35
Professional Code of Ethics of Peruvian Psychologists, 316–317
professional codes
   appearance of competence within, 47
   professional experience in, 48
   standards of conduct and, 51
professional limitations, recognition of, 87–88, 352–353
professional relationships, 85,
professions, 11
   expectations from, 19
   psychology as, 395–396
   responsibility of, 57–58
   social legitimacy of, 57
Protection of Personal and Property Rights Act, 417
Protocol of the Framework Agreement of Ethical Principles for the Professional Practice of Psychology in the Mercosur and Associated Countries, 16, 26, 122, 400
proximity
   to dialogue, 70–71
   ethics of, 70–72
   globalization and, 114
   to Other, 70
PSSA. *See* Psychological Society of South Africa
PsychINFO, 212, 377
psychological associations, xxiv, 19. *See also* professional associations
   in Africa, 103
   in Argentina, 399
   binding power of, 91
   in Brazil, 311
   in Canada, 110–111
   civil law and, 294
   in Colombia, 312
   in Europe, 341
   expulsion from, 92, 98
   international, 466
   in Latin America, 308–309
   law and, 58–59
   law *versus*, 137–138
   mediation and, 94
   membership rates, 98
   in Mexico, 314
   in Peru, 316
   in South America, 308–309
   strong, 345
   support for, 341
   terminating membership from, 92, 98
Psychological Ethics and National Security (PENS) Task Force, 234–235, 387–388
Psychological Practices Act, 358
Psychological Society of South Africa (PSSA), 104
   Universal Declaration of Ethical Principles for Psychologists and, 127
psychological treatment
   access to, 163–164
   expanded access to, 162

for indigenous cultures, 179–180
political influence on, 180
psychologist-client relationship, 31
  bias, in ethics codes, 248–249
  cross-cultural, 32
  cultural relationship between, 176
  ethics of utility and, 68
  financial arrangements in, 353–354
  in Russian ethics code, 435, 435–436
  termination of, 352
psychologists
  autonomy of, 87
  awareness of ethics codes by, 96
  business, 243
  consulting, 243
  cooperation with disciplinary procedures of, 98
  cross-jurisdictional mobility of, 323
  definition of, 233
  GNP and, 376
  legal obligations of, 59–60
  management, 243
  membership rates of, 98
  in military, 233–234
  misattribution of utility by, 68
  occupational health, 243
  qualifications of, 353
  ratio of, 377, 378
  RxP for, 321–322
  scope of, 322
  sexual abuse by, 58–59
  surveys of, in New Zealand, 412–413
  as testing professionals, 220–222
Psychologists Committee of Mercosur and Associated Countries, 400
Psychologist's Law (Romania), 381
Psychologist Statute (Taiwan), 329, 329–330
psychology. *See also specific psychology subfields*
  applied, 74, 242–243, 244
  clinical, 60, 76, 248, 388
  confidence in, 50
  curtailment of, 396–399
  deontological codes in, 247–248
  early regulation of, 121
  forensic, 105, 232, 248
  growth of, 247, 376, 452
  history of, 200
  image of, 50
  legalization of, in Argentina, 399–401
  legal status of, in Canada, 323
  legal status of, in Chinese societies, 329–330
  legal status of, in Europe, 338–341
  legal status of, in Oceania, 358–359
  legal status of, in US, 321–323
  in modern Russia, 434
  national development and, 378–380
  occupational, 243
  organizational, 218, 249
  as profession, 395–396
  recognition of, in Argentina, 398

  regulation of, 457–460
  re-organization of, in Russia, 425
  responsibility to, 350
  in Russia, 1990s, 430–431
  as science, 395
  in Soviet Union, 426
  in Turkey, 445–446
  values in, 375
  work, 243
Psychology Board of Australia, 364
Psychology Society of Buenos Aires, 395
psychometricians, 220–222
psycho-technics, 242
psychotherapy
  in Argentina, 396
  confidentiality and, 253
  Ethical Practice Model and, 253
  internet-based, 127
  learning and, 185
  as social control, 233
PTSD. *See* post-traumatic stress disorder
public
  code of ethics as coat-of-arms and, 49–50
  competence in interventions and, 48
  education, 203
  trust, 203
publications, 469–470
  ratio of, 379, 379
  in Russian ethics code, 436
  in Soviet Union, 428–429
Puerto Rico, 317–318
al-Qaeda, 233–234, 386, 388

Q

Qaujimanituqangit Principles, 386
qualitative research, 271
  doing no harm and, 275–276
  informed consent and, 271, 277
  participant selection for, 275
  proposals, 271–272
  protocols, 271
  RECs and, 271
  reviewing, 272
quality control audits, 272
quantitative methodologies, 194
Quebec, 385–386
Qur'an, 115, 246

R

racism, 179, 407–408, 408
rape, 36
Raven, Bertram, 398
Rawls, John, 47–48
Recommendations on Evaluative and Corrective Actions in Case of Complaints about Unethical Conduct, 342
records
  access to, 348
  client access to, 50, 50–51
  copy of, 50–51
  eHealth, 166

  electronic, 370
  honesty in, 353
  legal obligations and, 59–60
  online counseling, 166
  storage, in W/O Psychology, 254
  web-based interventions, 166
RECs. *See* Research Ethics Committees
reflection, 80–81, 83, 91
refugees, 77, 190–191. *See also* forced migrants
registration
  in Australia, 358–359
  boards, 359, 362
  in Hong Kong, 329, 333–334
  national, 370
regulation
  indicative *versus* functional, 459
  of research, 460
  self *versus* institutional, 458–459
Regulation for the Management of Mental Tests, 22
regulatory bodies, 31
  in Canada, 323
  in Denmark, 340
  developing, 459–460
  ethics codes and, 75
  measuring competence by, 33
  professional associations *versus*, 324
  regulatory bodies *versus*, 324
  in Spain, 340
  in US, 322
religion. *See also specific religions*
  migration and, 77–78
  moral philosophy and, 55
research. *See also international research; qualitative research*
  accountability in, 151
  in Argentina, 310
  biomedical, 270
  in Brazil, 312
  collaborative partnership and, 273–274
  community concerns after, 277
  confidentiality of proposal for, 147
  conflicts of interest in, 278
  COP and, 356
  criticism of, 50
  cross-cultural, 148, 150–151
  cultural perspectives on, 157
  deception in, 154
  democratic representation of study community and, 273–274
  to determine common standards, 138
  diverse methods of, 194
  on economic freedom, 391
  effect of, on interventions, 51
  elements of ethical, 273–278
  to eliminate discrimination, 157
  emerging challenges in, 460–461
  enhanced data collection for, 164
  ethical, 357
  ethical dilemmas and, 248
  ethical framework for, 273
  ethical oversight in, 79

research (Cont.)
  Ethical Principles of Psychologists and Code of Conduct and, 151
  ethical review of, 146
  of ethics, 315, 326, 356, 368–369
  falsified, 278
  favorable risk-benefit determination in, 275–276
  with forced migrants, 194–195
  as framework for ethics codes, 126
  growth of, 147
  guidelines for indigenous, 186
  with immigrants, 192–194
  indigenous psychology, 180–181, 186
  informed consent and, 276–277
  integrity, 278
  intervention availability after, 277–278
  IRB and, 331
  limitations, 148
  mediation and, 461
  methods studying ethics codes, 139–140
  mixed-methods, 185
  monitoring of, 270
  participants, 153–154
  in Peru, 316
  on political freedom, 391
  practices, 151
  regulation of, 460
  reporting of, 155–156
  scientific standards for, 146
  scientific validity of, 274
  scientists, 243
  in Soviet Union, 427, 428–429
  treatment outcome, 185–186
  in Turkey, 445
  US influence on, 157
  verification of, 147
research ethics
  as common standards, 138–139
  development of, 267–269
  in Russia, 431–432, 436
Research Ethics Committees (RECs), 268, 269
  capacity of, 272
  ethics training of, 278
  independent, 276
  limitations of, 270–271
  priorities of, 270
  qualitative research and, 271
  risk-benefit determination and, 275
  turnaround time of, 270
research participants
  children as, 154
  community-based, 194
  confidentiality of, 277
  from developing countries, 275
  discrimination of, 277
  ethical criteria for, 248
  in Europe, 352
  fair selection of, 275
  inducements for, 154, 275
  informed consent and, 271

Internet and, 164
IRB and, 331
potential exploitation of, 275
respect for, 277–278
rights of, 270
right to withdraw for, 277
research proposals, 460–461
  deviations from, 270–271
  qualitative, 271–272
  rejected, 270
Resnick, Robert, 236
respect
  in Europe, 347
  general, 85–86
  between psychologists, 347
  for research participants, 277–278
  in structure of *Universal Declaration of Ethical Principles for Psychologists*, 124
  for study communities, 277–278
  test use and, 205
respect for dignity, 4, 44, 85–86
  from 1st to 17th centuries, 7
  in 18th and 19th centuries, 10
  in APA Code, 151
  in *Canadian Code of Ethics for Psychologists*, 15–16
  before Common Era, 5
  across cultures, 33, 151
  in early to mid-20th century, 12–13
  ethical dilemmas of, 33–34
  as ethical principle, 120
  in ethical research, 273
  in Europe, 347–349
  IRBs and, 152
  in Mercado Común del Sur, 309
  in *Meta-Code of Ethics*, 16, 23, 44, 84
  in Mexico, 315
  in *NZ Code*, 414
  in South America, 16, 400
  in *Universal Declaration of Ethical Principles for Psychologists*, 17, 44, 124–125, 151
responsibility, 87
  in APA Code, 151
  collective, 177
  to community, 415
  context of, 85
  dependency and, 85
  in *Ethical Principles of Psychologists and Code of Conduct*, 44
  in Europe, 350–352
  extended, 87, 352
  general, 87
  in *Meta-Code of Ethics*, 16, 23, 44, 84, 350
  in Mexico, 315
  of professions, 57–58
  to psychology, 350
  in relationships, 71–72
  social, 247, 263
  for testing security, 216
  in test use, 206
  in *Universal Declaration of Ethical*

Principles for Psychologists, 44
responsibility to society, 4
  from 1st to 17th centuries, 9
  in 18th and 19th centuries, 11
  in *Canadian Code of Ethics for Psychologists*, 15–16
  before Common Era, 5–6
  across cultures, 151
  in early to mid-20th century, 14–15
  in *Ethical Standards of Psychologists*, 14–15
  in German ethics code, 346
  in Mexico, 315
  in *Nuremberg Code of Ethics in Medical Research*, 14
  in *NZ Code*, 414
  research participants and, 153–154
  social justice *versus*, 32
  in South America, 16
  in *Universal Declaration of Ethical Principles for Psychologists*, 17, 125, 151
responsible caring, 15–16, 120, 414
rights. *See also* human rights
  analysis of, 81
  animal, 140, 146, 147, 331, 351–352
  civil, 43, 61, 114, 117
  of clients, 407–408
  cultural, 117
  economic, 117
  of indigenous cultures, 405
  moral, 292
  natural, 116
  political, 377
  of research participants, 270
  social, 117
  solidarity, 117
  of vulnerable populations, 416–417
right to withdraw, 146
  as common standard theme, 140
  inclusion rate of, 147
  for research participants, 277
risk-benefit determination, 270, 275–276
risks
  eHealth, 165
  ethical decision-making and, 80
  ethical oversight and, 79
  ethics review and, 269–270
  online assessments and, 166, 168
Ritchie, James, 408
role conflicts, 354–355
Romania, 380–381
Roosevelt, Eleanor, 116, 117
Rosenzweig, Mark, 376
Royal Society of London, 246
rules. *See also* procedures
  acceptability of, 47
  bending of, 31
  binding power of, 47
  constituent, 44–45
  indigenous cultures and, 177
  interpretation of, 43
  judicial, 47

with moral standards, 203
standards as, 44
tactical, 44–45, 48
rules-compliance, 31, 38
Rules of Conduct Pertaining Specifically to Psychology, 385, 390
Russia, 424
in 1990s, 430–433
ethics code of, 434–436, 436–439
immigration in, 190
modern, 433–436
re-organization of psychology in, 425
Russian Psychological Society, 342–343, 425, 434, 434–436, 439
Russian Revolution, 117

S

Saddam Hussein, 387
SAM. *See* Society for Advancement of Management
sanctions, 92–93, 203
APA, 324–325
atonement *versus*, 94
in Brazil, 311
in Europe, 342
HKPS and, 333
in Mexico, 315
plagiarism, 261
power to impose, 98, 138
in Puerto Rico, 317
in Taiwan, 332
types of, 99
vignettes on, 99
Sati, Mustafa, 443
Sayyaf, Abu, 388
Scandinavian Code, 24
Schachter, Stanley, 245
science, 46
moral philosophy and, 54
psychological, 46, 138–139, 395
reliance on, 47
standards, 140, 146
universal truths and, 65
scientific evidence
ethics of procedure and, 69
professional insights *versus*, 47
in treatment outcome research, 185
of utility, 67–68
scientific method, 46
self-determination, 117, 120, 181, 349
self-interest orientation, 256
self-protection, 60, 66, 82
Serbia, 347
SERE. *See* Survival, Evasion, Resistance and Escape Program
Seventeen Rules of Enjuin, 6
sexual abuse, by psychologists, 58–59
sexual behavior, 261–262
sexual harassment, 261–262
sexual intimidation, 46
sexuality, 261
sexual orientation, 261
sexual relations, 57, 262, 354

Seymour, Fred, 406
Sherif, Muzaffer, 444
SHRM. *See* Society for Human Resources Management
SHUTi. *See* Sleep Healthy Using the Internet
Sleep Healthy Using the Internet (SHUTi), 163–164
Sloan Consortium, 217
Slovenia, 348
Smith, Alfredo, 398
social contracts, 19, 283
social control, 180, 233
social exclusion, 394
social inequality, 117, 152, 153
socialism, 55, 382
social justice, 32
economic transitions and, 391
ethical dilemmas in, 36–37
as ethical principle, 120
globalization and, 39, 114
human rights and, 130
language of, 130
market liberalization and, 419
in *NZ Code*, 414
political transitions and, 391
in South African ethics code, 385
social responsibility, 32, 247, 263, 309, 310–311
social services, 195, 195
society. *See also* responsibility to society
ethics codes and, 282–283
open, 376
welfare of, 32
Society for Advancement of Management (SAM), 253
Society for Human Resources Management (SHRM), 253
Socopi, 313
Soldz, Stephen, 236
South Africa, 104, 178, 385
South America, 16, 29, 105, 308–309
dictatorships in, 394
human rights in, 32
respect for dignity in, 400
social exclusion in, 394
Soviet Union, 424, 425–429
break-up of, 439
economic system of, 425–426
ethical standards in, 426–427
lack of ethics committees in, 427–428
law in, 427
political system of, 425–426
psychology in, 426
research in, 427, 428–429
Spain, 107
Catholic Church and, 246
confidentiality in, 348
ethics code of, 347
ethics committees in, 344
regulatory bodies in, 340
Spanish Psychological Association, 107, 247, 251

spiritual beliefs, 37, 183, 183, 409–410
stakeholders, 49, 51, 273–274
standards, 12, 20, 203–204. *See also* common standards; ethical standards
analysis of, 140
categories of, 43–44, 140
combined with principles, 136
comparisons of, 137
of competence, 42–43
of conduct, 51, 135
cultural differences among, 138
cultural interpretation of, 136–137
education, in Argentina, 400–401
enforcement of, 134
guidelines *versus*, 20
HPC and, 78–79, 79–80
incompatibility with informed consent of, 49
about informed consent, 49
infringements of, 91
intent of, 148
maintenance of, 91
moral, 203
need for, xix–xx
positive, 76
principles *versus*, 44
promotion of high, 351
recognition, 135
scientific, 140, 146, 147
testing, 207–208
test use, 138
in *Universal Declaration of Ethical Principles for Psychologists*, 126–127
universal *versus* common, 136–137
W/O Psychology, 262–263
Standards for Educational and Psychological Testing, 21, 202, 209, 210
statutory regulations, 78–79, 165, 458–459, 460. *See also* law
stereotypes, 156, 186
students
exploitation of, 355
extended responsibility to, 352
privacy of, 348
as research participants, 153–154
supervision of, 43
suicide, 99, 181
Sulaiman, Rajah, 388
Survival, Evasion, Resistance and Escape Program (SERE), 233
sustainability, 176–177, 419
Sweden, 24, 339, 344
Sweetland, Richard C., 212
Switzerland, 343, 346

T

Tahsin, Hoca, 443
Taiwan, 329–330, 332, 331–332, 335
Taiwan Counseling Psychology Association (TWCPA), 332
technology, 39
cheating, 216–217
cultural identity and, 127–128

technology (*Cont.*)
    ethical criteria for, 248
    ethics code development and, 139
    moral philosophy and, 55
    test development and, 224
    testing and, 215–217
    test security and, 217
telepsychology, 77, 455–456
Ten Commandments, 115, 203, 245–246
terrorism, 32, 39, 356, 386
    in Philippines, 388
    state, 398–399
Test Critiques (Keyser and Sweetland), 212
test development, 20–21, 200–201
    budgeting, 224, 228
    components of, 201
    ethics codes for, 202
    Federal Council of Psychology (Brazil) and, 208
    history of, 201
    impact of professional associations on, 208–209
    ITC and, 25
    with known security threats, 227
    national ethics codes and, 21
    standards, 207
    Standards for Educational and Psychological Testing and, 209
    technology and, 224
testing
    adaptations, 25, 206
    availability, 20–21, 201, 201
    bad, 222
    certification, 217
    companies, 212
    computerized, 216
    emerging challenges in, 455
    ethics codes affecting, 205–207
    guidelines, 206–207, 209–211, 221
    high-stakes, 217–218
    information sources, 211–212
    intellectual property and, 204
    international, 215
    Internet searches and, 211–212
    under known security threats, 222–223
    on-demand, 216, 224
    online, 216
    online proctoring, 227
    outdated, 223–224, 227–228
    pencil-and-paper, 223
    plagiarism of, 204
    pre-employment, 216, 225–226
    professionals, 220–222
    in Russian ethics code, 436, 438
    standards, national, 207–208
    standards, regional, 207–208
    technology and, 215–217
    translating, 204
    unproctored, 216, 219
    unsecure, 222
    W/O Psychology, 262–263
testing piracy, 218

braindump sites and, 222–223, 226–227
dealing with, 228–229
improper response to, 224–225
law and, 229
prevalence of, 218–219
types of, 221
testing security, 216, 219–220
    awareness of, 225
    budgeting, 224, 228
    ethical dilemmas with, 222–225
    Internet tools for, 225–226
    known threats to, 222–223, 226–227
    for outdated testing, 227–228
    plans, 228
    recommendations, 226
    responsibility for, 225
    solutions, 225–229
    specific threats to, 219–220
    technology and, 217
    threats, 218–220
Tests: A Comprehensive Reference for Assessment in Psychology, Education, and Business (Maddox), 212
Tests in Print (Geisinger), 212
test use, 20–21, 200–201
    acceptability and, 49
    children and, 202
    clinical, 205
    components of, 201
    confidentiality and, 205
    cross-cultural, 155
    cultural factors in, 156
    Dutch Institute of Psychology and, 209
    ethics codes for, 202
    good practices in, 25, 206
    guidelines, 206
    history of, 201–202
    IAAP and, 205
    impact of professional associations on, 208–209
    indigenous cultures and, 185
    international, 201
    international law and, 204
    ITC and, 25, 205–207
    IUPsyS and, 205
    Meta-Code of Ethics and, 23–24
    national ethics codes and, 21
    patterns, 201
    respect and, 205
    responsibility in, 206
    similarities in APA and CPS codes and, 22
    social, 205
    standards, 138, 207
    Standards for Educational and Psychological Testing and, 209
    Universal Declaration of Ethical Principles for Psychologists and, 205
    in World War II, 202
Te Whare Tapa Whā model, 183
theocracies, 384
Third Faces, 62, 67, 71

third party interests, 348
Thomas, David, 408
thought experiments, 47
Torres Strait Islanders, 364
torture
    in Argentina, 397
    COP and, 351
    at Guantanamo Bay, 236, 387
    interrogation *versus*, 232–233
    PENS report and, 387
    PTSD and, 236
Toulmin, Stephen, 245
Toward a Universal Declaration of a Global Ethic (Centre for Global Ethics), 31, 39
TPA. *See* Turkish Psychological Association
traditional healing, 30, 30
training. *See also* ethics training
    in Argentina, 395
    cultural awareness, 176
    of cultural diversity, 192
    eHealth, 167
    EuroPsy and, 340–341
    human rights, 235
    interrogation, 236
    organizational, 257
    for social services for immigrants, 195
translations
    of ethics codes, 148, 390
    research with immigrants and, 193–194
    of tests, 204
    of *UDHR*, 118
transparency
    in advertising, 353
    confidentiality *versus*, 49
    of methods, 283
Treaty of Waitangi, 175, 180–181, 366, 406, 422–423
    growing awareness of, 418
    influence of, on *NZ Code*, 414–415
    negotiations, 413
    nurses and, 407
    NZ Code and, 366–367, 405, 412
tribunals, 96, 97
Trilateral Forum on Professional Psychology, 314
trust
    earning, of indigenous cultures, 182
    ethics codes and, 19
    mutual, 71
    proximity to dialogue and, 70–71
    public, 203
Tunc, Mustafa Sekip, 444
Turhan, Mumtaz, 444
Turing, Alan, 261
Turkey, 107–108, 121
    education in, 445
    ethics code in, 446–448
    ethics committees in, 344
    ethics developments in, 448
    psychology in, 445–446

research in, 445
women in, 446
Turkish Psychological Association (TPA), 107–108, 282, 445–446
Turkish War of Independence, 444
Tuskegee syphilis study, 268
TWCPA. *See* Taiwan Counseling Psychology Association
Two Plus Four Treaty, 382

U

UDHR. *See* Universal Declaration of Human Rights
UK. *See* United Kingdom
UN. *See* United Nations
UNCROC. *See* United Nations Convention on the Rights of the Child
undocumented people, 191
UNESCO. *See* United Nations Educational, Scientific and Cultural Organization
unethical behavior
 best intentions and, 63, 64
 interests in, 92
 law and, 81
 legal, 61
 prevalence of, 458
 unlawful behavior *versus*, 258
 W/O Psychology and, 257
UNHCR. *See* United Nations High Commission on Refugees
United Kingdom (UK)
 ethics committees in, 343
 immigration and, 77
 licensing in, 339
 statutory regulations in, 78–79
United Nations (UN), 31, 39, 113
 adoption of *UDHR* and, 116–117
 charter of, 118
 Commission on Human Rights, 116
 Convention Against Torture, 233–234
 founding of, 116
 HDI, 376–377
 Principles of Medical Ethics, 235
 Refugee Convention, 191
United Nations Convention on the Rights of the Child (UNCROC), 417
United Nations Declaration on the Rights of Indigenous Peoples, 418
United Nations Educational, Scientific and Cultural Organization (UNESCO), 117
United Nations High Commission on Refugees (UNHCR), 190–191
United States (US), 21
 credentialing in, 321
 cross-cultural research and, 150–151
 cultural conditions in, 22
 current ethics research in, 326
 Declaration of Independence, 115
 ethical guidelines for international research and, 150

ethics codes, 325
ethics committees in, 324–325
ethics training in, 325–326
free market economy in, 247
immigration and, 77, 190
influence on research of, 157
legal status of psychology in, 321–323
licensing in, 322
professional associations in, 323–324
Puerto Rico and, 317
refugees in, 191
regulatory bodies in, 322
specific rules *versus* human values in, 31
statutory regulations in, 78
Universal Declaration of Ethical Principles for Psychologists and, 325
United States Embassy Beijing on Human Research Subject Protection, 153
Universal Declaration of Ethical Principles for Psychologists, 17, 31, 150, 151, 246, 248, 390
 adoption of, 113, 119–120, 122–123
 APS and, 361–362
 aspirational nature of, 134, 151
 authority for, 129
 Canadian Code of Ethics for Psychologists and, 325
 common moral framework and, 125
 compared to ethics before Common Era, 5–6
 competent caring for well-being in, 151
 content of, 123–125
 development of, 4, 454
 dictatorships and, 402
 empirical basis of, 125
 ethical dilemmas and, 39
 ethical principles in, 76
 gaps in, 151
 historical context for, 120–122
 human rights and, 292
 inclusiveness of, 77, 148
 integrity in, 50, 151
 international ethics codes and, 24–25
 international research and, 150–151
 minimizing bias and, 156
 moral-framework format and, 16
 national codes of ethics and, 319
 new applications for, 127
 principles categories in, 44
 promotion of, 127
 Psychologists Committee of Mercosur and Associated Countries and, 400
 purpose of, 120
 regional developments and, 355
 respect for dignity in, 151
 responsibility to society in, 151
 significance of, 125–127
 social justice in, 32
 standards in, 126–127
 structure of, 123–125
 target of, 129
 UDHR versus, 128–129
 US and, 325

Universal Declaration of Human Rights (*UDHR*), 31, 113
 adoption of, 116–117
 authority for, 129
 concept of human rights in, 114–115
 content of, 117–118
 as customary international law, 119
 drafting of, 116–117
 first generation human rights and, 117
 historical context for, 115–116
 Islam and, 119
 moral rights and, 292
 purpose of, 114
 ratification of, 115
 reasons for rejecting, 130
 significance of, 118–119
 structure of, 117–118
 target of, 129
 translations of, 118
 Universal Declaration of Ethical Principles for Psychologists versus, 128–129
universal declarations, 114, 119–120
universalism, 130, 269
Universidad Autónoma de México, 313
unlawful behavior, 258
US. *See* United States
utilitarianism, 244–245
utility
 ethics of, 66–68
 measuring, 67
 misattribution of, 68
 productivity *versus*, 68
 scientific evidence of, 67–68

V

values
 analysis of, 81
 common, 135
 common standards and, 137
 cultural restrictions on, 135
 emotionally-based sensitivity for, 56–57
 ethics of utility and, 68
 formulation *versus* practice, 58
 good reasons approach and, 245
 indigenous, 178
 individualist *versus* collectivist, 38
 moral discourse and, 53
 moral philosophy and, 55
 practical implications of, 414
 principles based on, 134–135
 professional ethics and, 57
 in psychology, 375
 rules bending and, 31
 threats to, 436
 universal, 29
Vasak, Karel, 117
Vedas, 115
verification, 140, 147, 147, 167
Veterans Administration hospitals, 202
vignettes, 28, 97, 245
 of competence ethical dilemmas, 33
 of ethical dilemmas, 32–33

of legal restrictions ethical dilemmas, 35–36
limitations of, 40
of professional boundaries ethical dilemmas, 34–35
of respect for dignity ethical dilemmas, 33–34
on sanctions, 99
sharing, 83
of social justice ethical dilemmas, 36–37
of status of women ethical dilemmas, 35
of underlying tensions, 37
violence
 among children, 37
 across cultures, 38
 in indigenous cultures, 181
 regional, 108
 against women, 35
virtues, 20, 203–204
von Hartmann, Eduard, 242
vulnerable populations, 276, 416, 416–417

W

Waitangi Tribunal, 180, 406–407
war, 32
Washington Post, 235
waterboarding, 236
Webb, Olive, 417
web-based interventions, 161. *See also* eHealth
 communication and, 163
 convenience and, 163
 crisis intervention for, 168
 e-mail and, 162–163
 emerging challenges in, 455–456
 geographic isolation and, 162
 meta-analyses of, 164
 records, 166
Welch, Bryant, 236
welfare
 of others, 120
 of society, 120, 125
Wellcome Trust, 153
West-East terminology, 29–30
West Germany, 382
WHO. *See* World Health Organization
Wittgenstein, Ludwig, 255
WMA. *See* World Medical Association
women
 oppression of, 38
 promotion for equality of, 157
 status of, 35
 in Turkey, 446
 violence against, 35
W/O Psychology. *See* Work and Organizational Psychology
Work and Organizational Psychology (W/O Psychology), 243
 casebooks, 250
 codes of conduct, 250
 confidentiality and, 251, 252–254
 deontological codes and, 248–249
 deontological complaints in, 252
 ethics code loyalties in, 250
 ethics in, 250–252
 lack of ethical literature in, 249
 literature, 258
 multifaced profile of, 257–259
 normative *versus* descriptive ethics and, 255–257
 personnel decisions and, 254
 plagiarism and, 260–261
 professional associations for, 253
 protocols, 262–263
 record storage and, 254
 standards, 262–263
 tasks, 257
 testing, 262–263
 unethical behavior and, 257
working conditions, 347
Working Party, 406, 411
working tools, 75
World Health Organization (WHO), 205, 377
World Intellectual Property Organization, 204
World Medical Association (WMA), 121, 268
World Psychiatric Association, 30
World Trade Organization, 204
worldviews, 38, 40, 176, 182
World War I, 201–202
World War II, 11–12, 116
 atrocities, 116, 120–121
 test use in, 202
written consent, 150
Wundt, Wilhelm, 426

Y

Yerkes, Robert, 201–202

Z

Zimbardo, Phil, 54, 235, 268